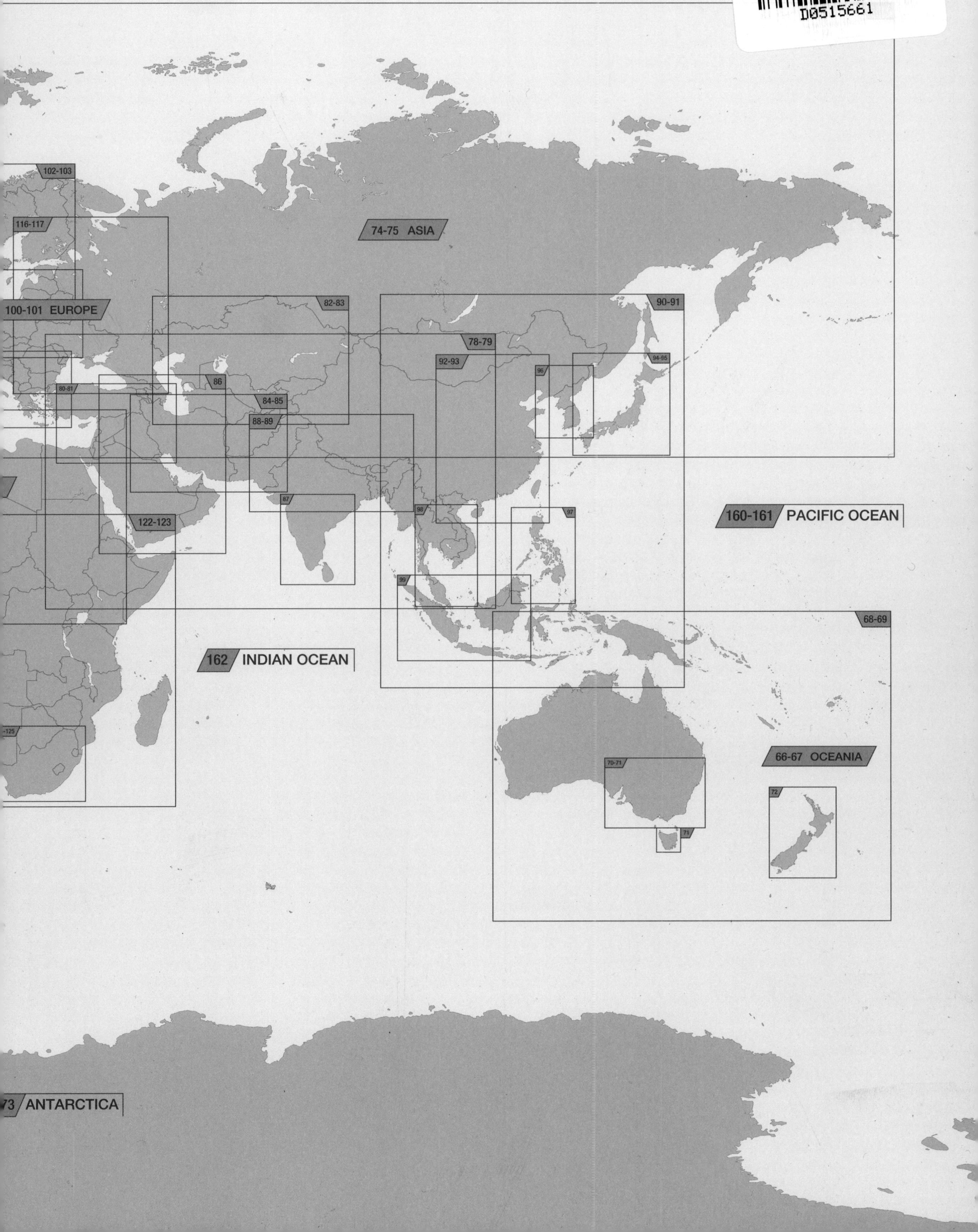

102-103

116-117

100-101 EUROPE

80-81

86

82-83

84-85

88-89

74-75 ASIA

78-79

92-93

96

90-91

94-95

87

98

97

122-123

160-161 PACIFIC OCEAN

162 INDIAN OCEAN

99

68-69

66-67 OCEANIA

-125

70-71

71

72

73 ANTARCTICA

D0515661

THE TIMES

ATLAS OF THE WORLD

REFERENCE EDITION

TIMES BOOKS

London

THE ✦ TIMES
ATLAS
OF THE
WORLD
REFERENCE EDITION

Times Books, 77-85 Fulham Palace Road, London W6 8JB

The Times is a registered trademark of Times Newspapers Ltd

First published 1995

Published as The Times Atlas of the World
New Generation Edition 1997

Second Edition 2002
Reprinted 2002 (twice), 2003

Copyright © Times Books Group Ltd 2002

Maps © Collins Bartholomew Ltd 2002

The contents of this edition of The Times Atlas of the World Reference Edition are believed correct at the time of printing. Nevertheless the publisher can accept no responsibility for errors or omissions, changes in the detail given or for any expense or loss thereby caused.

Printed and bound in the UK

British Library Cataloguing in Publication Data
A catalogue record for this book is available from the British Library
ISBN 0 00 712400 7
QH11650 Imp 004

The maps in this product are also available for purchase in digital format from Bartholomew Mapping Solutions
Tel: +44 (0) 141 306 3162, Fax: +44 (0) 141 306 3245
www.bartholomewmaps.com
e-mail: bartholomew@harpercollins.co.uk

www.harpercollins.co.uk
Visit the book lover's website

SATELLITE IMAGES

GEOGRAPHICAL INFORMATION

WORLD CITIES

ATLAS OF THE WORLD

TOTAL LAND AREA: 8 844 516 sq km / 3 414 887 sq miles (includes New Guinea and Pacific Island nations)

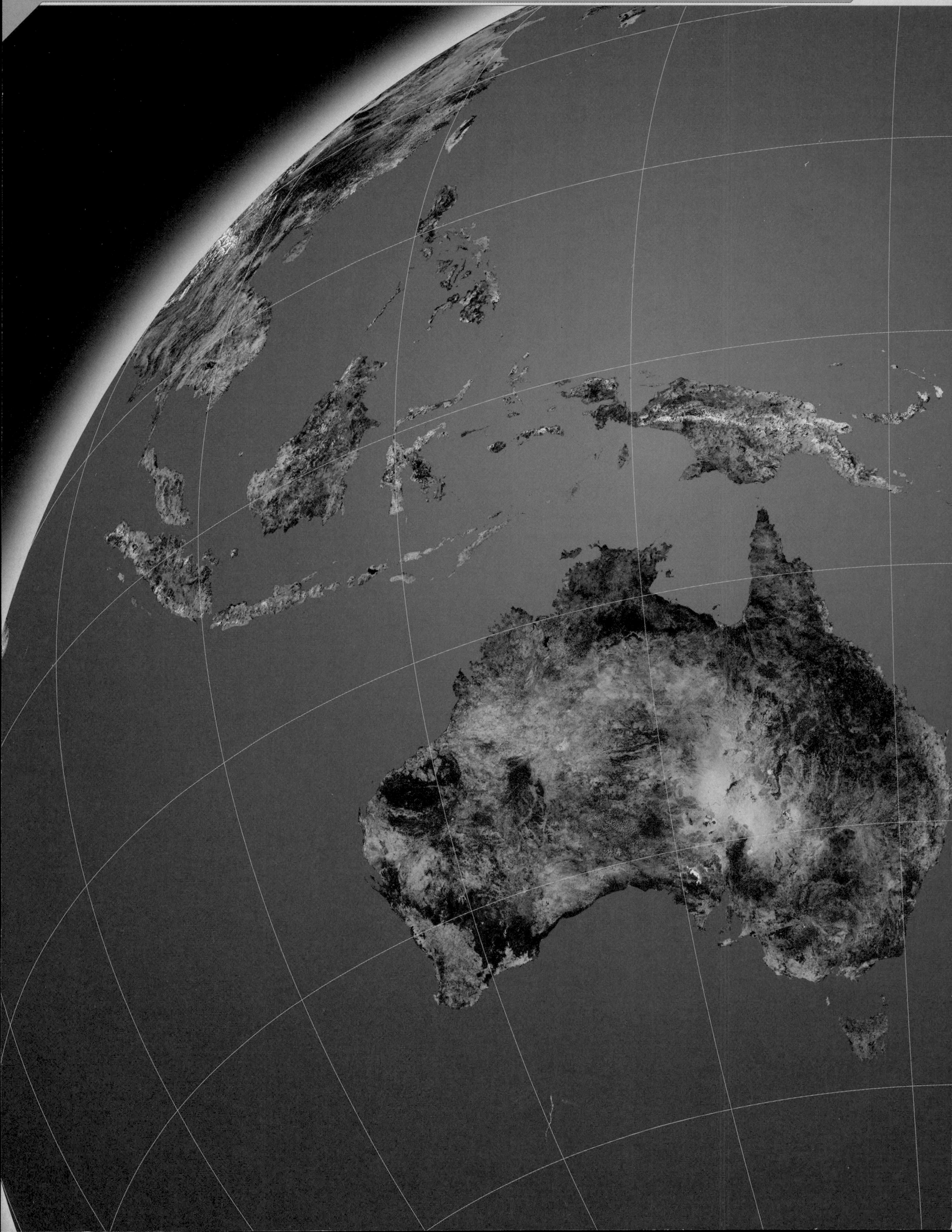

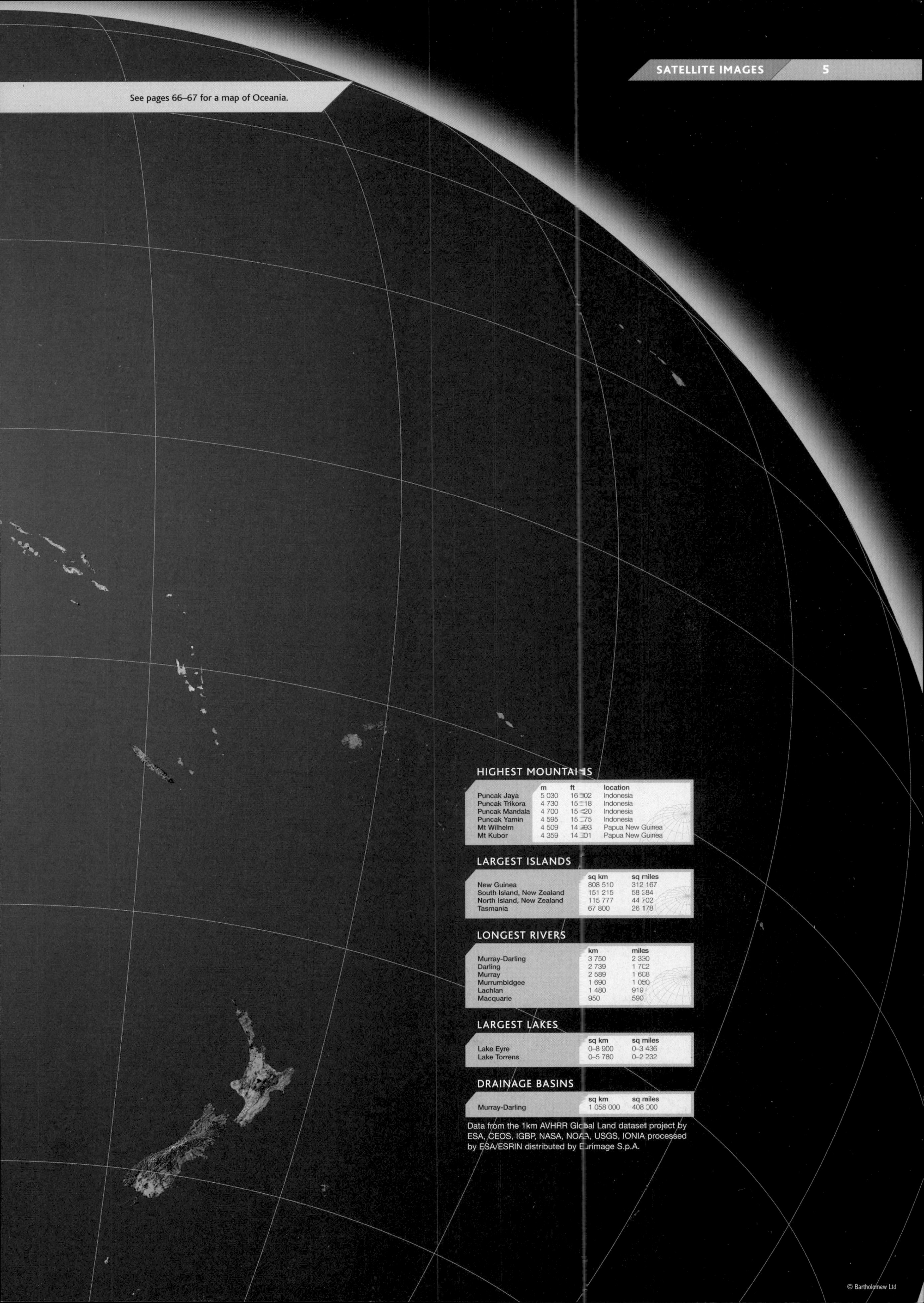

See pages 66–67 for a map of Oceania.

HIGHEST MOUNTAINS

	m	ft	location
Puncak Jaya	5 030	16 502	Indonesia
Puncak Trikora	4 730	15 518	Indonesia
Puncak Mandala	4 700	15 420	Indonesia
Puncak Yamin	4 595	15 075	Indonesia
Mt Wilhelm	4 509	14 793	Papua New Guinea
Mt Kubor	4 359	14 301	Papua New Guinea

LARGEST ISLANDS

	sq km	sq miles
New Guinea	808 510	312 167
South Island, New Zealand	151 215	58 384
North Island, New Zealand	115 777	44 702
Tasmania	67 800	26 178

LONGEST RIVERS

	km	miles
Murray-Darling	3 750	2 330
Darling	2 739	1 702
Murray	2 589	1 608
Murrumbidgee	1 690	1 050
Lachlan	1 480	919
Macquarie	950	590

LARGEST LAKES

	sq km	sq miles
Lake Eyre	0–8 900	0–3 436
Lake Torrens	0–5 780	0–2 232

DRAINAGE BASINS

	sq km	sq miles
Murray-Darling	1 058 000	408 000

Data from the 1km AVHRR Global Land dataset project by
ESA, CEOS, IGBP, NASA, NOAA, USGS, IONIA processed
by ESA/ESRIN distributed by Eurimage S.p.A.

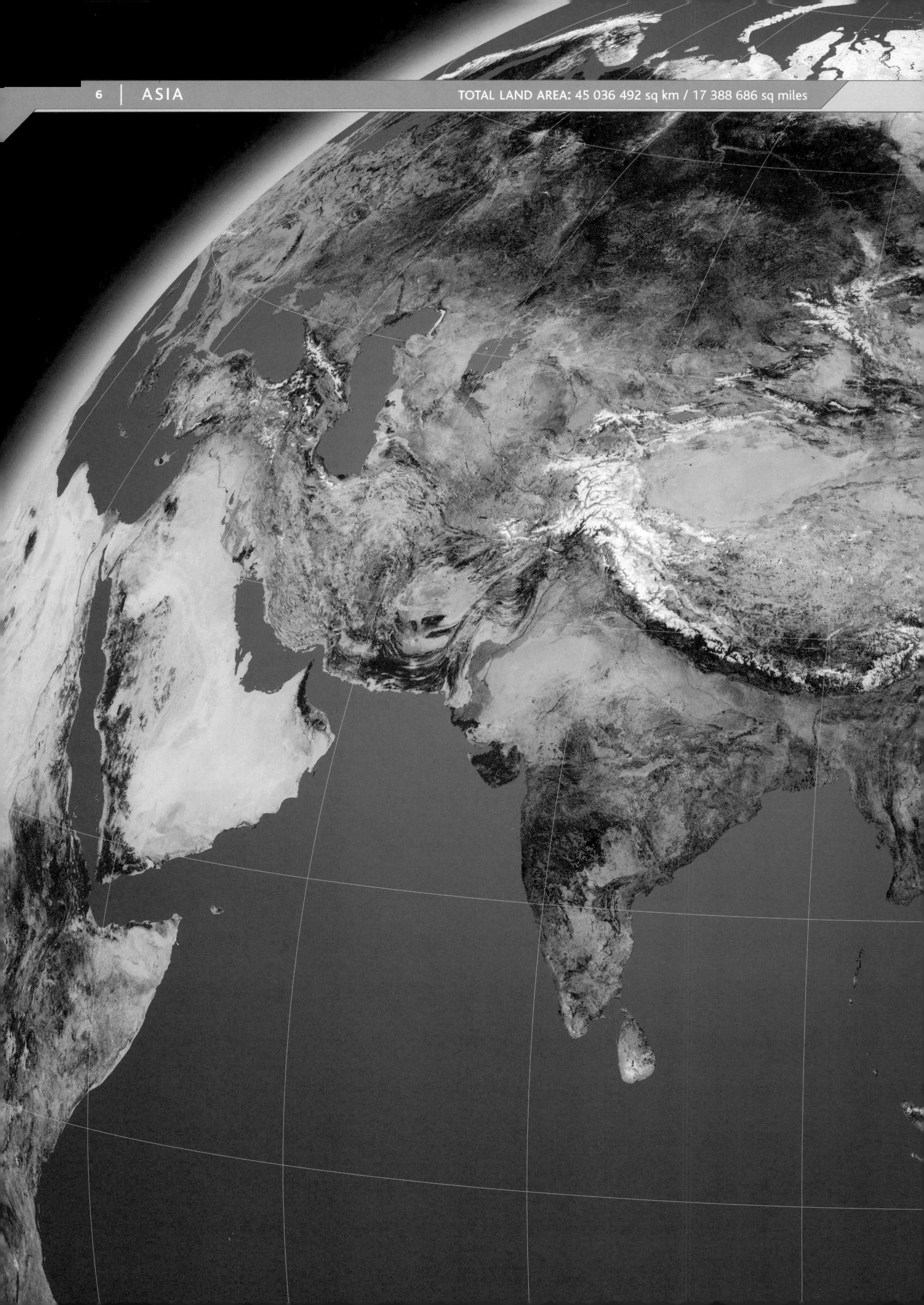

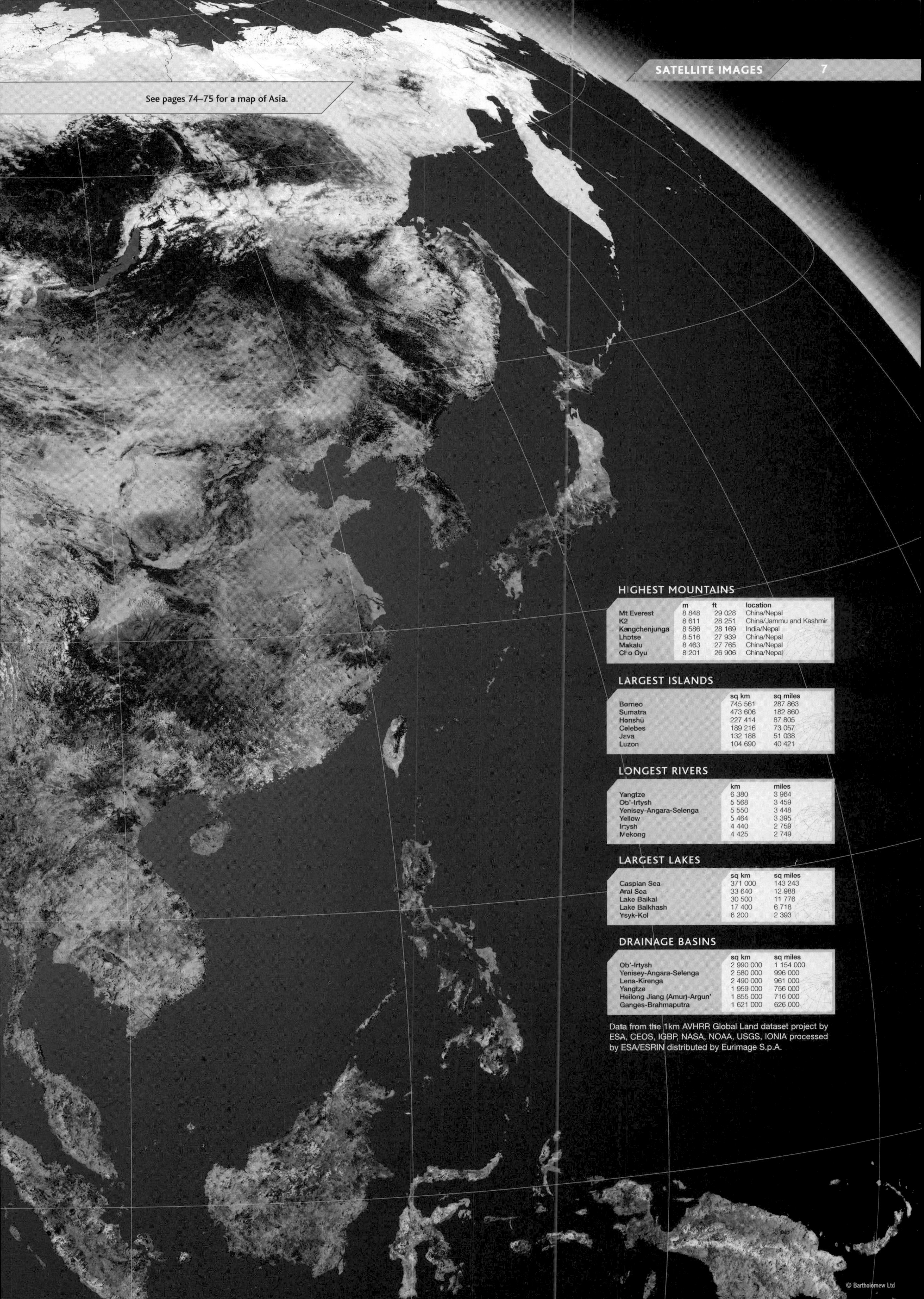

See pages 74–75 for a map of Asia.

HIGHEST MOUNTAINS

	m	ft	location
Mt Everest	8 848	29 028	China/Nepal
K2	8 611	28 251	China/Jammu and Kashmir
Kangchenjunga	8 586	28 169	India/Nepal
Lhotse	8 516	27 939	China/Nepal
Makalu	8 463	27 765	China/Nepal
Cho Oyu	8 201	26 906	China/Nepal

LARGEST ISLANDS

	sq km	sq miles
Borneo	745 561	287 863
Sumatra	473 606	182 860
Honshū	227 414	87 805
Celebes	189 216	73 057
Java	132 188	51 038
Luzon	104 690	40 421

LONGEST RIVERS

	km	miles
Yangtze	6 380	3 964
Ob'-Irtysh	5 568	3 459
Yenisey-Angara-Selenga	5 550	3 448
Yellow	5 464	3 395
Irtysh	4 440	2 759
Mekong	4 425	2 749

LARGEST LAKES

	sq km	sq miles
Caspian Sea	371 000	143 243
Aral Sea	33 640	12 988
Lake Baikal	30 500	11 776
Lake Balkhash	17 400	6 718
Ysyk-Kol	6 200	2 393

DRAINAGE BASINS

	sq km	sq miles
Ob'-Irtysh	2 990 000	1 154 000
Yenisey-Angara-Selenga	2 580 000	996 000
Lena-Kirenga	2 490 000	961 000
Yangtze	1 959 000	756 000
Heilong Jiang (Amur)-Argun'	1 855 000	716 000
Ganges-Brahmaputra	1 621 000	626 000

Data from the 1km AVHRR Global Land dataset project by ESA, CEOS, IGBP, NASA, NOAA, USGS, IONIA processed by ESA/ESRIN distributed by Eurimage S.p.A.

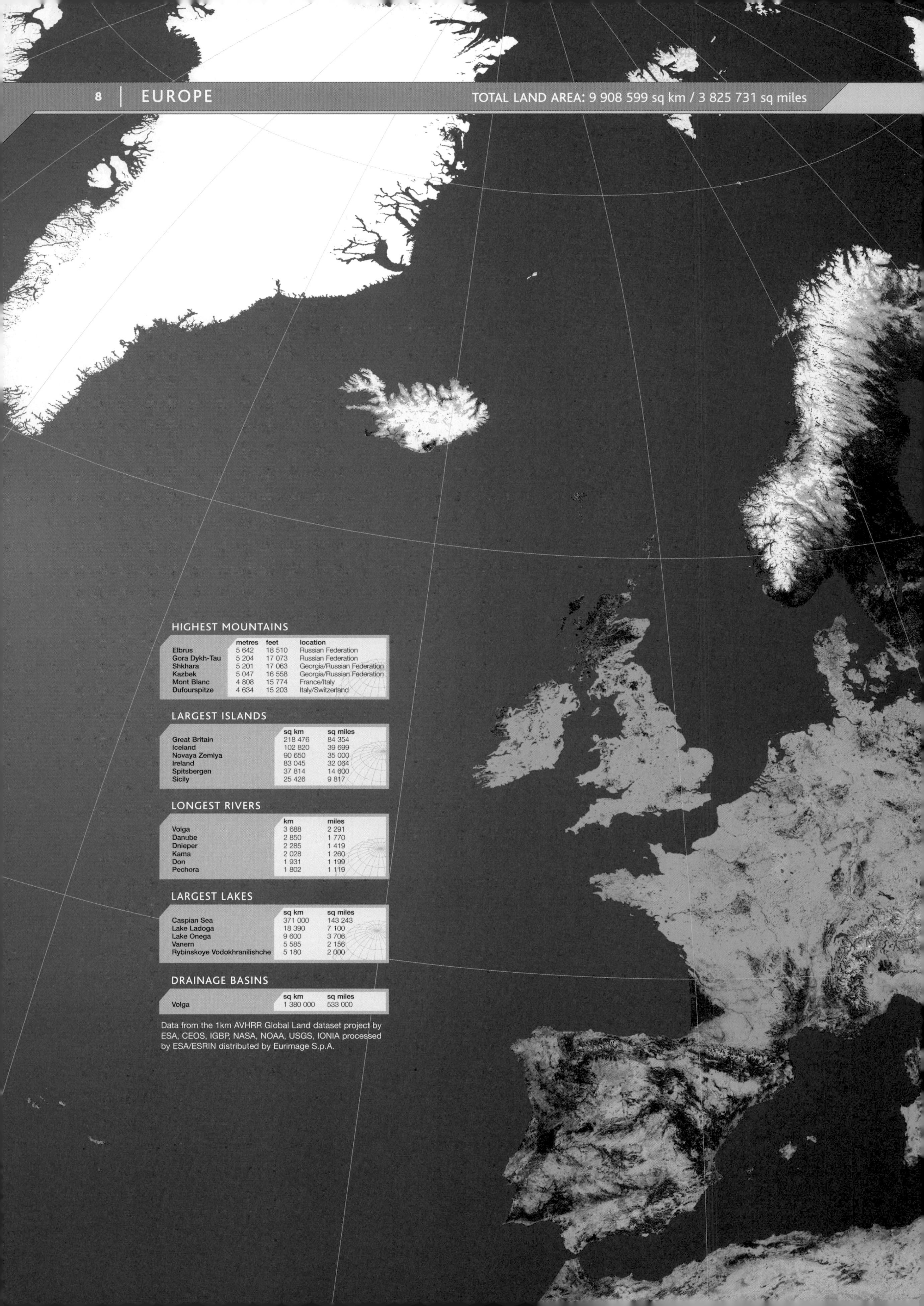

HIGHEST MOUNTAINS

	metres	feet	location
Elbrus	5 642	18 510	Russian Federation
Gora Dykh-Tau	5 204	17 073	Russian Federation
Shkhara	5 201	17 063	Georgia/Russian Federation
Kazbek	5 047	16 558	Georgia/Russian Federation
Mont Blanc	4 808	15 774	France/Italy
Dufourspitze	4 634	15 203	Italy/Switzerland

LARGEST ISLANDS

	sq km	sq miles
Great Britain	218 476	84 354
Iceland	102 820	39 699
Novaya Zemlya	90 650	35 000
Ireland	83 045	32 064
Spitsbergen	37 814	14 600
Sicily	25 426	9 817

LONGEST RIVERS

	km	miles
Volga	3 688	2 291
Danube	2 850	1 770
Dnieper	2 285	1 419
Kama	2 028	1 260
Don	1 931	1 199
Pechora	1 802	1 119

LARGEST LAKES

	sq km	sq miles
Caspian Sea	371 000	143 243
Lake Ladoga	18 390	7 100
Lake Onega	9 600	3 706
Vanern	5 585	2 156
Rybinskoye Vodokhranilishche	5 180	2 000

DRAINAGE BASINS

	sq km	sq miles
Volga	1 380 000	533 000

Data from the 1km AVHRR Global Land dataset project by ESA, CEOS, IGBP, NASA, NOAA, USGS, IONIA processed by ESA/ESRIN distributed by Eurimage S.p.A.

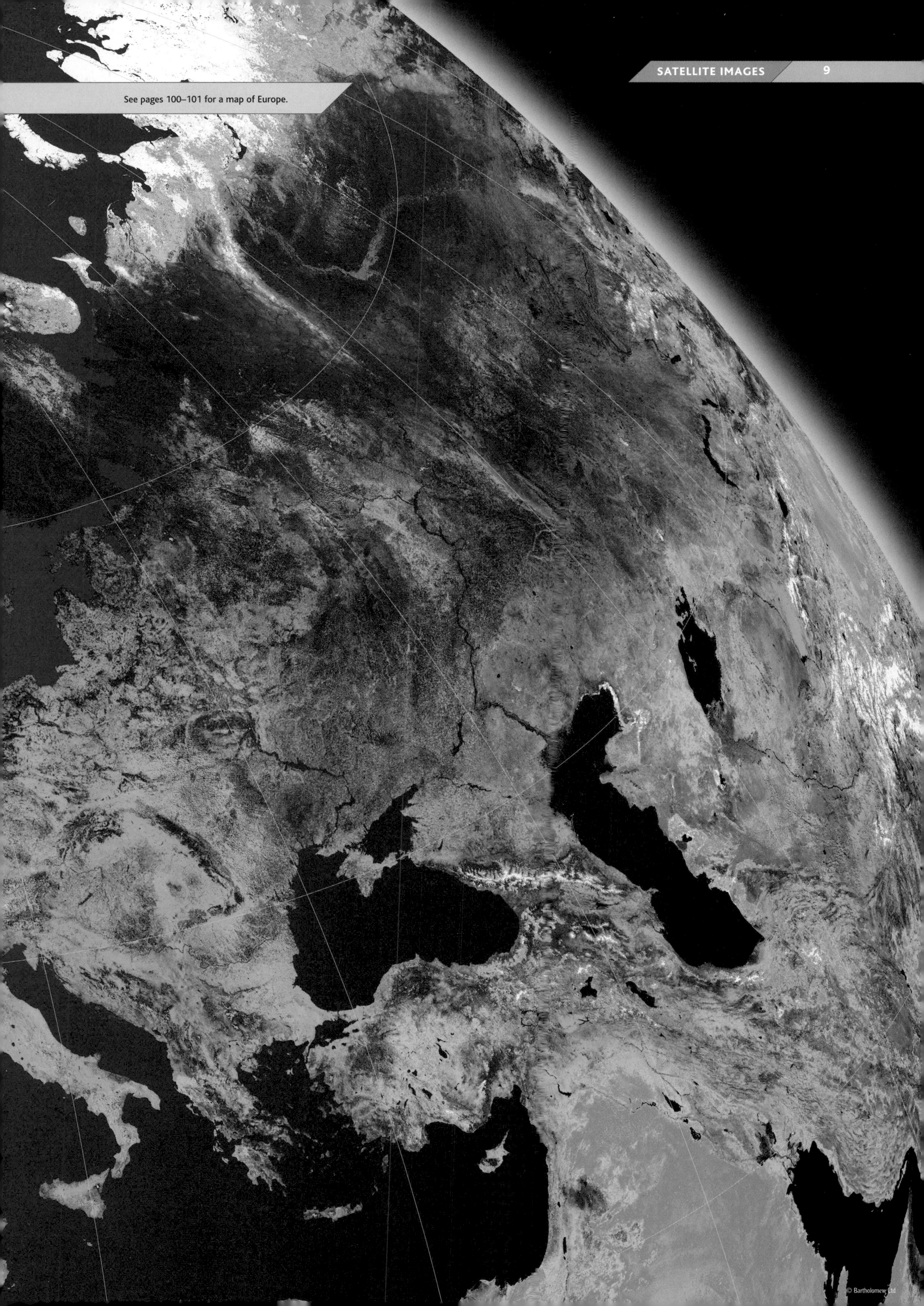

See pages 100–101 for a map of Europe.

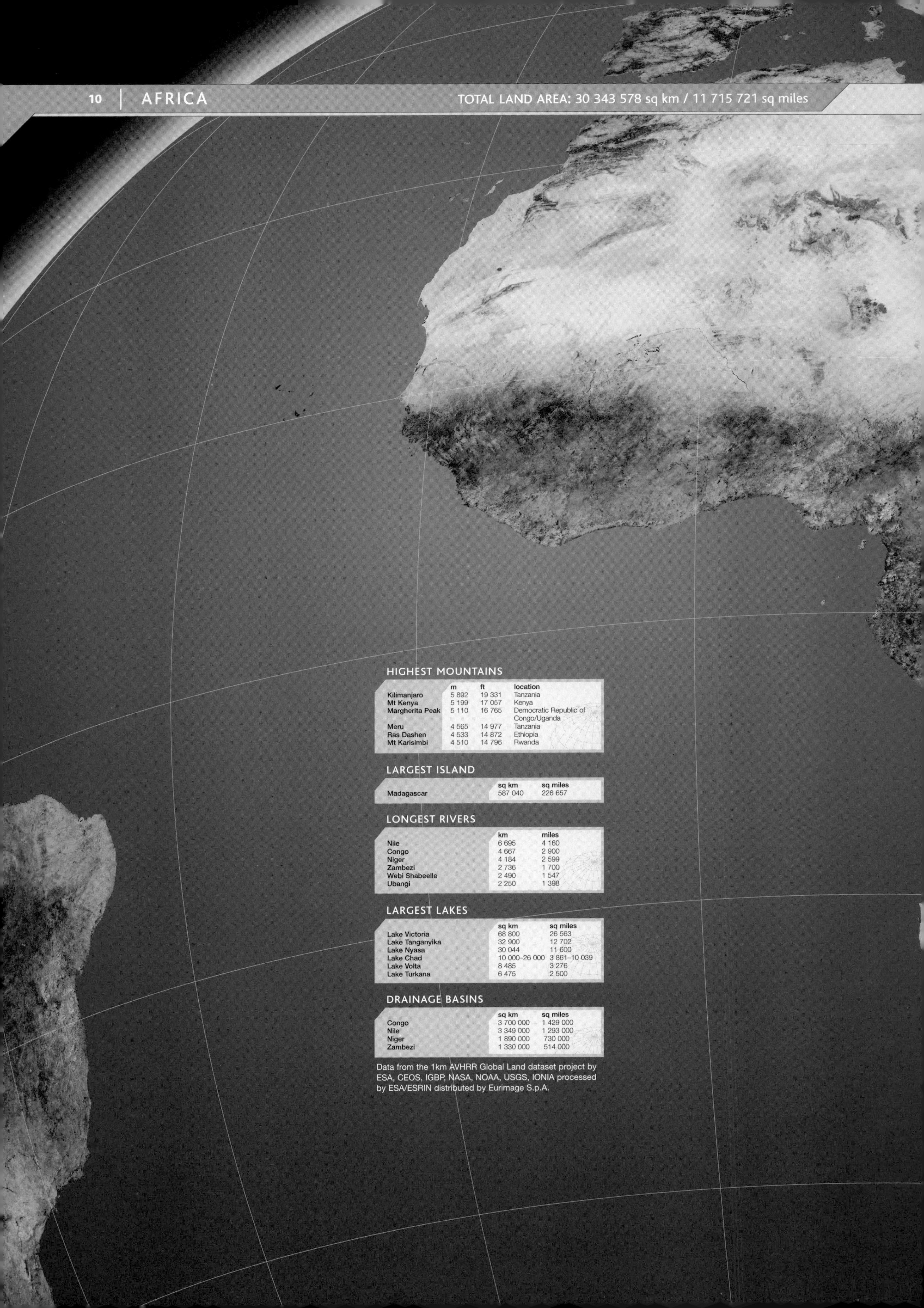

HIGHEST MOUNTAINS

	m	ft	location
Kilimanjaro	5 892	19 331	Tanzania
Mt Kenya	5 199	17 057	Kenya
Margherita Peak	5 110	16 765	Democratic Republic of Congo/Uganda
Meru	4 565	14 977	Tanzania
Ras Dashen	4 533	14 872	Ethiopia
Mt Karisimbi	4 510	14 796	Rwanda

LARGEST ISLAND

	sq km	sq miles
Madagascar	587 040	226 657

LONGEST RIVERS

	km	miles
Nile	6 695	4 160
Congo	4 667	2 900
Niger	4 184	2 599
Zambezi	2 736	1 700
Webi Shabeelle	2 490	1 547
Ubangi	2 250	1 398

LARGEST LAKES

	sq km	sq miles
Lake Victoria	68 800	26 563
Lake Tanganyika	32 900	12 702
Lake Nyasa	30 044	11 600
Lake Chad	10 000–26 000	3 861–10 039
Lake Volta	8 485	3 276
Lake Turkana	6 475	2 500

DRAINAGE BASINS

	sq km	sq miles
Congo	3 700 000	1 429 000
Nile	3 349 000	1 293 000
Niger	1 890 000	730 000
Zambezi	1 330 000	514 000

Data from the 1km AVHRR Global Land dataset project by ESA, CEOS, IGBP, NASA, NOAA, USGS, IONIA processed by ESA/ESRIN distributed by Eurimage S.p.A.

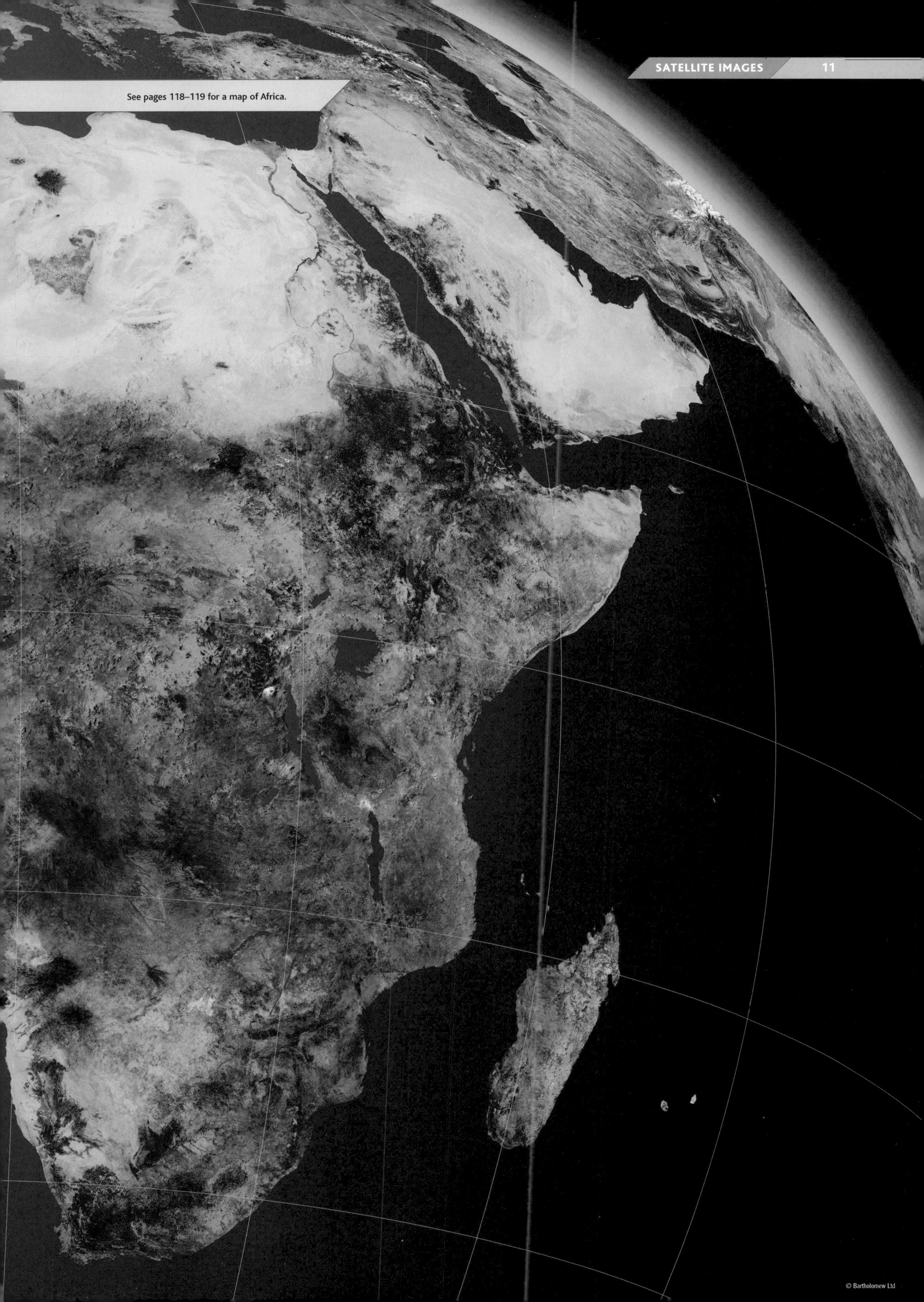

See pages 118–119 for a map of Africa.

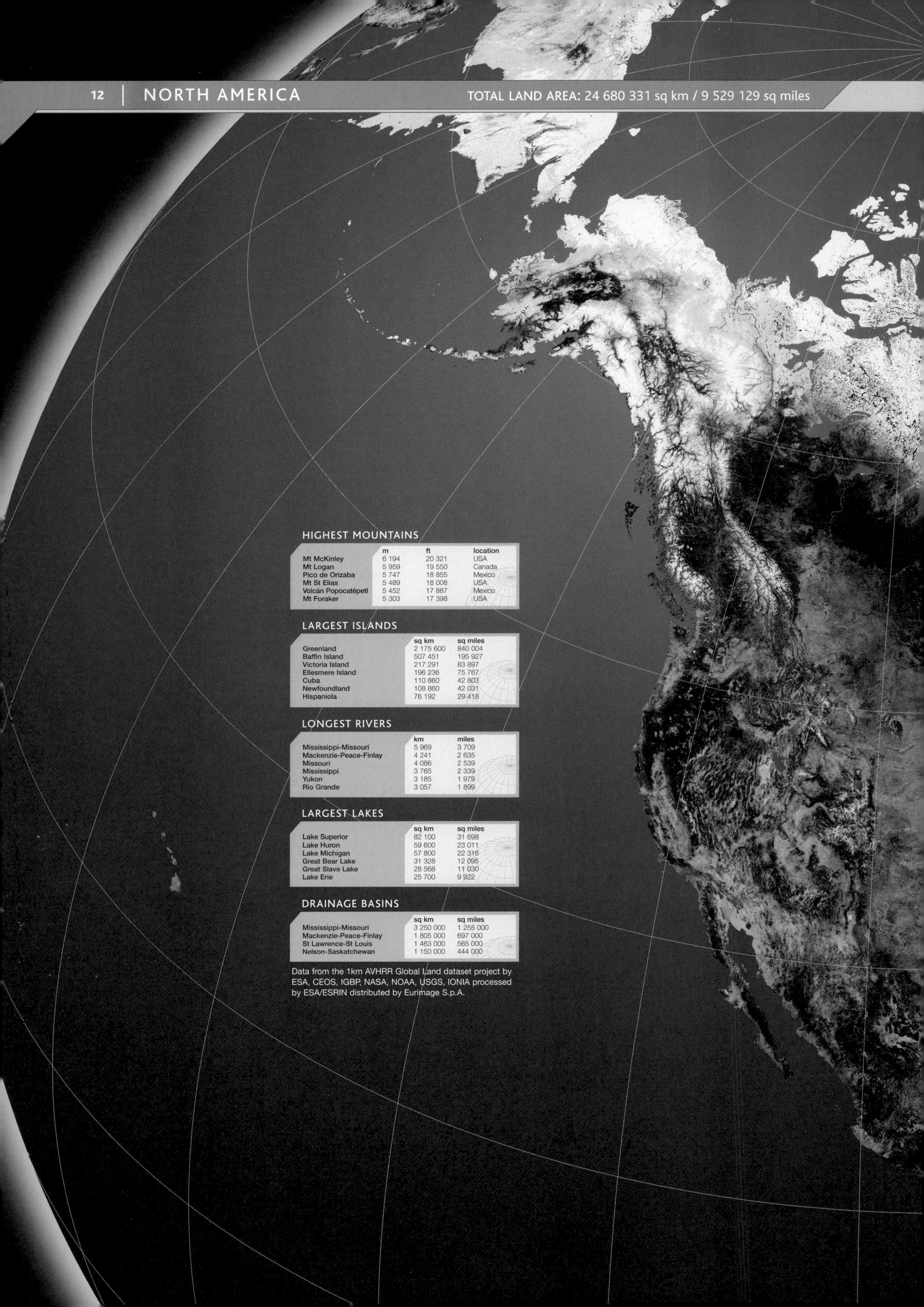

HIGHEST MOUNTAINS

	m	ft	location
Mt McKinley	6 194	20 321	USA
Mt Logan	5 959	19 550	Canada
Pico de Orizaba	5 747	18 855	Mexico
Mt St Elias	5 489	18 008	USA
Volcán Popocatépetl	5 452	17 887	Mexico
Mt Foraker	5 303	17 398	USA

LARGEST ISLANDS

	sq km	sq miles
Greenland	2 175 600	840 004
Baffin Island	507 451	195 927
Victoria Island	217 291	83 897
Ellesmere Island	196 236	75 767
Cuba	110 860	42 803
Newfoundland	108 860	42 031
Hispaniola	76 192	29 418

LONGEST RIVERS

	km	miles
Mississippi-Missouri	5 969	3 709
Mackenzie-Peace-Finlay	4 241	2 635
Missouri	4 086	2 539
Mississippi	3 765	2 339
Yukon	3 185	1 979
Rio Grande	3 057	1 899

LARGEST LAKES

	sq km	sq miles
Lake Superior	82 100	31 698
Lake Huron	59 600	23 011
Lake Michigan	57 800	22 316
Great Bear Lake	31 328	12 095
Great Slave Lake	28 568	11 030
Lake Erie	25 700	9 922

DRAINAGE BASINS

	sq km	sq miles
Mississippi-Missouri	3 250 000	1 255 000
Mackenzie-Peace-Finlay	1 805 000	697 000
St Lawrence-St Louis	1 463 000	565 000
Nelson-Saskatchewan	1 150 000	444 000

Data from the 1km AVHRR Global Land dataset project by
ESA, CEOS, IGBP, NASA, NOAA, USGS, IONIA processed
by ESA/ESRIN distributed by Eurimage S.p.A.

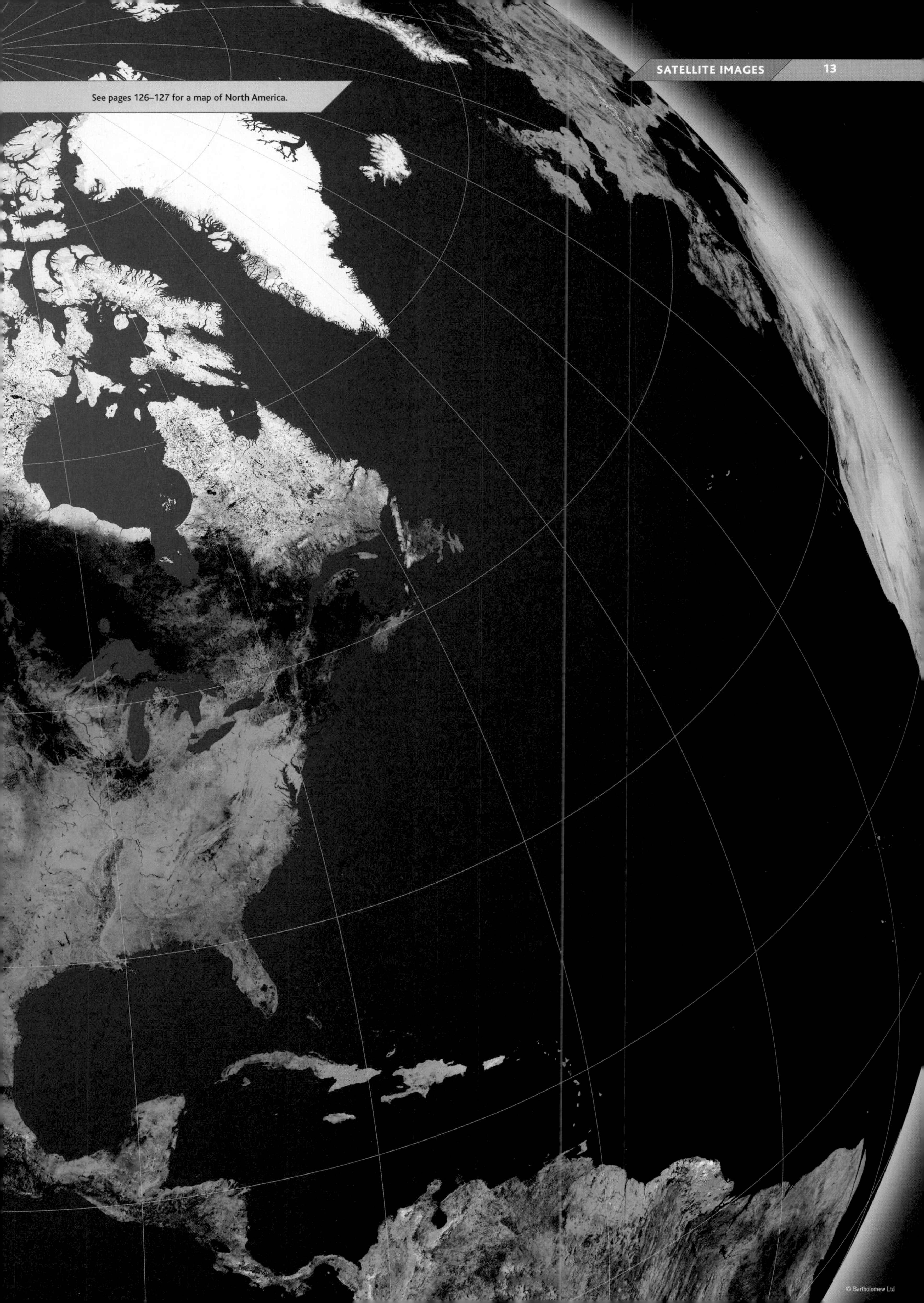

See pages 126–127 for a map of North America.

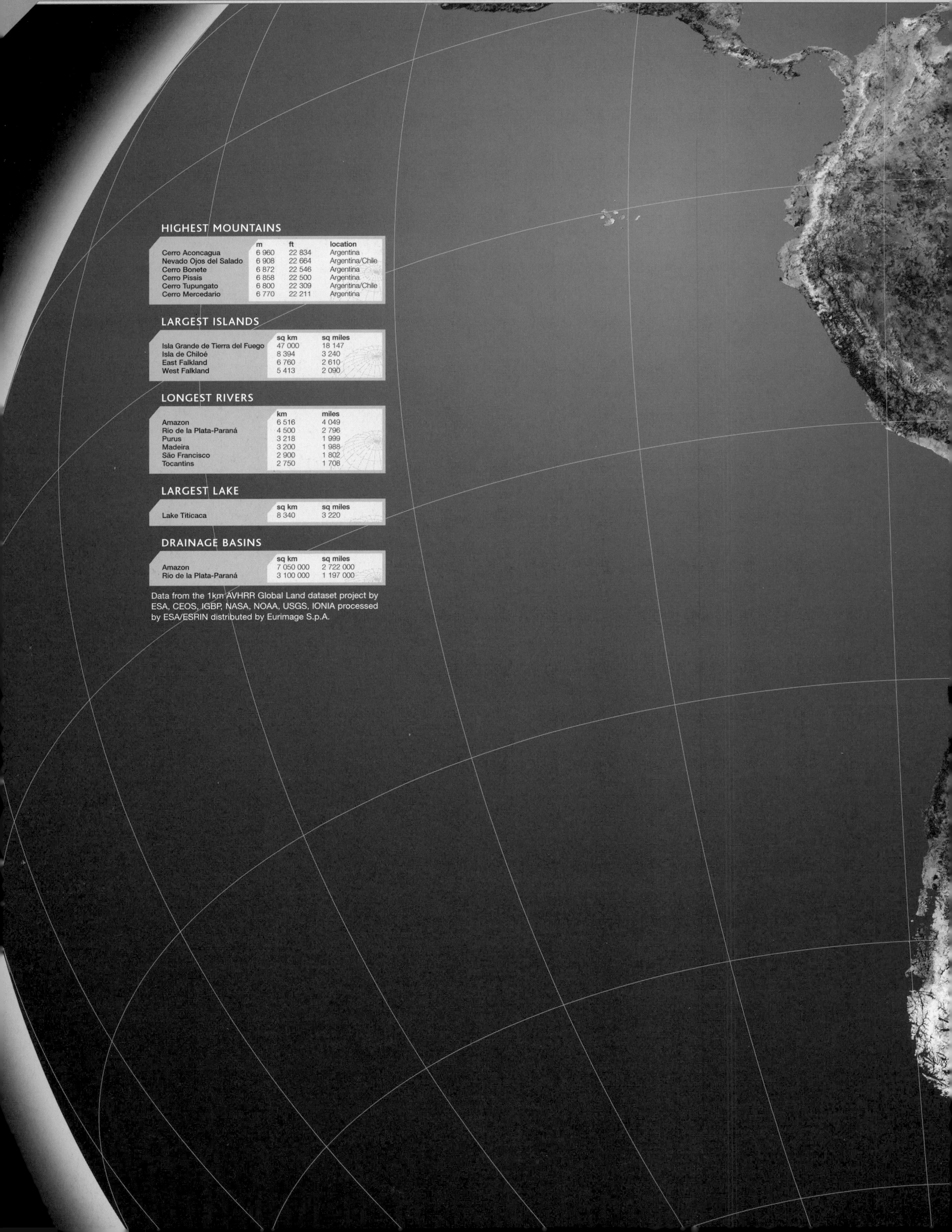

HIGHEST MOUNTAINS

	m	ft	location
Cerro Aconcagua	6 960	22 834	Argentina
Nevado Ojos del Salado	6 908	22 664	Argentina/Chile
Cerro Bonete	6 872	22 546	Argentina
Cerro Pissis	6 858	22 500	Argentina
Cerro Tupungato	6 800	22 309	Argentina/Chile
Cerro Mercedario	6 770	22 211	Argentina

LARGEST ISLANDS

	sq km	sq miles
Isla Grande de Tierra del Fuego	47 000	18 147
Isla de Chiloé	8 394	3 240
East Falkland	6 760	2 610
West Falkland	5 413	2 090

LONGEST RIVERS

	km	miles
Amazon	6 516	4 049
Rio de la Plata-Paraná	4 500	2 796
Purus	3 218	1 999
Madeira	3 200	1 988
São Francisco	2 900	1 802
Tocantins	2 750	1 708

LARGEST LAKE

	sq km	sq miles
Lake Titicaca	8 340	3 220

DRAINAGE BASINS

	sq km	sq miles
Amazon	7 050 000	2 722 000
Rio de la Plata-Paraná	3 100 000	1 197 000

Data from the 1km AVHRR Global Land dataset project by
ESA, CEOS, IGBP, NASA, NOAA, USGS, IONIA processed
by ESA/ESRIN distributed by Eurimage S.p.A.

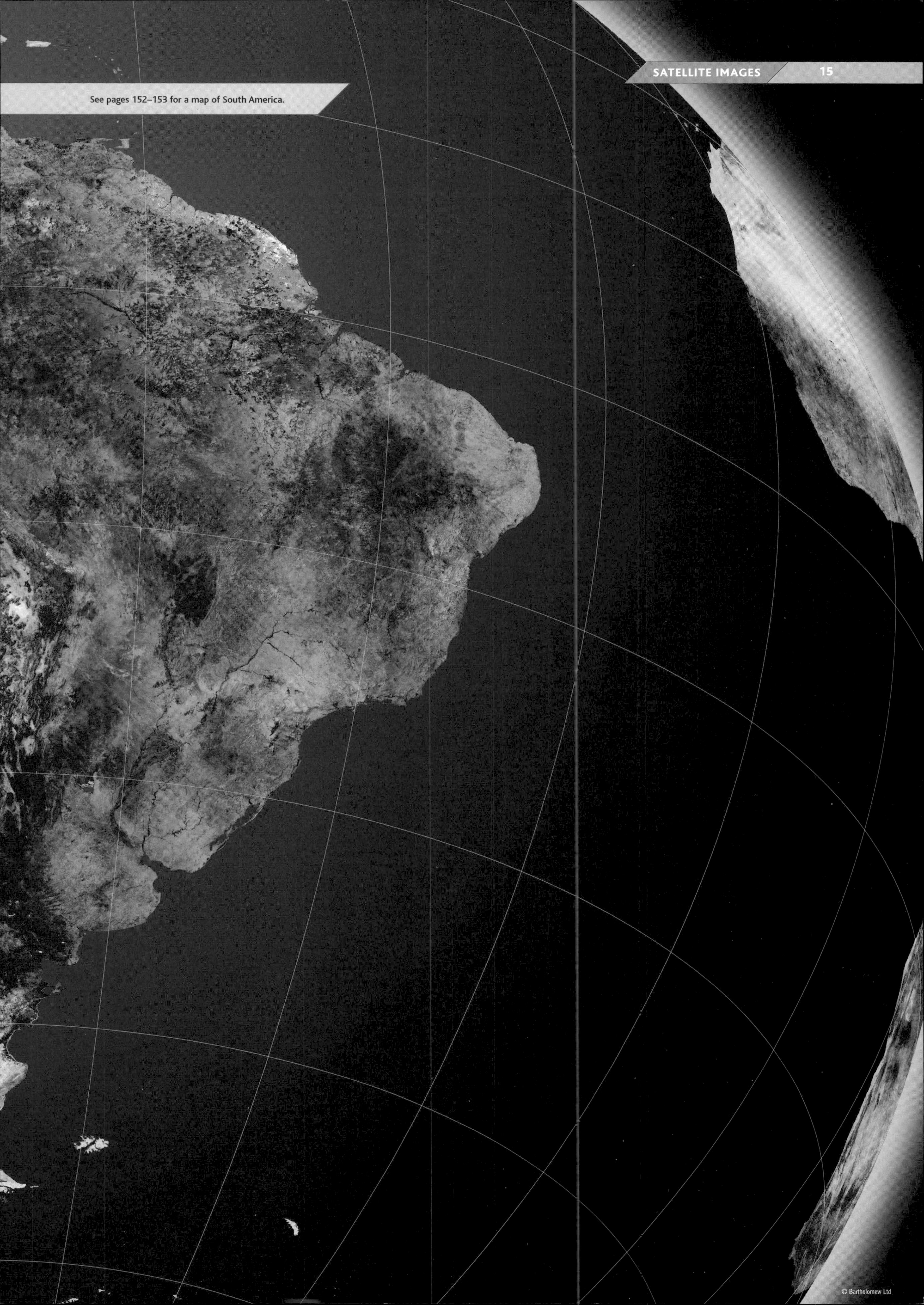

See pages 152–153 for a map of South America.

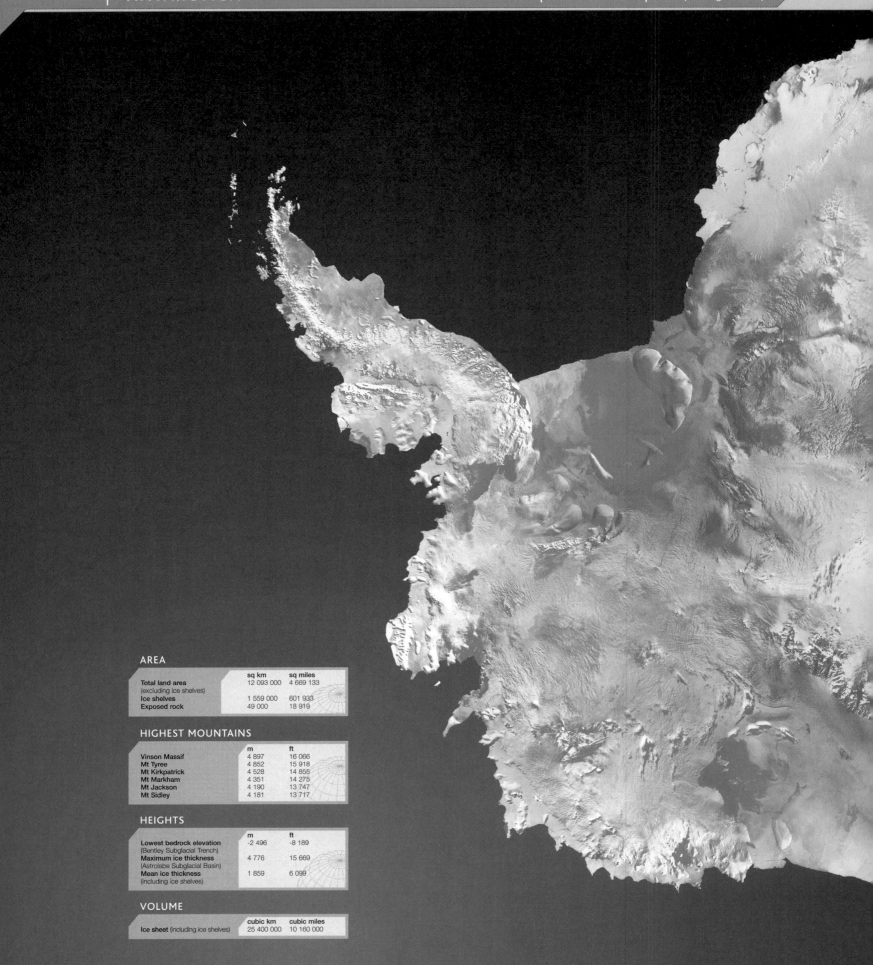

AREA

	sq km	sq miles
Total land area (excluding ice shelves)	12 093 000	4 669 133
Ice shelves	1 559 000	601 933
Exposed rock	49 000	18 919

HIGHEST MOUNTAINS

	m	ft
Vinson Massif	4 897	16 066
Mt Tyree	4 852	15 918
Mt Kirkpatrick	4 528	14 855
Mt Markham	4 351	14 275
Mt Jackson	4 190	13 747
Mt Sidley	4 181	13 717

HEIGHTS

	m	ft
Lowest bedrock elevation (Bentley Subglacial Trench)	-2 496	-8 189
Maximum ice thickness (Astrolabe Subglacial Basin)	4 776	15 669
Mean ice thickness (including ice shelves)	1 859	6 099

VOLUME

	cubic km	cubic miles
Ice sheet (including ice shelves)	25 400 000	10 160 000

See page 73 for a map of Antarctica.

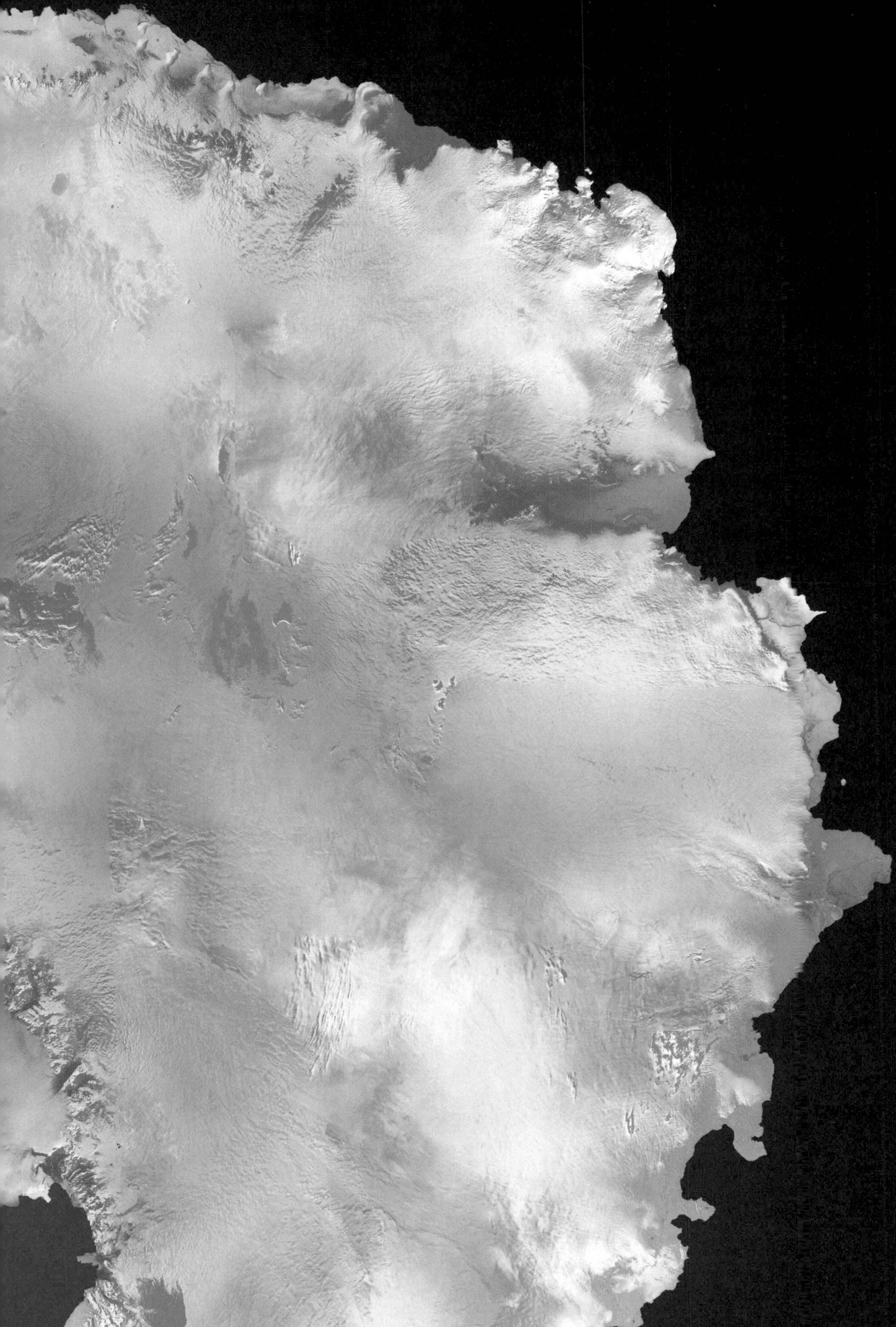

All independent countries and populated dependent and disputed territories are included in this list of the states and territories of the world; the list is arranged in alphabetical order by the conventional name form. For independent states, the full name is given below the conventional name, if this is different; for territories, the status is given. The capital city name is the same form as shown on the reference maps.

The statistics used for the area and population are the latest available and include estimates. The information on languages and religions is based on the latest information on 'de facto' speakers of the language or 'de facto' adherents to the religion. The information available on languages and religions varies greatly from country to country, some countries include questions in censuses others do not, in which case best estimates are used. The order of the languages and religions reflect their relative importance within the country; generally, languages or religions are included when more than one per cent of the population are estimated to be speakers or adherents.

Membership of selected international organizations is shown for each independent country. Dependent territories are not shown as having separate membership of these organizations.

ABBREVIATIONS

CURRENCIES

| CFA | Communauté Financière Africaine |
| CFP | Comptoirs Français du Pacifique |

ORGANIZATIONS

APEC	Asia-Pacific Economic Cooperation
ASEAN	Association of Southeast Asian Nations
CARICOM	Caribbean Community
CIS	Commonwealth of Independent States
Comm.	The Commonwealth
EU	European Union
OECD	Organization of Economic Cooperation and Development
OPEC	Organization of Petroleum Exporting Countries
SADC	Southern African Development Community
UN	United Nations

AFGHANISTAN
Islamic Emirate of Afghanistan

Area Sq Km	652 225
Area Sq Miles	251 825
Population	21 765 000
Capital	Kābul

Languages	Dari, Pushtu, Uzbek, Turkmen
Religions	Sunni Muslim, Shi'a Muslim
Currency	Afghani
Organizations	UN

Map page 85

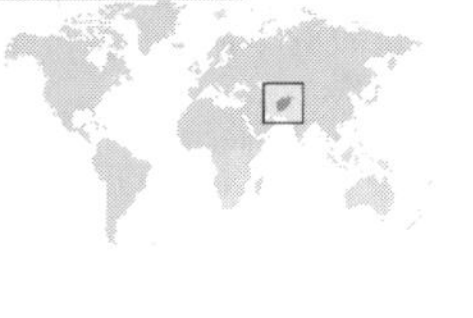

A landlocked country in central Asia with central highlands bordered by plains in the north and southwest and by the Hindu Kush mountains in the northeast. The climate is dry continental. Over the last twenty years war has disrupted the economy which was highly dependent on farming and livestock rearing. Most trade is with the former USSR, Pakistan and Iran.

ALBANIA
Republic of Albania

Area Sq Km	28 748
Area Sq Miles	11 100
Population	3 134 000
Capital	Tirana (Tiranë)

Languages	Albanian, Greek
Religions	Sunni Muslim, Albanian Orthodox, Roman Catholic
Currency	Lek
Organizations	UN

Map page 115

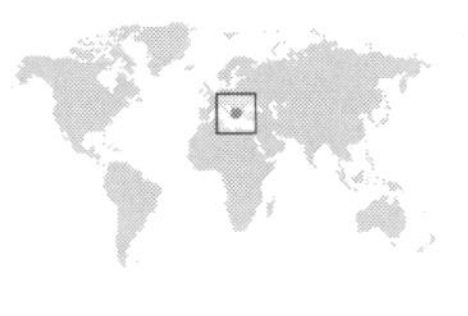

Albania lies in the Balkan Mountains in southeast Europe, bordering the Adriatic Sea. It is mountainous, with coastal plains where half the population live. The economy is based on agriculture and mining. Albania, one of the poorest countries in Europe, relies on foreign aid.

ALGERIA
Democratic and Popular Republic of Algeria

Area Sq Km	2 381 741
Area Sq Miles	919 595
Population	30 291 000
Capital	Algiers (Alger)

Languages	Arabic, French, Berber
Religions	Sunni Muslim
Currency	Algerian dinar
Organizations	OPEC, UN

Map page 120

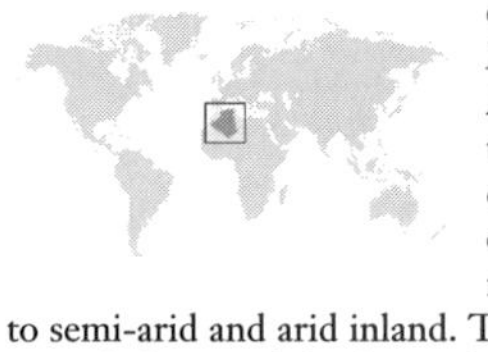

Algeria, the second largest country in Africa, lies on the Mediterranean coast of northwest Africa and extends southwards to the Atlas Mountains and the dry sandstone plateau and desert of the Sahara. The climate ranges from Mediterranean on the coast to semi-arid and arid inland. The most populated areas are the coastal plains and fertile northern slopes of the Atlas Mountains. Oil, natural gas and related products account for over ninety five per cent of export earnings. Agriculture employs about a quarter of the workforce, producing mainly food crops. The main trading partners are Italy, France and the USA.

American Samoa
United States Unincorporated Territory

Area Sq Km	197
Area Sq Miles	76
Population	68 000
Capital	Fagatogo

Languages	Samoan, English
Religions	Protestant, Roman Catholic
Currency	US dollar

Map page 67

Lying in the southwest Pacific Ocean, American Samoa consists of five main islands and two coral atolls. The largest island is Tutuila. Tuna and tuna products are the main exports and the main trading partner is the USA.

ANDORRA
Principality of Andorra

Area Sq Km	465
Area Sq Miles	180
Population	86 000
Capital	Andorra la Vella

Languages	Spanish, Catalan, French
Religions	Roman Catholic
Currency	Euro
Organizations	UN

Map page 111

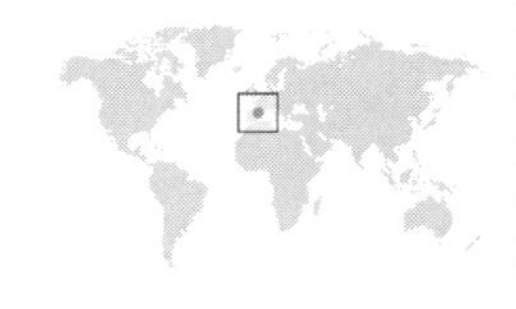

A landlocked state in southwest Europe, Andorra lies in the Pyrenees mountain range between France and Spain. It consists of deep valleys and gorges, surrounded by mountains. Tourism, encouraged by the development of ski resorts, is the mainstay of the economy. Banking is also an important economic activity.

ANGOLA
Republic of Angola

Area Sq Km	1 246 700
Area Sq Miles	481 354
Population	13 134 000
Capital	Luanda

Languages	Portuguese, Bantu, local languages
Religions	Roman Catholic, Protestant, traditional beliefs
Currency	Kwanza
Organizations	SADC, UN

Map page 120-121

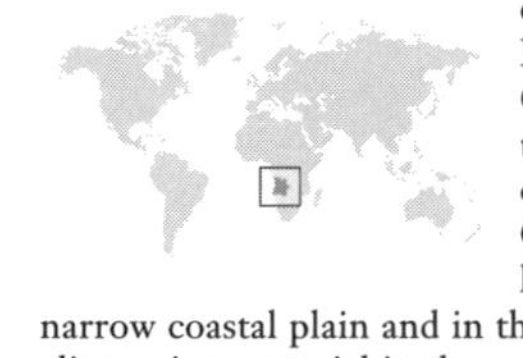

Angola lies on the Atlantic coast of southern central Africa. Its small northern province, Cabinda, is separated from the rest of the country by part of Democratic Republic of Congo. Much of Angola is high plateau. In the west is a narrow coastal plain and in the southwest is desert. The climate is equatorial in the north but desert in the south. Over eighty per cent of the population rely on subsistence agriculture. Angola is rich in minerals (particularly diamonds) and oil accounts for approximately ninety per cent of export earnings. The USA, South Korea and Portugal are its main trading partners.

Anguilla
United Kingdom Overseas Territory

Area Sq Km	155
Area Sq Miles	60
Population	11 000
Capital	The Valley

Languages	English
Religions	Protestant, Roman Catholic
Currency	East Caribbean dollar

Map page 149

Anguilla lies at the northern end of the Leeward Islands in the eastern Caribbean. Tourism and fishing form the basis of the economy.

ANTIGUA AND BARBUDA

Area Sq Km	442
Area Sq Miles	171
Population	65 000
Capital	St John's

Languages	English, Creole
Religions	Protestant, Roman Catholic
Currency	East Caribbean dollar
Organizations	CARICOM, Comm., UN

Map page 149

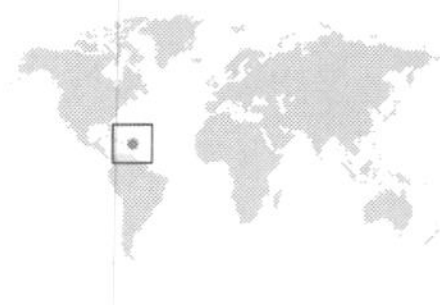

The state comprises the islands of Antigua, Barbuda and the tiny rocky outcrop of Redonda, in the Leeward Islands in the eastern Caribbean. Antigua, the largest and most populous island, is mainly hilly scrubland, with many beaches. The climate is tropical and the economy relies heavily on tourism. Most trade is with other eastern Caribbean states and the USA.

ARGENTINA
Argentine Republic

Area Sq Km	2 766 889
Area Sq Miles	1 068 302
Population	37 032 000
Capital	Buenos Aires

Languages	Spanish, Italian, Amerindian languages
Religions	Roman Catholic, Protestant
Currency	Argentinian peso
Organizations	UN

Map page 156

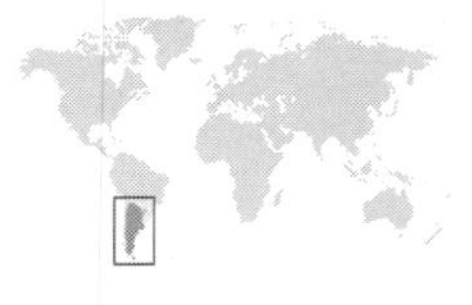

Argentina, the second largest country in South America, extends from Bolivia to Cape Horn and from the Andes mountains to the Atlantic Ocean. It has four geographical regions: the subtropical forests and swampland in the northeast; the temperate fertile plains or Pampas in the centre; the wooded foothills and valleys of the Andes in the west; and the cold, semi-arid plateaus of Patagonia, in the south. The highest mountain in South America, Cerro Aconcagua is in Argentina. Nearly ninety per cent of the population live in towns and cities. The country, which is remarkably self sufficient, is rich in natural resources including petroleum, natural gas, ores and precious metals. Agricultural products dominate exports, which also include motor vehicles and crude oil. Most trade is with Brazil and the USA.

ARMENIA
Republic of Armenia

Area Sq Km	29 800
Area Sq Miles	11 506
Population	3 787 000
Capital	Yerevan (Erevan)

Languages	Armenian, Azeri
Religions	Armenian Orthodox
Currency	Dram
Organizations	CIS, UN

Map page 81

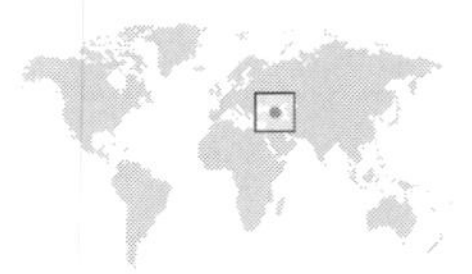

A landlocked state in southwest Asia, Armenia lies in the south of the Lesser Caucasus mountains. It is a mountainous country with a continental climate. One-third of the population live in the capital, Yerevan. Exports include diamonds, scrap metal and machinery. Many Armenians depend on remittances from nationals working abroad.

Aruba
Self-governing Netherlands Territory

Area Sq Km	193
Area Sq Miles	75
Population	101 000
Capital	Oranjestad

Languages	Papiamento, Dutch, English
Religions	Roman Catholic, Protestant
Currency	Aruban florin

Map page 157   The most southwesterly of the islands in the Lesser Antilles in the Caribbean, Aruba lies just off the coast of Colombia and Venezuela. Tourism, offshore finance and oil refining are the most important sectors of the economy. The USA is the main trading partner.

AUSTRALIA
Commonwealth of Australia

Area Sq Km	7 682 395
Area Sq Miles	2 966 189
Population	19 138 000
Capital	Canberra

Languages	English, Italian, Greek
Religions	Protestant, Roman Catholic, Orthodox
Currency	Australian dollar
Organizations	APEC, Comm., OECD, UN

Map page 68

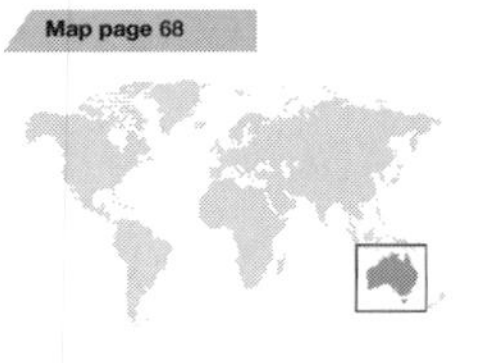

Australia, the world's sixth largest country, occupies the smallest, flattest and driest continent. The western half of the country is mostly arid plateaus, ridges and vast deserts. The central-eastern area comprises the lowlands of river systems draining into Lake Eyre, while to the east is the Great Dividing Range, a belt of ridges and plateaus running from Queensland to Victoria. Climatically, more than two-thirds of the country is arid or semi-

arid. The north is tropical monsoon, the east subtropical, and the southwest and southeast temperate. The majority of Australia's highly urbanized population live along the east, southeast and southwest coasts. Australia has vast mineral deposits and various sources of energy. It is among the world's leading producers of iron ore, bauxite, nickel, copper and uranium. It is a major producer of coal, and oil and natural gas are also being exploited. Although accounting for only five per cent of the workforce, agriculture continues to be an important sector of the economy with food and agricultural raw materials making up most of exports earnings. Fuel, ores and metals, and manufactured goods account for the remainder of exports. Japan and the USA are Australia's main trading partners.

Australian Capital Territory (Federal Territory)		
Area Sq Km (Sq Miles) 2 400 (927)	Population 313 400	Capital Canberra

New South Wales (State)		
Area Sq Km (Sq Miles) 801 600 (309 499)	Population 6 516 600	Capital Sydney

Northern Territory (Territory)		
Area Sq Km (Sq Miles) 1 346 200 (519 771)	Population 196 900	Capital Darwin

Queensland (State)		
Area Sq Km (Sq Miles) 1 727 200 (666 876)	Population 3 612 300	Capital Brisbane

South Australia (State)		
Area Sq Km (Sq Miles) 984 000 (379 925)	Population 1 501 400	Capital Adelaide

Tasmania (State)		
Area Sq Km (Sq Miles) 67 800 (26 178)	Population 470 300	Capital Hobart

Victoria (State)		
Area Sq Km (Sq Miles) 227 600 (87 877)	Population 4 816 100	Capital Melbourne

Western Australia (State)		
Area Sq Km (Sq Miles) 2 525 500 (975 101)	Population 1 904 100	Capital Perth

AUSTRIA
Republic of Austria

Area Sq Km 83 855	Languages German, Croatian, Turkish
Area Sq Miles 32 377	Religions Roman Catholic, Protestant
Population 8 080 000	Currency Euro
Capital Vienna (Wien)	Organizations EU, OECD, UN

Map page 112

Two-thirds of Austria, a landlocked state in central Europe, lies within the Alps, with low mountains to the north. The only lowlands are in the east. The Danube river valley in the northeast contains almost all the agricultural land and most of the population. Although the climate varies with altitude, in general summers are warm and winters cold with heavy snowfalls. Manufacturing industry and tourism are the most important sectors of the economy. Exports are dominated by manufactured goods. Germany is Austria's main trading partner.

AZERBAIJAN
Azerbaijani Republic

Area Sq Km 86 600	Languages Azeri, Armenian, Russian, Lezgian
Area Sq Miles 33 436	Religions Shi'a Muslim, Sunni Muslim, Russian and Armenian Orthodox
Population 8 041 000	Currency Azerbaijani manat
Capital Baku	Organizations CIS, UN

Map page 81

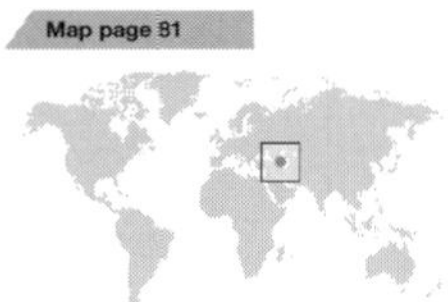

Azerbaijan lies to the southeast of the Caucasus mountains, on the Caspian Sea. Its region of Naxçıvan is separated from the rest of the country by part of Armenia. It has mountains in the northeast and west, valleys in the centre and a low coastal plain. The climate is continental. It is rich in energy and mineral resources. Oil production, onshore and offshore, is the main industry and the basis of heavy industries. Agriculture is important, with cotton and tobacco the main cash crops. War with Armenia has reduced output.

THE BAHAMAS
Commonwealth of The Bahamas

Area Sq Km 13 939	Languages English, Creole
Area Sq Miles 5 382	Religions Protestant, Roman Catholic
Population 304 000	Currency Bahamian dollar
Capital Nassau	Organizations CARICOM, Comm., UN

Map page 149

The Bahamas, an archipelago made up of approximately seven hundred islands and over two thousand cays, lies to the northeast of Cuba and east of the Florida coast of the USA. Twenty-two islands are inhabited, and

two-thirds of the population live on the main island of New Providence. The climate, warm for much of the year, experiences heavy rainfall in the summer. Tourism is the islands' main industry. Offshore banking, insurance and ship registration are major foreign exchange earners.

BAHRAIN
State of Bahrain

Area Sq Km 691	Languages Arabic, English
Area Sq Miles 267	Religions Shi'a Muslim, Sunni Muslim, Christian
Population 640 000	Currency Bahraini dinar
Capital Manama (Al Manāmah)	Organizations UN

Map page 84

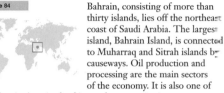

Bahrain, consisting of more than thirty islands, lies off the northeast coast of Saudi Arabia. The largest island, Bahrain Island, is connected to Muharraq and Sitrah islands by causeways. Oil production and processing are the main sectors of the economy. It is also one of the Gulf region's major banking and communications centres.

BANGLADESH
People's Republic of Bangladesh

Area Sq Km 143 998	Languages Bengali, English
Area Sq Miles 55 598	Religions Sunni Muslim, Hindu
Population 137 439 000	Currency Taka
Capital Dhaka (Dacca)	Organizations Comm., UN

Map page 89

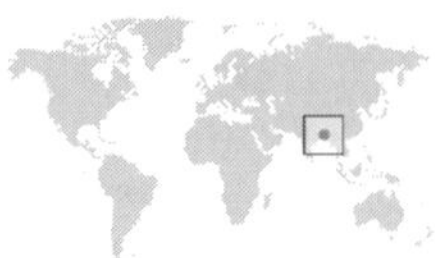

The south Asian state of Bangladesh is in the northeast of the Indian subcontinent, on the Bay of Bengal. It consists almost entirely of the low-lying alluvial plains and the deltas of the Ganges and Brahmaputra river. The southwest is swampy, with mangrove forests in the delta area. The north, northeast and southeast have low forested hills. Bangladesh is one of the world's most densely populated and least developed countries. The economy is based on agriculture although the garment industry is the main export sector. Floods and cyclones during the summer monsoon season frequently cause devastating flooding and crop destruction. The country relies on large-scale foreign aid and remittances from workers abroad.

BARBADOS

Area Sq Km 430	Languages English, Creole
Area Sq Miles 166	Religions Protestant, Roman Catholic
Population 267 000	Currency Barbados dollar
Capital Bridgetown	Organizations CARICOM, Comm., UN

Map page 149

The most easterly of the Caribbean islands, Barbados is small and densely populated. It has a tropical climate and is subject to hurricanes. The economy is based on tourism, financial services, light industries and sugar production.

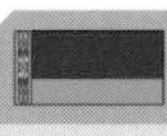

BELARUS
Republic of Belarus

Area Sq Km 207 600	Languages Belorussian, Russian
Area Sq Miles 80 155	Religions Belorussian Orthodox, Roman Catholic
Population 10 187 000	Currency Belarus rouble
Capital Minsk	Organizations CIS, UN

Map page 113

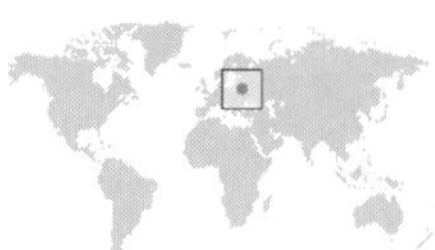

Belarus, a landlocked state in eastern Europe, consists of low hills and plains, with many lakes, rivers and, in the south, extensive marshes. Forests cover approximately one-third of the country. It has a continental climate. Agriculture contributes one-third of national income, with beef cattle and grains as the major products. Manufacturing industries produce a range of items, from construction equipment to textiles. The Russian Federation and Ukraine are the main trading partners.

BELGIUM
Kingdom of Belgium

Area Sq Km 30 520	Languages Dutch (Flemish), French (Walloon), German
Area Sq Miles 11 784	Religions Roman Catholic, Protestant
Population 10 249 000	Currency Euro
Capital Brussels (Bruxelles)	Organizations EU, OECD, UN

Map page 108

Belgium lies on the North Sea coast of western Europe. Beyond low sand dunes and a narrow belt of reclaimed land fertile plains extend to the Sambre-Meuse river valley. The land rises to the forested Ardennes plateau in the southeast.

Belgium has mild winters and cool summers. It is densely populated and has a highly urbanized population. With few mineral resources, Belgium imports raw materials for processing and manufacture. The agricultural sector is small, but provides for most food needs. A large services sector reflects Belgium's position as the home base for over eight hundred international institutions. The headquarters of the EU are in the capital, Brussels.

BELIZE

Area Sq Km 22 965	Languages English, Spanish, Mayan, Creole
Area Sq Miles 8 867	Religions Roman Catholic, Protestant
Population 226 000	Currency Belize dollar
Capital Belmopan	Organizations CARICOM, Comm., UN

Map page 151

Belize lies on the Caribbean coast of central America and includes numerous cays and a large barrier reef offshore. Belize's coastal areas are flat and swampy. To the southwest are the Maya Mountains. Tropical jungle covers much of the country and the climate is humid tropical, tempered by sea breezes. The economy is based primarily on agriculture, forestry and fishing. Exports include raw sugar, orange concentrate and bananas.

BENIN
Republic of Benin

Area Sq Km 112 620	Languages French, Fon, Yoruba, Adja, local languages
Area Sq Miles 43 483	Religions Traditional beliefs, Roman Catholic, Sunni Muslim
Population 6 272 000	Currency CFA franc
Capital Porto-Novo	Organizations UN

Map page 120

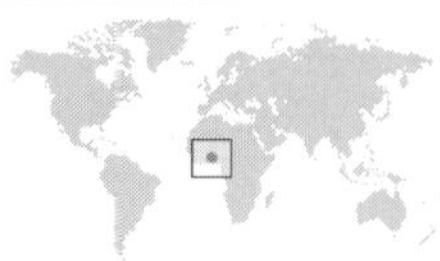

Benin is in west Africa, on the Gulf of Guinea. The climate is tropical in the north, equatorial in the south. The economy is based mainly on agriculture and transit trade. Agricultural products account for two-thirds of export earnings. Oil, produced offshore, is also a major export.

Bermuda
United Kingdom Overseas Territory

Area Sq Km 54	Languages English
Area Sq Miles 21	Religions Protestant, Roman Catholic
Population 63 000	Currency Bermuda dollar
Capital Hamilton	

Map page 149   In the Atlantic Ocean to the east of the USA, Bermuda comprises a group of small islands. The climate is warm and humid. The economy is based on tourism, insurance and shipping.

BHUTAN
Kingdom of Bhutan

Area Sq Km 46 620	Languages Dzongkha, Nepali, Assamese
Area Sq Miles 18 000	Religions Buddhist, Hindu
Population 2 085 000	Currency Ngultrum, Indian rupee
Capital Thimphu	Organizations UN

Map page 89

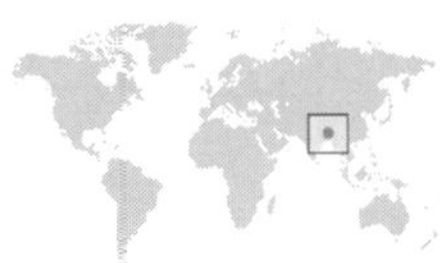

Bhutan lies in the eastern Himalaya mountains, between China and India. It is mountainous in the north, with fertile valleys. The climate ranges between permanently cold in the far north and subtropical in the south. Most of the population is involved in livestock raising and subsistence farming. Bhutan is the world's largest producer of cardamom and tourism is an increasingly important foreign currency earner.

BOLIVIA
Republic of Bolivia

Area Sq Km 1 098 581	Languages Spanish, Quechua, Aymara
Area Sq Miles 424 164	Religions Roman Catholic, Protestant, Baha'i
Population 8 329 000	Currency Boliviano
Capital La Paz/Sucre	Organizations UN

Map page 154

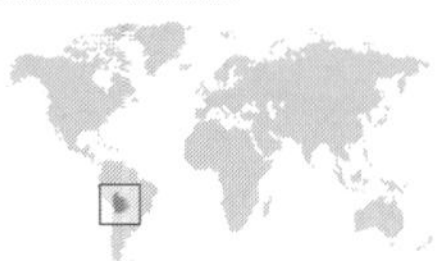

Bolivia is a landlocked state in central South America. Most Bolivians live in the high plateau within the Andes mountains. The lowlands range between dense rainforest in the northeast and semi-arid grasslands in the southeast. Bolivia is rich in minerals (zinc, tin and gold) and sales generate approximately half of export income. Natural gas, gold, timber and soya beans are also exported. The USA is the main trading partner.

BOSNIA-HERZEGOVINA
Republic of Bosnia and Herzegovina

Area Sq Km	51 130	Languages	Bosnian, Serbian, Croatian
Area Sq Miles	19 741	Religions	Sunni Muslim, Serbian Orthodox, Roman Catholic, Protestant
Population	3 977 000	Currency	Marka
Capital	Sarajevo	Organizations	UN

Map page 114-115

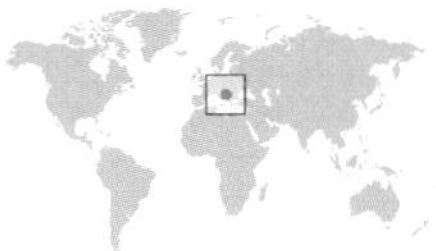

Bosnia-Herzegovina lies in the western Balkan Mountains of southern Europe, on the Adriatic Sea. It is mountainous, with ridges running northwest-southeast. The main lowlands are around the Sava valley in the north. Summers are warm, but winters can be very cold. The economy relies heavily on overseas aid.

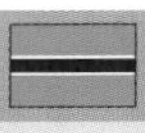

BOTSWANA
Republic of Botswana

Area Sq Km	581 370	Languages	English, Setswana, Shona, local languages
Area Sq Miles	224 468	Religions	Traditional beliefs, Protestant, Roman Catholic
Population	1 541 000	Currency	Pula
Capital	Gaborone	Organizations	Comm., SADC, UN

Map page 123

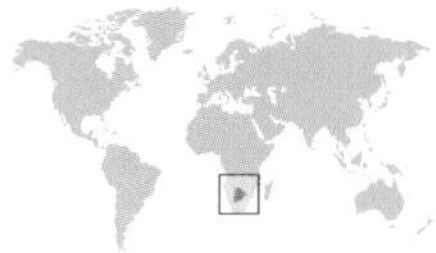

Botswana is a landlocked state in southern Africa. Over half of the country lies within the Kalahari Desert, with swamps to the north and salt-pans to the northeast. Most of the population live near the eastern border. The climate is subtropical, but drought-prone. The economy was founded on cattle rearing, and although beef remains an important export, the economy is now based on mining. Diamonds account for seventy per cent of export earnings. Copper-nickel matte is also exported. Most trade is with members of the Southern African Customs Union.

BRAZIL
Federative Republic of Brazil

Area Sq Km	8 547 379	Languages	Portuguese
Area Sq Miles	3 300 161	Religions	Roman Catholic, Protestant
Population	170 406 000	Currency	Real
Capital	Brasília	Organizations	UN

Map page 154-155

Brazil, in eastern South America, covers almost half of the continent, and is the world's fifth largest country. The northwest contains the vast basin of the Amazon. The centre west is largely a vast plateau of savanna and rock escarpments. The northeast is mostly semi-arid plateaus, while to the east and south are rugged mountains, fertile valleys and narrow, fertile coastal plains. The Amazon basin is hot, humid and wet; the rest of Brazil is cooler and drier, with seasonal variations. The northeast is drought-prone. Most Brazilians live in urban areas along the coast and on the central plateau. Brazil has well-developed agricultural, mining, and service sectors and the economy is larger than that of all other South American countries combined. Brazil is the world's largest producer of coffee and other agricultural crops include grains and sugar cane. Mineral production includes iron, aluminium, and gold. Manufactured goods include food products, transport equipment, machinery and industrial chemicals. The main trading partners are the USA and Argentina. Despite its natural wealth Brazil has a large external debt and a growing poverty gap.

BRUNEI
State of Brunei Darussalam

Area Sq Km	5 765	Languages	Malay, English, Chinese
Area Sq Miles	2 226	Religions	Sunni Muslim, Buddhist, Christian
Population	328 000	Currency	Brunei dollar
Capital	Bandar Seri Begawan	Organizations	APEC, ASEAN, Comm., UN

Map page 99

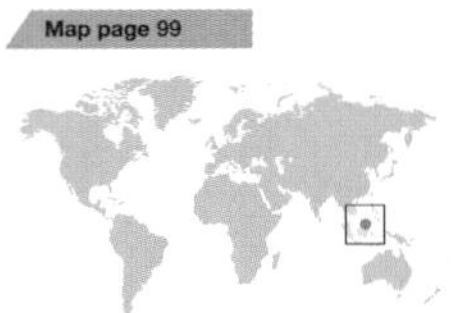

The southeast Asian oil-rich state of Brunei lies on the northwest coast of the island of Borneo, in the South China Sea. Its two enclaves are surrounded by the Malaysian state of Sarawak. Tropical rainforest covers over two-thirds of Brunei. The economy is dominated by oil and gas industries.

BULGARIA
Republic of Bulgaria

Area Sq Km	110 994	Languages	Bulgarian, Turkish, Romany, Macedonian
Area Sq Miles	42 855	Religions	Bulgarian Orthodox, Sunni Muslim
Population	7 949 000	Currency	Lev
Capital	Sofia (Sofiya)	Organizations	UN

Map page 115

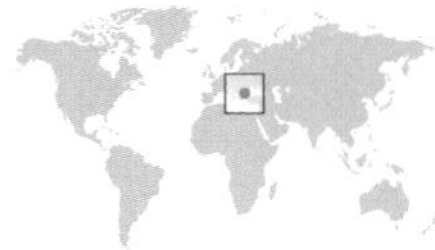

Bulgaria, in south Europe, borders the western shore of the Black Sea. The Balkan Mountains separate the Danube plains in the north from the Rhodope Mountains and the lowlands in the south. The economy has a strong agricultural base. Manufacturing industries include machinery, consumer goods, chemicals and metals. Most trade is with the Russian Federation, Italy and Germany.

BURKINA
Democratic Republic of Burkina Faso

Area Sq Km	274 200	Languages	French, Moore (Mossi), Fulani, local languages
Area Sq Miles	105 869	Religions	Sunni Muslim, traditional beliefs, Roman Catholic
Population	11 535 000	Currency	CFA franc
Capital	Ouagadougou	Organizations	UN

Map page 120

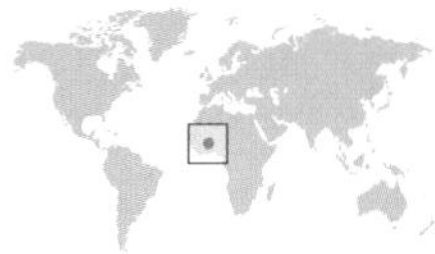

Burkina, a landlocked country in west Africa, lies within the Sahara desert to the north and the semi-arid savanna to the south. Rainfall is erratic and droughts are common. Livestock rearing and farming are the main economic activities and cotton, livestock, groundnuts and some minerals are exported. Burkina relies heavily on foreign aid, and is one of the poorest and least developed countries in the world.

BURUNDI
Republic of Burundi

Area Sq Km	27 835	Languages	Kirundi (Hutu, Tutsi), French
Area Sq Miles	10 747	Religions	Roman Catholic, traditional beliefs, Protestant
Population	6 356 000	Currency	Burundian franc
Capital	Bujumbura	Organizations	UN

Map page 122

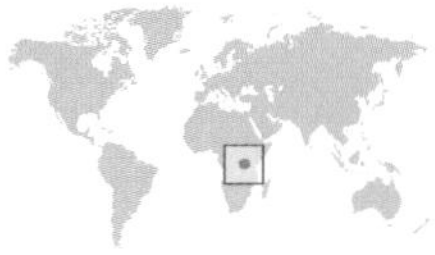

The densely populated east African state of Burundi consists of high plateaus rising from the shores of Lake Tanganyika in the southwest. It has a tropical climate and depends upon subsistence farming. Coffee is its main export and its main trading partners are Germany and Belgium.

CAMBODIA
Kingdom of Cambodia

Area Sq Km	181 000	Languages	Khmer, Vietnamese
Area Sq Miles	69 884	Religions	Buddhist, Roman Catholic, Sunni Muslim
Population	13 104 000	Currency	Riel
Capital	Phnom Penh	Organizations	ASEAN, UN

Map page 98

Cambodia lies in Southeast Asia, on the Gulf of Thailand and occupies the Mekong river basin, with the Tonle Sap (Great Lake) at its centre. The climate is tropical monsoon and forests cover half the country. Most of the population live on the plains and are engaged in farming (chiefly rice growing), fishing and forestry. The economy is recovering slowly following decades of civil war.

CAMEROON
Republic of Cameroon

Area Sq Km	475 442	Languages	French, English, Fang, Bamileke, local languages
Area Sq Miles	183 569	Religions	Roman Catholic, traditional beliefs, Sunni Muslim, Protestant
Population	14 876 000	Currency	CFA franc
Capital	Yaoundé	Organizations	UN

Map page 120-121

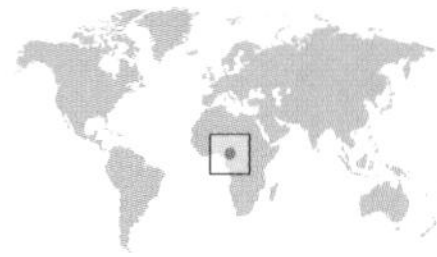

Cameroon is in west Africa, on the Gulf of Guinea. The coastal plains, southern and central plateaus are covered with tropical forest. Despite oil resources and favourable agricultural conditions Cameroon still faces problems of underdevelopment. Oil, timber and cocoa are the main exports and France is its main trading partner.

CANADA

Area Sq Km	9 970 610	Languages	English, French
Area Sq Miles	3 849 674	Religions	Roman Catholic, Protestant, Eastern Orthodox, Jewish
Population	30 757 000	Currency	Canadian dollar
Capital	Ottawa	Organizations	APEC, Comm., OECD, UN

Map page 128-129

The world's second largest country, Canada covers the northern two-fifths of North America and has coastlines on the Atlantic, Arctic and Pacific Oceans. In the west are the Coast Mountains, interior plateaus and the Rocky Mountains. In the centre lie the fertile prairies. Further east, covering about half the total land area, is the Canadian Shield, a relatively flat area of lowlands around Hudson Bay extending to Labrador on the east coast. The Shield is bordered to the south by the fertile Great Lakes-St Lawrence lowlands. In the far north climatic conditions are polar, while the rest of Canada has a continental climate. Most Canadians live in the urban areas around the Great Lakes-St Lawrence basin. Canada is rich in mineral and energy resources. Five per cent of the land is arable. Canada is among the world's leading producers of wheat, a leading exporter of wood from its vast coniferous forests, and of fish and seafood from its rich Atlantic and Pacific fishing grounds. It is a top producer of nickel, uranium, copper, iron ore, zinc and other minerals, as well as oil and natural gas. Its abundant raw materials are the basis for manufacturing industries. Main exports are machinery, motor vehicles, oil, timber, newsprint and paper, wood pulp and wheat. Since the 1989 free trade agreement with the USA and the 1994 North America Free Trade Agreement, trade with the USA has grown and now accounts for approximately seventy five per cent of imports and approximately eighty five per cent of exports.

Alberta (Province)		
Area Sq Km (Sq Miles) 661 190 (255 287)	Population 2 997 200	Capital Edmonton

British Columbia (Province)		
Area Sq Km (Sq Miles) 947 800 (365 948)	Population 4 063 800	Capital Victoria

Manitoba (Province)		
Area Sq Km (Sq Miles) 649 950 (250 947)	Population 1 147 900	Capital Winnipeg

New Brunswick (Province)		
Area Sq Km (Sq Miles) 73 440 (28 355)	Population 756 600	Capital Fredericton

Newfoundland (Province)		
Area Sq Km (Sq Miles) 405 720 (156 649)	Population 538 800	Capital St John's

Northwest Territories (Territory)		
Area Sq Km (Sq Miles) 1 432 320 (553 022)	Population 42 100	Capital Yellowknife

Nova Scotia (Province)		
Area Sq Km (Sq Miles) 55 490 (21 425)	Population 941 000	Capital Halifax

Nunavut (Territory)		
Area Sq Km (Sq Miles) 1 994 000 (769 888)	Population 27 700	Capital Iqaluit

Ontario (Province)		
Area Sq Km (Sq Miles) 1 068 580 (412 581)	Population 11 669 300	Capital Toronto

Prince Edward Island (Province)		
Area Sq Km (Sq Miles) 5 660 (2 185)	Population 138 900	Capital Charlottetown

Québec (Province)		
Area Sq Km (Sq Miles) 1 540 680 (594 860)	Population 7 372 400	Capital Québec

Saskatchewan (Province)		
Area Sq Km (Sq Miles) 652 330 (251 866)	Population 1 023 600	Capital Regina

Yukon Territory (Territory)		
Area Sq Km (Sq Miles) 483 450 (186 661)	Population 30 700	Capital Whitehorse

CAPE VERDE
Republic of Cape Verde

Area Sq Km	4 033	Languages	Portuguese, Creole
Area Sq Miles	1 557	Religions	Roman Catholic, Protestant
Population	427 000	Currency	Cape Verde escudo
Capital	Praia	Organizations	UN

Map page 120

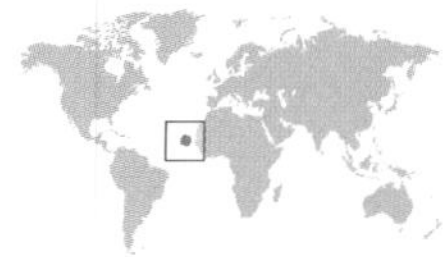

Cape Verde is a group of semi-arid volcanic islands lying off the coast of west Africa. The economy is based on fishing and subsistence farming, but relies on emigrant workers' remittances and foreign aid.

Cayman Islands
United Kingdom Overseas Territory

Area Sq Km	259	Languages	English
Area Sq Miles	100	Religions	Protestant, Roman Catholic
Population	38 000	Currency	Cayman Islands dollar
Capital	George Town		

Map page 149   This group of islands in the Caribbean, northwest of Jamaica has three main islands: Grand Cayman, Little Cayman and Cayman Brac. They form one of the world's major offshore financial centres. Tourism is also important to the economy.

CENTRAL AFRICAN REPUBLIC

Area Sq Km	622 436	Languages	French, Sango, Banda, Baya, local languages
Area Sq Miles	240 324	Religions	Protestant, Roman Catholic, traditional beliefs, Sunni Muslim
Population	3 717 000	Currency	CFA franc
Capital	Bangui	Organizations	UN

Map page 121

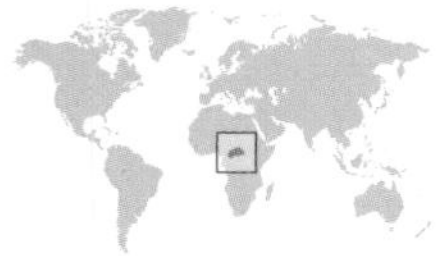

A landlocked country in central Africa, the Central African Republic is mainly savanna plateau, drained by the Ubangi and Chari river systems, with mountains to the east and west. The climate is tropical with high rainfall. Most of the population live in the south and west, and a majority of the workforce is involved in subsistence farming. Some cotton, coffee, tobacco and timber are exported, but diamonds account for approximately half of export earnings.

CHAD
Republic of Chad

Area Sq Km	1 284 000	Languages	Arabic, French, Sara, local languages
Area Sq Miles	495 755	Religions	Sunni Muslim, Roman Catholic, Protestant, traditional beliefs
Population	7 885 000	Currency	CFA franc
Capital	Ndjamena	Organizations	UN

Map page 121

Chad is a landlocked state of north central Africa. It consists of plateaus, the Tibesti mountains in the north and the Lake Chad basin in the west. Climatic conditions range from desert in the north to tropical forest in the southwest. The largely rural population live in the south and near Lake Chad. With few natural resources, Chad relies on subsistence farming, exports of raw cotton and foreign aid. The main trading partners are France, Portugal and Cameroon.

CHILE
Republic of Chile

Area Sq Km	756 945	Languages	Spanish, Amerindian languages
Area Sq Miles	292 258	Religions	Roman Catholic, Protestant
Population	15 211 000	Currency	Chilean peso
Capital	Santiago	Organizations	APEC, UN

Map page 156

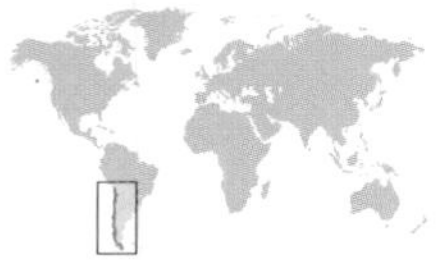

Chile lies along the Pacific coast of the southern half of South America. Between the Andes in the east and the lower coastal ranges, is a central valley, with a mild climate, where most Chileans live. To the north is the arid Atacama Desert, to the south is cold, wet forested grassland. Chile has considerable mineral resources and is the world's leading exporter of copper. Nitrates, molybdenum, gold and iron are also important. Agriculture (particularly viticulture), forestry and fishing are the most important activities.

CHINA
People's Republic of China

Area Sq Km	9 584 492	Languages	Mandarin, Wu, Cantonese, Hsiang, regional languages
Area Sq Miles	3 700 593	Religions	Confucian, Taoist, Buddhist, Christian, Sunni Muslim
Population	1 260 137 000	Currency	Yuan, Hong Kong dollar, Macau pataca
Capital	Beijing (Peking)	Organizations	APEC, UN

Map page 90

China, the world's most populous and fourth largest country, occupies almost the whole of east Asia, borders fourteen states and has coastlines on the Yellow, East China and South China Seas. It has an amazing variety of landscapes. The southwest contains the high Plateau of Tibet, flanked by the Himalaya and Kunlun Shan mountains. The north is mountainous with arid basins and extends from the Tien Shan and Altai Mountains and the vast Taklimakan in the west to the plateau and Gobi desert in the centre-east. East China is predominantly lowland and is divided broadly into the basins of the Yellow River in the north, the Yangtze in the centre and the Xi Jiang in the southeast. Climatic conditions and vegetation are as diverse as the topography: much of the country experiences temperate conditions, while southwest China has an extreme mountain climate, and the southeast enjoys a moist, warm subtropical climate. Nearly seventy per cent of China's huge population live in rural areas, and agriculture employs approximately half of the working population. The main crops are rice, wheat, soya beans, peanuts, cotton, tobacco and hemp. China is rich in coal, oil and natural gas and has the world's largest potential in hydroelectric power. It is a major world producer of iron ore, molybdenum, copper, asbestos and gold. Economic reforms from the early 1980's led to an explosion in manufacturing development concentrated on the 'coastal economic open region'. The main exports are machinery, textiles, footwear, toys and sports goods. Japan and the USA are the main trading partners.

Anhui (Province)
Area Sq Km (Sq Miles)	139 000 (53 668)	Population 62 370 000	Capital Hefei

Beijing (Municipality)
Area Sq Km (Sq Miles)	16 800 (6 487)	Population 12 570 000	Capital Beijing (Peking)

Chongqing (Municipality)
Area Sq Km (Sq Miles)	23 000 (8 880)	Population 30 750 000	Capital Chongqing

Fujian (Province)
Area Sq Km (Sq Miles)	121 400 (46 873)	Population 33 160 000	Capital Fuzhou

Gansu (Province)
Area Sq Km (Sq Miles)	453 700 (175 175)	Population 25 430 000	Capital Lanzhou

Guangdong (Province)
Area Sq Km (Sq Miles)	178 000 (68 726)	Population 72 700 000	Capital Guangzhou

Guangxi Zhuangzu Zizhiqu (Autonomous Region)
Area Sq Km (Sq Miles)	236 000 (91 120)	Population 47 130 000	Capital Nanning

Guizhou (Province)
Area Sq Km (Sq Miles)	176 000 (67 954)	Population 37 100 000	Capital Guiyang

Hainan (Province)
Area Sq Km (Sq Miles)	34 000 (13 127)	Population 7 620 000	Capital Haikou

Hebei (Province)
Area Sq Km (Sq Miles)	187 700 (72 471)	Population 66 140 000	Capital Shijiazhuang

Heilongjiang (Province)
Area Sq Km (Sq Miles)	454 600 (175 522)	Population 37 920 000	Capital Harbin

Henan (Province)
Area Sq Km (Sq Miles)	167 000 (64 479)	Population 93 870 000	Capital Zhengzhou

Hong Kong (Special Administrative Region)
Area Sq Km (Sq Miles)	1 075 (415)	Population 6 606 500	Capital Hong Kong

Hubei (Province)
Area Sq Km (Sq Miles)	185 900 (71 776)	Population 59 380 000	Capital Wuhan

Hunan (Province)
Area Sq Km (Sq Miles)	210 000 (81 081)	Population 65 320 000	Capital Changsha

Jiangsu (Province)
Area Sq Km (Sq Miles)	102 600 (39 614)	Population 72 130 000	Capital Nanjing

Jiangxi (Province)
Area Sq Km (Sq Miles)	166 900 (64 440)	Population 42 310 000	Capital Nanchang

Jilin (Province)
Area Sq Km (Sq Miles)	187 000 (72 201)	Population 26 580 000	Capital Changchun

Liaoning (Province)
Area Sq Km (Sq Miles)	147 400 (56 911)	Population 41 710 000	Capital Shenyang

Macau (Special Administrative Region)
Area Sq Km (Sq Miles)	17 (7)	Population 437 500	Capital Macau

Nei Mongol Zizhiqu Inner Mongolia (Autonomous Region)
Area Sq Km (Sq Miles)	1 183 000 (456 759)	Population 23 620 000	Capital Hohhot

Ningxia Huizu Zizhiqu (Autonomous Region)
Area Sq Km (Sq Miles)	66 400 (25 637)	Population 5 430 000	Capital Yinchuan

Qinghai (Province)
Area Sq Km (Sq Miles)	721 000 (278 380)	Population 5 100 000	Capital Xining

Shaanxi (Province)
Area Sq Km (Sq Miles)	205 600 (79 383)	Population 36 180 000	Capital Xi'an

Shandong (Province)
Area Sq Km (Sq Miles)	153 300 (59 189)	Population 88 830 000	Capital Jinan

Shanghai (Municipality)
Area Sq Km (Sq Miles)	6 300 (2 432)	Population 14 740 000	Capital Shanghai

Shanxi (Province)
Area Sq Km (Sq Miles)	156 300 (60 348)	Population 32 040 000	Capital Taiyuan

Sichuan (Province)
Area Sq Km (Sq Miles)	569 000 (219 692)	Population 85 500 000	Capital Chengdu

Tianjin (Municipality)
Area Sq Km (Sq Miles)	11 300 (4 363)	Population 9 590 000	Capital Tianjin

Xinjiang Uygur Zizhiqu Sinkiang (Autonomous Region)
Area Sq Km (Sq Miles)	1 600 000 (617 763)	Population 17 740 000	Capital Ürümqi

Xizang Zizhiqu Tibet (Autonomous Region)
Area Sq Km (Sq Miles)	1 228 400 (474 288)	Population 2 560 000	Capital Lhasa

Yunnan (Province)
Area Sq Km (Sq Miles)	394 000 (152 124)	Population 41 920 000	Capital Kunming

Zhejiang (Province)
Area Sq Km (Sq Miles)	101 800 (39 305)	Population 44 750 000	Capital Hangzhou

Christmas Island
Australian External Territory

Area Sq Km	135	Languages	English
Area Sq Miles	52	Religions	Buddhist, Sunni Muslim, Protestant, Roman Catholic
Population	2 195	Currency	Australian dollar
Capital	The Settlement		

Map page 91   The island is situated in the east of the Indian Ocean, to the south of Indonesia. The economy was formerly based on phosphate extraction, although reserves are nearly depleted. Tourism is developing and is the major employer.

Cocos Islands (Keeling Islands)
Australian External Territory

Area Sq Km	14	Languages	English
Area Sq Miles	5	Religions	Sunni Muslim, Christian
Population	637	Currency	Australian dollar
Capital	West Island		

Map page 91   The Cocos Islands consist of two coral atolls in the east Indian Ocean between Sri Lanka and Australia. Most of the population live on West Island and Home Island. Coconuts are the only cash crop and the main export.

COLOMBIA
Republic of Colombia

Area Sq Km	1 141 748	Languages	Spanish, Amerindian languages
Area Sq Miles	440 831	Religions	Roman Catholic, Protestant
Population	42 105 000	Currency	Colombian peso
Capital	Bogotá	Organizations	APEC, UN

Map page 157

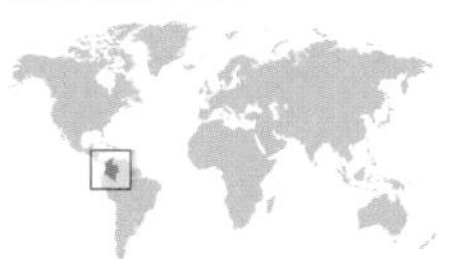

A state in northwest South America, Colombia has coastlines on the Pacific Ocean and the Caribbean Sea. Behind coastal plains lie three ranges of the Andes mountains, separated by high valleys and plateaus where most Colombians live. To the southeast are grasslands and the forests of the Amazon. Colombia has a tropical climate, although temperatures vary with altitude. Only five per cent of land is cultivable. Coffee (Colombia is the world's second largest producer), sugar, bananas, cotton and flowers are exported. Coal, nickel, gold, silver, platinum and emeralds (Colombia is the world's largest producer) are mined. Industry involves processing minerals and agricultural produce. Oil and its products are the main export and the main trading partner is the USA.

COMOROS
Federal Islamic Republic of the Comoros

Area Sq Km	1 862	Languages	Comorian, French, Arabic
Area Sq Miles	719	Religions	Sunni Muslim, Roman Catholic
Population	706 000	Currency	Comoros franc
Capital	Moroni	Organizations	UN

Map page 123

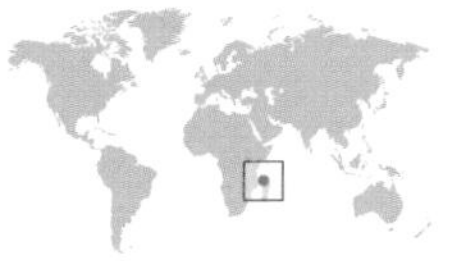

The state, in the Indian Ocean, off the east African coast comprises the three volcanic islands of Njazidja, Nzwani and Mwali, and some coral atolls. These tropical islands are mountainous, with poor soils and few natural resources. Subsistence farming predominates. Vanilla, cloves and ylang-ylang are exported and the economy relies heavily on workers' remittances from abroad.

© Bartholomew Ltd

CONGO
Republic of the Congo

Area Sq Km	342 000	
Area Sq Miles	132 047	Languages French, Kongo, Monokutuba, local languages
Population	3 018 000	Religions Roman Catholic, Protestant, traditional beliefs, Sunni Muslim
Capital	Brazzaville	Currency CFA franc
		Organizations UN

Map page 122

Congo, in central Africa, is mostly forest or savanna-covered plateaus drained by the Ubangi-Congo river systems. Sand dunes and lagoons line the short Atlantic coast. The climate is hot and tropical. Most Congolese live in the southern third of the country. Half of the workforce are farmers, growing food crops and cash crops including sugar, coffee, cocoa and oil palms. Oil and timber are the mainstays of the economy and oil makes up over fifty per cent of export revenues.

CONGO, DEMOCRATIC REPUBLIC OF

Area Sq Km	2 345 410	Languages French, Lingala, Swahili, Kongo, local languages
Area Sq Miles	905 568	
Population	50 948 000	Religions Christian, Sunni Muslim
Capital	Kinshasa	Currency Congolese franc
		Organizations SADC, UN

Map page 122-123

The central African state consists of the basin of the Congo river flanked by plateaus, with high mountain ranges to the east and a short Atlantic coastline to the west. The climate is tropical with rainforest close to the Equator and savanna to the north and south. Congo has fertile land which produces a range of food crops and cash crops, chiefly coffee. It has vast mineral resources with copper, cobalt and diamonds being the most important.

Cook Islands
Self-governing New Zealand Territory

Area Sq Km	293	Languages English, Maori
Area Sq Miles	113	Religions Protestant, Roman Catholic
Population	20 000	Currency New Zealand dollar
Capital	Avarua	

Map page 67

 These consist of groups of coral atolls and volcanic islands in the southwest Pacific Ocean. The main island is Rarotonga. Distance from foreign markets and few natural resources hinder development.

COSTA RICA
Republic of Costa Rica

Area Sq Km	51 100	Languages Spanish
Area Sq Miles	19 730	Religions Roman Catholic, Protestant
Population	4 024 000	Currency Costa Rican colón
Capital	San José	Organizations UN

Map page 150

Costa Rica, in Central America, has coastlines on the Caribbean Sea and the Pacific Ocean. From the tropical coastal plains, the land rises to mountains and a temperate central plateau where most of the population live. The economy depends on agriculture and tourism, with ecotourism becoming increasingly important. Main exports are textiles, coffee and bananas; almost half of all trade is with the USA.

CÔTE D'IVOIRE
Republic of Côte d'Ivoire

Area Sq Km	322 463	Languages French, Creole, Akan, local languages
Area Sq Miles	124 504	Religions Sunni Muslim, Roman Catholic, traditional beliefs, Protestant
Population	16 013 000	
Capital	Yamoussoukro	Currency CFA franc
		Organizations UN

Map page 120

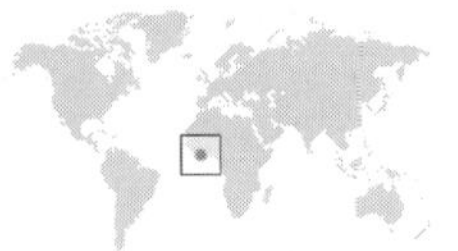

Côte d'Ivoire (Ivory Coast) is in west Africa, on the Gulf of Guinea. In the north are plateaus and savanna, in the south are low undulating plains and rainforest, with sand-bars and lagoons on the coast. Temperatures are warm, and rainfall is heavy in the south. Most of the workforce is engaged in farming. Côte d'Ivoire is a major producer of cocoa and coffee, and agricultural products (including cotton and timber) are the main exports. Oil and gas have begun to be exploited.

CROATIA
Republic of Croatia

Area Sq Km	56 538	Languages Croatian, Serbian
Area Sq Miles	21 829	Religions Roman Catholic, Serbian Orthodox, Sunni Muslim
Population	4 654 000	
Capital	Zagreb	Currency Kuna
		Organizations UN

Map page 114

 The south European state of Croatia has a long coastline on the Adriatic Sea with many offshore islands. Coastal areas have a Mediterranean climate, inland is colder and wetter. Croatia was once strong agriculturally and industrially, but conflict in 1991-1992, the loss of markets and a fall in tourist revenue have caused economic difficulties from which recovery has been slow.

CUBA
Republic of Cuba

Area Sq Km	110 860	Languages Spanish
Area Sq Miles	42 803	Religions Roman Catholic, Protestant
Population	11 199 000	Currency Cuban peso
Capital	Havana (La Habana)	Organizations UN

Map page 149

 Cuba comprises the island of Cuba, the largest island in the Caribbean, and many islets and cays. A fifth of Cubans live in and around Havana. Cuba is slowly recovering from the withdrawal of aid and subsidies from the former USSR. Sugar remains the basis of the economy, although tourism is developing and is, together with remittances from workers abroad, an important source of overseas revenue.

CYPRUS
Republic of Cyprus

Area Sq Km	9 251	Languages Greek, Turkish, English
Area Sq Miles	3 572	Religions Greek Orthodox, Sunni Muslim
Population	784 000	Currency Cyprus pound
Capital	Nicosia (Lefkosia)	Organizations Comm., UN

Map page 80

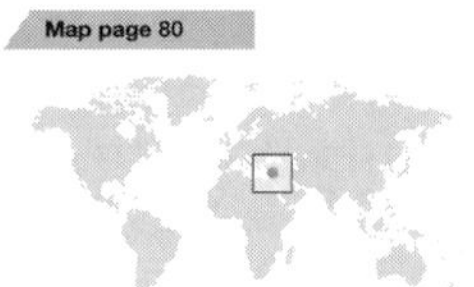

 The eastern Mediterranean island of Cyprus has hot dry summers and mild winters. The economy of the Greek south is based mainly on specialist agriculture and tourism, although shipping and offshore banking are also major sources of income. The Turkish north depends upon agriculture, tourism and aid from Turkey.

CZECH REPUBLIC

Area Sq Km	78 864	Languages Czech, Moravian, Slovak
Area Sq Miles	30 450	Religions Roman Catholic, Protestant
Population	10 272 000	Currency Czech koruna
Capital	Prague (Praha)	Organizations UN

Map page 112

 The landlocked Czech Republic in central Europe consists of rolling countryside, wooded hills and fertile valleys. The climate is temperate, but winters are fairly cold. The country has substantial reserves of coal and lignite, timber and some minerals, chiefly iron ore. It is highly industrialized and manufactured goods include industrial machinery, consumer goods, cars, iron and steel, chemicals and glass. Germany is the main trading partner.

DENMARK
Kingdom of Denmark

Area Sq Km	43 075	Languages Danish
Area Sq Miles	16 631	Religions Protestant
Population	5 320 000	Currency Danish krone
Capital	Copenhagen (København)	Organizations EU, OECD, UN

Map page 103

 In north Europe, Denmark occupies the Jutland peninsula and nearly five hundred islands in and between the North and Baltic Seas. The country is low-lying, with long, indented coastlines. The climate is cool and temperate, with rainfall throughout the year. A fifth of the population live around the capital, Copenhagen, on the largest of the islands, Zealand. Denmark's main natural resource is its agricultural potential; two thirds of the total area is fertile farmland or pasture. Agriculture is now high-tech and with forestry and fishing employs only around four per cent of the workforce. Denmark is self-sufficient in oil and natural gas, produced from fields in the North Sea. Manufacturing, largely based on imported raw materials, accounts for over half of allexports which include machinery, food, furniture, and pharmaceuticals. The main trading partners are Germany and Sweden.

DJIBOUTI
Republic of Djibouti

Area Sq Km	23 200	Languages Somali, Afar, French, Arabic
Area Sq Miles	8 958	Religions Sunni Muslim, Christian
Population	632 000	Currency Djibouti franc
Capital	Djibouti	Organizations UN

Map page 122

 Djibouti lies in northeast Africa, on the Gulf of Aden at the entrance to the Red Sea. Most of the country is semi-arid desert with high temperatures and low rainfall. More than two-thirds of the population live in the capital, Djibouti city. There is some camel, sheep and goat herding, but with few natural resources the economy is based on services and trade. Djibouti serves as a free trade zone in northern Africa and the port is a useful transshipment and refuelling destination. The port is linked by rail to Addis Ababa in Ethiopia.

DOMINICA
Commonwealth of Dominica

Area Sq Km	750	Languages English, Creole
Area Sq Miles	290	Religions Roman Catholic, Protestant
Population	71 000	Currency East Caribbean dollar
Capital	Roseau	Organizations CARICOM, Comm., UN

Map page 149

 Dominica is the most northerly of the Windward Islands in the eastern Caribbean. It is very mountainous and forested, with a coastline of steep cliffs. The climate is tropical and rainfall is abundant. Approximately a quarter of Dominicans live in the capital. The economy is based on agriculture, with bananas (the major export), coconuts and citrus fruits being the most important crops. Tourism is a developing industry.

DOMINICAN REPUBLIC

Area Sq Km	48 442	Languages Spanish, Creole
Area Sq Miles	18 704	Religions Roman Catholic, Protestant
Population	8 373 000	Currency Dominican peso
Capital	Santo Domingo	Organizations UN

Map page 149

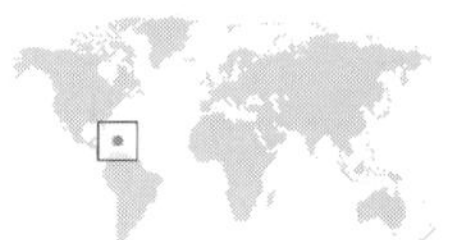

 The state occupies the eastern two-thirds of the Caribbean island of Hispaniola (the western third is Haiti). It has a series of mountain ranges, fertile valleys and a large coastal plain in the east. The climate is hot tropical, with heavy rainfall. Sugar, coffee and cocoa are the main cash crops. Nickel (the main export), and gold are mined, and there is some light industry. The USA is the main trading partner. Tourism is the main foreign exchange earner.

EAST TIMOR

Area Sq Km	14 874	Languages Portuguese, Tetun, English
Area Sq Miles	5 743	Religions Roman Catholic
Population	737 000	
Capital	Dili	

Map page 91

 The eastern part, and a small coastal enclave to the west, of the island Timor, which is part of the Indonesian archipelago to the north of Western Australia. A referendum in 1999 officially ended Indonesia's twenty three year occupation. East Timor was under a UN transitional administration until full independence.

ECUADOR
Republic of Ecuador

Area Sq Km	272 045	Languages	Spanish, Quechua, and other Amerindian languages
Area Sq Miles	105 037		
Population	12 646 000	Religions	Roman Catholic
Capital	Quito	Currency	US dollar
		Organizations	APEC, UN

Map page 154

Ecuador is in northwest South America, on the Pacific coast. It consists of a broad coastal plain, the high ranges of the Andes and the forested upper Amazon basin to the east. The climate is tropical, moderated by altitude. Most people live on the coast or in the mountain valleys. Ecuador is one of South America's main oil producers and mineral reserves include gold. Most of the workforce depends on agriculture. Petroleum, bananas, shrimps, coffee and cocoa are exported and the USA is the main trading partner.

EGYPT
Arab Republic of Egypt

Area Sq Km	1 000 250	Languages	Arabic
Area Sq Miles	386 199	Religions	Sunni Muslim, Coptic Christian
Population	67 884 000	Currency	Egyptian pound
Capital	Cairo (Al Qâhirah)	Organizations	UN

Map page 121

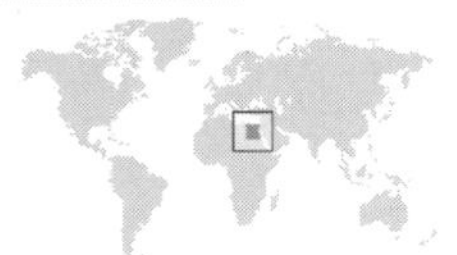

Egypt, on the eastern Mediterranean coast of North Africa, is mostly low-lying, with areas below sea level in the Qattara depression. It is a land of desert and semi-desert, except for the Nile valley, where ninety nine per cent of Egyptians live. The Sinai peninsula in the northeast of the country forms the only land bridge between Africa and Asia. The summers are hot, the winters mild and rainfall is negligible. Less than four per cent of land (chiefly around the Nile floodplain and delta) is cultivated. Farming employs about one-third of the workforce and cotton is the main cash crop. Egypt imports over half its food needs. There are oil and natural gas reserves, although nearly a quarter of electricity comes from hydro-electric power. Main exports are oil and oil products, cotton, textiles and clothing.

EL SALVADOR
Republic of El Salvador

Area Sq Km	21 041	Languages	Spanish
Area Sq Miles	8 124	Religions	Roman Catholic, Protestant
Population	6 278 000	Currency	El Salvador colón, US dollar
Capital	San Salvador	Organizations	UN

Map page 151

Located on the Pacific coast of central America, El Salvador consists of a coastal plain and volcanic mountains which enclose a densely populated plateau area. The coast is hot, with heavy summer rainfall, the highlands are cooler. Coffee (the chief export) and sugar are the main cash crops. The main trading partners are the USA, Guatemala and Honduras.

EQUATORIAL GUINEA
Republic of Equatorial Guinea

Area Sq Km	28 051	Languages	Spanish, French, Fang
Area Sq Miles	10 831	Religions	Roman Catholic, traditional beliefs
Population	457 000	Currency	CFA franc
Capital	Malabo	Organizations	UN

Map page 120

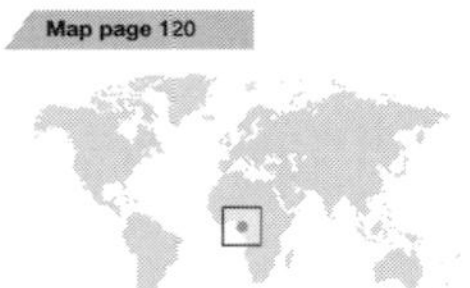

The state consists of Rio Muni, an enclave on the Atlantic coast of central Africa, and the islands of Bioco, Annobón and the Corisco group. Most of the population live on the coastal plain and upland plateau of Rio Muni. The capital city, Malabo, is on the fertile volcanic island of Bioco. The climate is hot, humid and wet. Oil production started in 1992 and oil is now the main export along with timber. The economy depends heavily on foreign aid.

ERITREA
State of Eritrea

Area Sq Km	117 400	Languages	Tigrinya, Tigre
Area Sq Miles	45 328	Religions	Sunni Muslim, Coptic Christian
Population	3 659 000	Currency	Nakfa
Capital	Asmara	Organizations	UN

Map page 122

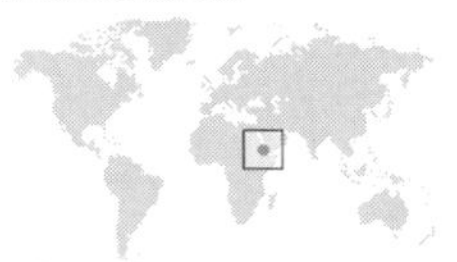

Eritrea, on the Red Sea coast of northeast Africa, consists of a high plateau in the north with a coastal plain which widens to the south. The coast is hot, inland is cooler. Rainfall is unreliable. The agricultural-based economy has suffered from over thirty years of war and occasional poor rains. Eritrea is one of the least developed countries in the world.

ESTONIA
Republic of Estonia

Area Sq Km	45 200	Languages	Estonian, Russian
Area Sq Miles	17 452	Religions	Protestant, Estonian and Russian Orthodox
Population	1 393 000	Currency	Kroon
Capital	Tallinn	Organizations	UN

Map page 103

Estonia is in north Europe, on the Gulf of Finland and the Baltic Sea. The land, over one-third of which is forested, is generally low-lying, with many lakes. The climate is temperate. Approximately one-third of Estonians live in the capital, Tallinn. Exported goods include machinery, wood products, textiles and food products. The main trading partners are the Russian Federation, Finland and Sweden.

ETHIOPIA
Federal Democratic Republic of Ethiopia

Area Sq Km	1 133 880	Languages	Oromo, Amharic, Tigrinya, local languages
Area Sq Miles	437 794	Religions	Ethiopian Orthodox, Sunni Muslim, traditional beliefs
Population	62 908 000	Currency	Birr
Capital	Addis Ababa (Ādīs Ābeba)	Organizations	UN

Map page 122

A landlocked country in northeast Africa, Ethiopia comprises a mountainous region in the west which is traversed by the Great Rift Valley. The east is mostly arid plateaus. The highlands are warm with summer rainfall. The east is hot and dry. Most people live in the centre-north. Civil war, continued conflict with Eritrea and poor infrastructure hamper economic development. Subsistence farming is the main activity, although droughts have led to frequent famines. Coffee is the main export and there is some light industry. Ethiopia is one of the least developed countries in the world.

Falkland Islands
United Kingdom Overseas Territory

Area Sq Km	12 170	Languages	English
Area Sq Miles	4 699	Religions	Protestant, Roman Catholic
Population	2 000	Currency	Falkland Islands pound
Capital	Stanley		

Map page 156

Lying in the southwest Atlantic Ocean, northeast of Cape Horn, two main islands, West and East Falkland and many smaller islands, form the overseas territory of the Falkland Islands. The economy is based on sheep farming and the sale of fishing licences.

Faroe Islands
Self-governing Danish Territory

Area Sq Km	1 399	Languages	Faroese, Danish
Area Sq Miles	540	Religions	Protestant
Population	46 000	Currency	Danish krone
Capital	Thorshavn (Tórshavn)		

Map page 102

A self governing territory, the Faroe Islands lie in the north Atlantic Ocean between the UK and Iceland. The islands benefit from the North Atlantic Drift which has a moderating effect on the climate. The economy is based on deep-sea fishing.

FIJI
Sovereign Democratic Republic of Fiji

Area Sq Km	18 330	Languages	English, Fijian, Hindi
Area Sq Miles	7 077	Religions	Christian, Hindu, Sunni Muslim
Population	814 000	Currency	Fiji dollar
Capital	Suva	Organizations	Comm., UN

Map page 69

The southwest Pacific republic of Fiji comprises two mountainous and volcanic islands, Vanua Levu and Viti Levu and over three hundred smaller islands. The climate is tropical and the economy is based on agriculture

(chiefly sugar, the main export), fishing, forestry, gold mining and tourism.

FINLAND
Republic of Finland

Area Sq Km	338 145	Languages	Finnish, Swedish
Area Sq Miles	130 559	Religions	Protestant, Greek Orthodox
Population	5 172 000	Currency	Euro
Capital	Helsinki (Helsingfors)	Organizations	EU, OECD, UN

Map page 102-103

Finland is in northern Europe, and nearly one-third of the country lies north of the Arctic Circle. It is low-lying, forests cover over seventy per cent of the land area and ten per cent is covered by lakes. Summers are short and warm, and winters are long and severe, particularly in the north. Most of the population live in the southern third of the country, along the coast or near the lakes. Timber is a major resource and there are important mineral resources, chiefly chromium. Main industries include metal working, electronics, paper and paper products and chemicals. The main trading partners are Germany, Sweden and the UK.

FRANCE
French Republic

Area Sq Km	543 965	Languages	French, Arabic
Area Sq Miles	210 026	Religions	Roman Catholic, Protestant, Sunni Muslim
Population	59 238 000	Currency	Euro
Capital	Paris	Organizations	EU, OECD, UN

Map page 110

France lies in western Europe and has coastlines on the Atlantic Ocean and the Mediterranean Sea. It includes the Mediterranean island of Corsica. Northern and western regions consist mostly of flat or rolling countryside, and include the major lowlands of the Paris basin, the Loire valley and the Aquitaine basin, drained by the Seine, Loire and Garonne river systems respectively. The centre-south is dominated by the Massif Central mountains. To the east, are the Vosges and Jura mountains and the Alps. In the southwest, the Pyrenees mountain range forms a natural border with Spain. The climate is mainly temperate with warm summers and cool winters. The Mediterranean coast has hot, dry summers and mild winters with some rainfall. Over seventy per cent of the population live in towns with almost a sixth of the population living in the Greater Paris area. The French economy has a substantial and varied agricultural base. France is a major producer of both fresh and processed food. There are relatively few mineral resources; it has coal reserves, some oil and natural gas, but it relies heavily on nuclear and hydroelectric power and imported fuels. France is one of the world's major industrial countries. Main industries include food processing, iron, steel and aluminium production, chemicals, cars, electronics and oil refining. The main exports are transport equipment, plastics and chemicals. Tourism is a major source of revenue and employment. Trade is predominantly with other EU countries.

French Guiana
French Overseas Department

Area Sq Km	90 000	Languages	French, Creole
Area Sq Miles	34 749	Religions	Roman Catholic
Population	165 000	Currency	Euro
Capital	Cayenne		

Map page 155

French Guiana, on the north coast of South America, is densely forested. The climate is tropical with high rainfall. Most people live in the coastal strip and agriculture is mostly subsistence farming. Forestry and fishing are important but mineral resources are largely unexploited and industry is limited. French Guiana depends upon French aid. The main trading partners are France and the USA.

French Polynesia
French Overseas Territory

Area Sq Km	3 265	Languages	French, Tahitian, Polynesian languages
Area Sq Miles	1 261	Religions	Protestant, Roman Catholic
Population	1 261	Currency	CFP franc
Capital	Papeete		

Map page 67

Extending over a vast area of the south Pacific Ocean, French Polynesia comprises more than one hundred and thirty islands and coral atolls. The main island groups are the Marquesas Islands, the Tuamotu Archipelago and the Society Islands. The capital, Papeete, is on Tahiti in the Society Islands. The climate is subtropical and tourism is an important industry. The main export is cultured pearls.

© Bartholomew Ltd

GABON
Gabonese Republic

Area Sq Km	267 667	Languages	French, Fang, local languages
Area Sq Miles	103 347	Religions	Roman Catholic, Protestant, traditional beliefs
Population	1 230 000	Currency	CFA franc
Capital	Libreville	Organizations	UN

Map page 122

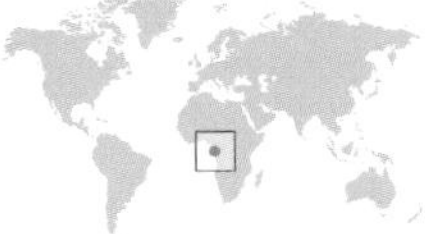

Gabon, on the Atlantic coast of central Africa consists of low plateaus, and a coastal plain lined with lagoons and mangrove swamps. The climate is tropical and rainforests cover over three-quarters of the land area. Over seventy per cent of the population live in towns. The economy is heavily dependent on oil, which accounts for approximately seventy-five per cent of exports. Manganese, uranium and timber are the other main exports. Agriculture is mainly at subsistence level.

THE GAMBIA
Republic of The Gambia

Area Sq Km	11 295	Languages	English, Malinke, Fulani, Wolof
Area Sq Miles	4 361	Religions	Sunni Muslim, Protestant
Population	1 303 000	Currency	Dalasi
Capital	Banjul	Organizations	Comm., UN

Map page 120

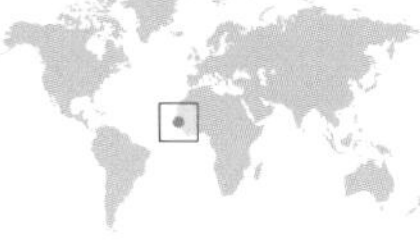

The Gambia, on the coast of west Africa, occupies a strip of land along the lower Gambia river. Sandy beaches are backed by mangrove swamps, beyond which is savanna. The climate is tropical, with rainfall in the summer. Over seventy per cent of Gambians are farmers, growing chiefly groundnuts (the main export), cotton, oil palms and food crops. Livestock rearing and fishing are important, while manufacturing is limited. Re-exports, mainly from Senegal, and tourism are major sources of income.

Gaza
Semi-autonomous region

Area Sq Km	363	Languages	Arabic
Area Sq Miles	140	Religions	Sunni Muslim, Shi'a Muslim
Population	3 191 000*	Currency	Israeli shekel
Capital	Gaza		

*Includes occupied West Bank

Map page 80 Gaza is a narrow strip of flat land on the southeast corner of the Mediterranean Sea, between Egypt and Israel. This Palestinian territory has limited autonomy from Israel.

GEORGIA
Republic of Georgia

Area Sq Km	69 700	Languages	Georgian, Russian, Armenian, Azeri, Ossetian, Abkhaz
Area Sq Miles	26 911		
Population	5 262 000	Religions	Georgian Orthodox, Russian Orthodox, Sunni Muslim
Capital	T'bilisi	Currency	Lari
		Organizations	CIS, UN

Map page 117

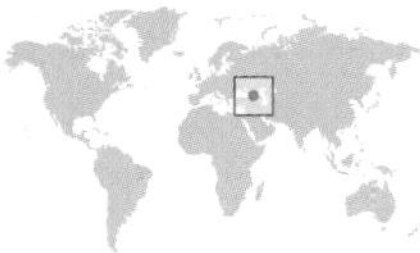

Georgia is in the northwest Caucasus area of southwest Asia, on the eastern coast of the Black Sea. Mountain ranges in the north and south flank the Kura and Rioni valleys. The climate is generally mild and subtropical along the coast. Agriculture is important, with tea, grapes, and citrus fruits the main crops. Mineral resources include manganese ore and coal. Main industries are steel, oil refining and machine building. The main trading partners are the Russian Federation and Turkey.

GERMANY
Federal Republic of Germany

Area Sq Km	357 028	Languages	German, Turkish
Area Sq Miles	137 849	Religions	Protestant, Roman Catholic
Population	82 017 000	Currency	Euro
Capital	Berlin	Organizations	EU, OECD, UN

Map page 112

The central European state of Germany borders nine countries and has coastlines on the North and Baltic Seas. Behind the indented coastline, and covering about one-third of the country, is the north German plain, a region of fertile farmland and sandy heaths drained by the country's major rivers. The central highlands are a belt of forested hills and plateaus which stretch from the Eifel region in the west to the Erzgebirge mountains along the border with the Czech Republic. Farther south the land rises to the Schwäbische Alb, and the high rugged

Schwarzwald (Black Forest) in the southwest. In the far south the Bavarian Alps form the border with Austria. The climate is temperate, with continental conditions in eastern areas. The population is highly urbanized with over eighty-five per cent living in cities and towns. With the exception of coal, lignite, potash and barite, Germany lacks minerals and other industrial raw materials. It has a small agricultural base, although a few products (chiefly wines and beers) enjoy an international reputation. Germany is the world's third ranking economy after the USA and Japan. Its industries are amongst the world's most technologically advanced. Exports include machinery, vehicles and chemicals. The majority of trade is with other countries in the EU, the USA and Japan

Baden-Württemberg (State)
Area Sq Km (Sq Miles)	35 751 (13 804)	Population	10 476 000	Capital	Stuttgart

Bayern (State)
Area Sq Km (Sq Miles)	70 552 (27 240)	Population	12 155 000	Capital	Munich (München)

Berlin (State)
Area Sq Km (Sq Miles)	891 (344)	Population	3 387 000	Capital	Berlin

Brandenburg (State)
Area Sq Km (Sq Miles)	29 476 (11 381)	Population	2 601 000	Capital	Potsdan

Bremen (State)
Area Sq Km (Sq Miles)	404 (156)	Population	663 000	Capital	Bremen

Hamburg (State)
Area Sq Km (Sq Miles)	755 (292)	Population	1 705 000	Capital	Hamburg

Hessen (State)
Area Sq Km (Sq Miles)	21 114 (8 152)	Population	6 052 000	Capital	Wiesbaden

Mecklenburg-Vorpommern (State)
Area Sq Km (Sq Miles)	23 170 (8 946)	Population	1 789 000	Capital	Schwerin

Niedersachsen (State)
Area Sq Km (Sq Miles)	47 612 (18 383)	Population	7 899 000	Capital	Hannover

Nordrhein-Westfalen (State)
Area Sq Km (Sq Miles)	34 079 (13 158)	Population	18 000 000	Capital	Düsseldorf

Rheinland-Pfalz (State)
Area Sq Km (Sq Miles)	19 853 (7 665)	Population	4 031 000	Capital	Mainz

Saarland (State)
Area Sq Km (Sq Miles)	2 570 (992)	Population	1 072 000	Capital	Saarbrücken

Sachsen (State)
Area Sq Km (Sq Miles)	18 413 (7 109)	Population	4 460 000	Capital	Dresden

Sachsen-Anhalt (State)
Area Sq Km (Sq Miles)	20 446 (7 894)	Population	2 649 000	Capital	Magdeburg

Schleswig-Holstein (State)
Area Sq Km (Sq Miles)	15 771 (6 089)	Population	2 777 000	Capital	Kiel

Thüringen (State)
Area Sq Km (Sq Miles)	16 171 (6 244)	Population	2 449 000	Capital	Erfurt

GHANA
Republic of Ghana

Area Sq Km	238 537	Languages	English, Hausa, Akan, local languages
Area Sq Miles	92 100	Religions	Christian, Sunni Muslim, traditional beliefs
Population	19 306 000	Currency	Cedi
Capital	Accra	Organizations	Comm., UN

Map page 120

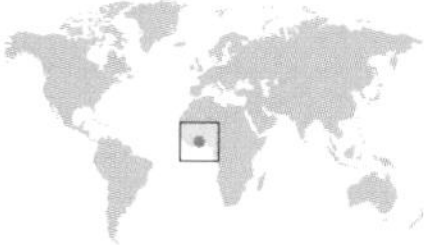

A west African state on the Gulf of Guinea, Ghana is a land of plains and low plateaus covered with savanna and rainforest. In the east is the Volta basin and Lake Volta. The climate is tropical, with the highest rainfalls in the south, where most of the population live. Agriculture employs around sixty per cent of the workforce. Main exports are gold, timber, cocoa, bauxite and manganese ore.

Gibraltar
United Kingdom Overseas Territory

Area Sq Km	7	Languages	English, Spanish
Area Sq Miles	3	Religions	Roman Catholic, Protestant, Sunni Muslim
Population	27 000	Currency	Gibraltar pound
Capital	Gibraltar		

Map page 111 Gibraltar lies on the south coast of Spain at the western entrance to the Mediterranean Sea. The economy depends on tourism, offshore banking and shipping services.

GREECE
Hellenic Republic

Area Sq Km	131 957	Languages	Greek
Area Sq Miles	50 949	Religions	Greek Orthodox, Sunni Muslim
Population	10 610 000	Currency	Euro
Capital	Athens (Athina)	Organizations	EU, OECD, UN

Map page 115

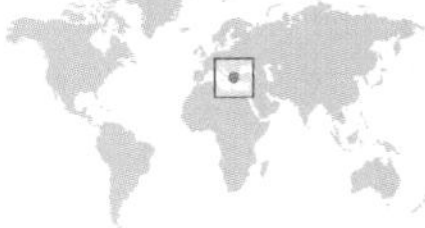

Greece comprises a mountainous peninsula in the Balkan region of southeast Europe and many islands in the Aegean, Ionian and Mediterranean Seas. The islands make up over one-fifth of its area. The main lowland areas are the plains of Thessalia in the centre and around Thessaloniki in the northeast. Summers are hot and dry. Winters are mild and wet, but colder in the north with heavy snowfalls in the mountains. One-third of Greeks live in the Athens area. Employment in agriculture accounts for approximately twenty per cent of the workforce and exports include citrus fruits, raisins, wine, olives and olive oil. Aluminium and nickel are mined and a wide range of manufactured goods are produced including food and tobacco, textiles, clothing, and chemicals. Tourism is an important industry and there is a large services sector. Most trade is with other EU countries.

Greenland
Self-governing Danish Territory

Area Sq Km	2 175 600	Languages	Greenlandic, Danish
Area Sq Miles	840 004	Religions	Protestant
Population	56 000	Currency	Danish krone
Capital	Nuuk (Godthåb)		

Map page 129

Situated to the northeast of North America between the Atlantic and Arctic Oceans, Greenland is the largest island in the world. It has a polar climate and over eighty per cent of the land area is permanent ice cap. The economy is based on fishing and fish processing.

GRENADA

Area Sq Km	378	Languages	English, Creole
Area Sq Miles	146	Religions	Roman Catholic, Protestant
Population	94 000	Currency	East Caribbean dollar
Capital	St George's	Organizations	CARICOM, Comm., UN

Map page 157

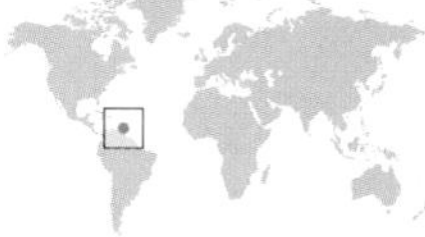

The Caribbean state comprises Grenada and the southern islands of The Grenadines. Grenada has wooded hills, beaches in the southwest, a warm climate and good rainfall. Agriculture is the main activity, with bananas, nutmeg and cocoa the main exports. Tourism is the main foreign exchange earner.

Guadeloupe
French Overseas Department

Area Sq Km	1 780	Languages	French, Creole
Area Sq Miles	687	Religions	Roman Catholic
Population	428 000	Currency	Euro
Capital	Basse-Terre		

Map page 149 Guadeloupe, in the Leeward Islands in the Caribbean, consists of two large islands, Basse-Terre and Grande-Terre, which are connected by a bridge, the smaller island of Marie Galante and a few outer islands. St Barthélemy and the northern part of the island of St Martin (Sint Maarten) island are dependencies of Guadeloupe. The climate is tropical, but is moderated by the trade winds. Bananas, sugar and rum are the main exports and tourism is a major source of income.

Guam
United States Unincorporated Territory

Area Sq Km	541	Languages	Chamorro, English, Tagalog
Area Sq Miles	209	Religions	Roman Catholic
Population	155 000	Currency	US dollar
Capital	Hagåtña		

Map page 91 Lying at the south end of the North Mariana Islands in the western Pacific Ocean, Guam has a humid tropical climate. The island has a large US military base and the economy relies on that and on tourism.

GUATEMALA
Republic of Guatemala

Area Sq Km	108 890	Languages	Spanish, Mayan languages
Area Sq Miles	42 043	Religions	Roman Catholic, Protestant
Population	11 385 000	Currency	Quetzal, US dollar
Capital	Guatemala City	Organizations	UN

Map page 151

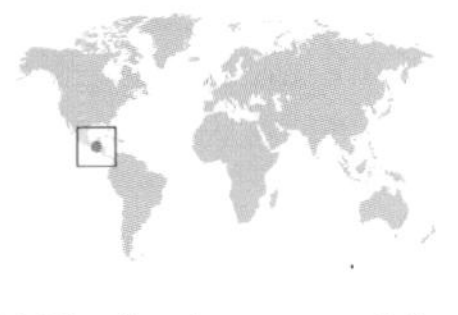

The most populous country in Central America after Mexico, Guatemala has long Pacific and short Caribbean coasts separated by a mountain chain which includes several active volcanoes. The climate is hot tropical in the lowlands and cooler in the highlands, where most of the population live. Farming is the main activity and coffee, sugar and bananas are the main exports. There is some manufacturing of clothing and textiles and the main trading partner is the USA.

Guernsey
United Kingdom Crown Dependency

Area Sq Km	78	Languages	English, French
Area Sq Miles	30	Religions	Protestant, Roman Catholic
Population	64 555	Currency	Pound sterling
Capital	St Peter Port		

Map page 110   One of the Channel Islands lying off the west coast of the Cherbourg peninsula in northern France.

GUINEA
Republic of Guinea

Area Sq Km	245 857	Languages	French, Fulani, Malinke, local languages
Area Sq Miles	94 926	Religions	Sunni Muslim, traditional beliefs, Christian
Population	8 154 000	Currency	Guinea franc
Capital	Conakry	Organizations	UN

Map page 120

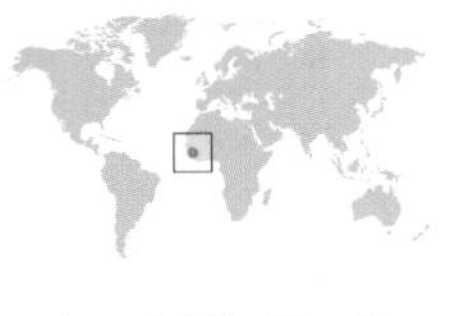

Guinea is in west Africa, on the Atlantic Ocean. There are mangrove swamps along the coast, inland are lowlands and the Fouta Djallon mountains and plateaus. To the east are savanna plains drained by the upper Niger river system. The southeast is hilly. The climate is tropical, with high coastal rainfall. Agriculture is the main activity employing nearly eighty per cent of the workforce, with coffee, bananas and pineapples the chief cash crops. There are huge reserves of bauxite which accounts for more than seventy per cent of total exports. Aluminium oxide, gold, coffee and diamonds are other major exports.

GUINEA-BISSAU
Republic of Guinea-Bissau

Area Sq Km	36 125	Languages	Portuguese, Crioulo, local languages
Area Sq Miles	13 948	Religions	Traditional beliefs, Sunni Muslim, Christian
Population	1 199 000	Currency	CFA franc
Capital	Bissau	Organizations	UN

Map page 120

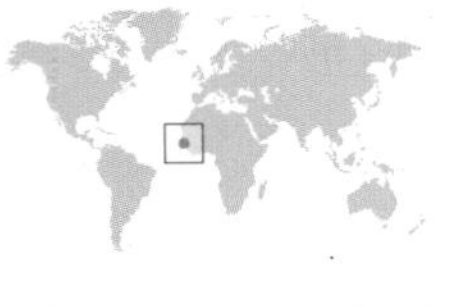

Guinea-Bissau, on the Atlantic coast of west Africa, includes the Bijagos Archipelago. The mainland coast is swampy and contains many estuaries. Inland are forested plains and to the east are savanna plateaus. The climate is tropical. The economy is based mainly on subsistence farming. There is little industry and timber and mineral resources are largely unexploited. Cashews account for seventy per cent of exports. Guinea-Bissau is one of the least developed countries in the world.

GUYANA
Co-operative Republic of Guyana

Area Sq Km	214 969	Languages	English, Creole, Amerindian languages
Area Sq Miles	83 000	Religions	Protestant, Hindu, Roman Catholic, Sunni Muslim
Population	761 000	Currency	Guyana dollar
Capital	Georgetown	Organizations	CARICOM, Comm., UN

Map page 154-155

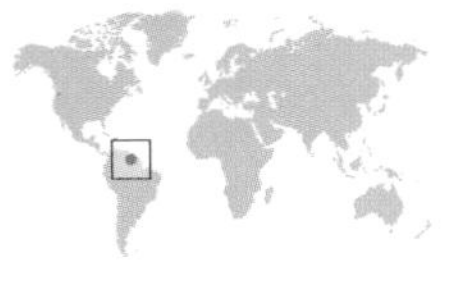

Guyana, on the north coast of South America, consists of highlands in the west, and savanna uplands in the southwest. Most of the country is densely forested. A lowland coastal belt supports crops and most of the population. The generally hot, humid and wet conditions are modified along the coast by sea breezes. The economy is based on agriculture, mining of bauxite and forestry. Sugar, bauxite, gold, rice and timber are the main exports.

HAITI
Republic of Haiti

Area Sq Km	27 750	Languages	French, Creole
Area Sq Miles	10 714	Religions	Roman Catholic, Protestant, Voodoo
Population	8 142 000	Currency	Gourde
Capital	Port-au-Prince	Organizations	CARICOM, UN

Map page 149

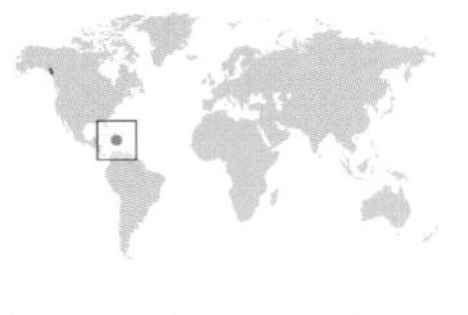

Haiti, occupying the western third of the Caribbean island of Hispaniola, is a mountainous state, with small coastal plains and a central valley. The Dominican Republic occupies the rest of the island. The climate is tropical, hottest in coastal areas. Haiti has few natural resources, is overpopulated and relies on exports of local crafts and coffee, and remittances from workers abroad.

HONDURAS
Republic of Honduras

Area Sq Km	112 088	Languages	Spanish, Amerindian languages
Area Sq Miles	43 277	Religions	Roman Catholic, Protestant
Population	6 417 000	Currency	Lempira
Capital	Tegucigalpa	Organizations	UN

Map page 150

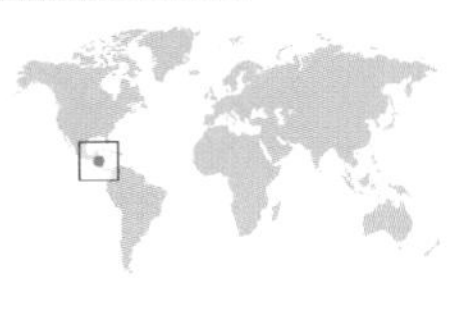

Honduras, in central America, is a mountainous and forested country with lowland areas along its long Caribbean and short Pacific coasts. Coastal areas are hot and humid with heavy summer rainfall, inland is cooler and drier. Most of the population live in the central valleys. Coffee and bananas are the main exports, along with shellfish and zinc. Industry involves mainly agricultural processing. Honduras was the country hardest hit by Hurricane Mitch in 1998 but has received significant foreign aid for reconstruction.

HUNGARY
Republic of Hungary

Area Sq Km	93 030	Languages	Hungarian
Area Sq Miles	35 919	Religions	Roman Catholic, Protestant
Population	9 968 000	Currency	Forint
Capital	Budapest	Organizations	OECD, UN

Map page 112-113

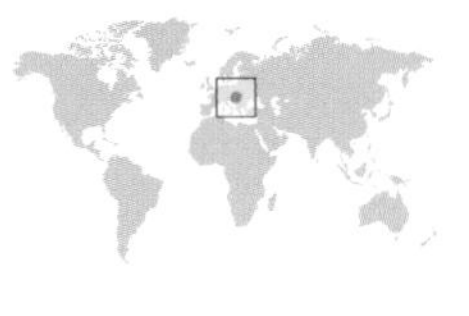

The Danube river flows north-south through central Hungary, a landlocked country in eastern Europe. In the east lies a great plain, flanked by highlands in the north and in the west low mountains and Lake Balaton separate a small plain and southern uplands. The climate is continental, with warm summers and cold winters. More than sixty per cent of the population live in urban areas, and one-fifth lives in the capital, Budapest. Some minerals and energy resources are exploited, chiefly bauxite, coal and natural gas. Hungary has an industrial economy. The main industries produce metals, machinery, transport equipment, chemicals and food products. The main trading partners are Germany and Austria.

ICELAND
Republic of Iceland

Area Sq Km	102 820	Languages	Icelandic
Area Sq Miles	39 699	Religions	Protestant
Population	279 000	Currency	Icelandic króna
Capital	Reykjavík	Organizations	OECD, UN

Map page 102

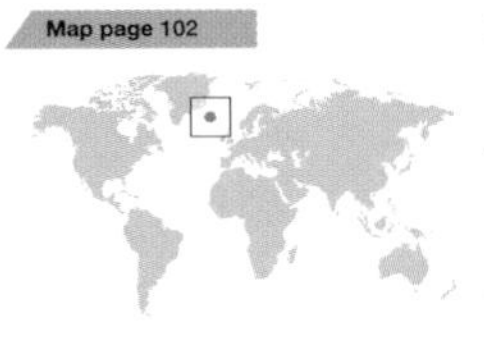

Iceland lies in the north Atlantic Ocean, near the Arctic Circle to the northwest of Scandinavia. The landscape is volcanic with numerous hot springs, geysers and approximately two hundred volcanoes. One-tenth of the country is covered by ice caps. Only coastal lowlands can be cultivated and settled, and over half of the population live in the Reykjavik area. The climate is mild, moderated by the North Atlantic Drift and southwesterly winds. The mainstay of the economy is fishing and fish processing, which account for seventy per cent of exports. Agriculture involves mainly sheep and dairy farming. Hydroelectric and geothermal energy resources are considerable. The main industries produce aluminium, ferro-silicon and fertilizers. Tourism, including ecotourism, is growing in importance.

INDIA
Republic of India

Area Sq Km	3 065 027	Languages	Hindi, English, many regional languages
Area Sq Miles	1 183 414	Religions	Hindu, Sunni Muslim, Shi'a Muslim, Sikh, Christian
Population	1 008 937 000	Currency	Indian rupee
Capital	New Delhi	Organizations	Comm., UN

Map page 78-79

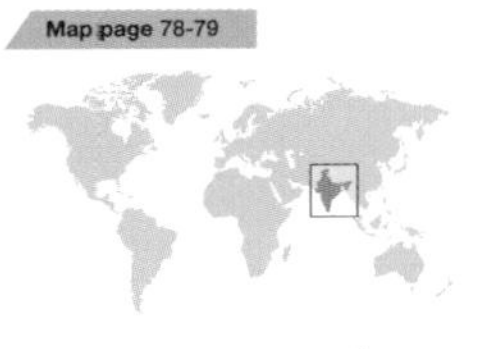

The south Asian country of India occupies a peninsula which juts out into the Indian Ocean between the Arabian Sea and the Bay of Bengal. The heart of the peninsula is the Deccan plateau, bordered on either side by ranges of hills, the Western Ghats and the Eastern Ghats, which fall away to narrow coastal plains. To the north is a broad plain, drained by the Indus, Ganges and Brahmaputra rivers and their tributaries. The plain is intensively farmed and is the country's most populous region. In the west is the Thar Desert and the Himalaya mountains, together with parts of the Karakoram and Hindu Kush ranges in the northwest, form India's northernmost border. The climate shows marked seasonal variation: the hot season from March to June; the monsoon season from June to October; and the cold season from November to February. Rainfall ranges between very high in the northeast Assam region to negligible in the Thar Desert. Temperatures range from very cold in the Himalaya to tropical heat over much of the south. Over seventy per cent of the huge population – the second largest in the world – is rural, although Mumbai and Kolkata (Calcutta) rank among the ten largest cities in the world. Agriculture, forestry and fishing account for a quarter of national output and two-thirds of employment. Much of the farming is on a subsistence basis and involves mainly rice and wheat growing. India is a major world producer of tea, sugar, jute, cotton and tobacco. Livestock is raised mainly for dairy products and hides. India has major reserves of coal, reserves of oil and natural gas and many minerals, including iron, manganese, bauxite, diamonds and gold. The manufacturing sector is large and diverse. The main products are chemicals and chemical products, textiles, iron and steel, food products, electrical goods and transport equipment; software and pharmaceuticals are also important. All the main manufactured products are exported, together with diamonds and jewellery. The USA, Germany, Japan and the UK are the main trading partners.

INDONESIA
Republic of Indonesia

Area Sq Km	1 919 445	Languages	Indonesian, local languages
Area Sq Miles	741 102	Religions	Sunni Muslim, Protestant, Roman Catholic, Hindu, Buddhist
Population	212 092 000	Currency	Rupiah
Capital	Jakarta	Organizations	APEC, ASEAN, OPEC, UN

Map page 91

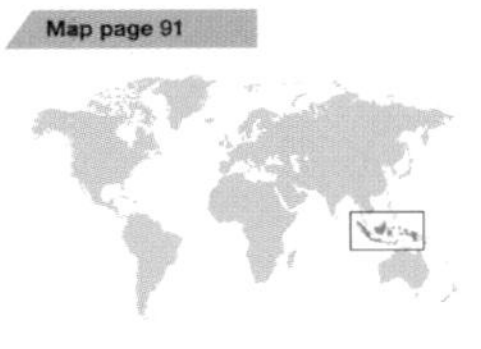

Indonesia, the largest and most populous country in Southeast Asia, consists of over thirteen thousand islands extending between the Pacific and Indian Oceans. Sumatra, Java, Celebes, Kalimantan (two-thirds of Borneo) and Irian Jaya (western New Guinea) make up ninety per cent of the land area. Most of Indonesia is mountainous and covered with rainforest or mangrove swamps, and there are over three hundred volcanoes, many active. Two-thirds of the population live in the lowland areas of the islands of Java and Madura. The climate is tropical monsoon. Agriculture is the largest sector of the economy and Indonesia is among the world's top producers of rice, palm oil, tea, coffee, rubber and tobacco. A wide range of goods are produced including textiles, clothing, cement, tin, fertilizer and vehicles. Main exports are oil, natural gas, timber products and clothing. Main trading partners are Japan, the USA and Singapore. Indonesia is a relatively poor country, and ethnic tensions and civil unrest often hinder economic development.

IRAN
Islamic Republic of Iran

Area Sq Km	1 648 000	Languages	Farsi, Azeri, Kurdish, regional languages
Area Sq Miles	636 296	Religions	Shi'a Muslim, Sunni Muslim
Population	70 330 000	Currency	Iranian rial
Capital	Tehrān	Organizations	OPEC, UN

Map page 84-85

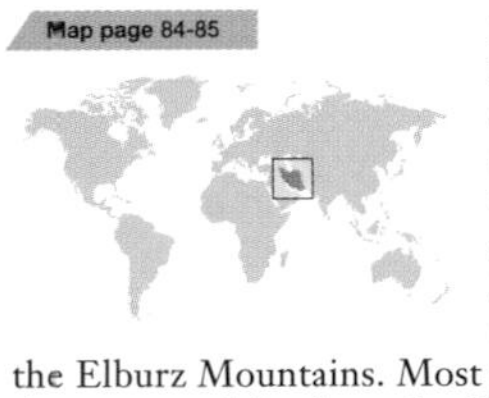

Iran is in southwest Asia and has coasts on The Gulf, the Gulf of Oman and the Caspian Sea. Eastern Iran is high plateau, with large salt pans and a vast sand desert. In the west the Zagros Mountains form a series of ridges and to the north lie the Elburz Mountains. Most farming and settlement is on the narrow plain along the Caspian Sea and in the foothills in the north and west. The climate is one of extremes, with hot summers and very cold winters. Most of the light rainfall falls in the winter months. Agriculture involves approximately one-third of the workforce. Wheat is the main crop but fruit (chiefly dates) and pistachio nuts are grown for export. Petroleum (the main export) and natural gas are Iran's leading natural resources. Manufactured goods include carpets, food products and construction materials.

© Bartholomew Ltd

IRAQ
Republic of Iraq

Area Sq Km	438 317	Languages	Arabic, Kurdish, Turkmen
Area Sq Miles	169 235	Religions	Shi'a Muslim, Sunni Muslim, Christian
Population	22 946 000	Currency	Iraqi dinar
Capital	Baghdād	Organizations	OPEC, UN

Map page 81

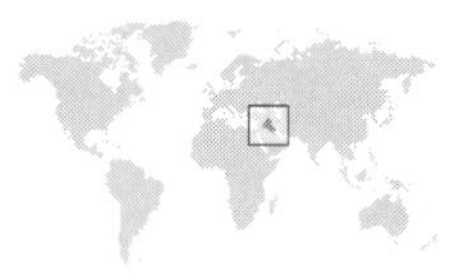

Iraq, in southwest Asia, has at its heart the lowland valley of the Tigris and Euphrates rivers. In the southeast, where the two rivers join, are marshes and the Shatt al Arab waterway. Northern Iraq is hilly, while western Iraq is desert. Summers are hot and dry, and winters are mild with light, unreliable rainfall. The Tigris-Euphrates valley contains most of the arable land. One in five of the population live in the capital, Baghdad. Defeat in the 1991 Gulf War and continued international sanctions have ruined the economy and caused considerable hardship. Oil is exported, almost all to Japan.

IRELAND, REPUBLIC OF

Area Sq Km	70 282	Languages	English, Irish
Area Sq Miles	27 136	Religions	Roman Catholic, Protestant
Population	3 803 000	Currency	Euro
Capital	Dublin (Baile Átha Cliath)	Organizations	EU, OECD, UN

Map page 107

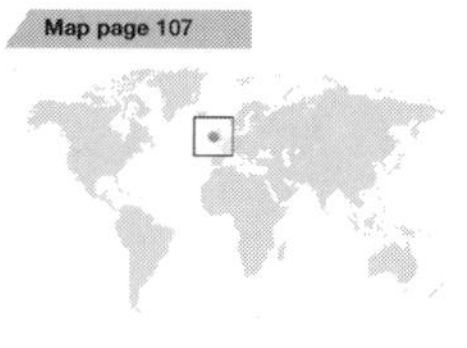

A state in northwest Europe, the Irish Republic occupies some eighty per cent of the island of Ireland. It is a lowland country of wide valleys, lakes and peat bogs, with isolated mountain ranges around the coast. The west coast is rugged and indented with many bays. The climate is mild due to the modifying effect of the North Atlantic Drift and rainfall is plentiful, although highest in the west. Nearly sixty per cent of the population live in urban areas, Dublin and Cork being the main cities. Resources include natural gas, peat, lead and zinc. Agriculture, the traditional mainstay, now employs less than ten per cent of the workforce and industry employs nearly thirty per cent. The main industries are electronics, pharmaceuticals and engineering as well as food processing, brewing and textiles. Service industries are expanding, with tourism a major foreign exchange earner. The UK is the main trading partner.

Isle of Man
United Kingdom Crown Dependency

Area Sq Km	572	Languages	English
Area Sq Miles	221	Religions	Protestant, Roman Catholic
Population	77 000	Currency	Pound sterling
Capital	Douglas		

Map page 104

The Isle of Man lies in the Irish Sea between England and Northern Ireland. The island is self-governing although the UK is responsible for its defence and foreign affairs. The island is not part of the EU, but has a special relationship with the EU which allows for free trade.

ISRAEL
State of Israel

Area Sq Km	20 770	Languages	Hebrew, Arabic
Area Sq Miles	8 019	Religions	Jewish, Sunni Muslim, Christian, Druze
Population	6 040 000	Currency	Shekel
Capital	Jerusalem (Yerushalayim) (El Quds)	Organizations	UN

Map page 80

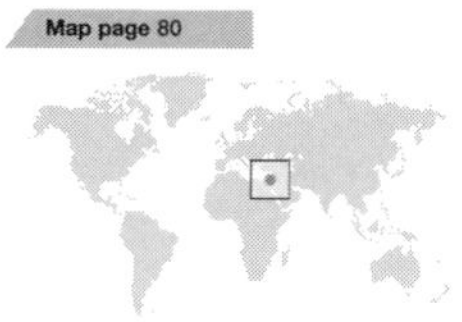

Israel lies on the Mediterranean coast of southwest Asia. Beyond the coastal Plain of Sharon are the hills and valleys of Samaria with the Galilee highlands to the north. In the east is a rift valley, which extends from Lake Tiberias to the Gulf of Aqaba and contains the Jordan river and Dead Sea. In the south is the Negev, a triangular semi-desert plateau. Most of the population live on the coastal plain or in northern and central areas. Much of Israel has warm summers and mild, wet winters. Southern Israel is hot and dry. Agricultural production was boosted by the inclusion of the West Bank in 1967. Manufacturing makes the largest contribution to the economy and tourism is also important. Israel's main exports are machinery and transport equipment, software, diamonds, clothing, fruit and vegetables. The country relies heavily on foreign aid. Territorial disputes over the West Bank and Gaza have still to be completely resolved.

ITALY
Italian Republic

Area Sq Km	301 245	Languages	Italian
Area Sq Miles	116 311	Religions	Roman Catholic
Population	57 530 000	Currency	Euro
Capital	Rome (Roma)	Organizations	EU, OECD, UN

Map page 114-115

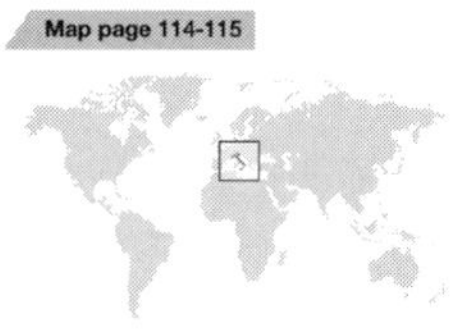

Most of the south European state of Italy occupies a peninsula which juts out into the Mediterranean Sea. It includes the islands of Sicily and Sardinia and approximately seventy much smaller islands in the surrounding seas. Italy is mountainous, dominated by two high ranges, the Alps, which form its northern border, and the various ranges of the Apennines, which run almost the full length of the peninsula. Many of Italy's mountains are of volcanic origin and its active volcanoes are Vesuvius, near Naples, Etna and Stromboli. The main lowland area, the Po river valley in the northeast, is the main agricultural and industrial area and is the most populous region. Italy has a Mediterranean climate although northern Italy experiences colder and wetter winters, with heavy snow in the Alps. Italy's natural resources are limited and only about twenty per cent of the land is suitable for cultivation. The economy is fairly diversified. Some oil, natural gas and coal are produced, but most fuels and minerals used by industry must be imported. Agriculture is important, with cereals, vines, fruit and vegetables the main crops. Italy is the world's largest wine producer. The north is the centre of Italian industry, especially around Turin, Milan and Genoa. Italy's leading manufactured goods include industrial and office equipment, domestic appliances, cars, textiles, clothing, leather goods, chemicals and metal products. Italy has a strong services sector. With over twenty-five million visitors a year, tourism is a major employer and accounts for five per cent of the national income. Finance and banking are also important. Most trade is with other EU countries.

JAMAICA

Area Sq Km	10 991	Languages	English, Creole
Area Sq Miles	4 244	Religions	Protestant, Roman Catholic
Population	2 576 000	Currency	Jamaican dollar
Capital	Kingston	Organizations	CARICOM, Comm., UN

Map page 149

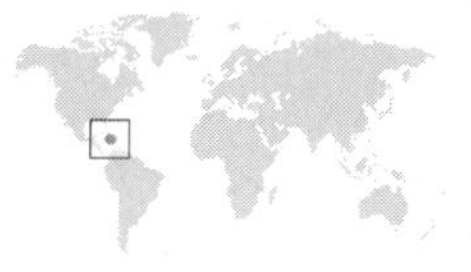

Jamaica, the third largest Caribbean island, has beaches and densely populated coastal plains traversed by hills and plateaus rising to the forested Blue Mountains in the east. The climate is tropical, but cooler and wetter on high ground. The economy is based on tourism, agriculture, mining and light manufacturing. Bauxite, aluminium oxide, sugar and bananas are the main exports. The USA is the main trading partner. Jamaica receives foreign aid.

Jammu and Kashmir
Disputed territory (India/Pakistan)

Area Sq Km	222 236	Population	13 000 000
Area Sq Miles	85 806	Capital	Srinagar

Map page 88   A disputed region in the north of Pakistan and India to the west of the Karakoram and Himalaya mountain ranges. The 'Line of Control' separates the northern, Pakistani controlled area and the southern, Indian controlled area.

JAPAN

Area Sq Km	377 727	Languages	Japanese
Area Sq Miles	145 841	Religions	Shintoist, Buddhist, Christian
Population	127 096 000	Currency	Yen
Capital	Tōkyō	Organizations	APEC, OECD, UN

Map page 94-95

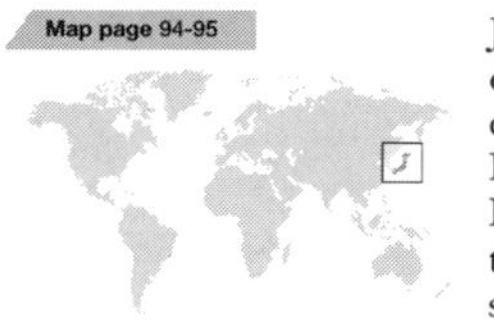

Japan, lies in the Pacific Ocean off the coast of east Asia and consists of four main islands – Hokkaidō, Honshū, Shikoku and Kyūshū – and more than three thousand smaller islands in the surrounding Sea of Japan, East China Sea and Pacific Ocean. The central island of Honshū accounts for sixty per cent of the total land area and contains eighty per cent of the population. Behind the long and deeply indented coastline, nearly three quarters of Japan is mountainous and heavily forested. Japan has over sixty active volcanoes, and is subject to frequent earthquakes and typhoons. The climate is generally temperate maritime, with warm summers and mild winters, except in western Hokkaidō and northwest Honshū, where the winters are very cold with heavy snow. Japan has few natural resources. It has a limited land area of which only fourteen per cent is suitable for cultivation. Production of its few industrial raw materials, coal, oil, natural gas, lead, zinc and copper, is insufficient for its industry and most raw materials must be imported, including about ninety per cent of energy requirements. Japan is the world's second largest industrial economy, with a range of modern heavy and light industries centred mainly around the major ports of Yokohama, Ōsaka and Tōkyō. It is the world's largest manufacturer of cars, motorcycles and merchant ships, and a major producer of steel, textiles, chemicals and cement. It is a leading producer of many consumer durables, such as washing machines, and electronic equipment, chiefly office equipment and computers. Japan has a strong service sector, banking and finance are particularly important, and Tōkyō is one of the world's major stock exchanges. Owing to intensive agricultural production, Japan is seventy per cent self-sufficient in food. The main food crops are rice, barley, fruit, wheat and soya beans. Livestock raising (chiefly cattle, pigs and chickens) and fishing are also important. Japan has one of the largest fishing fleets in the world. A major trading nation, Japan has trade links with many countries in southeast Asia and in Europe, although its main trading partner is the USA.

Jersey
United Kingdom Crown Dependency

Area Sq Km	116	Languages	English, French
Area Sq Miles	45	Religions	Protestant, Roman Catholic
Population	89 136	Currency	Pound sterling
Capital	St Helier		

Map page 110   One of the Channel Islands lying off the west coast of the Cherbourg peninsula in northern France.

JORDAN
Hashemite Kingdom of Jordan

Area Sq Km	89 206	Languages	Arabic
Area Sq Miles	34 443	Religions	Sunni Muslim, Christian
Population	4 913 000	Currency	Jordanian dinar
Capital	'Ammān	Organizations	UN

Map page 80-81

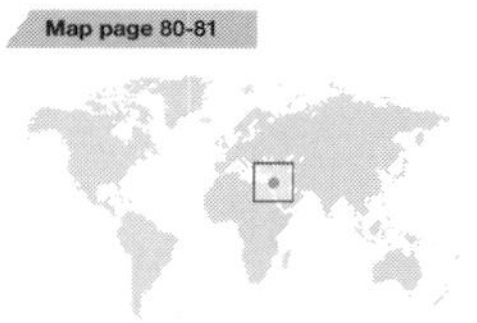

Jordan, in southwest Asia, is landlocked apart from a short coastline on the Gulf of Aqaba of the Red Sea. Much of the country is rocky desert plateaus and, to the west of the mountains, the land falls below sea level to the Dead Sea and Jordan river. The climate is hot and dry, and most of the population live in the northwest. Phosphates, potash, pharmaceuticals, fruit and vegetables are the main exports. The tourist industry is important and the economy relies on workers' remittances from abroad and foreign aid.

KAZAKHSTAN
Republic of Kazakhstan

Area Sq Km	2 717 300	Languages	Kazakh, Russian, Ukrainian, German, Uzbek, Tatar
Area Sq Miles	1 049 155	Religions	Sunni Muslim, Russian Orthodox, Protestant
Population	16 172 000	Currency	Tenge
Capital	Astana (Akmola)	Organizations	CIS, UN

Map page 82-83

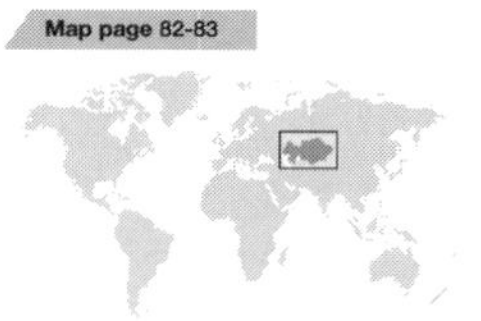

Stretching across central Asia, Kazakhstan covers a vast area of steppe and semi-desert. The land is flat in the west with large areas around the Caspian Sea, rising to mountains in the southeast. The climate is continental. Agriculture and livestock rearing are important and cotton and tobacco are the main cash crops. Kazakhstan is very rich in minerals, including coal, chromium, gold, molybdenum, lead and zinc and has substantial reserves of oil and gas. Mining, metallurgy, machine building and food processing are major industries. Oil, gas, and minerals are the main exports and the Russian Federation is the dominant trading partner.

KENYA
Republic of Kenya

Area Sq Km	582 646	Languages	Swahili, English, local languages
Area Sq Miles	224 961	Religions	Christian, traditional beliefs
Population	30 669 000	Currency	Kenyan shilling
Capital	Nairobi	Organizations	Comm., UN

Map page 122

Kenya is in East Africa, on the Indian Ocean. Inland beyond the coastal plains the land rises to plateaus interrupted by volcanic mountains. The Great Rift Valley runs north-south to the west of the capital, Nairobi.

Most of the population live in central Kenya. Conditions are tropical on the coast, semi-desert in the north and savanna in the south. Hydro-electric power from the Upper Tana river provides most of the electricity requirement. Agricultural products, mainly tea, coffee, fruit and vegetables, are the main exports. Light industry is important and tourism, oil refining and re-exports for landlocked neighbours are major foreign exchange earners.

KIRIBATI
Republic of Kiribati

Area Sq Km	717	Languages	Gilbertese, English
Area Sq Miles	277	Religions	Roman Catholic, Protestant
Population	83 000	Currency	Australian dollar
Capital	Bairiki	Organizations	Comm., UN

Map page 67

Kiribati, comprising coral islands in the Gilbert, Phoenix and Line groups and the volcanic island of Banaba, straddles the equator in the Pacific Ocean. Most of the population live on the Gilbert Islands, and the capital, Bairiki, is on Tarawa Island in this group. The climate is hot and the north is slightly wetter than the south. Copra and fish are exported. Kiribati relies on remittances from workers abroad and on foreign aid.

KUWAIT
State of Kuwait

Area Sq Km	17 818	Languages	Arabic
Area Sq Miles	6 880	Religions	Sunni Muslim, Shi'a Muslim, Christian, Hindu
Population	1 914 000	Currency	Kuwaiti dinar
Capital	Kuwait (Al Kuwayt)	Organizations	OPEC, UN

Map page 81

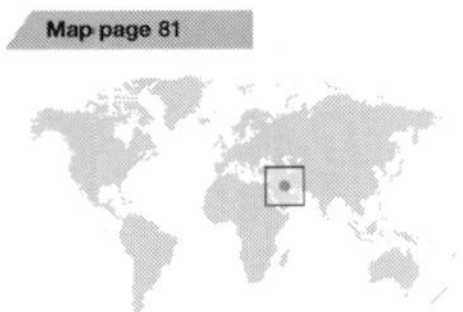

Kuwait lies on the northwest shores of The Gulf in southwest Asia. It is mainly low-lying desert, with irrigated areas along the bay, Kuwait Jun, where most of the population live. Summers are hot and dry, winters are cool with some rainfall. The oil industry, which accounts for eighty per cent of exports, has largely recovered from the damage caused by the Gulf War in 1991. Income is also derived from extensive overseas investments. Japan and the USA are the main trading partners.

KYRGYZSTAN
Kyrgyz Republic

Area Sq Km	198 500	Languages	Kyrgyz, Russian, Uzbek
Area Sq Miles	76 641	Religions	Sunni Muslim, Russian Orthodox
Population	4 921 000	Currency	Kyrgyz som
Capital	Bishkek (Frunze)	Organizations	CIS, UN

Map page 83

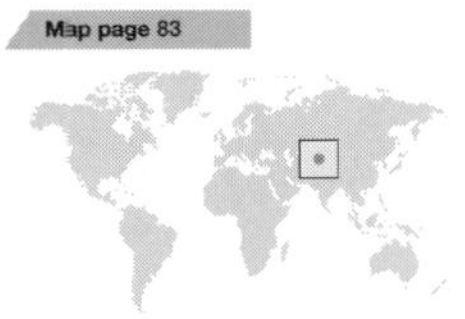

A landlocked central Asian state, Kyrgyzstan is rugged and mountainous, lying to the west of the Tien Shan mountain range. Most of the population live in the valleys of the north and west. Summers are hot and winters cold. Agriculture (chiefly livestock farming) is the main activity. Some oil and gas, coal, gold, antimony and mercury are produced. Manufactured goods include machinery, metals and metal products, which are the country's main exports. Most trade is with Germany, the Russian Federation, Kazakhstan and Uzbekistan.

LAOS
Lao People's Democratic Republic

Area Sq Km	236 800	Languages	Lao, local languages
Area Sq Miles	91 429	Religions	Buddhist, traditional beliefs
Population	5 279 000	Currency	Kip
Capital	Vientiane (Viangchan)	Organizations	ASEAN, UN

Map page 91

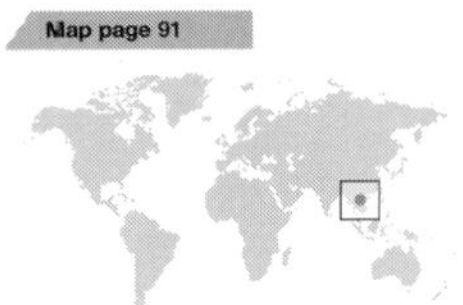

A landlocked country in southeast Asia, Laos is a land of mostly forested mountains and plateaus. The climate is tropical monsoon. Most people live in the Mekong river valley and the low plateau in the south, where food crops, chiefly rice, are grown. Electricity, from a hydro-electric plant on the Mekong, timber, coffee and tin are exported. Laos relies on foreign aid.

LATVIA
Republic of Latvia

Area Sq Km	63 700	Languages	Latvian, Russian
Area Sq Miles	24 595	Religions	Protestant, Roman Catholic, Russian Orthodox
Population	2 421 000	Currency	Lats
Capital	Rīga	Organizations	UN

Map page 103

Latvia is in north Europe, on the Baltic Sea and the Gulf of Rīga. The land is flat near the coast but hilly with woods and lakes inland. Latvia has a modified continental climate. One-third of the population live in the capital, Rīga. Crop and livestock farming are important. Latvia has few natural resources. Industries include food products, transport equipment, wood and wood products and textiles; these form most of the exports. The main trading partners are the Russian Federation and Germany.

LEBANON
Republic of Lebanon

Area Sq Km	10 452	Languages	Arabic, Armenian, French
Area Sq Miles	4 036	Religions	Shi'a Muslim, Sunni Muslim, Christian
Population	3 496 000	Currency	Lebanese pound
Capital	Beirut (Beyrouth)	Organizations	UN

Map page 80

Lebanon lies on the Mediterranean coast of southwest Asia. Beyond the coastal strip, where most of the population live, are two parallel mountain ranges, separated by the El Beqa'a valley. The 1975-1991 civil war crippled the traditional sectors of banking, commerce and tourism. Some fruit production and light industry survived and reconstruction of the infrastructure is under way. Financial service companies are beginning to return. Italy, France and UAE are the main trading partners.

LESOTHO
Kingdom of Lesotho

Area Sq Km	30 355	Languages	Sesotho, English, Zulu
Area Sq Miles	11 720	Religions	Christian, traditional beliefs
Population	2 035 000	Currency	Loti, South African rand
Capital	Maseru	Organizations	Comm., SADC, UN

Map page 125

Lesotho is a landlocked state surrounded by the Republic of South Africa. It is a mountainous country lying within the Drakensberg range. Farming and herding are the main activities. The economy depends heavily on South Africa for transport links and employment. A major hydropower plant completed in 1998 allows the sale of water to South Africa. Exports include manufactured goods (mainly clothing and road vehicles), food and live animals, wool and mohair.

LIBERIA
Republic of Liberia

Area Sq Km	111 369	Languages	English, Creole, local languages
Area Sq Miles	43 000	Religions	Traditional beliefs, Christian, Sunni Muslim
Population	2 913 000	Currency	Liberian dollar
Capital	Monrovia	Organizations	UN

Map page 120

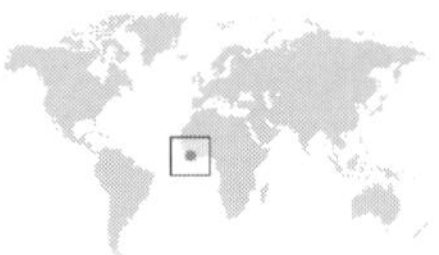

Liberia is on the Atlantic coast of west Africa. Beyond the coastal belt of sandy beaches and mangrove swamps the land rises to a forested plateau and highlands along the Guinea border. A quarter of the population live along the coast. The climate is hot with heavy rainfall. Liberia is rich in mineral resources and forests. The economy is based on the production and export of basic products. Exports include diamonds, iron ore, rubber and timber. Liberia has a huge international debt and relies heavily on foreign aid.

LIBYA
Socialist People's Libyan Arab Jamahiriya

Area Sq Km	1 759 540	Languages	Arabic, Berber
Area Sq Miles	679 362	Religions	Sunni Muslim
Population	5 290 000	Currency	Libyan dinar
Capital	Tripoli (Tarābulus)	Organizations	OPEC, UN

Map page 120-121

Libya lies on the Mediterranean coast of north Africa. The desert plains and hills of the Sahara dominate the landscape and the climate is hot and dry. Most of the population live in cities near the coast, where the climate is cooler with moderate rainfall. Farming and herding, chiefly in the northwest, are important but the main industry is oil. Libya is a major oil producer and oil accounts for virtually all of its export earnings. Italy and Germany are the main trading partners.

LIECHTENSTEIN
Principality of Liechtenstein

Area Sq Km	160	Languages	German
Area Sq Miles	62	Religions	Roman Catholic, Protestant
Population	33 000	Currency	Swiss franc
Capital	Vaduz	Organizations	UN

Map page 110

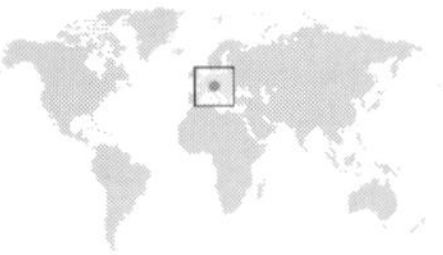

A landlocked state between Switzerland and Austria, Liechtenstein has an industrialized, free-enterprise economy. Low business taxes have attracted companies to establish offices which provide approximately one-third of state revenues. Banking is also important. Major products include precision instruments, ceramics and textiles.

LITHUANIA
Republic of Lithuania

Area Sq Km	65 200	Languages	Lithuanian, Russian, Polish
Area Sq Miles	25 174	Religions	Roman Catholic, Protestant, Russian Orthodox
Population	3 696 000	Currency	Litas
Capital	Vilnius	Organizations	UN

Map page 103

Lithuania is in northern Europe, on the eastern shores of the Baltic Sea. It is mainly lowland with many lakes, rivers and marshes. The climate is generally temperate. Agriculture, fishing and forestry are important, but manufacturing dominates the economy. The main exports are machinery, mineral products and chemicals. The Russian Federation and Germany are the main trading partners.

LUXEMBOURG
Grand Duchy of Luxembourg

Area Sq Km	2 586	Languages	Letzeburgish, German, French
Area Sq Miles	998	Religions	Roman Catholic
Population	437 000	Currency	Euro
Capital	Luxembourg	Organizations	EU, OECD, UN

Map page 108

Luxembourg, a small landlocked country in west Europe, borders Belgium, France and Germany. The hills and forests of the Ardennes dominate the north, with rolling pasture to the south, where the main towns, farms and industries are located. The iron and steel industry is important, however light industries (including textiles, chemicals and food products) are growing. Luxembourg is a major banking centre. Main trading partners are Belgium, Germany and France.

MACEDONIA (F.Y.R.O.M.)
Republic of Macedonia

Area Sq Km	25 713	Languages	Macedonian, Albanian, Turkish
Area Sq Miles	9 928	Religions	Macedonian Orthodox, Sunni Muslim
Population	2 034 000	Currency	Macedonian denar
Capital	Skopje	Organizations	UN

Map page 115

The Former Yugoslav Republic of Macedonia, is a landlocked state in southern Europe. Lying within the south Balkan Mountains, it is traversed northwest-southeast by the Vardar river valley. The climate is continental. The economy is based on industry, mining and agriculture, but the conflicts in the region have reduced trade and caused economic difficulties. Foreign aid and loans are now assisting in modernization and development of the country.

MADAGASCAR
Republic of Madagascar

Area Sq Km	587 041	Languages	Malagasy, French
Area Sq Miles	226 658	Religions	Traditional beliefs, Christian, Sunni Muslim
Population	15 970 000	Currency	Malagasy franc
Capital	Antananarivo	Organizations	UN

Map page 123

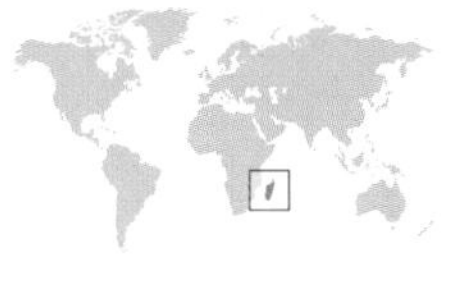

Madagascar lies off the east coast of southern Africa. The world's fourth largest island, it is mainly a high plateau with a coastal strip to the east and scrubby plain to the west. The climate is tropical with heavy rainfall in the north and east. Most people live on the plateau. Although the amount of arable land is limited the economy is based on agriculture. The main industries are agricultural processing, textile manufacturing and oil refining. Foreign aid is important. Exports include coffee, vanilla, cotton cloth, sugar and shrimps. France is the main trading partner.

MALAWI
Republic of Malawi

Area Sq Km	118 484	Languages	Chichewa, English, local languages
Area Sq Miles	45 747	Religions	Christian, traditional beliefs, Sunni Muslim
Population	11 308 000	Currency	Malawian kwacha
Capital	Lilongwe	Organizations	Comm., SADC, UN

Map page 123

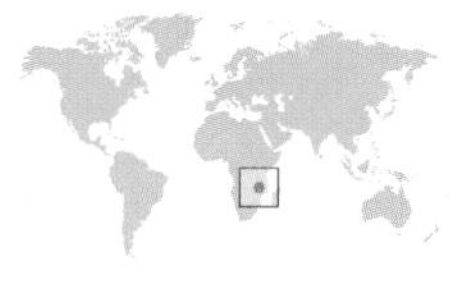

Landlocked Malawi in south Africa is a narrow hilly country at the southern end of the Great Rift Valley. One-fifth of the country is covered by Lake Nyasa. Most of the population live in rural areas in the southern regions. The climate is mainly subtropical with varying rainfall. The economy is predominantly agricultural. Tobacco, tea and sugar are the main exports. Malawi is one of the world's least developed countries and relies heavily on foreign aid. South Africa is the main trading partner.

MALAYSIA
Federation of Malaysia

Area Sq Km	332 965	Languages	Malay, English, Chinese, Tamil, local languages
Area Sq Miles	128 559	Religions	Sunni Muslim, Buddhist, Hindu, Christian, traditional beliefs
Population	22 218 000	Currency	Ringgit
Capital	Kuala Lumpur	Organizations	APEC, ASEAN, Comm., UN

Map page 99

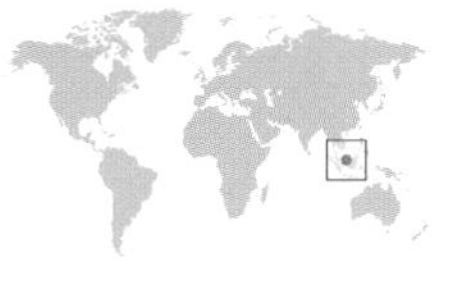

The Federation of Malaysia, in Southeast Asia, comprises two regions, separated by the South China Sea. The western region occupies the southern part of the Malay Peninsula, which has a chain of mountains dividing the eastern coastal strip from the wider plains to the west. East Malaysia, the states of Sabah and Sarawak in the north of the island of Borneo, is mainly rainforest-covered hills and mountains with mangrove swamps along the coast. Both regions have a tropical climate with heavy rainfall. About eighty per cent of the population live in the western part of the country, Peninsular Malaysia. The country is rich in natural resources and has reserves of minerals and fuels. It is an important producer of tin, oil, natural gas and tropical hardwoods. Agriculture forms a substantial part of the economy, but industry is the most important sector. The main exports are transport and electronic equipment, oil, chemicals, palm oil, wood and rubber. The main trading partners are Japan, the USA and Singapore.

MALDIVES
Republic of the Maldives

Area Sq Km	298	Languages	Divehi (Maldivian)
Area Sq Miles	115	Religions	Sunni Muslim
Population	291 000	Currency	Rufiyaa
Capital	Male	Organizations	Comm., UN

Map page 74

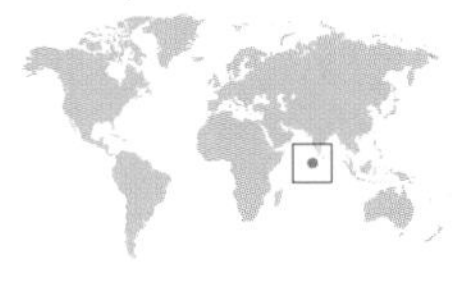

The Maldive archipelago comprises over a thousand coral atolls (around two hundred of which are inhabited), in the Indian Ocean, southwest of India. Over eighty per cent of the land area is less than one metre above sea level. The main atolls are North Male, South Male and Addu. The climate is hot, humid and monsoonal. There is little cultivation and almost all food is imported. Tourism has expanded rapidly and is the most important sector of the economy.

MALI
Republic of Mali

Area Sq Km	1 240 140	Languages	French, Bambara, local languages
Area Sq Miles	478 821	Religions	Sunni Muslim, traditional beliefs, Christian
Population	11 351 000	Currency	CFA franc
Capital	Bamako	Organizations	UN

Map page 120

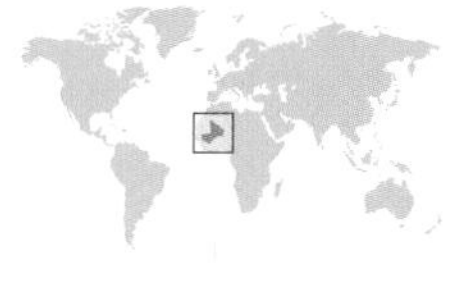

A landlocked state in west Africa, Mali is mostly low-lying with a few rugged hills in the northeast. Northern regions lie within the Sahara desert. To the south, around the Niger river, are marshes and savanna grassland. Rainfall is unreliable. Most people live along the Niger and Faléme rivers. Exports include cotton, livestock and gold. Mali is one of the least developed countries in the world and relies heavily on foreign aid.

MALTA
Republic of Malta

Area Sq Km	316	Languages	Maltese, English
Area Sq Miles	122	Religions	Roman Catholic
Population	390 000	Currency	Maltese lira
Capital	Valletta	Organizations	Comm., UN

Map page 114

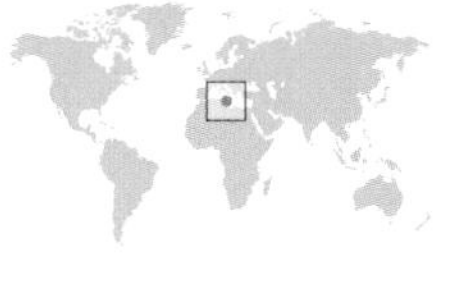

The islands of Malta and Gozo lie in the Mediterranean Sea, off the coast of south Italy. Malta, the main island, has low hills and an indented coastline. The islands have hot, dry summers and mild winters. The economy is dependent on foreign trade, tourism and the manufacture of electronics and textiles. Main trading partners are the USA, France and Italy.

MARSHALL ISLANDS
Republic of the Marshall Islands

Area Sq Km	181	Languages	English, Marshallese
Area Sq Miles	70	Religions	Protestant, Roman Catholic
Population	51 000	Currency	US dollar
Capital	Delap-Uliga-Djarrit	Organizations	UN

Map page 67

The Marshall Islands consist of over a thousand atolls, islands and islets, within two chains, in the north Pacific Ocean. The main atolls are Majuro (home to half the population), Kwajalein, Jaluit, Enewetak and Bikini. The climate is tropical with heavy autumn rainfall. About half the workforce is employed in farming or fishing. Tourism is a small source of foreign exchange and the islands depend heavily on US aid.

Martinique
French Overseas Department

Area Sq Km	1 079	Languages	French, Creole
Area Sq Miles	417	Religions	Roman Catholic, traditional beliefs
Population	383 000	Currency	Euro
Capital	Fort-de-France		

Map page 149

 Martinique, one of the Caribbean Windward Islands, has volcanic peaks in the north, a populous central plain, and hills and beaches in the south. The economy is based on sugar cane, bananas, oil refining and rum distilling. Tourism is a major source of foreign exchange and substantial aid is received from France. The main countries trading partners are France and Guadeloupe.

MAURITANIA
Islamic Arab and African Republic of Mauritania

Area Sq Km	1 030 700	Languages	Arabic, French, local languages
Area Sq Miles	397 955	Religions	Sunni Muslim
Population	2 665 000	Currency	Ouguiya
Capital	Nouakchott	Organizations	UN

Map page 120

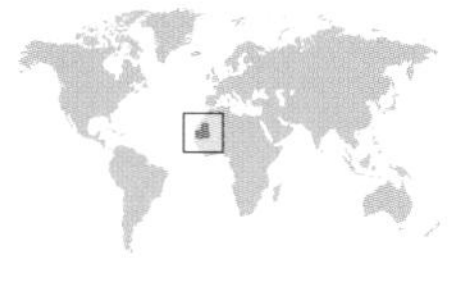

Mauritania is on the Atlantic coast of northwest Africa and lies almost entirely within the Sahara desert. Oases and a fertile strip along the Sénégal river to the south are the only areas suitable for cultivation. The climate is generally hot and dry. About a quarter of Mauritanians live in the capital, Nouakchott. Most of the workforce depends on livestock rearing and subsistence farming. There are large deposits of iron ore which account for more than half of total exports. Mauritania's coastal waters are among the richest fishing grounds in the world. Main trading partners are France, Japan and Italy.

MAURITIUS
Republic of Mauritius

Area Sq Km	2 040	Languages	English, Creole, Hindi, Bhojpuri, French
Area Sq Miles	788	Religions	Hindu, Roman Catholic, Sunni Muslim
Population	1 161 000	Currency	Mauritius rupee
Capital	Port Louis	Organizations	Comm., SADC, UN

Map page 119

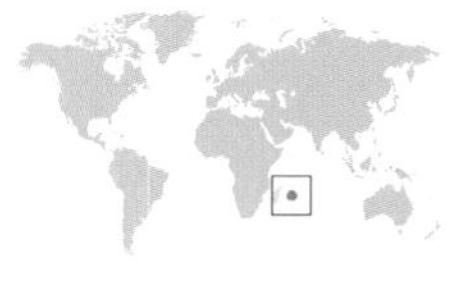

The state comprises Mauritius, Rodrigues and some twenty small islands in the Indian Ocean, east of Madagascar. The main island of Mauritius is volcanic in origin and has a coral coast rising to a central plateau. Most of the population live on the north and west sides of the island. The climate is warm and humid. The economy is based on sugar production, light manufacturing (chiefly clothing) and tourism.

Mayotte
French Territorial Collectivity

Area Sq Km	373	Languages	French, Mahorian
Area Sq Miles	144	Religions	Sunni Muslim, Christian
Population	144 944	Currency	Euro
Capital	Dzaoudzi		

Map page 123

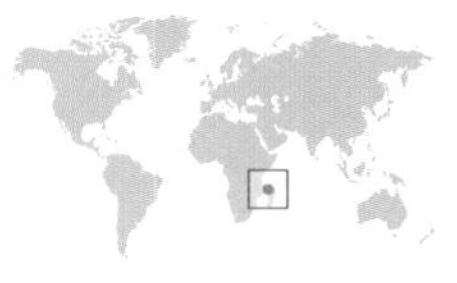

Lying in the Indian Ocean off the east coast of central Africa, Mayotte is geographically part of the Comoros archipelago. The economy is based on agriculture, but Mayotte depends heavily on aid from France.

MEXICO
United Mexican States

Area Sq Km	1 972 545	Languages	Spanish, Amerindian languages
Area Sq Miles	761 604	Religions	Roman Catholic, Protestant
Population	98 872 000	Currency	Mexican peso
Capital	Mexico City	Organizations	APEC, OECD, UN

Map page 150-151

The largest country in Central America, Mexico extends south from the USA to Guatemala and Belize, and from the Pacific Ocean to the Gulf of Mexico. The greater part of the country is high plateau flanked by the western and eastern ranges of the Sierra Madre mountains. The principal lowland is the Yucatán peninsula in the southeast. The climate varies with latitude and altitude: hot and humid in the lowlands, warm on the plateau and cool with cold winters in the mountains. The north is arid, while the far south has heavy rainfall. Mexico City is the second largest conurbation in the world and the country's centre of trade and industry. Agriculture involves a fifth of the workforce, crops include grains, coffee, cotton and vegetables. Mexico is rich in minerals, including copper, zinc, lead, tin, sulphur, and silver. It is one of the world's largest producers of oil, from vast oil and gas reserves in the Gulf of Mexico. The oil and petrochemical industries still dominate, but a variety of manufactured goods are now produced including iron and steel, motor vehicles, textiles, chemicals and food and tobacco products. Tourism is growing in importance. Over three-quarters of all trade is with the USA.

MICRONESIA, FEDERATED STATES OF
United Mexican States

Area Sq Km	701	Languages	English, Chuukese, Pohnpeian, local languages
Area Sq Miles	271	Religions	Roman Catholic, Protestant
Population	123 000	Currency	US dollar
Capital	Palikir	Organizations	UN

Map page 66-67

Micronesia comprises over six hundred atolls and islands of the Caroline Islands in the north Pacific Ocean. A third of the population live on Pohnpei. The climate is tropical with heavy rainfall. Fishing and subsistence farming are the main activities. Fish, garments and bananas are the main exports. Income is also derived from tourism and the licensing of foreign fishing fleets. The islands depend heavily on US aid.

MOLDOVA
Republic of Moldova

Area Sq Km	33 700	Languages	Romanian, Ukrainian, Gagauz, Russian
Area Sq Miles	13 012	Religions	Romanian Orthodox, Russian Orthodox
Population	4 295 000	Currency	Moldovan leu
Capital	Chişinău (Kishinev)	Organizations	CIS, UN

Map page 117

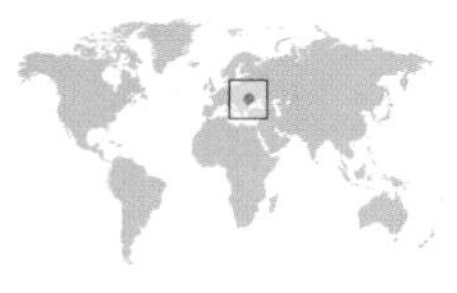

Moldova lies between Romania and Ukraine in east Europe. It consists of hilly steppe, drained by the Prut and Dniester rivers. Moldova has no mineral resources and the economy is mainly agricultural, with vegetables, tobacco, wine and fruit the chief products. Food processing, machinery and textiles are the main industries. The Russian Federation is the main trading partner.

MONACO
Principality of Monaco

Area Sq Km	2	Languages	French, Monegasque, Italian
Area Sq Miles	1	Religions	Roman Catholic
Population	33 000	Currency	Euro
Capital	Monaco-Ville	Organizations	UN

Map page 110

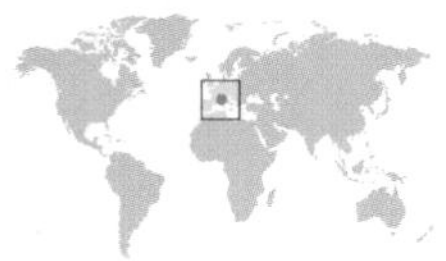

The principality occupies a rocky peninsula and a strip of land on France's Mediterranean coast. Monaco's economy depends on service industries (chiefly tourism, banking and finance) and light industry.

MONGOLIA

Area Sq Km	1 565 000	Languages	Khalka (Mongolian), Kazakh, local languages
Area Sq Miles	604 250	Religions	Buddhist, Sunni Muslim
Population	2 533 000	Currency	Tugrik (tögrög)
Capital	Ulan Bator (Ulaanbaatar)	Organizations	UN

Map page 90

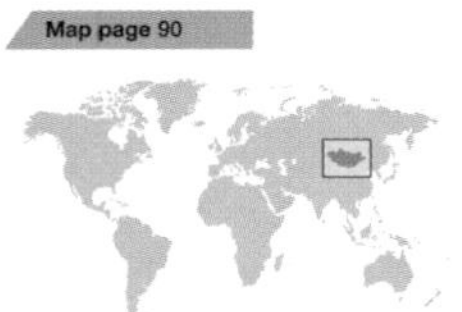

Mongolia is a landlocked country in east Asia between the Russian Federation and China. Much of it is high steppe, with mountains and lakes in the west and north. In the south is the Gobi desert. Mongolia has long, cold winters and short, mild summers. A quarter of the population live in the capital, Ulan Bator. Livestock breeding and agricultural processing are important. There are substantial mineral resources. Copper and textiles are the main exports. China and the Russian Federation are the main trading partners.

Montserrat
United Kingdom Overseas Territory

Area Sq Km	100	Languages	English
Area Sq Miles	39	Religions	Protestant, Roman Catholic
Population	4 000	Currency	East Caribbean dollar
Capital	Plymouth	Organizations	CARICOM

Map page 149

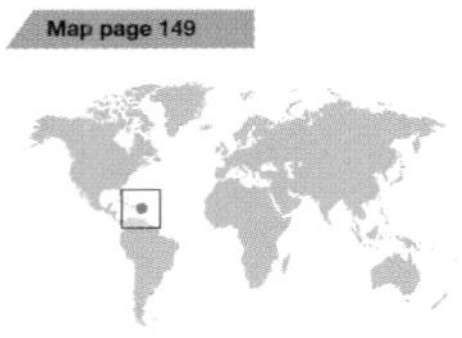

An island in the Leeward Island group in the Lesser Antilles in the Caribbean. From 1995 to 1997 the volcanoes in the Soufrière Hills erupted for the first time since 1630. Over sixty per cent of the island was covered in volcanic ash, the capital town was destroyed, many people emigrated and the remaining population moved to the north of the island. Reconstruction, funded by aid from the UK has begun.

MOROCCO
Kingdom of Morocco

Area Sq Km	446 550	Languages	Arabic, Berber, French
Area Sq Miles	172 414	Religions	Sunni Muslim
Population	29 878 000	Currency	Moroccan dirham
Capital	Rabat	Organizations	UN

Map page 120

Lying in the northwest corner of Africa, Morocco has both Atlantic and Mediterranean coasts. The Atlas Mountains separate the arid south and disputed region of Western Sahara from the fertile regions of the west and north, which

have a milder climate. Most Moroccans live on the Atlantic coastal plain. The economy is based mainly on agriculture, phosphate mining and tourism, the most important industries are food processing, textiles and chemicals. France is the main trading partner.

MOZAMBIQUE
Republic of Mozambique

Area Sq Km	799 380	Languages	Portuguese, Makua, Tsonga, local languages
Area Sq Miles	308 642	Religions	Traditional beliefs, Roman Catholic, Sunni Muslim
Population	18 292 000	Currency	Metical
Capital	Maputo	Organizations	Comm., SADC, UN

Map page 123

Mozambique lies on the east coast of southern Africa. The land is mainly a savanna plateau drained by the Zambezi and Limpopo rivers, with highlands to the north. Most people live on the coast or in the river valleys. In general the climate is tropical with winter rainfall, but droughts occur. The economy is based on subsistence agriculture. Exports include shrimps, cashews, cotton and sugar, but Mozambique relies heavily on aid, and remains one of the least developed countries in the world.

MYANMAR
Union of Myanmar

Area Sq Km	676 577	Languages	Burmese, Shan, Karen, local languages
Area Sq Miles	261 228	Religions	Buddhist, Christian, Sunni Muslim
Population	47 749 000	Currency	Kyat
Capital	Rangoon (Yangôn)	Organizations	ASEAN, UN

Map page 91

Myanmar is in Southeast Asia, bordering the Bay of Bengal and Andaman Sea. Most of the population live in the valley and delta of the Irrawaddy river, which is flanked on three sides by mountains and high plateaus. The climate is hot and monsoonal, and rainforest covers much of the land. Most of the workforce is employed in agriculture. Myanmar is rich in minerals, including zinc, lead, copper and silver. Political and social unrest and lack of foreign investment have affected economic development.

NAMIBIA
Republic of Namibia

Area Sq Km	824 292	Languages	English, Afrikaans, German, Ovambo, local languages
Area Sq Miles	318 261	Religions	Protestant, Roman Catholic
Population	1 757 000	Currency	Namibian dollar
Capital	Windhoek	Organizations	Comm., SADC, UN

Map page 123

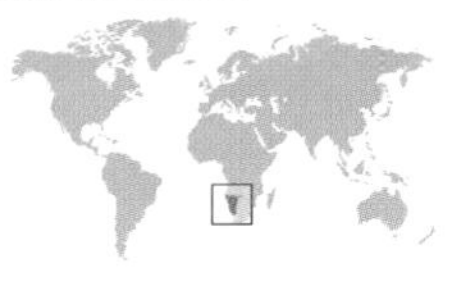

Namibia lies on the Atlantic coast of southern Africa. Mountain ranges separate the coastal Namib Desert from the interior plateau, bordered to the south and east by the Kalahari Desert. Namibia is hot and dry but some summer rain falls in the north and supports crops and livestock. Most of the workforce is employed in agriculture although the economy is based on mineral extraction, predominantly diamonds but also uranium, lead, zinc and silver. Fishing is increasingly important. The economy is closely linked to that of South Africa.

NAURU
Republic of Nauru

Area Sq Km	21	Languages	Nauruan, English
Area Sq Miles	8	Religions	Protestant, Roman Catholic
Population	12 000	Currency	Australian dollar
Capital	Yaren	Organizations	Comm., UN

Map page 69

Nauru is a coral island near the equator in the Pacific Ocean, it has a fertile coastal strip, a barren central plateau and a tropical climate. The economy is based on phosphate mining, but reserves are near exhaustion and replacement of this income is a serious long-term problem.

NEPAL
Kingdom of Nepal

Area Sq Km	147 181	Languages	Nepali, Maithili, Bhojpuri, English, local languages
Area Sq Miles	56 827	Religions	Hindu, Buddhist, Sunni Muslim
Population	23 043 000	Currency	Nepalese rupee
Capital	Kathmandu	Organizations	UN

Map page 88-89

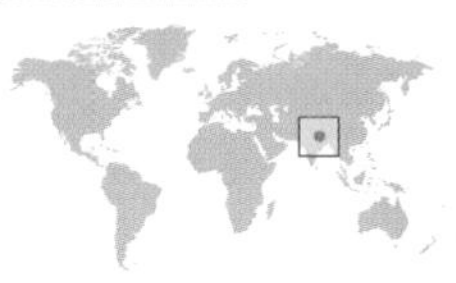

Nepal lies in the eastern Himalaya mountains between India and China. High mountains (including Everest) dominate northern Nepal. Most people live in the temperate central valleys and subtropical southern plains. The economy is based largely on agriculture and forestry. There is some manufacturing, chiefly textiles and carpets, and tourism is important. Nepal relies heavily on foreign aid.

NETHERLANDS
Kingdom of the Netherlands

Area Sq Km	41 526	Languages	Dutch, Frisian
Area Sq Miles	16 033	Religions	Roman Catholic, Protestant, Sunni Muslim
Population	15 864 000	Currency	Euro
Capital	Amsterdam/ The Hague	Organizations	EU, OECD, UN

Map page 108

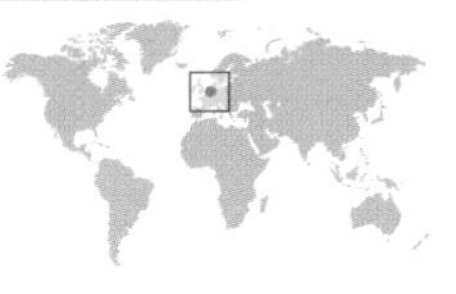

The Netherlands lies on the North Sea coast of west Europe. Apart from low hills in the far southeast, the land is flat and low-lying, much of it below sea level. The coastal region includes the delta of five rivers and polders (reclaimed land), protected by sand dunes, dykes and canals. The climate is temperate, with cool summers and mild winters. Rainfall is spread evenly throughout the year. The Netherlands is a densely populated and highly urbanized country, with the majority of the population living in the west Amsterdam-Rotterdam-The Hague area. Horticulture and dairy farming are important activities, although they employ less than four per cent of the workforce. The Netherlands ranks as the world's third agricultural exporter, and is a leading producer and exporter of natural gas from reserves in the North Sea. The economy is based mainly on international trade and manufacturing industry. The main industries produce food products, chemicals, machinery, electric and electronic goods and transport equipment. Germany is the main trading partner followed by other EU countries.

Netherlands Antilles
Self-governing Netherlands Territory

Area Sq Km	800	Languages	Dutch, Papiamento, English
Area Sq Miles	309	Religions	Roman Catholic, Protestant
Population	215 000	Currency	Netherlands Antilles guilder
Capital	Willemstad		

Map page 157

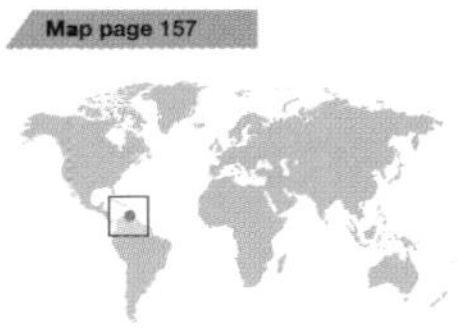

The territory comprises two separate island groups: Curaçao and Bonaire off the northern coast of Venezuela, and Saba, Sint Eustatius and the southern part of the island of Sint Maarten (St Martin) in the north Lesser Antilles. Tourism, oil refining and offshore finance are the mainstays of the economy and the main trading partners are the USA, Venezuela and Mexico.

New Caledonia
French Overseas Territory

Area Sq Km	19 058	Languages	French, local languages
Area Sq Miles	7 358	Religions	Roman Catholic, Protestant, Sunni Muslim
Population	215 000	Currency	CFP franc
Capital	Nouméa		

Map page 69

An island group lying in the southwest Pacific Ocean, with a sub-tropical climate. New Caledonia has over one-fifth of the world's nickel reserves and the main economic activity is metal mining. Tourism is also important to the economy. New Caledonia relies on aid from France.

NEW ZEALAND

Area Sq Km	270 534	Languages	English, Maori
Area Sq Miles	104 454	Religions	Protestant, Roman Catholic
Population	3 778 000	Currency	New Zealand dollar
Capital	Wellington	Organizations	APEC, Comm., OECD, UN

Map page 72

New Zealand comprises two main islands separated by the narrow Cook Strait, and a number of smaller islands. North Island, where three quarters of the population live, has mountain ranges, broad fertile valleys and a central plateau with hot springs and active volcanoes. South Island is also mountainous with the Southern Alps running its entire length. The only major lowland area is the Canterbury Plains in the centre east. The climate is generally temperate, although South Island has colder winters. Farming is the mainstay of the economy. New Zealand is one of the world's leading producers of meat (beef, lamb and mutton), wool and dairy products; fruit and fish are also important. Hydroelectric and geothermal power provide much of the country's energy needs. Other industries produce timber, wood pulp, iron, aluminium, machinery and chemicals. Tourism is the fastest growing sector of the economy. The main trading partners are Australia, the USA and Japan.

NICARAGUA
Republic of Nicaragua

Area Sq Km	130 000	Languages	Spanish, Amerindian languages
Area Sq Miles	50 193	Religions	Roman Catholic, Protestant
Population	5 071 000	Currency	Córdoba
Capital	Managua	Organizations	UN

Map page 153

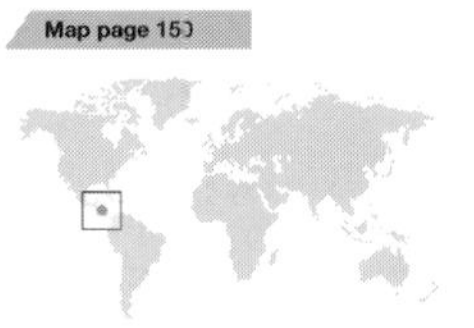

Nicaragua lies at the heart of Central America, with both Pacific and Caribbean coasts. Mountain ranges separate the east, which is largely rainforest, from the more developed western regions, including Lake Nicaragua and some active volcanoes. The highest land is in the north. The climate is tropical. Nicaragua is one of the western hemisphere's poorest countries and the economy is largely agricultural. Exports include coffee, seafood, cotton and bananas. The USA is the main trading partner. Nicaragua has a huge national debt and relies heavily on foreign aid.

NIGER
Republic of Niger

Area Sq Km	1 267 000	Languages	French, Hausa, Fulani, local languages
Area Sq Miles	489 191	Religions	Sunni Muslim, traditional beliefs
Population	10 832 000	Currency	CFA franc
Capital	Niamey	Organizations	UN

Map page 120-121

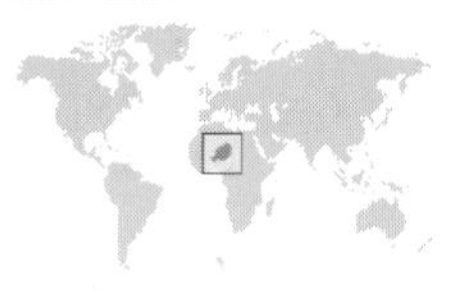

A landlocked state of west Africa, Niger lies mostly within the Sahara desert, but with savanna in the south and in the Niger valley area. The mountains of the Massif de l'Aïr dominate central regions. Much of the country is hot and dry. The south has some summer rainfall, although droughts occur. The economy depends on subsistence farming, herding, and uranium exports. Niger is one of the world's least developed countries and relies heavily on foreign aid. France is the main trading partner.

NIGERIA
Federal Republic of Nigeria

Area Sq Km	923 768	Languages	English, Hausa, Yoruba, Ibo, Fulani, local languages
Area Sq Miles	356 669	Religions	Sunni Muslim, Christian, traditional beliefs
Population	113 862 000	Currency	Naira
Capital	Abuja	Organizations	Comm., OPEC, UN

Map page 120-121

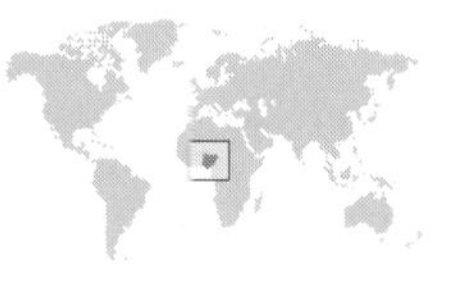

Nigeria is in west Africa, on the Gulf of Guinea, and is the most populous country in Africa. The Niger delta dominates coastal areas, fringed with sandy beaches, mangrove swamps and lagoons. Inland is a belt of rainforest which gives way to woodland or savanna on high plateaus. The far north is the semi-desert edge of the Sahara. The climate is tropical with heavy summer rainfall in the south but low rainfall in the north. Most of the population live in the coastal lowlands or in western Nigeria. More than half the workforce is involved in agriculture, mainly growing subsistence crops. Agricultural production, however, has failed to keep up with demand and Nigeria is now a net importer of food. Cocoa and rubber are the only significant export crops. The economy is heavily dependent on vast oil resources in the Niger delta and in shallow offshore waters, which account for over ninety per cent of export earnings. Nigeria also has natural gas reserves and some mineral deposits, but these are largely undeveloped. Industry involves mainly oil refining, chemicals (chiefly fertilizer), agricultural processing, textiles, steel manufacture and vehicle assembly. Political instability has left Nigeria with heavy debts, poverty and unemployment.

Niue
Self-governing New Zealand Territory

Area Sq Km	258	Languages	English, Polynesian
Area Sq Miles	100	Religions	Christian
Population	2 000	Currency	New Zealand dollar
Capital	Alofi		

Map page 69

Niue, one of the largest coral islands in the world, lies in the south Pacific Ocean about 500 kilometres (300 miles) east of Tonga. The economy depends on aid and remittances from New Zealand. The population is declining because of migration to New Zealand.

Norfolk Island
Australian External Territory

Area Sq Km	35	Languages	English
Area Sq Miles	14	Religions	Protestant, Roman Catholic
Population	2 000	Currency	Australian dollar
Capital	Kingston		

Map page 69

In the south Pacific Ocean, Norfolk Island lies between Vanuatu and New Zealand. Tourism is the mainstay of the economy and provides revenues for agricultural development.

Northern Mariana Islands
United States Commonwealth

Area Sq Km	477	Languages	English, Chamorro, local languages
Area Sq Miles	184	Religions	Roman Catholic
Population	73 000	Currency	US dollar
Capital	Capitol Hill		

Map page 91

A chain of islands in the northwest Pacific Ocean, extending over 550 kilometres (350 miles) north to south. The main island is Saipan. Tourism is a major industry employing approximately half the workforce.

NORTH KOREA
People's Democratic Republic of Korea

Area Sq Km	120 538	Languages	Korean
Area Sq Miles	46 540	Religions	Traditional beliefs, Chondoist, Buddhist
Population	22 268 000	Currency	North Korean won
Capital	P'yŏngyang	Organizations	UN

Map page 96

Occupying the northern half of the Korean peninsula in east Asia, North Korea is a rugged and mountainous country. The principal lowlands and the main agricultural areas are the plains in the southwest. More than half the population live in urban areas, mainly on the coastal plains. North Korea has a continental climate, with cold, dry winters and hot, wet summers. Approximately one-third of the workforce is involved in agriculture, mainly growing food crops on co-operative farms. A variety of minerals and ores, chiefly iron ore, are mined and are the basis of the country's heavy industry. Exports include minerals (lead, magnesite and zinc) and metal products (chiefly iron and steel). The economy has declined since 1991 when ties to the former USSR and eastern bloc collapsed, and there continue to be serious food shortages.

NORWAY
Kingdom of Norway

Area Sq Km	323 878	Languages	Norwegian
Area Sq Miles	125 050	Religions	Protestant, Roman Catholic
Population	4 469 000	Currency	Norwegian krone
Capital	Oslo	Organizations	OECD, UN

Map page 102-103

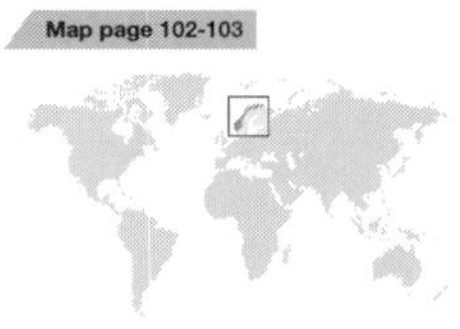

Norway stretches along the north and west coasts of Scandinavia, from the Arctic Ocean to the North Sea. Its extensive coastline is indented with fjords and fringed with many islands. Inland, the terrain is mountainous, with coniferous forests and lakes in the south. The only major lowland areas are along the North Sea and Skagerrak coasts, where most of the population live. The climate is modified by the effect of the North Atlantic Drift. Norway has vast petroleum and natural gas resources in the North Sea. It is one of west Europe's leading producers of oil and gas, and exports of oil account for approximately half of total export earnings. Related industries include engineering (oil and gas platforms) and petrochemicals. More traditional industries process fish, timber and minerals. Agriculture is limited, but fishing and fish farming are important. Norway is the world's leading exporter of farmed salmon. Merchant shipping and tourism are major sources of foreign exchange.

OMAN
Sultanate of Oman

Area Sq Km	309 500	Languages	Arabic, Baluchi, Indian languages
Area Sq Miles	119 499	Religions	Ibadhi Muslim, Sunni Muslim
Population	2 538 000	Currency	Omani riyal
Capital	Muscat (Masqat)	Organizations	UN

Map page 86

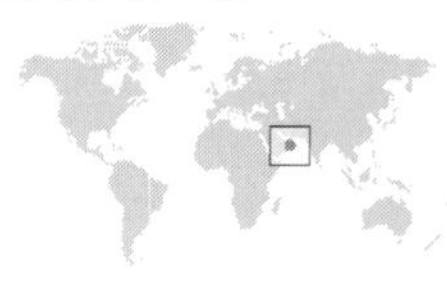

In southwest Asia, Oman occupies the east and southeast coasts of the Arabian Peninsula and an enclave north of the United Arab Emirates. Most of the land is desert, with mountains in the north and south. The climate is hot and mainly dry. Most of the population live on the coastal strip on the Gulf of Oman. The majority depend on farming and fishing, but the oil and gas industries dominate the economy, with approximately eighty per cent of export revenues coming from oil.

PAKISTAN
Islamic Republic of Pakistan

Area Sq Km	803 940	Languages	Urdu, Punjabi, Sindhi, Pushtu, English
Area Sq Miles	310 403	Religions	Sunni Muslim, Shi'a Muslim, Christian, Hindu
Population	141 256 000	Currency	Pakistani rupee
Capital	Islamabad	Organizations	Comm., UN

Map page 85

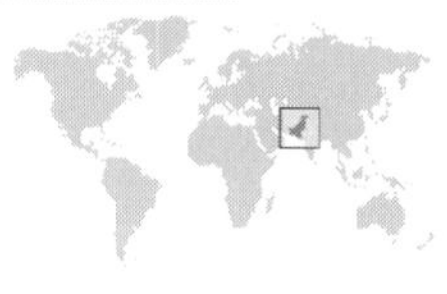

Pakistan is in the northwest part of the Indian subcontinent in south Asia, on the Arabian Sea. East and south Pakistan are dominated by the great basin of the Indus river system. This is the main agricultural area and contains most of the predominantly rural population. To the north the land rises to the mountains of the Karakoram, Hindu Kush and Himalaya. The west is semi-desert plateaus and mountain ranges. The climate ranges between dry desert, and tundra on the mountain tops. Temperatures are generally warm and rainfall is monsoonal. Agriculture the main sector of the economy, employs approximately half of the workforce and is dependent on extensive irrigation schemes. Pakistan is one of the world's leading producers of cotton and an important exporter of rice. Pakistan produces natural gas and has a variety of mineral deposits including coal and gold, but they are little developed. The main industries are textiles and clothing manufacture and food processing, with fabrics and ready-made clothing the leading exports. Pakistan also produces leather goods, fertilizers, chemicals, paper and precision instruments. The country depends heavily on foreign aid and remittances from Pakistanis working abroad.

PALAU
Republic of Palau

Area Sq Km	497	Languages	Palauan, English
Area Sq Miles	192	Religions	Roman Catholic, Protestant, traditional beliefs
Population	19 000	Currency	US dollar
Capital	Koror	Organizations	UN

Map page 91

Palau comprises over three hundred islands in the Caroline Islands in the west Pacific Ocean. The climate is tropical. The economy is based on farming, fishing and tourism. Palau is heavily dependent on US aid.

PANAMA
Republic of Panama

Area Sq Km	77 082	Languages	Spanish, English, Amerindian languages
Area Sq Miles	29 762	Religions	Roman Catholic, Protestant, Sunni Muslim
Population	2 856 000	Currency	Balboa
Capital	Panama City	Organizations	UN

Map page 150

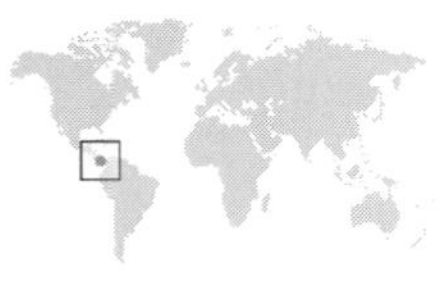

Panama is the most southerly state in Central America and has Pacific and Caribbean coasts. It is hilly, with mountains in the west and jungle near the Colombian border. The climate is tropical. Most people live on the drier Pacific coast. The economy is based mainly on services related to the canal: shipping, banking and tourism. Exports include bananas, shrimps, coffee, clothing and fish products. The USA is the main trading partner.

PAPUA NEW GUINEA
Independent State of Papua New Guinea

Area Sq Km	462 840	Languages	English, Tok Pisin (Creole), local languages
Area Sq Miles	178 704	Religions	Protestant, Roman Catholic, traditional beliefs
Population	4 809 000	Currency	Kina
Capital	Port Moresby	Organizations	Comm., UN

Map page 68

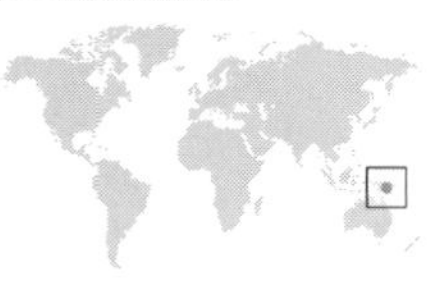

Papua New Guinea occupies the eastern half of the island of New Guinea and includes many island groups. It has a forested and mountainous interior, bordered by swampy plains, and a tropical monsoon climate. Most of the workforce are farmers. Timber, copra, coffee and cocoa are important, but exports are dominated by minerals, chiefly gold and copper. The country depends on foreign aid. Australia, Japan and Singapore are the main trading partners.

PARAGUAY
Republic of Paraguay

Area Sq Km	406 752	Languages	Spanish, Guaraní
Area Sq Miles	157 048	Religions	Roman Catholic, Protestant
Population	5 496 000	Currency	Guaraní
Capital	Asunción	Organizations	UN

Map page 156

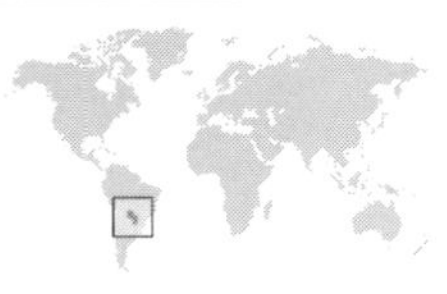

Paraguay is a landlocked country in central South America, bordering Bolivia, Brazil and Argentina. The Paraguay river separates a sparsely populated western zone of marsh and flat alluvial plains from a more developed, hilly and forested region to the east and south. The climate is subtropical. Virtually all electricity is produced by hydroelectric plants and surplus power is exported to Brazil and Argentina. The hydroelectric dam at Itaipu is the largest in the world. The mainstay of the economy is agriculture and agricultural industries. Exports include cotton, soya bean and edible oil products, timber and meat. Brazil and Argentina are the main trading partners.

PERU
Republic of Peru

Area Sq Km	1 285 216	Languages	Spanish, Quechua, Aymara
Area Sq Miles	496 225	Religions	Roman Catholic, Protestant
Population	25 662 000	Currency	Sol
Capital	Lima	Organizations	APEC, UN

Map page 154

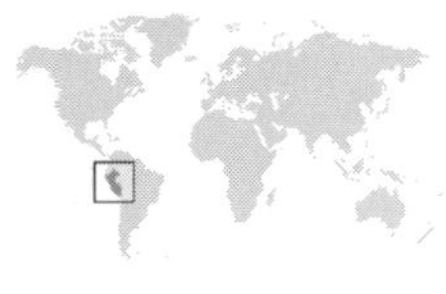

Peru lies on the Pacific coast of South America. Most Peruvians live on the coastal strip and the plateaus of the high Andes mountains. East of the Andes is the Amazon rainforest. The coast is temperate with low rainfall, while the east is hot, humid and wet. Agriculture involves one-third of the workforce, fishing is also important. Agriculture and fishing were both disrupted by the El Niño effect in the 1990s. Sugar cane, cotton, coffee and coca are the main cash crops. Copper and copper products, fishmeal, zinc products, coffee, petroleum and its products, and textiles are the main exports. The USA and the EU are the main trading partners.

PHILIPPINES
Republic of the Philippines

Area Sq Km	300 000	Languages	English, Pilipino, Cebuano, local languages
Area Sq Miles	115 831	Religions	Roman Catholic, Protestant, Sunni Muslim, Aglipayan
Population	75 653 000	Currency	Philippine peso
Capital	Manila	Organizations	APEC, ASEAN, UN

Map page 97

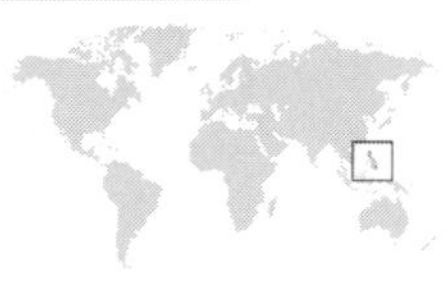

The Philippines, in Southeast Asia, consists of over seven thousand islands and atolls lying between the South China Sea and the Pacific Ocean. The islands of Luzon and Mindanao account for two-thirds of the land area. These and nine other fairly large islands are mountainous and forested, with active volcanoes. Earthquakes and annual tropical storms are common. Most people live in the plains on the larger islands or on the coastal strips. The climate is hot and humid with heavy monsoonal rainfall. Rice, coconuts, sugar cane, pineapples and bananas are the main agricultural crops; fishing is also important. Main exports are electronic equipment, machinery and transport equipment, garments and coconut products. Foreign aid and remittances from workers abroad are important to the economy, which faces problems of high population growth rate and high unemployment. The USA and Japan are the main trading partners.

Pitcairn Islands
United Kingdom Overseas Territory

Area Sq Km	45	Languages	English
Area Sq Miles	17	Religions	Protestant
Population	68	Currency	New Zealand dollar
Capital	Adamstown		

Map page 67

An island group in the southeast Pacific Ocean consisting of Pitcairn Island and three uninhabited islands. It was originally settled by mutineers from HMS Bounty.

POLAND
Polish Republic

Area Sq Km	312 683	Languages	Polish, German
Area Sq Miles	120 728	Religions	Roman Catholic, Polish Orthodox
Population	38 605 000	Currency	Złoty
Capital	Warsaw (Warszawa)	Organizations	OECD, UN

Map page 112-113

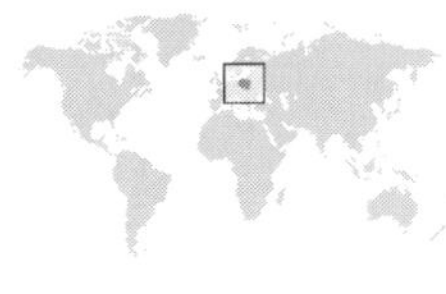

Poland lies on the Baltic coast of east Europe. The Odra and Vistula river deltas dominate the coast. Inland, much of Poland is low-lying with woods and lakes. In the south the land rises to the Sudety and western part of the Carpathian Mountains which border the Czech Republic and Slovakia respectively. The climate is continental. Around a quarter of the workforce is involved in agriculture. The economy is heavily industrialized, with mining and manufacturing accounting for forty per cent of national income. Poland is one of the world's major producers of coal, and also produces copper, zinc, lead, sulphur and natural gas. The main industries are machinery and transport equipment, ship building, metal and chemical production. Exports include machinery and transport equipment, manufactured goods, food and live animals. Germany is the main trading partner.

PORTUGAL
Portuguese Republic

Area Sq Km	88 940	Languages	Portuguese
Area Sq Miles	34 340	Religions	Roman Catholic, Protestant
Population	10 016 000	Currency	Euro
Capital	Lisbon (Lisboa)	Organizations	EU, OECD, UN

Map page 111

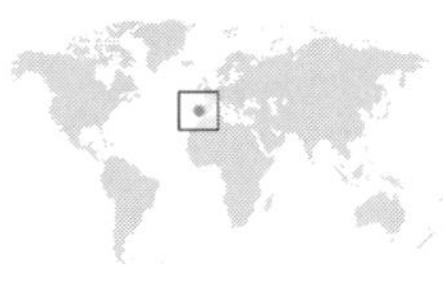

Portugal lies in the western part of the Iberian peninsula in southwest Europe, has an Atlantic coastline and is bordered by Spain to the north and east. The offshore island groups of the Azores and Madeira belong to Portugal. On the mainland the land north of the Tagus river is mostly highland with extensive forests of pine and cork. South of the river is undulating lowland. The climate in the north is cool and moist, the south is warmer, with dry, mild winters. Most Portuguese live near the coast and more than one-third of the total population live around the capital, Lisbon. Agriculture, fishing and forestry involve approximately ten per cent of the workforce. Mining and manufacturing are the main sectors of the economy. Portugal produces kaolin, copper, tin, zinc, tungsten and salt. Exports include textiles, clothing and footwear, electrical machinery and transport equipment, cork and wood products, and chemicals. Service industries, chiefly tourism and banking, are important to the economy as are remittances from workers abroad. Most trade is with other EU countries.

Puerto Rico
United States Commonwealth

Area Sq Km	9 104	Languages	Spanish, English
Area Sq Miles	3 515	Religions	Roman Catholic, Protestant
Population	3 915 000	Currency	US dollar
Capital	San Juan		

Map page 149

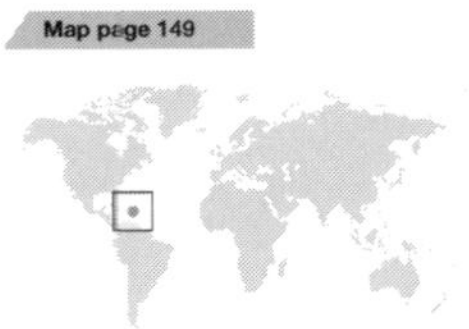

The Caribbean island of Puerto Rico has a forested, hilly interior, coastal plains and a tropical climate. Half of the population live in the San Juan area. The economy is based on manufacturing (chiefly chemicals, electronics and food), tourism and agriculture. The USA is the predominant trading partner.

QATAR
State of Qatar

Area Sq Km	11 437	Languages	Arabic
Area Sq Miles	4 416	Religions	Sunni Muslim
Population	565 000	Currency	Qatari riyal
Capital	Doha (Ad Dawḥah)	Organizations	OECD, UN

Map page 84

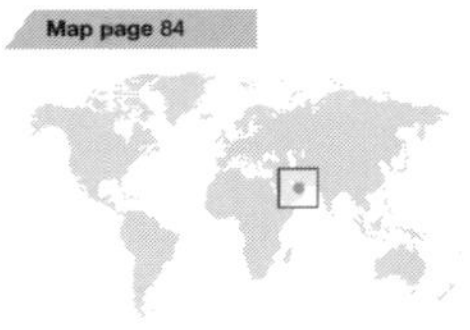

The emirate occupies a peninsula that extends northwards from east-central Saudi Arabia into The Gulf in southwest Asia. The land is flat and barren with sand dunes and salt pans. The climate is hot and mainly dry. Most people live in the Doha area. The economy is heavily dependent on oil and natural gas production and the oil-refining industry. Income also comes from overseas investment. Japan is the largest trading partner.

Réunion
French Overseas Department

Area Sq Km	2 551	Languages	French, Creole
Area Sq Miles	985	Religions	Roman Catholic
Population	721 000	Currency	Euro
Capital	St-Denis		

Map page 119

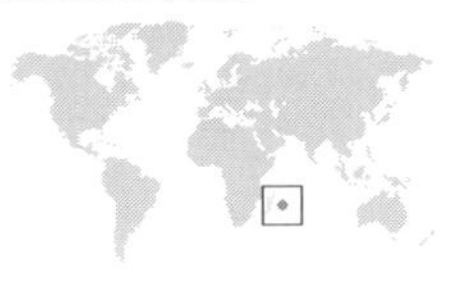

The Indian Ocean island of Réunion is mountainous, with coastal lowlands and a warm climate. The economy depends on tourism, French aid and exports of sugar.

ROMANIA

Area Sq Km	237 500	Languages	Romanian, Hungarian
Area Sq Miles	91 699	Religions	Romanian Orthodox, Protestant, Roman Catholic
Population	22 438 000	Currency	Romanian leu
Capital	Bucharest (Bucureşti)	Organizations	UN

Map page 115

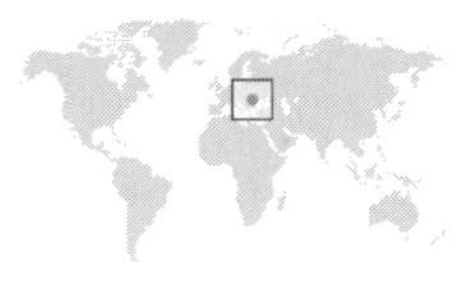

Romania lies in east Europe on the northwest coast of the Black Sea. Mountains separate the Transylvanian Basin at the centre of the country from the populous plains of the east and south and from the Danube delta. The climate is continental. Romania has mineral resources (zinc, lead, silver and gold), and oil and natural gas reserves. Economic reform, since the break up of the former U.S.S.R has been slow and sporadic, but measures to accelerate change were introduced in 1999. Agriculture employs over one-third of the workforce. The main exports are textiles, mineral products, chemicals, machinery and footwear. The most important trading partners are Germany and Italy.

© Bartholomew Ltd

RUSSIAN FEDERATION

Area Sq Km	17 075 400	Languages	Russian, Tatar, Ukrainian, local languages
Area Sq Miles	6 592 849	Religions	Russian Orthodox, Sunni Muslim, Protestant
Population	145 491 000	Currency	Russian rouble
Capital	Moscow (Moskva)	Organizations	APEC, CIS, UN

Map page 76-77

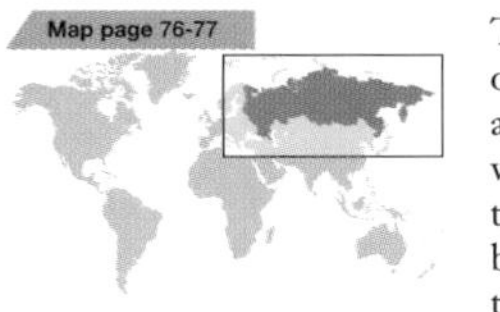

The Russian Federation occupies much of east Europe and all of north Asia, and is the world's largest state, nearly twice the size of the USA. It borders thirteen countries to the west and south and has long coastlines on the Arctic and Pacific Oceans to the north and east. The European section of the Russian Federation lies west of the Ural mountains. To the south the land rises to uplands and the Caucasus mountains on the border with Georgia and Azerbaijan. East of the Urals lie the flat West Siberian Plain and the Central Siberian Plateau. In the south is Lake Baikal, the world's deepest lake, and the Western and Southern Sayan mountain ranges on the border with Kazakhstan and Mongolia. Siberia is rugged and mountainous with many active volcanoes on the Kamchatka Peninsula. The country's major rivers are the Volga in the west and the Ob', Yenisey, Lena and Amur in Siberia. The climate and vegetation range between arctic tundra in the north and semi-arid steppe towards the Black and Caspian Sea coasts in the south. In general, the climate is continental with extreme temperatures. The majority of the population (the sixth largest in the world), and industry and agriculture are concentrated in European Russia.
The economy is heavily dependent on exploitation of raw materials and on heavy industry. Russia has a wealth of mineral resources, although they are often difficult to exploit because of the climate and remote locations. It is one of the world's leading producers of petroleum, natural gas and coal as well as iron ore, nickel, copper and bauxite, and many precious and rare metals. Forests cover over forty per cent of the land area and supply an important timber, paper and pulp industry. Approximately eight per cent of land is suitable for cultivation, but farming is generally inefficient and food, especially grain, must be imported. Fishing is important and Russia has a large fleet operating around the world. The transition to a market economy has been slow and difficult, with high unemployment and considerable underemployment. As well as mining and extractive industries there is a wide range of manufacturing industry from steel mills to aircraft and space vehicles, shipbuilding, synthetic fabrics, plastics, cotton fabrics, consumer durables, chemicals and fertilizers. Exports include fuels, metals, machinery, chemicals and forest products. The most important trading partners include Germany, the USA and Belarus.

RWANDA
Republic of Rwanda

Area Sq Km	26 338	Languages	Kinyarwanda, French, English
Area Sq Miles	10 169	Religions	Roman Catholic, traditional beliefs, Protestant
Population	7 609 000	Currency	Rwandan franc
Capital	Kigali	Organizations	UN

Map page 122

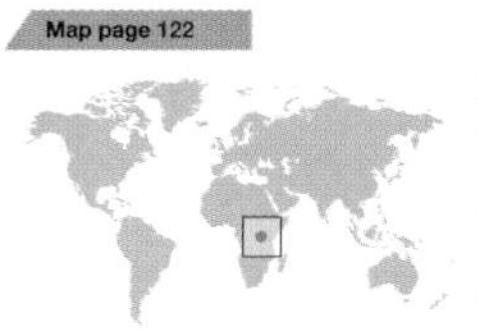

Rwanda, the most densely populated country in Africa, is situated in the mountains and plateaus to the east of the western branch of the Great Rift Valley in East Africa. The climate is warm with a summer dry season. Rwanda depends mainly on subsistence farming, coffee and tea exports, light industry and foreign aid.

St Helena and Dependencies
United Kingdom Overseas Territory

Area Sq Km	308	Languages	English
Area Sq Miles	119	Religions	Protestant, Roman Catholic
Population	6 000	Currency	St Helena pound
Capital	Jamestown		

Map page 118   St Helena and its dependencies Ascension and Tristan da Cunha are isolated island groups lying in the south Atlantic Ocean. The islands are volcanic in origin and fishing is the main activity. Ascension lies 1 300 kilometres (800 miles) to the northwest of St Helena and the Tristan da Cunha group lies 2 000 kilometres (1 250 miles) to the south. The economy relies on financial aid from the UK. Main trading partners are the UK and South Africa.

ST KITTS AND NEVIS
Federation of St Kitts and Nevis

Area Sq Km	261	Languages	English, Creole
Area Sq Miles	101	Religions	Protestant, Roman Catholic
Population	38 000	Currency	East Caribbean dollar
Capital	Basseterre	Organizations	CARICOM, Comm., UN

Map page 149

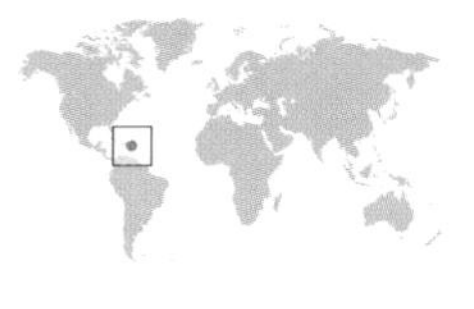

St Kitts and Nevis are in the Leeward Islands in the Caribbean Sea. Both volcanic islands are mountainous and forested with sandy beaches and a warm, wet climate. About three-quarters of the population live on St Kitts. Agriculture is the main activity, with sugar the main product. Tourism, manufacturing (chiefly garments and electronic components) and offshore banking are important activities.

ST LUCIA

Area Sq Km	616	Languages	English, Creole
Area Sq Miles	238	Religions	Roman Catholic, Protestant
Population	148 000	Currency	East Caribbean dollar
Capital	Castries	Organizations	CARICOM, Comm., UN

Map page 149

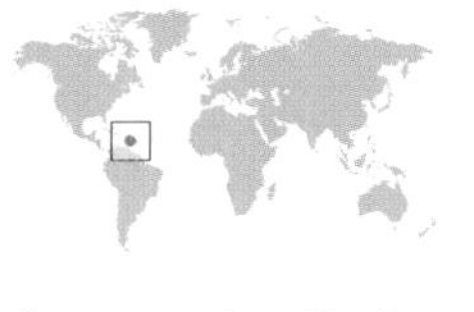

St Lucia, one of the Windward Islands in the Caribbean Sea, is a volcanic island with forested mountains, hot springs, sandy beaches and a wet tropical climate. Agriculture is the main activity, with bananas accounting for approximately forty per cent of export earnings. Tourism, agricultural processing and light manufacturing are increasingly important.

St Pierre and Miquelon
French Territorial Collectivity

Area Sq Km	242	Languages	French
Area Sq Miles	93	Religions	Roman Catholic
Population	7 000	Currency	Euro
Capital	St-Pierre		

Map page 129

A group of islands off the south coast of Newfoundland in east Canada. The islands are unsuitable for agriculture and fishing and fish processing are the most important activities. The islands rely heavily on financial assistance from France.

ST VINCENT AND THE GRENADINES

Area Sq Km	389	Languages	English, Creole
Area Sq Miles	150	Religions	Protestant, Roman Catholic
Population	112 000	Currency	East Caribbean dollar
Capital	Kingstown	Organizations	CARICOM, Comm., UN

Map page 149

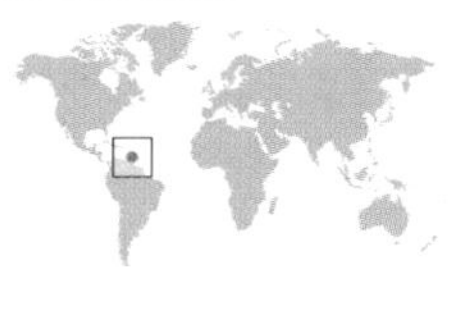

St Vincent, whose territory includes islets and cays in The Grenadines island group, is in the Windward Islands in the Caribbean Sea. St Vincent is forested and mountainous, with an active volcano, Soufrière. The climate is tropical and wet. The economy is based mainly on agriculture and tourism. Bananas account for approximately one-third of export earnings and arrowroot is also important. Most trade is with the USA and other CARICOM countries.

SAMOA
Independent State of Samoa

Area Sq Km	2 831	Languages	Samoan, English
Area Sq Miles	1 093	Religions	Protestant, Roman Catholic
Population	159 000	Currency	Tala
Capital	Apia	Organizations	Comm., UN

Map page 69

Samoa consists of two larger mountainous and forested islands, Savai'i and Upolu, and seven smaller islands in the south Pacific Ocean. Over half the population live on Upolu. The climate is tropical. The economy is based on agriculture, with some fishing and light manufacturing. Traditional exports are coconut products, fish and beer. Tourism is increasing, but the islands depend on workers' remittances from abroad and foreign aid.

SAN MARINO
Republic of San Marino

Area Sq Km	61	Languages	Italian
Area Sq Miles	24	Religions	Roman Catholic
Population	27 000	Currency	Euro
Capital	San Marino	Organizations	UN

Map page 114

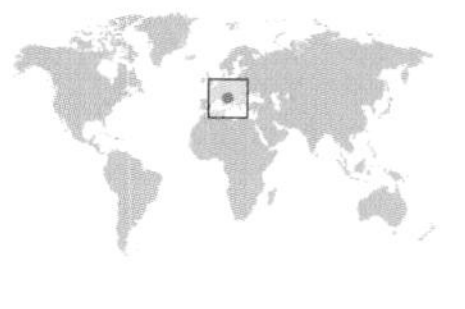

Landlocked San Marino lies in northeast Italy. A third of the population live in the capital. There is some agriculture and light industry. Most income comes from tourism and Italy is the main trading partner.

SÃO TOMÉ AND PRÍNCIPE
Democratic Republic of São Tomé and Príncipe

Area Sq Km	964	Languages	Portuguese, Creole
Area Sq Miles	372	Religions	Roman Catholic, Protestant
Population	138 000	Currency	Dobra
Capital	São Tomé	Organizations	UN

Map page 120

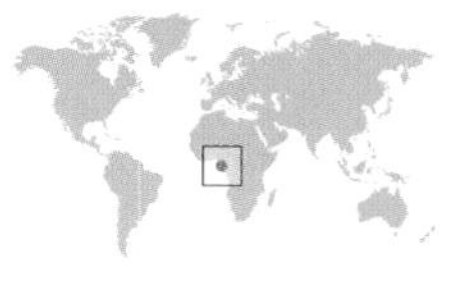

The two main islands and adjacent islets lie off the coast of west Africa in the Gulf of Guinea. São Tomé is the larger island with over ninety per cent of the population. Both São Tomé and Príncipe are mountainous and tree-covered, and have a hot and humid climate. The economy is heavily dependent on cocoa, which accounts for around ninety per cent of export earnings.

SAUDI ARABIA
Kingdom of Saudi Arabia

Area Sq Km	2 200 000	Languages	Arabic
Area Sq Miles	849 425	Religions	Sunni Muslim, Shi'a Muslim
Population	20 346 000	Currency	Saudi Arabian riyal
Capital	Riyadh (Ar Riyāḍ)	Organizations	OPEC, UN

Map page 86

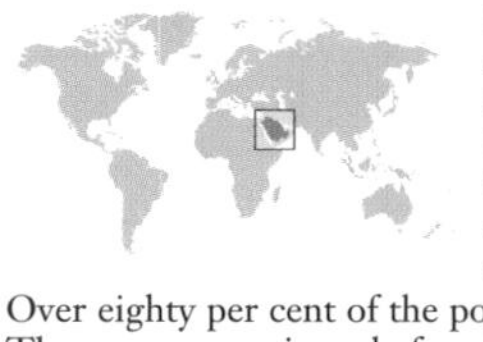

Saudi Arabia occupies most of the Arabian Peninsula in southwest Asia. The terrain is desert or semi-desert plateaus, which rise to mountains running parallel to the Red Sea in the west and slope down to plains in the southeast and along The Gulf in the east.
Over eighty per cent of the population live in urban areas. There are approximately four million foreign workers in Saudi Arabia employed mainly in the oil and service industries. Summers are hot, winters are warm and rainfall is low. Saudi Arabia has the world's largest reserves of oil and significant natural gas reserves, both onshore and in The Gulf. Crude oil and refined products account for over ninety per cent of export earnings. Other industries and irrigated agriculture are being encouraged, but most food and raw materials are imported. Saudi Arabia has important banking and commercial interests. Japan and the USA are the main export trading partners.

SENEGAL
Republic of Senegal

Area Sq Km	196 720	Languages	French, Wolof, Fulani, local languages
Area Sq Miles	75 954	Religions	Sunni Muslim, Roman Catholic, traditional beliefs
Population	9 421 000	Currency	CFA franc
Capital	Dakar	Organizations	UN

Map page 120

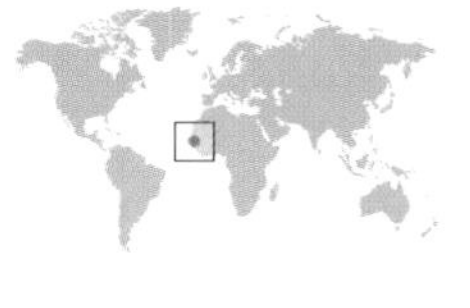

Senegal lies on the Atlantic coast of west Africa. The north is arid semi-desert, while the south is mainly fertile savanna bushland. The climate is tropical with summer rains, although droughts occur. One-fifth of the population live in and around Dakar, the capital and main port. Fish, groundnuts and phosphates are the main exports. France is the main trading partner.

SEYCHELLES
Republic of the Seychelles

Area Sq Km	455	Languages	English, French, Creole
Area Sq Miles	176	Religions	Roman Catholic, Protestant
Population	80 000	Currency	Seychelles rupee
Capital	Victoria	Organizations	Comm., SADC, UN

Map page 119

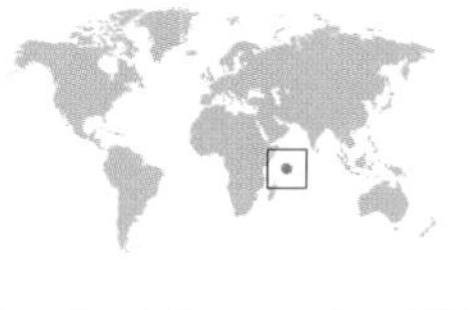

The Seychelles comprises an archipelago of over one hundred granitic and coral islands in the west Indian Ocean. Over ninety per cent of the population live on the main island, Mahé. The climate is hot and humid with heavy rainfall. The economy is based mainly on tourism, fishing and light manufacturing.

SIERRA LEONE
Republic of Sierra Leone

Area Sq Km	71 740	Languages	English, Creole, Mende, Temne, local languages
Area Sq Miles	27 699	Religions	Sunni Muslim, traditional beliefs
Population	4 405 000	Currency	Leone
Capital	Freetown	Organizations	Comm., UN

Map page 120

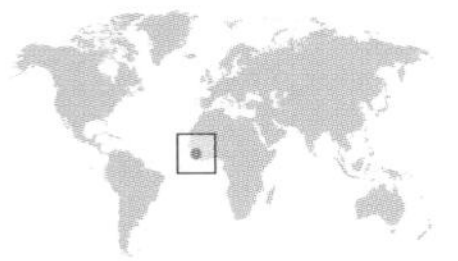

Sierra Leone lies on the Atlantic coast of west Africa. Its coast is heavily indented and lined with mangrove swamps. Inland is a forested area rising to savanna plateaus, with mountains to the northeast. The climate is tropical and rainfall is heavy. Most of the workforce is involved in subsistence farming. Cocoa and coffee are the main cash crops. Diamonds and rutile (titanium ore) are the main exports. The economy relies on substantial foreign aid.

SINGAPORE
Republic of Singapore

Area Sq Km	639	Languages	Chinese, English, Malay, Tamil
Area Sq Miles	247	Religions	Buddhist, Taoist, Sunni Muslim, Christian, Hindu
Population	4 018 000	Currency	Singapore dollar
Capital	Singapore	Organizations	APEC, ASEAN, Comm., UN

Map page 94

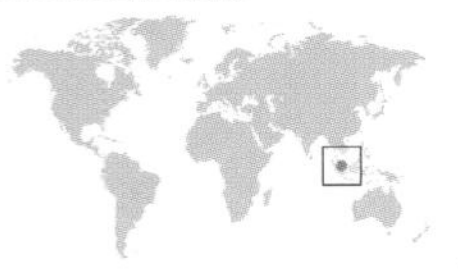

The state comprises the main island of Singapore and over fifty other islands, lying off the southern tip of the Malay Peninsula in Southeast Asia. Singapore is generally low-lying and includes land reclaimed from swamps and the sea. It is hot and humid, with heavy rainfall throughout the year. There are fish farms and vegetable gardens in the north and east of the island, but most food needs must be imported. Singapore also lacks mineral and energy resources. Manufacturing industries and services are the main sectors of the economy. Their rapid development has fuelled the nation's impressive economic growth over the last three decades. Main industries include electronics, oil refining, chemicals, pharmaceuticals, ship repair, food processing and textiles. Singapore is a major financial centre. Its port is one of the world's largest and busiest and acts as an entrepôt for neighbouring states. Tourism is also important. Japan, the USA and Malaysia are the main trading partners.

SLOVAKIA
Slovak Republic

Area Sq Km	49 035	Languages	Slovak, Hungarian, Czech
Area Sq Miles	18 933	Religions	Roman Catholic, Protestant, Orthodox
Population	5 399 000	Currency	Slovakian koruna
Capital	Bratislava	Organizations	UN

Map page 112-113

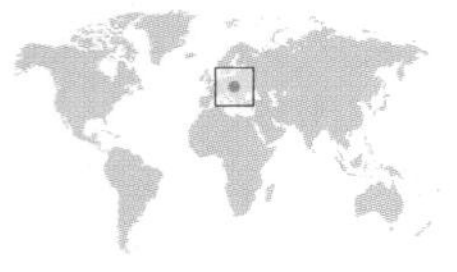

A landlocked country in central Europe, Slovakia is mountainous in the north, but low-lying in the southwest. The climate is continental. There is a range of manufacturing industries and the main exports are machinery and transport equipment, but during the 1990s there were continued economic difficulties and economic growth has been slow. Most trade is with EU countries and the Czech Republic.

SLOVENIA
Republic of Slovenia

Area Sq Km	20 251	Languages	Slovene, Croatian, Serbian
Area Sq Miles	7 819	Religions	Roman Catholic, Protestant
Population	1 988 000	Currency	Tólar
Capital	Ljubljana	Organizations	UN

Map page 114

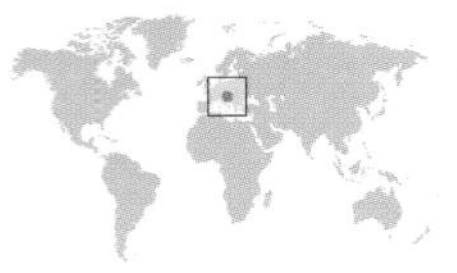

Slovenia lies in the northwest Balkan Mountains of south Europe and has a short coastline on the Adriatic Sea. It is mountainous and hilly, with lowlands on the coast and in the Sava and Drava river valleys. The climate is generally continental inland and Mediterranean nearer the coast. The main agricultural products are potatoes, grain and sugar beet. Main industries include metal processing, electronics and consumer goods. Trade has been re-orientated towards western markets and the main trading partners are Germany and Italy.

SOLOMON ISLANDS

Area Sq Km	28 370	Languages	English, Creole, local languages
Area Sq Miles	10 954	Religions	Protestant, Roman Catholic
Population	447 000	Currency	Solomon Islands dollar
Capital	Honiara	Organizations	Comm., UN

Map page 69

The state consists of the Solomon, Santa Cruz and Shortland Islands in the southwest Pacific Ocean. The six main islands are volcanic, mountainous and forested, although Guadalcanal, the most populous, has a large lowland area. The climate is generally hot and humid. Subsistence farming, forestry and fishing predominate. Exports include timber products, fish, copra and palm oil. The islands depend on foreign aid.

SOMALIA
Somali Democratic Republic

Area Sq Km	637 657	Languages	Somali, Arabic
Area Sq Miles	246 201	Religions	Sunni Muslim
Population	8 778 000	Currency	Somali shilling
Capital	Mogadishu (Muqdisho)	Organizations	UN

Map page 122

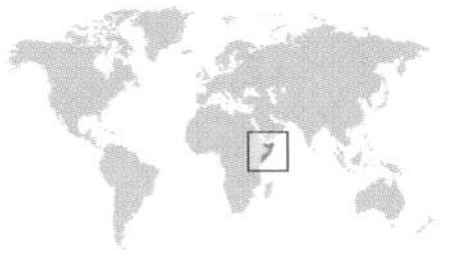

Somalia is in the north of east Africa, on the Gulf of Aden and the Indian Ocean. It consists of a dry scrubby plateau, rising to highlands in the north. The climate is hot and dry, but coastal areas and the Jubba and Webi Shabeelle river valleys support crops and most of the population. Subsistence farming and livestock rearing are the main activities. Exports include livestock and bananas. Frequent drought and civil war have prevented economic development. Somalia is one of the poorest and least developed countries in the world.

SOUTH AFRICA, REPUBLIC OF

Area Sq Km	1 219 090	Languages	Afrikaans, English, nine official languages
Area Sq Miles	470 693	Religions	Protestant, Roman Catholic, Sunni Muslim, Hindu
Population	43 309 000	Currency	Rand
Capital	Pretoria/ Cape Town	Organizations	Comm., SADC, UN

Map page 124-125

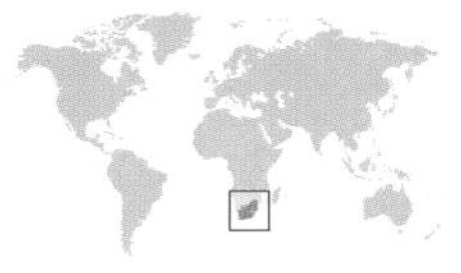

South Africa occupies most of the southern part of Africa. It borders five states, surrounds Lesotho and has a long coastline stretching from the Atlantic to the Indian Ocean. Much of the land is a vast plateau, covered with grassland or bush, drained by the Orange and Limpopo river systems. A fertile coastal plain rises to mountain ridges in the south and east, including Table Mountain near Cape Town and the Drakensberg range in the east. Gauteng is the most populous province, with Johannesburg and Pretoria its main cities. South Africa has warm summers and mild winters. Most of the country has rainfall in summer, but the coast around Cape Town has winter rains. South Africa is the largest and most developed economy in Africa, although wealth and economic control is unevenly distributed and unemployment is very high. Agriculture employs approximately one-third of the workforce and crops include fruit, wine, wool and maize. South Africa is rich in minerals. It is the world's main producer of gold and chromium and an important producer of diamonds; many other minerals are also mined. The main industries process minerals and agricultural produce, manufacture chemical products, electrical equipment and textiles, and assemble motor vehicles. Financial services are also important.

SOUTH KOREA
Republic of Korea

Area Sq Km	99 274	Languages	Korean
Area Sq Miles	38 330	Religions	Buddhist, Protestant, Roman Catholic
Population	46 740 000	Currency	South Korean won
Capital	Seoul (Sŏul)	Organizations	APEC, UN

Map page 96

The state consists of the southern half of the Korean peninsula in east Asia and many islands lying off the western and southern coasts in the Yellow Sea. The terrain is mountainous, although less rugged than that of North Korea. Population density is high and highly urbanized; most of the population live on the western coastal plains and in the river basins of the Han-gang in the northwest and the Naktong-gang in the southeast. South Korea has a continental climate, with hot, wet summers and dry, cold winters. Arable land is limited by the mountainous terrain, but because of intensive farming South Korea is nearly self-sufficient in food. Sericulture is important as is fishing, which contributes to exports. South Korea has few mineral resources, except for coal and tungsten. It has achieved high economic growth based mainly on export manufacturing. The main manufactured goods are cars, electronic and electrical goods, ships, steel, chemicals, and toys as well as textiles, clothing, footwear and food products. The USA and Japan are the main trading partners.

SPAIN
Kingdom of Spain

Area Sq Km	504 782	Languages	Castilian, Catalan, Galician, Basque
Area Sq Miles	194 897	Religions	Roman Catholic
Population	39 910 000	Currency	Euro
Capital	Madrid	Organizations	EU, OECD, UN

Map page 111

Spain occupies the greater part of the Iberian peninsula in southwest Europe, with coastlines on the Atlantic Ocean and the Mediterranean Sea. It includes the Balearic Islands in the Mediterranean Sea, the Canary Islands in the Atlantic Ocean, and two enclaves in north Africa, Ceuta and Melilla. Much of the mainland is a high plateau drained by the Duero, Tagus and Guadiana rivers. The plateau is interrupted by a low mountain range and bounded to the east and north by mountains, including the Pyrenees which form the border with France and Andorra. The main lowland areas are the Ebro basin in the northeast, the eastern coastal plains and the Guadalquivir basin in the southwest. Over three-quarters of the population live in urban areas. The plateau experiences hot summers and cold winters. Conditions are cooler and wetter to the north, and warmer and drier to the south. Agriculture involves about ten per cent of the workforce and fruit, vegetables and wine are exported. Fishing is an important industry and Spain has a large fishing fleet. Mineral resources include lead, copper, mercury and fluorspar. Some oil is produced, but Spain has to import most energy needs. The economy is based on manufacturing and services. The principal products are machinery, transport equipment, motor vehicles, food products and other manufactured goods. With approximately fifty million visitors each year, tourism is a major industry. Banking and commerce are also important. Approximately seventy per cent of trade is with other EU countries.

SRI LANKA
Democratic Socialist Republic of Sri Lanka

Area Sq Km	65 610	Languages	Sinhalese, Tamil, English
Area Sq Miles	25 332	Religions	Buddhist, Hindu, Sunni Muslim, Roman Catholic
Population	18 924 000	Currency	Sri Lankan rupee
Capital	Sri Jayewardenepura Kotte	Organizations	Comm., UN

Map page 87

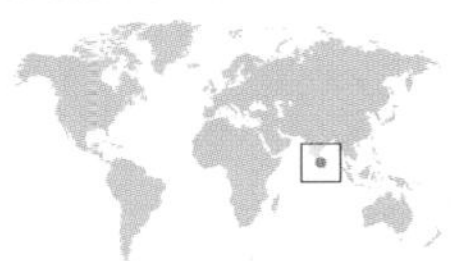

Sri Lanka lies in the Indian Ocean off the southeast coast of India in south Asia. It has rolling coastal plains with mountains in the centre-south. The climate is hot and monsoonal and most people live on the west coast. Manufactured goods (chiefly textiles and clothing), tea, rubber, copra and gems are exported. The economy relies on aid and overseas workers' remittances. The USA and the UK are the main trading partners.

SUDAN
Republic of the Sudan

Area Sq Km	2 505 813	Languages	Arabic, Dinka, Nubian, Beja, Nuer, local languages
Area Sq Miles	967 500	Religions	Sunni Muslim, traditional beliefs, Christian
Population	31 095 000	Currency	Sudanese dinar
Capital	Khartoum	Organizations	UN

Map page 121

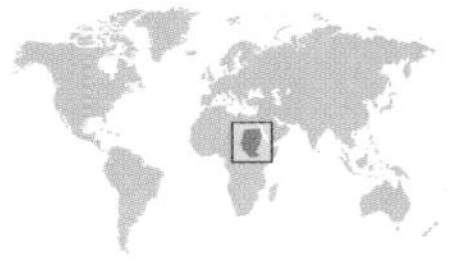

Africa's largest country, Sudan is located in the northeast of the continent, on the Red Sea. It lies within the upper Nile basin, much of which is arid plain but with swamps to the south. Mountains lie to the northeast, west and south. The climate is hot and arid with light summer rainfall, although droughts occur. Most of the population live along the Nile and are farmers and herders. Cotton, gum arabic, livestock and other agricultural products are exported. The government is working with foreign investors to develop oil resources but civil war in the south restricts the growth of the economy. Main trading partners are Saudi Arabia, China and Libya.

© Bartholomew Ltd

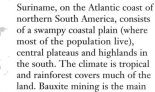

SURINAME
Republic of Suriname

Area Sq Km	163 820	Languages	Dutch, Surinamese, English, Hindi
Area Sq Miles	63 251	Religions	Hindu, Roman Catholic, Protestant, Sunni Muslim
Population	417 000	Currency	Suriname guilder
Capital	Paramaribo	Organizations	CARICOM, UN

Map page 155

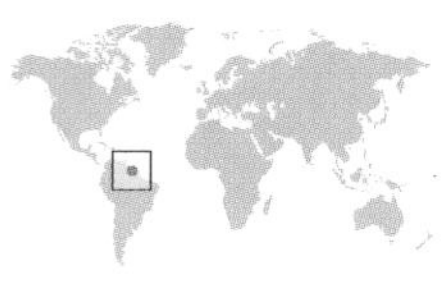

Suriname, on the Atlantic coast of northern South America, consists of a swampy coastal plain (where most of the population live), central plateaus and highlands in the south. The climate is tropical and rainforest covers much of the land. Bauxite mining is the main industry, and alumina and aluminium are the chief exports, with shrimps, rice, bananas and timber also exported. The main trading partners are The Netherlands, Norway and the USA.

SWAZILAND
Kingdom of Swaziland

Area Sq Km	17 364	Languages	Swazi, English
Area Sq Miles	6 704	Religions	Christian, traditional beliefs
Population	925 000	Currency	Emalangeni, South African rand
Capital	Mbabane	Organizations	Comm., SADC, UN

Map page 125

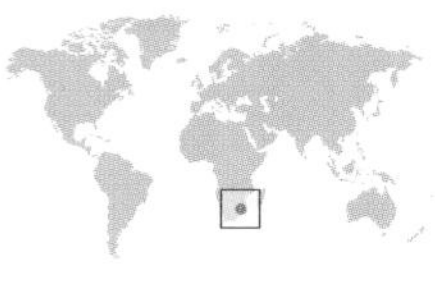

Landlocked Swaziland in southern Africa lies between Mozambique and South Africa. Savanna plateaus descend from mountains in the west towards hill country in the east. The climate is subtropical, but temperate in the mountains. Subsistence farming predominates. Asbestos and some diamonds are mined. Exports include sugar, fruit and wood pulp. Tourism and workers' remittances are important to the economy. Most trade is with South Africa.

SWEDEN
Kingdom of Sweden

Area Sq Km	449 964	Languages	Swedish
Area Sq Miles	173 732	Religions	Protestant, Roman Catholic
Population	8 842 000	Currency	Swedish krona
Capital	Stockholm	Organizations	EU, OECD, UN

Map page 102-103

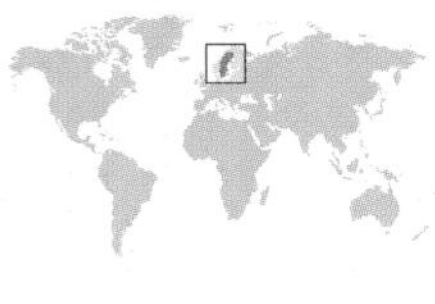

Sweden occupies the eastern part of the Scandinavian peninsula in north Europe and borders the North and Baltic Seas and the Gulf of Bothnia. Forested mountains cover the northern half of the country, part of which lies within the Arctic Circle. The southern part of the country is a lowland lake region, where most of the population live. Sweden has warm summers and cold winters which are more severe in the north. Natural resources include coniferous forests, mineral deposits and water resources. There is little agriculture, although some dairy products, meat, cereals and vegetables are produced in the south. The forests supply timber for export and for the important pulp, paper and furniture industries. Sweden is an important producer of iron ore and copper. Zinc, lead, silver and gold are also mined. Machinery and transport equipment, chemicals, pulp and wood, and telecommunications equipment are the main exports. The majority of trade is with other EU countries.

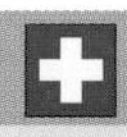

SWITZERLAND
Swiss Confederation

Area Sq Km	41 293	Languages	German, French, Italian, Romansch
Area Sq Miles	15 943	Religions	Roman Catholic, Protestant
Population	7 170 000	Currency	Swiss franc
Capital	Bern (Berne)	Organizations	OECD

Map page 110

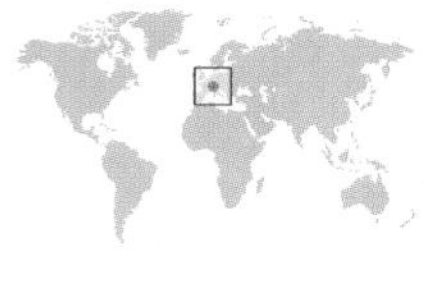

Switzerland is a mountainous landlocked country of west central Europe. The southern regions lie within the Alps mountain ranges, while the northwest is dominated by the Jura mountains. The rest of the land is a high plateau where most of the population live. The climate varies greatly, depending on altitude and relief, but in general summers are mild and winters are cold with heavy snowfalls. Switzerland has one of the highest standards of living in the world. It has few mineral resources and most food and industrial raw materials have to be imported. Manufacturing makes the largest contribution to the economy. Engineering is the most important industry, producing precision instruments and heavy machinery. Other important industries are chemicals and pharmaceuticals. Banking and financial services are very important and Zurich is one of the world's leading banking cities. Tourism, and international organizations based in Switzerland are also major foreign currency earners. Germany is the main trading partner.

SYRIA
Syrian Arab Republic

Area Sq Km	185 180	Languages	Arabic, Kurdish, Armenian
Area Sq Miles	71 498	Religions	Sunni Muslim, Shi'a Muslim, Christian
Population	16 189 000	Currency	Syrian pound
Capital	Damascus (Dimashq)	Organizations	UN

Map page 80-81

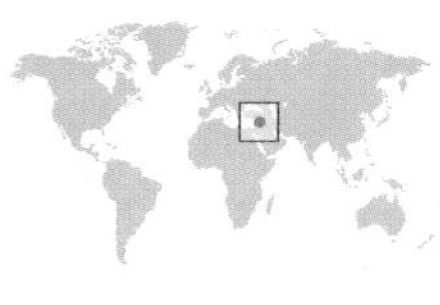

Syria is in southwest Asia, has a short coastline on the Mediterranean Sea and stretches inland to a plateau traversed northwest–southeast by the Euphrates river. Mountains flank the southwest borders with Lebanon and Israel. The climate is Mediterranean in coastal regions, hotter and drier inland. Most Syrians live on the coast or in the river valleys. Cotton, cereals and fruit are important products, but the main exports are petroleum and its products, and textiles.

TAIWAN
Republic of China

Area Sq Km	36 179	Languages	Mandarin, Min, Hakka, local languages
Area Sq Miles	13 969	Religions	Buddhist, Taoist, Confucian, Christian
Population	22 300 000	Currency	Taiwan dollar
Capital	T'aipei	Organizations	APEC

Map page 103

The east Asian state consists of the island of Taiwan, separated from mainland China by the Taiwan Strait, and several much smaller islands. Much of Taiwan is mountainous and forested. Densely populated coastal plains in the west contain the bulk of the population and most economic activity. Taiwan has a tropical monsoon climate, with warm, wet summers and mild winters. Agriculture is highly productive. Taiwan is virtually self-sufficient in food and exports some products. Coal, oil and natural gas are produced and a few minerals are mined but none of them are of great significance to the economy. Taiwan depends heavily on imports of raw materials and exports of manufactured goods. The main manufactured goods are electrical and electronic goods, including television sets, personal computers and calculators, textiles, fertilizers, clothing, footwear and toys. The main trading partners are the USA, Japan and Germany.

TAJIKISTAN
Republic of Tajikistan

Area Sq Km	143 100	Languages	Tajik, Uzbek, Russian
Area Sq Miles	55 251	Religions	Sunni Muslim
Population	6 087 000	Currency	Somoni
Capital	Dushanbe	Organizations	CIS, UN

Map page 83

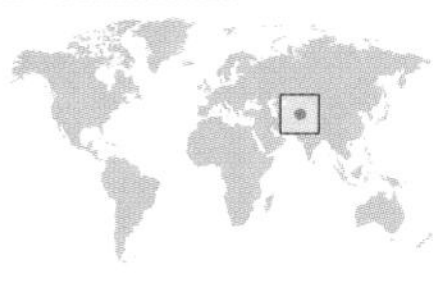

Landlocked Tajikistan in central Asia is a mountainous country, occupying the Alai Range and the Pamir mountains. In the less mountainous western areas summers are warm although winters are cold. Agriculture is the main sector of the economy, chiefly cotton growing and cattle breeding. Mineral deposits include lead, zinc, and uranium. Metal processing, textiles and clothing are the main manufactured goods. The main exports are aluminium and cotton. Uzbekistan, Liechtenstein and the Russian Federation, are the main trading partners.

TANZANIA
United Republic of Tanzania

Area Sq Km	945 087	Languages	Swahili, English, Nyamwezi, local languages
Area Sq Miles	364 900	Religions	Shi'a Muslim, Sunni Muslim, traditional beliefs, Christian
Population	35 119 000	Currency	Tanzanian shilling
Capital	Dodoma	Organizations	Comm., SADC, UN

Map page 122-123

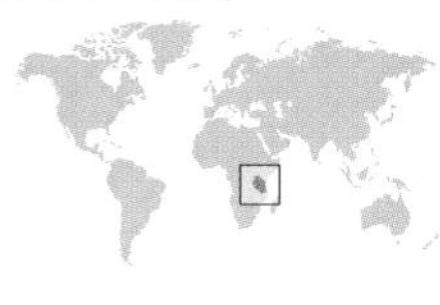

Tanzania lies on the coast of East Africa and includes the island of Zanzibar in the Indian Ocean. Most of the mainland is a savanna plateau lying east of the Great Rift Valley. In the north, near the border with Kenya, is Kilimanjaro, the highest mountain in Africa. The climate is tropical. The economy is predominantly based on agriculture which employs an estimated ninety per cent of the workforce. Agricultural processing and gold and diamond mining are the main industries, although tourism is growing. Coffee, cotton, cashew nuts and tobacco are the main exports, with cloves from Zanzibar. Most export trade is with India and the UK. Tanzania is one of the least developed countries in the world and depends heavily on foreign aid.

THAILAND
Kingdom of Thailand

Area Sq Km	513 115	Languages	Thai, Lao, Chinese, Malay, Mon-Khmer languages
Area Sq Miles	198 115	Religions	Buddhist, Sunni Muslim
Population	62 806 000	Currency	Baht
Capital	Bangkok (Krung Thep)	Organizations	APEC, ASEAN, UN

Map page 98

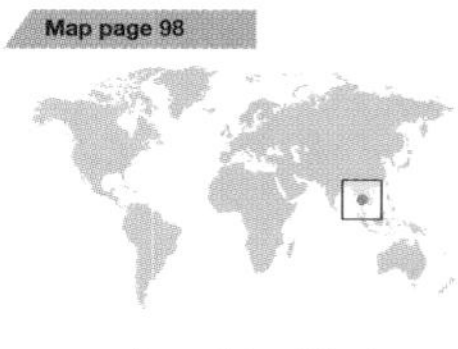

The largest country in the Indo-China peninsula, Thailand has coastlines on the Gulf of Thailand and the Andaman Sea. Central Thailand is dominated by the Chao Phraya river basin, which contains Bangkok, the capital city and centre of most economic activity. To the east is a dry plateau drained by tributaries of the Mekong river, while to the north, west and south, extending down most of the Malay peninsula, are forested hills and mountains. Many small islands line the coast. The climate is hot, humid and monsoonal. About half the workforce is involved in agriculture. Fish and fish processing are important. Thailand produces natural gas, some oil and lignite, minerals (chiefly tin, tungsten and barite) and gemstones. Manufacturing is the largest contributor to national income, with electronics, textiles, clothing and footwear, and food processing the main industries. With approximately seven million visitors a year, tourism is the major source of foreign exchange. Thailand is one of the world's leading exporters of rice and rubber, and a major exporter of maize and tapioca. Japan and the USA are the main trading partners.

TOGO
Republic of Togo

Area Sq Km	56 785	Languages	French, Ewe, Kabre, local languages
Area Sq Miles	21 925	Religions	Traditional beliefs, Christian, Sunni Muslim
Population	4 527 000	Currency	CFA franc
Capital	Lomé	Organizations	UN

Map page 120

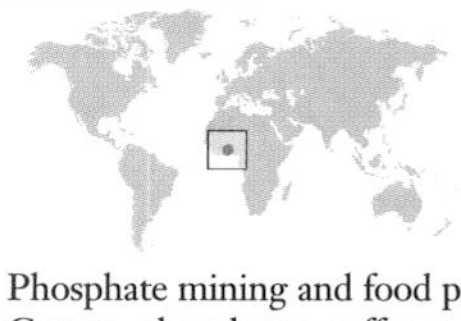

Togo is a long narrow country in west Africa with a short coastline on the Gulf of Guinea. The interior consists of plateaus rising to mountainous areas. The climate is tropical, drier inland. Agriculture is the mainstay of the economy. Phosphate mining and food processing are the main industries. Cotton, phosphates, coffee and cocoa are the main exports. Lomé, the capital, is an entrepôt trade centre.

Tokelau
New Zealand Overseas Territory

Area Sq Km	10	Languages	English, Tokelauan
Area Sq Miles	4	Religions	Christian
Population	1 000	Currency	New Zealand dollar

Map page 69   Tokelau consists of three atolls, Atafu, Nukunonu and Fakaofa, lying in the Pacific Ocean north of Samoa. Subsistence agriculture is the main activity, and the islands rely on aid from New Zealand.

TONGA
Kingdom of Tonga

Area Sq Km	748	Languages	Tongan, English
Area Sq Miles	289	Religions	Protestant, Roman Catholic
Population	99 000	Currency	Pa'anga
Capital	Nuku'alofa	Organizations	Comm., UN

Map page 69

Tonga comprises one hundred and seventy islands in the south Pacific Ocean, northeast of New Zealand. The three main groups are Tongatapu (where sixty per cent of Tongans live), Ha'apai and Vava'u. The climate is warm with good rainfall and the economy relies heavily on agriculture. Tourism and light industry are important to the economy. Exports include squash, fish, vanilla beans and root crops. Most trade is with New Zealand, Japan and Australia.

TRINIDAD AND TOBAGO
Republic of Trinidad and Tobago

Area Sq Km	5 130	Languages	English, Creole, Hindi
Area Sq Miles	1 981	Religions	Roman Catholic, Hindu, Protestant, Sunni Muslim
Population	1 294 000	Currency	Trinidad and Tobago dollar
Capital	Port of Spain	Organizations	CARICOM, Comm., UN

Map page 157

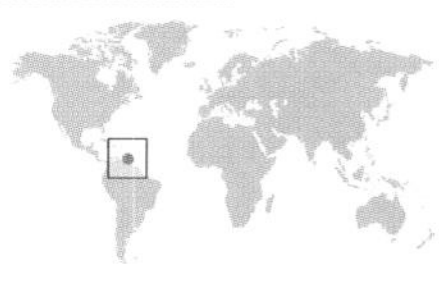

Trinidad, the most southerly Caribbean island, lies off the Venezuelan coast. It is hilly in the north, with a central plain. Tobago, to the northeast, is smaller, more mountainous and less developed. The climate is

tropical. The main crops are cocoa, sugar cane, coffee and fruit and vegetables. Oil and petrochemical industries dominate the economy. Tourism is also important. The USA is the main trading partner.

TUNISIA
Republic of Tunisia

Area Sq Km	164 150	Languages	Arabic, French
Area Sq Miles	63 379	Religions	Sunni Muslim
Population	9 459 000	Currency	Tunisian dinar
Capital	Tunis	Organizations	UN

Map page 120

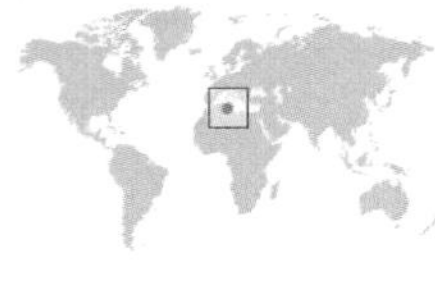

Tunisia is on the Mediterranean coast of north Africa. The north is mountainous with valleys and coastal plains, has a Mediterranean climate and is the most populous area. The south is hot and arid. Oil and phosphates are the main resources. The main crops are olives and citrus fruit. Tourism is an important industry. Exports include petroleum products, textiles, fruit and phosphorus. Most trade is with EU countries.

TURKEY
Republic of Turkey

Area Sq Km	779 452	Languages	Turkish, Kurdish
Area Sq Miles	300 948	Religions	Sunni Muslim, Shi'a Muslim
Population	66 668 000	Currency	Turkish lira
Capital	Ankara	Organizations	OECD, UN

Map page 80-81

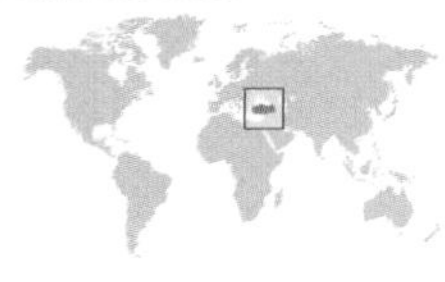

Turkey occupies the Asia Minor peninsula of southwest Asia and has coastlines on the Black, Mediterranean and Aegean Seas. It includes eastern Thrace, which is in southeast Europe and separated from the rest of the country by the Bosporus, the Sea of Marmara and Dardanelles. The Asian mainland consists of the semi-arid Anatolian plateau, flanked to the north, south and east by mountains. Over forty per cent of Turks live in central Anatolia and on the Marmara and Aegean coastal plains. The coast has a Mediterranean climate, but inland conditions are more extreme with hot, dry summers and cold, snowy winters. Agriculture involves approximately forty per cent of the workforce and products include cotton, grain, tobacco, fruit, nuts and livestock. Turkey is a leading producer of chromium, iron ore, lead, tin, borate, and barite; coal is also mined. The main manufactured goods are clothing, textiles, food products, steel and vehicles. Tourism is a major industry with nine million visitors a year. Germany and the USA are the main trading partners. Remittances from workers aboard are important to the economy.

TURKMENISTAN
Republic of Turkmenistan

Area Sq Km	488 100	Languages	Turkmen, Uzbek, Russian
Area Sq Miles	188 456	Religions	Sunni Muslim, Russian Orthodox
Population	4 737 000	Currency	Turkmen manat
Capital	Ashgabat (Ashkhabad)	Organizations	CIS, UN

Map page 82

Turkmenistan, in central Asia, comprises the plains of the Karakum Desert, the foothills of the Kopet Dag in the south, the Amudar'ya valley in the north and the Caspian Sea plains in the west. The climate is dry with extreme temperatures. The economy is based mainly on irrigated agriculture, chiefly cotton growing, and the production of natural gas and oil. Main exports are natural gas, oil and cotton fibre. Ukraine, Iran, Turkey and the Russian Federation are the main trading partners.

Turks and Caicos Islands
United Kingdom Overseas Territory

Area Sq Km	430	Languages	English
Area Sq Miles	166	Religions	Protestant
Population	17 000	Currency	US dollar
Capital	Grand Turk		

Map page 149 The territory consists of over forty low-lying islands and cays in the northern Caribbean region. Only eight islands are inhabited and two fifths of the population live on Grand Turk and Salt Cay. The climate is tropical. The economy is based on tourism, fishing and offshore banking.

TUVALU

Area Sq Km	25	Languages	Tuvaluan, English
Area Sq Miles	10	Religions	Protestant
Population	11 000	Currency	Australian dollar
Capital	Vaiaku	Organizations	Comm., UN

Map page 69

Tuvalu comprises nine low lying coral atolls in the south Pacific Ocean. One-third of the population live on Funafuti and most people depend on subsistence farming and fishing. The islands export copra, stamps and clothing, but rely heavily on foreign aid. Most trade is with Fiji, Australia and New Zealand.

UGANDA
Republic of Uganda

Area Sq Km	241 038	Languages	English, Swahili, Luganda, local languages
Area Sq Miles	93 065	Religions	Roman Catholic, Protestant, Sunni Muslim, traditional beliefs
Population	23 300 000	Currency	Ugandan shilling
Capital	Kampala	Organizations	Comm., UN

Map page 122

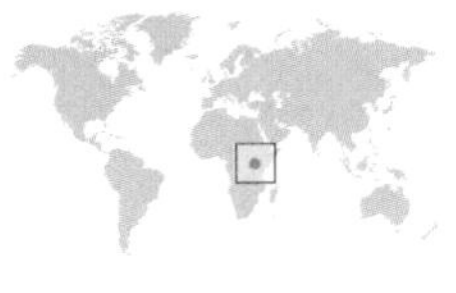

A landlocked country in east Africa, Uganda consists of a savanna plateau with mountains and lakes. The climate is warm and wet. Most people live in the southern half of the country. Agriculture employs around eighty per cent of the workforce and dominates the economy. Coffee, tea, fish and fish products are the main exports. Uganda relies heavily on aid.

UKRAINE

Area Sq Km	603 700	Languages	Ukrainian, Russian
Area Sq Miles	233 090	Religions	Ukrainian Orthodox, Ukrainian Catholic, Roman Catholic
Population	49 568 000	Currency	Hryvnia
Capital	Kiev (Kyiv)	Organizations	CIS, UN

Map page 117

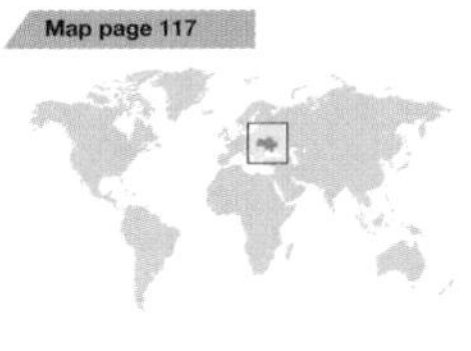

Ukraine lies on the Black Sea coast of east Europe. Much of the land is steppe, generally flat and treeless, with rich black soil drained by the river Dnieper. Along the border with Belarus are forested, marshy plains. The only uplands are the Carpathian Mountains in the west and smaller ranges on the Crimea peninsula. Summers are warm and winters are cold, with milder conditions in the Crimea area. About a quarter of the population live in the mainly industrial areas around Donets'k, Kiev and Dnipropetrovs'k. The Ukraine is rich in natural resources: fertile soil, substantial mineral and natural gas deposits, and forests. Agriculture and livestock raising are important, but mining and manufacturing are the most important sectors of the economy. Coal, iron and manganese mining, steel and metal production, machinery, chemicals and food processing are the main industries. The Russian Federation is the main trading partner.

UNITED ARAB EMIRATES
Federation of Emirates

Area Sq Km	83 600	Languages	Arabic, English
Area Sq Miles	32 278	Religions	Sunni Muslim, Shi'a Muslim
Population	2 606 000	Currency	UAE dirham
Capital	Abu Dhabi (Abū Ẓabī)	Organizations	OPEC, UN

Map page 84

The UAE lies on the Gulf coast of the Arabian Peninsula. Six emirates lie on The Gulf while the seventh, Fujairah, lies on the Gulf of Oman. Most of the land is flat desert with sand dunes and salt pans. The only hilly area is in the northeast. Over eighty per cent of the population live in three emirates - Abu Dhabi, Dubai and Sharjah. Summers are hot and winters are mild with occasional rainfall in coastal areas. Fruit and vegetables are grown in oases and irrigated areas, but the Emirates' wealth is based on extraction of hydrocarbons found in Abu Dhabi, Dubai, Sharjah and Ras al Khaimah. The UAE is one of the major oil producers in the Middle East. The tourist industry is increasing in importance. Dubai is an important entrepôt trade centre and the UAE's main trading partner is Japan.

Abu Dhabi (Emirate)

Area Sq Km (Sq Miles)	73 060 (28 209)	Population	928 360	Capital	Abu Dhabi (Abū Ẓabī)

Ajman (Emirate)

Area Sq Km (Sq Miles)	260 (100)	Population	118 812	Capital	Ajman

Dubai (Emirate)

Area Sq Km (Sq Miles)	3 900 (1 506)	Population	674 101	Capital	Dubai

Fujairah (Emirate)

Area Sq Km (Sq Miles)	1 300 (502)	Population	76 254	Capital	Fujairah

Ra's al Khaymah (Emirate)

Area Sq Km (Sq Miles)	1 700 (656)	Population	144 430	Capital	Ra's al Khaymah

Sharjah (Emirate)

Area Sq Km (Sq Miles)	2 600 (1 004)	Population	400 339	Capital	Sharjah

Umm al Qaywayn (Emirate)

Area Sq Km (Sq Miles)	780 (301)	Population	35 157	Capital	Umm al Qaywayn

UNITED KINGDOM
United Kingdom of Great Britain and Northern Ireland

Area Sq Km	244 082	Languages	English, Welsh, Gaelic
Area Sq Miles	94 241	Religions	Protestant, Roman Catholic, Muslim
Population	59 634 000	Currency	Pound sterling
Capital	London	Organizations	Comm., EU, OECD, UN

Map page 104-107

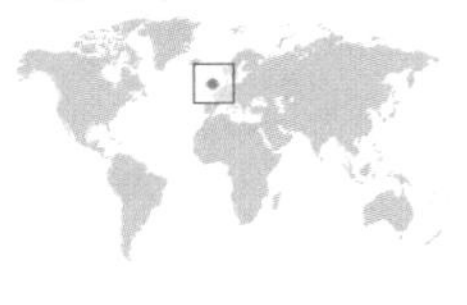

The United Kingdom, in northwest Europe, occupies the island of Great Britain, part of Ireland and many small adjacent islands. Great Britain comprises the countries of England, Scotland and Wales. England covers over half the land area and supports over four-fifths of the population, chiefly in the southeast region. The landscape is flat or rolling with some uplands, notably the Cheviot Hills on the Scottish border, the Pennines in the centre-north and the hills of the Lake District in the northwest. Scotland consists of southern uplands, central lowlands, highlands and islands. Wales is a land of mountains and river valleys. Northern Ireland contains uplands, plains and the UK's largest lake, Lough Neagh. The climate is mild, wet and variable. The UK has few mineral deposits, but has important energy resources. Agricultural activities involve sheep and cattle raising, dairy farming, and crop and fruit growing in the east and southeast. Productivity is high, but approximately one-third of food is imported. The UK produces petroleum and natural gas from reserves in the North Sea and is self-sufficient in energy in net terms. Major manufactured goods are food and drinks, motor vehicles and parts, aerospace equipment, machinery, electronic and electrical equipment, and chemicals and chemical products. However, the economy is dominated by service industries, including banking, insurance, finance and business services. London is one of the world's major financial centres. Tourism is a major industry, with approximately twenty five million visitors each year. International trade is also important, equivalent to one-third of national income. Over half of the UK's trade is with other EU countries.

England (Constituent country)

Area Sq Km (Sq Miles)	130 423 (50 357)	Population	49 997 100	Capital	London

Northern Ireland (Province)

Area Sq Km (Sq Miles)	14 121 (5 452)	Population	1 697 800	Capital	Belfast

Scotland (Constituent country)

Area Sq Km (Sq Miles)	78 772 (30 414)	Population	5 114 600	Capital	Edinburgh

Wales (Principality)

Area Sq Km (Sq Miles)	20 766 (8 018)	Population	2 946 200	Capital	Cardiff

UNITED STATES OF AMERICA
Federal Republic

Area Sq Km	9 809 378	Languages	English, Spanish
Area Sq Miles	3 787 422	Religions	Protestant, Roman Catholic, Sunni Muslim, Jewish
Population	283 230 000	Currency	US dollar
Capital	Washington DC	Organizations	APEC, OECD, UN

Map page 136-137

The USA comprises forty eight contiguous states in North America, bounded by Canada and Mexico, and the states of Alaska, to the northwest of Canada, and Hawaii, in the north Pacific Ocean. The populous eastern states consist

of the Atlantic coastal plain (which includes the Florida peninsula and the Gulf of Mexico coast) and the Appalachian Mountains. The central states form a vast interior plain drained by the Mississippi-Missouri river system. To the west lie the Rocky Mountains, separated from the Pacific coastal ranges by the intermontane plateaus. The coastal ranges in the west are prone to earthquakes. Hawaii is a group of some twenty volcanic islands in the north Pacific Ocean. Climatic conditions range between arctic in Alaska to desert in the intermontane plateaus. Most of the USA has a temperate climate, although the interior has continental conditions. The USA has abundant natural resources including major reserves of minerals and energy resources. The USA has the largest and most technologically advanced economy in the world, based on manufacturing and services. Although agriculture accounts for approximately two per cent of the national income, productivity is high and the USA is a net exporter of food, chiefly grains and fruit. Cotton is the major industrial crop. The USA produces iron ore, copper, lead, zinc, and many other minerals. It is a major producer of coal, petroleum and natural gas, although being the world's biggest energy user it imports significant quantities of petroleum and petroleum products. Manufacturing is diverse. The main industries are petroleum, steel, motor vehicles, aerospace, telecommunications, electronics, food processing, chemicals and consumer goods. Tourism is a major foreign currency earner with approximately forty-five million visitors a year. Other important service industries are banking and finance, and Wall Street in New York is a major stock exchange. Canada and Mexico are the main trading partners.

Alabama (State)
Area Sq Km (Sq Miles) 135 775 (52 423)   Population 4 447 100   Capital Montgomery

Alaska (State)
Area Sq Km (Sq Miles) 1 700 130 (656 424)   Population 626 932   Capital Juneau

Arizona (State)
Area Sq Km (Sq Miles) 295 274 (114 006)   Population 5 130 632   Capital Phoenix

Arkansas (State)
Area Sq Km (Sq Miles) 137 741 (53 182)   Population 2 673 400   Capital Little Rock

California (State)
Area Sq Km (Sq Miles) 423 999 (163 707)   Population 33 871 648   Capital Sacramento

Colorado (State)
Area Sq Km (Sq Miles) 269 618 (104 100)   Population 4 301 261   Capital Denver

Connecticut (State)
Area Sq Km (Sq Miles) 14 359 (5 544)   Population 3 405 565   Capital Hartford

Delaware (State)
Area Sq Km (Sq Miles) 6 446 (2 489)   Population 783 600   Capital Dover

District of Columbia (District)
Area Sq Km (Sq Miles) 176 (68)   Population 572 059   Capital Washington

Florida (State)
Area Sq Km (Sq Miles) 170 312 (65 758)   Population 15 982 378   Capital Tallahassee

Georgia (State)
Area Sq Km (Sq Miles) 153 951 (59 441)   Population 8 186 453   Capital Atlanta

Hawaii (State)
Area Sq Km (Sq Miles) 28 314 (10 932)   Population 1 211 537   Capital Honolulu

Idaho (State)
Area Sq Km (Sq Miles) 216 456 (83 574)   Population 1 293 953   Capital Boise

Illinois (State)
Area Sq Km (Sq Miles) 150 007 (57 918)   Population 12 419 293   Capital Springfield

Indiana (State)
Area Sq Km (Sq Miles) 94 327 (36 420)   Population 6 080 485   Capital Indianapolis

Iowa (State)
Area Sq Km (Sq Miles) 145 754 (56 276)   Population 2 926 324   Capital Des Moines

Kansas (State)
Area Sq Km (Sq Miles) 213 109 (82 282)   Population 2 688 418   Capital Topeka

Kentucky (State)
Area Sq Km (Sq Miles) 104 664 (40 411)   Population 4 041 769   Capital Frankfort

Louisiana (State)
Area Sq Km (Sq Miles) 134 273 (51 843)   Population 4 468 976   Capital Baton Rouge

Maine (State)
Area Sq Km (Sq Miles) 91 652 (35 387)   Population 1 274 923   Capital Augusta

Maryland (State)
Area Sq Km (Sq Miles) 32 134 (12 407)   Population 5 296 486   Capital Annapolis

Massachusetts (State)
Area Sq Km (Sq Miles) 27 337 (10 555)   Population 6 349 097   Capital Boston

Michigan (State)
Area Sq Km (Sq Miles) 250 737 (96 810)   Population 9 938 444   Capital Lansing

Minnesota (State)
Area Sq Km (Sq Miles) 225 181 (86 943)   Population 4 919 479   Capital St Paul

Mississippi (State)
Area Sq Km (Sq Miles) 125 443 (48 434)   Population 2 844 658   Capital Jackson

Missouri (State)
Area Sq Km (Sq Miles) 180 545 (69 709)   Population 5 595 211   Capital Jefferson City

Montana (State)
Area Sq Km (Sq Miles) 380 847 (147 046)   Population 902 195   Capital Helena

Nebraska (State)
Area Sq Km (Sq Miles) 200 356 (77 358)   Population 1 711 263   Capital Lincoln

Nevada (State)
Area Sq Km (Sq Miles) 286 367 (110 567)   Population 1 998 257   Capital Carson City

New Hampshire (State)
Area Sq Km (Sq Miles) 24 219 (9 351)   Population 1 235 786   Capital Concord

New Jersey (State)
Area Sq Km (Sq Miles) 22 590 (8 722)   Population 8 414 350   Capital Trenton

New Mexico (State)
Area Sq Km (Sq Miles) 314 937 (121 598)   Population 1 819 046   Capital Santa Fe

New York (State)
Area Sq Km (Sq Miles) 141 090 (54 475)   Population 18 976 457   Capital Albany

North Carolina (State)
Area Sq Km (Sq Miles) 139 396 (53 821)   Population 8 049 313   Capital Raleigh

North Dakota (State)
Area Sq Km (Sq Miles) 183 123 (70 704)   Population 642 200   Capital Bismarck

Ohio (State)
Area Sq Km (Sq Miles) 116 104 (44 828)   Population 11 353 140   Capital Columbus

Oklahoma (State)
Area Sq Km (Sq Miles) 181 048 (69 903)   Population 3 450 654   Capital Oklahoma City

Oregon (State)
Area Sq Km (Sq Miles) 254 819 (98 386)   Population 3 421 399   Capital Salem

Pennsylvania (State)
Area Sq Km (Sq Miles) 119 290 (46 058)   Population 12 281 054   Capital Harrisburg

Rhode Island (State)
Area Sq Km (Sq Miles) 4 002 (1 545)   Population 1 048 319   Capital Providence

South Carolina (State)
Area Sq Km (Sq Miles) 82 898 (32 007)   Population 4 012 012   Capital Columbia

South Dakota (State)
Area Sq Km (Sq Miles) 199 742 (77 121)   Population 754 844   Capital Pierre

Tennessee (State)
Area Sq Km (Sq Miles) 109 158 (42 146)   Population 5 689 283   Capital Nashville

Texas (State)
Area Sq Km (Sq Miles) 695 673 (268 601)   Population 20 851 820   Capital Austin

Utah (State)
Area Sq Km (Sq Miles) 219 900 (84 904)   Population 2 233 169   Capital Salt Lake City

Vermont (State)
Area Sq Km (Sq Miles) 24 903 (9 615)   Population 608 827   Capital Montpelier

Virginia (State)
Area Sq Km (Sq Miles) 110 771 (42 769)   Population 7 078 515   Capital Richmond

Washington (State)
Area Sq Km (Sq Miles) 184 674 (71 303)   Population 5 894 121   Capital Olympia

West Virginia (State)
Area Sq Km (Sq Miles) 62 758 (24 231)   Population 1 808 344   Capital Charleston

Wisconsin (State)
Area Sq Km (Sq Miles) 169 652 (65 503)   Population 5 363 675   Capital Madison

Wyoming (State)
Area Sq Km (Sq Miles) 253 347 (97 818)   Population 493 782   Capital Cheyenne

URUGUAY
Oriental Republic of Uruguay

Area Sq Km	176 215	Languages Spanish
Area Sq Miles	68 037	Religions Roman Catholic, Protestant, Jewish
Population	3 337 000	Currency Uruguayan peso
Capital	Montevideo	Organizations UN

Map page 159

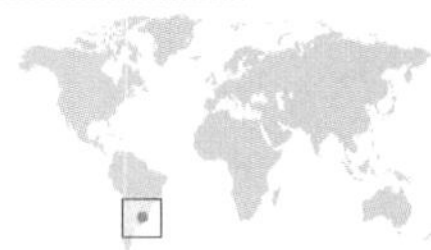

Uruguay, on the Atlantic coast of central South America, is a low-lying land of prairies. The coast and the River Plate estuary in the south are fringed with lagoons and sand dunes. Almost half of the population live in the capital, Montevideo. Uruguay has warm summers and mild winters. The economy is based on cattle and sheep ranching, and the main industries produce food products, textiles, and petroleum products. Meat, wool, hides, textiles and agricultural products are the main exports. Brazil and Argentina are the main trading partners.

UZBEKISTAN
Republic of Uzbekistan

Area Sq Km	447 400	Languages Uzbek, Russian, Tajik, Kazakh
Area Sq Miles	172 742	Religions Sunni Muslim, Russian Orthodox
Population	24 881 000	Currency Uzbek som
Capital	Tashkent	Organizations CIS, UN

Map page 82-83

A landlocked country of central Asia, Uzbekistan consists mainly of the flat Kyzylkum Desert. High mountains and valleys are found towards the southeast borders with Kyrgyzstan and Tajikistan. Most settlement is in the basin around Fergana. The climate is hot and dry. The economy is based mainly on irrigated agriculture, chiefly cotton production. Uzbekistan is rich in minerals including gold, copper, lead, zinc and uranium and it has the largest gold mine in the world. Industry specializes in fertilizers and machinery for cotton harvesting and textile manufacture. The Russian Federation is the main trading partner.

VANUATU
Republic of Vanuatu

Area Sq Km	12 190	Languages English, Bislama (Creole), French
Area Sq Miles	4 707	Religions Protestant, Roman Catholic, traditional beliefs
Population	197 000	Currency Vatu
Capital	Port Vila	Organizations Comm., UN

Map page 69

Vanuatu occupies an archipelago of approximately eighty islands in the southwest Pacific. Many of the islands are mountainous, of volcanic origin and densely forested. The climate is tropical with heavy rainfall. Half of the population live on the main islands of Éfaté

and Espíritu Santo, and the majority of people live by farming. Copra, beef, timber, vegetables and cocoa are the main exports. Tourism is becoming important to the economy. Australia, Japan and Germany are the main trading partners.

VATICAN CITY
Vatican City State

Area Sq Km	0.5	Languages	Italian
Area Sq Miles	0.2	Religions	Roman Catholic
Population	480	Currency	Euro
Capital	Vatican City		

Map page 114

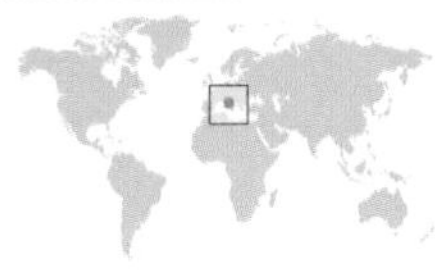

The world's smallest sovereign state, the Vatican City occupies a hill to the west of the river Tiber in the Italian capital, Rome. It is the headquarters of the Roman Catholic church and income comes from investments, voluntary contributions and tourism.

VENEZUELA
Republic of Venezuela

Area Sq Km	912 050	Languages	Spanish, Amerindian languages
Area Sq Miles	352 144	Religions	Roman Catholic, Protestant
Population	24 170 000	Currency	Bolívar
Capital	Caracas	Organizations	OPEC, UN

Map page 157

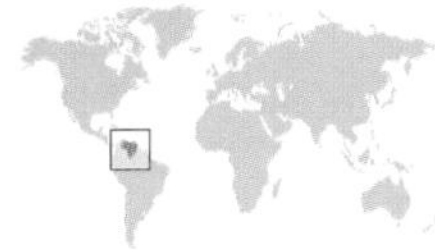

Venezuela is in north South America, on the Caribbean Sea. The oil-rich area of Lake Maracaibo lies at the western end of its coastline with the swampy Orinoco Delta to the east. Mountain ranges run parallel to the coast then turn southwestwards to form the northern extension of the Andes. Central Venezuela is lowland grasslands drained by the Orinoco river system. To the south are the Guiana Highlands which contain Angels Falls, the world's highest waterfall. Almost ninety per cent of the population live in towns, mostly in the mountainous coastal areas. The climate is tropical, with summer rainfall. Temperatures are lower in the mountains. Farming is important, particularly cattle ranching and dairy farming. Coffee, maize, rice and sugar cane are the main crops. Venezuela is a major oil producer, and sales account for approximately seventy five per cent of export earnings. Aluminium, iron ore, copper and gold are also mined and manufactured goods include petrochemicals, aluminium, steel, textiles and food products. The USA and Puerto Rico are the main trading partners.

VIETNAM
Socialist Republic of Vietnam

Area Sq Km	329 565	Languages	Vietnamese, Thai, Khmer, Chinese, local languages
Area Sq Miles	127 246	Religions	Buddhist, Taoist, Roman Catholic, Cao Dai, Hoa Hao
Population	78 137 000	Currency	Dong
Capital	Ha Nôi	Organizations	APEC, ASEAN, UN

Map page 91

Vietnam lies in Southeast Asia, on the west coast of the South China Sea. The Red River delta lowlands in the north are separated from the huge Mekong delta in the south by long, narrow coastal plains backed by the mountainous and forested terrain of the Annam Plateau. Most of the population live in the river deltas. The climate is tropical, with summer monsoon rains. Over three-quarters of the workforce are involved in agriculture, forestry and fishing. Rice is the main crop; coffee, tea and rubber are important cash crops. Vietnam is the world's second largest rice exporter. Oil, coal and copper are produced and the main industries are food processing, clothing and footwear, cement and fertilizers. Exports include oil, coffee, rice, clothing, fish and fish products. Japan and Singapore are the main trading partners.

Virgin Islands (UK)
United Kingdom Overseas Territory

Area Sq Km	153	Languages	English
Area Sq Miles	59	Religions	Protestant, Roman Catholic
Population	24 000	Currency	US dollar
Capital	Road Town		

Map page 149 The Caribbean territory comprises four main islands and over thirty islets at the eastern end of the Virgin Islands group. Apart from the flat coral atoll of Anegada, the islands are volcanic in origin and hilly. The climate is subtropical and tourism is the main industry.

Virgin Islands (USA)
United States Unincorporated Territory

Area Sq Km	352	Languages	English, Spanish
Area Sq Miles	136	Religions	Protestant, Roman Catholic
Population	121 000	Currency	US dollar
Capital	Charlotte Amalie		

Map page 149

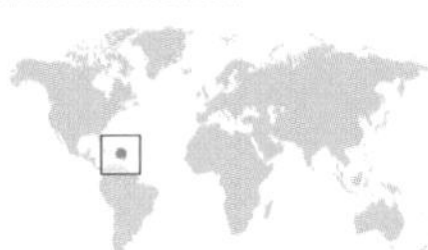

The territory consists of three main islands and over fifty islets in the Caribbean's western Virgin Islands. The islands are hilly, of volcanic origin and the climate is subtropical. The economy is based on tourism, with some manufacturing, including a major oil refinery on St Croix.

Wallis and Futuna Islands
French Overseas Territory

Area Sq Km	274	Languages	French, Wallisian, Futunian
Area Sq Miles	106	Religions	Roman Catholic
Population	14 000	Currency	CFP franc
Capital	Matā'utu		

Map page 69

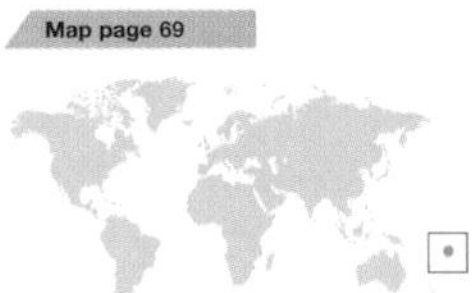

The south Pacific territory comprises the volcanic islands of the Wallis archipelago and Hoorn Islands. The climate is tropical. The islands depend on subsistence farming, the sale of licences to foreign fishing fleets, remittances from abroad and French aid.

West Bank
Disputed territory

Area Sq Km	5 860	Languages	Arabic, Hebrew
Area Sq Miles	2 263	Religions	Sunni Muslim, Jewish, Shi'a Muslim, Christian
		Currency	Jordanian dinar, Israeli shekel

Map page 80

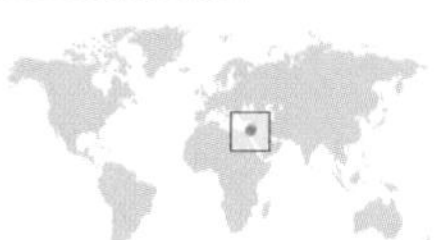

The territory consists of the west bank of the river Jordan and parts of Judea and Samaria. The land was annexed by Israel in 1967, but some areas have been granted self-government under agreements between Israel and the Palestine Liberation Organization.

Western Sahara
Disputed territory

Area Sq Km	266 000	Languages	Arabic
Area Sq Miles	102 703	Religions	Sunni Muslim
Population	252 000	Currency	Moroccan dirham
Capital	Laâyoune		

Map page 120

Situated on the northwest coast of Africa, the territory of Western Sahara is controlled by Morocco. The land is low, flat desert with higher land in the northeast. There is little cultivation and only approximately twenty per cent of the land is pasture. Livestock herding, fishing and phosphate mining are the main activities. All trade is controlled by Morocco.

YEMEN
Republic of Yemen

Area Sq Km	527 968	Languages	Arabic
Area Sq Miles	203 850	Religions	Sunni Muslim, Shi'a Muslim
Population	18 349 000	Currency	Yemeni riyal
Capital	San'a'	Organizations	UN

Map page 86

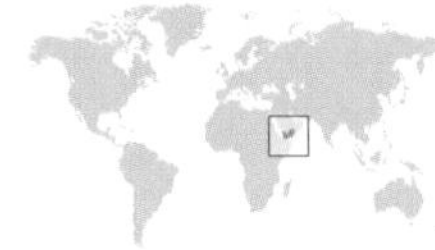

Yemen occupies the southwestern Arabian Peninsula, on the Red Sea and the Gulf of Aden. Beyond the Red Sea coastal plain the land rises to a mountain range and then descends to desert plateaus. Much of Yemen is hot and arid, but rainfall in the west supports crops and most settlement. Farming and fishing are the main activities, with cotton the main cash crop. The main exports are crude oil, fish, coffee and dried fruit. Despite its oil resources Yemen is one of the poorest countries in the Arab World. Main trading partners are Thailand, China, South Korea and Saudi Arabia.

YUGOSLAVIA
Federal Republic of Yugoslavia

Area Sq Km	102 173	Languages	Serbian, Albanian, Hungarian
Area Sq Miles	39 449	Religions	Serbian Orthodox, Montenegrin Orthodox, Sunni Muslim
Population	10 552 000	Currency	Yugoslav dinar
Capital	Belgrade (Beograd)	Organizations	UN

Map page 115

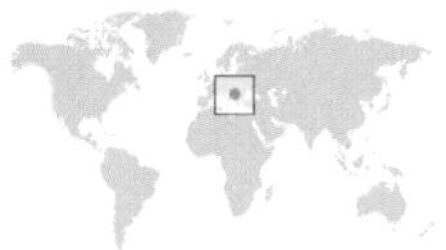

The south European state comprises two of the former Yugoslav republics, Serbia and the much smaller Montenegro. The landscape is for the most part rugged, mountainous and forested. Northern Serbia is low-lying and is drained by the Danube river system. The climate is Mediterranean on the coast and continental inland. Since 1991 the economy has been seriously affected by war, trade embargoes and economic sanctions.

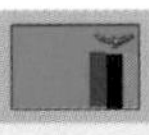

ZAMBIA
Republic of Zambia

Area Sq Km	752 614	Languages	English, Bemba, Nyanja, Tonga, local languages
Area Sq Miles	290 586	Religions	Christian, traditional beliefs
Population	10 421 000	Currency	Zambian kwacha
Capital	Lusaka	Organizations	Comm., SADC, UN

Map page 123

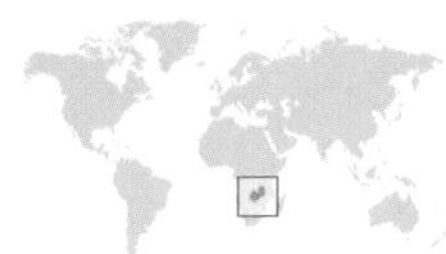

A landlocked state in south central Africa, Zambia borders seven countries. It is dominated by high savanna plateaus and is bordered by the Zambezi river in the south. The climate is tropical with a rainy season from November to May. Agriculture employs approximately eighty per cent of the workforce, but is mainly at subsistence level. Copper mining is the mainstay of the economy, although reserves are declining. Copper and cobalt are the main exports and most trade is with South Africa.

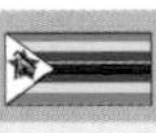

ZIMBABWE
Republic of Zimbabwe

Area Sq Km	390 759	Languages	English, Shona, Ndebele
Area Sq Miles	150 873	Religions	Christian, traditional beliefs
Population	12 627 000	Currency	Zimbabwean dollar
Capital	Harare	Organizations	Comm., SADC, UN

Map page 123

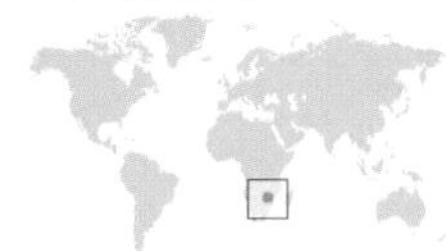

Zimbabwe, a landlocked state in south central Africa, consists of high plateaus flanked by the Zambezi river valley and Lake Kariba in the north and the Limpopo river in the south. Most of the population live in central Zimbabwe. There are significant mineral resources including gold, nickel, copper, asbestos, platinum and chromium. Agriculture is a major sector of the economy and crops include tobacco, maize, sugar cane, and cotton. Beef cattle are also important. Exports include tobacco, gold, ferroalloys, nickel and cotton. South Africa is the main trading partner.

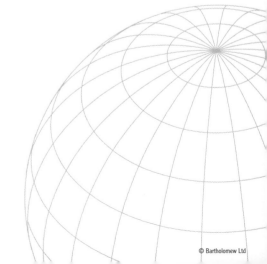

DISTRIBUTION OF MAJOR EARTHQUAKES AND VOLCANOES

Winkel Tripel Projection
scale approximately 1:95 000 000

●	'Deadliest' earthquakes
●	Earthquakes of magnitude >=7.5
○	Earthquakes of magnitude 5.5–7.5
▲	'Major' Volcanoes
▲	Other volcanoes

DEADLIEST EARTHQUAKES 1900–2001

Year	Location	Deaths
1905	Kangra, India	19 000
1907	west of Dushanbe, Tajikistan	12 000
1908	Messina, Italy	110 000
1915	Abruzzo, Italy	35 000
1917	Bali, Indonesia	15 000
1920	Ningxia Province, China	200 000
1923	Tōkyō, Japan	142 807
1927	Qinghai Province, China	200 000
1932	Gansu Province, China	70 000
1933	Sichuan Province, China	10 000
1934	Nepal/India	10 700
1935	Quetta, Pakistan	30 000
1939	Chillán, Chile	28 000
1939	Erzincan, Turkey	32 700
1948	Ashgabat, Turkmenistan	19 800
1962	northwest Iran	12 225
1970	Huánuco Province, Peru	66 794
1974	Yunnan and Sichuan Provinces, China	20 000
1975	Liaoning Province, China	10 000
1976	central Guatemala	22 778
1976	Hebei Province, China	242 000
1978	Khorāsān Province, Iran	20 000
1980	Ech Chélif, Algeria	11 000
1988	Spitak, Armenia	25 000
1990	Manjil, Iran	50 000
1999	Kocaeli (Izmit), Turkey	17 000
2001	Gujarat, India	20 000

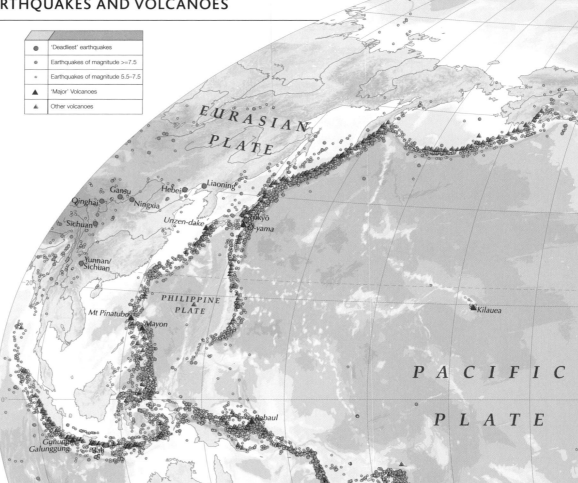

San Andreas Fault, California, USA

RICHTER SCALE

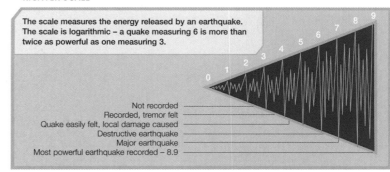

The scale measures the energy released by an earthquake.
The scale is logarithmic – a quake measuring 6 is more than
twice as powerful as one measuring 3.

Not recorded
Recorded, tremor felt
Quake easily felt, local damage caused
Destructive earthquake
Major earthquake
Most powerful earthquake recorded – 8.9

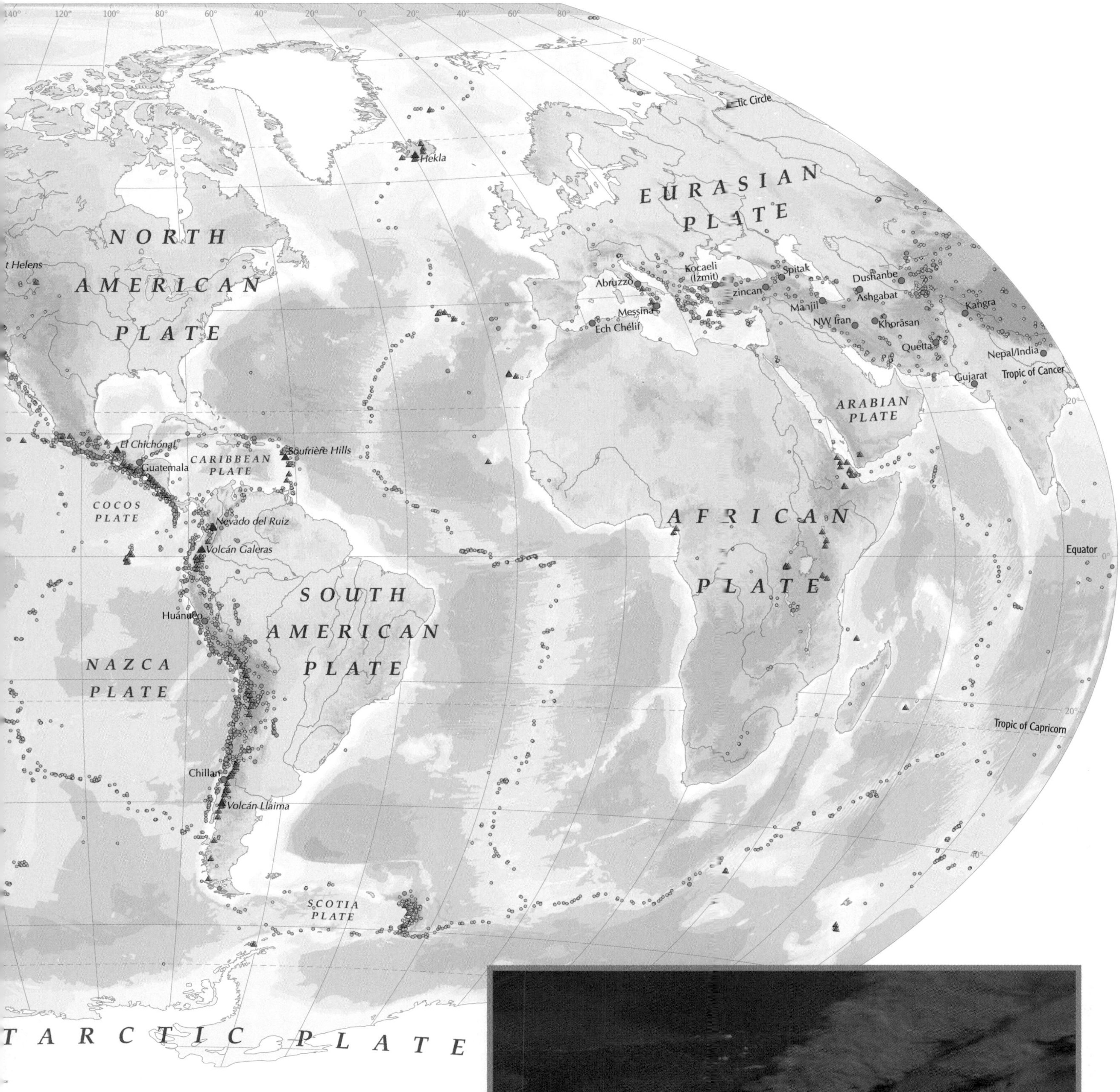

MAJOR VOLCANIC ERUPTIONS SINCE 1980

Date	Volcano	Country
1980	Mt St Helens	USA
1982	El Chichónal	Mexico
1982	Gunung Galunggung	Indonesia
1983	Kilauea	Hawaii
1983	Ō-yama	Japan
1985	Nevado del Ruiz	Colombia
1991	Hekla	Iceland
1991	Mt Pinatubo	Philippines
1991	Unzen-dake	Japan
1993	Mayon	Philippines
1993	Volcán Galeras	Colombia
1994	Volcán Llaima	Chile
1994	Rabaul	Papua New Guinea
1997	Soufrière Hills	Montserrat

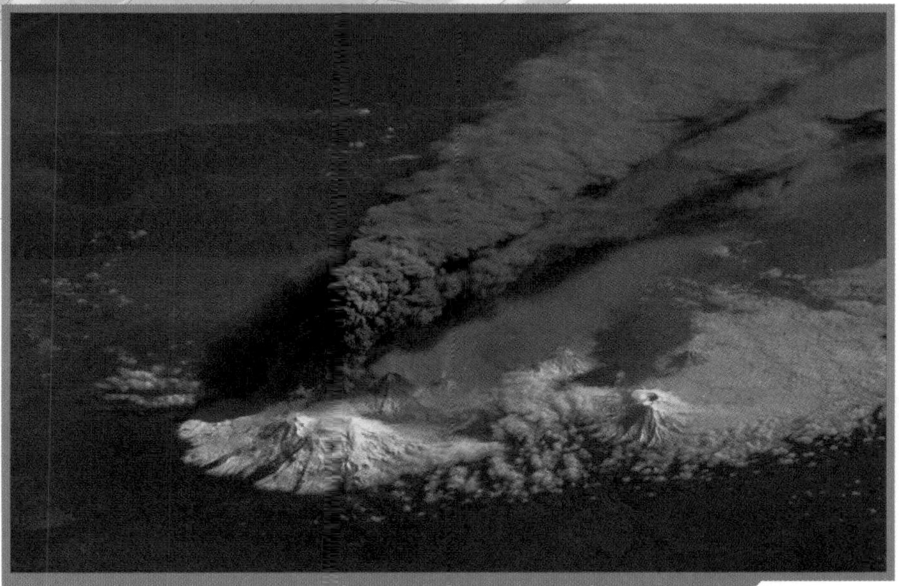

Klyuchevskaya Volcano, Kamchatka Peninsula, Russian Federation

© Bartholomew Ltd

CONTINENTAL LAND COVER COMPOSITION

%
100
80
60
40
20

South America
North America
Eurasia
Australia
Antarctica
Africa

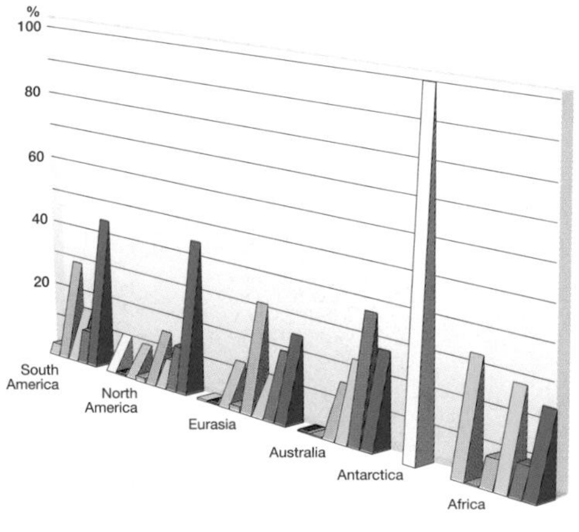

WORLD LAND COVER

Goode Interrupted Homolosine Projection
scale approximately 1:117 000 000
Map courtesy of IGBP, JRC and USGS

GLOBAL LAND COVER COMPOSITION

Wetland 0.9%
Urban 0.2%
Snow/Ice 11.4%
Forest/Woodland 27.5%
Barren 12.6%
Grass/Savanna 14.0%
Crops/Mosaic 19.2%
Shrubland 14.2%

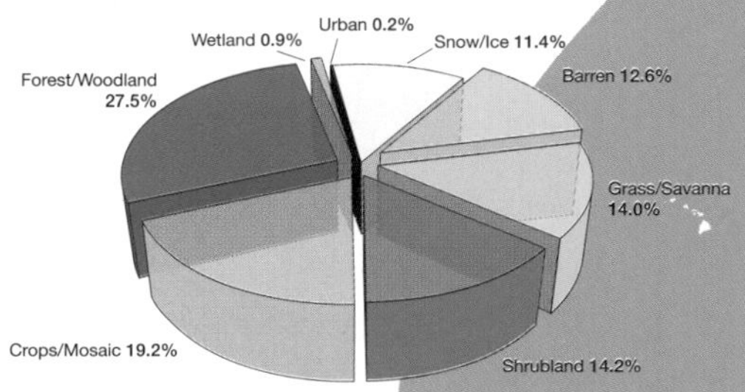

LAND COVER GRAPHS – CLASSIFICATION

Class description	IGBP/DISCover classes
Forest/Woodland	1 Evergreen needleleaf forest
	2 Evergreen broadleaf forest
	3 Deciduous needleleaf forest
	4 Deciduous broadleaf forest
	5 Mixed forest
Shrubland	6 Closed shrublands
	7 Open shrublands
Grass/Savanna	8 Woody savannas
	9 Savannas
	10 Grasslands
Wetland	11 Permanent wetlands
Crops/Mosaic	12 Croplands
	14 Cropland/Natural vegetation mosaic
Urban	13 Urban and built-up
Snow/Ice	15 Snow and Ice
Barren	16 Barren or sparsely vegetated

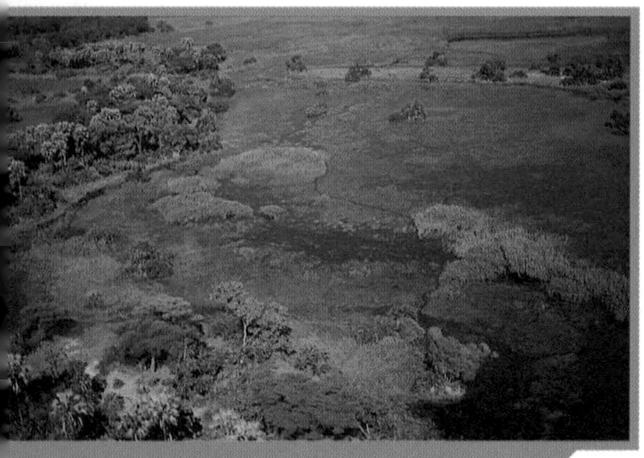

Wetland, Okavango Delta, Botswana

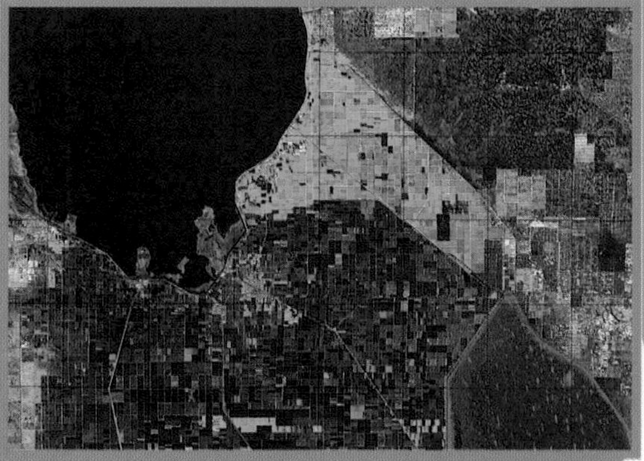

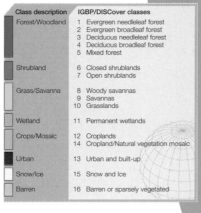

Crops/Mosaic, Florida, USA

MAJOR CLIMATIC REGIONS AND SUB-TYPES

Köppen classification system
Winkel Tripel Projection
scale 1:170 000 000

• Weather extreme location

A Rainy climate with no winter: coolest month above 18°C (64.4°F).

B Dry climates; limits are defined by formulae based on rainfall effectiveness:

BS Steppe or semi-arid climate.

BW Desert or arid climate.

*****C** Rainy climates with mild winters: coolest month above 0°C (32°F), but

below 18°C (64.4°F); warmest month above 10°C (50°F).

*****D** Rainy climates with severe winters: coldest month below 0°C (32°F);

warmest month above 10°C (50°F).

E Polar climates with no warm season: warmest month below 10°C (50°F).

ET Tundra climate: warmest month

below 10°C (50°F) but above 0°C (32°F).

EF Perpetual frost: all months below 0°C (32°F).

a Warmest month above 22°C (71.6°F).

b Warmest month below 22°C (71.6°F).

c Less than four months over 10°C (50°F).

d As 'c', but with severe cold: coldest month below -38°C (-36.4°F).

f Constantly moist rainfall throughout the year.

*****h** Warmer dry: all months above 0°C (32°F).

*****k** Cooler dry: at least one month below 0°C (32°F).

m Monsoon rain: short dry season, but is compensated by heavy rains during rest of the year.

n Frequent fog.

s Dry season in summer.

w Dry season in winter.

***** Modification of Köppen definition

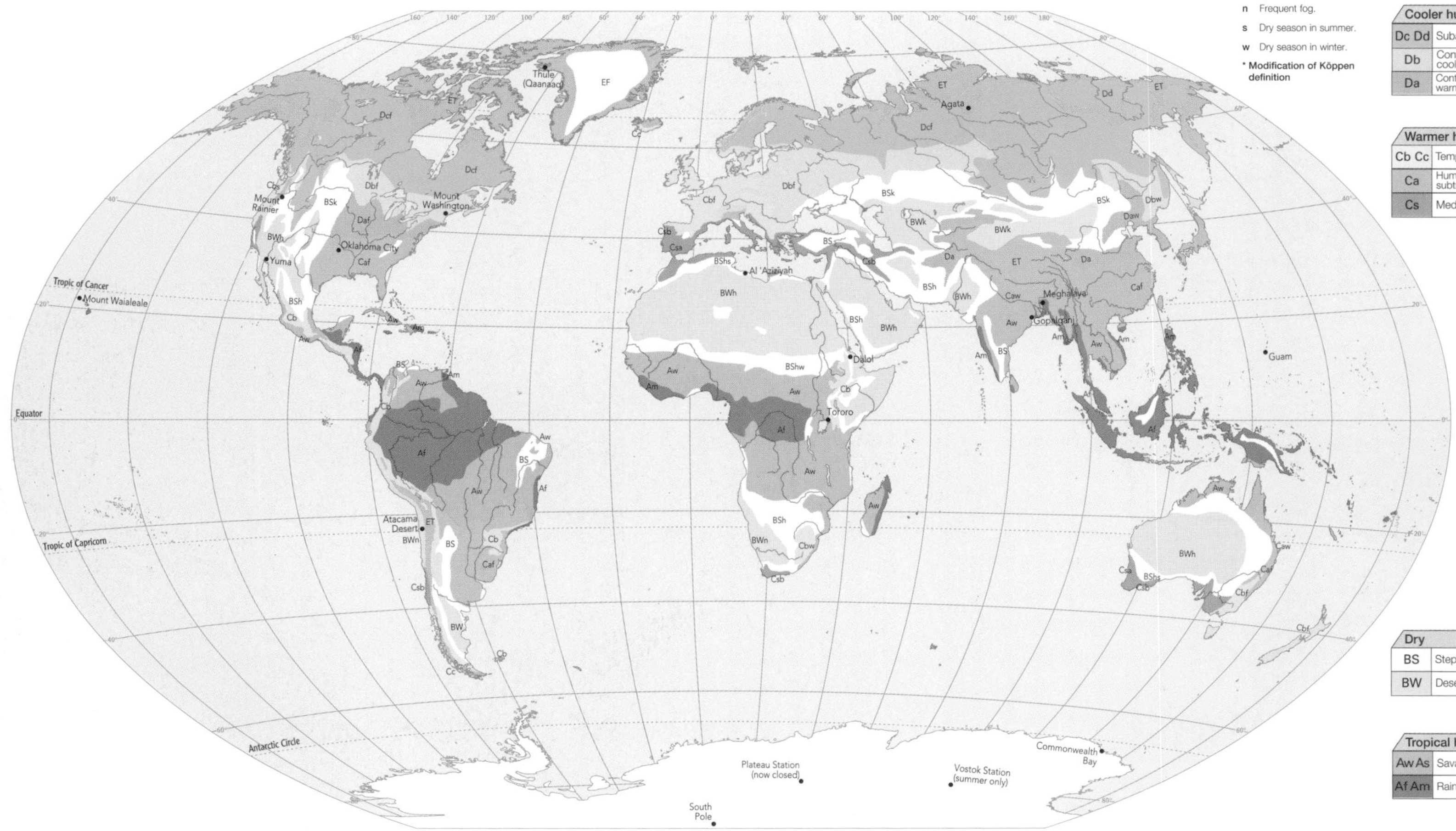

Polar	
EF	Ice cap
ET	Tundra

Cooler humid	
Dc Dd	Subarctic
Db	Continental cool summer
Da	Continental warm summer

Warmer humid	
Cb Cc	Temperate
Ca	Humid subtropical
Cs	Mediterranean

Dry	
BS	Steppe
BW	Desert

Tropical humid	
Aw As	Savanna
Af Am	Rain forest

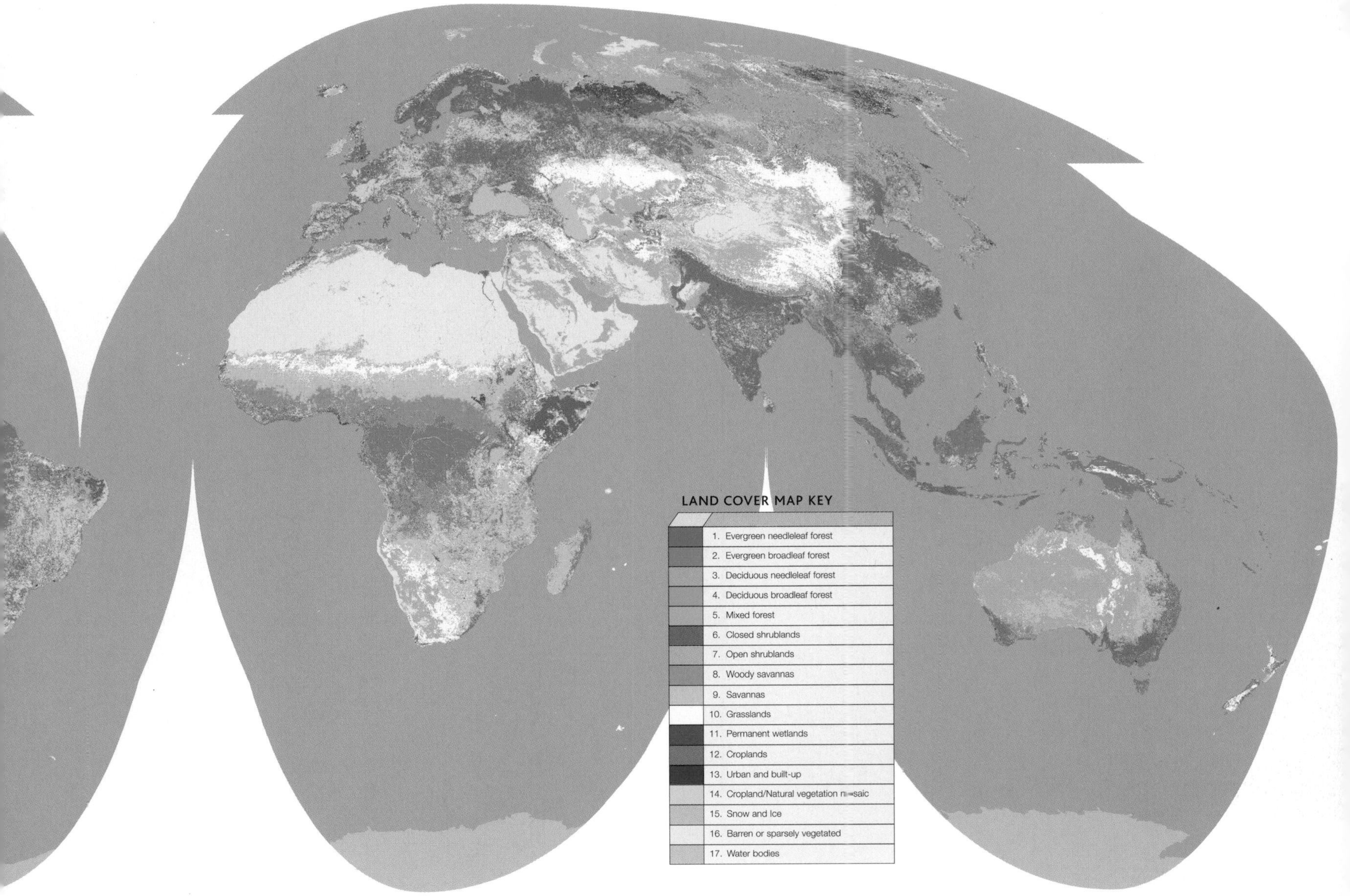

LAND COVER MAP KEY

1.	Evergreen needleleaf forest
2.	Evergreen broadleaf forest
3.	Deciduous needleleaf forest
4.	Deciduous broadleaf forest
5.	Mixed forest
6.	Closed shrublands
7.	Open shrublands
8.	Woody savannas
9.	Savannas
10.	Grasslands
11.	Permanent wetlands
12.	Croplands
13.	Urban and built-up
14.	Cropland/Natural vegetation mosaic
15.	Snow and ice
16.	Barren or sparsely vegetated
17.	Water bodies

WORLD WEATHER EXTREMES

Highest shade temperature	57.8°C/136°F Al 'Azīzīyah, Libya (13th September 1922)
Hottest place – Annual mean	34.4°C/93.9°F Dalol, Ethiopia
Driest place – Annual mean	0.1 mm/0.004 inches Atacama Desert, Chile
Most sunshine – Annual mean	90% Yuma, Arizona, USA (over 4 000 hours)
Least sunshine	Nil for 182 days each year, South Pole
Lowest screen temperature	-89.2°C/-128.6°F Vostok Station, Antarctica (21st July 1983)
Coldest place – Annual mean	-56.6°C/-69.9°F Plateau Station, Antarctica
Wettest place – Annual mean	11 873 mm/467.4 inches Meghalaya, India
Most rainy days	Up to 350 per year Mount Waialeale, Hawaii, USA
Windiest place	322 km per hour/200 miles per hour in gales, Commonwealth Bay, Antarctica

Highest surface wind speed	
– High altitude	372 km per hour/231 miles per hour Mount Washington, New Hampshire, USA (12th April 1934)
– Low altitude	333 km per hour/207 miles per hour Thule (Qaanaaq), (Greenland 8th March 1972)
– Tornado	512 km per hour/318 miles per hour Oklahoma City, Oklahoma, USA (3rd May 1999)
Greatest snowfall	31 102 mm/1 224.5 inches Mount Rainier, Washington, USA (19th February 1971 – 18th February 1972)
Heaviest hailstones	1kg/2.21 lb Gopalganj, Bangladesh (14th April 1986)
Thunder-days – Average	251 days per year Tororo, Uganda
Highest barometric pressure	1083.8 mb Agata, Siberia, Russian Federation (31st December 1968)
Lowest barometric pressure	870 mb 483 km/300 miles west of Guam, Pacific Ocean (12th October 1979)

TRACKS OF TROPICAL STORMS

Wind speeds often over 160 km per hour

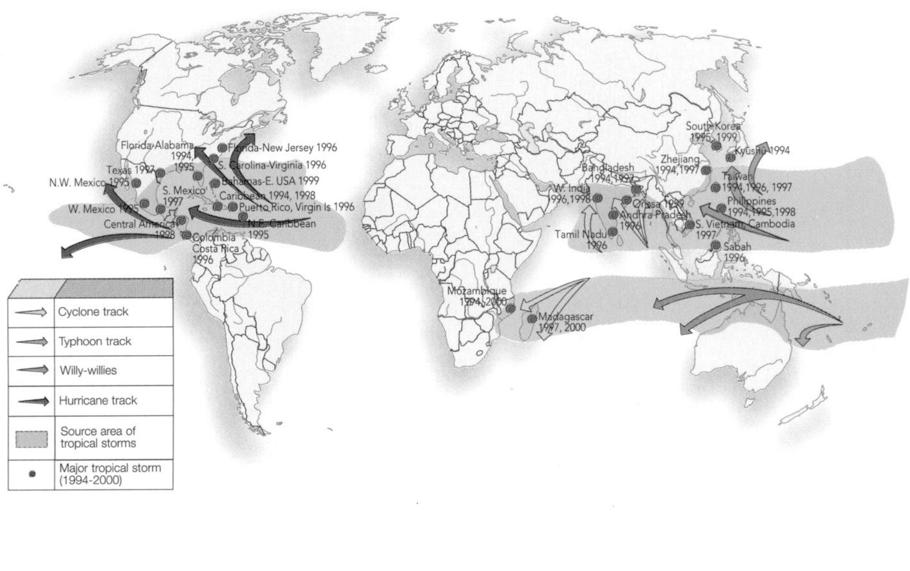

→	Cyclone track
→	Typhoon track
→	Willy-willies
→	Hurricane track
	Source area of tropical storms
•	Major tropical storm (1994-2000)

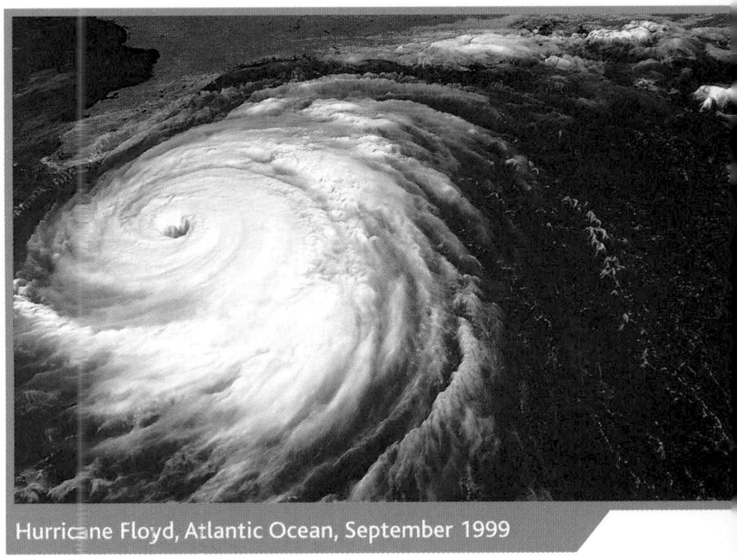

Hurricane Floyd, Atlantic Ocean, September 1999

WORLD POPULATION DISTRIBUTION AND THE WORLD'S MAJOR CITIES

Goode Interrupted Homolosine Projection
scale approximately 1:109 000 000

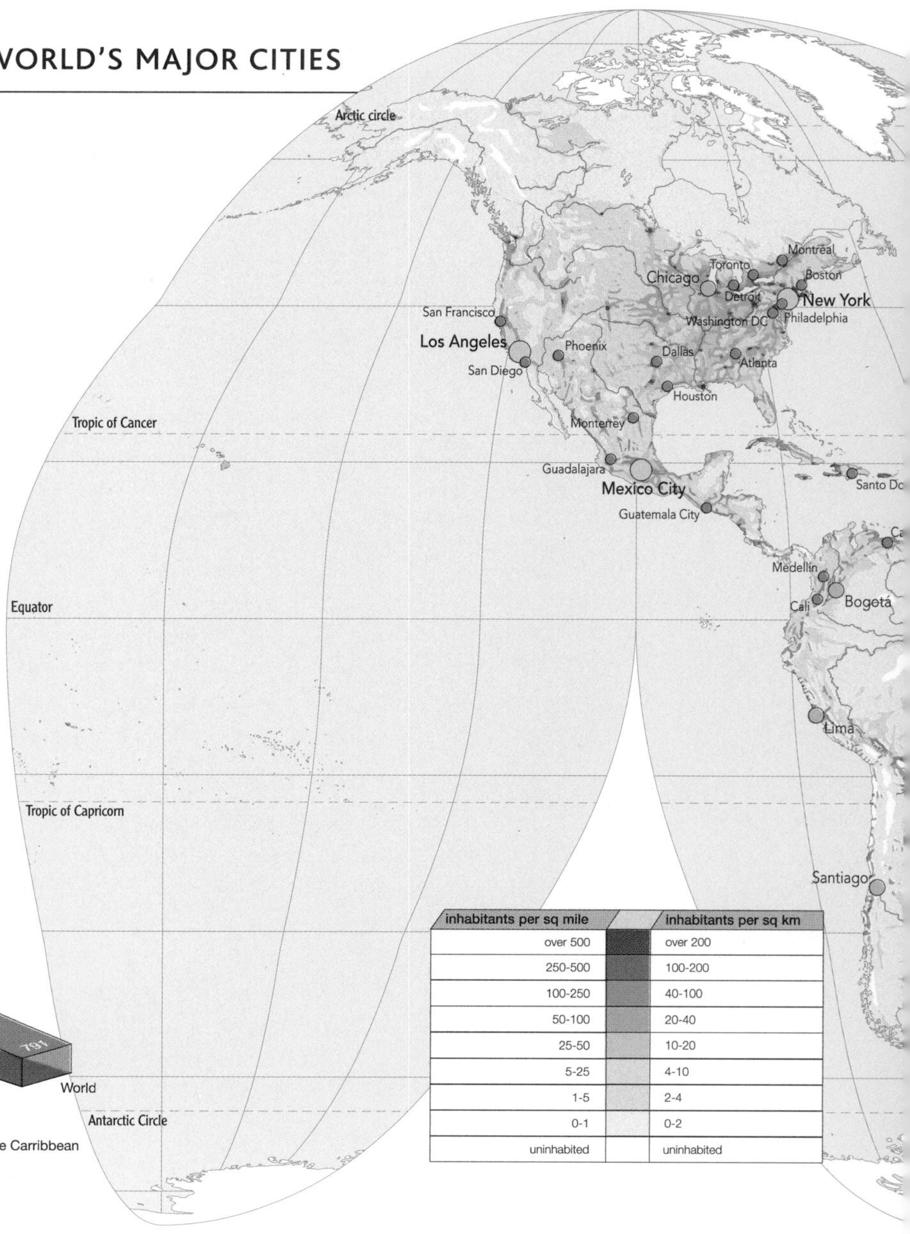

TEN MOST POPULOUS COUNTRIES 2000

	Country	Population
1.	China	1 260 137 000
2.	India	1 008 937 000
3.	United States of America	283 230 000
4.	Indonesia	212 092 000
5.	Brazil	170 406 000
6.	Russian Federation	145 491 000
7.	Pakistan	141 256 000
8.	Bangladesh	137 439 000
9.	Japan	127 096 000
10.	Nigeria	113 862 000

WORLD POPULATION GROWTH BY CONTINENT 1750–2050

inhabitants per sq mile	inhabitants per sq km
over 500	over 200
250-500	100-200
100-250	40-100
50-100	20-40
25-50	10-20
5-25	4-10
1-5	2-4
0-1	0-2
uninhabited	uninhabited

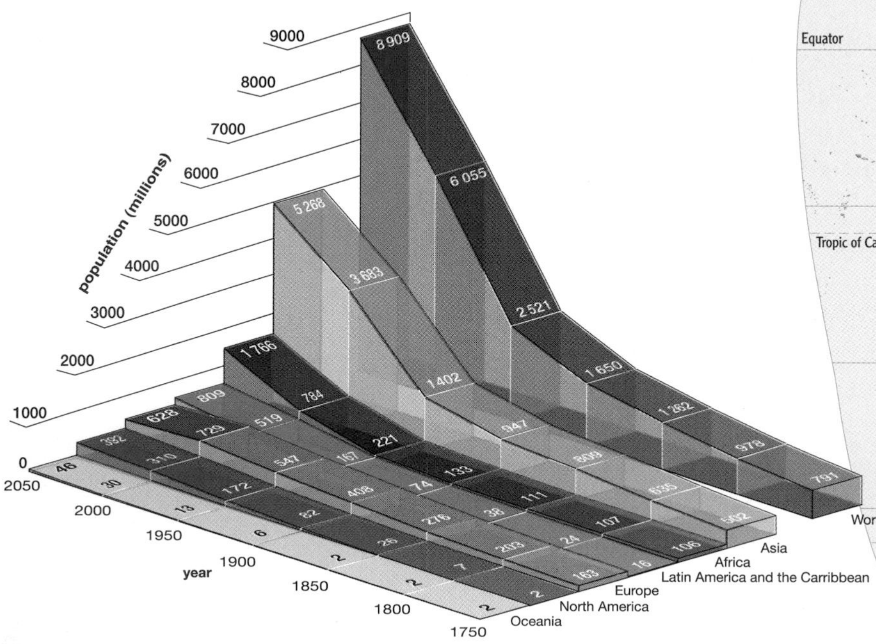

POPULATION CHANGE 1995–2000

Average annual rate of population change

	per cent
	5.7 – 7.5
	2.9 – 5.6
	1.5 – 2.8
	0.8 – 1.4
increase	0.0 – 0.7
decrease	-0.7 – -0.1
	-3.0 – -0.8
	no data

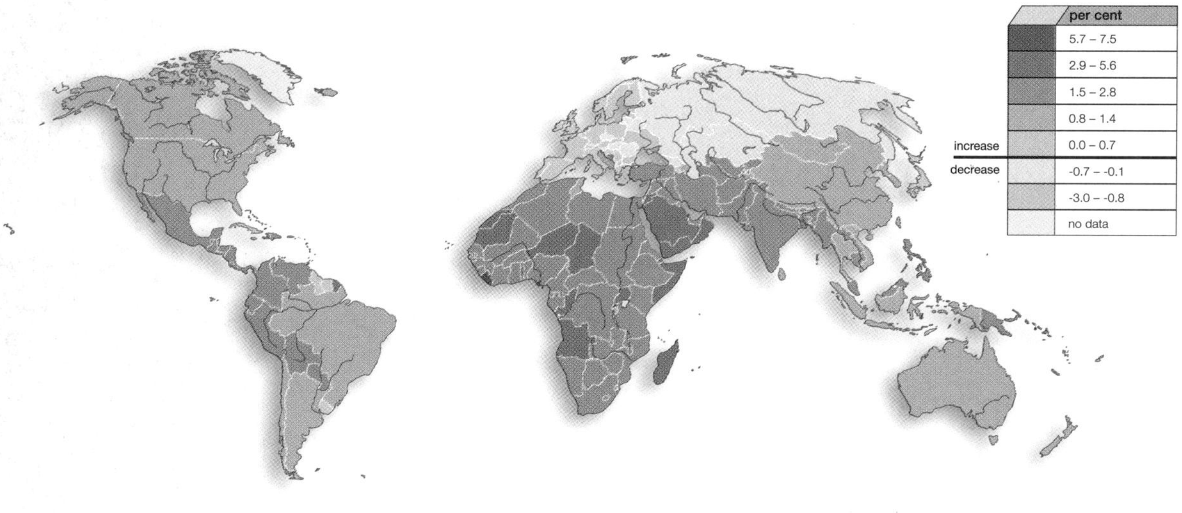

KEY POPULATION STATISTICS FOR MAJOR REGIONS

	Population (millions) 2000	Growth (per cent)	Infant mortality rate	Total fertility rate	Life expectancy (years)
World	6 055	1.33	57	2.7	65
More developed regions	1 188	0.28	9	1.6	75
Less developed regions	4 867	1.59	63	3.0	63
Africa	784	2.37	87	5.1	51
Asia	3 683	1.38	57	2.6	66
Europe	729	0.03	12	1.4	73
Latin America and the Caribbean	519	1.57	36	2.7	69
North America	310	0.85	7	1.9	77
Oceania	30	1.30	24	2.4	74

THE WORLD'S LARGEST CITIES 2000

City	Country	Population
Tōkyō	Japan	26 444 000
Mexico City	Mexico	18 131 000
Mumbai (Bombay)	India	18 066 000
São Paulo	Brazil	17 755 000
New York	United States of America	16 640 000
Lagos	Nigeria	13 427 000
Los Angeles	United States of America	13 140 000
Kolkata (Calcutta)	India	12 918 000
Shanghai	China	12 887 000
Buenos Aires	Argentina	12 560 000
Dhaka	Bangladesh	12 317 000
Karachi	Pakistan	11 794 000
Delhi	India	11 695 000
Jakarta	Indonesia	11 018 000
Ōsaka	Japan	11 013 000
Manila	Philippines	10 870 000
Beijing	China	10 839 000
Rio de Janeiro	Brazil	10 582 000
Cairo	Egypt	10 552 000
Seoul	South Korea	9 888 000
Paris	France	9 624 000
İstanbul	Turkey	9 451 000
Moscow	Russian Federation	9 321 000
Tianjin	China	9 156 000
London	United Kingdom	7 640 000
Lima	Peru	7 443 000
Bangkok	Thailand	7 281 000
Tehrān	Iran	7 225 000
Chicago	United States of America	6 951 000
Hong Kong	China	6 927 000
Hyderabad	India	6 842 000
Chennai	India	6 648 000
Essen	Germany	6 541 000
Bogotá	Colombia	6 288 000
Lahore	Pakistan	6 040 000
Bangalore	India	5 561 000
Santiago	Chile	5 538 000
Chongqing	China	5 312 000
Wuhan	China	5 169 000
St Petersburg	Russian Federation	5 133 000
Kinshasa	Dem. Rep. of Congo	5 064 000
Shenyang	China	4 828 000
Baghdād	Iraq	4 797 000
Toronto	Canada	4 651 000
Ho Chi Minh City	Vietnam	4 615 000
Philadelphia	United States of America	4 402 000
Milan	Italy	4 251 000
Rangoon	Myanmar	4 196 000
Belo Horizonte	Brazil	4 170 000
Ahmadabad	India	4 160 000

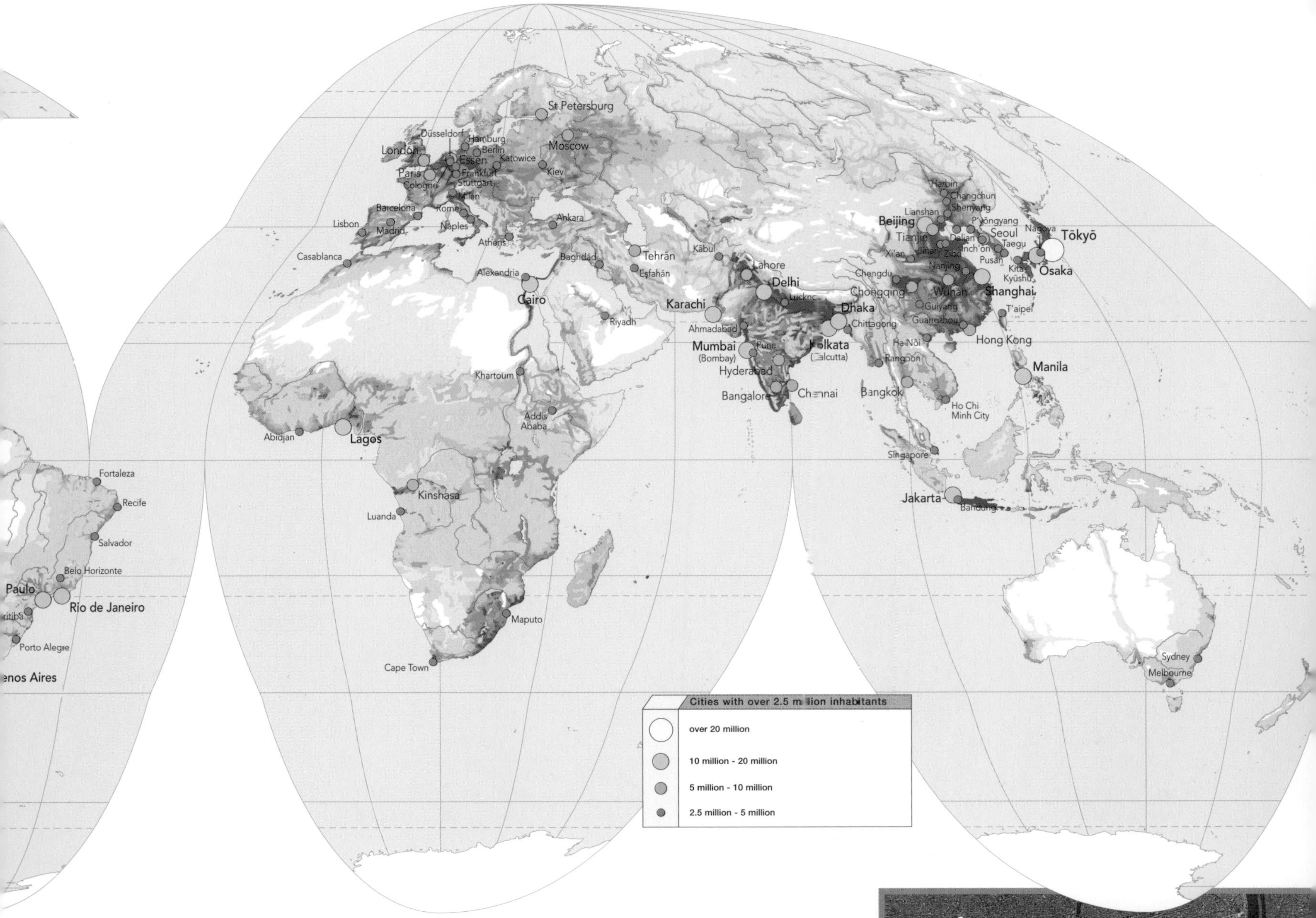

St Petersburg
Düsseldorf
London   Hamburg
Essen   Berlin   Katowice
Paris   Cologne
Frankfurt   Kiev
Barcelona   Stuttgart
Lisbon   München
Madrid   Rome
Naples   Athens
Casablanca   Ankara
Alexandria   Baghdad
Cairo   Tehrān   Kābul
Esfahān
Riyadh
Khartoum
Addis
Ababa
Abidjan   Lagos
Kinshasa
Luanda
Maputo
Cape Town

Moscow

Harbin
Changchun
Lanshan   Shenyang
Beijing   Pyongyang   Nagoya   Tōkyō
Tianjin   Dalian   Seoul   Kital   Osaka
Xi'an   Inch'ōn Taegu   Kyūshū
Nanjing   Pusan
Chengdu   Shanghai
Chongqing   Wuhan   Taipei
Guiyang   Guangzhou
Chittagong   Ha Nôi   Hong Kong
Rangoon
Lahore   Manila
Delhi   Lucknc
Karachi
Dhaka
Ahmadabad   Pune   Kolkata
Mumbai   Hyderabad   (Calcutta)
(Bombay)
Bangalore   Chennai   Bangkok   Ho Chi
Minh City
Singapore
Jakarta
Bandung

Fortaleza
Recife
Salvador
Belo Horizonte
Paulo
Rio de Janeiro
ritiba
Porto Alegre
enos Aires

Sydney
Melbourne

Cities with over 2.5 million inhabitants	
○	over 20 million
○	10 million - 20 million
○	5 million - 10 million
•	2.5 million - 5 million

LEVEL OF URBANIZATION

Percentage of total population living in urban areas 2000

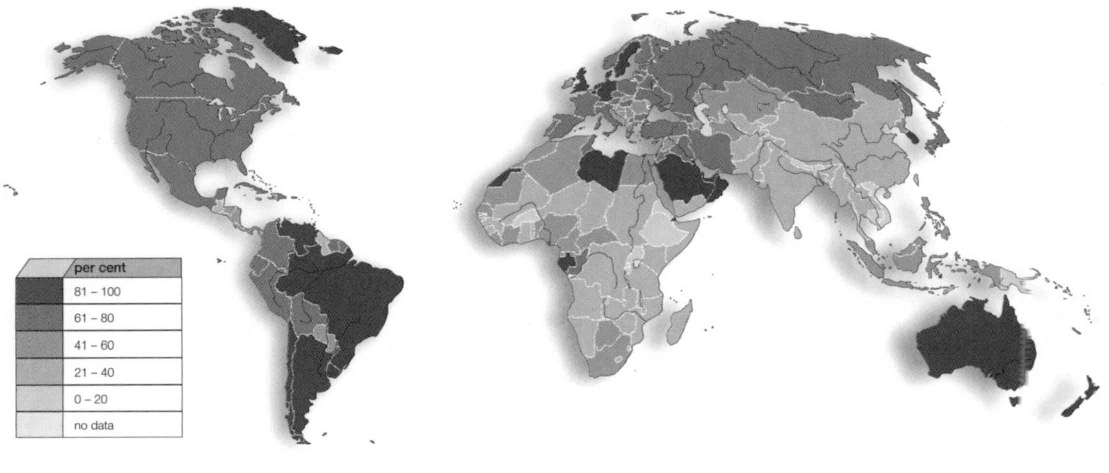

per cent	
	81 – 100
	61 – 80
	41 – 60
	21 – 40
	0 – 20
	no data

THE GROWTH OF CITIES

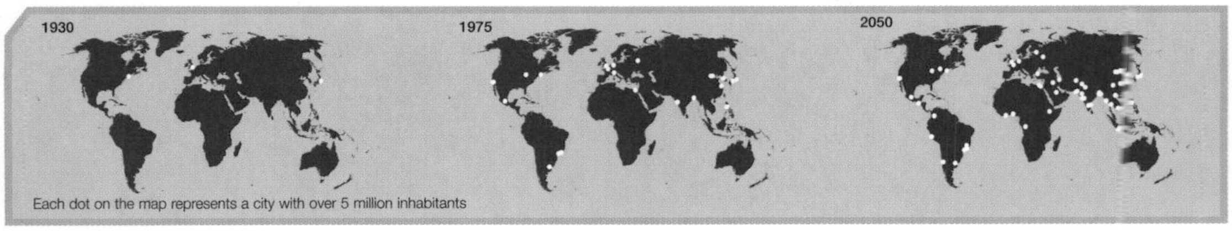

1930   1975   2050

Each dot on the map represents a city with over 5 million inhabitants

Tōkyō, Japan

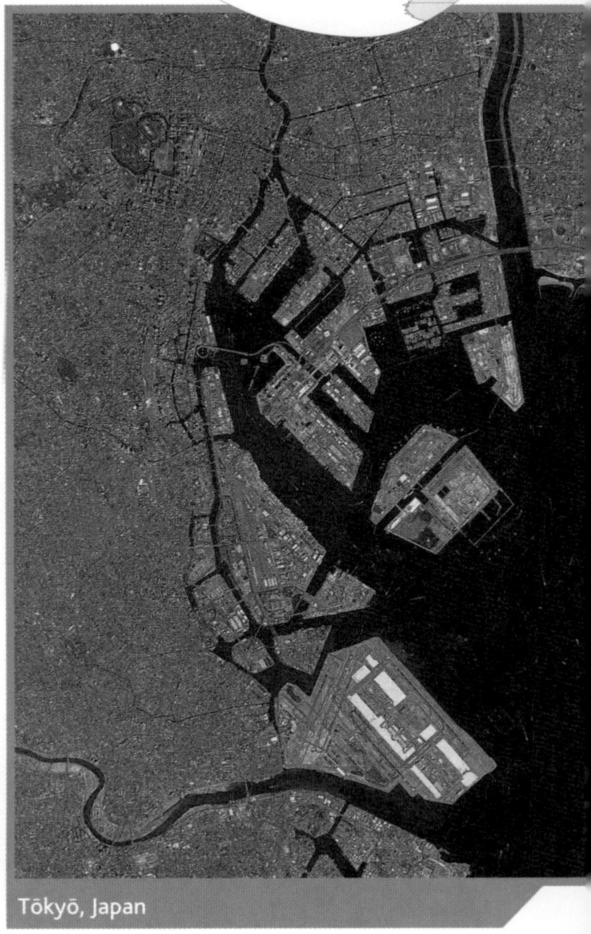

BUSIEST SCHEDULED INTERNATIONAL PASSENGER AIR ROUTES 1999

Briesemeister Projection
scale approximately 1:145 000 000

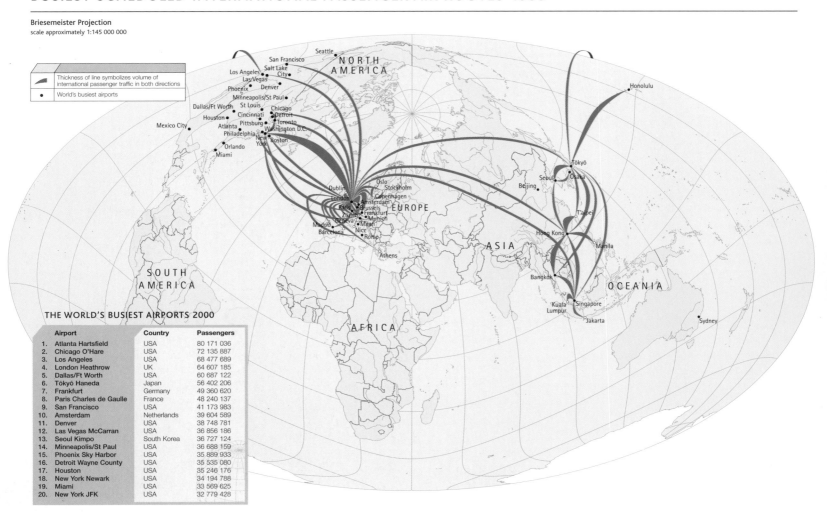

THE WORLD'S BUSIEST AIRPORTS 2000

	Airport	Country	Passengers
1.	Atlanta Hartsfield	USA	80 171 036
2.	Chicago O'Hare	USA	72 135 887
3.	Los Angeles	USA	68 477 689
4.	London Heathrow	UK	64 607 185
5.	Dallas/Ft Worth	USA	60 687 122
6.	Tōkyō Haneda	Japan	56 402 206
7.	Frankfurt	Germany	49 360 620
8.	Paris Charles de Gaulle	France	48 240 137
9.	San Francisco	USA	41 173 983
10.	Amsterdam	Netherlands	39 604 589
11.	Denver	USA	38 748 781
12.	Las Vegas McCarran	USA	36 856 186
13.	Seoul Kimpo	South Korea	36 727 124
14.	Minneapolis/St Paul	USA	36 688 159
15.	Phoenix Sky Harbor	USA	35 889 933
16.	Detroit Wayne County	USA	35 535 080
17.	Houston	USA	35 246 176
18.	New York Newark	USA	34 194 788
19.	Miami	USA	33 569 625
20.	New York JFK	USA	32 779 428

INTERNATIONAL TELECOMMUNICATIONS TRAFFIC 1999

Each band is proportional to the total annual traffic on the public telephone network in both directions
©TeleGeography, Inc.   www.telegeography.com

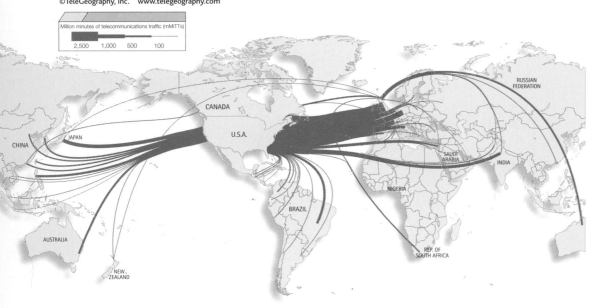

WORLD TELECOMMUNICATIONS EQUIPMENT

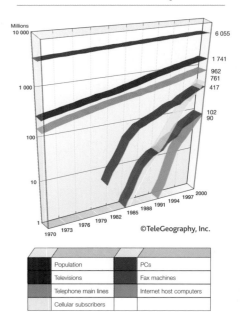

©TeleGeography, Inc.

Population	PCs
Televisions	Fax machines
Telephone main lines	Internet host computers
Cellular subscribers	

INTERNATIONAL TELECOMMUNICATIONS INDICATORS BY REGION 2000

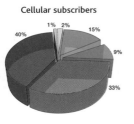

Telephone main lines

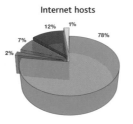

Cellular subscribers

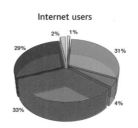

Internet hosts

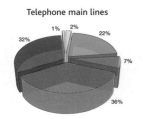

Internet users

| USA and Canada |
| South America and the Caribbean |
| Asia |
| Europe |
| Oceania |
| Africa |

© Bartholomew Ltd

CITY PLANS

CONTENTS

KEY TO CITY PLANS

Built-up area	Cemetery	Marsh
Park/Open space	Water	River/Canal

Road	Administrative boundary	General place of interest
Railway	Airport	Place of worship

Academic/ Municipal building	
Transport location	

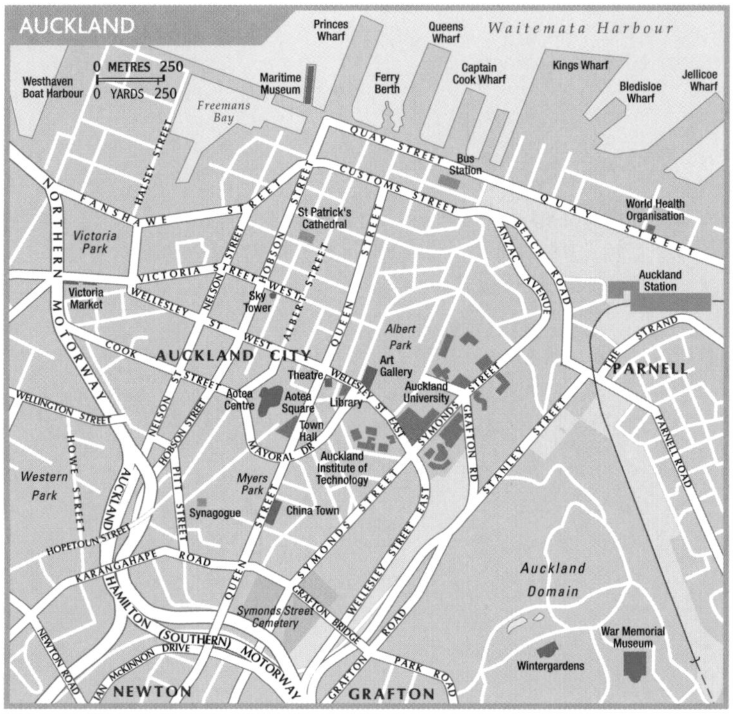
AUCKLAND
0 METRES 250
0 YARDS 250
Waitemata Harbour
Westhaven Boat Harbour
Princes Wharf
Queens Wharf
Maritime Museum
Ferry Berth
Captain Cook Wharf
Kings Wharf
Bledisloe Wharf
Jellicoe Wharf
Freemans Bay
QUAY STREET
Bus Station
CUSTOMS STREET
World Health Organisation
St Patrick's Cathedral
Victoria Park
Victoria Market
Sky Tower
Auckland Station
AUCKLAND CITY
Albert Park
Art Gallery
Auckland University
PARNELL
Theatre
Aotea Centre
Aotea Square
Library
Town Hall
Auckland Institute of Technology
Western Park
Myers Park
Synagogue
China Town
Auckland Domain
Symonds Street Cemetery
War Memorial Museum
Wintergardens
NEWTON
GRAFTON
KARANGAHAPE ROAD
HAMILTON (SOUTHERN) MOTORWAY
NORTHERN MOTORWAY
FANSHAWE STREET
VICTORIA STREET WEST
WELLESLEY ST
WELLINGTON STREET
HOPETOUN STREET
STANLEY STREET
THE STRAND

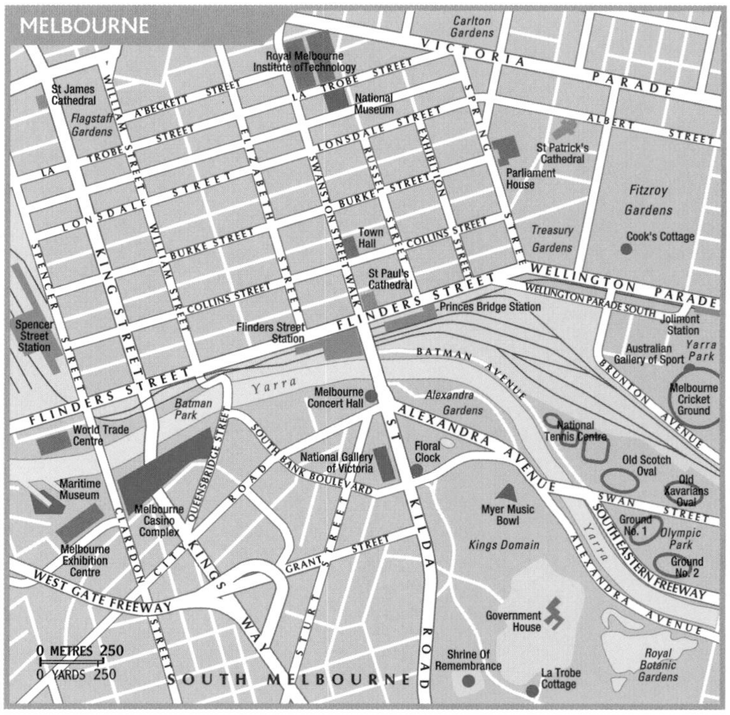
MELBOURNE
Carlton Gardens
Royal Melbourne Institute of Technology
VICTORIA PARADE
St James Cathedral
National Museum
Flagstaff Gardens
LA TROBE STREET
LONSDALE STREET
BURKE STREET
COLLINS STREET
FLINDERS STREET
St Patrick's Cathedral
Parliament House
Fitzroy Gardens
Treasury Gardens
Cook's Cottage
Town Hall
St Paul's Cathedral
WELLINGTON PARADE
Princes Bridge Station
Spencer Street Station
Flinders Street Station
Jolimont Station
Australian Gallery of Sport
Yarra Park
Melbourne Cricket Ground
Yarra
Batman Park
Melbourne Concert Hall
Alexandra Gardens
ALEXANDRA AVENUE
National Tennis Centre
Old Scotch Oval
World Trade Centre
National Gallery of Victoria
Floral Clock
Maritime Museum
Melbourne Casino Complex
Myer Music Bowl
Kings Domain
Olympic Park
Ground No. 1
Ground No. 2
Melbourne Exhibition Centre
WEST GATE FREEWAY
SOUTH EASTERN FREEWAY
Government House
Shrine Of Remembrance
La Trobe Cottage
Royal Botanic Gardens
0 METRES 250
0 YARDS 250
SOUTH MELBOURNE
ST KILDA ROAD
KINGS WAY

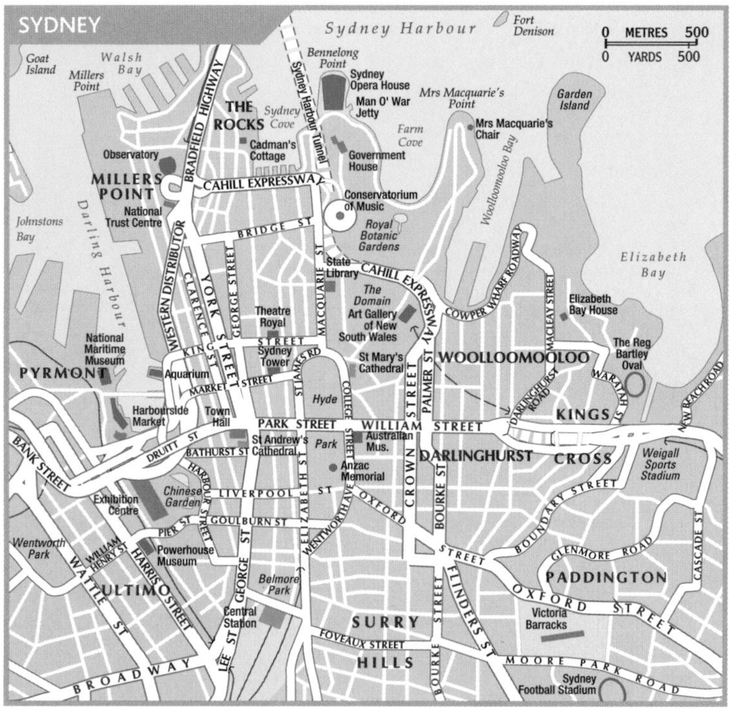
SYDNEY
Sydney Harbour
Fort Denison
0 METRES 500
0 YARDS 500
Goat Island
Walsh Bay
Millers Point
Bennelong Point
Sydney Opera House
Man O' War Jetty
Mrs Macquarie's Point
Garden Island
THE ROCKS
Sydney Cove
Cadman's Cottage
Farm Cove
Mrs Macquarie's Chair
Observatory
Government House
MILLERS POINT
CAHILL EXPRESSWAY
National Trust Centre
Conservatorium of Music
Johnstons Bay
Darling Harbour
Royal Botanic Gardens
Woolloomooloo Bay
Elizabeth Bay
State Library
The Domain
Art Gallery of New South Wales
Elizabeth Bay House
Theatre Royal
Sydney Tower
St Mary's Cathedral
WOOLLOOMOOLOO
National Maritime Museum
The Reg Bartley Oval
PYRMONT
Aquarium
KINGS CROSS
Harbourside Market
Town Hall
PARK STREET
WILLIAM STREET
St Andrew's Cathedral
Hyde Park
Australian Mus.
DARLINGHURST
Anzac Memorial
Weigall Sports Stadium
Chinese Garden
Exhibition Centre
LIVERPOOL ST
GOULBURN ST
Wentworth Park
Powerhouse Museum
ULTIMO
PADDINGTON
Belmore Park
OXFORD STREET
Central Station
SURRY HILLS
Victoria Barracks
FOVEAUX STREET
MOORE PARK ROAD
Sydney Football Stadium
BROADWAY

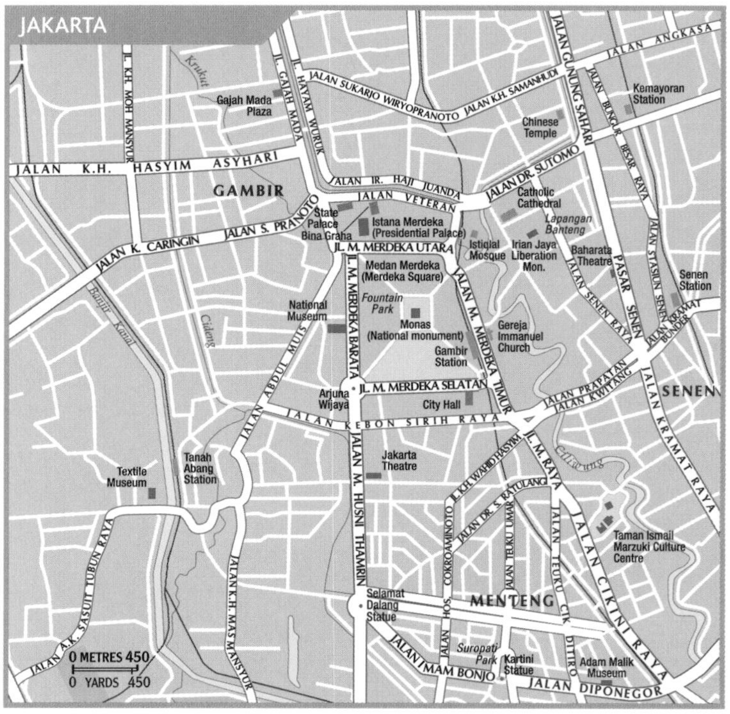
JAKARTA
JALAN ANGKASA
Kemayoran Station
Gajah Mada Plaza
Chinese Temple
JALAN K.H. HASYIM ASYHARI
GAMBIR
Catholic Cathedral
State Palace
Bina Graha
Istana Merdeka (Presidential Palace)
Lapangan Banteng
Istiqlal Mosque
Irian Jaya Liberation Mon.
Baharata Theatre
Senen Station
JL. M. MERDEKA UTARA
Medan Merdeka (Merdeka Square)
Fountain Park
National Museum
Monas (National monument)
Gambir Station
Gereja Immanuel Church
SENEN
Arjuna Wijaya
JL. M. MERDEKA SELATAN
City Hall
Jakarta Theatre
Textile Museum
Tanah Abang Station
Taman Ismail Marzuki Culture Centre
Selamat Datang Statue
MENTENG
Suropati Park
Kartini Statue
Adam Malik Museum
0 METRES 450
0 YARDS 450
JALAN DIPONEGORO

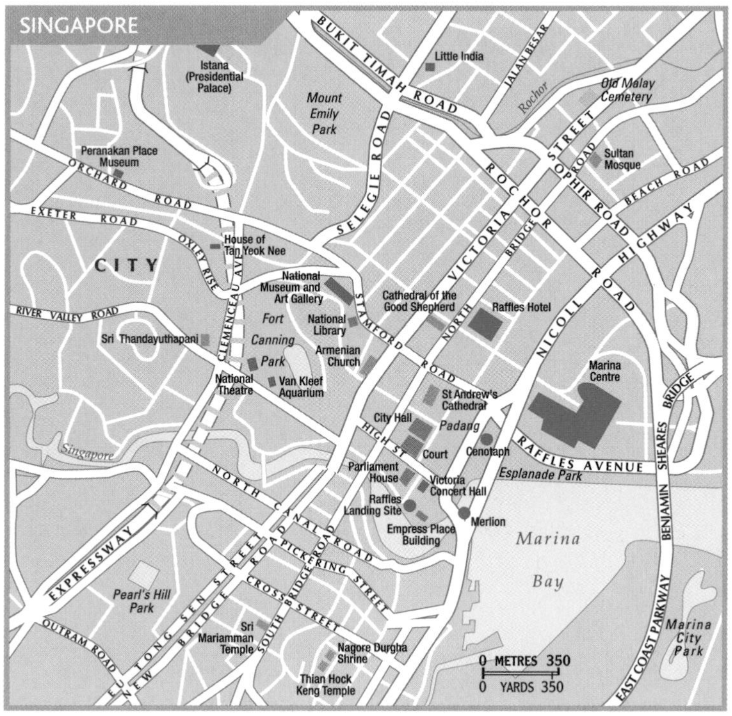
SINGAPORE
BUKIT TIMAH ROAD
Little India
Istana (Presidential Palace)
Mount Emily Park
Old Malay Cemetery
Sultan Mosque
Peranakan Place Museum
ORCHARD ROAD
EXETER ROAD
House of Tan Yeok Nee
CITY
National Museum and Art Gallery
Cathedral of the Good Shepherd
Raffles Hotel
RIVER VALLEY ROAD
Fort Canning Park
National Library
Sri Thandayuthapani
Armenian Church
Marina Centre
National Theatre
Van Kleef Aquarium
St Andrew's Cathedral
City Hall
Padang
Court
Cenotaph
RAFFLES AVENUE
Esplanade Park
Singapore
Parliament House
Victoria Concert Hall
Raffles Landing Site
Empress Place Building
Merlion
Marina Bay
EXPRESSWAY
Pearl's Hill Park
Sri Mariamman Temple
Nagore Durgha Shrine
Thian Hock Keng Temple
0 METRES 350
0 YARDS 350
Marina City Park
EAST COAST PARKWAY
BENJAMIN SHEARES BRIDGE
NICOLL HIGHWAY

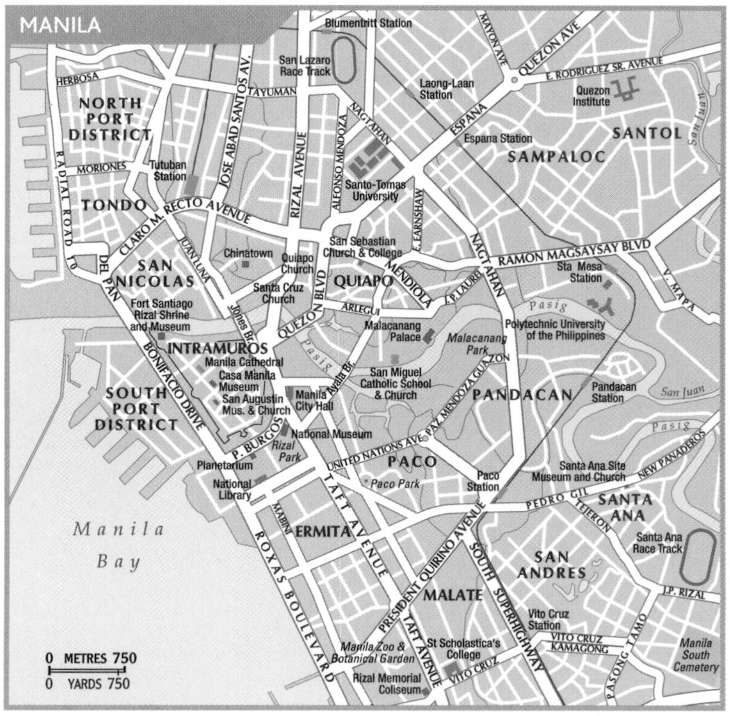
MANILA
Blumentritt Station
San Lazaro Race Track
Laong-Laan Station
Quezon Institute
NORTH PORT DISTRICT
SANTOL
Espana Station
SAMPALOC
Tutuban Station
Santo Tomas University
TONDO
C.M. RECTO AVENUE
San Sebastian Church & College
RAMON MAGSAYSAY BLVD
Sta Mesa Station
SAN NICOLAS
Chinatown
Quiapo Church
QUIAPO
Santa Cruz Church
Fort Santiago
Rizal Shrine and Museum
Polytechnic University of the Philippines
Malacanang Palace
Malacanang Park
INTRAMUROS
Manila Cathedral
Casa Manila Museum
San Augustin Mus. & Church
Manila City Hall
San Miguel Catholic School & Church
PANDACAN
Pandacan Station
SOUTH PORT DISTRICT
National Museum
Pasig
PACO
Paco Park
Paco Station
Planetarium
Rizal Park
Santa Ana Site Museum and Church
National Library
SANTA ANA
Manila Bay
ERMITA
Santa Ana Race Track
SAN ANDRES
MALATE
Vito Cruz Station
Manila Zoo & Botanical Garden
St Scholastica's College
Rizal Memorial Coliseum
Manila South Cemetery
ROXAS BOULEVARD
TAFT AVENUE
0 METRES 750
0 YARDS 750

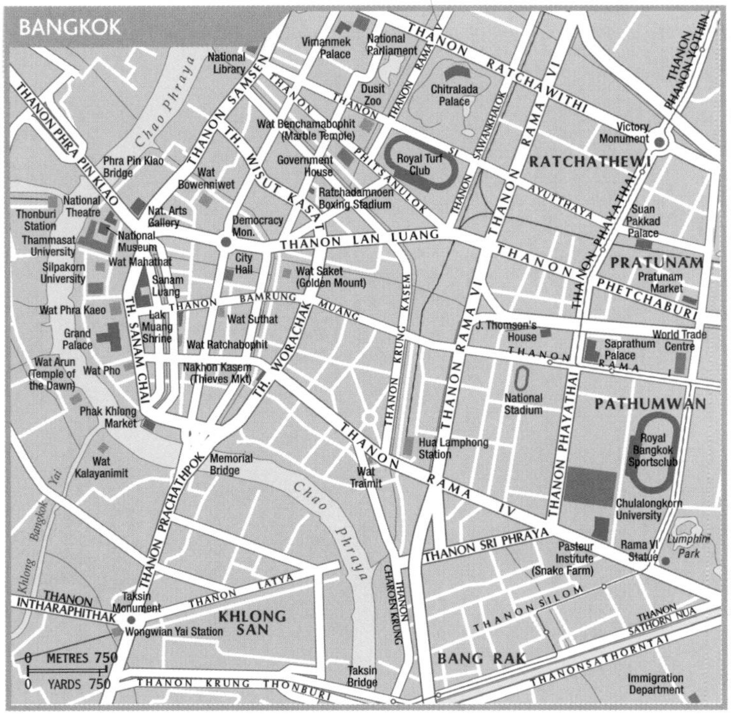

BANGKOK

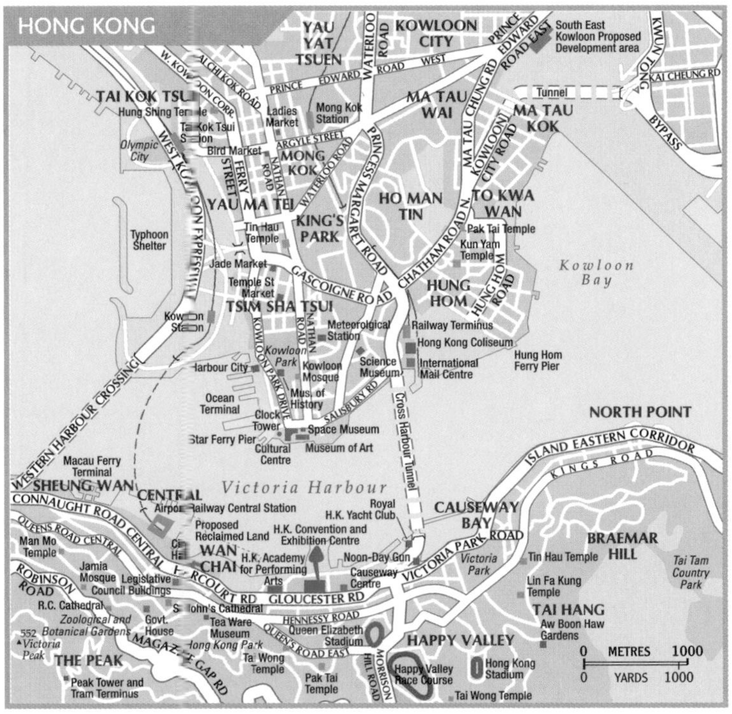

HONG KONG

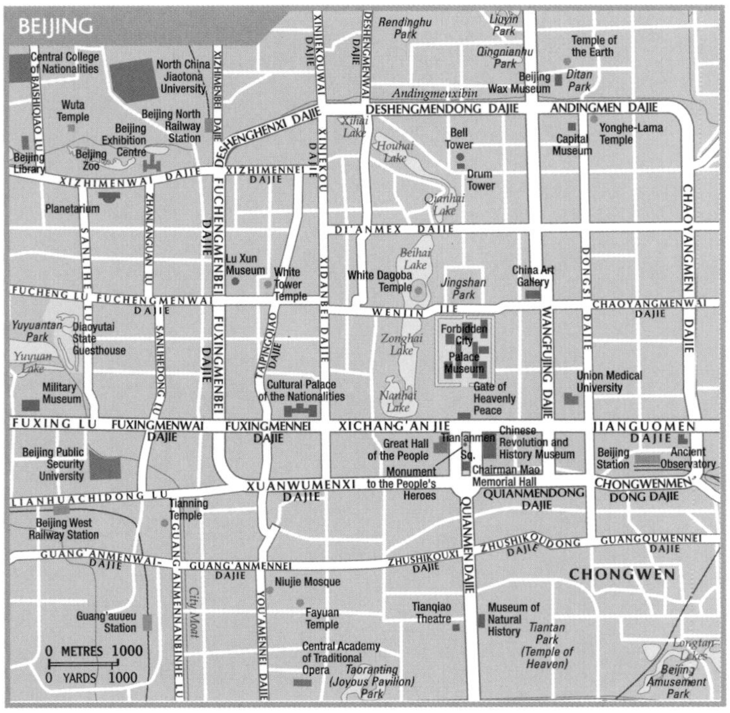

BEIJING

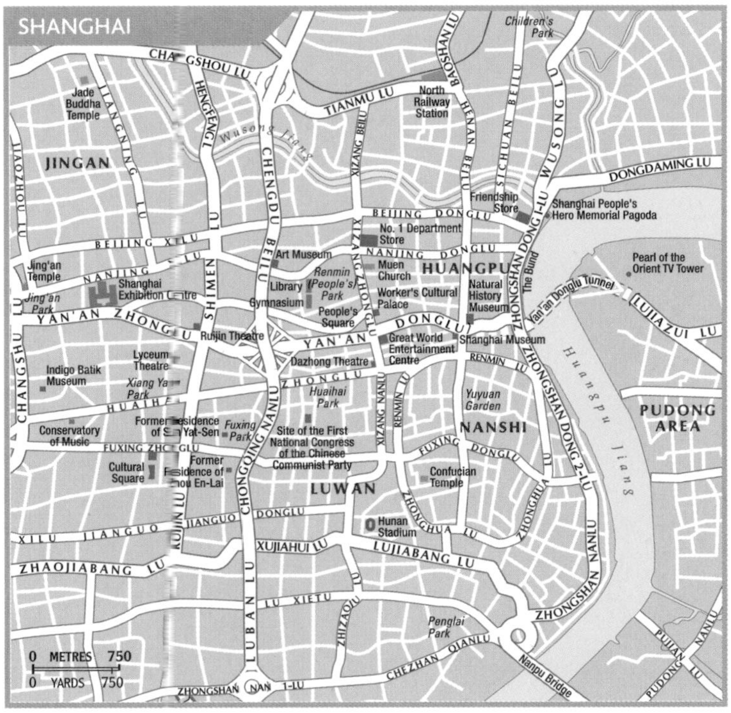

SHANGHAI

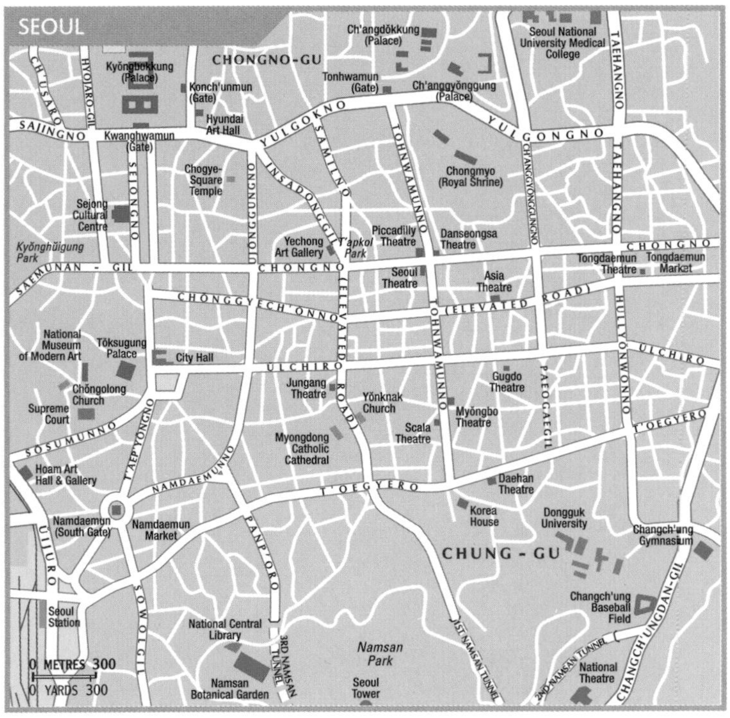

SEOUL

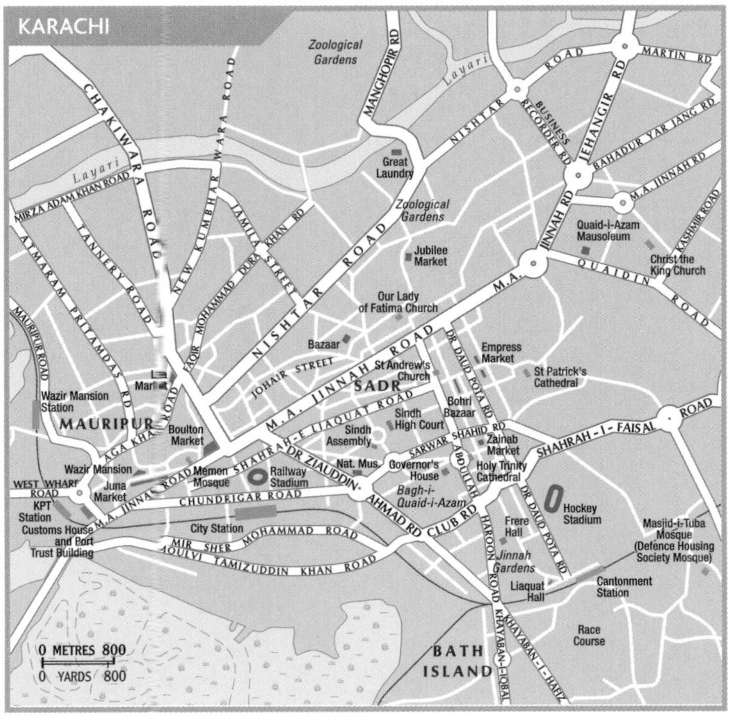

KARACHI

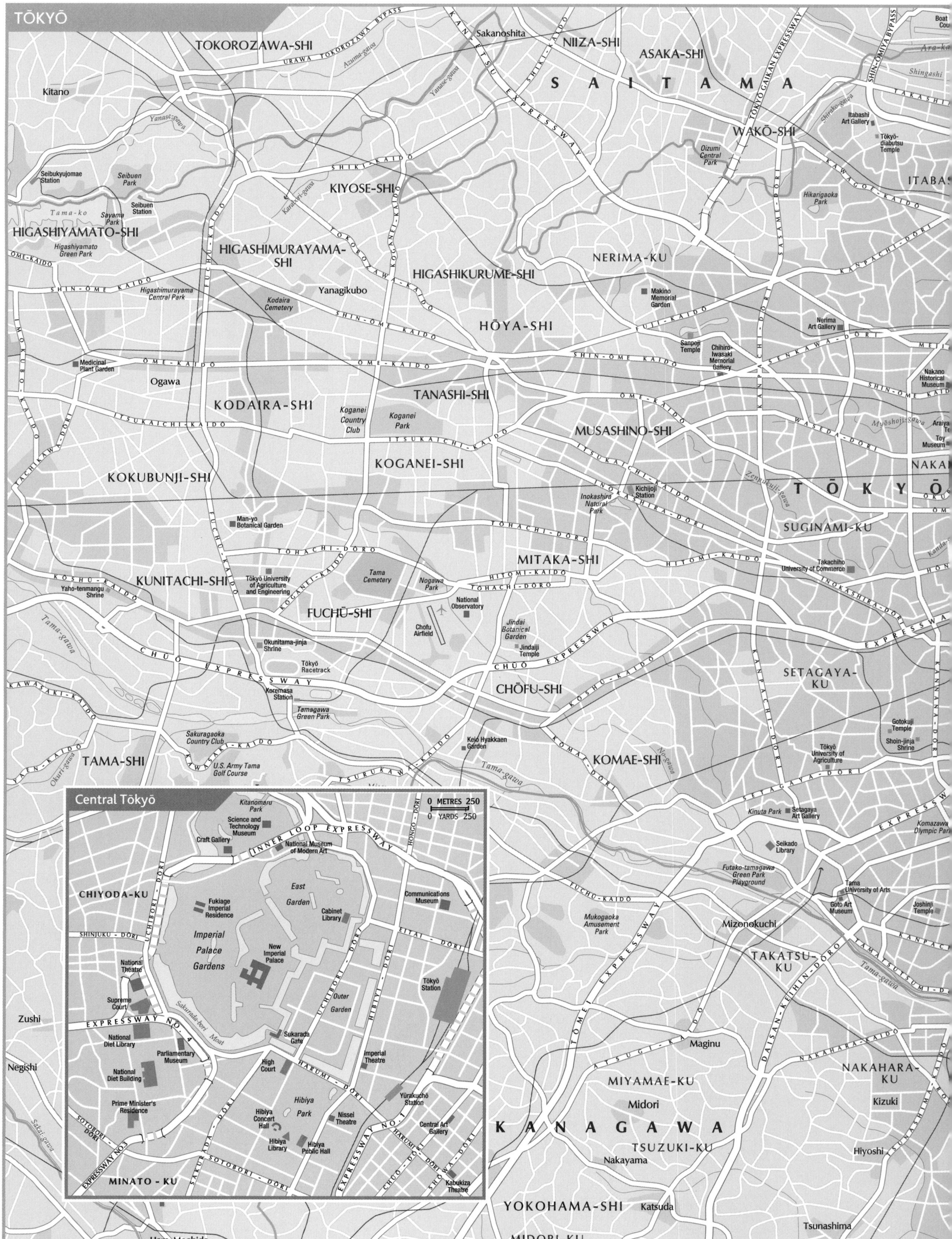

TŌKYŌ

TOKOROZAWA-SHI

Sakanoshita

NIIZA-SHI

ASAKA-SHI

Boat Course

Ara-kawa

SAITAMA

Shingashi

Kitano

UKAWA TOKOROZAWA BYPASS

Azuma-gawa

Yanase-gawa

KANETSU EXPRESSWAY

TOKYO GAIKAN EXPRESSWAY

SHIN-OMIYA BYPASS

TAKASHIMA

WAKŌ-SHI

Oizumi Central Park

Itabashi Art Gallery

ITABAS

Tōkyō-diabutsu Temple

KAWAGOE-KAIDO

Seibukyujomae Station

Seibuen Park

SHIKAKAIDO

Kashiwa-gawa

KIYOSE-SHI

Hikarigaoka Park

OME-KAIDO

Tama-ko

Sayama Park

Seibuen Park

Seibuen Station

HIGASHIYAMATO-SHI

HIGASHIMURAYAMA-SHI

HIGASHIKURUME-SHI

NERIMA-KU

Makino Memorial Garden

YUJI-KAIDO

Nerima Art Gallery

KANPACHI-DORI

Higashiyamato Green Park

Higashimurayama Central Park

Yanagikubo

HŌYA-SHI

Kodaira Cemetery

SHIN-OME-KAIDO

Sanpeji Temple

Chihiro Iwasaki Memorial Gallery

Nakano Historical Museum

MEI

Medicinal Plant Garden

OME-KAIDO

OME-KAIDO

SHIN-OME-KAIDO

TENKAWA-DORI

Ogawa

KODAIRA-SHI

TANASHI-SHI

WASED-DORI

Myōshōji-gawa

Araiya Te

Toy Museum

KOGANEI-SHI

Koganei Country Club

Koganei Park

MUSASHINO-SHI

Zenpukuji-gawa

TŌKYŌ

KOKUBUNJI-SHI

ITSUKAICHI-KAIDO

ITSUKAICHI-KAIDO

INO

Inokashira Natural Park

Kichijoji Station

INOKASHIRA-DORI

SUGINAMI-KU

NAKA

Man-yo Botanical Garden

TOHACHI-DORO

HITOMI-KAIDO

Takachiho University of Commerce

KUNITACHI-SHI

Tama Cemetery

Nogawa Park

MITAKA-SHI

Tōkyō University of Agriculture and Engineering

TOHACHI-DORO

National Observatory

HITOMI-KAIDO

Yaho-tenmangu Shrine

KOSHU-KAIDO

KOGANEI-KAIDO

FUCHŪ-SHI

Chofu Airfield

Jindai Botanical Garden

EXPRESSWAY

Tama-gawa

Okunitama-jinja Shrine

Jindaiji Temple

SETAGAYA-KU

CHŪŌ EXPRESSWAY

CHŪŌ EXPRESSWAY

Tōkyō Racetrack

Koremasa Station

KOSHU-KAIDO

KAWASAKI-KAIDO

Tamagawa Green Park

CHŌFU-SHI

KOMAZAWA-DORI

Gotokuji Temple

Shoin-jinja Shrine

Sakuragaoka Country Club

Keio Hyakkaen Garden

KOMAE-SHI

Tōkyō University of Agriculture

TAMA-SHI

TWO-KAIDO

U.S. Army Tama Golf Course

Okuri-gawa

TSURUKAWA-KAIDO

Tama-gawa

Nogawa

DORI

YEN-KAIDO

Mi

Kinuta Park

Setagaya Art Gallery

Komazawa Olympic Park

Seikado Library

Futako-tamagawa Green Park Playground

Tama University of Arts

Goto Art Museum

Joshinji Temple

FUCHU-KAIDO

Mukogaoka Amusement Park

Mizonokuchi

TAKATSU-KU

KANPACHI-DORI

TOMEI EXPRESSWAY

DAISAN-KEIHIN-DORI

Tama-gawa

Maginu

MIYAMAE-KU

Midori

NAKAHARA-KU

Kizuki

KANAGAWA

TSUZUKI-KU

Nakayama

YOKOHAMA-SHI

Katsuda

Hiyoshi

MIDORI-KU

Tsunashima

Hara-Machida

Central Tōkyō

0 METRES 250
0 YARDS 250

Kitanomaru Park

HONGO-DORI

Science and Technology Museum

Craft Gallery

INNER LOOP EXPRESSWAY

National Museum of Modern Art

CHIYODA-KU

East Garden

Communications Museum

Fukiage Imperial Residence

Cabinet Library

EITAI-DORI

Imperial Palace Gardens

SHINJUKU-DORI

SHIBORI-DORI

Zushi

National Theatre

New Imperial Palace

HIBIYA-DORI

Tōkyō Station

Supreme Court

Sakurada-bori Moat

Outer Garden

EXPRESSWAY NO. 4

National Diet Library

Parliamentary Museum

Sukarada Gate

Negishi

National Diet Building

High Court

Imperial Theatre

Prime Minister's Residence

Hibiya Park

Yūrakuchō Station

SOTOBORI-DORI

Hibiya Concert Hall

Nissel Theatre

Central Art Gallery

Sai-

SOTOBORI-DORI

SOTOBORI-DORI

Hibiya Library

Hibiya Public Hall

CHUO-DORI

HARUMI-DORI

EXPRESSWAY NO. 1

MINATO-KU

EXPRESSWAY NO. 3

Kabukiza Theatre

SHIO

DORI

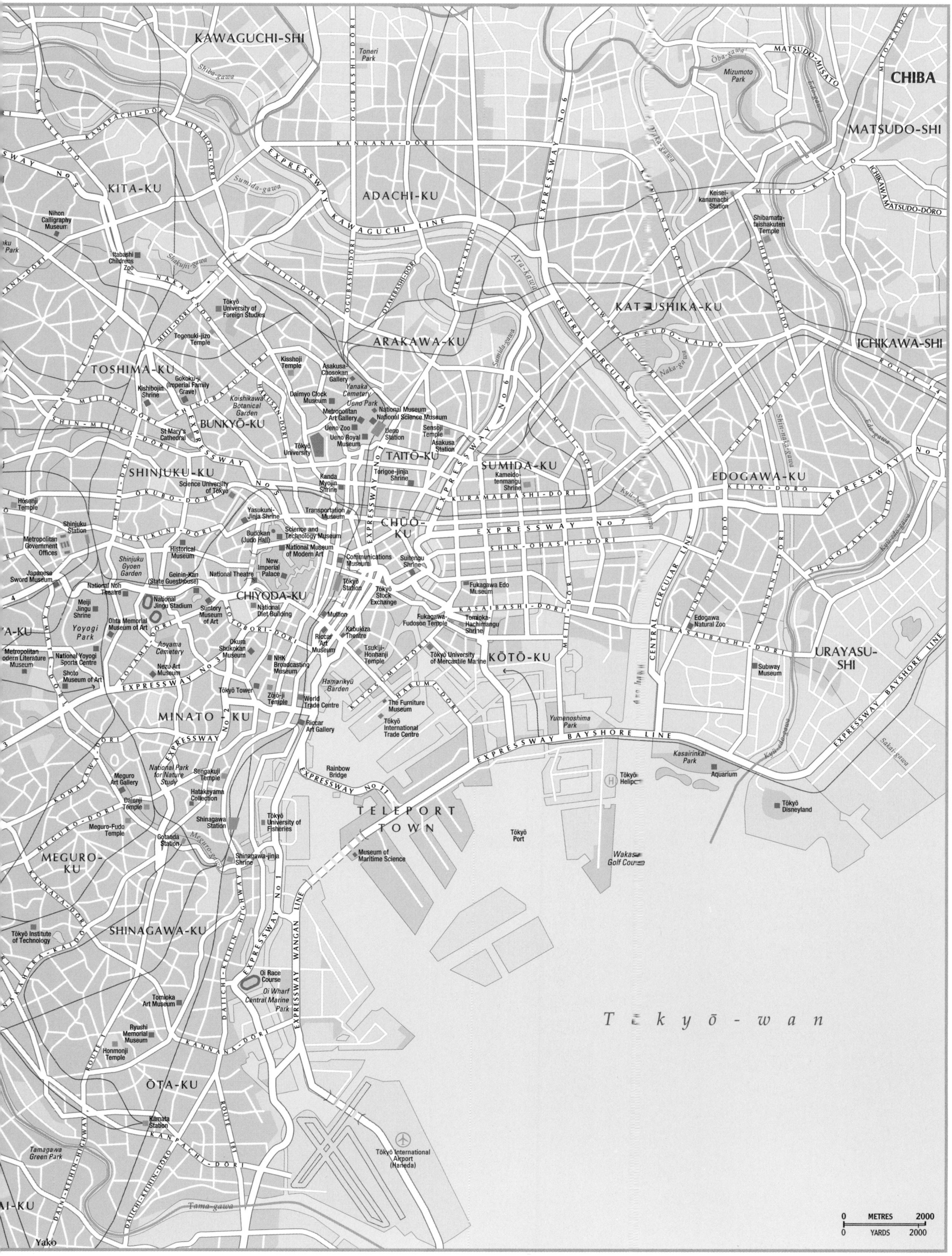

CHIBA

MATSUDO-SHI

KAWAGUCHI-SHI

Toneri Park

Mizumoto Park

Oba-gawa

MATSUDO-MISATO

KITA-KU

Shiba-gawa

KANNANA-DORI

ADACHI-KU

Keisei-kanamachi Station

ICHIKAWA-MATSUDO-DORO

Nihon Calligraphy Museum

Shakujii-gawa

Shibamata-taishakuten Temple

ICHIKAWA-SHI

Itabashi Childrens Zoo

Tokyo University of Foreign Studies

Togenuki-jizo Temple

KAT USHIKA-KU

ROUTE 14

TOSHIMA-KU

Kishibojin Shrine

Gokoku-ji (Imperial Family Grave)

Kisshoji Temple

Asakusa-Chosokan Gallery

Yanaka Cemetery

Ueno Park

National Museum

ARAKAWA-KU

Koishikawa Botanical Garden

Daimyo Clock Museum

Metropolitan Art Gallery

National Science Museum

BUNKYŌ-KU

St Mary's Cathedral

Ueno Zoo

Tokyo University

Ueno Station

Ueno Royal Museum

Sensoji Temple

Asakusa Station

SHINJUKU-KU

Science University of Tokyo

Kanda Myojin Shrine

TAITŌ-KU

SUMIDA-KU

Kameido tenmangu Shrine

Hosenji Temple

OKUBO-DORI

Torigoe-jinja Shrine

KURAMAEBASHI-DORI

EDOGAWA-KU

Shinjuku Station

Yasukuni-Jinja Shrine

Transportation Museum

CHŪŌ-KU

EXPRESSWAY No 7

Metropolitan Government Offices

Budokan (Judo Hall)

Science and Technology Museum

SHIN-OHASHI-DORI

Japanese Sword Museum

Historical Museum

National Museum of Modern Art

Communications Museum

Suitengu Shrine

Fukagawa Edo Museum

National Theatre

Geinin-Kan (State Guesthouse)

New Imperial Palace

Tokyo Station

Tokyo Stock Exchange

KASAIBASHI-DORI

Edogawa Natural Zoo

Shinjuku Gyoen Garden

CHIYODA-KU

National Diet Building

Mullion

Tomioka-Hachimangu Shrine

National Noh Theatre

National Jingu Stadium

Suntory Museum of Art

Riccar Art Museum

Kabukiza Theatre

Fukagawa-Fudoson Temple

Meiji Jingu Shrine

Ohta Memorial Museum of Art

Aoyama Cemetery

Okura Shukokan Museum

Tsukiji-Honganji Temple

Tokyo University of Mercantile Marine

KŌTŌ-KU

Subway Museum

URAYASU-SHI

Yoyogi Park

Nezu Art Museum

NHK Broadcasting Museum

Metropolitan Modern Literature Museum

National Yoyogi Sports Centre

Tokyo Tower

Hamarikyū Garden

The Furniture Museum

Shoto Museum of Art

Zōjō-ji Temple

World Trade Centre

Tokyo International Trade Centre

Yumenoshima Park

MINATO-KU

Riccar Art Gallery

Rainbow Bridge

Tokyo Helipc

Kasairinkai Park

Aquarium

National Park for Nature Study

Sengakuji Temple

Hatakeyama Collection

EXPRESSWAY BAYSHORE LINE

Meguro Art Gallery

Zuishoji Temple

Shinagawa Station

Tokyo Disneyland

Meguro-Fudo Temple

TELEPORT TOWN

Gotanda Station

Tokyo Port

Waka su Golf Cou se

MEGURO-KU

Shinagawa-jinja Shrine

Tokyo University of Fisheries

Museum of Maritime Science

Tōkyō Institute of Technology

SHINAGAWA-KU

Oi Race Course

Oi Wharf Central Marine Park

Tomioka Art Museum

Ryushi Memorial Museum

Honmonji Temple

Tōkyō - wan

ŌTA-KU

Kamata Station

Tamagawa Green Park

Tōkyō International Airport (Haneda)

Tama-gawa

Yako

0 METRES 2000
0 YARDS 2000

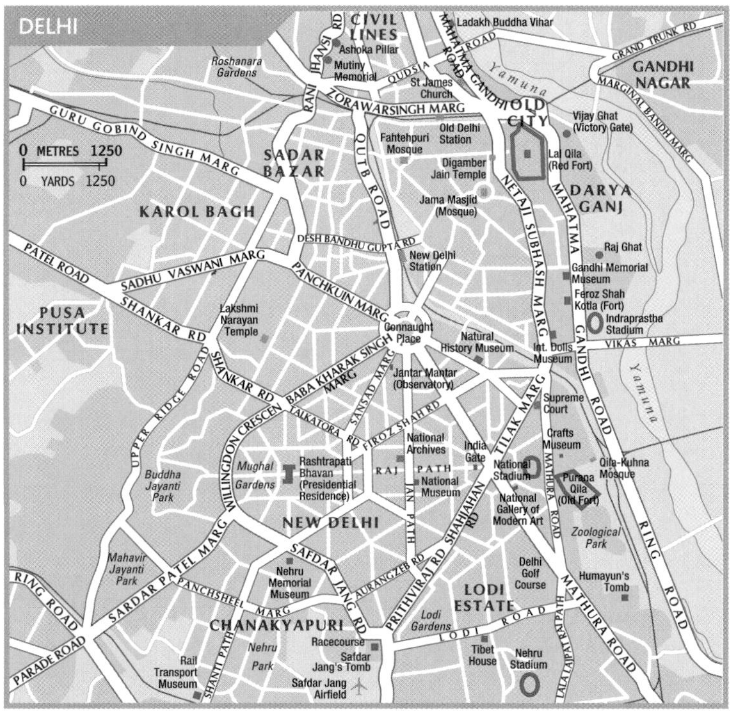
DELHI
CIVIL LINES
Roshanara Gardens
Ashoka Pillar
Mutiny Memorial
Ladakh Buddha Vihar
GANDHI NAGAR
St James Church
Yamuna
OLD CITY
Old Delhi Station
Fahtehpuri Mosque
Digamber Jain Temple
Lal Qila (Red Fort)
Vijay Ghat (Victory Gate)
Jama Masjid (Mosque)
DARYA GANJ
SADAR BAZAR
KAROL BAGH
0 METRES 1250
0 YARDS 1250
New Delhi Station
Raj Ghat
Gandhi Memorial Museum
Feroz Shah Kotla (Fort)
Indraprastha Stadium
PUSA INSTITUTE
Lakshmi Narayan Temple
Connaught Place
Natural History Museum
Int. Dolls Museum
Jantar Mantar (Observatory)
Supreme Court
Crafts Museum
National Archives
India Gate
National Stadium
Purana Qila (Old Fort)
Qila-Kuhna Mosque
Mughal Gardens
Rashtrapati Bhavan (Presidential Residence)
National Museum
National Gallery of Modern Art
Zoological Park
Buddha Jayanti Park
NEW DELHI
Mahavir Jayanti Park
Nehru Memorial Museum
Delhi Golf Course
Humayun's Tomb
LODI ESTATE
Lodi Gardens
CHANAKYAPURI
Nehru Park
Racecourse
Safdar Jang's Tomb
Safdar Jang Airfield
Rail Transport Museum
Tibet House
Nehru Stadium
RING ROAD
MATHURA ROAD
PARADE ROAD

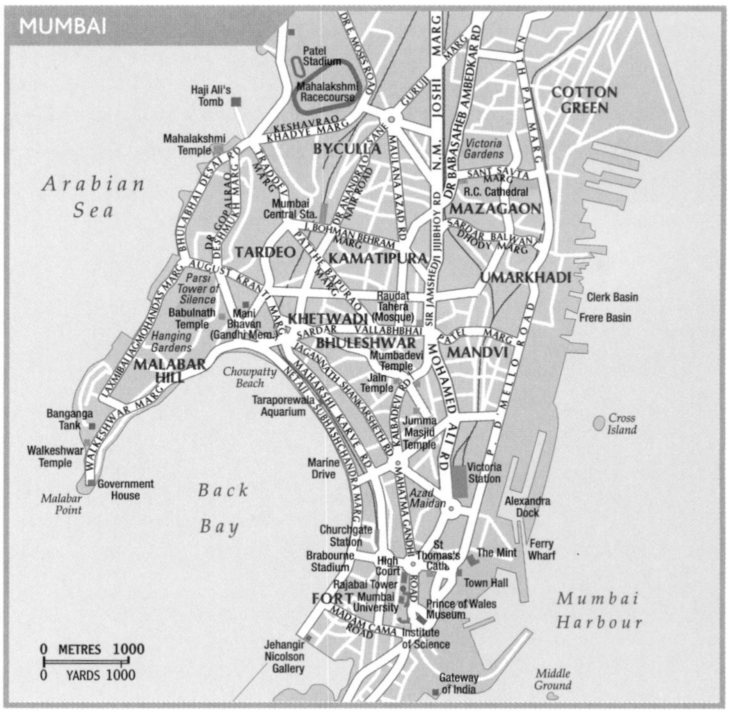
MUMBAI
Patel Stadium
Mahalakshmi Racecourse
Haji Ali's Tomb
Mahalakshmi Temple
COTTON GREEN
BYCULLA
Victoria Gardens
R.C. Cathedral
MAZAGAON
Arabian Sea
Mumbai Central Sta.
TARDEO
KAMATIPURA
UMARKHADI
Parsi Tower of Silence
Babulnath Temple
Hanging Gardens
Mani Bhavan (Gandhi Mem.)
KHETWADI
Raudat Tahera (Mosque)
BHULESHWAR
Mumbadevi Temple
MANDVI
Clerk Basin
Frere Basin
MALABAR HILL
Chowpatty Beach
Taraporewala Aquarium
Jain Temple
Jumma Masjid
Cross Island
Banganga Tank
Walkeshwar Temple
Government House
Malabar Point
Back Bay
Marine Drive
Azad Maidan
Victoria Station
Alexandra Dock
Churchgate Station
Brabourne Stadium
High Court
St Thomas's Cath.
The Mint
Ferry Wharf
Rajabai Tower
FORT
Mumbai University
Town Hall
Prince of Wales Museum
Institute of Science
Mumbai Harbour
0 METRES 1000
0 YARDS 1000
Jehangir Nicolson Gallery
Gateway of India
Middle Ground

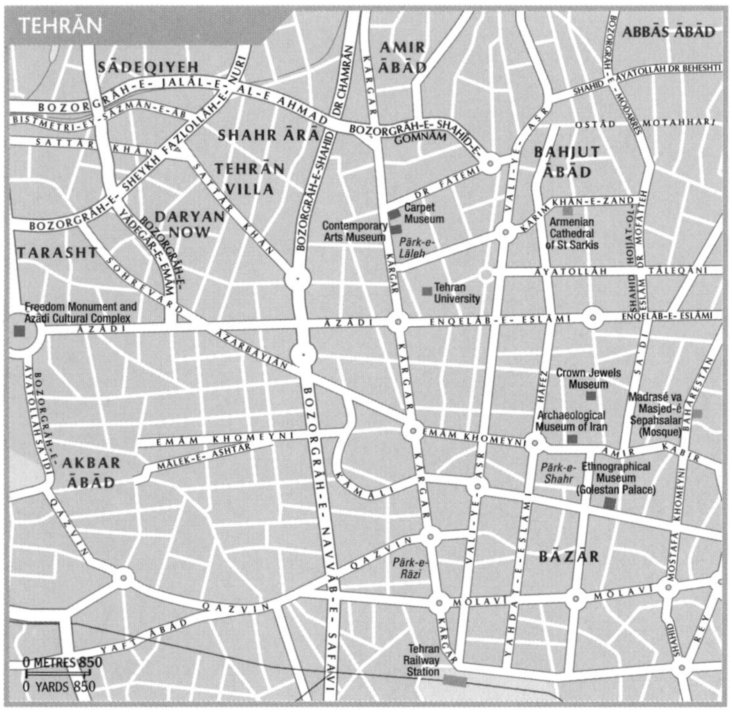
TEHRĀN
ABBĀS ĀBĀD
SĀDEQIYEH
AMIR ĀBĀD
SHAHR ĀRĀ
TEHRĀN VILLA
BAHJUT ĀBĀD
DARYAN NOW
Carpet Museum
Contemporary Arts Museum
Armenian Cathedral of St Sarkis
Pārk-e-Lāleh
TARASHT
Tehran University
Freedom Monument and Azādi Cultural Complex
ĀZĀDI
Crown Jewels Museum
Madrasé va Masjed-é-Sepahsalar (Mosque)
Archaeological Museum of Iran
AKBAR ĀBĀD
EMĀM KHOMEYNI
Ethnographical Museum (Golestan Palace)
Pārk-e-Shahr
BĀZĀR
Pārk-e-Rāzi
QAZVIN
Tehran Railway Station
0 METRES 850
0 YARDS 850

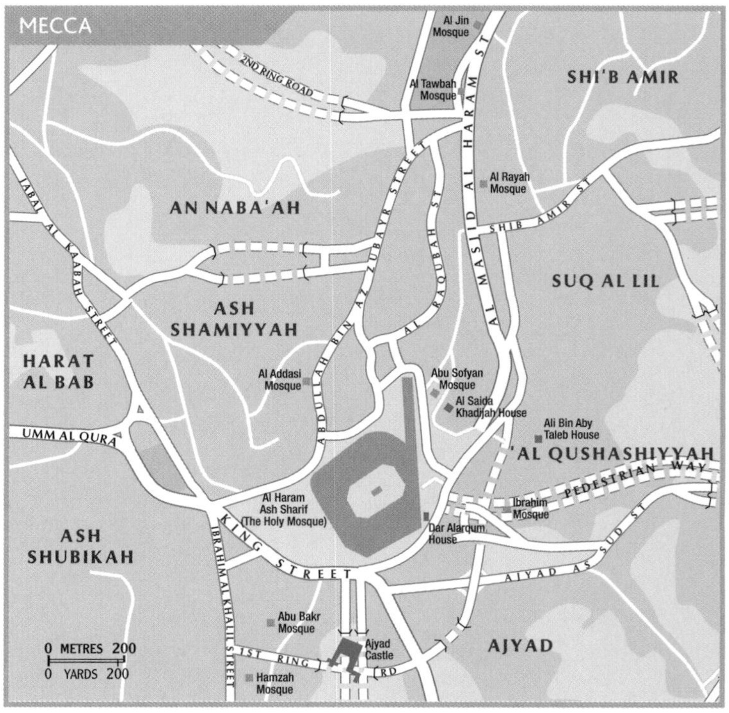
MECCA
Al Jin Mosque
2ND RING ROAD
Al Tawbah Mosque
SHI'B AMIR
Al Rayah Mosque
AN NABA'AH
ASH SHAMIYYAH
SUQ AL LIL
HARAT AL BAB
Al Addasi Mosque
Abu Sofyan Mosque
Al Saida Khadijah House
Ali Bin Aby Taleb House
UMM AL QURĀ
'AL QUSHASHIYYAH
PEDESTRIAN WAY
Al Haram Ash Sharif (The Holy Mosque)
Ibrahim Mosque
Dar Alarqum House
ASH SHUBIKAH
KING STREET
Abu Bakr Mosque
Ajyad Castle
AJYAD
0 METRES 200
0 YARDS 200
Hamzah Mosque

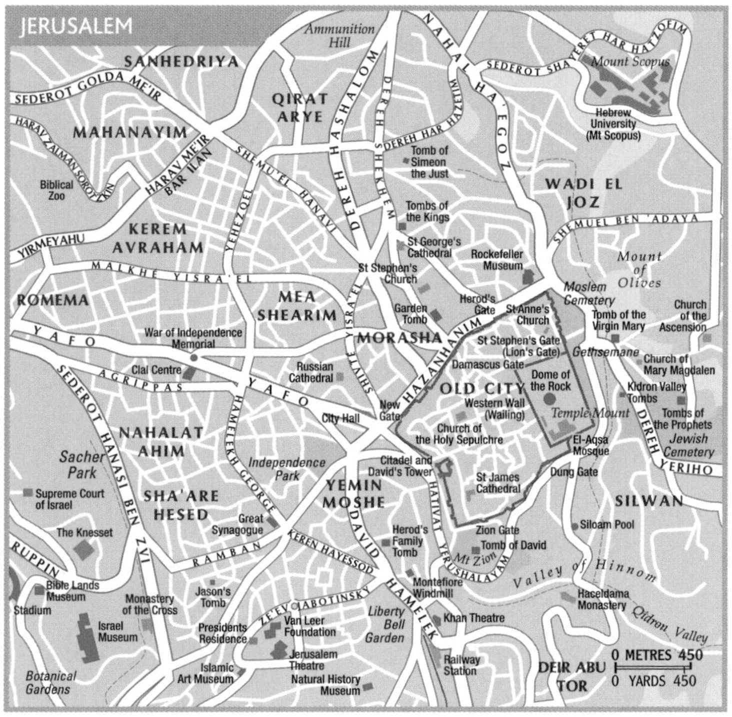
JERUSALEM
Ammunition Hill
SANHEDRIYA
Mount Scopus
QIRAT ARYE
MAHANAYIM
Hebrew University (Mt Scopus)
Tomb of Simeon the Just
Biblical Zoo
WADI EL JOZ
Tombs of the Kings
KEREM AVRAHAM
St George's Cathedral
Rockefeller Museum
Mount of Olives
ROMEMA
MEA SHEARIM
St Stephen's Church
Herod's Gate
St Anne's Church
Moslem Cemetery
Tomb of the Virgin Mary
Church of the Ascension
War of Independence Memorial
Garden Tomb
MORASHA
St Stephen's Gate (Lion's Gate)
Gethsemane
Church of Mary Magdalen
Clal Centre
Russian Cathedral
Damascus Gate
OLD CITY
Dome of the Rock
Kidron Valley Tombs
City Hall
New Gate
Western Wall (Wailing)
Temple Mount
Tombs of the Prophets
Jewish Cemetery
NAHALAT AHIM
Church of the Holy Sepulchre
El-Aqsa Mosque
Sacher Park
Independence Park
Citadel and David's Tower
Dung Gate
Supreme Court of Israel
SHA'ARE HESED
YEMIN MOSHE
St James Cathedral
SILWAN
The Knesset
Great Synagogue
Siloam Pool
Zion Gate
Herod's Family Tomb
Tomb of David
Mt Zion
Valley of Hinnom
Bible Lands Museum
Stadium
Monastery of the Cross
Jason's Tomb
Montefiore Windmill
Haceldama Monastery
Israel Museum
Presidents Residence
Van Leer Foundation
Liberty Bell Garden
Khan Theatre
Qidron Valley
Jerusalem Theatre
Islamic Art Museum
Natural History Museum
Railway Station
Botanical Gardens
DEIR ABU TOR
0 METRES 450
0 YARDS 450

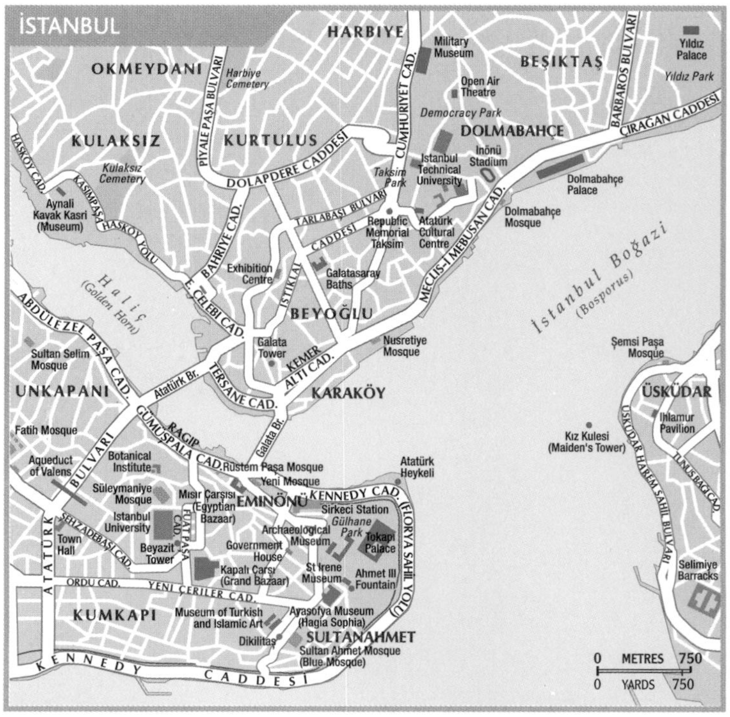
İSTANBUL
HARBIYE
Military Museum
Yıldız Palace
Yıldız Park
OKMEYDANI
Harbiye Cemetery
Open Air Theatre
BEŞIKTAŞ
Democracy Park
KULAKSIZ
KURTULUS
DOLMABAHÇE
Kulaksız Cemetery
İstanbul Technical University
İnönü Stadium
Dolmabahçe Palace
Aynali Kavak Kasri (Museum)
Taksim Park
Dolmabahçe Mosque
Republic Memorial Taksim
Atatürk Cultural Centre
Haliç (Golden Horn)
Exhibition Centre
Galatasaray Baths
İstanbul Boğazi (Bosporus)
BEYOĞLU
Galata Tower
Nusretiye Mosque
Sultan Selim Mosque
Şemsi Paşa Mosque
UNKAPANI
KARAKÖY
ÜSKÜDAR
Fatih Mosque
İhlamur Pavilion
Aqueduct of Valens
Botanical Institute
Rüstem Paşa Mosque
Yeni Mosque
Atatürk Heykeli
Kız Kulesi (Maiden's Tower)
Süleymaniye Mosque
Mısır Çarşısı (Egyptian Bazaar)
EMİNÖNÜ
Sirkeci Station
Gülhane Park
İstanbul University
Archaeological Museum
Topkapı Palace
Town Hall
Beyazit Tower
Government House
Kapalı Çarşı (Grand Bazaar)
St Irene Museum
Ahmet III Fountain
Selimiye Barracks
KUMKAPI
Museum of Turkish and Islamic Art
Ayasofya Museum (Hagia Sophia)
Dikilitaş
SULTANAHMET
Sultan Ahmet Mosque (Blue Mosque)
KENNEDY CADDESI
0 METRES 750
0 YARDS 750

ATHENS
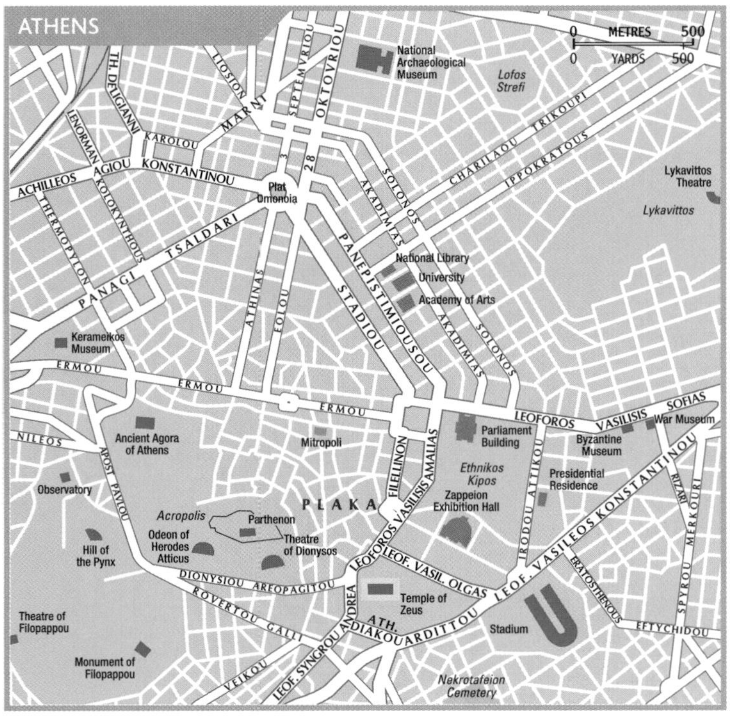

MOSCOW
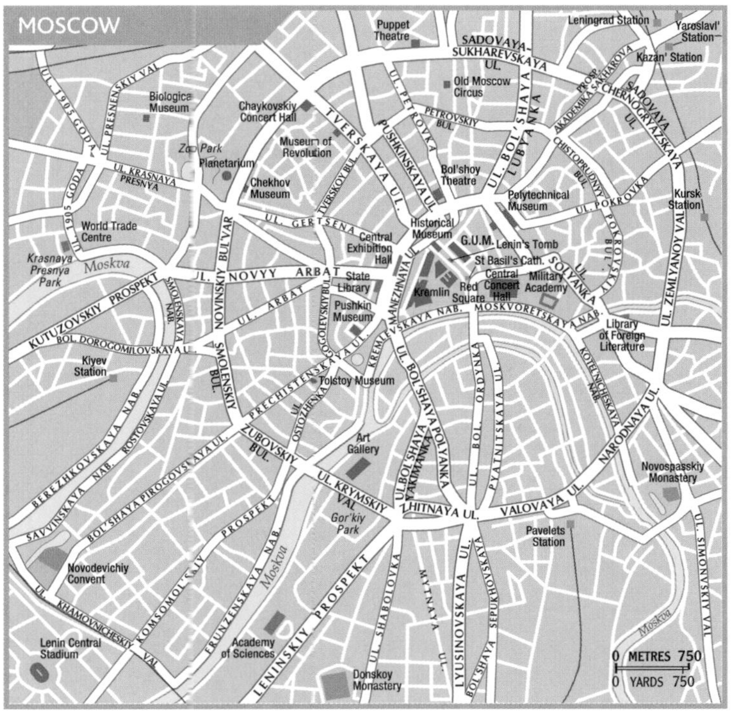

ST PETERSBURG
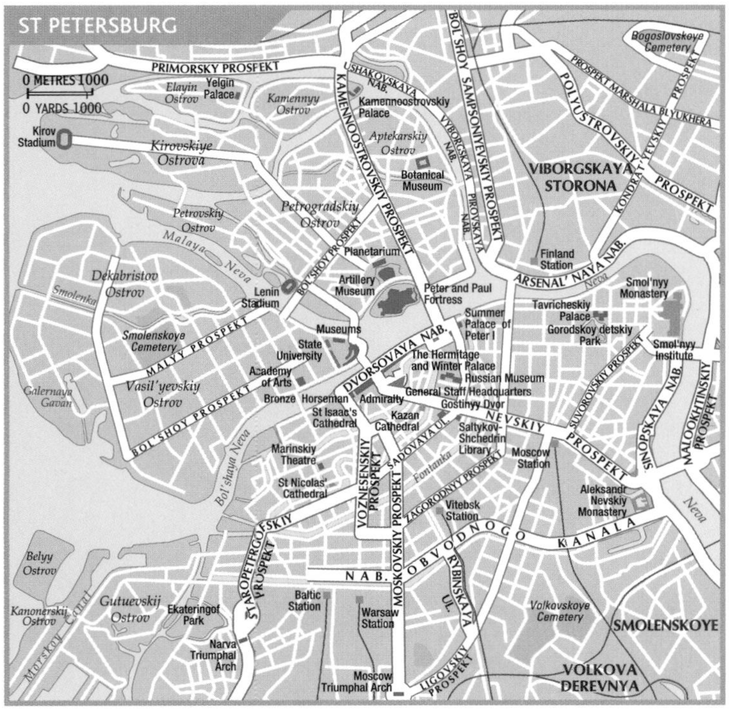

BERLIN
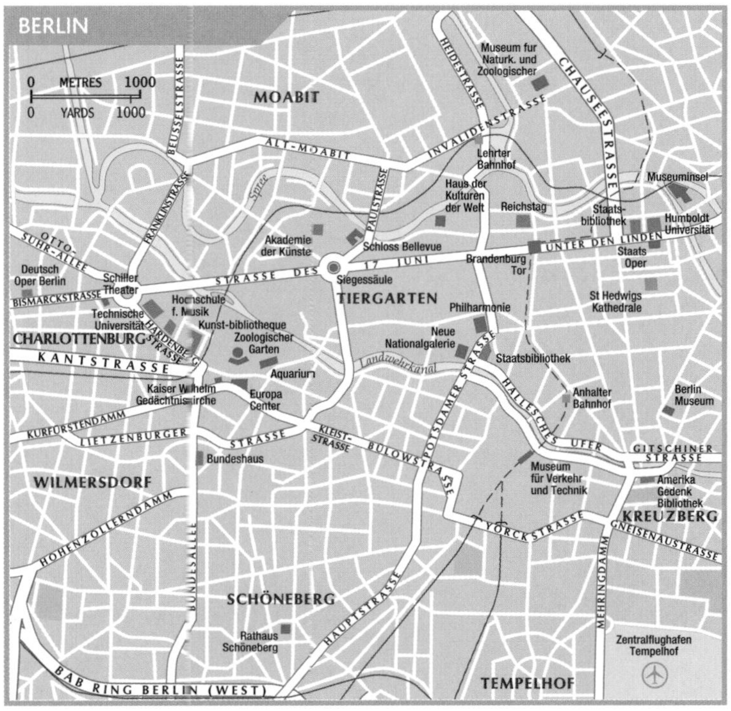

BRUSSELS
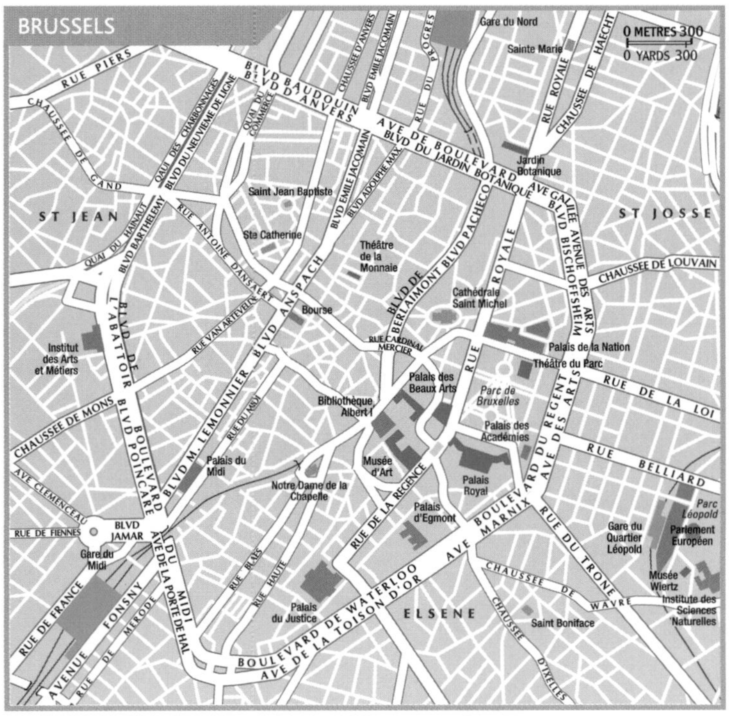

AMSTERDAM
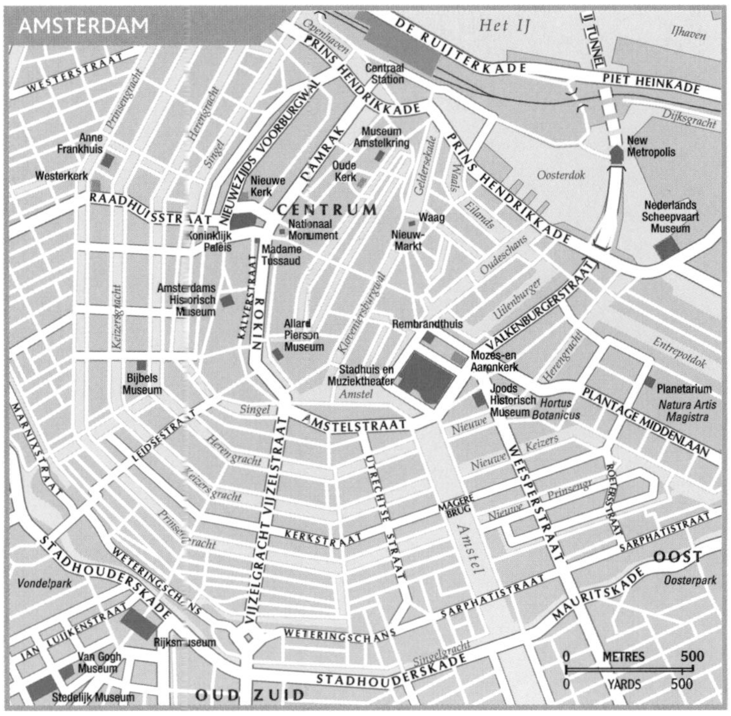

© Bartholomew Ltd

LONDON

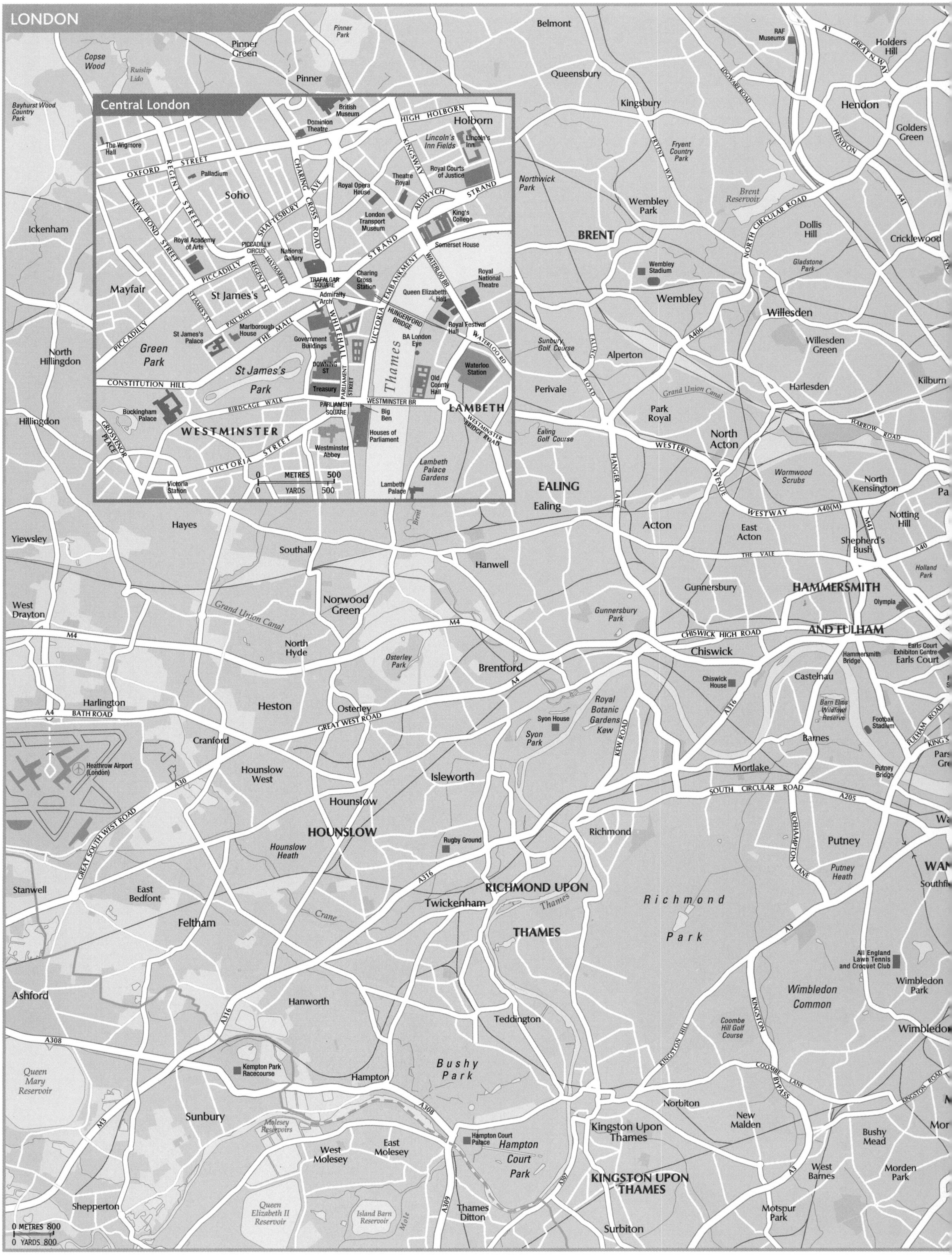

Central London

The Wigmore Hall
OXFORD STREET
NEW BOND STREET
REGENT STREET
Palladium
Soho
Dominion Theatre
British Museum
HIGH HOLBORN
Holborn
Lincoln's Inn Fields
Lincoln's Inn
KINGSWAY
CHARING CROSS ROAD
SHAFTESBURY AVE
Royal Opera House
Theatre Royal
Royal Courts of Justice
ALDWYCH
STRAND
Royal Academy of Arts
National Gallery
PICCADILLY CIRCUS
HAYMARKET
REGENT ST
London Transport Museum
King's College
Northwick Park
Somerset House
Mayfair
PICCADILLY
St James's
PALL MALL
TRAFALGAR SQUARE
Admiralty Arch
Charing Cross Station
STRAND
WATERLOO BRIDGE
VICTORIA EMBANKMENT
Queen Elizabeth Hall
Royal National Theatre
Marlborough House
THE MALL
St James's Palace
Government Buildings
WHITEHALL
HUNGERFORD BRIDGE
BA London Eye
Royal Festival Hall
WATERLOO RD
Green Park
CONSTITUTION HILL
St James's Park
BIRDCAGE WALK
DOWNING ST
Thames
Old County Hall
Waterloo Station
Buckingham Palace
GROSVENOR PLACE
Treasury
PARLIAMENT STREET
PARLIAMENT SQUARE
Big Ben
WESTMINSTER BR
LAMBETH
WESTMINSTER
Westminster Abbey
Houses of Parliament
WESTMINSTER BRIDGE ROAD
VICTORIA STREET
Victoria Station
Lambeth Palace Gardens
Lambeth Palace

METRES 500
YARDS 500

Belmont
RAF Museums
AT
GREAT N. WAY
Holders Hill
Pinner Park
Pinner Green
Copse Wood
Ruislip Lido
Pinner
Queensbury
Kingsbury
EDGWARE ROAD
Hendon
Golders Green
Bayhurst Wood Country Park
Fryent Country Park
HENDON
M1
Ickenham
Wembley Park
Brent Reservoir
BRENT
NORTH CIRCULAR ROAD
Dollis Hill
Cricklewood
North Hillingdon
Wembley Stadium
Wembley
Gladstone Park
Willesden
Hillingdon
Sunbury Golf Course
EALING ROAD
Alperton
Grand Union Canal
Willesden Green
Harlesden
Kilburn
HARROW ROAD
Perivale
Park Royal
North Acton
Hayes
Ealing Golf Course
EALING
Ealing
HANGER LANE
WESTERN AVENUE
Wormwood Scrubs
North Kensington
Yiewsley
Southall
Hanwell
Acton
East Acton
THE VALE
WESTWAY A40(M)
Notting Hill
Shepherd's Bush
A40
Holland Park
West Drayton
M4
Grand Union Canal
Norwood Green
M4
Gunnersbury
HAMMERSMITH
Olympia
North Hyde
Osterley Park
Brentford
A4
Gunnersbury Park
CHISWICK HIGH ROAD
AND FULHAM
Harlington
BATH ROAD A4
Heston
Osterley
GREAT WEST ROAD
Chiswick
Chiswick House
Hammersmith Bridge
Earls Court Exhibition Centre
Earls Court
Castelnau
Cranford
Syon House
Syon Park
Royal Botanic Gardens Kew
KEW ROAD
Barn Elms Wildfowl Reserve
Barnes
Football Stadium
FULHAM PALACE RD
KING'S
Stanwell
GREAT SOUTH WEST ROAD
Heathrow Airport (London)
A30
Hounslow West
Isleworth
Mortlake
SOUTH CIRCULAR ROAD
A205
Putney Bridge
Putney
Hounslow
HOUNSLOW
A316
Richmond
ROEHAMPTON LANE
WAN
East Bedfont
Hounslow Heath
Rugby Ground
A316
RICHMOND UPON
Richmond Park
Putney Heath
Southfi
Stanwell
Feltham
Crane
Twickenham
Thames
THAMES
A3
Wimbledon Common
Ashford
A316
Hanworth
Teddington
All England Lawn Tennis and Croquet Club
Wimbledon Park
Queen Mary Reservoir
Kempton Park Racecourse
A308
Bushy Park
Coombe Hill Golf Course
KINGSTON HILL
Wimbledon
A3
Sunbury
Molesey Reservoirs
Hampton
Hampton Court Palace
Hampton Court Park
Norbiton
COOMBE BYPASS
KINGSTON ROAD
M3
West Molesey
East Molesey
Kingston Upon Thames
New Malden
Bushy Mead
Mor
A308
Thames Ditton
KINGSTON UPON THAMES
West Barnes
Morden Park
Shepperton
Queen Elizabeth II Reservoir
Island Barn Reservoir
Mole
Surbiton
Motspur Park

0 METRES 800
0 YARDS 800

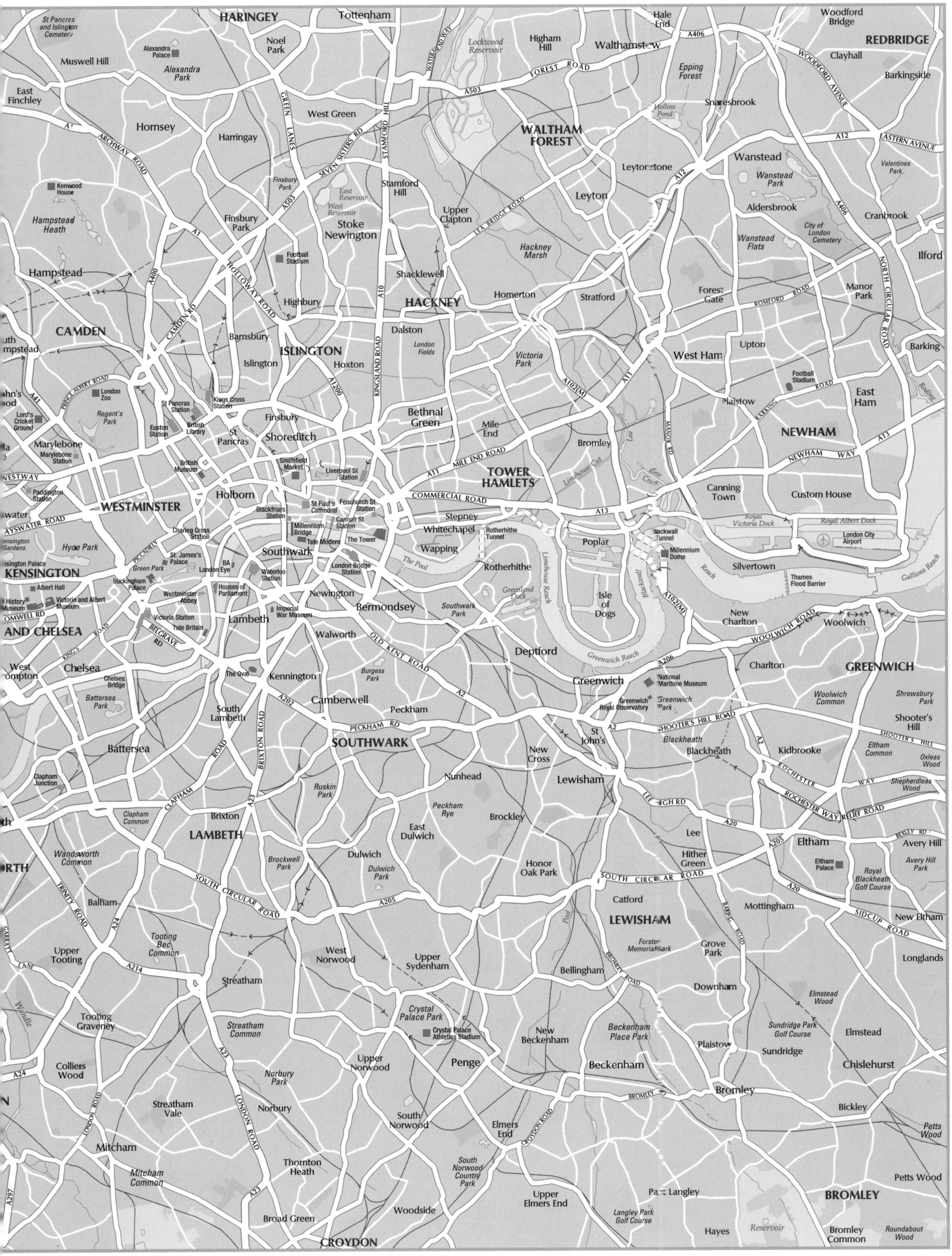
HARINGEY
Tottenham
St Pancras and Islington Cemetery
Muswell Hill
Alexandra Palace
Alexandra Park
Noel Park
Lockwood Reservoir
Higham Hill
Walthamstow
Hale End
A406
Woodford Bridge
REDBRIDGE
Clayhall
WOODFORD AVENUE
Barkingside
East Finchley
FOREST ROAD
A503
Epping Forest
Snaresbrook
Hollow Pond
Hornsey
GREEN LANES
West Green
STAMFORD HILL
SEVEN SISTERS RD
WALTHAM FOREST
ARCHWAY ROAD
Harringay
A12
EASTERN AVENUE
Wanstead
Wanstead Park
Valentines Park
Leytonstone
Kenwood House
Finsbury Park
East Reservoir
West Reservoir
Stamford Hill
Upper Clapton
LEA BRIDGE ROAD
Leyton
Aldersbrook
Cranbrook
Hampstead Heath
A503
A1
Finsbury Park
Stoke Newington
Hackney Marsh
Wanstead Flats
City of London Cemetery
A406
Ilford
Football Stadium
A10
Shacklewell
Hampstead
HOLLOWAY ROAD
A400
CAMDEN RD
Highbury
HACKNEY
Homerton
Stratford
Forest Gate
ROMFORD ROAD
Manor Park
NORTH CIRCULAR ROAD
CAMDEN
Barnsbury
Islington
ISLINGTON
Hoxton
Dalston
London Fields
Victoria Park
West Ham
Upton
Barking
PRINCE ALBERT ROAD
London Zoo
Regent's Park
Lord's Cricket Ground
A41
St Pancras Station
Kings Cross Station
KINGSLAND ROAD
A1200
A102(M)
A11
Football Stadium
BARKING ROAD
Roding
Plaistow
East Ham
Marylebone
Marylebone Station
Euston Station
British Library
St Pancras
Finsbury
Shoreditch
Bethnal Green
Mile End
MILE END ROAD
Bromley
MANOR RD
NEWHAM
NEWHAM WAY
A13
British Museum
Smithfield Market
Liverpool St Station
A11
TOWER HAMLETS
Limehouse Cut
Lea
Canning Town
Custom House
Paddington Station
WESTMINSTER
Holborn
St Paul's Cathedral
Fenchurch St Station
COMMERCIAL ROAD
A13
BAYSWATER ROAD
Blackfriars Station
Cannon St Station
Stepney
Royal Victoria Dock
Royal Albert Dock
London City Airport
Charing Cross Station
Millennium Bridge
Tate Modern
The Tower
Whitechapel
Rotherhithe Tunnel
Wapping
Blackwall Tunnel
Poplar
Millennium Dome
Hyde Park
PICCADILLY
St. James's Palace
Green Park
Southwark
The Pool
Rotherhithe
Limehouse Reach
Reach
Silvertown
Gallions Reach
KENSINGTON
BA London Eye
Waterloo Station
London Bridge Station
Blackwall
Albert Hall
Buckingham Palace
Houses of Parliament
Westminster Abbey
Newington
Greenland Dock
Isle of Dogs
Thames Flood Barrier
Victoria and Albert Museum
Imperial War Museum
Bermondsey
Southwark Park
Victoria Station
Tate Britain
Lambeth
A102(M)
New Charlton
AND CHELSEA
BELGRAVE RD
Walworth
OLD KENT ROAD
Deptford
WOOLWICH ROAD
Woolwich
KING'S ROAD
Greenwich Reach
A206
West Brompton
Chelsea
Chelsea Bridge
The Oval
Kennington
Burgess Park
A2
Greenwich
National Maritime Museum
Charlton
GREENWICH
Battersea Park
South Lambeth
A202
Camberwell
Peckham
Greenwich Royal Observatory
Greenwich Park
Woolwich Common
Shrewsbury Park
Shooter's Hill
PECKHAM RD
A2
SHOOTER'S HILL ROAD
Battersea
SOUTHWARK
BRIXTON ROAD
St John's
New Cross
Blackheath
Kidbrooke
Eltham Common
Oxleas Wood
Clapham Junction
Ruskin Park
Nunhead
Lewisham
ROCHESTER WAY
Shepherdleas Wood
Peckham Rye
Brockley
CLAPHAM
A23
Clapham Common
Brixton
LAMBETH
East Dulwich
Lee
A20
RELIEF ROAD
Eltham
BEXLEY RD
Avery Hill
Avery Hill Park
Wandsworth Common
Brockwell Park
Dulwich
Dulwich Park
Honor Oak Park
Hither Green
SOUTH CIRCULAR ROAD
A205
Eltham Palace
Royal Blackheath Golf Course
TRINITY ROAD
Balham
A24
A205
Catford
LEWISHAM
Mottingham
SIDCUP ROAD
New Eltham
Tooting Bec Common
Upper Tooting
A214
West Norwood
Upper Sydenham
Grove Park
BROMLEY ROAD
Longlands
Streatham
Bellingham
Downham
Elmstead Wood
Wandle
Tooting Graveney
Streatham Common
Crystal Palace Park
Crystal Palace Athletics Stadium
New Beckenham
Beckenham Place Park
Sundridge Park Golf Course
Elmstead
Plaistow
Sundridge
Colliers Wood
Upper Norwood
Penge
Beckenham
Chislehurst
A24
Norbury Park
BROMLEY
Bromley
Streatham Vale
LONDON ROAD
Norbury
South Norwood
Elmers End
CROYDON ROAD
Bickley
Petts Wood
Mitcham
Mitcham Common
Thornton Heath
South Norwood Country Park
Petts Wood
A297
A23
Upper Elmers End
Park Langley
BROMLEY
Broad Green
Woodside
Langley Park Golf Course
Hayes
Reservoir
Bromley Common
Roundabout Wood
CROYDON

PARIS

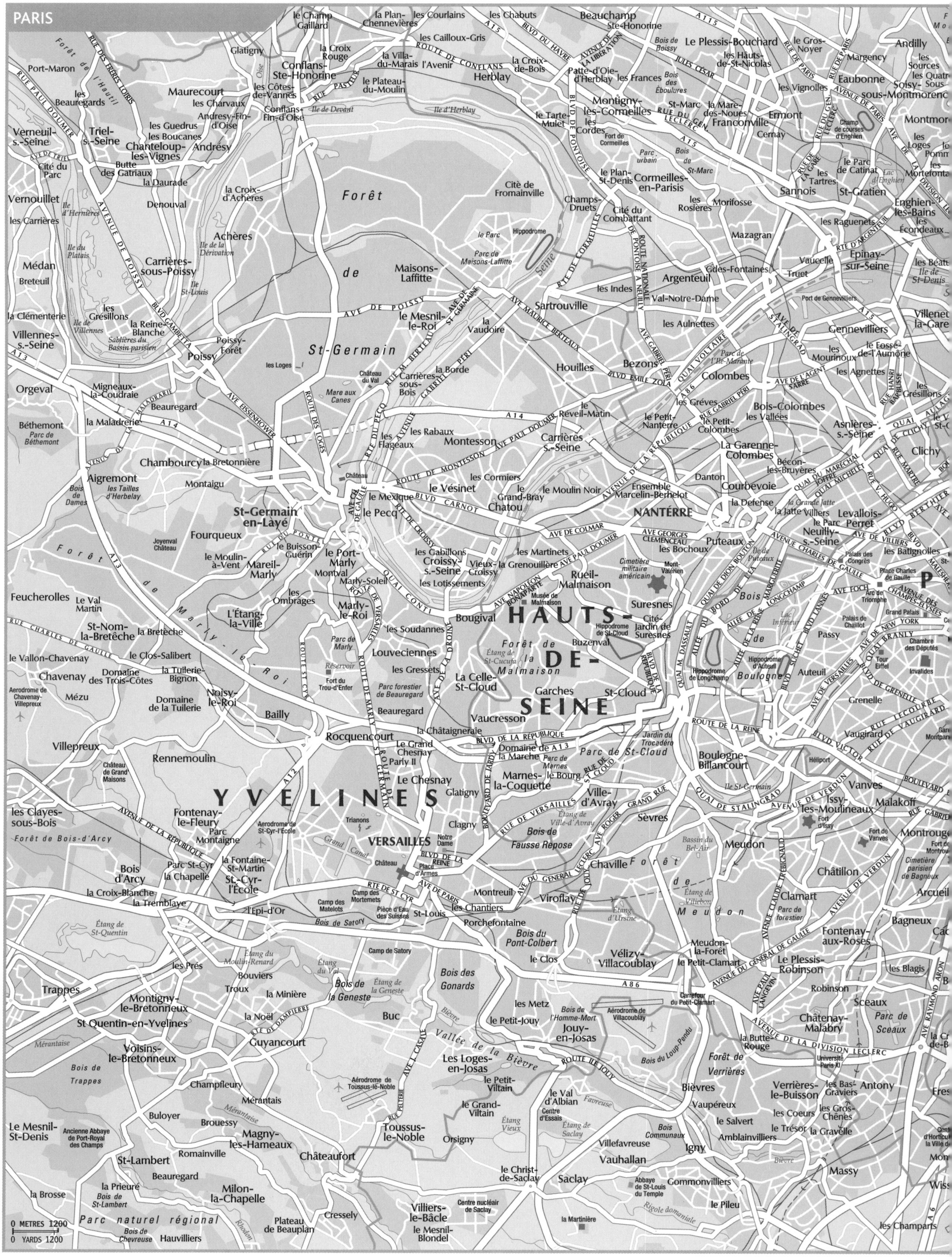
Conflans-Ste-Honorine
Herblay
Montigny-lès-Cormeilles
Franconville
Ermont
Eaubonne
Andilly
Sannois
St-Gratien
Enghien-les-Bains
Forêt de St-Germain
Maisons-Laffitte
Achères
Carrières-sous-Poissy
Poissy
Médan
Villennes-s.-Seine
Orgeval
Verneuil-s.-Seine
Triel-s.-Seine
Chanteloup-les-Vignes
Andrésy
Maurecourt
Sartrouville
Argenteuil
Epinay-sur-Seine
Gennevilliers
Colombes
Bezons
Houilles
Bois-Colombes
Asnières-s.-Seine
Clichy
La Garenne-Colombes
Courbevoie
Levallois-Perret
Neuilly-s.-Seine
Puteaux
NANTERRE
Rueil-Malmaison
Suresnes
Chatou
le Vésinet
Montesson
Carrières-s.-Seine
le Pecq
St-Germain-en-Laye
Fourqueux
Chambourcy
Aigremont
Mareil-Marly
le Port-Marly
Marly-le-Roi
L'Étang-la-Ville
St-Nom-la-Bretêche
Feucherolles
Chavenay
Louveciennes
Bougival
La Celle-St-Cloud
Vaucresson
Garches
St-Cloud
HAUTS-DE-SEINE
Bois de Boulogne
Boulogne-Billancourt
Sèvres
Meudon
Issy-les-Moulineaux
Vanves
Malakoff
Montrouge
Clamart
Châtillon
Bagneux
Fontenay-aux-Roses
Le Plessis-Robinson
Châtenay-Malabry
Sceaux
Antony
Verrières-le-Buisson
Massy
Bièvres
Igny
Vélizy-Villacoublay
Viroflay
Chaville
Ville-d'Avray
Marnes-la-Coquette
Le Chesnay
Rocquencourt
VERSAILLES
YVELINES
Bailly
Noisy-le-Roi
Villepreux
Rennemoulin
Fontenay-le-Fleury
St-Cyr-l'École
Bois d'Arcy
les Clayes-sous-Bois
Trappes
Montigny-le-Bretonneux
St-Quentin-en-Yvelines
Voisins-le-Bretonneux
Guyancourt
Buc
Jouy-en-Josas
Les Loges-en-Josas
Toussus-le-Noble
Châteaufort
Magny-les-Hameaux
Saclay
Villiers-le-Bâcle
Milon-la-Chapelle
Le Mesnil-St-Denis
Parc naturel régional
0 METRES 1200
0 YARDS 1200

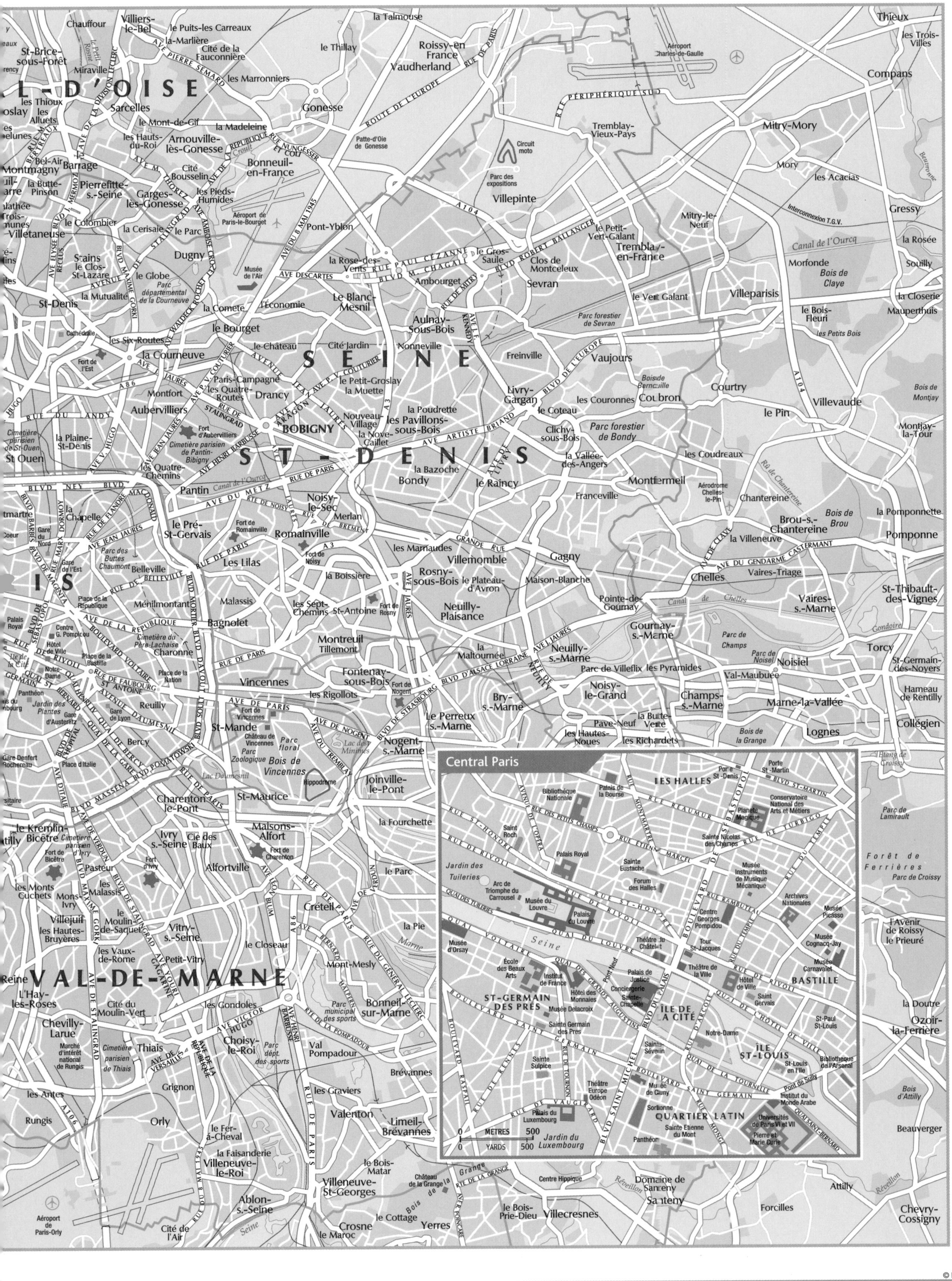
Chauffour
Villiers-le-Bel
le Puits-les Carreaux
la Marlière
Cité de la Fauconnière
la Talmouse
le Thillay
Roissy-en France
Vaudherland
Aéroport Charles-de-Gaulle
Thieux
les Trois-Villes
Compans
St-Brice-sous-Forêt
Miraville
AVE PIERRE SEMARD
les Marronniers
L-D'OISE
les Thioux
Sarcelles
Gonesse
ROUTE DE L'EUROPE
RTE PÉRIPHÉRIQUE SUD
le Mont-de-Gif
la Madeleine
les Hauts-du-Roi
Arnouville-lès-Gonesse
Patte-d'Oie de Gonesse
Circuit moto
Tremblay-Vieux-Pays
Mitry-Mory
Bel-Air
Montmagny
Barrage
Cité Bousselin
Bonneuil-en-France
Parc des expositions
Mory
les Acacias
la Butte-Pinson
Pierrefitte-s.-Seine
Garges-lès-Gonesse
les Pieds-Humides
Villepinte
Interconnexion T.G.V.
Gressy
le Colombier
Villetaneuse
Aéroport de Paris-le-Bourget
A104
Mitry-le-Neuf
la Cerisaie
le Parc
Pont-Yblon
le Petit-Vert-Galant
Tremblay-en-France
Canal de l'Ourcq
la Rosée
Stains
le Clos-St-Lazare
Dugny
AVE DU 8 MAI 1945
la Rose-des-Vents
RUE PAUL CEZANNE
le Gros-Saule
BLVD ROBERT BALLANGER
Clos de Montceleux
Morfonde
Bois de Claye
Souilly
le Globe
Parc départemental de la Courneuve
Musée de l'Air
AVE DESCARTES
BLVD M. CHAGALL
Ambourget
Sevran
la Mutualité
St-Denis
la Comete
l'Économie
Le Blanc-Mesnil
Aulnay-Sous-Bois
le Vert Galant
Villeparisis
la Closerie
Mauperthuis
le Bois-Fleuri
Parc forestier de Sevran
les Petits Bois
Cathédrale
les Six-Routes
le Bourget
le Château
Cité Jardin
Nonneville
la Courneuve
Fort de l'Est
SEINE
Freinville
Vaujours
BLVD DE L'EUROPE
Paris-Campagne
les Quatre-Routes
Drancy
le Petit-Groslay
la Muette
Livry-Gargan
Bois de Bernouille
Coubron
Courtry
Bois de Montjay
Montfort
A86
Aubervilliers
RUE DE STALINGRAD
la Poudrette
les Pavillons-sous-Bois
le Coteau
les Couronnes
le Pin
Villevaude
RUE DU LANDY
Fort d'Aubervilliers
BOBIGNY
Nouveau-Village
la Nove-Caillet
AVE ARTISTE BRIAND
Clichy-sous-Bois
Parc forestier de Bondy
Montjay-la-Tour
Cimetière parisien de St-Ouen
la Plaine-St-Denis
Cimetière parisien de Pantin-Bobigny
ST-DENIS
la Vallée-des-Angers
les Coudreaux
St Ouen
les Quatre-Chemins
la Bazoche
Bondy
le Raincy
Montfermeil
Aérodrome Chelles-le-Pin
Chantereine
BLVD NEY
Pantin
RUE DE PARIS
Noisy-le-Sec
Merlan
Franceville
Bois de Brou
la Pomponnette
la Chapelle
le Pré-St-Gervais
Fort de Romainville
Romainville
Brou-s.-Chantereine
Pomponne
Gare du Nord
Parc des Buttes Chaumont
Gare de l'Est
les Marnaudes
GRANDE RUE
Villemomble
la Villeneuve
AVE DU GENDARME CASTERMANT
Fort de Noisy
les Lilas
Gagny
Belleville
la Boissière
Rosny-sous-Bois
le Plateau-d'Avron
Maison-Blanche
Chelles
Vaires-Triage
Vaires-s.-Marne
St-Thibault-des-Vignes
Place de la République
Ménilmontant
Malassis
les Sept-Chemins
St-Antoine
Fort de Rosny
Neuilly-Plaisance
Pointe-de-Gournay
Canal de Chelles
Gournay-s.-Marne
Parc de Champs
Gondoire
Palais Royal
Centre G. Pompidou
Hôtel de Ville
Cimetière du Père-Lachaise
Charonne
Bagnolet
Montreuil
Tillemont
la Maltournée
Neuilly-s.-Marne
Parc de Noisel
Noisiel
Torcy
Île de la Cité
Notre-Dame
Place de la Bastille
AVE DE LA RÉPUBLIQUE
BOULEVARD VOLTAIRE
Place de la Nation
Fontenay-sous-Bois
Fort de Nogent
BLVD D'ALSACE LORRAINE
Parc de Villeflix
les Pyramides
Val-Maubuée
St-Germain-des-Noyers
Panthéon
Jardin des Plantes
Gare d'Austerlitz
Gare de Lyon
Vincennes
les Rigollots
BLVD DE STRASBOURG
Bry-s.-Marne
Noisy-le-Grand
Champs-s.-Marne
Marne-la-Vallée
Hameau de Rentilly
Reuilly
AVE DE PARIS
Fort de Vincennes
St-Mandé
AVE DE NOGENT
Le Perreux-s.-Marne
Pave-Neuf
la Butte-Verte
Bois de la Grange
Lognes
Collégien
Gare Denfert Rochereau
Place d'Italie
Bercy
Château de Vincennes
Parc Zoologique
Parc floral
Bois de Vincennes
Lac des Minimes
Nogent-s.-Marne
les Hautes-Noues
les Richardets
Lac Daumesnil
Hippodrome
Joinville-le-Pont
Étang de Croissy
Charenton-le-Pont
St-Maurice
la Fourchette
Parc de Lamirault
le Kremlin-Bicêtre
Cimetière parisien d'Ivry
Fort de Bicêtre
Ivry-s.-Seine
Cité des Baux
Maisons-Alfort
Fort de Charenton
Pasteur
Fort d'Ivry
Alfortville
le Parc
Forêt de Ferrières
Parc de Croissy
les Monts Cuchets
les Malassis
Mons-Ivry
Créteil
Villejuif
les Hautes-Bruyères
le Moulin-de-Saquet
Vitry-s.-Seine
la Pie
Marne
l'Avenir de Roissy
le Prieuré
le Closeau
les Vaux-de-Rome
Petit-Vitry
Mont-Mesly
VAL-DE-MARNE
L'Hay-les-Roses
Cité du Moulin-Vert
les Gondoles
Parc municipal des sports
Bonneuil-sur-Marne
la Doutre
Ozoir-la-Ferrière
Chevilly-Larue
Marché d'intérêt national de Rungis
Cimetière parisien de Thiais
Thiais
Choisy-le-Roi
Parc dépt. des sports
Val Pompadour
Grignon
Brévannes
Bois d'Attilly
les Antes
les Graviers
Rungis
Orly
Valenton
Limeil-Brévannes
Beauverger
le Fer-à-Cheval
la Faisanderie
Villeneuve-le-Roi
le Bois-Matar
Château de la Grange
Centre Hippique
Domaine de Sanceny
Santeny
Attilly
Villeneuve-St-Georges
Aéroport de Paris-Orly
Ablon-s.-Seine
le Bois-Prie-Dieu
Villecresnes
Forcilles
Chevry-Cossigny
Cité de l'Air
Seine
le Cottage
Crosne
Yerres
le Maroc
Central Paris
LES HALLES
Porte St-Denis
Porte St-Martin
Bibliothèque Nationale
Palais de la Bourse
Conservatoire National des Arts et Métiers
Planète Magique
RUE RÉAUMUR
RUE ST-HONORÉ
AVENUE DE L'OPÉRA
RUE DES PETITS CHAMPS
RUE DE TURBIGO
Saint Roch
Sainte Nicolas des Champs
RUE DE RIVOLI
Palais Royal
Sainte Eustache
Musée Instruments de Musique Mécanique
Jardin des Tuileries
Arc de Triomphe du Carrousel
Forum des Halles
Archives Nationales
Musée du Louvre
Palais du Louvre
Centre Georges Pompidou
Musée Picasso
QUAI DES TUILERIES
QUAI VOLTAIRE
QUAI DU LOUVRE
Musée d'Orsay
Théâtre du Châtelet
Tour St-Jacques
Musée Cognacq-Jay
Seine
École des Beaux Arts
Institut de France
Hôtel des Monnaies
Pont Neuf
Palais de Justice
Conciergerie
Sainte-Chapelle
Théâtre de la Ville
Hôtel de Ville
Musée Carnavalet
BASTILLE
ST-GERMAIN DES PRÉS
Musée Delacroix
ÎLE DE LA CITÉ
Saint Gervais
Sainte Germain des Prés
Notre-Dame
Saint-Paul St-Louis
Sainte Séverin
ÎLE ST-LOUIS
Saint Sulpice
Théâtre Europe Odéon
Musée de Cluny
St-Louis en l'Île
Bibliothèque de l'Arsenal
Pont de Sully
Institut du Monde Arabe
Palais du Luxembourg
Sorbonne
QUARTIER LATIN
Universités de Paris VI et VII
Pierre et Marie Curie
Sainte Etienne du Mont
Panthéon
Jardin du Luxembourg
BLVD SAINT MICHEL
BOULEVARD SAINT GERMAIN
BOULEVARD RASPAIL
RUE DE VAUGIRARD
METRES 0 500
YARDS 0 500

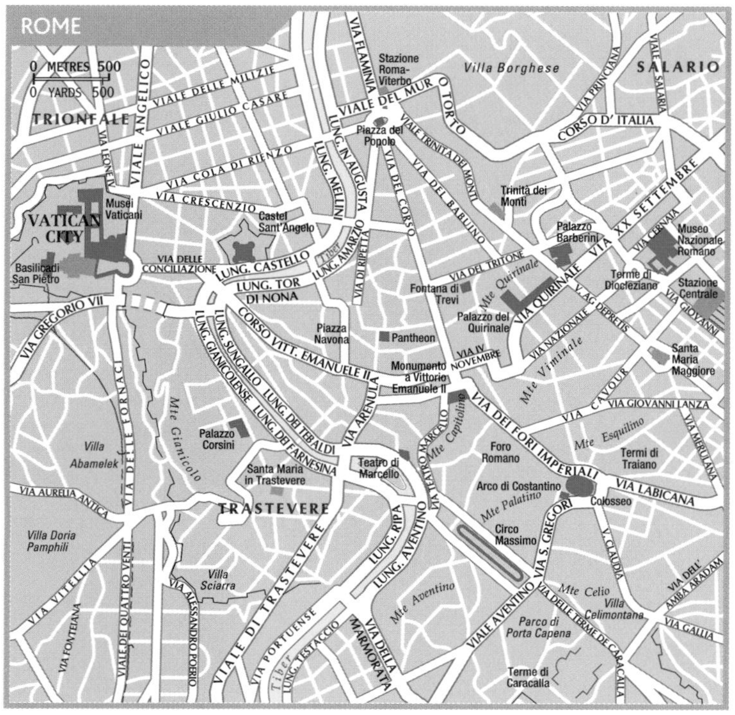
ROME
0 METRES 500
0 YARDS 500
TRIONFALE
VATICAN CITY
Musei Vaticani
Basilica di San Pietro
Castel Sant'Angelo
Stazione Roma-Viterbo
Villa Borghese
SALARIO
Piazza del Popolo
Trinità dei Monti
Palazzo Barberini
Museo Nazionale Romano
Terme di Diocleziano
Stazione Centrale
Fontana di Trevi
Palazzo del Quirinale
Piazza Navona
Pantheon
Santa Maria Maggiore
Monumento a Vittorio Emanuele II
Palazzo Corsini
Santa Maria in Trastevere
Teatro di Marcello
Foro Romano
Termi di Traiano
Arco di Costantino
Colosseo
Circo Massimo
TRASTEVERE
Villa Abamelek
Villa Doria Pamphili
Villa Sciarra
Mte Aventino
Mte Celio
Villa Celimontana
Parco di Porta Capena
Terme di Caracalla
Mte Gianicolo
Mte Palatino
Mte Capitolino
Mte Esquilino
Mte Viminale
Mte Quirinale
VIALE DELLE MILIZIE
VIALE GIULIO CESARE
VIALE ANGELICO
VIA COLA DI RIENZO
VIA CRESCENZIO
VIA DELLE CONCILIAZIONE
LUNG. CASTELLO
LUNG. TOR DI NONA
VIA GREGORIO VII
CORSO VITT. EMANUELE II
VIA DEI FORI IMPERIALI
VIA LABICANA
VIA CAVOUR
VIA GIOVANNI LANZA
VIA NAZIONALE
VIA XX SETTEMBRE
CORSO D'ITALIA
VIALE DEL MURO TORTO
VIA DEL CORSO
VIA DEL TRITONE
VIA AURELIA ANTICA
VIALE DI TRASTEVERE
VIA PORTUENSE
VIALE AVENTINO
VIA DI SAN GREGORIO
VIA FLAMINIA
VIA SALARIA
VIA NOMENTANA

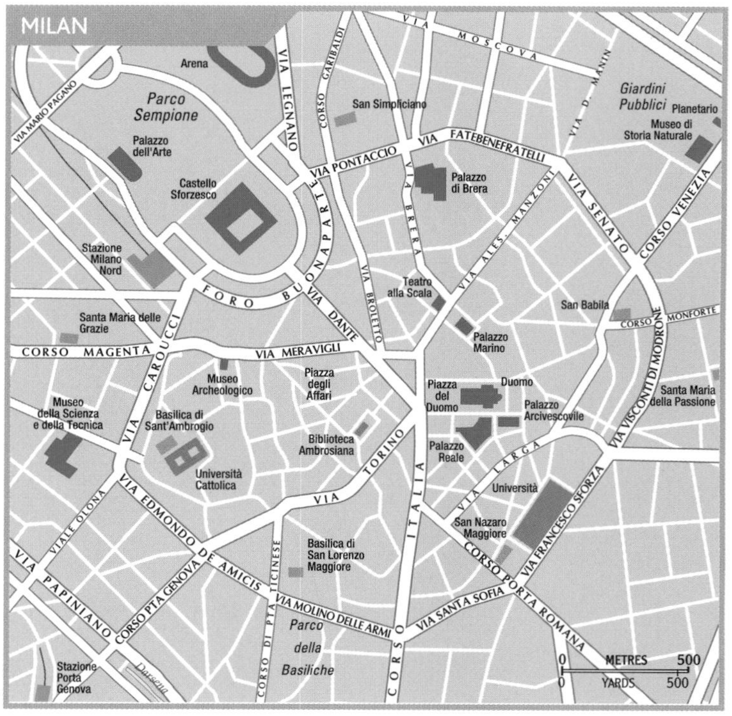
MILAN
Arena
Parco Sempione
Palazzo dell'Arte
Castello Sforzesco
San Simpliciano
Palazzo di Brera
Giardini Pubblici
Planetario
Museo di Storia Naturale
Stazione Milano Nord
Teatro alla Scala
Santa Maria delle Grazie
San Babila
Palazzo Marino
Museo della Scienza e della Tecnica
Museo Archeologico
Piazza degli Affari
Piazza del Duomo
Duomo
Palazzo Arcivescovile
Santa Maria della Passione
Basilica di Sant'Ambrogio
Biblioteca Ambrosiana
Palazzo Reale
Università Cattolica
Università
San Nazaro Maggiore
Basilica di San Lorenzo Maggiore
Parco della Basiliche
Stazione Porta Genova
0 METRES 500
0 YARDS 500
VIA MOSCOVA
VIA FATEBENEFRATELLI
VIA PONTACCIO
VIA LEGNANO
CORSO GARIBALDI
VIA BRERA
VIA MANZONI
VIA SENATO
CORSO VENEZIA
CORSO MONFORTE
FORO BUONAPARTE
VIA DANTE
CORSO MAGENTA
VIA MERAVIGLI
VIA CARDUCCI
VIA TORINO
VIA EDMONDO DE AMICIS
VIA MOLINO DELLE ARMI
CORSO ITALIA
VIA SANTA SOFIA
CORSO PORTA ROMANA
VIA FRANCESCO SFORZA
VIA VISCONTI DI MODRONE
VIALE PAPINIANO
CORSO PTA GENOVA
VIA MARIO PAGANO

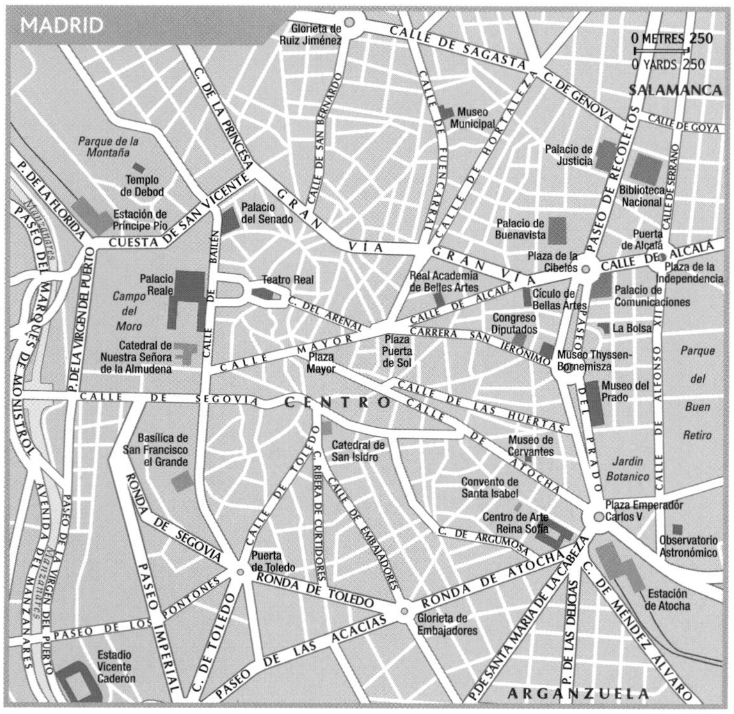
MADRID
0 METRES 250
0 YARDS 250
Glorieta de Ruiz Jiménez
CALLE DE SAGASTA
C. DE GENOVA
SALAMANCA
CALLE DE GOYA
Museo Municipal
Palacio de Justicia
Parque de la Montaña
Templo de Debod
Estación de Príncipe Pío
Palacio del Senado
Biblioteca Nacional
Palacio de Buenavista
Puerta de Alcalá
Plaza de la Cibeles
Plaza de la Independencia
Palacio Real
Campo del Moro
Teatro Real
Real Academia de Bellas Artes
Círculo de Bellas Artes
Palacio de Comunicaciones
Congreso Diputados
La Bolsa
Catedral de Nuestra Señora de la Almudena
Plaza Mayor
Plaza Puerta de Sol
Museo Thyssen-Bornemisza
Parque del Buen Retiro
Museo del Prado
CENTRO
Basílica de San Francisco el Grande
Catedral de San Isidro
Museo de Cervantes
Jardín Botanico
Convento de Santa Isabel
Centro de Arte Reina Sofía
Plaza Emperador Carlos V
Observatorio Astronómico
Puerta de Toledo
Estación de Atocha
Glorieta de Embajadores
Estadio Vicente Caderon
ARGANZUELA
GRAN VÍA
CALLE MAYOR
CALLE DE ALCALÁ
PASEO DE RECOLETOS
PASEO DEL PRADO
CALLE DE SEGOVIA
RONDA DE SEGOVIA
RONDA DE TOLEDO
RONDA DE ATOCHA
PASEO DE LAS ACACIAS
PASEO IMPERIAL
CALLE DE TOLEDO
CALLE DE BAILÉN
CALLE DE LA PRINCESA
CUESTA DE SAN VICENTE
CALLE DEL ARENAL
CARRERA SAN JERÓNIMO
CALLE DE LAS HUERTAS
CALLE DE ATOCHA
C. DE ARGUMOSA
C. DE MÉNDEZ ÁLVARO
CALLE DE SERRANO
P. DE LA FLORIDA
P. DE LA VIRGEN DEL PUERTO
PASEO DE LOS PONTONES

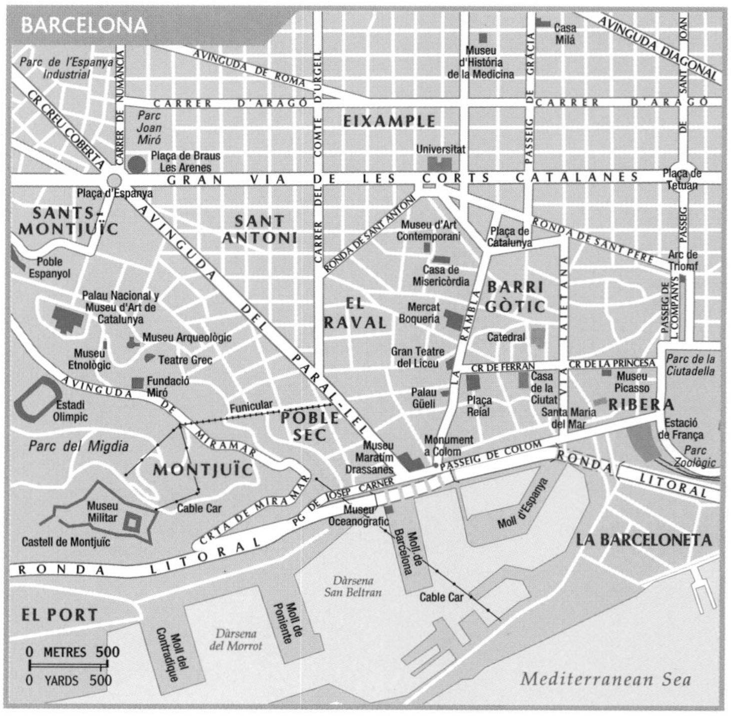
BARCELONA
Parc de l'Espanya Industrial
AVINGUDA DE ROMA
CARRER D'ARAGÓ
Casa Milà
Museu d'Història de la Medicina
AVINGUDA DIAGONAL
Parc Joan Miró
EIXAMPLE
Universitat
Plaça de Braus Les Arenes
GRAN VIA DE LES CORTS CATALANES
Plaça de Tetuan
Plaça d'Espanya
SANTS-MONTJUÏC
SANT ANTONI
Museu d'Art Contemporani
Plaça de Catalunya
RONDA DE SANT PERE
Arc de Triomf
Poble Espanyol
Casa de Misericòrdia
Palau Nacional y Museu d'Art de Catalunya
EL RAVAL
Mercat Boqueria
BARRI GÒTIC
Museu Arqueològic
Teatre Grec
Catedral
Museu Etnològic
Gran Teatre del Liceu
Parc de la Ciutadella
Fundació Miró
Estadi Olímpic
Palau Güell
Plaça Reial
Casa de la Ciutat
Museu Picasso
Santa Maria del Mar
RIBERA
Estació de França
Parc Zoològic
Funicular
POBLE SEC
Parc del Migdia
MONTJUÏC
Museu Marítim Drassanes
Monument a Colom
PASSEIG DE COLOM
RONDA LITORAL
Museu Militar
Cable Car
Castell de Montjuïc
Museu Oceanogràfic
Moll de Barcelona
Moll d'Espanya
LA BARCELONETA
Dàrsena San Beltran
EL PORT
Moll de Ponent
Moll del Contradique
Dàrsena del Morrot
0 METRES 500
0 YARDS 500
Mediterranean Sea
AVINGUDA DEL PARAL·LEL
CARRER DE SANT ANTONI
RONDA DE SANT ANTONI
LA RAMBLA
VIA LAIETANA

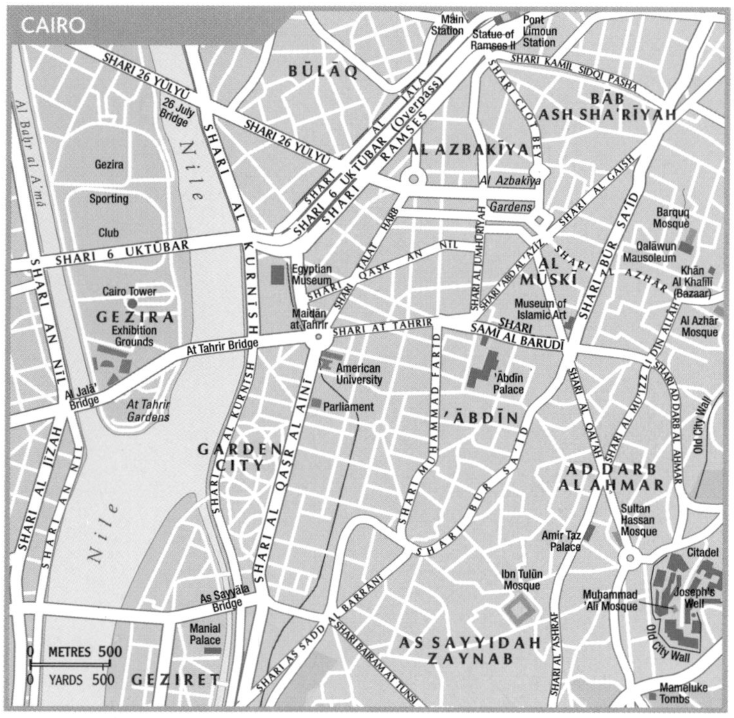
CAIRO
Main Station
Statue of Ramses II
Pont Limoun Station
BŪLĀQ
SHARI 26 YULYU
26 July Bridge
BĀB ASH SHA'RĪYAH
AL AZBAKĪYA
Al Azbakiya Gardens
Gezira
Sporting Club
Nile
Barquq Mosque
Qalawun Mausoleum
Khan Al Khalili (Bazaar)
SHARI 6 UKTUBAR
Egyptian Museum
AL MUSKI
Cairo Tower
GEZIRA Exhibition Grounds
Maidan at Tahrir
Museum of Islamic Art
Al Azhar Mosque
At Tahrir Bridge
American University
'Abdin Palace
Al Jala' Bridge
At Tahrir Gardens
Parliament
'ĀBDĪN
GARDEN CITY
AD DARB AL AHMAR
City Wall
Sultan Hassan Mosque
Amir Taz Palace
Citadel
Ibn Tulun Mosque
Muhammad 'Ali Mosque
Joseph's Well
As Sayyala Bridge
Manial Palace
AS SAYYIDAH ZAYNAB
Old City Wall
0 METRES 500
0 YARDS 500
GEZIRET
Mameluke Tombs
SHARI RAMSES
SHARI AL KURNISH
SHARI AL QASR AL AINI
SHARI AT TAHRIR
SHARI AL AZHAR
SHARI BUR SA'ID
SHARI AL GAISH
SHARI QASR AN NIL
SHARI AN NIL
SHARI AL JIZAH
Al Bahr al A'ma

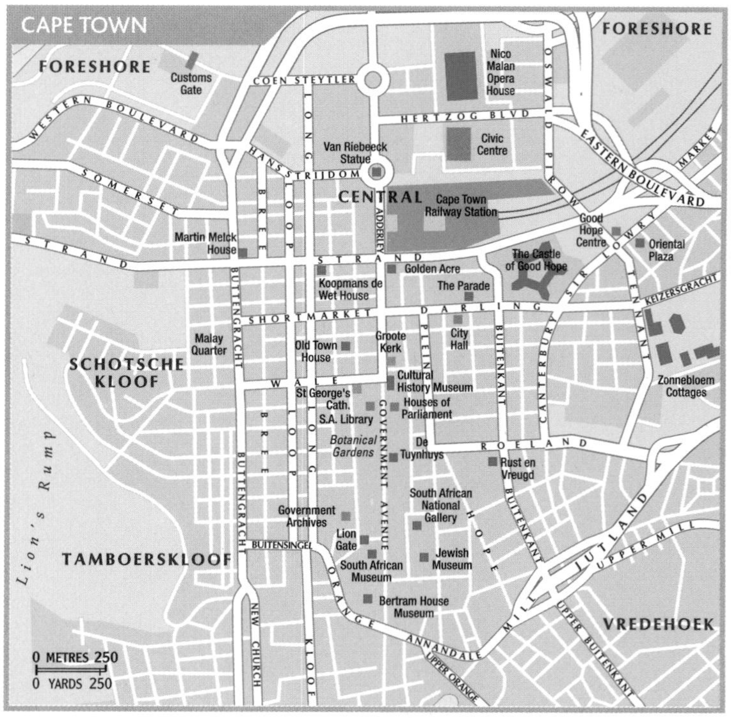
CAPE TOWN
FORESHORE
Customs Gate
COEN STEYTLER
Nico Malan Opera House
HERTZOG BLVD
WESTERN BOULEVARD
Civic Centre
Van Riebeeck Statue
HANS STRIJDOM
EASTERN BOULEVARD
SOMERSET
CENTRAL
Cape Town Railway Station
Good Hope Centre
Oriental Plaza
STRAND
Martin Melck House
The Castle of Good Hope
Golden Acre
The Parade
Koopmans de Wet House
KEIZERSGRACHT
SHORTMARKET
DARLING
Malay Quarter
Groote Kerk
City Hall
Old Town House
SCHOTSCHE KLOOF
WALE
Cultural History Museum
St George's Cath.
S.A. Library
Houses of Parliament
Zonnebloem Cottages
Botanical Gardens
De Tuynhuys
ROELAND
Rust en Vreugd
Lion's Rump
South African National Gallery
Government Archives
Lion Gate
Jewish Museum
TAMBOERSKLOOF
South African Museum
Bertram House Museum
BUITENSINGEL
UPPER MILL
JUTLAND
VREDEHOEK
ANNANDALE
UPPER ORANGE
0 METRES 250
0 YARDS 250
BREE
LONG
LOOP
BUITENGRACHT
ADDERLEY
BUITENKANT
GOVERNMENT AVENUE
HOPE
ORANGE
KLOOF
NEW CHURCH
CANTERBURY
OSWALD PIROW
MARKET

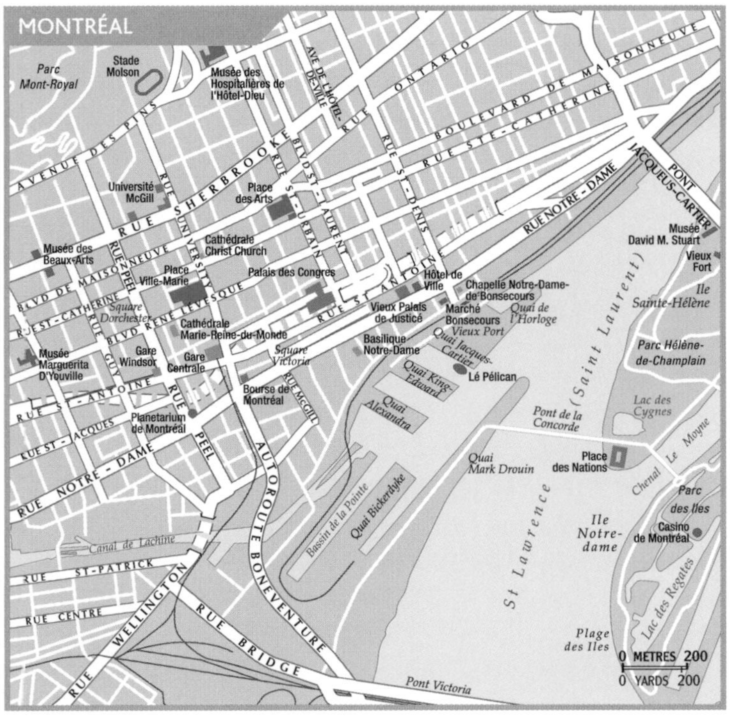

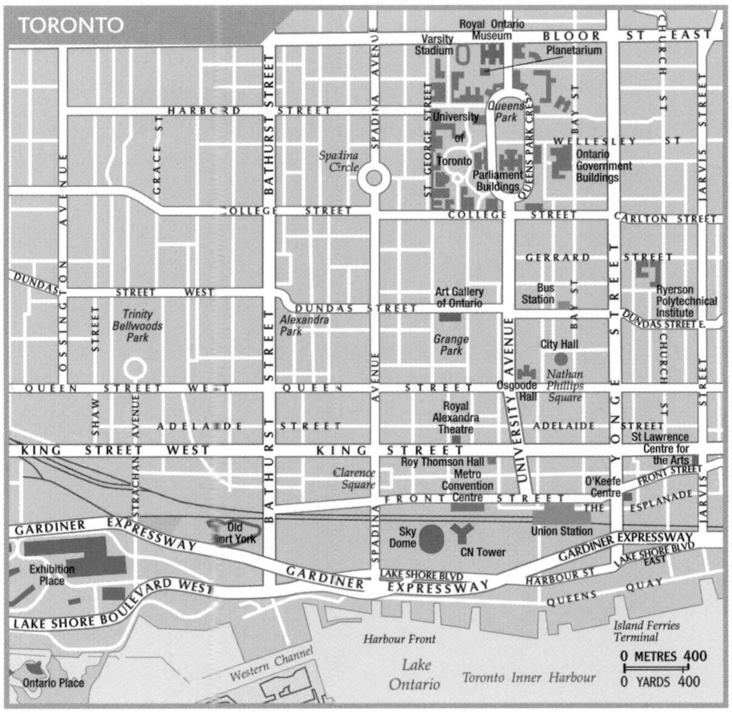

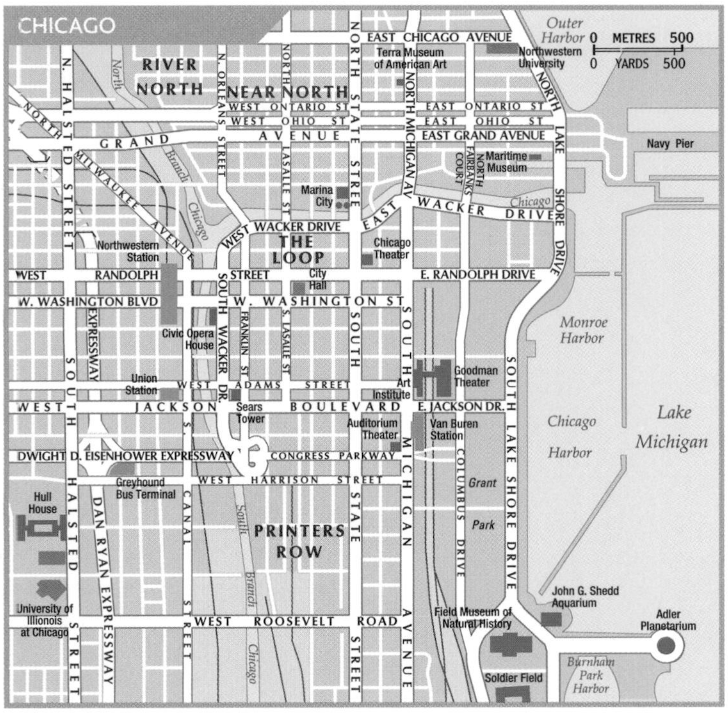

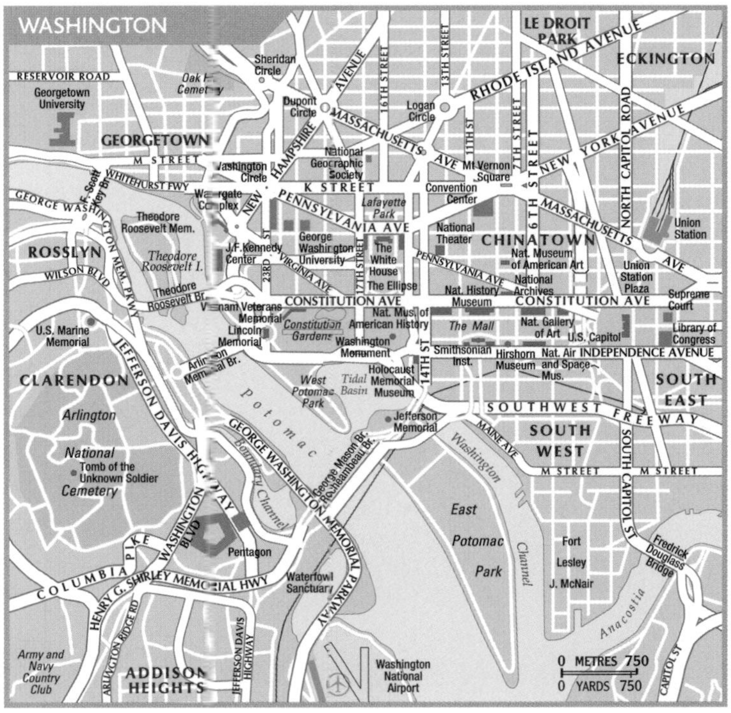

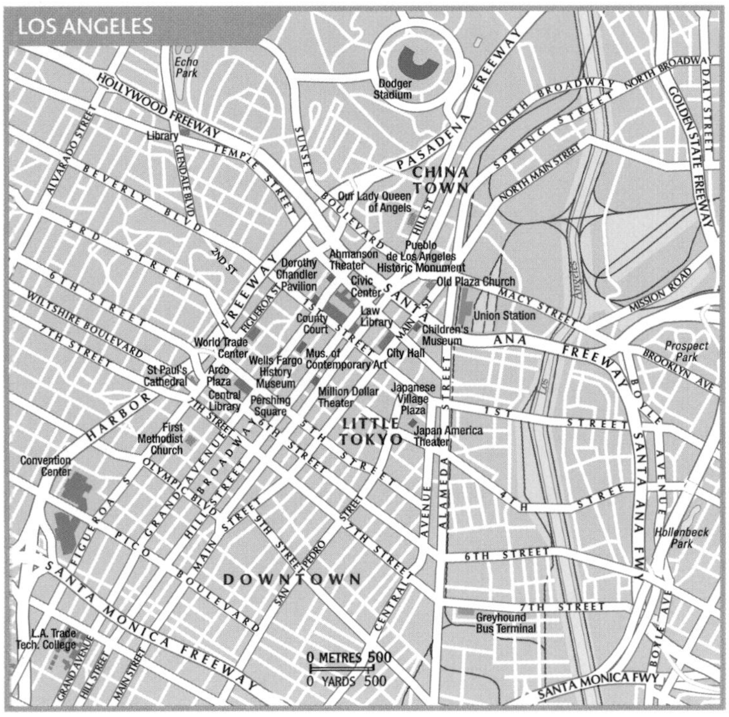

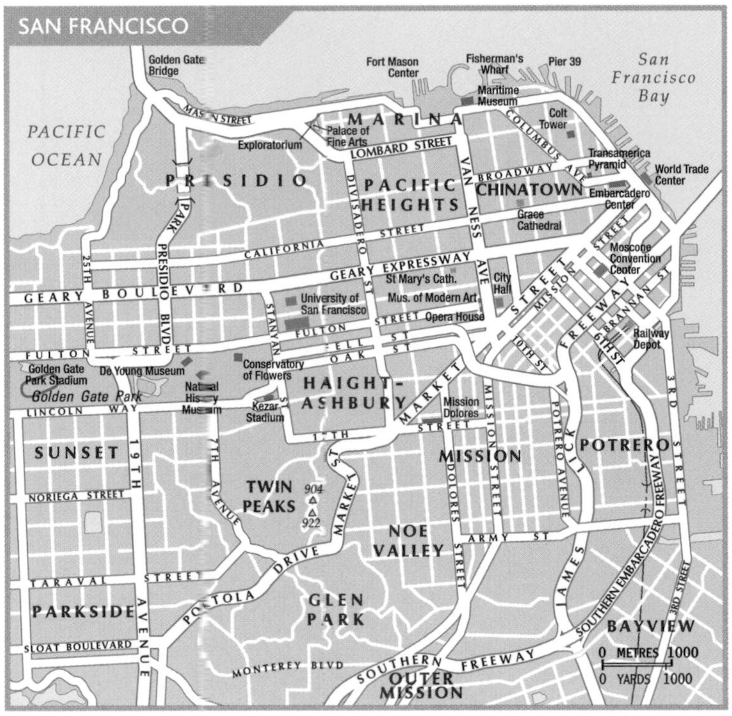

© Bartholomew Ltd

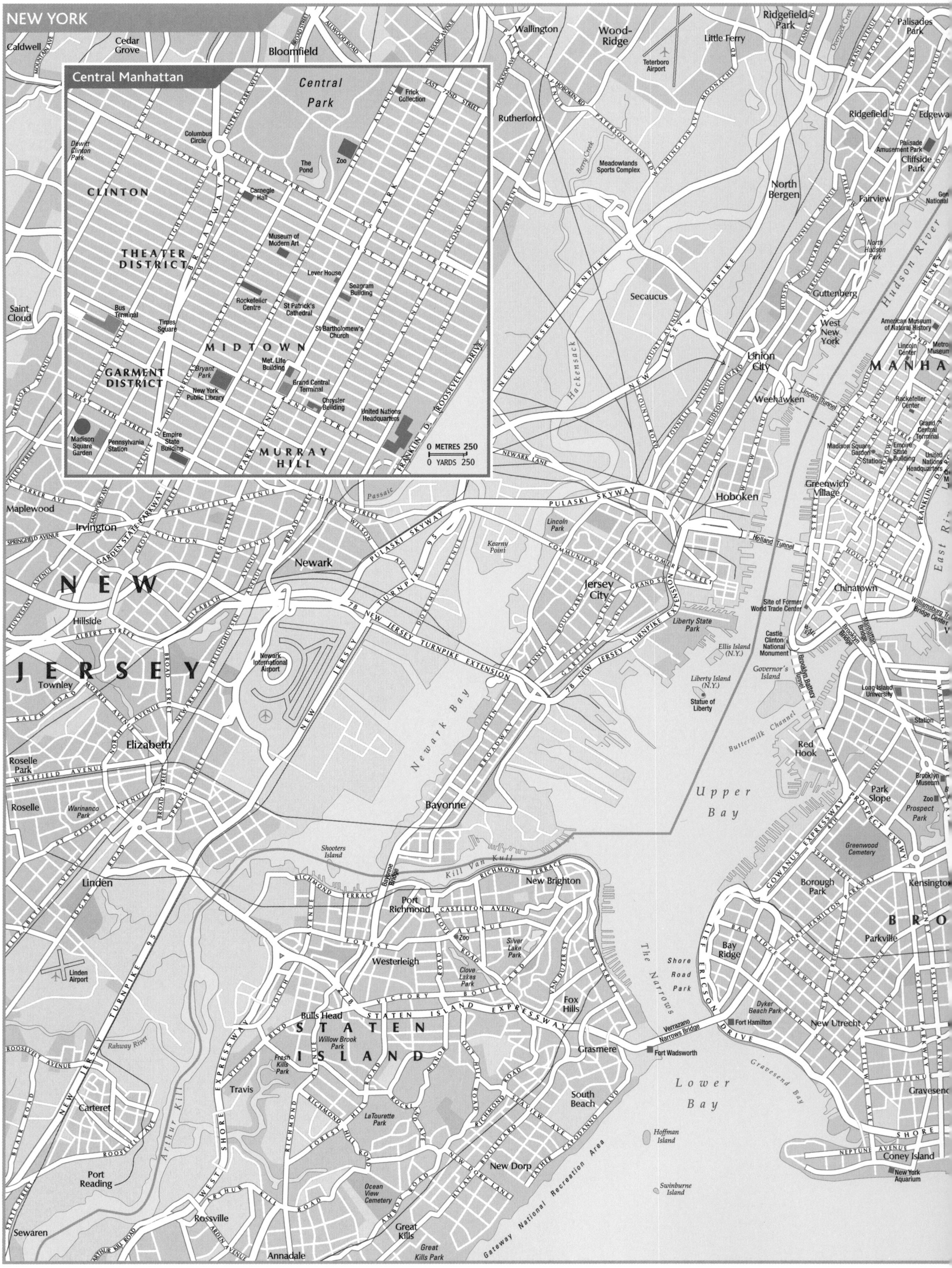

NEW YORK

Central Manhattan

Central Park

Frick Collection

Dewitt Clinton Park

Columbus Circle

CLINTON

The Pond

Zoo

Carnegie Hall

Museum of Modern Art

THEATER DISTRICT

Lever House

Seagram Building

Rockefeller Centre

St Patrick's Cathedral

St Bartholomew's Church

Saint Cloud

Bus Terminal

Times Square

MIDTOWN

Met. Life Building

GARMENT DISTRICT

Bryant Park

New York Public Library

Grand Central Terminal

Chrysler Building

United Nations Headquarters

Madison Square Garden

Pennsylvania Station

Empire State Building

MURRAY HILL

| 0 METRES | 250 |
| 0 YARDS | 250 |

Caldwell

Cedar Grove

Bloomfield

Wallington

Wood-Ridge

Little Ferry

Ridgefield Park

Palisades Park

Teterboro Airport

Rutherford

Ridgefield

Edgewater

Palisade Amusement Park

Cliffside Park

North Bergen

Fairview

North Hudson Park

Meadowlands Sports Complex

Secaucus

Guttenberg

West New York

American Museum of Natural History

Metro

Union City

Lincoln Center

MANHA

Weehawken

Lincoln Tunnel

Rockefeller Center

Grand Central Terminal

Maplewood

Passaic

PULASKI SKYWAY

Hoboken

Madison Square Garden

Empire State Building

United Nations Headquarters

Irvington

Lincoln Park

Holland Tunnel

Greenwich Village

Kearny Point

Newark

Jersey City

Chinatown

NEW

Site of Former World Trade Center

Williamsburg

Hillside

Liberty State Park

Castle Clinton National Monument

JERSEY

Newark International Airport

Ellis Island (N.Y.)

Governor's Island

Long Island University

Townley

Liberty Island (N.Y.)

Statue of Liberty

Buttermilk Channel

Station

Elizabeth

Red Hook

Roselle Park

Newark Bay

Upper Bay

Brooklyn Museum

Roselle

Warinanco Park

Park Slope

Zoo Prospect Park

Bayonne

Greenwood Cemetery

Borough Park

Kensington

Linden

Shooters Island

GOWANUS EXPRESSWAY

Bayonne Bridge

Kill Van Kull

RICHMOND TERRACE

New Brighton

Shore Road Park

Bay Ridge

BRO

Port Richmond

CASTLETON AVENUE

Parkville

Linden Airport

Zoo

Silver Lake Park

The Narrows

Fort Hamilton

New Utrecht

Westerleigh

Clove Lakes Park

Dyker Beach Park

Rahway River

STATEN ISLAND EXPRESSWAY

Fox Hills

Verrazano Narrows Bridge

Gravesend Bay

Gravesend

Bulls Head

STATEN

Willow Brook Park

Grasmere

Fort Wadsworth

Carteret

Fresh Kills Park

ISLAND

South Beach

Lower Bay

SHORE

Travis

LaTourette Park

Hoffman Island

NEPTUNE AVENUE

Coney Island

Port Reading

Ocean View Cemetery

New Dorp

Swinburne Island

New York Aquarium

Sewaren

Rossville

Annadale

Great Kills

Great Kills Park

Gateway National Recreation Area

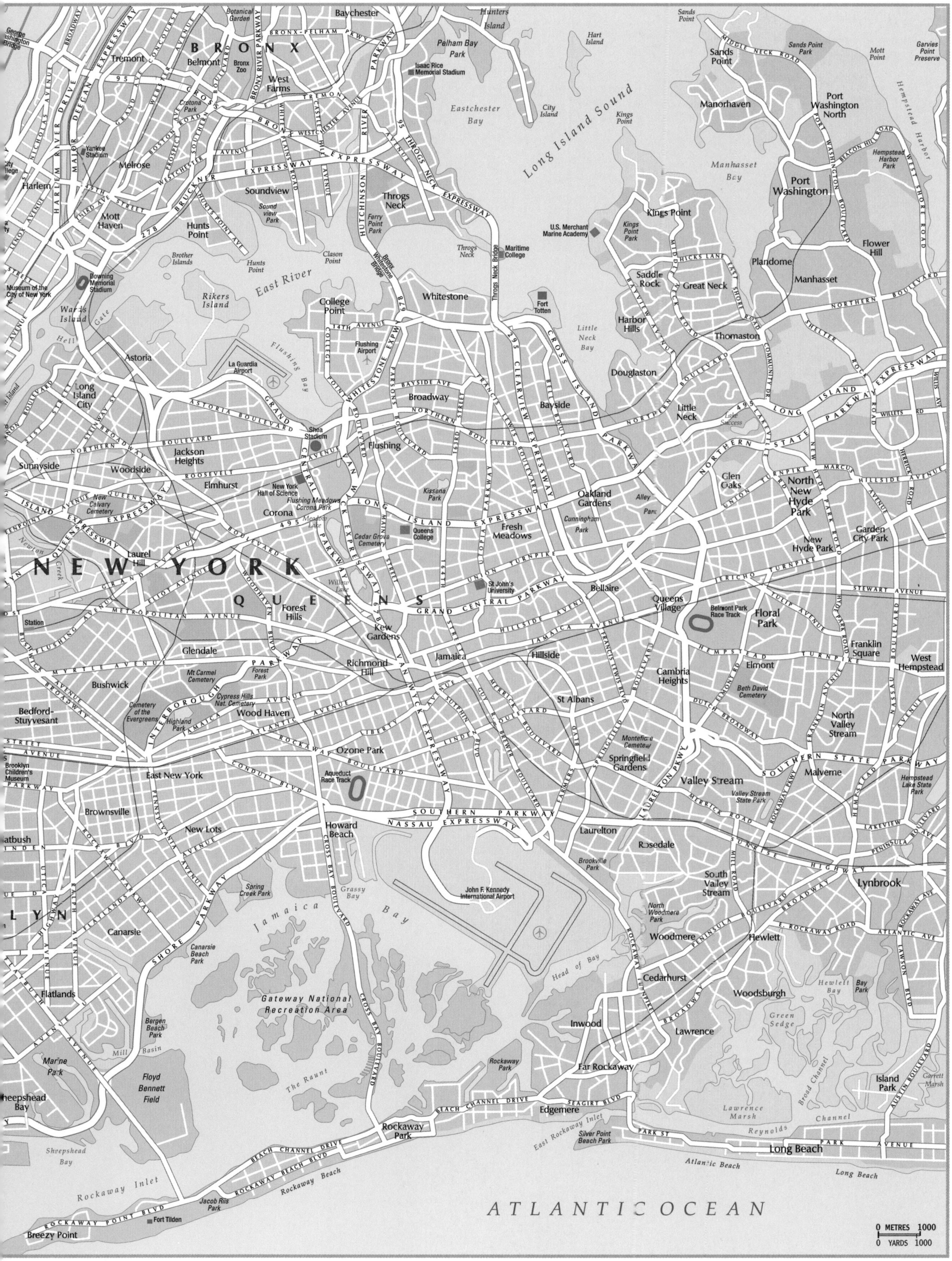
BRONX
Botanical Garden
Baychester
Hunters Island
Hart Island
Sands Point
Sands Point Park
Mott Point
Garvies Point Preserve
Tremont
Belmont
Bronx Zoo
West Farms
Pelham Bay Park
Isaac Rice Memorial Stadium
Eastchester Bay
City Island
Long Island Sound
Kings Point
Manorhaven
Port Washington North
Hempstead Harbor
Manhasset Bay
Port Washington
Hempstead Harbor Park
Yankee Stadium
Melrose
Harlem
Soundview
Soundview Park
Throgs Neck
Ferry Point Park
Mott Haven
Hunts Point
Kings Point
Kings Point Park
U.S. Merchant Marine Academy
Maritime College
Throgs Neck
Flower Hill
Plandome
Manhasset
Brother Islands
Hunts Point
Clason Point
Downing Memorial Stadium
Museum of the City of New York
East River
Rikers Island
Ward's Island
Hell Gate
College Point
Whitestone
Fort Totten
Saddle Rock
Great Neck
Harbor Hills
Thomaston
Little Neck Bay
Astoria
La Guardia Airport
Flushing Airport
Flushing Bay
Douglaston
Long Island City
Broadway
Bayside
Little Neck
Lake Success
Shea Stadium
Jackson Heights
Flushing
Sunnyside
Woodside
Elmhurst
New York Hall of Science
Flushing Meadows Corona Park
Kissena Park
Oakland Gardens
Alley Pond
Glen Oaks
North New Hyde Park
New Calvary Cemetery
Corona
Meadow Lake
Queens College
Cedar Grove Cemetery
Fresh Meadows
Cunningham Park
New Hyde Park
Garden City Park
Laurel Hill
NEW YORK
Newtown Creek
QUEENS
Willow Lake
St John's University
Bellaire
Queens Village
Belmont Park Race Track
Floral Park
Forest Hills
Kew Gardens
Station
Glendale
Jamaica
Hillside
Richmond Hill
Franklin Square
West Hempstead
Elmont
Bushwick
Mt Carmel Cemetery
Forest Park
Cambria Heights
Cypress Hills Nat. Cemetery
Cemetery of the Evergreens
Beth David Cemetery
Bedford-Stuyvesant
St Albans
Highland Park
Wood Haven
North Valley Stream
Montefiore Cemetery
Ozone Park
Springfield Gardens
Brooklyn Children's Museum
East New York
Aqueduct Race Track
Valley Stream
Malverne
Valley Stream State Park
Hempstead Lake State Park
Brownsville
Howard Beach
Laurelton
New Lots
Rosedale
Brookville Park
Lynbrook
Spring Creek Park
Grassy Bay
John F. Kennedy International Airport
South Valley Stream
North Woodmere Park
Jamaica Bay
Canarsie
Woodmere
Hewlett
Canarsie Beach Park
Head of Bay
Cedarhurst
Hewlett Bay
Bay Park
Flatlands
Gateway National Recreation Area
Woodsburgh
Green Sedge
Bergen Beach Park
Inwood
Lawrence
Mill Basin
Marine Park
Floyd Bennett Field
Rockaway Park
Far Rockaway
The Raunt
Broad Channel
Island Park
Garrett Marsh
Sheepshead Bay
Edgemere
Lawrence Marsh
Channel
Rockaway Park
Silver Point Beach Park
East Rockaway Inlet
Reynolds
Long Beach
Sheepshead Bay
Atlantic Beach
Long Beach
Rockaway Inlet
Rockaway Beach
Jacob Riis Park
ATLANTIC OCEAN
Fort Tilden
Breezy Point
CROSS BRONX EXPRESSWAY
BRUCKNER EXPRESSWAY
THROGS NECK EXPRESSWAY
HUTCHINSON RIVER PARKWAY
BRONX RIVER PARKWAY
MIDDLE NECK ROAD
NORTHERN BOULEVARD
LONG ISLAND EXPRESSWAY
GRAND CENTRAL PARKWAY
CROSS ISLAND PARKWAY
CLEARVIEW EXPRESSWAY
VAN WYCK EXPRESSWAY
NORTHERN STATE PARKWAY
JERICHO TURNPIKE
HEMPSTEAD TURNPIKE
SOUTHERN STATE PARKWAY
SOUTHERN PARKWAY
NASSAU EXPRESSWAY
ATLANTIC AVENUE
MYRTLE AVENUE
SHORE PARKWAY
CROSS BAY BOULEVARD
BEACH CHANNEL DRIVE
ROCKAWAY BEACH BLVD
ROCKAWAY POINT BLVD
PARK AVENUE
0 METRES 1000
0 YARDS 1000

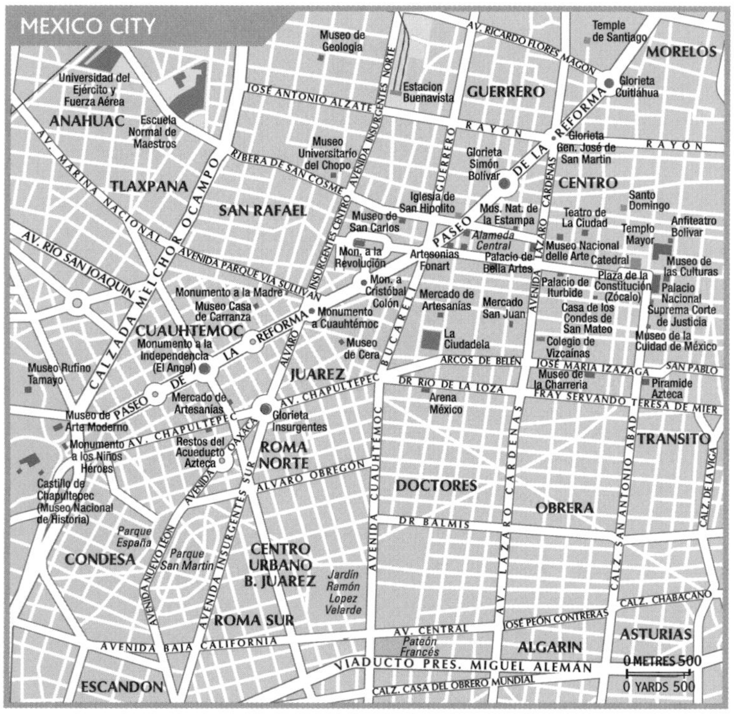

MEXICO CITY

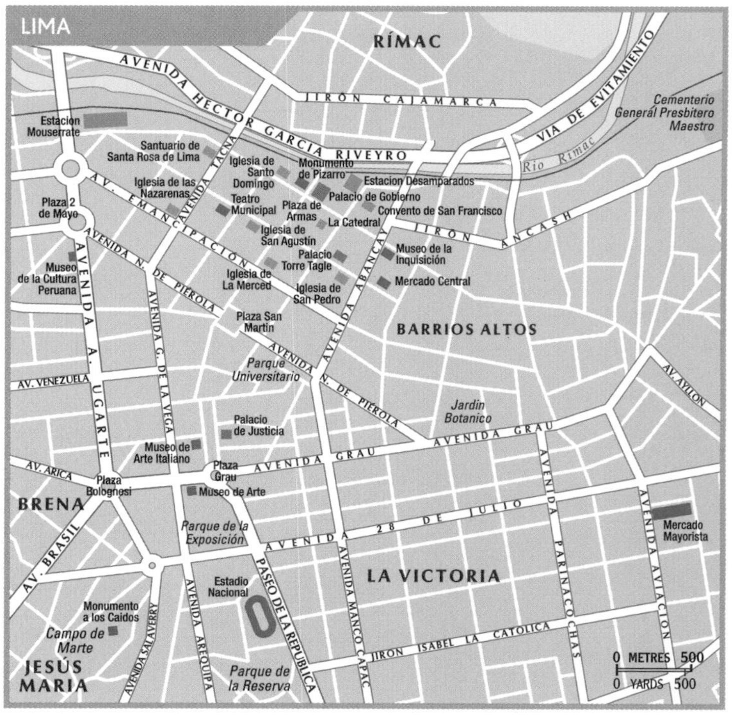

LIMA

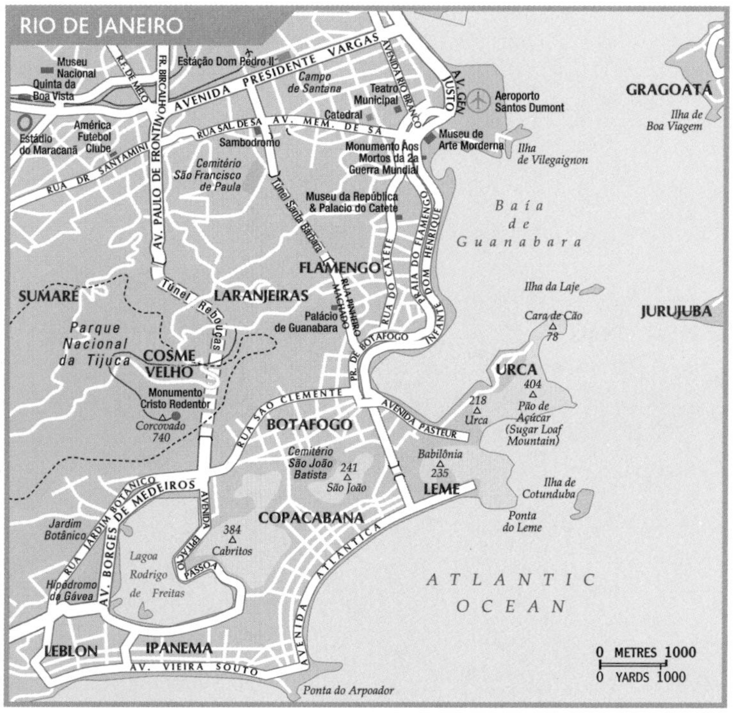

RIO DE JANEIRO

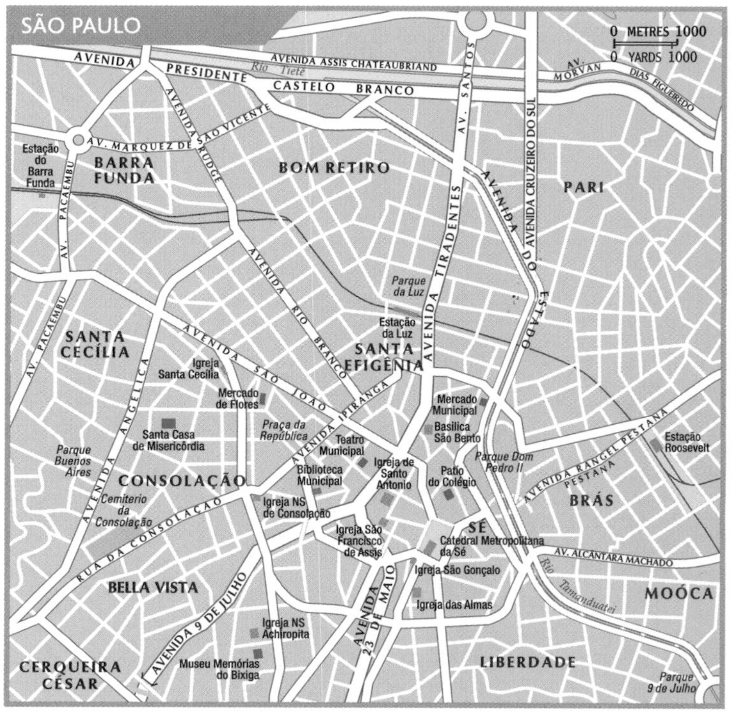

SÃO PAULO

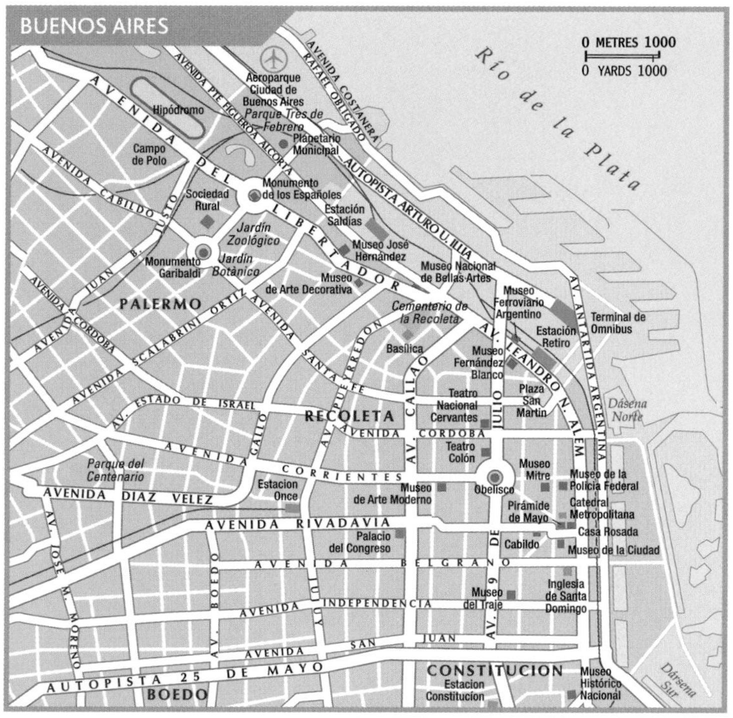

BUENOS AIRES

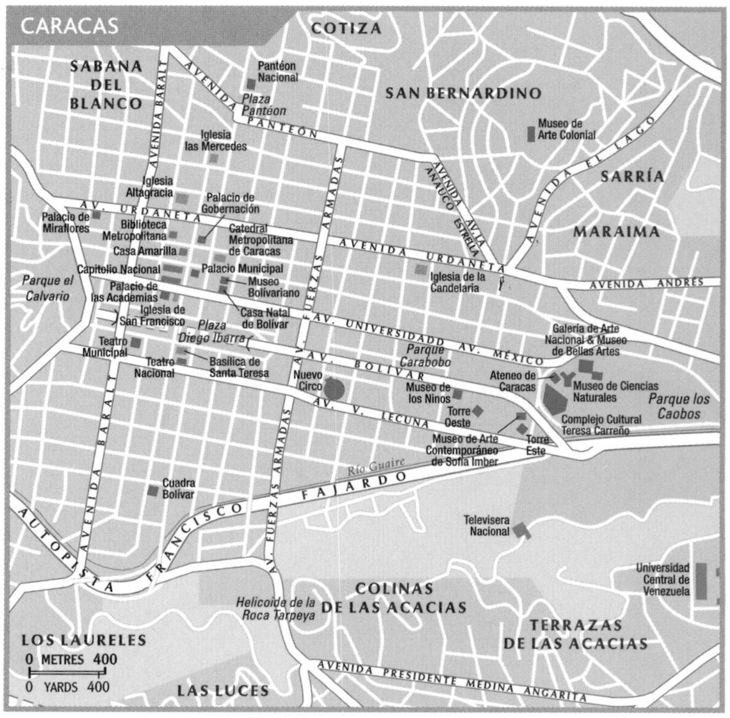

CARACAS

RELIEF

Contour intervals used in layer-colouring for land height and sea depth

Reference maps
Metres / Feet

Metres	Feet
6000	19686
5000	16404
4000	13124
3000	9843
2000	6562
1000	3281
500	1640
200	656
0	0

Land below sea level

Metres	Feet
200	656
2000	6562
4000	13124
6000	19686

1234 △ Summit Height in metres

Ocean maps
Metres / Feet

Metres	Feet
4000	13124
2000	6562
1000	3281
500	1640
200	656
0	0
200	656
2000	6562
3000	9843
4000	13124
5000	16404
6000	19686
7000	22967
9000	29529

123 · Ocean deep Depth in metres

LAND AND WATER FEATURES

— River

----- Impermanent river/Wadi

++++++ Canal

··········· Flood dyke

———— Coral reef

·········· Escarpment

— Dam/Barrage

⊐⊏ 123 Pass Height in metres

1234 ▲ Volcano Height in metres

‖ Waterfall

˅ Oasis

Lake

Salt lake/Lagoon

Dry salt lake/Salt pan

Impermanent lake

Impermanent salt lake

Marsh

Sandy desert/Dunes

Rocky desert

Lava field

Ice cap/Glacier

TRANSPORT

Motorway Shown on large-scale maps only

Main Road

Other road

----- Track

·—·—· Road tunnel

Main Railway

Other railway

→―+―← Railway tunnel

✈ Main airport

✈ Regional airport

ATLAS OF THE WORLD

CITIES AND TOWNS

Population	National Capital	Administrative Capital Shown for selected countries only	Other City or Town
over 5 million	**Beijing** ◨	**Tianjin** ⊙	**New York** ⊙
1 million to 5 million	**Seoul** ◨	**Lagos** ⊙	**Barranquilla** ⊙
500 000 to 1 million	**Bangui** ◨	**Douala** ◎	**Memphis** ◎
100 000 to 500 000	Wellington ◻	Mansa ○	Mara ○
50 000 to 100 000	Port of Spain ◻	Lubango ○	Arecibo ○
10 000 to 50 000	Malabo ◻	Chinhoyi ○	El Tigre ○
under 10 000	Roseau ◻	Ati ○	Soledad ○

STYLES OF LETTERING

Cities and towns are explained above

Country	**FRANCE**
Overseas Territory/Dependency	**Guadeloupe**
Disputed Territory	AKSAI CHIN
Administrative name Shown for selected countries only	SCOTLAND
Area name	PATAGONIA

Island	*Gran Canaria*
Lake	*Lake Erie*
Mountain	*Mont Blanc*
River	*Thames*
Region	*LAPPLAND*

BOUNDARIES

·—·—· International boundary

◂-◂-◂ Disputed international boundary/ alignment unconfirmed

····· Ceasefire line

·—·—· Administrative boundary

MISCELLANEOUS SYMBOLS

-------- National park

············ Reserve

ⁿⁿⁿⁿⁿⁿ Ancient wall

∴ Site of specific interest

Built-up area

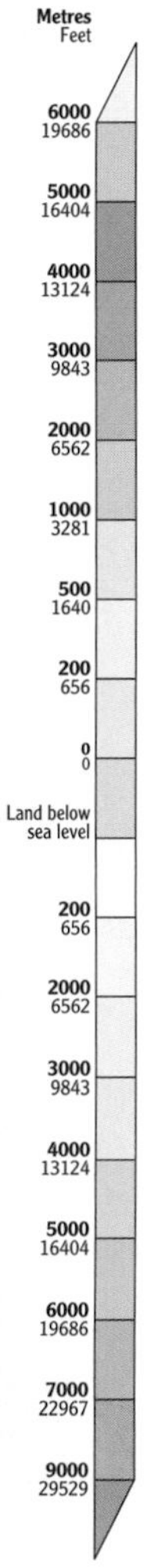

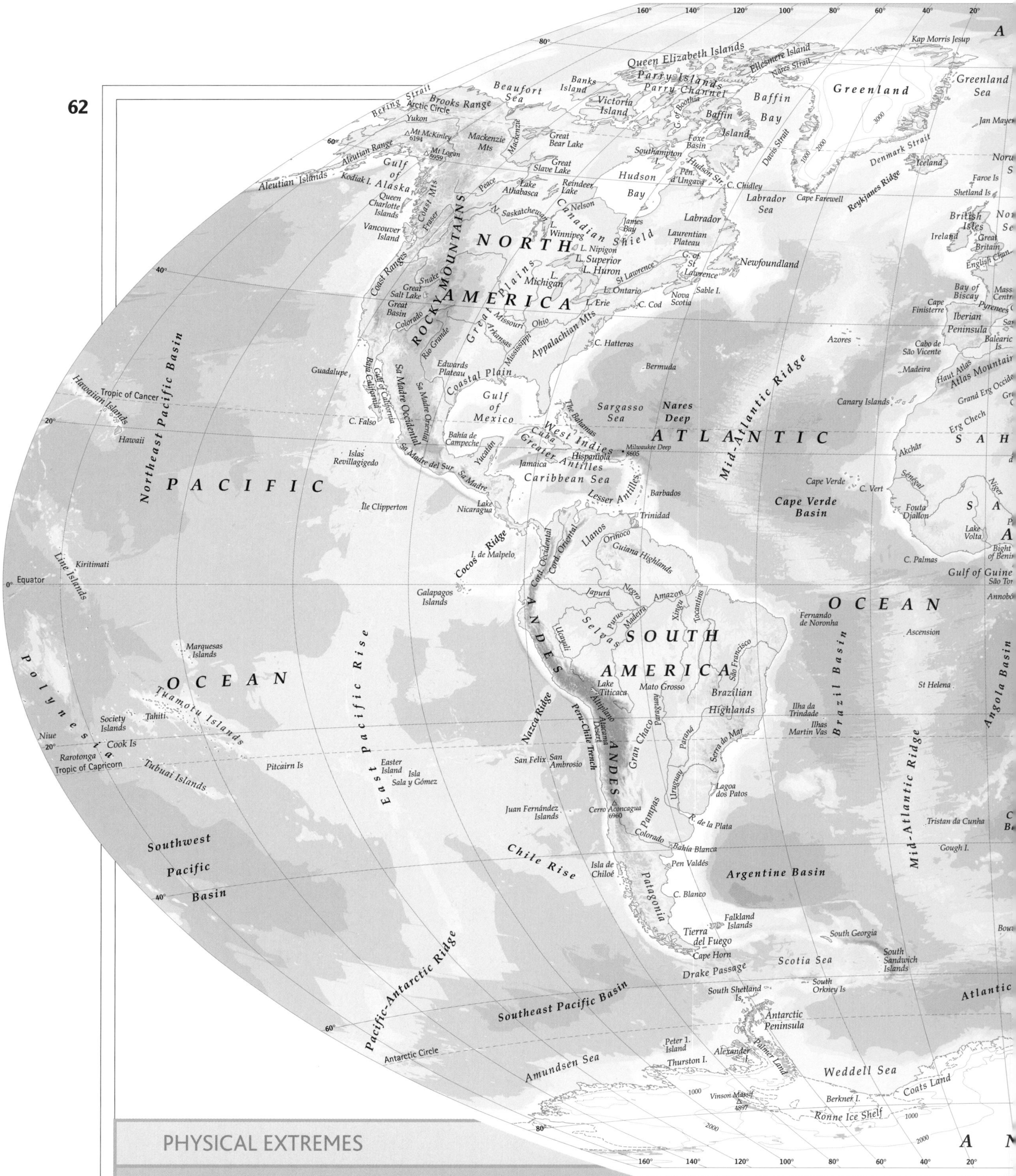

PHYSICAL EXTREMES

EARTH'S DIMENSIONS

Mass	5.974 X 10^21 tonnes	Equatorial diameter	12 756 km (7 926 miles)
Total area	509 450 000 sq km/196 672 000 sq miles	Polar diameter	12 714 km (7 900 miles)
Land area	149 450 000 sq km/57 688 000 sq miles	Equatorial circumference	40 075 km (24 903 miles)
Water area	360 000 000 sq km/138 984 000 sq miles	Meridional circumference	40 008 km (24 861 miles)
Volume	1 083 207 X 10^6 cu km/259 875 X 10^6 cu miles		

HIGHEST MOUNTAINS

	Location	Height metres	feet
Mt Everest	China/Nepal	8 848	29 028
K2	China/Jammu and Kashmir	8 611	28 251
Kangchenjunga	India/Nepal	8 586	28 169
Lhotse	China/Nepal	8 516	27 939
Makalu	China/Nepal	8 463	27 765
Cho Oyu	China/Nepal	8 201	26 906
Dhaulagiri	Nepal	8 167	26 794
Manaslu	Nepal	8 163	26 781
Nanga Parbat	Jammu and Kashmir	8 126	26 660
Annapurna I	Nepal	8 091	26 545

LONGEST RIVERS

	Location	Length km	miles
Nile	Africa	6 695	4 160
Amazon	South America	6 516	4 049
Yangtze	Asia	6 380	3 964
Mississippi-Missouri	North America	5 969	3 709
Ob'-Irtysh	Asia	5 568	3 459
Yenisey-Angara-Selenga	Asia	5 550	3 448
Yellow	Asia	5 464	3 395
Congo	Africa	4 667	2 900
Río de la Plata-Paraná	South America	4 500	2 796
Irtysh	Asia	4 440	2 759

LARGEST ISLANDS

	Location	Area sq km	sq miles
Greenland	North America	2 175 600	840 004
New Guinea	Oceania	808 510	312 167
Borneo	Asia	745 561	287 863
Madagascar	Africa	587 040	266 657
Baffin Island	North America	507 451	195 927
Sumatra	Asia	473 606	182 860
Honshū	Asia	227 414	87 805
Great Britain	Europe	218 476	84 354
Victoria Island	North America	217 291	83 897
Ellesmere Island	North America	196 236	75 767

LARGEST LAKES

	Location
Caspian Sea	Asia/Europe
Lake Superior	North America
Lake Victoria	Africa
Lake Huron	North America
Lake Michigan	North America
Aral Sea	Asia
Lake Tanganyika	Africa
Great Bear Lake	North America
Lake Baikal	Asia
Lake Nyasa	Africa

Metres / Feet

6000 / 19686
5000 / 16404
4000 / 13124
3000 / 9843
2000 / 6562
1000 / 3281
500 / 1640
200 / 656
0 / 0

Land below sea level

200 / 656
2000 / 6562
3000 / 9843
4000 / 13124
5000 / 16404
6000 / 19686
7000 / 22967
9000 / 29529

1:80 000 000

OCEANS AND SEAS

OCEAN DEEPS

Milwaukee Deep, Atlantic Ocean	8 605 metres/28 231 feet
Java Trench, Indian Ocean	7 125 metres/23 376 feet
Challenger Deep, Pacific Ocean	10 920 metres/35 826 feet
Mean ocean depth	3 554 metres/11 660 feet

Area	
sq km	sq miles
371 000	143 243
82 100	31 698
68 800	26 563
59 600	23 011
57 800	22 316
33 640	12 988
32 900	12 702
31 328	12 095
30 500	11 776
30 044	11 600

ATLANTIC OCEAN

	Area		Maximum depth	
	sq km	sq miles	metres	feet
Atlantic Ocean	86 557 000	33 420 000	8 605	28 231
Arctic Ocean	9 485 000	3 662 000	5 450	17 880
Caribbean Sea	2 512 000	970 000	7 680	25 196
Mediterranean Sea	2 510 000	969 000	5 121	16 800
Gulf of Mexico	1 544 000	596 000	3 504	11 495
Hudson Bay	1 233 000	476 000	259	849
North Sea	575 000	222 000	661	2 168
Black Sea	508 000	196 000	2 245	7 365
Baltic Sea	382 000	147 000	460	1 509

INDIAN OCEAN

	Area		Maximum depth	
	sq km	sq miles	metres	feet
Indian Ocean	73 427 000	28 350 000	7 125	23 376
Bay of Bengal	2 172 000	839 000	4 500	14 763
Red Sea	453 000	175 000	3 040	9 973
The Gulf	238 000	92 000	73	239

PACIFIC OCEAN

	Area		Maximum depth	
	sq km	sq miles	metres	feet
Pacific Ocean	166 241 000	64 186 000	10 920	35 826
South China Sea	2 590 000	1 000 000	5 514	18 090
Bering Sea	2 261 000	873 000	4 150	13 615
Sea of Okhotsk	1 392 000	537 000	3 363	11 033
East China Sea and Yellow Sea	1 202 000	464 000	2 717	8 913
Sea of Japan	1 013 000	391 000	3 743	12 280

© Bartholomew Ltd

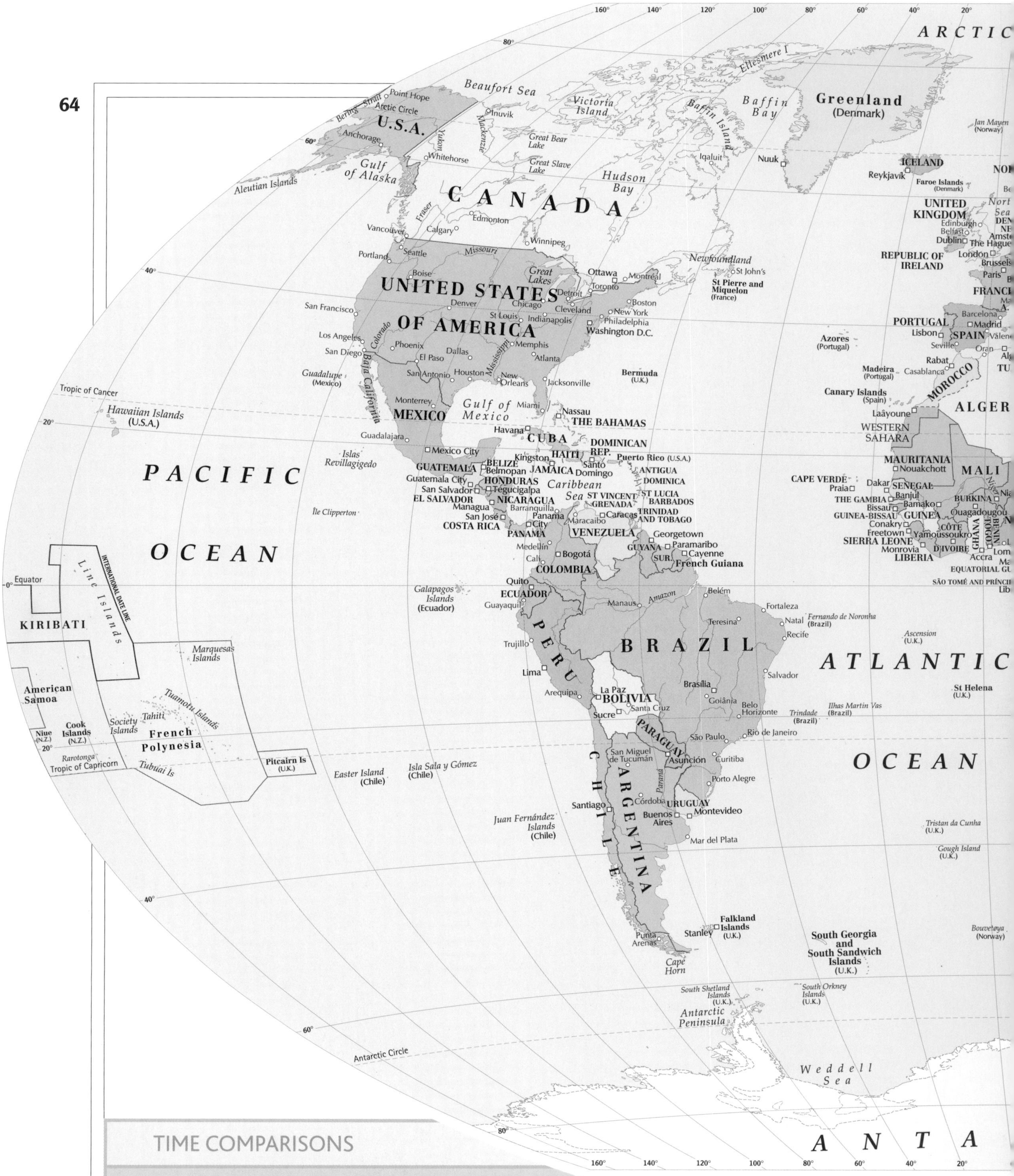

TIME COMPARISONS

Time varies around the world due to the earth's rotation causing different parts of the world to be in light or darkness at any one time. To account for this, the world is divided into twenty-four Standard Time Zones based on 15° intervals of longitude.

The table below gives examples of times observed at different parts of the world when it is 12 noon in the zone at the Greenwich Meridian (0° longitude). Daylight Saving Time, normally one hour ahead of local Standard Time, observed by certain countries for parts of the year, is not considered.

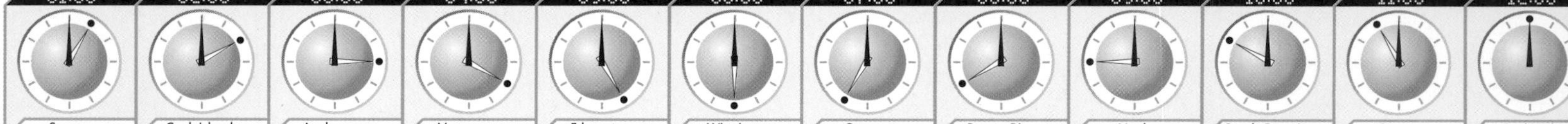

01:00	02:00	03:00	04:00	05:00	06:00	07:00	08:00	09:00	10:00	11:00	12:00
Samoa American Samoa	Cook Islands Hawaiian Islands Society Islands Tahiti	Anchorage	Vancouver Seattle San Francisco Los Angeles Pitcairn Islands	Edmonton Denver	Winnipeg Chicago Dallas Houston Monterrey Mexico City San Salvador San José Easter Island	Ottawa Toronto New York Philadelphia Washington D.C. Havana Bogotá Quito Lima	Puerto Rico Caracas Manaus La Paz Sucre Asunción	Nuuk Recife Brasília Rio de Janeiro São Paulo Montevideo Buenos Aires	South Georgia and South Sandwich Islands	Azores Cape Verde	Reykjavik Dublin London Rabat Nouakchott Dakar Freetown Accra Lomé

Winkel Tripel Projection

1:80 000 000

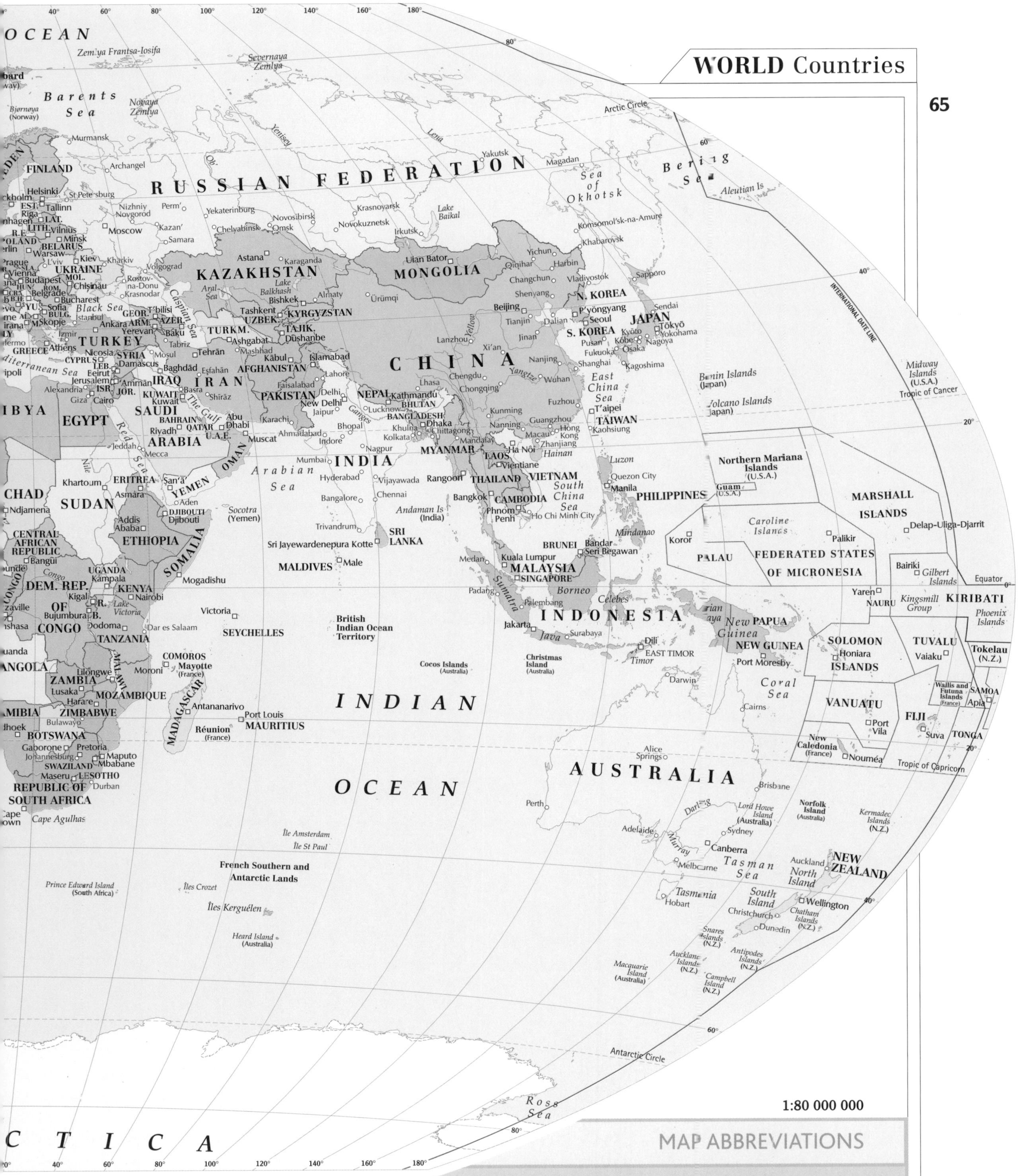

MAP ABBREVIATIONS

A.	ANDORRA	B.	BURUNDI	CR.	CROATIA	ISR.	ISRAEL	M.	MACEDONIA	SL.	SLOVENIA	TURKM.	TURKMENISTAN

A. ANDORRA
AL. ALBANIA
ARM. ARMENIA
AUST. AUSTRIA
AZER. AZERBAIJAN

B. BURUNDI
BEL. BELGIUM
B.H. BOSNIA-HERZEGOVINA
BULG. BULGARIA

CR. CROATIA
CZ.R. CZECH REPUBLIC
EST. ESTONIA
GEOR. GEORGIA
HUN. HUNGARY

ISR. ISRAEL
JOR. JORDAN
L. LUXEMBOURG
LAT. LATVIA
LEB. LEBANON
LITH. LITHUANIA

M. MACEDONIA
MOL. MOLDOVA
NETH. NETHERLANDS
R. RWANDA
R.F. RUSSIAN FEDERATION
ROM. ROMANIA

SL. SLOVENIA
SLA. SLOVAKIA
SUR. SURINAME
SW. SWITZERLAND
TAJIK. TAJIKISTAN

TURKM. TURKMENISTAN
U.A.E. UNITED ARAB EMIRATES
U.S.A. UNITED STATES OF AMERICA
UZBEK. UZBEKISTAN
YU. YUGOSLAVIA

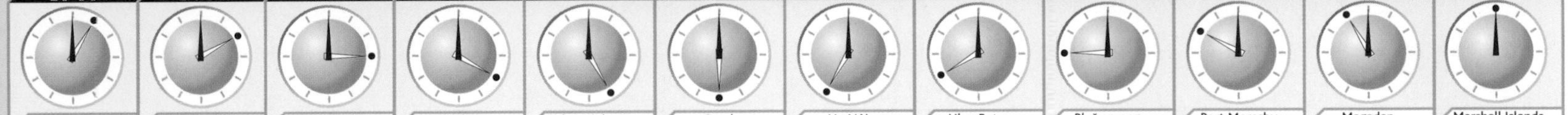

13:00	14:00	15:00	16:00	17:00	18:00	19:00	20:00	21:00	22:00	23:00	00:00
Oslo Berlin Paris Madrid Rome Algiers Abuja Kinshasa Luanda	Helsinki Kiev Ankara Jerusalem Cairo Kigali Harare Pretoria Cape Town	St Petersburg Moscow Baghdād Qatar Riyadh Addis Ababa Mogadishu Dodoma Antananarivo	T'bilisi Yerevan Baku Abu Dhabi Muscat Seychelles Mauritius	Yekaterinburg Ashgabat Bishkek Tashkent Islamabad Karachi	Omsk Almaty Bhutan Dhaka	Ha Nôi Vientiane Bangkok Phnom Penh Ho Chi Minh City Jakarta	Ulan Bator Beijing T'ai-pei Hong Kong Manila Kuala Lumpur Singapore Perth	P'yŏngyang Seoul Tōkyō Ōsaka Palau	Port Moresby Brisbane Sydney Canberra Melbourne	Magadan Solomon Islands Vanuatu New Caledonia	Marshall Islands Tuvalu Fiji Auckland Wellington

© Bartholomew Ltd

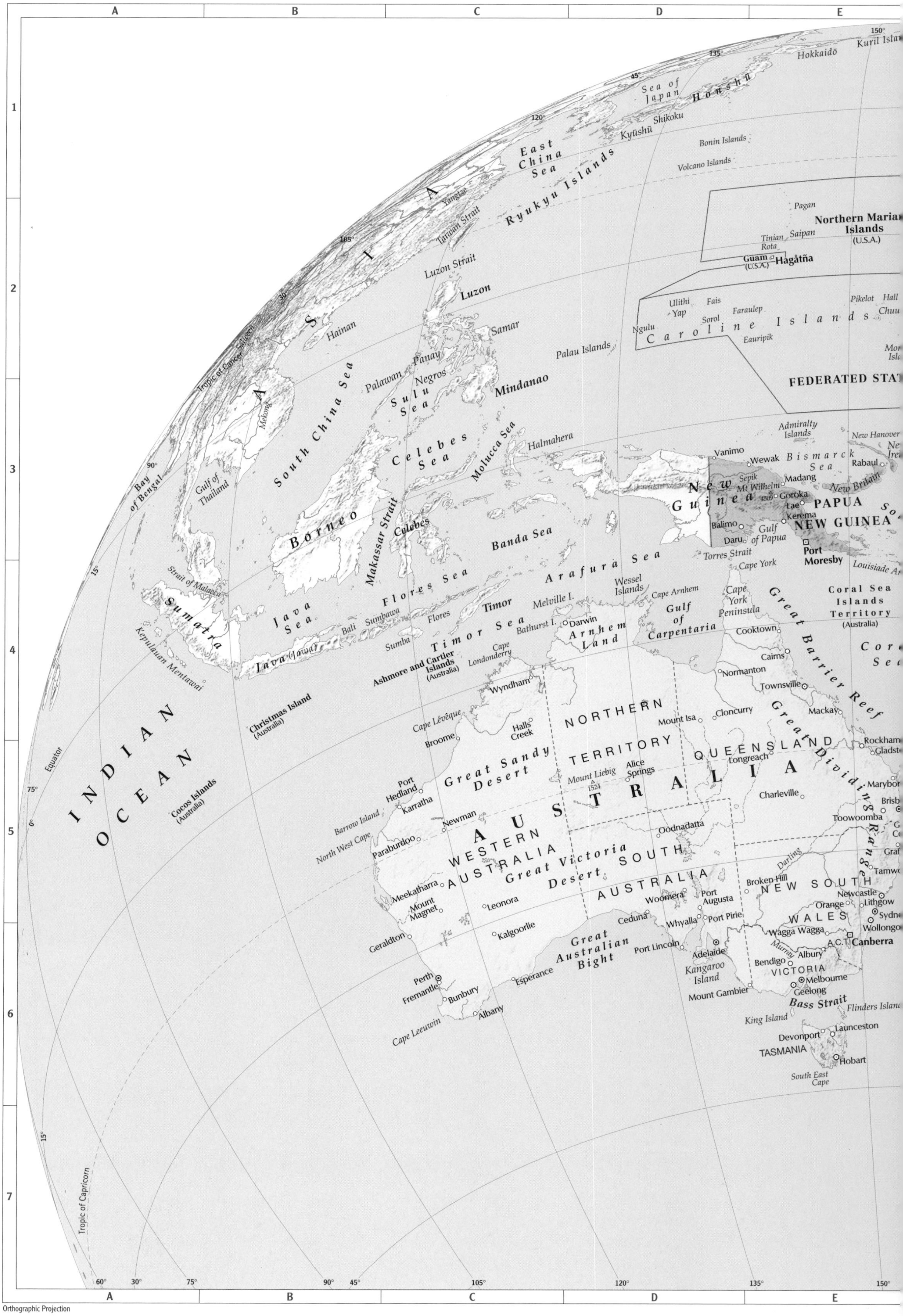

A | B | C | D | E

ASIA

Hokkaidō

Kuril Islam

Sea of Japan

Honshū

East China Sea

Shikoku

Kyūshū

Bonin Islands

Ryukyu Islands

Volcano Islands

Pagan

Northern Marian Islands (U.S.A.)

Tinian
Rota
Saipan

Guam (U.S.A.) Hagåtña

Luzon Strait

Taiwan Strait

Yangtze

Luzon

Hainan

Samar

Ulithi Fais
Yap Sorol Faraulep
Ngulu Eauripik

Pikelot Hall
Chuu

Caroline Islands

Mor
Isla

Tropic at Cancer

Mekong

Palawan Panay

Negros

Sulu Sea

Mindanao

Palau Islands

FEDERATED STAT

South China Sea

Gulf of Thailand

Celebes Sea

Molucca Sea

Halmahera

Admiralty Islands

New Hanover

New Ire

Bay of Bengal

Vanimo Wewak

Bismarck Sea

Rabaul

New Britai

Borneo

Makassar Strait

Celebes

Banda Sea

New Guinea

Sepik
Mt Wilhelm
Goroka
Lae
Kerema

Madang

PAPUA

NEW GUINEA

Strait of Malacca

Java Sea

Flores Sea

Arafura Sea

Balimo
Daru Gulf of Papua

Port Moresby

So

Louisiade Ar

Sumatra

Bali Sumbawa

Flores

Timor

Timor Sea

Wessel Islands

Cape Arnhem

Cape York Peninsula

Coral Sea Islands Territory (Australia)

Cor
Se

Kepulauan Mentawai

Java (Jawa)

Sumba

Cape Londonderry

Melville I.
Bathurst I. Darwin

Arnhem Land

Gulf of Carpentaria

Cooktown

Great Barrier Reef

Ashmore and Cartier Islands (Australia)

Wyndham

Cairns

Normanton

Townsville

Mackay

Christmas Island (Australia)

Cape Lévêque

Broome

Halls Creek

NORTHERN

TERRITORY

Mount Isa

Cloncurry

QUEENSLAND

Longreach

Great Dividing Range

Rockham
Gladst

INDIAN

OCEAN

Equator

Cocos Islands (Australia)

Port Hedland

Karratha

Newman

Great Sandy Desert

Mount Liebig
1524 Alice Springs

Charleville

Maryboro

Brisb

Barrow Island
North West Cape
Paraburdoo

AUSTRALIA

WESTERN AUSTRALIA

Great Victoria Desert

SOUTH

Oodnadatta

Toowoomba

C

Darling

Graf

Tamwo

Meekatharra

Mount Magnet

Leonora

AUSTRALIA

Woomera

Port Augusta

Broken Hill

NEW SOUTH

Newcastle

Lithgow

Orange
Wagga Wagga

Sydne

Wollongo

Geraldton

Kalgoorlie

Great Australian Bight

Ceduna

Whyalla Port Pirie

Port Lincoln

Adelaide

A.C.T. Canberra

WALES

Kangaroo Island

Murray Albury

Bendigo

VICTORIA

Melbourne

Perth

Fremantle

Bunbury

Albany

Geelong

Mount Gambier

Bass Strait

Flinders Islan

Cape Leeuwin

King Island

Devonport

Launceston

TASMANIA

Hobart

Tropic of Capricorn

South East Cape

A | B | C | D | E

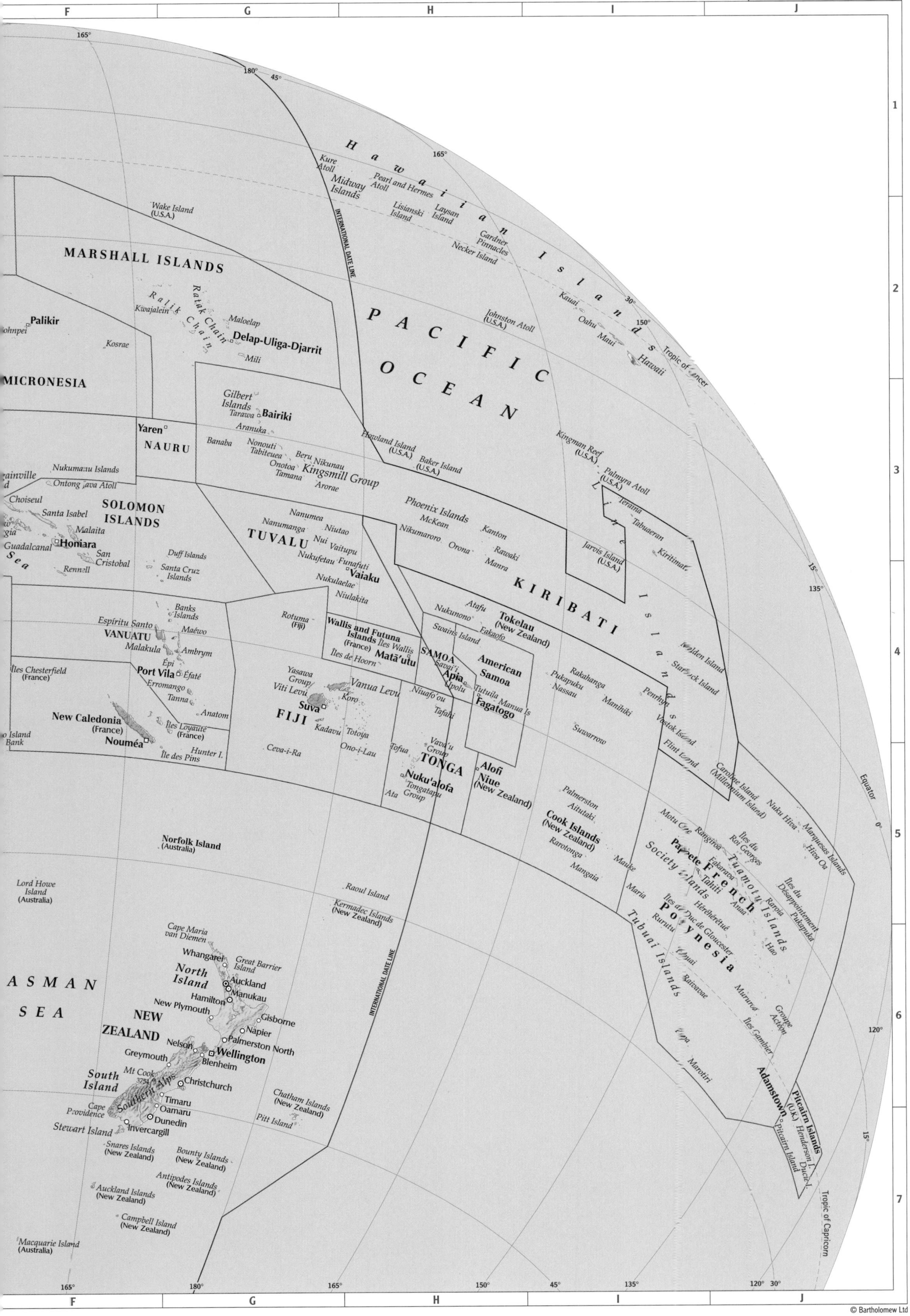

F G H I J

165° 180° 45° 165°

Ha wai ia n Is la n d s

Kure Atoll
Pearl and Hermes Atoll
Midway Islands
Lisianski Island
Laysan Island
Gardner Pinnacles
Necker Island

INTERNATIONAL DATE LINE

Wake Island (U.S.A.)

MARSHALL ISLANDS

Ralik Chain
Ratak Chain
Kwajalein
Maloelap
Delap-Uliga-Djarrit
Mili

Palikir
Pohnpei
Kosrae

MICRONESIA

Yaren°
NAURU

Gilbert Islands
Tarawa **Bairiki**
Aranuka
Banaba
Nonouti
Tabiteuea
Beru Nikunau
Onotoa
Tamana
Arorae
Kingsmill Group

PACIFIC OCEAN

Johnston Atoll (U.S.A.)

Kauai
Oahu
Maui
Hawaii
30°
150°
Tropic of Cancer

Kingman Reef (U.S.A.)
Palmyra Atoll (U.S.A.)
Teraina
Tabuaeran
Kiritimati

Howland Island (U.S.A.)
Baker Island (U.S.A.)

Phoenix Islands
McKean
Kanton
Nikumaroro
Orona
Manra
Rawaki

Jarvis Island (U.S.A.)

L i n e   I s l a n d s

15°
135°

KIRIBATI

Nukuma:u Islands
ainville
d
Ontong Java Atoll
Choiseul
Santa Isabel
San Cristobal
Rennell
Malaita
Guadalcanal
Homara
gia

SOLOMON ISLANDS

Sea

Duff Islands
Santa Cruz Islands

Nanumea
Nanumanga
Niutao
Nui
Vaitupu
Nukufetau
Funafuti
Vaiaku
Nukulaelae
Niulakita

TUVALU

Banks Islands
Espíritu Santo
VANUATU
Maéwo
Malakula
Ambrym
Epi
Efaté
Port Vila
Erromango
Tanna
Anatom

Rotuma (Fiji)

Wallis and Futuna Islands (France)
Îles Wallis
Mata'utu
Îles de Hoorn

Nukunono
Tokelau (New Zealand)
Swains Island
Fakaofo
Atafu

SAMOA
Savai'i
Apia
Upolu

American Samoa
Tutuila Manua Is.
Fagatogo

Rakahanga
Manihiki
Pukapuka
Nassau

Penrhyn
Starbuck Island

Suwarrow

Vostok Island

Flint Island

Îles Chesterfield (France)

o Island Bank

New Caledonia (France)
Nouméa
Îles Loyauté (France)
Hunter I.
Île des Pins

Yasawa Group
Viti Levu
Vanua Levu
Koro
Kadavu
Ono-i-Lau
Totoya
Suva
FIJI
Ceva-i-Ra

Niuafo'ou
Tafahi
Vava'u Group
Tofua
Nuku'alofa
Tongatapu Group
Ata
TONGA

Alofi
Niue (New Zealand)

Palmerston
Aitutaki
Cook Islands (New Zealand)
Rarotonga
Mangaia
Manke
Maria

Caroline Island (Millennium Island)
Nuku Hiva
Marquesas Islands
Hiva Oa
Îles du
Roti Georges
Îles du Désappointement
Rangiroa
Fakarava
Papeete
Tahiti
Hao
Motu One
Mehetia
Îles du Duc de Gloucester
Society Islands
French Polynesia
Rurutu
Tubuai
Raivavae
Tupai
Îles Gambier
Tuamotu Islands
Groupe Actéon
Mangareva
Îles Gambier
Marutea
Marotiri
Adamstown
Pitcairn Islands (U.K.) Henderson I. Ducie I.
Pitcairn Island

Equator 0°

120°

15°

Norfolk Island (Australia)

Lord Howe Island (Australia)

Raoul Island
Kermadec Islands (New Zealand)

INTERNATIONAL DATE LINE

Cape Maria van Diemen
Whangarei
Great Barrier Island
North Island
Auckland
Manukau
Hamilton
New Plymouth
Gisborne
Napier
NEW ZEALAND
Nelson
Greymouth
Wellington
Blenheim
Palmerston North

TASMAN SEA

Mt Cook 3754
Southern Alps
South Island
Cape Providence
Timaru
Oamaru
Dunedin
Invercargill
Christchurch

Chatham Islands (New Zealand)
Pitt Island

Stewart Island
Snares Islands (New Zealand)
Bounty Islands (New Zealand)
Auckland Islands (New Zealand)
Antipodes Islands (New Zealand)
Campbell Island (New Zealand)

Macquarie Island (Australia)

165° 180° 165° 150° 45° 135° 120° 30°

Tropic of Capricorn

Miles Km
1200 2000
1600
800 1200
800
400 400
0 0

1:32 000 000

© Bartholomew Ltd

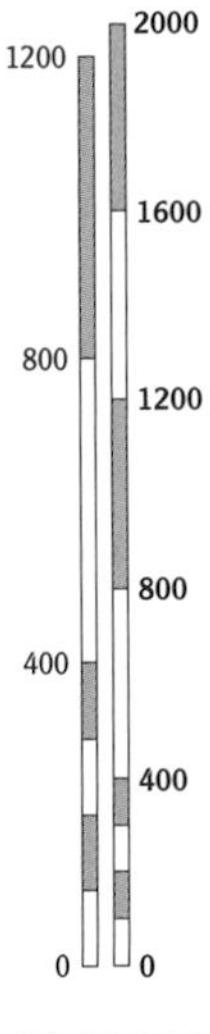

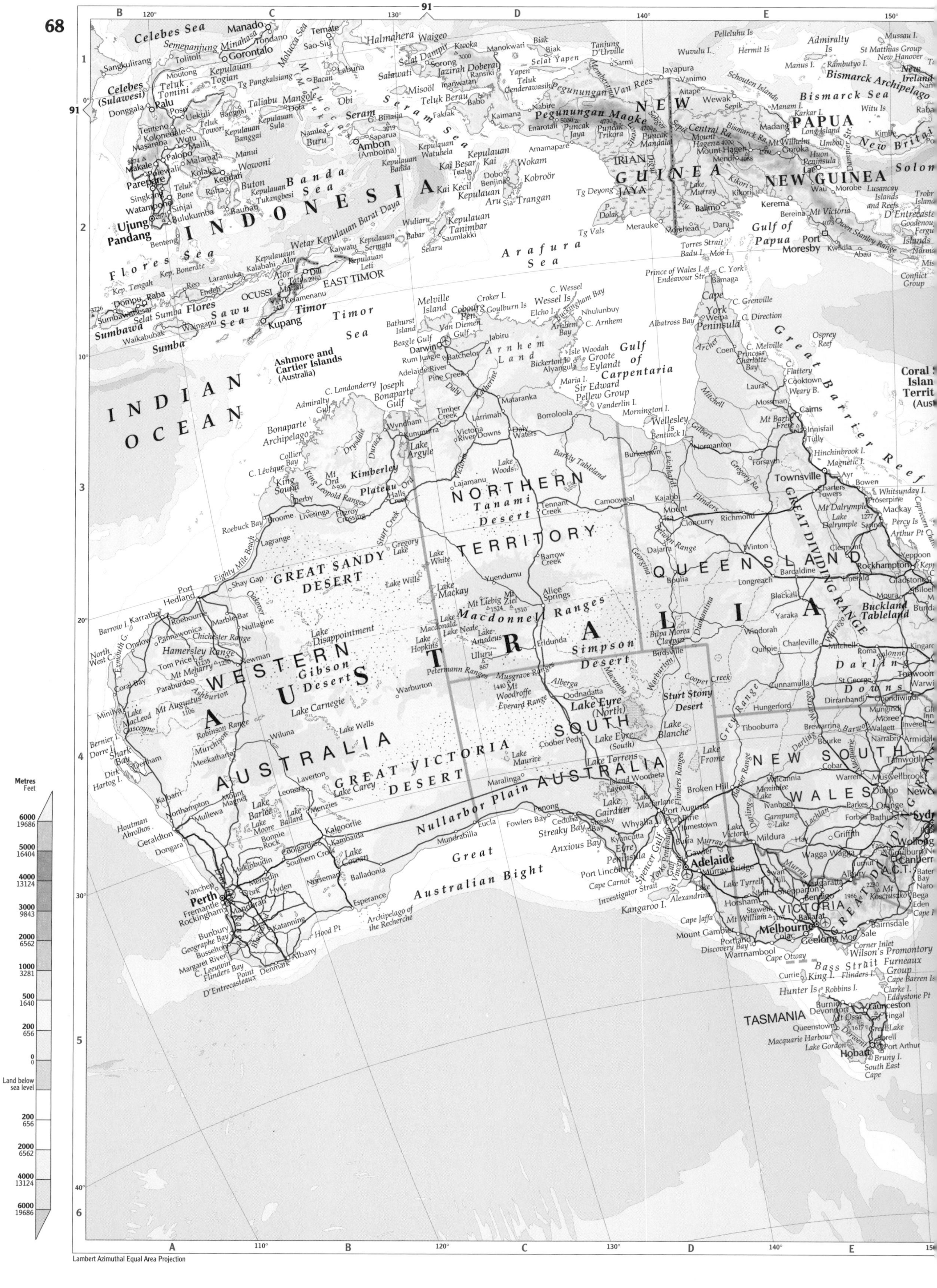

91

B 120° C 130° 91 D 140° E 150°

1

Celebes Sea Manado Ternate Halmahera Waigeo Pelleluhu Is Admiralty Is Mussau I.
Semenanjung Minahasa Tondano Sao-Siu Kwoka Manokwari Biak Tanjung D'Urville Wuvulu I. Hermit Is St Matthias Group New Hanover
Sangkulirang Tolitoli Molucca Sea Selat Dampir Sorong Yapen Teluk Cenderawasih Sarmi Jayapura Vanimo Schouten Islands Manus I. Rambutyo I. Bismarck Archipelago
Moutong Togian Tg Pangkalsiang Bacan Labuna Iazirah Doberai Ranski Pegunungan Van Rees Wewak Karkar I. Witu Is Long Island New

91 0°

Celebes Donggala Poso Obi Misool Teluk Berau Babo Kaimana Enarotali Puncak Trikora Mount Hagen 4000 Huon Peninsula New Britain
(Sulawesi) Uekuli Banggai Kepulauan Sula Seram Sea Fakfak Jaya Puncak Mandala Mendi Mt Wilhelm Coroka Solon
Tenteng Kolonedale Wotu Salili Tovori Banggai Seram Bintija NEW Mt Hagen 4050 Morobe Lusancay
Masamba Palopo Kolaka Wowoni Namlea Buru Saparua Amamapare GUINEA Wau Islands and Reefs
Makale Palevu Kendari Manui Ambon Kepulauan Kai Besar Wokam IRIAN Kerema Mt Victoria D'Entrecaste
Parepare Teluk Bone Raha Buton (Amboina) Banda Kai Kecil Benjini JAYA Kikori Goodenou
Singkang Sinjai Bulukumba Kepulauan Banda Sea Kepulauan Kai Dobo Aru Sia-Trangan Lake Murray Daru Gulf of Fergu
Ujung Pandang Watampone Tukangbesi Wuliaru Tanimbar Tg Deyong Dolak Morehead Papua Port Islands
Benteng Flores Sea Selat Babar Saumlakki Tg Vals Merauke Torres Strait Moresby Norma

2

Flores Sea Kep. Bonerate Wetar Kepulauan Sermata Leti Seru Arafura Sea Prince of Wales I. C. York Cape C. Grenville Conflict Group
Kep. Tengah Raba Kalabahi Alor Kepulauan Saumlakki Endeavour Str Badu I. Moa I. York Weipa C. Direction
Dompu Larantuka Dili Kefamenanu Melville Croker I. C. Wessel Wessel Is Bamaga Peninsula Albatross Bay Laura Osprey Reef
Sumbawa Selat Sumba Flores Kupang Timor Kalabahi Island Cobourg Pen. Goulburn Is Elcho I. Buckingham Bay Nhulunbuy C. Melville Princess Charlotte Bay Great Barrier Reef
Waikabubak Sawu Sea OCUSSI EAST TIMOR Bathurst Van Diemen Arnhem C. Arnhem Weary B. Cooktown Coral
Sumba Waingapu Timor Sea Island Beagle Gulf Darwin Land Isle Woodah Gulf of Mossman Island
Waikabubak Kupang Ashmore and Cartier Islands Rum Jungle Batchelor Jabiru Groote Eylandt Carpentaria Cairns Territory
(Australia) Adelaide River Pine Creek Maria I. Sir Edward Pellew Group Innisfail (Aus
INDIAN C. Londonderry Joseph Bonaparte Gulf Daly Katherine Larrimah Borroloola Vanderlin I. Mornington I. Mt Bartle Frere Tully
OCEAN Admiralty Gulf Wyndham Kununurra Timber Creek Mataranka Wellesley Is Bentinck I. Hinchinbrook I. Magnetic I.
Bonaparte Drysdale Victoria River Downs Daly Waters Normanton Ayr Townsville
Archipelago Lake Argyle Lake Woods Burketown Mitchell Bowen Whitsunday I.
C. Lévêque King Sound Mt Ord 936 Halls Creek Lajamanu Tennant Creek Camooweal Kajabbi Gilbert Richmond Proserpine Capricorn
Collier Bay Kimberley Plateau NORTHERN Barkly Tableland Mount Isa Cloncurry Mackay
Derby King Leopold Ranges Ord Tanami Creek Flinders Ra. Percy Is

3

Roebuck Bay Broome Fitzroy Crossing Sturt Creek TERRITORY Barrow Creek Kajabbi QUEENSLAND GREAT DIVIDING RANGE Rockhampton Yeppon
Lagrange Liveringa Gregory Lake Desert Yuendumu Boulia Dajarra Winton Clermont Gladstone
Eighty Mile Beach Lake White Lake Alice Springs Georgina Longreach Bardaldine Emerald Buckland
Port Hedland Shay Gap GREAT SANDY DESERT Lake Wills Lake Mackay Mt Liebig Mt Ziel 1524 1510 Macdonnell Ranges Barrow Creek Blackall Tableland
Karratha Roebourne Marble Bar Nullagine Lake Disappointment Macdonald Lake Neale Uluru 867 Simpson Desert Birdsville Windorah Quilpie Charleville Roma Bonnie
North West C. Onslow Pannawonica Chichester Range Lake Mt Woodroffe Musgrave Ranges Alberga Sturt Stony Cooper Creek Cunnamulla St George Toowoo
Barrow I. Hamersley Range WESTERN Gibson Warburton Petermann Ranges Everard Range Oodnadatta Desert Clayton Hungerford Dirranbandi Darling Downs
Exmouth Gulf Tom Price Mt Meharry 1235 Desert Erldunda Lake Eyre (North) Tibooburra Bourke Moree Narrabri Armidale
Coral Bay Paraburdoo AUSTRALIA Lake Carnegie Warburton Lake Eyre (South) Lake Blanche Brewarrina Walgett

4

Minilya Mt Augustus 1106 Mt Ashburton Lake Wells SOUTH Lake Frome NEW SOUTH Cobar Tamworth
Carnarvon Robinson Range Wiluna Lake Carnegie Coober Pedy Lake Torrens Menindee Nyngan Dubbo WALES
Bernier I. Mt MacLeod Murchison Meekatharra Laverton Lake Maurice AUSTRALIA Marree Flinders Ranges Broken Hill Ivanhoe Warren Forbes Orange
Shark Bay Dirk Hartog I. Leonora Maralinga Lake Gairdner Island Lagoon Woomera Port Augusta Wilcannia Hay Lachlan Bathurst Sydn
Denham Kalbarri Northampton Lake Barlee Menzies GREAT VICTORIA Lake Carey Ceduna Whyalla Yunta Mildura Griffith Wollong
Houtman Abrolhos Geraldton Mullewa Lake Moore Kalgoorlie DESERT Nullarbor Plain Streaky Bay Eyre Peninsula Port Pirie Victoria Wagga Wagga Canberra
Dongara Lake Ballard Kambalda Eucla Fowlers Bay Kimba AUSTRALIA Port Lincoln Jamestown Lake Victoria Balranald A.C.T. Bate
Northam Merredin Coolgardie Mundabilla Anxious Bay Yorketown Murray Bridge Swan Hill Shepparton Mt Kosciuszko Eden
Yanchep York Southern Cross Lake Cowan Great Cape Carnot Spencer Gulf Adelaide Murray Bendigo 2230 Narow
Perth Hyden Norseman Balladonia Australian Bight Investigator Strait Alexandrina Horsham VICTORIA Ballarat

5

Fremantle Brookton Esperance Kangaroo I. Cape Jaffa Stawell 1986 Albury
Rockingham Narrogin Archipelago of the Recherche Mount Gambier Lake Tyrrell Seymour Bairnsdale
Bunbury Katanning Hood Pt Portland Colac Melbourne Sale
Geographe Bay Busselton Warrnambool Geelong Moe Corner Inlet Wilson's Promontory
Margaret River Nannup Cape Otway Discovery Bay Furneaux Group
C. Leeuwin Denmark Albany Currie King I. Bass Strait Flinders I. Cape Barren I.
Flinders Bay D'Entrecasteaux Hunter Is Robbins I. Clarke I. Eddystone Pt
Burnie Devonport Launceston Fingal
TASMANIA Queenstown Mt Ossa 1617 Great Lake
Macquarie Harbour Lake Gordon Hobart Port Arthur
South East Cape Bruny I.

6

A 110° B 120° C 130° D 140° E 150°

Lambert Azimuthal Equal Area Projection

Metres Feet
6000 19686
5000 16404
4000 13124
3000 9843
2000 6562
1000 3281
500 1640
200 656
0 0
Land below sea level
200 656
2000 6562
4000 13124
6000 19686

INDONESIA NEW GUINEA PAPUA Banda Sea Seram Sea Flores Sea

AUSTRALIA WESTERN AUSTRALIA NORTHERN TERRITORY QUEENSLAND SOUTH AUSTRALIA NEW SOUTH WALES VICTORIA TASMANIA

Arnhem Land Gulf of Carpentaria Great Dividing Range Great Sandy Desert Gibson Desert Great Victoria Desert Simpson Desert Nullarbor Plain Great Australian Bight

Lake Eyre Lake Torrens Lake Gairdner Lake Frome Lake Argyle Lake Mackay Lake Disappointment Lake Carnegie

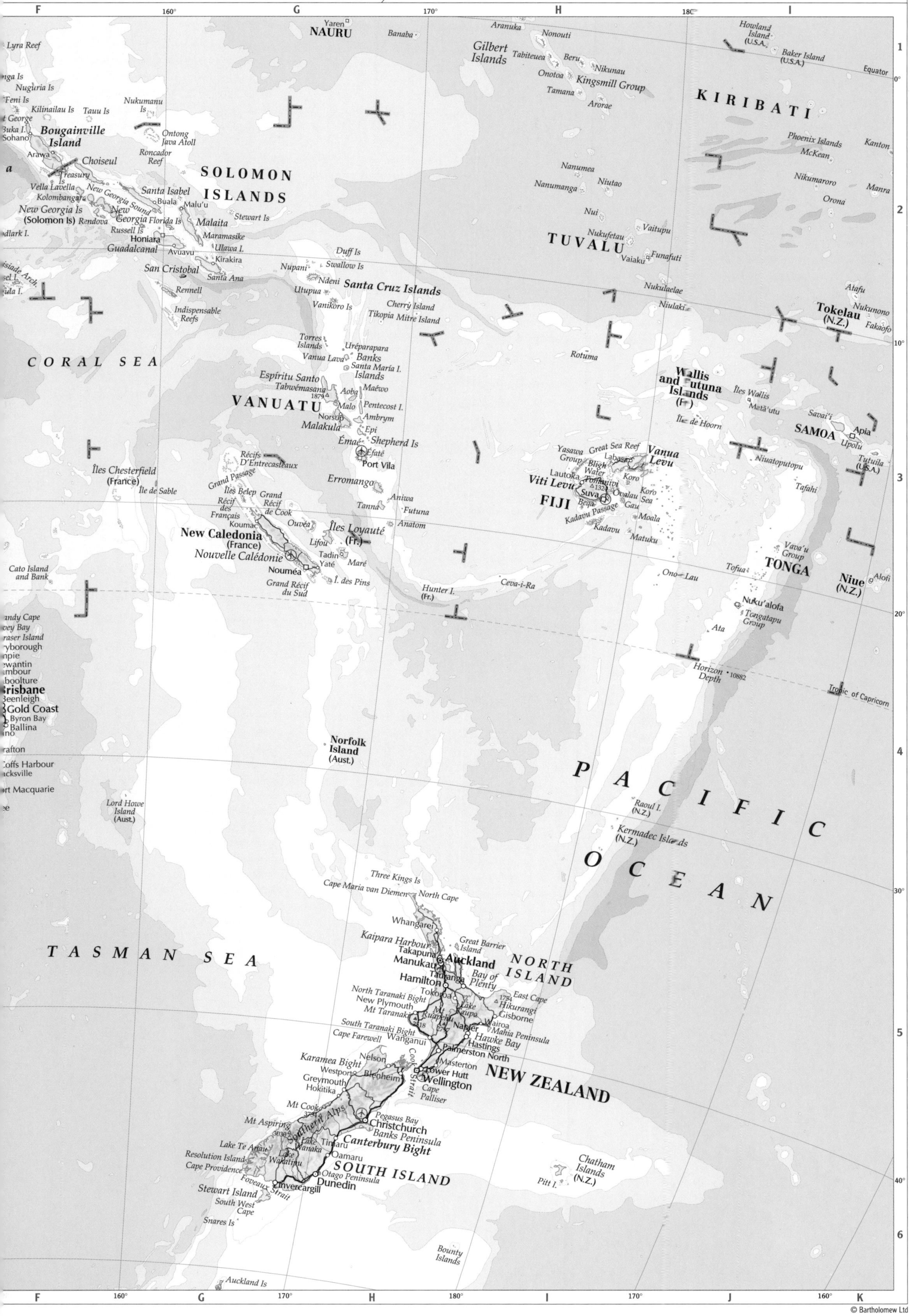

F 160° **G** 170° **H** 180° **I**

Lyra Reef
NAURU   Yaren
Banaba
Aranuka   Nonouti
Howland
Island
(U.S.A.)
Baker Island
(U.S.A.)
Gilbert
Islands
Tabiteuea
Beru
Nikunau
Equator   0°

onga Is
Nuguria Is
Nukumanu
Is
Onotoa   Tamana
Arorae
KIRIBATI

Feni Is
Kilinailau   Tauu Is
Ontong
Java Atoll
Roncador
Reef
Kingsmill Group
Phoenix Islands
McKean
Kanton

Buka I.
Bougainville
Island
Sohano
Arawa
Choiseul
SOLOMON
ISLANDS
Nanumea
Niutao
Nikumaroro
Manra
Orona

a
Treasury
Vella Lavella
New Georgia
Is
Santa Isabel
Buala
Malu'u
Stewart Is
Nanumanga
Nui
TUVALU

New Georgia Is
(Solomon Is)
Rendova
New
Georgia
Florida Is
Malaita
Maramasike
Nui
Nukufetau
Vaitupu
Atafu
Nukunono

dlark I.
Honiara
Guadalcanal
Avuavu
Ulawa I.
Kirakira
Nupani
Swallow Is
Vaiaku   Funafuti
Nukulaelae
Tokelau
(N.Z.)
Fakaofo

sidade Arch.
San Cristobal
Santa Ana
Rennell
Ndeni
Santa Cruz Islands
Niulaki
Nukunono

el I.
da I.
Indispensable
Reefs
Utupua
Vanikoro Is
Cherry Island
Tikopia Mitre Island
Rotuma
Wallis
and Futuna
Islands
(Fr.)
Îles Wallis
SAMOA
Apia
Upolu

CORAL SEA
Torres
Islands
Uréparapara
Banks
Islands
Espíritu Santo
Tabwémasana
1874
VANUATU
Malo
Aoba   Maêwo
Pentecost I.
Île de Hoorn
Meta'utu
Savai'i
Tafahi
Tutuila
(U.S.A.)

Îles Chesterfield
(France)
Île de Sable
Norsup
Malakula
Ambrym
Épi
Émaé   Shepherd Is
Yasawa
Group
Great Sea Reef
Vanua
Levu
Niuatoputapu

Récifs
D'Entrecasteaux
Grand Passage
Port Vila
Éfaté
Bligh
Water
Labasa
Lautoka
Viti Levu
Koro
Koro
Sea
Ovalau
FIJI   Suva
Gau
Niuafo'ou
Tafahi

Îles Belep   Grand
Récif
de Cook
Récif
des
Français
Koumac
Erromango
Tanna
Aniwa
Futuna
Anatom
Kadavu Passage
Bega
Kadavu
Matuku
Moala
Vava'u
Group
TONGA
Niue
(N.Z.)   Alofi

New Caledonia
(France)
Nouvelle Calédonie
Nouméa
Lifou
Îles Loyauté
(Fr.)
Tadin
Maré
Yaté
Ouvéa   Hunter I.
(Fr.)
Ceva-i-Ra
Ono-Lau
Tofua   Nuku'alofa
Tongatapu
Group

Cato Island
and Bank
Grand Récif
du Sud
Î. des Pins   Ata
Horizon
Depth   10882
Tropic of Capricorn

andy Cape
vey Bay
raser Island
yborough
mpie
ewantin
mbour
boolture
Brisbane
Beenleigh
Gold Coast
Byron Bay
Ballina
no

Norfolk
Island
(Aust.)
PACIFIC

rafton
offs Harbour
acksville
rt Macquarie
e
Lord Howe
Island
(Aust.)
OCEAN
Raoul I.
(N.Z.)
Kermadec Islands
(N.Z.)

Three Kings Is
Cape Maria van Diemen   North Cape
Whangarei   Miles   Km

TASMAN SEA
Kaipara Harbour
Takapuna
Manukau   Auckland
Hamilton
Great Barrier
Island
Bay of
Plenty
Tauranga
East Cape
Hikurangi
Gisborne
NORTH
ISLAND   800   1400
1200

North Taranaki Bight
New Plymouth
Mt Taranaki
Tokoroa
Rotorua
Lake
Taupo
Wairoa
Mahia Peninsula
Napier
Hawke Bay   600   1000
800

South Taranaki Bight
Cape Farewell   Wanganui
Palmerston North
Hastings   400   600

Karamea Bight
Nelson
Westport   Blenheim
Masterton
Lower Hutt
Wellington
Cape
Palliser
NEW ZEALAND   200   400

Greymouth
Hokitika   Cook
Strait   200

Mt Cook
Southern Alps
Mt Aspiring
Pegasus Bay
Christchurch
Banks Peninsula
Canterbury Bight
Chatham
Islands
(N.Z.)   0   0

Lake Te Anau
Resolution Island
Cape Providence
Lake
Wanaka
Lake
Tinaru
Wakatipu
Timaru
Oamaru
Otago Peninsula
Dunedin
SOUTH ISLAND
Pitt I.

Stewart Island
South West
Cape
Foveaux
Strait
Invercargill
Snares Is
Bounty
Islands

Auckland Is

F 160° **G** 170° **H** 180° **I** 170° **J** 160° **K**

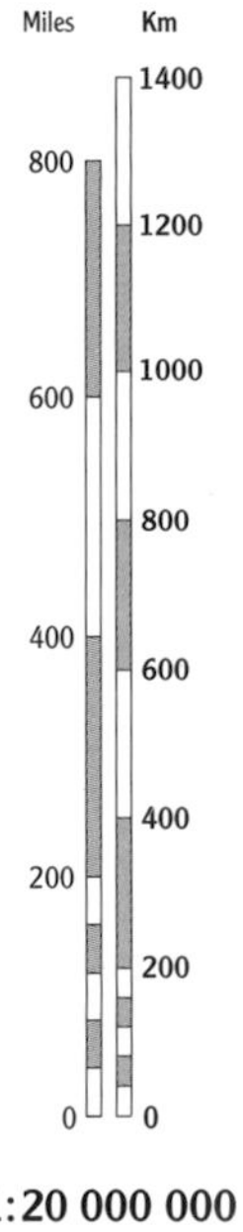

© Bartholomew Ltd

1:20 000 000

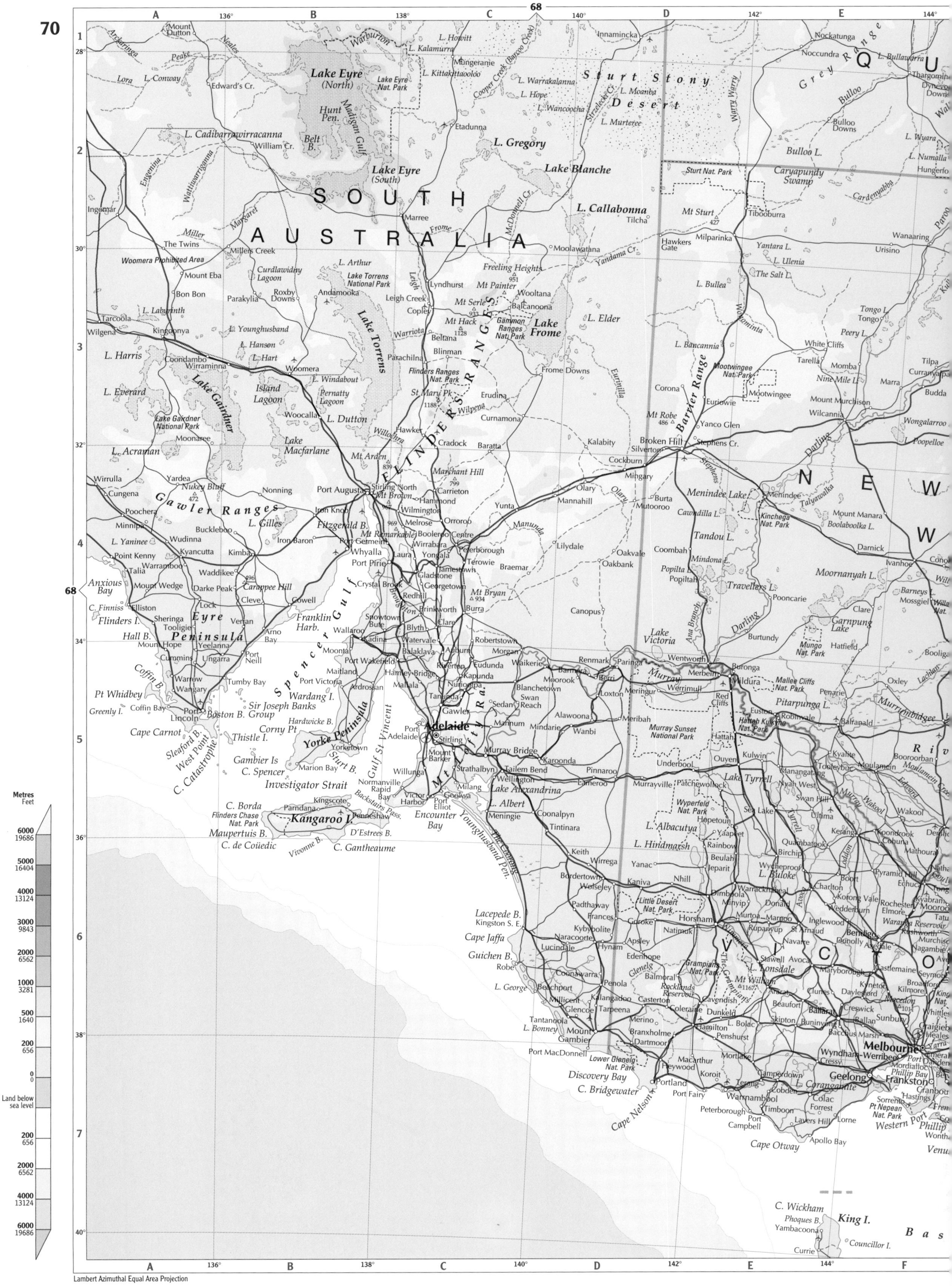

A 136° B 138° C **68** 140° D 142° E 144°

1

Archaringa · Mount Dutton · Nealles · Warburton · L. Howitt · L. Kalamurra · Innamincka · Nockatunga · Noccundra · Bullawarra · Thargomi

Peake · 28° · L. Kittakittaooldoo · Cooper Creek (Barcoo Creek) · Mungeranie · **Sturt Stony** · Grey Range · Q · U · Dynevo

Lora · Conway · Edward's Cr. · Lake Eyre Nat. Park · **Lake Eyre (North)** · L. Warrakalanna · C. Moanba · **Desert** · Warry Warry · Bulloo · L. Wyara · Numalla

Ingomar · L. Cadibarrawirracanna · William Cr. · Hunt Pen. · Madigan Gulf · L. Hope · L. Wancoocha · L. Murteree · Bulloo Downs · Bulloo L. · Hungerfo

2 · Wattipurrtganna · Belt B. · **Lake Eyre (South)** · **L. Gregory** · McDonnell Cr. · Sturt Nat. Park · Caryapundy Swamp · Cardenabba

Eninerina · Marsaret · Millers Gulf · Marree · **Lake Blanche** · Strzelecki Cr.

SOUTH · **L. Callabonna** · Mt Sturt 427 · Tiboobura · Wanaaring · Paroo

Miller · Frome · Tilcha · Hawkers Gate · Milparinka · Yantara L. · Urisino

30° · The Twins · Millers Creek · Moolawatana · Yandama Cr. · L. Ulenia

AUSTRALIA · L. Arthur · Freeling Heights · The Salt L. · L. Bullea

Woomera Prohibited Area · Mount Eba · Curdlawidny Lagoon · Lake Torrens National Park · Leigh · Lyndhurst · Mt Painter 951 · Wooltana · L. Elder · Tongo L. · Tongo

Bon Bon · Parakylia · Roxby Downs · Andamooka · Leigh Creek · Mt Serle 933 · Balcanoona · Peery L.

Tarcoola · Wilgena · Kingoonya · L. Younghusband · L. Hanson · Warriota · Mt Hack 1128 · Gammon Ranges Nat. Park · **Lake Frome** · L. Baucannia · White Cliffs · Nine Mile L.

3 · L. Harris · Coondambo · Wirraminna · L. Hart · Woomera · Parachilna · Blinman · Frome Downs · Corona · Euriowie · Momba · Curranyalpa

L. Everard · Island Lagoon · L. Windabout · Flinders Ranges Nat. Park · St Mary Pk 1188 · Erudina · Eurinilla · Mootwingee Nat. Park · Mootwingee · Mount Murchison · Budda

L. Acraman · Lake Gairdner National Park · Pernatty Lagoon · Willochra · Hawker · Wilpena · Curnamona · Mt Robe 486 · Yanco Glen · Wilcannia · Wongalarroo

32° · L. Acraman · Moonaree · Woocalla · L. Dutton · Cradock · Baratta · Kalabity · Broken Hill · Stephens Cr. · Poopelloe

Wirrulla · Yardea · Nukey Bluff 472 · Lake Macfarlane · Mt Arden 839 · Marchant Hill 799 · Cockburn · Silverton · Darling

Cungena · Nonning · **Gawler Ranges** · Port Augusta · Stirling North · Mt Brown 970 · Carrieton · Mingary · Burta · Menindee Lake · Menindee

Poochera · Iron Knob · Wilmington · Hammond · Yunta · Olary · Mutooroo · Cawdilla L. · Kinchega Nat. Park · Boolaboolka L.

Minnipa · Buckleboo · L. Gilles · Fitzgerald B. · Melrose · Ororoo · Centre · Manunda · Mannahill · Tandou L. · Mount Manara

4 · L. Yaninee · Wudinna · Iron Baron · Mt Remarkable 960 · Wirrabara · Peterborough · Lilydale · Oakvale · Coombah · Darnick · Ivanho

Warramboo · Kyancutta · Kimba · Port Germein · Laura · Yongala · Terowie · Braemar · Oakbank · Popilta L. · Travellers L. · Moornanyah L.

Talia · Waddikee · Carappee Hill · Whyalla · Jamestown · Gladstone · Georgetown · Mt Bryan 934 · Canopus · Popiltah · Barnes

Point Kenny · Warramboo · Darke Peak · Cleve · Cowell · Port Pirie · Crystal Brook · Redhill · Burra · Pooncarie · Clare · Garnpung Lake · Mossgiel

68 · Anxious Bay · Mount Wedge · Franklin Harb. · Snowtown · Brinkworth · Mungo Nat. Park · Hatfield

C. Finniss · Elliston · **Eyre** · Arno Bay · Wallaroo · Blyth · Clare · Lake Victoria · Burtundy · Booliga

Flinders I. · Sheringa · Tooligie · Verran · Yeelanna · Kadina · Watervale · Morgan · Ana Branch · Darling

34° · Hall B. · Mount Hope · **Peninsula** · Port Neill · Moonta · Port Wakefield · Balaklava · Auburn · Renmark · Paringa · Wentworth · Robinvale

Cummins · Ungarra · Tumby Bay · Maitland · Port Victoria · Hamley Bridge · Riverton · Eudunda · Barmera · Berri · Murray · Buronga

Coffin B. · Wangary · Port Broughton · Ardrossan · Mallala · Kapunda · Nuriootpa · Moorook · Loxton · Merbein · Wildura · Mallee Cliffs Nat. Park · Oxley

Pt Whidbey · **Spencer Gulf** · Wardang I. · Tanunda · Sedan · Swan Reach · Blanchetown · Meringur · Werrimull · Red Cliffs · Penarie · Murrumbidgee

Greenly I. · Coffin Bay · Port Lincoln · Hardwicke B. · **Yorke Peninsula** · Gawler · Alawoona · Mannum · Mindarie · Wanbi · Euston · Robinvale · Balranald · Riv

5 · Cape Carnot · Boston B. Group · Sir Joseph Banks · Corny Pt · **Gulf St Vincent** · **Adelaide** · Stirling · Murray Bridge · Karoonda · Meribah · Murray Sunset National Park · Hattah

Sleaford B. · Thistle I. · Yorketown · Port Adelaide · Mannum · Pinnaroo · Underbool · Ouyen · Kulwin · Kyalite · Moulamein

West Point · Gambier Is · C. Spencer · Sturt B. · Mount Barker · Murray Bridge · Lameroo · Murrayville · Patchewollock · Lake Tyrrell · Nyah West · Swan Hill · Wakool

C. Catastrophe · **Investigator Strait** · Normanville · Strathalbyn · Tailem Bend · Wyperfeld Nat. Park · Sea Lake · Ultima

Pandana · Rapid Bay · Victor Harbor · Wellington · Lake Alexandrina · Coonalpyn · Hopetoun · Quambatook · Koondrook · Den

C. Borda · Kingscote · Backstairs Pass · Willunga · Goolwa · Milang · L. Albert · Tintinara · L. Albacutya · Birchip · Cohuna · Mathoura

Flinders Chase Nat. Park · **Kangaroo I.** · Penneshaw · Encounter Bay · Meningie · Keith · L. Hindmarsh · Rainbow · Beulah · Wycheproof · Pyramid Hill · Echuca

6 · Maupertuis B. · D'Estrees B. · Youghusband Pen. · Wirrega · Yanac · Nhill · Jeparit · Warracknabeal · Charlton · Kerang · Donald · Rochester

C. de Couedic · Vivonne B. · C. Gantheaume · Bordertown · Wolseley · Kaniva · Dimboola · L. Buloke · Wycheproof · Kerang · Mooro

Lacepede B. · Kingston S. E. · Padthaway · Little Desert Nat. Park · Horsham · Murtoa · Rupanyup · Marnoo · St Arnaud · Navarre · Wara

Cape Jaffa · Naracoorte · Apsley · Edenhope · Grampians Nat. Park · **The Grampians** · Mt William 1167 · Stawell · Avoca · Maryborough · Castlemaine · Seymo

Guichen B. · Robe · Lucindale · Coonawarra · Penola · Balmoral · Rocklands Reservoir · Cavendish · Ararat · Beaufort · Clunes · Daylesford · Kilmor

VICTORIA

L. George · Beachport · Millicent · Kalangadoo · Casterton · Coleraine · Dunkeld · Skipton · Ballan · Sunbury

38° · L. Bonney · Mount Gambier · Glencoe · Tarpeena · Merino · Hamilton · Buninyong · **Ballarat** · Bacchus Marsh

Port MacDonnell · Lower Glenelg Nat. Park · Branxholme · Penshurst · Mortlake · Wyndham · Werribee · **Melbourne** · Frankston

Discovery Bay · Heywood · Koroit · Macarthur · Camperdown · Geelong · Phillip Bay · Geelong · Frankston

C. Bridgewater · Portland · Port Fairy · Warrnambool · Terang · Colac · Corangamite · Sorrento · Hastings · Bass

7 · Cape Nelson · Port Campbell · Peterborough · Timboon · Forrest · Lavers Hill · Lorne · Pt Nepean Nat. Park · Western Port · Wontha

Cape Otway · Apollo Bay · Venus

C. Wickham · Phoques B. · **King I.** · Bass

40° · Yambacoona · Councillor I. · Currie

A 136° B 138° C 140° D 142° E 144° F

Lambert Azimuthal Equal Area Projection

Metres Feet

6000 19686
5000 16404
4000 13124
3000 9843
2000 6562
1000 3281
500 1640
200 656
0 0

Land below sea level

200 656
2000 6562
4000 13124
6000 19686

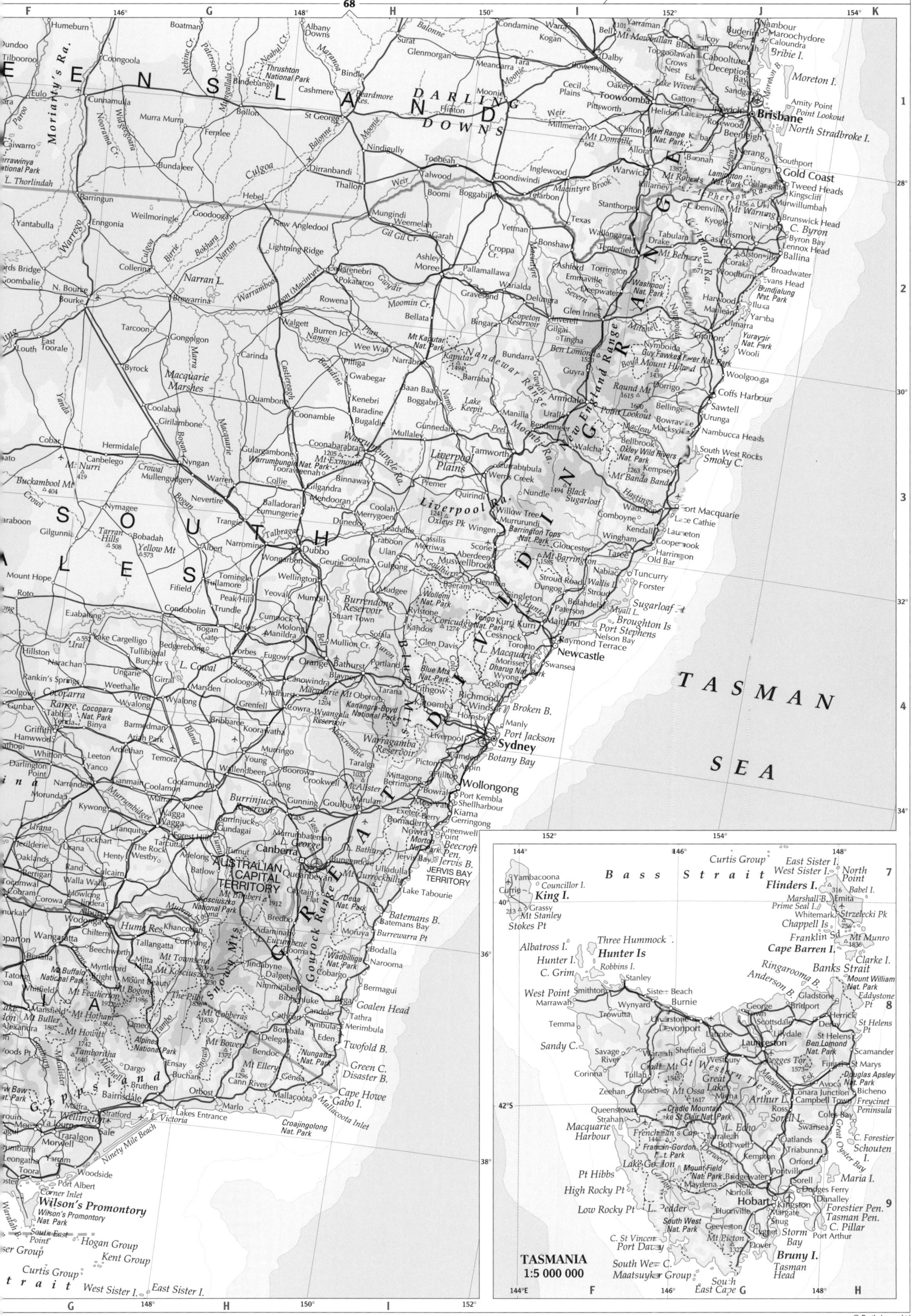

T A S M A N

S E A

TASMANIA
1:5 000 000

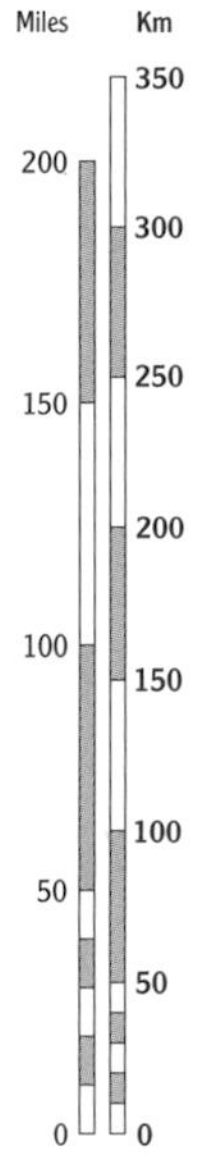

Miles   Km
350
200 ─
          300
150 ─
          250
          200
100 ─
          150
50 ─   100
          50
0 ─   0

1:5 000 000

© Bartholomew Ltd

NEW ZEALAND

72

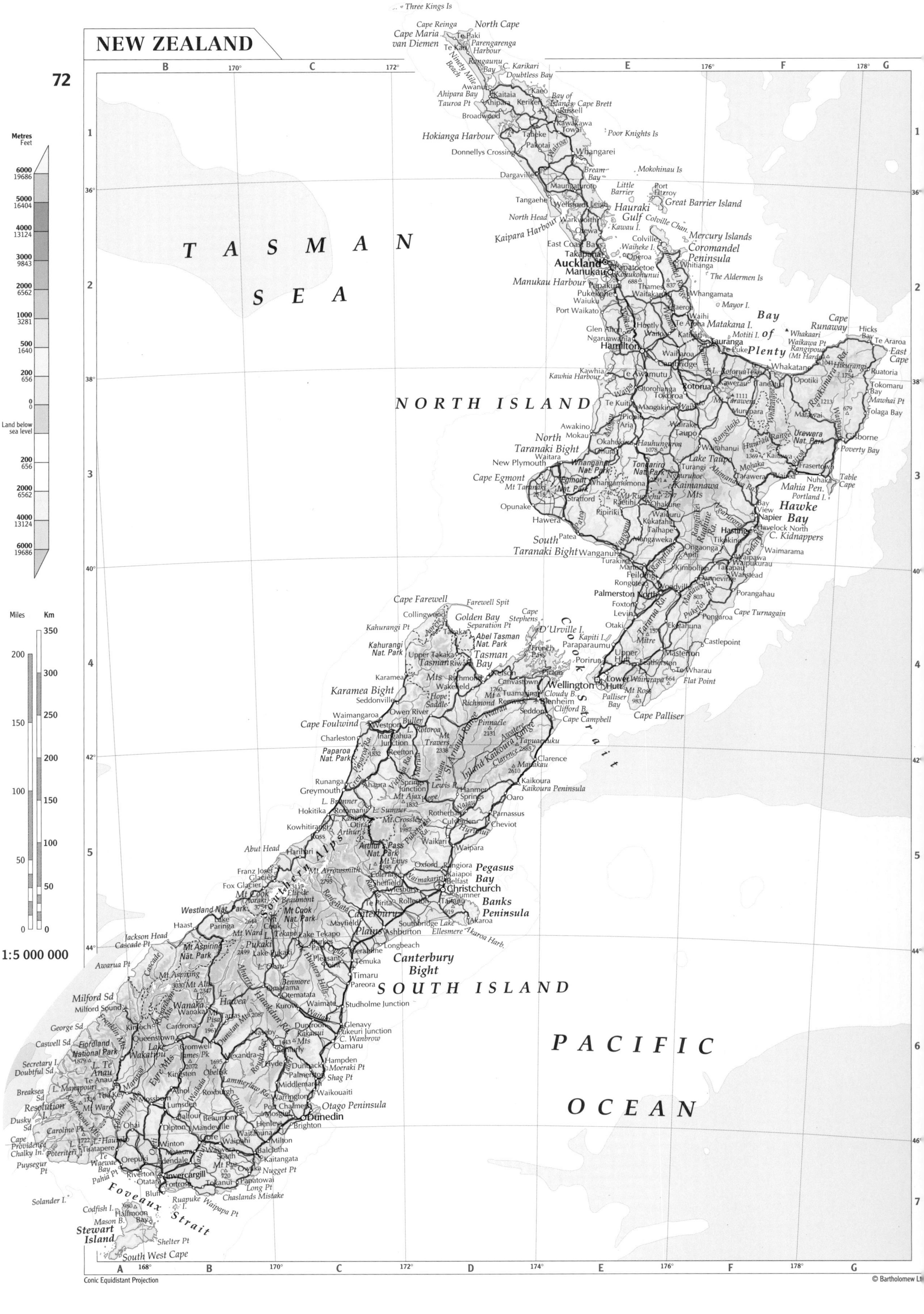

Metres / Feet

6000 / 19686
5000 / 16404
4000 / 13124
3000 / 9843
2000 / 6562
1000 / 3281
500 / 1640
200 / 656
0 / 0

Land below sea level

200 / 656
2000 / 6562
4000 / 13124
6000 / 19686

Miles / Km

200 / 350
300
150 / 250
200
100 / 150
50 / 100
50
0 / 0

1:5 000 000

TASMAN SEA

PACIFIC OCEAN

NORTH ISLAND

SOUTH ISLAND

Three Kings Is
Cape Reinga   North Cape
Cape Maria van Diemen   Te Paki   Parengarenga Harbour
Te Kao   Rangaunu Bay
Ninety Mile Beach   C. Karikari   Doubtless Bay
Awanui   Kaeo   Bay of Islands   Cape Brett
Ahipara Bay   Kaitaia   Kerikeri   Russell
Tauroa Pt   Ahipara   Kawakawa   Poor Knights Is
Broadwood   Towai
Hokianga Harbour   Taheke   Whangarei
Pakotai
Donnellys Crossing   Bream Bay   Mokohinau Is
Dargaville   Maunganui   Little Barrier   Port Fitzroy
Tangaehe   Wellsford Leigh   Great Barrier Island
North Head   Warkworth   Colville Chan.
Kaipara Harbour   Otewa   Kawau I.   Mercury Islands
East Coast Bay   Waiheke I.   Colville   Coromandel Peninsula
Takapuna   Oneroa   Whitianga
Auckland   Papatoetoe   The Aldermen Is
Manukau   Kohukohunui   Thames
Manukau Harbour   Pukekohe   Waitakaruru   Whangamata
Papakura   Mayor I.
Waiuku   Maeroa   Bay of Plenty
Port Waikato   Te Aroha   Matakana I.   Cape Runaway
Glen Afton   Waihou   Katikati   Whakaari   Hicks Bay
Ngaruawahia   Tauranga   Te Araroa
Hamilton   Waiharoa   Puke   East Cape
Cambridge   Rotorua   Whakatane   Ruatoria
Kawhia   Te Awamutu   Awakeri   Opotiki   Tokomaru Bay
Kawhia Harbour   Otorohanga   Rotorua   Tauranga   Mawhai Pt
Te Kuiti   Mangakino   Tolaga Bay
Pirongia   Urewera Nat. Park   Gisborne
Awakino   Taupo   Poverty Bay
North Taranaki Bight   Mokau   Okahukura   Hauhungaroa
New Plymouth   Waitara   Lake Taupo   Frasertown   Table Cape
Cape Egmont   Whangamomona   Tongariro Nat. Park   Mahia Pen.
Mt Taranaki   Egmont Nat. Park   Ngauruhoe   Portland I.
Opunake   Stratford   Mt Ruapehu   **Hawke Bay**
Hawera   Raetihi   Ohakune   Bay View   **Napier**
South Taranaki Bight   Patea   Waiouru   Hastings
Wanganui   Taihape   Havelock North
Turakina   C. Kidnappers
Marton   Waipawa   Waimarama
Feilding   Kimbolton   Dannevirke
Rongotea   Waih, Woodville   Porangahau
Palmerston North
Foxton   Cape Turnagain
Levin   Pongaroa
Otaki   Eketahuna
Cook Strait   Paraparaumu   Masterton   Castlepoint
D'Urville I.   Porirua   Upper Hutt   Carterton   Flat Point
Cape Stephens   French Pass   Kapiti I.   Greytown
Separation Pt   Picton   **Wellington**   Lower Hutt   Martinborough
Golden Bay   Cloudy B.   Palliser Bay   Mt Ross   Cape Palliser
Cape Farewell   Farewell Spit   Nelson   Blenheim   Wairarapa

Collingwood   Takaka   Havelock   Clifford B.
Kahurangi Pt   Motueka   Renwick   Cape Campbell
Kahurangi Nat. Park   Upper Takaka   Richmond   Seddon
Abel Tasman Nat. Park   Wakefield   Clarence
Tasman Bay   Tuamarina
Karamea   Richmond Mts   Awatere
Karamea Bight   Murchison   Inland Kaikoura Range
Seddonville   Hope Saddle   St Arnaud   Kaikoura
Waimangaroa   Owen River   Kekerengu
Westport   Buller   Manakau
Cape Foulwind   Inangahua Junction   Lewis Pass   Hanmer Springs   Kaikoura Peninsula
Charleston   Reefton   Oaro
Paparoa Nat. Park   Springs Junction   Rotherham   Parnassus
Runanga   Ahaura   Culverden   Cheviot
Greymouth   Mt Crossley   Waiau   Waipara
Hokitika   L. Brunner   L. Sumner   Oxford   Rangiora   **Pegasus Bay**
Kowhitirangi   Rotomanu   Kaiapoi   Belfast
Ross   Kaniere   Arthur's Pass Nat. Park   Sheffield   **Christchurch**
Otira   Darfield   Lincoln   Sumner
Abut Head   Arthur's Pass   Rolleston   **Banks Peninsula**
Harihari   Te Pirita   Akaroa
Franz Josef Glacier   Mt Arrowsmith   Oxford   Akaroa Harb.
Fox Glacier   Methven   Southbridge   Lake Ellesmere
Westland Nat. Park   Rakaia   Ashburton
Mt Cook   Mt Cook Nat. Park   Mayfield   Canterbury Plains
Haast   Mt Ward   Lake Tekapo   Rangitata   **Canterbury Bight**
Jackson Head   Cascade Pt   Geraldine   Temuka
Mt Aspiring   Mt Aspiring Nat. Park   Fairlie   Pleasant Point
Awarua Pt   Lake Pukaki   Timaru
Milford Sd   Wanaka   Pareora
Milford Sound   Lake Wanaka   Benmore   Waimate
George Sd   Cardrona   Omarama   Studholme Junction
Caswell Sd   Queenstown   Otematata   Glenavy
Fiordland National Park   Lake Wakatipu   Kurow   Pukeuri Junction
Secretary I.   Cromwell   Duntroon   Oamaru
Doubtful Sd   Lake Hawea   Alexandra   C. Wanbrow
Te Anau   Clyde   Hyde   Hampden
Breaksea Sd   L. Te Anau   Roxburgh   Dunback   Moeraki Pt
Resolution   Te Anau   Ranfurly   Palmerston   Shag Pt
Dusky Sd   Eyre Mts   Middlemarch   Waikouaiti
Caroline Pk   Lumsden   Warrington
Cape Providence   Garston   Beaumont   Port Chalmers
Chalky In.   Lawrence   Mosgiel   Otago Peninsula
Poteriteri   Dipton   Mandeville   Henley   **Dunedin**   Brighton
Puysegur Pt   Winton   Milton
Te Waewae Bay   Gore   Waitahuna   Balclutha
Riverton   Edendale   Mataura   Kaitangata
Pahia Pt   Otautau   Clinton   Owaka   Nugget Pt
Tuatapere   Invercargill   Fortrose   Papatowai   Long Pt
Orepuki   Tokanui   Chaslands Mistake
Solander I.   Bluff   Waipapa Pt
Codfish I.   Foveaux Strait   Ruapuke I.
Halfmoon Bay   Mason B.
Stewart Island   Shelter Pt
South West Cape

Conic Equidistant Projection   © Bartholomew Ltd

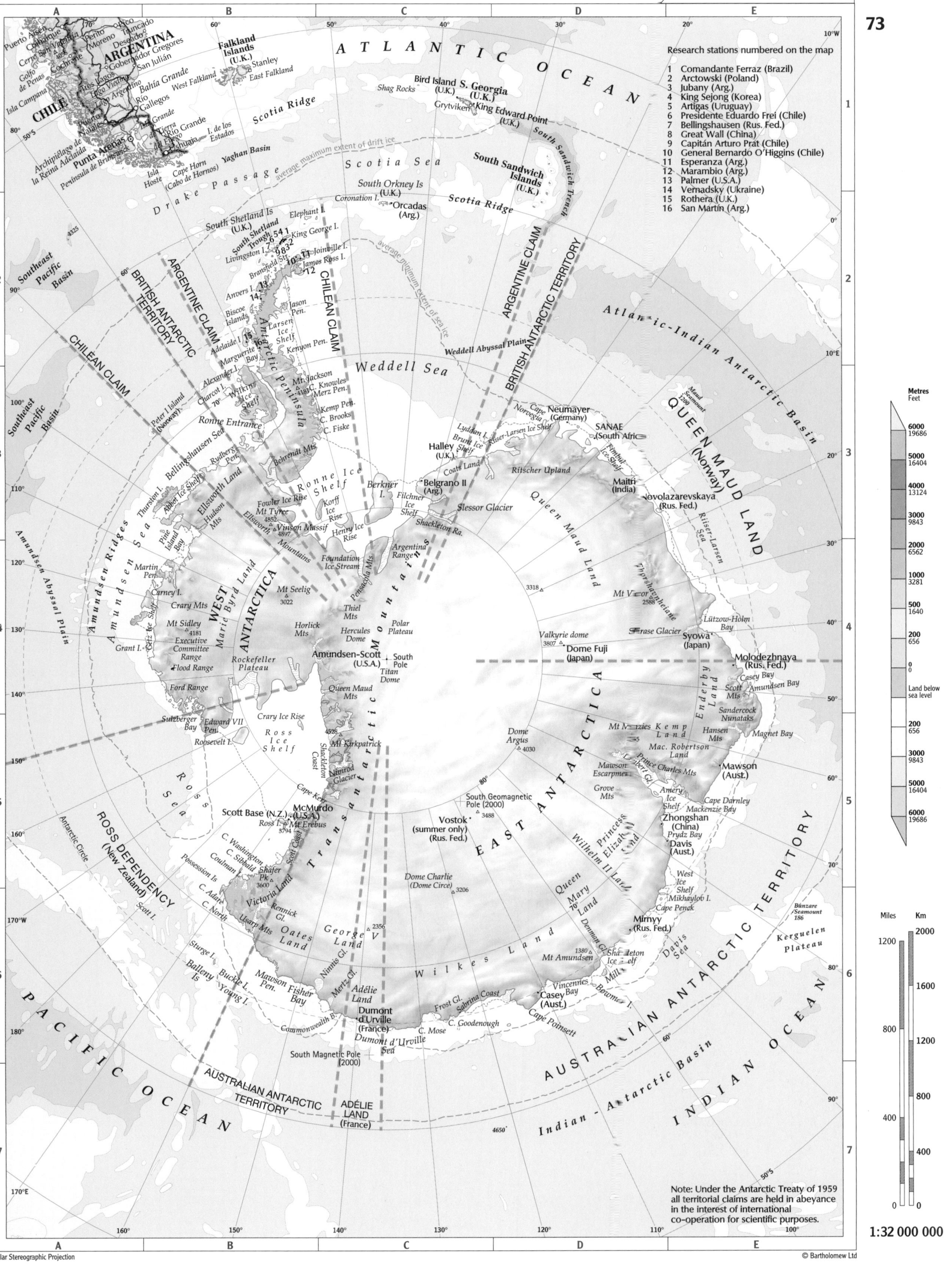

Research stations numbered on the map

1 Comandante Ferraz (Brazil)
2 Arctowski (Poland)
3 Jubany (Arg.)
4 King Sejong (Korea)
5 Artigas (Uruguay)
6 Presidente Eduardo Frei (Chile)
7 Bellingshausen (Rus. Fed.)
8 Great Wall (China)
9 Capitán Arturo Prat (Chile)
10 General Bernardo O'Higgins (Chile)
11 Esperanza (Arg.)
12 Marambio (Arg.)
13 Palmer (U.S.A.)
14 Vernadsky (Ukraine)
15 Rothera (U.K.)
16 San Martín (Arg.)

Note: Under the Antarctic Treaty of 1959
all territorial claims are held in abeyance
in the interest of international
co-operation for scientific purposes.

Metres
Feet

6000
19686

5000
16404

4000
13124

3000
9843

2000
6562

1000
3281

500
1640

200
656

0
0

Land below
sea level

200
656

3000
9843

5000
16404

6000
19686

Miles   Km

1200   2000

         1600

800   1200

         800

400   400

0   0

1:32 000 000

Polar Stereographic Projection

© Bartholomew Ltd

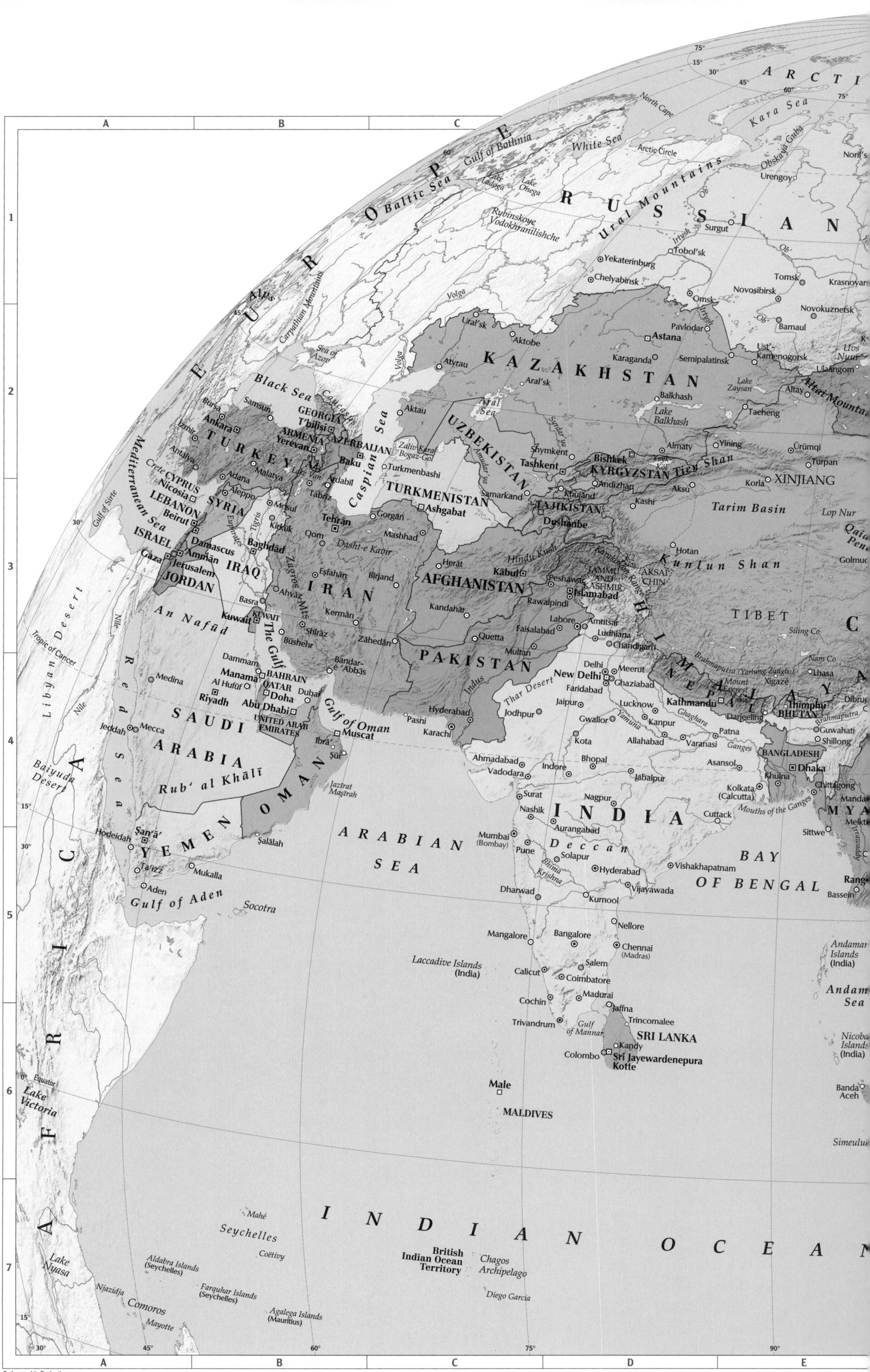

A B C D E

1

2

EUROPE

Alps
Carpathian Mountains
Ural Mountains

North Cape
Kara Sea
ARCTIC

Baltic Sea
Gulf of Bothnia
White Sea
Arctic Circle
Obskaja Guba
Noril'sk

Lake Ladoga
Lake Onega
Rybinskoye Vodokhranilishche
Urengoy

R U S S I A N

Volga
Irtysh
Tobol'sk
Surgut
Ob'

Yekaterinburg
Chelyabinsk
Tomsk
Krasnoyarsk

Novosibirsk
Novokuznetsk

Omsk
Pavlodar
Barnaul

Ust'-Kamenogorsk
Uvs Nuur
Ulaangom

Sea of Azov
Ural'sk
Aktobe
Astana
Semipalatinsk
Altay
Altai Mountains

Black Sea
Atyrau
K A Z A K H S T A N
Karaganda
Lake Zaysan
Taacheng

Bursa
Caucasus
Caspian Sea
Aral'sk
Aral Sea
Balkhash
Lake Balkhash

İzmir
Ankara
GEORGIA
T'bilisi
AZERBAIJAN
Aktau
UZBEKISTAN
Shymkent
Almaty
Yining
Ürümqi

TURKEY
ARMENIA
Yerevan
Baku
Zaliv Kara-Bogaz-Gol
Amudar'ya
Tashkent
Bishkek
Issyk Kul
KYRGYZSTAN
Tien Shan
Turpan

Antalya
Adana
Lake Van
Tabriz
Turkmenbashi
Samarkand
Andizhan
Aksu
Korla
XINJIANG

Crete
CYPRUS
Nicosia
Aleppo
Mosul
TURKMENISTAN
Khujand
Kashi
Tarim Basin
Lop Nur

Mediterranean Sea
LEBANON
Beirut
SYRIA
Kirkūk
Tigris
Ashgabat
TAJIKISTAN
Dushanbe
Kunlun Shan
Qaidam Pendi

Gulf of Sirte
ISRAEL
Damascus
Baghdad
Tehran
Qom
Mashhad
Herāt
Hindu Kush
Karakoram Range
K2
AKSAI CHIN
Hotan
Golmud

Gaza
Amman
IRAQ
Esfahān
Birjand
AFGHANISTAN
Peshawar
JAMMU AND KASHMIR
TIBET

Jerusalem
JORDAN
Basra
IRAN
Ahvaz
Kermān
Zāhedān
Kandahār
Rawalpindi
Islamabad
HIMALAYA
Siling Co

Tropic of Cancer
An Nafūd
Kuwait
KUWAIT
Shiraz
Kābul
Quetta
Lahore
Amritsar
Ludhiana
Nam Co
Lhasa

Libyan Desert
Zagros Mtns
Būshehr
Bandar-e 'Abbās
PAKISTAN
Faisalabad
Multan
Chandigarh
Brahmaputra (Yarlung Zangbo)
Xigaze

Nile
Dammam
The Gulf
Dubai
Indus
Delhi
Meerut
Mount Everest
BHUTAN

Medina
Manama
BAHRAIN
QATAR
Pashi
New Delhi
Ghaziabad
Kathmandu
NEPAL
Thimphu

Al Hufūf
Doha
Abu Dhabi
UNITED ARAB EMIRATES
Muscat
Faridabad
Lucknow
Kanpur
Darjeeling
Guwahati

Riyadh
Gulf of Oman
Ibra'
Jaipur
Gwalior
Ghaghara
Patna
Brahmaputra
Shillong

SAUDI
Jeddah
Mecca
Sur
Jodhpur
Thar Desert
Kota
Yamuna
Varanasi
Asansol
BANGLADESH
Dhaka

ARABIA
Jazīrat Maşīrah
Hyderabad
Karachi
Ahmadabad
Allahabad
Ganges
Khulna
Chittagong

Baiyuda Desert
Rub' al Khālī
OMAN
Vadodara
Indore
Bhopal
Jabalpur
Kolkata (Calcutta)
MYA

Red Sea
YEMEN
San'ā'
Salālah
Surat
Nagpur
Cuttack
Mouths of the Ganges
Mandalay

Hodeidah
Mumbai (Bombay)
Nashik
I N D I A
Aurangabad
Deccan
Bhima
Krishna
BAY
Sittwe
Meiktila

Ta'izz
Mukalla
Pune
Solapur
Hyderabad
Vishakhapatnam
OF BENGAL
Rang

Aden
ARABIAN
Dharwad
Vijayawada
Bassein

Gulf of Aden
Socotra
SEA
Kurnool
Nellore

Mangalore
Bangalore
Chennai (Madras)
Andaman Islands (India)

Laccadive Islands (India)
Calicut
Salem
Coimbatore
Andaman Sea

Cochin
Madurai
Jaffna
Trincomalee
Nicobar Islands (India)

Trivandrum
Gulf of Mannar
SRI LANKA
Banda Aceh

Colombo
Kandy
Sri Jayewardenepura Kotte

Male
Simeulue

MALDIVES

AFRICA
Equator
Lake Victoria

Lake Nyasa

I N D I A N   O C E A N

Mahé
Seychelles
Coëtivy
British Indian Ocean Territory
Chagos Archipelago

Aldabra Islands (Seychelles)

Njazidja
Farquhar Islands (Seychelles)
Comoros
Diego Garcia

Mayotte
Agalega Islands (Mauritius)

OCEAN

CENTRAL SIBERIAN
PLATEAU

Nizhnyaya Tunguska

FEDERATION

Bratsk
Irkutsk
Ulan-Ude
Hövsgöl Nuur
Biyastay
MONGOLIA
Dalandzadgad

Lena
Ust'-Kut
Bodaybo
Mirnyy
Vilyuy
Tiksi
Lena

Verkhoyanskiy Khrebet
Yakutsk
Aldan
Stanovoy Khrebet
Tynda
Amur
Heilong Jiang
Argun
Hailar
Huhhot
Da Hinggan Ling

Susuman
Arctic Circle
Khrebet Kolymskiy
Ugol'nyye Kopi

Bering Strait

Magadan

Sea of Okhotsk

Kamchatka Peninsula
Petropavlovsk-Kamchatskiy

BERING SEA
Pribilof Islands

Aleutian Islands

Komsomol'sk-na-Amure
Blagoveshchensk
Khabarovsk
Sakhalin
Yuzhno-Sakhalinsk
Korsakov
Kuril Islands

GOBI
Ulan Bator
Jargalant
Buir Nur
Bu-Nur
INNER MONGOLIA
Baotou
Datong
Hohhot
Yellow (Huang He)
Beijing
Tianjin
Shijiazhuang
Handan
Taiyuan

Changchun
Jilin
Shenyang
Fushun
Anshan
Dalian
Korea Bay
Bo Hai

Qiqihar
Daqing
Jiamusi
Harbin
Lake Khanka
Vladivostok
Ch'ŏngjin

Wakkanai
Hokkaidō
Sapporo
Hakodate
Akita
Sendai

NORTH KOREA
P'yŏngyang
Seoul
SOUTH KOREA
Taejŏn
Taegu
Pusan
Kwangju

Sea of Japan (East Sea)

Kanazawa
Honshū
Tōkyō
Yokohama
Kōbe Kyōto
Ōsaka

JAPAN

Yumen
Wuhai
Yinchuan
Lanzhou
Xi'an
Zhengzhou
Jining
Xuzhou
Huainan
Nanjing

Yantai
Zibo
Jinan
Qingdao
Yellow Sea

Kita-Kyūshū
Fukuoka
Nagasaki
Kumamoto
Kagoshima
Kyūshū
Shikoku
Hiroshima

Chengdu
Nanchong
Neijiang
Yibin
Chongqing
Panzhihua
Guiyang
Yangtze (Chang Jiang)
Yueyang
Changsha
Hengyang
Suizhou
Wuhan
Hefei
Nanchang
Quzhou
Wuxi
Shanghai
Ningbo
Wenzhou
East China Sea

CHINA

Qinghai Hu
Xining

Kunming
Qujing
Guiyang
Liuzhou
Nanning
Xun Jiang
Guangzhou
Macau
Hong Kong
Zhanjiang
Haikou
Hainan

Fuzhou
Xiamen
Meizhou
Shantou
Taiwan Strait
T'aipei
TAIWAN
T'aitung

Okinawa
Ryukyu Islands

Bonin Islands (Japan)

PACIFIC

Volcano Islands (Japan)

Tropic of Cancer

OCEAN

MYANMAR
Chiang Mai
Louangphrabang
Ha Nôi
Hai Phong
Gulf of Tongking
LAOS
Vientiane
Huê
Da Nang
VIETNAM
THAILAND
Nakhon Ratchasima
Bangkok
Tonle Sap
CAMBODIA
Phnom Penh
Mergui
Gulf of Thailand
Sihanoukville
Nha Trang
Ho Chi Minh City
Mae Nam Nan
Mekong

Paracel Islands

SOUTH CHINA SEA

Spratly Islands

Batan Islands
Luzon Strait
Aparri
Luzon
PHILIPPINES
Quezon City
Manila
Naga
Mindoro
Masbate
Samar
Panay
Iloilo
Cebu
Surigao
Negros
Palawan
Dipolog
Sulu Sea
Mindanao
Zamboanga
Davao

Northern Mariana Islands
Pagan
Saipan
Tinian
Rota
Guam

Yap
Caroline Islands
Chuuk

PALAU
Koror

Mortlock Islands

Nakhon Si Thammarat
George Town
Kota Bharu
Ipoh
Kuala Lumpur
Putrajaya
Singapore
Strait of Malacca
Medan

Kota Kinabalu
Sandakan
Sabah
Sulu Archipelago
Kepulauan Talaud
Kepulauan Sangir

MALAYSIA
BRUNEI
Bandar Seri Begawan
SARAWAK
Kuching
Sibu
Sri Aman
Pontianak
Borneo

Celebes Sea
Manado
Molucca Sea
Halmahera
Celebes
Sea
Seram Sea
Buru
Seram

Jazirah Doberai
Manokwari
IRIAN
Puncak Jaya
JAYA
New Guinea
Jayapura

Bismarck Archipelago
Bismarck Sea
New Britain
Solomon Sea

Sumatra
Siberut
Pulau Mentawai
Padang
Bangka
Palembang
Bengkulu
Enggano
Tanjungkarang-Telukbetung
Selat Sunda
Jakarta
Bandung
Java
Yogyakarta
Semarang
Madura
Surabaya
Bali
Bali Sea
Lombok
Sumbawa
Flores Sea
Sumba
Sawu Sea

Kepulauan Lingga

Balikpapan
Makassar Strait
Ketapang
Barito
Banjarmasin
Ujung Pandang
Parepare
Palu
Kepulauan Sula
Moluccas
Buton

INDONESIA
Java Sea

Raba
Flores

Wetar
OCUSSI
Dili
EAST TIMOR
Timor
Kupang

Kepulauan Tanimbar
Kepulauan Aru

Banda Sea

Arafura Sea
Torres Strait

Cape York Peninsula
CORAL SEA

Gulf of Papua

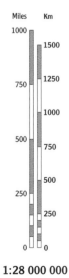

Miles | Km
1000 — 1500
750 — 1250
— 1000
500 — 750
250 — 500
— 250
0 — 0

1:28 000 000

© Bartholomew Ltd

ARCTIC
BARENTS SEA
Kara Sea (Karskoye More)
Norwegian Sea
North Sea
Baltic Sea
Gulf of Bothnia
White Sea (Beloye More)
Sea of Azov
Caspian Sea
Aral Sea
Lake Balkhash
Svalbard (Norway)
Spitsbergen
Nordaustlandet
Zemlya Frantsa-Iosifa
Novaya Zemlya
Faroe Islands (Denmark)
Shetland Islands
Orkney Islands
UNITED KINGDOM
NORWAY
SWEDEN
FINLAND
DENMARK
ESTONIA
LATVIA
LITHUANIA
POLAND
BELARUS
UKRAINE
GEORGIA
ARMENIA
AZERBAIJAN
TURKEY
IRAN
TURKMENISTAN
UZBEKISTAN
KAZAKHSTAN
KYRGYZSTAN
TAJIKISTAN
AFGHANISTAN
RUSSIAN
West Siberian Plain
Zapadno Sibirskaya Ravnina
Kazakhskiy Melkosopochnik
Karakum Desert
Kyzylkum Desert
Ustyurt Plateau
Tarim Basin (Tarim Pendi)
TIEN SHAN
Hindu Kush
Ural Mountains
Gydanskiy Poluostrov
Yamal Peninsula
Kola Peninsula
Moscow
St Petersburg
Stockholm
Helsinki
Oslo
Copenhagen
Riga
Vilnius
Minsk
Kiev
Warsaw
Tallinn
Murmansk
Archangel
Nizhniy Novgorod
Kazan'
Samara
Volgograd
Rostov-na-Donu
Astrakhan'
Yekaterinburg
Perm'
Chelyabinsk
Ufa
Orenburg
Omsk
Novosibirsk
Tomsk
Krasnoyarsk
Barnaul
Novokuznetsk
Kemerovo
Surgut
Tyumen'
Vorkuta
Karaganda
Astana (Akmola)
Almaty
Bishkek
Tashkent
Dushanbe
Ashgabat
Tehran
Baku
Tbilisi
Yerevan
Mashhad
Eşfahan
Ürümqi
Samarkand
Bukhara
Aktobe
Semipalatinsk
Pavlodar
Metres
Feet
6000 19686
5000 16404
4000 13124
3000 9843
2000 6562
1000 3281
500 1640
200 656
0 0
Land below sea level
200 656
2000 6562
4000 13124
6000 19686
113
78
Conic Equidistant Projection

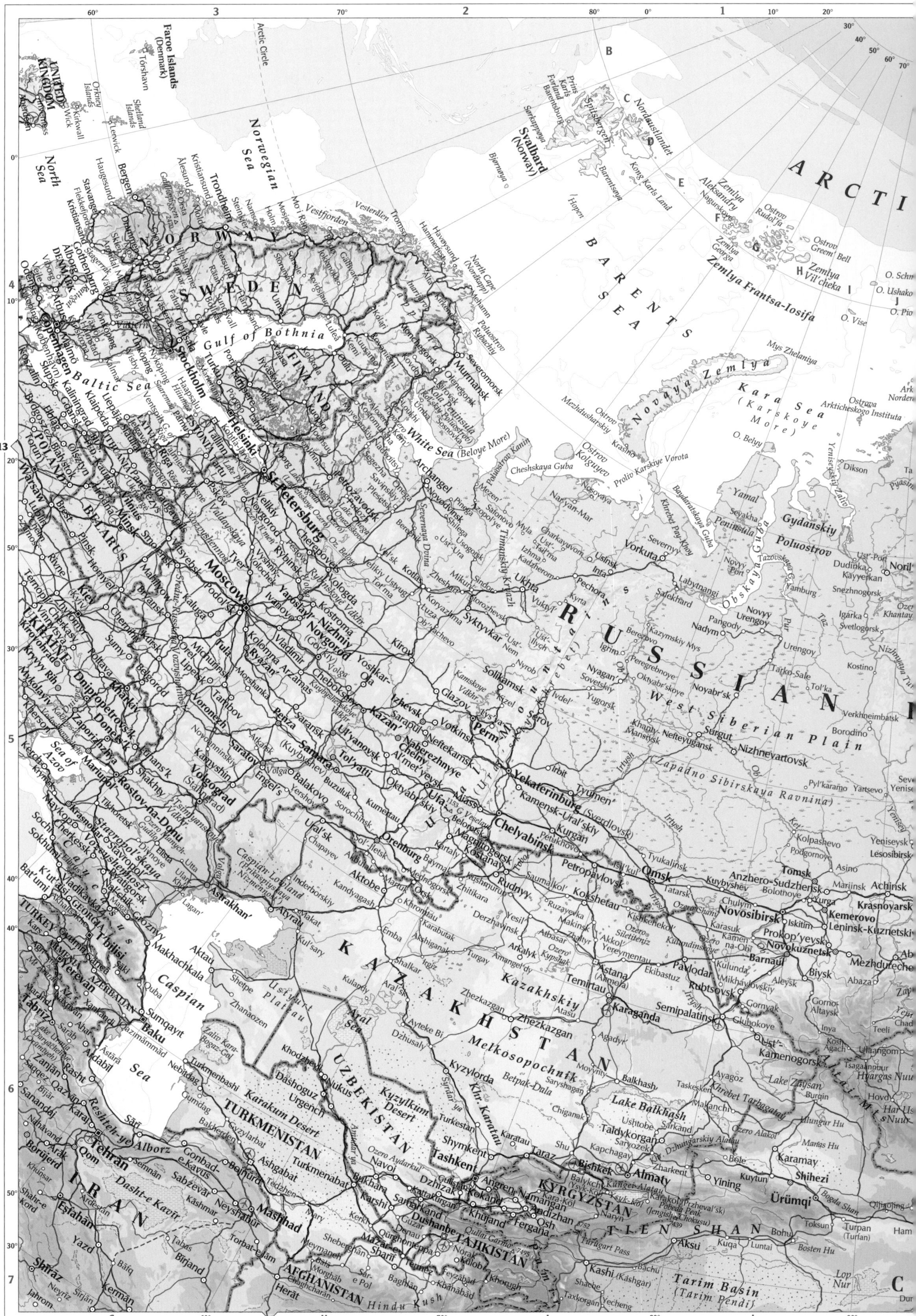

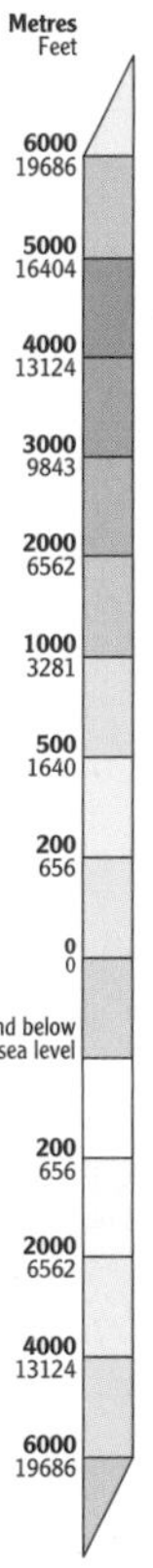

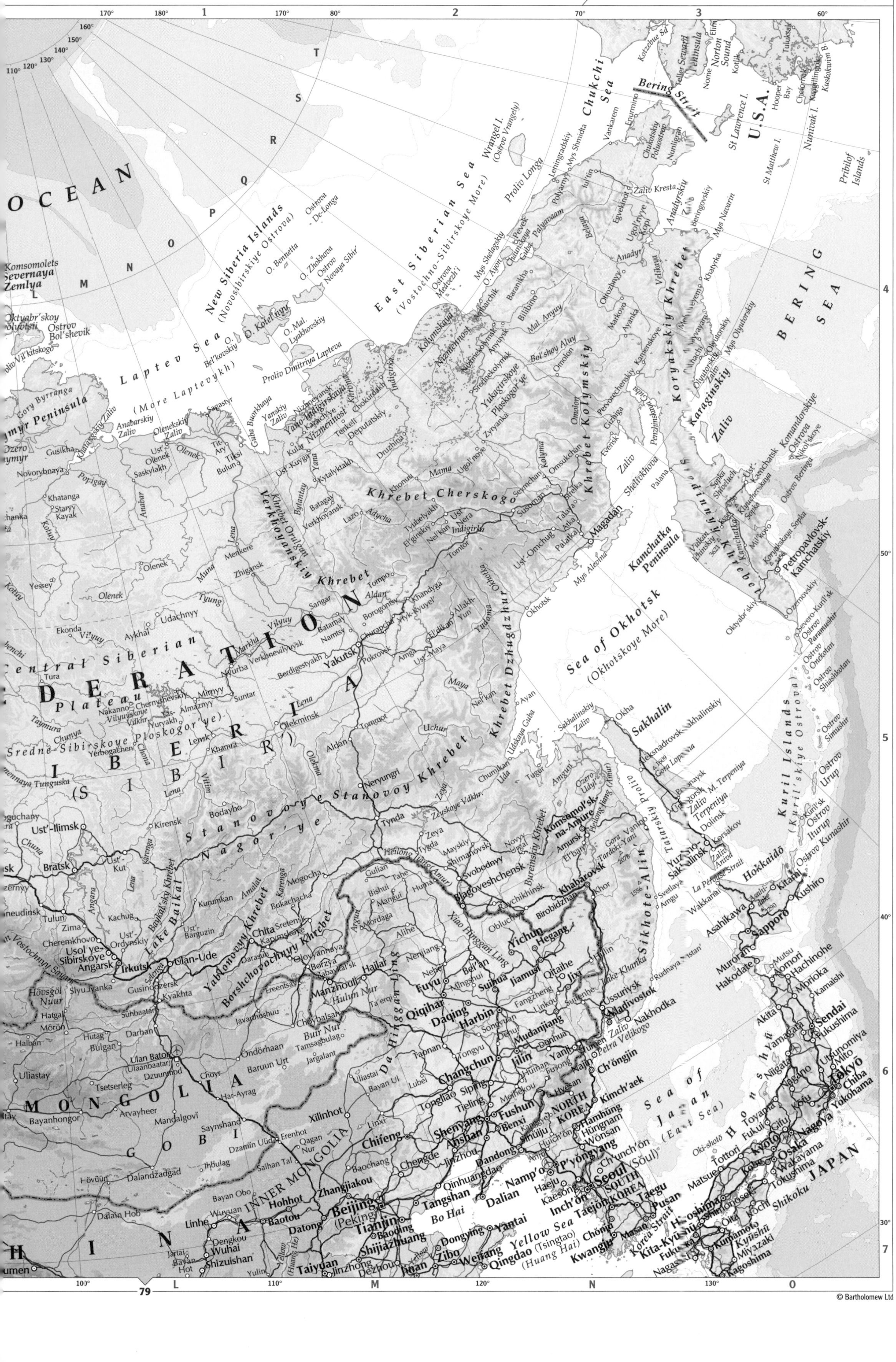
OCEAN
New Siberia Islands
(Novosibirskiye Ostrova)
Laptev Sea
(More Laptevykh)
East Siberian Sea
(Vostochno-Sibirskoye More)
Wrangel I.
(Ostrov Vrangelya)
Chukchi Sea
Bering Strait
U.S.A.
BERING SEA
Koryakskiy Khrebet
Khrebet Cherskogo
Verkhoyanskiy Khrebet
Khrebet Kolymskiy
Kamchatka Peninsula
Petropavlovsk-Kamchatskiy
Sea of Okhotsk
(Okhotskoye More)
Magadan
Yakutsk
Central Siberian Plateau
FEDERATION
SIBERIA
(SIBIR')
Stanovoy Khrebet
Stanovoye Nagor'ye
Sakhalin
Kuril Islands
(Kuril'skiye Ostrova)
Lake Baikal
Irkutsk
Khabarovsk
Vladivostok
Hokkaidō
Sapporo
Sea of Japan
(East Sea)
Honshū
Tōkyō
JAPAN
MONGOLIA
GOBI
INNER MONGOLIA
CHINA
Beijing
(Peking)
Tianjin
Harbin
Shenyang
NORTH KOREA
P'yŏngyang
SOUTH KOREA
Seoul
(Sŏul)
Bo Hai
Yellow Sea
(Huang Hai)
Shikoku
Kyūshū

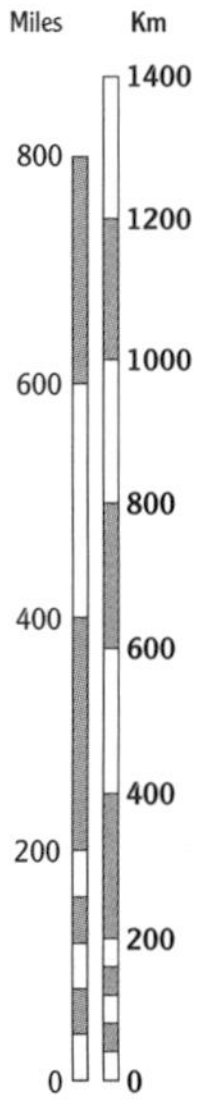
Miles
Km
800
600
400
200
0
1400
1200
1000
800
600
400
200
0

1:21 000 000

© Bartholomew Ltd

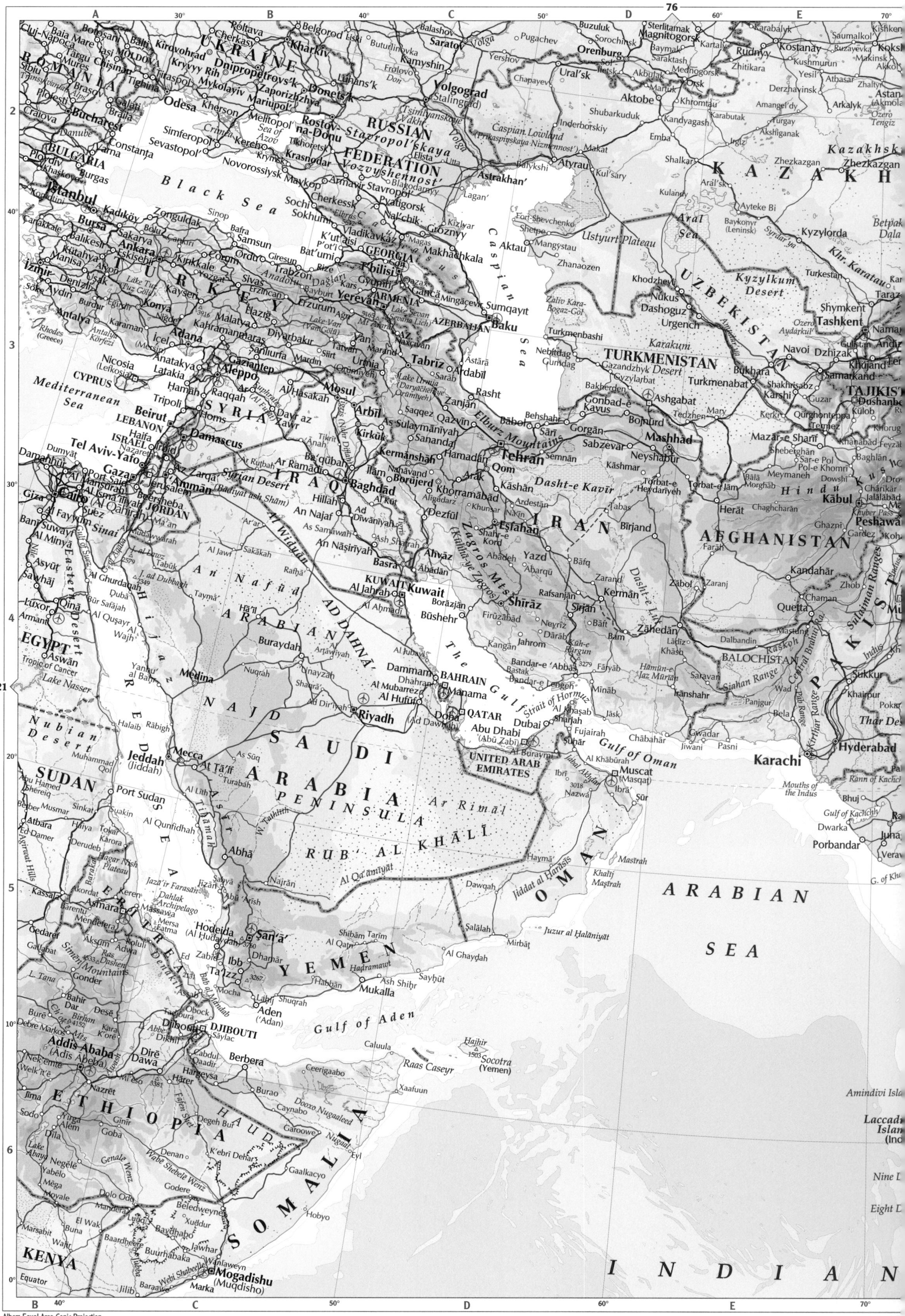

A 30° B 40° C 50° D 76 60° E 70°

Metres / Feet

6000 / 19686
5000 / 16404
4000 / 13124
3000 / 9843
2000 / 6562
1000 / 3281
500 / 1640
200 / 656
0
Land below sea level
200 / 656
2000 / 6562
4000 / 13124
6000 / 19686

121

RUSSIAN FEDERATION

Poltava · Cherkasy · Kharkiv · Liski · Balashov · Buzuluk · Sterlitamak · Magnitogorsk · Karabalyk · Saumalkol'

Kirovohrad · Kryvyy Rih · Dnipropetrovs'k · Donets'k · Luhans'k · Saratov · Volga · Pugachev · Orenburg · Baymak · Kartaly · Rudnyy · Kostanay

ROMANIA · MOLDOVA · UKRAINE · Zaporizhzhya · Mariupol' · Rostov na-Donu · Frolovo · Don · Kamyshin · Ural'sk · Sel · Saraktash · Mednogorsk · Orsk · Khromtau · Amangel'dy · Arkalyk

Cluj-Napoca · Baia Mare · Iaşi · Bălţi · Tighina · Cherkasy · Belgorod

Buchares · Brăila · Galaţi · Odesa · Kherson · Melitopol' · Berdyans'k · Taganrog · Volgograd (Stalingrad) · Yershov · Astrakhan' · Atyrau · Emba · Makat · Shalkar · Zhezkazgan

Black Sea · Simferopol' · Sevastopol' · Kerch · Novorossiysk · Maykop · Armavir · Stavropol' · Elista · Caspian Lowland · Inderborskiy · Kulangy · Kul'sary · Aral Sea

BULGARIA · Burgas · Istanbul · Kadıköy · Zonguldak · Bafra · Samsun · Sochi · Sokhumi · Nal'chik · Grozny · Kizlyar · Aktau · Ustyurt Plateau

KAZAKHSTAN

TURKEY · Ankara · Sivas · Trabzon · Rize · Batumi · GEORGIA · Tbilisi · Gyumri · ARMENIA · Yerevan · Makhachkala · Caspian Sea · Fort-Shevchenko · Zhanaozen · Aral

Izmir · Konya · Kayseri · Erzincan · Erzurum · Kars · Gäncä · Mingäçevir · Sumqayıt · Baku · Turkmenbashi · UZBEKISTAN · Nukus · Shymkent

CYPRUS · Nicosia · Latakia · Aleppo · Gaziantep · Diyarbakır · Van · Tabrīz · Ardabīl · AZERBAIJAN · Türkmenbaşy · TURKMENISTAN · Dashoguz · Urgench · Tashkent

Mediterranean Sea · Beirut · Damascus · SYRIA · Raqqah · Mosul · Arbīl · As Sulaymānīyah · Sanandaj · Qazvīn · Rasht · Karakum Desert · Ashgabat · Bukhara · Samarkand · TAJIKISTAN

LEBANON · ISRAEL · Tel Aviv-Yafo · Amman · JORDAN · Baghdad · IRAQ · Karbalā' · An Najaf · Kirkūk · Hamadān · Tehran · Qom · Semnān · Mashhad · Herāt · AFGHANISTAN · Kabul · Peshawar

EGYPT · Cairo · Suez · Sinai · Al Jawf · An Nafūd · ARABIAN · Esfahān · IRAN · Yazd · Kermān · Zāhedān · Kandahār · Quetta · PAKISTAN

Aswān · Tropic of Cancer · Lake Nasser · Medina · NAJD · KUWAIT · Kuwait · Shīrāz · Būshehr · Bandar-e 'Abbās · Strait of Hormuz · BALOCHISTAN · Karachi

Nubian Desert · Jeddah · Mecca · SAUDI ARABIA · AD DAHNĀ' · Dammam · Manama · BAHRAIN · Doha · QATAR · Abu Dhabi · UNITED ARAB EMIRATES · Muscat · Gulf of Oman · Hyderabad

SUDAN · Port Sudan · RED SEA · Abhā · RUB' AL KHĀLĪ · OMAN · Şalālah · Mouths of the Indus

ERITREA · Asmara · Massawa · YEMEN · Şan'ā' · Ta'izz · Aden · Mukalla · Socotra (Yemen) · **ARABIAN SEA**

ETHIOPIA · Addis Ababa · DJIBOUTI · Djibouti · Berbera · **Gulf of Aden** · Raas Caseyr

SOMALIA · Mogadishu (Muqdisho) · Gaalkacyo

KENYA · Equator · **INDIAN OCEAN**

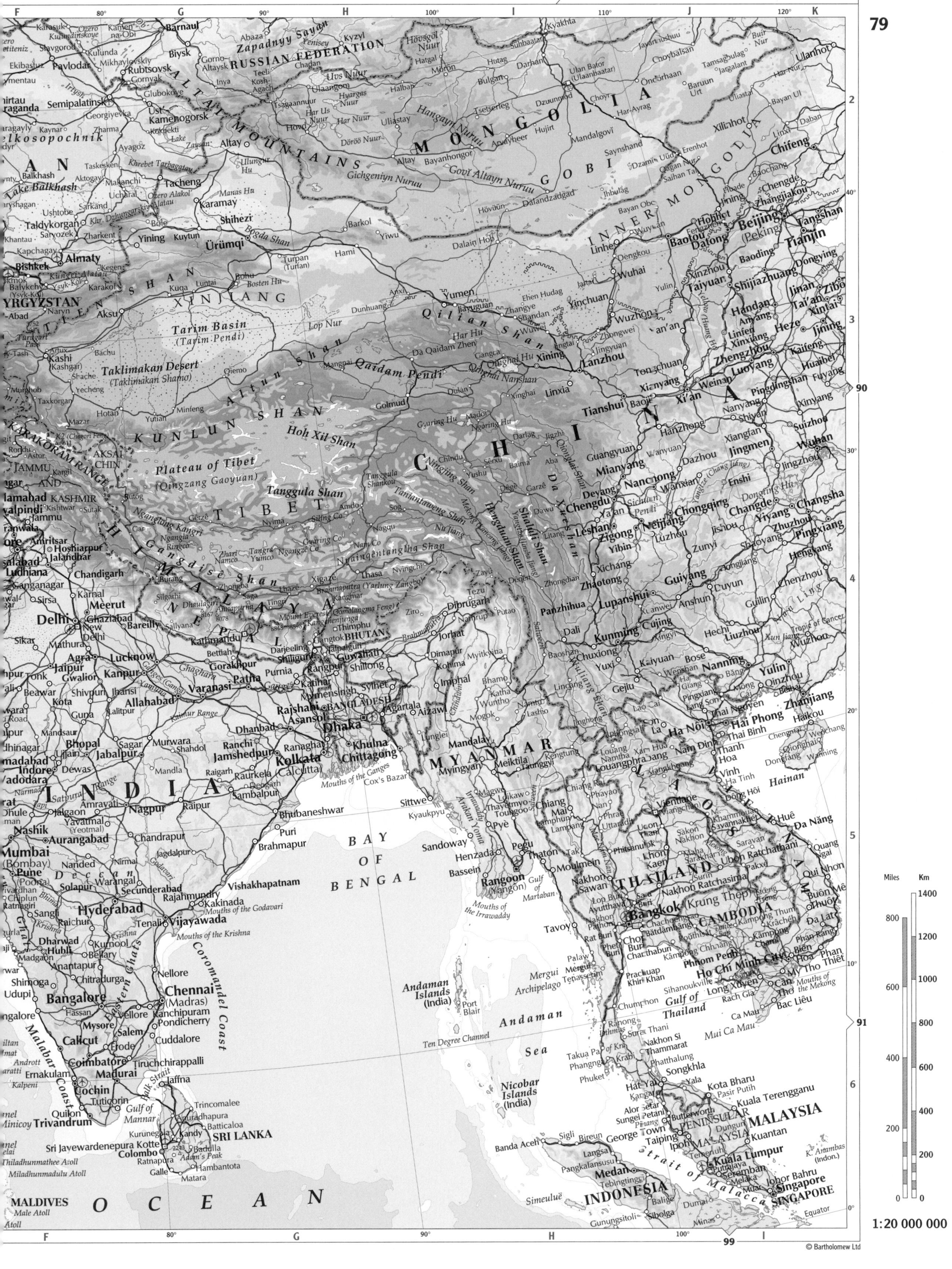

RUSSIAN FEDERATION

MONGOLIA

INNER MONGOLIA

GOBI

XINJIANG

Tarim Basin
(Tarim Pendi)

Taklimakan Desert
(Taklimakan Shamo)

TIEN SHAN

KUNLUN SHAN

ALTUN SHAN

Qilian Shan

Qaidam Pendi

Plateau of Tibet
(Qingzang Gaoyuan)

TIBET

C H I N A

Hoh Xil Shan

Tanggula Shan

KARAKORAM RANGE

AKSAI CHIN

KASHMIR

JAMMU
AND

HIMALAYA

NEPAL

BHUTAN

BANGLADESH

Dhaka

I N D I A

Deccan

Eastern Ghats

Western Ghats

Coromandel Coast

Malabar Coast

MYANMAR

THAILAND

CAMBODIA

MALAYSIA

PENINSULAR MALAYSIA

Singapore

INDONESIA

BAY
OF
BENGAL

Andaman
Islands
(India)

Nicobar
Islands
(India)

Andaman
Sea

Gulf of
Thailand

Ten Degree Channel

O C E A N

SRI LANKA

MALDIVES

Mouths of the Ganges

Mouths of the Irrawaddy

Mouths of the Godavari

Mouths of the Krishna

Mouths of the Mekong

Beijing
Peking

Tianjin

Delhi

New Delhi

Mumbai
(Bombay)

Kolkata
(Calcutta)

Chennai
(Madras)

Bangalore

Hyderabad

Bangkok
Krung Thep

Rangoon
(Yangon)

Ha Noi

Phnom Penh

Ho Chi Minh City

Kuala Lumpur

Hainan

Tropic of Cancer

Equator

Miles Km

1400

800   1200

1000

600   800

400   600

200   400

200

0   0

1:20 000 000

© Bartholomew Ltd

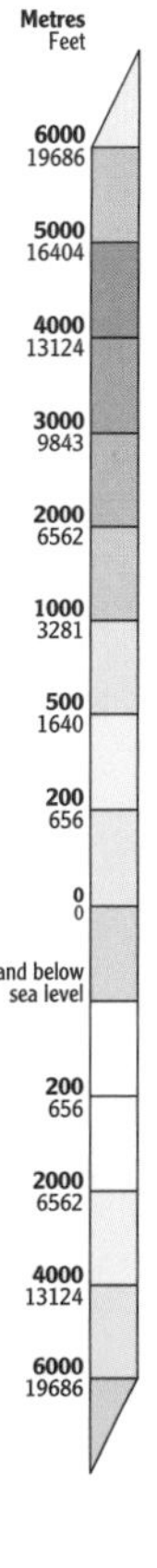

Metres
Feet
6000
19686
5000
16404
4000
13124
3000
9843
2000
6562
1000
3281
500
1640
200
656
0
0
Land below sea level
200
656
2000
6562
4000
13124
6000
19686

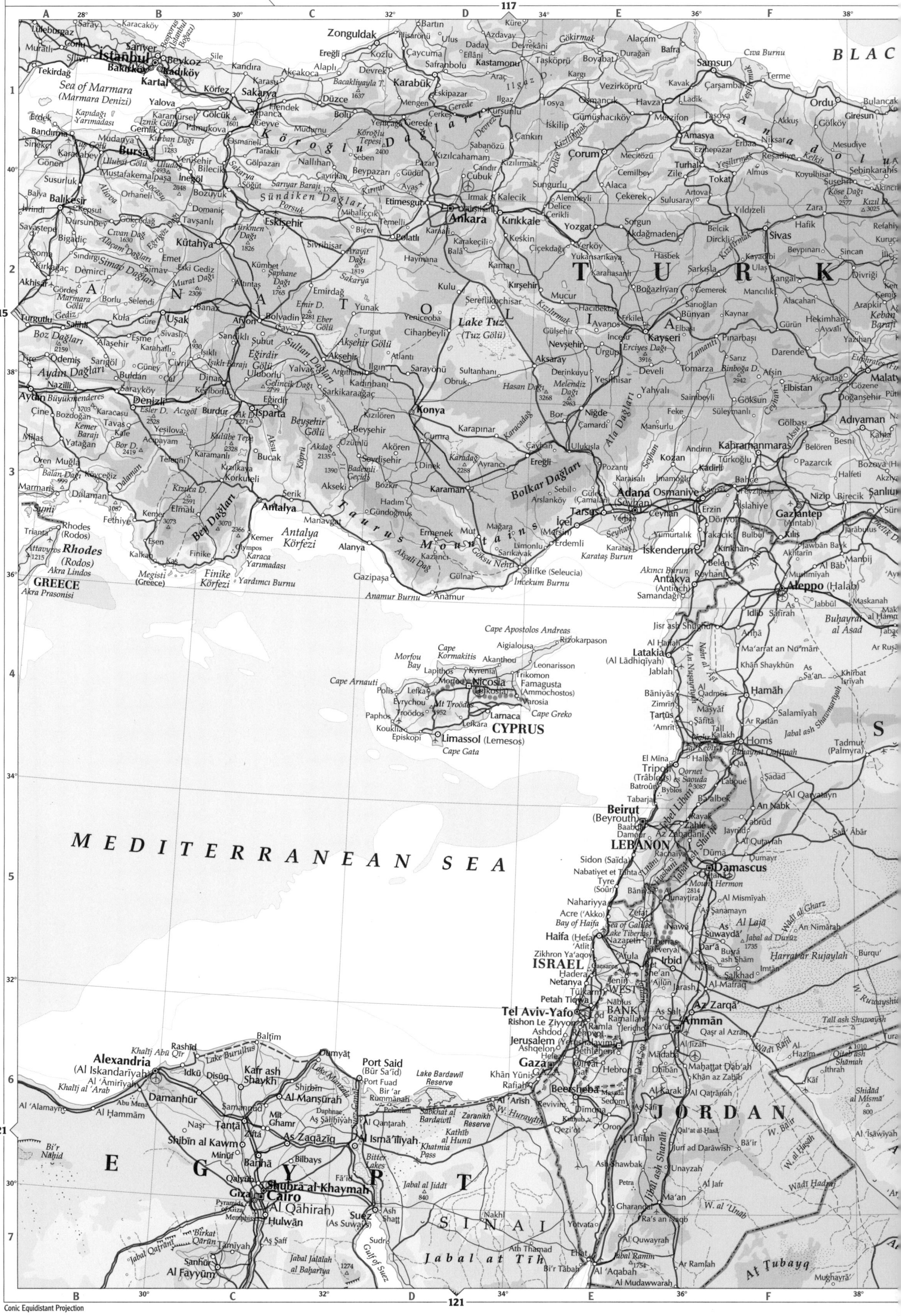

BLAC
TURKEY
A N A T O L I A
Köroğlu Dağları
Taurus Mountains
Sea of Marmara
(Marmara Denizi)
İstanbul
Bursa
Ankara
Konya
Eskişehir
Kütahya
Afyon
Antalya
Adana
Kayseri
Sivas
Samsun
Zonguldak
Karabük
Balıkesir
Denizli
Aydın
Isparta
Mersin
Gaziantep
Kahramanmaraş
İskenderun
Lake Tuz
(Tuz Gölü)
Antalya Körfezi
Rhodes
(Rodos)
GREECE
Cape Apostolos Andreas
Nicosia
CYPRUS
Limassol (Lemesos)
Larnaca
Famagusta
Cape Gata
Cape Arnauti
M E D I T E R R A N E A N   S E A
Antakya
Aleppo (Halab)
Latakia
Hamāh
Homs
Tripoli
Beirut
(Beyrouth)
LEBANON
Damascus
Sidon (Saïda)
Tyre
Haifa
ISRAEL
Tel Aviv-Yafo
Jerusalem
WEST BANK
Gaza
Beersheba
Irbid
Ammān
JORDAN
Al 'Aqabah
Alexandria
(Al Iskandarīyah)
Port Said
(Būr Sa'īd)
Cairo
Al Qāhirah
Giza
Suez
(As Suways)
Gulf of Suez
E G Y P T
S I N A I
Jabal at Tīh
Conic Equidistant Projection

SEA

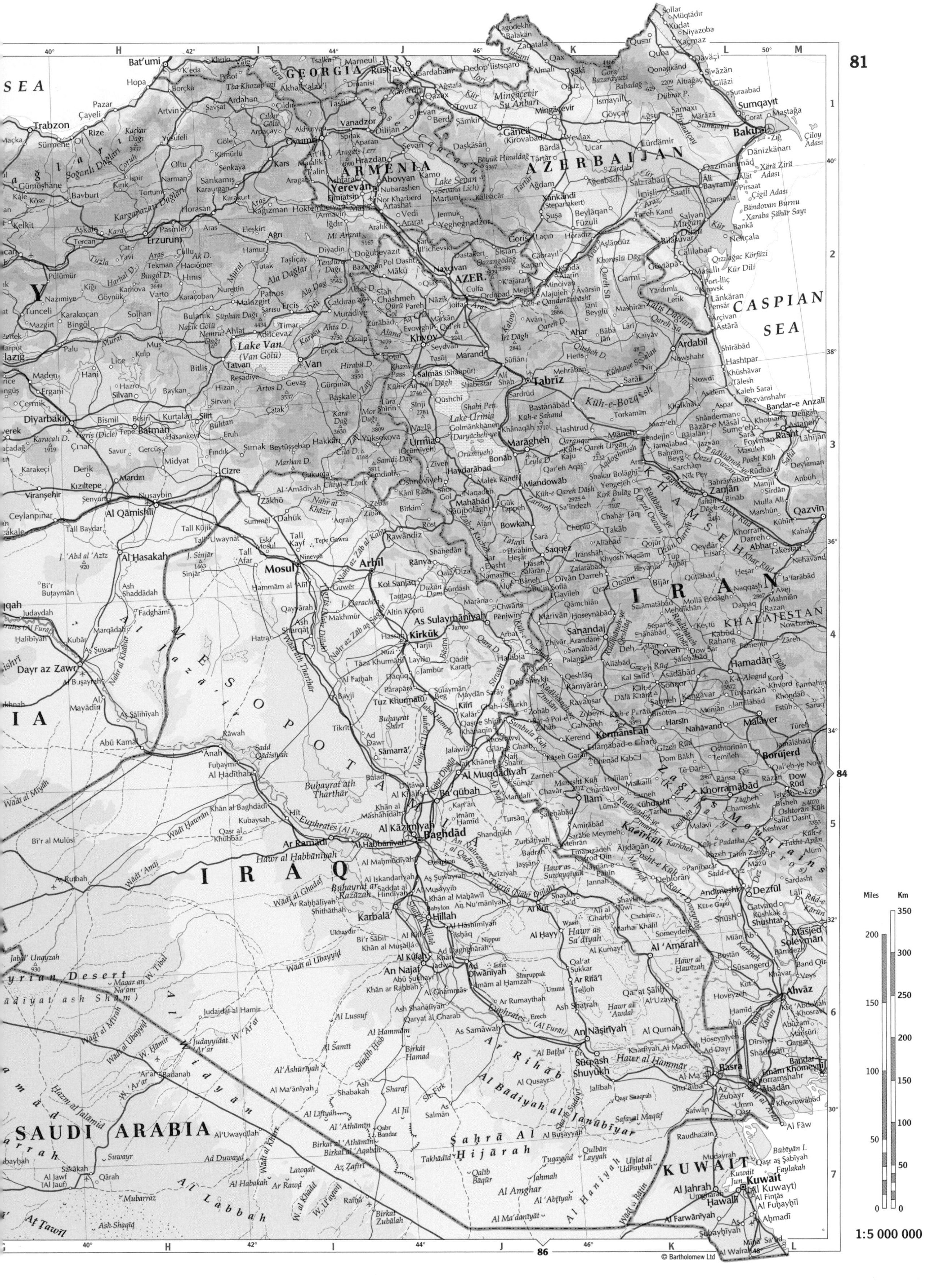

GEORGIA

ARMENIA

AZERBAIJAN

AZER.

CASPIAN SEA

Trabzon
Rize
Erzurum
Yerevan
Baku
Tabrīz

Y

Lake Van
(Van Gölü)
Van

Diyarbakır
Batman
Mardin

Lake Urmia
(Daryācheh-ye
Orūmīyeh)

Urmia
(Orūmīyeh)

Ardabīl

IRAN

KHAMSEH

Mosul
Arbīl

Kirkūk
As Sulaymānīyah

Zanjān
Qazvīn
Abhar

KHALAJESTAN

Dayr az Zawr

Hamadān

Borūjerd

Khorramābād

IA

MESOPOTAMIA

Sāmarrā'

Kermānshāh

Baghdad
Al Kāzimīyah
Ar Ramādī

Zagros Mountains

IRAQ

Karbalā'
Hillah

Dezfūl

An Najaf
Al Kūfah

Masjed
Soleymān

Ahvāz

Syrian Desert

An Nāşirīyah

Basra
Ābādān
Khorramshahr

SAUDI ARABIA

Şahrā Al Hijārah

KUWAIT

Kuwait
(Al Kuwayt)

Miles   Km
200   350
        300
150   250
        200
100   150
50   100
        50
0   0

1:5 000 000

84

86

© Bartholomew Ltd

RUSSIAN FEDERATION
SAMARSKAYA OBLAST'
SARATOVSKAYA OBLAST'
ORENBURGSKAYA OBLAST'
ZAPADNYY KAZAKHSTAN
AKTYUBINSKAYA OBLAST'
KOSTANAYSKAYA OBLAST'
ATYRAUSKAYA OBLAST'
MANGISTAUSKAYA OBLAST'
KYZYLORDINSKAYA OBLAST'
KAZA
UZBEKISTAN
TURKMENISTAN
IRAN
CASPIAN SEA
ARAL SEA
O. Vozrozhdeniya
(ARAL'SKOYE MORE)
Ryn-Caspian Lowland
(Prikaspiyskaya Nizmennost')
Peski
Obshchiy Syrt
Turgayskaya Stolovaya Strana
Turgayskaya
Peski Priaral'skiye Karakumy
Ustyurt Plateau
Poluostrov Buzachi
Poluostrov Mangyshlak
Uval Karabaur
Zaliv Kara-Bogaz-Gol
KYZYLKUM DESERT
KARAKUM DESERT
(PESKI KARAKUMY)
Zaunguzskiye Karakumy
TURAN LOWLAND
KARA KUMY
Samara
Tol'yatti
Syzran'
Novokuybyshevsk
Chapayevsk
Buguruslan
Sterlitamak
Beloretsk
Magnitogorsk
Troitsk
Kostanay
Rudnyy
Balakovo
Vol'sk
Buzuluk
Orenburg
Orsk
Novotroitsk
Ural'sk
Aktobe
Atyrau
Aktau
Baku
Sumqayıt
Nukus
Urgench
Dashoguz
Turkmenbashi
Nebitdag
Ashgabat
Turkmenabat
Bukhara
Navoi
Gorgān
Bojnūrd
Shīrvān
Quchan
Mary
Bayramaly
Sari
Amol
Babol
Ghaem Shahr
Kazalinsk
Aral'sk
Shalkar
Emba
Kandyagash
Metres
Feet
6000
19686
5000
16404
4000
13124
3000
9843
2000
6562
1000
3281
500
1640
200
656
0
0
Land below sea level
200
656
2000
6562
4000
13124
6000
19686
A
B
C
D
E
48°
52°
56°
60°
64°
44°
40°
1
2
3
4
5
Conic Equidistant Projection

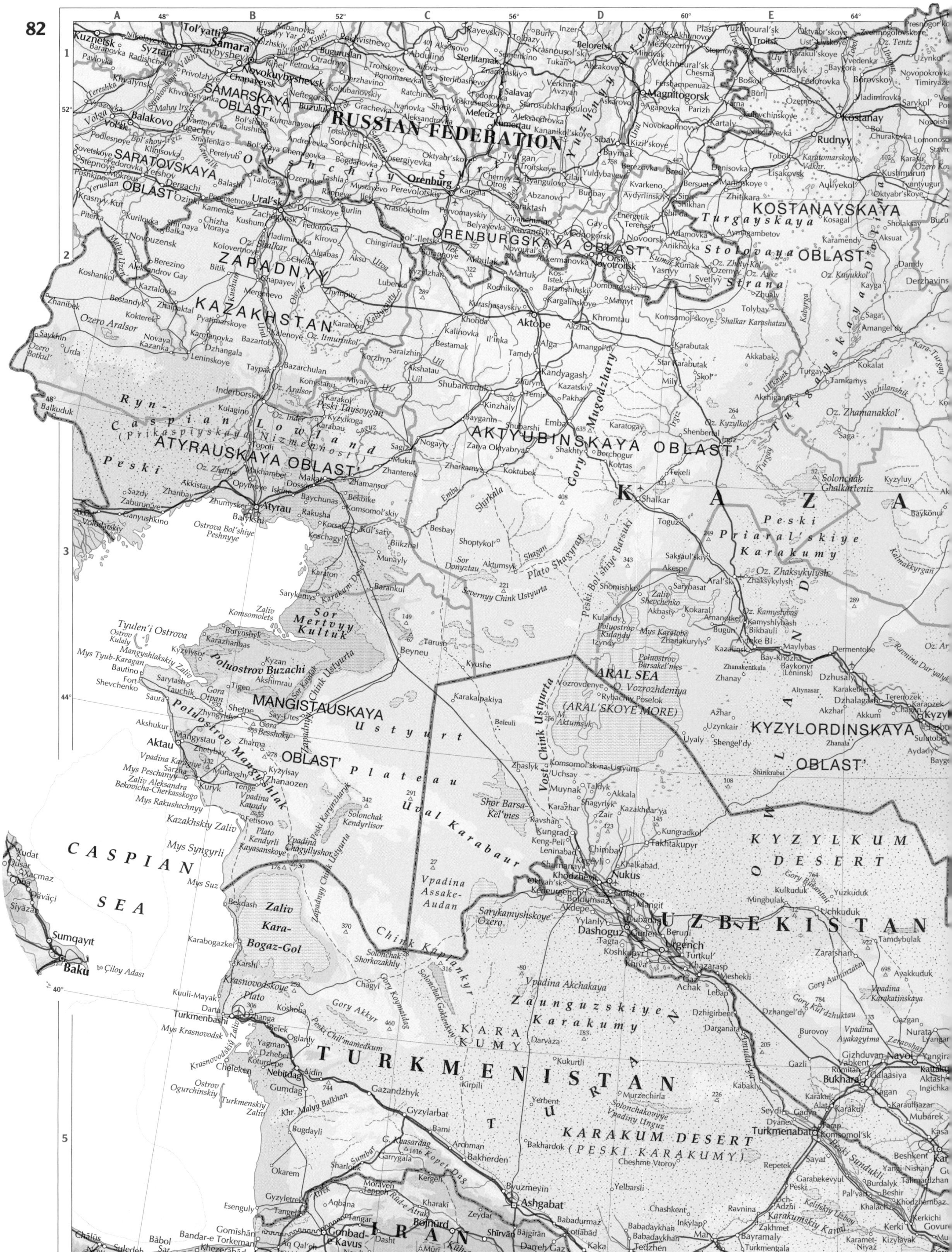

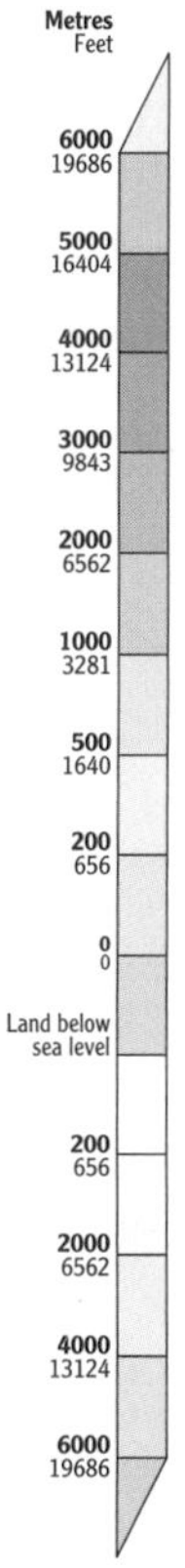

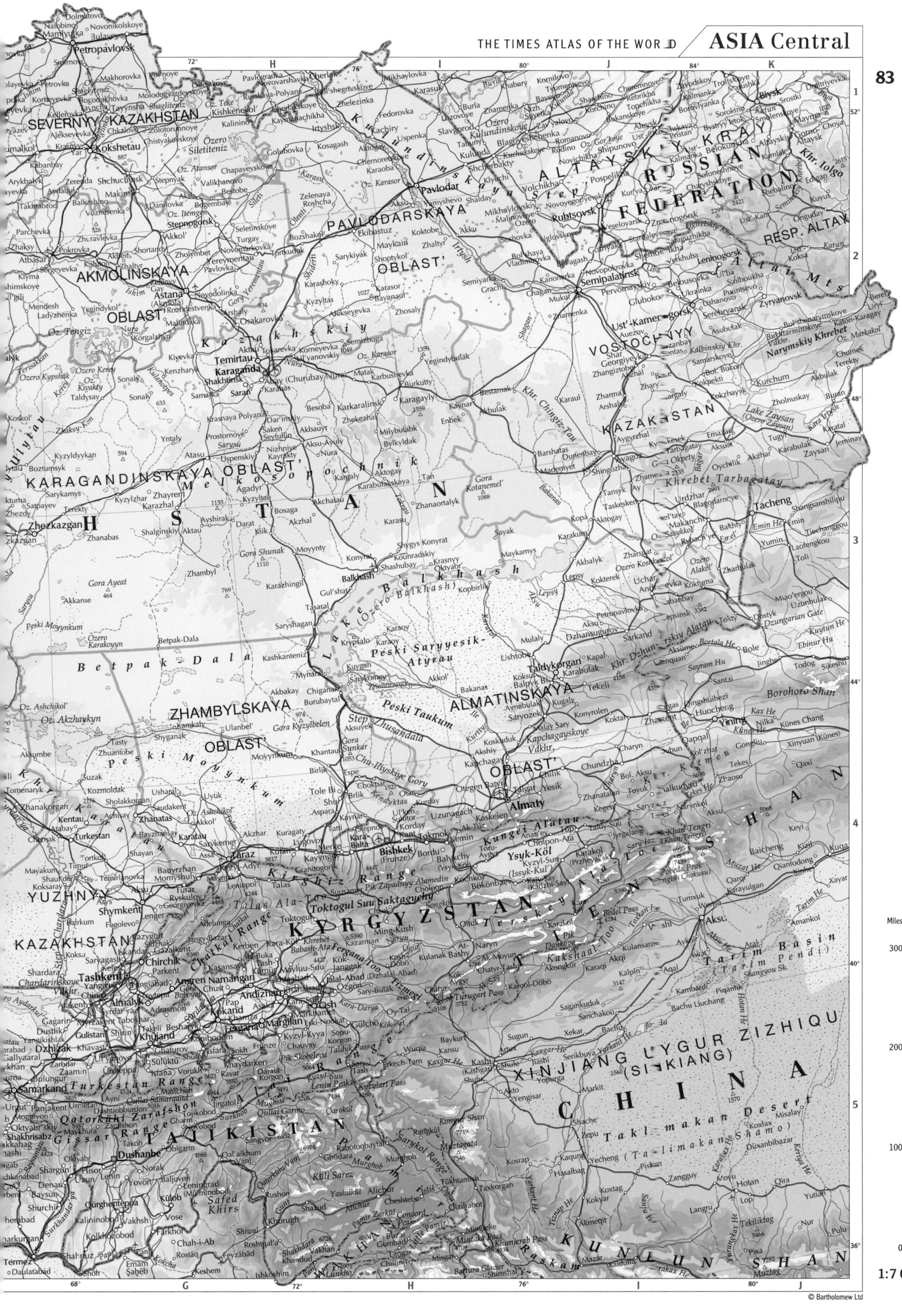
SEVERNYY KAZAKHSTAN
AKMOLINSKAYA OBLAST'
PAVLODARSKAYA OBLAST'
KARAGANDINSKAYA OBLAST'
ZHAMBYLSKAYA OBLAST
ALMATINSKAYA OBLAST'
VOSTOCHNYY KAZAKHSTAN
YUZHNYY KAZAKHSTAN
KAZAKHSTAN
ALTAYSKIY KRAY
RUSSIAN FEDERATION
RESP. ALTAY
KYRGYZSTAN
TAJIKISTAN
CHINA
XINJIANG UYGUR ZIZHIQU (SINKIANG)
Petropavlovsk
Kokshetau
Astana (Akmola)
Pavlodar
Semipalatinsk
Ust'-Kamenogorsk
Rubtsovsk
Barnaul
Biysk
Karaganda
Temirtau
Zhezkazgan
Balkhash
Taldykorgan
Almaty
Bishkek (Frunze)
Taraz
Shymkent
Tashkent
Andizhan
Namangan
Osh
Fergana
Kokand
Khujand
Samarkand
Dushanbe
Kulob
Termez
Aksu
Kashi (Kashgar)
Yining
Tacheng
Hotan
Yecheng
Lake Balkhash (Ozero Balkhash)
Lake Zaysan (Ozero Zaysan)
Ysyk-Köl (Issyk-Kul')
Kazakhskiy Melkosopochnik
Betpak-Dala
Peski Moyynkum
Peski Taukum
Peski Saryyesik-Atyrau
Kulundinskaya Step'
Altai Mts
Narymskiy Khrebet
Khrebet Tarbagatay
Dzungarian Gate
Khr. Dzhungarskiy Alatau
Kirghiz Range
Talas Ala-Too
Fergana Too Tizmegi
Alai Range
Turkestan Range
Gissar Range
Pamir
T I E N S H A N
Borohoro Shan
Tarim Basin (Tarim Pendi)
Taklimakan Desert (Taklimakan Shamo)
K U N L U N S H A N
Miles Km
1:7 000 000
© Bartholomew Ltd

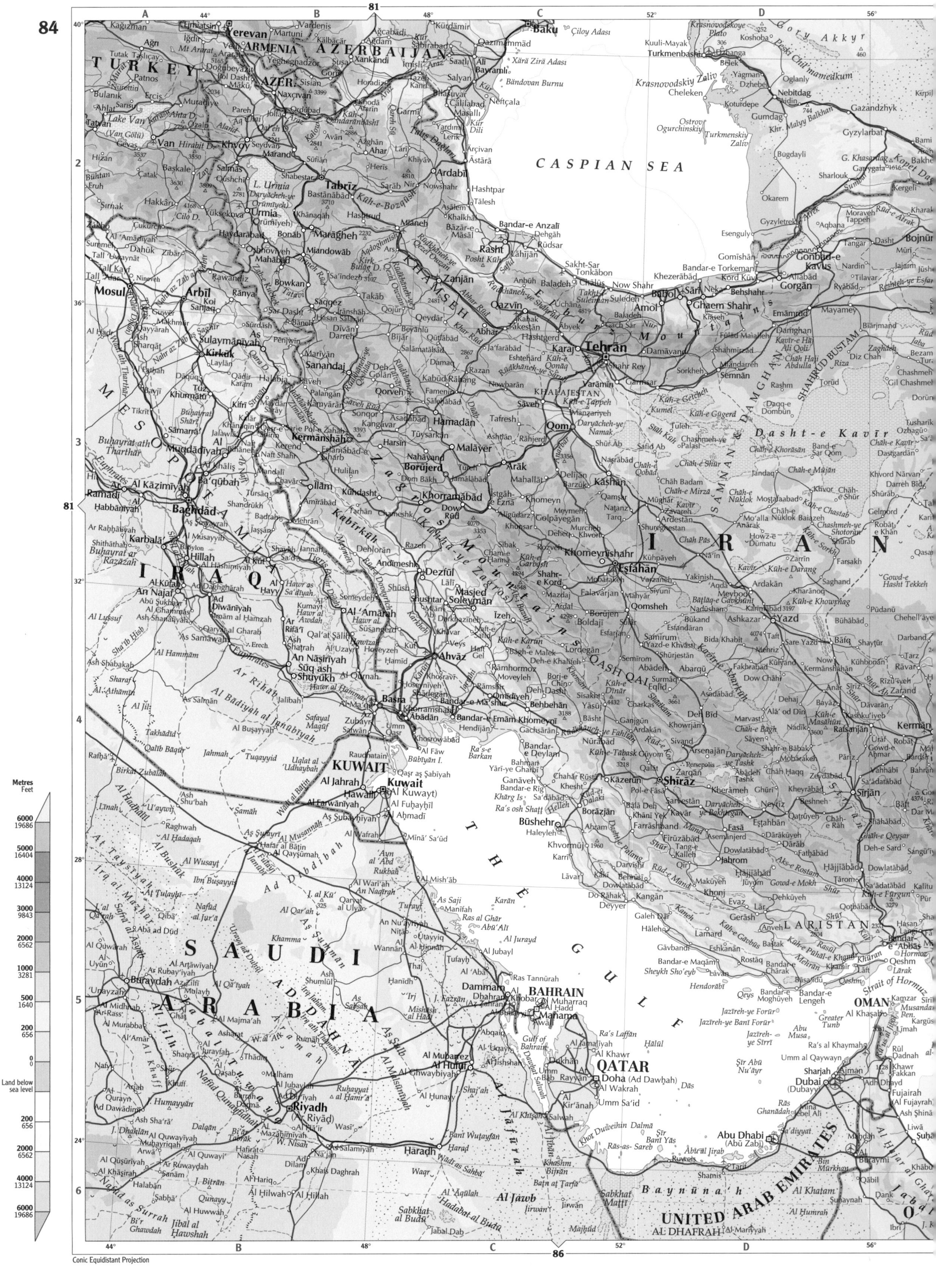

Map: Iran, Iraq and Arabian Peninsula

A   44°   81   B   48°   C   52°   D   56°

CASPIAN SEA

THE GULF

Countries
TURKEY
ARMENIA
AZERBAIJAN
AZER.
TURKMENISTAN
IRAN
IRAQ
KUWAIT
SAUDI ARABIA
BAHRAIN
QATAR
UNITED ARAB EMIRATES
OMAN
MESOPOTAMIA
KHAMSEH
KHUZESTAN
LARISTAN
QASHQAI
Dasht-e Kavir
AL DHAFRAH
BAYNUNAH

Selected place names
Yerevan, Baku, Turkmenbashi, Nebitdag, Van, Tabrīz, Urmia, Mosul, Arbīl, Kirkūk, Sulaymānīyah, Sanandaj, Rasht, Qazvīn, Tehrān, Karaj, Gorgān, Sārī, Āmol, Bābol, Hamadān, Kermānshāh, Baghdād, Karbalā', Hillah, An Najaf, Ad Dīwānīyah, As Samāwah, An Nāsirīyah, Basra, Ahvāz, Khorramābād, Borūjerd, Arāk, Qom, Kāshān, Eşfahān, Shahr-e Kord, Yazd, Kermān, Shīrāz, Kāzerūn, Būshehr, Borāzjān, Kuwait (Al Kuwayt), Al Jahrah, Al Ahmadī, Buraydah, Riyadh (Ar Riyāḍ), Dammām, Al Khubar, Dhahran, BAHRAIN, Manama, Al Muharraq, Al Hufūf, Al Mubarrez, Doha (Ad Dawḥah), Al Wakrah, Umm Sa'īd, Abu Dhabi (Abū Zabī), Dubai (Dubayy), Sharjah, Ajman, Al Fujairah, Al Khaimah, OMAN, Al Khasab, Bandar-e 'Abbās, Qeshm, Strait of Hormuz

Scale (Metres / Feet)
Metres	Feet
6000	19686
5000	16404
4000	13124
3000	9843
2000	6562
1000	3281
500	1640
200	656
0	0
Land below sea level	
200	656
2000	6562
4000	13124
6000	19686

Conic Equidistant Projection

44°   B   48°   C   52°   86   D   56°

THE GULF, IRAN AND AFGHANISTAN

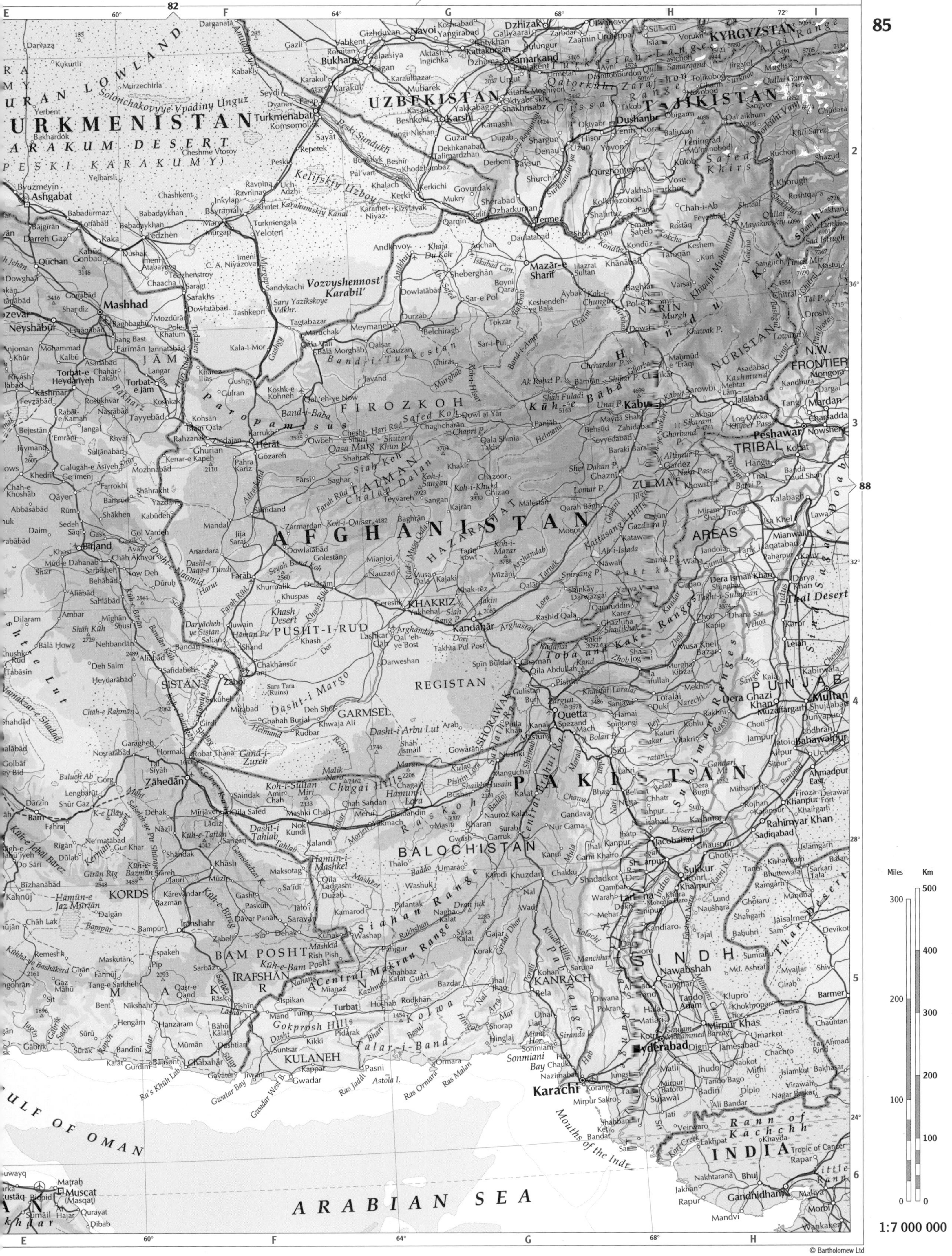

TURKMENISTAN

UZBEKISTAN

TAJIKISTAN

KYRGYZSTAN

KARAKUM DESERT

(PESKI KARAKUMY)

TURAN LOWLAND

Ashgabat

Mashhad

Neyshābūr

AFGHANISTAN

Herāt

FIROZKOH

Safed Koh

Kābul

Peshawar

TRIBAL AREAS

N.W. FRONTIER

NURISTAN

Mazār-e Sharif

Kandahār

REGISTAN

Zābul

Zāhedān

SISTĀN

KORDS

BALOCHISTAN

PAKISTAN

Quetta

PUNJAB

Multan

Bahawalpur

Sukkur

Khairpur

SINDH

Nawabshah

Hyderabad

Mirpur Khas

Karachi

BAM POSHT

MAKRAN

Central Makran Range

Siahan Range

KULANEH

Gwadar

Turbat

GULF OF OMAN

Muscat (Masqat)

Matrah

ARABIAN SEA

INDIA

Tropic of Cancer

Rann of Kachchh

Mouths of the Indus

Miles	Km
300	500
	400
200	300
	200
100	100
0	0

1:7 000 000

© Bartholomew Ltd

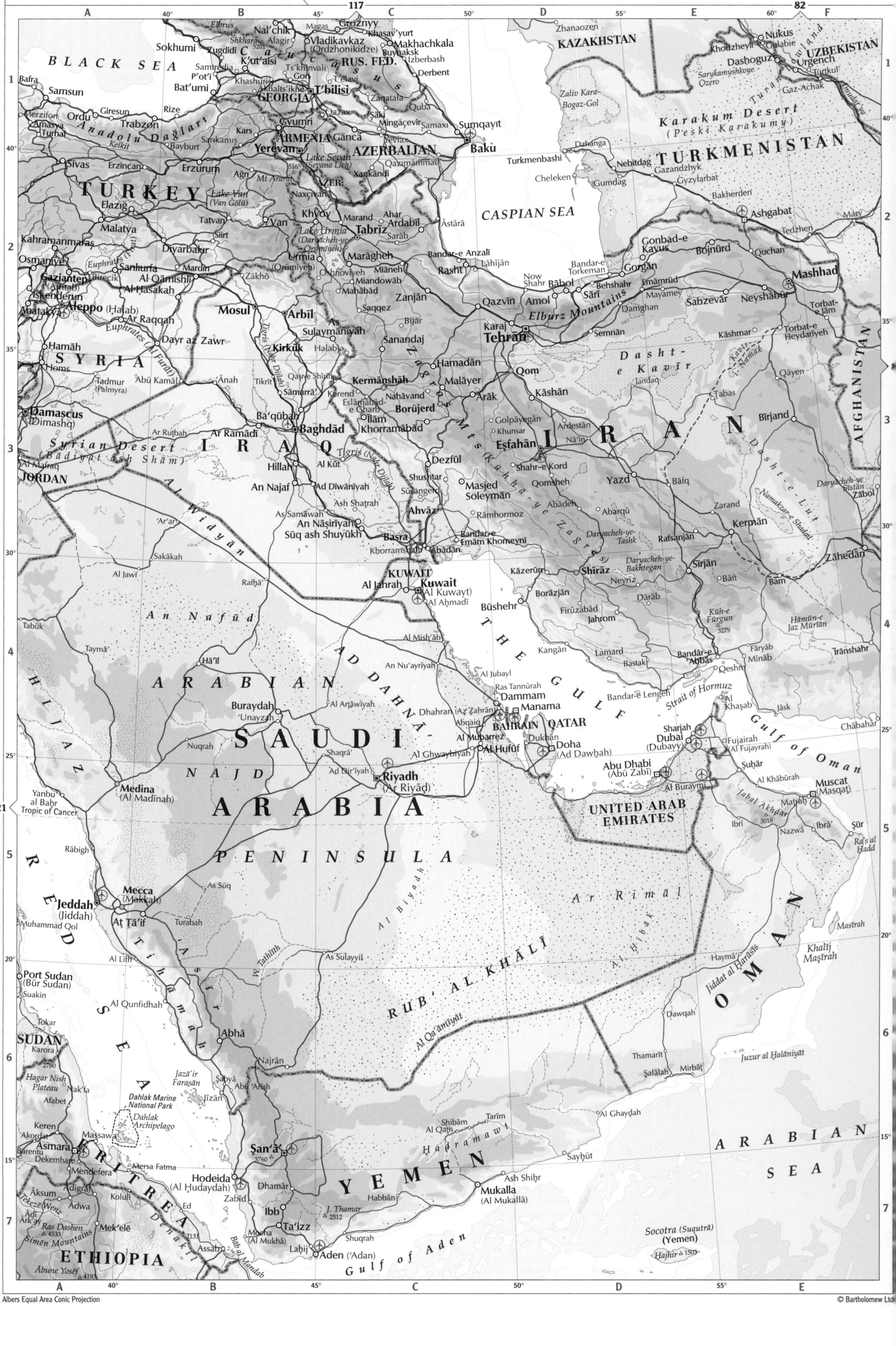

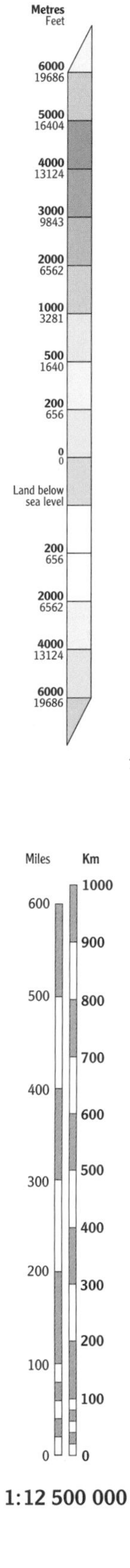

1 : 12 500 000

Albers Equal Area Conic Projection

© Bartholomew Ltd

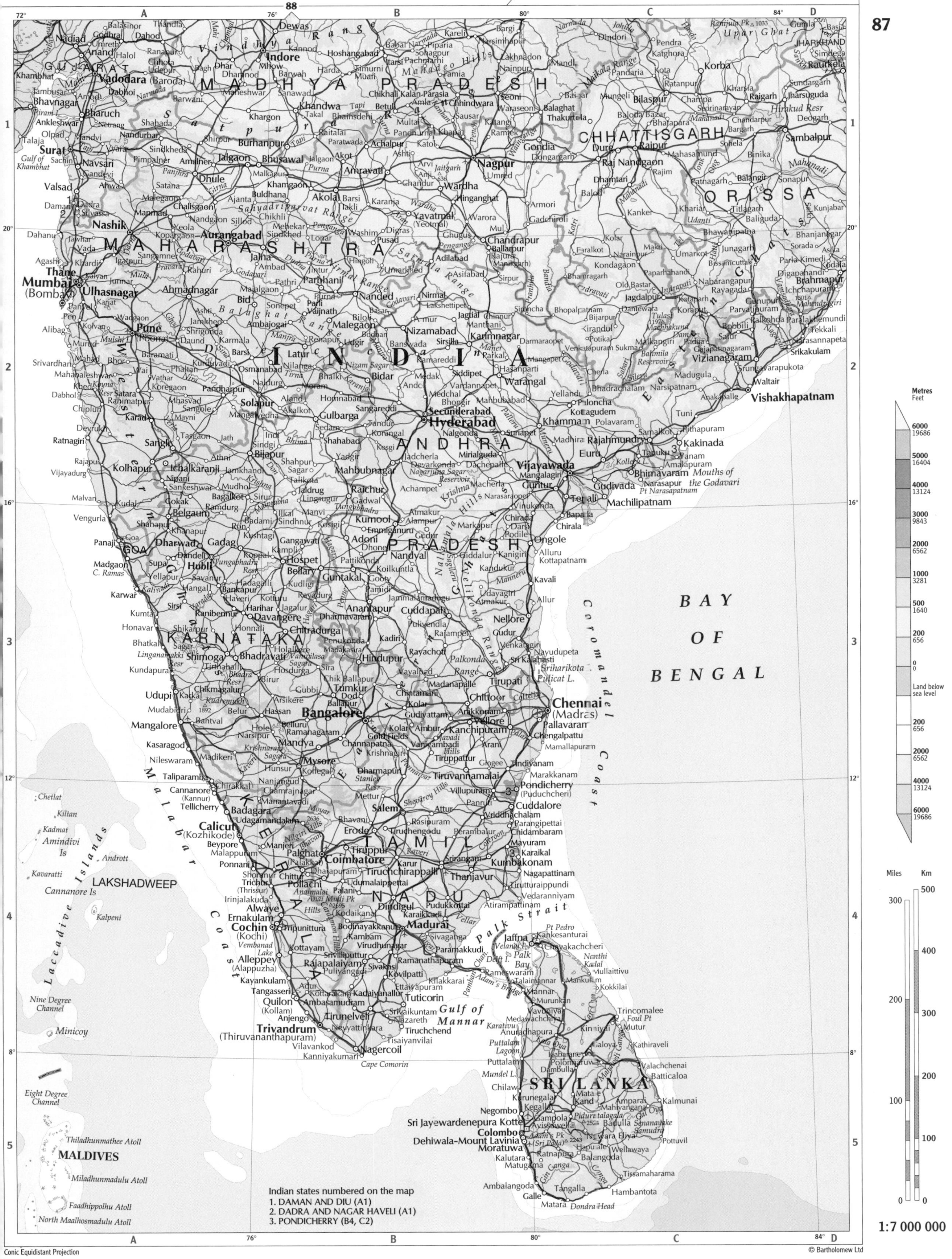

INDIA South AND SRI LANKA

Indian states numbered on the map
1. DAMAN AND DIU (A1)
2. DADRA AND NAGAR HAVELI (A1)
3. PONDICHERRY (B4, C2)

1:7 000 000

Conic Equidistant Projection

© Bartholomew Ltd

Metres
Feet

6000	19686
5000	16404
4000	13124
3000	9843
2000	6562
1000	3281
500	1640
200	656
0	0

Land below
sea level

200	656
2000	6562
4000	13124
6000	19686

Miles   Km
300   500
        400
200   300
        200
100   100
0   0

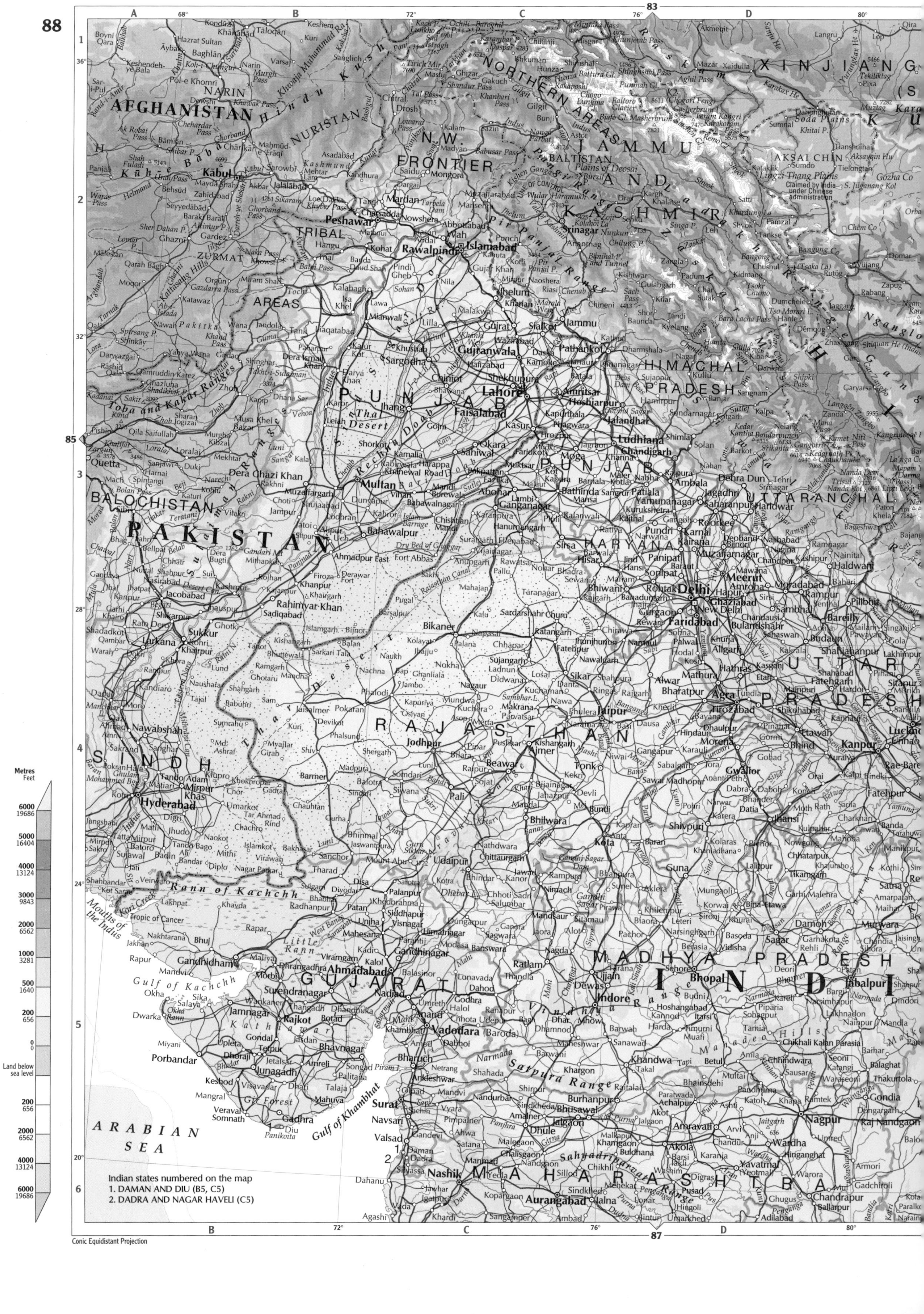

AFGHANISTAN

PAKISTAN

INDIA

NARIN

NURISTAN

N.W. FRONTIER

TRIBAL AREAS

ZURMAT

NORTHERN AREAS

JAMMU AND KASHMIR

BALTISTAN

XINJIANG

AKSAI CHIN
Claimed by India under Chinese administration

Kābul
Peshawar
Rawalpindi
Islamabad
Jammu
Srinagar

HIMACHAL PRADESH

BALOCHISTAN

Quetta

PUNJAB

Tha Desert

Lahore
Amritsar
Faisalabad
Multan
Ludhiana
Chandigarh

PUNJAB

HARYANA

UTTARANCHAL

Debra Dun
Haridwar

Delhi
New Delhi
Meerut
Faridabad

SINDH

Sukkur
Larkana
Hyderabad
Mirpur Khas

Bikaner

RAJASTHAN

Jaipur
Jodhpur
Ajmer
Kota
Udaipur

Tropic of Cancer

Rann of Kachchh

Little Rann

Mouths of the Indus

Gulf of Kachchh

Bhuj
Gandhidham
Jamnagar
Rajkot
Porbandar
Junagadh
Bhavnagar

GUJARAT

Ahmadabad
Gandhinagar
Vadodara (Baroda)
Surat
Navsari
Valsad

UTTAR PRADESH

Agra
Gwalior
Jhansi
Kanpur
Lucknow
Bareilly
Moradabad

MADHYA PRADESH

Indore
Bhopal
Ujjain
Ratlam
Jabalpur
Nagpur

Satpura Range

Vindhya Range

Narmada

Khandwa
Burhanpur
Jalgaon

MAHARASHTRA

Nashik
Aurangabad
Amravati
Akola
Wardha
Chandrapur

ARABIAN SEA

Gulf of Khambhat

Indian states numbered on the map
1. DAMAN AND DIU (B5, C5)
2. DADRA AND NAGAR HAVELI (C5)

Metres	Feet
6000	19686
5000	16404
4000	13124
3000	9843
2000	6562
1000	3281
500	1640
200	656
0	0

Land below sea level

200	656
2000	6562
4000	13124
6000	19686

Conic Equidistant Projection

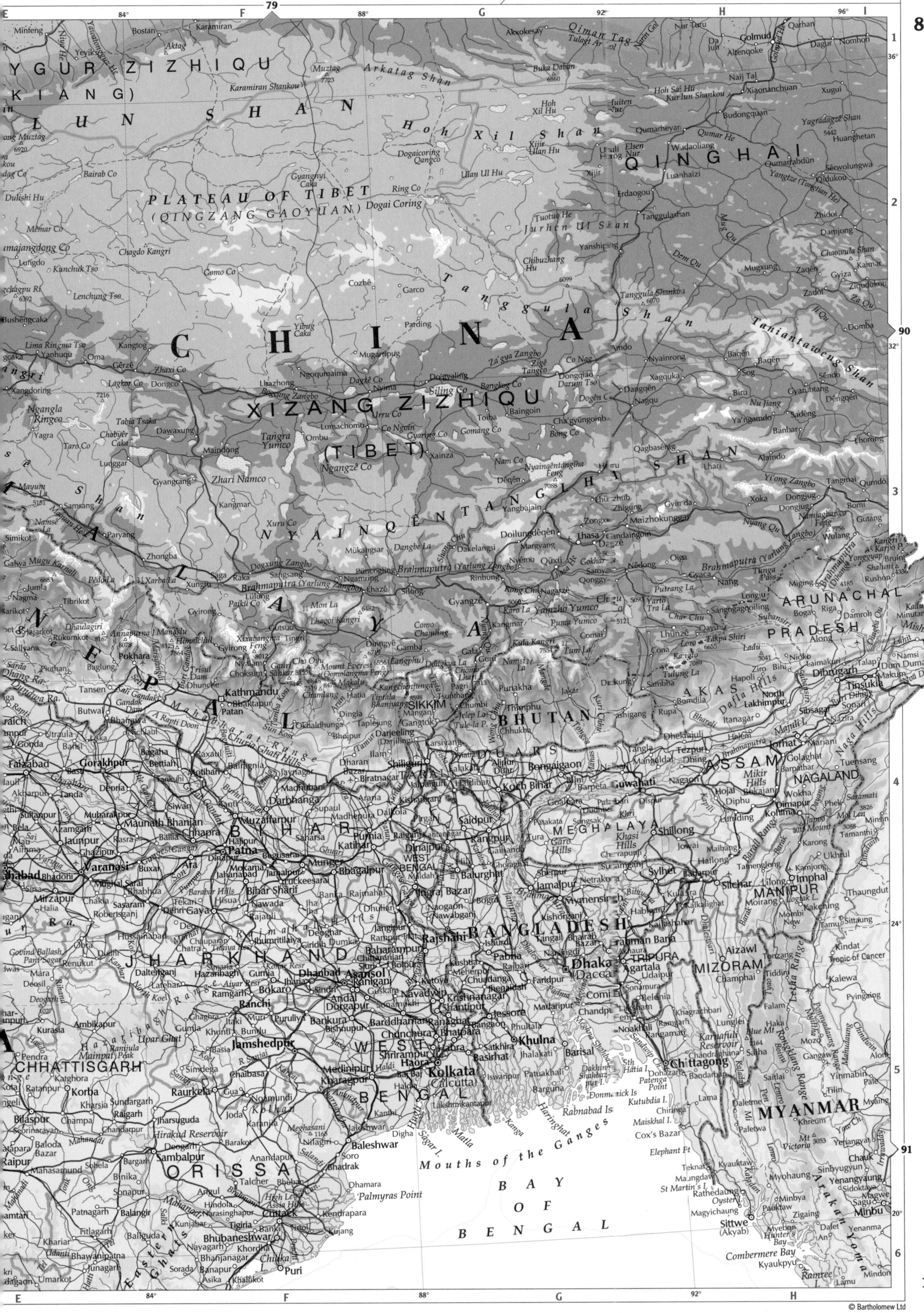
CHINA
XIZANG ZIZHIQU
(TIBET)
QINGHAI
PLATEAU OF TIBET
(QINGZANG GAOYUAN)
Hoh Xil Shan
Tanggula Shan
NYAINQÊNTANGLHA SHAN
NEPAL
SIKKIM
BHUTAN
ARUNACHAL PRADESH
ASSAM
NAGALAND
MEGHALAYA
MANIPUR
MIZORAM
TRIPURA
BANGLADESH
BIHAR
JHARKHAND
WEST BENGAL
ORISSA
CHHATTISGARH
MYANMAR
Brahmaputra (Yarlung Zangbo)
Kathmandu
Lhasa
Thimphu
Dhaka (Dacca)
Kolkata (Calcutta)
Patna
Guwahati
Shillong
Imphal
Chittagong
Khulna
Ranchi
Jamshedpur
Cuttack
Bhubaneshwar
Puri
Sittwe (Akyab)
Mount Everest
Mouths of the Ganges
BAY OF BENGAL
Tropic of Cancer

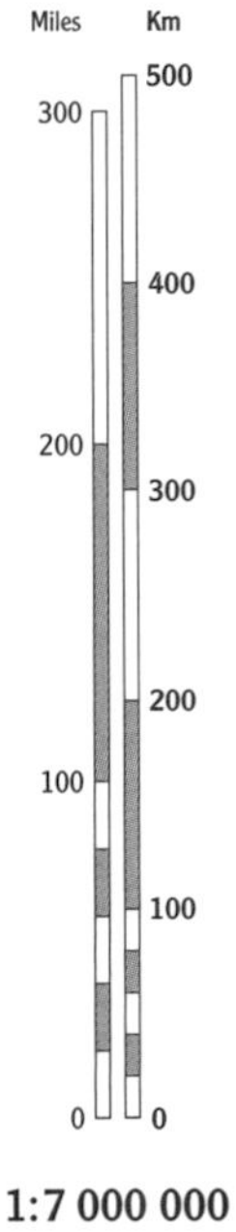
Miles
Km
300
200
100
0
500
400
300
200
100
0

1:7 000 000

SEA OF OKHOTSK (OKHOTSKOYE MORE)

RUSSIAN FEDERATION

MONGOLIA

CHINA

INNER MONGOLIA

XINJIANG

TIBET

INDIA

BHUTAN

JAPAN

NORTH KOREA

SOUTH KOREA

Sea of Japan (East Sea)

Yellow Sea (Huang Hai)

EAST CHINA SEA

Ryukyu Islands (Nansei-shotō)

Bonin Islands (Ogasawara-shotō) (Japan)

Volcano Is (Kazan-rettō) (Japan)

Tropic of Cancer

GOBI

ALTAI MOUNTAINS

Metres / Feet

Metres	Feet
6000	19686
5000	16404
4000	13124
3000	9843
2000	6562
1000	3281
500	1640
200	656
0	0

Land below sea level

Metres	Feet
200	656
2000	6562
4000	13124
6000	19686

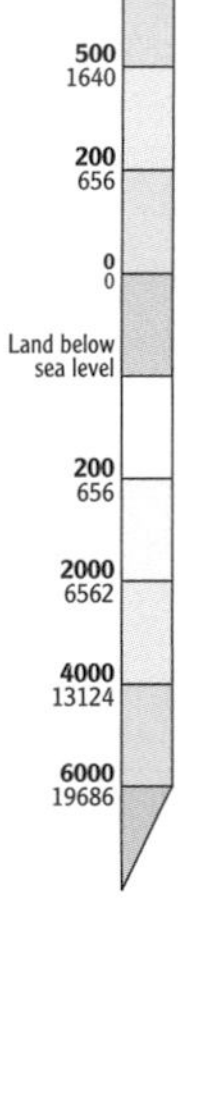

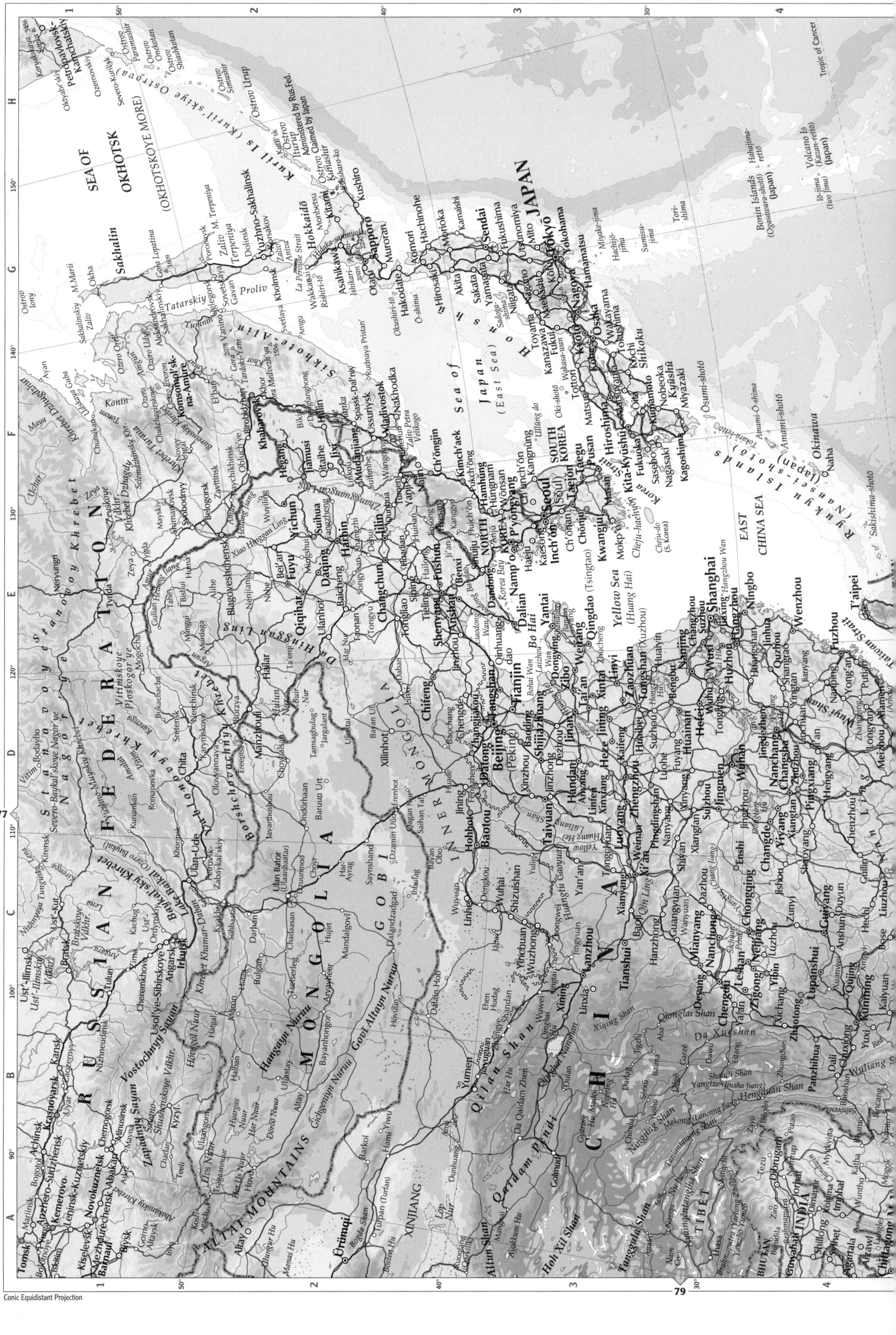

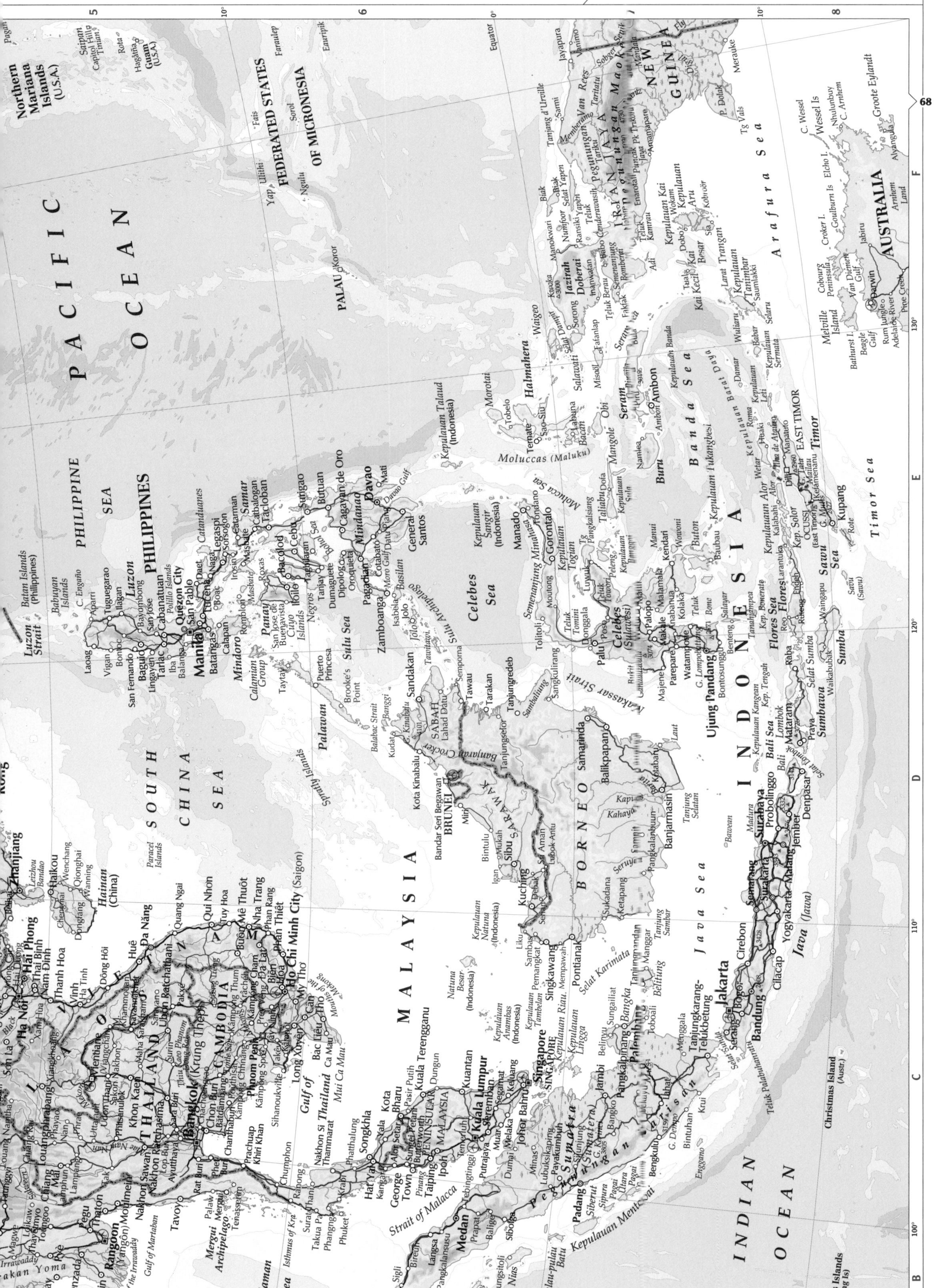

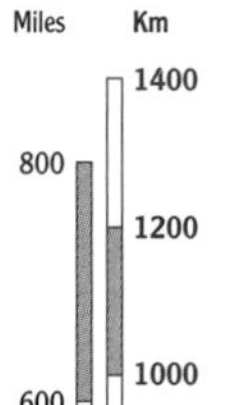

PACIFIC OCEAN

Northern Mariana Islands (U.S.A.)

Saipan
Tinian
Rota (U.S.A.)
Guam (U.S.A.)

FEDERATED STATES OF MICRONESIA

PALAU
Koror

PHILIPPINE SEA

PHILIPPINES

Luzon Strait

Batan Islands (Philippines)

Laoag
Vigan
Baguio
Lingayen
San Fernando
Tarlac
Cabanatuan
Quezon City
MANILA
Batangas
Calapan
Mindoro
Calamian Group
Palawan

Puerto Princesa
Brooke's Point
Balabac Strait

SOUTH CHINA SEA

Paracel Islands

Spratly Islands

Hong Kong
Zhanjiang
Haikou
Hainan (China)

Hải Phòng
Hà Nội
V I E T N A M
Thanh Hoa
Vinh
Đà Nẵng
Qui Nhon
Nha Trang
Phan Thiết
Ho Chi Minh City (Saigon)

L A O S
Vientiane
C A M B O D I A
Phnom Penh

T H A I L A N D
BANGKOK

Gulf of Thailand

Andaman Sea

Rangoon (Yangôn)

George Town
Taiping
Ipoh
KUALA LUMPUR
M A L A Y S I A
PENINSULAR MALAYSIA
Johor Bahru
SINGAPORE
Singapore

Strait of Malacca

Medan

INDIAN OCEAN

S u m a t e r a (Sumatra)

Padang
Palembang
Jakarta
Bandung
J a v a (Jawa)
Yogyakarta
Semarang
Surakarta
Surabaya
Malang
Denpasar
Bali

BRUNEI
Bandar Seri Begawan

SARAWAK
Kuching
SABAH
Kota Kinabalu
Sandakan
Tawau

B O R N E O

Banjarmasin
Balikpapan
Samarinda

Java Sea

I N D O N E S I A

Ujung Pandang
Celebes (Sulawesi)
Celebes Sea

Manado
Gorontalo
Palu
Kendari

Sulu Sea

Zamboanga
Davao
Cotabato
General Santos
Mindanao
Cagayan de Oro
Butuan
Surigao

Cebu
Bacolod
Iloilo
Panay
Negros
Samar
Tacloban
Legaspi

Moluccas (Maluku)

Halmahera
Ternate
Buru
Seram
Ambon
Banda Sea

Flores Sea
Flores
Sumba
Sumbawa
Lombok

Kupang
Timor
Timor Sea
EAST TIMOR
Dili

Arafura Sea

IRIAN JAYA
NEW GUINEA
Jayapura

AUSTRALIA
Darwin
Arnhem Land
Groote Eylandt
Gulf of Carpentaria

Equator

1:20 000 000

Miles / Km

800 / 1400
600 / 1200
400 / 1000
200 / 800
0 / 600
/ 400
/ 200
/ 0

© Bartholomew Ltd

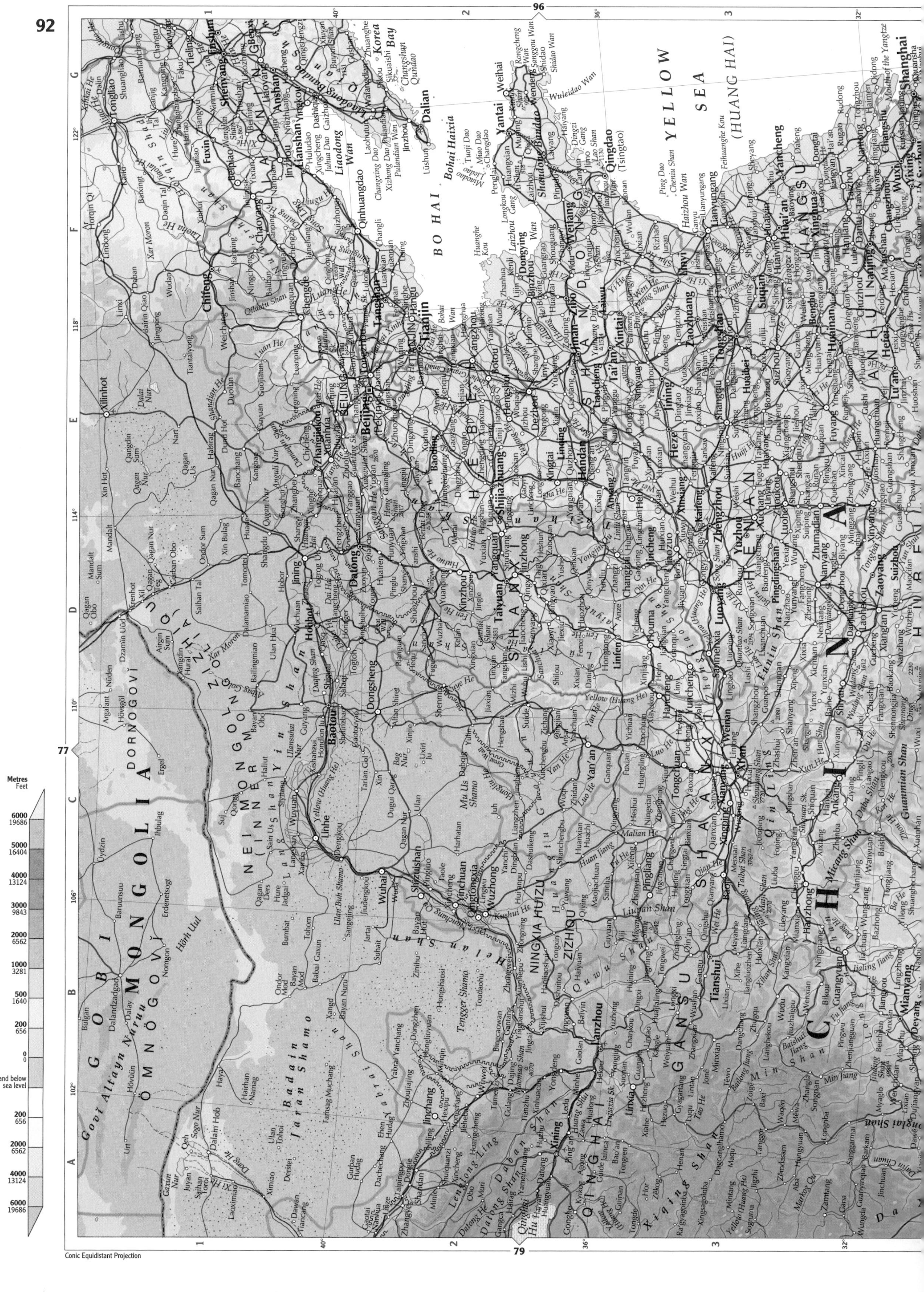

BO HAI

YELLOW SEA (HUANG HAI)

Korea Bay

Liaodong Wan

GOBI

MONGOLIA

DORNOGOVĬ

ÖMNÖGOVĬ

NEI MONGOL ZIZHIQU

NEIMENGGU

NINGXIA HUIZU ZIZHIQU

GANSU

QINGHAI

SHANXI

SHAANXI

HEBEI

SHANDONG

HENAN

JIANGSU

ANHUI

Beijing (Peking)

Tianjin

Shenyang

Anshan

Dalian

Yantai

Weihai

Qingdao (Tsingtao)

Lianyungang

Shijiazhuang

Taiyuan

Datong

Baotou

Hohhot

Yinchuan

Lanzhou

Xining

Xi'an

Zhengzhou

Luoyang

Kaifeng

Handan

Jinan

Zibo

Xuzhou

Bengbu

Huainan

Nanjing

Wuxi

Shanghai

Conic Equidistant Projection

Metres / Feet

6000 / 19686
5000 / 16404
4000 / 13124
3000 / 9843
2000 / 6562
1000 / 3281
500 / 1640
200 / 656
0 / 0
Land below sea level
200 / 656
2000 / 6562
4000 / 13124
6000 / 19686

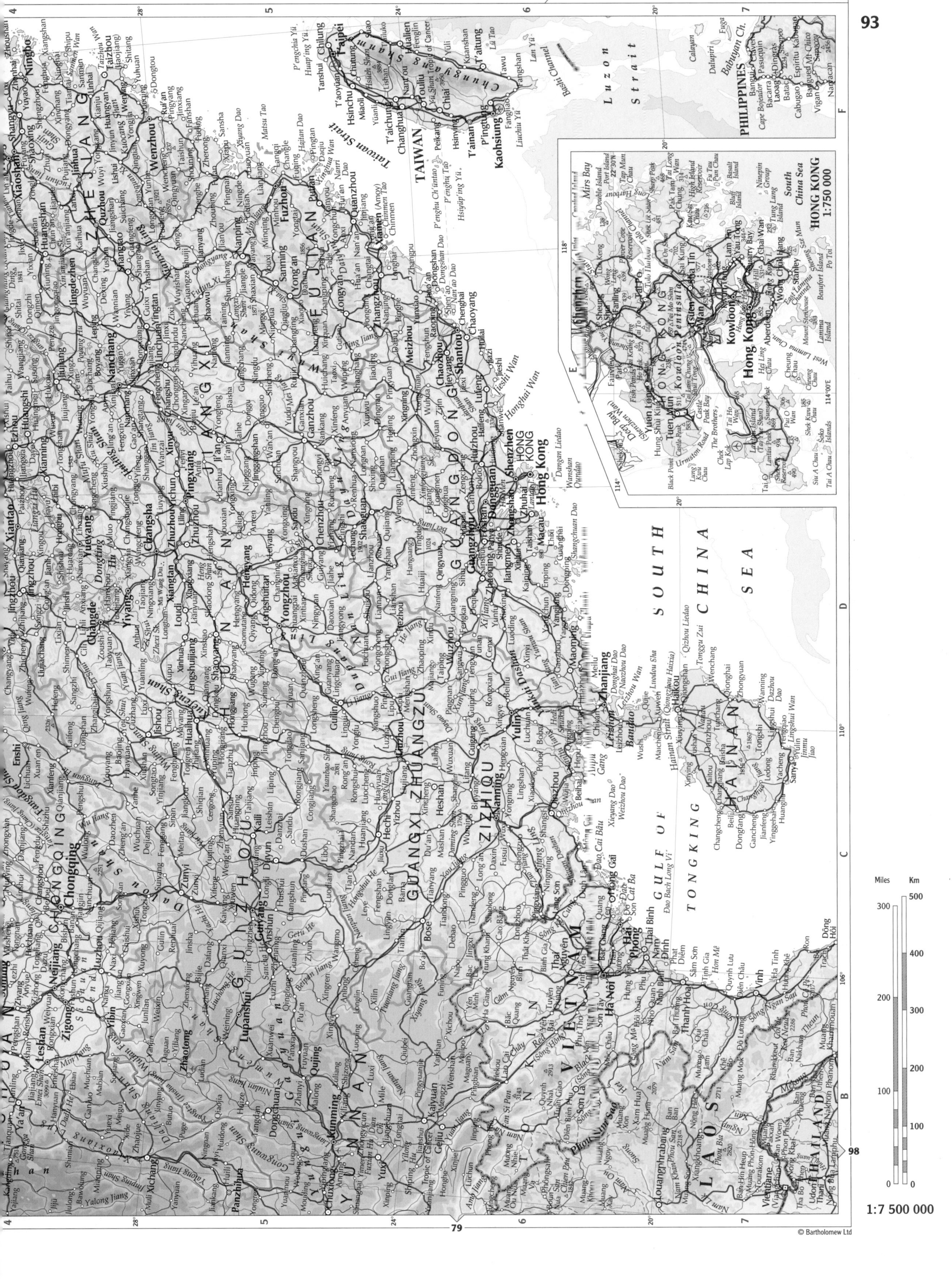

PHILIPPINES

TAIWAN

HONG KONG
1:750 000

ZHEJIANG

FUJIAN

JIANGXI

HUNAN

GUANGDONG

GUANGXI ZHUANGZU ZIZHIQU

GUIZHOU

HAINAN

SOUTH CHINA SEA

GULF OF TONGKING

VIETNAM

LAOS

THAILAND

YUNNAN

CHONGQING

1:7 500 000

RUSSIAN FEDERATION

Sakhalin

La Pérouse Strait

HOKKAIDŌ

Kuril Islands

Administered by Rus. Fed. Claimed by Japan

Korsakov
Novikovo
Gornozavodsk
Ostrov Moneron
Anivo
Zaliv Anivo
Mys Aniva
Mys Kril'on

Shiretoko-misaki
Wakkanai
Rishiri-tō
Rebun-tō
Noshappu-misaki
Shōga-misaki
Esashi
Hamatonbetsu
Teshio
Monbetsu
Ōmu
Nayoro
Shibetsu
Rumoi
Asahikawa
Bibai
Otaru
Sapporo
Chitose
Tomakomai
Muroran
Noboribetsu
Uchiura-wan
Mori
Hakodate
Matsumae

Abashiri
Kitami
Kushiro
Obihiro
Hiroo
Erimo-misaki
Urakawa
Samani

Hidaka-sammyaku

HONSHŪ

Aomori
Hachinohe
Misawa
Hirosaki
Noshiro
Akita
Honjō
Sakata
Tsuruoka

Miyako
Kamaishi
Kesennuma
Ishinomaki

RUSSIAN FEDERATION

PRIMORSKIY KRAY

Svetlaya
Kuznetsovo
Maksimovka
Amgu
Mys Belkina
Terney
Mys Yegorova
Plastun
Kavalerovo
Dal'negorsk
Ol'ga
Vladimir
Mys Nizmennyy

Luchegorsk
Bikin
Lesopil'noye
Vostok
Dal'nerechensk
Novopokrovka
Roshchino
Glubinnoye
Kirovskiy
Gornyy
Samarka
Chuguyevka
Arsen'yev
Anuchino
Arkhipovka
Lazo
Uglekamensk
Valentin
Preobrazheniye

Spassk-Dal'niy
Chernigovka
Yakovlevka
Sergeyevka
Smolyaninovo
Nakhodka

Ussuriysk
Artem
Vladivostok
Mys Gamova
Zaliv Petra Velikogo

SEA OF JAPAN
(EAST SEA)

CHINA

HEILONGJIANG

Hegang
Jiamusi
Shuangyashan
Jixi
Mishan
Mudanjiang
Hulin

JILIN

Yanji
Helong
Dunhua

NORTH KOREA

Ch'ŏngjin
Najin
Kimch'aek
Tanch'ŏn

Conic Equidistant Projection

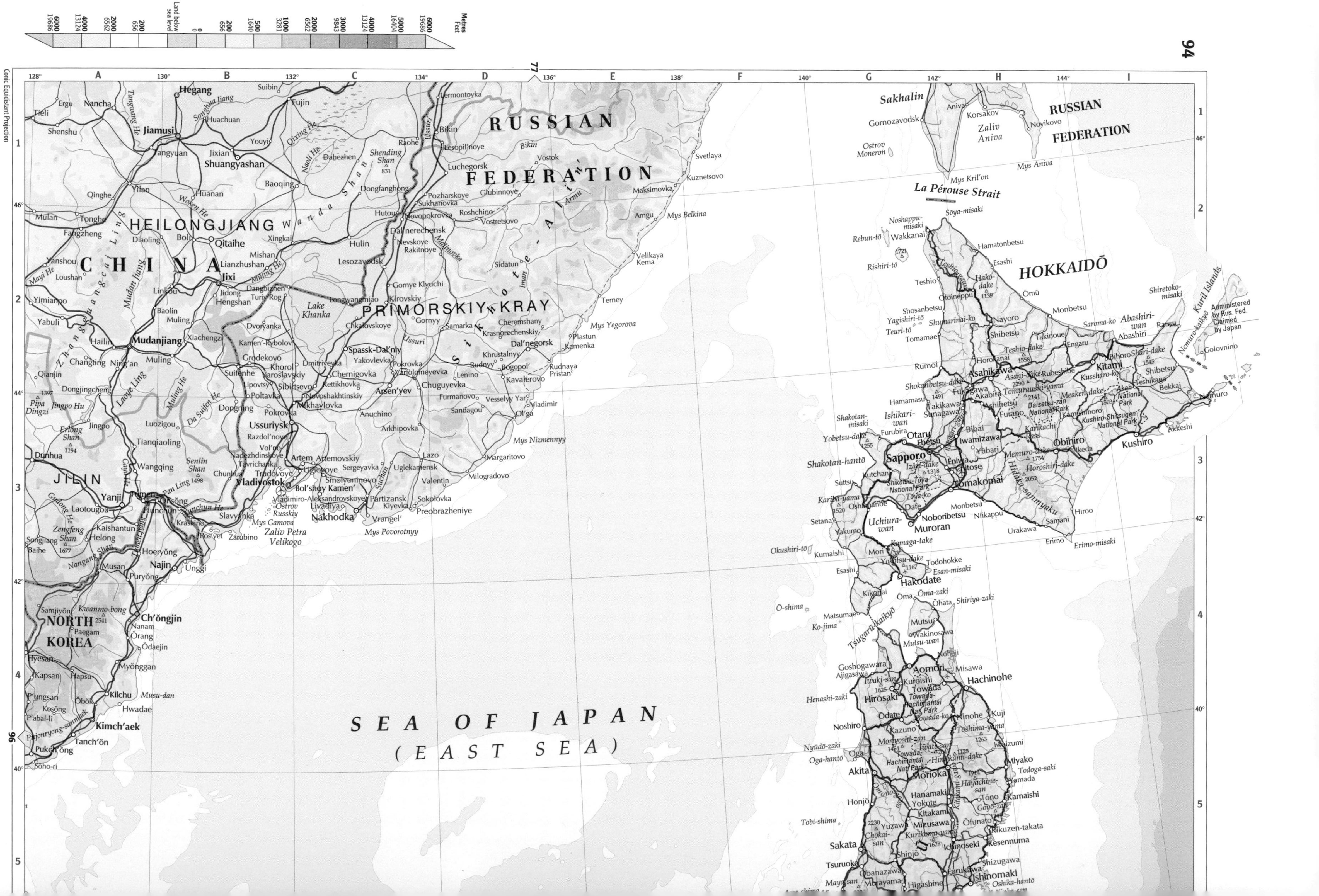

Metres / Feet
6000 / 19686
5000 / 16404
4000 / 13124
3000 / 9843
2000 / 6562
1000 / 3281
500 / 1640
200 / 656
0
Land below sea level
200 / 656
2000 / 6562
4000 / 13124
6000 / 19686

77

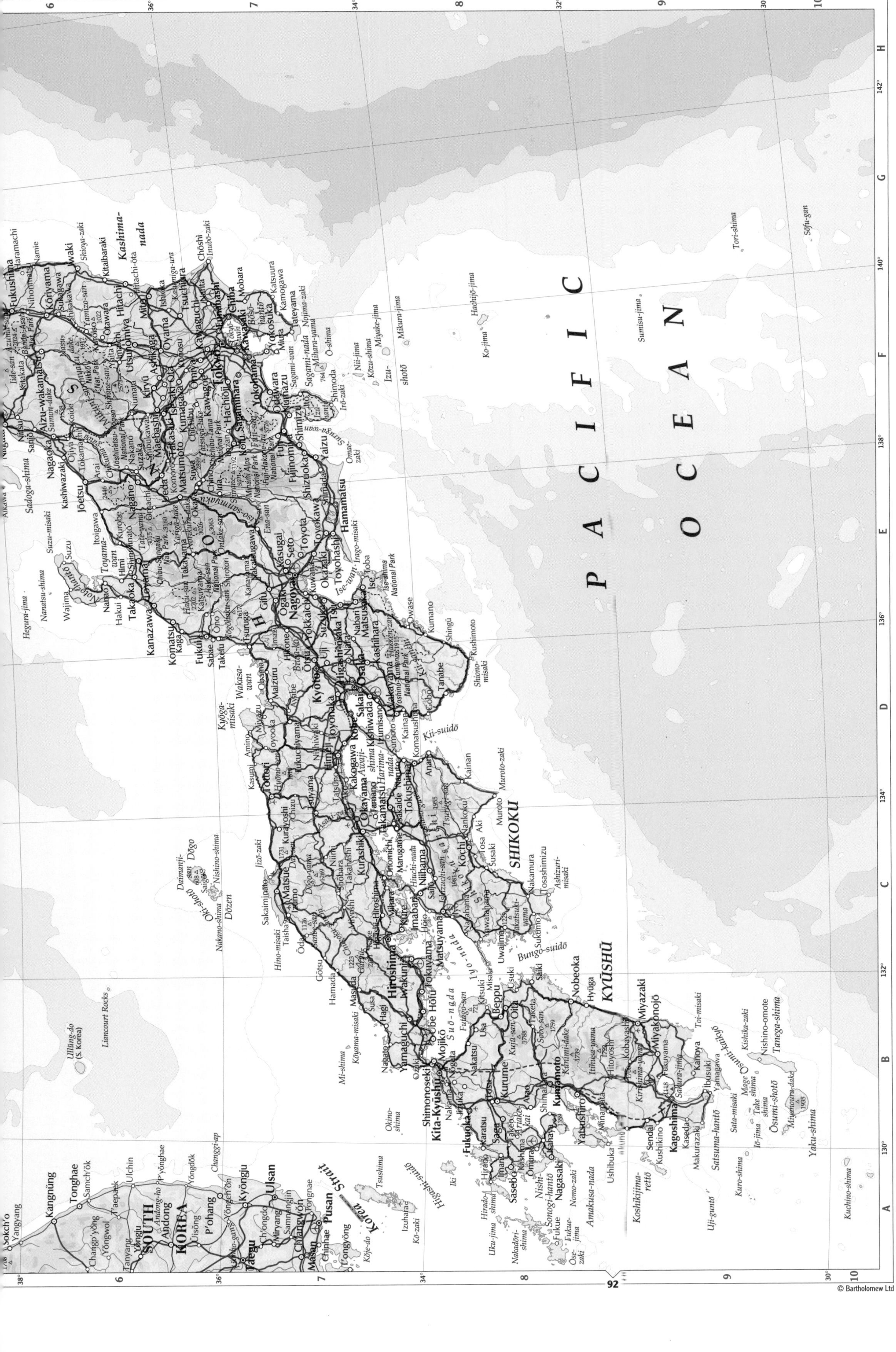

PACIFIC

OCEAN

SHIKOKU

KYŪSHŪ

SOUTH
KOREA

Korea Strait

Miles	Km
200	350
	300
150	250
	200
100	150
50	100
	50
0	0

1:5 000 000

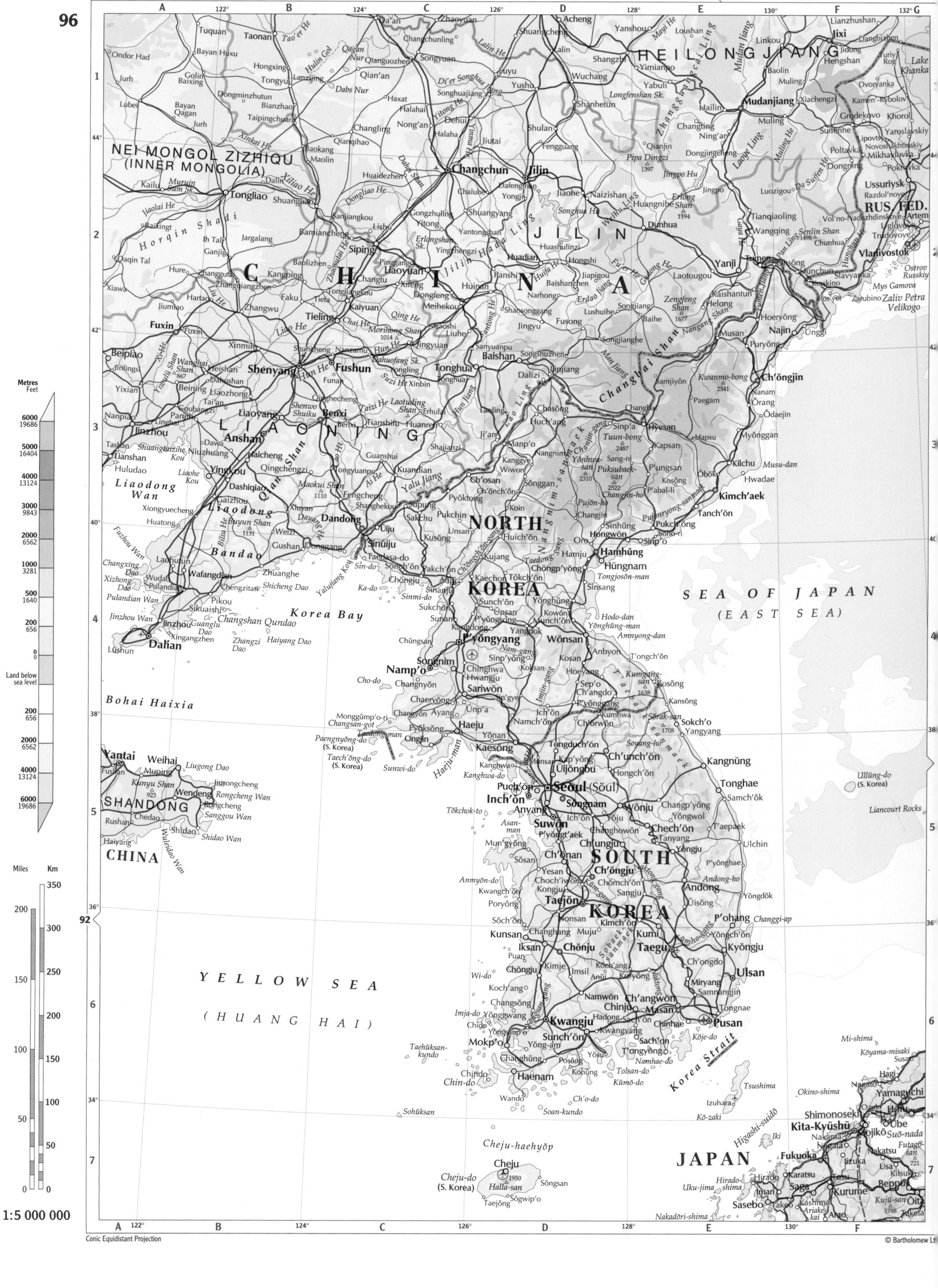

CHINA Northeast, NORTH KOREA AND SOUTH KOREA

HEILONGJIANG

NEI MONGOL ZIZHIQU
(INNER MONGOLIA)

CHINA

JILIN

RUS. FED.

LIAONING

NORTH
KOREA

SEA OF JAPAN
(EAST SEA)

Liaodong
Wan

Korea Bay

Bohai Haixia

SHANDONG

CHINA

YELLOW SEA
(HUANG HAI)

SOUTH
KOREA

JAPAN

1:5 000 000

Conic Equidistant Projection

© Bartholomew Ltd

Metres / Feet

6000 / 19686
5000 / 16404
4000 / 13124
3000 / 9843
2000 / 6562
1000 / 3281
500 / 1640
200 / 656
0 / 0

Land below sea level

200 / 656
2000 / 6562
4000 / 13124
6000 / 19686

Miles / Km

200 / 350
/ 300
150 / 250
/ 200
100 / 150
/ 100
50 / 50
0 / 0

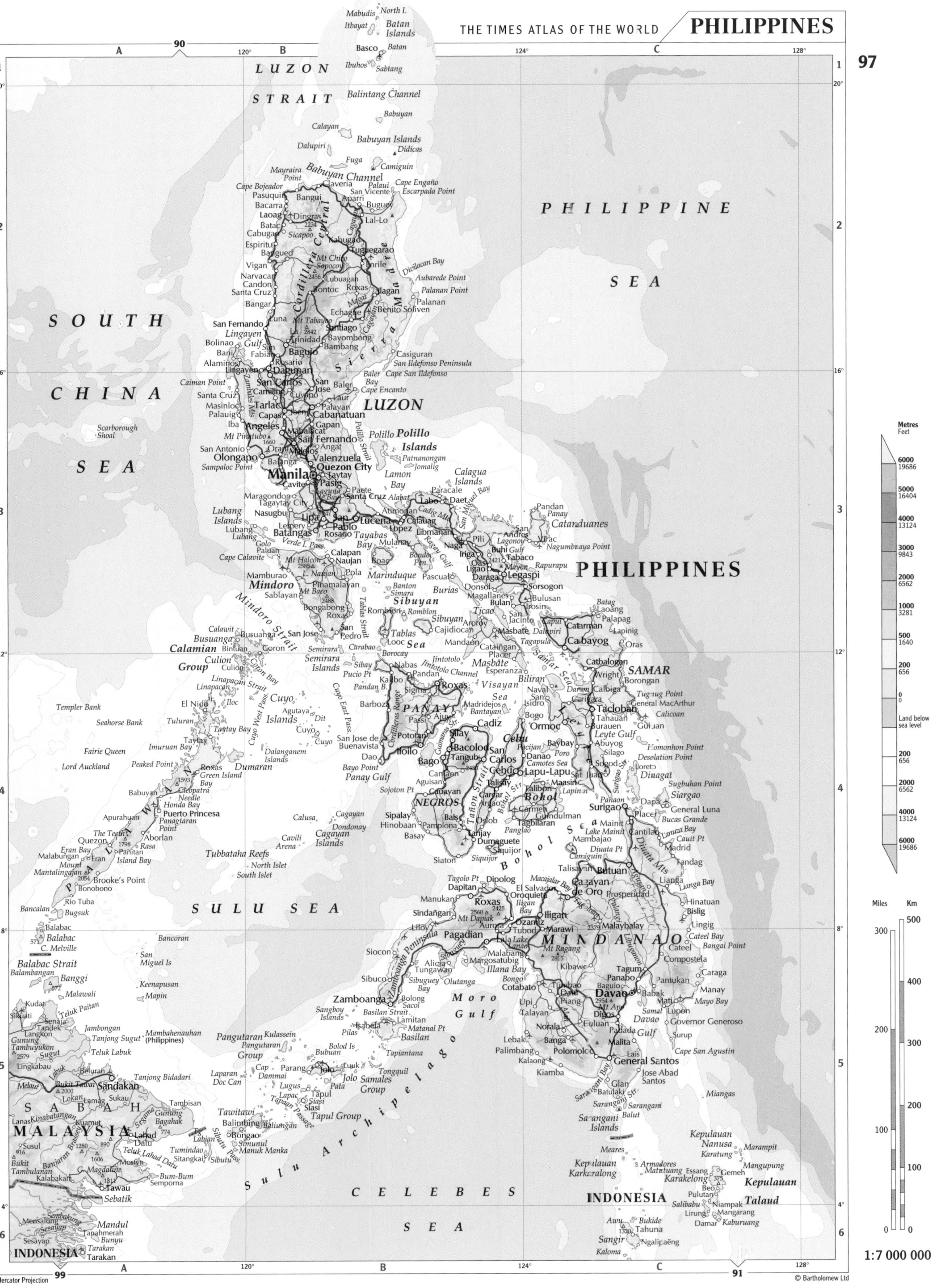

PHILIPPINE SEA

SOUTH CHINA SEA

LUZON STRAIT

Balintang Channel

LUZON

Cordillera Central

Sierra Madre

Lingayen Gulf

Manila

Quezon City

Polillo Islands

Lamon Bay

Mindoro

Mindoro Strait

Calamian Group

Cuyo Islands

Cuyo West Pass.

Cuyo East Pass.

Sibuyan Sea

PANAY

Visayan Sea

SAMAR

NEGROS

Cebu

Bohol

Bohol Sea

SULU SEA

Leyte Gulf

Zamboanga Peninsula

MINDANAO

Davao

Moro Gulf

General Santos

PHILIPPINES

Sulu Archipelago

SABAH
MALAYSIA

Sandakan
Tawau

INDONESIA

CELEBES SEA

Kepulauan Talaud

Metres	Feet
6000	19686
5000	16404
4000	13124
3000	9843
2000	6562
1000	3281
500	1640
200	656
0	0
Land below sea level	
200	656
2000	6562
4000	13124
6000	19686

Miles / Km

300 / 500
400
200 / 300
100 / 200
100
0 / 0

1:7 000 000

THAILAND, CAMBODIA AND PENINSULAR MALAYSIA
THAILAND
CAMBODIA
LAOS
VIETNAM
MYANMAR
CHINA
HAINAN
MALAYSIA
PENINSULAR MALAYSIA
INDONESIA
GULF OF TONGKING
GULF OF THAILAND
SOUTH CHINA SEA
STRAIT OF MALACCA
Mergui Archipelago
Bangkok (Krung Thep)
Vientiane (Viangchan)
Phnom Penh
Ho Chi Minh City (Saigon)
Kuala Lumpur
Singapore
Chiang Mai
Nakhon Ratchasima
Ubon Ratchathani
Hat Yai
Songkhla
George Town
Pinang
Ipoh
Kuantan
Johor Bahru
Medan
Sumatra
Mekong
Tonle Sap
Bight of Bangkok
Isthmus of Kra
Cardamom Range
Mouths of the Mekong
Kepulauan Anambas
Kepulauan Natuna
SINGAPORE 1:550 000
Strait of Singapore
Selat Johor
Metres
Feet
6000
19686
5000
16404
4000
13124
3000
9843
2000
6562
1000
3281
500
1640
200
656
0
Land below sea level
Miles
Km
1:7 500 000
Mercator Projection
99
© Bartholomew Ltd

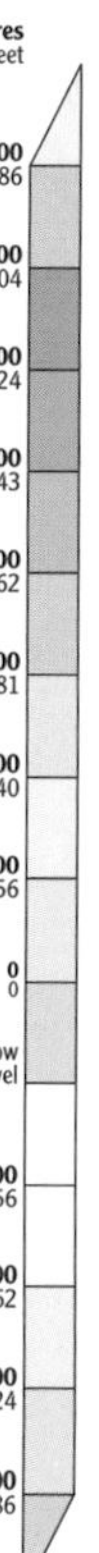

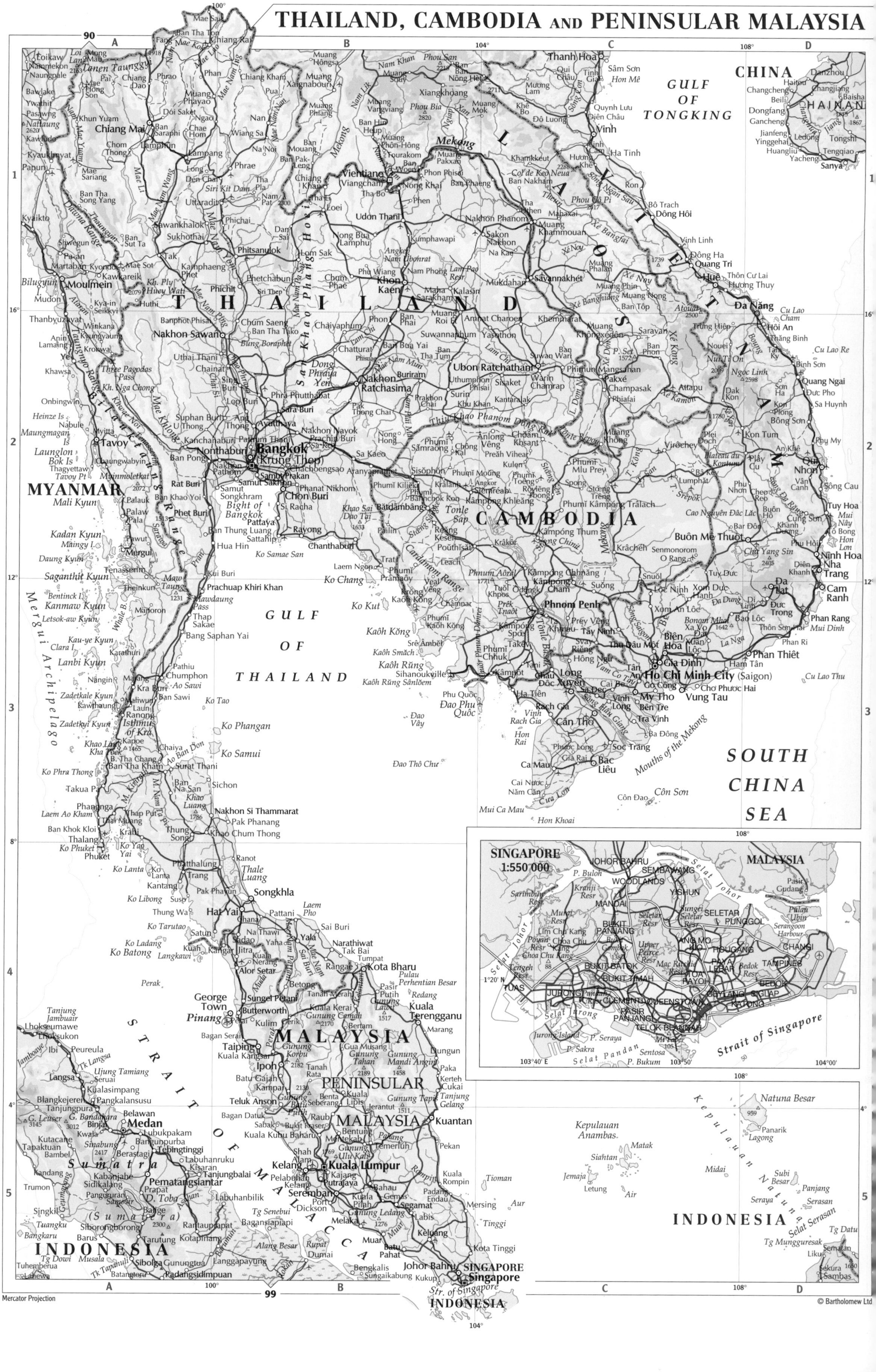

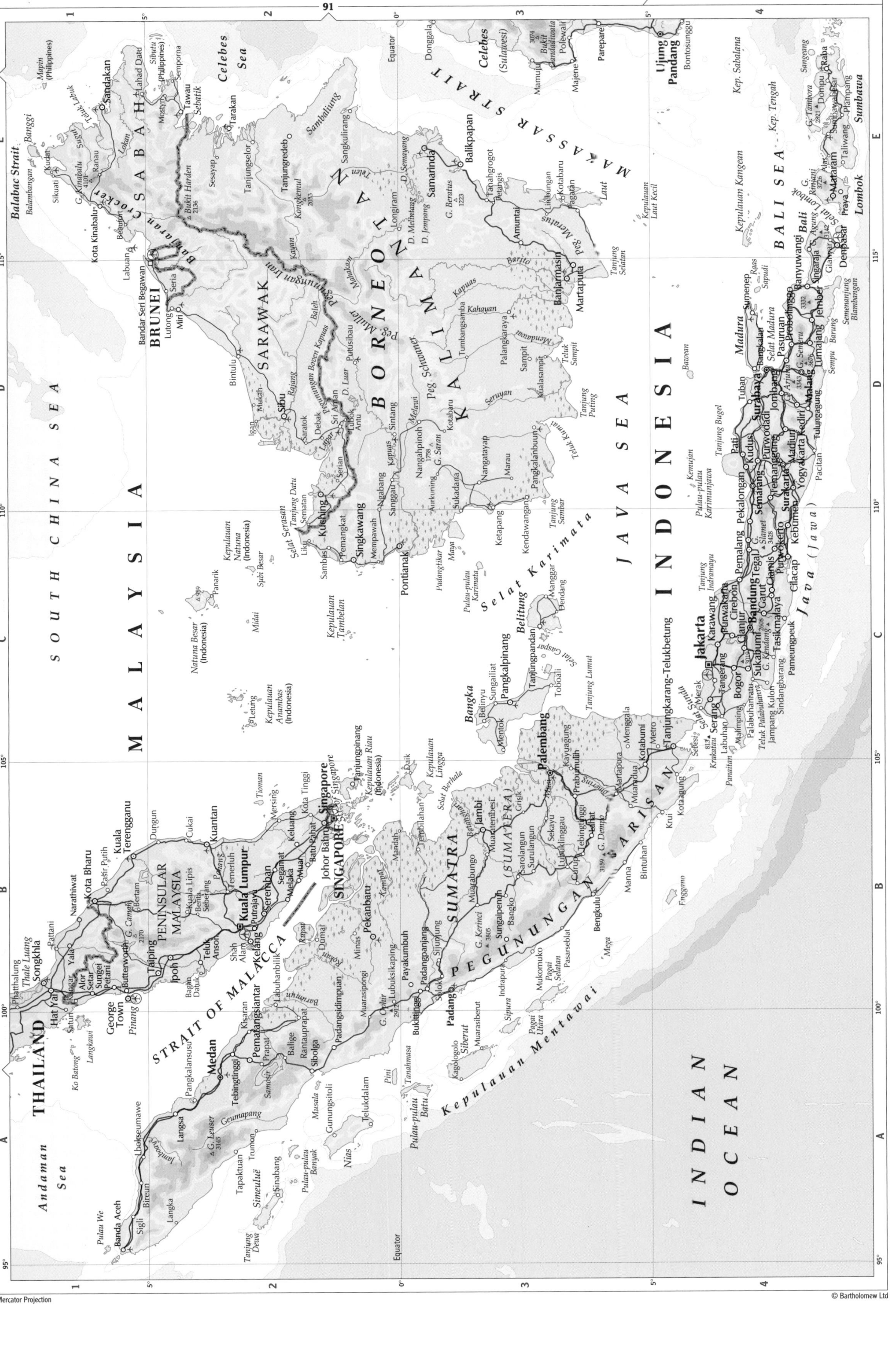

Balabac Strait

Andaman Sea

THAILAND

MALAYSIA

PENINSULAR MALAYSIA

Kuala Lumpur

Singapore

SINGAPORE

SOUTH CHINA SEA

Celebes Sea (Sulawesi)

MAKASSAR STRAIT

SABAH

Kota Kinabalu

BRUNEI

Bandar Seri Begawan

SARAWAK

BORNEO

KALIMANTAN

Balikpapan

Samarinda

Banjarmasin

Pontianak

Kuching

STRAIT OF MALACCA

Medan

SUMATRA (SUMATERA)

Padang

Palembang

PEGUNUNGAN BARISAN

JAVA SEA

INDONESIA

Jakarta

Bandung

JAVA (Jawa)

Semarang

Surabaya

Madura

BALI SEA

Bali

Denpasar

Lombok

Mataram

Sumbawa

Ujung Pandang

INDIAN OCEAN

Kepulauan Mentawai

Equator

Mercator Projection

© Bartholomew Ltd

1:10 000 000

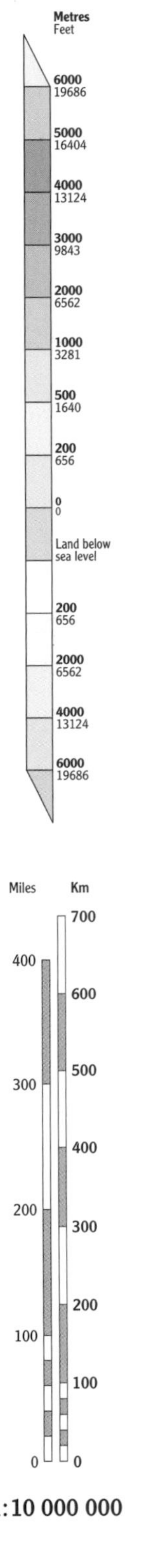

Metres / Feet

6000 / 19686
5000 / 16404
4000 / 13124
3000 / 9843
2000 / 6562
1000 / 3281
500 / 1640
200 / 656
0
Land below sea level
200 / 656
2000 / 6562
4000 / 13124
6000 / 19686

Miles / Km

400 / 700
600
300 / 500
400
200 / 300
200
100 / 100
0 / 0

A   75°   75°   60°   45°   30°   15°   B   0°   15°   30°   C   45°   60°   D   75°   E

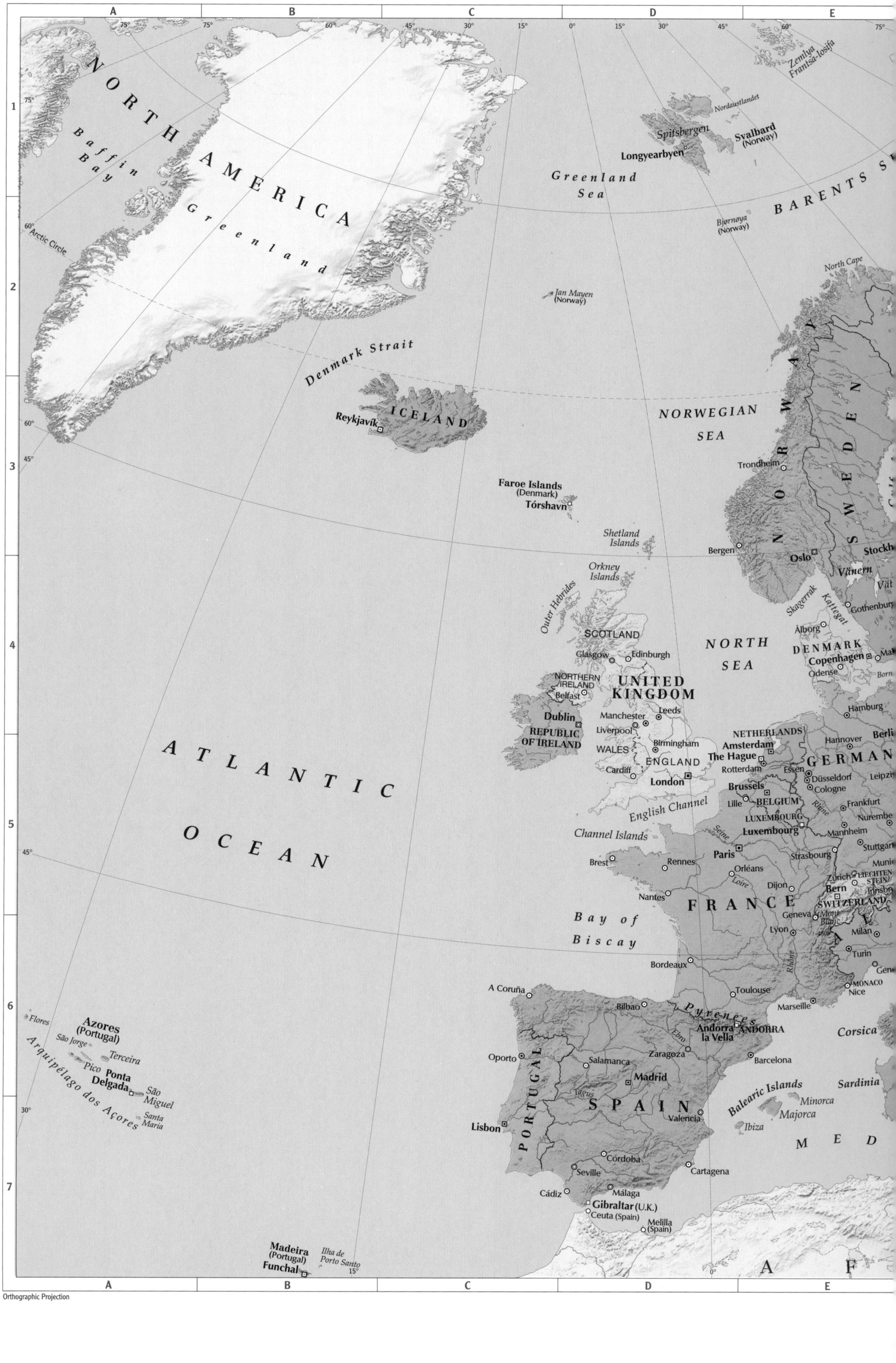

NORTH AMERICA

Baffin Bay

Greenland

Zemlya
Frantsa-Iosifa

Nordaustlandet

Spitsbergen   **Svalbard**
(Norway)

Longyearbyen

*Greenland
Sea*

BARENTS S

1

60° *Arctic Circle*

Bjørnøya
(Norway)

North Cape

2

Jan Mayen
(Norway)

Denmark Strait

NORWEGIAN

SEA

N O R W A Y

Trondheim

S W E D E N

60°

ICELAND

Reykjavík

3   45°

Faroe Islands
(Denmark)
Tórshavn

Bergen

Oslo   Stockh

Vänern   Vät

*Shetland
Islands*

*Orkney
Islands*

Skagerrak   Gothenburg

Ålborg

DENMARK

NORTH

SEA

Copenhagen

Odense   Born

Outer Hebrides

4

SCOTLAND

Glasgow   Edinburgh

NORTHERN
IRELAND   **UNITED
KINGDOM**

Hamburg

GERMAN

Belfast

Dublin   Manchester   Leeds

Liverpool   Birmingham

NETHERLANDS   Hannover   Berli

Amsterdam

REPUBLIC
OF IRELAND   WALES   ENGLAND   **The Hague**   Essen   Leipzi

Rotterdam   Düsseldorf

Cardiff   **London**   **Brussels**   Cologne   Frankfurt

BELGIUM   Nurembe

English Channel   Lille   **LUXEMBOURG**

ATLANTIC   *Channel Islands*   **Luxembourg**   Mannheim   Stuttga

5   Brest   Rennes   **Paris**   Strasbourg

Orléans   Zürich LIECHTEN-
STEIN

OCEAN   *Loire*   Dijon   **Bern**   Innsbru

Nantes   Geneva   SWITZERLAND

45°   F R A N C E   *Mont
Blanc*   A

Milan

Bay of   *Rhône*   Lyon   Turin   Gen

Biscay   Bordeaux   MONACO
Nice

6   A Coruña   Toulouse   Marseille

Pyrenees   Corsica

Bilbao   **Andorra
la Vella** ANDORRA

Flores

Azores
(Portugal)   *Terceira*   Zaragoza   Barcelona

São Jorge   *Ebro*

Pico   **Ponta
Delgada**   Oporto   Salamanca

Arquipélago dos Açores   São
Miguel   **Madrid**   Balearic Islands   Sardinia

30°   Santa
Maria   S P A I N   Minorca

Valencia   Majorca

P O R T U G A L   *Tagus*   Ibiza

Lisbon   M E D

Córdoba

7   Cartagena

Seville

Cádiz   Málaga

Gibraltar (U.K.)   A

Ceuta (Spain)

Melilla
(Spain)

Madeira
(Portugal)   Ilha de
Porto Santo   F

Funchal   15°   0°

A   B   C   D   E

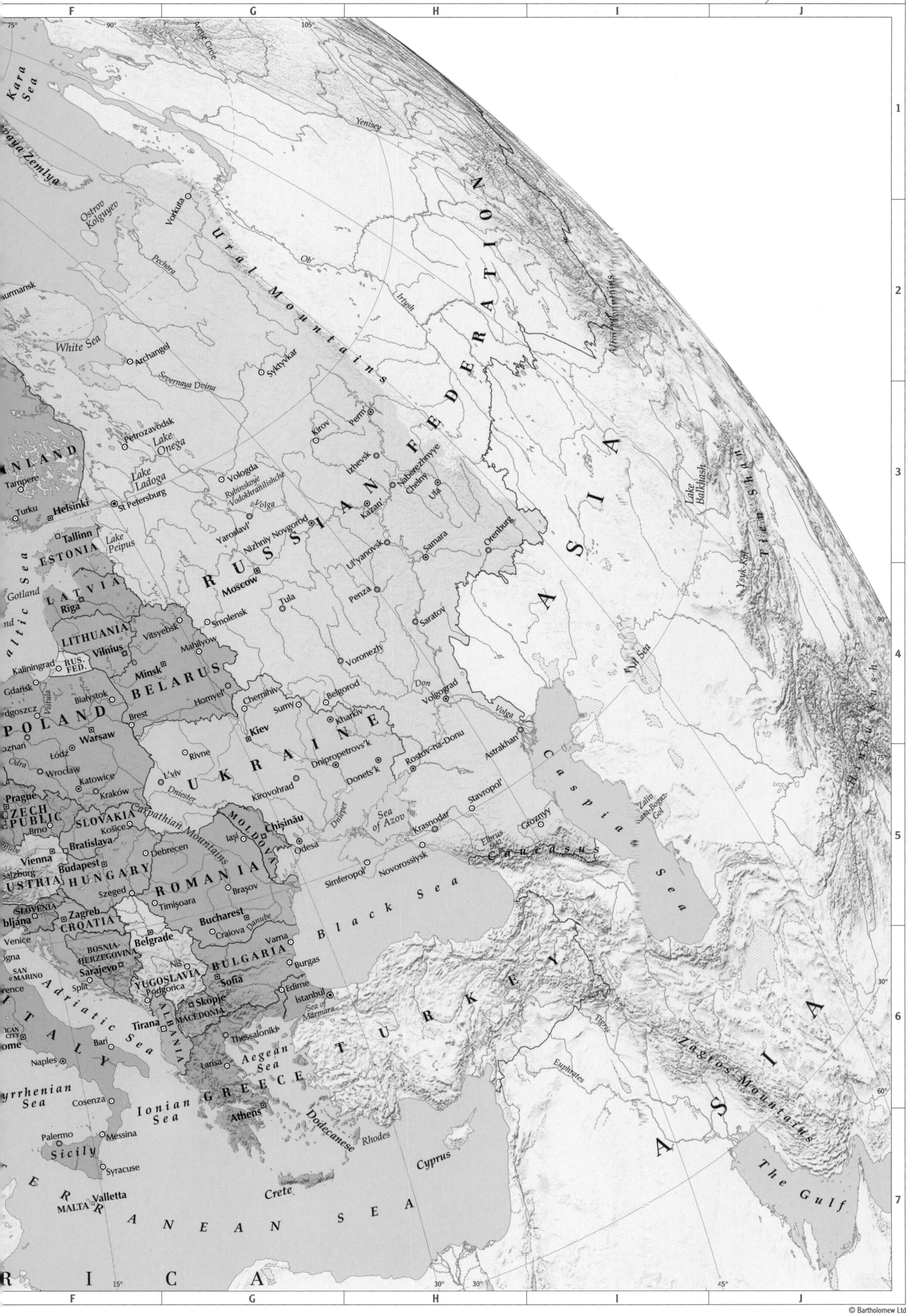

Kara Sea

Novaya Zemlya

Ostrov Kolguyev

Murmansk

White Sea

Archangel

FINLAND

Tampere

Turku

Helsinki

Lake Onega

Petrozavodsk

Severnaya Dvina

Syktyvkar

Vorkuta

Pechora

Ob'

Yenisey

Arctic Circle

Ural Mountains

RUSSIAN FEDERATION

A S I A

Altai Mountains

Irtysh

Kirov

Perm'

Izhevsk

Nabarezhnyye Chelny

Ufa

Lake Balkhash

ESTONIA

Tallinn

Lake Peipus

Gotland

LATVIA

Riga

LITHUANIA

Vilnius

Kaliningrad RUS. FED.

Gdańsk

Bydgoszcz

POLAND

Poznań

Łódź

Wrocław

Katowice

Prague

CZECH REPUBLIC

Brno

Vienna

AUSTRIA

St Petersburg

Lake Ladoga

Vologda

Rybinskoye Vodokhranilishche

Yaroslavl'

Volga

Nizhniy Novgorod

Moscow

Tula

Kazan'

Ul'yanovsk

Samara

Orenburg

Tian Shan

Ysyk-Köl

Hindu Kush

Vitsyebsk

Mahilyow

Homyel'

Chernihiv

Sumy

Belgorod

Don

Volgograd

Saratov

Penza

Voronezh

Bialystok

Brest

BELARUS

Minsk

Warsaw

Rivne

L'viv

UKRAINE

Kiev

Kharkiv

Dnipropetrovs'k

Donets'k

Rostov-na-Donu

Astrakhan

Caspian Sea

Set

Odra

Kraków

SLOVAKIA

Košice

Bratislava

Debrecen

HUNGARY

Budapest

Szeged

Dniester

Kirovohrad

MOLDOVA

Iaşi

Chişinău

Sea of Azov

Dnieper

Odesa

Krasnodar

Stavropol'

Grozny

Elbrus

C a u c a s u s

Zaliv Kara-Boga z-Gol

Salzburg

SLOVENIA

Ljubljana

Venice

Zagreb

CROATIA

ROMANIA

Timişoara

Bucharest

Craiova

Danube

Brașov

Simferopol

Novorossiysk

B l a c k   S e a

C a s p i a n   S e a

SAN MARINO

ITALY

Rome

Naples

BOSNIA-HERZEGOVINA

Sarajevo

Split

Belgrade

Niš

YUGOSLAVIA

Podgorica

Varna

BULGARIA

Burgas

Sofia

Edirne

Istanbul

Sea of Marmara

T U R K E Y

A S I A

Tigris

Euphrates

Zagros Mountains

Adriatic Sea

VATICAN CITY

Bari

Tirana

ALBANIA

Skopje

MACEDONIA

Thessaloniki

Aegean Sea

Larisa

Cosenza

Ionian Sea

GREECE

Athens

Dodecanese

Rhodes

Cyprus

The Gulf

Palermo

Messina

Sicily

Syracuse

Tyrrhenian Sea

MALTA

Valletta

Crete

M E D I T E R R A N E A N   S E A

A F R I C A

© Bartholomew Ltd

Miles   Km

800

1200

600

1000

800

400

600

400

200

200

0   0

1:17 500 000

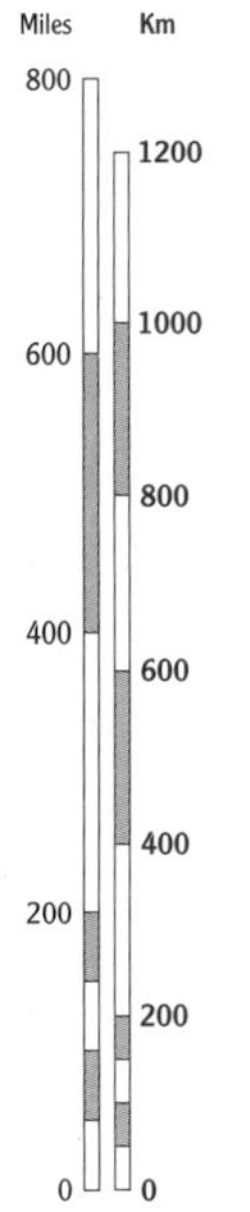

BARENTS SEA

MURMANSKAYA OBLAST'

RUSSIAN FEDERATION

RESP. KARELIYA

F I N L A N D

L A P P L A N D

POHJANMAA / ÖSTERBOTTEN

BOTHNIA

N O R R B O T T E N

V Ä S T E R B O T T E N

Murmansk

North Cape (Nordkapp)

Magerøya

Sørøya

Ringvassøy

Kvaløya

Senja

Andøya

Hinnøya

Langøya

Austvågøy

Vesterålen

Lofoten

Moskenesøy

Værøy

Røst

Varangerfjorden

Porsangen

Tanafjorden

Laksefjorden

Vadsø

Vardø

Kirkenes

Hammerfest

Alta

Karasjok

Kautokeino

Ivalo

Inari

Rovaniemi

Kemi

Tornio

Oulu

Luleå

Boden

Piteå

Skellefteå

Umeå

Kiruna

Gällivare

Jokkmokk

Arvidsjaur

Storuman

Kilpisjärvi

Tromsø

Narvik

Bodø

Mo i Rana

Mosjøen

Sandnessjøen

Brønnøysund

Namsos

Steinkjer

Trondheim

Vatnajökull

Hofsjökull

Langjökull

Mýrdalsjökull

ICELAND
1:5 000 000

Reykjavík

Akureyri

Ísafjörður

Vestmannaeyjar

Grímsey

Faxaflói

Breiðafjörður

Arctic Circle

Faroe Islands (Denmark)
1:5 000 000

Tórshavn

Eysturoy

Streymoy

Vágar

Suðuroy

N O R W E G I A N   S E A

Kristiansund

Ålesund

Conic Equidistant Projection

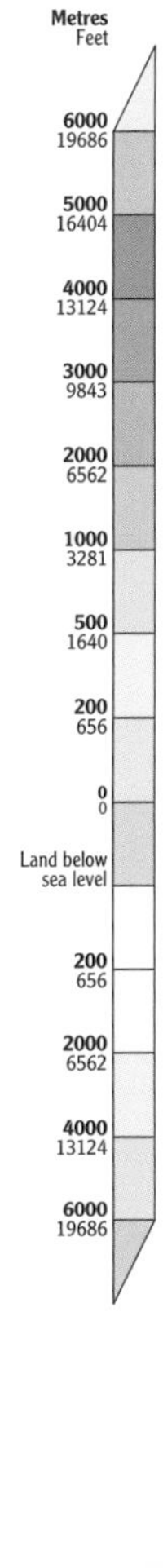

Metres / Feet
6000 / 19686
5000 / 16404
4000 / 13124
3000 / 9843
2000 / 6562
1000 / 3281
500 / 1640
200 / 656
0
Land below sea level
200 / 656
2000 / 6562
4000 / 13124
6000 / 19686

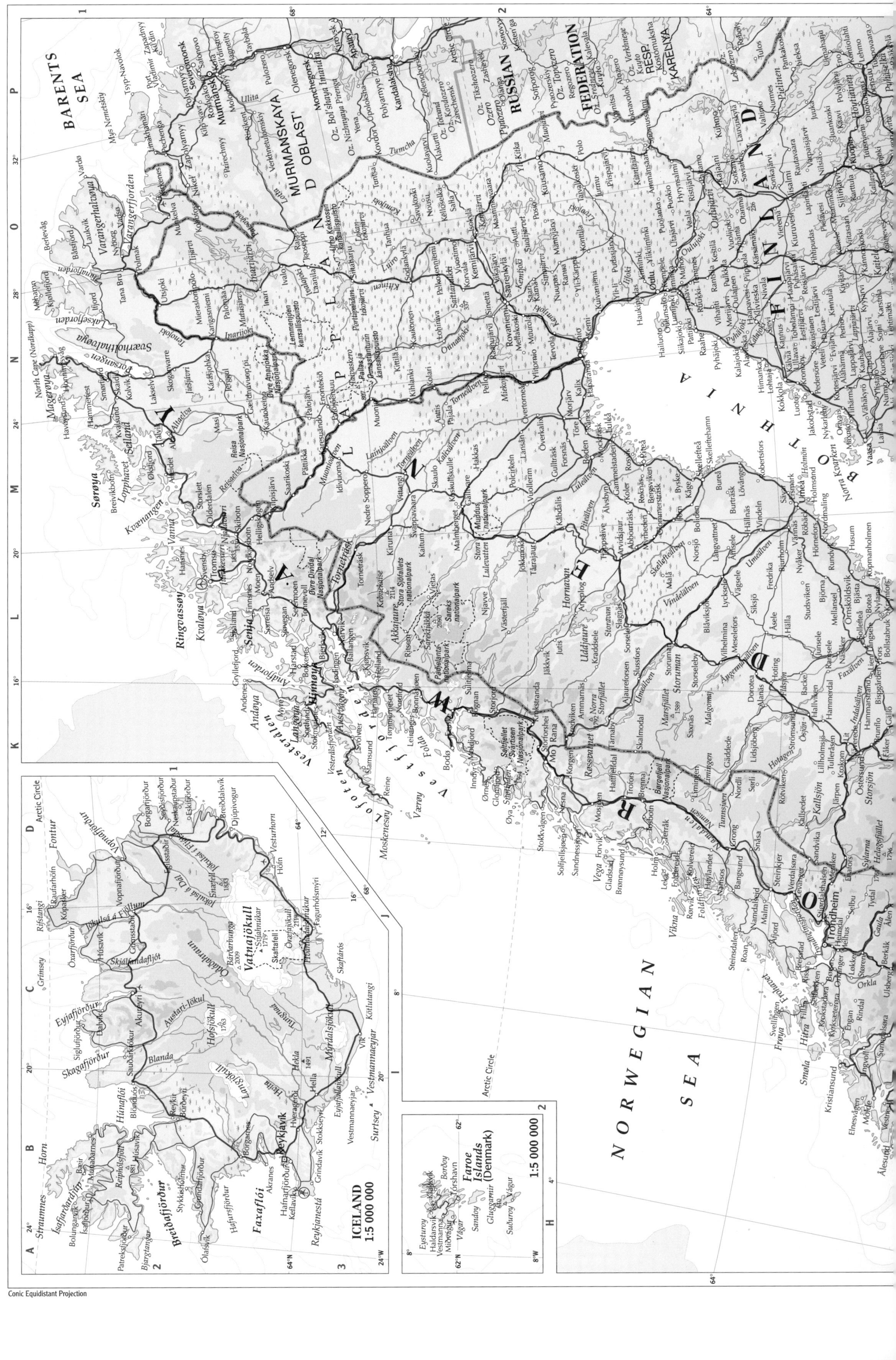

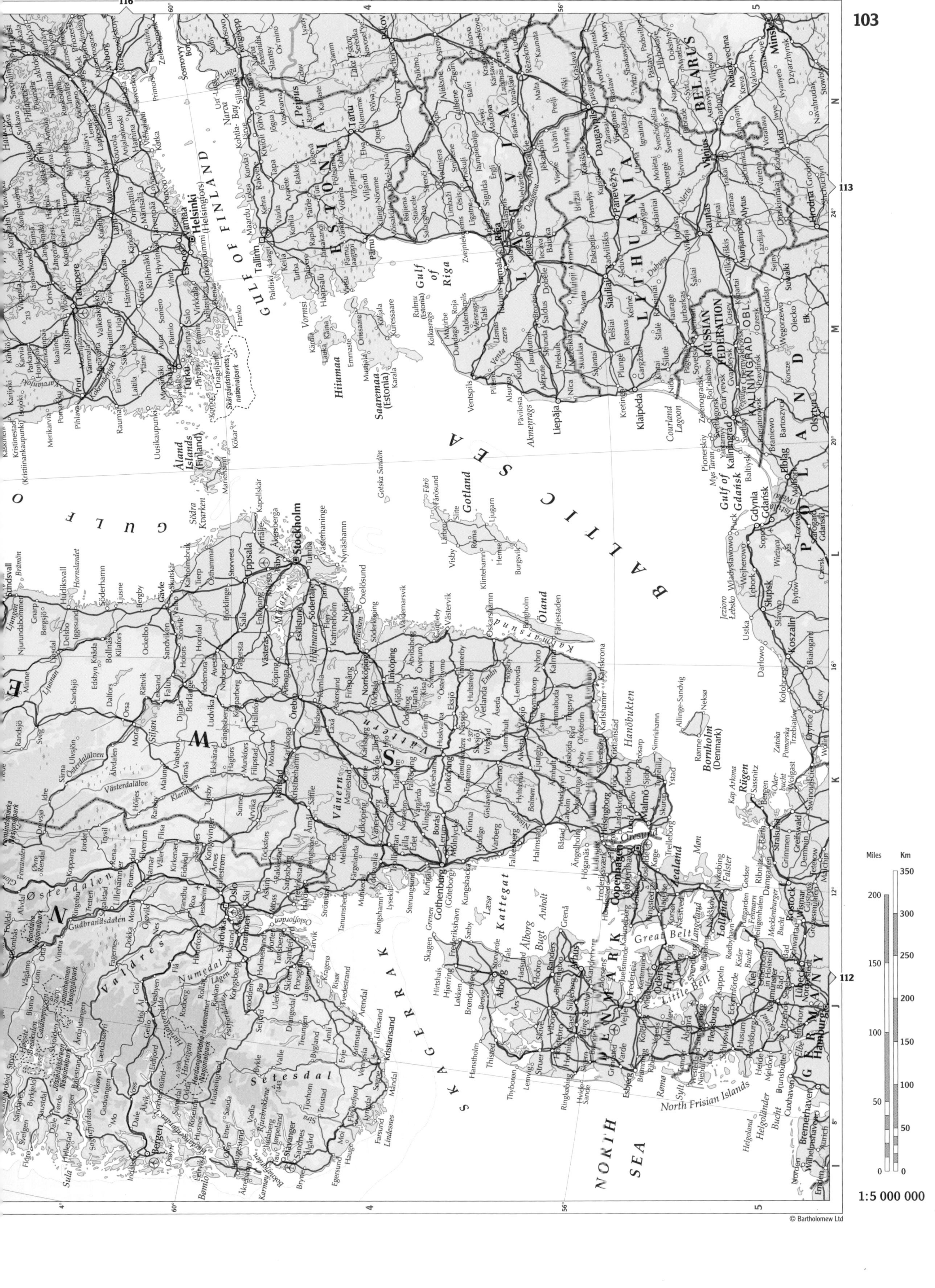
GULF OF FINLAND
BALTIC SEA
SKAGERRAK
Kattegat
NORTH SEA
Gulf of Riga
GULF OF BOTHNIA
ESTONIA
LATVIA
LITHUANIA
BELARUS
RUSSIAN FEDERATION
KALININGRAD OBL'
POLAND
GERMANY
DENMARK
SWEDEN
FINLAND
Helsinki
Tallinn
Riga
Vilnius
Minsk
Stockholm
Oslo
Copenhagen
Gotland
Öland
Saaremaa
Hiiumaa
Bornholm (Denmark)
Åland Islands (Finland)
Miles
Km
116
113
112

1:5 000 000

© Bartholomew Ltd

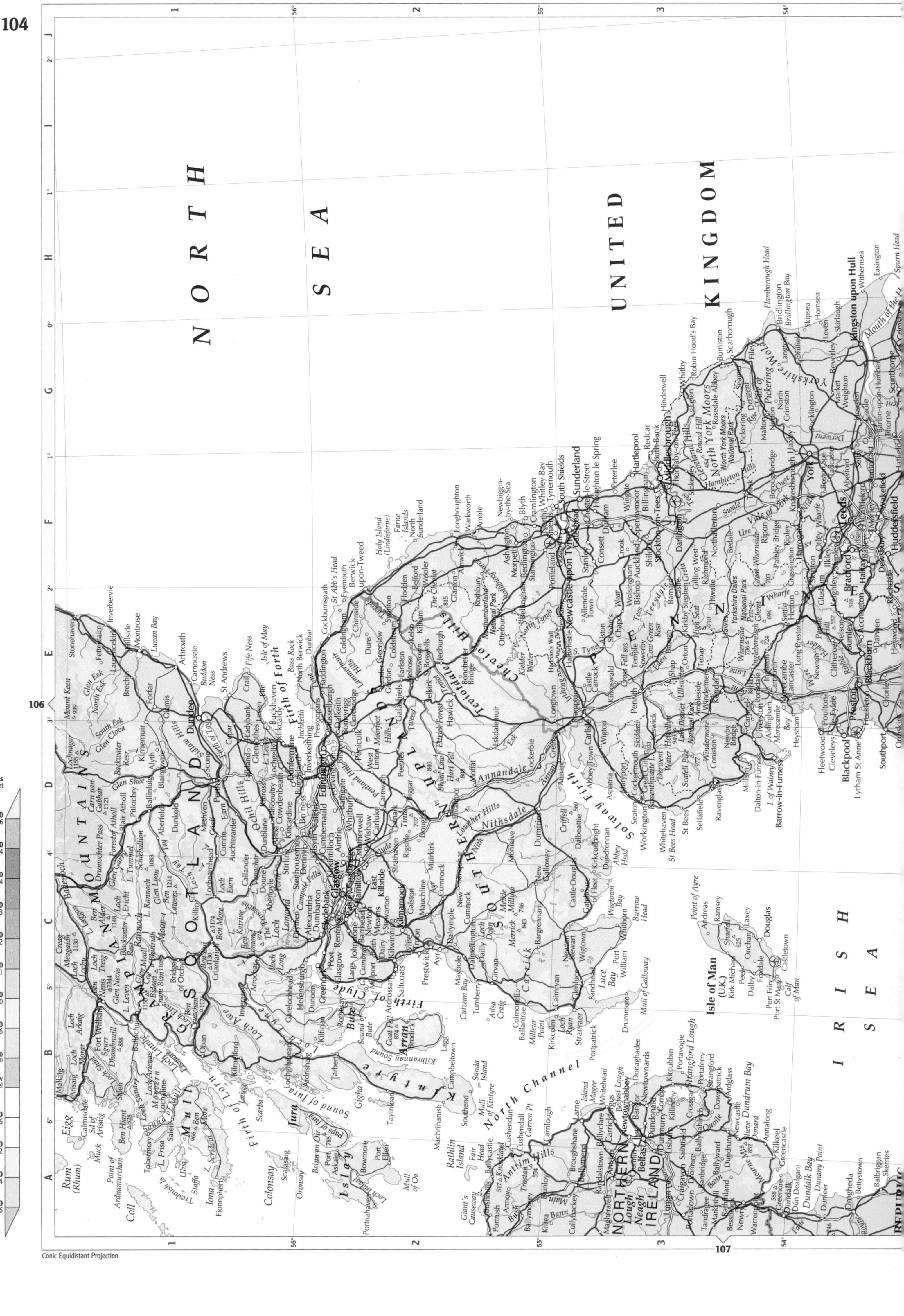

NORTH SEA

UNITED KINGDOM

Metres
Feet

6000 19686
5000 16404
4000 13124
3000 9843
2000 6562
1000 3281
500 1640
200 656
0 0

Land below
sea level

200 656
2000 6562
4000 13124
6000 19686

GRAMPIAN MOUNTAINS

SCOTLAND

SOUTHERN UPLANDS

Glasgow
Edinburgh

Firth of Forth

Firth of Clyde

Mull of Kintyre

Isle of Man
(U.K.)

Douglas

NORTHERN IRELAND

Belfast

IRISH SEA

North Channel

PENNINES

North York Moors
National Park

Kingston upon Hull

Leeds
Bradford

Blackpool
Preston

Lake District
National Park

Solway Firth

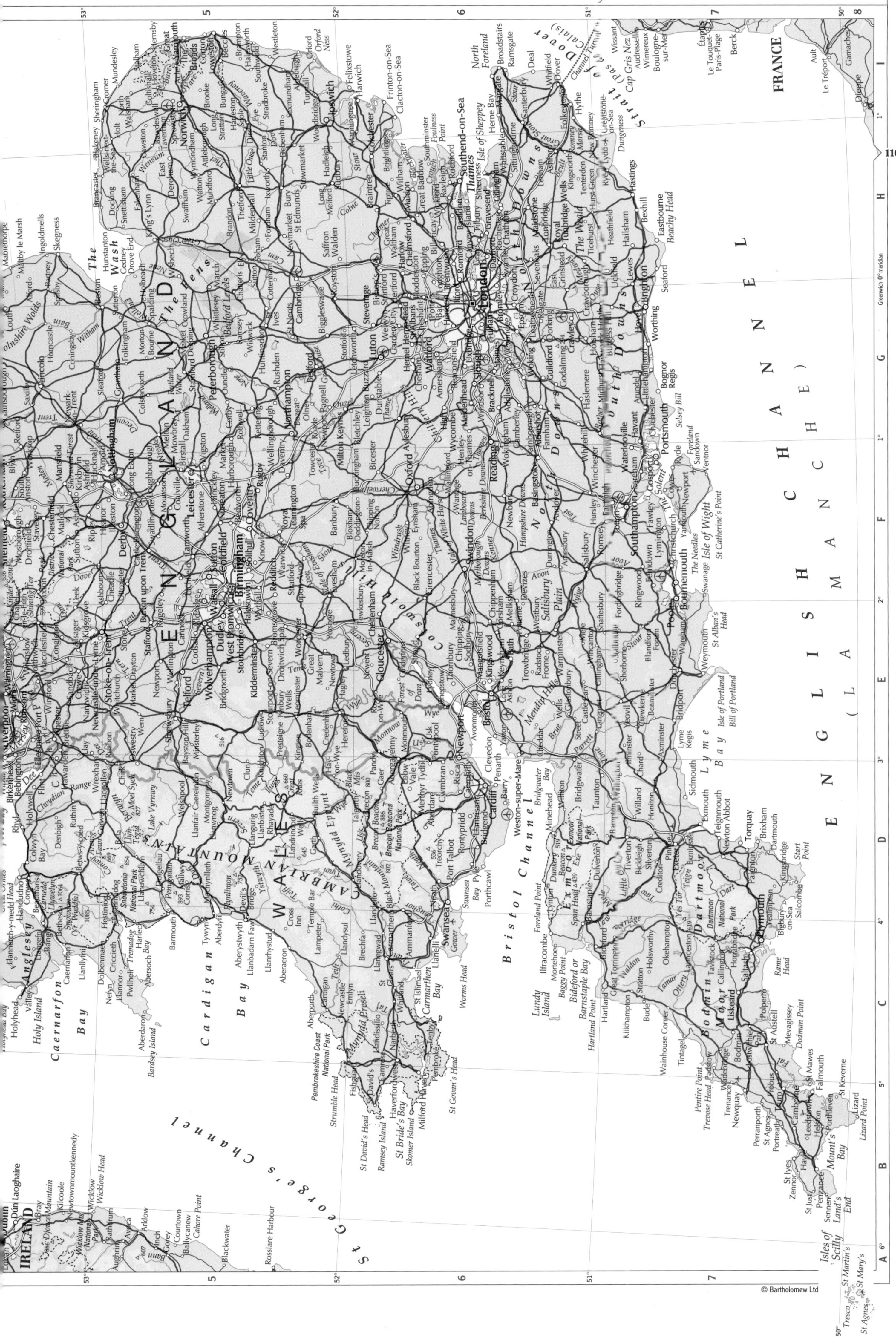

ENGLAND
WALES
IRELAND
FRANCE
ENGLISH CHANNEL
(LA MANCHE)
Bristol Channel
St George's Channel
Cardigan Bay
Caernarfon Bay
Strait of Dover (Pas de Calais)
The Wash
London
Birmingham
Bristol
Cardiff
Swansea
Plymouth
Southampton
Portsmouth
Brighton
Norwich
Ipswich
Cambridge
Oxford
Leicester
Nottingham
Coventry
Stoke-on-Trent
Liverpool
Chester
Exeter
Dublin
Isle of Wight
Isles of Scilly
Lundy Island
Anglesey
Dartmoor
Exmoor
Bodmin Moor
Salisbury Plain
Cotswold Hills
Chiltern Hills
North Downs
South Downs
Cambrian Mountains
Greenwich 0° meridian
110

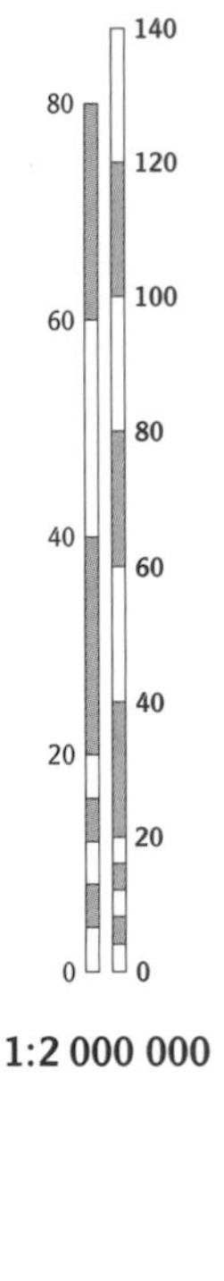

Miles
Km
0
20
40
60
80
0
20
40
60
80
100
120
140

1:2 000 000

A 7° B 6° C 5° D 4° E 3° F 2° G

Fair Isle

ATLANTIC OCEAN

Papa Westray
North Ronaldsay
Mull Head
Westray
Rousay
Sanday
Sanday Sound
Whitehall
Stronsay
Eday
Brough Head
Birsay
Orkney Islands
Tingwall
Shapinsay
Auskerry
Stromness
Mainland
Kirkwall
Gritley
St Mary's
Scapa Flow
Burray
Hoy
South Ronaldsay
Lyness
Burwick

Rona
Gealldruig Mhor
Sula Sgeir
Gralisgeir

Sule Skerry
Sule Stack

Pentland Firth
Dunnet Head
I. of Stroma
Duncansby Head
Cape Wrath
Durness
Strathy Point
Strathy
Scrabster
Dunnet Bay
John o' Groats
Loch Hope
Tongue
Bettyhill
Thurso
Halkirk
Mybster
Wick
Loch Inchard
Loch Laxford
Ben Hope 927
Ben Loyal
Loch Naver
Strath of Kildonan
Loch Watten
Sinclair's Bay
Handa Island
Foinaven 915
764
Loch More
Strathnaver
Watten
Scourie
Point of Stoer
Unapool
Ben Klibreck 961
Kinbrace
Latheron
Rubha Coigeach
Lochinver
Ben More Assynt 998
Loch Shin
Helmsdale
Summer Isles
Achiltibuie
Canisp 846
Elphin
Lairg
Strath Fleet
Brora
Greenstone Pt
Ledmore
Loch Lurgainn
Ullapool
Bonar Bridge
Golspie
Butt of Lewis
Port Ness
Muirneag 248
Tolsta Head
Loch a' Tuath
Portnaguran
Carloway
Stornoway
Eye Peninsula
Garrynahine
West Loch Roag
Great Bernera
Flannan Isles
Mealasta I.
Isle of Lewis
Kebock Head
Scarp
Loch Langavat
Clisham 799
Outer Hebrides
Tarbert
Shiant Islands
The Minch
Gruinard Bay
An Teallach 1062
Beinn Dearg 1084
Strathcarron
Tarbat Ness
Taransay
Harris
Northton
Scalpay
Rubha Reidh
Gairloch
Loch Maree
Liathach 1054
Sgurr Mor 1110
Loch Fannich
Garve
Dingwall
Ben Wyvis 1046
Cromarty
Rubha Hunish
Kilmaluag
Loch Shiel
Moray Firth
Lossiemouth
Cullen
Portsoy
Troup Head
Fraserburgh
Pabbay
Bernera
Boreray
Baile Mhartainn
Sound of Harris
Lochmaddy
Rodel
Uig
The Storr 719
Portree
Applecross
Craig
Achnasheen
Muir of Ord
Beauly
Inverness
Nairn
Cawdor
Forres
Elgin
Kinloss
Fochabers
Keith
Huntly
Turriff
New Deer
Peterhead
Knock
Banff
Macduff
Aberchirder
Strichen
Rattray Head
Sd of Monach
North Uist
Monach Islands
Benbecula
Sd of Berneray
Loch Snizort
Borve
Bracadale
Raasay
Sd of Raasay
Lochcarron
Kyle of Lochalsh
Carn Eighe 1183
Glen Cannich
Strathconon
Black Isle
Tomatin
Findhorn
Grantown-on-Spey
Dava
Rothes
Dufftown
Insch
Oldmeldrum
Mossat
Inverurie
Kintore
Newburgh
Westhill
Ellon
Cruden Bay
New Pitsligo
Hill of Dudwick
South Uist
Lochboisdale
Cuillin Hills
Sligachan
Broadford
Scalpay
Sgurr Alasdair 993
Bla Bheinn 928
Soay
Loch Eishort
Knoydart
A'Chralaig 1120
Glen Affric
Glen Moriston
Fort Augustus
Loch Ness
Monadhliath Mountains
Kingussie
Strathdearn
Foyers
Aviemore
Cairn Gorm 1245
Strathspey
Cairngorm Mountains
1291
1309
Ben Avon
Cock Bridge
Tomintoul
Glen
Don
Tillyfourie
Torphins
Kemnay
Dyce
Aberdeen
Fuday
Eriskay
Canna
Rum (Rhum)
Eigg
Galmisdale
Sd of Arisaig
Eilean Shona
Point of Ardnamurchan
Ben Hiant 528
Ardvasar
Sound of Sleat
L. Hourn
Quoich
Loch Arkaig
Loch Lochy
Laggan
Creag Meagaidh 1130
Ben Alder 1148
Loch Treig
Badenoch
Drumochter Pass
Carn nan Gabhar 1121
Forest of Atholl
Ben Macdui 1309
Cairn Toul 1291
Lochnagar 1155
Braemar
Ballater
Mount Keen 939
Glen Esk
North Esk
Stonehaven
Aboyne
Banchory
Newtonhill
Portlethen
Barra
Vatersay
Sandray
Pabbay
Mingulay
Berneray
Castlebay
Arisaig
Mallaig
Loch Morar
Loch Nevis
Loch Shiel
Ben Nevis 1344
Fort William
Glen Nevis
Loch Leven
Glen Coe
Blackwater Resr
Bidean nam Bian 1141
Loch Ericht
Rannoch
Schiehallion 1083
Pitlochry
Blair Atholl
L. Tummel
Glen Garry
L. Rannoch
Glen Lyon
Aberfeldy
Killiecrankie
Dunkeld
Backwater Resr
Brechin
Laurencekirk
Marykirk
Inverbervie
Tannadice
Montrose
Muck
Tiree
Coll
Treshnish Isles
Staffa
Iona
Fionnphort
Ulva
Salen
Tobermory
Loch Frisa
Sound of Mull
Morvern
Lochaline
Ben More 966
Mull
Loch Scridain
Loch Spelve
Kinlochleven
Ballachulish
Loch Linnhe
Lismore
Loch Etive
Ben Cruachan 1130
Rannoch Moor
Ben Lawers 1214
Tay
Killin
Loch Tay
Kenmore
Sidlaw Hills
Glamis
Forfar
Kirriemuir
Alyth
Blairgowrie
Coupar Angus
Scone
Dundee
Carnoustie
Buddon Ness
Arbroath
Lunan Bay
NORTH SEA
Firth of Lorn
Oban
Kilmelford
Luing
Scarba
Jura
Colonsay
Scalasaig
Oronsay
Islay
Bowmore
Port Askaig
Portnahaven
Port Ellen
Crianlarich
Tyndrum
Ben More 1174
Ben Vorlich 985
Comrie
Crieff
Methven
Perth
Firth of Tay
Cupar
St Andrews
Luncarty
Loch Earn
Lochearnhead
Callander
Doune
Auchterarder
Falkland
Ladybank
Fife Ness
Pitscottie
Beinn an Oir 785
Page of Jura
Sound of Jura
Argyll Forest
Loch Fyne
Loch Awe
Inveraray
Loch Katrine
The Trossachs
Loch Venachar
Ben Ledi
Aberfoyle
Loch Lomond
Drymen
Stirling
Alloa
Dollar
Kinross
Loch Leven
Glenrothes
Leslie
Leven
Elie
Crail
Isle of May
Ben Lomond 974
Arrochar
Gartmore
Campsie Fells
Denny
Falkirk
Linlithgow
Cowdenbeath
Dunfermline
Kincardine
Burntisland
Inchkeith
North Berwick
Dunbar
Bass Rock
St Abb's Head
Gigha
Tarbert
West Loch Tarbert
Ardrishaig
Lochgilphead
Helensburgh
Dumbarton
Clydebank
Renfrew
Glasgow
Kilsyth
Kirkintilloch
Cumbernauld
Coatbridge
Airdrie
Bathgate
Whitburn
Livingston
Penicuik
Dalkeith
Edinburgh
Musselburgh
Prestonpans
Tranent
Haddington
Lammermuir Hills
Coldingham
Eyemouth
Berwick-upon-Tweed
Holy Island (Lindisfarne)
Farne Is.
Bute
Rothesay
Cumbrae
Sd of Bute
Largs
Millport
Dunoon
Greenock
Gourock
Firth of Clyde
Paisley
Barrhead
Johnstone
Beith
Dalry
Kilwinning
Kilbirnie
East Kilbride
Hamilton
Motherwell
Wishaw
Carluke
Lanark
Carnwath
Biggar
West Linton
Peebles
Galashiels
Earlston
Kelso
Coldstream
Duns
Greenlaw
Swinton
Chirnside
Coll
Kilmarnock
Galston
Newmilns
Strathaven
Darvel
Muirkirk
Douglas
Rigside
Broad Law 840
Tweed
Selkirk
Melrose
St Boswells
Jedburgh
Wooler
Belford
Arran
Goat Fell 874
Brodick
Lamlash
Holy I.
Ardrossan
Saltcoats
Stevenston
Irvine
Troon
Prestwick
Ayr
Mauchline
Cumnock
Sorn
New Cumnock
Sanquhar
Moffat
Ettrick
White Coomb
Hart Fell 808
Teviotdale
Hawick
Denholm
Bonchester Bridge
The Cheviot 815
Cheviot Hills
Otterburn
Rothbury
Kintyre
Machrihanish
Campbeltown
Southend
Mull of Kintyre
Sanda Island
Rathlin Island
Fair Head
Ballycastle
North Channel
Culzean Bay
Maybole
Dalrymple
Turnberry
Girvan
Dailly
Loch Doon
Dalmellington
Carsphairn
New Galloway
Nithsdale
Thornhill
Dumfries
Lockerbie
Ecclefechan
Langtown
Gretna
Brampton
Haltwhistle
Hadrian's Wall
Northumberland National Park
Kielder Water
Bellingham
Newcastle upon Tyne
Malin Head
Inishtrahull
Inishowen
Malin
Ailsa Craig
Milleur Point
Ballantrae
Barrhill
Carrick
Merrick 843
Bargrennan
Colmonell
Meikle Millyea 746
New Galloway
Castle Douglas
Criffel 569
Solway Firth
Abbey Town
Wigton
Kirkswald
Penrith
Ullswater
Crook
Bishop Auckland
Buncrana
Londonderry
Claudy
Strabane
Sion Mills
Newtownstewart
Sperrin Mts
Sawel Mt 683
Omagh
Cookstown
Pomeroy
Sixmilecross
NORTHERN IRELAND
Coleraine
Portstewart
Portrush
Bushmills
Giant's Causeway
Armoy
Ballymoney
Kilrea
Garvagh
Maghera
Magherafelt
Moneymore
Draperstown
REP. OF IRELAND
Slieve Snaght 615
Lough Foyle
Eglinton
Limavady
Ballykelly
Ringsend
Dunloy
Cushendall
Garron Pt
Cushendun
Trostan 554
Antrim Mts
Carnlough
Ballymena
Broughshane
Larne
Island Magee
Whitehead
Carrickfergus
Belfast Lough
Bangor
Donaghadee
Newtownards
Dundonald
Ballyclare
Ballymena
Randalstown
Antrim
Newtownabbey
Belfast
Crumlin
Lough Neagh
UNITED KINGDOM
ENGLAND
Carlisle
Wigtown
Whithorn
Burrow Head
Mull of Galloway
Luce Bay
Port William
Sandhead
Stranraer
Portpatrick
Kirkcolm
Cairnryan
Newton Stewart
Wigtown Bay
Kirkcudbright
Dundrennan
Dalbeattie
Abbey Head

Metres / Feet
6000 / 19686
5000 / 16404
4000 / 13124
3000 / 9843
2000 / 6562
1000 / 3281
500 / 1640
200 / 656
0
Land below sea level
200 / 656
2000 / 6562
4000 / 13124
6000 / 19686

Shetland Islands
Herma Ness
Haroldswick
Unst
Baltasound
Point of Fethaland
Cullivoe
Yell
Belmont
Fetlar
The Isbister
Gloup
Funzie
St Magnus Bay
Ronas Hill
Mid Yell
Out Skerries
Papa Stour
Brae
Vidlin
Whalsay
Walls
Voe
Laxo
South Nesting Bay
Foula
Scalloway
Bressay
Isle of Noss
West Burra
Lerwick
Sandwick
Cunningsburgh
Scousburgh
Sumburgh
Sumburgh Head
1:2 000 000

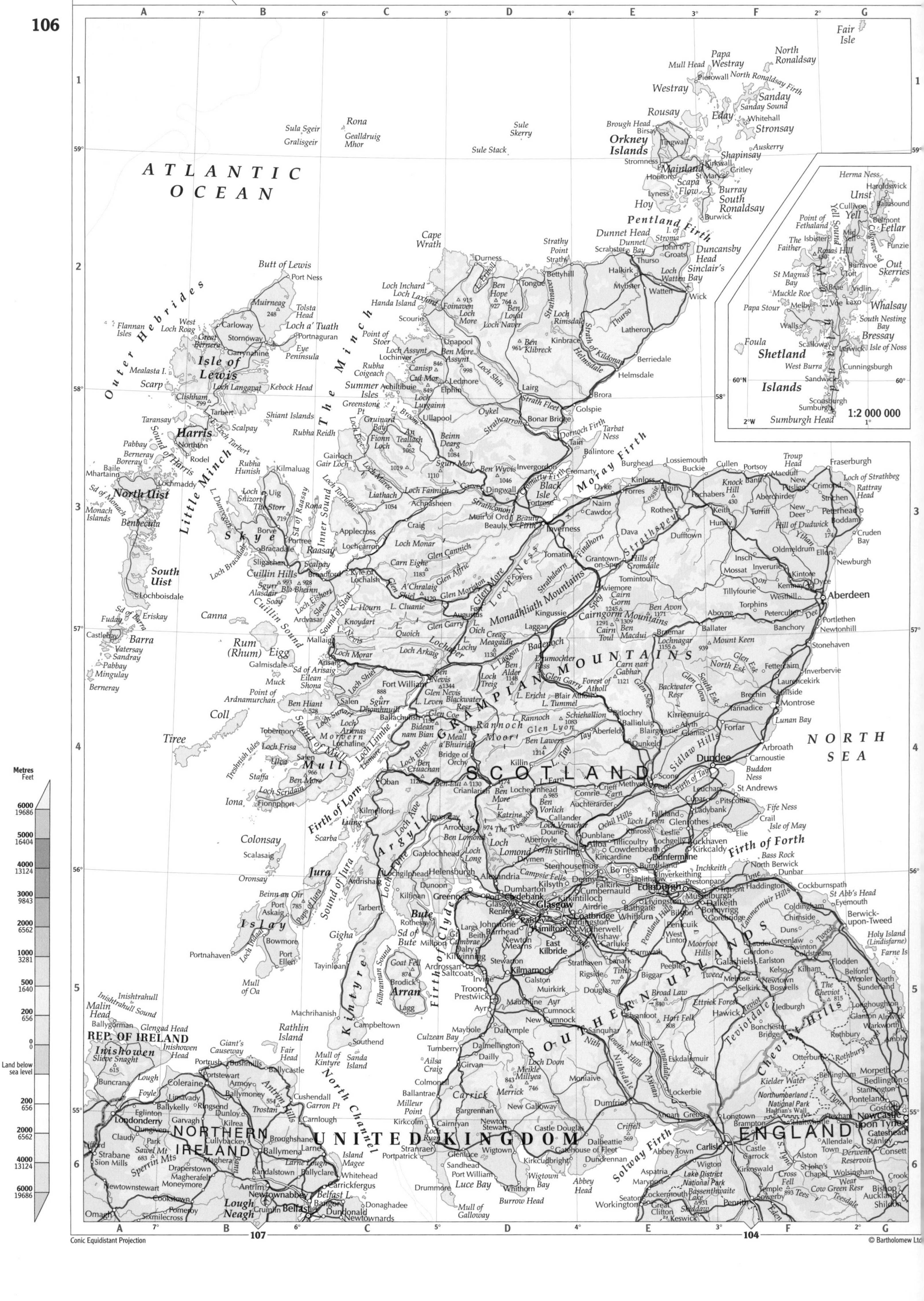

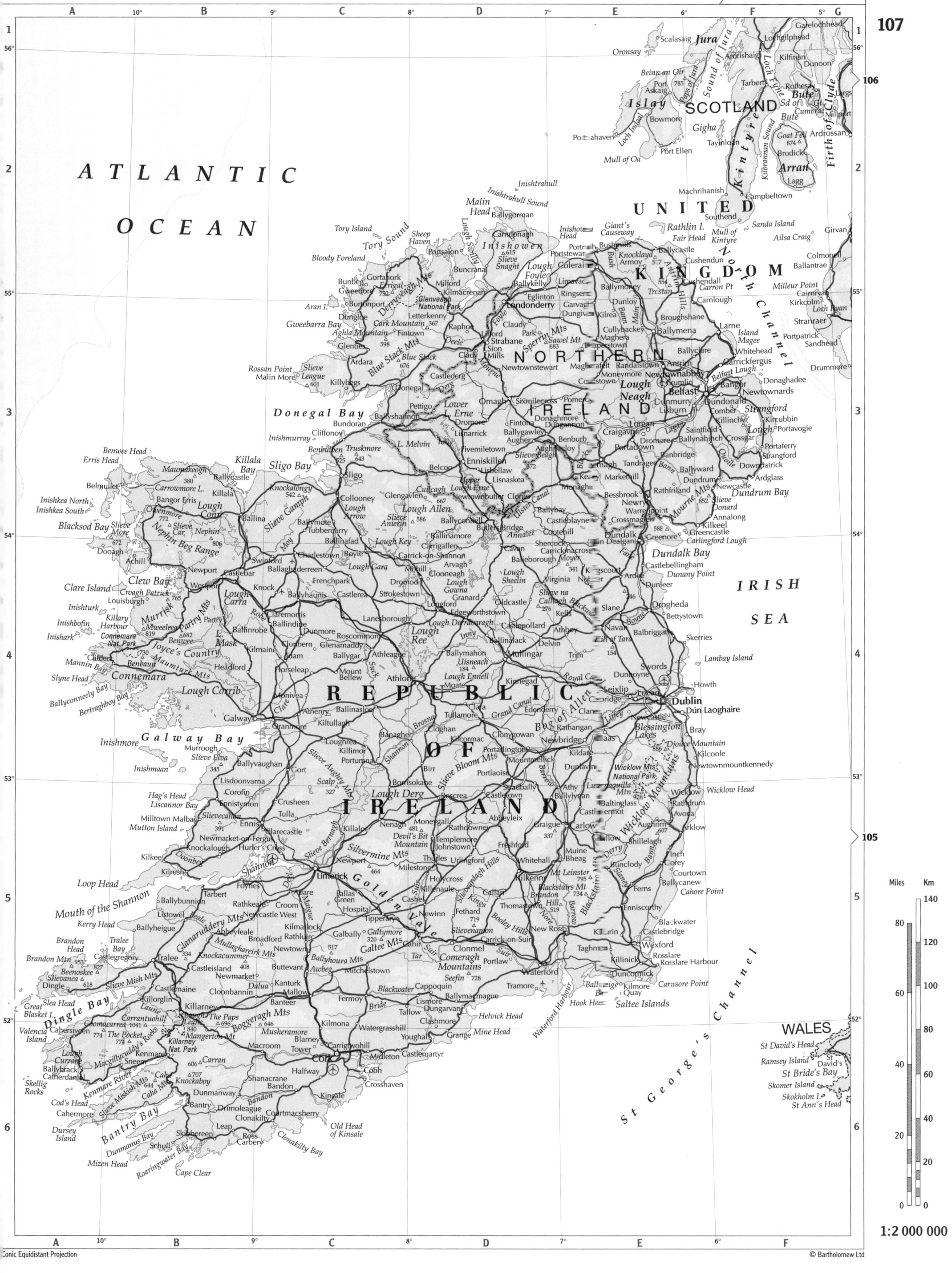

107

106

105

ATLANTIC

OCEAN

SCOTLAND

UNITED

KINGDOM

NORTHERN

IRELAND

IRISH

SEA

REPUBLIC

OF

IRELAND

WALES

St George's Channel

Miles   Km

1:2 000 000

Conic Equidistant Projection

© Bartholomew Ltd

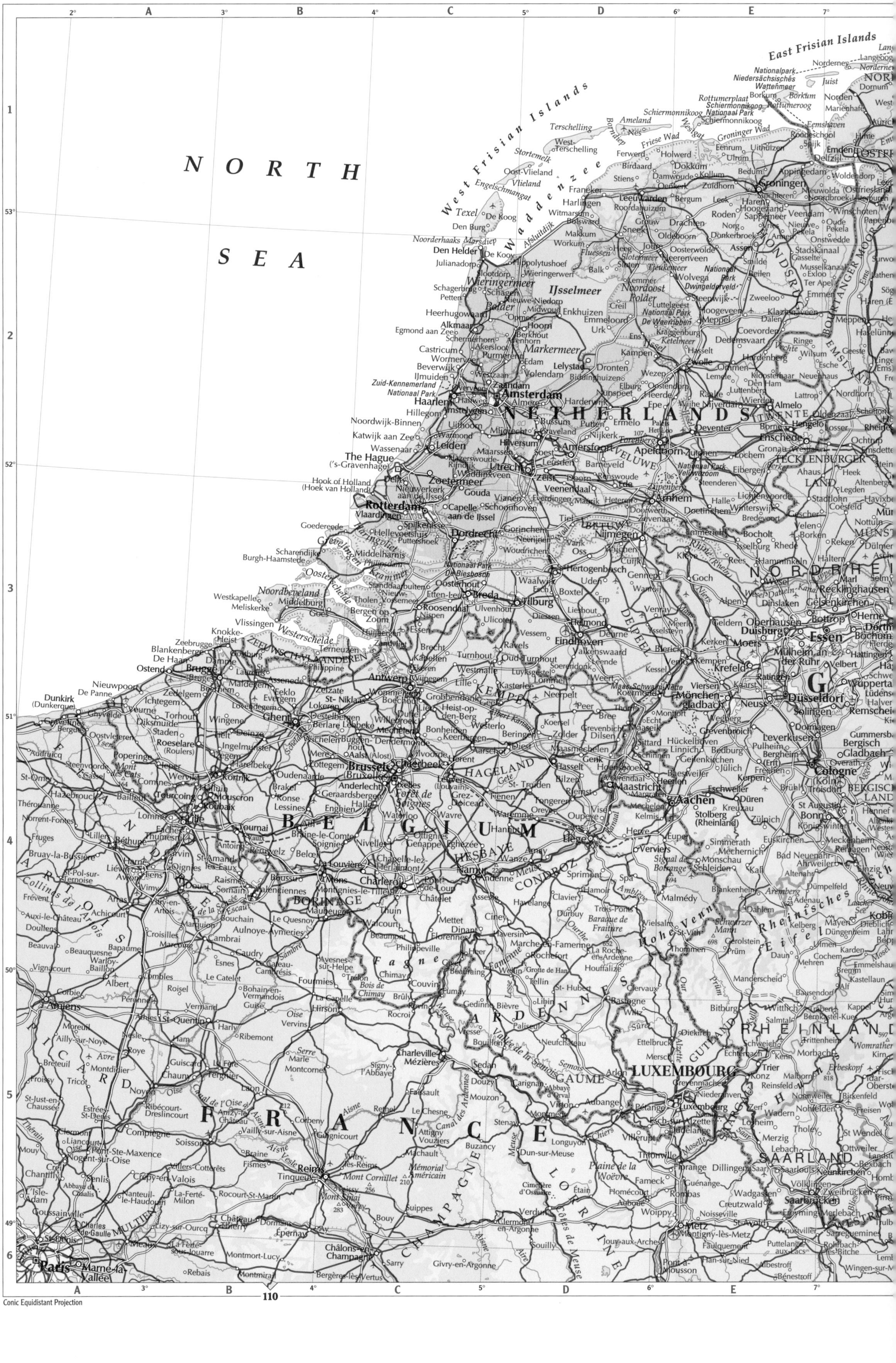

NORTH

SEA

West Frisian Islands

East Frisian Islands

NETHERLANDS

BELGIUM

FRANCE

LUXEMBOURG

SAARLAND

RHEINLAND

NORDRHE

Amsterdam
Haarlem
The Hague ('s-Gravenhage)
Rotterdam
Utrecht
Leiden
Zoetermeer
Delft
Dordrecht
Breda
Tilburg
Eindhoven
Nijmegen
Arnhem
Apeldoorn
Deventer
Enschede
Hengelo
Almelo
Zwolle
Groningen
Leeuwarden
Assen
Alkmaar
Den Helder
Hilversum
Amersfoort

Antwerp
Brussels / Bruxelles
Gent / Ghent
Brugge / Bruges
Ostend
Kortrijk
Roeselare
Mons
Charleroi
Namur
Liège
Hasselt
Maastricht
Aachen
Düsseldorf
Mönchengladbach
Neuss
Krefeld
Duisburg
Essen
Cologne / Köln
Leverkusen
Bonn
Wuppertal

Dunkirk (Dunkerque)
De Panne
Tournai
Lille
Roubaix
Tourcoing
Valenciennes
Cambrai
Douai
Arras
Amiens
St-Quentin
Laon
Soissons
Reims
Épernay
Châlons-en-Champagne
Verdun
Metz
Thionville
Saarbrücken
Luxembourg
Arlon
Trier
Sedan
Charleville-Mézières

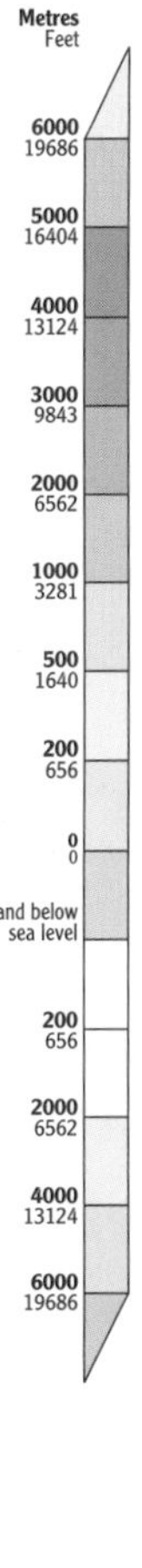

Metres / Feet
6000 / 19686
5000 / 16404
4000 / 13124
3000 / 9843
2000 / 6562
1000 / 3281
500 / 1640
200 / 656
0 / 0
Land below sea level
200 / 656
2000 / 6562
4000 / 13124
6000 / 19686

Paris

Conic Equidistant Projection

BELGIUM, NETHERLANDS AND GERMANY North

Miles   Km

1:2 000 000

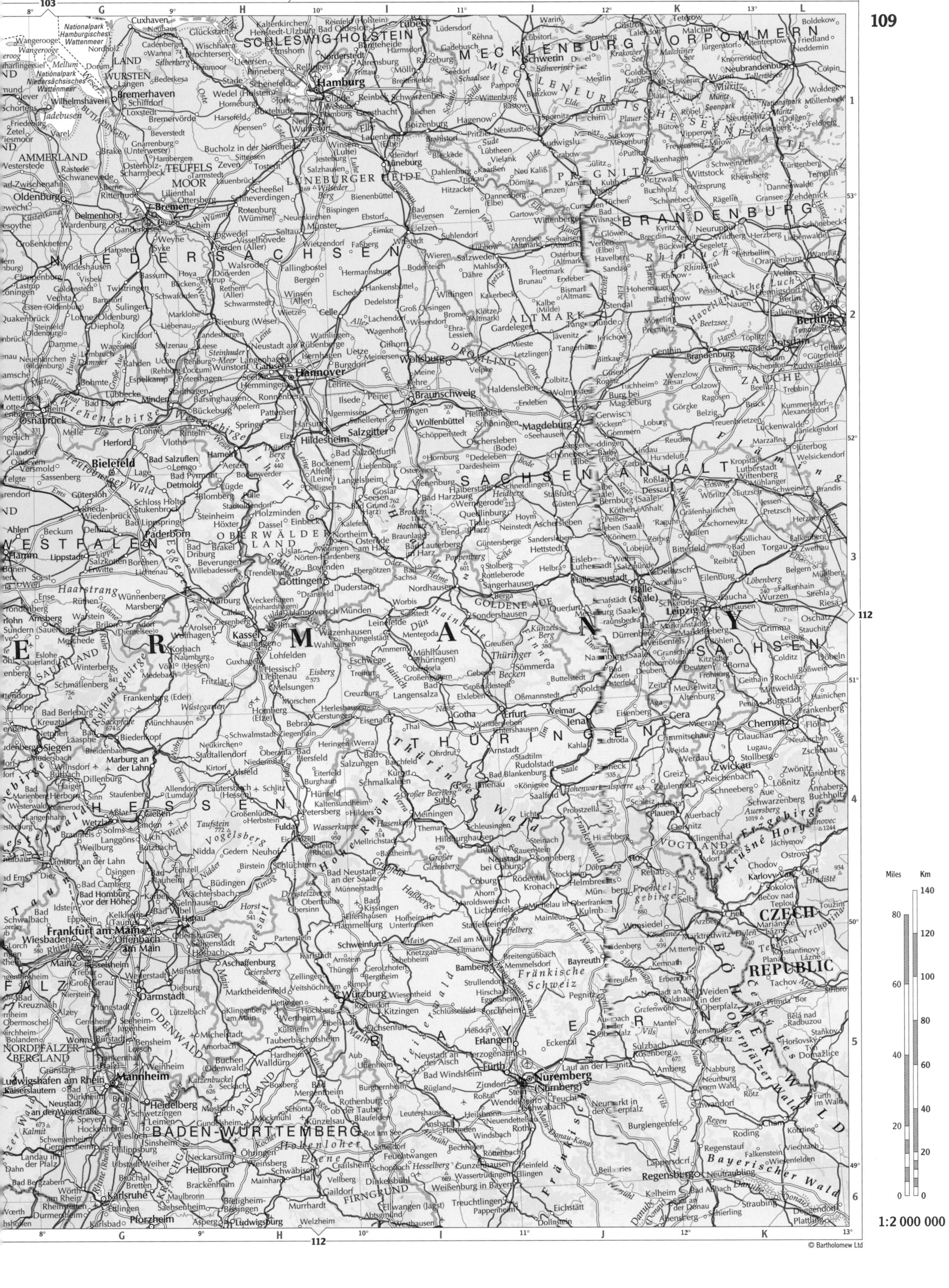

© Bartholomew Ltd

FRANCE

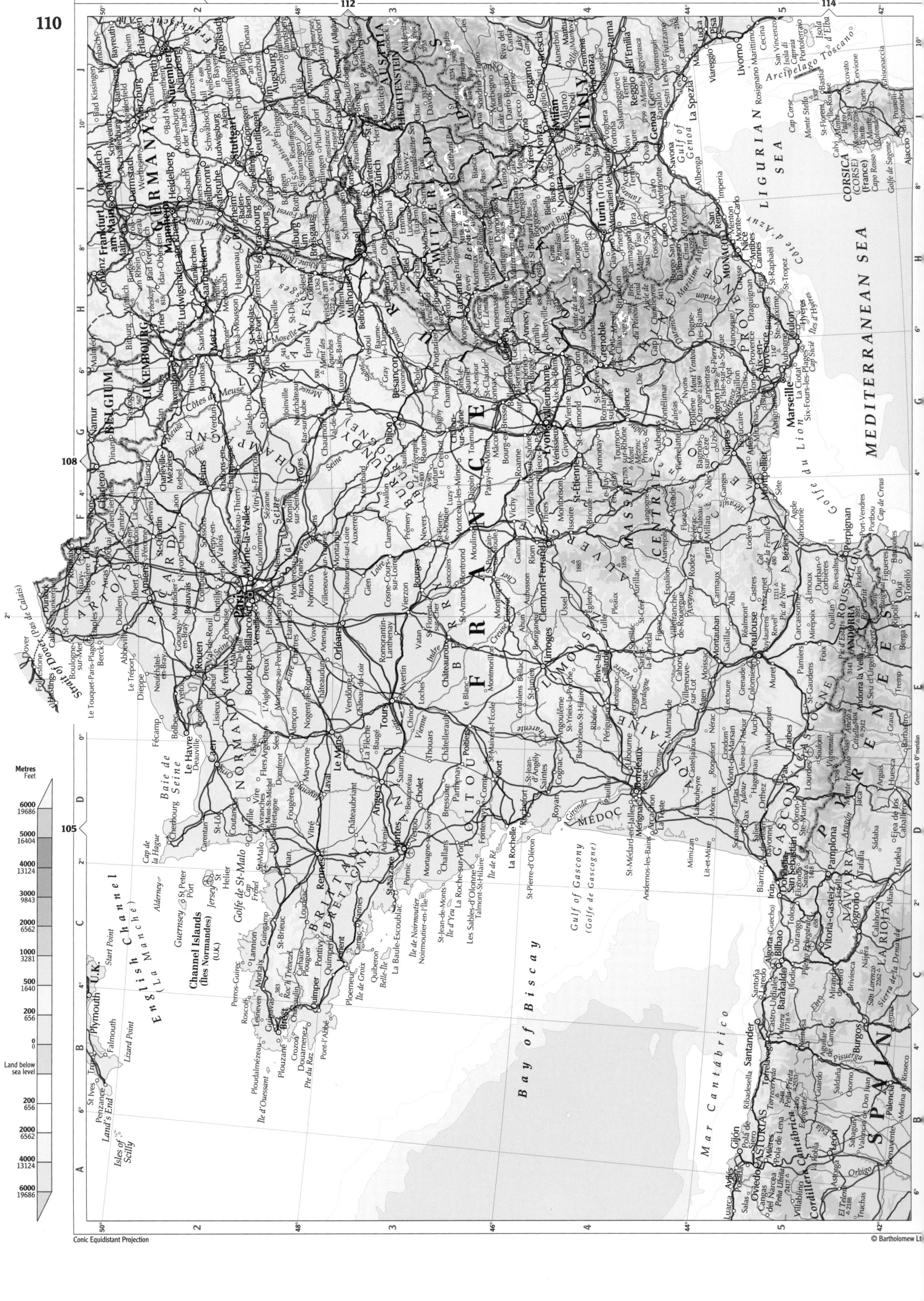

FRANCE
BELGIUM
LUXEMBOURG
GERMANY
SWITZERLAND
LIECHTENSTEIN
AUSTRIA
ITALY
MONACO
ANDORRA
SPAIN
U.K.
CORSICA (CORSE) (France)
MEDITERRANEAN SEA
LIGURIAN SEA
Bay of Biscay
Gulf of Gascony (Golfe de Gascogne)
English Channel (La Manche)
Channel Islands (Îles Normandes) (U.K.)
Mar Cantábrico
Golfe du Lion
Strait of Dover (Pas de Calais)
Paris
Lyon
Marseille
Toulouse
Bordeaux
Nantes
Lille
Strasbourg
Nice
Metres
Feet
6000 19686
5000 16404
4000 13124
3000 9843
2000 6562
1000 3281
500 1640
200 656
0 0
Land below sea level
200 656
2000 6562
4000 13124
6000 19686
105
108
112
114
Greenwich 0° meridian
Conic Equidistant Projection
© Bartholomew Lt

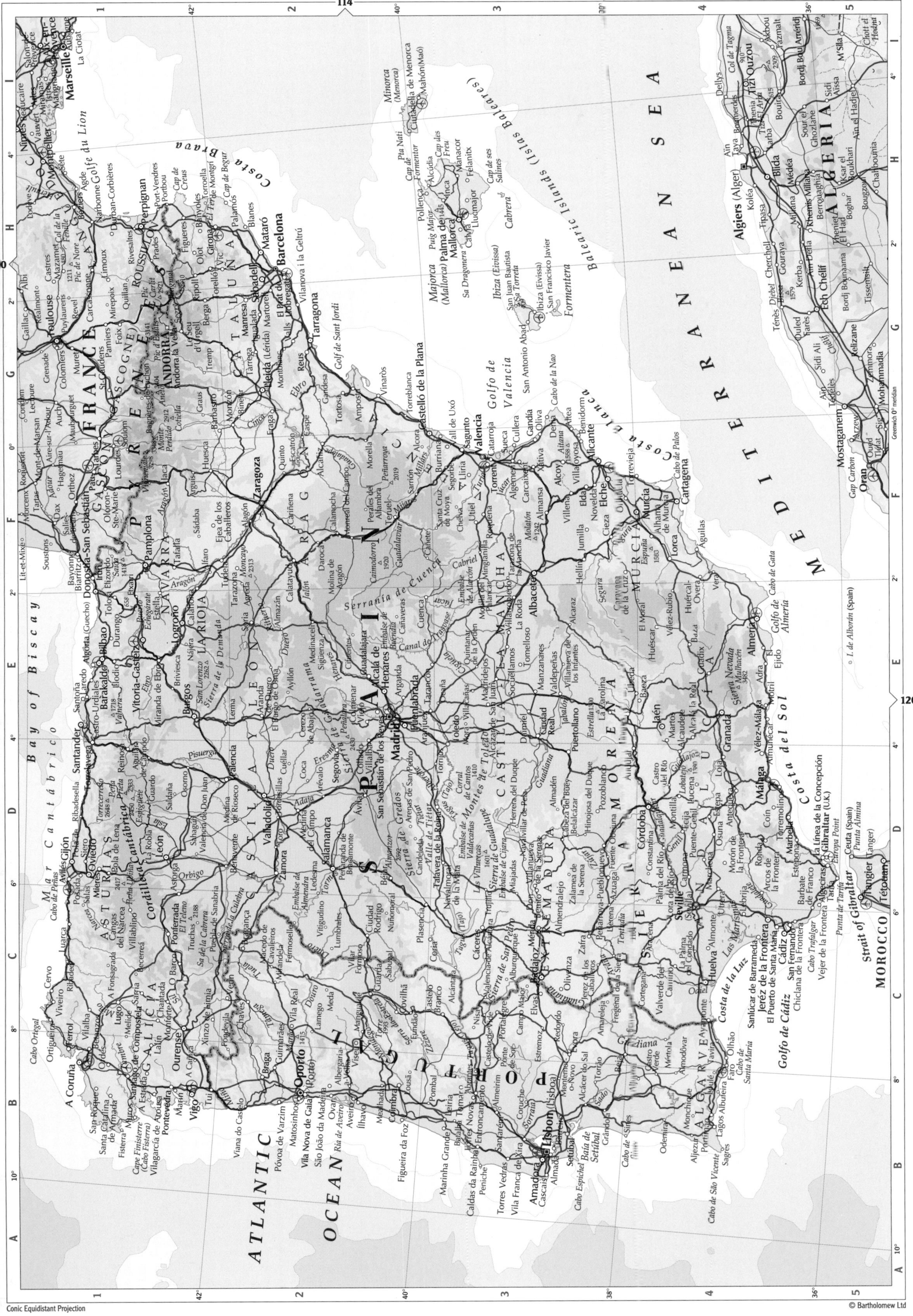

114
120

1:5 000 000

Conic Equidistant Projection

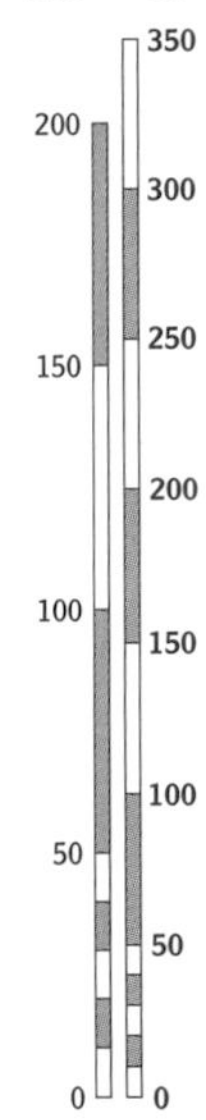

© Bartholomew Ltd

Miles Km

ATLANTIC OCEAN

Bay of Biscay

Mar Cantábrico

FRANCE

PYRENEES

GASCOGNE

ROUSSILLON

CATALUÑA

Golfe du Lion

Costa Brava

ANDORRA

Barcelona

Zaragoza

Pamplona

NAVARRA

LA RIOJA

Bilbao

Donostia-San Sebastián

Santander

Gijón

Oviedo

ASTURIAS

GALICIA

A Coruña

Vigo

Pontevedra

Ourense

Lugo

Oporto (Porto)

Vila Nova de Gaia

PORTUGAL

Lisboa

Setúbal

ALGARVE

Faro

Sevilla

Huelva

Golfo de Cádiz

Cádiz

Strait of Gibraltar

MOROCCO

Tánger (Tanger)

Tetouan

ANDALUCÍA

Málaga

Costa del Sol

Granada

Córdoba

Jaén

Gibraltar (U.K.)

Ceuta (Spain)

SIERRA MORENA

EXTREMADURA

Badajoz

Cáceres

CASTILLA-LA MANCHA

Ciudad Real

Albacete

MURCIA

Murcia

Cartagena

Alicante

Costa Blanca

VALENCIA

Valencia

Golfo de Valencia

Saguntó

Castelló de la Plana

Ebro

Tarragona

Reus

Lleida (Lérida)

SPAIN

Madrid

CASTILLA Y LEÓN

Valladolid

León

Salamanca

Zamora

Burgos

Toledo

Sierra de Gredos

Sierra de Guadarrama

MEDITERRANEAN SEA

Balearic Islands (Islas Baleares)

Menorca

Mahón (Maó)

Majorca (Mallorca)

Palma de Mallorca

Ibiza (Eivissa)

Formentera

Cabrera

ALGERIA

Algiers (Alger)

Oran

Mostaganem

Tizi Ouzou

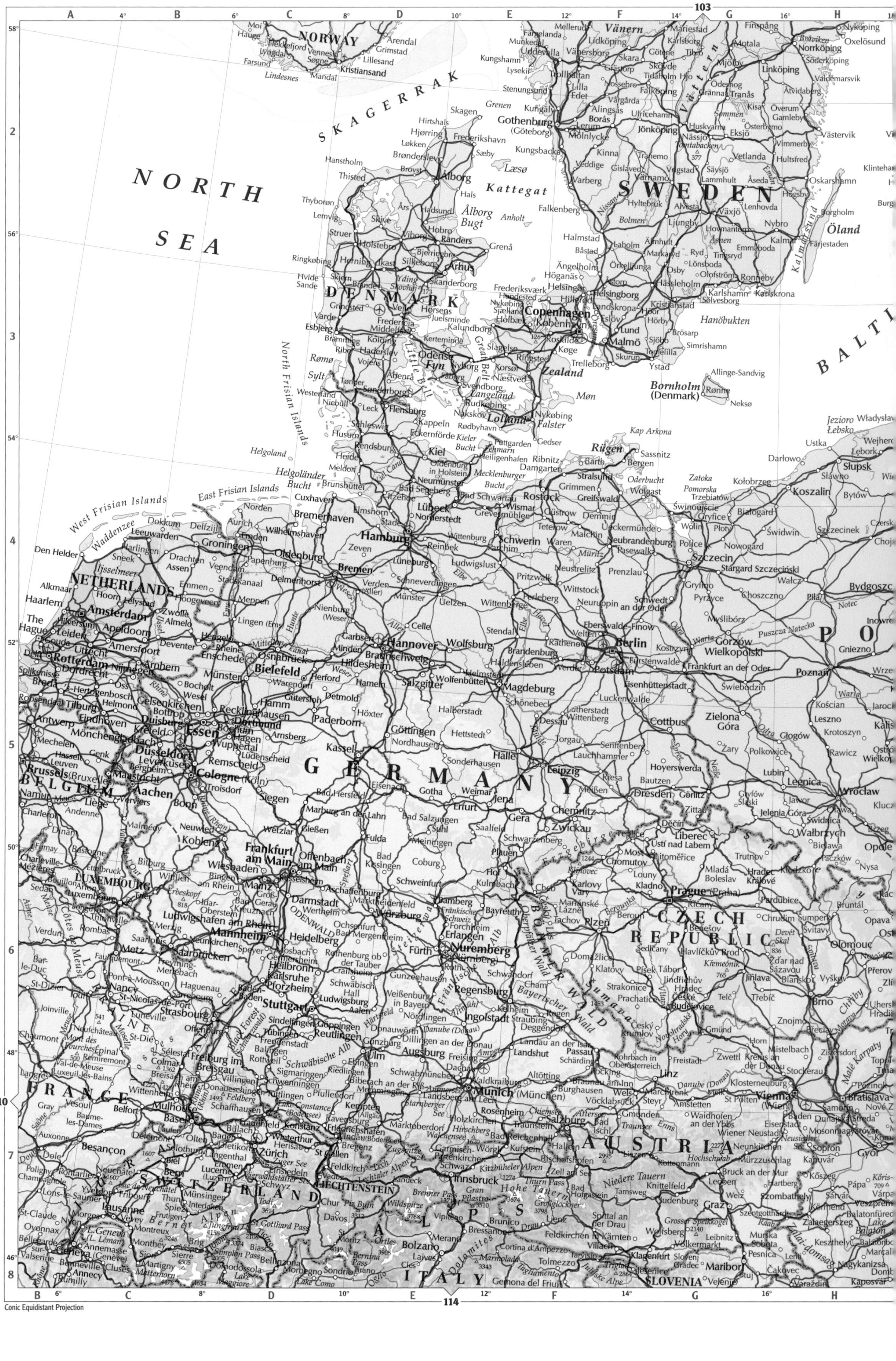

103

A 4° B 6° C 8° D 10° E 12° F 14° G 16° H 18°

NORWAY

NORTH

SEA

SKAGERRAK

Kattegat

DENMARK

Ålborg Bugt

Hanöbukten

Vänern

Vättern

SWEDEN

Öland

BALTIC

Copenhagen
København
Malmö

Zealand

Fyn

Lolland

Bornholm
(Denmark)

Rügen

North Frisian Islands

Helgoland

West Frisian Islands   East Frisian Islands

Waddenzee

NETHERLANDS

Amsterdam
Rotterdam
The Hague

BELGIUM

Brussels
(Bruxelles)

LUXEMBOURG
Luxembourg

Hamburg
Bremen
Hannover
Berlin
Potsdam
Magdeburg
Leipzig
Dresden

GERMANY

Cologne
(Köln)
Bonn
Frankfurt
am Main
Mainz
Mannheim
Stuttgart
Nuremberg
(Nürnberg)
Munich (München)

Szczecin

POLAND

Zielona
Góra

Wrocław

PRAGUE (Praha)

CZECH
REPUBLIC

Danube (Donau)

FRANCE

Strasbourg

SWITZERLAND

LIECHTENSTEIN

AUSTRIA

Vienna
(Wien)

Innsbruck

ALPS

ITALY

SLOVENIA

Graz

Conic Equidistant Projection

110

114

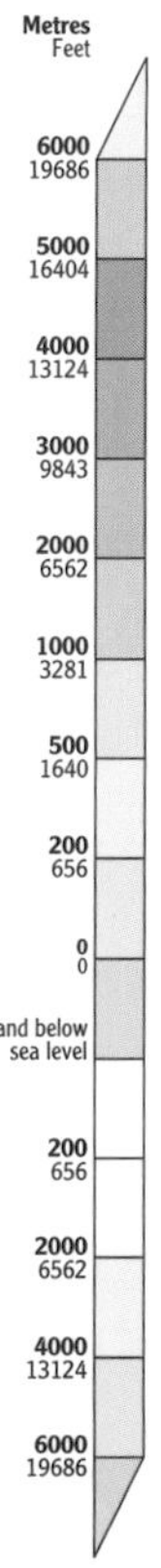

Metres
Feet

6000 19686
5000 16404
4000 13124
3000 9843
2000 6562
1000 3281
500 1640
200 656
0 0

Land below
sea level

200 656
2000 6562
4000 13124
6000 19686

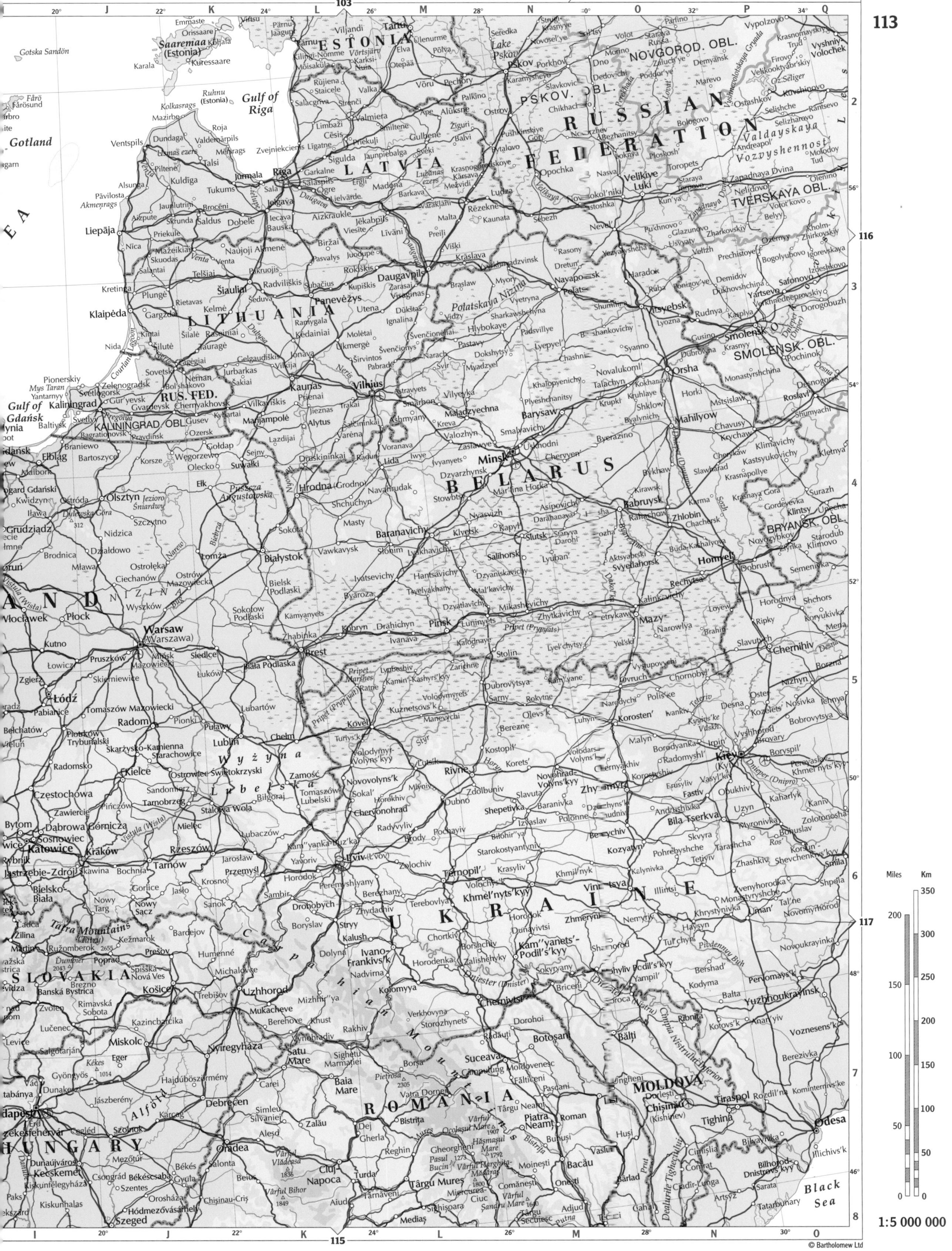
ESTONIA
LATVIA
LITHUANIA
BELARUS
UKRAINE
ROMANIA
MOLDOVA
SLOVAKIA
HUNGARY
RUSSIAN FEDERATION
RUS. FED.
KALININGRAD OBL.
PSKOV. OBL.
NOVGOROD. OBL.
TVERSKAYA OBL.
SMOLENSK. OBL.
BRYANSK. OBL.
Gulf of Riga
Gulf of Gdańsk
Gotland
Black Sea
Carpathian Mountains
Tatra Mountains
Warsaw (Warszawa)
Minsk
Vilnius
Riga
Kiev
Chişinău (Kishinev)
103
115
116
117
Miles
Km
1:5 000 000
© Bartholomew Ltd

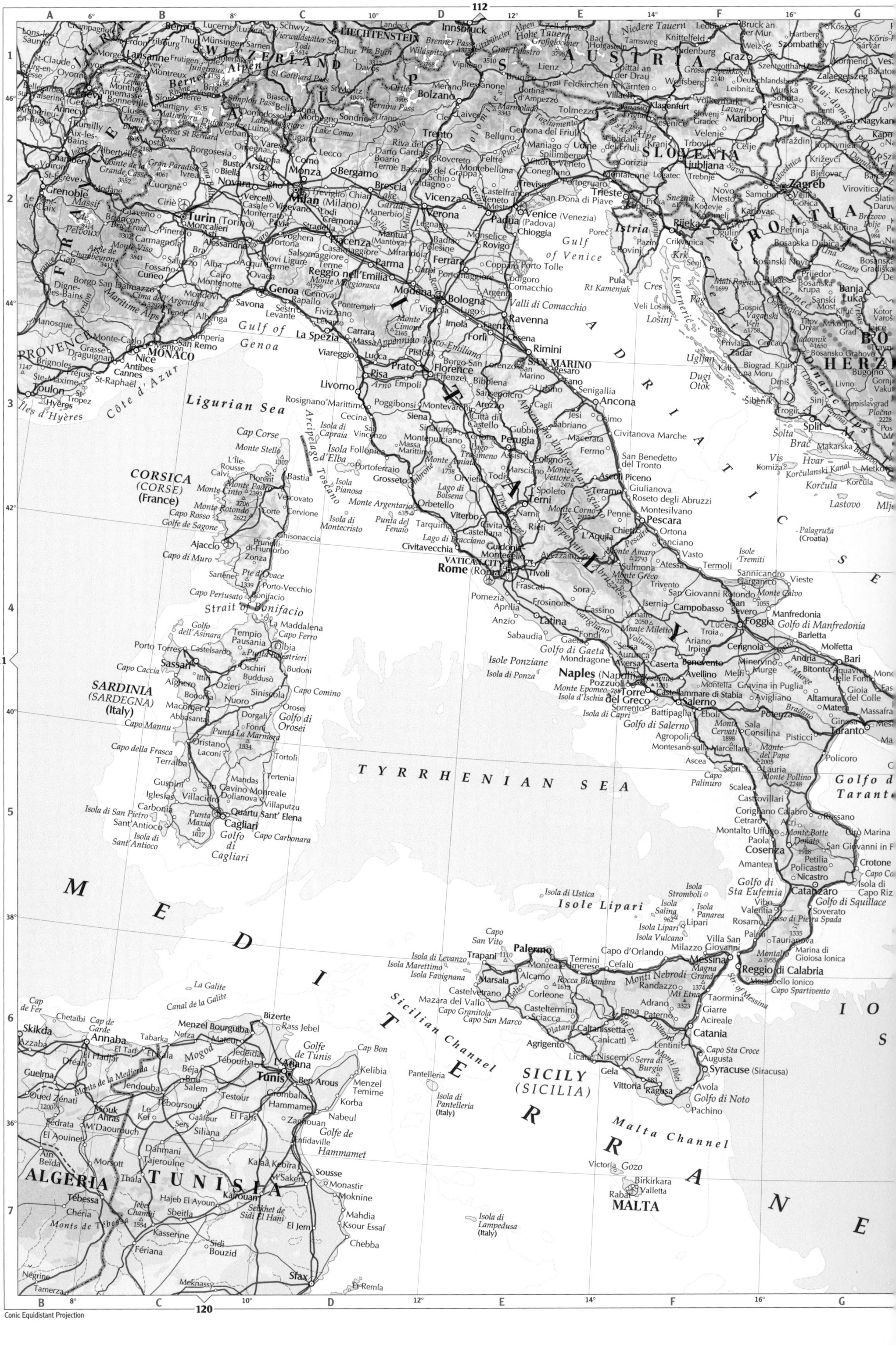

112

A 6° B 8° C 10° D 112 E 12° F 14° G 16°

LIECHTENSTEIN
SWITZERLAND
AUSTRIA
FRANCE
SLOVENIA
CROATIA

Bern
Lausanne
Geneva
Grenoble
Turin (Torino)
Milan (Milano)
Monza
Bergamo
Brescia
Verona
Vicenza
Padua (Padova)
Venice (Venezia)
Trieste
Ljubljana
Zagreb
Maribor

Novara
Pavia
Piacenza
Cremona
Parma
Reggio nell'Emilia
Modena
Bologna
Ferrara
Rovigo

Genoa
Savona
Monaco
Nice
Cannes
Antibes
San Remo
Imperia

Gulf of
Genoa

Gulf
of Venice

Istria

Pula

ADRIATIC

Zadar

Split

DALMATIA

BO
HERZ

Ligurian Sea

La Spezia
Carrara
Massa
Pisa
Livorno
Lucca
Pistoia
Prato
Florence
Empoli

CORSICA
(CORSE)
(France)
Ajaccio
Bastia
Calvi
Corte
Monte Cinto 2706
Monte Rotondo 2622

Strait of Bonifacio

Isola d'Elba
Grosseto

SARDINIA
(SARDEGNA)
(Italy)

Sassari
Oristano
Cagliari
Nuoro
Olbia

Golfo
di
Cagliari

Siena
Arezzo
Perugia
Terni
Viterbo
Civitavecchia

VATICAN CITY
Rome (Roma)
Tivoli
Frosinone
Latina
Anzio

ITALY

Pescara
L'Aquila
Chieti
Ancona
San Marino
Rimini
Ravenna
Forlì

Campobasso
Foggia
Bari
Barletta
Andria

Naples (Napoli)
Salerno
Caserta
Benevento
Avellino
Torre del Greco

Golfo di
Taranto
Taranto

Potenza
Matera

TYRRHENIAN SEA

Isole Lipari
Isola di Ustica
Stromboli

Cosenza
Catanzaro
Reggio di Calabria
Messina

MEDITERRANEAN

Palermo
Trapani
Marsala
Termini Imerese
Cefalù
Agrigento
Caltanissetta
Enna
Catania
Syracuse (Siracusa)
Gela
Ragusa

SICILY
(SICILIA)

Sicilian Channel

Pantelleria
Isola di Pantelleria
(Italy)

Malta Channel

MALTA
Valletta
Victoria Gozo
Birkirkara

Isola di
Lampedusa
(Italy)

ALGERIA
TUNISIA

Skikda
Annaba
Guelma
Bizerte
Tunis
Ben Arous
Sousse
Monastir
Kairouan
Sfax
Mahdia

Canal de la Galite
La Galite

Cap Bon
Golfe de Tunis
Golfe de
Hammamet

Tébessa

Metres
Feet
6000 19686
5000 16404
4000 13124
3000 9843
2000 6562
1000 3281
500 1640
200 656
0
Land below
sea level
200 656
2000 6562
4000 13124
6000 19686

Conic Equidistant Projection

B 8° C 10° D 12° E 14° F 16° G

120

ITALY AND THE BALKANS

1:5 000 000

HUNGARY
ROMANIA
MOLDOVA
UKRAINE
YUGOSLAVIA
SRBIJA (SERBIA)
VOJVODINA
KOSOVO
CRNA GORA (MONTENEGRO)
BULGARIA
MACEDONIA (F. Y. R. O. M.)
ALBANIA
GREECE
TURKEY
BLACK SEA
AEGEAN SEA
Sea of Marmara (Marmara Denizi)
Krytiko Pelagos
Mirtoö Pelagos
Thrakiko Pelagos
Ionian Islands (Ionioi Nisoi)
Strait of Otranto
Gulf of Corinth
Cyclades (Kyklades)
Dodecanese (Dodekanisos)
CARPATHIAN MTS
Transylvanian Alps (Carpații Meridionali)
Balkan Mountains (Stara Planina)
Rhodope Mountains
Bucharest (București)
Belgrade (Beograd)
Sofia (Sofiya)
Skopje
Tirana (Tiranë)
Athens (Athina)
İstanbul
Thessaloniki
Crete (Kriti)
Rhodes (Rodos)
Lesbos (Lesvos)
Chios
Limnos
Corfu (Kerkyra)
Kefallonia
Evvoia
Kythira
İzmir
Bursa
Constanța
Varna
Odesa
Sarajevo
Subotica
Timișoara
Cluj-Napoca
Iași
Plovdiv
Edirne
Patras
Larisa
Iraklion
Miles
Km
100
200
250
300
350

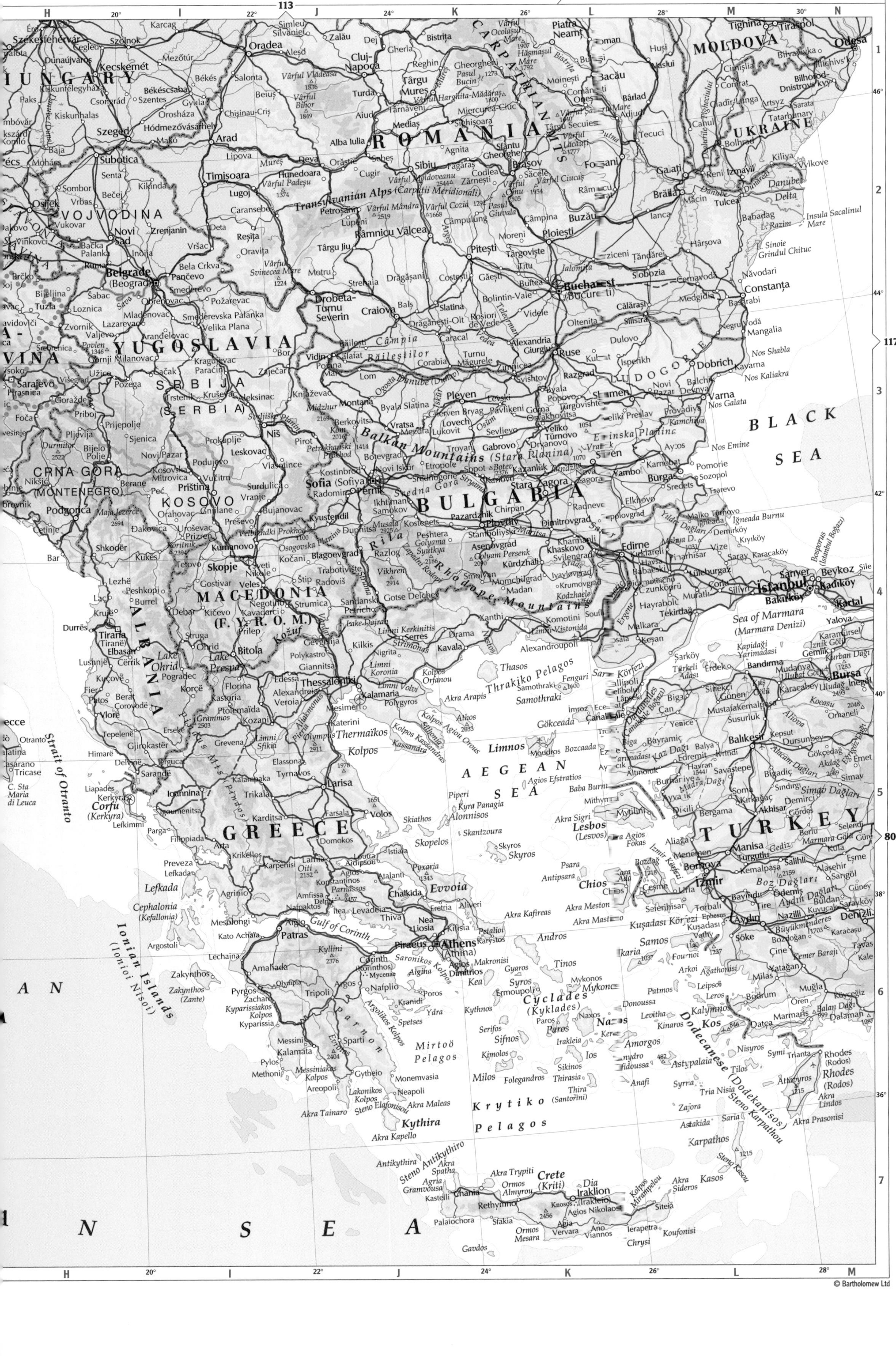

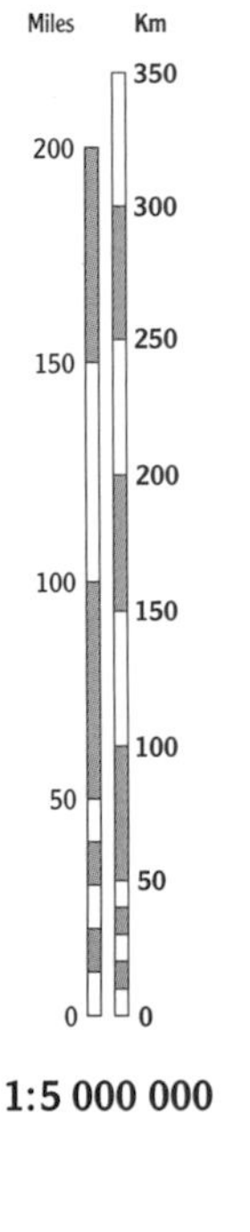

76

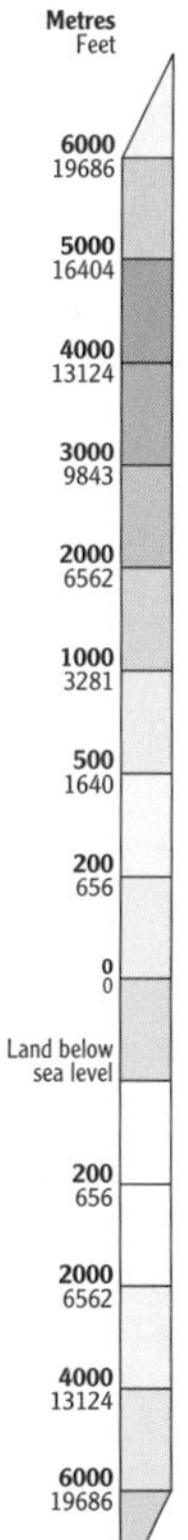

Metres
Feet

6000
19686

5000
16404

4000
13124

3000
9843

2000
6562

1000
3281

500
1640

200
656

0

Land below
sea level

200
656

2000
6562

4000
13124

6000
19686

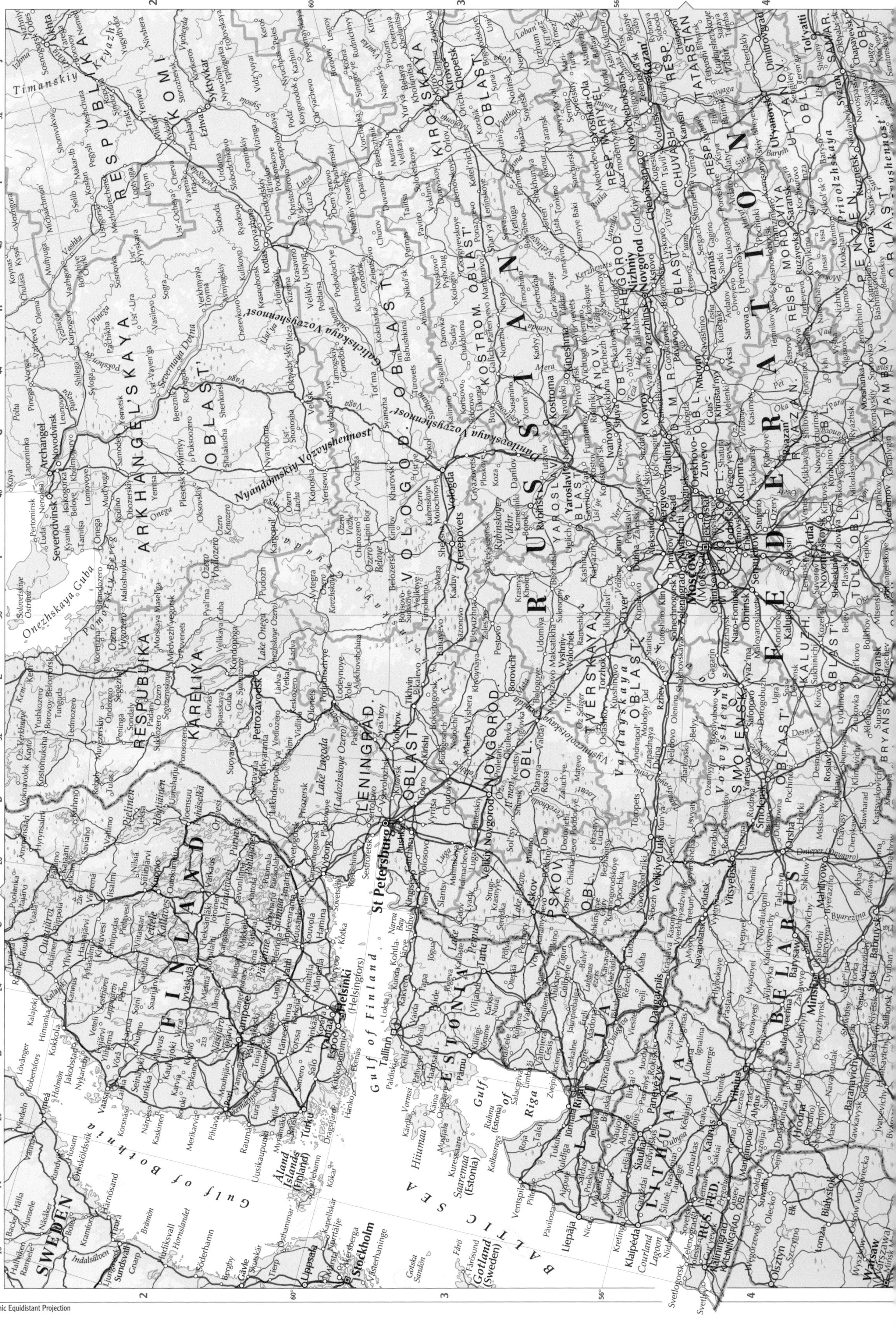

102

Conic Equidistant Projection

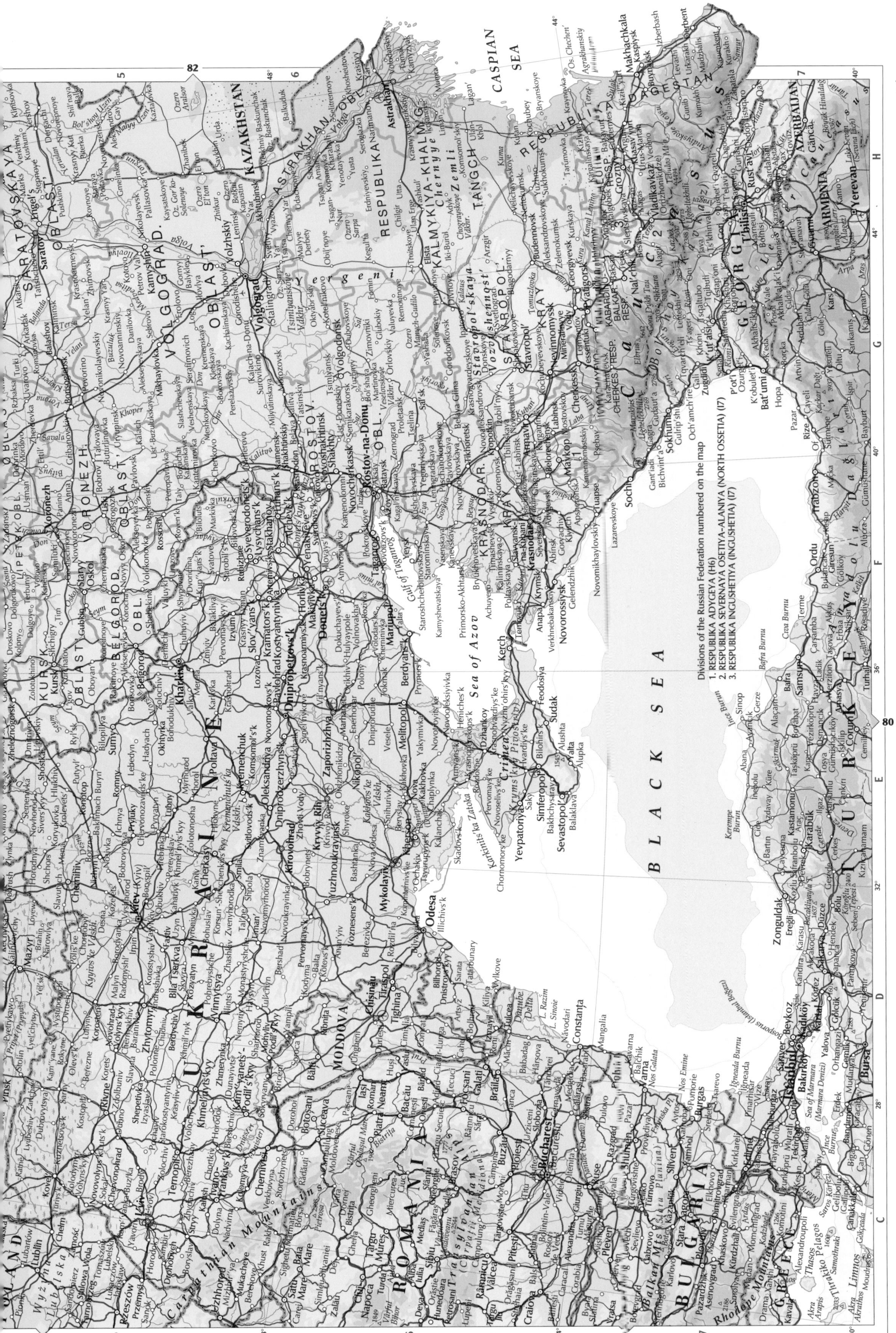

BLACK SEA

CASPIAN SEA

Sea of Azov

Gulf of Taganrog

KAZAKHSTAN

SARATOVSKAYA OBLAST'

VOLGOGRAD OBLAST'

ASTRAKHAN OBL.

RESPUBLIKA KALMYKIYA-KHALM'G TANGCH

VORONEZH OBLAST'

LIPETSK OBL.

KURSK OBL.

BELGOROD OBL.

ROSTOV OBL.

STAVROPOL' KRAY

KRASNODAR KRAY

DAGESTAN RESPUBLIKA

KABARDINO-BALKAR. RESP.

CHECHEN RESPUBLIKA

KARACHAYEVO-CHERKESS. RESP.

U K R A I N E

MOLDOVA

ROMANIA

BULGARIA

T U R K E Y

GEORGIA

ARMENIA

AZERBAIJAN

GREECE

POLAND

Caucasus

Yergeni

Carpathian Mountains

Transylvanian Alps

Balkan Mts.

Rhodope Mountains

Astrakhan', Volgograd (Stalingrad), Saratov, Voronezh, Belgorod, Kursk, Kharkiv, Rostov-na-Donu, Shakhty, Novocherkassk, Taganrog, Mariupol', Donets'k, Makiyivka, Horlivka, Luhans'k, Dnipropetrovs'k, Zaporizhzhya, Kryvyy Rih, Mykolaïv, Odesa, Illichivs'k, Chişinău, Tiraspol, Tighina, Iaşi, Bacău, Galaţi, Brăila, Buzău, Bucharest (Bucureşti), Ploieşti, Piteşti, Craiova, Constanţa, Varna, Burgas, İstanbul, Bursa, Samsun, Ordu, Trabzon, Batumi, Sokhumi, Sochi, Tuapse, Novorossiysk, Gelendzhik, Anapa, Krymsk, Krasnodar, Armavir, Cherkessk, Pyatigorsk, Nal'chik, Vladikavkaz, Groznyy, Makhachkala, Derbent, Tbilisi, Yerevan, Gäncä

Divisions of the Russian Federation numbered on the map
1. RESPUBLIKA ADYGEYA (H6)
2. RESPUBLIKA SEVERNAYA OSETIYA-ALANIYA (NORTH OSSETIA) (I7)
3. RESPUBLIKA INGUSHETIYA (INGUSHETIA) (I7)

Miles
300
200
100
0

Km
500
400
300
200
100
0

1:7 000 000

© Bartholomew Ltd

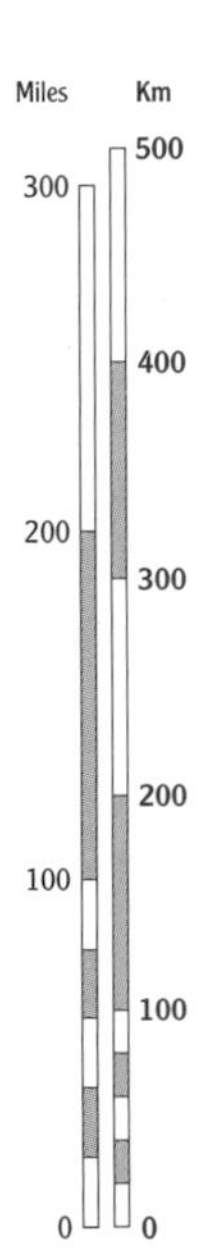

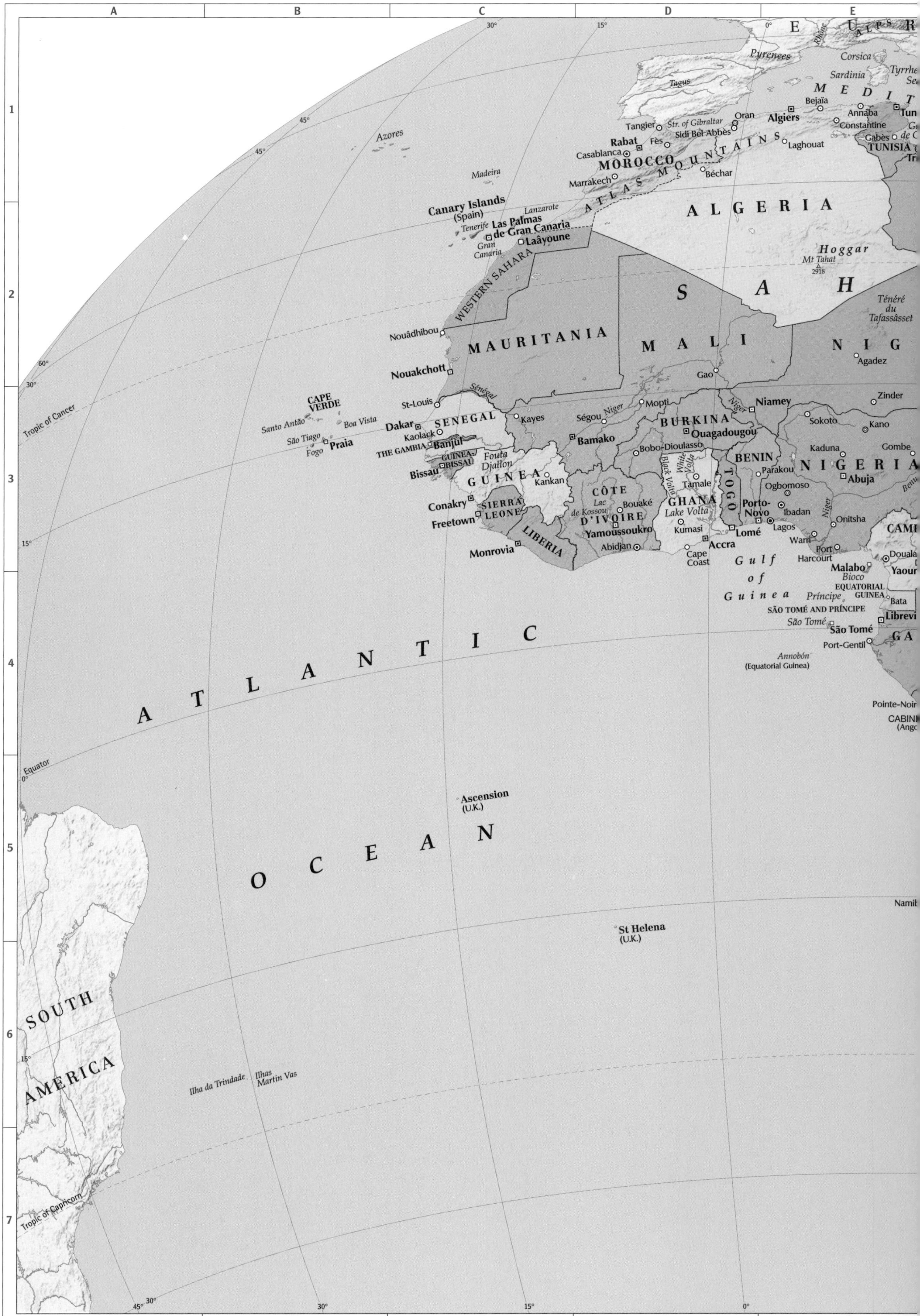

E U R O
Pyrenees
Rhône
ALPS
R
Corsica
Tagus
Sardinia
Tyrrhe
Sea
M E D I T
Bejaïa
Annaba
Tun
Tangier
Str. of Gibraltar
Oran
Algiers
Constantine
Rabat
Fès
Sidi Bel Abbès
Casablanca
Gabes
de G
Laghouat
TUNISIA
Tr
Marrakech
Béchar

A T L A S   M O U N T A I N S
A L G E R I A

Madeira

Azores

45°
45°
45°

Canary Islands
(Spain)
Lanzarote
Tenerife
Las Palmas
de Gran Canaria
Gran
Canaria
Laâyoune
Hoggar
Mt Tahat
2918
S A H
H A
Ténéré
du
Tafassâsset

WESTERN SAHARA

60°

Nouâdhibou

MAURITANIA
M A L I
N I G
Agadez

30°
Nouakchott
Gao
Zinder
Tropic of Cancer
Senegal
Niamey

St-Louis
Ségou
Niger
Mopti
CAPE
VERDE
Kayes
Sokoto
Kano
Santo Antão
Boa Vista
Dakar
SENEGAL
BURKINA
Kaduna
Gombe
São Tiago
Kaolack
Ouagadougou
Fogo
Praia
Banjul
Bamako
Bobo-Dioulasso
THE GAMBIA
GUINEA-
BISSAU
Fouta
Djallon
NIGERIA
BENIN
Bissau
Parakou
GUINEA
Kankan
CÔTE
Abuja
15°
Conakry
SIERRA
LEONE
D'IVOIRE
Lac
de Kossou
Tamale
Ogbomoso
Freetown
Bouaké
GHANA
TOGO
Porto-
Novo
Ibadan
Onitsha
LIBERIA
Yamoussoukro
Kumasi
Lomé
Lagos
CAM
Monrovia
Abidjan
Accra
Warri
Port
Harcourt
Douala
Yaou
Cape
Coast
Malabo
Bioco
Librevi
EQUATORIAL
GUINEA
Bata
Gulf
o f
Guinea
Príncipe
SÃO TOMÉ AND PRÍNCIPE
São Tomé
GA
São Tomé
Port-Gentil
Annobón
(Equatorial Guinea)
Pointe-Noir
CABIN
(Ango

A T L A N T I C

Ascension
(U.K.)

O C E A N

Namil

St Helena
(U.K.)

SOUTH

15°

AMERICA

Ilha da Trindade
Ilhas
Martin Vas

Tropic of Capricorn
45° 30°
30°
15°

Orthographic Projection

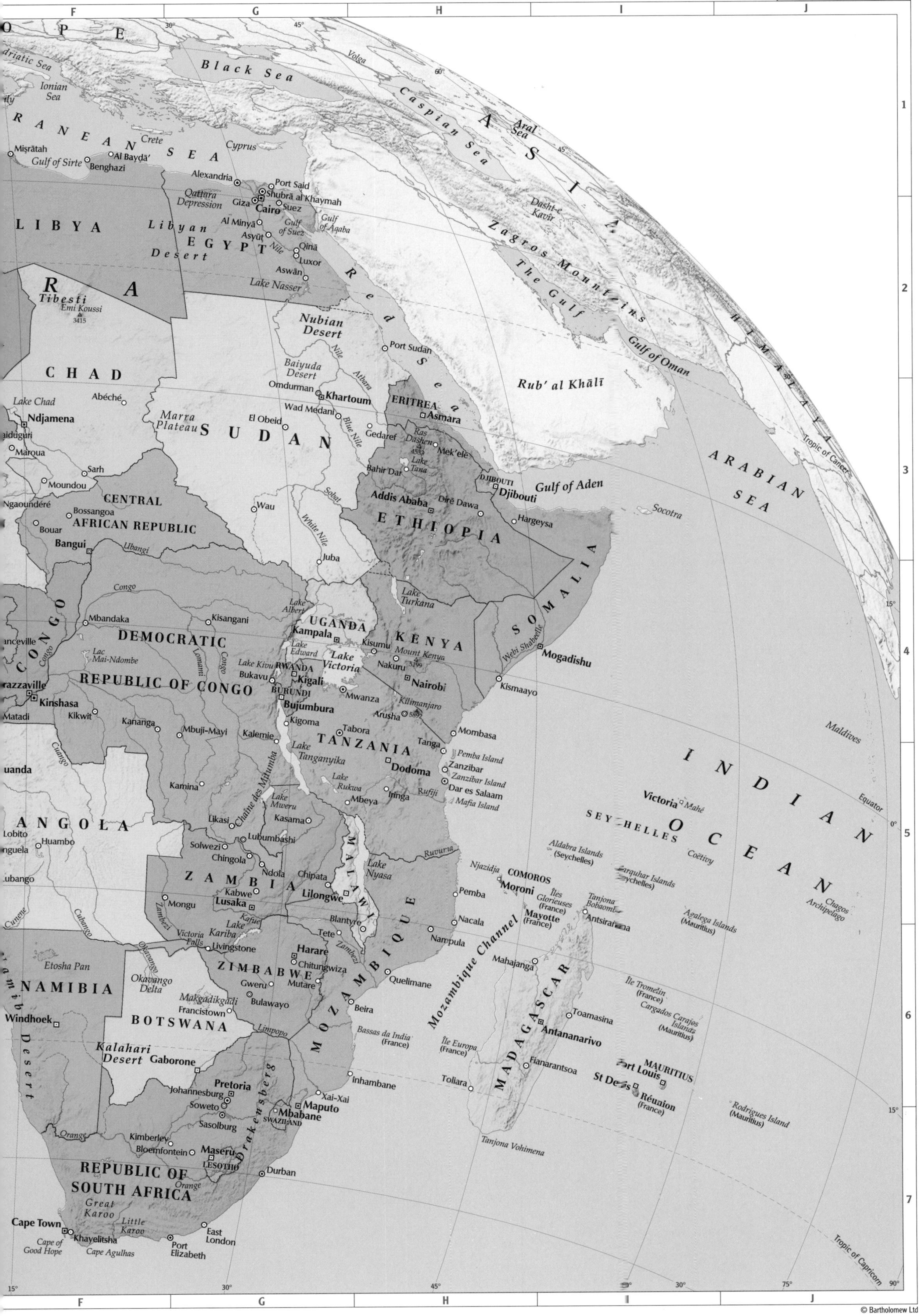

OPE

F G H I J

Black Sea
Volga
Caspian Sea
Aral Sea
Adriatic Sea
Ionian Sea
Crete
Cyprus
ASIA
Dasht-e Kavir

MEDITERRANEAN SEA

Mişrātah
Gulf of Sirte
Al Baydā'
Benghazi
Alexandria
Port Said
Shubrā al Khaymah
Giza
Cairo
Suez
Al Minyā
Gulf of Suez
Gulf of Aqaba
Asyūt
Qina
Luxor
Aswān
Lake Nasser

LIBYA
Libyan Desert
EGYPT

Zagros Mountains
The Gulf
Gulf of Oman
HIMALAYA

R
Tibesti
Emi Koussi
3415
CHAD

Red Sea

Rub' al Khālī

ARABIAN SEA

Tropic of Cancer

Lake Chad
Abéché
Ndjamena
aiduguri
Marqua
Moundou
Sarh
Ngaoundéré
Bossangoa
Bouar
Bangui
CENTRAL AFRICAN REPUBLIC

Marra Plateau
SUDAN
El Obeid
Omdurman
Khartoum
Wad Medani
Baiyuda Desert
Nubian Desert
Port Sudan
Gedaref
Atbara
Blue Nile
Nile

ERITREA
Asmara
Ras Dashen 4533
Mek'elē
Bahir Dar
Lake Tana
DJIBOUTI
Djibouti
Gulf of Aden
Addis Ababa
Dirē Dawa
Hargeysa
ETHIOPIA

Socotra

Wau
White Nile
Sobat
Juba
Ubangi
Congo

DEMOCRATIC
Mbandaka
Kisangani
Lac Mai-Ndombe
anceville
Congo
Lomami
Lake Albert
Lake Edward
Lake Kivu
UGANDA
Kampala
RWANDA
Kigali
Bukavu
BURUNDI
Bujumbura
Kisumu
Nakuru
Lake Turkana
Lake Victoria
KENYA
Mount Kenya 5199
Nairobi
Webi Shabeelle
SOMALIA
Mogadishu

Kismaayo

razzaville
Kinshasa
Matadi
Kikwit
Kananga
Mbuji-Mayi
Kalemie
Kamina
Lukuga
Mwanza
Arusha
Kilimanjaro 5895
Kigoma
Tabora
Dodoma
TANZANIA
Lake Tanganyika
Lake Rukwa
Iringa
Mbeya
Rufiji
Tanga
Mombasa
Pemba Island
Zanzibar
Zanzibar Island
Dar es Salaam
Mafia Island

INDIAN OCEAN

Maldives

Equator

uanda
ANGOLA
Lobito
nguela
Lubango
Cuango
Likasi
Chaîne des Mitumba
Kasama
Lake Mweru
Lubumbashi
Solwezi
Chingola
Ndola
Chipata
MALAWI
Lake Nyasa
Ruvuma
Njazidja
COMOROS
Moroni
Pemba
Nacala
Mahé
Victoria
SEY-CHELLES
Coëtivy
OCEAN

Aldabra Islands (Seychelles)
Îles Glorieuses (France)
Farquhar Islands (Seychelles)
Tanjona Bobaomby
Antsiranana
Agalega Islands (Mauritius)
Chagos Archipelago

ZAMBIA
Mongu
Kabwe
Lusaka
Kafue
Zambezi
Victoria Falls
Lake Kariba
Livingstone
Tete
Blantyre
Quelimane
Nampula
Mayotte (France)

Cunene
Cubango
Zambezi
Etosha Pan
NAMIBIA
Okavango Delta
Makgadikgadi
Harare
Chitungwiza
Mutare
ZIMBABWE
Gweru
Bulawayo
MOZAMBIQUE
Beira
Bassas da India (France)
Île Europa (France)
Mahajanga
Mozambique Channel
MADAGASCAR
Toamasina
Île Tromelin (France)
Cargados Carajos Islands (Mauritius)
Rodrigues Island (Mauritius)
MAURITIUS
Port Louis
Réunion (France)
St Denis
Antananarivo
Fianarantsoa
Toliara
Inhambane

Windhoek
BOTSWANA
Kalahari Desert
Gaborone
Limpopo
Drakensberg
Pretoria
Johannesburg
Soweto
Sasolburg
SWAZILAND
Mbabane
Maputo
Xai-Xai
Kimberley
Bloemfontein
Maseru
LESOTHO
Durban

ambb Desert

Orange
REPUBLIC OF SOUTH AFRICA
Great Karoo
Little Karoo
Cape Town
Khayelitsha
Cape of Good Hope
Cape Agulhas
Port Elizabeth
East London

1
2
3
4
5
6
7

30°
45°
60°
45°
30°
45°
15°
0°
15°
75°
90°
Tropic of Capricorn

Miles Km
1000 1500
750 1250
  1000
500 750
  500
250 250
0 0

1:28 000 000

© Bartholomew Ltd

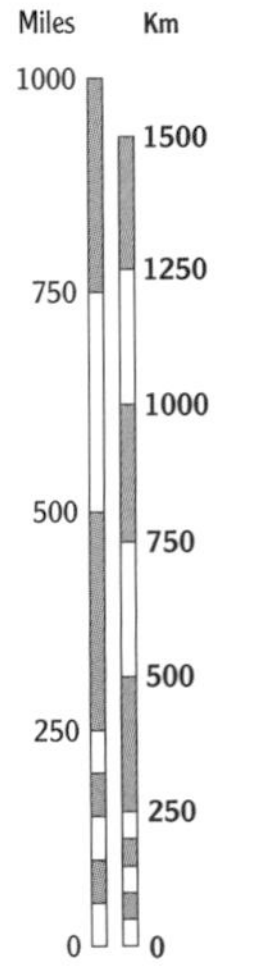

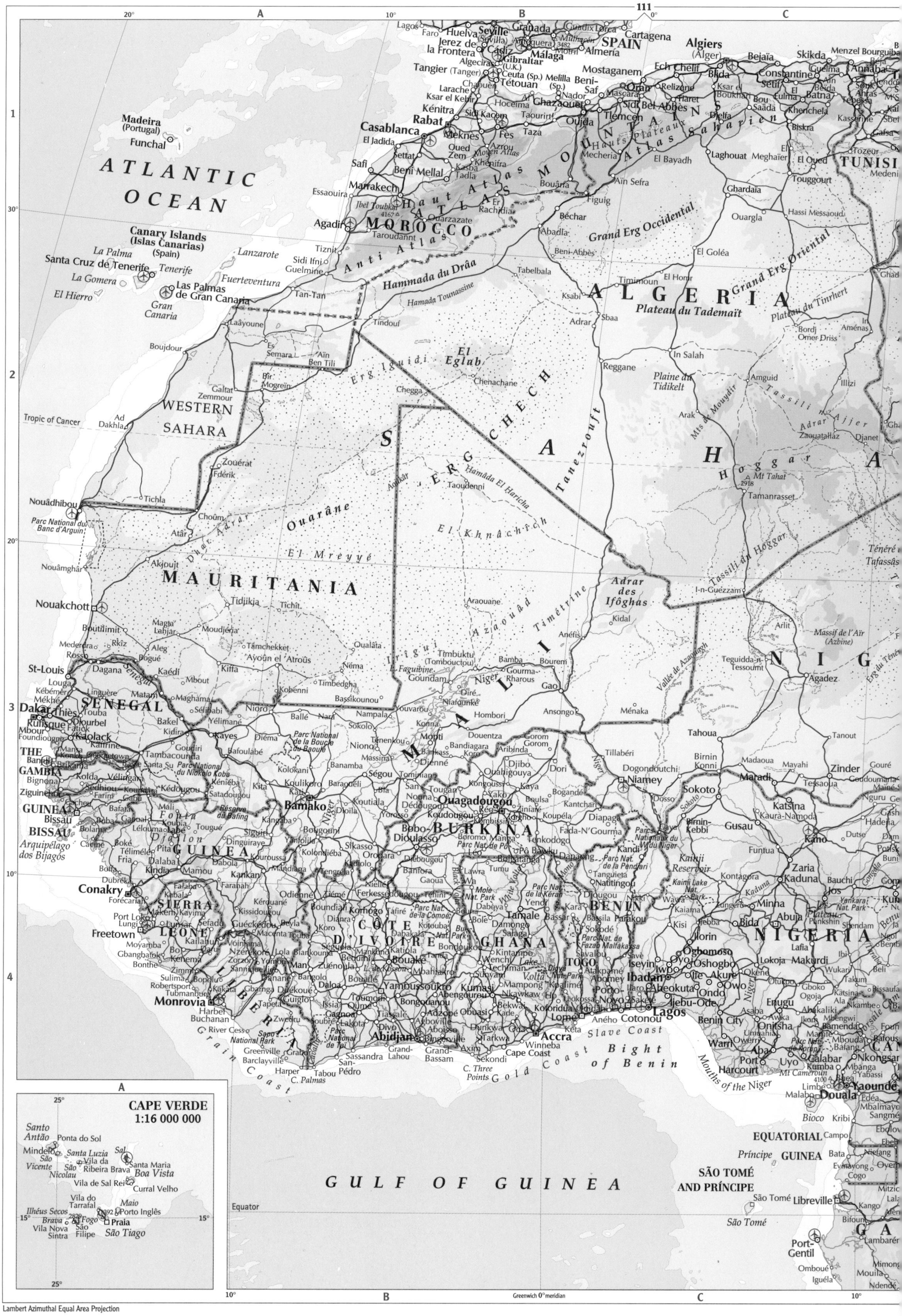

ATLANTIC
OCEAN

Madeira
(Portugal)
Funchal

Canary Islands
(Islas Canarias)
(Spain)
Santa Cruz de Tenerife
La Palma
Tenerife
La Gomera
El Hierro
Gran
Canaria
Las Palmas
de Gran Canaria
Lanzarote
Fuerteventura

Tropic of Cancer

WESTERN
SAHARA

SPAIN
Lagos
Faro Huelva Seville Granada Guadix Lorca Cartagena
Jerez de Cádiz Antequera Murcia Almería Algiers Skikda Menzel Bourguiba
la Frontera Málaga (Alger) Bejaïa Annaba
Tangier (Tanger) Gibraltar Almería Constantine Guelma
Ceuta (Sp.) Melilla Mostaganem Ech Chelif Sétif Batna
Algeciras Tétouan (Sp.) Beni- Relizane Bou Khenchela
Larache Chaouen Saf Mascara Saâda Biskra
Ksar el Kebir Hoceima Oujda Sidi Bel Abbès ATLAS
Kénitra Sidi Kacem Taourirt Tlemcen Saharien El Oued
Rabat Meknès Fès Taza Hauts Plateaux Touggourt
Casablanca Azrou Mecheria Atlas Laghouat Meghaïer
El Jadida Oued Figuig Aïn Sefra Ghardaïa TUNISIA
Safi Zem Khenifra Béchar Medenine
Settat Tadla Bou'arfa El Bayadh Ouargla
Beni Mellal Ifran Hassi Messaoud
Essaouira HAUT ATLAS Er Abadla Grand Erg Occidental
Marrakech Rachidia Ouarzazate El Goléa
Agadir Ibel Toubkal Timimoun El Homr
Taroudannt 4167 Anti Atlas Bordj
Hammada du Drâa Tabelbala Reggane Omer Driss
Tiznit Adrar Amguid
Sidi Ifni Ksabi In Salah Plateau du Tinrhert
Guelmine Hamada Tounassine Arak Illizi
Tan-Tan ALGERIA Mts du Mouydir
Laâyoune Plateau du Tademaït Tassili n'Ajjer
Boujdour Plaine du Adrar n'Ajjer
Tindouf Tidikelt Zaouatallaz Djanet
Es Erg Iguidi El Chenachane Hoggar
Semara Eglab In Guezzam Ténéré
Aïn Chegga Taoudenni Mt Tahat Tafassâsset
Ben Tili Erg Hamâda El Haricha 2918
Bîr ERG CHECH SAHARA
Mogrein Taoudenni Tamanrasset
Choûm Ouarâne El Khnâch'ch Adrar NIGER
Tichla des Arlit
Zouérat Ifôghas Massif de l'Aïr
Fdérik El Mreyyé (Azbine)
Nouâdhibou Kidal Agadez

MAURITANIA

Nouâmghâr Akjoujt Aïn Teguidda-
Nouakchott Tidjikja Tîchît Anéfis n-Tessoumt

Parc National du
Banc d'Arguin
Atâr

Timbédgha
Tamchekket Néma Timbouctou Gourma Niger Vallée de Azaouagh
Moudjéria 'Ayoûn el 'Atroûs (Tombouctou) Rharous Gao
Boutilimit Qualâta Diré Bamba Bourem
Tidjikja Kiffa Timbédgha Goundam Tahoua Tanout
Magta Lahjar Kobenni Diafarabé Niafunké Ansongo Ménaka Birni Madaoua
Bogué Bassikounou Youvarou Hombori Konni Madaoua
Kaédi Nampala Douentza Tillabéri Tahoua Zinder Gouré
St-Louis Dagana Nioro Sokolo Monti Bandiagara Dogondoutchi
Rosso Sélibabi Nara Niono Aribinda Gorom Dosso
Mbout Diéma Balé Ségou Djibo Dori Niamey Sokoto Maradi
Maghama Yélimané Ténenkou Mopti Kongoussi Kaya Bogandé Birnin Katsina
Magha Kayes Kidira Parc National Macina Djenné Ouahigouya Fada-N'Gourma Kebbi
Matam de la Boucle Banamba Tougan Boulsa Diapaga Kandi
Linguère du Baoulé Koulikoro Massina Kantchari Niamey
Louga Bakel Diéma Kolokani Ouagadougou Kaïnji Gusau
SENEGAL Nioro BURKINA Reservoir Kano
Thiès Bafoulabé Bamako Koutiala Dédougou Bobo- Koupéla Kaïmji Kano
Dakar Kita Bougouni Sikasso Dioulasso Pô Bawku Kainji Lake Kontagora Kaduna
Mbour Kidal Satadougou Kangaba Kolondiéba Orodara Léo Tenkodogo Parc Nat. Bauchi
Foundiougne Kaolack Kédougou Koussanar Banfora Gaoua Diébougou du Minna Jos
Kaffrine Réserve Dinguiraye Gaoua Pama Zorgo Abuja Yankari
THE Farim du Baoulé Siguiri Ferkessédougou Tenkodogo W du Niger Kaiama Plateau
GAMBIA Bafatá Kolokani Kankan Korhogo Tafiré Parc Nat. Jebba Kontagora
Banjul Tambacounda Kouroussa Tingréla Boundiali Parc Nat. de la Pendjari Ilorin NIGERIA
Bignona Kédougou Siguiri Odienné Katiola de la Comoé Kaïama Oshogbo Lafia
Ziguinchor GUINEA Mandiana Séguéla Bouna Mole Djougou Ogbomoso Iseyin Lokoja Makurdi
GUINEA- Bissau Dabola Kouroussa Beyla Bouaké Nat. Park Bassila Parakou Akure Okene Wukari
BISSAU Koundara Kindia Faranah Kankan Touba Koutouba Tamale Kara Save Ibadan Benin Bida
Bolama Mamou Dabola Kérouané Man Zuénoula Daboya Salaga BENIN Abeokuta Ondo Owo Gboko
Arquipélago Télimélé Dinguiraye Macenta Gagnoa COTE Kintampo Sokodé TOGO Ijebu-Ode Ondo
dos Bijagós Pita GUINEA Kissidougou D'IVOIRE Atakpamé Iwo Asaba Onitsha Bamenda
Boké Dalaba Gueckédou Gagnoa GHANA Volta Abomey Porto- Lagos Enugu Mamfe
Fria Mamou Kérouané Man Daloa   Sunyani Wenchi Kumasi Bekwai Pobé Novo Ikeja CAMEROON
Conakry Faranah Zuénoula Tumu Techiman Mampong Anécho Benin City Calabar Kumba
Dubréka Nzérékoré Duékoué Koforidua Cotonou Warri Port Uyo
Forécariah SIERRA Voinjama Issia Koumé Obuasi Keta Harcourt Bioko
Makeni LEONE Kailahun Gagnoa Abengourou Dunkwa Slave Coast Limbe 4100
Port Loko Sefadu Séguéla Divo Abidjan Winneba Accra Malabo Douala
Kambia Koidu Gbarnga Tabou Grand- Cape Coast Bight Bafang
Lunsar Kayima Bong Lahou Sékondi Gold Coast of Benin Mouths of the Niger Edéa
Freetown Moyamba Zimmi Sassandra Axim C. Three Kribi
SIERRA Kenema Zwedru Grand- Points
LEONE Bonthe Greenville Tabou Bassam EQUATORIAL Ebolowa
Sulima Tiama River Cess C. Palmas GUINEA
Robertsport Sapo Barclayville São Tomé Bata Mbini
Monrovia Buchanan National Harper Príncipe GUINEA Ntoum
LIBERIA Park Grain Coast SÃO TOMÉ Evinayong Cogo
Harbel AND PRÍNCIPE São Tomé Libreville
Robertsport Tapeta Grand Cess GABON
Tubmanburg Parc Port-Gentil
Kakata National
de Taï

GULF OF GUINEA

Equator Greenwich 0° meridian

CAPE VERDE
1:16 000 000

Santo
Antão Ponta do Sol
Mindelo Sal
São Santa Luzia Santa Maria
Vicente Nicolau Vila da Boa Vista
Ribeira Brava
Vila do Curral Velho
Tarrafal Maio
Ilhéus Secos Vila do Porto Inglês
Brava Tarrafal Praia
Vila Nova Fogo São São Tiago
Sintra Filipe

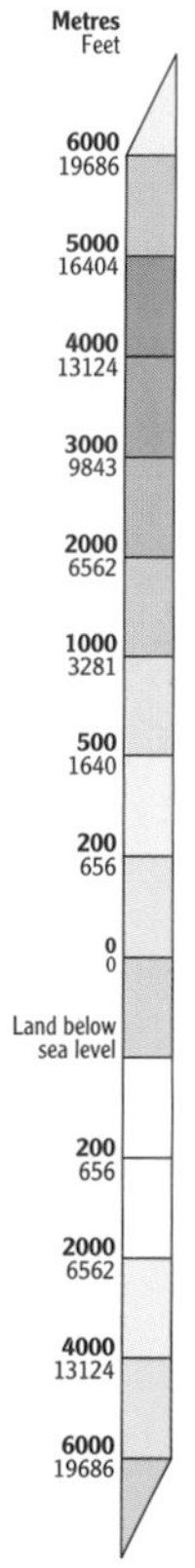

Metres
Feet
6000
19686
5000
16404
4000
13124
3000
9843
2000
6562
1000
3281
500
1640
200
656
0
Land below
sea level
200
656
2000
6562
4000
13124
6000
19686

Lambert Azimuthal Equal Area Projection

80

86

2

3

122

4

5

1:16 000 000

Header / Sea labels

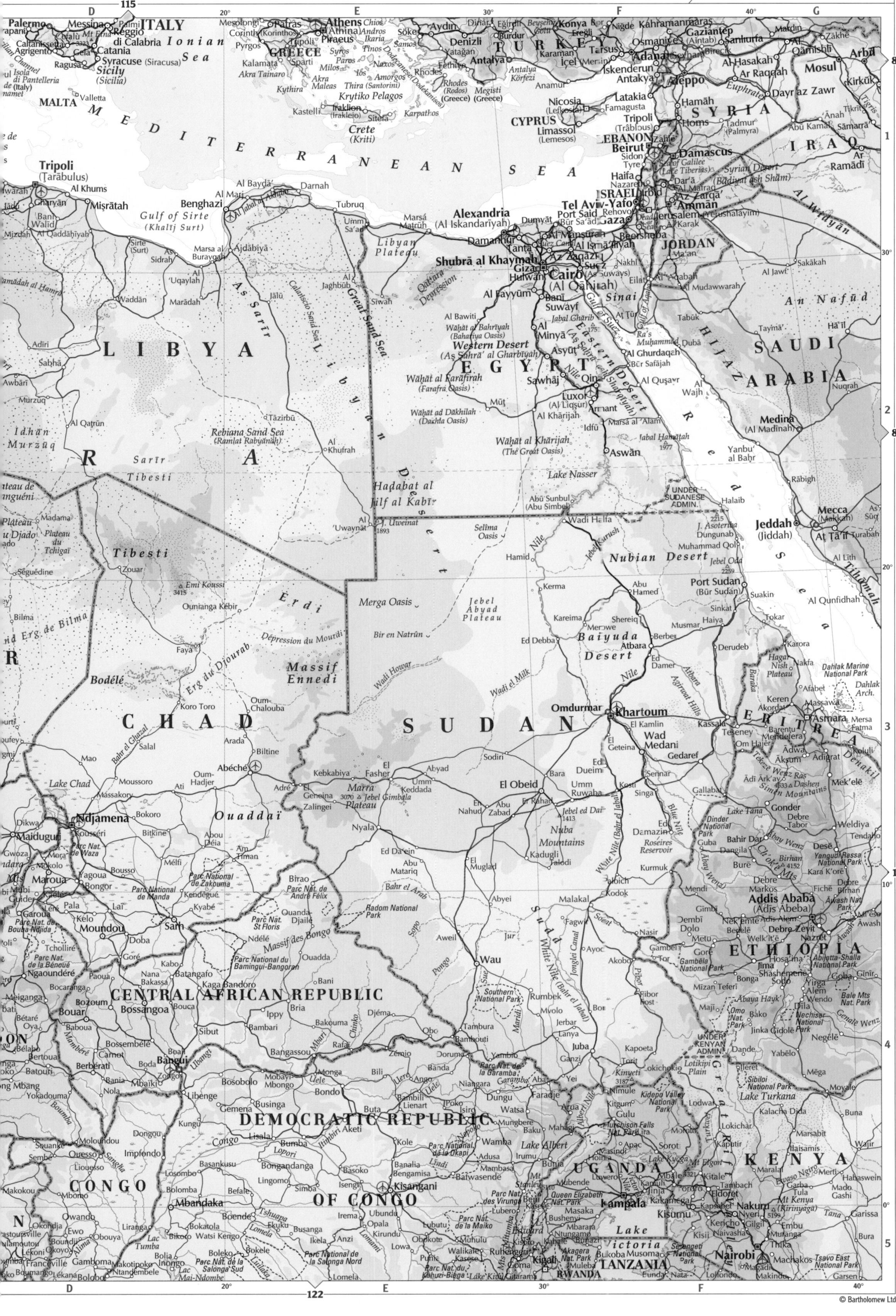

MEDITERRANEAN SEA

Ionian Sea

Countries

ITALY
GREECE
TURKEY
CYPRUS
SYRIA
LEBANON
ISRAEL
JORDAN
IRAQ
SAUDI ARABIA
HIJAZ
LIBYA
EGYPT
CHAD
SUDAN
ERITREA
ETHIOPIA
CENTRAL AFRICAN REPUBLIC
DEMOCRATIC REPUBLIC OF CONGO
CONGO
UGANDA
KENYA
TANZANIA
RWANDA
MALTA

Major cities and places

Palermo, Messina, Reggio di Calabria, Catania, Syracuse (Siracusa), Ragusa, Sicily (Sicilia), Caltanissetta, Agrigento, Gela, Mt Etna
Tripoli (Ṭarābulus), Al Khums, Mişrātah, Benghazi, Al Bayda, Darnah, Tubruq, Ajdābiyā, Sirte (Surt), Marsa al Burayqah
Athens (Athina), Piraeus, Corinth (Korinthos), Patras, Sparti, Kalamata
Alexandria (Al Iskandarīyah), Marsá Maṭrūh, Damanhūr, Ṭanṭā, Cairo (Al Qāhirah), Gizaḥ, Shubrā al Khaymah, Hulwān, Al Fayyūm, Banī Suwayf, Al Minyā, Asyūṭ, Sawhāj, Qinā, Luxor (Al Uqṣur), Al Khārijah, Aswān
Ankara references: Konya, Kähramanmaraş, Gaziantep, Şanlıurfa, Mardin, Adana, Mersin, Iskenderun, Antakya, Aleppo, Hamāh, Homs, Tripoli (Ṭrābulus), Latakia, Famagusta, Nicosia (Lefkosia), Limassol (Lemesos)
Beirut, Sidon, Tyre, Haifa, Tel Aviv-Yafo, Jerusalem (Yerushalayim), Gaza, Amman, Damascus, Az Zarqā, Al Karak, Ma'ān
Mosul, Kirkūk, Arbīl, Al Hasakah, Al Raqqah, Dayr az Zawr, Ar Ramādī
Medina (Al Madīnah), Mecca (Makkah), Jeddah (Jiddah), Aṭ Ṭā'if, Yanbu' al Baḥr, Rābigh, Al Lith, Al Qunfidhah
Khartoum, Omdurman, Wad Medani, El Obeid, El Fasher, Port Sudan (Būr Sudān), Kassala, Gedaref, Atbara, Berber, Nyala, Wau, Malakal, Juba, El Geneina, Zalingei, Kadugli, Ed Damazin
Asmara, Massawa, Keren, Mek'elē, Gonder, Bahir Dar, Dese, Addis Ababa (Ādīs Ābeba), Gambēla, Nazrēt
Ndjamena, Maiduguri, Sarh, Abéché, Moundou, Faya
Bangui, Bossangoa, Bouar, Bambari, Bangassou
Kisangani, Mbandaka, Bumba, Buta
Kampala, Nairobi, Kisumu, Nakuru, Eldoret
Lake Chad, Lake Nasser, Lake Tana, Lake Albert, Lake Turkana, Lake Victoria

Physical features

Western Desert, Libyan Desert, Eastern Desert, Nubian Desert, Baiyuda Desert, Great Sand Sea, Rebiana Sand Sea (Ramlat Rabyānah), As Sarīr, Tibesti, Emi Koussi 3415, Massif Ennedi, Erdi, Qattara Depression, Libyan Plateau, Jebel Abyad Plateau, Marra Plateau, Nuba Mountains, Simen Mountains, Dashen 4533, Red Sea, Gulf of Sirte (Khalīj Surt), Gulf of Suez, An Nafūd, Blue Nile, White Nile, Nile

Miles / Km
600 / 1000
400
200
0

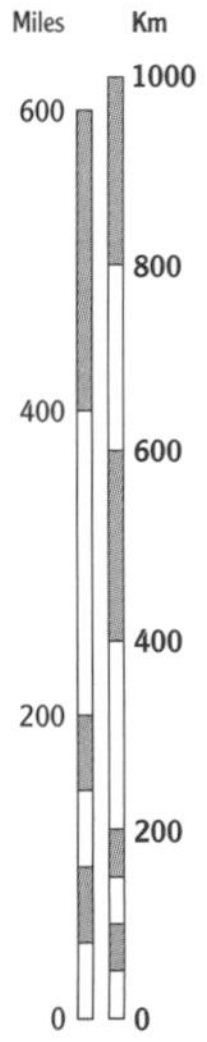

Metres / Feet

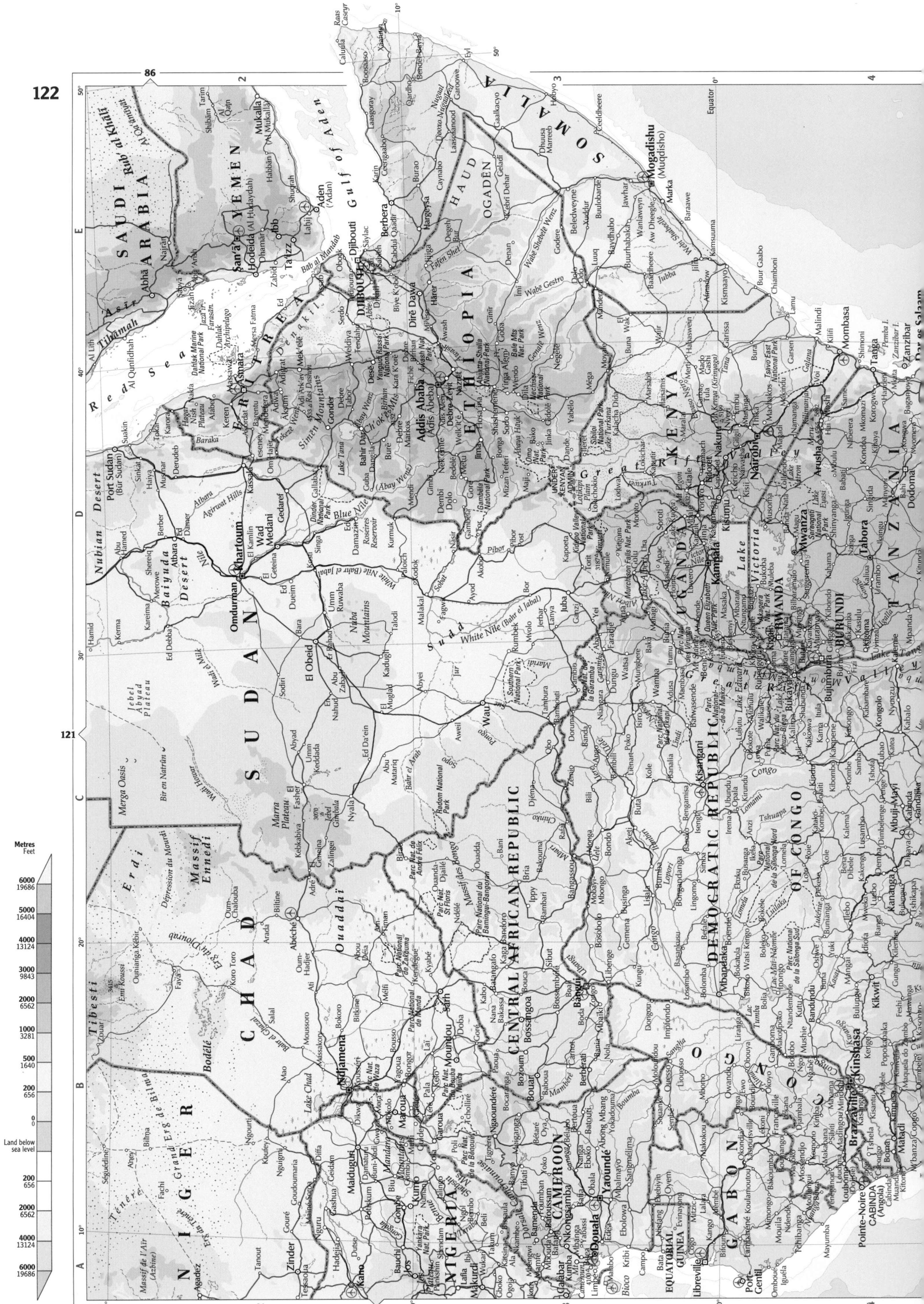

Metres	Feet
6000	19686
5000	16404
4000	13124
3000	9843
2000	6562
1000	3281
500	1640
200	656
0	0

Land below sea level

200	656
2000	6562
4000	13124
6000	19686

SAUDI ARABIA
Rub' al Khālī

YEMEN
Ṣan'ā'
Aden (Adan)
Gulf of Aden
Mukalla (Al Mukallā)

Red Sea

SOMALIA
Mogadishu (Muqdisho)
HAUD
OGADEN
Berbera
Hargeysa
Burao

DJIBOUTI
ERITREA
Asmara
Massawa

ETHIOPIA
Addis Ababa (Ādīs Ābeba)
Gonder
Dirē Dawa
Harēr
Lake Tana
Simēn Mountains

SUDAN
Khartoum
Omdurman
Port Sudan (Būr Sūdān)
Atbara
Berber
El Obeid
El Fasher
Nyala
Wad Medani
Gedaref
Kassala

Nubian Desert
Bayuda Desert
White Nile (Bahr el Jabal)
Blue Nile
Nuba Mountains
Sudd

KENYA
Nairobi
Lake Turkana (Lake Rudolf)
Marsabit
Mombasa
Malindi
Great Rift Valley

UGANDA
Kampala
Lake Victoria
Lake Albert
Lake Edward

RWANDA
Kigali

BURUNDI
Bujumbura

TANZANIA
Mwanza
Arusha
Tabora
Tanga
Zanzibar
Lake Eyasi

DEMOCRATIC REPUBLIC OF CONGO
Kinshasa
Kisangani
Congo

CONGO
Brazzaville
Pointe-Noire

GABON
Libreville
Port-Gentil

EQUATORIAL GUINEA
Bata
Bioco
Malabo

CAMEROON
Yaoundé
Douala
Maroua
Ngaoundéré

CENTRAL AFRICAN REPUBLIC
Bangui
Bossangoa
Bouar
Bambari

CHAD
Ndjamena
Moundou
Sarh
Abéché
Lake Chad
Tibesti
Emi Koussi
Faya
Ennedi
Ouaddaï

NIGER
Agadez
Zinder
Ténéré
Massif de l'Aïr (Azbine)
Grand Erg de Bilma

NIGERIA
Kano
Maiduguri
Makurdi

CABINDA (Angola)

Lambert Azimuthal Equal Area Projection

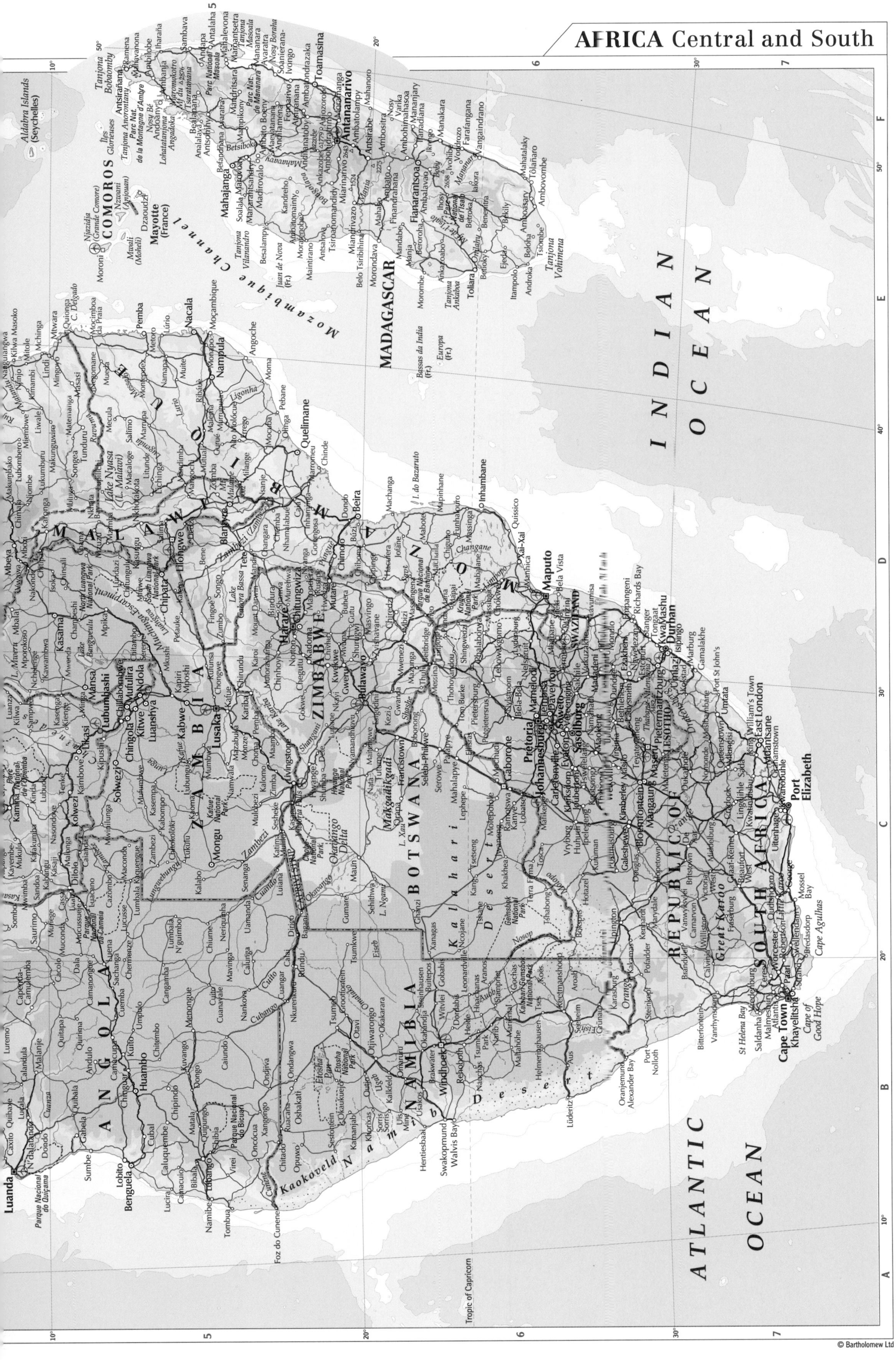

ATLANTIC

OCEAN

INDIAN

OCEAN

MADAGASCAR

COMOROS

Aldabra Islands
(Seychelles)

Mozambique Channel

Luanda

A N G O L A

N A M I B I A

Kalahari   Desert

B O T S W A N A

Z A M B I A

ZIMBABWE

M O Z A M B I Q U E

M A L A W I

REPUBLIC OF   SOUTH AFRICA

LESOTHO

SWAZILAND

Windhoek

Lusaka

Harare

Maputo

Pretoria

Johannesburg

Gaborone

Bloemfontein

Durban

Cape Town

Port
Elizabeth

East London

Tropic of Capricorn

Miles   Km

600

400

200

1000

800

600

400

200

0

1:16 000 000

© Bartholomew Ltd

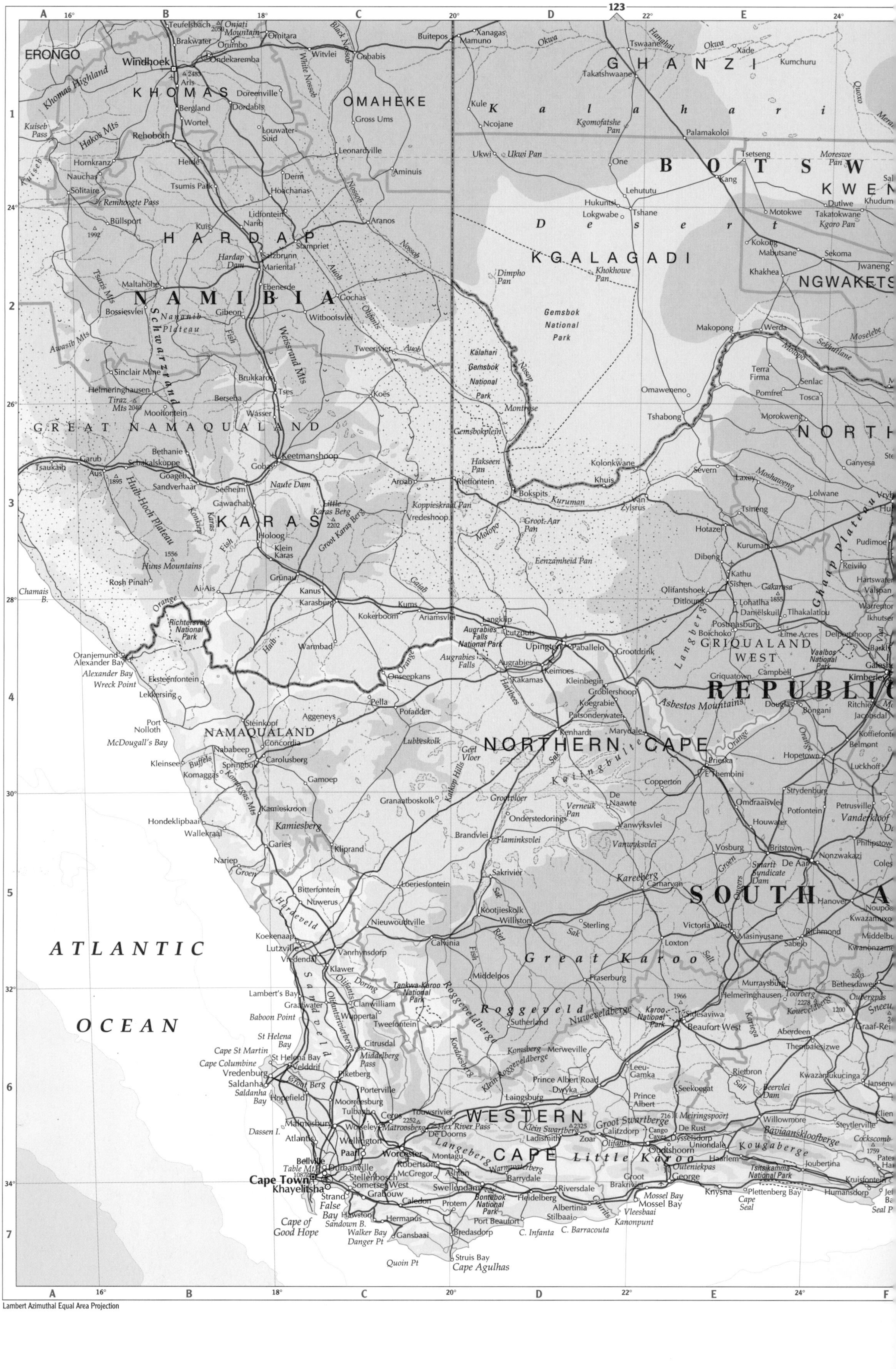

A 16° B 18° C 20° D 123 22° E 24°

ERONGO

Teufelsbach
Onjati Mountain 2039
Brakwater
Omitara
Buitepos
Xanagas
Mamuno
Okwa
Tswaanhai
Hanghai
Okwa
Xade
Kumchuru

Windhoek
2485
Aris
Ondekaremba
Witvlei
Gobabis
G H A N Z I
Takatshwaane
Quoxo

KHOMAS
Bergland
Wortel
Doreenville
Dordabis
Gross Ums
O M A H E K E
Kule
Ncojane
K a l a h a r i
Kgomofatshe Pan
Palamakoloi
Tsetseng
Moreswe Pan
B O T S W
KWEN
Khudum

Khomas Highland
Rehoboth
Heide
Louwater-Suid
Leonardville
Ukwi
Ukwi Pan
One
Lehututu
Lokgwabe
Tshane
Kang
Hukuntsi
Kokong
Mabutsane
Sekoma
Khakhea
Jwaneng
NGWAKETS

Kuiseb Pass
Hornkranz
Nauchas
Solitaire
Remhoogte Pass
Lidfontein
Narib
Aranos
D e s e r t
K G A L A G A D I
Dimpho Pan
Khokhowe Pan
Khakhea
Takatokwane
Kgaro Pan

HAKOS Mts
Büllsport
1992
Tsumis Park
Hoachanas
Derm
Salzbrunn
Stampriet

HARDAP
Hardap Dam
Mariental
Maltahöhe
Ebenerde
Gochas
Gemsbok National Park
Makopong
Werda
Moselebe
Sehitwa

N A M I B I A
Bossiesvlei
Gibeon
Witbooisvlei
Tweerivier
Kalahari
Gemsbok National Park
Omaweneno
Terra Firma
Senlac
Tosca
Pomfret
Morokweng
N O R T H

Namib Plateau
Schwarzrand
Brukkaros
Koes
Monthsa
Gemsbokplein
Tshabong

Sinclair Mine
Helmeringhausen
Tiraz Mts 2040
Moolfontein
Berseba
Tses
Wasser
Hakseen Pan
Kolonkwane
Khuis
Severn
Laxey
Moshaweng
Ganyesa

G R E A T N A M A Q U A L A N D
Bethanie
Schakalskuppe
Goageb
Keetmanshoop
Rietfontein
Bokspits
Kuruman
Van Zylsrus
Tsineng
Lolwane

Tsaukaib
Garub
Aus 1895
Sandverhaar
Gobas
Naute Dam
Koppieskraal Pan
Groot-Aar Pan
Hotazel
Kuruman
Dibeng
Reivilo
Pudimoe

Huib-Hoch Plateau
Seeheim
Gawachab
Little Karas Berg 2202
Groot Karas Berg
Vredeshoop
Molopo
Eenzamheid Pan
Kathu
Sishen
Gakarosa
Ghaap Plateau
Hartswater

K A R A S
1556
Holoog
Klein Karas
Grünau
Aroab
Rietfontein
Olifantshoek 1855
Lohatlha
Danielskuil
Tlhakalatlou
Postmasburg
Boichoko
Lime Acres
Delportshoop

Hüns Mountains
Rosh Pinah
Ai-Ais
Kanus
Karasburg
Kokerboom
Ariamsvlei
Langklip
Kakamas
Keimoes
Groblershoop
G R I Q U A L A N D W E S T
Griquatown
Campbell
Vaalbos National Park
Kimberle

Chamais B.
Orange
Richtersveld National Park
Kums
Augrabies Falls National Park
Upington
Paballelo
Grootdrink
Douglas
Ritchie
Jacobsdal

Oranjemund
Alexander Bay
Alexander Bay Wreck Point
Eksteenfontein
Lekkersing
Warmbad
Pella
Pofadder
Augrabies Falls
Augrabies
Keimoes
Koegabie
Putsonderwater
R E P U B L I C

Port Nolloth
McDougall's Bay
Steinkopf
Aggeneys
Onseepkans
Kenhardt
Marydale
Prieska
Hopetown
Luckhoff

Kleinsee
Buffels
N A M A Q U A L A N D
Nababeep
Concordia
Springbok
Carolusberg
Gamoep
Lubbeskolk
Geel Vloer
N O R T H E R N C A P E
Orange
E'Thembini
Bongani
Belmont
Koffiefonte

Komaggas
Kamieskroon
Kamiesberg
Granaatboskolk
Grootploer
Verneuk Pan
De Naawte
Copperton
Omdraaisvlei
Strydenburg
Petrusvill
Vanderkl
D

Hondeklipbaai
Wallekraal
Garies
Kliprand
Brandvlei
Flaminksvlei
Onderstedorings
Vanwyksvlei
Vanwyksvlei
Vosburg
Houwater
Potfontein
Philipstow

Nariep
Groen
Bitterfontein
Nuwerus
Sakrivier
Kareeberg
Carnarvon
De Aar
Hanover
Nonzwakazi
Noupo
Coles

Hardeveld
Nieuwoudtville
Kootjieskolk
Williston
Sterling
Victoria West
Masinyusane
Sabelo
Richmond
Middelbu
Kwanon

S O U T H A

A T L A N T I C
Koekenaap
Lutzville
Vanrhynsdorp
Calvinia
Riet
Loxton
G r e a t K a r o o
Murraysburg
Helmeringhausen
Toorberg 2278
Oubergpas
2503
Graaf-Rei

O C E A N
Klawer
Vredendal
Doring
Middelpos
Fraserburg
Roggeveldberge
Sutherland
Nuweveldberge
Karoo National Park
Beaufort West
Aberdeen
Thembalesizwe
Kwanonza

Lambert's Bay
Graafwater
Clanwilliam
Tankwa-Karoo National Park
Koedoesberg
Komsberg
Merweville
1966
Prince Albert Road
Leeu-Gamka
Riethron
Beervlei Dam
Kwazamukucinga

Baboon Point
Wuppertal
Tweefontein
R o g g e v e l d
Dwyka
Prince Albert
Seekoegat
Salt
Willowmore
Steytlerville

St Helena Bay
Citrusdal
Klein Aggeneisberge
Laingsburg
716
Meiringspoort
Willowmore
St Helena Bay
Cape St Martin
Cape Columbine
Vredenburg
Veldrif
Middelberg Pass
Piketberg
Porterville
Groot Swartberg
Calitzdorp
Cango Caves
De Rust
Bavaanskloofberge
Cockscomb

Saldanha
Hopefield
Groot Berg
Tulbagh
Ceres
Touwsrivier
W E S T E R N
Klein Swartberg 2325
Zoar
Olifant
Oudtshoorn
Uniondale
Kougaberge
1759
Joubertina
Pater

Saldanha Bay
Dassen I.
Malmesbury
Worcester
Matroosberg 2252
Hex River Pass
De Doorns
C A P E
Langeberg
L i t t l e K a r o o
Groot
Brakrivier
Outeniekpas
Tsitsikamma National Park
Kruisfonte

Atlantis
Paarl
Wellington
Robertson
Montagu
Oudtshoorn
Outeniquas
Mossel Bay
Knysna
Cape Seal
Plettenberg Bay
Humansdor

Bellville
Durbanville
Stellenbosch
McGregor
Ashton
Narmmelberg
Swellendam
Heidelberg
Riversdale
Mossel Bay
Seal Pt.

Cape Town
Khayelitsha
Table Mtn
Somerset West
Barrydale
Bredasdorp
Bontebok National Park
Port Beaufort
Stilbaai
Albertinia
Vleesbaai
Kanonpunt
Cape Seal

Strand
Grabouw
Caledon
Protem
C. Infanta
C. Barracouta
False Bay
Hawston
Hermanus
Struis Bay

Cape of Good Hope
Sandown B.
Walker Bay
Danger Pt
Gansbaai
Bredasdorp
Struis Bay
Cape Agulhas
Quoin Pt

Scale bar (left side):

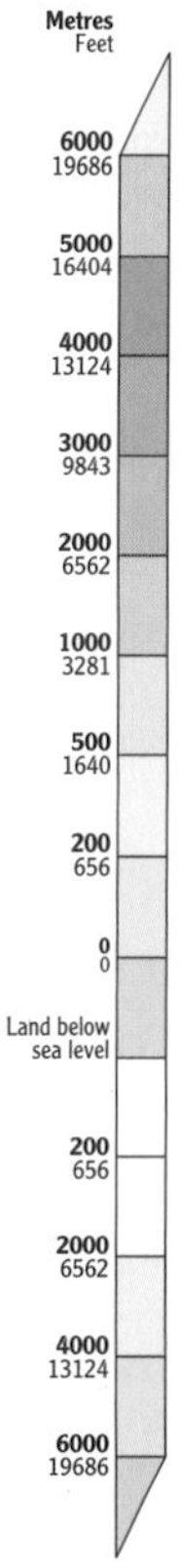

Metres
Feet
6000 19686
5000 16404
4000 13124
3000 9843
2000 6562
1000 3281
500 1640
200 656
0 0
Land below sea level
200 656
2000 6562
4000 13124
6000 19686

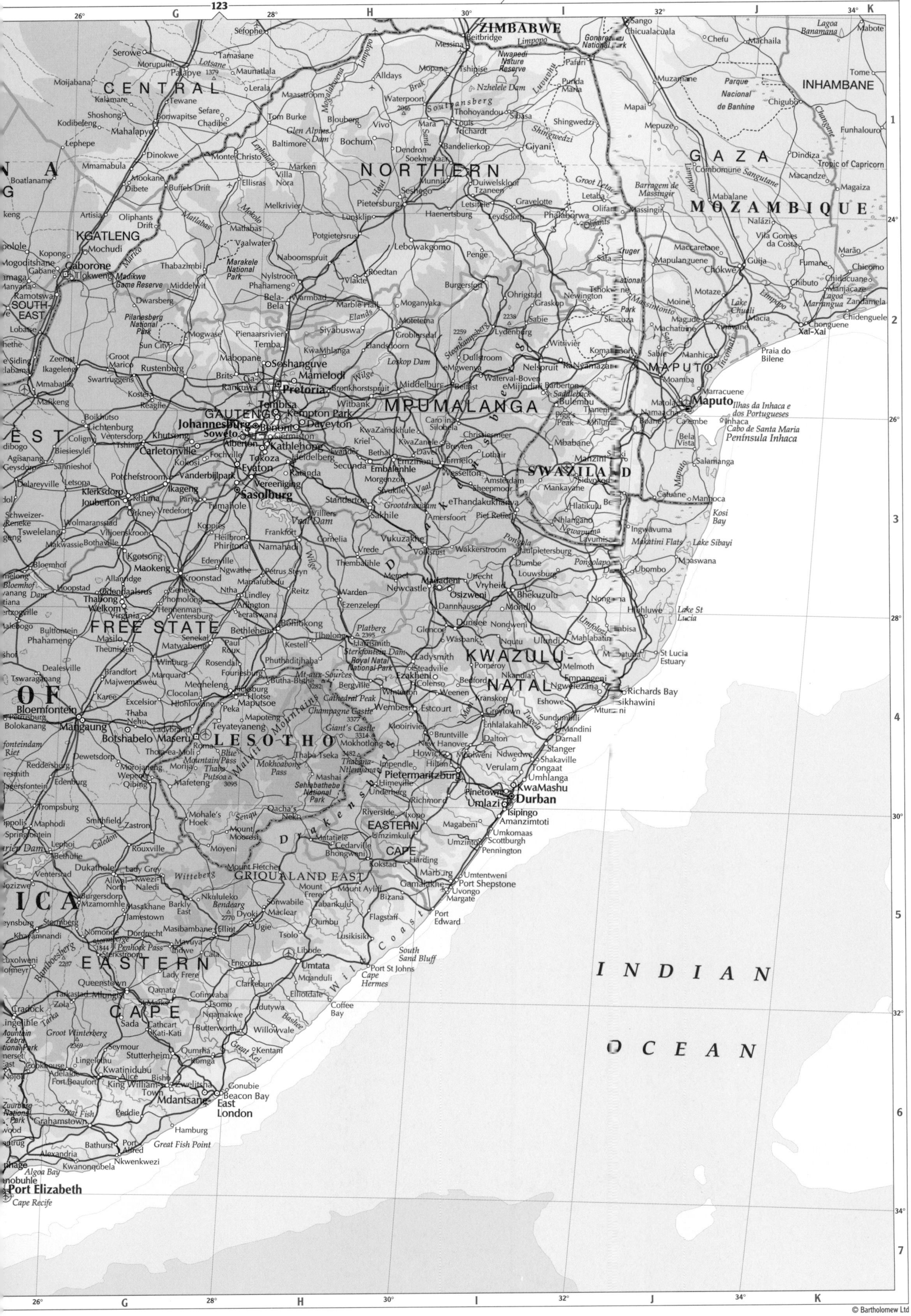

ZIMBABWE
MOZAMBIQUE
GAZA
INHAMBANE
MAPUTO
Maputo
NORTHERN
MPUMALANGA
GAUTENG
Pretoria
Johannesburg
Soweto
SWAZILAND
KWAZULU-NATAL
Durban
Pietermaritzburg
Richards Bay
FREE STATE
Bloemfontein
LESOTHO
Maseru
EASTERN CAPE
East London
Port Elizabeth
Grahamstown
Umtata
Kimberley
Welkom
Kroonstad
Ladysmith
Newcastle
Pietersburg
Nelspruit
Witbank
Standerton
Sasolburg
Vereeniging
Vanderbijlpark
Klerksdorp
Potchefstroom
Rustenburg
Gaborone
KGATLENG
CENTRAL
SOUTH-EAST
Messina
Beitbridge
Louis Trichardt
Thohoyandou
Phalaborwa
Tzaneen
Port Shepstone
Kokstad
Queenstown
King William's Town
Bisho
Mdantsane
Drakensberg
Maloti Mountains
Vaal Dam
Tropic of Capricorn
INDIAN OCEAN
Lake St Lucia
Kosi Bay
Lake Sibayi
Great Fish Point
Cape Recife
Algoa Bay
Wild Coast
Cape Hermes
Port St Johns
Giant's Castle
Champagne Castle
Thabana Ntlenyana
Bloemhof Dam
Parque Nacional de Banhine
Ilhas da Inhaca e dos Portugueses
Península Inhaca
Cabo de Santa Maria

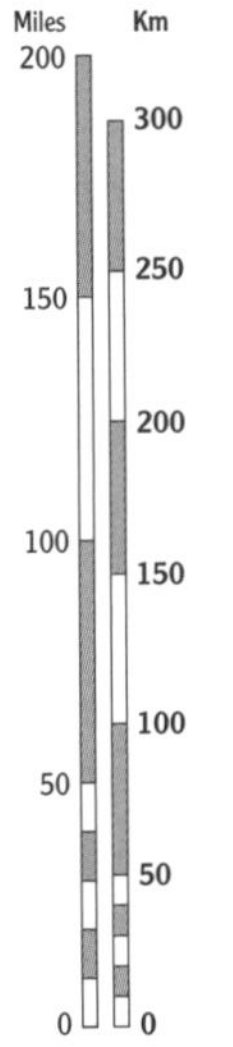

Miles
Km
200
150
100
50
0
300
250
200
150
100
50
0

1:5 000 000

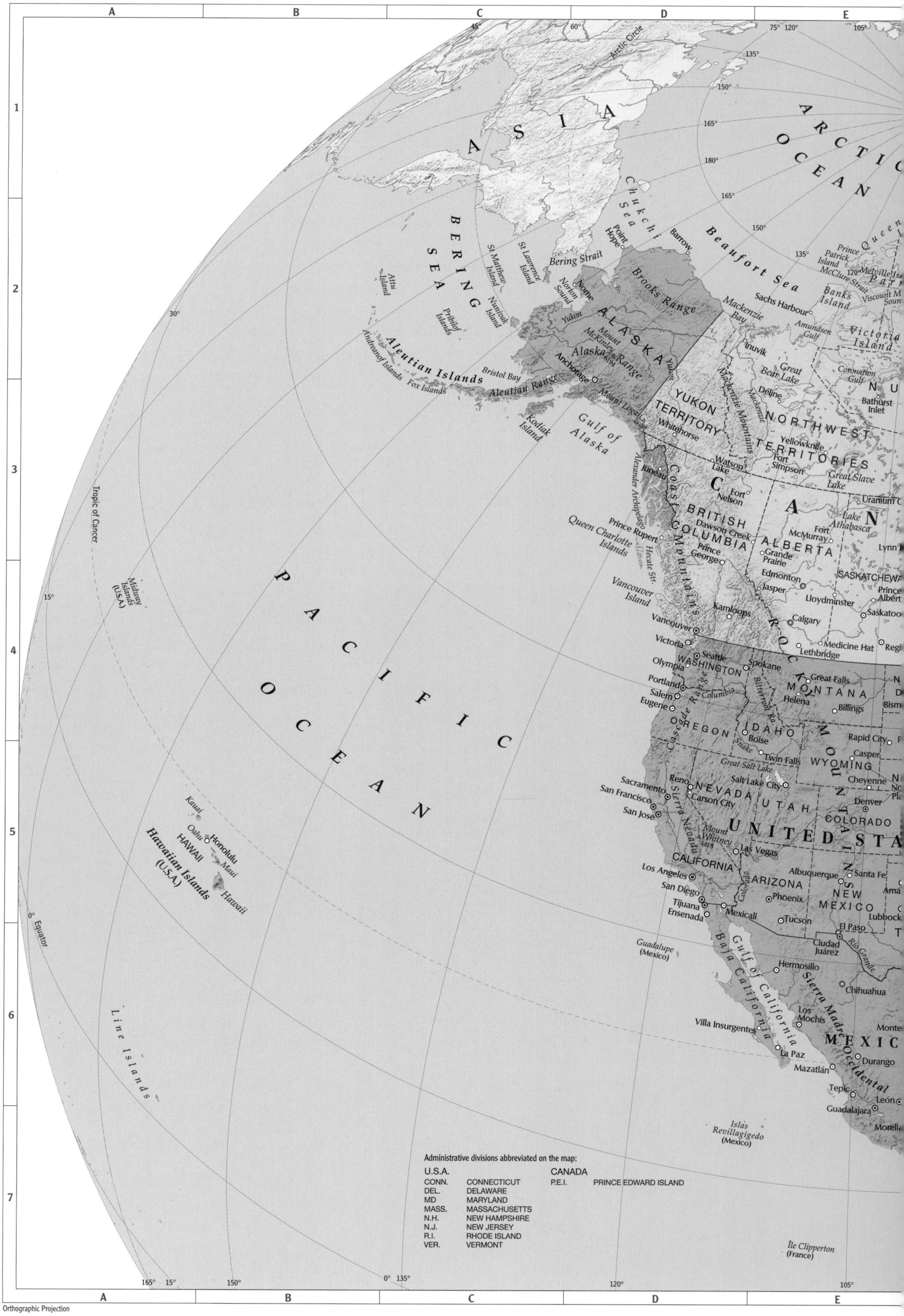

A B C D E

ASIA

ARCTIC OCEAN

Arctic Circle

45° 60° 75° 120° 105°

135°

165°

150°

180°

165°

Chukchi Sea

BERING SEA

Bering Strait

Barrow

Point Hope

Beaufort Sea

150°

135°

Queen

Prince Patrick Island

McClure Strait

Metville Is.

120°

Viscount M
Sound

St. Matthew Island

St. Lawrence Island

Nunivak Island

Nome

Norton Sound

BROOKS RANGE

Sachs Harbour

Banks Island

Victoria Island

Attu Island

Pribilof Islands

30°

ALASKA

Mount McKinley 6194

Alaska Range

Mackenzie Bay

Amundsen Gulf

NU

Aleutian Islands

Anchorage

Yukon

Inuvik

Great Bear Lake

Coronation Gulf

Bathurst Inlet

Andreanof Islands Fox Islands

Bristol Bay

Aleutian Range

YUKON TERRITORY

Déline

Mount Logan

Kodiak Island

Gulf of Alaska

Whitehorse

Mackenzie Mountains

NORTHWEST TERRITORIES

Yellowknife

Fort Simpson

Great Slave Lake

Tropic of Cancer

Juneau

Watson Lake

CAN

Fort Nelson

Uranium C

Coast Mountains

Alexander Archipelago

BRITISH COLUMBIA

Dawson Creek

McMurray

Lake Athabasca

ALBERTA

Lynn

15°

Midway Islands (U.S.A.)

Prince Rupert

Queen Charlotte Islands

Hecate Str.

Prince George

Grande Prairie

Edmonton

Jasper

Lloydminster

Prince Albert

SASKATCHEW

PACIFIC

Vancouver Island

Rocky Mountains

Kamloops

Calgary

Saskato

Vancouver

Victoria

Medicine Hat

Lethbridge

Regi

Seattle

Spokane

WASHINGTON

Olympia

Great Falls

Portland

Columbia

MONTANA

Bism

OCEAN

Salem

Helena

Billings

Eugene

Cascade Range

Bitterroot Range

IDAHO

OREGON

Boise

Rapid City

Snake

Twin Falls

Casper

WYOMING

Kauai

Oahu Honolulu

Reno

Great Salt Lake

Salt Lake City

Cheyenne

N

Sacramento

San Francisco

Carson City

NEVADA

Denver

HAWAII

Maui

Sierra Nevada

Mount Whitney 4418

UTAH

COLORADO

UNITED STA

San Jose

Las Vegas

Hawaiian Islands (U.S.A.)

Hawaii

CALIFORNIA

Santa Fe

Los Angeles

Albuquerque

ARIZONA

San Diego

NEW

Equator

Tijuana

Mexicali

Phoenix

MEXICO

Lubbock

Ensenada

Tucson

El Paso

T

Guadalupe (Mexico)

Ciudad Juárez

Rio Grande

Baja California

Hermosillo

Gulf of California

Chihuahua

Line Islands

Los Mochis

Sierra Madre Occidental

Villa Insurgentes

MEXICO

La Paz

Monte

Durango

Mazatlán

Tepic

León

Guadalajara

Islas Revillagigedo (Mexico)

Morelia

Administrative divisions abbreviated on the map:

U.S.A.
CONN. CONNECTICUT
DEL. DELAWARE
MD MARYLAND
MASS. MASSACHUSETTS
N.H. NEW HAMPSHIRE
N.J. NEW JERSEY
R.I. RHODE ISLAND
VER. VERMONT

CANADA
P.E.I. PRINCE EDWARD ISLAND

Île Clipperton (France)

165° 15° 150° 0° 135° 120° 105°

A B C D E

Orthographic Projection

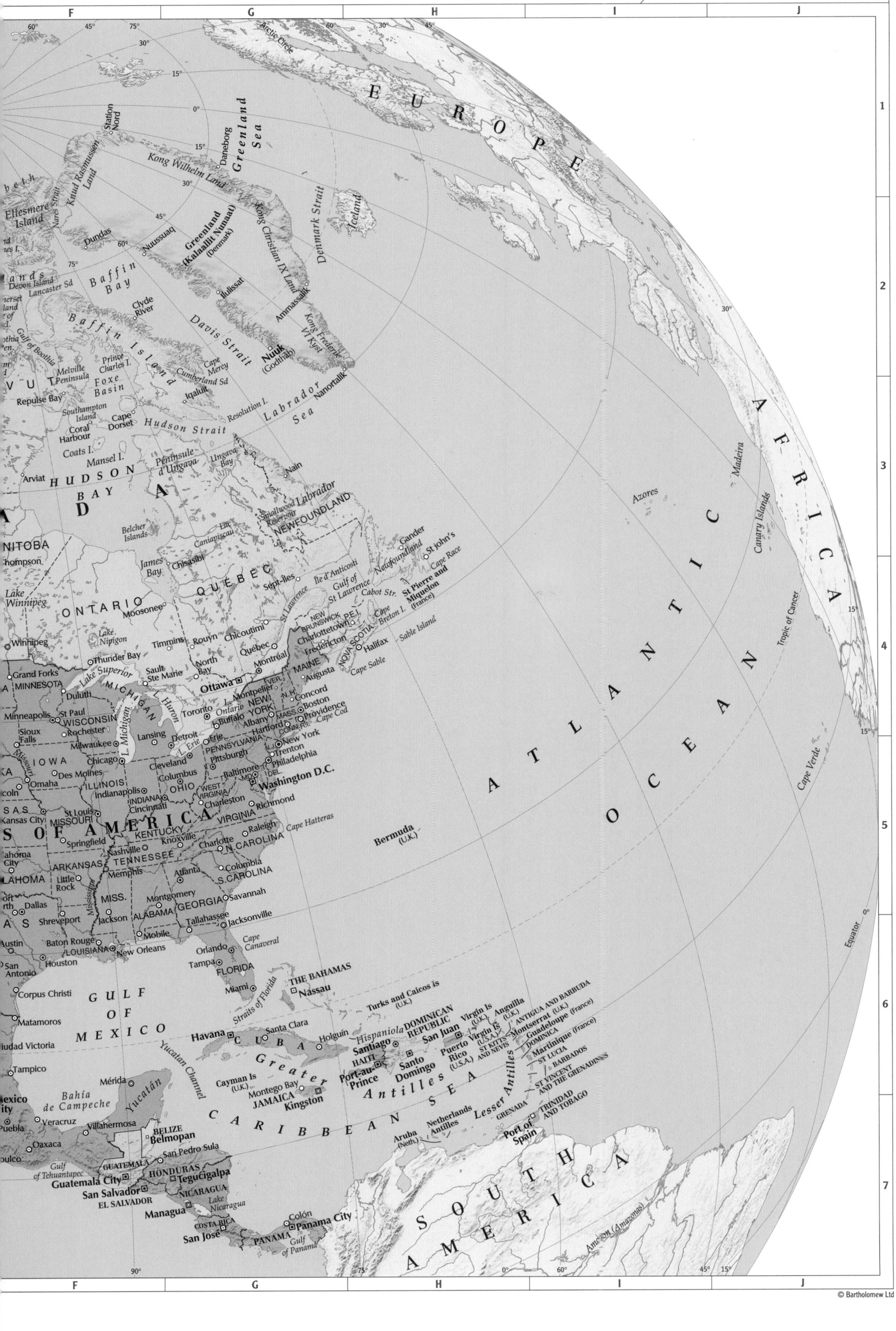

EUROPE

Station
Nord

Knud Rasmussen
Land

Kong Wilhelm Land

Daneborg

Greenland
Sea

Arctic Circle

Ellesmere
Island

Dundas

Nuussuaq

Greenland
(Kalaallit Nunaat)
(Denmark)

Kong Christian IX Land

Denmark Strait

Iceland

Devon Island
Lancaster Sd

Baffin
Bay

Clyde
River

Baffin Island

Davis Strait

Ilulissat

Nuuk
(Godthåb)

Kong Frederik
VI Kyst

Ammassalik

Gulf of
Boothia

Melville
Peninsula

Prince
Charles I.

Foxe
Basin

Cape
Mercy

Cumberland Sd

Repulse Bay

Southampton
Island

Coral
Harbour

Cape
Dorset

Igaluit

Labrador
Sea

Resolution I.

Nanortalik

Coats I.

Mansel I.

Hudson Strait

Arviat

HUDSON

BAY

Péninsule
d'Ungava

Ungava
Bay

Nain

NITOBA

hompson

Belcher
Islands

James
Bay

Chisasibi

Smallwood
Reservoir

Labrador

NEWFOUNDLAND

Gander

Netufoundland

St John's

Cape Race

Lake
Winnipeg

ONTARIO

QUÉBEC

Lac
Caniapiscau

Sept-Îles

Île d'Anticosti

Gulf of
St Lawrence

Cabot Str.

St Pierre and
Miquelon
(France)

Winnipeg

Moosonee

Timmins

Rouyn

Chicoutimi

Québec

St Lawrence

NEW
BRUNSWICK
Charlottetown
Fredericton

P.E.I.

Cape
Breton I.

Sable Island

Thunder Bay

Lake
Nipigon

Sault
Ste Marie

North
Bay

Montréal

MAINE
Augusta

NOVA
SCOTIA

Halifax

Cape Sable

Grand Forks

MINNESOTA

Duluth

St Paul

MICHIGAN

L. Huron

Ottawa

Ontario

Toronto

L. Ontario

Buffalo

Montpelier
NEW

Concord

VT

N.H.

Boston

Minneapolis

WISCONSIN

Rochester

Lansing

Detroit

L. Erie

Albany

Hartford

MASS.

Providence

Cape Cod

Sioux
Falls

Milwaukee

Chicago

Cleveland

Erie

Pittsburgh

PENNSYLVANIA

New York

Trenton

IOWA

Des Moines

ILLINOIS

Indianapolis

INDIANA

Columbus

OHIO

Philadelphia

coln

Omaha

St Louis

MISSOURI

Cincinnati

WEST
VIRGINIA

Baltimore

MD.

DEL.

Washington D.C.

KA

Kansas City

S OF AMERICA

Springfield

KENTUCKY

Charleston

Richmond

VIRGINIA

ahoma
City

Nashville

Knoxville

Raleigh

Cape Hatteras

LAHOMA

Little
Rock

ARKANSAS

TENNESSEE

Memphis

Charlotte

N. CAROLINA

Columbia

S. CAROLINA

rth

Dallas

MISS.

Montgomery

GEORGIA

Savannah

A S

Shreveport

Jackson

ALABAMA

Atlanta

Austin

Baton Rouge

LOUISIANA

Mobile

Tallahassee

Jacksonville

San
Antonio

Houston

New Orleans

Orlando

Cape
Canaveral

Corpus Christi

GULF

Tampa

FLORIDA

Matamoros

OF

Miami

Straits of Florida

THE BAHAMAS

Nassau

iudad
Victoria

MEXICO

Havana

CUBA

Santa Clara

Holguín

Turks and Caicos Is
(U.K.)

Tampico

Mérida

Yucatán Channel

CUBA

Santiago

Hispaniola

DOMINICAN
REPUBLIC

HAITI

Port-au-
Prince

Santo
Domingo

San Juan

Puerto
Rico
(U.S.A.)

Virgin Is
(U.K.)

Virgin Is
(U.S.A.)

Anguilla
(U.K.)

ANTIGUA AND BARBUDA

ST KITTS
AND NEVIS

Montserrat (U.K.)

Guadeloupe (France)

DOMINICA

Martinique (France)

ST LUCIA

BARBADOS

Mexico
ity

Bahía
de Campeche

Yucatán

Cayman Is
(U.K.)

Montego Bay

JAMAICA

Kingston

Greater

Antilles

Lesser Antilles

CARIBBEAN SEA

ST VINCENT
AND THE GRENADINS

GRENADA

TRINIDAD
AND TOBAGO

Puebla

Veracruz

Villahermosa

Aruba
(Neth.)

Netherlands
Antilles

Port of
Spain

Oaxaca

Gulf
of Tehuantepec

BELIZE

Belmopan

San Pedro Sula

HONDURAS

Am on (Amazonas)

GUATEMALA

oulco

Guatemala City

Tegucigalpa

San Salvador

EL SALVADOR

NICARAGUA

Managua

Lake
Nicaragua

Colón

Panama City

COSTA RICA

PANAMA

Gulf
of Panama

San José

SOUTH

AMERICA

ATLANTIC

OCEAN

AFRICA

Madeira

Azores

Canary Islands

Tropic of Cancer

Cape Verde

Bermuda
(U.K.)

Equator

Miles | Km

1200 | 2000

1600

800 | 1200

400 | 800

400

0 | 0

© Bartholomew Ltd

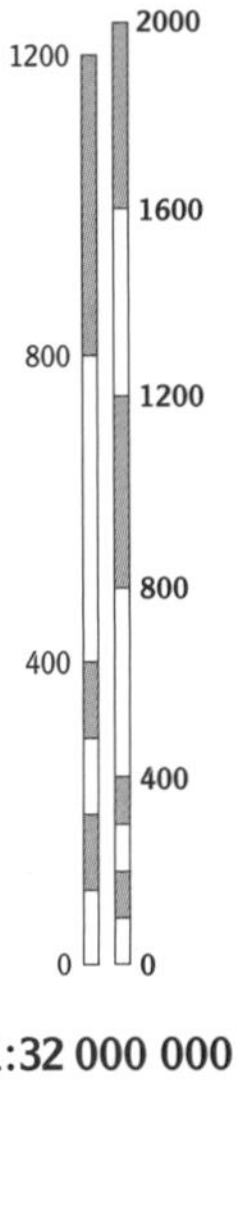

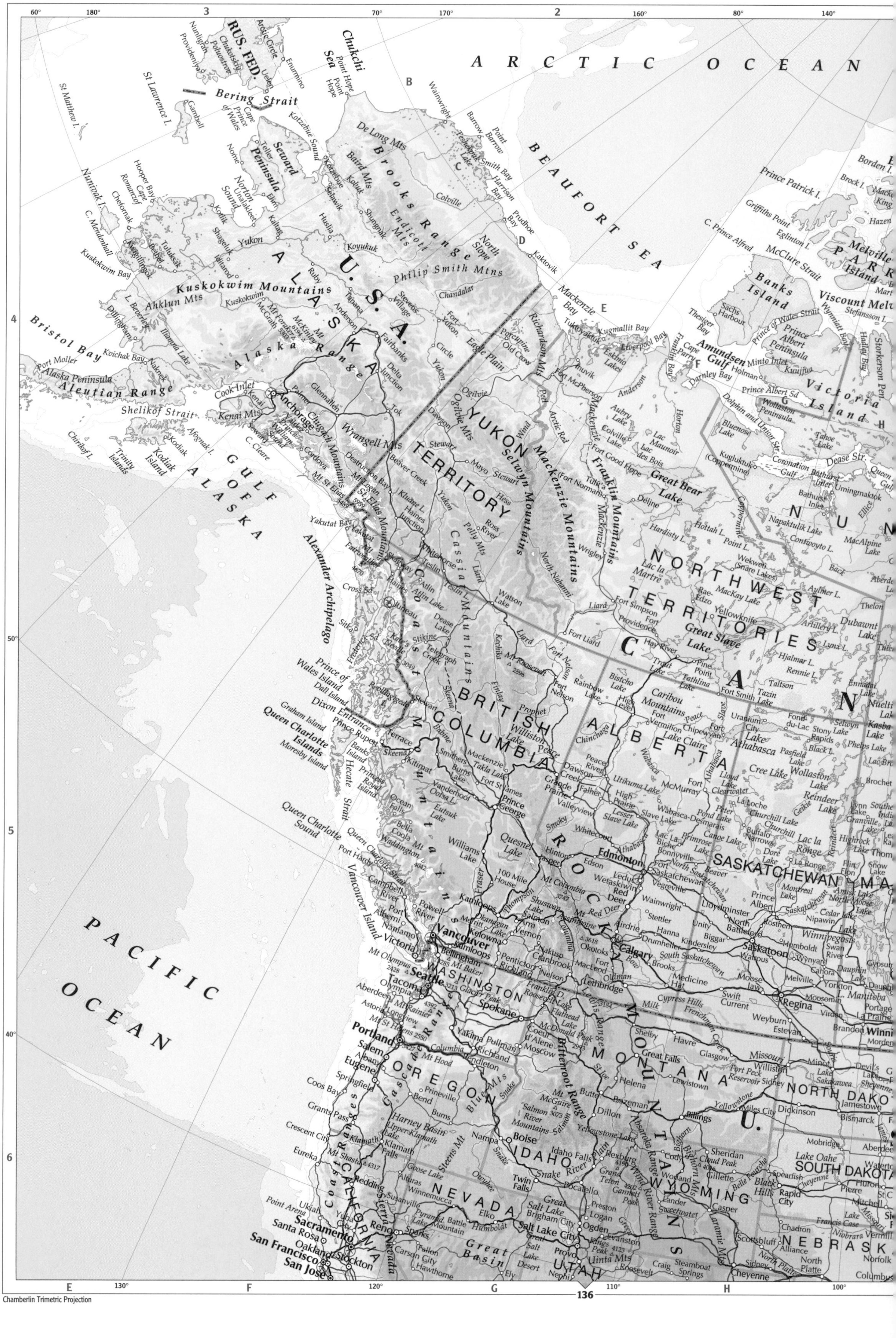

ARCTIC OCEAN

BEAUFORT SEA

RUS. FED.

Bering Strait

Chukchi Sea

U.S.A.

ALASKA

Brooks Range

Alaska Range

Kuskokwim Mountains

YUKON TERRITORY

NORTHWEST TERRITORIES

Great Bear Lake

Great Slave Lake

GULF OF ALASKA

Aleutian Range

Bristol Bay

Kodiak Island

Alexander Archipelago

Queen Charlotte Islands

BRITISH COLUMBIA

ALBERTA

SASKATCHEWAN

MANITOBA

Anchorage

Edmonton

Calgary

Regina

Winnipeg

Saskatoon

Vancouver

Victoria

Seattle

Tacoma

Portland

Salem

Eugene

WASHINGTON

OREGON

IDAHO

MONTANA

WYOMING

NORTH DAKOTA

SOUTH DAKOTA

NEBRASKA

NEVADA

UTAH

CALIFORNIA

Sacramento

San Francisco

Oakland

San Jose

Stockton

PACIFIC OCEAN

Great Basin

Salt Lake City

Boise

Great Salt Lake

Helena

Billings

Cheyenne

ROCKY MOUNTAINS

Metres / Feet

6000 19686
5000 16404
4000 13124
3000 9843
2000 6562
1000 3281
500 1640
200 656
0
Land below sea level
200 656
2000 6562
4000 13124
6000 19686

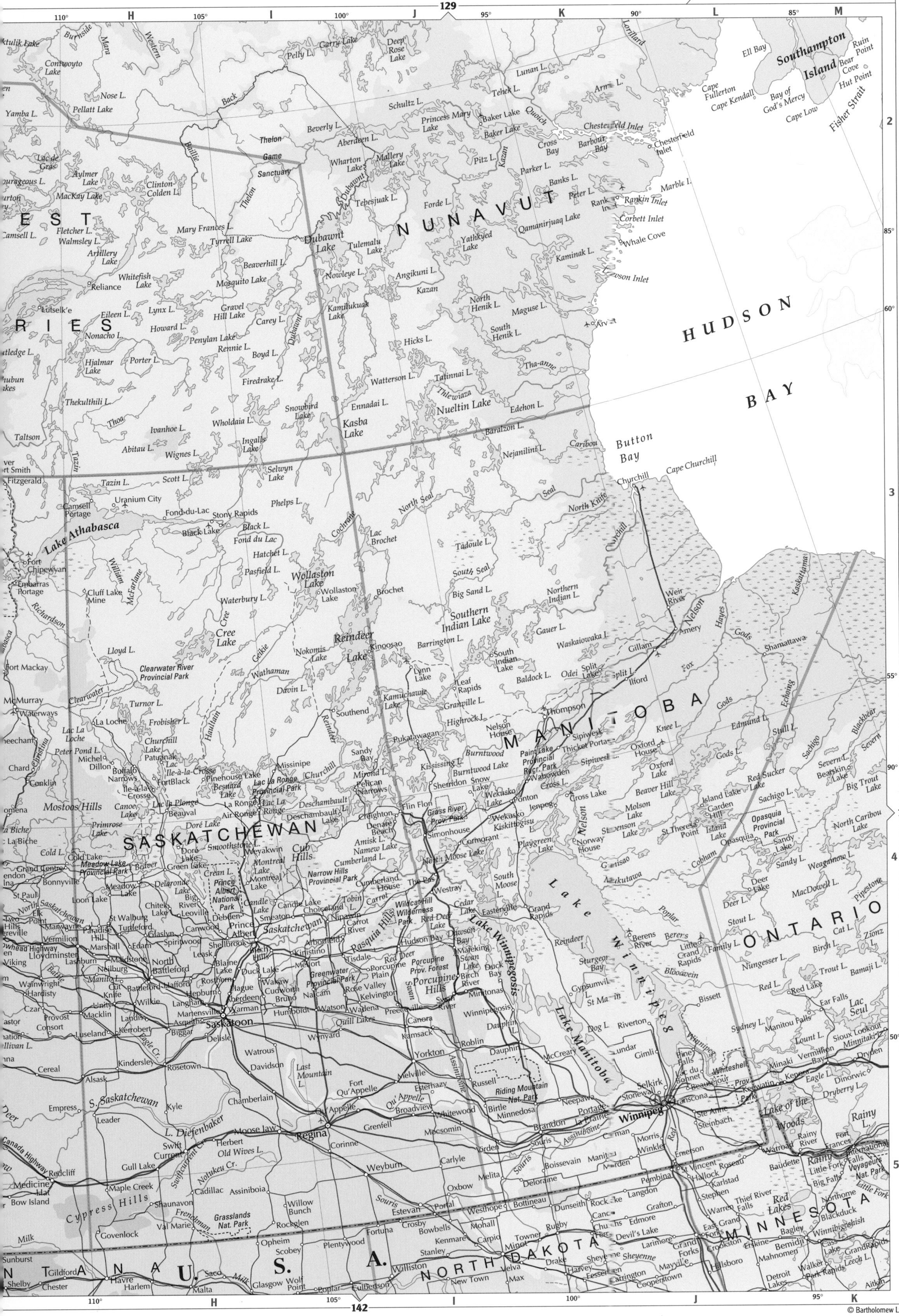

NUNAVUT

HUDSON

BAY

Southampton Island

Ell Bay
Cape Fullerton
Cape Kendall
Bay of God's Mercy
Cape Low
Fisher Strait
Bear Point
Ruin Cove
Hut Point

Cape Churchill
Churchill
Button Bay

NORTH WEST TERRITORIES

Lake Athabasca

Uranium City
Fond-du-Lac

Wollaston Lake

Reindeer Lake

Southern Indian Lake

MANITOBA

SASKATCHEWAN

ONTARIO

Lake Winnipeg

Lake Winnipegosis

Lake Manitoba

Cree Lake

McMurray
Waterways

Prince Albert National Park

Saskatoon

North Battleford

Regina
Moose Jaw
Swift Current

Medicine Hat

Cypress Hills

Winnipeg
Selkirk
Portage la Prairie
Brandon
Dauphin
Yorkton

Lake of the Woods

MINNESOTA

NORTH DAKOTA

U. S. A.

MONTANA

Riding Mountain Nat. Park

Grasslands Nat. Park

Clearwater River Provincial Park

Grass River Prov. Park

Opasquia Provincial Park

Miles   Km
300 ┐ ┌ 500
     │ │ 400
200 ┤ ┤ 300
     │ │ 200
100 ┤ ┤ 100
  0 ┘ └ 0

1:7 000 000

© Bartholomew Ltd

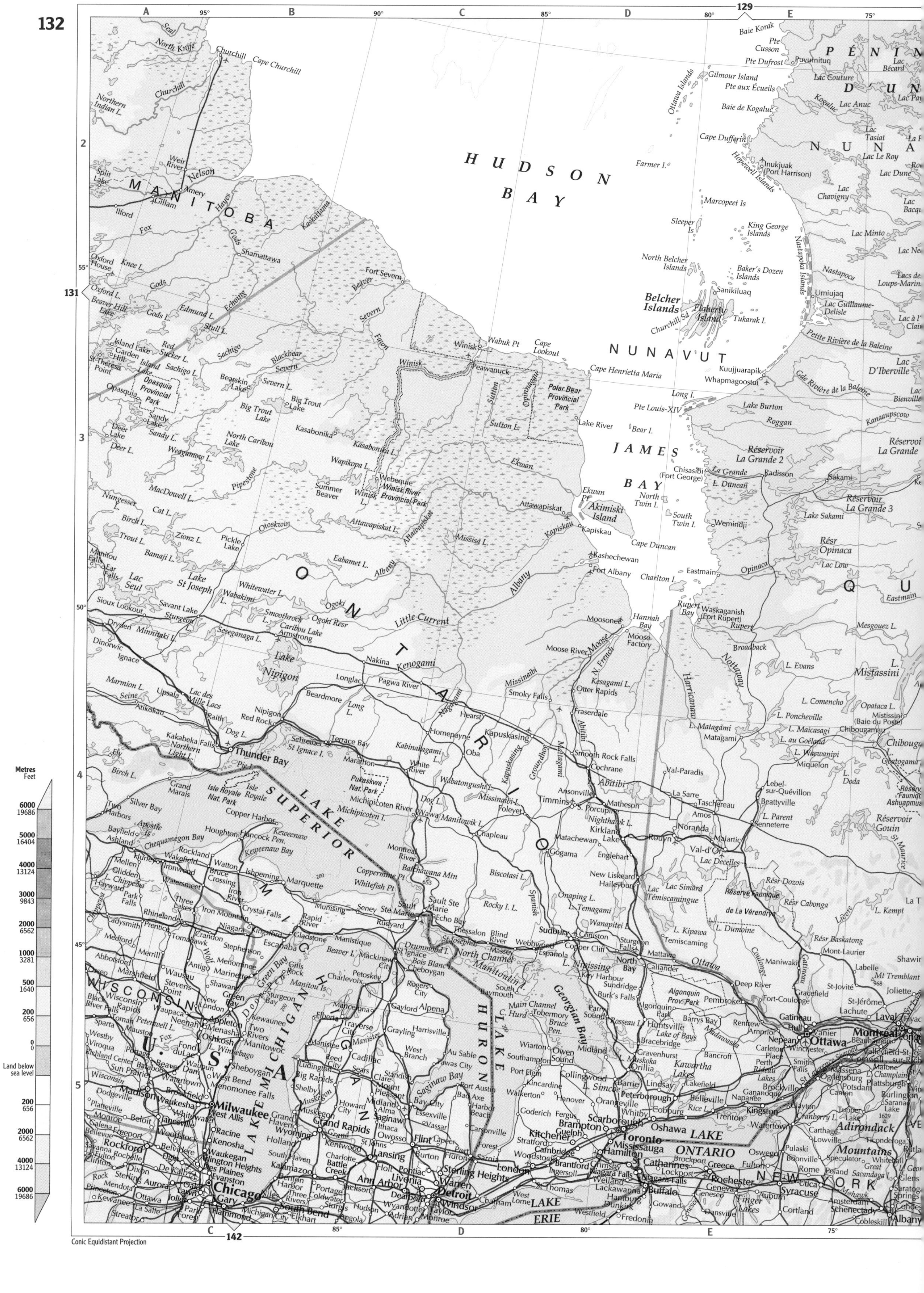
HUDSON BAY
JAMES BAY
MANITOBA
ONTARIO
NUNAVUT
WISCONSIN
MICHIGAN
NEW YORK
U.S.A.
LAKE SUPERIOR
LAKE MICHIGAN
LAKE HURON
LAKE ERIE
LAKE ONTARIO
Georgian Bay
North Channel
Belcher Islands
Akimiski Island
Churchill
Cape Churchill
Nelson
Gillam
Fort Severn
Winisk
Peawanuck
Cape Henrietta Maria
Polar Bear Provincial Park
Opasquia Provincial Park
Winisk River Provincial Park
Attawapiskat
Kapiskau
Kashechewan
Fort Albany
Moosonee
Moose Factory
Chisasibi (Fort George)
Radisson
Réservoir La Grande 2
Réservoir La Grande 3
Eastmain
Waskaganish (Fort Rupert)
Kuujjuarapik
Whapmagoostui
Sanikiluaq
Inukjuak (Port Harrison)
Umiujaq
Lake Nipigon
Lac Seul
Lake St Joseph
Thunder Bay
Nipigon
Hearst
Kapuskasing
Cochrane
Timmins
Kirkland Lake
Rouyn
Val-d'Or
Amos
Chibougamau
Lac Mistassini
Sudbury
North Bay
Sault Ste Marie
Marquette
Green Bay
Milwaukee
Madison
Chicago
Gary
South Bend
Grand Rapids
Lansing
Flint
Detroit
Windsor
London
Kitchener
Hamilton
Toronto
Mississauga
Oshawa
Kingston
Ottawa
Montréal
Buffalo
Rochester
Syracuse
Adirondack Mountains
Isle Royale Nat. Park
Pukaskwa Nat. Park
Algonquin Prov. Park
Réserve Faunique de La Vérendrye
Metres
Feet
6000 19686
5000 16404
4000 13124
3000 9843
2000 6562
1000 3281
500 1640
200 656
0 0
Land below sea level
200 656
2000 6562
4000 13124
6000 19686
129
131
142
Conic Equidistant Projection

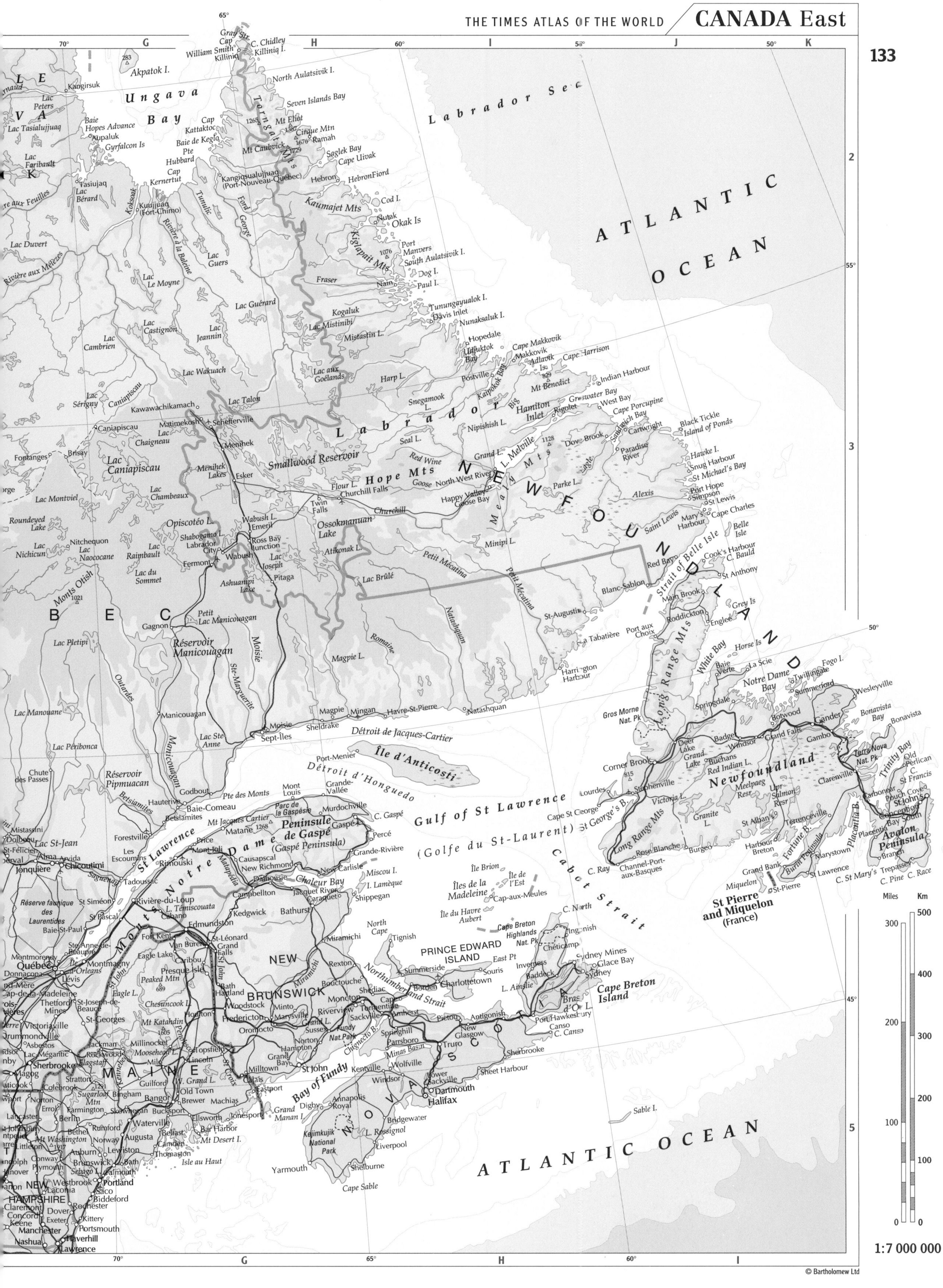

ATLANTIC

OCEAN

Labrador Sea

Ungava Bay

ATLANTIC OCEAN

Labrador

NEWFOUNDLAND

QUEBEC

Gulf of St Lawrence
(Golfe du St-Laurent)

Cabot Strait

St Pierre and Miquelon (France)

Newfoundland

Notre Dame Bay

Long Range Mts

Corner Brook

Gander

St John's

Avalon Peninsula

Cape Breton Island

PRINCE EDWARD ISLAND

Charlottetown

NOVA SCOTIA

Halifax

NEW BRUNSWICK

Fredericton

MAINE

NEW HAMPSHIRE

Bay of Fundy

Gulf of St Lawrence

Île d'Anticosti

Peninsule de Gaspé (Gaspé Peninsula)

St Lawrence

Notre Dame Mts

Québec

Miles Km

300   500

       400

200   300

       200

100

       100

0   0

1:7 000 000

© Bartholomew Ltd

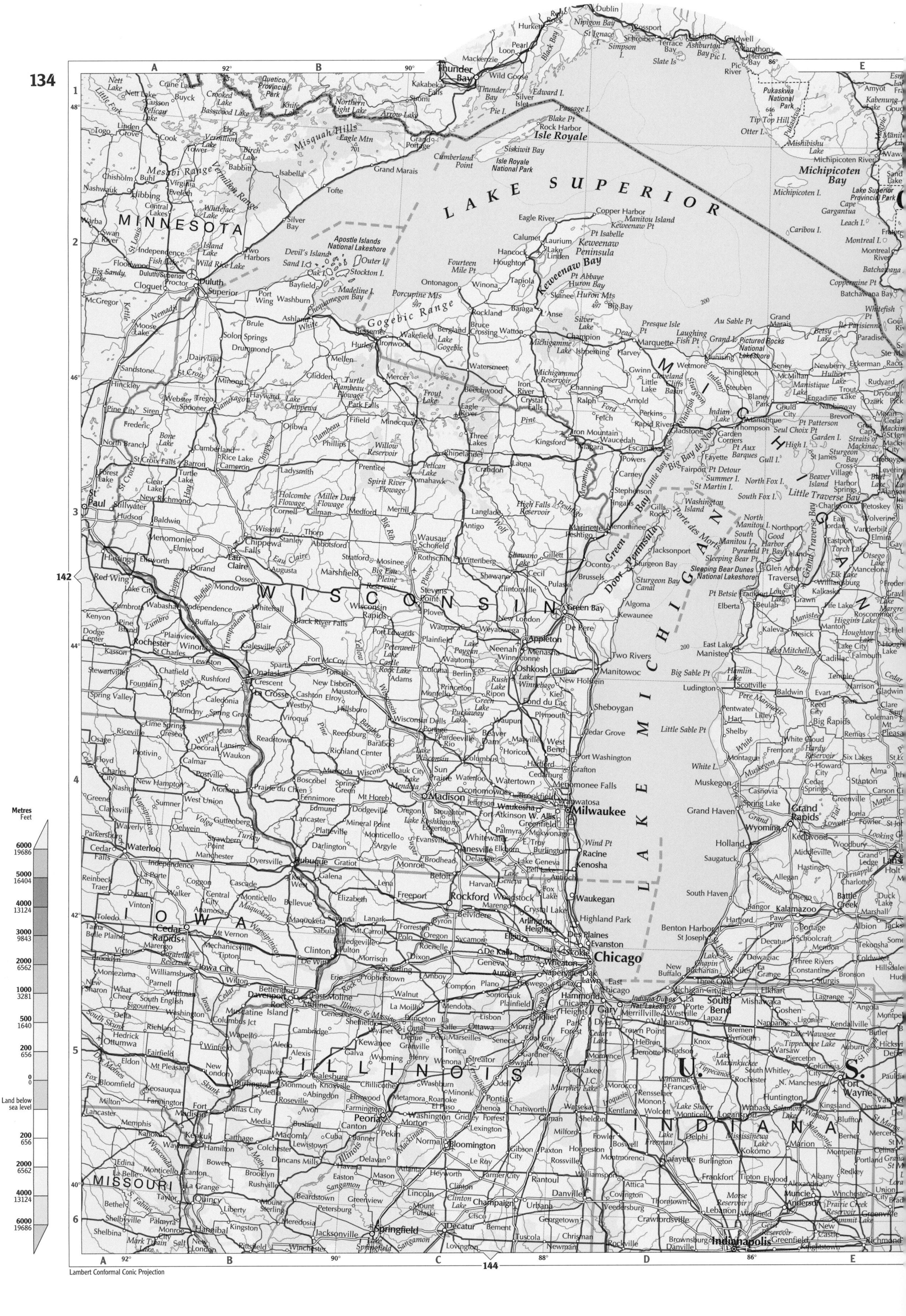

LAKE SUPERIOR

MINNESOTA

WISCONSIN

IOWA

ILLINOIS

MISSOURI

MICHIGAN

INDIANA

U.S.

LAKE MICHIGAN

Isle Royale
Isle Royale National Park

Thunder Bay

Apostle Islands National Lakeshore

Keweenaw Peninsula
Keweenaw Bay

Mesabi Range
Vermilion Range
Gogebic Range

Duluth
Superior

Chicago

Milwaukee
Madison
Green Bay
Oshkosh
Appleton
Eau Claire
La Crosse
Wausau
Rockford

Cedar Rapids
Davenport
Iowa City
Des Moines

Peoria
Bloomington
Decatur
Springfield

Indianapolis
Fort Wayne
South Bend
Gary

Grand Rapids
Wyoming
Holland
Kalamazoo
Battle Creek

Door Peninsula

Metres / Feet

6000 / 19686
5000 / 16404
4000 / 13124
3000 / 9843
2000 / 6562
1000 / 3281
500 / 1640
200 / 656
0 / 0
Land below sea level
200 / 656
2000 / 6562
4000 / 13124
6000 / 19686

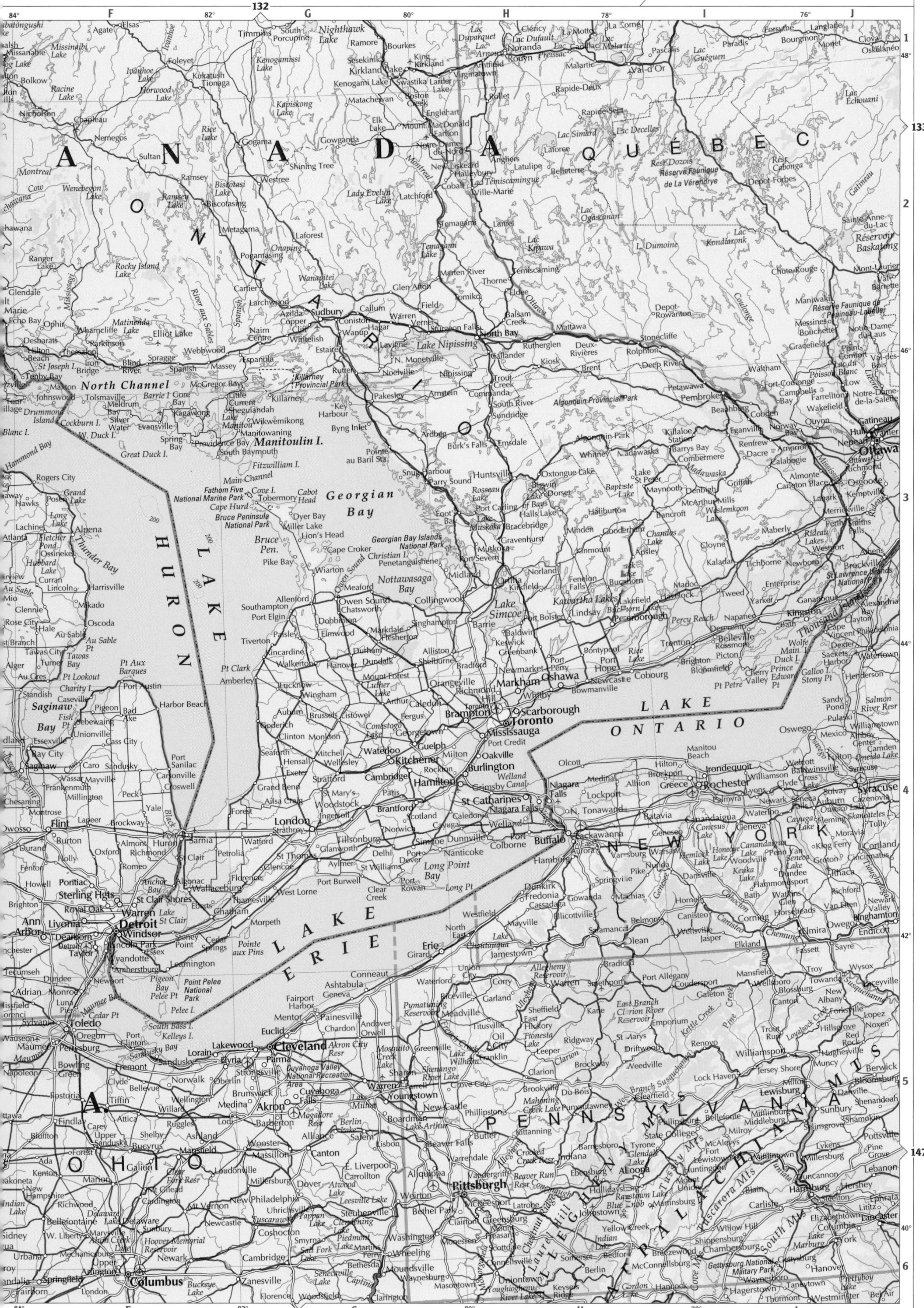

CANADA
ONTARIO
QUÉBEC
NEW YORK
PENNSYLVANIA
OHIO
LAKE HURON
LAKE ONTARIO
LAKE ERIE
Georgian Bay
North Channel
Manitoulin I.
Saginaw Bay
Bruce Pen.
Lake Nipissing
Lake Simcoe
Long Point Bay
Thousand Islands
Algonquin Provincial Park
Killarney Provincial Park
Fathom Five National Marine Park
Bruce Peninsula National Park
Georgian Bay Islands National Park
Point Pelee National Park
St Lawrence Islands National Park
Réserve Faunique de La Vérendrye
Réserve Faunique de Papineau-Labelle
Cuyahoga Valley National Recreation Area
Gettysburg National Military Park
ALLEGHENY MTS
APPALACHIAN MTS
Toronto
Ottawa
Gatineau
Hull
Sudbury
North Bay
Timmins
Kirkland Lake
Rouyn-Noranda
Val-d'Or
Sault
Pembroke
Kingston
Belleville
Peterborough
Oshawa
Markham
Scarborough
Brampton
Mississauga
Oakville
Burlington
Hamilton
St Catharines
Niagara Falls
Kitchener
Waterloo
Guelph
Cambridge
Brantford
London
Sarnia
Port Huron
Windsor
Detroit
Toledo
Cleveland
Akron
Youngstown
Erie
Buffalo
Rochester
Syracuse
Binghamton
Pittsburgh
Altoona
Harrisburg
Lancaster
Columbus
Mansfield
Flint
Saginaw
Ann Arbor
Owen Sound
Barrie
Orillia
Huntsville
Parry Sound
Brockville
Watertown
Oswego
Elmira
Williamsport
State College
Johnstown
Wheeling
Canton
Sandusky
1:3 500 000
Miles
Km

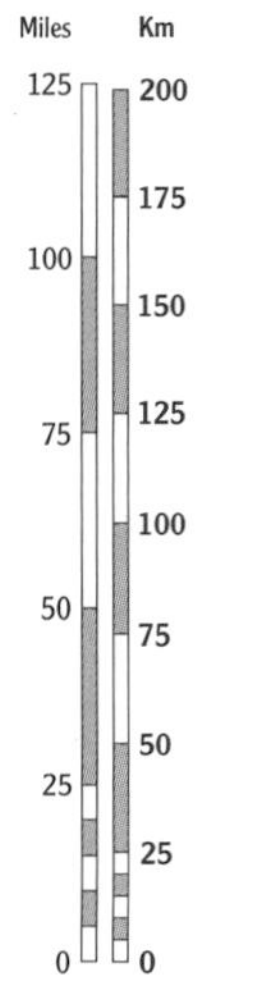

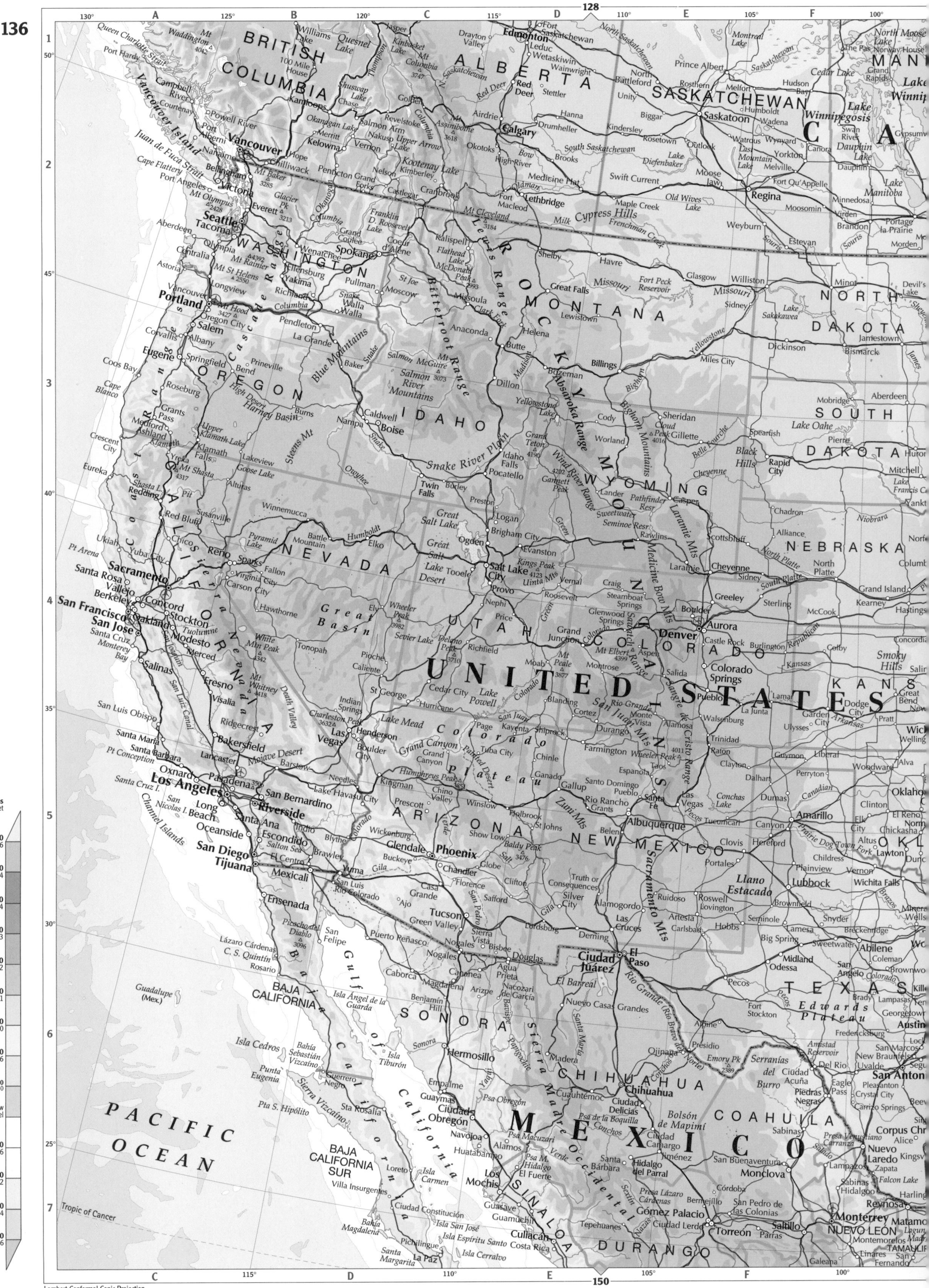

Map — Western United States, Western Canada, and Northern Mexico

Metres / Feet (elevation scale)

Metres	Feet
6000	19686
5000	16404
4000	13124
3000	9843
2000	6562
1000	3281
500	1640
200	656
0	0

Land below sea level

Metres	Feet
200	656
2000	6562
4000	13124
6000	19686

Lambert Conformal Conic Projection

Major labels include:

BRITISH COLUMBIA, ALBERTA, SASKATCHEWAN, MANITOBA, WASHINGTON, OREGON, IDAHO, MONTANA, WYOMING, NORTH DAKOTA, SOUTH DAKOTA, NEBRASKA, NEVADA, UTAH, COLORADO, KANSAS, CALIFORNIA, ARIZONA, NEW MEXICO, OKLAHOMA, TEXAS, UNITED STATES, MEXICO, BAJA CALIFORNIA, BAJA CALIFORNIA SUR, SONORA, CHIHUAHUA, COAHUILA, SINALOA, DURANGO, NUEVO LEÓN, TAMAULIPAS, PACIFIC OCEAN, ROCKY MOUNTAINS, Sierra Nevada, Great Basin, Snake River Plain, Gulf of California

Cities: Vancouver, Victoria, Seattle, Tacoma, Olympia, Spokane, Portland, Salem, Eugene, Sacramento, San Francisco, Oakland, San Jose, Fresno, Los Angeles, Long Beach, San Diego, Tijuana, Las Vegas, Phoenix, Tucson, Mexicali, Ensenada, Hermosillo, Ciudad Obregón, Culiacán, Chihuahua, Ciudad Juárez, El Paso, Albuquerque, Santa Fe, Denver, Aurora, Colorado Springs, Pueblo, Salt Lake City, Provo, Boise, Calgary, Edmonton, Saskatoon, Regina, Bismarck, Rapid City, Reno, Monterrey, Torreón, Gómez Palacio, Saltillo

Tropic of Cancer

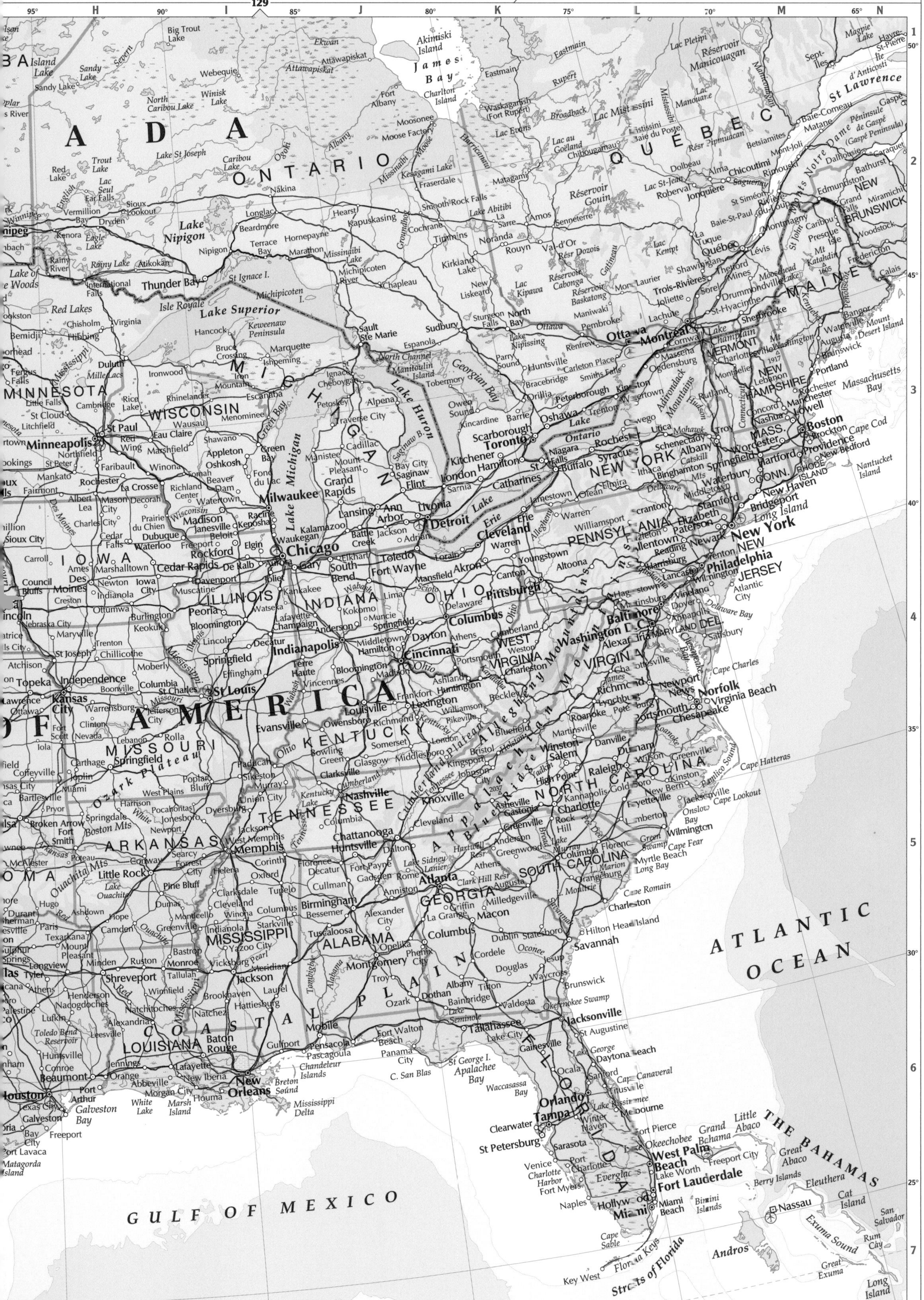

CANADA

ONTARIO

QUÉBEC

MAINE

NEW BRUNSWICK

St Lawrence

James Bay

Lake Superior

Lake Huron

Lake Michigan

Lake Erie

Lake Ontario

MICHIGAN

WISCONSIN

MINNESOTA

IOWA

ILLINOIS

INDIANA

OHIO

PENNSYLVANIA

NEW YORK

VERMONT

NEW HAMPSHIRE

MASS.

CONN.

RHODE ISLAND

NEW JERSEY

DEL.

MARYLAND

WEST VIRGINIA

VIRGINIA

KENTUCKY

MISSOURI

KANSAS

ARKANSAS

OKLAHOMA

TENNESSEE

NORTH CAROLINA

SOUTH CAROLINA

GEORGIA

ALABAMA

MISSISSIPPI

LOUISIANA

FLORIDA

OF AMERICA

Ozark Plateau

COASTAL PLAIN

Appalachian Mountains

Allegheny Mountains

Blue Ridge

Cumberland Plateau

ATLANTIC OCEAN

GULF OF MEXICO

THE BAHAMAS

Minneapolis · St Paul · Milwaukee · Chicago · Detroit · Cleveland · Columbus · Cincinnati · Indianapolis · St Louis · Kansas City · Memphis · Nashville · Atlanta · Birmingham · New Orleans · Houston · Galveston · Jacksonville · Orlando · Tampa · St Petersburg · Miami · Fort Lauderdale · West Palm Beach · Washington D.C. · Baltimore · Philadelphia · New York · Boston · Providence · Hartford · Buffalo · Pittsburgh · Toronto · Ottawa · Montréal · Québec

Tropic of Cancer

Straits of Florida

Key West

Miles	Km
500	800
400	700
	600
300	500
	400
200	300
	200
100	100
0	0

1:12 000 000

© Bartholomew Ltd

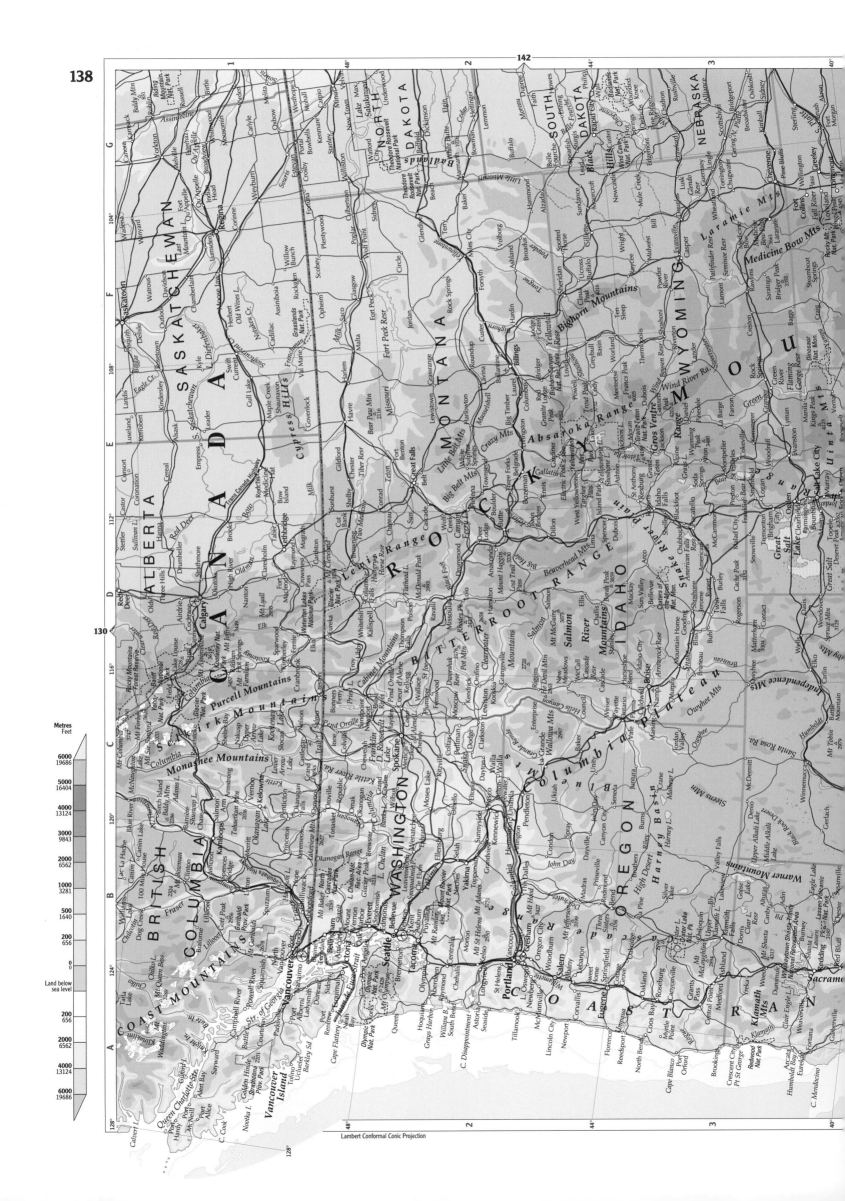
142
130
Metres
Feet
6000
19686
5000
16404
4000
13124
3000
9843
2000
6562
1000
3281
500
1640
200
656
0
0
Land below
sea level
200
656
2000
6562
4000
13124
6000
19686
Lambert Conformal Conic Projection
C A N A D A
ALBERTA
SASKATCHEWAN
BRITISH COLUMBIA
NORTH DAKOTA
SOUTH DAKOTA
NEBRASKA
MONTANA
WYOMING
IDAHO
WASHINGTON
OREGON
COAST MOUNTAINS
ROCKY
BITTERROOT RANGE
Columbia Plateau
Snake River Plain
Vancouver Island
Calgary
Regina
Saskatoon
Vancouver
Victoria
Seattle
Tacoma
Spokane
Portland
Salem
Eugene
Boise
Billings
Great Falls
Salt Lake City
Cheyenne
Kamloops
Kelowna
Lethbridge
Medicine Hat
Moose Jaw
Red Deer
Bighorn Mountains
Absaroka Range
Wind River Ra.
Monashee Mountains
Purcell Mountains
Selkirk Mountains
Cypress Hills
Black Hills
Badlands
Laramie Mts
Medicine Bow Mts
Great Salt Lake
Harney Basin
High Desert
Owyhee Mts
Salmon River Mountains
Blue Mts
Cascade Range
Klamath Mts
Sacramento

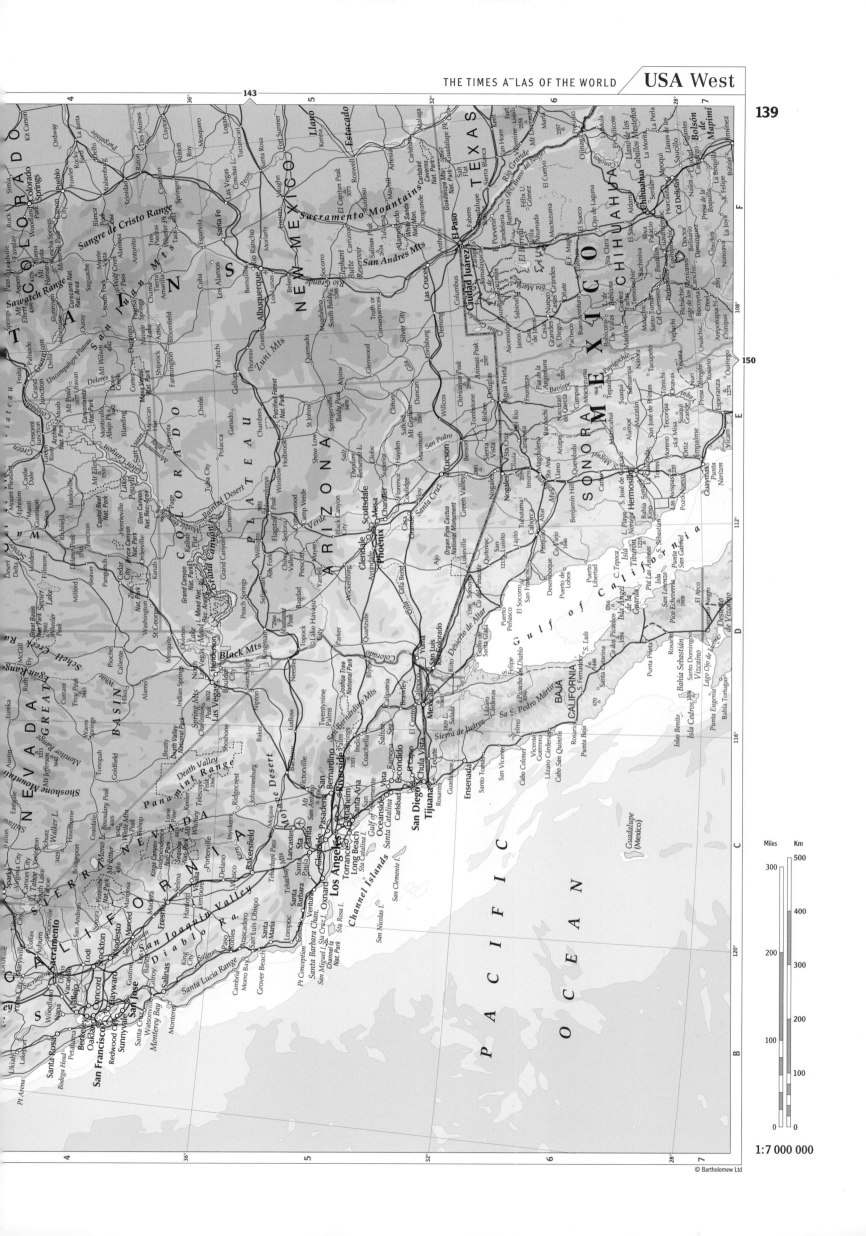
143
150
COLORADO
NEVADA
CALIFORNIA
ARIZONA
NEW MEXICO
TEXAS
MEXICO
SONORA
CHIHUAHUA
BAJA CALIFORNIA
GREAT BASIN
COLORADO PLATEAU
SIERRA NEVADA
PACIFIC OCEAN
Gulf of California
Channel Islands
Mojave Desert
Death Valley
San Joaquin Valley
Sangre de Cristo Range
San Juan Mts
Sacramento Mountains
San Andres Mts
Llano Estacado
Bolsón de Mapimí
Grand Canyon
Lake Powell
Painted Desert
San Francisco
Oakland
San Jose
Sacramento
Stockton
Modesto
Fresno
Bakersfield
Los Angeles
Long Beach
Riverside
San Bernardino
Santa Ana
San Diego
Tijuana
Mexicali
Ensenada
Las Vegas
Henderson
Phoenix
Mesa
Scottsdale
Glendale
Tucson
Yuma
Flagstaff
Albuquerque
Santa Fe
El Paso
Ciudad Juárez
Chihuahua
Hermosillo
Guaymas
Nogales
Colorado Springs
Pueblo
Miles
Km
0
100
200
300
400
500
1:7 000 000
© Bartholomew Ltd

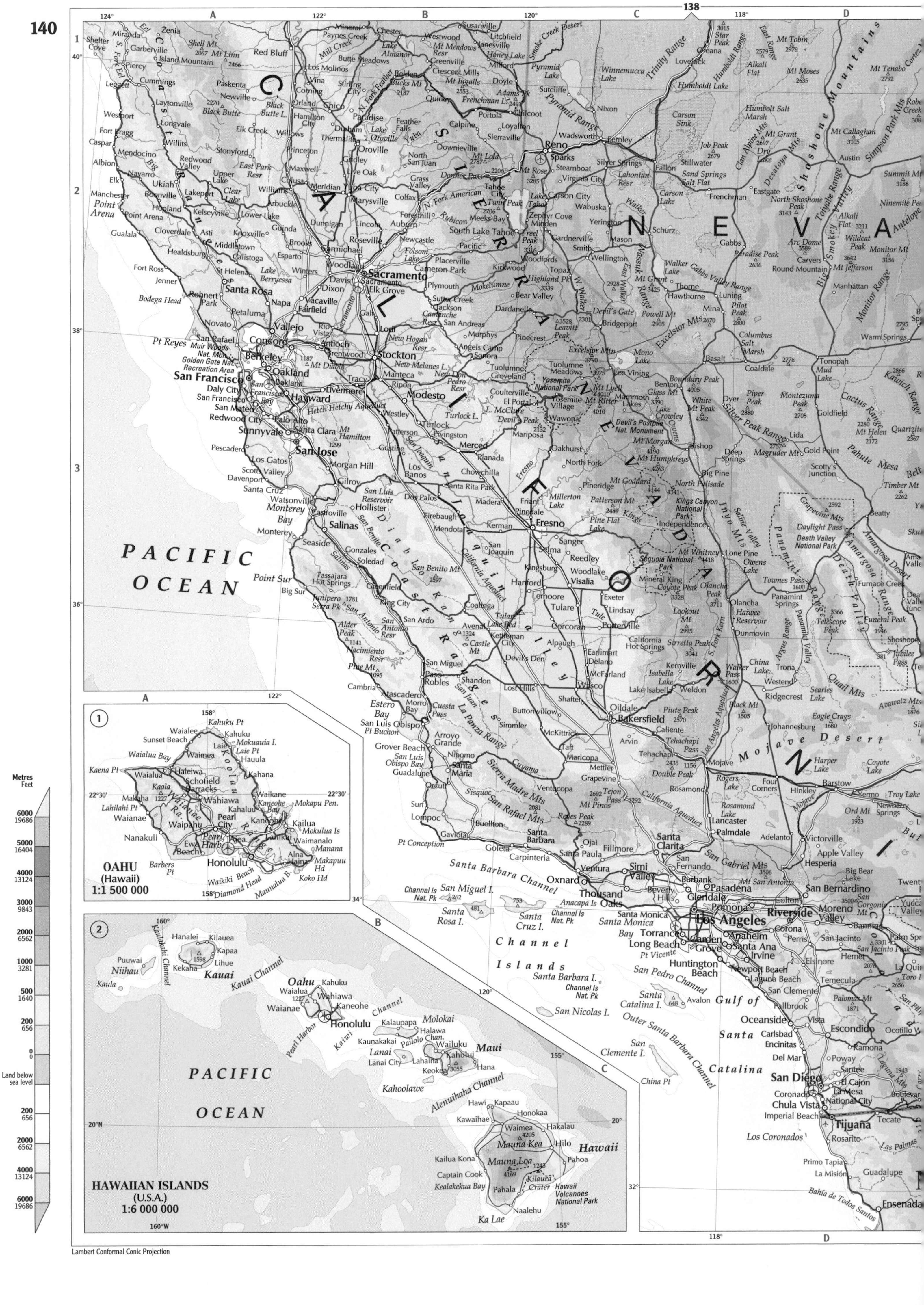

PACIFIC
OCEAN

PACIFIC
OCEAN

OAHU
(Hawaii)
1:1 500 000

HAWAIIAN ISLANDS
(U.S.A.)
1:6 000 000

Metres
Feet

6000
19686

5000
16404

4000
13124

3000
9843

2000
6562

1000
3281

500
1640

200
656

0
0

Land below
sea level

200
656

2000
6562

4000
13124

6000
19686

Lambert Conformal Conic Projection

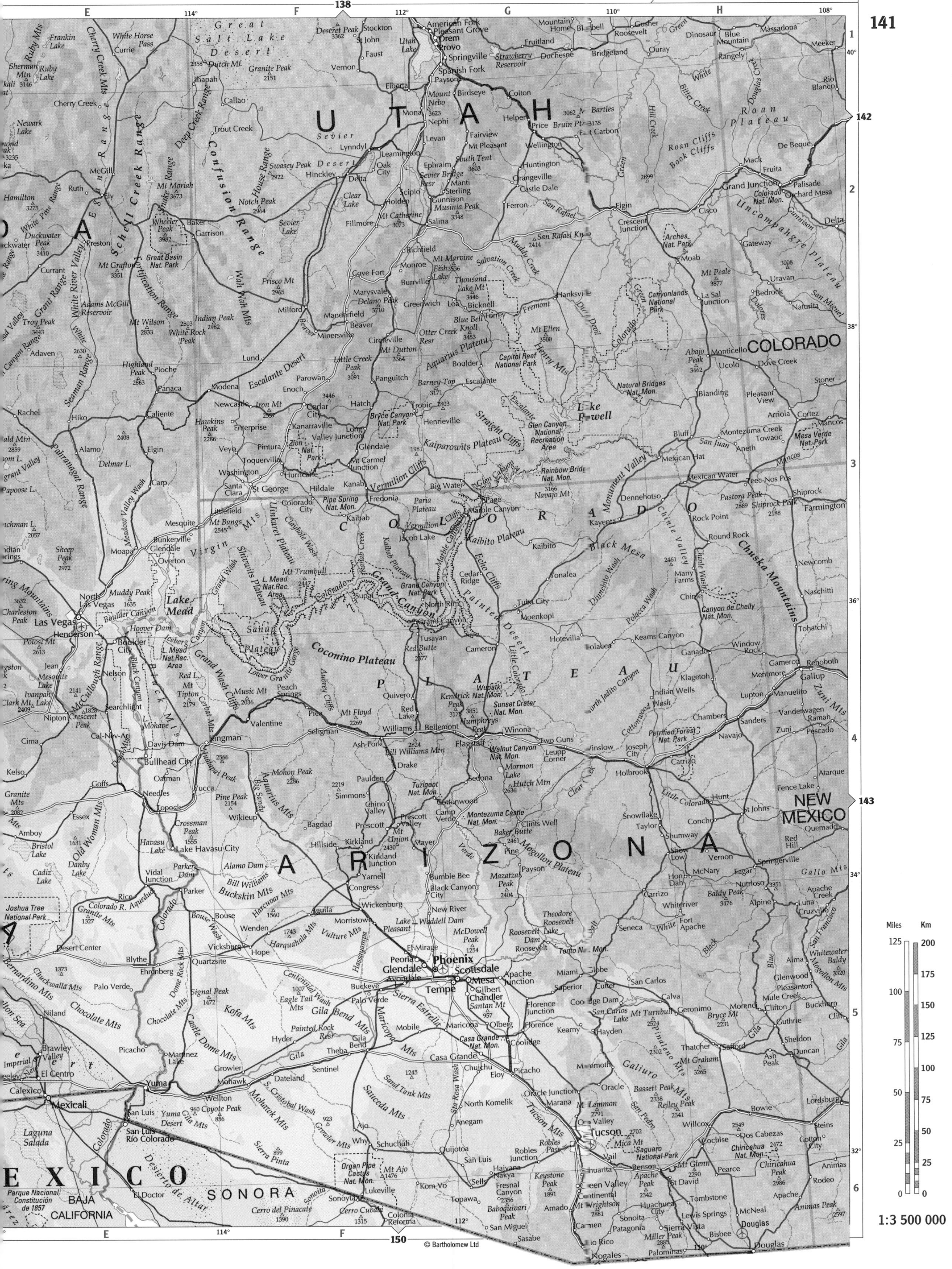
E
F
G
H
114°
112°
110°
108°
138
142
143
150
40°
38°
36°
34°
32°
1
2
3
4
5
6
UTAH
COLORADO
NEW MEXICO
ARIZONA
MEXICO
SONORA
BAJA CALIFORNIA
COLORADO PLATEAU
Great Salt Lake Desert
Sevier Desert
Escalante Desert
Painted Desert
Little Colorado
Lake Powell
Lake Mead
Grand Canyon
Coconino Plateau
Kaibab Plateau
Kaiparowits Plateau
Aquarius Plateau
Mogollon Plateau
Black Mesa
Chuska Mountains
Roan Plateau
Uncompahgre Plateau
Roan Cliffs
Book Cliffs
Vermilion Cliffs
Echo Cliffs
Straight Cliffs
Henry Mts
Confusion Range
House Range
Wah Wah Mts
Snake Range
Schell Creek Range
Deep Creek Range
Grand Wash Cliffs
Virgin Mts
Black Mts
Hualapai Peak
Aquarius Mts
Bill Williams Mts
Buckskin Mts
Harcuvar Mts
Harquahala Mts
Vulture Mts
Gila Bend Mts
Maricopa Mts
Sierra Estrella
Sand Tank Mts
Sauceda Mts
Growler Mts
Mohawk Mts
Castle Dome Mts
Kofa Mts
Chocolate Mts
Galiuro Mts
Pinaleno Mts
Chiricahua Peak
Desierto de Altar
Salt Lake City
Provo
Orem
Spanish Fork
Nephi
Delta
Richfield
Salina
Manti
Price
Helper
Green River
Moab
Monticello
Blanding
Bluff
Mexican Hat
Cedar City
St George
Kanab
Page
Tuba City
Kayenta
Flagstaff
Williams
Sedona
Prescott
Kingman
Bullhead City
Lake Havasu City
Parker
Yuma
Phoenix
Glendale
Scottsdale
Mesa
Tempe
Chandler
Casa Grande
Tucson
Nogales
Douglas
Bisbee
Tombstone
Benson
Willcox
Safford
Globe
Show Low
Holbrook
Winslow
St Johns
Springerville
Gallup
Farmington
Shiprock
Grand Junction
Delta
Cortez
Durango
Las Vegas
North Las Vegas
Henderson
Boulder City
Mesquite
Caliente
Pioche
Ely
Mexicali
Calexico
El Centro
San Luis Rio Colorado
Canyonlands National Park
Arches Nat. Park
Capitol Reef National Park
Bryce Canyon Nat. Park
Zion Nat. Park
Grand Canyon Nat. Park
Glen Canyon National Recreation Area
Great Basin Nat. Park
Petrified Forest Nat. Park
Saguaro National Park
Organ Pipe Cactus Nat. Mon.
Chiricahua Nat. Mon.
Canyon de Chelly Nat. Mon.
Natural Bridges Nat. Mon.
Rainbow Bridge Nat. Mon.
Mesa Verde Nat. Park
Joshua Tree National Park
Parque Nacional Constitución de 1857
Mt Graham 3265
Humphreys Peak 3851
Mt Peale 3877
© Bartholomew Ltd
Miles
Km
1:3 500 000

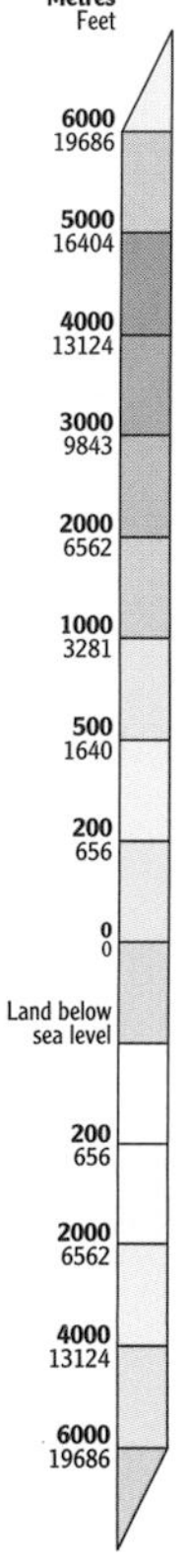

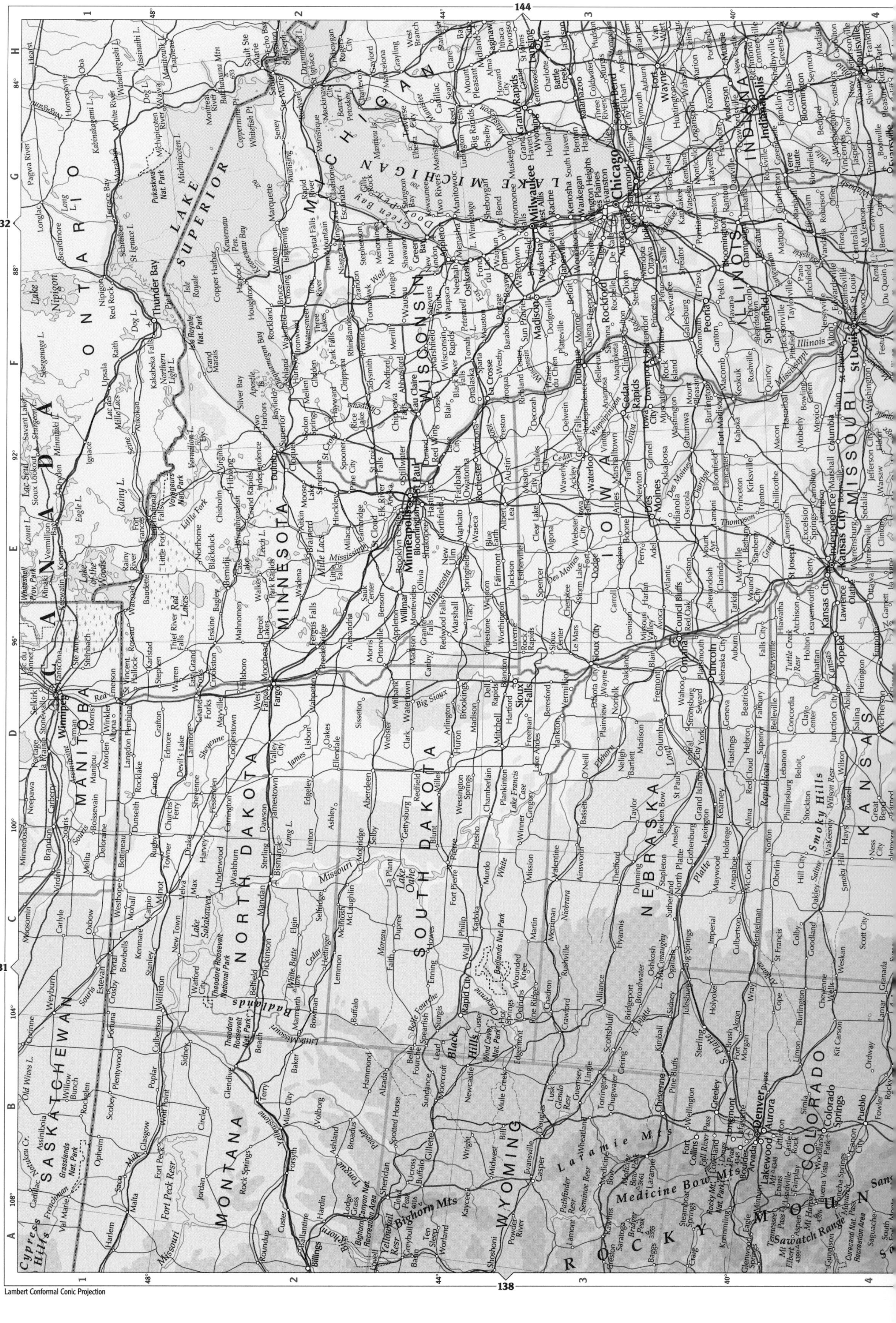

Lambert Conformal Conic Projection

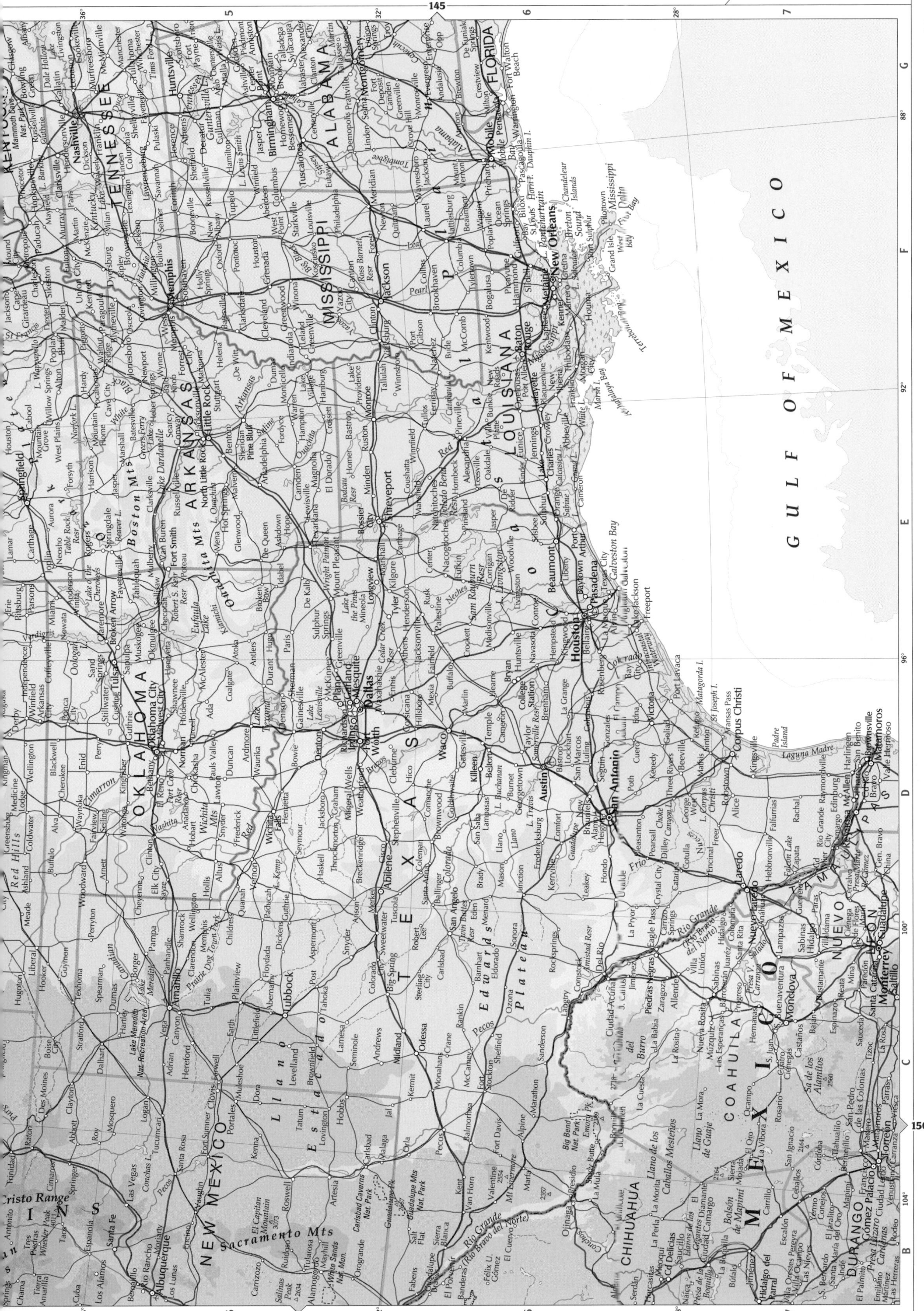

KENTUCKY
TENNESSEE
ALABAMA
FLORIDA
MISSISSIPPI
ARKANSAS
LOUISIANA
OKLAHOMA
TEXAS
NEW MEXICO
COAHUILA
NUEVO LEON
CHIHUAHUA
DURANGO
MEXICO

GULF OF MEXICO

Nashville, Memphis, Little Rock, North Little Rock, Pine Bluff, Birmingham, Huntsville, Mobile, New Orleans, Baton Rouge, Jackson, Shreveport, Monroe, Texarkana, Tulsa, Oklahoma City, Norman, Dallas, Fort Worth, Waco, Austin, San Antonio, Houston, Pasadena, Beaumont, Corpus Christi, Laredo, Nuevo Laredo, Matamoros, Brownsville, McAllen, Monterrey, Saltillo, Albuquerque, Santa Fe, Amarillo, Lubbock, Midland, Odessa, Wichita Falls, Abilene

Sangre de Cristo Range
Sacramento Mts
Guadalupe Mts
Edwards Plateau
Llano Estacado
Ozark Plateau
Boston Mts
Ouachita Mts
Rio Grande (Rio Bravo del Norte)
Big Bend Nat. Park
Carlsbad Caverns Nat. Park
Laguna Madre
Padre Island

Miles Km
300   500
       400
200   300
       200
100   100
0   0

1:7 000 000

© Bartholomew Ltd

145 139 150 143

ROCKY MOUNTAINS

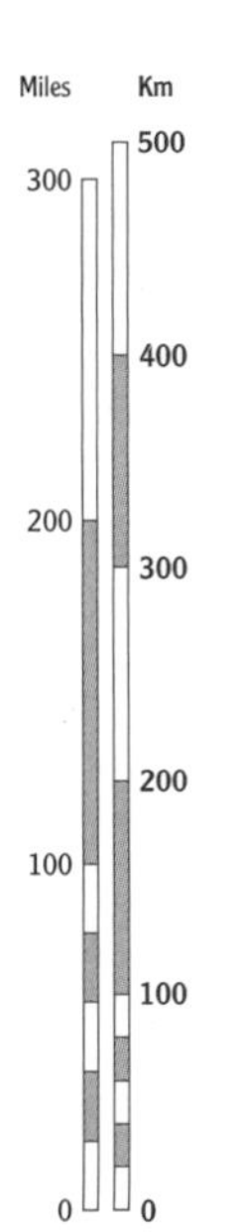

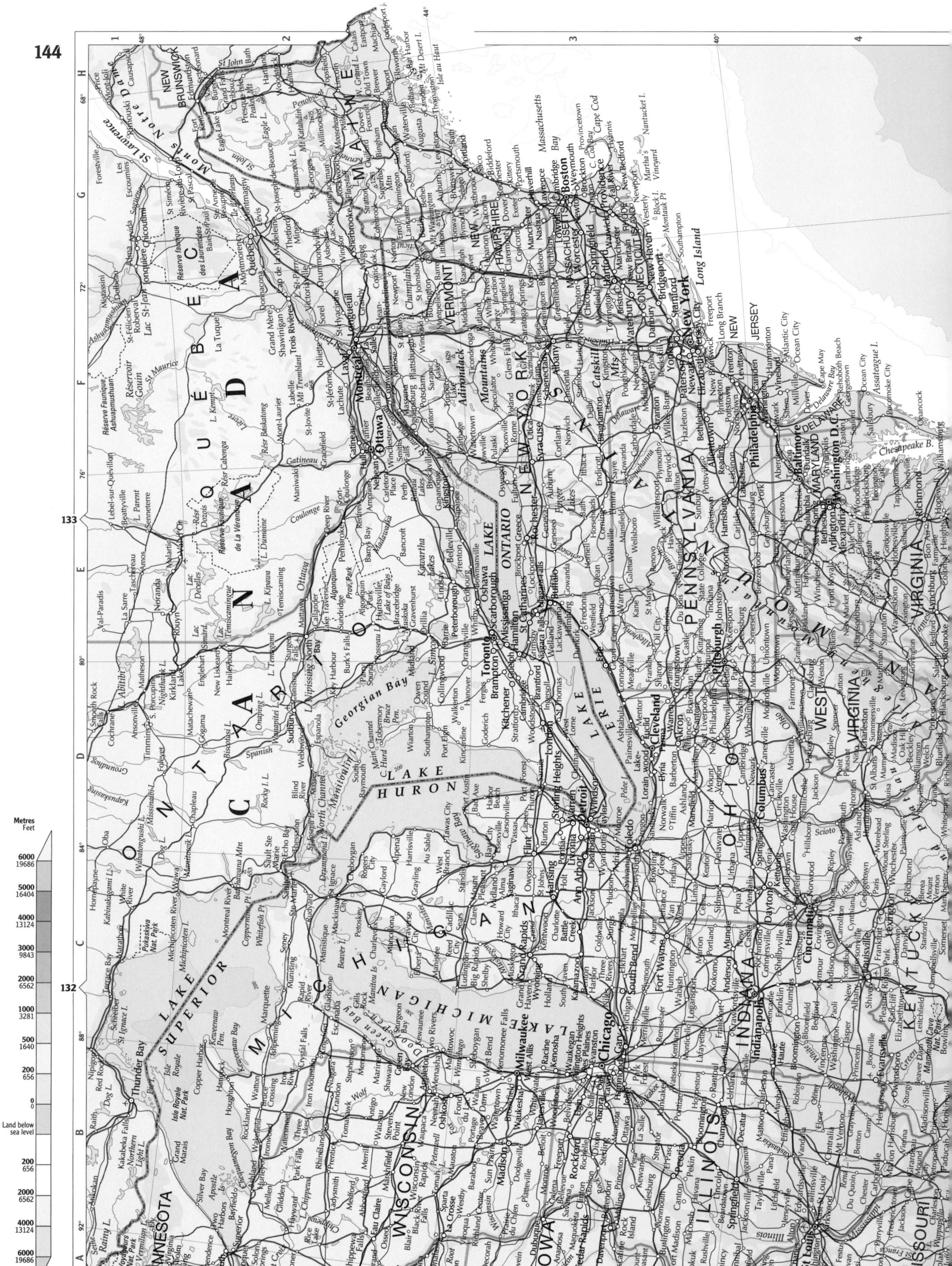

Metres
Feet

6000
19686

5000
16404

4000
13124

3000
9843

2000
6562

1000
3281

500
1640

200
656

0
0

Land below
sea level

200
656

2000
6562

4000
13124

6000
19686

Lambert Conformal Conic Projection

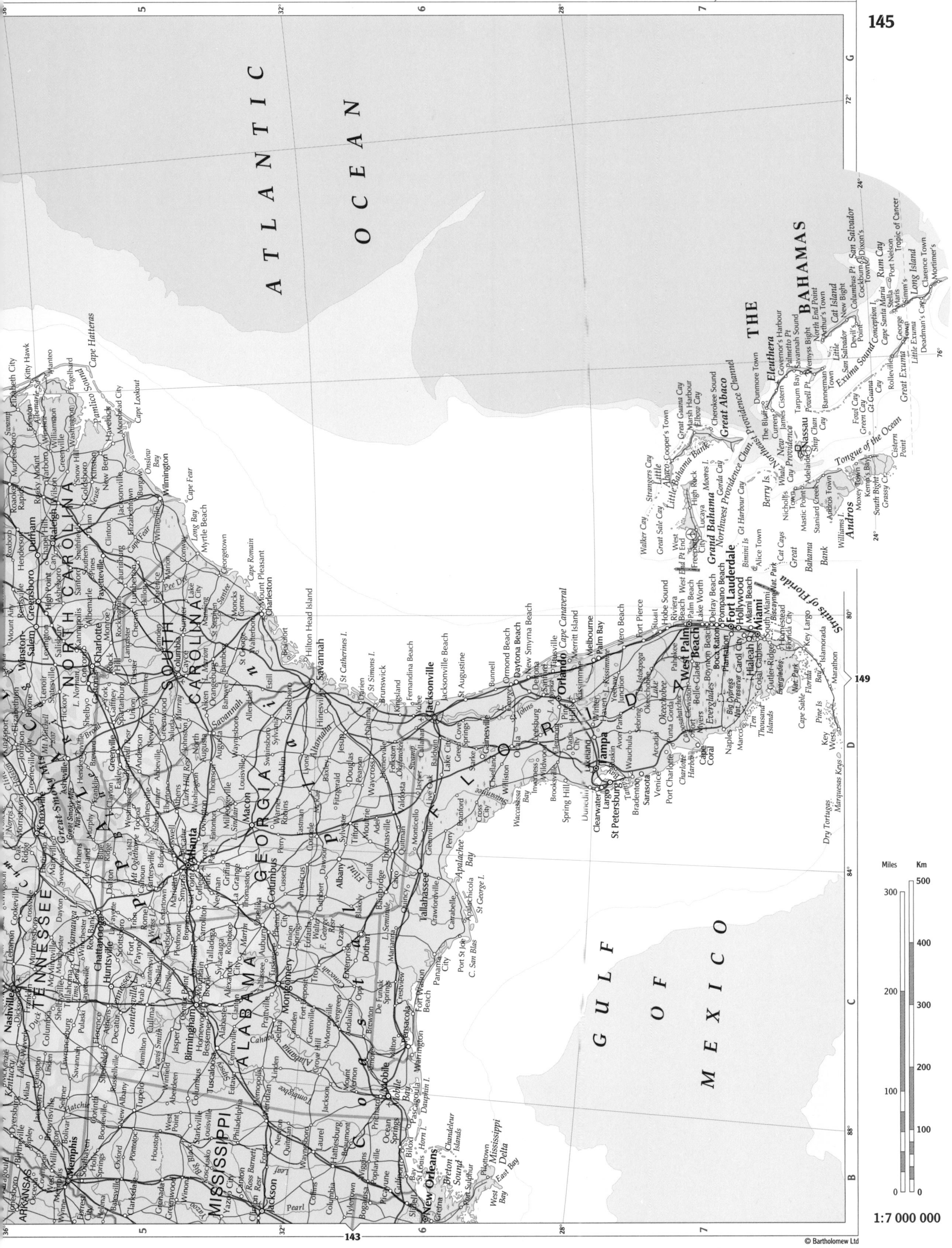

A T L A N T I C

O C E A N

G U L F

O F

M E X I C O

THE BAHAMAS

NORTH CAROLINA

SOUTH CAROLINA

GEORGIA

FLORIDA

ALABAMA

MISSISSIPPI

TENNESSEE

ARKANSAS

Miles	Km
300	500
	400
200	300
	200
100	100
0	0

1:7 000 000

© Bartholomew Ltd

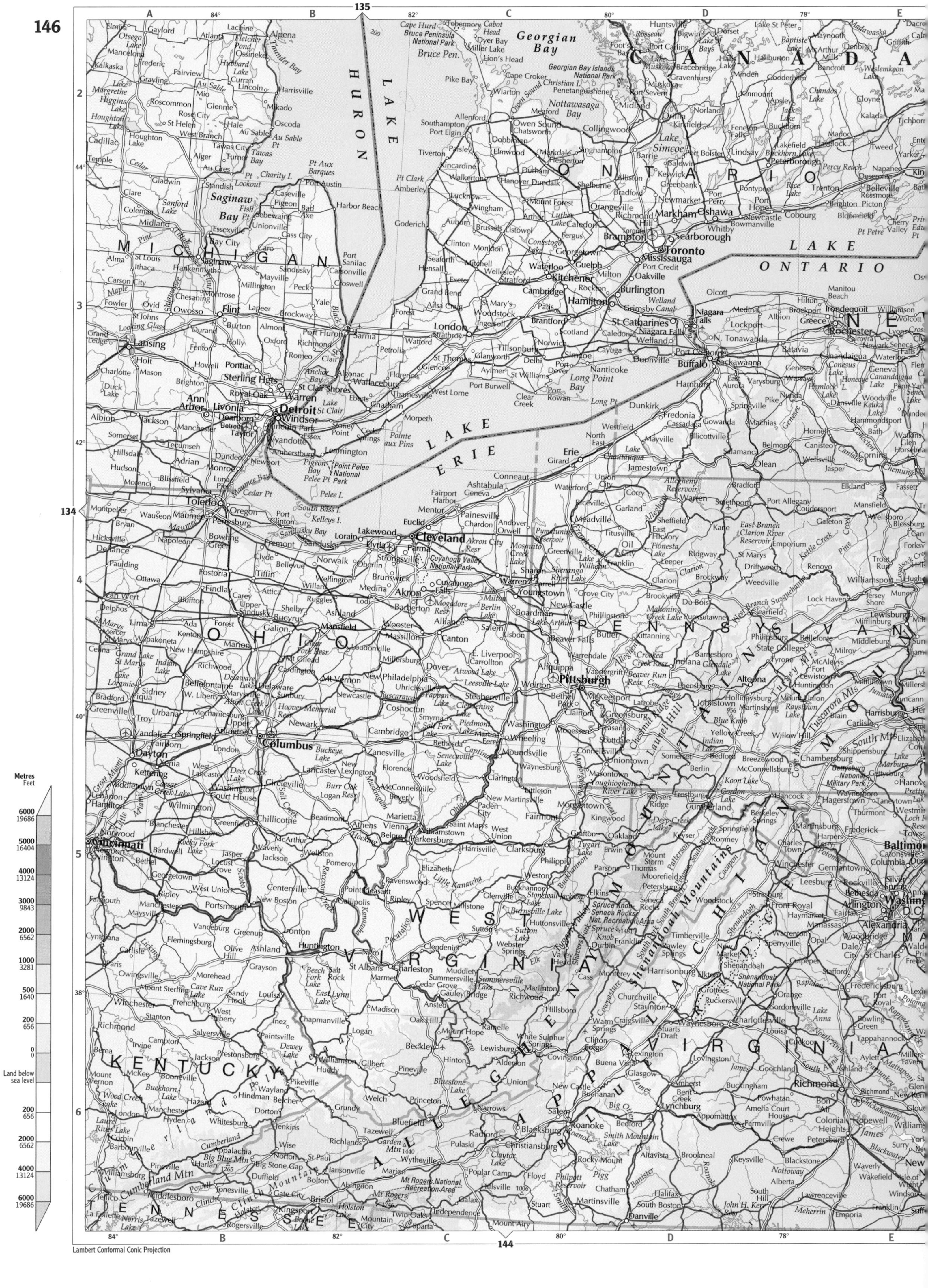

Lambert Conformal Conic Projection

1:3 500 000

1:3 500 000

© Bartholomew Ltd

QUÉBEC
NEW YORK
VERMONT
NEW HAMPSHIRE
MAINE
MASSACHUSETTS
CONNECTICUT
RHODE ISLAND
NEW JERSEY
DELAWARE
CANADA
NEW BRUNSWICK
ATLANTIC OCEAN
Lake Champlain
Adirondack Mountains
Catskill Mountains
Green Mountains
White Mountains
Long Island Sound
Block Island Sound
Long Island
Massachusetts Bay
Cape Cod Bay
Cape Cod
Nantucket Sound
Nantucket Island
Martha's Vineyard
Buzzards Bay
Delaware Bay
Chesapeake Bay
Boston
New York
Philadelphia
Albany
Hartford
Providence
Springfield
Worcester
Portland
Manchester
Concord
Syracuse
Burlington
Bangor
Augusta
Trenton
Newark
Atlantic City
Norfolk
Virginia Beach
Portsmouth
Chesapeake
Acadia Nat. Park
Fire Island National Seashore
Cape Cod National Seashore
Gateway National Recreational Area
Assateague Island National Seashore
Delaware Water Gap Nat. Rec. Area
Chamberlain Lake
Moosehead Lake
Mt Katahdin
Miles
Km
25
75
100
125
150
175
200

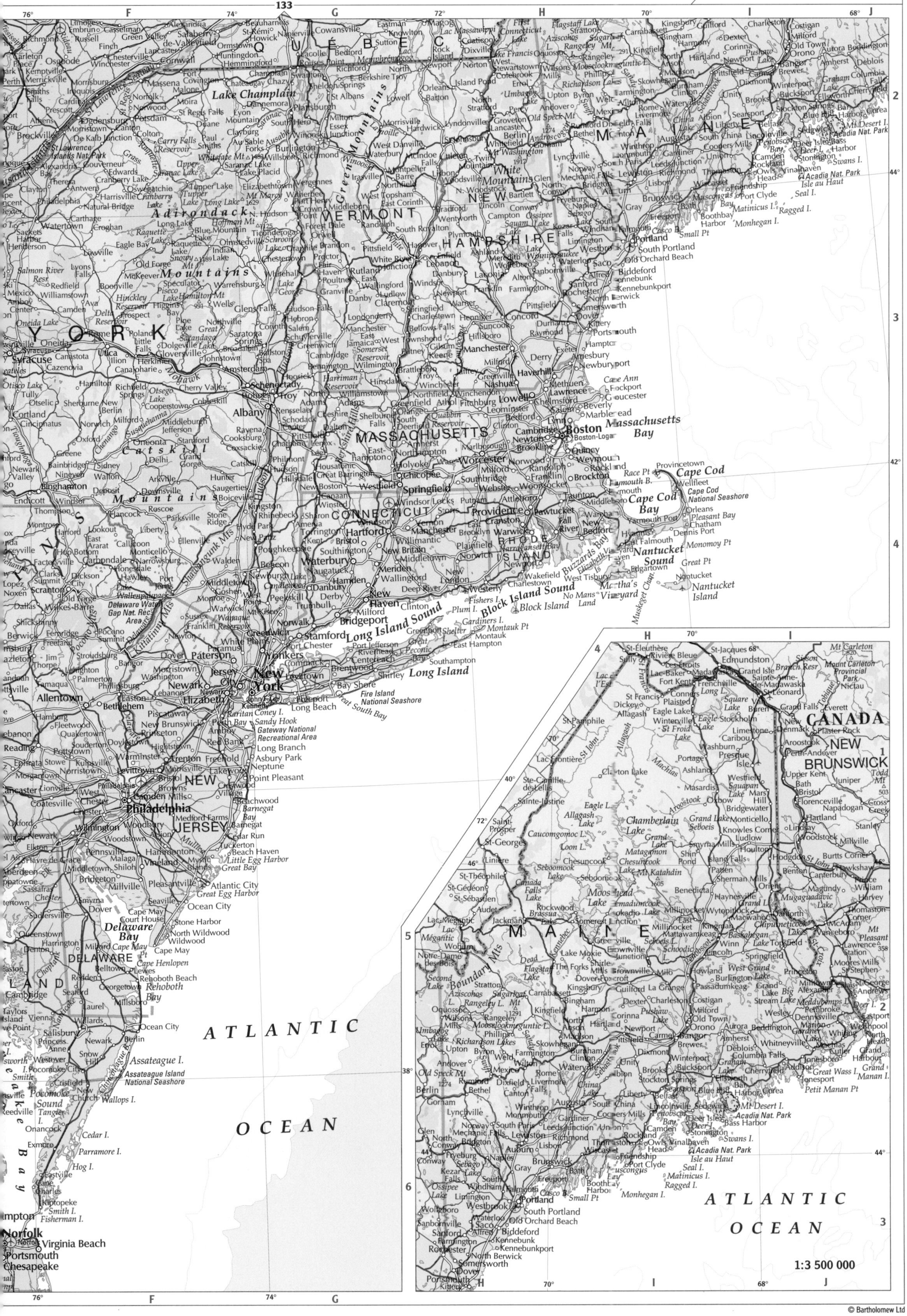

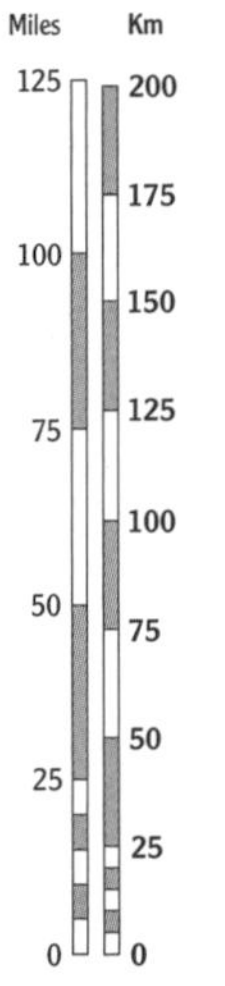

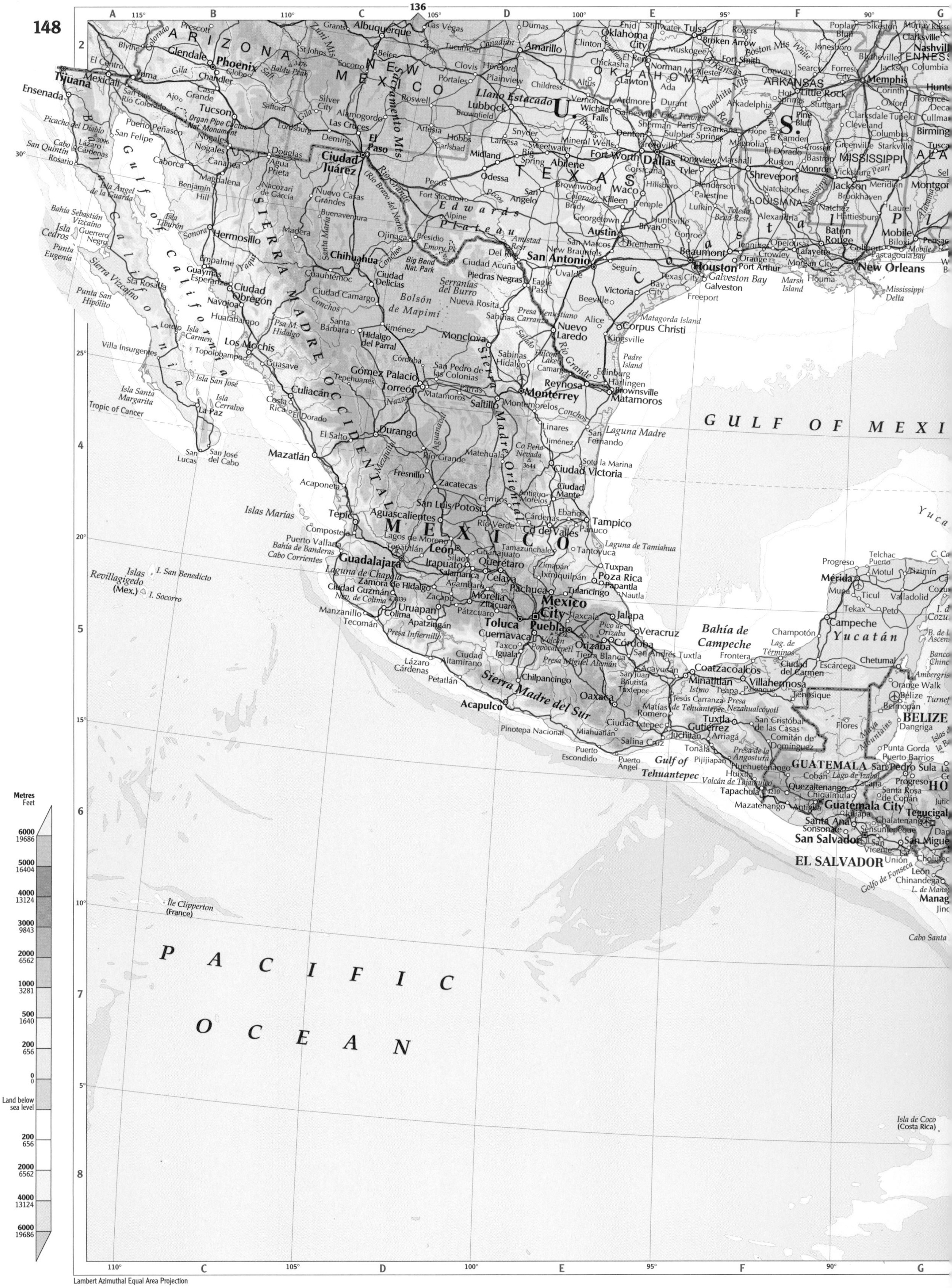

136

A 115° B 110° C 105° D 100° E 95° F 90° G

PACIFIC

OCEAN

GULF OF MEXI

Metres
Feet

6000
19686

5000
16404

4000
13124

3000
9843

2000
6562

1000
3281

500
1640

200
656

0
0

Land below
sea level

200
656

2000
6562

4000
13124

6000
19686

Lambert Azimuthal Equal Area Projection

110° 105° 100° 95° 90°
C D E F G

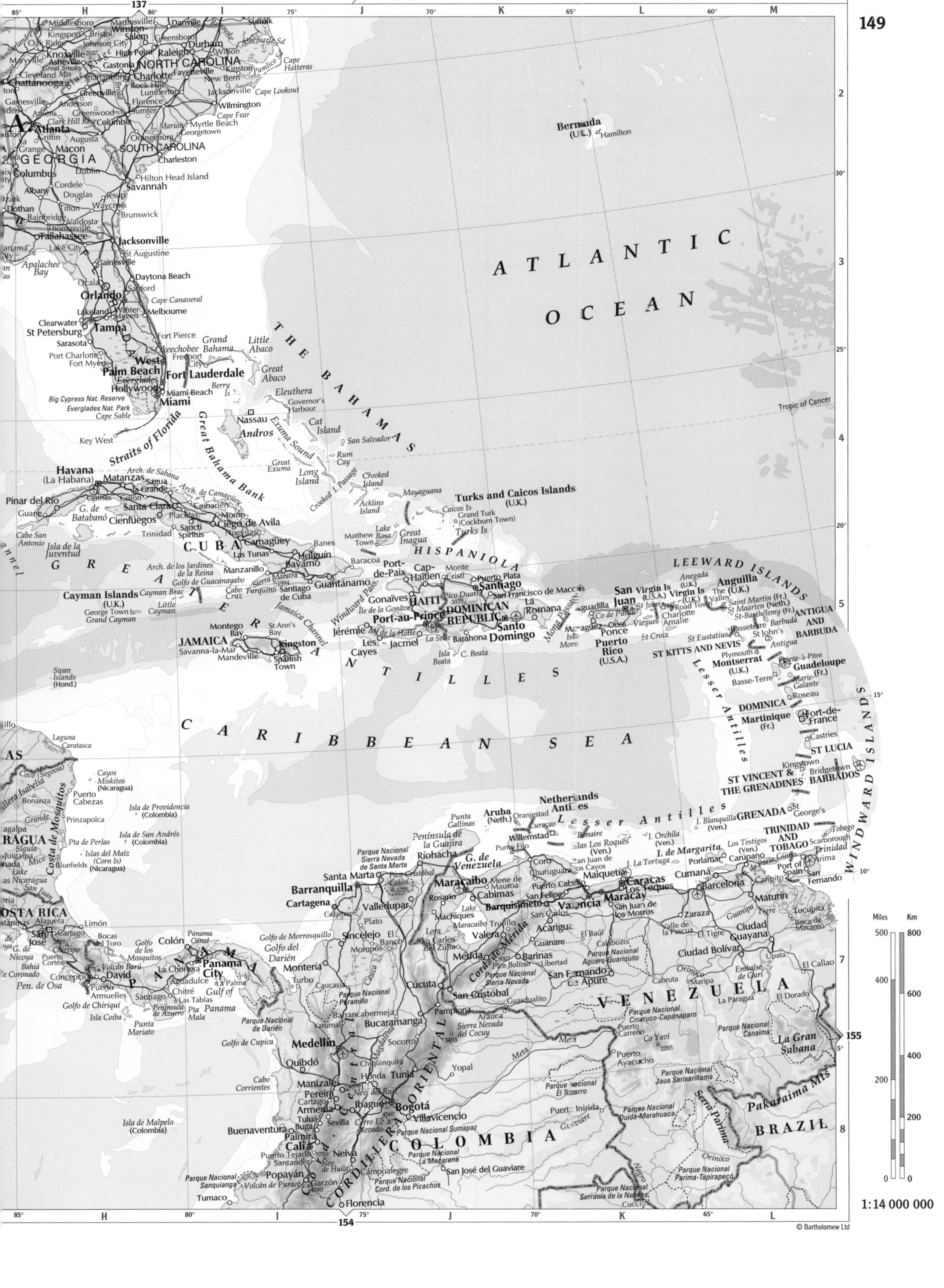
ATLANTIC OCEAN
CARIBBEAN SEA
GREATER ANTILLES
THE BAHAMAS
Lesser Antilles
LEEWARD ISLANDS
WINDWARD ISLANDS
Tropic of Cancer
NORTH CAROLINA
SOUTH CAROLINA
GEORGIA
CUBA
HISPANIOLA
HAITI
DOMINICAN REPUBLIC
JAMAICA
Cayman Islands (U.K.)
Turks and Caicos Islands (U.K.)
Bermuda (U.K.)
Hamilton
Puerto Rico (U.S.A.)
San Juan
Netherlands Antilles
Aruba (Neth.)
ANTIGUA AND BARBUDA
ST KITTS AND NEVIS
DOMINICA
Guadeloupe (Fr.)
Martinique (Fr.)
ST LUCIA
ST VINCENT & THE GRENADINES
BARBADOS
GRENADA
TRINIDAD AND TOBAGO
VENEZUELA
COLOMBIA
PANAMA
BRAZIL
Havana (La Habana)
Miami
Nassau
Kingston
Port-au-Prince
Santo Domingo
Caracas
Bogotá
Panama City
Maracaibo
Barranquilla
Medellín
Cali
Straits of Florida
Windward Passage
Mona Passage
Jamaica Channel
Great Bahama Bank
Miles
Km

1:14 000 000

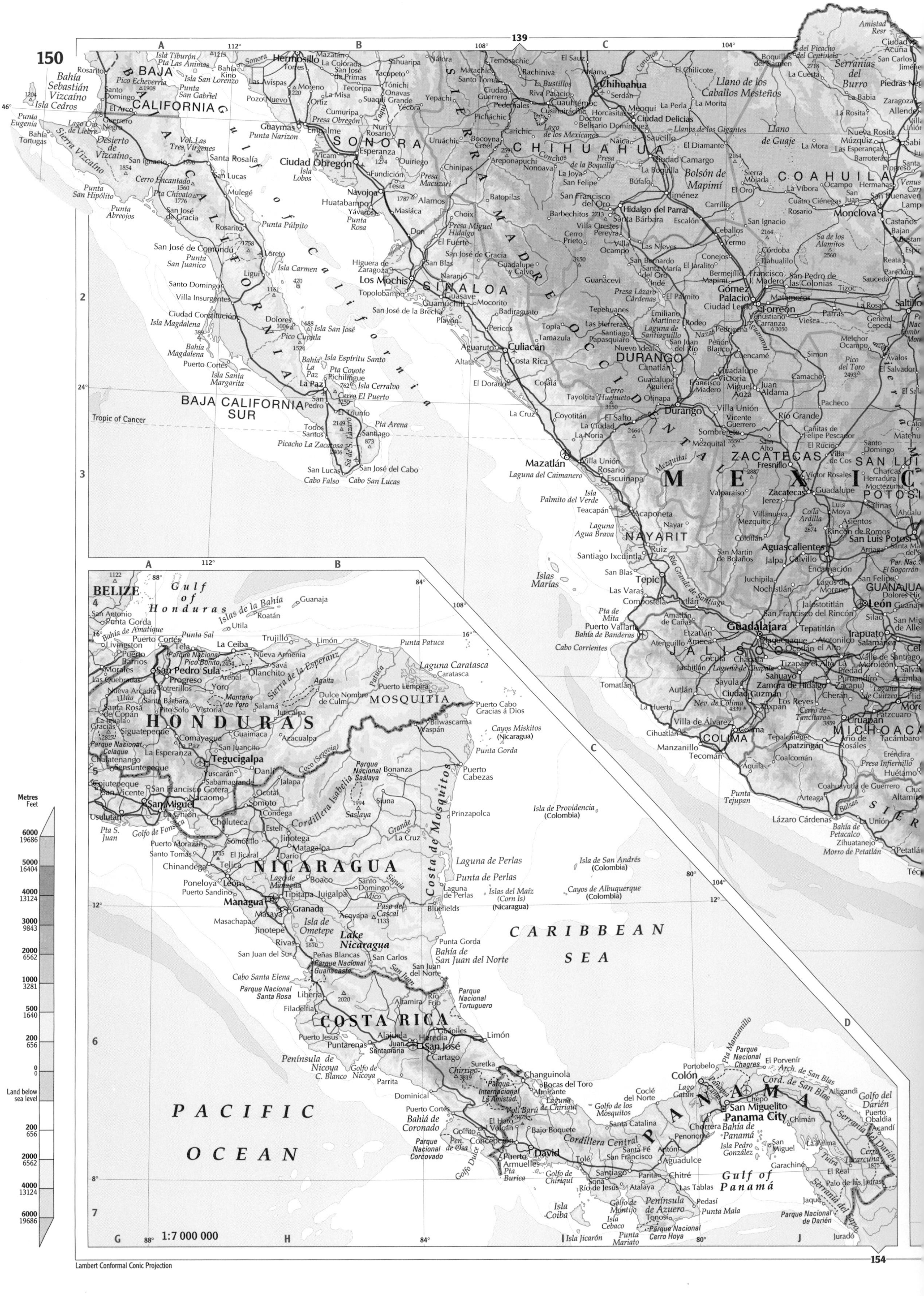

PACIFIC

OCEAN

CARIBBEAN

SEA

BAJA

CALIFORNIA

SONORA

CHIHUAHUA

COAHUILA

SINALOA

DURANGO

BAJA CALIFORNIA
SUR

M E X I C O

ZACATECAS

SAN LUI
POTOSI

NAYARIT

GUANAJUA

JALISCO

COLIMA

MICHOAC

BELIZE

Gulf
of
Honduras

HONDURAS

MOSQUITIA

Tegucigalpa

NICARAGUA

Lake
Nicaragua

Managua

COSTA RICA

San José

PANAMA

Panama City

Tropic of Cancer

Metres
Feet

6000
19686

5000
16404

4000
13124

3000
9843

2000
6562

1000
3281

500
1640

200
656

0

Land below
sea level

200
656

2000
6562

4000
13124

6000
19686

1:7 000 000

Lambert Conformal Conic Projection

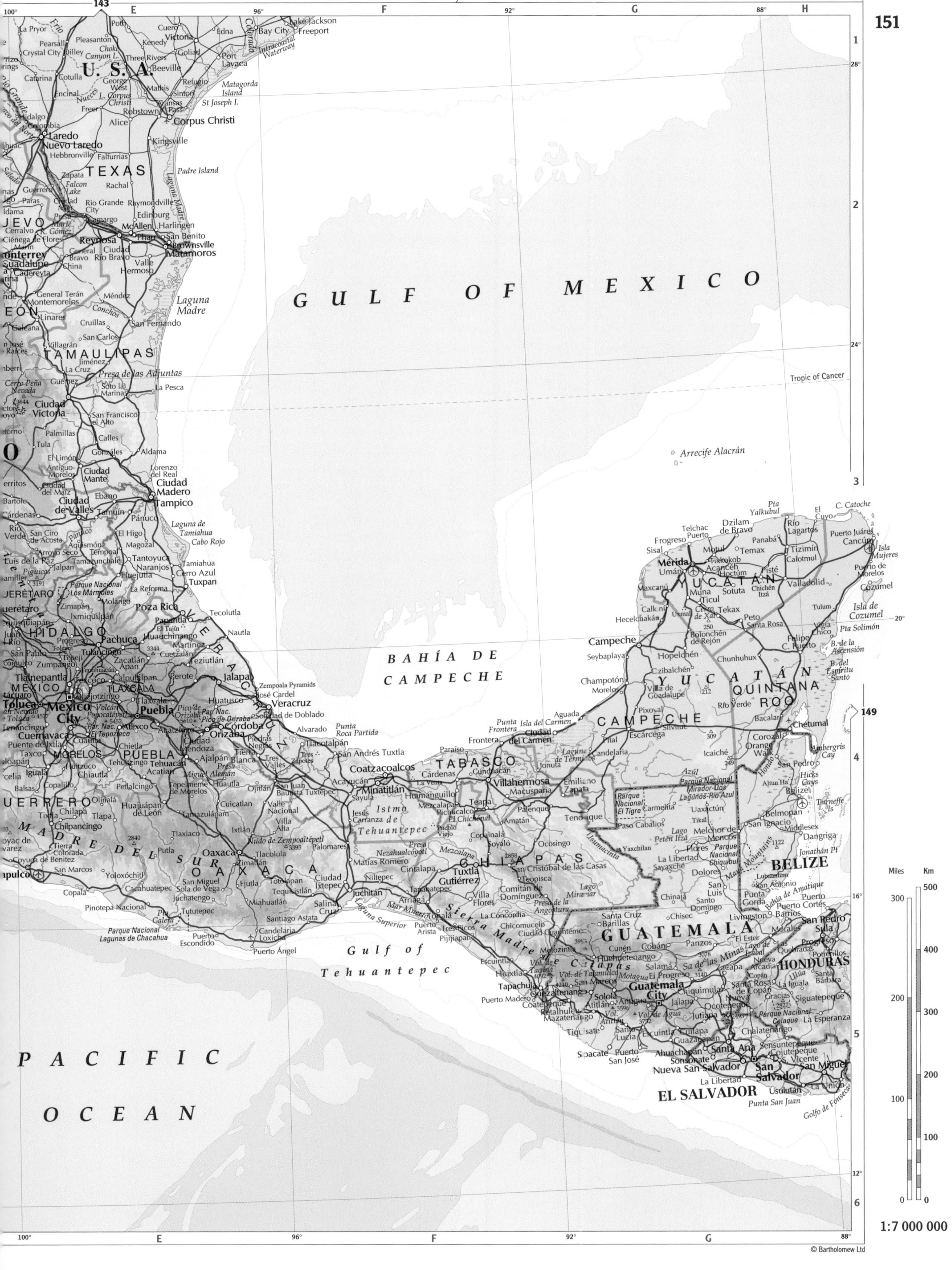

GULF OF MEXICO

U.S.A.

TEXAS

TAMAULIPAS

BAHÍA DE CAMPECHE

GUATEMALA

HONDURAS

EL SALVADOR

BELIZE

YUCATÁN

QUINTANA ROO

CAMPECHE

TABASCO

CHIAPAS

OAXACA

PUEBLA

MORELOS

GUERRERO

HIDALGO

VERACRUZ

TLAXCALA

Mexico City

PACIFIC OCEAN

Gulf of Tehuantepec

149

Miles   Km
300   500

200   400
        300

        200
100
        100
0   0

1 : 7 000 000

© Bartholomew Ltd

A B C D E F G

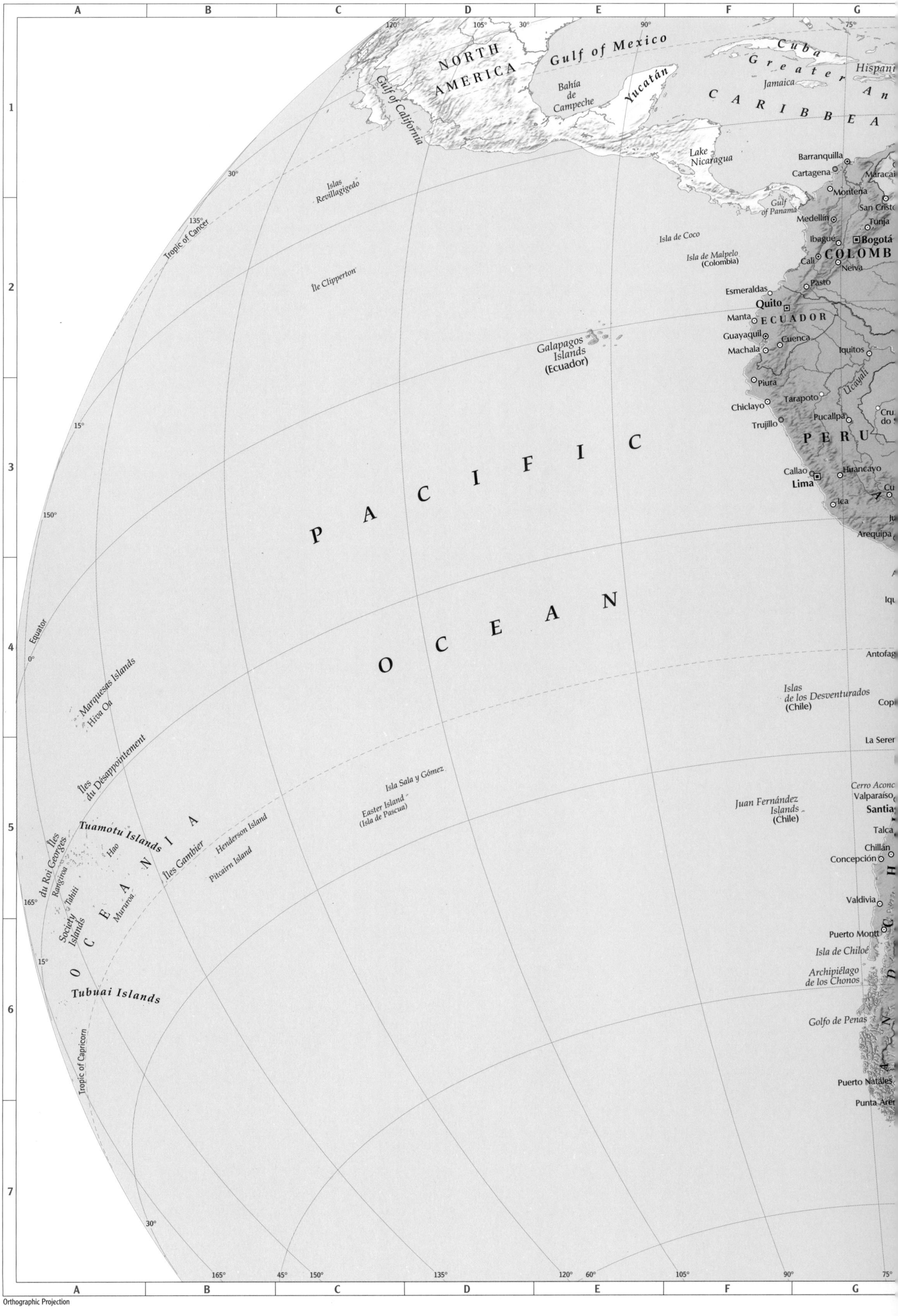

NORTH
AMERICA

Gulf of Mexico

Cuba

Greater

Hispan

CARIBBEA

Jamaica

Gulf of California

Bahía
de
Campeche

Yucatán

Lake
Nicaragua

Barranquilla

Cartagena

Maracai

Monteria

San Crist

Gulf
of Panama

Medellín

Turja

Ibagué

Bogotá

Islas
Revillagigedo

Isla de Coco

Isla de Malpelo
(Colombia)

COLOMB

Cali

Neiva

Tropic of Cancer

Esmeraldas

Pasto

Quito

Île Clipperton

Manta

ECUADOR

Guayaquil

Cuenca

Machala

Iquitos

Galapagos
Islands
(Ecuador)

Piura

Ucayali

Tarapoto

Chiclayo

Pucallpa

Cru

do

Trujillo

P E R U

Callao

Huancayo

Cu

Lima

A

Ica

15°

P A C I F I C

150°

Antofag

O C E A N

Islas
de los Desventurados
(Chile)

Copi

Equator

Marquesas Islands

Hiva Oa

La Seren

Îles
du Désappointement

Isla Sala y Gómez

Cerro Aconc

Valparaíso

Easter Island
(Isla de Pascua)

Juan Fernández
Islands
(Chile)

Santia

O C E A N I A

Tuamotu Islands

Henderson Island

Talca

Chillán

Îles
du Roi Georges

Îles

Hao

Îles Gambier

Concepción

Rangiroa

Pitcairn Island

165°

Tahiti

Mururoa

Valdivia

Society
Islands

Puerto Montt

15°

Isla de Chiloé

O C E A N I A

Archipiélago
de los Chonos

Tubuai Islands

Golfo de Penas

Tropic of Capricorn

Puerto Natales

Punta Aren

30°

165° 45° 150° 135° 120° 60° 105° 90°

A B C D E F G

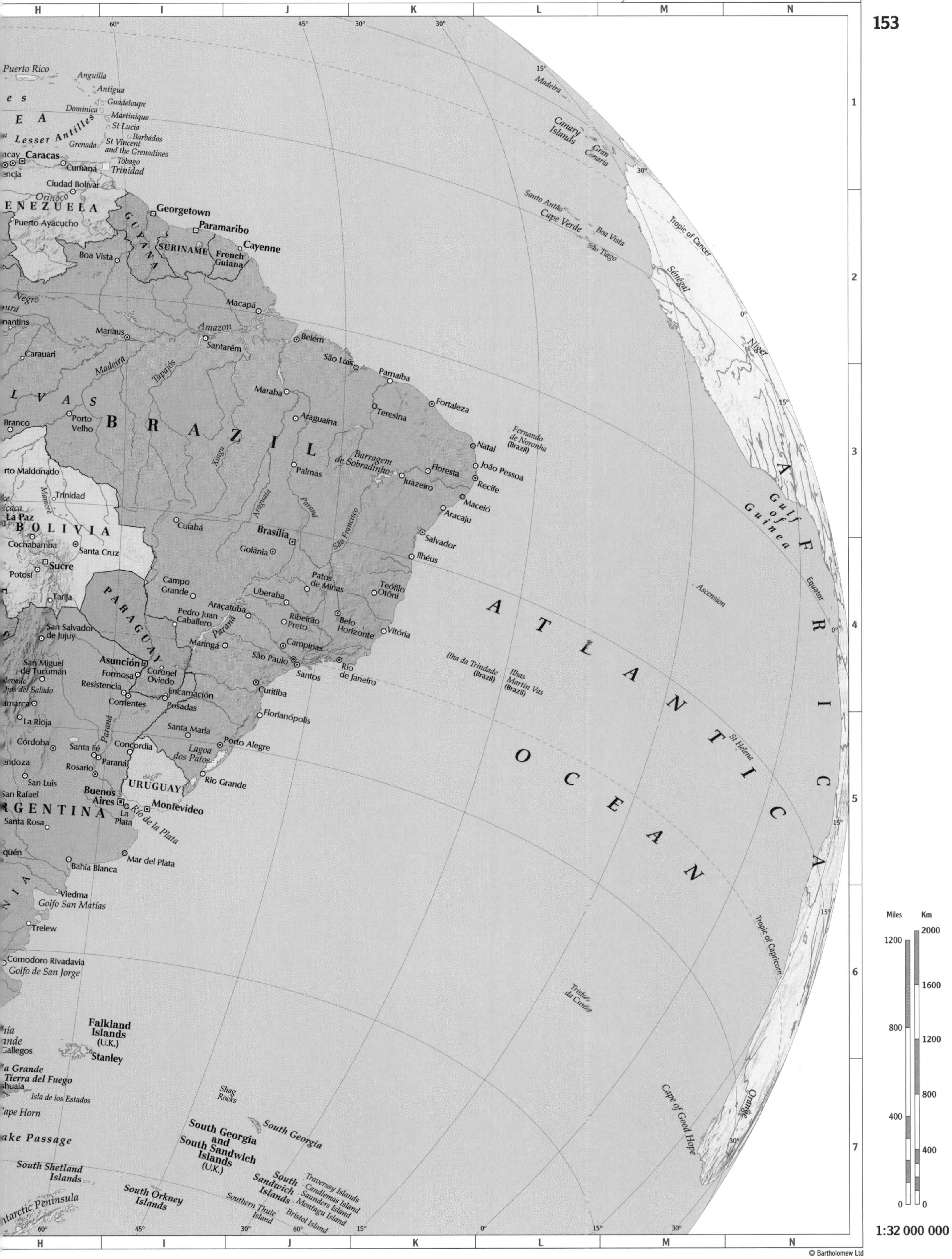
Puerto Rico
Anguilla
Antigua
Guadeloupe
Dominica
Martinique
St Lucia
Lesser Antilles
Barbados
Grenada
St Vincent and the Grenadines
Tobago
Trinidad
Caracas
Cumaná
Ciudad Bolívar
Orinoco
VENEZUELA
Puerto Ayacucho
Georgetown
GUYANA
Paramaribo
SURINAME
Cayenne
French Guiana
Boa Vista
Negro
Macapá
Amazon
Manaus
Santarém
Belém
São Luís
Parnaíba
Carauari
Madeira
Tapajós
Marabá
Fortaleza
Teresina
Araguaína
Porto Velho
Branco
BRAZIL
Xingu
Natal
Barragem de Sobradinho
Palmas
Floresta
João Pessoa
Recife
Juàzeiro
Maceió
Aracaju
Fernando de Noronha (Brazil)
rto Maldonado
Mamoré
Trinidad
La Paz
BOLIVIA
Cuiabá
Araguaia
Paraná
São Francisco
Brasília
Goiânia
Salvador
Ilhéus
Cochabamba
Santa Cruz
Sucre
Potosí
Tarija
Campo Grande
PARAGUAY
Patos de Minas
Uberaba
Teófilo Otôni
Araçatuba
Pedro Juan Caballero
Ribeirão Preto
Belo Horizonte
Vitória
San Salvador de Jujuy
Maringá
Campinas
São Paulo
Rio de Janeiro
Santos
San Miguel de Tucumán
Asunción
Formosa
Coronel Oviedo
Resistencia
Corrientes
Encarnación
Posadas
Curitiba
Florianópolis
La Rioja
Santa Maria
Córdoba
Santa Fé
Concordia
Paraná
Porto Alegre
Rosario
Lagoa dos Patos
San Luis
URUGUAY
Rio Grande
Buenos Aires
Montevideo
La Plata
Río de la Plata
ARGENTINA
Santa Rosa
Mar del Plata
Bahía Blanca
Viedma
Golfo San Matías
Trelew
Comodoro Rivadavia
Golfo de San Jorge
Falkland Islands (U.K.)
Stanley
Tierra del Fuego
Isla de los Estados
Cape Horn
Drake Passage
South Shetland Islands
Antarctic Peninsula
South Orkney Islands
Shag Rocks
South Georgia
South Georgia and South Sandwich Islands (U.K.)
South Sandwich Islands
Traversay Islands
Candlemas Island
Saunders Island
Montagu Island
Bristol Island
Southern Thule Island
Madeira
Canary Islands
Gran Canaria
Santo Antão
Cape Verde
Boa Vista
São Tiago
Tropic of Cancer
Sénégal
Niger
Gulf of Guinea
AFRICA
Equator
Ascension
ATLANTIC OCEAN
Ilha da Trindade (Brazil)
Ilhas Martin Vas (Brazil)
St Helena
Tropic of Capricorn
Tristan da Cunha
Cape of Good Hope
Orange
Miles
Km
1:32 000 000

© Bartholomew Ltd

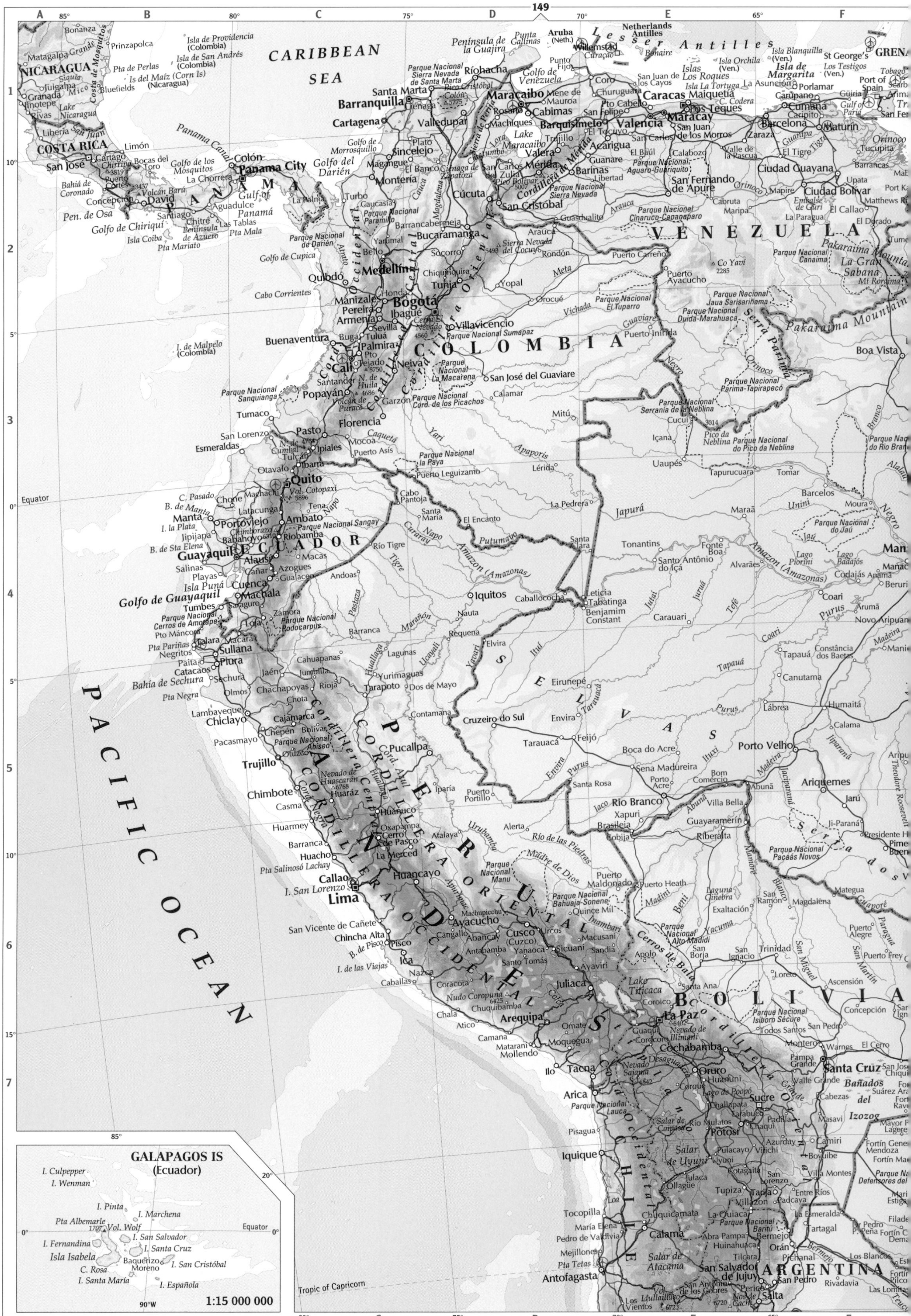

149

Map labels

CARIBBEAN SEA

PACIFIC OCEAN

NICARAGUA
COSTA RICA
PANAMA
COLOMBIA
ECUADOR
PERU
VENEZUELA
BOLIVIA
ARGENTINA

Lesser Antilles

Netherlands Antilles

Selected place names: San José, Limón, Colón, Panama City, Panamá, David, Cartagena, Barranquilla, Santa Marta, Maracaibo, Cabimas, Caracas, Maracay, Valencia, Barquisimeto, Barcelona, Cumaná, Maturín, Mérida, San Cristóbal, Cúcuta, Bucaramanga, Medellín, Quibdó, Bogotá, Manizales, Pereira, Armenia, Ibagué, Cali, Buenaventura, Popayán, Pasto, Florencia, Villavicencio, Puerto Carreño, Ciudad Bolívar, Ciudad Guayana, San Fernando de Apure, Boa Vista, Tumaco, Esmeraldas, Quito, Manta, Portoviejo, Guayaquil, Ambato, Riobamba, Cuenca, Machala, Loja, Iquitos, Leticia, Tabatinga, Cruzeiro do Sul, Rio Branco, Porto Velho, Ariquemes, Chiclayo, Trujillo, Chimbote, Huaraz, Lima, Callao, Huancayo, Ayacucho, Cusco (Cuzco), Pucallpa, Juliaca, Arequipa, Puno, Tacna, Arica, Iquique, La Paz, Cochabamba, Sucre, Potosí, Oruro, Santa Cruz, Antofagasta, Calama, Salta, San Salvador de Jujuy

Cordillera Occidental, Cordillera Oriental, Cordillera Central

Lake Titicaca, Salar de Uyuni, Salar de Atacama

Amazon (Amazonas), Río Negro, Orinoco

Equator

Tropic of Capricorn

Scale legend

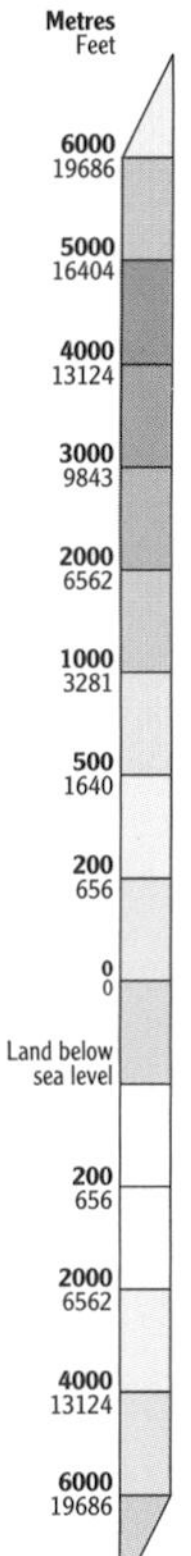

Metres / Feet

6000 19686
5000 16404
4000 13124
3000 9843
2000 6562
1000 3281
500 1640
200 656
0
Land below sea level
200 656
2000 6562
4000 13124
6000 19686

Inset

GALAPAGOS IS
(Ecuador)

I. Culpepper, I. Wenman, I. Pinta, I. Marchena, I. Fernandina, Isla Isabela, Vol. Wolf, Pta Albemarle, Baquerizo Moreno, I. Santa Cruz, I. San Salvador, I. San Cristóbal, I. Santa María, I. Española

1:15 000 000

Lambert Azimuthal Equal Area Projection

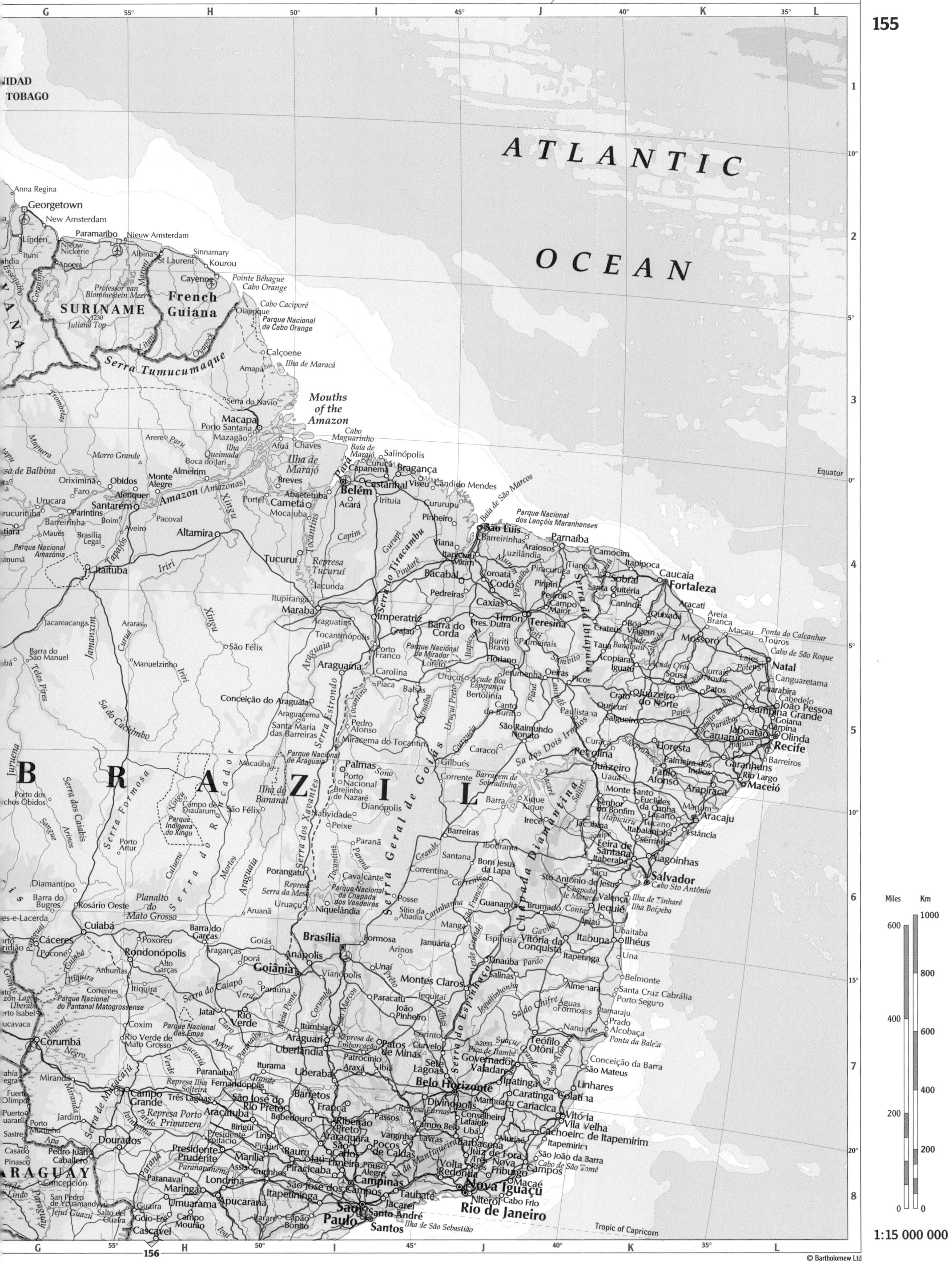

ATLANTIC

OCEAN

NIDAD
TOBAGO

Anna Regina
Georgetown
New Amsterdam
Linden
Ituni
Paramaribo Nieuw Amsterdam
Nieuw Nickerie
Apoera Albina St Laurent Sinnamary
Kourou
Cayenne

Professor van
Blommestein Meer
1230
SURINAME French
Juliana Top Guiana

Pointe Béhague
Cabo Orange
Oiapoque
Parque Nacional
de Cabo Orange

Serra Tumucumaque

Calçoene
Ilha de Maracá
Amapá

Mouths
of the
Amazon

Serra do Navio
Macapá
Porto Santana
Mazagão Afuá Chaves
Ilha
Queimada
Boca do Jari
Ilha de
Marajó

Cabo
Maguarinho
Baía de
Marajó
Salinópolis
Bragança
Capanema
Viseu Cândido Mendes

Equator

Morro Grande
Almeirim
Oriximiná Óbidos Monte
Alegre
Breves Castanhal
Portel Belém
Abaetetuba
Acará
Irituia

Baía de São Marcos
Parque Nacional
dos Lençóis Maranhenses

Faro
Urucará Santarém
Afenquer
Parintins Boim
Maués Brasília
Legal
Altamira
Veiro
Pacoval
Cametá
Mocajuba
Capim

Pinheiro
Cururupu
São Luís
Barreirinhas
Parnaíba
Camocim

Amazon (Amazonas)
Xingu

Parque Nacional
Amazônia
Itaituba

Tapajós Iriri

Tucuruí
Represa
Tucuruí

Jacundá

Araosos
Viana Luzilândia
Itapicuru Mirim Coroatá Piracuruca Itapipoca
Caucaia
Bacabal Codó Piripiri Pedro II
Sobral Santa Quitéria Fortaleza
Pedreiras Caxias Campo Canindé
Maior Aracati
Jacareacanga Araras Manuelzinho
São Félix
Maraba Imperatriz
Tocantinópolis Grajaú
Barra do
Corda
Pres. Dutra
Teresina
Buriti
Bravo
Palmeirais
Floriano
Crateús Boa
Viagem
Quixadá
Taua Mossoró
Macau Ponta do Calcanhar
Touros

Conceição do Araguaia
Porto
Franco
Carolina
Loreto
Uruçuí
Açude Boa
Esperança
Bertolínia
Picos
Iguatu Currais
Novos Lajes
Natal
Canguaretama

Piaca Balsas
Canto
do Burití
Jerumenha
Oeiras
Crato
Juazeiro
do Norte
João Pessoa
Cabedelo
Campina Grande

Santa Maria
das Barreiras
Pedro
Afonso
Miracema do Tocantins
São Raimundo
Nonato
Paulista
Salgueiro
Quixeru
Jaboatão
Caruaru
Olinda
Recife

Parque Nacional
de Araguaia
Macaúba
Palmas
Porto
Nacional
Gilbués
Floresta
Palmares
Rio Largo
Maceió

Ilha do
Bananal
Brejinho
de Nazaré
Dianópolis
Barra
Petrolina
Juazeiro
Monte
santo
Garanhuns
Barreiros

São Félix
Natividade
Peixe
Corrente
Barragem de
Sobradinho
Xique
Xique
Senhor
do Bonfim
Euclides
da Cunha
Arapiraca
Aracaju

Paraná
Barreiras
Irecê
Jacobina
Tucano
Itabaianinha
Estância

Porangatu
Santana
Bom Jesus
da Lapa
Feira de
Santana
Alagoinhas

Diamantino
Rosário Oeste
Uruaçu
Posse
Sítio da
Abadia
Sto Antônio de Jesus
Itaberaba
Cachoeira
Valença
Salvador
Cabo Sto Antônio

Cuiabá
Barra do
Garças
Goiás
Brasília
Formosa
Januária
Guanambi
Brumado
Jequié
Ilha de Tinharé
Ilha Boipeba

Rondonópolis
Anápolis
Montes Claros
Ubaitaba
Itabuna
Ilhéus

Goiânia
Unaí
Salinas
Vitória da
Conquista
Itapetinga
Una

Jataí
Rio
Verde
Paracatu
João
Pinheiro
Almenara
Belmonte
Santa Cruz Cabrália
Porto Seguro

Araguari
Uberlândia
Curvelo
Teófilo
Otoni
Nanuque
Itamaraju
Alcobaça
Ponta da Baleia

Corumbá
Patos
de Minas
Governador
Valadares
Ipatinga
São Mateus

Campo
Grande
Uberaba
Sete
Lagoas
Belo Horizonte
Caratinga
Cariacica
Colatina
Linhares

São José do
Rio Preto
Ribeirão
Preto
Divinópolis
Conselheiro
Lafaiete
Vitória
Vila
Velha

Dourados
Franca
Barbacena
Cachoeiro de Itapemirim

Presidente
Prudente
Marília
Bauru
Juiz de Fora
São João da Barra
Campos

Londrina
Campinas
Taubaté
Nova Iguaçu
Niterói Cabo Frio

Maringá
São
Paulo
Santo André
Rio de Janeiro

 PARAGUAY
Santos
Ilha de São Sebastião
Tropic of Capricorn

B R A Z I L

Miles Km
600 1000
800
400 600
400
200 200
0 0

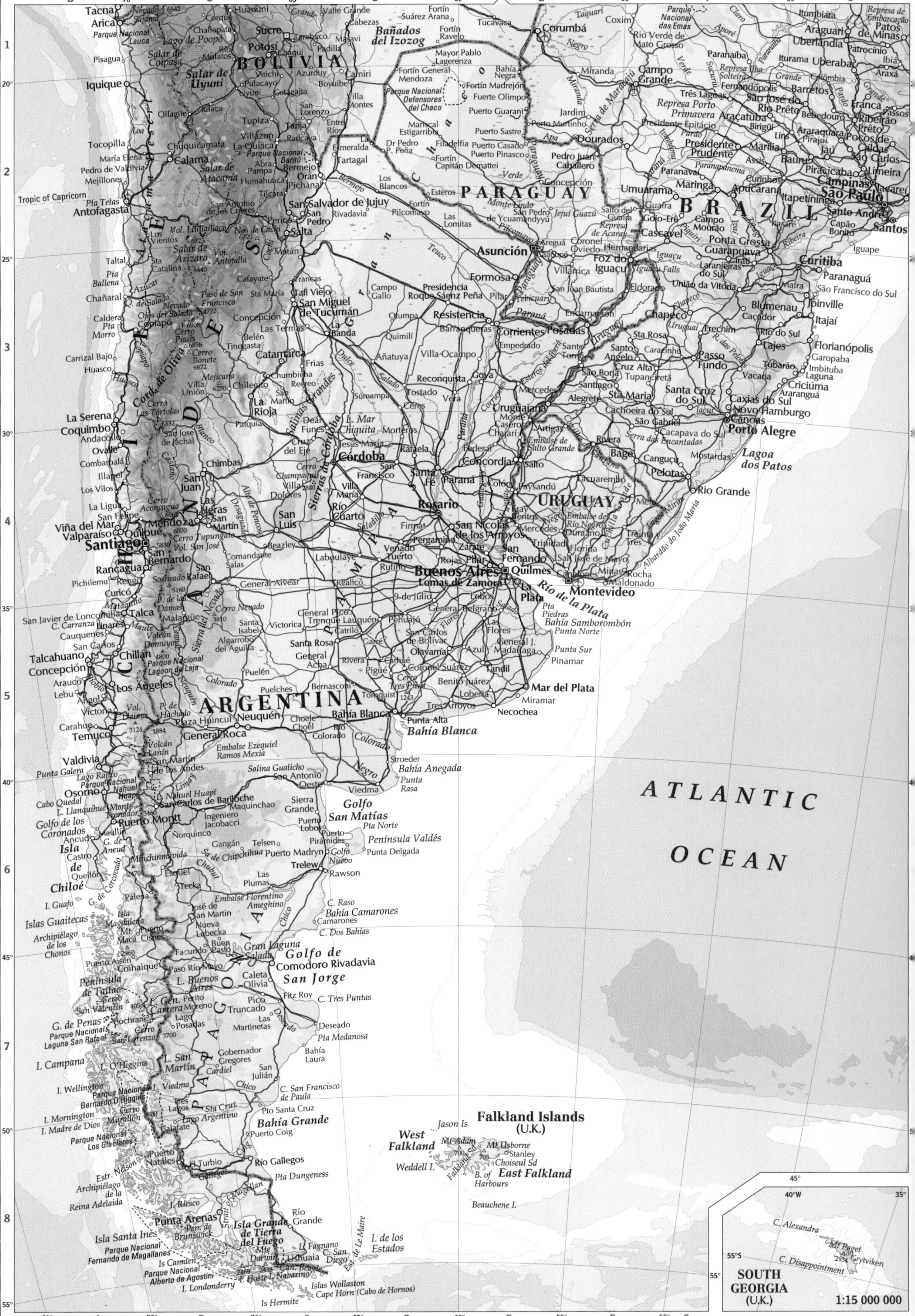
SOUTH AMERICA South
156
155
BOLIVIA
PARAGUAY
BRAZIL
URUGUAY
ARGENTINA
CHILE
ANDES
PATAGONIA
PAMPAS
Gran Chaco
ATLANTIC
OCEAN
Tropic of Capricorn
Falkland Islands
(U.K.)
West Falkland
East Falkland
Stanley
SOUTH GEORGIA
(U.K.)
Grytviken
Río de la Plata
Buenos Aires
Montevideo
Santiago
Asunción
Sucre
La Paz
Córdoba
Rosario
Mendoza
Valparaíso
Concepción
Antofagasta
Iquique
Arica
Tacna
Salta
San Miguel de Tucumán
Corrientes
Posadas
Resistencia
Mar del Plata
Bahía Blanca
Neuquén
Puerto Montt
Comodoro Rivadavia
Río Gallegos
Punta Arenas
Ushuaia
Cape Horn (Cabo de Hornos)
Isla Grande de Tierra del Fuego
Isla de Chiloé
Golfo San Matías
Golfo de San Jorge
Bahía Grande
Península Valdés
Porto Alegre
Lagoa dos Patos
Curitiba
São Paulo
Santos
Campo Grande
Corumbá
Florianópolis
Salar de Uyuni
Lago de Poopó
Bañados del Izozog
Metres
Feet
6000
19686
5000
16404
4000
13124
3000
9843
2000
6562
1000
3281
500
1640
200
656
0
0
Land below sea level
Miles
Km
1:15 000 000
Lambert Azimuthal Equal Area Projection
© Bartholomew

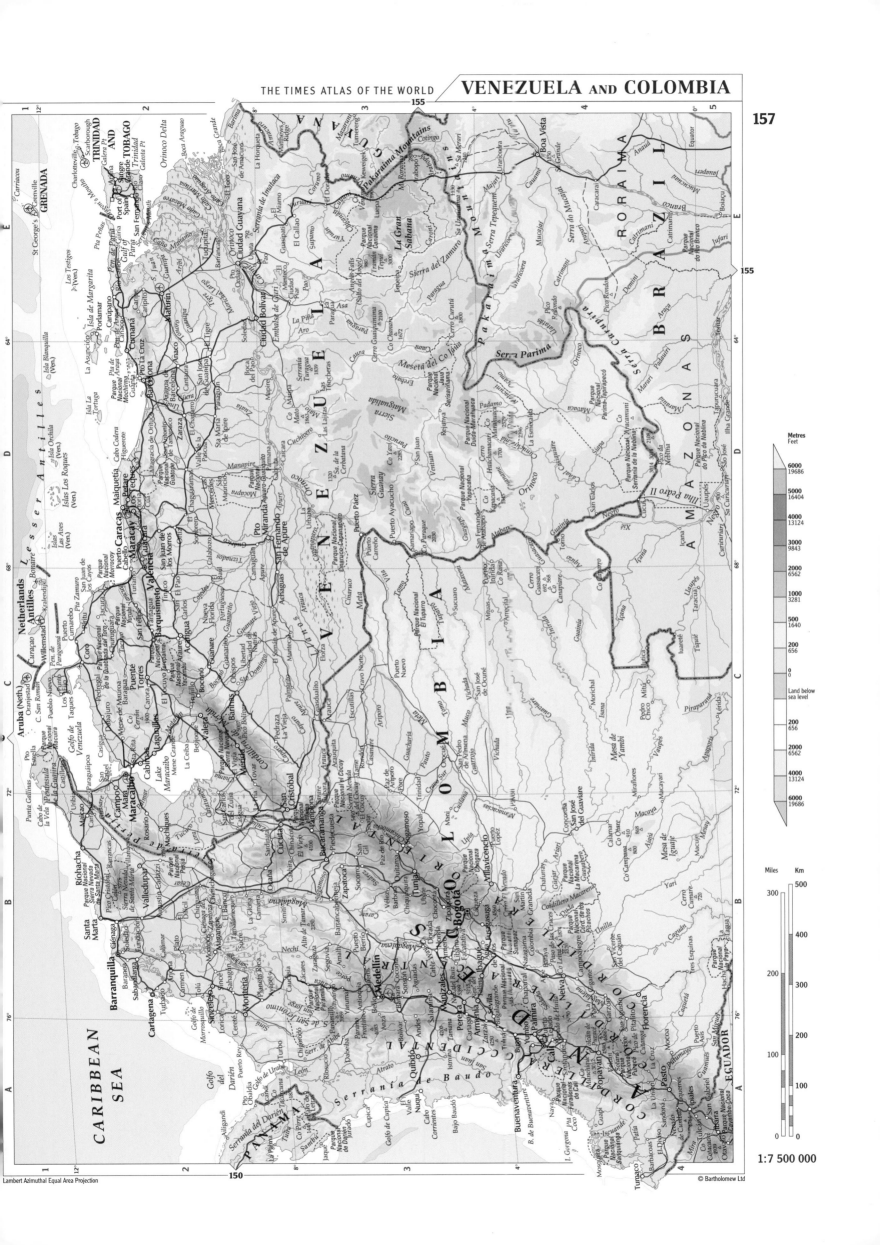

Lambert Azimuthal Equal Area Projection

© Bartholomew Ltd

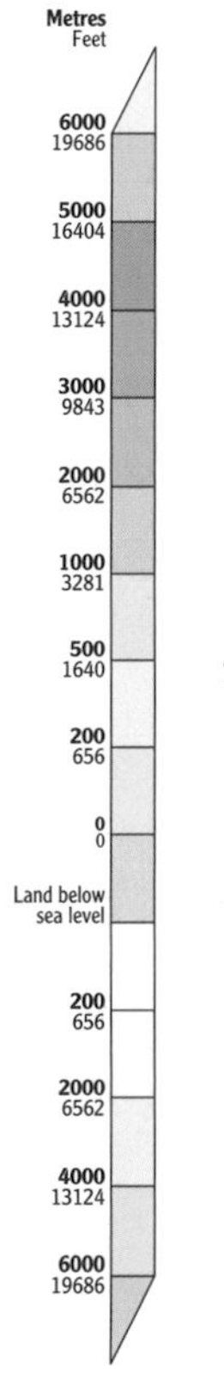

1:7 500 000

Lambert Azimuthal Equal Area Projection

© Bartholomew Ltd

Metres
Feet
6000
19686
16404
4000
13124
3000
9843
2000
6562
1000
3281
1640
200
656
Land below sea level
200
656
2000
6562
4000
13124
6000
19686
Miles
Km
300
400
200
300
200
100
100
ATLANTIC
OCEAN
Tropic of Capricorn
BAHIA
MINAS GERAIS
GOIÁS
SÃO PAULO
RIO DE JANEIRO
PARANÁ
MATO GROSSO DO SUL
MATO GROSSO
PARAGUAY
ARG.
DISTRITO FEDERAL
Salvador
Brasília
Belo Horizonte
Rio de Janeiro
São Paulo
Curitiba
Goiânia
Vitória
Campo Grande
Cuiabá
Santos
Campinas
Uberlândia
Londrina
Ilhéus
Montes Claros
155
156

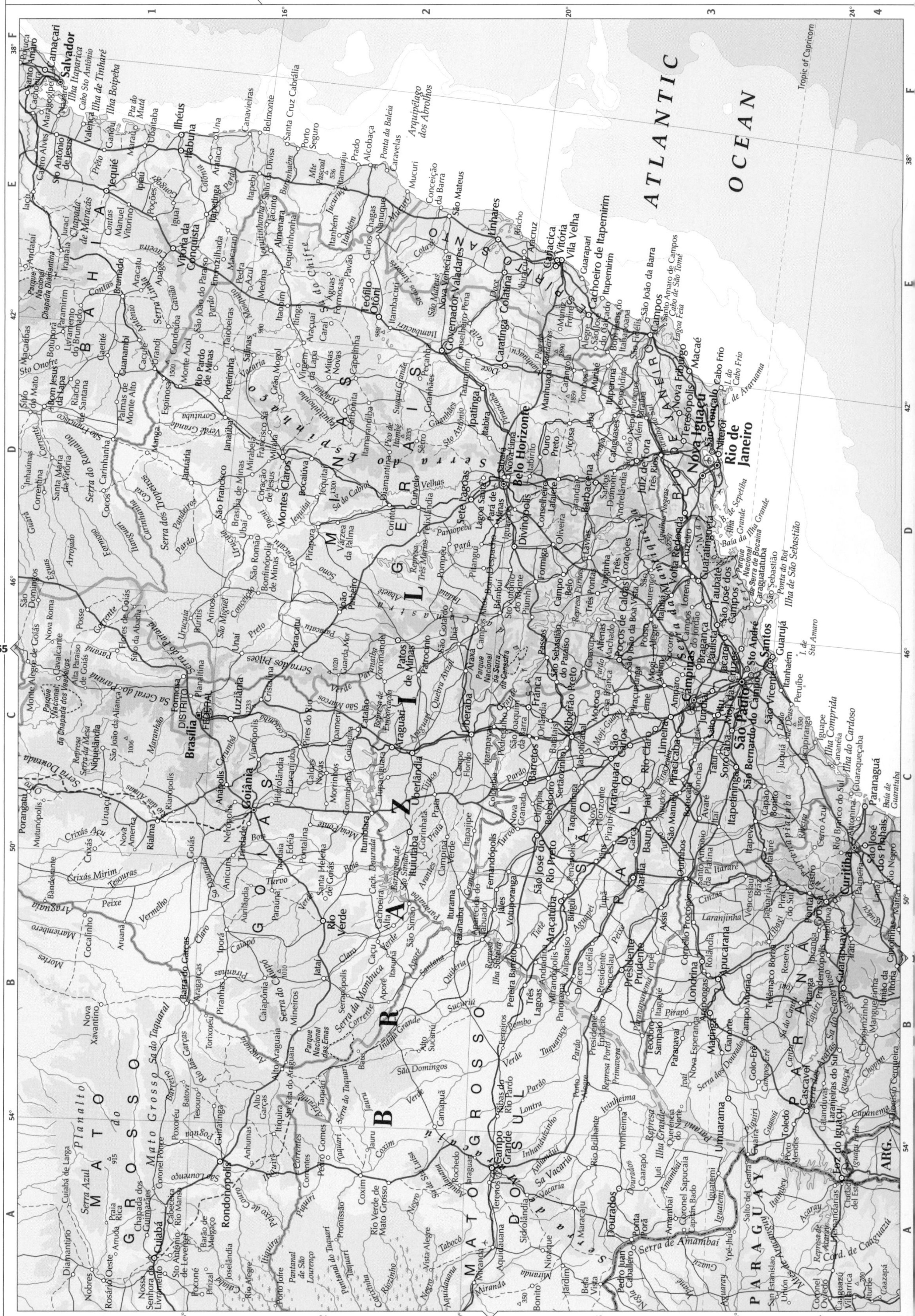

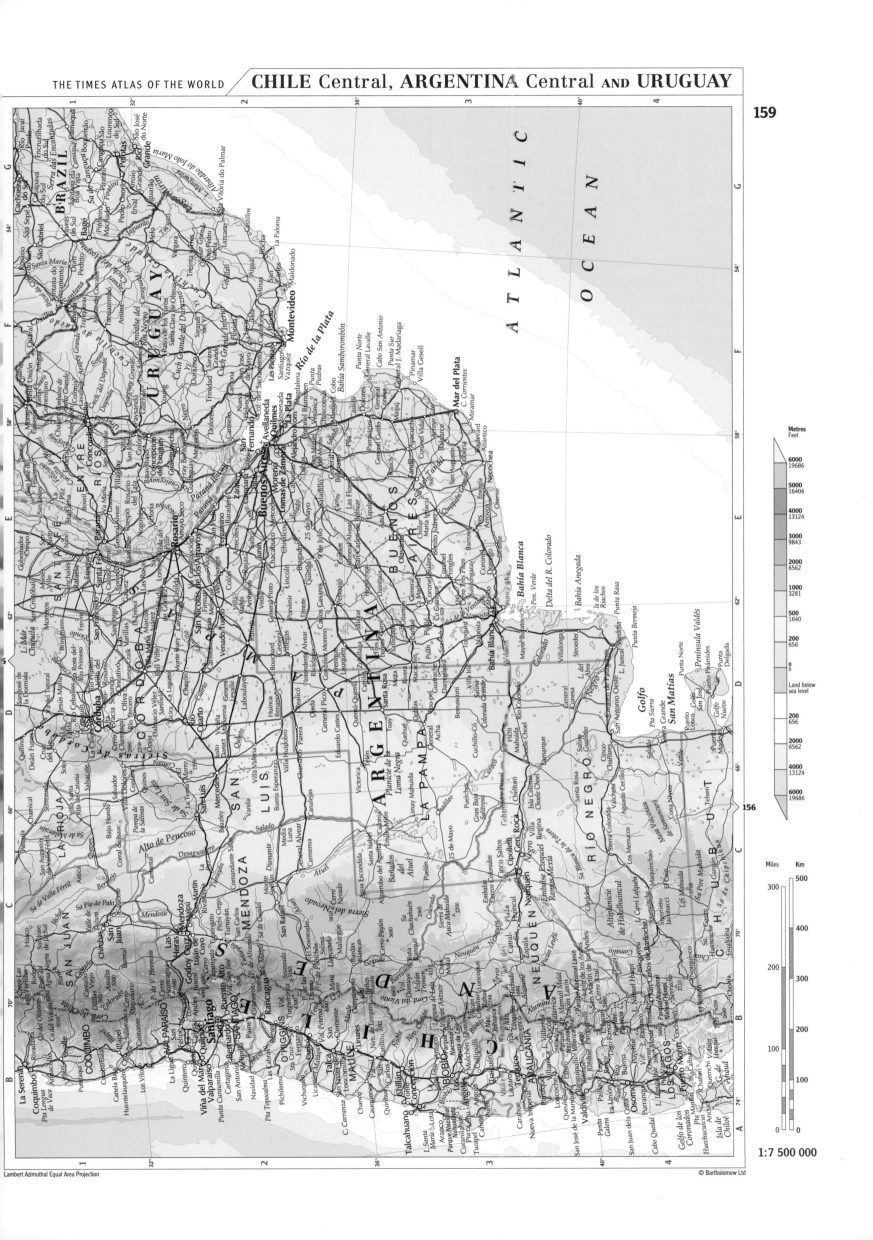

Lambert Azimuthal Equal Area Projection

© Bartholomew Ltd

1:7 500 000

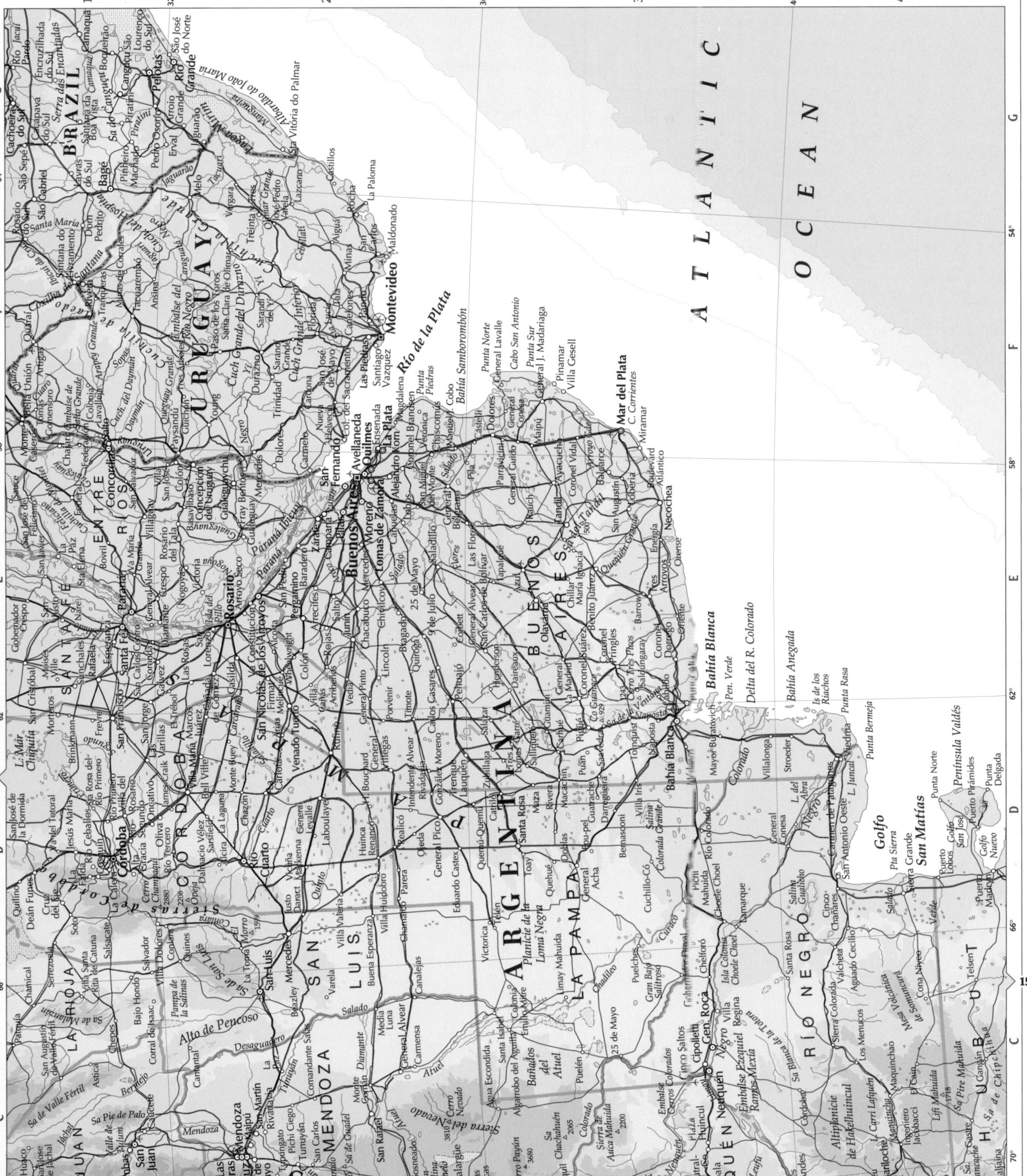

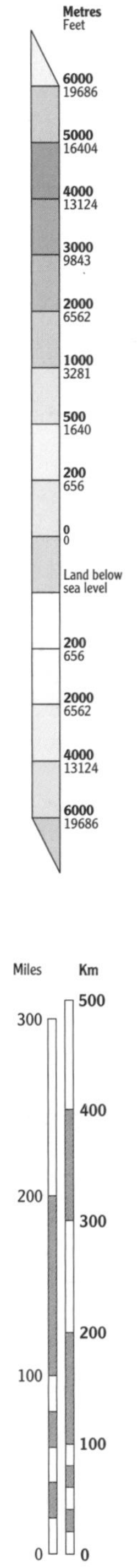

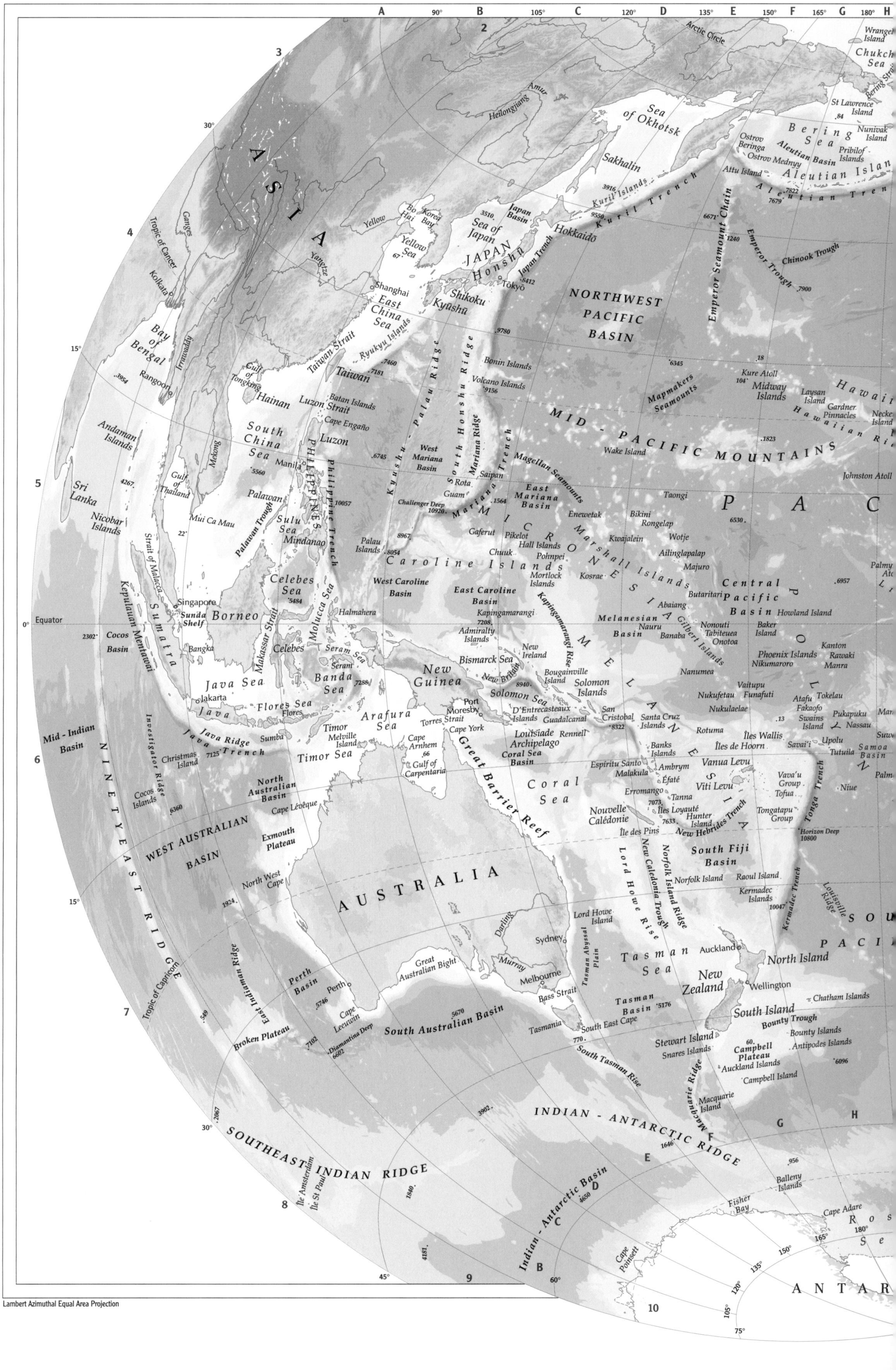

ASIA

Arctic Circle
Wrangel Island
Chukchi Sea

Sea of Okhotsk
St Lawrence Island .84
Bering Sea
Ostrov Beringa
Ostrov Mednyy
Nunivak Island
Pribilof Islands
Aleutian Basin
Attu Island
Aleutian Islands
.7822 .7679
Aleutian Trench

Amur
Heilongjiang
Sakhalin
Kuril Islands .3916
Kuril Trench
.6671 .1240
Emperor Seamount Chain
Emperor Trough .7900
Chinook Trough

Tropic of Cancer
Ganges
Kolkata
Yellow
Bo Hai
Korea Bay
Yellow Sea
Japan Basin
.3510
.9550
.67
Sea of Japan
Hokkaido
JAPAN
Honshu
Japan Trench
.8412
Tōkyō
.9780
NORTHWEST PACIFIC BASIN

Bay of Bengal
Irrawaddy
.3954
Rangoon
Gulf of Tongking
Hainan
Shanghai
East China Sea
Kyūshū
Shikoku
Taiwan Strait
Ryukyu Islands
.7181 .7460
Taiwan
Bonin Islands
.6345
South Honshu Ridge
.18
Kure Atoll
Mapmakers Seamounts
.104
Midway Islands
Laysan Island
Gardner Pinnacles
Necker Island
Hawaii
Hawaiian Ridge

Andaman Islands
South China Sea
Luzon Strait
Batan Islands
Cape Engaño
Luzon
Kyūshū - Palau Ridge
West Mariana Basin
.6745
Mariana Ridge
Volcano Islands
.9156
MID - PACIFIC MOUNTAINS
.1823
Wake Island
Johnston Atoll
PAC

Sri Lanka
Nicobar Islands
Gulf of Thailand
Mekong
Mui Ca Mau
.4267
Manila
PHILIPPINES
.5560
Palawan
Palawan Trough
Sulu Sea
Mindanao
.22
.10057
Philippine Trench
Saipan
Rota
Guam .1564
East Mariana Basin
Magellan Seamounts
Taongi
.6530
MICRONESIA
Enewetak
Gaferut
Pikelot
Pohnpei
Hall Islands
Chuuk
.8054 .8967
West Caroline Basin
Caroline Islands
East Caroline Basin
Kwajalein
Wotje
Ailinglapalap
Marshall Islands
Bikini
Rongelap
Majuro
Central Pacific Basin
.6957
Palmy
Challenger Deep .10920
Mariana Trench

Strait of Malacca
Kepulauan Mentawai
Sumatra
Singapore
Sunda Shelf
Borneo
Celebes Sea
.5484
Halmahera
Molucca Sea
West Caroline Basin
Kapingamarangi
.7208
Admiralty Islands
Kapingamarangi Rise
Mortlock Islands
Kosrae
Melanesian Basin
Abaiang
Butaritari
Nauru
Banaba
Gilbert Islands
Nonouti
Tabiteuea
Onotoa
Baker Island
Howland Island
Kanton
Phoenix Islands
Rawaki
Nikumaroro
Manra

Equator
Cocos Basin
.2302
Bangka
Celebes
Seram Sea
Seram
Java Sea
Banda Sea
.7288
Bismarck Sea
New Ireland
New Britain
Bougainville Island
.8940
Solomon Islands
Solomon Sea
New Guinea
POL
Nanumea
Nukufetau
Vaitupu
Funafuti
Nukulaelae
Atafu
Fakaofo
Tokelau
Swains Island
Pukapuka
Nassau
Suwa

Mid - Indian Basin
Jakarta
Java
Flores Sea
Flores
Arafura Sea
Timor
Melville Island
Sumba
Torres Strait
Cape York
Port Moresby
D'Entrecasteaux Islands
Guadalcanal
San Cristobal .8322
Santa Cruz Islands
Rotuma
Îles de Hoorn
Îles Wallis
.13
Samoa Basin
Tutuila
Upolu
Savai'i
MELANESIA

Java Ridge
Java Trench
.7125
Christmas Island
Cocos Islands
.6360
Timor Sea
North Australian Basin
Cape Arnhem .66
Gulf of Carpentaria
Coral Sea Basin
Louisiade Archipelago
Rennell
Banks Islands
Espiritu Santo
Malakula
Ambrym
Éfaté
Vanua Levu
Vava'u Group
Tofua
Viti Levu
Niue
Tonga Trench
Palm

Investigator Ridge
Cape Lévêque
Exmouth Plateau
North West Cape
.1924
Erromango
Tanna
Nouvelle Calédonie
Île des Pins
.7073
Îles Loyauté
Hunter Island
.7633
New Hebrides Trench
Horizon Deep .10800
Tongatapu Group
SOUTH

WEST AUSTRALIAN BASIN
AUSTRALIA
Great Barrier Reef
Coral Sea
Lord Howe Rise
New Caledonia Trough
Norfolk Island Ridge
South Fiji Basin
Norfolk Island
Raoul Island
Kermadec Islands
.10047
Kermadec Trench
Louisville Ridge
.6096
PACIF

Broken Plateau
East Indiaman Ridge
Perth Basin
.5746
Perth
Cape Leeuwin
Darling
Murray
Sydney
Melbourne
Bass Strait
Great Australian Bight
.5670
Tasmania
Tasman Abyssal Plain
Lord Howe Island
Auckland
North Island
Wellington
Chatham Islands
South Island
Bounty Trough
Bounty Islands
Antipodes Islands
.6096
Tasman Sea
Tasman Basin .5176
New Zealand

Tropic of Capricorn
.549
Diamantina Deep .6602
.7102
South Australian Basin
South East Cape
.770
South Tasman Rise
Stewart Island
Snares Islands
Campbell Plateau
Auckland Islands
Campbell Island
.60

The Amsterdam
Île St Paul
.2067
.3902
.1646
INDIAN - ANTARCTIC RIDGE
.956
Balleny Islands
.1348

SOUTHEAST INDIAN RIDGE
.4181
Indian - Antarctic Basin
.4650
Cape Poinsett
Fisher Bay
Cape Adare
Ross Sea

ANTAR

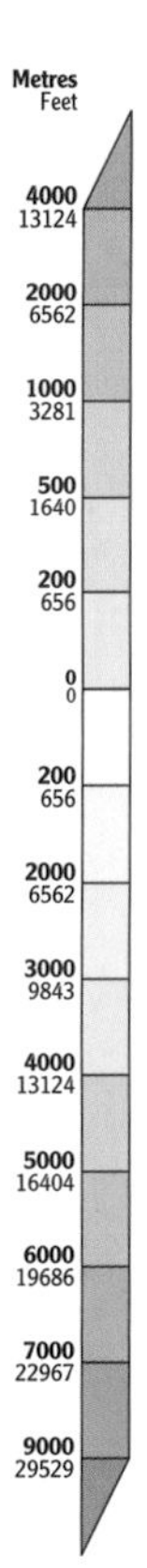

Metres / Feet
4000 / 13124
2000 / 6562
1000 / 3281
500 / 1640
200 / 656
0 / 0
200 / 656
2000 / 6562
3000 / 9843
4000 / 13124
5000 / 16404
6000 / 19686
7000 / 22967
9000 / 29529

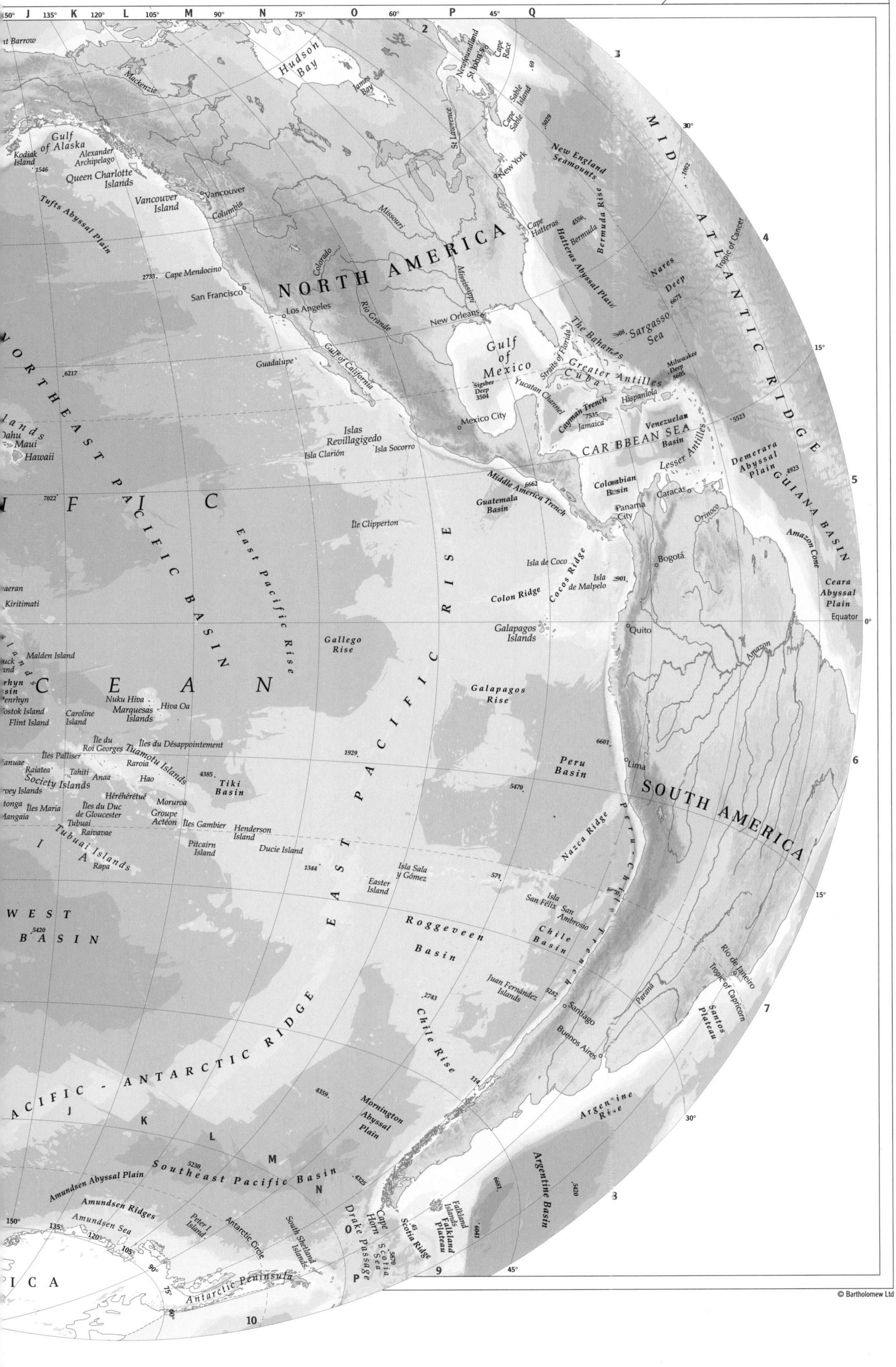

© Bartholomew Ltd

F 30° G 45° H 60° I 75° J 90° K 105° L 120° M 135° N 150° O

ASIA

Black Sea 2210
Caspian Sea 1025
Aral Sea
Tigris
Euphrates
The Gulf
Gulf of Oman 3694
Indus
Karachi
Ganges
Kolkata
Red Sea 3039
Tropic of Cancer
Mastrah
Arabian Basin
Mumbai
Arabian Sea
Bay of Bengal 3954
Rangoon
Irrawaddy
Guangzhou
Gulf of Tongking
Hainan
Mekong
Yellow
Yellow Sea 67
Bo Hai
Korea Bay
Shanghai
East China Sea
Japan Basin 3510
Sea of Japan
Hokkaido 9550
Tokyo 8412
Shikoku
Kyūshū
Ryukyu Islands
Taiwan Strait
Taiwan 7181
Ryukyu Trench 7460
Kyūshū-Palau Ridge
Batan Islands
Luzon Strait
Cape Engaño
Luzon
Manila
Philippine Basin 6745
PHILIPPINES
Philippine Trench 10057
Palau 5054
Mindanao
Celebes Sea 5484
Halmahera
Molucca Sea
Aden
Gulf of Aden
Socotra 5803
1481
Laccadive Islands
Chagos-Laccadive Ridge
Sri Lanka
Gulf of Mannar
Andaman Islands
Andaman Basin 4267
Gulf of Thailand
Nicobar Islands
Maldives 4735
Strait of Malacca
Sumatra
South China Sea 5560
Palawan
Palawan Trough
Sulu Sea
Somali Basin 5060
Seychelles
Amirante Islands 5273
Mascarene Plateau
Diego Garcia
Chagos Archipelago
Vema Trench 6402
5406
MID-INDIAN BASIN 5421
Cocos Basin 2302
Kepulauan Mentawai
Singapore
Sunda Shelf
Bangka
Borneo
Jakarta
Java Sea
Celebes
Makassar Strait
Seram Sea
Seram
Banda Sea 7288
Equator
Mombasa
Pemba Island
Zanzibar Island
Mafia Island
Aldabra Islands
Farquhar Islands
Agalega Islands
Mascarene Basin
Île Tromelin
Cargados Carajos Islands
Rodrigues Island
MID-INDIAN RIDGE
NINETYEAST RIDGE
Investigator Ridge 6360
Cocos Islands
Christmas Island
Java Ridge 7125
Java Trench
Sumba
Flores Sea
Flores
Timor
North Australian Basin
Timor Sea
Arafura Sea
New Guinea
AFRICA
Njazidja
Comoros
Mayotte
Mascarene Plain
Madagascar 5194
Mauritius
Réunion
INDIAN OCEAN
WEST AUSTRALIAN BASIN
Exmouth Plateau
Cape Lévêque
Gulf of Carpentaria
Mozambique Channel
Madagascar Basin 6400
Tropic of Capricorn
MID-INDIAN RIDGE
2067
NINETYEAST RIDGE 549
East Indiaman Ridge 1924
North West Cape
AUSTRALIA
Durban
Natal Basin 6291
1207
Madagascar Ridge
SOUTHWEST INDIAN RIDGE
Crozet Basin 5195
Île Amsterdam
Île St Paul
Broken Plateau 3745
7102
Perth Basin 5746
Perth
Naturaliste Plateau
Diamantina Deep 6602
SOUTHEAST INDIAN RIDGE
South Australian Basin 5670
Great Australian Bight
Darling
Sydney
Melbourne
Bass Strait
Mozambique Ridge
Agulhas Plateau 5371
Agulhas Basin 6195
Crozet Plateau
Prince Edward Islands
Îles Crozet
4590
Îles Kerguélen
Kerguelen Plateau
Heard Island
McDonald Islands
4181
1840
3902
INDIAN-ANTARCTIC RIDGE
Tasmania
South East Cape
770
South Tasman Rise
Tasman Sea
Tasman Abyssal Plain
South Island
New Zealand
Stewart Island
Atlantic-Indian Ridge
Bouvetøya
5790
Conrad Rise 230
Banzare Seamount 186
6972
Enderby Abyssal Plain
Atlantic-Indian Antarctic Basin
INDIAN-ANTARCTIC BASIN 4650
Davis Sea
Cape Darnley
Vincennes Bay
Cape Poinsett
956
1566
Macquarie Ridge
Macquarie Island
Campbell Plateau
Auckland Islands
Campbell Island
Antipodes Islands 6696
Bounty Islands
Maud Seamount 1208
Lützow-Holm Bay
F 15° E
Cape Norvegia
ANTARCTICA
South Pole
Pacific-Antarctic Ridge
Cape North
Cape Adare
Coulman Island
Fisher Bay
Ross Sea
Antarctic Circle
American-Antarctic Ridge
South Sandwich Trench 8325
Scotia Ridge
South Sandwich Islands
South Georgia
Scotia Sea
South Orkney Islands
Weddell Sea
Weddell Abyssal Plain
Antarctic Peninsula

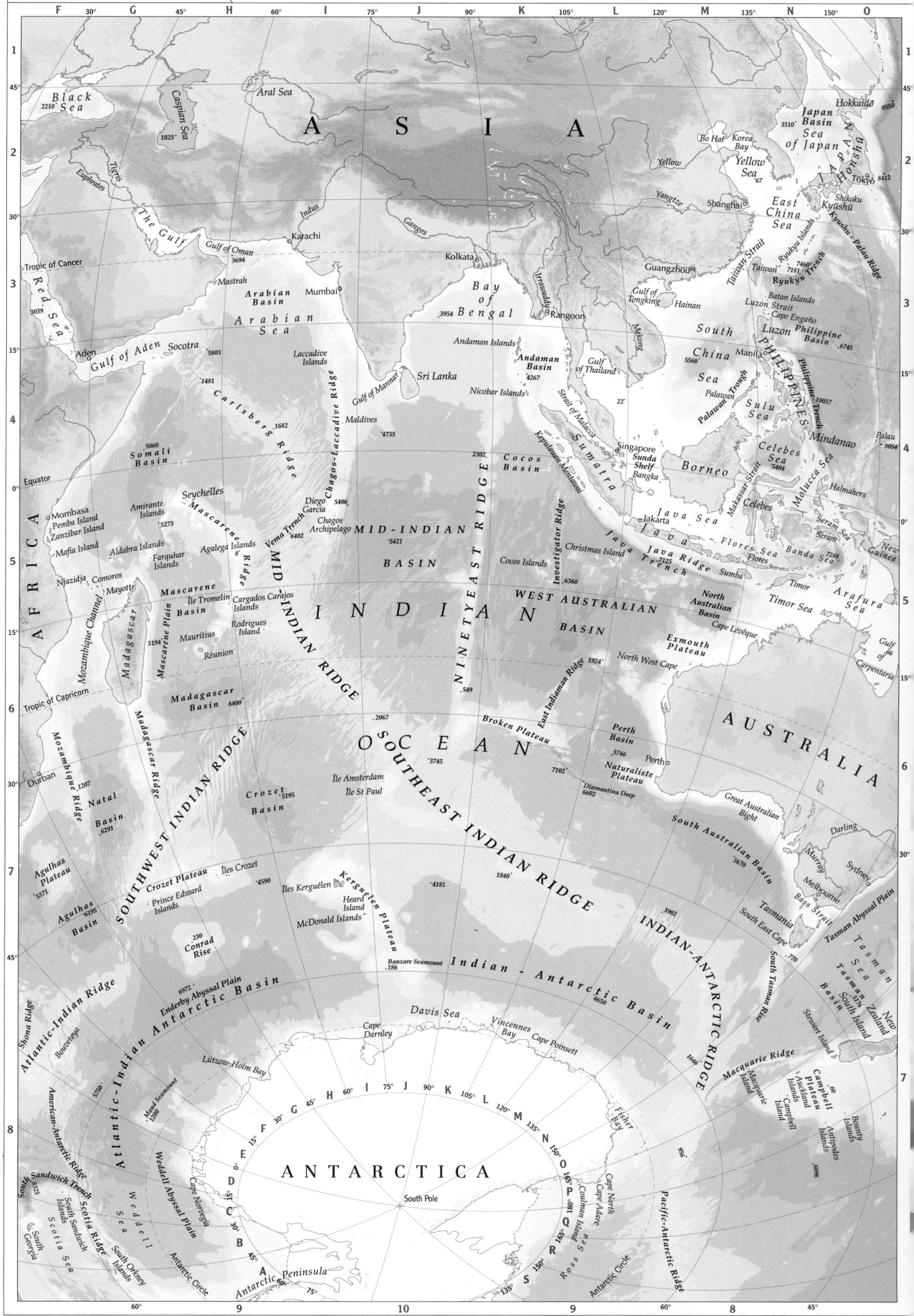

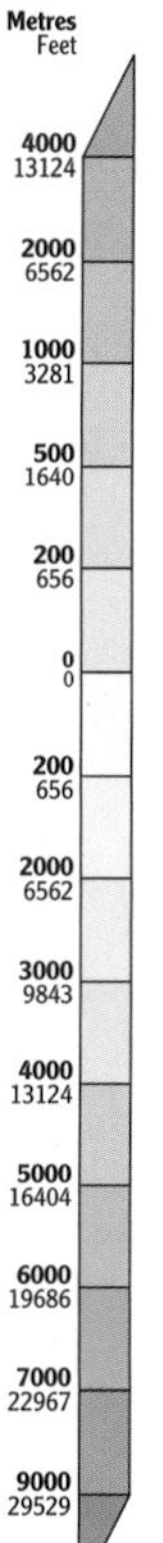

Metres / Feet
4000 13124
2000 6562
1000 3281
500 1640
200 656
0 0
200 656
2000 6562
3000 9843
4000 13124
5000 16404
6000 19686
7000 22967
9000 29529

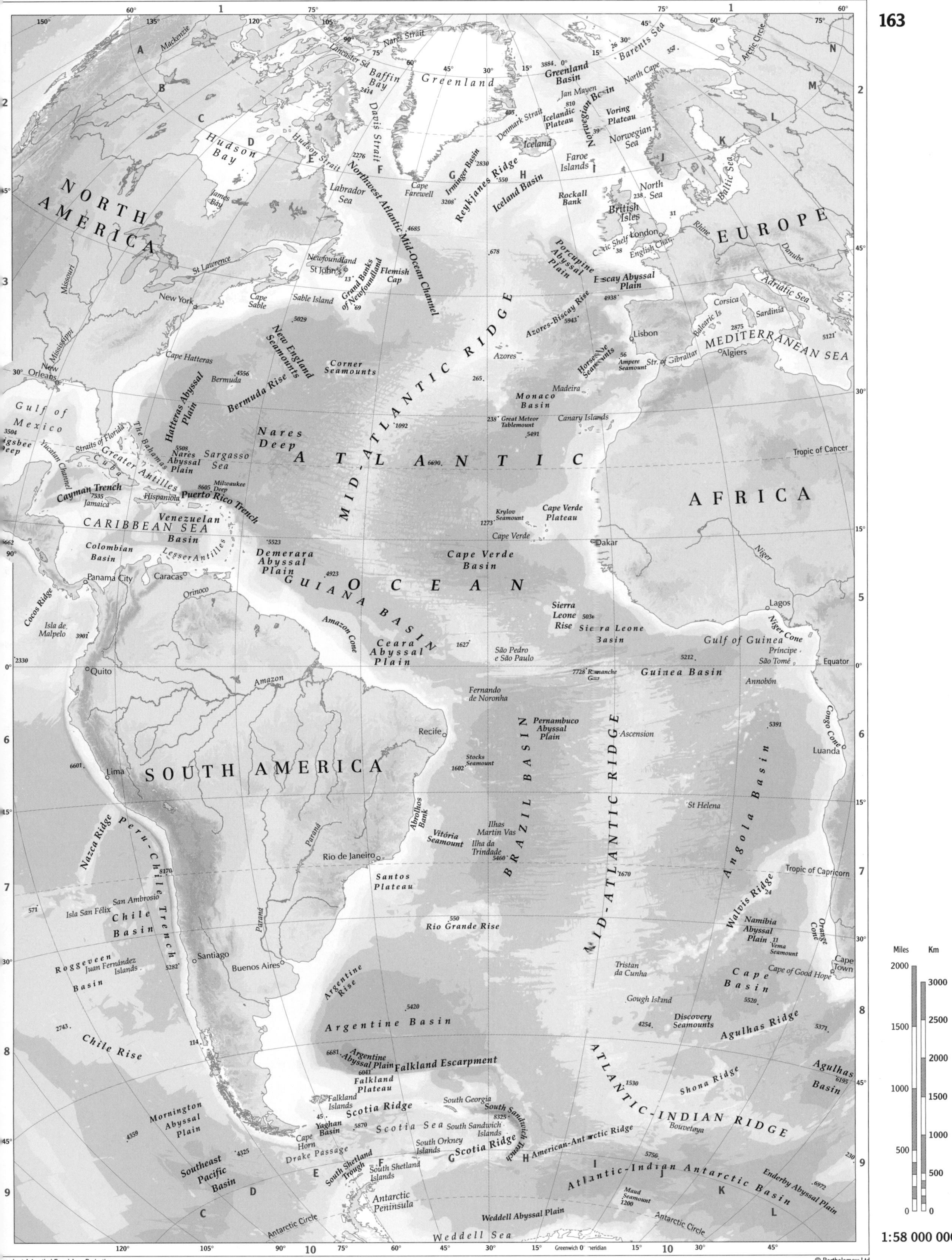
NORTH AMERICA
SOUTH AMERICA
EUROPE
AFRICA
ATLANTIC OCEAN
MID-ATLANTIC RIDGE
Greenland
Iceland
British Isles
Hudson Bay
James Bay
Baffin Bay
Davis Strait
Hudson Strait
Labrador Sea
Cape Farewell
Irminger Basin
Reykjanes Ridge
Iceland Basin
Greenland Basin
Jan Mayen
Norwegian Basin
Icelandic Plateau
Denmark Strait
Voring Plateau
Norwegian Sea
Faroe Islands
Rockall Bank
North Sea
Barents Sea
North Cape
Baltic Sea
Arctic Circle
Nares Strait
Lancaster Sd
Northwest Atlantic Mid-Ocean Channel
Newfoundland
St John's
Grand Banks of Newfoundland
Flemish Cap
Porcupine Abyssal Plain
Celtic Shelf
London
English Chan.
Biscay Abyssal Plain
Azores-Biscay Rise
Rhine
Danube
Adriatic Sea
Corsica
Sardinia
Balearic Is
MEDITERRANEAN SEA
Algiers
Lisbon
Str. of Gibraltar
Ampere Seamount
Horseshoe Seamounts
Azores
Madeira
Monaco Basin
Canary Islands
Great Meteor Tablemount
St Lawrence
Missouri
Mississippi
New York
Cape Sable
Sable Island
New England Seamounts
Corner Seamounts
Cape Hatteras
Bermuda
Bermuda Rise
Hatteras Abyssal Plain
Nares Deep
Nares Abyssal Plain
Sargasso Sea
New Orleans
Gulf of Mexico
Sigsbee Deep
Straits of Florida
The Bahamas
Yucatan Channel
Greater Antilles
Cuba
Cayman Trench
Jamaica
Hispaniola
Puerto Rico Trench
Milwaukee Deep
Venezuelan Basin
CARIBBEAN SEA
Colombian Basin
Lesser Antilles
Panama City
Caracas
Orinoco
Cocos Ridge
Isla de Malpelo
Demerara Abyssal Plain
GUIANA BASIN
Amazon Cone
Ceara Abyssal Plain
Krylov Seamount
Cape Verde
Cape Verde Plateau
Cape Verde Basin
Dakar
Niger
Tropic of Cancer
Sierra Leone Rise
Sierra Leone Basin
Lagos
Niger Cone
Gulf of Guinea
Príncipe
São Tomé
Equator
São Pedro e São Paulo
Romanche Gap
Guinea Basin
Annobón
Quito
Amazon
Fernando de Noronha
Recife
Pernambuco Abyssal Plain
Ascension
Congo Cone
Luanda
Stocks Seamount
Lima
BRAZIL BASIN
Angola Basin
St Helena
Abrolhos Bank
Vitória Seamount
Ilhas Martin Vas
Ilha da Trindade
Rio de Janeiro
Santos Plateau
Paraná
Tropic of Capricorn
Walvis Ridge
Namibia Abyssal Plain
Vema Seamount
Orange Cone
Nazca Ridge
Peru-Chile Trench
San Ambrosio
Isla San Félix
Chile Basin
Rio Grande Rise
Santiago
Buenos Aires
Juan Fernández Islands
Roggeveen Basin
Tristan da Cunha
Cape Town
Cape of Good Hope
Cape Basin
Argentine Rise
Gough Island
Discovery Seamounts
Agulhas Ridge
Argentine Basin
Chile Rise
Argentine Abyssal Plain
Falkland Escarpment
Falkland Plateau
Falkland Islands
ATLANTIC-INDIAN RIDGE
Agulhas Basin
Shona Ridge
Bouvetøya
Mornington Abyssal Plain
Scotia Ridge
South Georgia
South Sandwich Trench
South Sandwich Islands
Yaghan Basin
Cape Horn
Scotia Sea
South Orkney Islands
Drake Passage
American-Antarctic Ridge
Atlantic-Indian Antarctic Basin
Enderby Abyssal Plain
Southeast Pacific Basin
South Shetland Trough
South Shetland Islands
Antarctic Peninsula
Maud Seamount
Weddell Abyssal Plain
Weddell Sea
Antarctic Circle
Greenwich Meridian
Miles
Km

1:58 000 000

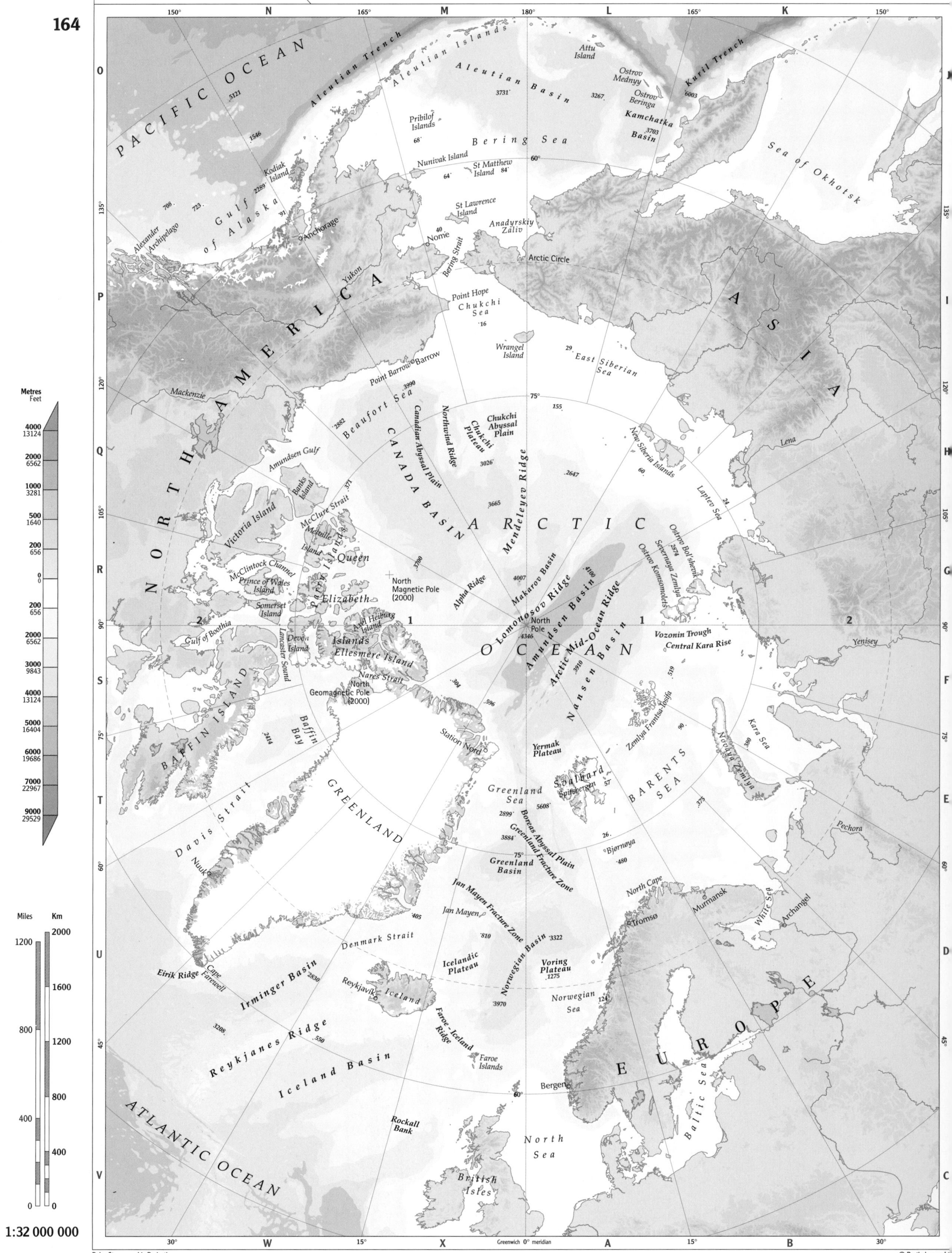

Metres
Feet

4000
13124

2000
6562

1000
3281

500
1640

200
656

0

200
656

2000
6562

3000
9843

4000
13124

5000
16404

6000
19686

7000
22967

9000
29529

Miles   Km

1200   2000

1600

800   1200

800

400   400

400

0   0

1:32 000 000

Polar Stereographic Projection

© Bartholomew Lt

PACIFIC OCEAN

NORTH AMERICA

ASIA

ARCTIC OCEAN

GREENLAND

EUROPE

ATLANTIC OCEAN

Aleutian Trench
Aleutian Islands
Aleutian Basin
Attu Island
Ostrov Mednyy
Kuril Trench
Ostrov Beringa
Kamchatka Basin
Bering Sea
Sea of Okhotsk
Pribilof Islands
Nunivak Island
St Matthew Island
St Lawrence Island
Anadyrskiy Zaliv
Arctic Circle
Nome
Bering Strait
Yukon
Point Hope
Chukchi Sea
Wrangel Island
East Siberian Sea
New Siberia Islands
Laptev Sea
Lena
Point Barrow Barrow
Beaufort Sea
Northwind Ridge
Canadian Abyssal plain
Chukchi Plateau
Chukchi Abyssal Plain
CANADA BASIN
Mendeleyev Ridge
Mackenzie
Amundsen Gulf
Ostrov Bol'shevik
Severnaya Zemlya
Ostrov Komsomolets
Banks Island
Victoria Island
McClure Strait
Melville Island
Queen
North Magnetic Pole (2000)
Alpha Ridge
Makarov Basin
Lomonosov Ridge
North Pole
Amundsen Basin
Arctic Mid-Ocean Ridge
Vozonin Trough
Central Kara Rise
Yenisey
McClintock Channel
Prince of Wales Island
Somerset Island
Elizabeth
Axel Heiburg Island
Islands
Nansen Basin
Gulf of Boothia
Devon Island
Lancaster Sound
Ellesmere Island
Nares Strait
North Geomagnetic Pole (2000)
Station Nord
Yermak Plateau
Zemlya Frantsa-Iosifa
Kara Sea
Novaya Zemlya
BARENTS SEA
BAFFIN ISLAND
Baffin Bay
Greenland Sea
Svalbard
Spitsbergen
Davis Strait
Nuuk
Greenland Abyssal Plain
Bjørnøya
North Cape
Pechora
Murmansk
Archangel
White Sea
Denmark Strait
Jan Mayen Fracture Zone
Jan Mayen
Boreas Abyssal Plain
Greenland Fracture Zone
Greenland Basin
Norwegian Basin
Voring Plateau
Tromsø
Irminger Basin
Eirik Ridge
Cape Farewell
Reykjavik
Iceland
Icelandic Plateau
Norwegian Sea
Reykjanes Ridge
Faroe-Iceland Ridge
Faroe Islands
Bergen
Baltic Sea
Iceland Basin
Rockall Bank
North Sea
British Isles

INTRODUCTION TO THE INDEX

The index includes all names shown on the reference maps in the atlas. Each entry includes the country or geographical area in which the feature is located, a page number and an alphanumeric reference. Additional entry details and aspects of the index are explained below.

REFERENCING

Names are referenced by page number and by grid reference. The grid reference relates to the alphanumeric values which appear in the margin of each map. These reflect the graticule on the map – the letter relates to longitude divisions, the number to latitude divisions.

Names are generally referenced to the largest scale map page on which they appear. For large geographical features, including countries, the reference is to the largest scale map on which the feature appears in its entirety, or on which the majority of it appears.

Rivers are referenced to their lowest downstream point – either their mouth or their confluence with another river. The river name will generally be positioned as close to this point as possible.

Entries relating to names appearing on insets are indicated by a small box symbol: □ followed by a grid reference if the inset has its own alphanumeric values.

ALTERNATIVE NAMES

Alternative names appear as cross-references and refer the user to the index entry for the form of the name used on the map.

For rivers with multiple names – for example those which flow through several countries – all alternative name forms are included within the main index entries, with details of the countries in which each form applies.

ADMINISTRATIVE QUALIFIERS

Administrative divisions are included in an entry to differentiate duplicate names – entries of exactly the same name and feature type within the one country – where these division names are shown on the maps. In such cases, duplicate names are alphabetized in the order of the administrative division names. Additional qualifiers are included for names within selected geographical areas, to indicate more clearly their location.

DESCRIPTORS

Entries, other than those for towns and cities, include a descriptor indicating the type of geographical feature. Descriptors are not included where the type of feature is implicit in the name itself, unless there is a town or city of exactly the same name.

NAME FORMS AND ALPHABETICAL ORDER

Name forms are as they appear on the maps, with additional alternative forms included as cross-references. Names appear in full in the index, although they may appear in abbreviated form on the maps.

The German character ß is alphabetized as 'ss'. Names beginning with Mac or Mc are alphabetized exactly as they appear. The terms Saint, Sainte, etc, are abbreviated to St, Ste, etc, but alphabetized as if in the full form.

NUMERICAL ENTRIES

Entries beginning with numerals appear at the beginning of the index, in numerical order. Elsewhere, numerals are alphabetized before 'a'.

PERMUTED TERMS

Names beginning with generic, geographical terms are permuted – the descriptive term is placed after, and the index alphabetized by, the main part of the name. For example, Lake Superior is indexed as Superior, Lake; Mount Everest as Everest, Mount. This policy is applied to all languages. Permuting has not been applied to names of towns, cities or administrative divisions beginning with such geographical terms. These remain in their full form, for example, Lake Isabella, USA.

INDEX ABBREVIATIONS

admin. dist.	administrative district	IN	Indiana	plat.	plateau
admin. div.	administrative division	Indon.	Indonesia	P.N.G.	Papua New Guinea
admin. reg.	administrative region	is	islands	Port.	Portugal
Afgh.	Afghanistan	Kazakh.	Kazakhstan	prov.	province
AK	Alaska	KS	Kansas	pt	point
AL	Alabama	KY	Kentucky	Qld	Queensland
Alg.	Algeria	Kyrg.	Kyrgyzstan	Que.	Québec
Alta	Alberta	l.	lake	r.	river
AR	Arkansas	LA	Louisiana	reg.	region
Arg.	Argentina	lag.	lagoon	Rep. of Ireland	Republic of Ireland
aut. comm.	autonomous community	Lith.	Lithuania	res.	reserve
aut. reg.	autonomous region	Lux.	Luxembourg	resr	reservoir
aut. rep.	autonomous republic	MA	Massachusetts	RI	Rhode Island
AZ	Arizona	Madag.	Madagascar	r. mouth	river mouth
Azer.	Azerbaijan	Man.	Manitoba	Rus. Fed.	Russian Federation
b.	bay	MD	Maryland	S.	South
Bangl.	Bangladesh	ME	Maine	S.A.	South Australia
B.C.	British Columbia	Mex.	Mexico	S. Africa	Republic of South Africa
Bol.	Bolivia	MI	Michigan	salt l.	salt lake
Bos.-Herz.	Bosnia-Herzegovina	MN	Minnesota	Sask.	Saskatchewan
Bulg.	Bulgaria	MO	Missouri	SC	South Carolina
c.	cape	Moz.	Mozambique	SD	South Dakota
CA	California	MS	Mississippi	sea chan.	sea channel
Cent. Afr. Rep.	Central African Republic	MT	Montana	Sing.	Singapore
CO	Colorado	mt.	mountain	Switz.	Switzerland
Col.	Colombia	mts	mountains	Tajik.	Tajikistan
CT	Connecticut	N.	North, Northern	Tanz.	Tanzania
Czech Rep.	Czech Republic	nat. park	national park	Tas.	Tasmania
DC	District of Columbia	N.B.	New Brunswick	terr.	territory
DE	Delaware	NC	North Carolina	Thai.	Thailand
Dem. Rep. Congo	Democratic Republic of Congo	ND	North Dakota	TN	Tennessee
depr.	depression	NE	Nebraska	Trin. and Tob.	Trinidad and Tobago
des.	desert	Neth.	Netherlands	Turkm.	Turkmenistan
Dom. Rep.	Dominican Republic	Neth. Antilles	Netherlands Antilles	TX	Texas
English Chan.	English Channel	Nfld.	Newfoundland	U.A.E.	United Arab Emirates
Equat. Guinea	Equatorial Guinea	NH	New Hampshire	U.K.	United Kingdom
esc.	escarpment	NJ	New Jersey	Ukr.	Ukraine
est.	estuary	NM	New Mexico	U.S.A.	United States of America
Eth.	Ethiopia	N.S.	Nova Scotia	UT	Utah
Fin.	Finland	N.S.W.	New South Wales	Uzbek.	Uzbekistan
FL	Florida	N.W.T.	Northwest Territories	VA	Virginia
for.	forest	N.Z.	New Zealand	Venez.	Venezuela
Fr. Guiana	French Guiana	NV	Nevada	Vic.	Victoria
Fr. Polynesia	French Polynesia	NY	New York	vol.	volcano
g.	gulf	OH	Ohio	vol. crater	volcanic crater
GA	Georgia	OK	Oklahoma	VT	Vermont
Guat.	Guatemala	Ont.	Ontario	W.	Western
hd	headland	OR	Oregon	W.A.	Western Australia
HI	Hawaii	PA	Pennsylvania	WA	Washington
Hond.	Honduras	Pak.	Pakistan	WI	Wisconsin
i.	island	Para.	Paraguay	WV	West Virginia
IA	Iowa	P.E.I.	Prince Edward Island	WY	Wyoming
ID	Idaho	pen.	peninsula	Y.T.	Yukon Territory
IL	Illinois	Phil.	Philippines	Yugo.	Yugoslavia

1

159 E2 9 de Julio Arg.
159 E3 25 de Mayo Arg.
159 E2 25 de Mayo Arg.
130 E4 100 Mile House Canada

A

108 E4 Aachen Germany
112 E6 Aalen Germany
108 C4 Aalst Belgium
108 C4 Aarschot Belgium
92 A3 Aba China
122 D3 Aba Dem. Rep. Congo
120 C4 Aba Nigeria
84 B5 Abā ad Dūd Saudi Arabia
84 D4 Ābādān Iran
84 D4 Ābādeh Iran
84 D4 Ābādeh Tashk Iran
120 B1 Abadla Alg.
158 D2 Abaeté r. Brazil
155 I4 Abaetetuba Brazil
160 G6 Abaiang atoll Kiribati
139 E4 Abajo Peak mt. U.S.A.
120 C4 Abakaliki Nigeria
90 B1 Abakan Rus. Fed.
90 A1 Abakanskiy Khrebet mts Rus. Fed.
117 E7 Abana Turkey
154 D6 Abancay Peru
84 D4 Abarkūh, Kavīr-e des. Iran
84 D4 Abarqū Iran
94 I2 Abashiri Japan
94 I2 Abashiri-wan b. Japan
68 E3 Abau P.N.G.
83 H2 Abay Kazakh.
122 D3 Abaya, Lake l. Eth.
Ābaya Hāyk' l. Eth. see Abaya, Lake
121 F3 Ābay Wenz r. Eth. alt. Azraq, Bahr el (Sudan); conv. Blue Nile
76 K4 Abaza Rus. Fed.
85 E3 Abbāsābād Iran
114 C4 Abbasanta Sardinia Italy
134 C2 Abbaye, Point U.S.A.
108 A5 Abbaye de Chaalis France
108 D5 Abbaye d'Orval Belgium
122 E2 Abbe, Lake Eth.
110 E1 Abbeville France
143 E6 Abbeville LA U.S.A.
145 D5 Abbeville SC U.S.A.
107 B5 Abbeyfeale Rep. of Ireland
106 E6 Abbey Head hd U.K.
107 D5 Abbeyleix Rep. of Ireland
104 D3 Abbey Town U.K.
102 L2 Abborrträsk Sweden
73 A3 Abbot Ice Shelf Antarctica
130 E5 Abbotsford Canada
134 B3 Abbotsford U.S.A.
139 F4 Abbott U.S.A.
88 C2 Abbottabad Pak.
81 H3 'Abd al 'Azīz, Jabal hill Syria
81 K5 Ābdānān Iran
82 C1 Abdulino Rus. Fed.
121 E3 Abéché Chad
72 D4 Abel Tasman National Park N.Z.
120 B4 Abengourou Côte d'Ivoire
103 J5 Åbenrå Denmark
109 J6 Abensberg Germany
120 C4 Abeokuta Nigeria
105 C5 Aberaeron U.K.
106 F3 Aberchirder U.K.
71 H5 Abercrombie r. Australia
105 D6 Aberdare U.K.
105 C5 Aberdaron U.K.
71 I4 Aberdeen Australia
131 H4 Aberdeen Canada
93 □ Aberdeen Hong Kong China
124 F6 Aberdeen S. Africa
106 F3 Aberdeen U.K.
147 E5 Aberdeen MD U.S.A.
143 F5 Aberdeen MS U.S.A.
142 D2 Aberdeen SD U.S.A.
138 B2 Aberdeen WA U.S.A.
131 I2 Aberdeen Lake Canada
105 C5 Aberdyfi U.K.
106 E4 Aberfeldy U.K.
104 F4 Aberford U.K.
106 D4 Aberfoyle U.K.
105 D6 Abergavenny U.K.
143 C5 Abernathy U.S.A.
105 C5 Aberporth U.K.
105 C5 Abersoch U.K.
105 C5 Aberystwyth U.K.
86 B6 Abhā Saudi Arabia
83 H2 Abhar Iran
84 C2 Abhar Rūd r. Iran
121 F3 Abiad, Bahr el r. Sudan/Uganda alt. Jebel, Bahr el; conv. White Nile
84 C3 Ab-i Bazuft r. Iran
157 A2 Abibe, Serranía de mts Col.
120 B4 Abidjan Côte d'Ivoire
85 H3 Ab-i-Istada l. Afgh.
122 D3 Abijatta-Shalla National Park Eth.
84 E3 Ab-i-Kavir salt flat Iran
142 D4 Abilene KS U.S.A.
143 D5 Abilene TX U.S.A.
105 F6 Abingdon U.K.
134 B5 Abingdon IL U.S.A.
146 C6 Abingdon VA U.S.A.
117 F6 Abinsk Rus. Fed.
85 G2 Ab-i-Safed r. Afgh.
154 C5 Abiseo, Parque Nacional nat. park Peru
131 H2 Abitau Lake Canada
132 E4 Abitibi r. Canada
132 E4 Abitibi, Lake Canada
81 J5 Ab Naft r. Iraq
88 C3 Abohar India
120 B4 Aboisso Côte d'Ivoire
120 C4 Abomey Benin
121 D4 Abong Mbang Cameroon
97 A4 Aborlan Phil.
121 D3 Abou Déia Chad
81 J1 Abovyan Armenia
106 F3 Aboyne U.K.
86 C4 Abqaiq Saudi Arabia
159 D4 Abra, Lago del l. Arg.
111 B3 Abrantes Port.
156 C2 Abra Pampa Arg.
150 A2 Abreojos, Punta pt Mex.
158 E2 Abrolhos, Arquipélago dos is Brazil
163 G7 Abrolhos Bank sea feature S. Atlantic Ocean
138 E2 Absaroka Range mts U.S.A.
109 H6 Absberg Germany
84 C5 Abū 'Alī i. Saudi Arabia
85 H3 Abū al Jirab i. U.A.E.
86 B6 Abū 'Arīsh Saudi Arabia
86 D5 Abu Dhabi U.A.E.
121 F3 Abu Hamed Sudan
120 C4 Abuja Nigeria
81 H4 Abū Kamāl Syria
121 D3 Abū Matariq Sudan
84 D5 Abu Musa i. Iran
154 E6 Abunã r. Bol.
154 E5 Abunã Brazil
86 A7 Abune Yosēf mt. Eth.
80 C5 Abū Qīr, Khalīj b. Egypt
79 F4 Abu Road India
Abu Simbel Egypt see Abū Şunbul
81 J6 Abū Şukhayr Iraq
121 F2 Abū Şunbul Egypt

72 C5 Abut Head hd N.Z.
97 C4 Abuyog Phil.
121 E3 Abu Zabad Sudan
Abū Żabī U.A.E. see Abu Dhabi
81 L6 Abūzam Iran
121 E3 Abyad Sudan
121 E4 Abyei Sudan
84 C2 Abyek Iran
82 D1 Abzakovo Rus. Fed.
82 D2 Abzanovo Rus. Fed.
147 I2 Acadia National Park U.S.A.
150 D3 Acambaro Mex.
151 G3 Acancéh Mex.
157 A2 Acandí Col.
111 B1 A Cañiza Spain
151 E4 Acaponeta Mex.
151 E5 Acapulco Mex.
155 I4 Acará Brazil
155 J4 Acaraú r. Brazil
158 A4 Acaray r. Para.
156 C3 Acaray, Represa de resr Para.
157 C2 Acarigua Venez.
151 E4 Acatlan Mex.
110 F5 Acatzingo Mex.
151 F4 Acayucan Mex.
120 B4 Accra Ghana
104 E4 Accrington U.K.
157 C3 Achaguas Venez.
88 D5 Achalpur India
87 B2 Achampet India
77 S3 Achayvayam Rus. Fed.
96 D1 Acheng China
108 A4 Achicourt France
107 B4 Achill Head hd Rep. of Ireland
107 A4 Achill Island Rep. of Ireland
106 C2 Achiltibuie U.K.
109 H1 Achim Germany
90 B1 Achinsk Rus. Fed.
83 G4 Achisay Kazakh.
106 C3 Achnasheen U.K.
106 C3 A'Chralaig mt. U.K.
117 F6 Achuyevo Rus. Fed.
80 B3 Acıgöl l. Turkey
80 B3 Acıpayam Turkey
114 F6 Acireale Sicily Italy
142 E3 Ackley U.S.A.
149 J4 Acklins Island Bahamas
105 I5 Acle U.K.
159 B2 Aconcagua r. Chile
159 B2 Aconcagua, Cerro mt. Arg.
155 K5 Acopiara Brazil
111 B1 A Coruña Spain
150 H6 Acoyapa Nicaragua
114 C2 Acqui Terme Italy
70 A4 Acraman, Lake salt flat Australia
80 E5 Acre Israel
114 C3 Acri Italy
112 I7 Ács Hungary
67 M4 Actéon, Groupe is Fr. Polynesia
146 B4 Ada OH U.S.A.
143 D5 Ada OK U.S.A.
111 D2 Adaja r. Spain
156 B8 Adam, Mount hill Falkland Is
71 H4 Adaminaby Australia
82 D2 Adamovka Rus. Fed.
147 G3 Adams MA U.S.A.
134 C4 Adams WI U.S.A.
138 B2 Adams, Mount U.S.A.
87 B4 Adam's Bridge reef India/Sri Lanka
130 F4 Adams Lake Canada
141 E2 Adams McGill Reservoir U.S.A.
140 B2 Adams Mountain U.S.A.
87 C5 Adam's Peak Sri Lanka
'Adan Yemen see Aden
80 E3 Adana Turkey
107 E3 Adare Rep. of Ireland
73 A5 Adare, Cape Antarctica
141 E2 Adaven U.S.A.
81 J5 Ad Daghgharah Iraq
86 C5 Ad Dahnā' des. Saudi Arabia
120 A2 Ad Dakhla W. Sahara
Ad Dammām Saudi Arabia see Dammam
84 B5 Ad Dawādimī Saudi Arabia
Ad Dawhah Qatar see Doha
81 I4 Ad Dawr Iraq
81 K6 Ad Dayr Iraq
84 B5 Ad Dibdībah plain Saudi Arabia
84 B6 Ad Dilam Saudi Arabia
86 C5 Ad Dir'īyah Saudi Arabia
122 D3 Addis Ababa Eth.
147 J2 Addison U.S.A.
81 J6 Ad Dīwānīyah Iraq
105 G6 Addlestone U.K.
81 I6 Ad Duwayd well Saudi Arabia
145 D6 Adel GA U.S.A.
142 E3 Adel IA U.S.A.
70 C5 Adelaide Australia
145 E7 Adelaide Bahamas
125 G6 Adelaide S. Africa
73 B2 Adelaide I. Antarctica
68 D1 Adelaide River Australia
140 D4 Adelanto U.S.A.
71 H5 Adelong Australia
83 G4 Adenau Uzbek.
86 C7 Aden Yemen
86 D7 Aden, Gulf of Somalia/Yemen
108 E4 Adenau Germany
109 I1 Adendorf Germany
91 F1 Adh Dhayd U.A.E.
122 D2 Ādī Ārk'ay Eth.
122 D2 Ādīgrat Eth.
88 D6 Adilabad India
81 I2 Adilcevaz Turkey
138 B3 Adin U.S.A.
121 D2 Adiri Libya
147 F2 Adirondack Mountains U.S.A.
Adīs Ābeba Eth. see Addis Ababa
122 D3 Ādīs Alem Eth.
80 G3 Adiyaman Turkey
113 M7 Adjud Romania
133 I3 Adlavik Islands Canada
68 B4 Admiralty Gulf Australia
129 J2 Admiralty Inlet Canada
130 C3 Admiralty Island Canada
130 C3 Admiralty Island National Monument – Kootznoowoo Wilderness nat. park U.S.A.
68 E2 Admiralty Islands P.N.G.
88 B3 Adoni India
109 K4 Adorf Germany
109 G3 Adorf (Diemelsee) Germany
110 D5 Adour r. France
111 E4 Adra Spain
114 F5 Adrano Sicily Italy
120 B2 Adrar Alg.
120 A2 Adrar Alg.
85 F3 Adraskand r. Afgh.
83 G4 Adrasman Tajik.
121 E3 Adré Chad
114 D2 Adria Italy
134 E4 Adrian MI U.S.A.
143 C5 Adrian TX U.S.A.
114 E2 Adriatic Sea Europe
88 C4 Adur India
122 C3 Adusa Dem. Rep. Congo
77 O3 Adycha r. Rus. Fed.
117 F6 Adygeya, Respublika aut. rep. Rus. Fed.
117 H6 Adyk Rus. Fed.
120 B4 Adzopé Côte d'Ivoire
115 K6 Aegean Sea Greece/Turkey
109 H2 Aerzen Germany
111 B1 A Estrada Spain
81 J3 Afan Iran
85 F3 Afghanistan country Asia
122 E3 Afgooye Somalia
103 J4 Afjord Norway
122 E3 Afmadow Somalia
128 C4 Afognak Island U.S.A.

111 C1 A Fonsagrada Spain
118 Africa
80 F3 'Afrin, Nahr r. Syria/Turkey
80 F2 Afşin Turkey
108 D2 Afsluitdijk barrage Neth.
138 E3 Afton U.S.A.
155 H4 Afuá Brazil
80 E5 'Afula Israel
80 C2 Afyon Turkey
109 K4 Aga Germany
120 C3 Agadez Niger
120 B1 Agadir Morocco
83 H2 Agadyr' Kazakh.
119 I5 Agalega Islands Mauritius
150 H5 Agalta nat. park Hond.
82 D1 Agapovka Rus. Fed.
89 G5 Agartala India
88 C6 Agashi India
135 F2 Agate Canada
115 L6 Agathonisi i. Greece
120 B4 Agboville Côte d'Ivoire
81 K1 Ağcabədi Azer.
81 K2 Ağdam Azer.
110 F5 Agde France
110 E4 Agen France
124 C4 Aggeneys S. Africa
108 F4 Agger r. Germany
88 D5 Aghil Pass China
107 C3 Aghla Mountain h. Rep. of Ireland
115 K7 Agia Vervara Greece
80 C2 Ağın Turkey
115 K5 Agios Dimitrios Greece
115 K5 Agios Efstratios i. Greece
115 L5 Agios Fokas, Akra pt Greece
115 J4 Agios Konstantinos Greece
115 K7 Agios Nikolaos Greece
115 J4 Agiou Orous, Kolpos b. Greece
125 F3 Agisanang S. Africa
120 B4 Agnibilékrou Côte d'Ivoire
115 K2 Agnita Romania
92 A2 Agong China
88 D3 Agra India
117 H7 Agrakhanskiy Poluostrov pen. Rus. Fed.
111 F2 Agreda Spain
81 I2 Ağrı Turkey
115 I5 Agria Gramvousa i. Greece
114 F6 Agrigento Sicily Italy
115 I5 Agrinio Greece
159 B3 Agrio r. Arg.
114 F4 Agropoli Italy
81 J1 Ağstafa Azer.
81 L1 Ağsu Azer.
151 G5 Agua, Volcán de vol. Guat.
157 C3 Agua Brava, Laguna lag. Mex.
150 C2 Aguada Mex.
157 B3 Aguada Col.
157 B3 Agua de Dios Col.
149 K5 Aguadilla Puerto Rico
150 I6 Aguadulce Panama
150 C3 Agua Escondida Arg.
148 C2 Aguanaval r. Mex.
159 C1 Agua Negra, Paso del pass Arg./Chile
158 B3 Aguapeí r. Brazil
158 C2 Agua Prieta Mex.
157 D2 Aguaray Guazú r. Para.
157 D2 Aguaro-Guariquito, Parque Nacional nat. park Venez.
150 C2 Aguaruto Mex.
151 E2 Aguascalientes Mex.
150 D3 Aguascalientes state Mex.
158 B2 Águas Formosas Brazil
158 C3 Agudos Brazil
141 F5 Aguila U.S.A.
111 D2 Aguilar de Campóo Spain
111 F4 Águilas Spain
124 D7 Agulhas, Cape S. Africa
163 K9 Agulhas Basin sea feature Southern Ocean
158 C3 Agulhas Negras mt. Brazil
162 F7 Agulhas Plateau sea feature Southern Ocean
163 J8 Agulhas Ridge sea feature S. Atlantic Ocean
99 K4 Agung, Gunung vol. Indon.
97 C4 Agusan r. Phil.
97 B4 Agutaya Phil.
84 B2 Ahar Iran
72 C5 Ahaura N.Z.
108 F2 Ahaus Germany
72 F3 Ahimanawa Range mts N.Z.
88 D1 Ahipara N.Z.
72 D1 Ahipara Bay N.Z.
128 B4 Ahklun Mountains U.S.A.
81 I2 Ahlat Turkey
109 F3 Ahlen Germany
88 C5 Ahmadabad India
87 A2 Ahmadnagar India
88 B3 Ahmadpur East Pak.
84 C4 Ahram Iran
109 I1 Ahrensburg Germany
81 L6 Āhū Iran
102 N3 Ähtäri Fin.
151 G5 Ahuachapán El Salvador
150 D3 Ahualulco Mex.
110 F3 Ahun France
72 B6 Ahuriri r. N.Z.
84 C4 Ahvāz Iran
124 B5 Ai-Ais Namibia
92 D1 Aibag Gol r. China
82 C5 Aidin Turkm.
80 □¹ Aiea U.S.A.
80 C4 Aigialousa Cyprus
115 J6 Aigina i. Greece
115 J5 Aigio Greece
110 H4 Aigle de Chambeyron mt. France
159 F2 Aiguá Uruguay
96 C3 Ai He r. China
95 F5 Aikawa Japan
145 D5 Aiken U.S.A.
150 G6 Ailigandí Panama
160 G6 Ailinglaplap atoll Marshall Is
108 A5 Ailly-sur-Noye France
135 G4 Ailsa Craig Canada
106 C5 Ailsa Craig i. U.K.
158 D2 Aimorés Brazil
158 E2 Aimorés, Serra dos hills Brazil
110 G2 Ain r. France
120 B1 Aïn Beïda Alg.
120 B2 'Aïn Ben Tili Mauritania
120 B1 Aïn Defla Alg.
120 B1 Aïn el Hadjel Alg.
120 B1 Aïn Sefra Alg.
142 D3 Ainsworth U.S.A.
Aintab Turkey see Gaziantep
111 H4 Aïn Taya Alg.
120 B2 Aïn Tédélès Alg.
157 B4 Aipe Col.
98 C5 Air i. Indon.
130 D4 Airdrie Canada
106 E5 Airdrie U.K.
110 D5 Aire-sur-l'Adour France
110 E1 Aire-sur-la-Lys France
129 L3 Air Force Island Canada
92 D1 Airgin Sum China
131 H3 Ai Shan hill China
92 F2 Ai Shan hill China
83 G3 Aishihik China
130 B2 Aishihik Lake Canada
110 G2 Aisne r. France
111 J2 Aitana mt. Spain
68 E2 Aitape P.N.G.
142 E2 Aitkin U.S.A.
82 C1 Aitova Rus. Fed.
67 □ Aitutaki i. Pacific Ocean
113 K7 Aiud Romania
110 G5 Aix-en-Provence France

110 G4 Aix-les-Bains France
89 H5 Aiyar Reservoir India
89 H5 Aizawl India
103 N4 Aizkraukle Latvia
103 M4 Aizpute Latvia
95 F6 Aizu-wakamatsu Japan
114 B2 Ajaccio Corsica France
157 B4 Ajají r. Col.
151 E4 Ajalpan Mex.
87 A1 Ajanta India
102 K2 Ajaureforsen Sweden
72 C3 Ajax, Mount N.Z.
80 E5 'Ajlun Jordan
84 C4 Ajman U.A.E.
88 C4 Ajmer India
141 F5 Ajo, Mount U.S.A.
97 B4 Ajuy Phil.
94 H3 Akabira Japan
87 B2 Akalkot India
94 I3 Akan National Park Japan
80 D4 Akanthou Cyprus
72 D5 Akaroa N.Z.
72 D5 Akaroa Harbour N.Z.
89 H3 Akas reg. India
83 H3 Akbakay Kazakh.
83 I3 Akbalyk Kazakh.
89 E4 Akbarpur India
83 H2 Akbasty Kazakh.
83 H2 Akbauyr Kazakh.
83 I3 Akbeit Kazakh.
111 I4 Akbou Alg.
83 I2 Akbulak Vostochnyy Kazakhstan Kazakh.
83 K2 Akbulak Vostochnyy Kazakhstan Kazakh.
82 C2 Akbulak Rus. Fed.
80 F2 Akçadağ Turkey
81 G3 Akçakale Turkey
80 C1 Akçakoca Turkey
80 D3 Akçalı Dağ mt. Turkey
82 D4 Akchakaya, Vpadina depr. Turkm.
83 H3 Akchatau Kazakh.
80 C2 Akdağ mt. Turkey
80 B3 Ak Dağ mt. Turkey
81 H2 Ak Dağ mts Turkey
80 E2 Akdağmadeni Turkey
103 L4 Åkersberga Sweden
108 C2 Akersloot Neth.
122 C3 Aketi Dem. Rep. Congo
81 I1 Akhalk'alak'i Georgia
117 G7 Akhalts'ikhe Georgia
89 G5 Akhaura Bangl.
121 E1 Akhdar, Jabal al mts Libya
86 E5 Akhdar, Jabal mts Oman
80 A2 Akhisar Turkey
80 D3 Akhtarin Syria
117 H5 Akhtubinsk Rus. Fed.
81 H1 Akhuryan Armenia
95 C8 Aki Japan
80 E3 Akımcı Burun pt Turkey
80 G1 Akıncılar Turkey
94 G5 Akita Japan
120 A3 Akjoujt Mauritania
83 I2 Akkabak Kazakh.
102 L2 Akkajaure l. Sweden
82 D4 Akkala Uzbek.
83 G3 Akkanse Kazakh.
117 H5 Akkermanovka Rus. Fed.
94 I3 Akkeshi Japan
80 E5 'Akko Israel see Acre
83 H3 Akkol' Almatinskaya Oblast' Kazakh.
83 H2 Akkol' Atyrauskaya Oblast' Kazakh.
83 G4 Akkol' Zhambylskaya Oblast' Kazakh.
82 B3 Akku Kazakh.
83 I2 Akkum Kazakh.
80 F1 Akkuş Turkey
82 F1 Akkyr, Gory hills Turkm.
88 D4 Aklera India
103 M4 Akmenrags pt Latvia
88 D1 Akmeqit China
Akmola Kazakh. see Astana
Akmolinskaya Oblast' admin. div. Kazakh.
81 I2 Ak-Moyun Kyrg.
95 D7 Akō Japan
121 F4 Akobo Sudan
88 D5 Akola India
83 I4 Akongkür China
122 D2 Akordat Eritrea
89 D5 Akot India
129 M3 Akpatok Island Canada
83 I3 Akqi China
102 B2 Akranes Iceland
117 C7 Akrathos, Akra pt Greece
103 I4 Akrehamn Norway
85 G3 Ak Robat Pass Afgh.
138 G3 Akron CO U.S.A.
146 A4 Akron OH U.S.A.
146 D3 Akron City Reservoir U.S.A.
88 D2 Aksai Chin terr. Asia
80 D2 Aksaray Turkey
83 H4 Ak-Say r. Kyrg.
117 F6 Aksay Rus. Fed.
81 □¹ Aksayqin Hu l. China/Jammu and Kashmir
80 C2 Akşehir Turkey
80 C2 Akşehir Gölü l. Turkey
80 C3 Akseki Turkey
70 D5 Aksenovo, Lake Australia
81 J6 Aks-e Rostam r. Iran
82 C2 Akshatau Kazakh.
82 E2 Akshiganak Kazakh.
82 E2 Akshimrau Kazakh.
83 I4 Akshiy China
83 I3 Aksu Almatinskaya Oblast' Kazakh.
83 J4 Aksu Xinjiang China
83 J4 Aksu Xinjiang China
83 I3 Aksu Almatinskaya Oblast' Kazakh.
83 I1 Aksu Pavlodarskaya Oblast' Kazakh.
81 G1 Aksu Severnyy Kazakhstan Kazakh.
80 C3 Aksu r. Turkey
83 I4 Aksu Yuzhnyy Kazakhstan Kazakh.
82 C2 Aksu Zapadnyy Kazakhstan Kazakh.
82 C2 Aksu r. Kazakh.
80 B3 Aksu r. Turkey
82 C2 Aksu-Ayuly Kazakh.
83 H2 Aksu He r. China
83 H3 Aksüme China
83 H3 Aksuyek Kazakh.
83 G2 Aktas Kazakh.
80 D3 Aktaş Dağı mt. Turkey
83 G3 Aktash Kazakh.
83 I3 Aktau Karagandinskaya Oblast' Kazakh.
83 H2 Aktau Karagandinskaya Oblast' Kazakh.
82 D2 Aktau Mangistauskaya Oblast' Kazakh.

83 I5 Akto China
82 D2 Aktobe Kazakh.
83 H2 Aktogay Karagandinskaya Oblast' Kazakh.
83 H1 Aktogay Pavlodarskaya Oblast' Kazakh.
83 I3 Aktogay Vostochnyy Kazakhstan Kazakh.
83 H3 Aktogay Karagandinskaya Oblast' Kazakh.
83 J2 Akzhal Vostochnyy Kazakhstan Kazakh.
82 D2 Akzhar Aktyubinskaya Oblast' Kazakh.
82 F3 Akzhar Kzyl-Ordinskaya Oblast' Kazakh.
83 J3 Akzhar Vostochnyy Kazakhstan Kazakh.
83 F3 Akzhaykyn, Ozero salt l. Kazakh.
80 G3 Akziyaret Turkey
103 J3 Ål Norway
84 C5 Al 'Abā Saudi Arabia
145 C6 Alabama state U.S.A.
145 C6 Alabama r. U.S.A.
145 C5 Alabaster U.S.A.
81 J7 'Abţiyah well Iraq
83 G4 Ala-Buka Kyrg.
80 E1 Alaca Turkey
80 F2 Alaçam Turkey
80 E1 Alacahan Turkey
80 A2 Alaçam Turkey
80 E3 Alaçam Dağları mts Turkey
151 D3 Alacrán, Arrecife atoll Mex.
81 I2 Ala Dağ mt. Turkey
81 I2 Ala Dağı mts Turkey
80 E3 Ala Dağlar mts Turkey
81 H7 Alagir Rus. Fed.
155 K6 Alagoinhas Brazil
111 F2 Alagón Spain
97 C5 Alah r. Phil.
102 M3 Alahärmä Fin.
84 C4 Al Aḩmadī Kuwait
83 I3 Alai Range mts Asia
120 A3 Alak Mauritania
102 M3 Alajärvi Fin.
88 D3 Alaknanda r. India
83 H3 Alakol', Ozero salt l. Kazakh.
102 O2 Alakurtti Rus. Fed.
81 H5 Al 'Alamayn Egypt
81 I4 Al 'Amādīyah Iraq
84 D4 Al'Amār Saudi Arabia
81 K6 Al 'Amārah Iraq
89 H3 Alamdo China
83 H4 Alamedin, Pik Zapadnyy mt. Kyrg.
81 J7 Al Amghar waterhole Iraq
97 A2 Alaminos Phil.
80 B6 Al 'Āmirīyah Egypt
141 E3 Alamo U.S.A.
141 E4 Alamo Dam U.S.A.
139 F5 Alamogordo U.S.A.
143 D6 Alamo Heights U.S.A.
139 E6 Alamos Sonora Mex.
150 D2 Alamos Sonora Mex.
139 F4 Alamosa U.S.A.
87 B3 Alampur India
102 K2 Alanäs Sweden
Åland is Fin. see Åland Islands
109 J1 Aland r. Germany
87 B2 Aland India
84 B2 Aland r. Iran
103 L3 Åland Islands is Fin.
98 B5 Alang Besar i. Indon.
134 E3 Alanson U.S.A.
80 D3 Alanya Turkey
88 C2 Alappuzha India see Alleppey
80 E7 Al 'Aqabah Jordan
84 A4 Al 'Aqabah, Gulf of g.
111 D2 Alar del Rey Spain
111 F3 Albacete Spain
70 D5 Albacutya, Lake Australia
81 J6 Al Bādiyah al Janūbīyah hill Iraq
115 J1 Alba Iulia Romania
132 C3 Albanel, Lake Canada
118 Albania country Europe
71 G8 Albany Australia
133 I3 Albany r. Canada
145 C5 Albany GA U.S.A.
134 E5 Albany IN U.S.A.
145 C4 Albany KY U.S.A.
147 G3 Albany NY U.S.A.
138 B2 Albany OR U.S.A.
143 D5 Albany TX U.S.A.
71 H1 Albany Downs Australia
159 D2 Albardão do João Maria coastal area Brazil
84 B5 Al Barrah Saudi Arabia
Al Başrah Iraq see Basra
68 D3 Albatross Bay Australia
71 F8 Albatross Island Australia
121 E1 Al Bawīţī Egypt
121 E2 Al Baydā' Libya
154 □ Albemarle, Punta pt Galapagos Is Ecuador
145 E5 Albemarle Sound sea chan. U.S.A.
114 C2 Albenga Italy
111 E2 Alberche r. Spain
71 G4 Alberga watercourse Australia
111 B2 Albergaria-a-Velha Port.
110 F2 Albert France
70 C5 Albert, Lake Australia
122 C3 Albert, Lake Dem. Rep. Congo/Uganda
130 G4 Alberta prov. Canada
124 D7 Albertinia S. Africa
108 C4 Albert Kanal canal Belgium
142 E3 Albert Lea U.S.A.
122 D3 Albert Nile r. Sudan/Uganda

156 B8 Alberto de Agostini, Parque Nacional nat. park Chile
125 H3 Alberton S. Africa
108 E6 Albertville France
71 G6 Albi France
155 H2 Albina Suriname
147 I2 Albion ME U.S.A.
134 E4 Albion MI U.S.A.
146 B3 Albion NY U.S.A.
111 E5 Alborán, Isla de i. Spain
103 J4 Ålborg Denmark
103 J4 Ålborg Bugt b. Denmark
Alborz, Reshteh-ye mts Iran see Elburz Mountains
130 F4 Albreda Canada
84 C5 Al Budayyi' Bahrain
111 B4 Albufeira Port.
150 I5 Albuquerque, Cayos de is Col.
86 E5 Al Buraymi Oman
111 C3 Alburquerque Spain
111 E3 Alcácer do Sal Port.
111 D3 Alcalá de Henares Spain
111 E4 Alcalá la Real Spain
114 E6 Alcamo Sicily Italy
111 F2 Alcañiz Spain
111 C3 Alcántara Spain
111 D4 Alcaraz Spain
111 D4 Alcázar de San Juan Spain
117 F5 Alchevs'k Ukr.
159 D2 Alcira Arg.
158 D2 Alcobaça Brazil
111 F2 Alcora Spain
159 E2 Alcorta Arg.
111 D4 Alcoy Spain
111 H3 Alcúdia Spain
123 E4 Aldabra Islands Seychelles
150 C1 Aldama Chihuahua Mex.
151 D3 Aldama Tamaulipas Mex.
77 N4 Aldan Rus. Fed.
77 O3 Aldan r. Rus. Fed.
105 I5 Aldeburgh U.K.
110 D2 Alderney i. U.K.
140 B2 Alder Peak mt. U.S.A.
105 G6 Aldershot U.K.
146 C6 Alderson U.S.A.
84 D6 Al Dhafrah reg. U.A.E.
105 E5 Aldridge U.K.
120 A3 Aleg Mauritania
158 E3 Alegre Brazil
158 E3 Alegre Brazil
159 E2 Alejandro Korn Arg.
116 E4 Alekhovshchina Rus. Fed.
82 B4 Aleksandra Bekovicha-Cherkassogo, Zaliv b. Kazakh.
82 C1 Aleksandrovka Orenburgskaya Oblast' Rus. Fed.
82 D1 Aleksandrovka Respublika Bashkortostan Rus. Fed.
117 H6 Aleksandrovskoye Rus. Fed.
77 P4 Aleksandrovsk-Sakhalinskiy Rus. Fed.
76 I1 Aleksandry, Zemlya i. Rus. Fed.
83 I1 Alekseyevka Kokshetauskaya Oblast' Kazakh.
83 H2 Alekseyevka Pavlodarskaya Oblast' Kazakh.
117 F5 Alekseyevka Belgorodskaya Oblast' Rus. Fed.
117 F5 Alekseyevka Belgorodskaya Oblast' Rus. Fed.
117 G5 Alekseyevskaya Rus. Fed.
116 F4 Aleksin Rus. Fed.
115 I3 Aleksinac Yugo.
122 B4 Alèmbé Gabon
158 D3 Além Paraíba Brazil
103 J3 Ålen Norway
110 E2 Alençon France
155 H4 Alenquer Brazil
140 □² Alenuihaha Channel U.S.A.
80 F3 Aleppo Syria
154 D6 Alerta Peru
130 D4 Alert Bay Canada
110 G4 Alès France
113 K7 Aleşd Romania
114 C2 Alessandria Italy
102 I3 Ålesund Norway
160 G2 Aleutian Basin sea feature Bering Sea
126 C2 Aleutian Islands AK U.S.A.
160 H2 Aleutian Trench sea feature N. Pacific Ocean
77 Q4 Alevina, Mys c. Rus. Fed.
147 J2 Alexander U.S.A.
130 B3 Alexander Archipelago is U.S.A.
124 B4 Alexander Bay Namibia/S. Africa
124 B4 Alexander Bay S. Africa
145 C5 Alexander City U.S.A.
73 A2 Alexander Island Antarctica
71 H6 Alexandra Australia
72 B6 Alexandra N.Z.
115 J4 Alexandreia Greece
121 E1 Alexandria Egypt
113 L3 Alexandria Romania
125 G5 Alexandria S. Africa
106 D5 Alexandria U.K.
143 E6 Alexandria LA U.S.A.
142 D2 Alexandria MN U.S.A.
146 E4 Alexandria VA U.S.A.
70 C5 Alexandrina, Lake Australia
115 K4 Alexandroupoli Greece
133 I3 Alexis r. Canada
130 E4 Alexis Creek Canada
83 J1 Aley r. Rus. Fed.
108 F4 Alf Germany
111 F1 Alfaro Spain
81 K7 Al Farwānīyah Kuwait
81 L7 Al Fatḩah Iraq
81 L7 Al Faw Iraq
121 F2 Al Fayyūm Egypt
158 D3 Alfenas Brazil
109 H2 Alfeld (Leine) Germany
113 J7 Alföld plain Hungary
105 H4 Alford U.K.
147 J2 Alfred Canada
84 C4 Al Fuḩayḩil Kuwait
Al Fujayrah U.A.E. see Fujairah
81 J6 Al Furāt r. Iraq/Syria alt. Fırat (Turkey); conv. Euphrates
82 C2 Alga Kazakh.
103 I4 Ålgård Norway
159 B4 Algarrobo del Aguila Arg.
116 B4 Algarve reg. Port.
111 D4 Algeciras Spain
111 F3 Algemesí Spain
Alger Alg. see Algiers
135 E3 Alger U.S.A.
118 Algeria country Africa
109 H2 Algermissen Germany
81 J6 Al Ghammās Iraq

84 B5	Al Ghaţ Saudi Arabia
86 D6	Al Ghaydah Yemen
114 C4	Alghero *Sardinia* Italy
121 F2	Al Ghurdaqah Egypt
84 C4	Al Ghwaybīyah Saudi Arabia
120 C1	Algiers Alg.
125 F6	Algoa Bay S. Africa
134 D3	Algoma U.S.A.
142 E3	Algona U.S.A.
135 F4	Algonac U.S.A.
135 H3	Algonquin Park Canada
	Algonquin Provincial Park Canada
111 E1	Algorta Spain
81 J4	Al Habakah *well* Saudi Arabia
81 I5	Al Habbānīyah Iraq
84 B4	Al Hadaqah *well* Saudi Arabia
84 C5	Al Hadd Bahrain
84 A4	Al Hadhālīl *plat.* Saudi Arabia
81 I4	Al Hadīthah Iraq
80 F4	Al Haffah Syria
84 B5	Al Hā'ir Saudi Arabia
84 E6	Al Hajar Oman
84 C5	Al Hajar al Gharbī *mts* Oman
81 G6	Al Hamād *reg.* Jordan/Saudi Arabia
121 D2	Al Hamādah al Hamrā' *plat.* Libya
111 F4	Alhama de Murcia Spain
80 B6	Al Hammām Egypt
81 I6	Al Hammām *well* Iraq
84 B4	Al Hariq Saudi Arabia
81 J7	Al Harīq Saudi Arabia
84 B6	Al Hariq Saudi Arabia
81 G6	Al Harrah *reg.* Saudi Arabia
81 H3	Al Hasakah Syria
81 J5	Al Hāshimīyah Iraq
80 F6	Al Hazīm Jordan
84 B5	Al Hillah Saudi Arabia
84 B6	Al Hilwah Saudi Arabia
84 C5	Al Hinnah Saudi Arabia
120 B1	Al Hoceima Morocco
	Al Hudaydah Yemen *see* Hodeida
86 C4	Al Hufūf Saudi Arabia
84 D6	Al Humrah *reg.* U.A.E.
84 C5	Al Hunayy Saudi Arabia
84 B6	Al Huwwah Saudi Arabia
81 K3	'Alīābād Iran
81 K4	'Alīābād Iran
82 D7	'Alīābād Iran
83 E3	'Alīābād Iran
85 E4	'Alīābād Iran
115 L5	Aliağa Turkey
115 J4	Aliakmonas *r.* Greece
81 K5	'Alī al Gharbī Iraq
87 A2	Alibag India
84 B4	Ali Bandar Pak.
81 L2	Äli Bayramlı Azer.
111 F3	Alicante Spain
125 G6	Alice S. Africa
130 D3	Alice Arm Canada
128 D6	Alice Springs Australia
145 E7	Alice Town Bahamas
83 H5	Alichur Tajik.
83 H5	Alichur *r.* Tajik.
97 B5	Alicia Phil.
88 D4	Aligarh India
84 C3	Alīgūdarz Iran
90 E1	Alihe China
122 B4	Alima *r.* Congo
103 K4	Alingsås Sweden
80 B2	Alioova *r.* Turkey
88 B3	Alipur Pak.
89 G4	Alipur Duar India
146 C4	Aliquippa U.S.A.
122 E2	Al Sabieh Djibouti
80 F6	Al 'Īsāwīyah Saudi Arabia
81 J2	Al Shah Iran
	Al Iskandarīyah Egypt *see* Alexandria
81 J5	Al Iskandarīyah Iraq
121 F1	Al Ismā'īlīyah Egypt
115 K5	Aliveri Greece
125 G5	Aliwal North S. Africa
130 C4	Alix Canada
80 F6	Al Jafr Jordan
81 E2	Al Jāfūrah *des.* Saudi Arabia
121 E2	Al Jaghbūb Libya
81 K7	Al Jahrah Kuwait
84 C5	Al Jamaliyah Qatar
84 C6	Al Jawb *reg.* Saudi Arabia
86 A4	Al Jawf Saudi Arabia
121 D1	Al Jawsh Libya
81 G3	Al Jazā'ir Iraq/Syria
111 B4	Aljezur Port.
84 C5	Al Jibān *reg.* Saudi Arabia
81 I6	Al Jill *well* Iraq
84 C5	Al Jilh *esc.* Saudi Arabia
	Al Jīzah Egypt *see* Giza
80 E6	Al Jīzah Jordan
81 J6	Al Jubayl Saudi Arabia
84 C5	Al Jubaylah Saudi Arabia
84 C5	Al Jurayd *i.* Saudi Arabia
84 B5	Al Jurayfah Saudi Arabia
111 B4	Aljustrel Port.
80 E6	Al Karak Jordan
81 J5	Al Khābūrah Iraq
86 E5	Al Khābūrah Oman
81 J5	Al Khāliş Iraq
121 F2	Al Khārijah Egypt
84 E4	Al Khaşab Oman
84 A4	Al Khatam *reg.* U.A.E.
84 D6	Al Khawr Qatar
84 C5	Al Khiṣah *well* Saudi Arabia
84 C5	Al Khobar Saudi Arabia
84 B5	Al Khuff *reg.* Saudi Arabia
121 D1	Al Khums Libya
84 C5	Al Kifl Iraq
81 J5	Al Kirānah Qatar
108 C2	Alkmaar Neth.
81 K5	Al Kūfah Iraq
81 K5	Al Kumayt Iraq
81 K5	Al Kūt Iraq
	Al Kuwayt Kuwait *see* Kuwait
81 H7	Al Labbah *plain* Saudi Arabia
	Al Lādhiqīyah Syria *see* Latakia
147 I1	Allagash U.S.A.
147 I1	Allagash *r.* U.S.A.
147 I1	Allagash Lake U.S.A.
89 E4	Allahabad India
80 F5	Al Lajā *lava field* Syria
77 M4	Allakh-Yun' Rus. Fed.
125 G3	Allanridge S. Africa
125 H1	Alldays S. Africa
134 E4	Allegan U.S.A.
146 D4	Allegheny *r.* U.S.A.
146 C6	Allegheny Mountains U.S.A.
146 D4	Allegheny Reservoir U.S.A.
107 C3	Allen, Lough *l.* Rep. of Ireland
145 D5	Allendale U.S.A.
104 E3	Allendale Town U.K.
150 D1	Allende Mex.
150 D2	Allende *Nuevo León* Mex.
109 J4	Allendorf (Lumda) Germany
135 G4	Allenford Canada
147 F4	Allentown U.S.A.
87 B4	Alleppey India
109 J2	Aller *r.* Germany
142 C3	Alliance NE U.S.A.
146 C3	Alliance OH U.S.A.
81 I6	Al Lifīyah *well* Iraq
103 K5	Allinge-Sandvig Denmark
131 K3	Alliston Canada
86 B5	Al Lith Saudi Arabia
106 E4	Alloa U.K.
71 J2	Allora Australia
81 I8	Al Lussuf *well* Iraq
133 F4	Alma Canada

134 E4	Alma *MI* U.S.A.
142 D3	Alma *NE* U.S.A.
141 H5	Alma *NM* U.S.A.
81 I6	Al Ma'āniyah Iraq
	Alma-Ata Kazakh. *see* Almaty
111 B3	Almada Port.
81 J7	Al Ma'daniyat *well* Iraq
111 D3	Almadén Spain
81 K6	Al Madīnah Iraq
	Al Madīnah Saudi Arabia *see* Medina
80 F5	Al Mafraq Jordan
81 J5	Al Mahmūdīyah Iraq
84 B5	Al Majma'ah Saudi Arabia
81 K1	Almalı Azer.
84 C5	Al Malsūnīyah *reg.* Saudi Arabia
83 G4	Almalyk Uzbek.
	Al Manāmah Bahrain *see* Manama
140 B1	Almanor, Lake U.S.A.
111 F3	Almansa Spain
121 F2	Al Mansūrah Egypt
111 D2	Almanzor *mt.* Spain
81 K6	Al Maqil Iraq
84 D6	Al Mariyyah U.A.E.
121 E1	Al Marj Libya
158 C1	Almas, Rio das *r.* Brazil
83 H3	Almatinskaya Oblast' *admin. div.* Kazakh.
83 I4	Almaty Kazakh.
81 H4	Al Mawşil Iraq *see* Mosul
84 B5	Al Mayādīn Syria
84 B5	Al Mazāhimīyah Saudi Arabia
111 E2	Almazán Spain
77 M3	Almaznyy Rus. Fed.
155 I4	Almeirim Brazil
111 B3	Almeirim Port.
108 E2	Almelo Neth.
158 E2	Almenara Brazil
111 C2	Almendra, Embalse de *resr* Spain
111 C3	Almendralejo Spain
108 D2	Almere Neth.
111 E4	Almería Spain
111 E4	Almería, Golfo de *b.* Spain
76 K7	Al'met'yevsk Rus. Fed.
103 K4	Älmhult Sweden
84 B5	Al Midhnab Saudi Arabia
111 D5	Almina, Punta de Morocco
121 F2	Al Minyā Egypt
150 I6	Almirante Panama
86 C4	Al Mish'āb Saudi Arabia
111 B4	Almodôvar Port.
135 F4	Almont U.S.A.
135 I3	Almonte Canada
111 C4	Almonte Spain
88 D4	Almora India
80 E7	Al Mudawwarah Jordan
84 C5	Al Muharraq Bahrain
	Al Mukallā Yemen *see* Mukalla
	Al Mukhā Yemen *see* Mocha
111 E4	Almuñécar Spain
81 J5	Al Muqdādīyah Iraq
84 B5	Al Murabba Saudi Arabia
80 F1	Almus Turkey
84 B4	Al Musannah *ridge* Saudi Arabia
81 J5	Al Musayyib Iraq
115 K7	Almyrou, Ormos *b.* Greece
140 □1	Alna Haina U.S.A.
104 F2	Alnwick U.K.
89 H9	Alon Myanmar
89 H3	Along India
115 J5	Alonnisos *i.* Greece
91 E7	Alor *i.* Indon.
91 E7	Alor, Kepulauan *is* Indon.
99 B1	Alor Setar Malaysia
	Alost Belgium *see* Aalst
88 C5	Alot India
102 O2	Alozero Rus. Fed.
108 D3	Alpaugh U.S.A.
108 E3	Alpen Germany
135 F3	Alpena U.S.A.
164 P1	Alpha Ridge *sea feature* Arctic Ocean
141 H5	Alpine *AZ* U.S.A.
143 C6	Alpine *TX* U.S.A.
138 E3	Alpine *WY* U.S.A.
114 C1	Alps *mts* Europe
86 C4	Al Qa'āmīyāt *reg.* Saudi Arabia
121 D1	Al Qaddāhīyah Libya
80 F4	Al Qadmūs Syria
84 B5	Al Qā'īyah *well* Saudi Arabia
81 H3	Al Qāmishlī Syria
80 D6	Al Qantarah Egypt
84 B5	Al Qar'ah *well* Saudi Arabia
80 F4	Al Qaryatayn Syria
84 B5	Al Qaşab Saudi Arabia
86 C6	Al Qaţn Yemen
80 F6	Al Qaţrānah Jordan
121 D2	Al Qaţrūn Libya
84 B4	Al Qayşūmah Saudi Arabia
80 E5	Al Qunayţirah Syria
84 A5	Al Qunfidhah Saudi Arabia
84 A5	Al Qurayn Saudi Arabia
81 K6	Al Qurnah Iraq
121 F2	Al Quşayr Egypt
81 J6	Al Quşayr Iraq
80 F5	Al Quţayfah Syria
84 A5	Al Qūşūrīyah Saudi Arabia
84 A5	Al Quwayʿ Saudi Arabia
84 B5	Al Quwayyah Saudi Arabia
80 F6	Al Quwayrah Jordan
110 H2	Alsace *reg.* France
105 E4	Alsager U.K.
81 I6	Al Samīt *well* Iraq
131 H4	Alsask Canada
109 H4	Alsfeld Germany
109 J3	Alsleben (Saale) Germany
104 E3	Alston U.K.
71 J2	Alstonville Australia
103 M4	Alsunga Latvia
102 M1	Alta Norway
72 B6	Alta, Mount N.Z.
102 M1	Altaelva *r.* Norway
157 D2	Altagracia de Orituco Venez.
79 G2	Altai Mountains China/Mongolia
145 D6	Altamaha *r.* U.S.A.
155 I4	Altamira Brazil
151 H5	Altamira Costa Rica
114 G4	Altamura Italy
92 C2	Altan Shiret China
158 C1	Alta Paraíso de Goiás Brazil
150 B2	Altata Mex.
146 C4	Altavista U.S.A.
79 G2	Altay China
90 B2	Altay Mongolia
92 K2	Altay, Respublika *aut. rep.* Rus. Fed.
83 K2	Altayskiy Rus. Fed.
	Altayskiy Kray *admin. div.* Rus. Fed.
111 F3	Altea Spain
102 M1	Alteidet Norway
108 H4	Altenahr Germany
109 K4	Altenberge Germany
109 L1	Altenburg Germany
	Altenkirchen (Westerwald) Germany
89 H1	Altenqoke China
109 L1	Altentreptow Germany
85 H3	Altin Köprü Iraq
80 C2	Altıntaş Turkey
158 C1	Altinoluk Turkey
138 D3	Altiplano *plain* Bol.
109 J2	Altmark *reg.* Germany
109 I5	Altmühl *r.* Germany
158 B2	Alto Araguaia Brazil
111 F2	Alto del Moncayo *mt.* Spain
159 C2	Alto de Pencoso *hill* Arg.

157 B3	Alto de Tamar *mt.* Col.
158 B2	Alto Garças Brazil
123 D5	Alto Molócuè Moz.
143 D5	Alton *MO* U.S.A.
147 H3	Alton *NH* U.S.A.
142 D1	Altona Canada
146 D4	Altoona U.S.A.
158 B2	Alto Sucuriú Brazil
112 F6	Altötting Germany
105 E4	Altrincham U.K.
109 K1	Alt Schwerin Germany
151 H5	Altun Ha *tourist site* Belize
90 A3	Altun Shan *mts* China
138 B3	Alturas U.S.A.
143 D5	Altus U.S.A.
82 E3	Altynasar *tourist site* Kazakh.
80 G1	Alucra Turkey
103 N4	Alūksne Latvia
81 L5	Alūm Iran
84 B4	Alun Creek Lake U.S.A.
159 B3	Aluminé Arg.
159 B3	Aluminé, Lago *l.* Arg.
117 E6	Alupka Ukr.
121 D1	Al 'Uqaylah Libya
84 C5	Al 'Uqayr Saudi Arabia
	Al 'Uqşur Egypt *see* Luxor
117 E6	Alushta Ukr.
81 J4	'Alūt Iran
121 E2	Al 'Uwaynāt Libya
84 B6	Al 'Uwayqīlah Saudi Arabia
84 A5	Al 'Uyūn Saudi Arabia
81 K6	Al 'Uzayr Iraq
143 D4	Alva U.S.A.
81 L4	Alvand, Kūh-e *mt.* Iran
151 F4	Alvarado Mex.
159 C2	Alvarado, Paso de *pass* Chile
158 B2	Alvares Brazil
103 J3	Ålvdal Norway
103 K3	Älvdalen Sweden
103 K4	Alvesta Sweden
103 I3	Ålvik Norway
103 L3	Alvik Sweden
143 E6	Alvin U.S.A.
102 M2	Älvsbyn Sweden
76 K7	Al Wafrah Kuwait
78 B4	Al Wajh Saudi Arabia
84 C5	Al Wakrah Qatar
88 D4	Al Wannān Saudi Arabia
85 B5	Al Wari'ah Saudi Arabia
87 B4	Alwaye India
81 H5	Al Widyān *plat.* Iraq/ Saudi Arabia
84 A4	Al Wusayt *well* Saudi Arabia
68 D3	Alyangula Australia
106 E4	Alyth U.K.
103 N5	Alytus Lith.
138 F2	Alzada U.S.A.
108 E4	Alzette *r.* Lux.
109 G5	Alzey Germany
157 E3	Amacuro *r.* Guyana/Venez.
68 D4	Amadeus, Lake *salt flat* Australia
129 K3	Amadjuak Lake Canada
141 G6	Amado U.S.A.
111 B3	Amadora Port.
95 A8	Amakusa-nada *b.* Japan
103 K4	Åmål Sweden
87 C2	Amalapuram India
157 B3	Amalfi Col.
124 F3	Amalia S. Africa
115 I6	Amaliada Greece
88 C5	Amalner India
91 F7	Amamapare Indon.
158 A3	Amambaí Brazil
158 A3	Amambaí *r.* Brazil
158 A3	Amambaí, Serra de *hills* Brazil/Para.
90 E4	Amami-Ō-shima *i.* Japan
90 E4	Amami-shotō *is* Japan
82 D2	Amangel'dy Kazakh.
82 F2	Amangel'dy Kazakh.
83 J4	Amankol Kazakh.
82 E3	Amanotkel' Kazakh.
114 G5	Amantea Italy
155 H3	Amapá Brazil
155 H3	Amapá *state* Brazil
140 D3	Amargosa Desert U.S.A.
140 D3	Amargosa Range *mts* U.S.A.
140 D3	Amargosa Valley U.S.A.
143 C5	Amarillo U.S.A.
114 F3	Amaro, Monte *mt.* Italy
80 E1	Amasya Turkey
151 F4	Amatán Mex.
150 C3	Amatique, Bahía de *b.* Guat.
150 C3	Amatlán de Cañas Mex.
108 D4	Amay Belgium
155 H4	Amazon *r.* S. America *alt.* Amazonas/Para.
155 I3	Amazon, Mouths of the *est.* Brazil
157 D4	Amazonas *state* Brazil
155 H4	Amazonas *r.* S. America *conv.* Amazon
163 F5	Amazon Cone *sea feature* S. Atlantic Ocean
155 G4	Amazónia, Parque Nacional *nat. park* Brazil
88 C6	Ambad India
87 B2	Ambajogai India
88 D3	Ambala India
87 C5	Ambalangoda Sri Lanka
123 E6	Ambalavao Madag.
123 E5	Ambanja Madag.
85 E4	Ambar Iran
77 R3	Ambarchik Rus. Fed.
80 B2	Ambarcık Turkey
154 C4	Ambato Ecuador
123 E5	Ambato Boeny Madag.
123 E5	Ambato Finandrahana Madag.
123 E5	Ambatolampy Madag.
123 E5	Ambatomainty Madag.
123 E5	Ambatondrazaka Madag.
109 J5	Amberg Germany
151 H4	Ambergris Cay *i.* Belize
110 G4	Ambérieu-en-Bugey France
89 G3	Amberley Canada
88 D4	Ambikapur India
123 E5	Ambilobe Madag.
130 C3	Ambition, Mount Canada
104 F2	Amble U.K.
104 D4	Ambleside U.K.
108 D4	Amblève *r.* Belgium
123 E6	Amboasary Madag.
123 E5	Ambohidratrimo Madag.
123 E6	Ambohimahasoa Madag.
91 E7	Ambon Indon.
91 E7	Ambon *i.* Indon.
123 E6	Ambositra Madag.
123 E6	Ambovombe Madag.
140 D4	Amboy *CA* U.S.A.
134 C5	Amboy *IL* U.S.A.
123 B4	Amboy Center U.S.A.
123 B4	Ambriz Angola
69 G2	Ambrym *i.* Vanuatu
87 B3	Ambur India
150 D1	Ameca Mex.
150 D3	Ameca *r.* Mex.
151 E4	Amealco Mex.
147 G4	Amelia Court House U.S.A.
147 G4	Amelia U.S.A.
158 C3	American, North Fork *r.* U.S.A.
163 H9	American-Antarctic Ridge *sea feature* S. Atlantic Ocean
138 D3	American Falls U.S.A.
138 D3	American Falls Reservoir U.S.A.
141 G1	American Fork U.S.A.
67 H4	American Samoa *terr.* Pacific Ocean
145 C5	Americus U.S.A.

108 D2	Amersfoort Neth.
125 H3	Amersfoort S. Africa
105 G6	Amersham U.K.
131 K3	Amery Canada
143 F4	Amery Ice Shelf Antarctica
142 E3	Ames U.S.A.
105 F6	Amesbury U.K.
147 H3	Amesbury U.S.A.
89 E4	Amethi India
115 J5	Amfissa Greece
77 O3	Amga Rus. Fed.
90 F2	Amgu Rus. Fed.
120 C2	Amguid Alg.
90 F1	Amgun' *r.* Rus. Fed.
133 H4	Amherst Canada
147 G3	Amherst *MA* U.S.A.
147 I2	Amherst *NY* U.S.A.
146 D6	Amherst *VA* U.S.A.
135 F4	Amherstburg Canada
110 F2	Amiens France
81 H5	'Āmij, Wādī *watercourse* Iraq
87 A4	Amindivi Islands India
95 D7	Aminuo Japan
124 C1	Aminuis Namibia
84 B3	Amirabad Iran
163 M6	Amirante Islands Seychelles
162 H5	Amirante Trench *sea feature* Indian Ocean
85 E4	Amir Chah Pak.
131 I4	Amisk Lake Canada
150 I6	Amistad, Parque Internacional La *nat. park* Costa Rica/Panama
143 C6	Amistad Reservoir Mex./U.S.A.
71 J1	Amity Point Australia
88 D5	Amla India
103 J4	Åmli Norway
105 C4	Amlwch U.K.
81 I5	'Ammān Jordan
80 E6	'Ammān Jordan
102 O2	Ämmänsaari Fin.
129 O3	Ammassalik Greenland
109 I1	Ammern Germany
109 I3	Ammern Germany
112 E7	Ammochostos Cyprus *see* Famagusta
88 D4	Amnyong-dan *hd* N. Korea
93 B6	Amo Jiang *r.* China
84 D2	Amol Iran
109 H5	Amorbach Germany
115 K6	Amorgos *i.* Greece
132 E4	Amos Canada
	Amoy China *see* Xiamen
87 C5	Amparai India
122 E6	Amparo Brazil
112 E6	Amper *r.* Germany
163 I3	Ampere Seamount *sea feature* N. Atlantic Ocean
111 I3	Amposta Spain
88 B5	Amravati India
88 B5	Amreli India
80 E4	'Amrīt Syria
88 C3	Amritsar India
88 D3	Amroha India
102 L2	Åmsele Sweden
108 C2	Amstelveen Neth.
108 C2	Amsterdam Neth. (City Plan 55)
125 I3	Amsterdam S. Africa
146 F3	Amsterdam U.S.A.
162 J7	Amsterdam, Île *i.* Indian Ocean
112 G6	Amstetten Austria
121 E3	Am Timan Chad
82 D3	Amudar'ya *r.* Turkm./Uzbek.
129 H2	Amund Ringnes Island Canada
73 C5	Amundsen, Mount Antarctica
161 K10	Amundsen Abyssal Plain *sea feature* Southern Ocean
164 B1	Amundsen Basin *sea feature* Arctic Ocean
73 B4	Amundsen Bay Antarctica
73 B4	Amundsen Glacier Antarctica
128 F2	Amundsen Gulf Canada
161 K10	Amundsen Ridge *sea feature* Southern Ocean
73 B4	Amundsen-Scott *research station* Antarctica
73 A3	Amundsen Sea Antarctica
99 C2	Amuntai Indon.
90 E2	Amur *r.* China/Rus. Fed. *alt.* Heilong Jiang
77 M2	Amurzet Rus. Fed.
117 F6	Amvrosiyivka Ukr.
134 E1	Amyot Canada
89 H4	An Myanmar
161 J7	Anaa *atoll* Fr. Polynesia
91 E7	Anabanua Indon.
77 M2	Anabar *r.* Rus. Fed.
70 D4	Ana Branch *r.* Australia
140 C4	Anacapa Islands U.S.A.
157 D2	Anaco Venez.
138 D3	Anaconda U.S.A.
138 C1	Anacortes U.S.A.
143 D5	Anadarko U.S.A.
80 F1	Anadolu Dağları *mts* Turkey
77 S3	Anadyr' Rus. Fed.
77 T3	Anadyr' *r.* Rus. Fed.
115 K6	Anadyrskiy Zaliv *b.* Rus. Fed.
115 K6	Anafi *i.* Greece
158 E1	Anagé Brazil
81 I5	'Ānah Iraq
140 D5	Anaheim U.S.A.
130 D4	Anahim Lake Canada
151 D2	Anáhuac Mex.
87 B4	Anai Mudi Peak India
87 C2	Anakapalle India
123 E5	Analalava Madag.
154 F4	Anamã Brazil
99 C2	Anambas, Kepulauan *is* Indon.
134 A2	Anamosa U.S.A.
80 D3	Anamur Turkey
80 D3	Anamur Burnu *pt* Turkey
95 D8	Anan Japan
88 C5	Anand India
89 F5	Anandapur India
87 B2	Anantapur India
88 C2	Anantnag Jammu and Kashmir
84 C3	Anār Iran
84 C3	Anarbar *r.* Iran
84 B3	Anārak Iran
83 I3	Anārbār Afgh.
96 C5	Anatolia *reg.* Turkey
82 F3	Anatom Afgh.
156 C3	Anatuya Arg.
159 B3	Añelo Arg.
157 E4	Anauá *r.* Brazil
106 E6	Anayaza *valley* U.K.
109 I3	Ancenis France
128 B2	Anchorage U.S.A.
146 E5	Annapolis U.S.A.
133 G5	Annapolis Royal Canada
80 F3	Ancol Italy
159 B5	Ancud Chile
159 B5	Ancud, Golfo de *g.* Chile
90 C1	Anda China
154 B4	Andacollo Chile
102 I3	Åndalsnes Norway
111 D4	Andalucía *aut. comm.* Spain
143 C6	Andalusia U.S.A.
79 M5	Andaman and Nicobar Islands *union terr.* India
162 K4	Andaman Basin *sea feature* Indian Ocean
79 H5	Andaman Islands India
79 H5	Andaman Sea Asia

70 B3	Andamooka Australia
123 E5	Andapa Madag.
158 E1	Aracruz Brazil
102 L1	Andenes Norway
108 D4	Andenne Belgium
108 C4	Anderlecht Belgium
110 D4	Andernos-les-Bains France
128 F3	Anderson *r.* Canada
128 D3	Anderson *AK* U.S.A.
134 E5	Anderson *IN* U.S.A.
145 D5	Anderson *SC* U.S.A.
71 G8	Anderson Bay Australia
154 E5	Andes *mts* S. America
102 L1	Andfjorden *sea chan.* Norway
87 B3	Andhra Pradesh *state* India
123 E5	Andilamena Madag.
123 E5	Andilanatoby Madag.
84 D3	Andīmeshk Iran
80 F3	Andırın Turkey
117 H7	Andiyskoye Koysu *r.* Rus. Fed.
83 H4	Andkhui Afgh.
85 G2	Andkhvoy Afgh.
123 E5	Andoany Madag.
154 C4	Andoas Peru
87 B2	Andol India
95 C6	Andong S. Korea
95 C6	Andong-ho *l.* S. Korea
111 G1	Andorra *country* Europe
111 G1	Andorra la Vella Andorra
105 F6	Andover U.K.
147 H2	Andover *ME* U.S.A.
146 C4	Andover *OH* U.S.A.
102 K1	Andøya *i.* Norway
158 B3	Andradina Brazil
117 D5	Andrushivka Ukr.
102 L1	Andselv Norway
111 D3	Andújar Spain
123 B5	Andulo Angola
120 E3	Anéfis Mali
149 L5	Anegada *i.* Virgin Is (U.K.)
159 D4	Anegada, Bahía *b.* Arg.
120 C4	Aného Togo
111 H3	Aneto *mt.* Spain
121 D3	Aney Niger
123 E5	Angadoka, Lohatanjona *hd* Madag.
90 A3	Angara *r.* Rus. Fed.
90 C1	Angarsk Rus. Fed.
103 K3	Ånge Sweden
148 E3	Ángel de la Guarda, Isla *i.* Mex.
97 B3	Angeles Phil.
103 K4	Ängelholm Sweden
140 B2	Angels Camp U.S.A.
102 L3	Ångermanälven *r.* Sweden
110 D3	Angers France
131 J2	Angikuni Lake Canada
98 B2	Angkor Cambodia
105 C4	Anglesey *i.* U.K.
143 E6	Angleton U.S.A.
135 H2	Angliers Canada
98 □1	Ang Mo Kio Sing.
122 C4	Ango Dem. Rep. Congo
123 D5	Angoche Moz.
159 B3	Angol Chile
123 B5	Angola *country* Africa
134 E5	Angola U.S.A.
163 I7	Angola Basin *sea feature* S. Atlantic Ocean
110 E4	Angoulême France
82 F2	Angren Uzbek.
98 B2	Ang Thong Thai.
149 L5	Anguilla *terr.* Caribbean Sea
93 C4	Anguli Nur *l.* China
92 E1	Anguo China
158 A3	Anhandui *r.* Brazil
103 J4	Anholt *i.* Denmark
93 C4	Anhua China
92 A2	Anhui *prov.* China
158 A2	Anhumas Brazil
158 C2	Anicuns Brazil
82 E2	Anikhovka Rus. Fed.
141 H6	Animas U.S.A.
98 A2	Anin Myanmar
90 H1	Aniva, Mys *c.* Rus. Fed.
90 D2	Aniva, Zaliv *b.* Rus. Fed.
69 G3	Aniwa *i.* Vanuatu
108 B5	Anizy-le-Château France
103 N3	Anjalankoski Fin.
87 B4	Anjengo India
93 C5	Anji China
84 B3	Anjir Iran
84 B3	Anjira Iran
	Anjouan *i.* Comoros *see* Nzwani
95 C5	Anju N. Korea
92 E6	Ankang China
80 D2	Ankara Turkey
123 E5	Ankazoabo Madag.
123 E5	Ankazobe Madag.
98 D2	An Khê Vietnam
88 C5	Anklesvar India
109 L1	Anklam Germany
88 C2	Ankleshwar India
93 C4	Anlong China
98 C2	Ânlong Vêng Cambodia
92 F4	Anlu China
89 G5	Anmyŏn-do *i.* S. Korea
135 I3	Ann *r.* Canada
117 C5	Ann, Lake U.S.A.
146 E5	Anna U.S.A.
109 L4	Annaberg-Buchholtz Germany
84 A5	An Nabk Syria
86 B4	An Nafūd *des.* Saudi Arabia
81 I5	An Nahrawan al Qadīm *canal* Iraq
81 J6	An Najaf Iraq
107 F3	Annalee *r.* Rep. of Ireland
108 C4	Annan U.K.
106 E6	Annan *r.* U.K.
146 E5	Annapolis U.S.A.
133 G5	Annapolis Royal Canada
89 E3	Annapurna I *mt.* Nepal
84 C6	An Naqīrah *well* Saudi Arabia
134 F4	Ann Arbor U.S.A.
155 G2	Anna Regina Guyana
81 K6	An Nāşirīyah Iraq
110 G4	Annecy France
108 D5	Annemasse France
108 H3	Annen Neth.
147 K1	Anne's Island U.S.A.
84 B5	An Nimāsh Syria
93 B5	Anning China
145 C5	Anniston U.S.A.
118 G4	Annobón *i.* Equat. Guinea
110 G4	Annonay France

86 C4	An Nu'ayrīyah Saudi Arabia
81 J5	An Nu'mānīyah Iraq
80 F4	An Nuşayrīyah, Jabal *mts* Syria
142 E2	Anoka U.S.A.
123 E5	Anorontany, Tanjona *hd* Madag.
115 K7	Ano Viannos Greece
93 D6	Anpu China
93 C6	Anpu Gang *b.* China
93 E4	Anqing China
92 F2	Anqiu China
93 D5	Anren China
108 D4	Ans Belgium
92 C2	Ansai China
109 I5	Ansbach Germany
71 K7	Anser Group *is* Australia
96 A5	Anshan China
93 B5	Anshun China
159 C1	Ansilta *mt.* Arg.
156 E4	Ansina Uruguay
142 D3	Ansley U.S.A.
143 D5	Anson U.S.A.
132 C3	Ansonville Canada
146 C5	Ansted U.S.A.
88 D4	Anta India
154 D6	Antabamba Peru
80 F3	Antakya Turkey
123 F5	Antalaha Madag.
80 C3	Antalya Turkey
80 C3	Antalya Körfezi *g.* Turkey
123 E5	Antananarivo Madag.
73	Antarctica
73 B2	Antarctic Peninsula Antarctica
106 C3	An Teallach *mt.* U.K.
140 D2	Antelope Range *mts* U.S.A.
111 D4	Antequera Spain
139 F5	Anthony U.S.A.
120 B2	Anti Atlas *mts* Morocco
110 H5	Antibes France
133 H4	Anticosti, Île d' *i.* Canada
134 C3	Antigo U.S.A.
133 H4	Antigonish Canada
149 L5	Antigua *i.* Antigua and Barbuda
151 G5	Antigua Guat.
149 L5	Antigua and Barbuda *country* Caribbean Sea
151 E3	Antiguo-Morelos Mex.
115 J7	Antikythira *i.* Greece
115 J7	Antikythiro, Steno *sea chan.* Greece
	Antioch Turkey *see* Antakya
140 B3	Antioch *CA* U.S.A.
134 C4	Antioch *IL* U.S.A.
157 B3	Antioquia Col.
67 G7	Antipodes Islands N.Z.
115 K5	Antipsara *i.* Greece
143 E5	Antlers U.S.A.
156 B2	Antofagasta Chile
156 C3	Antofalla, Volcán *vol.* Arg.
108 B4	Antoing Belgium
150 I6	Antón Panama
158 C3	Antonina Brazil
158 C1	Antônio *r.* Brazil
139 F4	Antonito U.S.A.
107 E2	Antrim U.K.
123 E5	Antsalova Madag.
123 E5	Antsirabe Madag.
123 E5	Antsirañana Madag.
123 E5	Antsohihy Madag.
102 N2	Änttis Sweden
159 B3	Antuco Chile
159 B3	Antuco, Volcán *vol.* Chile
108 C3	Antwerp Belgium
108 C3	Antwerpen Belgium
70 A4	Anxious Bay Australia
92 C2	Anyang China
96 D5	Anyang S. Korea
90 A3	A'nyêmaqên Shan *mts* China
93 C5	Anyi China
93 E5	Anyuan China
77 R3	Anyuysk Rus. Fed.
157 B3	Anzá Col.
90 A1	Anze China
122 C4	Anzi Dem. Rep. Congo
114 E4	Anzio Italy
69 G3	Aoba *i.* Vanuatu
98 A3	Ao Kham, Laem *pt* Thai.
94 E4	Aomori Japan
88 D3	Aonla India
	Aoraki mt. N.Z. *see* Cook, Mount
	Aoraki N.Z. *see* Mount Cook
98 C2	Aôral, Phnum *mt.* Cambodia
72 C4	Aorangi mt. N.Z.
114 B2	Aosta Italy
120 B2	Aoukâr *reg.* Mali/Mauritania
155 G8	Apa *r.* Brazil
141 H5	Apache U.S.A.
141 H6	Apache Creek U.S.A.
141 G6	Apache Junction U.S.A.
141 H5	Apache Peak U.S.A.
145 C6	Apalachee Bay U.S.A.
145 C6	Apalachicola U.S.A.
151 E4	Apan Mex.
81 J1	Aparan Armenia
158 B3	Aparecida do Tabuado Brazil
97 C5	Aparri Phil.
102 P2	Apatity Rus. Fed.
150 D4	Apatzingán Mex.
103 N4	Ape Latvia
108 E2	Apeldoorn Neth.
109 G1	Apen Germany
109 H1	Apensen Germany
88 F3	Api *mt.* Nepal
69 I3	Apia Samoa
72 E3	Api N.Z.
97 C5	Apo, Mount *vol.* Phil.
155 H6	Apoera Suriname
109 J3	Apolda Germany
128 D6	Apollo Bay Australia
154 E6	Apolo Bol.
158 D1	Aporé Brazil
158 B2	Aporé *r.* Brazil
144 B2	Apostle Islands National Lakeshore *res.* U.S.A.
80 E4	Apostolos Andreas, Cape Cyprus
146 C5	Appalachia U.S.A.
114 E3	Appalachian Mountains U.S.A.
114 D2	Appennino Tosco-Emiliano *mts* Italy
114 E3	Appennino Umbro-Marchigiano *mts* Italy
71 I5	Appin Australia
108 E1	Appingedam Neth.
106 E5	Applecross U.K.
134 C3	Appleton *MN* U.S.A.
134 C3	Appleton *WI* U.S.A.
146 D6	Apple Valley U.S.A.
146 D6	Appomattox U.S.A.
117 F6	Apsheronsk Rus. Fed.
70 D6	Apsley Australia

135 H3 **Apsley** Canada
110 G5 **Apt** France
158 B3 **Apucarana** Brazil
97 A4 **Apurahuan** Phil.
157 D3 **Apure** r. Venez.
154 D6 **Apurímac** r. Peru
121 F2 **Aqaba, Gulf of** Asia
83 I4 **Aqal** China
84 D2 **Aqbana** Iran
85 G2 **Aqchah** Afgh.
84 B2 **Aq Chai** r. Iran
84 D3 **'Aqdā** Iran
84 B2 **Aqdoghmish** r. Iran
81 J3 **Āq Kān Dāgh, Kūh-e** mt. Iran
82 C5 **Āq Qal'eh** Iran
81 I3 **'Aqrah** Iraq
141 F4 **Aquarius Mountains** U.S.A.
141 G3 **Aquarius Plateau** U.S.A.
114 G3 **Aquaviva delle Fonti** Italy
158 A3 **Aquidauana** Brazil
158 A2 **Aquidauana** r. Brazil
150 D4 **Aquila** Mex.
157 D4 **Aquio** r. Col.
151 E3 **Aquismón** Mex.
110 D4 **Aquitaine** reg. France
89 F4 **Ara** India
85 G4 **Arab** Afgh.
145 C5 **Arab** U.S.A.
121 E3 **Arab, Bahr el** watercourse Sudan
80 B6 **'Arab, Khalīj al** b. Egypt
85 E3 **'Arabābād** Iran
162 I4 **Arabian Basin** sea feature Indian Ocean
78 E5 **Arabian Sea** Indian Ocean
157 E3 **Araboó** Venez.
157 E3 **Arabopó** r. Venez.
80 D1 **Araç** Turkey
157 E4 **Araça** r. Brazil
155 K6 **Aracaju** Brazil
157 D4 **Aracamuni, Cerro** mt. Venez.
158 A4 **Aracanguy, Montes de** hills Para.
155 K4 **Aracati** Brazil
158 E1 **Aracatu** Brazil
158 B3 **Araçatuba** Brazil
111 C4 **Aracena** Spain
158 E2 **Aracruz** Brazil
158 D2 **Araçuaí** Brazil
158 D2 **Araçuaí** r. Brazil
115 I1 **Arad** Romania
121 E3 **Arada** Chad
68 D2 **Arafura Sea** Australia/Indon.
160 D6 **Arafura Shelf** sea feature Australia/Indon.
158 B1 **Aragarças** Brazil
158 I1 **Aragats** Armenia
81 J1 **Aragats Lerr** mt. Armenia
111 F2 **Aragón** r. Spain
111 F1 **Aragón** reg. Spain
155 I5 **Araguacema** Brazil
157 D2 **Aragua de Barcelona** Venez.
155 I5 **Araguaia** Brazil
155 H6 **Araguaia, Parque Nacional de** nat. park Brazil
155 I5 **Araguaína** Brazil
157 E2 **Araguao, Boca** est. Venez.
157 E2 **Araguao, Caño** r. Venez.
158 C2 **Araguari** Brazil
158 C2 **Araguari** r. Brazil
155 I5 **Araguatins** Brazil
117 H7 **Aragvi** r. Georgia
95 F6 **Arai** Japan
155 J4 **Araiosos** Brazil
120 C2 **Arak** Alg.
84 C3 **Arāk** Iran
Araks r. Armenia/Turkey see **Araz**
89 H5 **Arakan Yoma** mts Myanmar
87 B3 **Arakkonam** India
83 J4 **Aral** China
81 J2 **Aralık** Turkey
82 D3 **Aral Sea** salt l. Kazakh./Uzbek.
82 E3 **Aral'sk** Kazakh.
Aral'skoye More salt l. Kazakh./Uzbek. see **Aral Sea**
82 B2 **Aralsor, Ozero** l. Kazakh.
82 C2 **Aralsor, Ozero** salt l. Kazakh.
84 B5 **Aramah** plat. Saudi Arabia
151 E2 **Aramberri** Mex.
88 D6 **Aran** r. India
81 K4 **Arandān** Iran
115 I2 **Arandelovac** Yugo.
87 B3 **Araní** India
107 C3 **Aran Island** Rep. of Ireland
107 B4 **Aran Islands** Rep. of Ireland
111 E2 **Aranjuez** Spain
123 D6 **Aranos** Namibia
143 D7 **Aransas Pass** U.S.A.
158 B2 **Arantes** r. Brazil
69 H1 **Aranuka** i. Kiribati
98 B2 **Aranyaprathet** Thai.
95 B8 **Arao** Japan
155 G6 **Araouane** Mali
142 D3 **Arapahoe** U.S.A.
157 E4 **Arapari** r. Brazil
159 F1 **Arapey Grande** r. Uruguay
155 K5 **Arapiraca** Brazil
115 K4 **Arapis, Akra** pt Greece
80 C2 **Arapkir** Turkey
158 B3 **Arapongas** Brazil
89 F4 **A Rapti Doon** r. Nepal
86 B3 **'Ar'ar** Saudi Arabia
81 I6 **'Ar'ar** watercourse Iraq/Saudi Arabia
156 G3 **Araranguá** Brazil
158 C3 **Araraquara** Brazil
155 H5 **Araras** Brazil
158 B4 **Araras, Serra das** mts Brazil
81 J2 **Ararat** Armenia
70 E6 **Ararat** Australia
81 J1 **Ararat, Mount** Turkey
89 F4 **Araria** India
158 D3 **Araruama, Lago de** lag. Brazil
81 I2 **Aras** Turkey
81 I1 **Aras** r. Turkey alt. **Araks** (Armenia/Turkey), alt. **Araz** (Azerbaijan)
158 E1 **Arataca** Brazil
157 C3 **Arauca** Col.
157 C3 **Arauca** r. Venez.
159 B3 **Araucanía** admin. reg. Chile
159 B3 **Arauco** Chile
157 C3 **Arauquita** Col.
157 C2 **Araure** Venez.
88 C4 **Aravalli Range** mts India
103 N4 **Aravete** Estonia
69 F2 **Arawa** P.N.G.
158 C2 **Araxá** Brazil
157 D2 **Araya, Península de** pen. Venez.
80 C2 **Araya, Punta de** pt Venez.
80 C2 **Arayıt Dağı** mt. Turkey
81 L2 **Araz** r. Asia alt. **Araks** (Armenia/Turkey), alt. **Aras** (Turkey)
81 J4 **Arbat** Iraq
116 I1 **Arbazh** Rus. Fed.
81 J3 **Arbīl** Iraq
103 K4 **Arboga** Sweden
131 I4 **Arborfield** Canada
106 F4 **Arbroath** U.K.
140 A2 **Arbuckle** U.S.A.
85 F4 **Arbu Lut, Dasht-e** des. Afgh.
110 D4 **Arcachon** France
145 D7 **Arcadia** U.S.A.
158 A3 **Arcata** U.S.A.
140 D2 **Arc Dome** mt. U.S.A.
151 D4 **Arcelia** Mex.
116 G1 **Archangel** Rus. Fed.
68 E3 **Archer** r. Australia
141 H2 **Arches National Park** U.S.A.
82 D5 **Archman** Turkm.
81 L2 **Ārçivan** Azer.

70 A2 **Arckaringa** watercourse Australia
138 D3 **Arco** U.S.A.
111 D4 **Arcos de la Frontera** Spain
129 J2 **Arctic Bay** Canada
164 B1 **Arctic Mid-Ocean Ridge** sea feature Arctic Ocean
164 **Arctic Ocean**
128 E3 **Arctic Red** r. Canada
84 C2 **Ardabīl** Iran
81 I1 **Ardahan** Turkey
84 C4 **Ardakān** Iran
84 D3 **Ardakān** Iran
84 C4 **Ardal** Iran
103 I3 **Årdalstangen** Norway
107 C3 **Ardara** Rep. of Ireland
115 K4 **Ardas** r. Bulg.
116 H4 **Ardatov** Nizhegorodskaya Oblast' Rus. Fed.
116 H4 **Ardatov** Respublika Mordoviya Rus. Fed.
135 G3 **Ardbeg** Canada
107 F4 **Ardee** Rep. of Ireland
70 B4 **Arden, Mount** hill Australia
108 D5 **Ardennes** reg. Belgium
108 C5 **Ardennes, Canal des** France
84 D3 **Ardestān** Iran
107 F3 **Ardglass** U.K.
111 C3 **Ardila** r. Port.
71 G5 **Ardlethan** Australia
143 D5 **Ardmore** U.S.A.
106 B4 **Ardnamurchan, Point of** U.K.
70 B5 **Ardrishaig** U.K.
106 C4 **Ardrossan** Australia
106 D5 **Ardrossan** U.K.
106 C3 **Ardvasar** U.K.
159 E2 **Areco** r. Arg.
155 K4 **Areia Branca** Brazil
108 E4 **Aremberg** hill Germany
97 B4 **Arena** reef Phil.
140 A2 **Arena, Point** U.S.A.
150 B3 **Arena, Punta** pt Mex.
150 H5 **Arenal** Hond.
112 D2 **Arenas de San Pedro** Spain
103 J4 **Arendal** Norway
109 J2 **Arendsee (Altmark)** Germany
105 D5 **Arenig Fawr** hill U.K.
115 J6 **Areopoli** Greece
150 C2 **Areponapuchi** Mex.
154 D7 **Arequipa** Peru
155 H4 **Arere** Brazil
111 D2 **Arévalo** Spain
114 D3 **Arezzo** Italy
80 G5 **'Arfajah** well Saudi Arabia
92 D1 **Argalant** Mongolia
111 E2 **Arganda** Spain
97 B4 **Argao** Phil.
114 D2 **Argenta** Italy
110 D2 **Argentan** France
114 D3 **Argentario, Monte** hill Italy
114 D2 **Argentera, Cima del** mt. Italy
110 F5 **Argenthal** Germany
156 C5 **Argentina** country S. America
73 B3 **Argentina Range** mts Antarctica
163 F9 **Argentine Abyssal Plain** sea feature S. Atlantic Ocean
163 G8 **Argentine Basin** sea feature S. Atlantic Ocean
163 G8 **Argentine Rise** sea feature S. Atlantic Ocean
156 B8 **Argentino, Lago** l. Arg.
115 K2 **Argeş** r. Romania
85 G4 **Arghandab** r. Afgh.
85 G4 **Arghastan** r. Afgh.
80 C2 **Argıthanı** Turkey
115 J5 **Argolikos Kolpos** b. Greece
115 J6 **Argos** Greece
115 I5 **Argostoli** Greece
111 F1 **Arguís** Spain
90 E1 **Argun'** r. China/Rus. Fed.
141 H7 **Argus Range** mts U.S.A.
68 C3 **Argyle, Lake** Australia
106 C4 **Argyll** reg. U.K.
103 J4 **Århus** Denmark
72 E3 **Aria** N.Z.
71 G5 **Ariah Park** Australia
95 B8 **Ariake-kai** b. Japan
123 B6 **Ariamsvlei** Namibia
114 F4 **Ariano Irpino** Italy
71 G8 **Ariari** r. Col.
159 D2 **Arias** Arg.
79 F6 **Ari Atoll** Maldives
157 E2 **Aribí** r. Venez.
112 B3 **Aribinda** Burkina
156 B5 **Arica** Chile
106 C4 **Arienas, Loch** l. U.K.
80 F4 **Ariḩā** Syria
158 C4 **Arikaree** r. U.S.A.
157 E2 **Arima** Trin. and Tob.
155 G6 **Arinos** r. Brazil
157 D4 **Ario de Rosáles** Mex.
157 C4 **Ariporo** r. Col.
154 F5 **Aripuanã** Brazil
154 F5 **Aripuanã** r. Brazil
158 E2 **Ariranhá** r. Brazil
124 B1 **Aris** Namibia
106 C4 **Arisaig, Sound of** sea chan. U.K.
130 D4 **Aristazabal Island** Canada
156 C2 **Arizaro, Salar de** salt flat Arg.
141 G4 **Arizona** state U.S.A.
105 G7 **Arundel** U.K.
81 J1 **'Arjah** Saudi Arabia
102 L2 **Arjeplog** Sweden
157 B2 **Arjona** Col.
99 D4 **Arjuna, Gunung** vol. Indon.
143 E5 **Arkadak** Rus. Fed.
143 E5 **Arkadelphia** U.S.A.
106 C4 **Arkaig, Loch** l. U.K.
83 F2 **Arkalyk** Kazakh.
143 E5 **Arkansas** r. U.S.A.
143 D5 **Arkansas** state U.S.A.
143 E4 **Arkansas City** U.S.A.
89 G1 **Arkatag Shan** mts China
116 E2 **Arkhangel'skaya Oblast'** admin. div. Rus. Fed.
116 F4 **Arkhangel'skoye** Rus. Fed.
94 C3 **Arkhipovka** Rus. Fed.
107 E5 **Arklow** Rep. of Ireland
109 L6 **Arkoí** i. Greece
111 F5 **Arkona, Kap** hd Germany
76 J2 **Arkticheskogo Instituta, Ostrova** is Rus. Fed.
147 F3 **Arkville** U.S.A.
110 G5 **Arles** France
125 I5 **Arlington** S. Africa
143 D5 **Arlington** TX U.S.A.
142 C4 **Arlington** SD U.S.A.
146 E5 **Arlington** VA U.S.A.
120 C3 **Arlit** Niger
108 B4 **Arlon** Belgium
107 E3 **Armadale** U.K.
107 D4 **Armagh** U.K.
121 F2 **Armant** Egypt
117 I6 **Armavir** Rus. Fed.
81 J1 **Armenia** country Asia
157 B3 **Armenia** Col.
108 A4 **Armentières** France
157 B3 **Armero** Col.
71 I3 **Armidale** Australia
88 E5 **Armori** India
107 E4 **Armoy** U.K.
130 D2 **Armstrong** B.C. Canada
132 C3 **Armstrong** Ont. Canada
151 H4 **Armstrong** r. Mex.
94 E1 **Armu** r. Rus. Fed.
87 B3 **Armur** India
117 E6 **Armyans'k** Ukr.
80 D4 **Arnaoutis, Cape** Cyprus see **Arnauti, Cape**

133 F1 **Arnaud** r. Canada
80 D4 **Arnauti, Cape** Cyprus
84 E4 **Arnes** Norway
143 D4 **Arnett** U.S.A.
108 D3 **Arnhem** Neth.
68 D3 **Arnhem, Cape** Australia
68 D3 **Arnhem Bay** Australia
68 D3 **Arnhem Land** reg. Australia
114 D2 **Arno** r. Italy
70 B4 **Arno Bay** Australia
105 F4 **Arnold** U.K.
134 D2 **Arnold** U.S.A.
135 I3 **Arnoux, Lac** l. Canada
135 I3 **Arnprior** Canada
109 G3 **Arnsberg** Germany
109 I4 **Arnstadt** Germany
109 H5 **Arnstein** Germany
141 F4 **Arntfield** Canada
123 B6 **Aroab** Namibia
109 H3 **Arolsen** Germany
114 C2 **Arona** Italy
147 J1 **Aroostook** Canada
147 I1 **Aroostook** r. Canada/U.S.A.
69 H2 **Arorae** i. Kiribati
97 B3 **Aroroy** Phil.
117 G7 **Arpaçay** r. Armenia/Turkey
81 I1 **Arpaçay** Turkey
85 G5 **Arra** r. Pak.
81 I5 **Ar Raḩḩāliyah** Iraq
81 I5 **Ar Ramādī** Iraq
80 E7 **Ar Ramlah** Jordan
106 C3 **Arran** i. U.K.
81 G4 **Ar Raqqah** Syria
110 F1 **Arras** France
84 B5 **Ar-Rass** Saudi Arabia
80 F4 **Ar Rastān** Syria
81 I7 **Ar Rawḑ** well Saudi Arabia
84 C5 **Ar Rayyān** Qatar
157 C2 **Arrecifal** Col.
159 F4 **Arrecifes** Arg.
151 F4 **Arriagá** Chiapas Mex.
151 F4 **Arriaga** r. San Luis Potosí Mex.
159 E2 **Arribeños** Arg.
81 K6 **Ar Rifā'ī** Iraq
81 J6 **Ar Rihāb** salt flat Iraq
86 D5 **Ar Rimāl** reg. Saudi Arabia
141 H3 **Arriba** U.S.A.
Ar Riyāḍ Saudi Arabia see **Riyadh**
106 D4 **Arrochar** U.K.
159 G2 **Arroio Grande** Brazil
158 D1 **Arrojado** r. Brazil
107 C3 **Arrow, Lough** l. Rep. of Ireland
134 B1 **Arrow Lake** Canada
138 D3 **Arrowrock Reservoir** U.S.A.
72 C5 **Arrowsmith, Mount** N.Z.
140 B4 **Arroyo Grande** U.S.A.
159 E2 **Arroyo Seco** Arg.
157 D4 **Arroyo Seco** Mex.
84 B5 **Ar Rubay'īyah** Saudi Arabia
158 A1 **Arruda** Brazil
81 J5 **Ar Rumaythah** Iraq
80 G4 **Ar Ruṣāfah** Syria
85 E6 **Ar Rustāq** Oman
84 B6 **Ar Ruwayḑah** Saudi Arabia
103 J4 **Ars** Denmark
84 B2 **Ars** Iran
84 D4 **Arsenajān** Iran
94 C2 **Arsen'yev** Rus. Fed.
83 H2 **Arshaly** Akmolinskaya Oblast' Kazakh.
83 J2 **Arshaly** Vostochnyy Kazakhstan Kazakh.
87 B3 **Arsikere** India
116 I3 **Arsk** Rus. Fed.
80 E3 **Arslanköy** Turkey
115 I5 **Arta** Greece
81 J2 **Artashat** Armenia
150 A1 **Arteaga** Mex.
94 C3 **Artem** Rus. Fed.
117 F5 **Artemivs'k** Ukr.
94 C3 **Artemovskiy** Rus. Fed.
110 D2 **Artenay** France
139 F5 **Artesia** U.S.A.
135 G4 **Arthur** r. Canada
70 C6 **Arthur, Lake** salt flat Australia
146 C4 **Arthur, Lake** U.S.A.
71 G8 **Arthur Lake** Australia
68 F4 **Arthur Point** Australia
72 C5 **Arthur's Pass** N.Z.
72 C5 **Arthur's Pass National Park** N.Z.
145 F7 **Arthur's Town** Bahamas
73 B1 **Artigas** research station Antarctica
159 F1 **Artigas** Uruguay
131 H2 **Artillery Lake** Canada
125 D2 **Artisia** Botswana
110 F1 **Artois** reg. France
108 A4 **Artois, Collines d'** hills France
81 I2 **Artos Dağı** mt. Turkey
80 F1 **Artova** Turkey
117 D6 **Artsyz** Ukr.
83 I5 **Artux** China
81 H1 **Artvin** Turkey
91 F7 **Aru, Kepulauan** is Indon.
122 D3 **Arua** Uganda
157 C1 **Aruba** terr. Caribbean Sea
154 F4 **Arumã** Brazil
89 F4 **Arun** r. Nepal
89 H3 **Arunachal Pradesh** state India
105 G7 **Arundel** U.K.
122 D3 **Arusha** Tanz.
142 B4 **Arvada** U.S.A.
107 D4 **Arvagh** Rep. of Ireland
90 C2 **Arvayheer** Mongolia
88 D5 **Arvi** India
131 K2 **Arviat** Canada
133 H4 **Arvida** Canada
102 L3 **Arvidsjaur** Sweden
103 K4 **Arvika** Sweden
140 C4 **Arvin** U.S.A.
84 B6 **Arwā'** Saudi Arabia
89 G4 **Arwal** India
83 G1 **Arxan** China
81 K2 **Arys** Kazakh.
82 C2 **Arys', Ozero** salt l. Kazakh.
116 H4 **Arzamas** Rus. Fed.
109 F5 **Arzberg** Germany
111 C5 **Arzew** Alg.
111 H6 **Arzgir** Rus. Fed.
109 K6 **Aš** Czech Rep.
120 C4 **Asaba** Nigeria
80 H3 **Asad, Buhayrat al** resr Syria
85 H3 **Asadābād** Afgh.
84 C3 **Asadābād** Iran
84 E3 **Asadābād** Iran
96 B5 **Asan-man** b. S. Korea
89 F5 **Asansol** India
108 H4 **Asbach** Germany
147 F5 **Asbury Park** U.S.A.
155 G4 **Ascea** Italy
107 E2 **Ascension** Bol.
151 H4 **Ascension, Bahía de la** b. Mex.
163 **Ascension** i. S. Atlantic Ocean
108 H5 **Aschaffenburg** Germany
109 J3 **Ascheberg** Germany
109 J2 **Aschersleben** Germany
114 E3 **Ascoli Piceno** Italy
103 K4 **Åseda** Sweden

102 L2 **Åsele** Sweden
115 K3 **Asenovgrad** Bulg.
84 C7 **Asharat** Saudi Arabia
80 J4 **Aswān** Egypt
68 B4 **Ashburton** watercourse Australia
72 C5 **Ashburton** N.Z.
134 D1 **Ashburton Bay** Canada
83 G4 **Aschikol', Ozero** salt l. Kazakh.
83 F3 **Aschikol', Ozero** salt l. Kazakh.
130 E4 **Ashcroft** Canada
80 E6 **Ashdod** Israel
143 E5 **Ashdown** U.S.A.
145 E5 **Asheboro** U.S.A.
145 D5 **Asheville** U.S.A.
71 I2 **Ashford** Australia
105 H6 **Ashford** U.K.
141 F4 **Ash Fork** U.S.A.
82 D5 **Ashgabat** Turkm.
94 H3 **Ashibetsu** Japan
95 F6 **Ashikaga** Japan
104 F2 **Ashington** U.K.
116 I3 **Ashit** r. Rus. Fed.
95 C5 **Ashizuri-misaki** pt Japan
84 D4 **Ashkazar** r. Iran
143 D4 **Ashland** KS U.S.A.
146 B5 **Ashland** KY U.S.A.
147 I1 **Ashland** ME U.S.A.
138 E2 **Ashland** MT U.S.A.
147 G7 **Ashland** NH U.S.A.
146 B4 **Ashland** OH U.S.A.
138 B3 **Ashland** OR U.S.A.
146 E6 **Ashland** VA U.S.A.
134 B2 **Ashland** WI U.S.A.
71 H2 **Ashley** Australia
142 D2 **Ashley** U.S.A.
116 C4 **Ashmyany** Belarus
141 H5 **Ash Peak** U.S.A.
80 E6 **Ashqelon** Israel
81 I6 **Ash Shabakah** Iraq
81 H3 **Ash Shaddādah** Syria
81 H6 **Ash Shanāfīyah** Iraq
81 J6 **Ash Shaqīq** well Saudi Arabia
84 B5 **Ash Sha'rā'** Saudi Arabia
Ash Shāriqah U.A.E. see **Sharjah**
81 I4 **Ash Sharqāṭ** Iraq
81 K6 **Ash Shaṭrah** Iraq
80 E6 **Ash Shaṭṭ** Egypt
80 E6 **Ash Shawbak** Jordan
84 C7 **Ash Shiḥr** Yemen
84 C5 **Ash Shiṇāṣ** Oman
84 B5 **Ash Shu'bah** Saudi Arabia
84 B5 **Ash Shumlūl** Saudi Arabia
87 A2 **Ashta** Maharashtra India
88 D5 **Ashti** Maharashtra India
84 C3 **Ashtiān** Iran
124 D6 **Ashton** S. Africa
138 E3 **Ashton** U.S.A.
129 L4 **Ashuanipi Lake** Canada
133 F2 **Ashuapmushuan** r. Canada
133 F2 **Ashuapmushuan, Réserve Faunique** res. Canada
145 C5 **Ashville** U.S.A.
80 F4 **'Āşī, Nahr al** r. Asia
74 **Asia**
150 D3 **Asientos** Mex.
87 D2 **Asifabad** India
87 D2 **Asika** India
77 Q3 **Asino** Rus. Fed.
116 D4 **Asipovichy** Belarus
84 B5 **'Asir** reg. Saudi Arabia
81 H2 **Aşkale** Turkey
116 H3 **Askarovo** Rus. Fed.
103 J4 **Askim** Norway
81 K2 **Aşlănduz** Iran
81 K2 **Aslānduz** Iran
103 I3 **Asker** Norway
103 J4 **Askersund** Sweden
81 K2 **Aspar** Iran
83 H3 **Aspara** Kazakh.
104 E3 **Aspatria** U.K.
139 F4 **Aspen** U.S.A.
109 H6 **Asperg** Germany
143 C5 **Aspermont** U.S.A.
72 B6 **Aspiring, Mount** N.Z.
131 H4 **Asquith** Canada
83 G4 **Assa** Kazakh.
80 C7 **As Sa'an** Syria
84 B5 **As Sabsab** well Saudi Arabia
80 C7 **Aş Şaff** Egypt
80 F3 **As Safirah** Syria
Aş Şaḥrā' al Gharbīyah Egypt see **Western Desert**
Aş Şaḥrā' ash Sharqīyah Egypt see **Eastern Desert**
84 C5 **As Saji** well Saudi Arabia
82 D4 **Assake-Audan, Vpadina** basin
84 B5 **As Salamīyah** Saudi Arabia
80 D6 **As Sālihīyah** Egypt
81 H4 **As Sālihīyah** Syria
81 J6 **As Salmān** Iraq
80 E6 **As Salt** Jordan
81 J6 **As Samāwah** Iraq
84 A4 **As Samāyn** Syria
121 E2 **Aş Şarīr** reg. Libya
147 F5 **Assateague Island** U.S.A.
147 F6 **Assateague Island National Seashore** res. U.S.A.
108 E1 **Assen** Neth.
108 E3 **Assenede** Belgium
108 C4 **Assesse** Belgium
89 F5 **Assia Hills** India
121 D1 **As Sidrah** Libya
131 H5 **Assiniboia** Canada
131 J5 **Assiniboine** r. Canada
130 F4 **Assiniboine, Mount** Canada
158 B3 **Assis** Brazil
114 E3 **Assisi** Italy
109 G4 **Aßlar** Germany
81 K7 **Aş Şubayḩīyah** Kuwait
84 A4 **Aş Şufayrī** well Saudi Arabia
80 F4 **Aş Şukhnah** Syria
81 I4 **As Sulaymānīyah** Iraq
86 C4 **As Sulayyil** Saudi Arabia
84 B6 **Aş Şulb** reg. Saudi Arabia
84 B5 **Aş Şummān** plat. Saudi Arabia
81 H4 **As Sūq** Saudi Arabia
81 H4 **Aş Şuwar** Syria
80 F7 **Aş Şuwayrah** Syria
85 E6 **As Suwayq** Oman
81 J4 **As Suwayrah** Iraq
As Suways Egypt see **Suez**
106 C2 **Assynt, Loch** l. U.K.
115 L6 **Astakida** i. Greece
83 G2 **Astana** Kazakh.
84 C2 **Astāneh** Iran
81 L2 **Astara** Azer.
81 L2 **Āstārā** Iran
114 C3 **Asti** Italy
115 L6 **Astipalaia** i. Greece
85 G3 **Astola Island** Pak.
88 C2 **Astor** Jammu and Kashmir
85 H3 **Astor** r. Pak.
111 C1 **Astorga** Spain
138 B2 **Astoria** U.S.A.
103 K4 **Åstorp** Sweden
117 H6 **Astrakhan'** Rus. Fed.
117 H6 **Astrakhanskaya Oblast'** admin. div. Rus. Fed.
103 M5 **Astravyets** Belarus
73 D3 **Astrid Ridge** sea feature Antarctica
111 C1 **Asturias** aut. comm. Spain
115 L6 **Astypalaia** i. Greece

83 J2 **Asubulak** Kazakh.
156 E3 **Asunción** Para.
80 J4 **Aswān** Egypt
121 F2 **Asyūt** Egypt
69 I4 **Ata** i. Tonga
157 D4 **Atabapo** r. Col./Venez.
83 G4 **Atabay** Kazakh.
Atacama, Desierto de des. Chile see **Atacama Desert**
156 C2 **Atacama, Salar de** salt flat Chile
156 C2 **Atacama Desert** des. Chile
83 G4 **Atakent** Kazakh.
120 C4 **Atakpamé** Togo
115 J5 **Atalanti** Greece
150 I7 **Atalaya** Panama
154 D6 **Atalaya** Peru
83 G1 **Atansor, Ozero** salt l. Kazakh.
120 A2 **Atâr** Mauritania
98 A1 **Ataran** r. Myanmar
141 H4 **Ataque** U.S.A.
140 B4 **Atascadero** U.S.A.
83 G2 **Atasu** Kazakh.
91 E7 **Ataúro, Ilha de** i. East Timor
121 F3 **Atbara** Sudan
83 G2 **Atbasar** Kazakh.
81 K5 **At-Bashy** Kyrg.
143 F6 **Atchafalaya Bay** U.S.A.
142 E4 **Atchison** U.S.A.
150 C3 **Atenguillo** Mex.
114 E3 **Aterno** r. Italy
114 F3 **Atessa** Italy
108 B4 **Ath** Belgium
131 G4 **Athabasca** Canada
128 C4 **Athabasca** r. Canada
129 I3 **Athabasca, Lake** Canada
107 E4 **Athboy** Rep. of Ireland
107 C4 **Athenry** Rep. of Ireland
135 J3 **Athens** Canada
115 J6 **Athens** Greece (City Plan 55)
145 C5 **Athens** AL U.S.A.
145 D5 **Athens** GA U.S.A.
146 B5 **Athens** OH U.S.A.
145 C5 **Athens** TN U.S.A.
143 E5 **Athens** TX U.S.A.
105 F5 **Atherstone** U.K.
68 E3 **Atherton** Australia
Athina Greece see **Athens**
107 C4 **Athleague** Rep. of Ireland
107 C4 **Athlone** Rep. of Ireland
87 A2 **Athni** India
72 I6 **Athol** N.Z.
146 D3 **Athol** U.S.A.
106 F4 **Atholl, Forest of** reg. U.K.
115 K4 **Athos** mt. Greece
80 E7 **Ath Thamad** Egypt
81 I4 **Ath Tharthar, Wādī** r. Iraq
121 E3 **Ati** Chad
154 D7 **Atico** Peru
133 H3 **Atikokan** Canada
133 H3 **Atikonak Lake** Canada
97 B3 **Atimonan** Phil.
87 B4 **Atirampattinam** India
151 G5 **Atitlán** l. Guat.
151 G5 **Atitlán, Volcán** vol. Guat.
150 D3 **Atizapán** Mex.
117 H5 **Atkarsk** Rus. Fed.
151 E4 **Atlacomulco** Mex.
145 C5 **Atlanta** GA U.S.A.
134 C5 **Atlanta** IL U.S.A.
135 E3 **Atlanta** MI U.S.A.
80 D2 **Atlanti** Turkey
142 E3 **Atlantic** U.S.A.
147 F5 **Atlantic City** U.S.A.
162 D9 **Atlantic-Indian-Antarctic Basin** sea feature S. Atlantic Ocean
162 D8 **Atlantic-Indian Ridge** sea feature Southern Ocean
163 **Atlantic Ocean**
125 B5 **Atlantis** S. Africa
120 C1 **Atlas Saharien** mts Alg.
130 C3 **Atlin** Canada
130 C3 **Atlin Lake** Canada
130 C3 **Atlin Provincial Park** Canada
80 E5 **'Atlit** Israel
151 E4 **Atlixco** Mex.
87 B3 **Atmakur** Andhra Pradesh India
87 B3 **Atmakur** Andhra Pradesh India
145 C6 **Atmore** U.S.A.
143 E5 **Atoka** U.S.A.
150 D3 **Atotonilco el Alto** Mex.
98 C1 **Atouat** mt. Laos
151 E4 **Atoyac de Álvarez** Mex.
89 E4 **Atrai** r. India
84 E2 **Atrak, Rūd-e** r. Iran/Turkm.
157 A3 **Atrato** r. Col.
84 E2 **Atrek** r. Iran/Turkm. alt. **Atrak, Rūd-e**, alt. **Etrek**
147 F5 **Atsion** U.S.A.
80 E6 **Aṭ Ṭafīlah** Jordan
86 B4 **Aṭ Ṭā'if** Saudi Arabia
98 C2 **Attapu** Laos
115 L6 **Attavyros** mt. Greece
132 D3 **Attawapiskat** Canada
132 D3 **Attawapiskat** r. Canada
132 D3 **Attawapiskat Lake** Canada
81 G7 **Aṭ Ṭawīl** mts Saudi Arabia
84 A4 **Aṭ Ṭaysīyah** plat. Saudi Arabia
109 G4 **Attendorn** Germany
112 F7 **Attersee** l. Austria
134 D5 **Attica** IN U.S.A.
146 B4 **Attica** OH U.S.A.
108 C5 **Attigny** France
147 H3 **Attleboro** U.S.A.
105 I5 **Attleborough** U.K.
80 F7 **Aṭ Ṭubayq** reg. Saudi Arabia
160 G2 **Attu Island** U.S.A.
84 B5 **Aṭ Ṭulayḩī** well Saudi Arabia
81 G7 **Aṭ Ṭūr** Egypt
87 B4 **Attur** India
159 C2 **Atuel** r. Arg.
103 K4 **Åtvidaberg** Sweden
146 C4 **Atwood Lake** U.S.A.
82 B3 **Atyrau** Kazakh.
82 B3 **Atyrauskaya Oblast'** admin. div. Kazakh.
109 I5 **Aub** Germany
108 C4 **Aubagne** France
108 B4 **Aubange** Belgium
97 B2 **Aubarede Point** Phil.
108 D5 **Auboué** France
147 F4 **Auburn** Canada
140 B2 **Auburn** CA U.S.A.
134 E5 **Auburn** IN U.S.A.
147 H2 **Auburn** ME U.S.A.
142 E3 **Auburn** NE U.S.A.
146 E3 **Auburn** NY U.S.A.
138 B2 **Auburn** WA U.S.A.
110 E4 **Aubusson** France
159 C3 **Auca Mahuida, Sierra de** mt. Arg.
111 C1 **Auce** Latvia
110 E4 **Auch** France
72 E2 **Auckland** N.Z. (City Plan 50)
69 G6 **Auckland Islands** N.Z.
109 J5 **Auerbach in der Oberpfalz** Germany

109 K4 **Auersberg** mt. Germany
83 J2 **Auezov** Kazakh.
107 D3 **Augher** U.K.
107 E3 **Aughnacloy** U.K.
107 C5 **Aughrim** Rep. of Ireland
124 D4 **Augrabies** S. Africa
124 D4 **Augrabies Falls** S. Africa
124 D4 **Augrabies Falls National Park** S. Africa
135 F3 **Au Gres** U.S.A.
112 E6 **Augsburg** Germany
114 F6 **Augusta** Sicily Italy
145 D5 **Augusta** GA U.S.A.
143 D4 **Augusta** KS U.S.A.
147 I2 **Augusta** ME U.S.A.
134 B3 **Augusta** WI U.S.A.
68 A4 **Augustus, Mount** Australia
82 F1 **Auliyekol'** Kazakh.
108 B4 **Aulnoye-Aymeries** France
105 I7 **Ault** France
82 E4 **Auminzatau, Gory** hills Uzbek.
123 B6 **Auob** watercourse Namibia
133 G3 **Aupaluk** Canada
98 C5 **Aur** i. Malaysia
103 M3 **Aura** Fin.
88 D4 **Auraiya** India
88 D4 **Aurangabad** India
108 F1 **Aurich** Germany
158 B2 **Aurilândia** Brazil
110 F4 **Aurillac** France
99 B5 **Aurkuning** Indon.
97 B5 **Aurora** Phil.
134 C5 **Aurora** CO U.S.A.
134 C5 **Aurora** IL U.S.A.
147 I2 **Aurora** ME U.S.A.
143 E4 **Aurora** MO U.S.A.
123 B6 **Aus** Namibia
135 F3 **Au Sable** U.S.A.
135 E3 **Au Sable** r. U.S.A.
147 G2 **Ausable** r. U.S.A.
147 G2 **Au Sable Forks** U.S.A.
134 D2 **Au Sable Point** MI U.S.A.
135 F3 **Au Sable Point** MI U.S.A.
106 F1 **Auskerry** i. U.K.
102 C2 **Austari-Jökulsá** r. Iceland
142 E3 **Austin** MN U.S.A.
143 D6 **Austin** TX U.S.A.
Australes, Îles is Fr. Polynesia see **Tubuai Islands**
73 B6 **Australian Antarctic Territory** reg. Antarctica
71 H5 **Australian Capital Territory** admin. div. Australia
112 F7 **Austria** country Europe
102 K1 **Austvågøy** i. Norway
102 N2 **Auttii** Fin.
110 D3 **Autun** France
110 F3 **Auxerre** France
108 A4 **Auxi-le-Château** France
110 G3 **Auxonne** France
147 F3 **Ava** U.S.A.
110 F3 **Avallon** France
133 J4 **Avalon Peninsula** Canada
150 D2 **Ávalos** Mex.
84 D3 **Avān** Iran
80 E2 **Avanos** Turkey
158 C3 **Avaré** Brazil
81 K2 **Āvārsīn** Iran
155 G4 **Avaviri** Brazil
70 E6 **Aveiro** Port.
111 B2 **Aveiro** Port.
155 H4 **Aveiro** Brazil
111 B2 **Aveiro, Ria de** est. Port.
159 E4 **Avellaneda** Arg.
114 F4 **Avellino** Italy
140 B3 **Avenal** U.S.A.
70 F6 **Avenel** Australia
108 A5 **Avesnes-sur-Helpe** France
114 F4 **Aversa** Italy
103 L3 **Avesta** Sweden
110 F3 **Aveyron** r. France
114 E3 **Avezzano** Italy
106 E4 **Aviemore** U.K.
114 F4 **Avigliano** Italy
110 G5 **Avignon** France
111 D2 **Ávila** Spain
111 D1 **Avilés** Spain
110 C4 **Avion** France
87 B5 **Avissawella** Sri Lanka
116 F2 **Avnyugskiy** Rus. Fed.
71 I5 **Avoca** r. Australia
70 E6 **Avoca** Australia
107 E5 **Avoca** Rep. of Ireland
114 F6 **Avola** Sicily Italy
105 F5 **Avon** r. England U.K.
105 F5 **Avon** r. England U.K.
105 E7 **Avon** r. England U.K.
147 H2 **Avondale** U.S.A.
105 D7 **Avonmouth** U.K.
145 D7 **Avon Park** U.S.A.
108 A5 **Avranches** France
110 F4 **Avre** r. France
69 G7 **Avuavu** Solomon Is
95 D7 **Awaji-shima** i. Japan
72 D1 **Awakino** N.Z.
84 C5 **Awālī** Bahrain
72 D1 **Awanui** N.Z.
122 B6 **Awarua Point** N.Z.
122 E3 **Āwash** Eth.
94 F5 **Awa-shima** i. Japan
122 E3 **Āwash National Park** Eth.
122 E2 **Awasib Mountains** Namibia
83 J4 **Awat** China
72 D5 **Awatere** r. N.Z.
121 D2 **Awbārī** Libya
107 D4 **Awbeg** r. Rep. of Ireland
81 K6 **'Awdah, Hawr al** l. Iraq
122 E3 **Aw Dheegle** Somalia
106 D4 **Awe, Loch** l. U.K.
94 H4 **Aweil** Sudan
120 C4 **Awka** Nigeria
97 C6 **Awu** mt. Indon.
99 C6 **Awu** vol. Indon.
129 I2 **Axel Heiberg Island** Canada
120 B4 **Axedale** Australia
105 E7 **Axminster** U.K.
108 B5 **Ay** France
95 F6 **Ayabe** Japan
159 D4 **Ayacucho** Arg.
154 D6 **Ayacucho** Peru
83 J3 **Ayagoz** watercourse Kazakh.
82 F4 **Ayagkaytma, Vpadina** depr. Uzbek.
82 F4 **Ayakkuduk** Uzbek.
90 A3 **Ayakkum Hu** l. China
111 C4 **Ayamonte** Spain
91 H1 **Ayan** Rus. Fed.
117 E7 **Ayancık** Turkey
96 C4 **Ayang** N. Korea
77 R3 **Ayanka** Rus. Fed.
157 B2 **Ayapel** Col.
80 D1 **Ayaş** Turkey
85 H2 **Ayaviri** Peru
83 H2 **Aydabol** Kazakh.
81 K6 **Aydarkul', Ozero** Uzbek.
82 F3 **Aydarly** Kazakh.

80 A3 Aydın Turkey
80 A2 Aydın Dağları mts Turkey
82 D2 Aydyrlinskiy Rus. Fed.
83 G3 Ayeat, Gora hill Kazakh.
98 □ Ayer Chawan, Pulau i. Sing.
98 □ Ayer Merbau, Pulau i. Sing.
Ayers Rock hill Australia see Uluru
83 J2 Aygyrzhal Kazakh.
82 E2 Ayke, Ozero i. Kazakh.
77 M3 Aykhal Rus. Fed.
116 I2 Aykino Rus. Fed.
83 J4 Aykol China
72 D5 Aylesbury N.Z.
105 G6 Aylesbury U.K.
146 E6 Aylett U.S.A.
111 E2 Ayllón Spain
135 G4 Aylmer Canada
131 H2 Aylmer Lake Canada
82 E2 Aymagambetov Kazakh.
83 I3 Aynabulak Kazakh.
84 C4 'Ayn al 'Abd well Saudi Arabia
83 G5 Ayni Tajik.
80 G3 'Ayn 'Īsá Syria
121 F4 Ayod Sudan
77 R3 Ayon, Ostrov i. Rus. Fed.
120 B3 'Ayoûn el 'Atroûs Mauritania
68 E3 Ayr Australia
106 D5 Ayr U.K.
106 D5 Ayr r. U.K.
80 D3 Ayrancı Turkey
104 C3 Ayre, Point of Isle of Man
83 G3 Ayshirak Kazakh.
83 E3 Ayteke Bi Kazakh.
115 L3 Aytos Bulg.
98 B2 Ayutthaya Thai.
115 L5 Ayvacık Turkey
80 F2 Ayvalı Turkey
115 L5 Ayvalık Turkey
150 H5 Azacualpa Hond.
89 E4 Azamgarh India
120 C3 Azaouad reg. Mali
120 C3 Azaouagh, Vallée de watercourse Mali/Niger
Azbine mts Niger see L'Aïr, Massif de
80 D1 Azdavay Turkey
81 K1 Azerbaijan country Asia
84 B2 Āzghān Iran
82 E3 Azhar Kazakh.
135 G2 Azilda Canada
147 H2 Aziscohos Lake U.S.A.
154 C4 Azogues Ecuador
76 F3 Azopol'ye Rus. Fed.
163 H3 Azores-Biscay Rise sea feature N. Atlantic Ocean
117 F6 Azov Rus. Fed.
117 F6 Azov, Sea of Rus. Fed./Ukr.
121 F3 Azraq, Bahr el r. Sudan alt. Abay Wenz (Ethiopia), conv. Blue Nile
120 B1 Azrou Morocco
139 F4 Aztec U.S.A.
111 D3 Azuaga Spain
156 B3 Azúcar r. Chile
150 I7 Azuero, Península de pen. Panama
159 E3 Azul Arg.
151 G4 Azúl r. Mex.
159 B4 Azul, Cerro mt. Arg.
154 C5 Azul, Cordillera mts Peru
158 A1 Azul, Serra hills Brazil
95 G6 Azuma-san vol. Japan
83 G4 Azurduy Bol.
114 B6 Azzaba Alg.
80 F5 Az Zabadānī Syria
81 I6 Az Zāfirī reg. Iraq
Az Zahrān Saudi Arabia see Dhahran
121 F1 Az Zaqāzīq Egypt
80 F5 Az Zarqā' Jordan
84 B5 Az Zilfī Saudi Arabia
81 K2 Az Zubayr Iraq

B

80 E5 Baabda Lebanon
80 F4 Ba'albek Lebanon
71 H3 Baan Baa Australia
122 E3 Baardheere Somalia
85 H3 Bābā, Kūh-e mts Afgh.
115 L5 Baba Burnu pt Turkey
81 L1 Babadağ mt. Azer.
115 M2 Babadag Romania
82 E5 Babadaykhan Turkm.
82 E5 Babadurmaz Turkm.
82 D5 Babadurmaz Turkm.
117 C7 Babaeski Turkey
154 C4 Babahoyo Ecuador
87 B1 Babai India
89 E3 Babai r. Nepal
92 B1 Babai Gaxun China
81 K2 Bābā Jān i. Phil.
122 E2 Bāb al Mandab strait Africa/Asia
91 E7 Babar i. Indon.
83 H4 Babash-Ata, Khrebet mt. Kyrg.
122 D4 Babati Tanz.
116 E3 Babayevo Rus. Fed.
134 B2 Babbitt U.S.A.
71 H7 Babel Island Australia
128 F4 Babine r. Canada
130 D4 Babine Lake Canada
91 F7 Babo Indon.
84 D2 Bābol Iran
84 D2 Bābol Sar Iran
124 C6 Baboon Point S. Africa
141 G6 Baboquivari Peak mt. U.S.A.
122 B3 Baboua Centr. Afr. Rep.
116 D4 Babruysk Belarus
88 B4 Babuhri India
88 C2 Babusar Pass Pak.
97 A4 Babuyan Phil.
91 J Babuyan i. Phil.
93 F7 Babuyan Channel Phil.
97 B2 Babuyan Islands Phil.
81 J5 Babylon Iraq
155 I4 Bacabal Brazil
80 C1 Bacakliyayla Tepesi mt. Turkey
151 G4 Bacalar Mex.
91 E7 Bacan i. Indon.
97 B2 Bacarra Phil.
113 M7 Bacău Romania
70 F6 Bacchus Marsh Australia
93 C6 Băc Giang Vietnam
150 C1 Bachiniva Mex.
93 C6 Bach Long Vi, Đảo i. Vietnam
83 I5 Bachu China
83 I5 Bachu Liuchang China
131 I1 Back r. Canada
113 H2 Bačka Palanka Yugo.
130 D2 Backbone Ranges mts Canada
102 L3 Backe Sweden
70 B5 Backstairs Passage sea chan. Australia
106 E4 Backwater Resr U.K.
93 B6 Bắc Lac Vietnam
98 C3 Băc Liêu Vietnam
93 C6 Băc Ninh Vietnam
97 B3 Baco, Mount Phil.
93 B4 Bacolod Phil.
93 B6 Băc Quang Vietnam
132 F2 Bacqueville, Lac l. Canada
109 K6 Bad Abbach Germany
109 F2 Bad Aibling Germany
87 A4 Badagara India
92 A1 Badain Jaran Shamo des. China
154 F4 Badajós, Lago l. Brazil
111 C3 Badajoz Spain
87 A3 Badami India

81 H6 Badanah Saudi Arabia
89 H4 Badarpur India
135 F4 Bad Axe U.S.A.
109 F5 Bad Bergzabern Germany
109 G3 Bad Berleburg Germany
109 I1 Bad Bevensen Germany
109 J4 Bad Blankenburg Germany
109 G4 Bad Camberg Germany
133 H4 Baddeck Canada
85 G4 Baddo r. Pak.
109 H3 Bad Driburg Germany
109 K3 Bad Düben Germany
109 G5 Bad Dürkheim Germany
109 I4 Bad Dürrenberg Germany
80 C3 Bademli Geçidi pass Turkey
109 F4 Bad Ems Germany
112 H6 Baden Austria
112 D7 Baden Switz.
109 G5 Baden-Baden Germany
106 D4 Badenoch reg. U.K.
109 G4 Baden-Württemberg admin. div. Germany
109 G2 Bad Essen Germany
133 I4 Badger Canada
109 I3 Bad Grund (Harz) Germany
109 I3 Bad Harzburg Germany
109 H4 Bad Hersfeld Germany
112 F7 Bad Hofgastein Austria
109 G4 Bad Homburg vor der Höhe Germany
114 D2 Badia Polesine Italy
88 B4 Badin Pak.
150 C2 Badiraguato Mex.
112 F7 Bad Ischl Austria
Bādiyat ash Shām Asia see Syrian Desert
109 I4 Bad Kissingen Germany
109 J3 Bad Kösen Germany
109 F5 Bad Kreuznach Germany
109 G3 Bad Laasphe Germany
142 G2 Badlands National Park U.S.A.
109 I3 Bad Langensalza Germany
109 I3 Bad Lauterberg im Harz Germany
109 G2 Bad Lippspringe Germany
109 F4 Bad Marienberg (Westerwald) Germany
109 H5 Bad Mergentheim Germany
109 H4 Bad Nauheim Germany
108 F4 Bad Neuenahr-Ahrweiler Germany
109 I4 Bad Neustadt an der Saale Germany
109 I1 Bad Oldesloe Germany
92 D4 Badong China
93 C6 Ba Đông Vietnam
109 H3 Bad Pyrmont Germany
81 J5 Badrah Iraq
112 F7 Bad Reichenhall Germany
109 I3 Bad Sachsa Germany
109 G2 Bad Salzdetfurth Germany
109 G2 Bad Salzuflen Germany
109 I4 Bad Salzungen Germany
109 G3 Bad Schwalbach Germany
112 E4 Bad Schwartau Germany
112 E4 Bad Segeberg Germany
68 E3 Badu Island Australia
87 C5 Badulla Sri Lanka
109 G4 Bad Vilbel Germany
109 I5 Bad Wilsnack Germany
109 I5 Bad Windsheim Germany
80 B1 Baerkoy Turkey
102 B1 Baeir Iceland
71 I4 Baerami Australia
108 F4 Baesweiler Germany
111 E4 Baeza Spain
120 D4 Bafang Cameroon
120 A3 Bafatá Guinea-Bissau
129 L2 Baffin Bay Canada/Greenland
129 K2 Baffin Island Canada
120 D4 Bafia Cameroon
120 A3 Bafing, Réserve du nat. park Mali
120 A3 Bafoulabé Mali
120 D4 Bafoussam Cameroon
84 D4 Bāfq Iran
80 E1 Bafra Turkey
80 E1 Bafra Burnu pt Turkey
84 D4 Bāft Iran
122 C3 Bafwasende Dem. Rep. Congo
97 A5 Bagahak, Gunung hill Sabah Malaysia
87 A2 Bagalkot India
122 D4 Bagamoyo Tanz.
99 B2 Bagan Datuk Malaysia
123 C5 Bagani Namibia
98 B4 Bagan Serai Malaysia
98 B5 Bagansiapiapi Indon.
83 J3 Bagar watercourse Kazakh.
141 F4 Bagdad U.S.A.
159 F1 Bagé Brazil
89 E4 Bageshwar India
138 F3 Baggs U.S.A.
80 B3 Baggy Point U.K.
88 C5 Bagh India
85 F2 Baghbaghū'īyeh Iran
81 J5 Baghdād Iraq
85 E4 Bāgh-e Bābū'īyeh Iran
84 C4 Bāgh-e Malek Iran
85 H2 Baghlān Afgh.
85 G3 Baghrān Afgh.
142 F2 Bagley U.S.A.
89 F4 Baglung Nepal
111 G1 Bagnères-de-Luchon France
110 E5 Bagnols-sur-Cèze France
89 F4 Bagnuiti r. Nepal
92 C2 Bag Nur l. China
97 B4 Bago Phil.
113 J3 Bagrationovsk Rus. Fed.
97 B2 Baguio Phil.
97 C5 Baguio Phil.
141 I3 Bahadurgarh India
145 D6 Bahamas, The country Caribbean Sea
89 G4 Baharampur India
Bahariya Oasis Egypt see Baḥrīyah, Wāḥāt al
99 B3 Bahau Malaysia
88 C3 Bahawalnagar Pak.
88 B3 Bahawalpur Pak.
80 F3 Bahçe Turkey
92 C4 Ba He r. China
88 D3 Baheri India
122 D4 Bahi Tanz.
155 E1 Bahia state Brazil
159 B3 Bahía Blanca Arg.
150 B3 Bahía Kino Mex.
156 C7 Bahía Laura Arg.
156 B3 Bahía Negra Para.
150 A2 Bahía Tortugas Mex.
122 D3 Bahir Dar Eth.
84 C4 Bahman Yārī-ye Gharbī Iran
89 F4 Bahraich India
84 C5 Bahrain country Asia
81 L3 Bahrāmābād Iran
84 D4 Bahrāmjerd Iran
121 F2 Baḥrīyah, Wāḥāt al oasis Egypt
85 F5 Bāhū Kalāt Iran
113 K7 Baia Mare Romania
84 D3 Baiazeh Iran
92 E4 Baicheng Jilin China
83 J4 Baicheng Xinjiang China
133 G4 Baie-Comeau Canada
Baie du Poste Canada see Mistissini
133 F4 Baie-St-Paul Canada
133 I4 Baie Verte Canada
88 E5 Baihar India
92 E2 Baihe Jilin China
92 D3 Baihe Shaanxi China

92 E1 Bai He r. China
90 C1 Baikal, Lake Rus. Fed.
106 A3 Baile Mhartainn U.K.
115 J2 Băileşti Romania
115 J2 Băileştii, Câmpia plain Romania
92 D1 Bailingmiao China
108 A4 Baillie U.S.A.
131 H2 Baillie r. Canada
92 B3 Bailong Jiang r. China
90 C3 Baima China
92 E4 Baima Jian mt. China
105 G4 Bain r. U.K.
145 C6 Bainbridge GA U.S.A.
147 F3 Bainbridge NY U.S.A.
89 G3 Baingoin China
80 F6 Ba'ir, Wādī watercourse Jordan
89 F4 Bairagnia India
107 G3 Baird Mountains U.S.A.
67 G3 Bairiki atoll Kiribati
92 F1 Bairin Qiao China
71 G6 Bairnsdale Australia
92 B4 Bais China
93 C7 Baisha Hainan China
93 F3 Baisha Jiangxi China
92 C4 Baisha Sichuan China
92 D3 Baishan China
96 D2 Baishanzhen China
93 B7 Bai Thuong Vietnam
96 A2 Baixingt China
92 B2 Baiyin China
121 F3 Baiyuda Desert Sudan
115 H1 Baja Hungary
150 A2 Baja California pen. Mex.
136 C6 Baja California state Mex.
150 A2 Baja California Sur state Mex.
81 L3 Bājalān Iran
88 E3 Bajan Mex.
85 E2 Baj Baj India
85 E2 Bājgīrān Iran
157 B3 Bajo Baudó Col.
150 I6 Bajo Boquete Panama
159 D1 Bajo Hondo Arg.
83 I3 Bakanas Kazakh.
83 I3 Bakanas watercourse Kazakh.
120 A3 Bakel Senegal
140 D4 Baker CA U.S.A.
138 F2 Baker MT U.S.A.
141 E2 Baker NV U.S.A.
138 C2 Baker OR U.S.A.
138 B1 Baker, Mount vol. U.S.A.
69 I1 Baker Island Pacific Ocean
130 C3 Baker Island Canada
131 J2 Baker Lake l. Canada
131 J2 Baker Lake Canada
132 E2 Baker's Dozen Islands Canada
140 C4 Bakersfield U.S.A.
98 C2 Bă Kêv Cambodia
82 D5 Bakharden Turkm.
85 F3 Bākharz mts Iran
88 B4 Bakhasar India
83 F3 Babyk Bi Kazakh.
117 E6 Bakhchysaray Ukr.
82 D5 Bakherden Turkm.
117 E5 Bakhmach Ukr.
84 D4 Bakhtegan, Daryācheh-ye l. Iran
83 J3 Bakhty Kazakh.
80 B1 Bakırköy Turkey
122 B3 Bakouma Centr. Afr. Rep.
122 B4 Bakoumba Gabon
117 G7 Baksan Rus. Fed.
81 L1 Baku Azer.
122 B3 Baku Dem. Rep. Congo
73 A4 Bakutis Coast Antarctica
80 D2 Balâ Turkey
105 D5 Bala U.K.
154 E6 Bala, Cerros de mts Bol.
97 A4 Balabac Phil.
97 A5 Balabac i. Phil.
99 E1 Balabac Strait strait Malaysia/Phil.
81 J4 Balad Iraq
84 C2 Baladeh Iran
84 C2 Balādeh Iran
84 C2 Bālā Deh Iran
87 A2 Balaghat India
87 A2 Balaghat Range hills India
81 K1 Balakän Azer.
116 I3 Balakhna Rus. Fed.
70 C5 Balaklava Australia
117 E6 Balaklava Ukr.
117 H4 Balakovo Rus. Fed.
85 F3 Balā Morghāb Afgh.
88 B4 Balan India
117 H5 Balanda r. Rus. Fed.
80 D3 Balan Dağı mt. Turkey
97 B3 Balanga Phil.
87 C5 Balangir India
87 C5 Balangoda Sri Lanka
82 C5 Balashov Rus. Fed.
88 C5 Balasinor India
112 H7 Balaton l. Hungary
112 H7 Balatonboglár Hungary
112 H7 Balatonfüred Hungary
155 G4 Balbina, Represa de resr Brazil
107 E4 Balbriggan Rep. of Ireland
70 D3 Balcanoona Australia
159 E3 Balcarce Arg.
115 M3 Balchik Bulg.
72 B7 Balclutha N.Z.
143 F5 Bald Knob U.S.A.
141 F6 Bald Mountain U.S.A.
131 J3 Baldock Lake Canada
145 D6 Baldwin FL U.S.A.
134 E4 Baldwin MI U.S.A.
134 A3 Baldwin WI U.S.A.
147 H5 Baldy Peak U.S.A.
111 H3 Baleares, Islas is Spain
Balearic Islands is Spain see Baleares, Islas
99 D2 Baleh r. Sarawak Malaysia
158 E2 Baleia, Ponta da pt Brazil
122 D3 Bale Mountains National Park Eth.
97 B3 Baler Phil.
97 B3 Baler Bay b. Phil.
89 F5 Baleshwar India
103 I3 Balestrand Norway
72 B6 Balfour N.Z.
99 C4 Bali i. Indon.
107 E4 Balieborough Rep. of Ireland
87 B2 Balige Indon.
89 H5 Baliguda India
92 F1 Balihan China
80 A2 Balıkesir Turkey
99 E3 Balikpapan Indon.
87 A5 Balimbing Indon.
89 H5 Balimo P.N.G.
112 D6 Balingen Germany
99 D2 Balingian Channel Phil.
106 D3 Balintore U.K.
94 E4 Bali Sea g. Indon.
97 B5 Baliungan i. Phil.
83 G5 Baljuvon Tajik.
85 D3 Balk Neth.
115 J3 Balkan Mountains Bulg./Yugo.
83 G1 Balkashino Kazakh.
85 E2 Balkh Afgh.
83 H3 Balkhash Kazakh.
83 H3 Balkhash, Lake l. Kazakh.

82 A3 Balkuduk Kazakh.
106 C4 Ballachulish U.K.
68 C5 Balladonia Australia
71 H3 Balladoran Australia
107 C4 Ballaghadderreen Rep. of Ireland
102 L1 Ballangen Norway
138 E2 Ballantine U.S.A.
106 D5 Ballantrae U.K.
70 E6 Ballarat Australia
68 C4 Ballard, Lake salt flat Australia
88 D6 Ballarpur India
106 E3 Ballater U.K.
120 B3 Balle Mali
156 B3 Ballena, Punta pt Chile
73 A6 Balleny Islands Antarctica
89 F4 Ballia India
71 J2 Ballina Australia
107 B3 Ballina Rep. of Ireland
107 D4 Ballinalack Rep. of Ireland
107 D4 Ballinamore Rep. of Ireland
107 C4 Ballinasloe Rep. of Ireland
143 D6 Ballinger U.S.A.
107 C4 Ballinluig U.K.
107 C6 Ballinrobe Rep. of Ireland
98 A3 Ban Don, Ao b. Thai.
107 A6 Ballybay Rep. of Ireland
107 B5 Ballybrack Rep. of Ireland
107 A6 Ballybunnion Rep. of Ireland
107 E3 Ballycanew Rep. of Ireland
107 B3 Ballycastle Rep. of Ireland
107 F3 Ballycastle Rep. of Ireland
107 A4 Ballyconneely Bay Rep. of Ireland
107 C4 Ballyconnell Rep. of Ireland
107 C4 Ballygar Rep. of Ireland
107 D3 Ballygawley U.K.
107 D2 Ballyhaunis Rep. of Ireland
107 B5 Ballyhoura Mountains Rep. of Ireland
107 E2 Ballykelly U.K.
107 D5 Ballylynan Rep. of Ireland
107 C5 Ballymacmague Rep. of Ireland
107 E2 Ballymahon Rep. of Ireland
107 E2 Ballymena U.K.
107 E2 Ballymoney U.K.
107 F3 Ballymote Rep. of Ireland
107 F3 Ballynahinch U.K.
107 B4 Ballyteige Bay Rep. of Ireland
107 B4 Ballyvaughan Rep. of Ireland
107 E3 Ballyward U.K.
70 D6 Balmoral Australia
143 C6 Balmorhea U.S.A.
85 G4 Balochistan prov. Pak.
78 E4 Balochistān reg. Pak.
88 E5 Balod India
88 C4 Baloda Bazar India
71 H2 Balonne r. Australia
88 C4 Balotra India
83 I3 Balpyk Bi Kazakh.
115 K2 Balş Romania
135 H2 Balsam Creek Canada
155 I5 Balsas Brazil
151 E5 Balsas Mex.
150 D4 Balsas r. Mex.
117 D6 Balta Ukr.
117 C6 Balti Moldova
103 L5 Baltic Sea g. Europe
121 E3 Baltim Egypt
123 D6 Baltinando, Parque Nacional de nat. park Moz.
98 B1 Ban Hin Heup Laos
107 B5 Baltimore Rep. of Ireland
124 B4 Baltimore S. Africa
146 E5 Baltimore U.S.A.
88 C2 Baltistan reg. Jammu and Kashmir
113 J3 Baltiysk Rus. Fed.
88 D2 Baltoro Glacier Pak.
84 C4 Baluch Ab well Iran
89 G4 Balurghat India
146 D6 Banister r. U.S.A.
80 A2 Balya Turkey
83 I4 Balykchy Kyrg.
82 B3 Balykshi Kazakh.
85 E2 Bām Iran
85 E2 Bām Iran
93 C5 Bama China
68 E3 Bamaga Australia
132 E3 Bamaji Lake Canada
120 B3 Bamako Mali
120 B3 Bamba Mali
97 B2 Bambang Phil.
122 A3 Bambari Centr. Afr. Rep.
109 I5 Bamberg Germany
122 C3 Bambili Dem. Rep. Congo
125 G5 Bamboesberg mts S. Africa
122 C3 Bambouti Centr. Afr. Rep.
158 D1 Bambuí Brazil
120 D4 Bamenda Cameroon
82 D5 Bami Turkm.
85 H3 Bāmīān Afgh.
92 C4 Bamiancheng China
122 C3 Bamingui-Bangoran, Parc National du nat. park Centr. Afr. Rep.
96 C2 Bamiancheng China
85 F5 Bampton U.K.
105 E7 Bampton U.K.
85 F5 Bampūr Iran
85 F5 Bampūr watercourse Iran
69 G2 Banaba i. Kiribati
155 K5 Banabuiu, Açude resr Brazil
154 F7 Bañados del Izozog swamp Bol.
107 D4 Banagher Rep. of Ireland
122 C3 Banalia Dem. Rep. Congo
125 J1 Banamana, Lagoa l. Moz.
120 A2 Banamba Mali
93 C4 Banan China
155 H6 Bananal, Ilha do i. Brazil
88 D4 Banapur India
88 B2 Banas r. India
90 D6 Banas, Ras pt Egypt
80 B2 Banaz Turkey
98 B1 Ban Ban Laos
107 H3 Banbar China
107 H3 Banbridge U.K.
105 F6 Banbury U.K.
106 F3 Banchory U.K.
135 H3 Bancroft Canada
122 C3 Banda Dem. Rep. Congo
88 E4 Banda India
91 E7 Banda, Kepulauan is Indon.
120 A2 Banc d'Arguin, Parc National du nat. park Mauritania
106 F3 Banchory U.K.
122 D3 Bancoran i. Phil.
135 I3 Bancroft U.S.A.
85 E3 Band Iran
122 C3 Banda Dem. Rep. Congo
88 E4 Banda India
91 E7 Banda, Kepulauan is Indon.
111 H1 Banda Banda, Mount Australia
88 B2 Banda Daud Shah Pak.
91 A5 Bandahara, Gunung mt. Indon.
162 J8 Banzare Seamount sea feature Indian Ocean
92 E1 Banzkow Germany
92 E2 Bandai-Asahi National Park Japan
92 E2 Baochang China
92 D3 Baoding China
92 B3 Baofeng China
92 C3 Baoji China

84 C2 Bandar-e Anzali Iran
84 D5 Bandar-e Chārak Iran
84 D5 Bandar-e Deylam Iran
84 C4 Bandar-e Emām Khomeynī Iran
84 D5 Bandar-e Lengeh Iran
84 D5 Bandar-e Maqām Iran
84 C4 Bandar-e Ma'shur Iran
84 D5 Bandar-e Moghūyeh Iran
88 D3 Bandarpunch mt. India
84 C4 Bandar-e Rīg Iran
84 D2 Bandar-e Torkeman Iran
99 D2 Bandar Seri Begawan Brunei
91 F7 Banda Sea Indon.
158 E2 Bandeirante Brazil
158 E3 Bandeiras, Pico de mt. Brazil
125 H1 Bandelierkop S. Africa
150 D3 Banderas, Bahía de b. Mex.
84 D3 Band-e Sar Qom Iran
88 E6 Bandia r. India
120 B3 Bandiagara Mali
80 A1 Bandırma Turkey
107 A6 Bandon Rep. of Ireland
107 C6 Bandon r. Rep. of Ireland
98 A3 Ban Don, Ao b. Thai.
81 L2 Bāndovan Burnu pt Azer.
81 L6 Band Qīr Iran
122 B4 Bandundu Dem. Rep. Congo
99 C4 Bandung Indon.
84 B3 Bāneh Iran
149 I4 Banes Cuba
130 F4 Banff Canada
106 F3 Banff U.K.
130 F4 Banff National Park Canada
120 B3 Banfora Burkina
122 C4 Banga Dem. Rep. Congo
97 C5 Banga Phil.
93 B7 Bangai Point Phil.
87 B3 Bangalore India
89 G5 Bangaon India
92 B2 Bangar China
122 C2 Bangassou Centr. Afr. Rep.
92 E2 Banga, Co salt l. China
99 E1 Banggi i. Sabah Malaysia
99 C3 Bangka i. Indon.
98 B3 Bangkalan Indon.
93 F3 Bangka i. Indon.
98 B2 Bangkok Thai.
(City Plan 51)
98 B2 Bangkok, Bight of b. Thai.
89 G5 Bangladesh country Asia
120 D2 Bangolo Côte d'Ivoire
88 D2 Bangong Co l. China
107 F3 Bangor Northern Ireland U.K.
105 C5 Bangor Wales U.K.
147 I2 Bangor ME U.S.A.
134 E4 Bangor MI U.S.A.
147 F4 Bangor PA U.S.A.
107 B3 Bangor Erris Rep. of Ireland
141 F3 Bangs, Mount U.S.A.
98 A3 Bang Saphan Yai Thai.
102 J2 Bangsund Norway
97 B2 Bangued Phil.
122 B3 Bangui Centr. Afr. Rep.
97 B2 Bangui Phil.
123 C5 Bangweulu, Lake Zambia
98 B1 Ban Hin Heup Laos
122 A3 Bania Centr. Afr. Rep.
85 E2 Bani Forūr, Jazīreh-ye i. Iran
88 C2 Banihal Pass and Tunnel Jammu and Kashmir
121 F2 Banī Suwayf Egypt
121 D1 Banī Walīd Libya
84 C5 Bani Wuṭayfān well Saudi Arabia
80 E4 Bāniyās Syria
80 E4 Bāniyās Syria
99 C4 Banjarmasin Indon.
120 A3 Banjul Gambia
81 L2 Bankä Azer.
87 A3 Bankapur India
122 D3 Bankass Mali
98 B2 Ban Khao Yoi Thai.
98 A3 Ban Khok Kloi Thai.
109 I5 Banki India
131 K2 Banks Island B.C. Canada
128 E4 Banks Island N.W.T. Canada
69 G3 Banks Islands Vanuatu
131 K2 Banks Lake Canada
72 D2 Banks Peninsula N.Z.
71 I8 Banks Strait Australia
89 F5 Bankura India
98 B1 Ban Mouang Laos
107 B5 Bann r. Rep. of Ireland
98 A3 Ban Nakham Laos
98 A3 Ban Na San Thai.
134 C4 Banner U.S.A.
145 E7 Bannerman Town Bahamas
159 B3 Baños Maule Chile
98 B1 Ban Pak-Leng Laos
98 B1 Ban Phaeng Thai.
98 B1 Ban Phai Thai.
98 B1 Ban Phon Laos
98 B2 Banphot Phisai Thai.
98 B1 Ban Pong Thai.
98 B1 Ban Sawi Thai.
98 A3 Ban Sut Ta Thai.
98 B1 Ban Suwan Wari Thai.
98 B1 Ban Thung Luang Thai.
97 B3 Banton i. Phil.
98 C1 Ban Tôp Laos
107 B6 Bantry Rep. of Ireland
107 B6 Bantry Bay Rep. of Ireland
87 A3 Bantval India
91 E7 Banda, Kepulauan is Indon.
120 C4 Banyo Cameroon
111 H1 Banyoles Spain
99 C4 Banyuwangi Indon.
73 C6 Banzare Coast Antarctica
162 J8 Banzare Seamount sea feature Indian Ocean
92 E1 Banzhou China
109 J1 Banzkow Germany
92 E2 Baochang China
92 D3 Baoding China
92 B3 Baofeng China
92 C3 Baoji China

93 C4 Baojing China
92 D4 Baokang Hubei China
92 B1 Baokang Nei Mongol China
96 B1 Baoqing China
96 E1 Baolin China
98 C3 Baolizhen China
98 D4 Bao Lôc Vietnam
94 C1 Baoqing China
90 B4 Baoshan China
92 D1 Baotou China
93 B4 Baoxing China
92 F3 Baoying China
88 C3 Bapatla India
87 C3 Bapatla India
108 A5 Bapaume France
135 H3 Baptiste Lake Canada
89 H2 Baqên China
93 E5 Baqiu China
81 J5 Baqûbah Iraq
154 □ Baquerizo Moreno Galapagos Is Ecuador
115 H3 Bar Yugo.
79 B4 Bara Sudan
122 E3 Baraawe Somalia
89 F4 Barabar Hills India
134 C4 Baraboo U.S.A.
134 B4 Baraboo r. U.S.A.
149 J4 Baracoa Cuba
159 C2 Baradero Arg.
71 H3 Baradine Australia
71 H3 Baradine r. Australia
134 C2 Baraga U.S.A.
157 C2 Baraguá Cuba
149 J5 Barahona Dom. Rep.
89 H4 Barail Range mts India
89 H4 Barak r. India
121 F3 Baraka watercourse Eritrea/Sudan
111 E1 Barakaldo Spain
85 H3 Baraki Barak Afgh.
87 D1 Barakot India
88 D2 Bara Lacha Pass India
131 J3 Baralzon Lake Canada
88 A2 Baramati India
88 D4 Baran India
85 F3 Bārān, Kūh-e mts Iran
116 C4 Baranavichy Belarus
77 R3 Baranikha Rus. Fed.
117 C5 Baranivka Ukr.
82 C3 Barankul Kazakh.
157 B2 Baranoa Col.
130 B3 Baranof Island U.S.A.
82 A1 Baranovka Rus. Fed.
120 B3 Barão de Melgaço Brazil
120 B3 Baraoueli Mali
108 D4 Baraque de Fraiture hill Belgium
91 F7 Barat Daya, Kepulauan is Indon.
70 C4 Baratta Australia
88 D3 Baraut India
158 B1 Barbacena Brazil
157 B4 Barbacoas Col.
149 M6 Barbados country Caribbean Sea
111 G1 Barbastro Spain
111 D1 Barbate de Franco Spain
150 C2 Barbechitos Mex.
125 I2 Barberton S. Africa
146 C4 Barberton U.S.A.
110 D4 Barbezieux-St-Hilaire France
157 B3 Barbosa Col.
131 K2 Barbour Bay Canada
146 B6 Barbourville U.S.A.
90 B4 Barbuda i. Antigua and Barbuda
109 J3 Barby (Elbe) Germany
68 D3 Barcaldine Australia
111 H2 Barcelona Spain
(City Plan 60)
157 E2 Barcelona Venez.
155 G4 Barcelos Brazil
109 I4 Barchfeld Germany
157 C2 Barclayville Liberia
114 G2 Barcs Hungary
81 K1 Bärdä Azer.
102 C2 Bárðarbunga mt. Iceland
159 C2 Bardas Blancas Arg.
90 D6 Bardawil, Sabkhat al lag. Egypt
89 F5 Barddhaman India
113 J6 Bardejov Slovakia
93 B6 Bar Đen Vietnam
105 C5 Bardsey Island U.K.
84 E4 Bardsīr Iran
144 C4 Bardstown U.S.A.
146 B5 Bardwell U.S.A.
88 E3 Bareilly India
76 D2 Barentsburg Svalbard
76 D2 Barentsøya i. Svalbard
76 D2 Barents Sea Arctic Ocean
122 D2 Barentu Eritrea
88 C3 Barga China
87 C1 Bargarh India
109 I1 Bargteheide Germany
89 G5 Barguna Bangl.
147 I2 Bar Harbor U.S.A.
114 G4 Bari Italy
98 C3 Ba Ria Vietnam
88 B3 Bari Doab lowland Pak.
157 E2 Barikot Nepal
157 E2 Barima r. Venez.
89 G5 Barisal Bangl.
99 B4 Barisan, Pegunungan mts Indon.
99 D3 Barito r. Indon.
154 F8 Baritú, Parque Nacional nat. park Arg.
84 B4 Barkā Oman
92 B4 Barkam China
103 N4 Barkava Latvia
130 D4 Barkerville Canada
145 D5 Barkley, Lake U.S.A.
130 D5 Barkley Sound inlet Canada
124 G5 Barkly East S. Africa
68 D3 Barkly Tableland reg. Australia
124 F4 Barkly West S. Africa
90 F2 Barkol China
113 M7 Bârlad Romania
110 H2 Bar-le-Duc France
70 C3 Barlee, Lake salt flat Australia
114 G4 Barletta Italy
71 G5 Barmedman Australia
70 D5 Barmera Australia
88 B4 Barmer India
105 C5 Barmouth U.K.
88 E4 Barnala India
105 F4 Barnard Castle U.K.
71 F3 Barnato Australia
82 F1 Barnaul Rus. Fed.
147 F4 Barnegat U.S.A.
147 F4 Barnegat Bay U.S.A.
146 C4 Barnesboro U.S.A.
131 N2 Barnes Icecap Canada
70 F4 Barney, Lake salt flat Australia
143 G4 Barney Top mt. U.S.A.
141 H3 Barnhart U.S.A.
105 F5 Barnsley U.K.
105 C6 Barnstaple U.K.
105 C6 Barnstaple Bay U.K. see Bideford Bay
109 G2 Barntorf Germany
145 D5 Barnwell U.S.A.
88 E5 Baroda India see Vadodara
89 H3 Baroghil Pass Afgh.
89 G4 Barpathar India
89 G4 Barpeta India

134	D3	**Barques, Point Aux** MI U.S.A.
135	F3	**Barques, Point Aux** MI U.S.A.
157	C2	**Barquisimeto** Venez.
155	J6	**Barra** Brazil
106	A4	**Barra** i. U.K.
106	A3	**Barra, Sound of** sea chan. U.K.
71	I3	**Barraba** Australia
124	D7	**Barracouta, Cape** hd S. Africa
155	G6	**Barra do Bugres** Brazil
155	I5	**Barra do Corda** Brazil
158	B1	**Barra de Garças** Brazil
155	G5	**Barra do São Manuel** Brazil
154	C6	**Barranca** Peru
154	C4	**Barranca** Peru
157	B3	**Barrancabermeja** Col.
159	B3	**Barrancas** r. Arg.
157	B2	**Barrancas** Col.
157	E2	**Barrancas** Venez.
156	E3	**Barranqueras** Arg.
157	B2	**Barranquilla** Col.
147	G2	**Barre** U.S.A.
159	C1	**Barreal** Arg.
155	J6	**Barreiras** Brazil
155	G4	**Barreirinha** Brazil
155	J4	**Barreirinhas** Brazil
158	B1	**Barreiro** r. Brazil
111	B3	**Barreiro** Port.
155	K5	**Barreiros** Brazil
158	C3	**Barretos** Brazil
130	G4	**Barrhead** Canada
106	D5	**Barrhead** U.K.
135	H3	**Barrie** Canada
135	F3	**Barrie Island** Canada
130	E4	**Barrière** Canada
70	D3	**Barrier Range** hills Australia
71	I4	**Barrington, Mount** Australia
131	I3	**Barrington Lake** Canada
71	F2	**Barringun** Australia
134	B3	**Barron** U.S.A.
150	D2	**Barroterán** Mex.
159	B3	**Barrow** Arg.
107	E5	**Barrow** r. Rep. of Ireland
128	C2	**Barrow** U.S.A.
128	C2	**Barrow, Point** c. U.S.A.
68	D4	**Barrow Creek** Australia
104	D3	**Barrow-in-Furness** U.K.
68	B4	**Barrow Island** Australia
129	I2	**Barrow Strait** Canada
105	D6	**Barry** U.K.
124	D6	**Barrydale** S. Africa
135	I3	**Barrys Bay** Canada
82	D3	**Barsakel'mes, Poluostrov** pen. Kazakh.
88	C3	**Barsalpur** India
83	I2	**Barshatas** Kazakh.
87	A2	**Barsi** India
88	D5	**Barsi Iakli** India
109	H2	**Barsinghausen** Germany
140	D4	**Barstow** U.S.A.
110	G2	**Bar-sur-Aube** France
112	F3	**Barth** Germany
155	G2	**Bartica** Guyana
80	D1	**Bartın** Turkey
68	D1	**Bartle Frere, Mount** Australia
141	G2	**Bartles, Mount** U.S.A.
137	G4	**Bartlesville** U.S.A.
142	D3	**Bartlett** NE U.S.A.
147	H2	**Bartlett** NH U.S.A.
130	F2	**Bartlett Lake** Canada
147	G2	**Barton** U.S.A.
104	G4	**Barton-upon-Humber** U.K.
113	J3	**Bartoszyce** Poland
150	I6	**Barú, Volcán** vol. Panama
99	D2	**Barumun** r. Indon.
98	A5	**Barus** Indon.
92	B1	**Baruunsuu** Mongolia
90	D2	**Baruun Urt** Mongolia
88	D5	**Barwah** India
88	C3	**Barwala** India
88	C5	**Barwani** India
71	H2	**Barwon** r. Australia
116	D4	**Barysaw** Belarus
116	H4	**Barysh** Rus. Fed.
116	H4	**Barysh** r. Rus. Fed.
84	C3	**Barzūk** Iran
84	D5	**Bāsa'īdū** Iran
98	C3	**Basăk, Tônlé** r. Cambodia
140	C2	**Basalt** U.S.A.
93	□	**Basalt Island** Hong Kong China
122	B3	**Basankusu** Dem. Rep. Congo
87	B2	**Basar** India
115	M2	**Basarabi** Romania
159	E2	**Basavilbaso** Arg.
97	B4	**Basay** Phil.
97	B1	**Basco** Phil.
112	C7	**Basel** Switz.
85	E5	**Bashākerd, Kūhhā-ye** mts Iran
130	G4	**Bashaw** Canada
125	H6	**Bashee** r. S. Africa
85	H3	**Bashgul** r. Afgh.
116	G4	**Bashmakovo** Rus. Fed.
84	C4	**Bāsht** Iran
117	E6	**Bashtanka** Ukr.
88	D4	**Basi** India
87	D1	**Basia** India
97	B5	**Basilan** i. Phil.
97	B5	**Basilan Strait** Phil.
105	H6	**Basildon** U.K.
138	E2	**Basin** U.S.A.
105	F6	**Basingstoke** U.K.
84	J4	**Bāsīra** r. Iraq
89	G5	**Basirhat** India
147	J2	**Baskahegan Lake** U.S.A.
81	J2	**Başkale** Turkey
135	J2	**Baskatong, Réservoir** resr Canada
117	H5	**Baskunchak, Ozero** l. Rus. Fed.
		Basle Switz. see Basel
88	D5	**Basoda** India
122	C3	**Basoko** Dem. Rep. Congo
81	K6	**Basra** Iraq
114	D2	**Bassano del Grappa** Italy
120	C4	**Bassar** Togo
123	D6	**Bassas da India** i. Indian Ocean
91	B5	**Bassein** Myanmar
103	A3	**Bassenthwaite Lake** U.K.
120	A3	**Basse Santa Su** Gambia
149	L5	**Basse-Terre** Guadeloupe
149	L5	**Basseterre** St Kitts and Nevis
142	D3	**Bassett** U.S.A.
141	G5	**Bassett Peak** mt. U.S.A.
147	I2	**Bass Harbor** U.S.A.
120	B3	**Bassikounou** Mauritania
120	C4	**Bassila** Benin
106	F4	**Bass Rock** i. U.K.
68	E5	**Bass Strait** Australia
109	G3	**Bassum** Germany
134	B1	**Basswood Lake** U.S.A.
103	K4	**Båstad** Sweden
84	D5	**Bastak** Iran
84	B2	**Bastānābād** Iran
109	I4	**Bastheim** Germany
89	E4	**Basti** India
114	C3	**Bastia** Corsica France
108	D4	**Bastogne** Belgium
143	F5	**Bastrop** LA U.S.A.
143	D6	**Bastrop** TX U.S.A.
85	G5	**Basul** r. Pak.
120	C4	**Bata** Equat. Guinea
149	H4	**Batabanó, Golfo de** b. Cuba
97	B2	**Batac** Phil.
97	C3	**Batag** i. Phil.
77	O3	**Batagay** Rus. Fed.
88	B2	**Batala** India
111	B3	**Batalha** Port.
98	C5	**Batam** i. Indon.
77	N3	**Batamay** Rus. Fed.
82	D2	**Batamshinskiy** Kazakh.
97	B1	**Batan** i. Phil.
122	B3	**Batangafo** Centr. Afr. Rep.
97	B3	**Batangas** Phil.
99	B3	**Batanghari** r. Indon.
98	A5	**Batangtoru** Indon.

97	B1	**Batan Islands** Phil.
158	C3	**Batatais** Brazil
134	C5	**Batavia** IL U.S.A.
146	D3	**Batavia** NY U.S.A.
117	F6	**Bataysk** Rus. Fed.
135	E2	**Batchawana** Canada
135	E2	**Batchawana** r. Canada
132	D4	**Batchawana Bay** Canada
135	E2	**Batchawana Mountain** Canada
68	D3	**Batchelor** Australia
98	B2	**Bătdâmbâng** Cambodia
71	I5	**Batemans Bay** b. Australia
71	I5	**Batemans Bay** Australia
143	F5	**Batesville** AR U.S.A.
143	F5	**Batesville** MS U.S.A.
116	D3	**Batetskiy** Rus. Fed.
133	G4	**Bath** N.B. Canada
135	I3	**Bath** Ont. Canada
105	E6	**Bath** U.K.
147	I3	**Bath** ME U.S.A.
146	E3	**Bath** NY U.S.A.
106	E5	**Bathgate** U.K.
88	D3	**Bathinda** India
71	H4	**Bathurst** Australia
133	G4	**Bathurst** Canada
125	G6	**Bathurst** S. Africa
71	H5	**Bathurst, Lake** Australia
128	H3	**Bathurst Inlet** inlet Canada
128	H3	**Bathurst Inlet** Canada
68	D3	**Bathurst Island** Australia
129	I2	**Bathurst Island** Canada
81	K7	**Bāṭin, Wādī al** watercourse Asia
84	D3	**Bāṭlāq-e Gavkhūnī** marsh Iran
104	F4	**Batley** U.K.
71	H5	**Batlow** Australia
81	H3	**Batman** Turkey
120	C1	**Batna** Alg.
98	C1	**Batong, Ko** is Thai.
143	F6	**Baton Rouge** U.S.A.
150	C2	**Batopilas** Mex.
121	D4	**Batouri** Cameroon
158	B1	**Batovi** Brazil
80	E4	**Batroûn** Lebanon
102	O1	**Båtsfjord** Norway
87	C5	**Batticaloa** Sri Lanka
114	F4	**Battipaglia** Italy
131	G4	**Battle** r. Canada
134	E4	**Battle Creek** U.S.A.
131	H4	**Battleford** Canada
138	C3	**Battle Mountain** U.S.A.
88	C1	**Battura Glacier** Jammu and Kashmir
99	A3	**Batu, Pulau-pulau** is Indon.
98	B4	**Batu Gajah** Malaysia
97	C5	**Batulaki** Phil.
81	H1	**Bat'umi** Georgia
99	B2	**Batu Pahat** Malaysia
98	B4	**Batu Putih, Gunung** mt. Malaysia
91	E7	**Baubau** Indon.
120	C3	**Bauchi** Nigeria
142	E1	**Baudette** U.S.A.
157	A3	**Baudó, Serranía de** mts Col.
110	F3	**Baugé** France
109	H5	**Bauland** reg. Germany
133	I3	**Bauld, Cape** hd Canada
88	C2	**Baume-les-Dames** France
158	C3	**Baunei** Italy
155	I6	**Bauru** Brazil
158	B2	**Baús** Brazil
108	E4	**Bausendorf** Germany
103	N4	**Bauska** Latvia
82	B3	**Bautino** Kazakh.
112	G5	**Bautzen** Germany
83	G4	**Bauyrzhan Momyshuly** Kazakh.
124	E6	**Baviaanskloofberge** mts S. Africa
136	E6	**Bavispe** r. Mex.
99	D4	**Bawean** i. Indon.
108	F2	**Bawinkel** Germany
120	B3	**Bawku** Ghana
98	A1	**Bawlake** Myanmar
93	A4	**Bawolung** China
92	B3	**Baxi** China
145	D6	**Baxley** U.S.A.
97	B3	**Bay, Laguna de** lag. Phil.
149	I4	**Bayamo** Cuba
88	D4	**Bayana** India
82	A2	**Bayanaul** Kazakh.
90	D3	**Bayan Har Shan** mts China
90	C2	**Bayanhongor** Mongolia
92	B2	**Bayan Hot** China
96	A1	**Bayan Huxu** China
92	B3	**Bayan Mod** China
92	B1	**Bayan Nuru** China
92	C1	**Bayan Obo** China
96	A1	**Bayan Ul** China
84	D4	**Bayāz** Iran
97	C4	**Baybay** Phil.
81	H1	**Bayburt** Turkey
135	F4	**Bay City** MI U.S.A.
143	D6	**Bay City** TX U.S.A.
76	H3	**Baydaratskaya Guba** Rus. Fed.
122	E3	**Baydhabo** Somalia
109	J1	**Bayeno** Rus. Fed.
134	B2	**Bayfield** U.S.A.
82	C2	**Baygakum** Kazakh.
82	F3	**Baygora** Kazakh.
82	E1	**Baygora** Kazakh.
115	L5	**Bayındır** Turkey
81	I4	**Bayjī** Iraq
		Baykal, Ozero l. Rus. Fed. see Baikal, Lake
90	C1	**Baykal'skiy Khrebet** mts Rus. Fed.
81	H2	**Baykan** Turkey
82	F3	**Bay-Khozha** Kazakh.
82	F3	**Baykonur** Kazakh.
82	D1	**Baykonyr** Kazakh.
81	D1	**Baykurt** China
84	D6	**Baynūna'h** reg. U.A.E.
97	B2	**Bayombong** Phil.
110	D5	**Bayonne** France
97	B4	**Bayo Point** Phil.
82	B1	**Bayramaly** Turkm.
115	L5	**Bayramiç** Turkey
109	J5	**Bayreuth** Germany
122	D3	**Bay Shore** U.S.A.
147	G4	**Bay Shore** U.S.A.
83	F5	**Baysun** Uzbek.
83	G4	**Baysuntau, Gory** mts Uzbek.
143	E6	**Baytown** U.S.A.
72	F3	**Bay View** N.Z.
83	G4	**Bayzhansay** Kazakh.
89	J5	**Bayingnies** Germany
82	B2	**Bazarchulan** Kazakh.
84	C2	**Bāzār-e Māsāl** Iran
81	J2	**Bāzārgān** Iran
117	H4	**Bazarnyy Karabulak** Rus. Fed.
96	A3	**Bazhou** China
123	C6	**Bazaruto, Ilha do** i. Moz.
80	C2	**Bazhong** China
92	E2	**Bazhou** China
85	F4	**Bazmān** Iran
85	F4	**Bazmān, Kūh-e** mt. Iran
98	C3	**Bé** r. Vietnam
123	E5	**Bé, Nosy** i. Madag.
142	C2	**Beach** U.S.A.
132	E5	**Beachburg** Canada
147	F5	**Beach Haven** U.S.A.
70	D6	**Beachport** Australia
105	H7	**Beachy Head** U.K.
147	G4	**Beacon** U.S.A.
125	G6	**Beacon Bay** S. Africa

93	□	**Beacon Hill** Hong Kong China
105	G6	**Beaconsfield** U.K.
156	C8	**Beagle, Canal** sea chan. Arg.
68	C3	**Beagle Gulf** Australia
123	E5	**Bealanana** Madag.
105	E7	**Beaminster** U.K.
138	E7	**Bear** r. U.S.A.
131	M2	**Bear Cove** b. Canada
132	C4	**Beardmore** Canada
73	B4	**Beardmore Glacier** Antarctica
71	H1	**Beardmore Reservoir** Australia
134	B5	**Beardstown** U.S.A.
132	D3	**Bear Island** Canada
130	D3	**Bear Lake** Canada
138	E3	**Bear Lake** U.S.A.
88	D4	**Bearma** r. India
138	E1	**Bear Paw Mountain** U.S.A.
73	A3	**Bear Peninsula** Antarctica
132	B2	**Bearskin Lake** Canada
140	B2	**Bear Valley** U.S.A.
88	C3	**Beas** r. India
88	C3	**Beas Dam** India
149	J5	**Beata, Cabo** c. Dom. Rep.
149	J5	**Beata, Isla** i. Dom. Rep.
142	D3	**Beatrice** U.S.A.
85	G3	**Beatton** r. Canada
130	D3	**Beatton River** Canada
132	D3	**Beatty** U.S.A.
132	E4	**Beattyville** Canada
110	G5	**Beaucaire** France
156	E8	**Beauchene Island** Falkland Is
70	E6	**Beaufort** Australia
98	C1	**Beaufort** Sabah Malaysia
145	D5	**Beaufort** r. Canada
128	E2	**Beaufort Sea** Canada/U.S.A.
124	E6	**Beaufort West** S. Africa
132	F4	**Beauharnois** Canada
106	D3	**Beauly** U.K.
106	D3	**Beauly Firth** est. U.K.
105	C4	**Beaumaris** U.K.
108	C4	**Beaumont** Belgium
72	B7	**Beaumont** N.Z.
143	F6	**Beaumont** U.S.A.
146	B5	**Beaumont** MS U.S.A.
143	E6	**Beaumont** TX U.S.A.
110	D3	**Beaune** France
110	D3	**Beaupréau** France
108	A4	**Beauquesne** France
131	J4	**Beauséjour** Canada
131	H3	**Beauval** Canada
108	A4	**Beauval** France
128	H4	**Beaver** r. B.C./Y.T. Canada
130	D2	**Beaver** r. Ont. Canada
141	F2	**Beaver** r. U.S.A.
141	F2	**Beaver** r. U.S.A.
130	A2	**Beaver Creek** Canada
144	C4	**Beaver Dam** KY U.S.A.
134	C4	**Beaver Dam** WI U.S.A.
146	C4	**Beaver Falls** U.S.A.
138	D2	**Beaverhead Mountains** U.S.A.
131	J4	**Beaver Hill Lake** Canada
134	E3	**Beaver Island** U.S.A.
143	E4	**Beaver Lake** resr U.S.A.
130	F3	**Beaverlodge** Canada
146	D4	**Beaver Run Reservoir** U.S.A.
88	C4	**Beawar** India
159	C2	**Beazley** Arg.
158	B3	**Bebedouro** Brazil
105	D4	**Bebington** U.K.
109	H4	**Bebra** Germany
132	F1	**Bécard, Lac** l. Canada
105	I5	**Beccles** U.K.
115	I2	**Bečej** Yugo.
111	C1	**Becerreá** Spain
120	B1	**Béchar** Alg.
109	I5	**Bechhofen** Germany
146	C5	**Beckley** U.S.A.
109	G3	**Beckum** Germany
104	F3	**Bedale** U.K.
108	E4	**Bedburg** Germany
147	I2	**Beddington** U.S.A.
122	E3	**Bedelê** Eth.
83	I4	**Bedel Pass** China/Kyrg.
109	G1	**Bederkesa** Germany
147	G2	**Bedford** Canada
125	G6	**Bedford** S. Africa
105	G5	**Bedford** U.K.
144	C4	**Bedford** IN U.S.A.
147	H3	**Bedford** MA U.S.A.
146	D6	**Bedford** VA U.S.A.
105	G5	**Bedford Levels** lowland U.K.
71	G4	**Bedgerebong** Australia
104	F2	**Bedlington** U.K.
98	□	**Bedok** Sing.
98	□	**Bedok Reservoir** Sing.
141	H2	**Bedrock** U.S.A.
108	E1	**Bedum** Neth.
88	D3	**Bedworth** U.K.
88	B3	**Beech Fork Lake** U.S.A.
145	B5	**Beech Fork Lake** U.S.A.
134	C2	**Beechwood** U.S.A.
71	G6	**Beechworth** Australia
73	K5	**Beecroft Peninsula** Australia
109	J2	**Beelitz** Germany
71	J1	**Beenleigh** Australia
107	A5	**Beenoskee** hd Rep. of Ireland
108	B3	**Beernem** Belgium
80	E6	**Beersheba** Israel
124	E6	**Beervlei Dam** S. Africa
71	J1	**Beerwah** Australia
109	G1	**Beetzee** l. Germany
143	D6	**Beeville** U.S.A.
122	C3	**Befale** Dem. Rep. Congo
123	E5	**Befandriana Avaratra** Madag.
71	H6	**Bega** Australia
88	B3	**Begari** r. Pak.
111	F2	**Begur, Cap de** pt Spain
89	F4	**Begusarai** India
85	D3	**Behābād** Iran
85	H3	**Béhague, Pointe** pt Fr. Guiana
84	C4	**Behbehān** Iran
130	C3	**Behm Canal** inlet U.S.A.
73	B3	**Behrendt Mts** Antarctica
84	D2	**Behshahr** Iran
85	G3	**Behsūd** Afgh.
90	E2	**Bei'an** China
93	C4	**Beibei** China
92	B4	**Beichuan** China
96	D4	**Beihai** China
96	C2	**Bei Jiang** r. China
92	E2	**Beijing** China (City Plan **51**)
92	E1	**Beijing** mun. China
108	E1	**Beilen** Neth.
93	C7	**Beili** China
92	B4	**Beilingries** Germany
96	D2	**Beining** China
106	D3	**Beinn an Oir** hill U.K.
106	D3	**Beinn Dearg** mt. U.K.
92	C4	**Beipan Jiang** r. China
96	A3	**Beipiao** China
123	C6	**Beira** Moz.
92	E3	**Beiru He** r. China
80	E5	**Beirut** Lebanon
76	I3	**Beira** Port.
109	K2	**Beitai Ding** mt. China
123	D6	**Beitbridge** Zimbabwe
106	D5	**Beith** U.K.
113	K7	**Beius** Romania
111	C3	**Beja** Port.
120	C1	**Béja** Tunisia
111	D4	**Béjar** Spain
115	D1	**Bejestān** Iran
84	D3	**Bekasi** Indon.
99	C4	**Bekdash** Turkm.
113	J7	**Békés** Hungary
113	J7	**Békéscsaba** Hungary

123	E6	**Bekily** Madag.
94	I3	**Bekkai** Japan
120	B4	**Bekwai** Ghana
89	E4	**Bela** India
85	G5	**Bela** Pak.
88	B3	**Belab** r. Pak.
125	H2	**Bela-Bela** S. Africa
121	D4	**Bélabo** Cameroon
115	I2	**Bela Crkva** Yugo.
83	J2	**Bel'agash** Kazakh.
123	E6	**Belair** U.S.A.
111	D3	**Belalcázar** Spain
109	L3	**Bělá nad Radbuzou** Czech Rep.
71	F4	**Belaraboon** Australia
113	M4	**Belarus** country Europe
158	A1	**Bela Vista** Brazil
123	D6	**Bela Vista** Moz.
77	S3	**Belaya** r. China
76	G5	**Belaya Glina** Rus. Fed.
98	B3	**Belaya Kalitva** Rus. Fed.
117	G5	**Belaya Kholunitsa** Rus. Fed.
113	I5	**Belchatów** Poland
146	B6	**Belcher** U.S.A.
129	J4	**Belcher Islands** Canada
85	G3	**Belchiragh** Afgh.
80	F2	**Belcik** Turkey
107	D3	**Belcoo** U.S.A.
120	B1	**Beni-Abbès** Alg.
111	B3	**Belden** U.S.A.
140	B1	**Belden** U.S.A.
122	E3	**Beledweyne** Somalia
155	I4	**Belém** Brazil
156	C3	**Belén** Arg.
80	F3	**Belen** Turkey
139	F5	**Belen** U.S.A.
69	G3	**Belep, Îles** is New Caledonia
82	D3	**Beleuli** tourist site Uzbek.
116	F4	**Belev** Rus. Fed.
72	D5	**Belfast** N.Z.
125	I2	**Belfast** S. Africa
107	F3	**Belfast** U.K.
147	I2	**Belfast** U.S.A.
107	F3	**Belfast Lough** inlet U.K.
142	C2	**Belfield** U.S.A.
104	F2	**Belford** U.K.
110	H3	**Belfort** France
87	A3	**Belgaum** India
109	L3	**Belgern** Germany
108	C4	**Belgium** country Europe
104	C4	**Belgorod** Rus. Fed.
73	B3	**Belgrano II** research station Antarctica
120	D4	**Beli** Nigeria
114	F6	**Belice** r. Sicily Italy
99	C3	**Belinyu** Indon.
99	C3	**Belitung** i. Indon.
151	G4	**Belize** Belize
151	G4	**Belize** country Central America
94	E2	**Belkina, Mys** pt Rus. Fed.
77	O2	**Bel'kovskiy, Ostrov** i. Rus. Fed.
71	I1	**Bell** Australia
130	D4	**Bella Bella** Canada
110	E3	**Bellac** France
130	D4	**Bella Coola** Canada
143	E6	**Bellaire** U.S.A.
87	B3	**Bellary** India
71	H2	**Bellata** Australia
159	F1	**Bella Unión** Uruguay
71	J3	**Bellbrook** Australia
146	B4	**Bellefontaine** U.S.A.
146	E4	**Bellefonte** U.S.A.
142	C2	**Belle Fourche** U.S.A.
142	C2	**Belle Fourche** r. U.S.A.
110	D3	**Bellegarde-sur-Valserine** France
145	D7	**Belle Glade** U.S.A.
110	C3	**Belle-Île** i. France
133	I3	**Belle Isle** Canada
133	I3	**Belle Isle, Strait of** Canada
141	G4	**Bellemont** U.S.A.
134	A5	**Belle Plaine** U.S.A.
135	I2	**Belleterre** Canada
135	I3	**Belleville** Canada
134	B4	**Belleville** IA U.S.A.
138	D3	**Belleville** ID U.S.A.
146	B6	**Belleville** U.S.A.
138	B2	**Bellevue** WA U.S.A.
71	J3	**Bellingen** Australia
104	E2	**Bellingham** U.K.
138	B1	**Bellingham** U.S.A.
73	B2	**Bellingshausen** research station Antarctica
73	A3	**Bellingshausen Sea** Antarctica
112	D7	**Bellinzona** Switz.
157	B3	**Bello** Col.
147	G3	**Bellows Falls** U.S.A.
88	B3	**Bellpat** Pak.
147	F5	**Belltown** U.S.A.
114	C1	**Belluno** Italy
87	B3	**Belluru** India
159	D2	**Bell Ville** Arg.
124	C6	**Bellville** S. Africa
109	G1	**Bell Germany
106	□	**Belmont** U.K.
146	D3	**Belmont** U.S.A.
158	E1	**Belmonte** Brazil
151	G4	**Belmopan** Belize
71	J2	**Belmore, Mount** Australia
107	B3	**Belmullet** Rep. of Ireland
158	D1	**Belo** Brazil
147	D2	**Beloeil** Canada
90	E1	**Belogorsk** Rus. Fed.
123	E6	**Beloha** Madag.
158	D2	**Belo Horizonte** Brazil
142	D4	**Beloit** KS U.S.A.
134	C4	**Beloit** WI U.S.A.
76	G3	**Belomorsk** Rus. Fed.
116	F3	**Beloomut** Rus. Fed.
89	G4	**Belonia** India
117	F6	**Belorechensk** Rus. Fed.
80	F2	**Belören** Turkey
82	D1	**Belrussia** country Europe see Belarus
123	E6	**Belo Tsiribihina** Madag.
83	J2	**Belousovka** Kazakh.
82	B1	**Belousovka** Kazakh.
116	F2	**Beloye, Ozero** l. Rus. Fed.
		Beloye More g. Rus. Fed. see White Sea
116	F2	**Belozersk** Rus. Fed.
146	C5	**Belpre** U.S.A.
138	E2	**Belt** U.S.A.
125	H4	**Beltana** Australia
68	B2	**Belt Bay** salt flat Australia
140	D3	**Belted Range** mts U.S.A.
87	A3	**Belur** India
95	A5	**Belvedere** Sabah Malaysia
134	C4	**Belvidere** U.S.A.
116	H4	**Belyando** Rus. Fed.
116	E4	**Belyy** Rus. Fed.
76	I2	**Belyy, Ostrov** i. Rus. Fed.
109	K2	**Belzig** Germany
124	C6	**Bement** U.S.A.
142	E2	**Bemidji** U.S.A.
108	E2	**Bemmel** Neth.
106	D4	**Ben Alder** mt. U.K.
120	E4	**Benalla** Australia
111	D1	**Benavente** Spain
106	A3	**Benbecula** i. U.K.
107	B4	**Benbaun** hill Rep. of Ireland
107	C3	**Benbulben** hill Rep. of Ireland
107	E3	**Benburb** U.K.

106	C4	**Ben Cruachan** mt. U.K.
138	B2	**Bend** U.S.A.
125	G5	**Bendearg** mt. S. Africa
71	I3	**Bendemeer** Australia
122	E3	**Bender-Bayla** Somalia
70	F6	**Bendigo** Australia
71	H6	**Beñdoc** Australia
123	D5	**Bene** Moz.
133	I3	**Benedict, Mount** Canada
123	E6	**Benenitra** Madag.
112	G6	**Benešov** Czech Rep.
114	F4	**Benevento** Italy
79	G5	**Bengal, Bay of** sea Asia
122	C4	**Bengamisa** Dem. Rep. Congo
92	B3	**Bengbu** China
121	E1	**Benghazi** Libya
92	F3	**Beng He** r. China
98	B3	**Bengkalis** Indon.
99	B3	**Bengkulu** Indon.
123	K4	**Bengtsfors** Sweden
123	B5	**Benguela** Angola
106	B4	**Ben Hiant** hill U.K.
164	E6	**Beni** r. Bol.
122	C3	**Beni** Dem. Rep. Congo
120	B1	**Beni-Abbès** Alg.
111	F3	**Benidorm** Spain
120	B1	**Beni Mellal** Morocco
120	C4	**Benin** country Africa
120	B1	**Benin City** Nigeria
120	B1	**Beni-Saf** Alg.
159	E3	**Benito Juárez** Arg.
139	F5	**Benito Soliven** Phil.
154	E4	**Benjamin Constant** Brazil
148	B2	**Benjamín Hill** Mex.
68	D2	**Benjina** Indon.
106	D2	**Ben Klibreck** mt. U.K.
106	D2	**Ben Lawers** mt. U.K.
71	I3	**Ben Lomond** mt. Australia
106	D4	**Ben Lomond** mt. U.K.
71	G8	**Ben Lomond National Park** Australia
106	D2	**Ben Loyal** hill U.K.
106	D4	**Ben Lui** mt. U.K.
106	B4	**Ben Macdui** mt. U.K.
106	D4	**Ben More** mt. Scotland U.K.
106	D4	**Ben More** mt. Scotland U.K.
72	C6	**Benmore, Lake** N.Z.
106	D2	**Ben More Assynt** mt. U.K.
77	P2	**Bennetta, Ostrov** i. Rus. Fed.
106	C4	**Ben Nevis** mt. U.K.
147	G3	**Bennington** U.S.A.
125	H3	**Benoni** S. Africa
109	G5	**Bensheim** Germany
141	G2	**Benson** AZ U.S.A.
142	E2	**Benson** MN U.S.A.
85	E5	**Bent** Iran
99	B2	**Benta Seberang** Malaysia
88	A3	**Bentinck Island** Australia
95	A9	**Bentinck Island** Myanmar
122	E3	**Bentiu** Sudan
146	E5	**Benton** AR U.S.A.
143	E5	**Benton** CA U.S.A.
134	B4	**Benton** IL U.S.A.
134	B4	**Benton Harbor** U.S.A.
98	C3	**Bên Tre** Vietnam
98	B5	**Bentung** Malaysia
120	D4	**Benue** r. Nigeria
106	D4	**Ben Vorlich** mt. U.K.
106	B3	**Benwee Head** hd Rep. of Ireland
106	B3	**Ben Wyvis** mt. U.K.
96	B3	**Benxi** Liaoning China
96	B3	**Benxi** Liaoning China
97	C5	**Beo** Indon.
		Beograd Yugo. see Belgrade
120	E5	**Béoumi** Côte d'Ivoire
95	B8	**Beppu** Japan
69	H3	**Beqa** i. Fiji
88	C4	**Berach** r. India
115	I5	**Berane** Yugo.
133	G2	**Bérard, Lac** l. Canada
88	D5	**Berasia** India
98	B2	**Berastagi** Indon.
115	H4	**Berat** Albania
99	E3	**Beratus, Gunung** mt. Indon.
91	F7	**Berau, Teluk** b. Indon.
121	F3	**Berber** Sudan
122	E2	**Berbera** Somalia
122	B3	**Berbérati** Centr. Afr. Rep.
82	D2	**Berchogur** Kazakh.
110	E1	**Berck** France
81	J1	**Berd** Armenia
77	N3	**Berdigestyakh** Rus. Fed.
90	A1	**Berdsk** Rus. Fed.
117	F6	**Berdyans'k** Ukr.
117	D5	**Berdychiv** Ukr.
146	A6	**Berea** U.S.A.
117	B5	**Berehove** Ukr.
69	L3	**Bereina** P.N.G.
131	J4	**Berens** r. Canada
131	J4	**Berens River** Canada
142	D3	**Beresford** U.S.A.
117	B5	**Berezhany** Ukr.
117	C5	**Berezne** Ukr.
116	K3	**Bereznik** Rus. Fed.
76	H4	**Berezniki** Rus. Fed.
76	I3	**Berezovo** Rus. Fed.
109	I3	**Berga** Germany
111	G1	**Berga** Spain
115	L5	**Bergama** Turkey
114	C2	**Bergamo** Italy
103	I3	**Bergby** Sweden
109	H2	**Bergen** Mecklenburg-Vorpommern Germany
103	I3	**Bergen** Niedersachsen Germany
102	M2	**Bergen** Norway
108	E2	**Bergen op Zoom** Neth.
110	E4	**Bergerac** France
108	E4	**Bergères-lès-Vertus** France
108	E3	**Bergheim (Erft)** Germany
108	F4	**Bergisch Gladbach** Germany
124	B1	**Bergland** Namibia
102	M2	**Bergsviken** Sweden
109	I5	**Bergtheim** Germany
108	E1	**Bergum** Neth.
125	H4	**Bergville** S. Africa
99	B3	**Berhala, Selat** sea chan. Indon.
77	S3	**Bering, Ostrov** i. Rus. Fed.
77	S4	**Beringovskiy** Rus. Fed.
75		**Bering Sea** Pacific Ocean
128	B3	**Bering Strait** strait
102	J3	**Berkåk** Norway
140	A3	**Berkeley** U.S.A.
146	D5	**Berkeley Springs** U.S.A.
73	G2	**Berkner Island** Antarctica
115	J3	**Berkovitsa** Bulg.
105	F6	**Berkshire Downs** hills U.K.
102	O1	**Berlevåg** Norway
111	D1	**Berlanga** Spain
109	G1	**Berlin** Germany
147	H2	**Berlin** NH U.S.A.
146	D5	**Berlin** PA U.S.A.
134	C4	**Berlin** WI U.S.A.
129	J2	**Berlinguet Inlet** Canada

146	C4	**Berlin Lake** U.S.A.
71	I6	**Bermagui** Australia
159	C4	**Bermeja, Punta** pt Arg.
150	D2	**Bermejillo** Mex.
159	C1	**Bermejo** r. Arg.
156	D2	**Bermejo** r. Arg./Bol.
154	F8	**Bermejo** Bol.
149	M2	**Bermuda** terr. Atlantic Ocean
163	E4	**Bermuda Rise** sea feature N. Atlantic Ocean
112	C7	**Bern** Switz.
139	F5	**Bernalillo** U.S.A.
156	A7	**Bernardo O'Higgins, Parque Nacional** nat. park Chile
159	D3	**Bernasconi** Arg.
109	J3	**Bernburg (Saale)** Germany
109	G1	**Berne** Germany
134	E5	**Berne** U.S.A.
112	C7	**Bernese Alpen** mts Switz.
150	C2	**Bernejillo** Mex.
106	A4	**Bernera** i. Scotland U.K.
106	A4	**Berneray** i. Scotland U.K.
129	J2	**Bernier Bay** Canada
68	B4	**Bernier Island** Australia
112	E7	**Bernina Pass** Switz.
108	F5	**Bernkastel-Kues** Germany
123	E6	**Beroroha** Madag.
112	F5	**Beroun** Czech Rep.
70	D5	**Berri** Australia
106	E2	**Berriedale** U.K.
71	F5	**Berrigan** Australia
71	I5	**Berrima** Australia
107	F4	**Berrouaghia** Alg.
71	I5	**Berry** Australia
110	E3	**Berry** reg. France
140	A2	**Berryessa, Lake** U.S.A.
145	E7	**Berry Islands** Bahamas
124	B3	**Berseba** Namibia
109	F2	**Bersenbrück** Germany
117	D5	**Bershad'** Ukr.
82	E1	**Bersuat** Rus. Fed.
99	B1	**Bertam** Malaysia
155	J5	**Bertolínia** Brazil
121	D4	**Bertoua** Cameroon
107	B4	**Bertraghboy Bay** Rep. of Ireland
69	H2	**Beru** i. Kiribati
82	E4	**Beruni** Uzbek.
154	F4	**Beruri** Brazil
104	F7	**Berwick** U.S.A.
147	E4	**Berwick** U.S.A.
104	F3	**Berwick-upon-Tweed** U.K.
130	F3	**Berwyn** Canada
105	D5	**Berwyn** hill U.K.
117	E6	**Beryslav** Ukr.
123	E6	**Besalampy** Madag.
110	H3	**Besançon** France
82	C3	**Besbay** Kazakh.
83	F5	**Besharyk** Uzbek.
82	F5	**Beshir** Turkm.
85	E5	**Beshkent** Uzbek.
84	B3	**Beshneh** Iran
81	H3	**Beşiri** Turkey
117	H7	**Beslan** Rus. Fed.
131	H3	**Besnard Lake** Canada
80	F3	**Besni** Turkey
83	H2	**Besoba** Kazakh.
134	B2	**Bessemer** AL U.S.A.
134	B2	**Bessemer** MI U.S.A.
83	H2	**Bessonky, Gora** hill Kazakh.
82	C2	**Bestamak** Aktyubinskaya Oblast' Kazakh.
83	I2	**Bestamak** Vostochnyy Kazakhstan Kazakh.
83	H1	**Bestobe** Kazakh.
111	B1	**Betanzos** Spain
121	D4	**Bétaré Oya** Cameroon
124	D5	**Bethal** S. Africa
124	B3	**Bethanie** Namibia
142	E3	**Bethany** Missouri U.S.A.
143	D5	**Bethany** OK U.S.A.
128	B3	**Bethel** AK U.S.A.
147	H2	**Bethel** ME U.S.A.
146	A5	**Bethel** OH U.S.A.
147	G4	**Bethel Park** U.S.A.
146	C4	**Bethesda** U.K.
105	C5	**Bethesda** U.K.
146	E5	**Bethesda** MD U.S.A.
124	F5	**Bethesdaweg** S. Africa
147	H4	**Bethlehem** U.S.A.
125	H4	**Bethlehem** S. Africa
80	E6	**Bethlehem** West Bank
125	H5	**Bethulie** S. Africa
108	A4	**Béthune** France
157	C2	**Betijoque** Venez.
123	E6	**Betioky** Madag.
98	B4	**Betong** Thai.
83	G3	**Betpak-Dala** Kazakh.
83	G3	**Betpak-Dala** plain Kazakh.
123	E6	**Betroka** Madag.
80	E5	**Bet She'an** Israel
133	G4	**Betsiamites** Canada
133	G4	**Betsiamites** r. Canada
123	E5	**Betsiboka** r. Madag.
134	D3	**Betsie, Point** U.S.A.
134	E2	**Betsy Lake** U.S.A.
108	B2	**Bettendorf** U.S.A.
89	F4	**Bettiah** India
107	E4	**Bettyhill** U.K.
107	E4	**Bettystown** Rep. of Ireland
88	D5	**Betul** India
108	E2	**Betuwe** reg. Neth.
105	D5	**Betws-y-coed** U.K.
108	E2	**Betzdorf** Germany
70	E6	**Beulah** Australia
134	D3	**Beulah** U.S.A.
105	H6	**Beult** r. U.K.
104	F4	**Beverley** U.K.
128	C4	**Beverley, Lake** U.S.A.
147	H3	**Beverly** MA U.S.A.
146	C5	**Beverly** OH U.S.A.
140	C4	**Beverly Hills** U.S.A.
134	C4	**Beverly Lake** Canada
109	G1	**Beverstedt** Germany
109	G1	**Beverungen** Germany
108	D2	**Beverwijk** Neth.
108	F5	**Bexbach** Germany
105	H7	**Bexhill** U.K.
84	B2	**Beyānlū** Iran
80	C3	**Bey Dağları** mts Turkey
80	C3	**Beykoz** Turkey
120	B4	**Beyla** Guinea
82	A2	**Beyneu** Kazakh.
80	F2	**Beypınarı** Turkey
80	F2	**Beypazarı** Turkey
80	C3	**Beyşehir** Turkey
80	C3	**Beyşehir Gölü** l. Turkey
84	E4	**Beytüşşebap** Turkey
84	E3	**Bezameh** Iran
110	F5	**Béziers** France
116	I3	**Bezhanitsy** Rus. Fed.
116	F3	**Bezhetsk** Rus. Fed.
89	E4	**Bhabhar** India
88	B4	**Bhabhar** India
88	B5	**Bhachau** India
89	E4	**Bhadarwah** India
87	C2	**Bhadrachalam** India
87	A3	**Bhadra Reservoir** India
88	A3	**Bhag** r. Pak.
89	F4	**Bhagalpur** India
88	G5	**Bhagirathi** r. India
89	E4	**Bhadgaon** Nepal see Bhaktapur
87	C2	**Bhadrachalam** India
88	D5	**Bhainsdehi** India

89 G4 **Bhairab Bazar** Bangl.
89 E4 **Bhairawa** Nepal
89 F4 **Bhaktapur** Nepal
87 B2 **Bhalki** India
90 B4 **Bhamo** Myanmar
87 C2 **Bhamragarh** India
88 D4 **Bhander** India
89 F6 **Bhanjanagar** India
88 C4 **Bhanpura** India
88 D5 **Bhanrer Range** *hills* India
89 H4 **Bharatpur** India
85 F5 **Bhari** *r.* Pak.
88 C5 **Bharuch** India
87 C1 **Bhatapara** India
87 A3 **Bhatkal** India
89 G5 **Bhatpara** India
87 B4 **Bhavani** India
87 B4 **Bhavani** *r.* India
88 C5 **Bhavnagar** India
87 C2 **Bhawana** Pak.
87 C2 **Bhawanipatna** India
125 I3 **Bhekuzulu** S. Africa
89 E3 **Bheri** *r.* Nepal
88 C4 **Bhilwara** India
87 B2 **Bhima** *r.* India
87 C2 **Bhimavaram** India
88 D4 **Bhind** India
88 C4 **Bhindar** India
89 E4 **Bhinga** India
88 C4 **Bhinmal** India
89 F4 **Bhojpur** Nepal
87 B2 **Bhongir** India
125 H5 **Bhongweni** S. Africa
88 D5 **Bhopal** India
87 C2 **Bhopalpatnam** India
87 A2 **Bhor** India
89 F5 **Bhuban** India
88 B5 **Bhuj** India
88 C5 **Bhusawal** India
89 G4 **Bhutan** *country* Asia
88 B4 **Bhuttewala** India
98 B1 **Bia, Phou** *mt.* Laos
84 E5 **Biabān** *mts* Iran
88 C2 **Biafo Glacier** Pak.
91 F7 **Biak** Indon.
91 F7 **Biak** *i.* Indon.
113 K4 **Biała Podlaska** Poland
112 G4 **Białogard** Poland
113 K4 **Białystok** Poland
120 B4 **Biankouma** Côte d'Ivoire
96 B1 **Bianzhao** China
88 D5 **Biaora** India
84 D2 **Biärjmand** Iran
114 D2 **Biarritz** France
85 B5 **Bi'r Tabrāk** *well* Saudi Arabia
112 D7 **Biasca** Switz.
94 G3 **Bibai** Japan
123 B5 **Bibala** Angola
71 H6 **Bibbenluke** Australia
114 D3 **Bibbiena** Italy
112 D6 **Biberach an der Riß** Germany
89 G4 **Bibiyana** *r.* Bangl.
112 E5 **Biblis** Germany
80 C2 **Biçer** Turkey
105 F6 **Bicester** U.K.
71 H8 **Bicheno** Australia
117 G7 **Bichvint'a** Georgia
68 D3 **Bickerton Island** Australia
105 D7 **Bickleigh** U.K.
141 G2 **Bicknell** U.S.A.
123 B5 **Bicuari, Parque Nacional do** *nat. park* Angola
87 A2 **Bid** India
120 C4 **Bida** Nigeria
97 K3 **Bidadari, Tanjung** *pt* Sabah Malaysia
84 D4 **Bida Khabit** Iran
82 D2 **Bidar** India
85 E6 **Bidbid** Oman
147 H3 **Biddeford** U.S.A.
108 D2 **Biddinghuizen** Neth.
106 C4 **Bidean nam Bian** *mt.* U.K.
105 C6 **Bideford** U.K.
105 C6 **Bideford Bay** U.K.
113 K4 **Biebrza** *r.* Poland
109 G4 **Biedenkopf** Germany
112 C7 **Biel** Switz.
112 H5 **Bielawa** Poland
109 G2 **Bielefeld** Germany
114 C2 **Biella** Italy
113 I6 **Bielsko-Biała** Poland
113 K4 **Bielsk Podlaski** Poland
109 I1 **Bienenbüttel** Germany
98 C3 **Biên Hoa** Vietnam
132 F2 **Bienville, Lac** *l.* Canada
125 F3 **Biesiesvlei** S. Africa
109 H6 **Bietigheim-Bissingen** Germany
108 D5 **Bièvre** Belgium
122 B4 **Bifoun** Gabon
133 I3 **Big** *r.* Canada
140 A2 **Big** *r.* U.S.A.
117 C7 **Biga** Turkey
80 D5 **Bigadiç** Turkey
115 L5 **Biga Yarımadası** *pen.* Turkey
134 D2 **Big Bay** U.S.A.
134 D3 **Big Bay de Noc** U.S.A.
140 D4 **Big Bear Lake** U.S.A.
138 E2 **Big Belt Mountains** U.S.A.
125 I3 **Big Bend** Swaziland
143 C6 **Big Bend National Park** U.S.A.
143 F5 **Big Black** *r.* U.S.A.
105 D7 **Bigbury-on-Sea** U.K.
145 D7 **Big Cypress National Preserve** *res.* U.S.A.
134 C3 **Big Eau Pleine Reservoir** U.S.A.
131 K5 **Big Falls** U.S.A.
131 H4 **Biggar** Canada
106 F5 **Biggar** U.K.
130 B3 **Bigger, Mount** Canada
105 G5 **Biggleswade** U.K.
138 D2 **Big Hole** *r.* U.S.A.
138 F2 **Bighorn** *r.* U.S.A.
138 E2 **Bighorn Canyon National Recreation Area** *res.* U.S.A.
138 F2 **Bighorn Mountains** U.S.A.
129 K3 **Big Island** Nunavut Canada
130 F2 **Big Island** N.W.T. Canada
147 J2 **Big Lake** U.S.A.
120 A3 **Bignona** Senegal
146 D6 **Big Otter** *r.* U.S.A.
140 C3 **Big Pine** U.S.A.
134 K4 **Big Rapids** U.S.A.
134 C3 **Big Rib** *r.* U.S.A.
130 C2 **Big River** Canada
134 D3 **Big Sable Point** U.S.A.
131 J3 **Big Sand Lake** Canada
141 F4 **Big Sandy** *r.* U.S.A.
140 D2 **Big Sioux** *r.* U.S.A.
140 D2 **Big Smokey Valley** U.S.A.
143 C5 **Big Spring** U.S.A.
142 C3 **Big Springs** U.S.A.
134 B6 **Big Sur** U.S.A.
88 B3 **Big Sur** *r.* U.S.A.
138 E2 **Big Timber** U.S.A.
132 B3 **Big Trout Lake** *l.* Canada
132 C3 **Big Trout Lake** Canada
141 G3 **Big Water** U.S.A.
135 H3 **Bigwin** Canada
114 F2 **Bihać** Bos.-Herz.
89 F4 **Bihar** *state* India
89 F4 **Bihar Sharif** India
113 K7 **Bihor, Vârful** *mt.* Romania
94 I3 **Bihoro** Japan
88 C4 **Biikzhal** Kazakh.
120 A3 **Bijagós, Arquipélago dos** *is* Guinea-Bissau
88 C4 **Bijainagar** India
82 B3 **Bijapur** India
84 B3 **Bijar** Iran
87 C2 **Bijarpur** India
115 H2 **Bijeljina** Bos.-Herz.

115 H3 **Bijelo Polje** Yugo.
93 B5 **Bijie** China
89 G4 **Bijni** India
88 D3 **Bijnor** India
88 B3 **Bijnot** Pak.
84 C5 **Bijrān, Khashm** *hill* Saudi Arabia
88 C3 **Bikaner** India
82 E3 **Bikbauli** Kazakh.
90 F2 **Bikin** Rus. Fed.
94 D1 **Bikin** *r.* Rus. Fed.
160 G5 **Bikini** *i.* Marshall Is
122 B4 **Bikoro** Dem. Rep. Congo
92 B3 **Bikou** China
92 C4 **Bilara** India
87 C1 **Bilaspur** India
81 L2 **Biläsuvar** Azer.
117 D5 **Bila Tserkva** Ukr.
98 A2 **Bilauktaung Range** *mts*
111 E1 **Bilbao** Spain
80 C6 **Bilbays** Egypt
115 H3 **Bileća** Bos.-Herz.
80 B1 **Bilecik** Turkey
113 K5 **Biłgoraj** Poland
122 C4 **Bilharamulo** Tanz.
117 D6 **Bilhorod-Dnistrovs'kyy** Ukr.
122 C3 **Bili** Dem. Rep. Congo
77 R3 **Bilibino** Rus. Fed.
97 C4 **Biliran** *i.* Phil.
90 B4 **Biliu He** *r.* China
138 F3 **Bill** U.S.A.
105 H6 **Billericay** U.K.
163 J2 **Billingford** U.K.
104 F3 **Billingham** U.K.
138 E2 **Billings** U.S.A.
105 E7 **Bill of Portland** *hd* U.K.
141 F4 **Bill Williams** *r.* U.S.A.
141 F4 **Bill Williams Mountain** U.S.A.
121 D3 **Bilma** Niger
68 F4 **Biloela** Australia
117 E6 **Bilohirs'k** Ukr.
113 M5 **Bilohir'ya** Ukr.
87 B2 **Biloli** India
117 E5 **Bilopillya** Ukr.
117 F5 **Bilovods'k** Ukr.
145 B6 **Biloxi** U.S.A.
68 D4 **Bilpa Morea Claypan** *salt flat* Australia
106 E5 **Bilston** U.K.
121 E3 **Biltine** Chad
98 A1 **Bilugyun Island** Myanmar
150 I5 **Bilwascarma** Nicaragua
116 I4 **Bilyarsk** Rus. Fed.
117 D6 **Bilyayivka** Ukr.
108 D4 **Bilzen** Belgium
71 H5 **Bimberi, Mount** Australia
145 E7 **Bimini Islands** Bahamas
81 L3 **Bināb** Iran
88 D4 **Bina-Etawa** India
91 F7 **Binaija, Gunung** *mt.* Indon.
80 F2 **Binboğa Daği** *mt.* Turkey
71 G1 **Bindebango** Australia
71 H1 **Bindle** Australia
123 B4 **Bindu** Dem. Rep. Congo
123 D5 **Bindura** Zimbabwe
111 G2 **Binefar** Spain
71 I2 **Bingara** N.S.W. Australia
71 H2 **Bingara** Qld Australia
92 B2 **Bingcaowan** China
109 F5 **Bingen am Rhein** Germany
120 B4 **Bingerville** Côte d'Ivoire
147 I2 **Bingham** U.S.A.
147 F3 **Binghamton** U.S.A.
80 F3 **Bingöl** Turkey
81 H2 **Bingöl Daği** *mt.* Turkey
93 C6 **Binh Gia** Vietnam
98 D2 **Binh Son** Vietnam
89 H4 **Bini** India
87 C1 **Binika** India
98 A5 **Binjai** Indon.
84 D5 **Bin Mūrkhan** *well* U.A.E.
71 H3 **Binnaway** Australia
98 C5 **Bintan** *i.* Indon.
97 B3 **Bintuan** Phil.
71 H4 **Bintuhan** Indon.
99 D2 **Bintulu** Sarawak Malaysia
92 C3 **Binxian** China
71 G5 **Binya** Australia
93 C6 **Binyang** China
92 F2 **Binzhou** China
159 B3 **Biobío** *admin. reg.* Chile
159 B3 **Biobío** *r.* Chile
120 C4 **Bioco** *i.* Equat. Guinea
114 G3 **Biokovo** *mts* Croatia
85 F5 **Bīrag, Kūh-e** *mts* Iran
81 H5 **Bi'r al Mulūsi** Iraq
116 F2 **Birandozero** Rus. Fed.
122 C2 **Birao** Centr. Afr. Rep.
80 C2 **Bi'r ar Rummānah** Egypt
89 F4 **Biratnagar** Nepal
80 G3 **Bi'r Buțayman** Syria
130 G3 **Birch** *r.* Canada
131 H4 **Birch Hills** Canada
70 E5 **Birchip** Australia
130 F4 **Birch Island** Canada
132 B3 **Birch Lake** Canada
134 B2 **Birch Lake** Canada
130 G3 **Birch Mountains** Canada
138 C3 **Birch River** Canada
100 D1 **Birch'ran** Canada
73 C1 **Bird Island** *research station* Antarctica
141 G2 **Birdseye** U.S.A.
68 D4 **Birdsville** Australia
80 F3 **Birecik** Turkey
121 E3 **Bir en Natrûn** *well* Sudan
84 B6 **Bi'r Ghawdah** *well* Saudi Arabia
122 D2 **Birhan** *mt.* Eth.
158 B3 **Birigüí** Brazil
85 E3 **Birjand** Iran
81 I6 **Birkat al 'Aqabah** *well* Iraq
81 I6 **Birkat al 'Athāmin** *well* Iraq
81 J6 **Birkat Hamad** *well* Iraq
84 C6 **Birkat Zubālah** *waterhole* Saudi Arabia
108 C5 **Birkenfeld** Germany
105 D4 **Birkenhead** U.K.
81 J3 **Birkim** Iraq
114 F7 **Birkirkara** Malta
83 H3 **Birlik** Kazakh.
105 F5 **Birmingham** U.K.
145 C5 **Birmingham** U.S.A.
120 A2 **Bir Mogreïn** Mauritania
80 B6 **Bi'r Nāḥid** *oasis* Egypt
120 C3 **Birnin-Kebbi** Nigeria
120 C3 **Birnin Konni** Niger
90 F2 **Birobidzhan** Rus. Fed.
107 D4 **Birr** Rep. of Ireland
71 G2 **Birrie** *r.* Australia
81 I5 **Bi'r Sābil** Iraq
106 F1 **Birsay** U.K.
159 F1 **Birstall** U.K.
114 H4 **Birstein** Germany
80 D7 **Bi'r Tābah** Egypt
131 I4 **Birtle** Canada
89 H3 **Biru** China
87 A2 **Birur** India
103 N4 **Biržai** Lith.
141 H5 **Bisbee** U.S.A.
114 D4 **Biscay, Bay of** *sea* France/Spain
163 I3 **Biscay Abyssal Plain** *sea feature* N. Atlantic Ocean
145 D7 **Biscayne National Park** U.S.A.
112 F7 **Bischofshofen** Austria
73 B2 **Biscoe Islands** Antarctica
135 F2 **Biscotasi Lake** Canada
135 F2 **Biscotasing** Canada
123 D5 **Bishan** China
81 S5 **Bishek** Iran
83 J4 **Bishkek** Kyrg.
89 F5 **Bishnupur** India

125 G6 **Bisho** S. Africa
140 C3 **Bishop** U.S.A.
104 F3 **Bishop Auckland** U.K.
105 H6 **Bishop's Stortford** U.K.
81 G4 **Bishri, Jabal** *hill* Syria
120 C1 **Biskra** Alg.
97 C4 **Bislig** Phil.
142 C2 **Bismarck** U.S.A.
68 E2 **Bismarck Archipelago** *is* P.N.G.
68 E2 **Bismarck Range** *mts* P.N.G.
68 E2 **Bismarck Sea** P.N.G.
109 J2 **Bismark (Altmark)** Germany
81 H3 **Bismil** Turkey
103 J3 **Bismo** Norway
81 K4 **Bisotūn** Iran
102 L3 **Bispgården** Sweden
109 I1 **Bispingen** Germany
111 G4 **Bissa, Djebel** *mt.* Alg.
87 C2 **Bissamcuttak** India
120 A3 **Bissau** Guinea-Bissau
120 D4 **Bissaula** Nigeria
131 J4 **Bissett** Canada
130 F3 **Bistcho Lake** Canada
113 L7 **Bistrita** Romania
113 M7 **Bistrița** *r.* Romania
108 E5 **Bitburg** Germany
108 F5 **Bitche** France
82 D2 **Bītik** Kazakh.
81 J2 **Bitlis** Turkey
115 I4 **Bitola** Macedonia
114 G4 **Bitonto** Italy
84 B6 **Biţrān, Jabal** *hill* Saudi Arabia
141 H2 **Bitter Creek** *r.* U.S.A.
109 K3 **Bitterfeld** Germany
125 H5 **Bitterfontein** S. Africa
80 D6 **Bitter Lakes** Egypt
138 D2 **Bitterroot Range** *mts* U.S.A.
117 J2 **Bittkau** Germany
117 J2 **Bityug** *r.* Rus. Fed.
121 D3 **Biu** Nigeria
95 D7 **Biwa-ko** *l.* Japan
83 K1 **Biya** *r.* Rus. Fed.
92 D3 **Biyang** China
97 K6 **Biyo'K'obë** Eth.
83 K1 **Biysk** Rus. Fed.
125 H5 **Bizana** S. Africa
120 C1 **Bizerte** Tunisia
85 C1 **Bizhanābād** Iran
102 L3 **Bjargtangar** *hd* Iceland
114 G2 **Bjelovar** Croatia
102 L1 **Bjerkvik** Norway
103 J4 **Bjerringbro** Denmark
103 J3 **Björklinge** Sweden
103 J3 **Bjorli** Norway
102 L3 **Björna** Sweden
76 C2 **Bjørnøya** *i.* Svalbard
120 B3 **Bla** Mali
106 B3 **Bla Bheinn** *mt.* U.K.
141 H5 **Black** *r.* AZ U.S.A.
135 F4 **Black** *r.* WI U.S.A.
134 B3 **Black** *r.* WI U.S.A.
93 B6 **Black** *r.* Vietnam
68 E4 **Blackall** Australia
132 C1 **Black Bay** Canada
132 B3 **Blackbear** *r.* Canada
105 E4 **Black Bourton** U.K.
104 E4 **Blackburn** U.K.
71 J1 **Blackbutt** Australia
140 A2 **Black Butte** U.S.A.
140 A2 **Black Butte Lake** U.S.A.
141 F4 **Black Canyon** U.S.A.
141 F4 **Black Canyon City** U.S.A.
142 E2 **Blackduck** U.S.A.
70 D4 **Blackfalds** Canada
138 D3 **Blackfoot** U.S.A.
141 F4 **Black Foot** *r.* U.S.A.
142 D2 **Black Hills** *reg.* U.S.A.
131 H3 **Black Lake** *l.* Canada
131 H3 **Black Lake** Canada
135 E3 **Black Lake** Canada
141 G3 **Black Mesa** *plat.* U.S.A.
105 D6 **Black Mountain** U.S.A.
140 D4 **Black Mountain** U.S.A.
105 D6 **Black Mountains** U.K.
141 E4 **Black Mountains** U.S.A.
124 B3 **Black Nossob** *watercourse* Namibia
93 □ **Black Point** Hong Kong China
104 D4 **Blackpool** U.K.
134 B3 **Black River Falls** U.S.A.
138 C3 **Black Rock Desert** U.S.A.
146 C5 **Blacksburg** U.S.A.
117 F7 **Black Sea** Asia/Europe
107 A3 **Blacksod Bay** Rep. of Ireland
107 E5 **Blackstairs Mountains** Rep. of Ireland
146 E6 **Blackstone** U.S.A.
71 I3 **Black Sugarloaf** *mt.* Australia
133 I3 **Black Tickle** Canada
120 B4 **Black Volta** *r.* Africa
107 D5 **Blackwater** *r.* Rep. of Ireland
107 A3 **Blackwater** *r.* Rep. of Ireland
107 D4 **Blackwater** *r.* Rep. of Ireland/U.K.
105 H6 **Blackwater** *r.* U.K.
130 E2 **Blackwater Lake** Canada
104 D4 **Blackwater Reservoir** U.K.
143 D4 **Blackwell** U.S.A.
68 D5 **Blackwood** *r.* Australia
83 J3 **Blagodarnoye** Kazakh.
117 G6 **Blagodarnyy** Rus. Fed.
115 J3 **Blagoevgrad** Bulg.
83 I1 **Blagoveshchenka** Rus. Fed.
90 B1 **Blagoveshchensk** Rus. Fed.
130 E4 **Blain** U.S.A.
135 I3 **Blaine** U.S.A.
131 H4 **Blaine Lake** Canada
134 D3 **Blair** NE U.S.A.
134 D3 **Blair** WI U.S.A.
106 E4 **Blair Atholl** U.K.
106 E4 **Blairgowrie** U.K.
145 D6 **Blakely** U.S.A.
105 I5 **Blakeney** U.K.
134 C1 **Blake Point** U.S.A.
99 **Blambangan, Semenanjung** *pen.* Indon.
110 H4 **Blanc, Mont** *mt.* France/Italy
159 C3 **Blanca, Bahía** *b.* Arg.
159 C3 **Blanca de la Totora, Sierra** *hills* Arg.
139 F4 **Blanca Peak** *mt.* U.S.A.
70 C2 **Blanche, Lake** *salt flat* Australia
146 D5 **Blanchester** U.S.A.
70 C2 **Blanchetown** Australia
159 C3 **Blanco** *r.* Arg.
154 F6 **Blanco** *r.* Bol.
158 C1 **Blanco** *r.* Arg.
155 H6 **Blanco, Cabo** *c.* Costa Rica
138 A3 **Blanco, Cape** U.S.A.
133 I3 **Blanc-Sablon** Canada
71 G4 **Bland** *r.* Australia
102 B2 **Blanda** *r.* Iceland
141 H3 **Blandford Forum** U.K.
89 F3 **Blanding** U.S.A.
111 H2 **Blanes** Spain
134 C2 **Blaney Park** U.S.A.
98 A5 **Blangkejeren** Indon.
108 B3 **Blankenberge** Belgium
108 E4 **Blankenheim** Germany
157 D2 **Blanquilla, Isla** *i.* Venez.
113 H6 **Blansko** Czech Rep.
123 D5 **Blantyre** Malawi
105 G7 **Blarney** Rep. of Ireland
109 H5 **Blaufelden** Germany
102 L2 **Blåviksjön** Sweden
71 H4 **Blayney** Australia

109 I1 **Bleckede** Germany
72 H4 **Blenheim** N.Z.
108 E3 **Blerick** Neth.
107 E4 **Blessington Lakes** Rep. of Ireland
105 G5 **Bletchley** U.K.
120 C1 **Blida** Alg.
185 E5 **Blies** *r.* Germany
69 H3 **Bligh Water** *b.* Fiji
123 D5 **Blind River** Canada
68 C3 **Blinman** Australia
138 D3 **Bliss** U.S.A.
135 F5 **Blissfield** U.S.A.
147 H4 **Block Island** U.S.A.
147 H4 **Block Island Sound** *sea chan.* U.S.A.
125 G4 **Bloemfontein** S. Africa
125 G3 **Bloemhof** S. Africa
125 F3 **Bloemhof Dam** S. Africa
102 B2 **Blönduós** Iceland
147 F5 **Bloodsworth Island** U.S.A.
131 J4 **Bloodvein** *r.* Canada
107 C2 **Bloody Foreland** *pt* Rep. of Ireland
135 I4 **Bloomfield** Canada
134 A5 **Bloomfield** IA U.S.A.
147 F4 **Bloomfield** IN U.S.A.
139 F4 **Bloomfield** NM U.S.A.
134 C5 **Bloomington** IL U.S.A.
147 H4 **Bloomington** IN U.S.A.
142 E2 **Bloomington** MN U.S.A.
146 E4 **Bloomsburg** U.S.A.
146 E4 **Blossburg** U.S.A.
129 P3 **Blosseville Kyst** Greenland
125 H1 **Blouberg** S. Africa
105 F5 **Bloxham** U.K.
141 H5 **Blue** *r.* U.S.A.
141 G1 **Bluebell** U.S.A.
142 E3 **Blue Earth** U.S.A.
146 C6 **Bluefield** U.S.A.
150 I5 **Bluefields** Nicaragua
147 I2 **Blue Hill** U.S.A.
89 H5 **Blue Knob** *hill* U.S.A.
141 H1 **Blue Mountain** India
147 F3 **Blue Mountain Lake** U.S.A.
71 I4 **Blue Mountain Pass** U.S.A.
138 C2 **Blue Mountains** Australia
71 I4 **Blue Mountains National Park** Australia
121 F3 **Blue Nile** *r.* Sudan
alt. Ābay Wenz (Ethiopia),
alt. Azraq, Bahr (Sudan)
128 G3 **Bluenose Lake** Canada
146 D6 **Blue Ridge** *mts* U.S.A.
130 F4 **Blue River** Canada
140 D2 **Blue Springs** U.S.A.
106 B3 **Blue Stack** *r.* Rep. of Ireland
107 C3 **Blue Stack Mountains** Rep. of Ireland
146 C6 **Bluestone Lake** U.S.A.
72 B7 **Bluff** N.Z.
141 H3 **Bluff** U.S.A.
93 □ **Bluff Island** Hong Kong China
134 E5 **Bluffton** IN U.S.A.
146 B4 **Bluffton** OH U.S.A.
156 G3 **Blumenau** Brazil
142 C2 **Blunt** U.S.A.
138 B3 **Bly** U.S.A.
70 C4 **Blyth** England U.K.
104 F2 **Blyth** England U.K.
141 E5 **Blythe** U.S.A.
143 F5 **Blytheville** U.S.A.
103 J4 **Bø** Norway
120 A4 **Bo** Sierra Leone
97 B3 **Boac** Phil.
150 H5 **Boaco** Nicaragua
155 J5 **Boa Esperança, Açude** *resr* Brazil
92 A3 **Bo'ai** China
93 C6 **Bo'ai** China
122 B3 **Boali** Centr. Afr. Rep.
146 C4 **Boane** Moz.
146 C4 **Boardman** U.S.A.
125 I1 **Boatlaname** Botswana
71 G1 **Boatman** Australia
155 K5 **Boa Viagem** Brazil
157 F4 **Boa Vista** Brazil
120 □ **Boa Vista** *i.* Cape Verde
71 G4 **Bobadah** Australia
93 D6 **Bobai** China
123 E5 **Bobaomby, Tanjon** *c.* Madag.
87 C2 **Bobbili** India
123 C6 **Bobonong** Botswana
83 G4 **Boboyob, Gora** *mt.* Uzbek.
117 D5 **Bobrovytsya** Ukr.
117 E5 **Bobrynets'** Ukr.
123 E6 **Boby** *mt.* Madag.
157 D2 **Boca del Pao** Venez.
149 L7 **Boca de Macareo** Venez.
154 C2 **Boca do Jari** Brazil
155 H4 **Boca do Acre** Brazil
158 D2 **Bocaiúva** Brazil
157 C2 **Bocanó** *r.* Venez.
122 B3 **Bocaranga** Centr. Afr. Rep.
145 D7 **Boca Raton** U.S.A.
150 I6 **Bocas del Toro** Panama
113 I6 **Bochnia** Poland
108 D7 **Bocholt** Germany
108 D7 **Bochum** Germany
125 H1 **Bochum** S. Africa
109 I2 **Bockenem** Germany
157 C2 **Bocono** Venez.
122 B3 **Boda** Centr. Afr. Rep.
71 I6 **Bodalla** Australia
77 N3 **Bodaybo** Rus. Fed.
143 F5 **Bodcau Reservoir** U.S.A.
106 G3 **Boddam** U.K.
109 J3 **Bode** *r.* Germany
140 D2 **Bodega Head** U.S.A.
121 D3 **Bodélé** *reg.* Chad
102 M2 **Boden** Sweden
105 **Bodenham** U.K.
Bodensee *l.* Germany/Switz. *see* Constance, Lake
109 I2 **Bodenteich** Germany
109 H3 **Bodenwerder** Germany
87 B2 **Bodhan** India
105 C7 **Bodmin** U.K.
105 C7 **Bodmin Moor** U.K.
102 K2 **Bodø** Norway
115 L6 **Bodrum** Turkey
122 B3 **Boende** Dem. Rep. Congo
120 A4 **Boffa** Guinea
89 H4 **Boga** India
143 F6 **Bogalusa** U.S.A.
71 G4 **Bogan** *r.* Australia
71 G4 **Bogan Gate** Australia
120 B3 **Bogandé** Burkina
68 E4 **Bogantungan** Australia
80 E2 **Boğazlıyan** Turkey
89 E3 **Bogcang Zangbo** *r.* China
82 C1 **Bogda Shan** *mts* China
90 A2 **Bogdanovich** Rus. Fed.
149 K6 **Bogdo** Venez.
81 H1 **Bogda** Turkey
81 L7 **Bogra** Bangl.
84 B2 **Bogorodsk** Rus. Fed.

116 E4 **Bogolyubovo** Rus. Fed.
71 G6 **Bogong, Mount** Australia
94 D2 **Bogopol'** Rus. Fed.
99 C4 **Bogor** Indon.
116 G3 **Bogorodsk** Rus. Fed.
116 I3 **Bogorodskoye** Rus. Fed.
157 B3 **Bogotá** Col.
90 A1 **Bogotol** Rus. Fed.
89 G4 **Bogra** Bangl.
77 K2 **Boguchany** Rus. Fed.
117 G5 **Boguchar** Rus. Fed.
120 A3 **Bogué** Mauritania
92 F2 **Bo Hai** *g.* China
96 A4 **Bohai Haixia** *sea chan.* China
110 F7 **Bohain-en-Vermandois** France
92 E2 **Bohai Wan** *b.* China
109 K3 **Böhlen** Germany
125 H4 **Bohlokong** S. Africa
109 J4 **Böhmer Wald** *mts* Germany
109 G2 **Bohmte** Germany
117 E5 **Bohodukhiv** Ukr.
97 C4 **Bohol** *i.* Phil.
97 C4 **Bohol Sea** Phil.
94 B1 **Bohol Strait** Phil.
79 G4 **Bohu** China
117 D5 **Bohuslav** Ukr.
158 E1 **Boi, Ponta do** *pt* Brazil
89 A1 **Boiaçu** Brazil
158 E1 **Boipeba, Ilha** *i.* Brazil
158 E1 **Bois** *r.* Brazil
128 F3 **Bois, Lac des** *l.* Canada
128 E3 **Bois Blanc Island** U.S.A.
138 G3 **Boise** U.S.A.
131 I5 **Boissevain** Canada
141 G1 **Boituelong** S. Africa
109 I1 **Boizenburg** Germany
84 E2 **Bojnūrd** Iran
89 F5 **Bokaro** India
122 B4 **Bokatola** Dem. Rep. Congo
120 A3 **Bolama** Guinea-Bissau
88 A3 **Bolan** *r.* Pak.
84 A3 **Bolan Pass** Pak.
110 E2 **Bolbec** France
81 L4 **Boldājī** Iran
109 I1 **Boldekow** Germany
82 D4 **Boldumsaz** Turkm.
83 J3 **Bole** China
120 B4 **Bole** Ghana
120 B4 **Boleko** Dem. Rep. Congo
120 B3 **Bolgatanga** Ghana
117 D6 **Bolhrad** Ukr.
94 B2 **Boli** China
122 B4 **Bolia** Dem. Rep. Congo
102 M2 **Boliden** Sweden
97 B3 **Bolinao** Phil.
115 K2 **Bolintin-Vale** Romania
157 A3 **Bolívar** Col.
154 C5 **Bolívar** Peru
143 E5 **Bolívar** MO U.S.A.
145 B5 **Bolivar** TN U.S.A.
157 C2 **Bolívar, Pico** *mt.* Venez.
154 E7 **Bolivia** *country* S. America
81 J5 **Bolkar Dağları** *mts* Turkey
116 F4 **Bolkhov** Rus. Fed.
110 G1 **Bollène** France
103 L3 **Bollnäs** Sweden
71 G2 **Bollon** Australia
102 L3 **Bollstabruk** Sweden
103 K4 **Bolmen** *l.* Sweden
117 H7 **Bolnisi** Georgia
122 B4 **Bolobo** Dem. Rep. Congo
114 D2 **Bologna** Italy
103 O3 **Bologoye** Rus. Fed.
116 E3 **Bologoye** Rus. Fed.
122 B3 **Bolokanang** S. Africa
122 B3 **Bolomba** Dem. Rep. Congo
151 G3 **Bolonchén de Rejón** Mex.
93 B5 **Bolong** China
76 J4 **Bolotnoye** Rus. Fed.
98 C2 **Bolovens, Phouphieng** *plat.* Laos
89 F5 **Bolpur** India
114 D3 **Bolsena, Lago di** *l.* Italy
116 E3 **Bolsena** Rus. Fed.
82 F1 **Bol'shakovo** Rus. Fed.
117 F5 **Bol'shaya Chernigovka** Rus. Fed.
82 F1 **Bol'shaya Churakova** Kazakh.
82 B1 **Bol'shaya Glushitsa** Rus. Fed.
102 P2 **Bol'shaya Imandra, Ozero** *l.* Rus. Fed.
81 L1 **Bol'shaya Kinel'** *r.* Rus. Fed.
117 G6 **Bol'shaya Martynovka** Rus. Fed.
94 C3 **Bol'shaya Vladimirovka** Kazakh.
145 D7 **Bol'shegrivskoye** Rus. Fed.
83 H1 **Bol'shenarymskoye** Kazakh.
77 L2 **Bol'shevik, Ostrov** *i.* Rus. Fed.
82 B1 **Bol'shiye Barsuki, Peski** *des.* Kazakh.
116 H2 **Bol'shiye Chirki** Rus. Fed.
82 B3 **Bol'shiye Peshnyye, Ostrova** *is* Kazakh.
77 R3 **Bol'shoy Aluy** *r.* Rus. Fed.
82 B2 **Bol'shoy Bukon'** Kazakh.
82 B2 **Bol'shoy Irgiz** *r.* Rus. Fed.
94 C3 **Bol'shoy Kamen'** Rus. Fed.
Bol'shoy Kavkaz *mts* Asia/Europe *see* Caucasus
117 I5 **Bol'shoy Uzen'** *r.* Rus. Fed.
104 D1 **Bolsward** Neth.
104 E4 **Bolton** U.K.
80 C1 **Bolu** Turkey
102 B1 **Bolungarvík** Iceland
93 E6 **Boluo** China
80 B1 **Bolvadin** Turkey
122 B4 **Boma** Dem. Rep. Congo
71 I4 **Bomaderry** Australia
88 C2 **Bombala** Australia
Bombay India *see* Mumbai
91 F7 **Bomberai, Semenanjung** Indon.
154 D5 **Bom Comércio** Brazil
158 D2 **Bom Despacho** Brazil
89 H4 **Bomdila** India
93 H4 **Bomi** China
158 D1 **Bom Jesus da Lapa** Brazil
158 E1 **Bom Jesus do Itabapoana** Brazil
103 I4 **Bømlo** *i.* Norway
121 D1 **Bon, Cap** *c.* Tunisia
84 B2 **Bonāb** Iran
90 A2 **Bon Air** U.S.A.
149 K6 **Bonaire** *i.* Neth. Antilles
150 H5 **Bonanza** Nicaragua
68 C3 **Bonaparte Archipelago** *is* Australia
106 F3 **Bonar Bridge** U.K.
133 J4 **Bonavista** Canada
133 J4 **Bonavista Bay** Canada
70 D6 **Bon Bon** Australia
106 F5 **Bonchester Bridge** U.K.
122 B3 **Bondo** Dem. Rep. Congo
97 B3 **Bondoc Peninsula** Phil.

120 B4 **Bondoukou** Côte d'Ivoire
91 E7 **Bone, Teluk** *b.* Indon.
134 A3 **Bone Lake** U.S.A.
109 F3 **Bönen** Germany
91 E7 **Bonerate, Kepulauan** *is* Indon.
106 E4 **Bo'ness** U.K.
158 D2 **Bonfinópolis de Minas** Brazil
122 D3 **Bonga** Eth.
97 B3 **Bongabong** Phil.
89 G4 **Bongaigaon** India
122 C3 **Bongandanga** Dem. Rep. Congo
124 H3 **Bongani** S. Africa
89 A5 **Bong Co** *l.* China
97 C5 **Bongo** *i.* China
122 C3 **Bongo, Massif des** *mts* Centr. Afr. Rep.
123 E5 **Bongolava** *mts* Madag.
121 D3 **Bongor** Chad
120 B3 **Bongouanou** Côte d'Ivoire
98 D2 **Bông Son** Vietnam
114 C4 **Bonifacio** Corsica France
114 C4 **Bonifacio, Strait of** *strait* France/Italy
90 G4 **Bonin Islands** Japan
158 A3 **Bonito** Brazil
108 F4 **Bonn** Germany
102 K2 **Bonnåsjøen** Norway
138 C1 **Bonners Ferry** U.S.A.
110 H3 **Bonneville** France
70 D6 **Bonney, Lake** Australia
68 B5 **Bonnie Rock** Australia
106 E5 **Bonnyrigg** U.K.
130 G4 **Bonnyville** Canada
114 C4 **Bonorva** Sardinia Italy
71 I2 **Bonshaw** Australia
120 A4 **Bonthe** Sierra Leone
99 B2 **Bontoc** Phil.
91 E7 **Bontosunggu** Indon.
125 G1 **Bonwapitse** Botswana
141 H2 **Book Cliffs** U.S.A.
70 E4 **Boolaboolka Lake** Australia
70 C4 **Booleroo Centre** Australia
107 D5 **Booley Hills** Rep. of Ireland
68 B4 **Booligal** Australia
71 H2 **Boomi** Australia
71 J1 **Boonah** Australia
142 E3 **Boone** IA U.S.A.
145 D4 **Boone** NC U.S.A.
146 B6 **Booneville** KY U.S.A.
145 F5 **Booneville** MS U.S.A.
140 A2 **Boonville** CA U.S.A.
146 F4 **Boonville** IN U.S.A.
142 E4 **Boonville** MO U.S.A.
147 F3 **Boonville** NY U.S.A.
71 H5 **Booroorban** Australia
71 H5 **Boorowa** Australia
70 E6 **Boort** Australia
122 E2 **Bosaaso** Somalia
145 D7 **Boothbay Harbor** U.S.A.
128 I2 **Boothia, Gulf of** Canada
129 I2 **Boothia Peninsula** Canada
105 E4 **Bootle** U.K.
120 A4 **Bopolu** Liberia
109 F4 **Boppard** Germany
159 G1 **Boqueirão** Brazil
150 D1 **Boquillas del Carmen** Mex.
109 K5 **Bor** Czech Rep.
80 E3 **Bor** Turkey
80 E3 **Bor** Sudan
115 J2 **Bor** Yugo.
138 D2 **Boraha, Nosy** *i.* Madag.
138 D2 **Borah Peak** *mt.* U.S.A.
103 K4 **Boraphet, Bung** *l.* Thai.
103 K4 **Borås** Sweden
84 C4 **Borāzjān** Iran
155 G4 **Borba** Brazil
155 K5 **Borborema, Planalto da** *plat.* Brazil
109 K5 **Borchen** Germany
73 H1 **Borchgrevink Coast** Antarctica
81 H1 **Borçka** Turkey
70 D6 **Borda, Cape** *pt* Australia
80 B3 **Bor Daği** *mt.* Turkey
114 D2 **Bordeaux** France
133 H4 **Borden** Canada
128 G2 **Borden Island** Canada
70 D6 **Borden Peninsula** Canada
70 D6 **Bordertown** Australia
102 B1 **Bordeyri** Iceland
111 I4 **Bordj Bou Arréridj** Alg.
111 H5 **Bordj Bounaama** Alg.
105 G5 **Bordj Omer Driss** Alg.
102 □ **Bordoy** *i.* Faroe Is
83 H4 **Bordu** Kyrg.
106 A3 **Boreray** *i.* U.K.
102 B2 **Borgarfjörður** Iceland
102 B2 **Borgarnes** Iceland
102 □ **Børgefjell Nasjonalpark** *nat. park* Norway
143 C5 **Borger** U.S.A.
103 L4 **Borgholm** Sweden
114 B2 **Borgo San Dalmazzo** Italy
114 C2 **Borgo San Lorenzo** Italy
108 B3 **Borinage** *reg.* Belgium
117 O5 **Borisoglebsk** Rus. Fed.
116 F4 **Borisovka** Rus. Fed.
116 F3 **Borisovo-Sudskoye** Rus. Fed.
117 G7 **Borjomi** Georgia
109 F2 **Borken** Germany
102 L1 **Borkenes** Norway
108 E1 **Borkum** Germany
108 E1 **Borkum** *i.* Germany
103 K3 **Borlänge** Sweden
80 C2 **Borlu** Turkey
109 H3 **Borna** Germany
108 E2 **Borne** Neth.
71 □ **Borneo** *i.* Asia
103 K5 **Bornholm** *i.* Denmark
115 L5 **Bornova** Turkey
97 B4 **Borocay** *i.* Phil.
76 J3 **Borodino** Rus. Fed.
117 D5 **Borodyanka** Ukr.
77 O3 **Borogontsy** Rus. Fed.
116 B3 **Borohoro Shan** *mts* China
120 B3 **Boromo** Burkina
97 C4 **Borongan** Phil.
130 B3 **Boroughbridge** U.K.
141 D1 **Borovan** Bulg.
102 J3 **Borovichi** Rus. Fed.
116 F3 **Borovichi** Rus. Fed.
116 E1 **Borovoy** Respublika Kareliya Rus. Fed.
116 J2 **Borovoy** Respublika Komi Rus. Fed.
82 F1 **Borovskoye** Kazakh.
107 D5 **Borris** Rep. of Ireland
107 D5 **Borrisokane** Rep. of Ireland
71 H1 **Borroloola** Australia
102 K3 **Børsa** Norway
117 D5 **Borshchiv** Ukr.
90 C2 **Borshchovochnyy Khrebet** *mts* Rus. Fed.
84 E3 **Bortala He** *r.* China
81 L4 **Borūjerd** Iran
106 A3 **Borve** U.K.
117 D5 **Boryslav** Ukr.
117 D5 **Boryspil'** Ukr.
117 E5 **Borzna** Ukr.
90 D1 **Borzya** Rus. Fed.
82 B3 **Bosaga** Kazakh.
114 G2 **Bosanska Dubica** Bos.-Herz.

114 G2 **Bosanska Gradiška** Bos.-Herz.
114 G2 **Bosanska Krupa** Bos.-Herz.
114 G2 **Bosanska Novi** Bos.-Herz.
114 G2 **Bosanska Grahovo** Bos.-Herz.
134 B4 **Boscobel** U.S.A.
93 C6 **Bose** China
125 F4 **Boshof** S. Africa
82 E1 **Boskol'** Kazakh.
114 G2 **Bosnia-Herzegovina** *country* Europe
122 B3 **Bosobolo** Dem. Rep. Congo
95 G7 **Bōsō-hantō** *pen.* Japan
80 B1 **Bosporus** *strait* Turkey
122 B3 **Bossangoa** Centr. Afr. Rep.
122 B3 **Bossembélé** Centr. Afr. Rep.
143 E5 **Bossier City** U.S.A.
124 B2 **Bossiesvlei** Namibia
89 F1 **Bostan** China
81 K6 **Bostān** Iran
82 B2 **Bostandyk** Kazakh.
90 A2 **Bosten Hu** *l.* China
105 G5 **Boston** U.K.
147 H5 **Boston** U.S.A.
70 A5 **Boston Bay** Australia
135 H1 **Boston Creek** Canada
147 H5 **Boston-Logan** *airport* U.S.A.
143 E5 **Boston Mountains** U.S.A.
104 F4 **Boston Spa** U.K.
134 D5 **Boswell** U.S.A.
88 B5 **Botad** India
71 I4 **Botany Bay** Australia
102 L3 **Boteå** Sweden
115 K3 **Botev** *mt.* Bulg.
115 J3 **Botevgrad** Bulg.
125 G3 **Bothaville** S. Africa
102 L3 **Bothnia, Gulf of** Fin./Sweden
71 G9 **Bothwell** Australia
117 H5 **Botkul', Ozero** *l.* Kazakh./Rus. Fed.
113 M7 **Botoşani** Romania
92 E2 **Botou** China
98 C1 **Bô Trach** Vietnam
125 G4 **Botshabelo** S. Africa
123 C6 **Botswana** *country* Africa
114 G5 **Botte Donato, Monte** *mt.* Italy
102 M2 **Bottenviken** *g.* Fin./Sweden
104 G4 **Botterford** U.K.
142 C1 **Bottineau** U.S.A.
108 E3 **Bottrop** Germany
158 D1 **Botuporã** Brazil
133 J4 **Botwood** Canada
120 B4 **Bouaflé** Côte d'Ivoire
120 B4 **Bouaké** Côte d'Ivoire
122 B3 **Bouar** Centr. Afr. Rep.
120 B1 **Bouârfa** Morocco
121 D4 **Bouba Ndjida, Parc National de** *nat. park* Cameroon
122 B3 **Bouca** Centr. Afr. Rep.
108 B4 **Bouchain** France
147 G2 **Boucherville** Canada
135 J2 **Bouchette** Canada
133 H4 **Bouctouche** Canada
69 F2 **Bougainville Island** P.N.G.
120 B3 **Bougouni** Mali
108 D5 **Bouillon** Belgium
111 H4 **Bouira** Alg.
120 A2 **Boujdour** W. Sahara
138 F3 **Boulder** *CO* U.S.A.
138 D2 **Boulder** *MT* U.S.A.
141 G3 **Boulder** *UT* U.S.A.
141 E3 **Boulder Canyon** U.S.A.
141 E4 **Boulder City** U.S.A.
140 D5 **Boulevard** U.S.A.
159 E3 **Boulevard Atlántico** Arg.
68 D4 **Boulia** Australia
110 F2 **Boulogne-Billancourt** France
108 B4 **Boulogne-sur-Mer** France
120 B3 **Boulsa** Burkina
122 B4 **Boumango** Gabon
121 D4 **Boumba** *r.* Cameroon
111 H4 **Boumerdes** Alg.
120 B4 **Bouna** Côte d'Ivoire
147 H2 **Boundary Mountains** U.S.A.
140 C3 **Boundary Peak** *mt.* U.S.A.
120 B4 **Boundiali** Côte d'Ivoire
122 B4 **Boundji** Congo
98 D1 **Boung** *r.* Vietnam
93 A6 **Boun Nua** Laos
138 E3 **Bountiful** U.S.A.
69 H6 **Bounty Islands** N.Z.
160 G9 **Bounty Trough** *sea feature* S. Pacific Ocean
120 B3 **Bourem** Mali
110 E4 **Bourganeuf** France
110 G3 **Bourg-en-Bresse** France
110 F3 **Bourges** France
147 F2 **Bourget** Canada
135 J1 **Bourgmont** Canada
Bourgogne *reg.* France *see* **Burgundy**
71 F3 **Bourke** Australia
135 G1 **Bourkes** Canada
105 G5 **Bourne** U.K.
105 F7 **Bournemouth** U.K.
108 F2 **Bourtanger Moor** *reg.* Germany
120 C1 **Bou Saâda** Alg.
114 C6 **Bou Salem** Tunisia
141 E5 **Bouse** U.S.A.
141 E5 **Bouse Wash** *r.* U.S.A.
121 D3 **Bousso** Chad
108 B4 **Boussu** Belgium
120 A3 **Boutilimit** Mauritania
163 J9 **Bouvetøya** *terr.* Atlantic Ocean
108 C5 **Bouy** France
109 H3 **Bovenden** Germany
99 D2 **Boven Kapuas, Pegunungan** *mts* Malaysia
159 E1 **Bovril** Arg.
131 G4 **Bow** *r.* Canada
142 C1 **Bowbells** U.S.A.
68 E4 **Bowen** Australia
134 B5 **Bowen** U.S.A.
71 H6 **Bowen, Mount** Australia
71 I1 **Bowenville** Australia
160 G2 **Bowers Ridge** *sea feature* Bering Sea
141 H5 **Bowie** *AZ* U.S.A.
143 D5 **Bowie** *TX* U.S.A.
131 G5 **Bow Island** Canada
84 B2 **Bowkan** Iran
144 C4 **Bowling Green** *KY* U.S.A.
142 F4 **Bowling Green** *MO* U.S.A.
146 B4 **Bowling Green** *OH* U.S.A.
146 E5 **Bowling Green** *VA* U.S.A.
142 C2 **Bowman** U.S.A.
130 C4 **Bowman, Mount** Canada
73 C6 **Bowman Island** Antarctica
73 B3 **Bowman Peninsula** Antarctica
135 H4 **Bowmanville** Canada
106 B5 **Bowmore** U.K.
71 I5 **Bowral** Australia
71 J3 **Bowraville** Australia
130 E4 **Bowron** *r.* Canada
130 E4 **Bowron Lake Provincial Park** Canada
109 H5 **Boxberg** Germany
92 F2 **Boxing** China
108 D3 **Boxtel** Neth.
80 E1 **Boyabat** Turkey
93 E4 **Boyang** China
71 J3 **Boyd** *r.* Australia
131 I2 **Boyd Lake** Canada
130 G4 **Boyle** Canada
107 C4 **Boyle** Rep. of Ireland
107 E4 **Boyne** *r.* Rep. of Ireland
85 G2 **Boyni Qara** Afgh.
145 D7 **Boynton Beach** U.S.A.
138 E3 **Boysen Reservoir** U.S.A.
154 F8 **Boyuibe** Bol.
81 J1 **Böyük Hinaldağ** *mt.* Azer.
83 J2 **Bozashy** Kazakh.
115 L5 **Bozcaada** *i.* Turkey
80 A2 **Boz Dağları** *mts* Turkey

80 B3 **Bozdoğan** Turkey
105 G5 **Bozeat** U.K.
138 E2 **Bozeman** U.S.A.
92 E3 **Bozhou** China
80 D3 **Bozkır** Turkey
122 B3 **Bozoum** Centr. Afr. Rep.
80 D3 **Bozova** Turkey
84 B2 **Bozqūsh, Kūh-e** *mts* Iran
83 H2 **Bozshakol'** Kazakh.
83 F2 **Boztumsyk** Kazakh.
80 C2 **Bozüyük** Turkey
114 B2 **Bra** Italy
73 B2 **Brabant Island** Antarctica
114 G3 **Brač** *i.* Croatia
106 B3 **Bracadale** U.K.
106 B3 **Bracadale, Loch** *b.* U.K.
114 E3 **Bracciano, Lago di** *l.* Italy
135 H3 **Bracebridge** Canada
102 K3 **Bräcke** Sweden
109 H5 **Brackenheim** Germany
105 G6 **Bracknell** U.K.
114 D2 **Bradano** *r.* Italy
145 D7 **Bradenton** U.S.A.
135 H3 **Bradford** Canada
104 F4 **Bradford** U.K.
146 A4 **Bradford** *OH* U.S.A.
146 D4 **Bradford** *PA* U.S.A.
147 G3 **Bradford** *VT* U.S.A.
143 D6 **Brady** U.S.A.
130 B3 **Brady Glacier** U.S.A.
70 C4 **Brae** U.K.
70 C4 **Braemar** Australia
106 E3 **Braemar** U.K.
111 B2 **Braga** Port.
159 E2 **Bragado** Arg.
155 I4 **Bragança** Brazil
111 C2 **Bragança** Port.
158 C3 **Bragança Paulista** Brazil
117 D5 **Brahin** Belarus
109 I1 **Brahlstorf** Germany
89 G5 **Brahmanbaria** Bangl.
87 D1 **Brahmani** *r.* India
89 G4 **Brahmapur** India
89 G4 **Brahmaputra** *r.* Asia
    alt. Dihang (India),
    alt. Yarlung Zangbo (China)
115 L2 **Brăila** Romania
108 B5 **Braine** France
108 C4 **Braine-le-Comte** Belgium
142 E2 **Brainerd** U.S.A.
105 H6 **Braintree** U.K.
125 H1 **Brak** *r.* S. Africa
109 G1 **Brake (Unterweser)** Germany
108 B4 **Brakel** Belgium
109 H3 **Brakel** Germany
123 B6 **Brakwater** Namibia
130 E4 **Bralorne** Canada
103 D5 **Bramming** Denmark
111 J5 **Brämön** *i.* Sweden
135 H4 **Brampton** Canada
104 E3 **Brampton** *England* U.K.
105 I5 **Brampton** *England* U.K.
109 G2 **Bramsche** Germany
105 H5 **Brancaster** U.K.
133 J4 **Branco** *r.* Brazil
157 A3 **Branco** *r.* Brazil
103 J3 **Brandbu** Norway
103 J5 **Brande** Denmark
109 K2 **Brandenburg** Germany
109 K2 **Brandenburg** *admin. div.* Germany
125 G4 **Brandfort** S. Africa
109 L3 **Brandis** Germany
131 J5 **Brandon** Canada
105 H5 **Brandon** U.K.
142 D3 **Brandon** *SD* U.S.A.
147 G3 **Brandon** *VT* U.S.A.
107 A5 **Brandon Head** Rep. of Ireland
107 E5 **Brandon Hill** Rep. of Ireland
107 A5 **Brandon Mountain** Rep. of Ireland
124 D5 **Brandvlei** S. Africa
145 D6 **Branford** U.S.A.
113 I3 **Braniewo** Poland
73 B2 **Bransfield Strait** Antarctica
135 G4 **Brantford** Canada
70 D6 **Branxholme** Australia
133 H4 **Bras d'Or Lake** Canada
154 E6 **Brasiléia** Brazil
158 C1 **Brasília** Brazil
158 D2 **Brasília de Minas** Brazil
158 A4 **Brasília Legal** Brazil
113 M3 **Braslaw** Belarus
115 K2 **Braşov** Romania
97 A5 **Brassey, Banjaran** *mts* Sabah Malaysia
147 I2 **Brassua Lake** U.S.A.
112 H6 **Bratislava** Slovakia
90 C1 **Bratsk** Rus. Fed.
90 C1 **Bratskoye Vodokhranilishche** *resr* Rus. Fed.
147 G3 **Brattleboro** U.S.A.
112 F6 **Braunau am Inn** Austria
109 G4 **Braunfels** Germany
109 I3 **Braunlage** Germany
109 J2 **Braunschweig** Germany
120 □ **Brava** *i.* Cape Verde
103 L4 **Bräviken** *inlet* Sweden
151 E2 **Bravo del Norte, Rio** *r.* Mex./U.S.A.
    alt. Rio Grande
141 E5 **Brawley** U.S.A.
107 E4 **Bray** Rep. of Ireland
130 F4 **Brazeau** *r.* Canada
155 H6 **Brazil** *country* S. America
163 H7 **Brazil Basin** *sea feature* S. Atlantic Ocean
143 D5 **Brazos** *r.* U.S.A.
122 B4 **Brazzaville** Congo
115 H2 **Brčko** Bos.-Herz.
143 D5 **Breaux Bridge** U.S.A.
72 A6 **Breaksea Sound** *inlet* N.Z.
72 E1 **Bream Bay** N.Z.
72 E1 **Bream Head** N.Z.
105 C6 **Brechfa** U.K.
106 F4 **Brechin** U.K.
108 C3 **Brecht** Belgium
142 D2 **Breckenridge** *MN* U.S.A.
143 D5 **Breckenridge** *TX* U.S.A.
112 H6 **Břeclav** Czech Rep.
105 D6 **Brecon** U.K.
105 D6 **Brecon Beacons** *hills* U.K.
105 D6 **Brecon Beacons National Park** U.K.
108 C3 **Breda** Neth.
124 D7 **Bredasdorp** S. Africa
71 H5 **Breddin** Australia
109 K2 **Breddin** Germany
108 E3 **Bredevoort** Neth.
102 K3 **Bredviken** Norway
82 E1 **Bredy** Rus. Fed.
108 D4 **Bree** Belgium
146 D5 **Breezewood** U.S.A.
112 D7 **Bregenz** Austria
102 A2 **Breiðafjörður** *b.* Iceland
102 A2 **Breiðdalsvík** Iceland
109 G4 **Breidenbach** Germany
112 C6 **Breisach am Rhein** Germany
109 I1 **Breitenfelde** Germany
105 I5 **Breitengüßbach** Germany
102 M1 **Breivikbotn** Norway
155 I6 **Brejinho de Nazaré** Brazil
102 J3 **Brekstad** Norway
109 G1 **Bremen** Germany
145 C5 **Bremen** *GA* U.S.A.
134 D5 **Bremen** *IN* U.S.A.
109 G1 **Bremerhaven** Germany
138 B2 **Bremerton** U.S.A.
109 H1 **Bremervörde** Germany
143 E6 **Brenham** U.S.A.
109 K2 **Brenna** Germany
112 E7 **Brenner Pass** Austria/Italy

135 H2 **Brent** Canada
114 D2 **Brenta** *r.* Italy
105 H6 **Brentwood** U.K.
140 B3 **Brentwood** *CA* U.S.A.
147 G4 **Brentwood** *NY* U.S.A.
114 D2 **Brescia** Italy
114 D1 **Bressanone** Italy
106 □ **Bressay** *i.* U.K.
110 D3 **Bressuire** France
117 B4 **Brest** Belarus
110 B2 **Brest** France
    Bretagne *reg.* France *see* **Brittany**
110 A5 **Breteuil** France
143 F6 **Breton Sound** *b.* U.S.A.
72 E1 **Brett, Cape** N.Z.
109 G5 **Bretten** Germany
105 E4 **Bretton** U.K.
145 D5 **Brevard** U.S.A.
155 H4 **Breves** Brazil
134 E2 **Brevort** U.S.A.
71 G2 **Brewarrina** Australia
147 I2 **Brewer** U.S.A.
138 C1 **Brewster** U.S.A.
143 G6 **Brewton** U.S.A.
125 H3 **Breyten** S. Africa
113 I6 **Brezno** Slovakia
114 G2 **Brezovo Polje** *hill* Croatia
122 C3 **Bria** Centr. Afr. Rep.
110 H4 **Briançon** France
71 G5 **Bribbaree** Australia
71 J1 **Bribie Island** Australia
117 C5 **Briceni** Moldova
110 H4 **Bric Froid** *mt.* France/Italy
107 C5 **Bride** *r.* Rep. of Ireland
141 G1 **Bridgeland** U.S.A.
105 D6 **Bridgend** U.K.
106 D4 **Bridge of Orchy** U.K.
140 C2 **Bridgeport** *CA* U.S.A.
147 G4 **Bridgeport** *CT* U.S.A.
142 C3 **Bridgeport** *NE* U.S.A.
138 E2 **Bridger** U.S.A.
138 F3 **Bridger Peak** *mt.* U.S.A.
147 F5 **Bridgeton** U.S.A.
149 M6 **Bridgetown** Barbados
71 A8 **Bridgetown** Australia
133 H4 **Bridgewater** Canada
147 J1 **Bridgewater** U.S.A.
70 D7 **Bridgewater, Cape** *hd* Australia
105 E5 **Bridgnorth** U.K.
105 D6 **Bridgwater** U.K.
105 D6 **Bridgwater Bay** U.K.
104 G3 **Bridlington** U.K.
104 G3 **Bridlington Bay** U.K.
71 G8 **Bridport** Australia
105 E7 **Bridport** U.K.
112 C7 **Brig** Switz.
104 G3 **Brigg** U.K.
138 D3 **Brigham City** U.S.A.
71 G6 **Bright** Australia
105 I6 **Brightlingsea** U.K.
105 I3 **Brighton** U.K.
72 C6 **Brighton** N.Z.
105 G7 **Brighton** U.K.
135 F4 **Brighton** U.K.
110 H5 **Brignoles** France
120 A3 **Brikama** Gambia
109 G2 **Brilon** Germany
114 G4 **Brindisi** Italy
159 D1 **Brinkmann** Arg.
70 C4 **Brinkworth** Australia
133 H4 **Brion, Île** *i.* Canada
110 F4 **Brioude** France
133 F3 **Brisay** Canada
71 J1 **Brisbane** Australia
147 J1 **Bristol** Canada
105 E6 **Bristol** U.K.
147 G4 **Bristol** *CT* U.S.A.
147 F4 **Bristol** *PA* U.S.A.
146 B6 **Bristol** *TN* U.S.A.
128 B4 **Bristol Bay** U.S.A.
105 C6 **Bristol Channel** *est.* U.K.
73 C1 **Bristol Island** Atlantic Ocean
141 E4 **Bristol Lake** U.S.A.
141 E4 **Bristol Mountains** U.S.A.
73 A2 **British Antarctic Territory** *reg.* Antarctica
130 D3 **British Columbia** *prov.* Canada
129 J1 **British Empire Range** *mts* Canada
74 C7 **British Indian Ocean Territory** *terr.* Indian Ocean
163 J6 **British Isles** N. Atlantic Ocean
125 G2 **Brits** S. Africa
124 E5 **Britstown** S. Africa
110 C2 **Brittany** *reg.* France
110 E4 **Brive-la-Gaillarde** France
111 E1 **Briviesca** Spain
105 D7 **Brixham** U.K.
83 H4 **Brlik** Kazakh.
112 H6 **Brno** Czech Rep.
145 D5 **Broad** *r.* U.S.A.
147 F3 **Broadalbin** U.S.A.
132 E3 **Broadback** *r.* Canada
70 F6 **Broadford** Australia
107 C5 **Broadford** Rep. of Ireland
106 C3 **Broadford** U.K.
105 I6 **Broadstairs** U.K.
71 I2 **Broadview** Australia
142 C3 **Broadwater** U.S.A.
71 J2 **Broadwater** Australia
72 D1 **Broadwood** N.Z.
103 M4 **Broceni** Latvia
131 I3 **Brochet** Canada
131 I3 **Brochet, Lac** *l.* Canada
109 I3 **Brocken** *mt.* Germany
122 G2 **Brock Island** Canada
146 E3 **Brockport** U.S.A.
147 H3 **Brockton** U.S.A.
135 J3 **Brockville** Canada
135 F4 **Brockway** *MI* U.S.A.
146 D4 **Brockway** *PA* U.S.A.
129 J2 **Brodeur Peninsula** Canada
134 C4 **Brodhead** U.S.A.
106 C5 **Brodick** U.K.
113 I4 **Brodnica** Poland
117 C5 **Brody** Ukr.
143 E4 **Broken Arrow** U.S.A.
71 I4 **Broken Bow** *NE* U.S.A.
143 E5 **Broken Bow** *OK* U.S.A.
70 D3 **Broken Hill** Australia
162 K7 **Broken Plateau** *sea feature* Indian Ocean
109 I2 **Bromary** U.K.
113 C4 **Bromley** U.K.
105 G6 **Bromsgrove** U.K.
103 J4 **Brønderslev** Denmark
125 H2 **Bronkhorstspruit** S. Africa
102 K2 **Brønnøysund** Norway
134 E5 **Bronson** U.S.A.
97 A4 **Brooke's Point** Phil.
134 C4 **Brookfield** U.S.A.
143 F6 **Brookhaven** U.S.A.
138 B3 **Brookings** *OR* U.S.A.
142 D2 **Brookings** *SD* U.S.A.
147 H3 **Brookline** U.S.A.
134 A3 **Brooklyn** *IA* U.S.A.
134 A5 **Brooklyn** *IL* U.S.A.
142 E2 **Brooklyn Center** U.S.A.
146 D6 **Brookneal** U.S.A.
131 G4 **Brooks** Canada
145 C6 **Brooks** *CA* U.S.A.
147 I2 **Brooks** *ME* U.S.A.
133 I4 **Brooks** Canada
128 C3 **Brooks Range** *mts* U.S.A.
145 D6 **Brooksville** U.S.A.
146 C6 **Brookville** U.S.A.
71 A6 **Brookton** Australia
141 H3 **Brookville Lake** U.S.A.
70 B4 **Brooloo** Australia
140 B3 **Brooloo** Australia
88 D3 **Brookville** U.S.A.
107 C4 **Broomehill** Australia
89 F5 **Broome** Australia
105 I5 **Broom, Loch** *inlet* U.K.
146 D4 **Broom, Loch** *inlet* U.K.

103 K5 **Brösarp** Sweden
107 D4 **Brosna** *r.* Rep. of Ireland
138 B3 **Brothers** U.S.A.
93 □ **Brothers, The** *is* Hong Kong China
104 E3 **Brough** U.K.
104 E1 **Brough Head** *hd* U.K.
107 E3 **Broughshane** U.K.
70 C4 **Broughton** *r.* Australia
71 J4 **Broughton Islands** Australia
    Broughton Island Canada *see* **Qikiqtarjuaq**
113 O5 **Brovary** Ukr.
103 J4 **Brovst** Denmark
70 C4 **Brown, Mount** Australia
143 C5 **Brownfield** U.S.A.
138 D1 **Browning** U.S.A.
134 D6 **Brownsburg** U.S.A.
147 F5 **Browns Mills** U.S.A.
145 B5 **Brownsville** *TN* U.S.A.
143 D7 **Brownsville** *TX* U.S.A.
146 C5 **Brownville** U.S.A.
147 I2 **Brownville Junction** U.S.A.
143 D6 **Brownwood** U.S.A.
113 N4 **Broxa** Belarus
110 F1 **Bruay-la-Bussière** France
134 C2 **Bruce Crossing** U.S.A.
132 D4 **Bruce Peninsula** Canada
135 G3 **Bruce Peninsula National Park** Canada
109 G5 **Bruchsal** Germany
109 K2 **Brück** Germany
112 G7 **Bruck an der Mur** Austria
105 E6 **Brue** *r.* U.K.
    Bruges Belgium *see* **Brugge**
108 B3 **Brugge** Belgium
109 G5 **Brühl** Germany
108 E4 **Brühl** Germany
141 G2 **Bruin Point** *mt.* U.S.A.
89 I3 **Bruint** India
124 C2 **Brukkaros** Namibia
134 B2 **Brule** *r.* U.S.A.
133 H3 **Brûlé, Lac** *l.* Canada
108 C5 **Brûly** Belgium
158 E1 **Brumado** Brazil
103 J3 **Brumunddal** Norway
90 D2 **Bruni** *r.* Mongolia
123 B6 **Brunau** Germany
138 D3 **Bruneau** *r.* U.S.A.
99 D2 **Brunei** *country* Asia
102 K3 **Brunflo** Sweden
114 D1 **Brunico** Italy
72 C5 **Brunner, Lake** N.Z.
109 I2 **Bruns** Germany
112 D4 **Brunsbüttel** Germany
145 D6 **Brunswick** *GA* U.S.A.
147 I3 **Brunswick** *ME* U.S.A.
146 C4 **Brunswick** *OH* U.S.A.
156 B8 **Brunswick, Peninsula de** *pen.* Chile
71 J2 **Brunswick Head** Australia
112 H6 **Bruntál** Czech Rep.
73 A3 **Brunt Ice Shelf** Antarctica
125 H4 **Bruntville** S. Africa
71 G9 **Bruny Island** Australia
138 G3 **Brush** U.S.A.
108 C4 **Brussels** Belgium
    (City Plan 55)
135 G4 **Brussels** Canada
134 D3 **Brussels** U.S.A.
113 N5 **Brusyliv** Ukr.
71 G6 **Bruthen** Australia
    Bruxelles Belgium *see* **Brussels**
146 A4 **Bryan** *OH* U.S.A.
143 D6 **Bryan** *TX* U.S.A.
70 C4 **Bryan, Mount** Australia
73 A3 **Bryan Coast** Antarctica
116 E4 **Bryansk** Rus. Fed.
116 E4 **Bryanskaya Oblast'** *admin. div.* Rus. Fed.
117 H6 **Bryanskoye** Rus. Fed.
141 F3 **Bryce Canyon Nat. Park** U.S.A.
141 H5 **Bryce Mountain** U.S.A.
103 I4 **Bryne** Norway
117 F6 **Bryukhovetskaya** Rus. Fed.
113 H5 **Brzeg** Poland
69 F2 **Buala** Solomon Is
120 A3 **Buba** Guinea-Bissau
81 L7 **Būbiyān Island** Kuwait
97 B5 **Bubuan** *i.* Phil.
80 C3 **Bucak** Turkey
157 B3 **Bucaramanga** Col.
97 C4 **Bucas Grande** *i.* Phil.
120 A4 **Buchanan** Liberia
134 D5 **Buchanan** *MI* U.S.A.
146 D6 **Buchanan** *VA* U.S.A.
143 D6 **Buchanan, Lake** U.S.A.
129 K2 **Buchan Gulf** Canada
133 I4 **Buchans** Canada
115 L2 **Bucharest** Romania
109 I1 **Büchen** Germany
109 H5 **Buchen (Odenwald)** Germany
109 K1 **Buchholz** Germany
109 H1 **Buchholz in der Nordheide** Germany
140 B4 **Buchon, Point** U.S.A.
113 L7 **Bucin, Pasul** *pass* Romania
71 J3 **Buckamboo Mountain** Australia
109 H2 **Buckeburg** Germany
109 H2 **Bücken** Germany
141 F5 **Buckeye** U.S.A.
146 B5 **Buckeye Lake** U.S.A.
105 F4 **Buckhannon** U.S.A.
107 E5 **Buckhannon** *r.* U.S.A.
106 E4 **Buckhaven** U.K.
122 D4 **Buckhorn** Canada
135 H3 **Buckhorn** Canada
141 H3 **Buckhorn Lake** U.S.A.
146 B6 **Buckhorn Lake** U.S.A.
106 F3 **Buckie** U.K.
135 J3 **Buckingham** Canada
105 G6 **Buckingham** U.K.
146 D6 **Buckingham** U.S.A.
68 D3 **Buckingham Bay** Australia
68 E4 **Buckland Tableland** *reg.* Australia
70 B4 **Buckleboo** Australia
73 A6 **Buckle Island** Antarctica
141 F4 **Buckskin Mountains** U.S.A.
140 B3 **Bucks Mountain** U.S.A.
147 I2 **Bucksport** U.S.A.
    Bucureşti Romania *see* **Bucharest**
162 K7 **Brecon Plateau** *sea feature* Indian Ocean
146 B5 **Bucyrus** U.S.A.
113 O4 **Buda-Kashalyova** Belarus
113 I7 **Budapest** Hungary
88 D3 **Budaun** India
73 D3 **Budd Coast** Antarctica
104 F4 **Buddon Ness** *pt* U.K.
114 C4 **Buddusò** Sardinia Italy
105 C7 **Bude** U.K.
117 H6 **Budennovsk** Rus. Fed.
109 H4 **Büdesheim** Germany
88 D5 **Budni** India
116 E3 **Budogoshch'** Rus. Fed.
114 C4 **Budoni** Sardinia Italy
84 C2 **Budū', Sabkhat al** *salt pan* Saudi Arabia
120 C4 **Buea** Cameroon
140 B4 **Buellton** U.S.A.
159 E4 **Buena Esperanza** Arg.
157 A4 **Buenaventura** Col.
148 C3 **Buenaventura** Mex.
157 A4 **Buenaventura, Bahía de** *b.* Col.
139 F4 **Buena Vista** *CO* U.S.A.
146 D6 **Buena Vista** *VA* U.S.A.
111 E4 **Buendia, Embalse de** *resr* Spain

159 B4 **Bueno** *r.* Chile
159 E2 **Buenos Aires** Arg.
    (City Plan 64)
159 E3 **Buenos Aires** *prov.* Arg.
156 B7 **Buenos Aires, Lago** *l.* Arg./Chile
156 C7 **Buen Pasto** Arg.
150 C2 **Búfalo** Mex.
130 G3 **Buffalo** *r.* Canada
146 D3 **Buffalo** *NY* U.S.A.
143 D6 **Buffalo** *OK* U.S.A.
142 C2 **Buffalo** *SD* U.S.A.
143 D6 **Buffalo** *TX* U.S.A.
134 B3 **Buffalo** *WI* U.S.A.
138 F2 **Buffalo** *WY* U.S.A.
134 B3 **Buffalo** *r.* U.S.A.
71 G6 **Buffalo, Mount** Australia
130 F3 **Buffalo Head Hills** Canada
130 F2 **Buffalo Lake** Canada
131 H3 **Buffalo Narrows** Canada
124 B4 **Buffels** *watercourse* S. Africa
125 G1 **Buffels Drift** S. Africa
115 K2 **Buftea** Romania
145 D6 **Buford** U.S.A.
115 K2 **Bug** *r.* Poland
130 D4 **Buga** Col.
157 A4 **Buga** Col.
68 E3 **Bugalagrande** Col.
71 H3 **Bugaldie** Australia
82 C5 **Bugdayli** Turkm.
108 C3 **Buggenhout** Belgium
114 G2 **Bugojno** Bos.-Herz.
97 A4 **Bugsuk** *i.* Phil.
97 B2 **Buguey** Phil.
82 E3 **Buguy'** Kazakh.
82 C1 **Buguruslan** Rus. Fed.
84 D4 **Buḩābād** Iran
123 D5 **Buhera** Zimbabwe
97 B3 **Buhi** Phil.
138 D3 **Buhl** *ID* U.S.A.
134 A2 **Buhl** *MN* U.S.A.
81 I3 **Bühtan** *r.* Turkey
113 M7 **Buhuşi** Romania
105 D5 **Builth Wells** U.K.
120 D4 **Bui National Park** Ghana
116 I4 **Buinsk** Rus. Fed.
81 K4 **Bu'in Soflā** Iran
90 D2 **Buir Nur** *l.* Mongolia
123 B6 **Buitepos** Namibia
115 I3 **Bujanovac** Yugo.
122 C4 **Bujumbura** Burundi
90 D1 **Buka Daban** *mt.* China
69 F2 **Buka Island** P.N.G.
81 H4 **Bükänd** Iran
83 J1 **Bukanskoye** Rus. Fed.
82 E4 **Bukantau, Gory** *hills* Uzbek.
122 C4 **Bukavu** Dem. Rep. Congo
82 F5 **Bukhara** Uzbek.
83 K2 **Bukhtarminskoye Vodkhranilishche** *resr* Kazakh.
97 C6 **Bukide** *i.* Indon.
98 □ **Bukit Batok** Sing.
98 B5 **Bukit Fraser** Malaysia
98 □ **Bukit Panjang** Sing.
98 □ **Bukit Timah** Sing.
99 B3 **Bukittinggi** Indon.
122 D4 **Bukoba** Tanz.
98 □ **Bukum, Pulau** *i.* Sing.
91 F7 **Bula** Indon.
116 I4 **Bula** *r.* Rus. Fed.
112 D7 **Bülach** Switz.
71 H4 **Bulahdelal** Australia
80 G1 **Bulan** Phil.
88 D3 **Bulandshahr** India
81 I2 **Bulanik** Turkey
123 C6 **Bulawayo** Zimbabwe
83 G6 **Bulayevo** Kazakh.
80 F3 **Buldan** Turkey
88 D5 **Buldhana** India
125 I2 **Bulembu** Swaziland
90 C2 **Bulgan** Mongolia
92 B1 **Bulgan** Mongolia
115 K3 **Bulgaria** *country* Europe
70 E1 **Bullawarra, Lake** *salt flat* Australia
70 D4 **Bulloo** *watercourse* Australia
72 D4 **Bulloo, Lake** *salt flat* Australia
123 G6 **Bulloo Downs** Australia
120 A4 **Bullom** Namibia
98 □ **Buloh, Pulau** *i.* Sing.
70 E6 **Buloke, Lake** Australia
125 G4 **Bultfontein** S. Africa
97 C5 **Buluan** Phil.
68 C2 **Bulukumba** Indon.
77 N2 **Bulun** Rus. Fed.
122 C4 **Bulungu** Dem. Rep. Congo
122 C4 **Bulungu** Dem. Rep. Congo
82 B3 **Bulungur** Uzbek.
97 C3 **Bulusan** Phil.
122 D3 **Bumba** Dem. Rep. Congo
92 B1 **Bumbat** China
141 F4 **Bumble Bee** U.S.A.
97 A5 **Bum-Bum** *i.* Malaysia
122 D4 **Buna** Kenya
122 D4 **Buna** Kenya
92 D4 **Bunazi** Tanz.
107 C2 **Bunbeg** Rep. of Ireland
68 B5 **Bunbury** Australia
107 E5 **Bunclody** Rep. of Ireland
107 D2 **Buncrana** Rep. of Ireland
122 D4 **Bunda** Tanz.
68 F4 **Bundaberg** Australia
71 I2 **Bundaleer** Australia
71 I3 **Bundarra** Australia
88 C4 **Bundi** India
107 C3 **Bundoran** Rep. of Ireland
89 F5 **Bundu** India
105 I5 **Bungay** U.K.
71 H4 **Bungendore** Australia
73 C6 **Bunger Hills** Antarctica
95 C8 **Bungo-suidō** *sea chan.* Japan
122 D3 **Bunia** Dem. Rep. Congo
122 C4 **Bunianga** Dem. Rep. Congo
120 D3 **Buni-Yadi** Nigeria
88 C2 **Bunji** Jammu and Kashmir
141 E3 **Bunkerville** U.S.A.
143 E6 **Bunkie** U.S.A.
145 D6 **Bunnell** U.S.A.
80 D2 **Bünyan** Turkey
99 F1 **Bunyu** *i.* Indon.
77 O2 **Buorkhaya, Guba** *b.* Rus. Fed.
122 D4 **Bura** Kenya
83 K2 **Burang** China
88 B5 **Burhanpur** India

133 I4 **Burgeo** Canada
125 G5 **Burgersdorp** S. Africa
125 I2 **Burgersfort** S. Africa
109 H4 **Burgess Hill** U.K.
112 F6 **Burghausen** Germany
106 E3 **Burghead** U.K.
108 B3 **Burgh-Haamstede** Neth.
114 F6 **Burgio, Serra di** *hills* Sicily Italy
109 K5 **Burglengenfeld** Germany
111 E1 **Burgos** Spain
109 K4 **Burgstädt** Germany
103 L4 **Burgsvik** Sweden
110 G3 **Burgundy** *reg.* France
90 B3 **Burhan Budai Shan** *mts* China
115 L5 **Burhaniye** Turkey
88 D5 **Burhanpur** India
89 F4 **Burhi Gandak** *r.* India
97 B3 **Burias** *i.* Phil.
82 D2 **Buribay** Rus. Fed.
150 I6 **Burica, Punta** *pt* Costa Rica
89 H4 **Buri Dihing** *r.* India
89 E4 **Buri Gandak** *r.* Nepal
128 C4 **Burin Peninsula** Canada
98 B2 **Buriram** Thai.
155 J5 **Buriti Bravo** Brazil
158 C1 **Buritis** Brazil
85 G4 **Burj** Pak.
73 A3 **Burke Island** Antarctica
72 C6 **Burkes Pass** N.Z.
68 D3 **Burketown** Australia
120 B3 **Burkina** *country* Africa
135 H3 **Burk's Falls** Canada
83 I1 **Burkutty** Kazakh.
83 I1 **Burla** Rus. Fed.
83 I1 **Burla** *r.* Rus. Fed.
82 E1 **Burli** Kazakh.
82 C2 **Burlin** Kazakh.
142 C4 **Burlington** *CO* U.S.A.
134 B5 **Burlington** *IA* U.S.A.
134 D5 **Burlington** *IN* U.S.A.
147 I2 **Burlington** *ME* U.S.A.
147 G2 **Burlington** *VT* U.S.A.
134 C4 **Burlington** *WI* U.S.A.
82 D1 **Burly** Rus. Fed.
    Burma Asia *see* **Myanmar**
143 D6 **Burnet** U.S.A.
138 B3 **Burney** U.S.A.
147 I2 **Burnham** U.S.A.
71 F8 **Burnie** Australia
104 G3 **Burniston** U.K.
104 E4 **Burnley** U.K.
140 B3 **Burns** U.S.A.
146 C5 **Burnside** *r.* Canada
146 C5 **Burns Lake** U.S.A.
106 E4 **Burntisland** U.K.
131 I3 **Burntwood** *r.* Canada
131 I3 **Burntwood Lake** Canada
70 E5 **Buronga** Australia
82 E4 **Burovoy** Uzbek.
80 D5 **Burqin** China
80 J5 **Burqu'** Jordan
70 C4 **Burra** Australia
106 □ **Burravoe** U.K.
106 F2 **Burray** *i.* U.K.
115 I4 **Burrel** Albania
71 H4 **Burrendong Reservoir** Australia
71 H3 **Burren Jct.** Australia
115 I5 **Burewarra Point** Australia
111 F3 **Burriana** Spain
71 H5 **Burrinjuck** Australia
71 H5 **Burrinjuck Reservoir** Australia
150 D1 **Burro, Serranías del** *mts* Mex.
146 B5 **Burr Oak Reservoir** U.S.A.
106 D4 **Burrow Head** U.K.
141 J1 **Burrville** U.S.A.
80 B1 **Bursa** Turkey
    Būr Sa'īd Egypt *see* **Port Said**
109 G5 **Bürstadt** Germany
    Būr Sudan Sudan *see* **Port Sudan**
70 D4 **Burta** Australia
134 E3 **Burt Lake** U.S.A.
135 F4 **Burton** U.S.A.
132 E3 **Burton, Lac** *l.* Canada
107 C3 **Burtonport** Rep. of Ireland
105 F5 **Burton upon Trent** U.K.
102 M2 **Burträsk** Sweden
71 J1 **Burtts Corner** Canada
71 F8 **Burundy** Australia
122 C4 **Burundi** *country* Africa
83 H3 **Buraybtal** Kazakh.
80 C6 **Burullus, Lake** *lag.* Egypt
122 D4 **Bururi** Burundi
130 B2 **Burwash Landing** Canada
106 F2 **Burwick** U.K.
117 E5 **Buryn'** Ukr.
83 H1 **Burynshyk** Kazakh.
105 H5 **Bury St Edmunds** U.K.
122 C4 **Burzil Pass** Jammu and Kashmir
122 C4 **Busanga** Dem. Rep. Congo
107 E2 **Bush** *r.* U.K.
84 C4 **Būshehr** Iran
89 E2 **Bushengcaka** China
122 D4 **Bushenyi** Uganda
104 E5 **Bushmill** U.S.A.
98 □ **Busing, Pulau** *i.* Sing.
122 C3 **Businga** Dem. Rep. Congo
80 L5 **Buṣrá ash Shām** Syria
68 A5 **Busselton** Australia
108 D2 **Bussum** Neth.
150 D2 **Bustamante** Mex.
150 C1 **Bustillos, Lago** Mex.
114 C2 **Busto Arsizio** Italy
97 A3 **Busuanga** Phil.
97 A3 **Busuanga** *i.* Phil.
122 C3 **Buta** Dem. Rep. Congo
159 B3 **Buta Ranquil** Arg.
122 C4 **Butare** Rwanda
160 G6 **Butaritari** *atoll* Kiribati
70 B4 **Bute** Australia
106 C5 **Bute** *i.* U.K.
70 B4 **Bute, Sound of** *sea chan.* U.K.
130 D4 **Bute Inlet** Canada
125 I4 **Butha-Buthe** Lesotho
109 I2 **Butjadingen** *reg.* Germany
146 E4 **Butler** *PA* U.S.A.
146 A5 **Butler Bridge** Rep. of Ireland
145 C5 **Butler** U.S.A.
91 E7 **Buton** *i.* Indon.
109 K1 **Bütow** Germany
138 D2 **Butte** U.S.A.
109 I4 **Buttelstedt** Germany
140 B2 **Butte Meadows** U.S.A.
99 B1 **Butterworth** Malaysia
125 H6 **Butterworth** S. Africa
130 D5 **Buttle Lake** Canada
130 B2 **Button Bay** Canada
140 C4 **Buttonwillow** U.S.A.
93 B5 **Butuo** China
97 C4 **Butuan** Phil.
117 G5 **Buturlinovka** Rus. Fed.
89 E3 **Butwal** Nepal
109 G5 **Butzbach** Germany
109 J1 **Bützow** Germany
122 E4 **Buur Gaabo** Somalia
122 E3 **Buurhabaka** Somalia
89 F4 **Buxar** India
109 H1 **Buxtehude** Germany
105 F5 **Buxton** U.K.
116 J3 **Buy** Rus. Fed.
134 A1 **Buyck** U.S.A.
117 H7 **Buynaksk** Rus. Fed.

80 A3 Büyük Ağrı Daği mt. Turkey see Ararat, Mount
96 B3 Büyükmenderes r. Turkey
82 B3 Buyun Shan mt. China
82 B3 Buzachi, Poluostrov pen. Kazakh.
83 H5 Buzai Gumbad Afgh.
108 C5 Buzancy France
115 L2 Buzău Romania
123 C5 Búzi Moz.
82 C1 Buzuluk Rus. Fed.
117 G5 Buzuluk r. Rus. Fed.
68 E3 Buzuluk r. Kazakh.
147 H4 Buzzards Bay U.S.A.
115 K3 Byala Bulg.
115 J3 Byala Slatina Bulg.
113 N4 Byalynichy Belarus
128 H2 Byam Martin Island Canada
116 C4 Byaroza Belarus
116 C4 Byaroza Belarus
80 E4 Byblos Lebanon
112 I4 Bydgoszcz Poland
116 D4 Byerazino Belarus
138 F4 Byers U.S.A.
113 N3 Byeshankovichy Belarus
103 I4 Bygland Norway
103 I4 Bykhaw Belarus
103 I4 Bykle Norway
83 H2 Bylkyldak Kazakh.
129 K2 Bylot Island Canada
135 G3 Byng Inlet Canada
73 B5 Byrd Glacier Antarctica
103 I3 Byrkjelo Norway
71 G3 Byrock Australia
134 C4 Byron IL U.S.A.
147 H2 Byron ME U.S.A.
71 J2 Byron, Cape hd Australia
71 J2 Byron Bay Australia
77 L2 Byrranga, Gory mts Rus. Fed.
102 M2 Byske Sweden
83 K1 Bystryy Istok Rus. Fed.
77 O3 Bytantay r. Rus. Fed.
113 I5 Bytom Poland
112 H3 Bytów Poland
82 D5 Byuzmeyin Turkm.

C

156 E3 Caacupé Para.
158 A4 Caagazú, Cordillera de hills Para.
158 A4 Caaguazú Para.
158 A3 Caarapó Para.
158 A4 Caazapá Para.
154 C6 Caballas Peru
154 D4 Caballococha Peru
97 B3 Cabanatuan Phil.
123 G4 Cabano Canada
122 E2 Cabdul Qaadir Somalia
158 A1 Cabeceira Rio Manso Brazil
155 L5 Cabedelo Brazil
111 D3 Cabeza del Buey Spain
154 F7 Cabezas Bol.
159 E3 Cabildo Arg.
157 C2 Cabimas Venez.
123 C4 Cabinda Angola
122 B4 Cabinda prov. Angola
138 C1 Cabinet Mountains U.S.A.
157 B3 Cable Way pass Col.
158 D3 Cabo Frio Brazil
158 E3 Cabo Frio, Ilha do i. Brazil
132 E4 Cabonga, Réservoir resr Canada
143 E4 Cabool U.S.A.
71 J1 Caboolture Australia
155 H3 Cabo Orange, Parque Nacional de nat. park Brazil
154 C4 Cabo Pantoja Peru
148 B2 Caborca Mex.
135 G3 Cabot Head pt Canada
133 I4 Cabot Strait Canada
158 D1 Cabral, Serra do mts Brazil
81 K2 Cäbrayil Azer.
111 F3 Cabrera r. Spain
111 F3 Cabrera i. Spain
157 D3 Cabruta Venez.
97 B2 Cabugao Phil.
156 F3 Caçador Brazil
151 E4 Cacahuatepec Mex.
115 I3 Čačak Yugo.
159 G1 Cacapava do Sul Brazil
146 D5 Cacapon r. U.S.A.
157 B3 Cáceres Col.
114 C4 Caccia, Capo pt Sardinia Italy
155 G7 Cáceres Brazil
111 C3 Cáceres Spain
138 D3 Cache Peak mt. U.S.A.
120 A3 Cacheu Guinea-Bissau
156 C3 Cachi r. Arg.
154 C5 Cachi, Nevados de mt. Arg.
155 H5 Cachimbo, Serra do hills Brazil
157 B3 Cáchira Col.
158 E1 Cachoeira Brazil
158 D2 Cachoeira Alta Brazil
159 G1 Cachoeira do Sul Brazil
158 E3 Cachoeiro de Itapemirim Brazil
120 A3 Cacine Guinea-Bissau
155 H3 Caciporé, Cabo c Brazil
123 B5 Cacolo Angola
122 B4 Caconda Angola
140 D3 Cactus Range mts U.S.A.
158 B2 Caçu Brazil
158 D1 Caculé Brazil
113 I6 Čadca Slovakia
109 H1 Cadenberge Germany
151 D2 Caderetya Mex.
70 A2 Cadibarrawirracanna, Lake salt flat Australia
97 B3 Cadig Mountains Phil.
135 H1 Cadillac Que. Canada
131 H5 Cadillac Sask. Canada
134 E3 Cadillac U.S.A.
97 B4 Cadiz Phil.
111 C4 Cádiz Spain
111 C4 Cádiz, Golfo de g. Spain
141 E4 Cadiz Lake U.S.A.
110 D2 Caen France
105 C4 Caernarfon U.K.
105 C4 Caernarfon Bay U.K.
105 D6 Caerphilly U.K.
146 B5 Caesar Creek Lake U.S.A.
80 E5 Caesarea Israel
158 D1 Caetité Brazil
156 C3 Cafayate Arg.
97 B4 Cagayan r. Phil.
97 C4 Cagayan r. Phil.
97 C4 Cagayan de Oro Phil.
97 B4 Cagayan Islands Phil.
114 C5 Cagli Italy
114 C5 Cagliari Sardinia Italy
114 C5 Cagliari, Golfo di b. Sardinia Italy
157 B4 Caguán r. Col.
107 B6 Caha hill Rep. of Ireland
145 C5 Cahaba r. U.S.A.
107 A6 Caha Mountains Rep. of Ireland
107 A6 Cahersiveen Rep. of Ireland
107 D5 Cahir Rep. of Ireland
123 D5 Cahora Bassa, Lago de resr Moz.
107 C5 Cahore Point Rep. of Ireland
110 E4 Cahors France
154 C5 Cahuapanas Peru
117 D6 Cahul Moldova
123 D5 Caia Moz.
155 G6 Caiabis, Serra dos hills Brazil
123 C5 Caianda Angola
158 B2 Caiapó r. Brazil
158 B2 Caiapônia Brazil
158 B2 Caiapó, Serra do mts Brazil
149 I4 Caibarién Cuba
93 C6 Cai Bầu, Đao i. Vietnam

98 C3 Cai Be Vietnam
157 D3 Caicara Venez.
149 J4 Caicos Islands Turks and Caicos Is
93 E4 Caidian China
159 B1 Caimanes Chile
97 A3 Caiman Point Phil.
111 F2 Caimodorro mt. Spain
98 C3 Cai Nước Vietnam
106 E3 Cairn Gorm mt. U.K.
106 E3 Cairngorm Mountains U.K.
106 C6 Cairnryan U.K.
71 H4 Cairns Australia
106 E3 Cairn Toul mt. U.K.
121 F1 Cairo Egypt (City Plan 60)
130 F3 Cairo IL U.S.A.
120 C4 Cairo Park U.S.A.
145 C6 Cairo U.S.A.
114 C2 Cairo Montenotte Italy
123 B5 Caiundo Angola
71 F2 Caiwarro Australia
154 C5 Cajamarca Peru
97 B3 Cajidiocan Phil.
114 G1 Čakovec Croatia
80 B2 Çal Turkey
125 G5 Cala S. Africa
120 C4 Calabar Nigeria
135 I3 Calabogie Canada
157 D2 Calabozo Venez.
115 J3 Calafat Romania
156 B8 Calafate Arg.
111 F1 Calahorra Spain
110 E1 Calais France
147 J2 Calais U.S.A.
154 F5 Calama Brazil
156 C2 Calama Chile
157 B2 Calamar Col.
157 B4 Calamar Col.
97 A4 Calamian Group is Phil.
111 F2 Calamocha Spain
123 B4 Calandula Angola
121 E2 Calanscio Sand Sea des. Libya
97 B3 Calapan Phil.
115 L2 Călărași Romania
111 F2 Calatayud Spain
97 B3 Calauag Phil.
97 B3 Calavite, Cape pt Phil.
97 A3 Calawit i. Phil.
97 B2 Calayan i. Phil.
97 C3 Calbayog Phil.
109 J3 Calbe (Saale) Germany
97 C4 Calbiga Phil.
159 B4 Calbuco Chile
155 K5 Calcanhar, Ponta do pt Brazil
143 E6 Calcasieu Lake U.S.A.
155 H3 Calçoene Brazil
— Calcutta India see Kolkata
111 B3 Caldas da Rainha Port.
158 C2 Caldas Novas Brazil
109 H3 Calden Germany
156 B3 Caldera Chile
81 I2 Çaldıran Turkey
138 C3 Caldwell U.S.A.
146 B3 Caledon Canada
125 G5 Caledon r. Lesotho/S. Africa
124 C7 Caledon S. Africa
135 H4 Caledonia Canada
134 B4 Caledonia U.S.A.
156 C7 Caleta Olivia Arg.
115 K2 Călimănești Romania
104 C5 Calf of Man i. U.K.
138 D2 Calgary Canada
145 C5 Calhoun U.S.A.
97 C4 Calicoan i. Phil.
87 A4 Calicut India
140 E3 Caliente CA U.S.A.
141 E3 Caliente NV U.S.A.
140 B3 California state U.S.A.
— California, Golfo de g. Mex. see California, Gulf of
150 B2 California, Gulf of Mex.
140 B2 California Aqueduct canal U.S.A.
140 C4 California Hot Springs U.S.A.
81 L2 Çälilabad Azer.
140 A2 Calistoga U.S.A.
124 D6 Calitzdorp S. Africa
151 G3 Calkiní Mex.
70 D2 Callabonna, Lake salt flat Australia
140 D2 Callaghan, Mount U.S.A.
146 E3 Callaghan U.S.A.
148 E3 Callaghan Mex.
148 C2 Callananen Mex.
157 C4 Canapiare, Cerro hill Col.
154 C4 Cañar Ecuador
107 D5 Callan Rep. of Ireland
135 H2 Callander Canada
106 D4 Callander U.K.
154 C6 Callao Peru
141 F2 Callao U.S.A.
151 E5 Calles Mex.
146 D3 Callicoon U.S.A.
105 C7 Callington U.K.
131 J4 Callum Canada
130 G4 Calmar Canada
134 B4 Calmar U.S.A.
141 E5 Cal-Nev-Ari U.S.A.
145 D7 Caloosahatchee r. U.S.A.
71 J1 Caloundra Australia
140 B2 Calpine U.S.A.
151 E4 Calpulálpan Mex.
114 F6 Caltanissetta Sicily Italy
134 C2 Calumet U.S.A.
123 B5 Calunga Angola
123 B5 Caluquembe Angola
122 E2 Caluula Somalia
130 D4 Calvert Island Canada
114 C3 Calvi Corsica France
111 H3 Calvià Spain
150 D4 Calvillo Mex.
124 E6 Calvinia S. Africa
114 F4 Calvo, Monte mt. Italy
105 H5 Cam r. U.K.
158 E1 Camaçari Brazil
140 B2 Camacho Reservoir U.S.A.
131 H4 Camacho Mex.
123 B5 Camacuio Angola
123 B5 Camacupa Angola
157 D2 Camaguán Venez.
149 I4 Camagüey Cuba
149 I4 Camagüey, Archipiélago de is Cuba
158 E1 Camamu Brazil
154 D7 Camaná Peru
123 C5 Camanongue Angola
158 B2 Camapuã Brazil
159 G1 Camaquã Brazil
159 G1 Camaquã r. Brazil
80 E3 Çamardı Turkey
151 D3 Camargo Mex.
156 C6 Camarones Mex.
156 C6 Camarones, Bahía b. Arg.
98 C3 Ca Mau Vietnam
99 B1 Camah, Gunung mt. Malaysia
— Camalan Turkey see Gülek
154 C7 Camaná Peru
123 C5 Camanongue Angola
158 B2 Camapuã Brazil
159 G1 Camaquã Brazil
159 G1 Camaquã r. Brazil
93 D6 Cangwu China
92 E2 Cangzhou China
157 B4 Caguán r. Col.
107 B6 Caha hill Rep. of Ireland
92 E2 Canaiapiscau r. Canada
133 G2 Caniapiscau r. Canada
133 G2 Caniapiscau Canada
133 G3 Caniapiscau, Lac resr Canada
114 E6 Canicattì Sicily Italy
130 E4 Canim Lake Canada
130 E4 Canim Lake l. Canada
155 I4 Canindé Brazil
155 J5 Canindé r. Brazil
97 B3 Canipaan Phil.
106 D2 Canisp hill U.K.
146 E3 Canisteo U.S.A.
146 E3 Canisteo r. U.S.A.
150 D3 Cañitas de Felipe Pescador Mex.
80 D1 Çankırı Turkey
97 B4 Canlaon Phil.
87 B4 Cannanore India
87 A4 Cannanore Islands India
110 H5 Cannes France
71 I5 Camden Australia

145 C5 Camden AL U.S.A.
147 I2 Camden ME U.S.A.
147 F5 Camden NJ U.S.A.
147 F3 Camden NY U.S.A.
145 D5 Camden SC U.S.A.
156 B8 Camden, Isla i. Chile
123 C5 Cameia, Parque Nacional da nat. park Angola
141 G4 Cameron AZ U.S.A.
143 E6 Cameron LA U.S.A.
142 E4 Cameron MO U.S.A.
143 D6 Cameron TX U.S.A.
134 B3 Cameron WI U.S.A.
130 F3 Cameron Hills Canada
140 B2 Cameron Park U.S.A.
120 C4 Cameroon country Africa
120 C4 Cameroon, Mont mt. Cameroon
155 I4 Cametá Brazil
97 B2 Camiguin i. Phil.
97 C5 Camiguin i. Phil.
97 B3 Camiling Phil.
145 C6 Camilla U.S.A.
154 F8 Camiri Bol.
155 J4 Camocim Brazil
68 D3 Camooweal Australia
97 C4 Camotes Sea g. Phil.
157 B4 Campana, Cerro hill Col.
156 A7 Campana, Isla i. Chile
159 B2 Campanario mt. Arg./Chile
130 D4 Campania Island Canada
124 E4 Campbell S. Africa
72 E4 Campbell, Cape N.Z.
67 F7 Campbell Island N.Z.
160 G9 Campbell Plateau sea feature S. Pacific Ocean
130 D4 Campbell River Canada
135 I3 Campbells Bay Canada
144 C4 Campbellsville U.S.A.
133 G4 Campbellton Canada
71 G8 Campbell Town Australia
106 C5 Campbeltown U.K.
151 G5 Campeche Mex.
151 G4 Campeche, Bahía de g. Mex.
70 E7 Camperdown Australia
115 K2 Câmpina Romania
155 K5 Campina Grande Brazil
158 C3 Campinas Brazil
158 B2 Campina Verde Brazil
120 C4 Campo Cameroon
157 B4 Campoalegre Col.
114 F4 Campobasso Italy
158 D3 Campo Belo Brazil
158 C2 Campo Florido Brazil
158 A3 Campo Gallo Arg.
158 A3 Campo Grande Brazil
155 J4 Campo Maior Brazil
111 C3 Campo Maior Port.
158 B3 Campo Mourão Brazil
158 E3 Campos Brazil
158 D3 Campos Altos Brazil
158 D3 Campos do Jordão Brazil
105 F5 Campsie Fells hills U.K.
146 B6 Campton KY U.S.A.
147 H3 Campton NH U.S.A.
115 K2 Câmpulung Romania
115 L7 Câmpulung Moldovenesc Romania
141 G4 Camp Verde U.S.A.
98 D3 Cam Ranh Vietnam
130 G4 Camrose Canada
105 B6 Camrose U.K.
131 G2 Camsell Lake Canada
131 H3 Camsell Portage Canada
80 C1 Çan Turkey
147 G3 Canaan U.S.A.
123 G3 Canada country N. America
164 O1 Canada Basin sea feature Arctic Ocean
159 E2 Cañada de Gómez Arg.
147 H2 Canada Falls Lake U.S.A.
143 C5 Canadian r. U.S.A.
157 E3 Canaima, Parque Nacional nat. park Venez.
147 F3 Canajoharie U.S.A.
117 C7 Çanakkale Turkey
124 C6 Çanakkale Boğazı strait Turkey see Dardanelles
159 C2 Canalejas Arg.
146 E3 Canandaigua U.S.A.
146 E3 Canandaigua Lake U.S.A.
148 B2 Cananea Mex.
158 A4 Cananéia Brazil
157 C4 Canapiare, Cerro hill Col.
154 C4 Cañar Ecuador
— Canarias, Islas is Atlantic Ocean see Canary Islands
— Canarias, Islas terr. Canary Islands
120 A1 Canary Islands is Atlantic Ocean
118 C2 Canary Islands terr. Atlantic Ocean
147 F3 Canastota U.S.A.
158 C2 Canastra, Serra da mts Brazil
150 D2 Canatlán Mex.
145 D6 Canaveral, Cape U.S.A.
111 E2 Cañaveras Spain
158 E1 Canavieiras Brazil
71 G3 Canbelego Australia
71 H5 Canberra Australia
138 B3 Canby CA U.S.A.
142 D2 Canby MN U.S.A.
151 E4 Candelaria Campeche Mex.
151 G4 Candelaria Chihuahua Mex.
139 F6 Candelaria r. Mex.
151 E5 Candelaria Loxicha Mex.
111 D2 Candeleda Spain
71 H6 Candelo Australia
155 I4 Cândido Mendes Brazil
80 E1 Çandır Turkey
131 H4 Candle Lake Canada
73 C1 Candlemas Island Atlantic Ocean
147 G4 Candlewood, Lake U.S.A.
142 D1 Cando U.S.A.
97 B3 Candon Phil.
159 B1 Canela Baja Chile
159 F2 Canelones Uruguay
159 B3 Cañete Chile
111 F2 Cañete Spain
154 C6 Cangallo Peru
123 B5 Cangamba Angola
111 C1 Cangas del Narcea Spain
124 E6 Cango Caves S. Africa
155 K5 Canguaretama Brazil
159 G1 Canguçu Brazil
159 G1 Canguçu, Serra do hills Brazil
93 D6 Cangwu China
92 E2 Cangzhou China

105 E5 Cannock U.K.
71 H6 Cann River Australia
156 F3 Canoas Brazil
131 H3 Canoe Lake Canada
158 B4 Canoinhas Brazil
139 F4 Canon City U.S.A.
70 D4 Canopus Australia
131 I4 Canora Canada
71 H4 Canowindra Australia
133 H4 Canso, Cape hd Canada
111 D1 Cantábrica, Cordillera mts Spain
110 B4 Cantábrico, Mar sea France/Spain
159 C2 Cantantal Arg.
157 D2 Cantaura Venez.
105 I6 Canterbury U.K.
72 C5 Canterbury Bight b. N.Z.
72 C5 Canterbury Plains N.Z.
98 C3 Cần Thơ Vietnam
97 C4 Cantilan Phil.
155 J5 Canto do Buriti Brazil
— Canton China see Guangzhou
134 B5 Canton IL U.S.A.
147 H2 Canton ME U.S.A.
142 F4 Canton MO U.S.A.
143 F5 Canton MS U.S.A.
146 F2 Canton NY U.S.A.
146 C4 Canton OH U.S.A.
146 E4 Canton PA U.S.A.
158 B4 Cantu r. Brazil
158 B4 Cantu, Serra do hills Brazil
159 E2 Cañuelas Arg.
155 G4 Canumã Brazil
71 J2 Canungra Australia
72 D4 Canvastown N.Z.
105 H6 Canvey Island U.K.
131 H4 Canwood Canada
143 C5 Canyon U.S.A.
138 C2 Canyon City U.S.A.
141 H3 Canyon de Chelly National Monument res. U.S.A.
138 D2 Canyon Ferry Lake U.S.A.
141 H2 Canyonlands National Park U.S.A.
130 D2 Canyon Ranges mts Canada
138 B3 Canyonville U.S.A.
93 C6 Cao Bằng Vietnam
96 C3 Cao He r. China
98 D2 Cao Nguyên Đắc Lắc plat. Vietnam
96 C2 Caoshi China
92 E3 Caoxian China
97 B3 Cap i. Phil.
157 D3 Capanaparo r. Venez.
155 I4 Capanema Brazil
158 B4 Capanema r. Brazil
158 C3 Capão Bonito Brazil
157 C3 Caparo r. Venez.
157 B4 Caparro, Cerro hill Brazil
97 B3 Capas Phil.
133 I4 Cap-aux-Meules Canada
133 G4 Cap-de-la-Madeleine Canada
71 H8 Cape Barren Island Australia
163 J8 Cape Basin sea feature S. Atlantic Ocean
133 H4 Cape Breton Highlands National Park Canada
133 H4 Cape Breton Island Canada
133 I3 Cape Charles Canada
147 E6 Cape Charles U.S.A.
120 B4 Cape Coast Ghana
147 H4 Cape Cod Bay U.S.A.
147 I4 Cape Cod National Seashore res. U.S.A.
145 D7 Cape Coral U.S.A.
135 G3 Cape Croker Canada
129 K3 Cape Dorset Canada
145 E5 Cape Fear r. U.S.A.
143 F4 Cape Girardeau U.S.A.
158 D2 Capelinha Brazil
108 C3 Capelle aan de IJssel Neth.
105 C4 Capel Llywelyn mt. U.K.
123 B4 Capenda-Camulemba Angola
133 I4 Cape St George Canada
133 I4 Cape St George Canada
124 C6 Cape Town S. Africa
120 Cape Verde country
163 G5 Cape Verde Basin sea feature N. Atlantic Ocean
163 G4 Cape Verde Plateau sea feature N. Atlantic Ocean
147 F2 Cape Vincent U.S.A.
71 H5 Cape York Peninsula Australia
149 J5 Cap-Haïtien Haiti
155 I4 Capim r. Brazil
141 G2 Capitol Reef National Park U.S.A.
73 Capitán Arturo Prat research station Antarctica
158 A3 Capitán Bado Para.
114 G3 Capljina Bos.-Herz.
114 F5 Capo d'Orlando Sicily Italy
107 D5 Cappoquin Rep. of Ireland
114 C4 Capraia, Isola di i. Italy
114 F4 Capri, Isola di i. Italy
123 C5 Caprivi Strip reg. Namibia
140 Captain Cook U.S.A.
71 H5 Captain's Flat Australia
97 C3 Capul i. Phil.
157 B3 Cáqueza Col.
97 B3 Carabao i. Phil.
115 K2 Caracal Romania
157 E2 Caracaraí Brazil
157 D2 Caracas Venez. (City Plan 64)
155 J5 Caracol Brazil
159 F2 Caraguatatuba r. Uruguay
158 C3 Caraguatatuba Brazil
159 B3 Carahue Chile
158 E2 Caraí Brazil
158 D3 Carandaí Brazil
158 D3 Carangola Brazil
115 J2 Caransebeş Romania
133 H4 Caraquet Canada
157 B4 Carare r. Col.
156 F3 Carazinho Brazil
107 B3 Carbery Canada
144 B4 Carbondale IL U.S.A.
133 J4 Carbondale PA U.S.A.
133 J4 Carbonear Canada
114 C5 Carbonia Sardinia Italy
133 J4 Carbonear Canada
142 D2 Carcaixent Spain
111 F3 Carcassonne France
130 C2 Carcross Canada
142 D2 Cardamom Range mts Cambodia
87 B4 Cardamon Hills India
146 C5 Cardenas MO U.S.A.
151 E3 Cárdenas Mex.
131 H1 Carrot r. Canada
70 D6 Cardiel, Lago l. Arg.

105 D6 Cardiff U.K.
105 C5 Cardigan U.K.
105 C5 Cardigan Bay U.K.
147 F2 Cardinal Canada
146 E4 Cardington U.S.A.
159 F2 Cardona Uruguay
158 C4 Cardoso, Ilha do i. Brazil
72 B6 Cardrona N.Z.
130 F3 Cardston Canada
113 K7 Carei Romania
110 D2 Carentan France
146 B4 Carey U.S.A.
68 C4 Carey, Lake salt flat Australia
131 I2 Carey Lake Canada
162 H6 Cargados Carajos Islands Mauritius
110 C2 Carhaix-Plouguer France
159 D3 Carhué Arg.
158 E3 Cariacica Brazil
157 E2 Cariaco Venez.
149 I5 Caribbean Sea Atlantic Ocean
130 E4 Cariboo Mountains Canada
131 J3 Caribou r. Man. Canada
130 D2 Caribou r. N.W.T. Canada
147 J1 Caribou U.S.A.
132 C3 Caribou Island Canada
129 J4 Caribou Lake Canada
130 F4 Caribou Mountains Canada
97 C4 Carigara Phil.
108 D5 Carignan France
71 G3 Carinda Australia
111 F2 Cariñena Spain
158 D1 Carinhanha Brazil
158 D1 Carinhanha r. Brazil
157 E2 Caripe Venez.
157 E2 Caripito Venez.
107 D3 Cark Mountain Rep. of Ireland
135 I3 Carleton Place Canada
125 G3 Carletonville S. Africa
138 C3 Carlin U.S.A.
107 E3 Carlingford Lough inlet Rep. of Ireland/U.K.
104 E3 Carlisle U.K.
146 A5 Carlisle KY U.S.A.
146 E4 Carlisle PA U.S.A.
106 D2 Carloway U.K.
140 D5 Carlsbad CA U.S.A.
139 F5 Carlsbad NM U.S.A.
143 C6 Carlsbad TX U.S.A.
139 F5 Carlsbad Caverns National Park U.S.A.
162 H4 Carlsberg Ridge sea feature Indian Ocean
73 J4 Carlson Inlet Antarctica
106 E5 Carluke U.K.
131 I5 Carlyle Canada
130 C2 Carmacks Canada
114 F2 Carmagnola Italy
131 J5 Carman Canada
105 C6 Carmarthen U.K.
105 C6 Carmarthen Bay U.K.
110 F4 Carmaux France
146 A5 Carmel U.S.A.
105 C4 Carmel Head hd U.K.
150 C2 Carmelita Guat.
159 E2 Carmelo Uruguay
148 D5 Carmen r. Mex.
141 G6 Carmen Mex.
97 C4 Carmen Phil.
159 D4 Carmen de Patagones Arg.
150 B2 Carmen, Isla i. Mex.
151 H5 Carmen, Isla del i. Mex.
159 D4 Carmen de Patagones Arg.
144 B4 Carmi U.S.A.
140 B2 Carmichael U.S.A.
111 C3 Carmona Spain
110 C3 Carnac France
68 A4 Carnarvon Australia
124 E5 Carnarvon S. Africa
107 D2 Carndonagh Rep. of Ireland
105 D4 Carnedd Llywelyn mt. U.K.
68 C4 Carnegie, Lake salt flat Australia
161 N6 Carnegie Ridge sea feature S. Pacific Ocean
106 D3 Carn Eighe mt. U.K.
73 A3 Carney Island Antarctica
104 E3 Carnforth U.K.
107 D3 Carnlough U.K.
106 E4 Carn nan Gabhar mt. U.K.
120 C4 Carnot Cent. Afr. Rep.
70 A5 Carnot, Cape hd Australia
106 F4 Carnoustie U.K.
107 E5 Carnsore Point Rep. of Ireland
106 E5 Carnwath U.K.
145 D7 Carol City U.S.A.
155 I5 Carolina Brazil
125 H3 Carolina S. Africa
67 I5 Caroline Island Kiribati
66 D2 Caroline Islands N. Pacific Ocean
72 A6 Caroline Peak mt. N.Z.
124 B4 Carolusberg S. Africa
157 C2 Caroni r. Venez.
157 E3 Caroní r. Venez.
157 C2 Carora Venez.
113 L6 Carpathian Mountains Romania/Ukr.
— Carpații Meridionali mts Romania see Transylvanian Alps
68 D3 Carpentaria, Gulf of Australia
110 G4 Carpentras France
114 D2 Carpi Italy
131 I5 Carpina Spain
155 K5 Carpina Brazil
130 E4 Carp Lake Provincial Park Canada
107 B4 Carra, Lough l. Rep. of Ireland
147 H2 Carrabassett U.S.A.
145 C6 Carrabelle U.S.A.
157 B3 Carraipía Col.
159 G2 Carahue Chile
158 E2 Caraí Brazil
158 D3 Carandaí Brazil
158 D3 Carangola Brazil
150 D2 Carranza, Presa Venustiano resr Mex.
157 E3 Carrao r. Venez.
114 D2 Carrara Italy
71 F5 Carrathool Australia
133 H4 Carraquet Canada
159 C2 Carrero, Cerro mt. Arg.
131 G4 Castor Canada
149 G3 Carriacou i. Grenada
106 D5 Carrickfergus U.K.
107 D4 Carrickmacross Rep. of Ireland
107 C4 Carrick-on-Shannon Rep. of Ireland
107 D5 Carrick-on-Suir Rep. of Ireland
107 C4 Carrieton Australia
107 C4 Carrigallen Rep. of Ireland
107 C6 Carrigaline Rep. of Ireland
107 D5 Carrizal Bajo Chile
141 H4 Carrizo AZ U.S.A.
141 H5 Carrizo Creek r. U.S.A.
143 C6 Carrizo Springs U.S.A.
139 F5 Carrizozo U.S.A.
142 D2 Carroll U.S.A.
144 C4 Carrollton GA U.S.A.
144 C4 Carrollton KY U.S.A.
142 E4 Carrollton MO U.S.A.
146 C4 Carrollton OH U.S.A.
131 H4 Carrot r. Man. Canada
131 H4 Carrot River Canada
107 B3 Carrowmore Lough l. Rep. of Ireland

147 F2 Carry Falls Reservoir U.S.A.
80 F1 Çarşamba Turkey
134 C3 Carson City MI U.S.A.
140 C2 Carson City NV U.S.A.
140 C2 Carson Lake U.S.A.
140 C2 Carson Sink l. U.S.A.
135 F4 Carsonville U.S.A.
159 B2 Cartagena Chile
111 F4 Cartagena Spain
157 B2 Cartagena Col.
157 B3 Cartago Col.
145 C5 Cartago Costa Rica
145 C5 Cartersville U.S.A.
134 B5 Carthage IL U.S.A.
143 E4 Carthage MO U.S.A.
147 F2 Carthage NY U.S.A.
143 E5 Carthage TX U.S.A.
135 G2 Cartier Canada
104 E3 Cartmel U.K.
133 J4 Cartwright Canada
155 K5 Caruaru Brazil
157 E2 Carúpano Venez.
140 A2 Carvers U.S.A.
108 A4 Carvin France
145 E5 Cary U.S.A.
70 E2 Caryapundy Swamp Australia
120 B1 Casablanca Morocco
158 C3 Casa Branca Brazil
139 E6 Casa de Janos Mex.
141 G5 Casa Grande U.S.A.
141 G5 Casa Grande National Monument res. U.S.A.
114 C2 Casale Monferrato Italy
114 C2 Casalmaggiore Italy
157 C3 Casanare r. Col.
115 H4 Casarano Italy
72 B6 Cascade N.Z.
134 B4 Cascade IA U.S.A.
138 C2 Cascade ID U.S.A.
138 D2 Cascade MT U.S.A.
72 B6 Cascade Point N.Z.
138 B3 Cascade Range mts Canada/U.S.A.
138 D2 Cascade Reservoir U.S.A.
111 B3 Cascais Port.
150 H6 Cascal, Paso del pass Nicaragua
158 B4 Cascavel Brazil
147 I3 Casco Bay U.S.A.
114 F4 Caserta Italy
135 F4 Caseville U.S.A.
73 C6 Casey research station Antarctica
73 D4 Casey Bay Antarctica
122 D2 Casey, Raas c. Somalia
107 D5 Cashel Rep. of Ireland
71 H1 Cashmere Australia
134 A3 Cashton U.S.A.
157 C2 Casigua Venez.
97 B2 Casiguran Phil.
159 E2 Casilda Arg.
72 A6 Casino Australia
154 C5 Casma Peru
134 C4 Casnovia U.S.A.
140 A2 Caspar U.S.A.
111 F2 Caspe Spain
138 F3 Casper U.S.A.
82 B2 Caspian Lowland Kazakh./Rus. Fed.
76 C2 Caspian Sea Asia/Europe
146 D5 Cass r. U.S.A.
135 F4 Cass r. U.S.A.
146 D5 Cassadaga U.S.A.
123 C5 Cassai Angola
135 F4 Cass City U.S.A.
108 A4 Cassel France
135 H1 Casselman Canada
130 D3 Cassiar Canada
130 D3 Cassiar Mountains Canada
71 H4 Cassilis Australia
114 E4 Cassino Italy
142 E2 Cass Lake U.S.A.
155 I4 Castanhal Brazil
159 C2 Castaño r. Arg.
150 C2 Castaños Mex.
159 C2 Castaño Viejo Arg.
110 E4 Casteljaloux France
114 F4 Castellammare di Stabia Italy
159 F3 Castelli Arg.
111 G2 Castelló de la Plana Spain
111 C3 Castelo Branco Port.
111 C3 Castelo de Vide Port.
114 E6 Casteltermini Sicily Italy
114 E6 Castelvetrano Sicily Italy
70 D6 Casterton Australia
133 G2 Castignon, Lac l. Canada
111 E3 Castilla - La Mancha aut. comm. Spain
111 D2 Castilla y León aut. comm. Spain
157 C2 Castilletes Col.
159 G2 Castillos Uruguay
107 B4 Castlebar Rep. of Ireland
106 A4 Castlebay U.K.
107 E3 Castlebellingham Rep. of Ireland
107 E3 Castleblayney Rep. of Ireland
107 D3 Castlederg Rep. of Ireland
104 F3 Castle Carrock U.K.
105 G5 Castle Cary U.K.
141 G2 Castle Dale U.S.A.
107 E5 Castledermot Rep. of Ireland
141 E5 Castle Dome Mountains U.S.A.
105 F5 Castle Donington U.K.
106 E6 Castle Douglas U.K.
130 F5 Castlegar Canada
107 B5 Castlegregory Rep. of Ireland
107 C6 Castleisland Rep. of Ireland
70 F6 Castlemaine Australia
107 B5 Castlemaine Rep. of Ireland
107 C6 Castlemartyr Rep. of Ireland
141 G4 Castle Mountain U.S.A.
93 Castle Peak hill Hong Kong China
72 F4 Castlepoint N.Z.
107 D4 Castlepollard Rep. of Ireland
107 C4 Castlerea Rep. of Ireland
71 H3 Castlereagh r. Australia
139 F4 Castle Rock U.S.A.
134 B4 Castle Rock Lake U.S.A.
104 C3 Castletown Isle of Man
107 C4 Castletown Rep. of Ireland
131 G4 Castor Canada
110 F5 Castres France
108 C2 Castricum Neth.
149 L6 Castries St Lucia
158 B3 Castro Brazil
159 B4 Castro Chile
111 D4 Castro del Río Spain
111 B3 Castro Verde Port.
114 G5 Castrovillari Italy
154 B5 Catacaos Peru
158 C3 Cataguases Brazil
143 E5 Catahoula Lake U.S.A.
80 E3 Çatak Turkey
158 C2 Catalão Brazil
111 G2 Cataluña aut. comm. Spain
156 C3 Catamarca Arg.
97 C4 Catanduanes i. Phil.
158 C3 Catanduva Brazil
114 F6 Catania Sicily Italy
114 G5 Catanzaro Italy
143 D6 Catarina U.S.A.
97 C4 Catarman Phil.
111 F3 Catarroja Spain
70 A5 Catastrophe, Cape hd Australia

157 B2 **Catatumbo** r. Venez.
93 C6 **Cat Ba, Dao** i. Vietnam
97 C4 **Catbalogan** Phil.
145 E7 **Cat Cays** is Bahamas
72 C5 **Cateel** Phil.
97 C5 **Cateel Bay** Phil.
125 J3 **Catembe** Moz.
71 H6 **Cathcart** Australia
125 G6 **Cathcart** S. Africa
125 H4 **Cathedral Peak** S. Africa
107 A6 **Catherdaniel** Rep. of Ireland
141 F2 **Catherine, Mount** U.S.A.
159 B3 **Catillo** Chile
148 E7 **Cat Island** Bahamas
132 B3 **Cat Lake** Canada
151 H3 **Catoche, Cabo** Mex.
146 E5 **Catonsville** U.S.A.
150 D3 **Catorce** Mex.
159 D3 **Catrilo** Chile
157 E4 **Catrimani** Brazil
157 E4 **Catrimani** r. Brazil
108 A4 **Cats, Mont des** hill France
147 G3 **Catskill** U.S.A.
147 F4 **Catskill Mountains** U.S.A.
125 J3 **Catuane** Moz.
157 E4 **Cauamé** r. Brazil
97 B4 **Cauayan** Phil.
133 H2 **Caubvick, Mount** Canada
157 B3 **Cauca** r. Col.
155 K4 **Caucaia** Brazil
157 B3 **Caucasia** Col.
117 G7 **Caucasus** mts Asia/Europe
159 C1 **Caucete** Arg.
147 I1 **Caucomgomoc Lake** U.S.A.
108 B4 **Caudry** France
97 C4 **Cauit Point** Phil.
159 B3 **Cauquenes** Chile
157 D2 **Caura** r. Venez.
133 G4 **Causapscal** Canada
110 G5 **Cavaillon** France
158 C1 **Cavalcante** Brazil
120 B4 **Cavally** r. Côte d'Ivoire
107 D4 **Cavan** Rep. of Ireland
143 F4 **Cave City** U.S.A.
158 E1 **Caveira** r. Brazil
70 E6 **Cavendish** Australia
158 B4 **Cavernoso, Serra do** mts Brazil
146 B5 **Cave Run Lake** U.S.A.
97 B4 **Cavili** reef Phil.
97 B3 **Cavite** Phil.
106 E3 **Cawdor** U.K.
70 D4 **Cawndilla Lake** Australia
105 I5 **Cawston** U.K.
155 J4 **Caxias** Brazil
156 F3 **Caxias do Sul** Brazil
123 B4 **Caxito** Angola
80 C2 **Çay** Turkey
145 D5 **Cayce** U.S.A.
80 D1 **Çaycuma** Turkey
81 H1 **Çayeli** Turkey
155 H3 **Cayenne** Fr. Guiana
80 C2 **Çayırhan** Turkey
149 I5 **Cayman Brac** i. Cayman Is
149 H5 **Cayman Islands** terr.
   Caribbean Sea
163 D4 **Cayman Trench** sea feature
   Caribbean Sea
122 E3 **Caynabo** Somalia
135 H4 **Cayuga** Canada
146 E3 **Cayuga Lake** U.S.A.
147 F3 **Cazenovia** U.S.A.
123 C5 **Cazombo** Angola
163 G6 **Ceara Abyssal Plain** sea feature
   S. Atlantic Ocean
150 I7 **Cebaco, Isla** i. Panama
150 C2 **Ceballos** Mex.
159 F2 **Cebollatí** r. Uruguay
97 B4 **Cebu** Phil.
97 B4 **Cebu** i. Phil.
134 C3 **Cecil** U.S.A.
71 I1 **Cecil Plains** Australia
114 D3 **Cedar** r. U.S.A.
134 A4 **Cedar** r. IA U.S.A.
142 C2 **Cedar** r. ND U.S.A.
134 D4 **Cedarburg** U.S.A.
142 C3 **Cedar City** U.S.A.
143 D5 **Cedar Creek Reservoir** U.S.A.
134 A4 **Cedar Falls** U.S.A.
134 D4 **Cedar Grove** WI U.S.A.
146 C5 **Cedar Grove** WV U.S.A.
147 F6 **Cedar Island** U.S.A.
131 I4 **Cedar Lake** Canada
133 G3 **Cedar Lake** U.S.A.
146 B4 **Cedar Point** U.S.A.
134 B5 **Cedar Rapids** U.S.A.
141 G3 **Cedar Ridge** U.S.A.
147 F5 **Cedar Run** U.S.A.
135 F4 **Cedar Springs** Canada
134 E4 **Cedar Springs** U.S.A.
145 C5 **Cedartown** U.S.A.
125 H5 **Cedarville** S. Africa
134 E3 **Cedarville** U.S.A.
150 A1 **Cedros, Isla** i. Mex.
68 D5 **Ceduna** Australia
122 E3 **Ceeldheere** Somalia
122 E2 **Ceerigaabo** Somalia
114 F5 **Cefalù** Sicily Italy
113 I7 **Cegléd** Hungary
79 E5 **Ceheng** China
80 E1 **Çekerek** Turkey
150 G5 **Celaque, Parque Nacional**
   nat. park Hond.
150 D3 **Celaya** Mex.
107 E4 **Celbridge** Rep. of Ireland
99 E3 **Celebes** i. Indon.
91 E6 **Celebes Sea** Indon./Phil.
146 A4 **Celina** U.S.A.
114 F1 **Celje** Slovenia
109 I2 **Celle** Germany
163 □ **Celtic Shelf** sea feature
   N. Atlantic Ocean
80 E1 **Cemilbey** Turkey
80 G2 **Çemişgezek** Turkey
91 F7 **Cenderawasih, Teluk** b. Indon.
141 F5 **Centennial Wash** r. U.S.A.
143 E6 **Center** U.S.A.
147 G4 **Centereach** U.S.A.
145 C5 **Center Point** U.S.A.
145 C5 **Centerville** AL U.S.A.
146 B5 **Centerville** OH U.S.A.
125 G1 **Central** admin. dist. Botswana
157 A4 **Central, Cordillera** mts Col.
150 I6 **Central, Cordillera**
   mts Panama
154 C5 **Central, Cordillera** mts Peru
97 B2 **Central, Cordillera** mts Phil.
122 D4 **Central African Republic**
   country Africa
85 G4 **Central Brahui Range** mts Pak.
134 B4 **Central City** IA U.S.A.
142 D3 **Central City** NE U.S.A.
134 B2 **Centralia** IL U.S.A.
138 B2 **Centralia** WA U.S.A.
134 A2 **Central Lakes** U.S.A.
85 G5 **Central Makran Range**
   mts Pak.
160 G5 **Central Pacific Basin**
   sea feature Pacific Ocean
157 B3 **Central Point** U.S.A.
68 E2 **Central Range** mts P.N.G.
76 E4 **Central Russian Upland**
   reg. Rus. Fed.
77 L3 **Central Siberian Plateau**
   Rus. Fed.
93 D6 **Cenxi** China
115 I5 **Cephalonia** i. Greece
141 E4 **Cerbat Mountains** U.S.A.
131 G4 **Cereal** Canada
156 D3 **Ceres** Arg.
124 C5 **Ceres** S. Africa
157 B2 **Cerezo** Col.
111 E2 **Cerezo de Abajo** Spain
114 F4 **Cerignola** Italy

80 D2 **Çerikli** Turkey
80 D1 **Çerkeş** Turkey
81 G2 **Çermelik Deresi** r. Syria
81 G2 **Çermik** Turkey
115 M2 **Cernavodă** Romania
151 E2 **Cerralvo** Mex.
150 D2 **Cerralvo, Isla** i. Mex.
115 H4 **Çërrik** Albania
151 D3 **Cerritos** Mex.
158 C4 **Cerro Azul** Brazil
151 E3 **Cerro Azul** Mex.
98 C2 **Cerro de Pasco** Peru
150 I7 **Cerro Hoya, Parque Nacional**
   nat. park Panama
157 D3 **Cerro Jáua, Meseta del** plat.
   Venez.
157 C2 **Cerrón, Cerro** mt. Venez.
150 C2 **Cerro Prieto** Mex.
159 C3 **Cerros Colorados, Embalse**
   resr Arg.
154 B4 **Cerros de Amotape, Parque**
   Nacional nat. park Peru
114 F4 **Cervati, Monte** mt. Italy
114 C3 **Cervione** Corsica France
111 C1 **Cervo** Spain
157 B2 **César** r. Col.
114 E2 **Cesena** Italy
103 N4 **Cēsis** Latvia
112 G6 **České Budějovice** Czech Rep.
112 G6 **Český Krumlov** Czech Rep.
109 K5 **Český Les** mts
   Czech Rep./Germany
115 L5 **Çeşme** Turkey
71 I4 **Cessnock** Australia
115 H3 **Cetinje** Yugo.
114 F5 **Cetraro** Italy
111 D5 **Ceuta** Spain
69 H4 **Ceva-i-Ra** reef Fiji
110 F4 **Cévennes** mts France
80 E3 **Ceyhan** Turkey
80 E3 **Ceyhan** r. Turkey
81 H3 **Ceylanpınar** Turkey
85 F5 **Chābahār** Iran
89 E3 **Chabyêr Caka** salt l. China
85 F4 **Chacabuco** Arg.
159 B4 **Chacao** Chile
159 C3 **Chachahuén, Sierra** mt. Arg.
154 C5 **Chachapoyas** Peru
116 D4 **Chachersk** Belarus
98 B2 **Chachoengsao** Thai.
88 B4 **Chachro** Pak.
96 C2 **Chaek** Kyrg.
96 C4 **Chaeryŏng** N. Korea
157 B4 **Chafurray** Col.
85 G4 **Chagai** Pak.
85 F4 **Chagai Hills** Afgh./Pak.
82 F3 **Chagan** Kzyl-Ordinskaya Oblast'
   Kazakh.
83 I2 **Chagan** Vostochnyy Kazakhstan
   Kazakh.
89 F2 **Chagdo Kangri** reg. China
85 G3 **Chaghcharān** Afgh.
83 G1 **Chaglinka** r. Kazakh.
110 D3 **Chagny** France
75 C7 **Chagos Archipelago** is
   British Indian Ocean Terr.
162 I5 **Chagos-Laccadive Ridge**
   sea feature Indian Ocean
162 I5 **Chagos Trench** sea feature
   Indian Ocean
116 I4 **Chagra** r. Rus. Fed.
150 J6 **Chagres, Parque Nacional**
   nat. park Panama
157 D2 **Chaguaramas** Venez.
82 C4 **Chagyl** Turkm.
85 F4 **Cha'gyüngoinba** China
85 F4 **Chahah Burjal** Afgh.
85 F3 **Chahchaheh** Afgh.
85 E3 **Chahār Rüstā'ī** Iran
85 E3 **Chahār Takāb** Iran
81 K3 **Chāh Bahār** Iran
84 D4 **Chāh Badam** Iran
84 D4 **Chāh-e Bāgh** well Iran
84 D3 **Chāh-e Kavīr** well Iran
84 D3 **Chāh-e Khorāsān** well Iran
84 D3 **Chāh-e Khoshāb** Iran
84 D3 **Chāh-e Mīrzā** well Iran
84 D4 **Chāh-e Mūjān** well Iran
84 D4 **Chāh-e Nūklok** Iran
84 D4 **Chāh-e Nūklok** well Iran
84 D3 **Chāh-e Qeyşar** well Iran
84 D3 **Chāh-e Qobād** well Iran
84 D4 **Chāh-e Rāh** Iran
84 D3 **Chāh-e Raḩmān** well Iran
84 E3 **Chāh-e Shūr** Iran
84 D4 **Chāh-e Shūr** well Iran
84 D3 **Chāh Haji Abdulla** well Iran
84 D3 **Chāh Ḩaqq** Iran
85 H2 **Chāh-i-Āb** Afgh.
81 J4 **Chāh-i-Shurkh** Iraq
85 E3 **Chāh Lak** Iran
84 D3 **Chāh Pas** well Iran
85 F4 **Chāh Sandan** Pak.
89 F3 **Chaibasa** India
133 G3 **Chaigneau, Lac** l. Canada
96 C2 **Chai He** r. China
98 B2 **Chainat** Thai.
98 B2 **Chai Si** r. Thai.
93 □ **Chai Wan** Hong Kong China
98 A3 **Chaiya** Thai.
98 B2 **Chaiyaphum** Thai.
159 F1 **Chajari** Arg.
89 H5 **Chakar** r. Pak.
85 H3 **Chakaria** Bangl.
85 F4 **Chakhānsūr** Afgh.
89 E4 **Chakia** India
88 D5 **Chakku** Pak.
115 J5 **Chalkida** Greece
83 I4 **Chalkudysu** Kazakh.
72 A7 **Chalky Inlet** N.Z.
110 D3 **Challans** France
154 D7 **Challapata** Bol.
160 E5 **Challenger Deep** sea feature
   N. Pacific Ocean
110 G2 **Châlons-en-Champagne**
   France
110 G3 **Chalon-sur-Saône** France
84 C2 **Chālūs** Iran
108 F5 **Cham** Germany
139 F4 **Chama** U.S.A.
157 C2 **Chama** r. Venez.
123 D5 **Chama** Zambia
159 D2 **Chamaico** Arg.
123 A3 **Chamais Bay** Namibia
85 G4 **Chaman** Pak.
88 D2 **Chamba** India
131 H4 **Chambeaux, Lac** l. Canada
131 H3 **Chamberlain** Canada
142 D3 **Chamberlain** U.S.A.
147 I1 **Chamberlain Lake** U.S.A.
141 H4 **Chambers** U.S.A.
146 E5 **Chambersburg** U.S.A.
110 G4 **Chambéry** France
123 D5 **Chambeshi** Zambia
110 G3 **Chambon-sur-Lac** France
110 G4 **Chamechaude** mt. France
142 F3 **Chamisal** U.S.A.
84 C3 **Chamishk** Iran

159 C1 **Chamical** Arg.
89 F4 **Chamlang** mt. Nepal
98 B3 **Châmnar** Cambodia
130 B2 **Champa** India
110 G2 **Champagne** reg. France
125 H4 **Champagne Castle** mt. S. Africa
110 G3 **Champagnole** France
134 C5 **Champaign** U.S.A.
159 D1 **Champaqui, Cerro** mt. Arg.
98 C2 **Champasak** Laos
89 H5 **Champhai** India
134 D2 **Champlain** U.S.A.
147 G2 **Champlain** U.S.A.
147 G2 **Champlain, Lake** l. Canada/U.S.A.
151 G4 **Champotón** Mex.
87 B4 **Chamrajnagar** India
116 H4 **Chamzinka** Rus. Fed.
98 B4 **Chana** Thai.
156 B3 **Chañaral** Chile
157 E3 **Chanaro, Cerro** mt. Venez.
159 B2 **Chanco** Chile
128 D3 **Chandalar** r. U.S.A.
87 C1 **Chandanpur** India
88 D3 **Chandausi** India
143 F6 **Chandeleur Islands** U.S.A.
88 E5 **Chandia** India
88 D3 **Chandigarh** India
141 G5 **Chandler** U.S.A.
135 I3 **Chandler** Canada
88 B3 **Chandpur** Bangl.
88 D3 **Chandpur** India
88 H5 **Chandraghona** Bangl.
88 D6 **Chandrapur** India
88 D5 **Chandur** India
98 B2 **Chang, Ko** i. Thai.
123 D6 **Changane** r. Moz.
123 D5 **Changara** Moz.
96 B3 **Changbai** China
96 B3 **Changbai Shan** mts
   China/N. Korea
93 C7 **Changcheng** China
96 C1 **Changchun** China
96 C1 **Changchunling** China
92 F2 **Changdao** China
96 D4 **Ch'angdo** N. Korea
92 E3 **Changfeng** China
96 D6 **Changgi-ap** pt S. Korea
96 D5 **Changhang** S. Korea
96 D6 **Changhowŏn** S. Korea
93 F5 **Changhua** Taiwan
96 C1 **Changhua Jiang** r. China
96 D5 **Changhŭng** S. Korea
98 □ **Changi** Sing.
93 C7 **Changjiang** China
93 E4 **Chang Jiang** r. China
   alt. Jinsha Jiang,
   alt. Tongtian He,
   alt. Zhi Qu,
   conv. Yangtze,
   long Yangtze Kiang
96 D3 **Changjin** N. Korea
96 D3 **Changjin-gang** r. N. Korea
96 D3 **Changjin-ho** N. Korea
93 F5 **Changle** China
93 C5 **Changli** China
96 B1 **Changling** China
93 D5 **Changning** China
96 C4 **Changnyŏn** N. Korea
92 E1 **Changping** China
92 F5 **Chang'yŏng** S. Korea
96 A4 **Changxing Dao** i. China
93 E5 **Changyang** China
92 F2 **Changyi** China
92 E3 **Changyuan** China
96 D3 **Changyŏn** N. Korea
92 C2 **Changzhou** China
115 K7 **Chania** Greece
92 B3 **Chankou** China
87 B3 **Channapatna** India
   Channel Islands terr.
   English Chan.
140 C5 **Channel Islands** U.S.A.
140 B5 **Channel Islands National Park**
   U.S.A.
133 I4 **Channel-Port-aux-Basques**
   Canada
105 I6 **Channel Tunnel** France/U.K.
134 C2 **Channing** U.S.A.
111 C1 **Chantada** Spain
98 B2 **Chanthaburi** Thai.
110 F2 **Chantilly** France
114 D7 **Chanute** U.S.A.
76 I4 **Chany, Ozero** salt l. Rus. Fed.
92 E4 **Chaobai Xinhe** r. China
92 E4 **Chaohu** China
92 E4 **Chaohu** l. China
98 B2 **Chao Phraya** r. Thai.
120 B1 **Chaouèn** Morocco
89 H2 **Chaowula Shan** mts China
93 E6 **Chaoyang** Guangdong China
92 E5 **Chaoyang** Liaoning China
93 E6 **Chaozhou** China
158 E1 **Chapada Diamantina, Parque**
   Nacional nat. park Brazil
158 A1 **Chapada dos Guimarães**
   Brazil
158 C1 **Chapada dos Veadeiros,**
   Parque Nacional da
   nat. park Brazil
151 E5 **Chapala** Mex.
150 D3 **Chapala, Laguna de** l. Mex.
157 B4 **Chaparral** Col.
82 B2 **Chapayev** Kazakh.
116 I4 **Chapayevsk** Rus. Fed.
83 H1 **Chapayevskoye** Kazakh.
156 F3 **Chapecó** Brazil
156 F3 **Chapecó** r. Brazil
105 F4 **Chapel-en-le-Frith** U.K.
145 D5 **Chapel Hill** U.S.A.
108 C4 **Chapelle-lez-Herlaimont**
   Belgium
105 F4 **Chapeltown** U.K.
134 D5 **Chapin** U.S.A.
135 F2 **Chapleau** Canada
116 F4 **Chaplygin** Rus. Fed.
117 E5 **Chaplynka** Ukr.
146 B6 **Chapmanville** U.S.A.
71 G8 **Chappell Islands** Australia
85 F4 **Chapri Pass** Afgh.
154 E7 **Chaqui** Bol.
88 D2 **Char** Jammu and Kashmir
150 D3 **Charcas** Mex.
89 H3 **Char Chu** r. China
73 **Charcot Island** Antarctica
131 G3 **Chard** Canada
105 E5 **Chard** U.K.
83 G4 **Chardara, Step'** plain Kazakh.
83 G4 **Chardarinskoye Vdkhr.** resr
   Kazakh./Uzbek.
81 K5 **Chārdāvol** Iran
146 C4 **Chardon** U.S.A.
110 D3 **Charente** r. France
85 H3 **Chari** r. Afgh.
142 D2 **Chariton** r. U.S.A.
135 F3 **Charity Island** U.S.A.
84 C4 **Charkas** Iran

76 G3 **Charkayuvom** Rus. Fed.
88 D4 **Charkhari** India
108 C4 **Charleroi** Belgium
134 A4 **Charles, Cape** pt U.S.A.
137 K4 **Charles City** U.S.A.
108 A5 **Charles de Gaulle** airport
   France
72 C4 **Charleston** N.Z.
144 B4 **Charleston** IL U.S.A.
142 I2 **Charleston** MO U.S.A.
143 F4 **Charleston** MO U.S.A.
146 E5 **Charleston** SC U.S.A.
146 C5 **Charleston** WV U.S.A.
141 E3 **Charleston Peak** mt. U.S.A.
107 C4 **Charlestown** Rep. of Ireland
147 G3 **Charlestown** NH U.S.A.
147 H4 **Charlestown** RI U.S.A.
146 E5 **Charles Town** U.S.A.
134 E3 **Charleville** Australia
130 E3 **Charleville-Mézières** France
134 A4 **Charlevoix, Lake** l. Canada
134 E4 **Charlotte** MI U.S.A.
145 D5 **Charlotte** NC U.S.A.
145 D7 **Charlotte Harbor** b. U.S.A.
133 H4 **Charlottetown** Canada
157 E2 **Charlotteville** Trin. and Tob.
70 E6 **Charlton** Australia
132 E3 **Charlton Island** Canada
88 B2 **Charsadda** Pak.
68 E3 **Charters Towers** Australia
110 E2 **Chartres** France
83 G4 **Charvakskoye Vdkhr.** resr
   Kazakh./Uzbek.
83 I4 **Charyn** Kazakh.
83 I4 **Charyn** r. Kazakh.
83 J1 **Charysh** r. Rus. Fed.
83 J2 **Charyshskoye** Rus. Fed.
159 E2 **Chascomús** Arg.
130 F4 **Chase** Canada
82 E5 **Chashkent** Turkm.
84 D3 **Chashmeh** ME Iran
84 D3 **Chashmeh-ye Palasi** Iran
84 D3 **Chashmeh-ye Shotoran**
   well Iran
116 D4 **Chashniki** Belarus
72 B7 **Chaslands Mistake** c. N.Z.
96 D3 **Chasŏng** N. Korea
84 D3 **Chāstāb, Kūh-e** mts Iran
110 D3 **Châteaubriant** France
110 E2 **Château-du-Loir** France
110 E2 **Châteaudun** France
147 F2 **Chateaugay** U.S.A.
147 G2 **Châteauguay** Canada
110 E3 **Châteaulin** France
110 E3 **Châteauneuf-sur-Loire** France
110 E3 **Châteauroux** France
108 E6 **Château-Salins** France
110 F2 **Château-Thierry** France
108 C4 **Châtelet** Belgium
110 E3 **Châtellerault** France
134 A4 **Chatfield** U.S.A.
105 H6 **Chatham** U.K.
147 H4 **Chatham** MA U.S.A.
147 G3 **Chatham** NY U.S.A.
146 D4 **Chatham** VA U.S.A.
69 I6 **Chatham Islands** N.Z.
160 H8 **Chatham Rise** sea feature
   S. Pacific Ocean
130 C4 **Chatham Sound** sea chan.
   Canada
130 C4 **Chatham Strait** U.S.A.
83 G4 **Chatkal** r. Kazakh.
83 G4 **Chatkal Range** mts Kyrg.
135 E4 **Chatsworth** Canada
105 G6 **Chatsworth** U.S.A.
145 C5 **Chattanooga** U.S.A.
76 F3 **Chatteris** U.K.
98 B2 **Chatturat** Thai.
83 H4 **Chatyr-Köl** l. Kyrg.
83 I4 **Chatyr-Tash** Kyrg.
98 C3 **Châu Đốc** Vietnam
88 B4 **Chauhtan** India
89 H5 **Chauk** Myanmar
88 E4 **Chauka** r. India
88 D3 **Chaukhamba** mts India
110 G2 **Chaumont** France
98 A2 **Chaungwabyin** Myanmar
77 R3 **Chaunskaya Guba** b. Rus. Fed.
110 F2 **Chauny** France
88 E5 **Chauparan** India
146 D3 **Chautauqua, Lake** l. U.S.A.
87 C4 **Chauvay** Kyrg.
116 D4 **Chavusy** Belarus
93 B6 **Chây** r. Vietnam
159 D2 **Chazón** Arg.
147 G2 **Chazy** U.S.A.
105 F5 **Cheadle** U.K.
146 D5 **Cheat** r. U.S.A.
109 L4 **Cheb** Czech Rep.
114 D7 **Chebba** Tunisia
116 H3 **Cheboksary** Rus. Fed.
134 E3 **Cheboygan** U.S.A.
117 H7 **Chechen', Ostrov** i. Rus. Fed.
117 H7 **Chechenskaya Respublika**
   aut. rep. Rus. Fed.
   Chechnia aut. rep. Rus. Fed. see
   Chechenskaya Respublika
96 C5 **Chechŏn** S. Korea
143 E5 **Checotah** U.S.A.
96 A5 **Chedao** China
105 E5 **Cheddar** U.K.
131 G3 **Cheecham** Canada
73 B5 **Cheetham, Cape** Antarctica
128 B3 **Chefornak** U.S.A.
125 J1 **Chefu** Moz.
120 B2 **Chegga** Mauritania
123 D5 **Chegutu** Zimbabwe
85 H3 **Chehardar Pass** Afgh.
96 C5 **Cheju** S. Korea
96 D7 **Cheju do** i. S. Korea
90 D7 **Cheju do** i. S. Korea
96 D7 **Cheju-do** i. S. Korea
96 D7 **Cheju-haehyŏp** sea chan.
   S. Korea
116 F4 **Chekhov** Rus. Fed.
138 B2 **Chelan, Lake** l. U.S.A.
82 C5 **Cheleken** Turkm.
159 C3 **Chelforó** Arg.
111 G4 **Chélif, Oued** r. Alg.
82 B2 **Chelkar** Kazakh.
113 K5 **Chełm** Poland
105 H5 **Chelmer** r. U.K.
113 I4 **Chełmno** Poland
147 H3 **Chelmsford** U.S.A.
105 H6 **Chelmsford** U.K.
105 E6 **Cheltenham** U.K.
111 F3 **Chelva** Spain
76 H4 **Chelyabinsk** Rus. Fed.
126 D2 **Chemba** Moz.
109 K4 **Chemnitz** Germany
146 E3 **Chemung** r. U.S.A.
85 H2 **Chenab** r. India/Pak.
120 B2 **Chenachane** Alg.
147 F3 **Chenango** r. U.S.A.
138 C2 **Cheney** U.S.A.
143 D4 **Cheney Reservoir** U.S.A.
87 B2 **Chengalpattu** India
92 E2 **Cheng'an** China
92 B3 **Chengbu** China
92 E1 **Chengde** China
93 B4 **Chengdu** China

92 C3 **Chenggu** China
93 E6 **Chenghai** China
92 C4 **Chengkou** China
91 D5 **Chengmai** China
96 B4 **Chengzitan** China
92 F3 **Cheniu Shan** i. China
87 D3 **Chennai** India
134 C5 **Chenoa** U.S.A.
93 D5 **Chenxi** China
93 D5 **Chenzhou** China
98 D2 **Cheo Reo** Vietnam
154 C5 **Chepén** Peru
159 C1 **Chepes** Arg.
150 J6 **Chepo** Panama
105 E6 **Chepstow** U.K.
116 I3 **Cheptsa** r. Rus. Fed.
110 F3 **Cher** r. France
134 B2 **Cheraw** Mex.
145 E5 **Cheraw** U.S.A.
110 D2 **Cherbourg** France
111 H4 **Cherchell** Alg.
116 I4 **Cherdakly** Rus. Fed.
90 C1 **Cheremkhovo** Rus. Fed.
83 J1 **Cheremnoye** Rus. Fed.
94 C2 **Cheremshany** Rus. Fed.
116 H2 **Cherevkovo** Rus. Fed.
114 B7 **Chéria** Alg.
117 E5 **Cherkasy** Ukr.
117 G6 **Cherkessk** Rus. Fed.
87 C2 **Cherla** India
83 H1 **Cherlak** Rus. Fed.
83 H1 **Cherlakskoye** Rus. Fed.
123 G4 **Chermenze** Angola
94 G3 **Chermoz** Rus. Fed.
117 F6 **Cherniivka** Ukr.
117 C5 **Cherniiv** Ukr.
90 B1 **Chernogorsk** Rus. Fed.
83 I1 **Chernoretskoye** Kazakh.
117 H3 **Chernovskoye** Rus. Fed.
117 E5 **Chernyakhiv** Ukr.
113 J3 **Chernyakhovsk** Rus. Fed.
117 F6 **Chernyanka** Rus. Fed.
116 I4 **Chernyshevskiy** Rus. Fed.
77 M3 **Chernyshevskiy** Rus. Fed.
117 H6 **Chernyye Zemli** reg. Rus. Fed.
82 C2 **Chernyy Otrog** Rus. Fed.
117 H5 **Chernyy Yar** Rus. Fed.
114 E3 **Cherokee** IA U.S.A.
143 D4 **Cherokee** OK U.S.A.
143 E4 **Cherokees, Lake o' the** U.S.A.
143 F4 **Cherokee Sound** Bahamas
89 G4 **Cherrapunji** India
141 E2 **Cherry Creek** U.S.A.
141 E1 **Cherry Creek Mountains** U.S.A.
135 H3 **Cherryfield** U.S.A.
69 G3 **Cherry Island** Solomon Is
147 F2 **Cherry Valley** Canada
147 F3 **Cherry Valley** U.S.A.
77 P3 **Cherskogo, Khrebet** mts
   Rus. Fed.
117 G5 **Chertkovo** Rus. Fed.
116 I2 **Cherva** Rus. Fed.
115 K3 **Cherven Bryag** Bulg.
117 C5 **Chervonohrad** Ukr.
117 E5 **Chervonozavods'ke** Ukr.
116 C4 **Chervyen'** Belarus
116 D4 **Cherykaw** Belarus
105 F6 **Cherwell** r. U.K.
135 E4 **Chesaning** U.S.A.
147 E6 **Chesapeake** U.S.A.
146 E6 **Chesapeake Bay** U.S.A.
105 G6 **Chesham** U.K.
147 G3 **Cheshire** U.S.A.
105 E4 **Cheshire Plain** U.K.
82 E5 **Cheshme Vtoroy** Turkm.
76 F3 **Cheshskaya Guba** b. Rus. Fed.
83 H5 **Cheshtebe** Tajik.
85 F3 **Chesht-e Sharīf** Afgh.
82 C1 **Chesma** Rus. Fed.
105 E4 **Chester** U.K.
140 B1 **Chester** CA U.S.A.
144 B4 **Chester** IL U.S.A.
138 E1 **Chester** MT U.S.A.
147 H3 **Chester** PA U.S.A.
146 E5 **Chester** PA U.S.A.
145 D5 **Chester** SC U.S.A.
147 G3 **Chester** VT U.S.A.
105 F4 **Chesterfield** U.K.
69 F3 **Chesterfield, Îles** is
   New Caledonia
131 K2 **Chesterfield Inlet** Canada
131 K2 **Chesterfield Inlet** inlet Canada
104 F3 **Chester-le-Street** U.K.
147 E5 **Chestertown** MD U.S.A.
147 G3 **Chestertown** NY U.S.A.
146 F2 **Chesterville** Canada
146 D5 **Chestnut Ridge** U.S.A.
147 I1 **Chesuncook** U.S.A.
147 I1 **Chesuncook Lake** U.S.A.
114 B6 **Chetaïbi** Alg.
133 H4 **Chéticamp** Canada
87 A4 **Chetlat** i. India
151 G4 **Chetumal** Mex.
130 E3 **Chetwynd** Canada
93 □ **Cheung Chau** Hong Kong China
93 □ **Cheung Chau** i. Hong Kong
   China
72 D5 **Cheviot** N.Z.
104 E2 **Cheviot Hills** U.K.
138 C1 **Chewelah** U.S.A.
143 D5 **Cheyenne** OK U.S.A.
138 F3 **Cheyenne** WY U.S.A.
142 C2 **Cheyenne** r. U.S.A.
142 C3 **Cheyenne Wells** U.S.A.
130 E4 **Chezacut** Canada
88 D4 **Chhapar** India
89 F4 **Chhapra** India
88 D5 **Chhatr** Pak.
88 D4 **Chhata** India
88 E5 **Chhatarpur** India
88 E5 **Chhindwara** India
88 D5 **Chhota Udepur** India
89 G6 **Chhukha** Bhutan
93 F5 **Chiai** Taiwan
122 A1 **Chiamboni** Kenya
98 A1 **Chiang Dao** Thai.
98 A1 **Chiang Khan** Thai.
98 A1 **Chiang Rai** Thai.
151 F5 **Chiapas** state Mex.
114 E2 **Chiari** Italy
151 F5 **Chiautla** Mex.
95 G7 **Chiba** Japan
123 C5 **Chibi** China
123 C5 **Chiboma** Angola
133 F4 **Chibougamau** Canada
133 F4 **Chibougamau, Lac** l. Canada
95 E6 **Chibu-Sangaku National Park**
   Japan
125 J2 **Chibuto** Moz.
89 D5 **Chibuzhang Hu** l. China
134 D5 **Chicago** U.S.A.
   (City Plan **61**)
134 D5 **Chicago Heights** U.S.A.
134 D5 **Chicago Ship Canal** U.S.A.
157 C2 **Chicamocha** r. Col.
157 B2 **Chicanán** r. Venez.
130 C3 **Chichagof** U.S.A.
130 C3 **Chichagof Island** U.S.A.
151 G4 **Chichén Itzá** tourist site Mex.
105 G7 **Chichester** U.K.
68 B4 **Chichester Range** mts Australia
95 F6 **Chichibu** Japan
95 F7 **Chichibu-Tama National Park**
   Japan
146 E6 **Chickahominy** r. U.S.A.

145 C5 **Chickamauga Lake** U.S.A.
143 D5 **Chickasha** U.S.A.
111 C4 **Chiclana de la Frontera** Spain
154 C5 **Chiclayo** Peru
156 C6 **Chico** r. Chubut Arg.
159 B4 **Chico** r. Chubut/Río Negro Arg.
156 C7 **Chico** r. Arg.
140 B2 **Chico** U.S.A.
125 K2 **Chicomo** Moz.
150 C2 **Chicomucelo** Mex.
147 G3 **Chicopee** U.S.A.
97 B2 **Chico Sapocoy, Mount** Phil.
133 F4 **Chicoutimi** Canada
125 I1 **Chicualacuala** Moz.
87 B3 **Chidambaram** India
125 K2 **Chidenguele** Moz.
133 H1 **Chidley, Cape** Canada
96 D6 **Chido** S. Korea
123 C5 **Chiducuane** Moz.
145 D6 **Chiefland** U.S.A.
112 F7 **Chieri** Italy
114 F3 **Chieti** Italy
92 F1 **Chifeng** China
158 E2 **Chifre, Serra do** mts Brazil
83 H3 **Chiganak** Kazakh.
133 G4 **Chignecto Bay** Canada
157 A3 **Chigorodó** Col.
123 D6 **Chigubo** Moz.
89 C3 **Chigu Co** l. China
150 C1 **Chihuahua** Mex.
150 C1 **Chihuahua** state Mex.
83 F3 **Chiili** Kazakh.
93 D5 **Chikan** China
89 D5 **Chik Ballapur** India
116 D3 **Chikhachevo** Rus. Fed.
88 D5 **Chikhali Kalan Parasia** India
88 D5 **Chikhli** India
87 A3 **Chikmagalur** India
95 H5 **Chikuma-gawa** r. Japan
130 E4 **Chilanko Forks** Canada
151 E4 **Chilapa** Mex.
87 B4 **Chilas** Jammu and Kashmir
87 B5 **Chilaw** Sri Lanka
130 E4 **Chilcotin** r. Canada
143 C5 **Childress** U.S.A.
156 B5 **Chile** country S. America
161 N8 **Chile Basin** sea feature
   S. Pacific Ocean
156 C3 **Chilecito** Arg.
161 N8 **Chile Rise** sea feature
   S. Pacific Ocean
159 B3 **Chillán** Chile
159 B3 **Chillán, Nevado** mts Chile
159 B3 **Chillar** Arg.
134 C5 **Chillicothe** IL U.S.A.
142 E4 **Chillicothe** MO U.S.A.
146 B5 **Chillicothe** OH U.S.A.
130 E5 **Chilliwack** Canada
159 B3 **Chiloé, Isla de** i. Chile
138 B3 **Chiloquin** U.S.A.
151 E4 **Chilpancingo** Mex.
105 G6 **Chiltern** U.K.
105 G6 **Chiltern Hills** U.K.
134 C3 **Chilton** U.S.A.
93 F6 **Chilung** Taiwan
88 D2 **Chilung Pass** India
123 D5 **Chimala** Tanz.
150 J6 **Chimán** Panama
108 C4 **Chimay** Belgium
108 C4 **Chimay, Bois de** for. Belgium
82 C4 **Chimbay** Uzbek.
154 C4 **Chimborazo** mt. Ecuador
154 C5 **Chimbote** Peru
157 B2 **Chimichaguá** Col.
123 D5 **Chimoio** Moz.
151 E2 **China** Mex.
161 K4 **China** country Asia
141 E4 **China Lake** CA U.S.A.
147 I2 **China Lake** ME U.S.A.
151 G4 **Chinajá** Guat.
150 J6 **Chinandega** Nicaragua
140 C5 **China Point** U.S.A.
147 I2 **Chinati Peak** U.S.A.
154 C6 **Chincha Alta** Peru
130 F4 **Chinchaga** r. Canada
148 E5 **Chinchorro, Banco** is Mex.
147 F6 **Chincoteague Bay** U.S.A.
123 D6 **Chinde** Moz.
96 D6 **Chin-do** i. S. Korea
96 D6 **Chindo** S. Korea
90 B3 **Chindu** China
89 H5 **Chindwin** r. Myanmar
88 C2 **Chineni** Jammu and Kashmir
157 B3 **Chingaza, Parque Nacional**
   nat. park Col.
96 C4 **Chinghwa** N. Korea
83 I2 **Chingirlau** Kazakh.
123 C5 **Chingola** Zambia
123 B5 **Chinguar** Angola
96 E6 **Chinhae** S. Korea
123 D5 **Chinhoyi** Zimbabwe
88 C2 **Chiniot** Pak.
150 B2 **Chinipas** Mex.
96 E6 **Chinju** S. Korea
122 C3 **Chinko** r. Centr. Afr. Rep.
141 H3 **Chinle** U.S.A.
141 H3 **Chinle Valley** valley U.S.A.
93 F5 **Chinmen** Taiwan
93 F5 **Chinmen Tao** i. Taiwan
87 B2 **Chinnur** India
95 H7 **Chino** Japan
110 E3 **Chinon** France
141 G5 **Chino Valley** U.S.A.
123 D5 **Chinsali** Zambia
87 B2 **Chintamani** India
114 E2 **Chioggia** Italy
115 L5 **Chios** Greece
115 L5 **Chios** i. Greece
123 D5 **Chipata** Zambia
159 B4 **Chipchihua, Sierra de** mts Arg.
123 B5 **Chipindo** Angola
123 D6 **Chipinge** Zimbabwe
105 E6 **Chippenham** U.K.
134 B3 **Chippewa, Lake** l. U.S.A.
134 B3 **Chippewa Falls** U.S.A.
134 A3 **Chippewa, Lake** l. U.S.A.
105 F6 **Chipping Norton** U.K.
105 F6 **Chipping Sodbury** U.K.
147 J2 **Chiputneticook Lakes**
   Canada/U.S.A.
154 C5 **Chiquián** Peru
157 B2 **Chiquinquirá** Col.
151 H5 **Chiquibul, Parque Nacional**
   nat. park Belize
151 G5 **Chiquimula** Guat.
157 B3 **Chiquinquirá** Col.
87 B3 **Chirala** India
87 A2 **Chirakkal** India
88 C3 **Chirawa** India
83 G4 **Chirchik** Uzbek.

123 D6 Chiredzi Zimbabwe
141 H5 Chiricahua National Monument res. U.S.A.
141 H6 Chiricahua Peak mt. U.S.A.
157 B2 Chiriguaná Col.
128 C4 Chirikof Island U.S.A.
150 I6 Chiriquí, Golfo de b. Panama
150 I6 Chiriquí, Laguna de b. Panama
105 D5 Chirk U.K.
106 F5 Chirnside U.K.
115 K3 Chirpan Bulg.
117 I6 Chirripó mt. Costa Rica
123 C5 Chirundu Zambia
132 E3 Chisasibi Canada
151 G5 Chisec Guat.
134 A2 Chisholm U.S.A.
88 C3 Chishtian Mandi Pak.
93 B4 Chishui China
117 D6 Chişinău Moldova
113 J7 Chişineu-Criş Romania
116 I4 Chistopol' Rus. Fed.
90 D1 Chita Rus. Fed.
123 D5 Chitado Angola
123 D5 Chitambo Zambia
122 C4 Chitato Angola
131 H4 Chitek Lake Canada
123 B5 Chitembo Angola
123 D5 Chitipa Malawi
123 C5 Chitokoloki Zambia
94 G3 Chitose Japan
87 B3 Chitradurga India
88 B2 Chitral Pak.
88 B2 Chitral r. Pak.
150 I7 Chitré Panama
89 G5 Chittagong Bangl.
89 F5 Chittaranjan India
88 C4 Chittaurgarh India
87 B3 Chittoor India
87 B4 Chittur India
123 D5 Chitungulu Zambia
123 D5 Chitungwiza Zimbabwe
123 C5 Chiume Angola
150 A2 Chivato, Punta pt Mex.
123 D5 Chivhu Zimbabwe
159 E2 Chivilcoy Arg.
93 D6 Chixi China
82 B2 Chizha Vtoraya Kazakh.
95 D7 Chizu Japan
83 G1 Chkalovo Kazakh.
116 G3 Chkalovskoye Rus. Fed.
94 C2 Chkalovskoye Rus. Fed.
98 □ Choa Chu Kang Sing.
98 □ Choa Chu Kang hill Sing.
95 C2 Chŏâm Khsant Cambodia
159 B1 Choapa r. Chile
123 C5 Chobe National Park Botswana
96 D5 Choch'iwŏn S. Korea
141 H5 Chocolate Mountains U.S.A.
157 B3 Chocontá Col.
96 C4 Cho-do i. N. Korea
96 D6 Cho-e-do i. S. Korea
109 K4 Chodov Czech Rep.
159 D3 Choele Choel Arg.
88 C2 Chogo Lungma Glacier Pak.
Chogori Feng mt. China/Jammu and Kashmir see K2
117 H6 Chograyskoye Vodokhranilishche resr Rus. Fed.
131 I4 Choiceland Canada
69 F2 Choiseul i. Solomon Is
156 E8 Choiseul Sound sea chan. Falkland Is
150 B2 Choix Mex.
112 H4 Chojnice Poland
94 G4 Chōkai-san vol. Japan
143 D6 Choke Canyon Lake U.S.A.
122 D2 Ch'ok'ē Mountains Eth.
83 H4 Chokpar Kazakh.
89 F3 Choksum China
77 P2 Chokurdakh Rus. Fed.
123 D6 Chókwé Moz.
110 D3 Cholet France
159 B4 Cholila Arg.
83 H4 Cholpon Kyrg.
83 H4 Cholpon-Ata Kyrg.
150 H5 Choluteca Hond.
123 C5 Choma Zambia
96 E5 Chŏmch'ŏn S. Korea
89 G4 Chomo Lhari mt. Bhutan
98 A1 Chom Thong Thai.
112 F5 Chomutov Czech Rep.
77 L3 Chona r. Rus. Fed.
96 D5 Ch'ŏnan S. Korea
98 B2 Chon Buri Thai.
96 D3 Ch'ŏnch'ŏn N. Korea
154 B4 Chone Ecuador
96 C4 Ch'ŏngch'ŏn-gang r. N. Korea
96 E5 Ch'ŏngdo S. Korea
96 E3 Ch'ŏngjin N. Korea
96 C5 Chŏngju N. Korea
96 B2 Chŏngju N. Korea
96 D4 Ch'ŏngju S. Korea
93 D4 Chongqing China
93 E5 Chongqing prov. China
93 E5 Chongren China
125 J2 Chonguene Moz.
123 C5 Chongwe Zambia
93 D6 Chongyang China
93 F5 Chongyang Xi r. China
93 E5 Chongyi China
93 D6 Chongzuo China
96 D6 Chŏnju S. Korea
89 F3 Cho Oyu mt. China/Nepal
98 C3 Chơ Phước Hai Vietnam
158 B4 Chopim r. Brazil
158 B4 Chopimzinho Brazil
147 F5 Choptank r. U.S.A.
88 B4 Chor Pak.
104 E4 Chorley U.K.
117 D5 Chornobyl' Ukr.
117 E6 Chornomors'ke Ukr.
117 C5 Chortkiv Ukr.
96 D4 Ch'ŏrwŏn S. Korea
96 C4 Ch'osan N. Korea
95 G7 Chōshi Japan
159 B3 Chos Malal Arg.
112 G4 Choszczno Poland
154 B5 Chota Peru
138 D2 Choteau U.S.A.
88 B3 Choti Pak.
120 A2 Choûm Mauritania
142 D4 Chowchilla U.S.A.
92 C1 Choyr Mongolia
90 C2 Choybalsan Mongolia
112 H6 Chřiby hill Czech Rep.
134 D6 Chrisman U.S.A.
125 I3 Chrissiesmeer S. Africa
67 D5 Christchurch N.Z.
105 F7 Christchurch U.K.
129 L2 Christian r. Canada
125 F3 Christiana S. Africa
135 G3 Christian Island Canada
146 C6 Christiansburg U.S.A.
Christianshåb Greenland see Qasigiannguit
130 C3 Christian Sound sea chan. U.S.A.
131 K3 Christina r. Canada
91 C8 Christmas Island terr. Indian Ocean
112 G6 Chrudim Czech Rep.
115 K7 Chrysi i. Greece
76 H5 Chu r. Kazakh.
89 G5 Chuadanga Bangl.
92 H4 Chuanshan China
123 C5 Chubbuck U.S.A.
159 C4 Chubut prov. Arg.
156 C6 Chubut r. Arg.

141 E5 Chuckwalla Mountains U.S.A.
117 D5 Chudniv Ukr.
116 D3 Chudovo Rus. Fed.
128 C4 Chugach Mountains U.S.A.
95 C7 Chūgoku-sanchi mts Japan
94 C2 Chuguyevka Rus. Fed.
138 F3 Chugwater U.S.A.
117 F5 Chuhuyiv Ukr.
141 G5 Chuichu U.S.A.
83 H3 Chu-Iliyskiye Gory mts Kazakh.
90 F1 Chukchagirskoye, Ozero l. Rus. Fed.
164 M1 Chukchi Plateau sea feature Arctic Ocean
77 U3 Chukchi Sea Rus. Fed./U.S.A.
116 G3 Chukhloma Rus. Fed.
77 T3 Chukotskiy Poluostrov pen. Rus. Fed.
116 H1 Chulasa Rus. Fed.
140 D5 Chula Vista U.S.A.
76 J4 Chulym Rus. Fed.
89 G4 Chumbi China
156 C5 Chumbicha Arg.
83 K2 Chumek Kazakh.
90 F1 Chumikan Rus. Fed.
98 B1 Chum Phae Thai.
98 B2 Chum Saeng Thai.
77 K4 Chuna r. Rus. Fed.
93 F4 Chun'an China
96 D5 Ch'unch'ŏn S. Korea
89 G5 Chunchura India
83 I4 Chundzha Kazakh.
96 D5 Ch'ungju S. Korea
Chungking China see Chongqing
96 C4 Chŭngsan N. Korea
85 H3 Chungur, Koh-i- hill Afgh.
93 F6 Chungyang Shanmo mts Taiwan
96 F2 Chunhua China
151 G4 Chunhuhux Mex.
77 L3 Chunya r. Rus. Fed.
81 K3 Chūpluī Iran
154 D7 Chuquibamba Peru
156 C6 Chuquicamata Chile
112 D7 Chur Switz.
77 O3 Churapcha Rus. Fed.
131 K3 Churchill Canada
131 J3 Churchill r. Man./Sask. Canada
133 H3 Churchill r. Nfld Canada
131 K3 Churchill, Cape Canada
133 H3 Churchill Falls Canada
131 K3 Churchill Lake Canada
128 C4 Churchill Peak mt. Canada
132 E2 Churchill Sound sea chan. Canada
142 D1 Churchs Ferry U.S.A.
146 D5 Churchville U.S.A.
89 F4 Churia Ghati Hills Nepal
116 H3 Churov Rus. Fed.
88 C3 Churu India
Churubay Nura Kazakh. see Abay
157 C2 Churuguara Venez.
88 D2 Chushul Jammu and Kashmir
141 H3 Chuska Mountains U.S.A.
83 G4 Chust Uzbek.
133 F4 Chute-des-Passes Canada
135 I2 Chute-Rouge Canada
135 J2 Chute-St-Philippe Canada
93 F5 Chutung Taiwan
67 E2 Chuuk is Micronesia
116 H4 Chuvashskaya Respublika aut. rep. Rus. Fed.
93 A5 Chuxiong China
98 D2 Chư Yang Sin mt. Vietnam
92 F3 Chuzhou China
81 M1 Chwārtā Iraq
117 D6 Ciadîr-Lunga Moldova
99 C4 Ciamis Indon.
99 C4 Cianjur Indon.
158 B3 Cianorte Brazil
114 F2 Čićarija mts Croatia
80 E2 Çiçekdağ Turkey
117 E7 Cide Turkey
113 J4 Ciechanów Poland
149 I4 Ciego de Avila Cuba
157 B2 Ciénaga Col.
151 D2 Ciénega de Flores Mex.
149 H4 Cienfuegos Cuba
111 E2 Cieza Spain
81 L2 Cigil Adası i. Azer.
111 E3 Cigüela r. Spain
80 D2 Cihanbeyli Turkey
150 C4 Cihuatlán Mex.
111 D3 Cíjara, Embalse de resr Spain
99 C4 Cilacap Indon.
81 I1 Çıldır Turkey
81 I1 Çıldır Gölü l. Turkey
93 E4 Cili China
81 J3 Cilo Dağı mt. Turkey
81 M1 Çiloy Adası i. Azer.
141 E4 Cima U.S.A.
139 F4 Cimarron U.S.A.
143 D4 Cimarron r. U.S.A.
117 D6 Cimişlia Moldova
114 G2 Cimone, Monte mt. Italy
81 H3 Çınar Turkey
157 D3 Cinaruco-Capanaparo, Parque Nacional nat. park Venez.
111 G2 Cinca r. Spain
146 C4 Cincinnati U.S.A.
146 C5 Cincinnatus U.S.A.
159 C4 Cinco Chañares Arg.
159 C3 Cinco Saltos Arg.
156 E6 Cinderford U.K.
80 B3 Çine Turkey
108 B3 Ciney Belgium
151 F4 Cintalapa Mex.
110 I5 Cinto, Monte mt. France
158 B3 Cinzas r. Brazil
159 C3 Cipolletti Arg.
128 G4 Circle AK U.S.A.
138 F2 Circle MT U.S.A.
146 B4 Circleville OH U.S.A.
141 F2 Circleville UT U.S.A.
99 C4 Cirebon Indon.
105 F6 Cirencester U.K.
114 F2 Ciriè Italy
114 G5 Cirò Marina Italy
133 H2 Cirque Mountain Canada
140 D3 Cisco IL U.S.A.
141 H2 Cisco UT U.S.A.
143 D5 Cisco TX U.S.A.
157 B3 Cisneros Col.
143 E7 Cistern Point Bahamas
114 G3 Citluk Bos.-Herz.
114 D2 Cittadella Italy
114 E3 Città di Castello Italy
115 K2 Ciucaş, Vârful mt. Romania
150 D4 Ciudad Altamirano Mex.
154 E2 Ciudad Bolívar Venez.
150 C2 Ciudad Camargo Mex.
150 B2 Ciudad Constitución Mex.
151 E5 Ciudad del Carmen Mex.
158 A4 Ciudad del Este Para.
150 C1 Ciudad Delicias Mex.
151 G5 Ciudad del Maíz Mex.
157 D2 Ciudad de Nutrias Venez.
151 E3 Ciudad de Valles Mex.
154 E2 Ciudad Guayana Venez.
150 C1 Ciudad Guerrero Mex.
150 D4 Ciudad Guzmán Mex.
151 E5 Ciudad Hidalgo Mex.
151 F4 Ciudad Ixtepec Mex.
150 D2 Ciudad Juárez Mex.
151 G4 Ciudad Lerdo Mex.
151 E3 Ciudad Madero Mex.
151 E3 Ciudad Mante Mex.

151 E4 Ciudad Mendoza Mex.
151 E2 Ciudad Mier Mex.
150 D2 Ciudad Obregón Mex.
157 E3 Ciudad Ojeda Venez.
111 E3 Ciudad Real Spain
151 D2 Ciudad Rio Bravo Mex.
111 C2 Ciudad Rodrigo Spain
111 H2 Ciutadella de Menorca Spain
80 F1 Çıva Burnu pt Turkey
80 F2 Cıvan Dağ mt. Turkey
114 E1 Cividale del Friuli Italy
114 E3 Civita Castellana Italy
114 E3 Civitanova Marche Italy
114 D3 Civitavecchia Italy
80 B2 Çivril Turkey
93 F4 Cixi China
81 I3 Cizre Turkey
105 I6 Clacton-on-Sea U.K.
107 D3 Clady U.K.
131 G3 Claire, Lake Canada
138 B3 Clair Engle Lake resr U.S.A.
146 D4 Clairton U.S.A.
110 F3 Clamecy France
140 D2 Clan Alpine Mountains U.S.A.
107 C5 Clane Rep. of Ireland
145 C5 Clanton U.S.A.
124 C5 Clanwilliam S. Africa
107 E4 Clara Rep. of Ireland
98 A3 Clara Island Myanmar
70 E4 Clare N.S.W. Australia
70 C4 Clare S.A. Australia
107 C4 Clare r. Rep. of Ireland
107 C4 Clare Island Rep. of Ireland
107 E4 Clare S.A. ... Clare r. Rep. of Ireland
107 C4 Clare r. Rep. of Ireland
137 I5 Clarecastle Rep. of Ireland
107 A4 Clare Island Rep. of Ireland
147 G3 Claremont U.S.A.
143 E4 Claremore U.S.A.
107 C4 Claremorris Rep. of Ireland
71 J2 Clarence r. Australia
73 D5 Clarence N.Z.
73 B1 Clarence Island Antarctica
145 F7 Clarence Town Bahamas
143 C5 Clarendon U.S.A.
133 K4 Clarenville Canada
130 G5 Claresholm Canada
134 E3 Clarinda U.S.A.
146 D4 Clarington U.S.A.
134 D4 Clarion U.S.A.
161 L4 Clarión, Isla i. Mex.
142 F2 Clark U.S.A.
125 H5 Clarkebury S. Africa
71 H8 Clarke Island Australia
136 D2 Clark Fork r. U.S.A.
145 D5 Clark Hill Reservoir U.S.A.
141 E3 Clark Mountain U.S.A.
135 G3 Clark Point Canada
143 F5 Clarksburg U.S.A.
143 F5 Clarksdale U.S.A.
147 H4 Clarks Summit U.S.A.
143 E4 Clarksville AR U.S.A.
134 A4 Clarksville IA U.S.A.
145 C4 Clarksville TN U.S.A.
158 B1 Claro r. Goiás Brazil
158 B2 Claro r. Goiás Brazil
107 D5 Clashmore Rep. of Ireland
107 D3 Claudy U.K.
97 B2 Claveria Phil.
108 D4 Clavier Belgium
142 D4 Clay Center U.S.A.
141 F3 Clayhole Wash r. U.S.A.
145 D5 Clayton GA U.S.A.
139 G4 Clayton NM U.S.A.
147 I1 Clayton NY U.S.A.
147 I1 Clayton Lake U.S.A.
107 D5 Clear, Cape Rep. of Ireland
135 G4 Clear Creek Canada
140 A2 Clear Creek r. U.S.A.
128 G4 Cleare, Cape U.S.A.
146 E3 Clearfield PA U.S.A.
138 E3 Clearfield UT U.S.A.
146 E5 Clear Fork Reservoir U.S.A.
130 A2 Clear Hills Canada
140 C2 Clear Lake CA U.S.A.
142 E2 Clear Lake IA U.S.A.
141 F2 Clear Lake UT U.S.A.
138 B3 Clear Lake Reservoir U.S.A.
130 C4 Clearwater r. Alta Canada
131 H3 Clearwater r. Sask. Canada
138 D2 Clearwater Mountains U.S.A.
131 H3 Clearwater River Provincial Park Canada
143 D5 Cleburne U.S.A.
138 B2 Cle Elum U.S.A.
104 G4 Cleethorpes U.K.
98 □ Clementi Sing.
146 C5 Clendenin U.S.A.
146 C4 Clendening Lake U.S.A.
97 A4 Cleopatra Needle mt. Phil.
135 H1 Cléricy Canada
71 D5 Clermont Australia
108 D5 Clermont France
108 A5 Clermont France
108 F3 Clermont-en-Argonne France
108 F3 Clermont-Ferrand France
119 I5 Clervaux Lux.
138 C2 Cléry r. Venez.
114 D1 Cles Italy
70 B4 Cleve Australia
105 E6 Clevedon U.K.
146 C4 Cleveland MS U.S.A.
146 C4 Cleveland OH U.S.A.
145 C5 Cleveland TN U.S.A.
138 D2 Cleveland, Mount U.S.A.
125 G6 Cleveland Cliffs Basin l. U.S.A.
104 F3 Cleveland Hills U.K.
104 D4 Cleveleys U.K.
145 D7 Clewiston U.S.A.
107 A4 Clifden Rep. of Ireland
71 H5 Cliffdale r. Australia
107 C6 Cliffoney Rep. of Ireland
72 E4 Clifford Bay N.Z.
71 I1 Clifton Australia
141 H5 Clifton U.S.A.
146 D6 Clifton Forge U.S.A.
130 E4 Clinch r. U.S.A.
146 B6 Clinch Mountain mts U.S.A.
130 E4 Clinton B.C. Canada
131 O4 Clinton Ont. Canada
147 G3 Clinton CT U.S.A.
134 C5 Clinton IL U.S.A.
134 C3 Clinton IA U.S.A.
147 I2 Clinton ME U.S.A.
134 E4 Clinton MO U.S.A.
131 H2 Clinton-Colden Lake Canada
134 C3 Clinton Lake U.S.A.
134 C3 Clintonville U.S.A.
148 C6 Clipperton, Île terr. Pacific Ocean
106 B3 Clisham hill U.K.
130 E4 Clive Lake Canada
107 E5 Cloghan Rep. of Ireland
107 C6 Clonakilty Rep. of Ireland
107 C6 Clonakilty Bay Rep. of Ireland
71 G4 Cloncurry Australia
107 E3 Clones Rep. of Ireland
107 D5 Clonmel Rep. of Ireland
107 E4 Cloonbannin Rep. of Ireland
107 D4 Cloone Rep. of Ireland
109 G2 Cloppenburg Germany

134 A2 Cloquet U.S.A.
138 F2 Cloud Peak mt. U.S.A.
72 E4 Cloudy Bay N.Z.
93 □ Cloudy Hill Hong Kong China
73 J1 Clova Canada
140 A2 Cloverdale U.S.A.
143 C5 Clovis U.S.A.
135 I3 Cloyne Canada
107 C6 Cloyne Rep. of Ireland
131 H3 Cluff Lake Mine Canada
113 K7 Cluj-Napoca Romania
105 D5 Clun r. U.K.
70 E6 Clunes Australia
105 H3 Cluses France
105 D5 Clwydian Range hills U.K.
130 G4 Clyde Canada
106 D5 Clyde r. U.K.
146 E3 Clyde NY U.S.A.
146 B5 Clyde OH U.S.A.
106 D5 Clyde, Firth of est. U.K.
106 D5 Clydebank U.K.
129 L2 Clyde River Canada
140 D5 Coachella U.S.A.
150 D4 Coahuayutla de Guerrero Mex.
150 C3 Coahuila state Mex.
130 D3 Coal r. Canada
134 C5 Coal City U.S.A.
150 D4 Coalcomán Mex.
140 D3 Coaldale U.S.A.
143 D5 Coalgate U.S.A.
140 B3 Coalinga U.S.A.
130 D3 Coal River Canada
105 F5 Coalville U.S.A.
154 F4 Coari Brazil
154 E4 Coari r. Brazil
137 I5 Coastal Plain U.S.A.
130 D4 Coast Mountains Canada
138 B2 Coast Ranges mts U.S.A.
106 E5 Coatbridge U.K.
151 G5 Coatepeque Guat.
147 F5 Coatesville U.S.A.
133 I4 Coaticook Canada
129 J3 Coats Island Canada
73 C3 Coats Land coastal area Antarctica
151 F4 Coatzacoalcos Mex.
146 E3 Cobalt Canada
151 G5 Cobán Guat.
71 G5 Cobar Australia
71 H6 Cobargo Australia
70 E7 Cobden Australia
135 I3 Cobden Canada
107 C6 Cóbh Rep. of Ireland
154 E6 Cobija Bol.
146 E3 Cobleskill U.S.A.
135 H4 Cobourg Canada
71 F1 Cobourg Peninsula Australia
71 F5 Cobram Australia
87 B4 Cochin India
141 H5 Cochise U.S.A.
130 D4 Cochrane Alta Canada
132 D4 Cochrane Ont. Canada
131 I3 Cochrane r. Canada
156 B7 Cochrane Chile
70 D4 Cockburn Australia
135 F3 Cockburn Island Canada
106 F5 Cockburnspath U.K.
145 F7 Cockburn Town Bahamas
129 L3 Cockburn Town Turks and Caicos Is Grand Turk
104 D3 Cockermouth U.K.
124 F6 Cockscomb mt. S. Africa
150 I6 Coclé del Norte Panama
150 H5 Coco r. Hond./Nicaragua
148 G7 Coco, Isla de i. Col.
157 A4 Coco, Punta pt Col.
141 F4 Coconino Plateau U.S.A.
71 G4 Cocoparra Range hills Australia
157 B3 Cocorná Col.
158 D1 Cocos Brazil
162 K4 Cocos Basin sea feature Indian Ocean
91 B8 Cocos Islands terr. Indian Ocean
161 N5 Cocos Ridge sea feature N. Pacific Ocean
150 D3 Cocula Mex.
157 B3 Cocuy, Sierra Nevada del mt. Col.
147 H4 Cod, Cape U.S.A.
154 F4 Codajás Brazil
157 D2 Codera, Cabo c. Venez.
72 A7 Codfish Island N.Z.
114 E2 Codigoro Italy
133 H2 Cod Island Canada
113 L7 Codlea Romania
155 J4 Codó Brazil
105 E5 Codsall U.K.
138 E2 Cody U.S.A.
107 A6 Cod's Head Rep. of Ireland
71 H3 Coen Australia
109 G3 Coesfeld Germany
138 C2 Coeur d'Alene U.S.A.
138 C2 Coeur d'Alene Lake U.S.A.
108 C2 Coevorden Neth.
125 H5 Coffee Bay S. Africa
143 E4 Coffeyville U.S.A.
70 A5 Coffin Bay Australia
70 A5 Coffin Bay b. Australia
71 J3 Coffs Harbour Australia
125 G6 Cofimvaba S. Africa
110 D4 Cognac France
120 B4 Cogo Equat. Guinea
146 E3 Cohocton r. U.S.A.
147 I2 Cohoes U.S.A.
71 F5 Cohuna Australia
150 I7 Coiba, Isla i. Panama
156 C7 Coig r. Arg.
106 C2 Coigeach, Rubha pt U.K.
156 B7 Coihaique Chile
87 B4 Coimbatore India
111 B2 Coimbra Port.
111 D4 Coín Spain
154 E7 Coipasa, Salar de salt flat Bol.
157 C2 Cojedes r. Venez.
151 H5 Cojutepeque El Salvador
70 E7 Colac Australia
158 E2 Colatina Brazil
109 J2 Colbitz Germany
154 D7 Colca r. Peru
142 C4 Colby U.S.A.
105 I6 Colchester U.K.
106 F5 Coldingham U.K.
109 H6 Colditz Germany
131 H4 Cold Lake Canada
131 H4 Cold Lake l. Canada
106 F5 Coldstream U.K.
135 G4 Coldwater Canada
143 C4 Coldwater KS U.S.A.
146 A5 Coldwater MI U.S.A.
143 F5 Coldwater r. U.S.A.
147 H2 Colebrook U.S.A.
134 D2 Coleman MI U.S.A.
143 D6 Coleman TX U.S.A.
125 H5 Colenso S. Africa
70 E7 Coleraine Australia
107 E2 Coleraine U.K.
72 C5 Coleridge, Lake N.Z.
87 B3 Coleroon r. India
124 E5 Colesberg S. Africa
140 C2 Colfax CA U.S.A.
138 C2 Colfax WA U.S.A.

106 □ Colgrave Sound sea chan. U.K.
125 G3 Coligny S. Africa
150 D4 Colima Mex.
150 D4 Colima state Mex.
150 D4 Colima, Nevado de vol. Mex.
106 B4 Coll i. U.K.
111 E2 Collado Villalba Spain
71 C7 Collarenebri Australia
145 C5 College Park U.S.A.
143 D6 College Station U.S.A.
71 H3 Collie Australia
71 H3 Collie Australia
135 G3 Collier Bay Australia
135 G3 Collingwood Canada
72 D4 Collingwood N.Z.
143 F6 Collins U.S.A.
144 B4 Collinsville U.S.A.
159 B3 Collipulli Chile
107 D2 Collooney Rep. of Ireland
110 H2 Colmar France
111 E2 Colmenar Viejo Spain
105 H6 Colne r. U.K.
71 C... Colo r. Australia
108 F4 Cologne Germany
134 C5 Coloma U.S.A.
158 C3 Colômbia Brazil
151 E2 Colombia Mex.
157 B3 Colombia country S. America
163 D5 Colombian Basin sea feature S. Atlantic Ocean
87 B5 Colombo Sri Lanka
110 E5 Colomiers France
159 E2 Colón Arg.
159 E2 Colón Arg.
149 H4 Colón Cuba
150 J6 Colón Panama
139 G4 Colonet, Cabo c. Mex.
159 B3 Colonia Choele Choel, Isla i. Arg.
159 F2 Colonia del Sacramento Uruguay
159 F1 Colonia Emilio Mitre Arg.
159 F1 Colonia Lavalleja Uruguay
146 E3 Colonial Heights U.S.A.
151 G5 Colonia Reforma Mex.
114 G5 Colonna, Capo pt Italy
161 M5 Colon Ridge sea feature Pacific Ocean
106 B4 Colonsay i. U.K.
159 C1 Colorado r. San Juan Arg.
La Pampa/Río Negro Arg.
159 C1 Colorado r. La Pampa/Río Negro Arg.
141 I5 Colorado r. Mex./U.S.A.
143 D6 Colorado r. U.S.A.
141 H2 Colorado state U.S.A.
159 B3 Colorado, Delta del Río Arg.
141 G5 Colorado City AZ U.S.A.
143 C5 Colorado City TX U.S.A.
141 H2 Colorado National Monument res. U.S.A.
141 I3 Colorado Plateau U.S.A.
141 E5 Colorado River Aqueduct canal U.S.A.
139 F4 Colorado Springs U.S.A.
150 D3 Colotlán Mex.
109 L1 Colpin Germany
105 I5 Colsterworth U.K.
105 I5 Coltishall U.K.
140 C4 Colton CA U.S.A.
147 F2 Colton NY U.S.A.
141 G2 Colton UT U.S.A.
142 C1 Columbia r. Canada/U.S.A.
146 E5 Columbia MD U.S.A.
142 E4 Columbia MO U.S.A.
143 F6 Columbia MS U.S.A.
146 E5 Columbia PA U.S.A.
145 D5 Columbia SC U.S.A.
145 C5 Columbia TN U.S.A.
129 K1 Columbia, Cape Canada
146 E5 Columbia, District of state U.S.A.
130 F4 Columbia, Mount Canada
134 C5 Columbia City U.S.A.
147 J2 Columbia Falls ME U.S.A.
138 D1 Columbia Falls MT U.S.A.
130 F4 Columbia Mountains Canada
138 C2 Columbia Plateau U.S.A.
124 B5 Columbine, Cape pt S. Africa
145 C5 Columbus GA U.S.A.
134 C5 Columbus IN U.S.A.
144 C4 Columbus MS U.S.A.
143 F5 Columbus MS U.S.A.
138 F2 Columbus MT U.S.A.
142 D3 Columbus NE U.S.A.
139 F6 Columbus NM U.S.A.
146 B4 Columbus OH U.S.A.
143 D6 Columbus TX U.S.A.
134 C4 Columbus WI U.S.A.
134 C4 Columbus Junction U.S.A.
145 F7 Columbus Point Bahamas
140 D2 Columbus Salt Marsh U.S.A.
130 F4 Colville Canada
72 E2 Colville N.Z.
128 C3 Colville r. U.S.A.
72 E2 Colville Channel N.Z.
130 E4 Colville Lake Canada
105 D4 Colwyn Bay U.K.
114 C2 Comacchio Italy
114 C2 Comacchio, Valli di lag. Italy
93 D4 Comai China
159 C4 Comallo r. Arg.
143 D6 Comanche U.S.A.
73 B1 Comandante Ferraz research station Antarctica
159 C4 Comandante Salas Arg.
113 K7 Comăneşti Romania
150 H5 Comayagua Hond.
159 B1 Combarbalá Chile
107 F3 Comber U.K.
135 ... Combermere Canada
89 H6 Combermere Bay Myanmar
108 A4 Combles France
125 J1 Combomune Moz.
71 J2 Comboyne Australia
132 E2 Commanda Canada
132 E2 Committee Bay Canada
73 B1 Commonwealth Bay Antarctica
114 C2 Como Italy
114 C2 Como, Lago di l. Italy
89 G3 Como Chamling l. China
159 C5 Comodoro Rivadavia Arg.
87 H2 Comorin, Cape India
119 I5 Comoros country Africa
110 E2 Compiègne France
150 D3 Compostela Mex.
97 A4 Compostela Phil.
117 D6 Comrat Moldova
106 F5 Comrie U.K.
143 D6 Comstock U.S.A.
93 B5 Con, Sông r. Vietnam
98 C1 Con Cuông Vietnam
120 A3 Conakry Guinea
159 C5 Cona Niyeo Arg.
71 G8 Conara Jct. Australia
158 D2 Conceição r. Brazil
158 E2 Conceição da Barra Brazil
153 E2 Conceição da Araguaia Brazil
155 I5 Conceição do Araguaia Brazil
154 D6 Concepción Bol.
159 B3 Concepción Chile

150 I6 Concepción Panama
156 E2 Concepción Para.
159 E2 Concepción del Uruguay Arg.
140 B4 Conception, Point U.S.A.
145 F7 Conception Island Bahamas
158 C3 Conchas Brazil
139 F5 Conchas Lake U.S.A.
141 H4 Concho U.S.A.
150 C2 Conchos r. Chihuahua Mex.
151 E2 Conchos r. Tamaulipas Mex.
140 A3 Concord CA U.S.A.
145 D5 Concord NC U.S.A.
147 H3 Concord NH U.S.A.
159 F1 Concordia Arg.
157 B4 Concordia Col.
124 E3 Concordia S. Africa
142 D4 Concordia U.S.A.
83 I1 Concord Peak Afgh.
71 I1 Condamine Australia
98 C3 Côn Đao Vietnam
150 H5 Condega Nicaragua
71 G4 Condobolin Australia
110 E5 Condom France
138 B2 Condon U.S.A.
108 D4 Condroz reg. Belgium
114 E2 Conegliano Italy
150 D4 Conejos Mex.
135 G4 Conestogo Lake Canada
146 E3 Conesus Lake U.S.A.
147 G4 Coney Island U.S.A.
68 F3 Conflict Group is P.N.G.
110 E3 Confolens France
141 H2 Confusion Range mts U.S.A.
93 D6 Conghua China
105 E4 Congleton U.K.
122 B4 Congo country Africa
122 B3 Congo r. Africa
122 C4 Congo, Democratic Republic of country Africa
163 J6 Congo Cone sea feature S. Atlantic Ocean
141 F4 Congress U.S.A.
159 B3 Conguillo, Parque Nacional nat. park Chile
105 G4 Coningsby U.K.
104 D3 Coniston Canada
104 D3 Coniston U.K.
131 H4 Conklin Canada
159 D2 Conlara Arg.
159 D2 Conlara r. Arg.
107 B3 Conn, Lough l. Rep. of Ireland
146 C4 Conneaut U.S.A.
147 G3 Connecticut r. U.S.A.
147 G3 Connecticut state U.S.A.
146 D4 Connellsville U.S.A.
107 B4 Connemara reg. Rep. of Ireland
144 C4 Conners Canada
134 C4 Connersville U.S.A.
68 D3 Conoble Australia
98 B2 Co Nôi Vietnam
146 E5 Conowingo U.S.A.
138 E2 Conrad U.S.A.
163 L9 Conrad Rise sea feature Southern Ocean
143 E6 Conroe U.S.A.
158 E2 Conselheiro Lafaiete Brazil
158 E2 Conselheiro Pena Brazil
104 F3 Consett U.K.
98 C3 Côn Sơn i. Vietnam
131 G4 Consort Canada
112 D7 Constance, Lake Germany/Switz.
154 F5 Constância dos Baetas Brazil
115 M2 Constanţa Romania
111 D4 Constantina Spain
120 C1 Constantine Alg.
128 C4 Constantine, Cape U.S.A.
141 E6 Constitución de 1857, Parque Nacional nat. park Mex.
138 D3 Contact U.S.A.
154 C5 Contamana Peru
158 E1 Contas r. Brazil
141 G6 Continental U.S.A.
151 G4 Contoy, Isla i. Mex.
135 G1 Contwoyto Lake Canada
143 E5 Conway AR U.S.A.
147 H3 Conway NH U.S.A.
145 E5 Conway SC U.S.A.
70 A2 Conway, Lake salt flat Australia
105 D4 Conwy U.K.
105 D4 Conwy r. U.K.
71 H4 Coober Pedy Australia
72 C5 Cook, Mount N.Z.
145 C4 Cookeville U.S.A.
128 C3 Cook Inlet sea chan. U.S.A.
67 I5 Cook Islands terr. Pacific Ocean
133 I3 Cook's Harbour Canada
107 E3 Cookstown U.K.
72 E4 Cook Strait N.Z.
71 H3 Cooktown Australia
71 G5 Coolabah Australia
71 H3 Coolah Australia
71 H5 Coolamon Australia
68 G5 Coolgardie Australia
71 H5 Coolgardie Australia
141 H6 Coolidge U.S.A.
141 H6 Coolidge Dam U.S.A.
71 H6 Cooma Australia
107 A6 Coomacarrea hill Rep. of Ireland
70 C2 Coombah Australia
70 A3 Coonalpyn Australia
71 H3 Coonamble Australia
70 A3 Coonawarra Australia
70 A3 Coondambo Australia
70 C2 Coongoola Australia
71 H3 Cooper Creek watercourse Australia
71 J3 Coopernook Australia
145 E7 Cooper's Town Bahamas
147 G2 Cooperstown NY U.S.A.
142 D2 Cooperstown ND U.S.A.
138 A3 Coos Bay U.S.A.
71 H5 Cootamundra Australia
107 E3 Cootehill Rep. of Ireland
159 B3 Copahue, Volcán mt. Chile
151 F4 Copainalá Mex.
151 G5 Copán tourist site Hond.
103 K5 Copenhagen Denmark
98 C1 Cô Pi, Phou mt. Laos/Vietnam
156 B3 Copiapó Chile
159 B... Copiapó r. Chile
114 G2 Copparo Italy
135 G2 Copper Cliff Canada
134 D2 Copper Harbor U.S.A.
Coppermine Canada see Kugluktuk
128 G3 Coppermine r. Canada
135 G2 Coppermine Point Canada
124 E... Copperton S. Africa
150 ... Coquihalla Highway Canada
159 B1 Coquimbo Chile
159 B1 Coquimbo admin. reg. Chile
115 J3 Corabia Romania
158 D1 Coração de Jesus Brazil
154 D6 Coracora Peru
71 J2 Coraki Australia
68 B4 Coral Bay Australia
145 D7 Coral Gables U.S.A.
129 J3 Coral Harbour Canada
69 F3 Coral Sea Coral Sea Is Terr.

82 C4 Darta Turkm.
105 H6 Dartford U.K.
70 D6 Dartmoor Australia
105 C7 Dartmoor reg. U.K.
105 C7 Dartmoor National Park U.K.
133 H5 Dartmouth Canada
105 D7 Dartmouth U.K.
104 F4 Darton U.K.
68 E2 Daru P.N.G.
120 A4 Daru Sierra Leone
89 G3 Darum Tso l. China
114 G2 Daruvar Croatia
82 D4 Darvaza Turkm.
84 D4 Darvīshī Iran
85 G4 Darvāzgāī Afgh.
104 E4 Darwen U.K.
85 G4 Darweshan Afgh.
68 D3 Darwin Australia
156 C8 Darwin, Monte mt. Chile
88 B3 Darya Khan Pak.
85 E4 Dārzīn Iran
85 H5 Dās i. U.A.E.
86 B3 Dasha China
82 D4 Dashoguz Turkm.
84 E2 Dasht Iran
85 F5 Dasht r. Pak.
84 C4 Dasht-e Palang r. Iran
85 F5 Dashtiari Iran
83 G5 Dashtiobburdon Tajik.
92 B3 Dashuikeng China
92 B2 Dashuitou China
88 C2 Daska Pak.
84 K1 Daşkäsän Azer.
88 C1 Daspar mt. Pak.
109 H3 Dassel Germany
124 C6 Dassen Island S. Africa
81 K2 Dastakert Armenia
84 E3 Dastgardān Iran
96 F2 Da Suifen He r. China
115 L6 Datça Turkey
94 G3 Date Japan
141 F5 Dateland U.S.A.
88 D4 Datia India
93 E5 Datian China
92 A2 Datong Qinghai China
92 D1 Datong Shanxi China
92 B2 Datong He r. China
92 A2 Datong Shan mts China
99 C2 Datu, Tanjung c. Indon./Malaysia
97 C5 Datu Piang Phil.
116 C3 Daugava r. Belarus/Latvia
    alt. Zakhodnyaya Dzvina,
    alt. Zapadnaya Dvina,
    conv. Western Dvina
103 N5 Daugavpils Latvia
85 G2 Daulatabad Afgh.
88 C6 Daulatabad India
108 E4 Daun Germany
87 A2 Daund India
98 A2 Daung Kyun i. Myanmar
131 I4 Dauphin Canada
110 G4 Dauphiné reg. France
143 F6 Dauphin Island U.S.A.
131 J4 Dauphin Lake Canada
88 D2 Dausa India
106 E3 Dava U.K.
82 A4 Däväçi Azer.
87 A3 Davangere India
97 C5 Davao Phil.
97 C5 Davao Gulf Phil.
84 C4 Dāvarān Iran
84 F5 Dāvar Panāh Iran
125 H3 Davel S. Africa
140 D2 Davenport CA U.S.A.
134 B5 Davenport IA U.S.A.
105 F5 Daventry U.K.
125 H3 Daveyton S. Africa
150 I6 David Panama
130 H4 Davidson Canada
131 I3 Davin Lake Canada
73 D5 Davis research station Antarctica
140 B2 Davis U.S.A.
141 E4 Davis Dam U.S.A.
133 H2 Davis Inlet Canada
73 D5 Davis Sea Antarctica
129 M3 Davis Strait Canada/Greenland
112 D7 Davos Switz.
96 B3 Dawa China
92 A1 Dawan China
89 F3 Dawaxung China
92 B4 Dawê China
92 E3 Dawen He r. China
98 A1 Dawna Range mts Myanmar/Thai.
86 D6 Dawqah Oman
128 E3 Dawson Canada
145 C6 Dawson U.S.A.
142 D2 Dawson ND U.S.A.
131 I4 Dawson Bay Canada
130 E3 Dawson Creek Canada
131 K2 Dawson Inlet Canada
130 D2 Dawson Range mts Canada
92 A4 Dawu Hubei China
90 C3 Dawu Sichuan China
110 D5 Dax France
93 C5 Daxin China
92 E2 Daxing China
93 A4 Da Xueshan mts China
89 H4 Dayang r. India
96 B4 Dayang He r. China
92 B3 Dayao Shan mts China
93 E4 Daye China
93 B4 Dayi China
70 F6 Daylesford Australia
140 D3 Daylight Pass U.S.A.
159 F1 Daymán r. Uruguay
159 F1 Daymán, Cuchilla del hills Uruguay
81 H4 Dayr az Zawr Syria
146 A5 Dayton OH U.S.A.
145 C5 Dayton TN U.S.A.
138 C2 Dayton WA U.S.A.
145 D6 Daytona Beach U.S.A.
93 E5 Dayu China
93 D5 Dayu Ling mts China
92 F3 Da Yunhe canal China
138 C2 Dayville U.S.A.
93 C4 Dazhou China
93 D7 Dazhou Dao i. China
93 B4 Dazu China
124 F5 De Aar S. Africa
147 K1 Dead r. ME U.S.A.
134 D2 Dead r. WI U.S.A.
147 F2 Deadman's Cay Bahamas
141 E4 Dead Mountains U.S.A.
80 C3 Dead Sea salt l. Asia
105 I6 Deal U.K.
125 F4 Dealesville S. Africa
130 D4 Dean r. Canada
93 A4 De'an China
105 E6 Dean, Forest of U.K.
159 D1 Deán Funes Arg.
135 F4 Dearborn U.S.A.
130 C3 Dease r. Canada
130 C3 Dease Lake Canada
128 H3 Dease Strait Canada
140 D3 Death Valley U.S.A.
140 D3 Death Valley Junction U.S.A.
140 D3 Death Valley National Park U.S.A.
110 E2 Deauville France
99 C2 Debak Sarawak Malaysia
93 C6 Debao China
115 I4 Debar Macedonia
131 H4 Debden Canada
105 I5 Debenham U.K.
141 H2 De Beque U.S.A.
108 C3 De Biesbosch, Nationaal Park nat. park Neth.
147 I2 Deblois U.S.A.
122 D2 Debre Birhan Eth.
113 J7 Debrecen Hungary
122 D2 Debre Markos Eth.
122 D2 Debre Tabor Eth.

122 D3 Debre Zeyit Eth.
145 C5 Decatur AL U.S.A.
145 C5 Decatur GA U.S.A.
134 C6 Decatur IL U.S.A.
134 C5 Decatur IN U.S.A.
134 E4 Decatur MI U.S.A.
87 B2 Deccan plat. India
135 H2 Decelles, Lac resr Canada
112 G5 Děčín Czech Rep.
134 B4 Decorah U.S.A.
105 F6 Deddington U.K.
109 I2 Dedeleben Germany
109 I2 Dedelstorf Germany
108 E2 Dedemsvaart Neth.
158 C4 Dedo de Deus mt. Brazil
81 K1 Dedop'listsqaro Georgia
120 B3 Dédougou Burkina
116 B3 Dedovichi Rus. Fed.
123 D5 Dedza Malawi
104 E4 Dee r. U.K.
105 E4 Dee r. England/Wales U.K.
106 F3 Dee r. Scotland U.K.
107 C5 Deel r. Rep. of Ireland
107 D3 Deele r. Rep. of Ireland
93 □ Deep Bay Hong Kong China
146 D5 Deep Creek Lake U.S.A.
141 F2 Deep Creek Range mts U.S.A.
135 I2 Deep River Canada
147 G4 Deep River U.S.A.
131 J1 Deep Rose Lake Canada
140 D3 Deep Springs U.S.A.
71 I2 Deepwater Australia
146 B5 Deer Creek Lake U.S.A.
147 J2 Deer Island Canada
133 I4 Deer Island U.S.A.
147 I2 Deer Isle U.S.A.
132 B3 Deer Lake l. Canada
133 I4 Deer Lake Nfld Canada
132 B3 Deer Lake Ont. Canada
138 D2 Deer Lodge U.S.A.
156 D2 Defensores del Chaco, Parque Nacional nat. park Para.
146 A4 Defiance U.S.A.
145 C6 De Funiak Springs U.S.A.
90 B3 Dêgê China
122 E3 Degeh Bur Eth.
109 K6 Deggendorf Germany
88 C3 Degh r. Pak.
108 A3 De Haan Belgium
84 D5 Dehaj Iran
85 F4 Dehak Iran
85 F5 Dehak Iran
84 D4 Deh-Dasht Iran
84 C4 Deh-e Khalīfeh Iran
84 C4 Deheq Iran
84 E4 Deh-e Sard Iran
84 C3 Dehgāh Iran
84 B3 Deh Golān Iran
87 B4 Dehiwala-Mount Lavinia Sri Lanka
84 D5 Dehkhoyeh Iran
84 D5 Dehlorān Iran
88 D3 Dehra Dun India
89 F4 Dehri India
85 E4 Deh Salm Iran
81 I4 Deh Sheykh Iran
85 F4 Deh Shū Afgh.
93 F5 Dehua China
96 C1 Dehui China
108 B4 Deinze Belgium
113 K7 Dej Romania
93 C4 Dejiang China
134 C5 De Kalb IL U.S.A.
143 E5 De Kalb TX U.S.A.
147 F2 De Kalb Junction U.S.A.
86 A4 Dekemhare Eritrea
122 C4 Dekese Dem. Rep. Congo
83 F3 Dekhkanabad Uzbek.
108 C1 De Koog Neth.
108 C2 De Kooy Neth.
140 C4 Delano U.S.A.
141 F2 Delano Peak mt. U.S.A.
67 G2 Delap-Uliga-Djarrit Marshall Is
85 F3 Delārām Afgh.
125 H4 Delareyville S. Africa
131 H4 Delaronde Lake Canada
134 C5 Delavan IL U.S.A.
134 C4 Delavan WI U.S.A.
146 E4 Delaware U.S.A.
147 F4 Delaware r. U.S.A.
147 F5 Delaware state U.S.A.
147 F5 Delaware Bay U.S.A.
147 F4 Delaware Water Gap National Recreational Area res. U.S.A.
109 G3 Delbrück Germany
71 H6 Delegate Australia
112 C7 Delémont Switz.
108 C2 Delft Neth.
87 B4 Delft Island Sri Lanka
108 E1 Delfzijl Neth.
123 E5 Delgado, Cabo pt Moz.
135 G4 Delhi Canada
90 B3 Delhi China
88 D3 Delhi India
    (City Plan 54)
139 F4 Delhi CO U.S.A.
147 F3 Delhi NY U.S.A.
81 I2 Delice Turkey
80 E2 Delice r. Turkey
80 E1 Delice r. Turkey
85 E4 Delījān Iran
130 E1 Déline Canada
109 I4 Delisle Canada
109 L3 Delitzsch Germany
109 H4 Delligsen Germany
134 B3 Dell Rapids U.S.A.
114 B1 Dellys Alg.
140 D5 Del Mar U.S.A.
141 E3 Delmar Lake U.S.A.
109 G1 Delmenhorst Germany
77 G1 De-Longa, Ostrova is Rus. Fed.
128 B3 De Long Mountains U.S.A.
131 I5 Deloraine Canada
135 H3 Deloro Canada
146 A4 Delphos U.S.A.
124 F4 Delportshoop S. Africa
115 I2 Delray Beach U.S.A.
139 E6 Del Rio Mex.
143 C6 Del Rio U.S.A.
103 L3 Delsbo Sweden
141 H2 Delta CO U.S.A.
141 F2 Delta IA U.S.A.
141 F2 Delta UT U.S.A.
128 D3 Delta Junction U.S.A.
147 F3 Delta Reservoir U.S.A.
150 □ Deltona U.S.A.
71 I2 Delungra Australia
107 I4 Delvin Rep. of Ireland
115 I5 Delvinë Albania
82 C1 Dema r. Rus. Fed.
122 C4 Demba Dem. Rep. Congo
122 D3 Dembī Dolo Eth.
163 F5 Demerara Abyssal Plain sea feature S. Atlantic Ocean
116 H2 Demidov Rus. Fed.
139 F5 Deming U.S.A.
157 E4 Demini r. Brazil
80 B2 Demirci Turkey
115 L4 Demirköy Turkey
109 M1 Demmin Germany
145 C5 Demopolis U.S.A.
134 D5 Demotte U.S.A.
99 B3 Dempo, Gunung vol. Indon.
116 H2 Dem'yanovo Rus. Fed.
77 P2 Demyansk Rus. Fed.
124 D5 De Naawte S. Africa
81 H1 Denakil reg. Eritrea
122 E3 Denan Eth.
131 J4 Denare Beach Canada
83 F5 Denau Uzbek.

135 I3 Denbigh Canada
105 D4 Denbigh U.K.
108 D1 Den Burg Neth.
98 B1 Den Chai Thai.
99 C3 Dendang Indon.
108 D2 Dendermonde Belgium
125 H1 Dendron S. Africa
92 C1 Dengkou China
89 H3 Dêngqên China
92 D3 Dengzhou China
Den Haag Neth. see The Hague
68 B4 Denham Australia
108 E2 Den Ham Neth.
108 D1 Den Helder Neth.
111 G3 Dénia Spain
70 F5 Deniliquin Australia
138 C3 Denio U.S.A.
142 E3 Denison IA U.S.A.
143 D5 Denison TX U.S.A.
82 E1 Denisovka Kazakh.
80 B3 Denizli Turkey
71 J4 Denman Australia
73 E2 Denman Glacier Antarctica
68 B5 Denmark Australia
103 J4 Denmark country Europe
129 P3 Denmark Strait strait Greenland/Iceland
147 H3 Dennehotso U.S.A.
147 H4 Dennis Port U.S.A.
106 E4 Denny U.K.
147 J2 Dennysville U.S.A.
99 E4 Denpasar Indon.
147 G4 Denton MD U.S.A.
143 D5 Denton TX U.S.A.
68 B5 D'Entrecasteaux, Point Australia
69 G3 D'Entrecasteaux, Récifs reef New Caledonia
68 F2 D'Entrecasteaux Islands P.N.G.
138 F4 Denver U.S.A.
89 F4 Deo India
88 D3 Deoband India
87 D1 Deogarh India
89 E5 Deogarh mt. India
89 F4 Deoghar India
88 D5 Deori India
89 F4 Deoria India
88 C2 Deosai, Plains of Pak.
88 E5 Deosil India
108 A3 De Panne Belgium
134 D3 De Pere U.S.A.
147 F3 Deposit U.S.A.
135 I2 Depot-Forbes Canada
135 I2 Depot-Rowanton Canada
134 C5 Depue U.S.A.
77 O3 Deputatskiy Rus. Fed.
89 G3 Dêqên China
90 B4 Dêqên China
93 D6 Deqing Guangdong China
93 F4 Deqing Zhejiang China
143 E5 De Queen U.S.A.
88 B3 Dera Bugti Pak.
88 B3 Dera Ghazi Khan Pak.
88 B3 Dera Ismail Khan Pak.
88 B3 Derawar Fort Pak.
81 I7 Derbent Rus. Fed.
83 J4 Derbent Uzbek.
71 G8 Derby Tas. Australia
68 D3 Derby W.A. Australia
105 F5 Derby U.K.
147 G4 Derby CT U.S.A.
143 D4 Derby KS U.S.A.
107 D5 Derg r. Rep. of Ireland/U.K.
107 C5 Derg, Lough l. Rep. of Ireland
117 F5 Derhachi Ukr.
143 E6 De Ridder U.S.A.
81 H3 Derik Turkey
80 D3 Derinkuyu Turkey
117 F6 Derkul r. Rus. Fed./Ukr.
124 C1 Derm Namibia
82 E3 Dermentobe Kazakh.
107 D4 Derravaragh, Lough l. Rep. of Ireland
107 E5 Derry r. Rep. of Ireland
94 B2 Derong China
107 C3 Derryveagh Mountains Rep. of Ireland
92 A1 Dêrstei China
121 F3 Derudeb Sudan
126 B5 De Rust S. Africa
114 G2 Derventa Bos.-Herz.
71 G9 Derwent r. Australia
104 F4 Derwent r. U.K.
104 E3 Derwent Reservoir U.K.
104 D3 Derwent Water l. U.K.
82 C1 Derzhavino Rus. Fed.
82 D2 Derzhavinsk Kazakh.
67 J5 Désappointement, Îles du is Fr. Polynesia
140 D2 Desatoya Mountains U.S.A.
135 F2 Desbarats Canada
131 I3 Deschambault Canada
131 I4 Deschambault Lake Canada
138 B2 Deschutes r. U.S.A.
122 D2 Desē Eth.
159 C7 Deseado Arg.
156 C7 Deseado r. Arg.
141 F1 Deseret Peak mt. U.S.A.
135 I3 Deseronto Canada
88 B3 Desert Canal Pak.
141 E5 Desert Center U.S.A.
130 G3 Desmarais Canada
142 E3 Des Moines IA U.S.A.
139 G4 Des Moines NM U.S.A.
134 E5 Des Moines r. U.S.A.
116 E3 Desna r. Rus. Fed.
117 D5 Desnogorsk Rus. Fed.
97 C4 Desolation Point Phil.
108 D3 Dessel Belgium
109 K3 Dessau Germany
135 H1 Destor Canada
70 B6 D'Estrees Bay Australia
130 B2 Destruction Bay Canada
115 I2 Deta Romania
123 C5 Dete Zimbabwe
109 I3 Detmold Germany
134 D3 Detour, Point U.S.A.
141 H3 De Tour Village U.S.A.
135 F4 Detroit U.S.A.
142 E2 Detroit Lakes U.S.A.
71 H5 Deua National Park Australia
109 K3 Deuben Germany
114 F1 Deutschlandsberg Austria
109 H3 Deutzen Germany
135 H2 Deux-Rivières Canada
115 J2 Deva Romania
89 H4 Devarkonda India
80 D3 Develi Turkey
108 E2 Deventer Neth.
104 E3 Deverill r. U.K.
112 H6 Devét Skal hill Czech Rep.
107 D5 Devil's Bit Mountain Rep. of Ireland
105 D5 Devil's Bridge U.K.
140 C2 Devil's Gate pass U.S.A.
134 B2 Devil's Island U.S.A.
142 D1 Devil's Lake U.S.A.
140 C3 Devil's Peak mt. U.S.A.
147 F2 Devil's Point Bahamas
140 C3 Devil's Postpile National Monument res. U.S.A.
105 F6 Devizes U.K.
88 C4 Devli India
115 K3 Devnya Bulg.
130 D4 Devon Canada
105 G5 Devon r. U.K.

129 I2 Devon Island Canada
71 G8 Devonport Australia
80 C1 Devrek Turkey
80 C1 Devrekâni Turkey
87 A2 Devrukh India
99 A2 Dewa, Tanjung pt Indon.
108 D5 Dewas India
108 E2 De Weerribben, Nationaal Park nat. park Neth.
125 G4 Dewetsdorp S. Africa
146 B5 Dewey Lake U.S.A.
143 F5 De Witt AR U.S.A.
134 B5 De Witt IA U.S.A.
104 F4 Dewsbury U.K.
93 E4 Dexing China
147 I2 Dexter ME U.S.A.
143 F4 Dexter MO U.S.A.
147 E2 Dexter NY U.S.A.
92 B4 Deyang China
84 J3 Deyhuk Iran
81 L3 Deylaman Iran
68 D2 Deyong, Tanjung pt Indon.
84 C5 Deyyer Iran
81 L6 Dez r. Iran
84 C3 Dezfūl Iran
92 E2 Dezhou China
84 B5 Dhahlān, Jabal hill Saudi Arabia
84 B5 Dhahran Saudi Arabia
89 G5 Dhaka Bangl.
89 H4 Dhaleswari r. Bangl.
89 H4 Dhaleswari r. India
86 B7 Dhamār Yemen
88 C5 Dhamara India
88 D5 Dhamnod India
87 C1 Dhamtari India
88 B5 Dhana Sar Pak.
89 F5 Dhanbad India
88 B5 Dhandhuka India
89 F4 Dhang Range mts Nepal
88 C5 Dhar India
120 A2 Dhar Adrar hills Mauritania
89 F4 Dhari India
88 B5 Dharan Nepal
87 B3 Dharapuram India
87 B3 Dharmapuri India
87 B3 Dharmavaram India
88 D2 Dharmshala India
87 A3 Dharwad India
89 E3 Dhasan r. India
88 E3 Dhaulagiri mt. Nepal
88 C4 Dhebar Lake India
89 H4 Dhekiajuli India
80 E6 Dhībān Jordan
89 H4 Dhing India
88 B5 Dhone India
88 C5 Dhoraji India
88 C5 Dhule India
89 F4 Dhulian India
89 F4 Dhunche Nepal
122 E3 Dhuusa Marreeb Somalia
140 D3 Diablo, Mount U.S.A.
148 A2 Diablo, Picacho del mt. Mex.
140 D3 Diablo Range mts U.S.A.
159 E2 Diamante Arg.
159 C2 Diamante r. Arg.
68 D4 Diamantina watercourse Australia
158 D2 Diamantina Brazil
155 J6 Diamantina, Chapada plat. Brazil
162 K7 Diamantina Deep sea feature Indian Ocean
158 D2 Diamantino Brazil
140 □1 Diamond Head hd U.S.A.
141 E2 Diamond Peak mt. U.S.A.
93 D6 Dianbai China
93 C4 Dian Chi l. China
93 C4 Dianjiang China
155 I6 Dianópolis Brazil
120 B4 Dianra Côte d'Ivoire
92 B2 Diaoling China
120 B3 Diapaga Burkina
88 E6 Dibaa India
122 C4 Dibaya Dem. Rep. Congo
122 E3 Dibeng S. Africa
125 G1 Dibete Botswana
89 H4 Dibrugarh India
143 C5 Dickens U.S.A.
142 C2 Dickinson U.S.A.
145 C4 Dickson U.S.A.
147 F4 Dickson City U.S.A.
81 H3 Dicle r. Turkey
    alt. Dijlah, Nahr (Iraq/Syria),
    conv. Tigris
97 B2 Didicas i. Phil.
88 C4 Didwana India
115 L4 Didymoteicho Greece
110 G4 Die France
108 F4 Dieblich Germany
120 B3 Diébougou Burkina
109 G5 Dieburg Germany
131 H4 Diefenbaker, Lake Canada
162 I5 Diego Garcia i. British Indian Ocean Terr.
108 E5 Diekirch Lux.
123 D6 Diéma Mali
109 H3 Diemel r. Germany
98 C1 Điện Biên Phu Vietnam
98 C1 Điện Châu Vietnam
98 C1 Điện Khanh Vietnam
109 G2 Diepholz Germany
110 E2 Dieppe France
122 C2 Di'er Nonchang Qu r. China
96 C2 Di'er Songhua Jiang r. China
108 D4 Diest Belgium
112 D7 Dietikon Switz.
109 G4 Diez Germany
121 D3 Diffa Niger
87 D3 Digapahandi India
110 H5 Digha India
110 H5 Digne-les-Bains France
110 G4 Digoin France
97 C5 Digos Phil.
88 D5 Digras India
88 B4 Digri Pak.
91 H4 Digul r. Indon.
120 B4 Digya National Park Ghana
89 H4 Dihang r. India
    alt. Yarlung Zangbo (China),
    conv. Brahmaputra
110 G5 Dijon France
81 J5 Dijlah, Nahr r. Iraq/Syria
    alt. Dicle (Turkey),
    conv. Tigris
122 E2 Dikhil Djibouti
115 L5 Dikili Turkey
108 A3 Diksmuide Belgium
76 J2 Dikson Rus. Fed.
121 D3 Dikwa Nigeria
85 E4 Dilaram Iran
68 C2 Dili East Timor
81 J1 Dilijan Armenia
98 D2 Di Linh Vietnam
109 G4 Dillenburg Germany
143 D6 Dilley U.S.A.
112 E6 Dillingen (Saar) Germany
109 J6 Dillingen an der Donau Germany
128 C4 Dillingham U.S.A.
131 I4 Dillon Canada
138 D2 Dillon MT U.S.A.
145 E5 Dillon SC U.S.A.
122 C4 Dilolo Dem. Rep. Congo
108 D3 Dilsen Belgium
81 J5 Diltāwa Iraq

89 H4 Dimapur India
Dimashq Syria see Damascus
122 C4 Dimbelenge Dem. Rep. Congo
120 B4 Dimbokro Côte d'Ivoire
70 E6 Dimboola Australia
115 K3 Dimitrovgrad Bulg.
116 I4 Dimitrovgrad Rus. Fed.
80 F6 Dimona Israel
124 D2 Dimpho Pan salt pan Botswana
97 C4 Dinagat i. Phil.
89 G4 Dinajpur Bangl.
110 C2 Dinan France
88 C2 Dinanagar India
108 C4 Dinant Belgium
89 F4 Dinapur India
80 D3 Dinar Turkey
84 C4 Dīnār, Kūh-e mt. Iran
114 G2 Dinara Planina mts Croatia see Dinaric Alps
114 G2 Dinaric Alps mts Croatia
121 F3 Dinder National Park Sudan
87 B3 Dindigul India
89 E5 Dindori India
92 E2 Dingbian China
89 H4 Dingba Qu r. China
123 B5 Dinge Angola
109 I3 Dingelstädt Germany
89 F4 Dingla Nepal
107 A5 Dingle Rep. of Ireland
107 A5 Dingle Bay Rep. of Ireland
97 B2 Dingras Phil.
92 E3 Dingtao China
120 A3 Dinguiraye Guinea
106 D3 Dingwall U.K.
92 D3 Dingxi China
92 E2 Dingxing China
92 E2 Dingyuan China
92 E2 Dingzhou China
93 C6 Dingzi Gang inlet China
98 C3 Đinh Lập Vietnam
109 I5 Dinkelsbühl Germany
141 H1 Dinnebito Wash r. U.S.A.
125 G1 Dinokwe Botswana
106 D3 Dinngyè China
141 H1 Dinosaur U.S.A.
138 E3 Dinosaur National Monument res. U.S.A.
108 E3 Dinslaken Germany
120 B3 Dioïla Mali
158 B4 Dionísio Cerqueira Brazil
120 A3 Diourbel Senegal
89 H4 Diphu India
88 B5 Diplo Pak.
92 E2 Dipolog Phil.
72 B6 Dipton N.Z.
120 E3 Diré Mali
68 E3 Direction, Cape Australia
122 E3 Dire Dawa Eth.
123 C5 Dirico Angola
68 E4 Dirk Hartog Island Australia
71 H2 Dirranbandi Australia
85 D3 Dīrsīyeh Iran
141 G2 Dirty Devil r. U.S.A.
88 C4 Disa India
156 □ Disappointment, Cape Atlantic Ocean
138 A2 Disappointment, Cape U.S.A.
68 C4 Disappointment, Lake salt flat Australia
71 H6 Disaster Bay Australia
70 D7 Discovery Bay Australia
93 □ Discovery Bay Hong Kong China
163 J8 Discovery Seamounts sea feature S. Atlantic Ocean
147 E6 Dismal Swamp U.S.A.
89 G4 Dispur India
105 I5 Diss U.K.
158 C1 Distrito Federal admin. dist. Brazil
80 D2 Disûq Egypt
97 □4 Dit i. Phil.
124 F6 Ditloung S. Africa
114 F6 Dittaino r. Sicily Italy
97 A4 Diuata Mountains Phil.
97 C4 Diuata Point Phil.
84 B3 Dīvān Darreh Iran
116 H4 Diveyevo Rus. Fed.
97 B3 Divilacan Bay Phil.
158 D3 Divinópolis Brazil
117 G6 Divnoye Rus. Fed.
120 B4 Divo Côte d'Ivoire
80 F3 Divriği Turkey
85 G5 Diwana Pak.
147 I1 Dixfield U.S.A.
140 B2 Dixon CA U.S.A.
134 C5 Dixon IL U.S.A.
130 C4 Dixon Entrance sea chan. Canada/U.S.A.
145 F7 Dixon's Bahamas
130 F3 Dixonville Canada
84 I2 Dixville Canada
81 J5 Diyālá, Nahr r. Iraq
81 H3 Diyarbakır Turkey
88 B4 Diyodar India
85 D2 Diz Chak Iran
120 D3 Djado, Plateau du Niger
122 B4 Djambala Congo
120 C2 Djanet Alg.
122 C3 Djéma Centr. Afr. Rep.
120 B3 Djenné Mali
120 B3 Djibo Burkina
122 E2 Djibouti country Africa
122 E2 Djibouti Djibouti
107 D4 Djouce Mountain Rep. of Ireland
120 C4 Djougou Benin
102 D2 Djúpivogur Iceland
103 K3 Djurås Sweden
82 D2 Dmanisi Georgia
77 P2 Dmitriya Lapteva, Proliv sea chan. Rus. Fed.
94 C2 Dmitriyevka Primorskiy Kray Rus. Fed.
83 K1 Dmitriyevka Respublika Altay Rus. Fed.
116 G4 Dmitriyevka Tambovskaya Oblast' Rus. Fed.
117 E4 Dmitriyev-L'govskiy Rus. Fed.
116 F3 Dmitrov Rus. Fed.
113 P7 Dnepr r. Europe see Dnieper
113 O5 Dnieper r. Europe
    alt. Dnepr (Rus. Fed.),
    alt. Dnipro (Ukraine),
    alt. Dnyapro (Belarus),
    conv. Dnieper
113 M6 Dniester r. Europe
    alt. Dnister (Rus. Fed.),
    alt. Nistru (Moldova),
    conv. Dniester
113 P7 Dnipro r. Ukraine
    alt. Dnepr (Rus. Fed.),
    alt. Dnyapro (Belarus),
    conv. Dnieper
117 E5 Dniprodzerzhyns'k Ukr.
117 E5 Dnipropetrovs'k Ukr.
117 E5 Dniprorudne Ukr.
113 M6 Dnister r. Ukr.
    alt. Nistru (Moldova),
    conv. Dniester
115 D3 Dno Rus. Fed.
113 P7 Dnyapro r. Belarus
    alt. Dnepr (Rus. Fed.),
    alt. Dnipro (Ukraine),
    conv. Dnieper

121 D4 Doba Chad
135 G3 Dobbinton Canada
103 M4 Dobele Latvia
109 L3 Döbeln Germany
91 F7 Doberai, Jazirah Indon.
159 D3 Doblas Arg.
115 G4 Dobo Indon.
114 H2 Doboj Bos.-Herz.
117 G4 Dobrinka Rus. Fed.
117 D4 Dobrush Belarus
97 A5 Doc Can reef Phil.
158 E2 Doce r. Brazil
105 H5 Docking U.K.
151 D5 Doctor Arroyo Mex.
150 C1 Doctor Belisario Domínguez Mex.
156 D2 Doctor Pedro P. Peña Para.
87 B3 Dod Ballapur India
115 L6 Dodecanese is Greece see Dodecanese
138 G2 Dodge U.S.A.
134 A3 Dodge Center U.S.A.
143 C4 Dodge City U.S.A.
71 G9 Dodges Ferry Australia
134 B4 Dodgeville U.S.A.
105 C7 Dodman Point U.K.
122 D4 Dodoma Tanz.
108 E3 Doetinchem Neth.
89 G3 Dogai Coring salt l. China
89 G2 Dogaicoring Qangco salt l. China
80 F2 Doğanşehir Turkey
130 E4 Dog Creek Canada
89 G3 Dogên Co l. China
132 D2 Dog Island Canada
138 E1 Dog Lake Canada
95 C6 Dōgo i. Japan
120 C3 Dogondoutchi Niger
95 C7 Dōgo-yama mt. Japan
81 J2 Doğubeyazıt Turkey
89 G3 Dogxung Zangbo r. China
89 G3 Do'gyaling China
86 H5 Doha Qatar
89 H5 Dohazari Bangl.
92 C1 Doilungdêqên China
98 A1 Doi Saket Thai.
155 J5 Dois Irmãos, Serra dos hills Brazil
115 J4 Dojran, Lake Greece/Macedonia
103 J3 Dokka Norway
108 E1 Dokkum Neth.
103 M3 Dokshytsy Belarus
117 F6 Dokuchayevs'k Ukr.
91 F7 Dolak, Pulau i. Indon.
133 F4 Dolbeau Canada
105 C5 Dolbenmaen U.K.
110 D2 Dol-de-Bretagne France
110 G3 Dole France
105 D5 Dolgellau U.K.
109 L1 Dolgen Germany
147 F3 Dolgeville U.S.A.
117 F4 Dolgorukovo Rus. Fed.
117 F4 Dolgoye Rus. Fed.
114 C5 Dolianova Sardinia Italy
90 B2 Dolinsk Rus. Fed.
Dolisie Congo see Loubomo
109 J6 Dollnstein Germany
83 B7 Dolmatovo Kazakh.
114 D1 Dolomites mts Italy
122 E3 Dolo Odo Eth.
159 F3 Dolores Arg.
151 G4 Dolores Guat.
159 E2 Dolores Uruguay
150 E2 Dolores Hidalgo Mex.
128 G3 Dolphin and Union Strait Canada
93 B7 Đô Lương Vietnam
117 E5 Dolyna Ukr.
80 E2 Domaniç Turkey
112 E6 Domažlice Czech Rep.
84 B3 Dom Bākh Iran
82 D2 Dombarovskiy Rus. Fed.
103 J3 Dombås Norway
112 I7 Dombóvár Hungary
73 C4 Dome Argus ice feature Antarctica
73 C5 Dome Circe ice feature Antarctica
130 E4 Dome Creek Canada
130 D2 Dome Peak mt. Canada
141 E5 Dome Rock Mountains U.S.A.
110 D2 Domfront France
149 L5 Dominica country Caribbean Sea
150 I6 Dominical Costa Rica
151 K5 Dominican Republic country Caribbean Sea
109 J1 Dömitz Germany
98 C2 Dom Noi, Lam r. Thai.
114 C1 Domodossola Italy
115 J5 Domokos Greece
159 F1 Dom Pedrito Brazil
99 E4 Dompu Indon.
159 C3 Domuyo, Volcán vol. Arg.
71 I2 Domville, Mount Australia
87 B2 Don r. India
150 B2 Don Mex.
116 G5 Don r. Rus. Fed.
106 F3 Don r. U.K.
107 I3 Donaghadee U.K.
107 I3 Donaghmore U.K.
70 E6 Donald Australia
112 G6 Donau r. Austria/Germany
    alt. Duna (Hungary),
    alt. Dunaj (Slovakia),
    alt. Dunărea (Romania),
    alt. Dunav (Yugoslavia),
    conv. Danube
112 D7 Donaueschingen Germany
112 E7 Donauwörth Germany
111 D3 Don Benito Spain
104 F4 Doncaster U.K.
123 D5 Dondo Moz.
123 B4 Dondo Angola
87 C5 Dondra Head c. Sri Lanka
107 C3 Donegal Rep. of Ireland
107 D3 Donegal Bay g. Rep. of Ireland
117 F6 Donets'k Ukr.
117 F5 Donets'kyy Kryazh hills Rus. Fed./Ukr.
93 D5 Dong r. China
68 D2 Dongara Australia
93 C6 Dongchuan China
89 F2 Dongco China
94 C7 Dongfang China
93 E3 Dongfanghong China
99 E3 Donggala Indon.
93 D6 Donggang China
93 D6 Donggu China
92 F3 Donggou China
92 A1 Donghai China
93 D6 Dong Hai sea China
95 A1 Dong He watercourse China
98 D1 Đông Hôi Vietnam
89 H2 Dongjiang Xizang China
89 H1 Dongjiang Xizang China
93 D5 Dongkou China

89 G4 **Dongkya La** pass India
93 C5 **Donglan** China
92 A2 **Dongle** China
96 C2 **Dongliao He** r. China
96 B1 **Dongminzhutun** China
92 B2 **Dongning** China
123 B5 **Dongo** Angola
122 B3 **Dongou** Congo
98 B2 **Dong Phraya Yen** esc. Thai.
93 D6 **Dongping** Guangdong China
92 E3 **Dongping** Shandong China
89 G3 **Dongqiao** China
93 E6 **Dongshan** China
93 E6 **Dongshan Dao** i. China
92 D2 **Dongsheng** China
92 F3 **Dongtai** China
92 F3 **Dongtai** r. China
93 D4 **Dongting Hu** l. China
93 F5 **Dongtou** China
93 E4 **Dongxiang** China
93 C4 **Dongyang** China
92 E2 **Dongzhen** China
92 B2 **Dongzhen** China
93 E4 **Dongzhi** China
130 B2 **Donjek** r. Canada
108 E1 **Donkerbroek** Neth.
89 G5 **Donmanick Islands** Bangl.
133 H4 **Donnacona** Canada
130 F3 **Donnelly** Canada
130 D1 **Donnellys Crossing** N.Z.
140 B2 **Donner Pass** U.S.A.
111 F1 **Donostia - San Sebastián** Spain
115 K6 **Donoussa** i. Greece
116 F4 **Donskoy** Rus. Fed.
117 G6 **Donskoye** Rus. Fed.
97 B3 **Donsol** Phil.
107 A4 **Dooagh** Rep. of Ireland
106 D5 **Doon, Loch** l. U.K.
107 B5 **Doonbeg** r. Rep. of Ireland
108 D2 **Doorn** Neth.
134 D3 **Door Peninsula** U.S.A.
108 D3 **Doorwerth** Neth.
124 □ **Dooxo Nugaaleed** valley Somalia
85 F4 **Dor** watercourse Afgh.
143 C5 **Dora** r. Afgh.
114 C2 **Dora Baltea** r. Italy
84 C5 **Do Rāhak** Iran
105 E7 **Dorchester** U.K.
123 B6 **Dordabis** Namibia
110 E4 **Dordogne** r. France
108 C3 **Dordrecht** Neth.
125 H4 **Dordrecht** S. Africa
131 H4 **Doré Lake** Canada
131 H4 **Doré Lake** l. Canada
114 C4 **Dorgali** Sardinia Italy
85 G4 **Dorī** r. Afgh.
120 B3 **Dori** Burkina
124 C5 **Doring** r. S. Africa
105 G6 **Dorking** U.K.
108 E3 **Dormagen** Germany
108 B5 **Dormans** France
106 D3 **Dornoch Firth** est. U.K.
92 C1 **Dornogovĭ** prov. Mongolia
108 F1 **Dornum** Germany
116 E4 **Dorogobuzh** Rus. Fed.
113 M7 **Dorohoi** Romania
90 B2 **Döröö Nuur** l. Mongolia
102 L2 **Dorotea** Sweden
68 B4 **Dorre Island** Australia
71 J3 **Dorrigo** Australia
138 B3 **Dorris** U.S.A.
120 D4 **Dorsale Camerounaise** slope Cameroon/Nigeria
135 H3 **Dorset** U.S.A.
108 F3 **Dortmund** Germany
80 F5 **Dörtyol** Turkey
109 G1 **Dorum** Germany
122 C3 **Doruma** Dem. Rep. Congo
84 E3 **Dorüneh** Iran
109 H2 **Dörverden** Germany
85 E4 **Do Sārī** Iran
156 C6 **Dos Bahías, Cabo** pt Arg.
141 H5 **Dos Cabezas** U.S.A.
154 C5 **Dos de Mayo** Peru
93 C6 **Do Son** Vietnam
140 B3 **Dos Palos** U.S.A.
109 K2 **Dosse** r. Germany
120 C3 **Dosso** Niger
82 C3 **Dossor** Kazakh.
83 J3 **Dostyk** Kazakh.
110 F1 **Douai** France
120 C4 **Douala** Cameroon
110 B2 **Douarnenez** France
93 □ **Double Island** Hong Kong China
140 C4 **Double Peak** mt. U.S.A.
110 H3 **Doubs** r. France
72 A6 **Doubtful Sound** inlet N.Z.
72 D1 **Doubtless Bay** N.Z.
120 B3 **Douentza** Mali
104 C3 **Douglas** Isle of Man
124 E4 **Douglas** S. Africa
106 E5 **Douglas** U.K.
130 C3 **Douglas** AK U.S.A.
141 H6 **Douglas** AZ U.S.A.
145 D6 **Douglas** GA U.S.A.
138 F3 **Douglas** WY U.S.A.
130 D4 **Douglas Channel** Canada
141 H2 **Douglas Creek** r. U.S.A.
110 F1 **Doullens** France
106 D4 **Doune** U.K.
158 C2 **Dourada, Cachoeira** waterfall Brazil
158 B3 **Dourada, Serra** hills Brazil
158 C1 **Dourada, Serra** mts Brazil
158 A3 **Dourados** Brazil
158 A3 **Dourados** r. Brazil
158 B3 **Dourados, Serra dos** hills Brazil
111 C2 **Douro** r. Port.
   alt. Duero (Spain)
108 D5 **Douzy** France
105 F4 **Dove** r. England U.K.
105 I5 **Dove** r. England U.K.
133 I3 **Dove Brook** Canada
141 H3 **Dove Creek** U.S.A.
71 G9 **Dover** Australia
105 I6 **Dover** U.K.
147 F5 **Dover** DE U.S.A.
147 H3 **Dover** NH U.S.A.
147 F4 **Dover** NJ U.S.A.
146 C4 **Dover** OH U.S.A.
105 I7 **Dover, Strait of** France/U.K.
147 I2 **Dover-Foxcroft** U.S.A.
84 B3 **Doveyrich, Rūd-e** r. Iran/Iraq
134 D6 **Dowagiac** U.S.A.
84 D4 **Dow Chāhī** Iran
85 E2 **Dowlatābād** Afgh.
98 A5 **Dowi, Tanjung** pt Indon.
85 E5 **Dowlatābād** Afgh.
85 G2 **Dowlatābād** Afgh.
84 D4 **Dowlatābād** Iran
84 E4 **Dowlatābād** Iran
84 E4 **Dowlatābād** Iran
85 F3 **Dowlatābād** Iran
85 G3 **Dowlat Yār** Afgh.
140 B2 **Downieville** U.S.A.
107 F3 **Downpatrick** U.K.
147 F3 **Downsville** U.S.A.
84 C3 **Dow Rūd** Iran
84 M4 **Dow Sar** Iran
85 H3 **Dowshi** Afgh.
140 B1 **Doyle** U.S.A.
147 F4 **Doylestown** U.S.A.
95 C6 **Dōzen** is Japan
135 I2 **Dozois, Réservoir** resr Canada
158 B3 **Dracena** Brazil
108 E1 **Drachten** Neth.
115 K2 **Drăgăneşti-Olt** Romania
157 E2 **Dragon's Mouths** strait Trin. and Tob./Venez.
103 M3 **Dragsfjärd** Fin.

110 H5 **Draguignan** France
117 C4 **Drahichyn** Belarus
71 J2 **Drake** Australia
141 F4 **Drake** AZ U.S.A.
131 I5 **Drake** ND U.S.A.
125 H5 **Drakensberg** mts Lesotho/S. Africa
125 I2 **Drakensberg** mts S. Africa
163 E9 **Drake Passage** S. Atlantic Ocean
115 K4 **Drama** Greece
103 J4 **Drammen** Norway
103 J4 **Drangedal** Norway
85 G5 **Drangme Chu** r. China
109 H3 **Dransfeld** Germany
107 E3 **Draperstown** U.K.
88 C2 **Dras** Jammu and Kashmir
112 F7 **Drau** r. Austria
130 G4 **Drayton Valley** Canada
114 B6 **Dréan** Alg.
109 H4 **Dreistelzberge** hill Germany
112 F5 **Dresden** Germany
116 D4 **Dretun'** Belarus
110 E2 **Dreux** France
103 K3 **Drevsjø** Norway
104 G3 **Driffield** U.K.
146 D4 **Driftwood** U.S.A.
107 B6 **Drimoleague** Rep. of Ireland
114 G3 **Drniš** Croatia
109 H1 **Drochtersen** Germany
107 E4 **Drogheda** Rep. of Ireland
117 B5 **Drohobych** Ukr.
105 E5 **Droitwich Spa** U.K.
89 G4 **Drokung** India
109 I2 **Drömling** reg. Germany
107 D3 **Dromod** Rep. of Ireland
107 E3 **Dromore** Northern Ireland U.K.
107 E3 **Dromore** Northern Ireland U.K.
105 F4 **Dronfield** U.K.
129 P2 **Dronning Louise Land** reg. Greenland
108 D2 **Dronten** Neth.
88 B2 **Drosh** Pak.
116 F3 **Droskovo** Rus. Fed.
71 F7 **Drouin** Australia
130 G4 **Drumheller** Canada
138 D2 **Drummond** MT U.S.A.
134 B2 **Drummond** WI U.S.A.
135 F3 **Drummond Island** U.S.A.
133 F4 **Drummondville** Canada
106 D6 **Drumochter, Pass of** U.K.
104 N5 **Druskininkai** Lith.
77 P3 **Druzhina** Rus. Fed.
115 K3 **Dryanovo** Bulg.
130 B3 **Dry Bay** U.S.A.
131 K5 **Dryberry Lake** Canada
134 E2 **Dryden** Canada
132 B4 **Dryden** U.S.A.
73 D5 **Drygalski Ice Tongue** Antarctica
73 D5 **Drygalski Island** Antarctica
140 D2 **Dry Lake** U.S.A.
106 D4 **Drymen** U.K.
68 C3 **Drysdale** r. Australia
84 C3 **Dūāb** r. Iran
93 C6 **Du'an** China
147 F2 **Duane** U.S.A.
149 J5 **Duarte, Pico** mt. Dom. Rep.
78 B4 **Dubā** Saudi Arabia
86 E4 **Dubai** U.A.E.
131 I2 **Dubawnt** r. Canada
131 I2 **Dubawnt Lake** Canada
78 B4 **Dubbagh, Jabal ad** mt. Saudi Arabia
71 H4 **Dubbo** Australia
134 D1 **Dublin** Canada
107 E4 **Dublin** Rep. of Ireland
145 D5 **Dublin** U.S.A.
116 F3 **Dubna** Rus. Fed.
117 C5 **Dubno** Ukr.
138 D2 **Dubois** ID U.S.A.
138 E3 **Dubois** WY U.S.A.
146 D4 **Du Bois** U.S.A.
117 H5 **Dubovka** Rus. Fed.
117 G6 **Dubovskoye** Rus. Fed.
81 L1 **Dübrar Pass** Azer.
120 A4 **Dubréka** Guinea
115 H3 **Dubrovnik** Croatia
117 D5 **Dubrovytsya** Ukr.
116 D4 **Dubrowna** Belarus
83 J4 **Dubun** Kazakh.
134 B4 **Dubuque** U.S.A.
103 M5 **Dubysa** r. Lith.
67 J6 **Duc de Gloucester, Îles du** i. Fr. Polynesia
93 B4 **Duchang** China
141 G1 **Duchesne** U.S.A.
67 J7 **Ducie Island** Pitcairn Is
145 C5 **Duck** r. U.S.A.
131 I4 **Duck Bay** Canada
131 H4 **Duck Lake** Canada
134 C1 **Duck Lake** U.S.A.
141 E2 **Duckwater** U.S.A.
141 E2 **Duckwater Peak** mt. U.S.A.
99 D2 **Đực Phô** Vietnam
98 D3 **Đực Trong** Vietnam
157 B4 **Duco** r. U.S.A.
108 E5 **Dudelange** Lux.
109 I3 **Duderstadt** Germany
89 G4 **Dudhi** India
76 J3 **Dudinka** Rus. Fed.
105 E5 **Dudley** U.K.
88 D6 **Dudna** r. India
106 F3 **Dudwick, Hill of** U.K.
120 B4 **Duékoué** Côte d'Ivoire
111 C2 **Duero** r. Spain
   alt. Douro (Portugal)
133 H1 **Dufault, Lac** l. Canada
73 B4 **Dufek Coast** Antarctica
108 C3 **Duffel** Belgium
132 E2 **Dufferin, Cape** hd Canada
146 B6 **Duffield** U.S.A.
69 G2 **Duff Islands** Solomon Is
132 E1 **Dufrost, Pointe** pt Canada
83 F5 **Dugab** Uzbek.
114 F3 **Dugi Otok** i. Croatia
92 C2 **Dugui Qarag** China
157 D4 **Duida, Cerro** mt. Venez.
108 E3 **Duisburg** Germany
157 B3 **Duitama** Col.
124 D5 **Duiwelskloof** S. Africa
92 A4 **Dujiangyan** China
81 J4 **Dukän Dam** Iraq
124 B4 **Dukathole** S. Africa
130 C4 **Duke Island** U.S.A.
78 C5 **Dukhän** Qatar
116 E4 **Dukhovshchina** Rus. Fed.
88 B3 **Duki** Pak.
103 N5 **Dūkštas** Lith.
85 E4 **Dūlab** Iran
90 B3 **Dulan** China
156 D3 **Dulce** r. Arg.
149 H5 **Dulce, Golfo** b. Costa Rica
148 H5 **Dulce Nombre de Culmí** Hond.
125 I3 **Dulini Hul** salt l. China
122 D3 **Dulishi** S. Africa
115 L3 **Dulovo** Bulg.
134 A2 **Duluth** U.S.A.
105 D6 **Dulverton** U.K.
80 D2 **Dūmā** Syria
97 C5 **Dumaguete** Phil.
96 B2 **Dumai** Indon.
97 B4 **Dumaran** i. Phil.
143 E5 **Dumas** AR U.S.A.
143 C5 **Dumas** TX U.S.A.

80 F5 **Dumayr** Syria
106 D5 **Dumbarton** U.K.
125 I3 **Dumbe** S. Africa
113 I6 **Ďumbier** mt. Slovakia
88 D2 **Dumchele** Jammu and Kashmir
89 H4 **Dum Duma** India
106 E5 **Dumfries** U.K.
89 F4 **Dumka** India
109 G2 **Dümmer** l. Germany
132 E4 **Dumoine, Lac** Canada
73 B6 **Dumont d'Urville** research station Antarctica
73 B6 **Dumont d'Urville Sea** Antarctica
108 E4 **Dümpelfeld** Germany
121 F1 **Dumyât** Egypt
109 I3 **Dün** ridge Germany
115 H1 **Duna** r. Hungary
   alt. Donau (Austria/Germany),
   alt. Dunaj (Slovakia),
   alt. Dunărea (Romania),
   alt. Dunav (Yugoslavia),
   conv. Danube
115 L3 **Dunaj** r. Slovakia
   alt. Donau (Austria/Germany),
   alt. Duna (Hungary),
   alt. Dunărea (Romania),
   alt. Dunav (Yugoslavia),
   conv. Danube
112 H7 **Dunajská Streda** Slovakia
113 I7 **Dunakeszi** Hungary
71 G9 **Dunalley** Australia
107 M2 **Dunany Point** Rep. of Ireland
   Dunărea r. Romania see Danube
   alt. Donau (Austria/Germany),
   alt. Duna (Hungary),
   alt. Dunaj (Slovakia),
   alt. Dunav (Yugoslavia),
   conv. Danube
113 I7 **Dunaújváros** Hungary
   Dunav r. Yugo. see Danube
   alt. Donau (Austria/Germany),
   alt. Duna (Hungary),
   alt. Dunaj (Slovakia),
   alt. Dunărea (Romania),
   conv. Danube
117 C5 **Dunayivtsi** Ukr.
72 C5 **Dunback** N.Z.
106 F4 **Dunbar** U.K.
106 D4 **Dunblane** U.K.
107 E4 **Dunboyne** Rep. of Ireland
130 E5 **Duncan** Canada
141 H5 **Duncan** AZ U.S.A.
143 D5 **Duncan** OK U.S.A.
132 D3 **Duncan, Cape** Canada
132 E3 **Duncan, Lac** l. Canada
146 E4 **Duncannon** U.S.A.
106 E2 **Duncansby Head** U.K.
134 B5 **Duncans Mills** U.S.A.
107 E5 **Duncormick** Rep. of Ireland
103 N4 **Dundaga** Latvia
107 E3 **Dundalk** Rep. of Ireland
146 E3 **Dundalk** U.S.A.
107 E4 **Dundalk Bay** Rep. of Ireland
129 L2 **Dundas** Greenland
130 C4 **Dundas, Lake** salt flat Australia
   Dún Dealgan Rep. of Ireland see Dundalk
125 I4 **Dundee** S. Africa
106 F4 **Dundee** U.K.
135 F5 **Dundee** MI U.S.A.
146 E3 **Dundee** NY U.S.A.
92 E1 **Dund Hot** China
107 F3 **Dundonald** U.K.
71 F1 **Dundoo** Australia
106 E3 **Dundrennan** U.K.
107 F3 **Dundrum** U.K.
107 F3 **Dundrum Bay** U.K.
72 C6 **Dunedin** N.Z.
145 D6 **Dunedin** U.S.A.
71 H4 **Dunedoo** Australia
106 E4 **Dunfermline** U.K.
107 E3 **Dungannon** U.K.
88 C5 **Dungarpur** India
107 D5 **Dungarvan** Rep. of Ireland
105 H7 **Dungeness** hd U.K.
156 C8 **Dungeness, Punta** pt Arg.
108 F4 **Düngenheim** Germany
107 E3 **Dungiven** U.K.
71 I4 **Dungog** Australia
122 C3 **Dungu** Dem. Rep. Congo
99 B2 **Dungun** Malaysia
121 F2 **Dungunab** Sudan
96 E2 **Dunhua** China
90 B2 **Dunhuang** China
70 E4 **Dunkeld** Australia
106 E4 **Dunkeld** U.K.
   Dunkerque France see Dunkirk
105 D6 **Dunkery Beacon** hill U.K.
110 F1 **Dunkirk** France
146 D3 **Dunkirk** U.S.A.
120 B4 **Dunkwa** Ghana
107 E4 **Dún Laoghaire** Rep. of Ireland
107 D4 **Dunlavin** Rep. of Ireland
107 E4 **Dunleer** Rep. of Ireland
107 E2 **Dunloy** U.K.
107 B6 **Dunmanus Bay** Rep. of Ireland
107 C7 **Dunmanway** Rep. of Ireland
149 E7 **Dunmore Town** Bahamas
140 D3 **Dunmovin** U.S.A.
130 D3 **Dunn** r. Canada
106 E2 **Dunnet Bay** U.K.
106 E2 **Dunnet Head** hd U.K.
131 I5 **Dunnigan** U.S.A.
142 C2 **Dunnigan** U.S.A.
135 H4 **Dunnville** Canada
70 E6 **Dunolly** Australia
106 D5 **Dunoon** U.K.
106 E5 **Dunragit** U.K.
104 E5 **Dunseith** U.S.A.
138 B3 **Dunsmuir** U.S.A.
105 G5 **Dunstable** U.K.
72 B6 **Dunstan Mountains** N.Z.
110 G2 **Dun-sur-Meuse** France
72 C6 **Duntroon** N.Z.
106 B3 **Dunvegan, Loch** inlet U.K.
88 B3 **Dunyapur** Pak.
92 C2 **Duolun** China
93 C4 **Duomula** China
135 H1 **Dupang Ling** mts China
115 J3 **Dupnitsa** Bulg.
142 B1 **Dupree** U.S.A.
144 B4 **Du Quoin** U.S.A.
68 E3 **Durack** r. Australia
80 E3 **Durağan** Turkey
110 H4 **Durance** r. France
135 F4 **Durand** MI U.S.A.
150 C2 **Durango** Mex.
111 E1 **Durango** Spain
141 G3 **Durango** U.S.A.
150 C2 **Durango** state Mex.
143 D5 **Durant** U.S.A.
156 E3 **Durazno** Uruguay
159 F1 **Durazno, Cuchilla Grande del** hills Uruguay
125 I4 **Durban** S. Africa
110 F5 **Durban-Corbières** France
124 D6 **Durbanville** S. Africa
146 D5 **Durbin** U.S.A.
108 E4 **Düren** Germany
89 E5 **Durg** India
104 F4 **Durham** U.K.

140 B2 **Durham** CA U.S.A.
145 E4 **Durham** NC U.S.A.
147 H3 **Durham** NH U.S.A.
117 O6 **Durleşti** Moldova
109 G6 **Durmersheim** Germany
115 H3 **Durmitor** mt. Yugo.
106 D2 **Durness** U.K.
115 H4 **Durrës** Albania
105 F6 **Durrington** U.K.
107 A6 **Dursey Island** Rep. of Ireland
80 B2 **Dursunbey** Turkey
85 F3 **Düruh** Iran
80 F5 **Durüz, Jabal ad** mt. Syria
68 D2 **D'Urville, Tanjung** pt Indon.
72 D5 **D'Urville Island** N.Z.
85 G3 **Durzab** Afgh.
85 G4 **Dushai** Pak.
82 D5 **Dushak** Turkm.
93 C5 **Dushan** China
83 H2 **Dushanbe** Tajik.
117 H7 **Dusheti** Georgia
72 A6 **Dusky Sound** inlet N.Z.
108 E3 **Düsseldorf** Germany
141 F1 **Dutch Mountain** U.S.A.
124 C1 **Dutlwe** Botswana
120 C3 **Dutse** Nigeria
70 B3 **Dutton, Lake** salt flat Australia
141 F2 **Dutton, Mount** mt. U.S.A.
116 H3 **Duvannoye** Rus. Fed.
133 F2 **Duvert, Lac** l. Canada
84 C5 **Duweihin, Khor** b. Saudi Arabia/U.A.E.
83 J5 **Düxanbibazar** China
93 C5 **Duyun** China
85 F5 **Duzab** Pak.
80 C3 **Düzce** Turkey
117 F5 **Dvorichna** Ukr.
94 B2 **Dvoryanka** Rus. Fed.
88 B5 **Dwarka** India
125 G2 **Dwarsberg** S. Africa
134 C5 **Dwight** U.S.A.
108 E2 **Dwingelderveld, Nationaal Park** nat. park Neth.
138 C2 **Dworshak Reservoir** U.S.A.
124 D6 **Dwyka** S. Africa
93 C5 **Dyanev** Turkm.
116 E4 **Dyat'kovo** Rus. Fed.
106 C3 **Dyce** U.K.
134 D5 **Dyer** IN U.S.A.
140 D3 **Dyer** NV U.S.A.
132 G3 **Dyer, Cape** Canada
135 G4 **Dyer Bay** Canada
145 B4 **Dyersburg** U.S.A.
134 B4 **Dyersville** U.S.A.
105 D5 **Dyfi** r. U.K.
106 E3 **Dyke** U.K.
117 G7 **Dykh-Tau, Gora** mt. Georgia/Rus. Fed.
109 K5 **Dyleň** hill Czech Rep.
113 I4 **Dylewska Góra** hill Poland
70 F2 **Dynow Downs** Australia
83 G5 **Dyoki** S. Africa
71 G9 **Dysart** Australia
134 A4 **Dysart** U.S.A.
124 E6 **Dysselsdorp** S. Africa
90 D2 **Dzamïn Üüd** Mongolia
123 E5 **Dzaoudzi** Mayotte
116 I3 **Dzerzhinsk** Rus. Fed.
113 M5 **Dzerzhyns'k** Ukr.
90 E1 **Dzhagdy, Khrebet** mts Rus. Fed.
82 F3 **Dzhalagash** Kazakh.
   Dzhalal-Abad Kyrg. see Jalal-Abad
82 C2 **Dzhanga** Turkm.
82 B2 **Dzhangala** Kazakh.
117 E6 **Dzhankoy** Ukr.
83 F5 **Dzharkurgan** Uzbek.
82 C5 **Dzhebel** Turkm.
83 F4 **Dzhigirbent** Turkm.
82 C4 **Dzhizak** Uzbek.
90 F1 **Dzhugdzhur, Khrebet** mts Rus. Fed.
83 H4 **Dzhuma** Uzbek.
79 F2 **Dzhungarskiy Alatau, Khrebet** mts China/Kazakh.
82 F3 **Dzhusaly** Kazakh.
113 J4 **Działdowo** Poland
151 G4 **Dzibalchén** Mex.
151 G3 **Dzilam de Bravo** Mex.
83 J3 **Dzungarian Gate** pass China/Kazakh.
90 C2 **Dzuunmod** Mongolia
116 C3 **Dzyaniskavichy** Belarus
117 F4 **Dzyarzhynsk** Belarus
113 M4 **Dzyatlavichy** Belarus

E

132 C3 **Eabamet Lake** Canada
141 H4 **Eagar** U.S.A.
133 I3 **Eagle** r. Canada
139 F4 **Eagle** U.S.A.
147 F3 **Eagle Bay** U.S.A.
140 D4 **Eagle Crags** mt. U.S.A.
131 H4 **Eagle Creek** r. Canada
134 B5 **Eagle Grove** U.S.A.
147 I1 **Eagle Lake** l. Canada
138 B3 **Eagle Lake** CA U.S.A.
147 I1 **Eagle Lake** l. U.S.A.
134 B2 **Eagle Mountain** U.S.A.
143 C6 **Eagle Pass** U.S.A.
132 D3 **Eagle Plain** Canada
134 C2 **Eagle River** MI U.S.A.
134 B2 **Eagle River** WI U.S.A.
130 C3 **Eaglesham** Canada
141 F5 **Eagle Tail Mountains** U.S.A.
132 B3 **Ear Falls** Canada
140 C3 **Earlimart** U.S.A.
106 F5 **Earlston** U.K.
134 C5 **Earl Park** U.S.A.
106 E4 **Earn** r. U.K.
106 D4 **Earn, Loch** l. U.K.
143 C5 **Earth** U.S.A.
104 H4 **Easington** U.K.
145 D5 **Easley** U.S.A.
73 C5 **East Antarctica** reg. Antarctica
146 E3 **East Aurora** U.S.A.
133 G3 **East Bay** Canada
105 H7 **Eastbourne** U.K.
147 I1 **East Branch Clarion River Reservoir** U.S.A.
72 G2 **East Cape** N.Z.
141 F5 **East Carbon City** U.S.A.
160 E5 **East Caroline Basin** sea feature N. Pacific Ocean
134 D5 **East Chicago** U.S.A.
90 D3 **East China Sea** Asia
72 B7 **East Coast Bays** N.Z.
146 A6 **East Corinth** U.S.A.
105 H5 **East Dereham** U.K.
152 □ **Easter Island** S. Pacific Ocean
125 G3 **Eastern Cape** prov. S. Africa
87 E7 **Eastern Desert** Egypt
88 B4 **Eastern Ghats** mts India
88 B4 **Eastern Nara** canal Pak.
   Eastern Transvaal prov. S. Africa see Mpumalanga
131 J4 **Easterville** Canada
156 E8 **East Falkland** i. Falkland Is
147 H4 **East Falmouth** U.S.A.
109 G1 **East Frisian Islands** Germany
147 G2 **East Grand Forks** U.S.A.
142 D1 **East Grand Forks** U.S.A.
105 G7 **East Grinstead** U.K.
147 G3 **Easthampton** U.S.A.
147 G4 **East Hampton** U.S.A.

146 D4 **East Hickory** U.S.A.
162 K6 **East Indiaman Ridge** sea feature Indian Ocean
147 G3 **East Jamaica** U.S.A.
134 C5 **East Jordan** U.S.A.
106 D5 **East Kilbride** U.K.
134 C3 **East Lake** U.S.A.
105 F7 **Eastleigh** U.K.
146 C4 **East Liverpool** U.S.A.
106 B3 **East Loch Tarbert** b. U.K.
125 H6 **East London** S. Africa
146 B5 **East Lynn Lake** U.S.A.
132 E3 **Eastmain** Canada
132 F3 **Eastmain** r. Canada
147 G2 **Eastman** Canada
145 D5 **Eastman** U.S.A.
160 F5 **East Mariana Basin** sea feature Pacific Ocean
147 I2 **East Millinocket** U.S.A.
134 C5 **East Moline** U.S.A.
134 C5 **Easton** IL U.S.A.
147 F4 **Easton** MD U.S.A.
147 F4 **Easton** PA U.S.A.
161 L8 **East Pacific Ridge** sea feature S. Pacific Ocean
161 L4 **East Pacific Rise** sea feature N. Pacific Ocean
140 A2 **East Park Reservoir** U.S.A.
133 H4 **East Point** Canada
145 C5 **East Point** U.S.A.
147 J2 **Eastport** ME U.S.A.
134 E3 **Eastport** MI U.S.A.
144 B4 **East St Louis** U.S.A.
   East Sea N. Pacific Ocean see Japan, Sea of
77 Q2 **East Siberian Sea** Rus. Fed.
71 H7 **East Sister Island** Australia
91 K7 **East Timor** terr. Asia
89 F4 **East Tons** r. India
71 F3 **East Toorale** Australia
134 C4 **East Troy** U.S.A.
147 F6 **Eastville** U.S.A.
140 C2 **East Walker** r. U.S.A.
147 G3 **East Wallingford** U.S.A.
145 D5 **Eatonton** U.S.A.
134 B3 **Eau Claire** U.S.A.
134 B3 **Eau Claire** r. U.S.A.
133 F2 **Eau Claire, Lac à l'** l. Canada
160 E5 **Eauripik** Micronesia
160 E5 **Eauripik Rise-New Guinea Rise** sea feature N. Pacific Ocean
151 E3 **Ébano** Mex.
105 D6 **Ebbw Vale** U.K.
120 D4 **Ebebiyin** Equat. Guinea
124 B2 **Ebenerde** Namibia
146 E4 **Ebensburg** U.S.A.
80 C2 **Eber Gölü** l. Turkey
109 I3 **Ebergötzen** Germany
112 F4 **Eberswalde-Finow** Germany
94 D3 **Ebetsu** Japan
93 B4 **Ebian** China
83 J3 **Ebinur Hu** salt l. China
114 F4 **Eboli** Italy
120 D4 **Ebolowa** Cameroon
81 J3 **Ebrähim Heşär** Iran
111 G2 **Ebro** r. Spain
109 I1 **Ebstorf** Germany
115 L4 **Eceabat** Turkey
97 B2 **Echague** Phil.
120 C1 **Ech Chélif** Alg.
111 E1 **Echégárate, Puerto** pass Spain
150 A1 **Echeverria, Pico** mt. Mex.
71 G9 **Echo, Lake** Australia
132 F1 **Echo Bay** N.W.T. Canada
135 E2 **Echo Bay** Ont. Canada
141 G3 **Echo Cliffs** U.S.A.
132 B3 **Echoing** r. Canada
135 J2 **Échouani, Lac** l. Canada
108 D3 **Echt** Neth.
108 E5 **Echternach** Lux.
70 E6 **Echuca** Australia
111 D4 **Écija** Spain
109 J5 **Eckental** Germany
112 D3 **Eckernförde** Germany
129 K2 **Eclipse Sound** sea chan. Canada
154 C4 **Ecuador** country S. America
108 D2 **Edam** Neth.
106 F1 **Eday** i. U.K.
121 F3 **Ed Da'ein** Sudan
121 F3 **Ed Damazin** Sudan
121 F3 **Ed Damer** Sudan
121 F3 **Ed Debba** Sudan
121 F3 **Ed Dueim** Sudan
71 H8 **Eddystone Point** Australia
108 D2 **Ede** Neth.
120 C4 **Edéa** Cameroon
158 C2 **Edéia** Brazil
70 F6 **Eden** Australia
104 E4 **Eden** r. U.K.
143 C6 **Eden** U.S.A.
124 E5 **Edenburg** S. Africa
72 B7 **Edendale** N.Z.
107 D4 **Edenderry** Rep. of Ireland
70 D6 **Edenhope** Australia
145 E4 **Edenton** U.S.A.
109 F1 **Edewecht** Germany
147 G2 **Edgartown** U.S.A.
142 C3 **Edgeley** U.S.A.
142 C2 **Edgemont** U.S.A.
64 C2 **Edgeøya** i. Svalbard
107 D4 **Edgeworthstown** Rep. of Ireland
80 E1 **Edincik** Turkey
106 E5 **Edinburgh** U.K.
117 C7 **Edirne** Turkey
147 G3 **Edison** U.S.A.
145 D5 **Edisto** r. U.S.A.
138 D2 **Edith, Mount** mt. U.S.A.
130 F4 **Edith Cavell, Mount** Canada
83 K2 **Ediz** Uzbek.
138 B2 **Edmonds** U.S.A.
130 G4 **Edmonton** Canada
134 C3 **Edmore** U.S.A.
133 G4 **Edmundston** Canada
143 D6 **Edna** U.S.A.
130 C3 **Edna Bay** U.S.A.
114 E5 **Edolo** Italy
80 D3 **Edremit** Turkey
80 A2 **Edremit Körfezi** b. Turkey
130 G4 **Edson** Canada
156 D3 **Eduardo Castex** Arg.
131 K2 **Edward** r. Canada
122 C4 **Edward, Lake** Dem. Rep. Congo/Uganda
73 B1 **Edward VIII Bay** Antarctica
147 H2 **Edward Island** Canada
134 A1 **Edward Island** Canada
70 A1 **Edwards Creek** Australia
143 C6 **Edwards Plateau** U.S.A.
130 B3 **Eek** U.S.A.
140 A1 **Eel** r. U.S.A.
108 E1 **Eemshaven** pt Neth.
124 E4 **Eenzamheid Pan** salt pan S. Africa
108 D3 **Eersel** Neth.
69 G3 **Éfaté** i. Vanuatu
80 D1 **Eflani** Turkey
114 D6 **Egadi, Isole** is Sicily Italy
135 H2 **Eganville** Canada
141 E2 **Egan Range** mts U.S.A.
113 J7 **Eger** Hungary
103 I4 **Egersund** Norway

109 G3 **Eggegebirge** hill Germany
109 J5 **Eggolsheim** Germany
108 C4 **Eghezée** Belgium
102 D2 **Egilsstaðir** Iceland
80 C3 **Eğirdir** Turkey
80 C3 **Eğirdir Gölü** l. Turkey
110 F4 **Égletons** France
107 D2 **Eglinton** U.K.
128 F2 **Eglinton Island** Canada
108 C2 **Egmond aan Zee** Neth.
72 D3 **Egmont, Cape** N.Z.
   Egmont, Mount vol. N.Z. see Taranaki, Mount
72 D3 **Egmont National Park** N.Z.
80 B2 **Eğrigöz Dağı** mts Turkey
104 G3 **Egton** U.K.
158 D1 **Éguas** r. Brazil
77 U3 **Egvekinot** Rus. Fed.
121 F2 **Egypt** country Africa
92 A2 **Ehen Hudag** China
112 D6 **Ehingen (Donau)** Germany
109 I2 **Ehra-Lessien** Germany
141 E5 **Ehrenberg** U.S.A.
109 I5 **Eibelstadt** Germany
108 E2 **Eibergen** Neth.
109 H4 **Eichenzell** Germany
109 I5 **Eichstätt** Germany
103 I3 **Eidfjord** Norway
103 I3 **Eidsvoll** Norway
108 E4 **Eifel** reg. Germany
106 B4 **Eigg** i. U.K.
87 A4 **Eight Degree Channel** India/Maldives
73 A3 **Eights Coast** Antarctica
71 F6 **Eighty Mile Beach** Australia
80 E7 **Eilat** Israel
71 F6 **Eildon** Australia
131 H2 **Eileen Lake** Canada
109 I2 **Eilenburg** Germany
109 I2 **Eimke** Germany
108 D3 **Eindhoven** Neth.
112 D7 **Einsiedeln** Switz.
163 D2 **Eirik Ridge** sea feature N. Atlantic Ocean
154 E5 **Eirunepé** Brazil
109 H2 **Eisberg** hill Germany
123 C5 **Eiseb** watercourse Namibia
109 I4 **Eisenach** Germany
109 J4 **Eisenberg** Germany
112 H7 **Eisenhüttenstadt** Germany
112 G7 **Eisenstadt** Austria
109 K4 **Eisfeld** Germany
106 B4 **Eishort, Loch** inlet U.K.
109 I4 **Eisleben Lutherstadt** Germany
109 H4 **Eislingen** Germany
   Eivissa see Ibiza
   Eivissa Spain see Ibiza
   Eivissa i. Spain see Ibiza
111 F1 **Ejea de los Caballeros** Spain
123 E6 **Ejeda** Madag.
81 J1 **Ejmiatsin** Armenia
151 E4 **Ejido** Mex.
103 M4 **Ekenäs** Fin.
108 C3 **Ekeren** Belgium
72 E4 **Eketahuna** N.Z.
83 H2 **Ekibastuz** Kazakh.
77 P3 **Ekonda** Rus. Fed.
103 K3 **Ekshärad** Sweden
103 K4 **Eksjö** Sweden
124 B4 **Eksteenfontein** S. Africa
122 C4 **Ekuku** Dem. Rep. Congo
132 D3 **Ekwan** r. Canada
132 D3 **Ekwan Point** Canada
115 J6 **Elafonisou, Steno** sea chan. Greece
125 H2 **Elandsdoorn** S. Africa
125 H2 **Elandsrivier** S. Africa
120 C1 **El Aouinet** Alg.
150 A1 **El Arco** Mex.
115 I5 **Elassona** Greece
81 G2 **Elazığ** Turkey
114 D3 **Elba, Isola d'** i. Italy
157 B2 **El Banco** Col.
150 C2 **El Barreal** salt l. Mex.
115 I4 **Elbasan** Albania
157 C2 **El Baúl** Venez.
120 C1 **El Bayadh** Alg.
109 I1 **Elbe** r. Germany
   alt. Labe (Czech Rep.)
139 F4 **Elbert, Mount** mt. U.S.A.
134 D3 **Elberta** MI U.S.A.
141 G2 **Elberta** UT U.S.A.
145 D5 **Elberton** U.S.A.
110 E2 **Elbeuf** France
80 F2 **Elbistan** Turkey
113 I3 **Elbląg** Poland
156 B4 **El Bolsón** Arg.
145 E7 **Elbow Cay** i. Bahamas
117 G7 **Elbrus** mt. Rus. Fed.
108 D2 **Elburg** Neth.
111 E2 **El Burgo de Osma** Spain
84 C2 **Elburz Mountains** mts Iran
159 C4 **El Cain** Arg.
140 E5 **El Cajon** U.S.A.
157 D2 **El Callao** Venez.
143 D6 **El Campo** U.S.A.
139 F5 **El Capitan Mountain** U.S.A.
140 E5 **El Centro** U.S.A.
154 F7 **El Cerro** Bol.
157 E3 **El Chaparro** Venez.
111 F3 **Elche** Spain
151 F4 **El Chichón** vol. Mex.
150 D1 **El Chilicote** Mex.
71 G3 **Elcho Island** Australia
157 B3 **El Cocuy** Col.
157 B3 **El Cocuy, Parque Nacional** nat. park Col.
151 G4 **El Cuyo** Mex.
109 J1 **Elde** r. Germany
135 H2 **Eldee** Canada
70 D3 **Elder, Lake** salt flat Australia
134 B4 **Eldon** IA U.S.A.
142 E4 **Eldon** MO U.S.A.
150 C2 **El Doctor** Mex.
156 E2 **Eldorado** Arg.
158 B3 **Eldorado** Brazil
150 D3 **El Dorado** Mex.
143 E5 **El Dorado** AR U.S.A.
143 D4 **El Dorado** KS U.S.A.
122 D3 **Eldoret** Kenya
140 C2 **Electric Peak** mt. U.S.A.
120 B2 **El Eglab** plat. Alg.
116 F3 **Elektrostal'** Rus. Fed.
154 D4 **El Encanto** Col.
139 F5 **Elephant Butte Reservoir** U.S.A.
73 B1 **Elephant Island** Antarctica
89 H5 **Elephant Point** Bangl.
81 I2 **Eleşkirt** Turkey
154 □ **El Estor** Guat.
114 C6 **El Eulma** Alg.
145 E7 **Eleuthera** i. Bahamas
114 C6 **El Fahs** Tunisia
121 F3 **El Fasher** Sudan
109 H4 **Elfershausen** Germany
150 B2 **El Fuerte** Mex.
121 F3 **El Geneina** Sudan
121 F3 **El Geteina** Sudan
106 F3 **Elgin** U.K.
134 B5 **Elgin** IL U.S.A.
142 C2 **Elgin** ND U.S.A.
141 G2 **Elgin** UT U.S.A.
77 P3 **El'ginskiy** Rus. Fed.

92 E4 Feidong China
92 F3 Feihuanghe Kou est. China
154 D5 Feijó Brazil
72 E4 Feilding N.Z.
155 K6 Feira de Santana Brazil
92 E4 Feixi China
80 E3 Feke Turkey
111 H3 Felanitx Spain
134 D3 Felch U.S.A.
100 L1 Feldberg Germany
112 D7 Feldberg mt. Germany
112 D7 Feldkirch Austria
112 G7 Feldkirchen in Kärnten Austria
159 E1 Feliciano r. Arg.
151 G4 Felipe C. Puerto Mex.
158 D2 Felixlândia Brazil
105 I6 Felixstowe U.K.
114 D1 Feltre Italy
103 J3 Femunden l. Norway
103 K3 Femundsmarka Nasjonalpark nat. park Norway
114 D3 Fenaio, Punta del pt Italy
141 H4 Fence Lake U.S.A.
135 H3 Fennimore U.S.A.
115 K4 Fengari mt. Greece
93 E4 Fengcheng Jiangxi China
96 C3 Fengcheng Liaoning China
93 C4 Fengdu China
93 C5 Fenggang China
96 D1 Fengguang China
93 F4 Fenghua China
93 C5 Fenghuang China
92 C4 Fengjie China
93 D6 Fengkai China
93 F6 Fenglin Taiwan
92 F2 Fengnan China
92 E1 Fengning China
92 E3 Fengqiu China
93 C5 Fengshan China
93 E6 Fengshun China
92 E3 Fengtai China
93 E4 Fengxin China
92 E3 Fengyang China
92 D1 Fengzhen China
92 D2 Fen He r. China
89 G5 Feni Bangl.
69 F2 Feni Islands P.N.G.
134 B4 Fennimore U.S.A.
123 E5 Fenoarivo Atsinanana Madag.
135 F4 Fenton U.S.A.
92 D2 Fenxi China
92 D2 Fenyang China
93 E5 Fenyi China
117 E6 Feodosiya Ukr.
114 B6 Fer, Cap de hd Alg.
85 E3 Ferdows Iran
83 G4 Fergana Uzbek.
83 H4 Fergana Too Tizmegi mts Kyrg.
135 G4 Fergus Canada
142 D2 Fergus Falls U.S.A.
68 F2 Fergusson Island P.N.G.
114 C7 Fériana Tunisia
120 B4 Ferkessédougou Côte d'Ivoire
114 E3 Fermo Italy
133 G3 Fermont Canada
111 C2 Fermoselle Spain
107 C5 Fermoy Rep. of Ireland
154 □ Fernandina, Isla i. Galapagos Is Ecuador
145 D6 Fernandina Beach U.S.A.
156 B8 Fernando de Magallanes, Parque Nacional nat. park Chile
163 G6 Fernando de Noronha i. Brazil
158 B3 Fernandópolis Brazil
138 B1 Ferndale U.S.A.
105 F7 Ferndown U.K.
130 F5 Fernie Canada
71 G2 Fernlee Australia
140 C2 Fernley U.S.A.
147 F4 Fernridge U.S.A.
107 E5 Ferns Rep. of Ireland
138 C2 Fernwood U.S.A.
114 D2 Ferrara Italy
158 B3 Ferreiros Brazil
143 F6 Ferriday U.S.A.
114 C4 Ferro, Capo pt Sardinia Italy
111 B1 Ferrol Spain
141 G2 Ferron U.S.A.
82 D1 Fershampenuaz Rus. Fed.
108 D1 Ferwerd Neth.
120 B1 Fès Morocco
122 B4 Feshi Dem. Rep. Congo
131 J5 Fessenden U.S.A.
142 F4 Festus U.S.A.
106 □ Fethaland, Point of U.K.
107 D6 Fethard Rep. of Ireland
80 B3 Fethiye Turkey
82 C4 Fetisovo Kazakh.
106 □ Fetlar i. U.K.
106 F4 Fettercairn U.K.
109 J5 Feucht Germany
109 I5 Feuchtwangen Germany
133 F2 Feuilles, Rivière aux r. Canada
80 F3 Fevzipaşa Turkey
85 H2 Feyzābād Afgh.
85 E3 Feyzābād Iran
105 D5 Ffestiniog U.K.
123 E6 Fianarantsoa Madag.
122 D3 Fiché Eth.
109 K4 Fichtelgebirge reg. Germany
125 G4 Ficksburg S. Africa
130 F4 Field B.C. Canada
135 G2 Field Ont. Canada
115 H4 Fier Albania
134 E3 Fife Lake U.S.A.
106 F4 Fife Ness pt U.K.
71 G4 Fifield Australia
134 B3 Fifield U.S.A.
110 F3 Figeac France
111 B2 Figueira da Foz Port.
111 H1 Figueres Spain
120 B1 Figuig Morocco
69 H3 Fiji country Pacific Ocean
150 H6 Filadelfia Costa Rica
156 D2 Filadelfia Para.
73 B3 Filchner Ice Shelf Antarctica
104 D3 Filey U.K.
115 I5 Filippiada Greece
103 K4 Filipstad Sweden
102 J3 Fillan Norway
140 C4 Fillmore CA U.S.A.
141 G4 Fillmore UT U.S.A.
147 F2 Finch Canada
106 F3 Findhorn r. U.K.
81 H3 Fındık Turkey
146 B4 Findlay U.S.A.
71 H8 Fingal Australia
135 E4 Finger Lakes U.S.A.
123 D5 Fingoè Moz.
80 C3 Finike Turkey
80 C3 Finike Körfezi b. Turkey
111 B1 Finisterre, Cape Spain
116 S5 Finland country Europe
103 M4 Finland, Gulf of Europe
130 D3 Finlay r. Canada
130 D3 Finlay, Mount Canada
71 H5 Finley Australia
109 J5 Finne ridge Germany
70 A4 Finniss, Cape pt Australia
102 L1 Finnmark Norway
103 K4 Finnsnes Norway
103 D3 Finspång Sweden
107 D3 Fintona Rep. of Ireland
107 C3 Fintown Rep. of Ireland
106 D3 Fionn Loch l. U.K.
106 B4 Fionnphort U.K.
81 J6 Fiordland National Park N.Z.
81 J6 Firat r. Turkey
alt. Al Furāt (Iraq/Syria),
conv. Euphrates
140 B3 Firebaugh U.S.A.
131 I2 Firedrake Lake Canada
147 G4 Fire Island National Seashore res. U.S.A.

Firenze Italy see Florence
81 J6 Firk, Sha'īb watercourse Iraq
159 E2 Firmat Arg.
110 G4 Firminy France
109 I6 Firngrund reg. Germany
113 P2 Firovo Rus. Fed.
88 B3 Firoza Pak.
88 D4 Firozabad India
85 G3 Firozkoh reg. Afgh.
88 C3 Firozpur India
147 H2 First Connecticut Lake U.S.A.
84 D4 Fīrūzābād Iran
88 C5 Fīrūzkūh Iran
88 B5 Fischbach Germany
123 B6 Fish r. Namibia
124 D5 Fish r. S. Africa
73 B6 Fisher Bay Antarctica
147 F6 Fisherman Island U.S.A.
131 M2 Fishers Island U.S.A.
105 D5 Fishguard U.K.
130 E2 Fish Lake Canada
134 A3 Fish Lake MN U.S.A.
141 G2 Fish Lake UT U.S.A.
135 F4 Fish Point U.S.A.
93 □ Fish Ponds l. Hong Kong China
73 B3 Fiske, Cape Antarctica
108 B5 Fismes France
111 B1 Fisterra Spain
111 B1 Fisterra, Cabo c. Spain see Finisterre, Cape
147 H3 Fitchburg U.S.A.
131 G3 Fitzgerald Canada
68 B5 Fitzgerald U.S.A.
70 B4 Fitzgerald Bay Australia
156 C7 Fitz Roy Arg.
68 C3 Fitzroy Crossing Australia
135 G3 Fitzwilliam Island Canada
107 D3 Fivemiletown U.K.
114 D2 Fivizzano Italy
122 C4 Fizi Dem. Rep. Congo
103 J3 Flå Norway
125 H5 Flagstaff S. Africa
141 F4 Flagstaff U.S.A.
147 H2 Flagstaff Lake U.S.A.
132 E2 Flaherty Island Canada
134 B3 Flambeau r. U.S.A.
104 G3 Flamborough Head hd U.K.
109 K2 Fläming hill Germany
139 E3 Flaming Gorge Reservoir l. U.S.A.
124 D5 Flaminksvlei salt pan S. Africa
108 A4 Flandre reg. France
106 A2 Flannan Isles i. U.K.
102 K2 Flåsjön l. Sweden
134 E4 Flat r. U.S.A.
72 E4 Flat Point N.Z.
143 F5 Flattery, Cape pt U.S.A.
138 A1 Flattery, Cape U.S.A.
102 L3 Flathead Lake U.S.A.
109 J2 Fleetmark Germany
104 D4 Fleetwood U.K.
147 F4 Fleetwood U.S.A.
103 I4 Flekkefjord Norway
146 E3 Fleming U.S.A.
147 G2 Flemingsburg U.S.A.
163 G2 Flemish Cap sea feature N. Atlantic Ocean
103 L4 Flen Sweden
112 D3 Flensburg Germany
110 D2 Flers France
135 G3 Flesherton Canada
131 H2 Fletcher Lake Canada
135 F3 Fletcher Pond l. U.S.A.
68 B5 Flinders r. Australia
68 B5 Flinders Bay Australia
70 B5 Flinders Chase National Park Australia
70 A4 Flinders Island S.A. Australia
71 H7 Flinders Island Tas. Australia
70 C3 Flinders Ranges mts Australia
70 C3 Flinders Ranges National Park Australia
131 I4 Flin Flon Canada
105 D4 Flint U.K.
135 F4 Flint r. GA U.S.A.
135 F4 Flint r. MI U.S.A.
161 I5 Flint i. Kiribati
71 H1 Flinton Australia
103 K3 Flisa Norway
109 L4 Flöha Germany
109 L4 Flöha r. Germany
73 A4 Flood Range mts Antarctica
134 A2 Floodwood U.S.A.
144 B4 Flora U.S.A.
110 F3 Florac France
108 E5 Florange France
135 F4 Florence Canada
114 D3 Florence Italy
145 C5 Florence AL U.S.A.
141 G5 Florence AZ U.S.A.
142 C4 Florence KS U.S.A.
138 A3 Florence OR U.S.A.
145 E5 Florence SC U.S.A.
141 G5 Florence Junction U.S.A.
147 H2 Florenceville Canada
157 B4 Florencia Col.
108 C4 Florennes Belgium
156 C6 Florentino Ameghino, Embalse resr Arg.
159 E2 Flores r. Arg.
151 G4 Flores Guat.
71 E7 Flores i. Indon.
158 C1 Flores de Goiás Brazil
91 D7 Flores Sea Indon.
155 K5 Floresta Brazil
155 J5 Floriano Brazil
156 F3 Florianópolis Brazil
159 F2 Florida Uruguay
145 D6 Florida U.S.A.
149 H4 Florida, Straits of strait Bahamas/U.S.A.
145 D7 Florida Bay U.S.A.
145 D7 Florida City U.S.A.
69 G2 Florida Islands Solomon Is
145 D7 Florida Keys is U.S.A.
115 H4 Florina Greece
103 I3 Florø Norway
130 H3 Flour Lake Canada
134 A4 Floyd IA U.S.A.
146 C5 Floyd VA U.S.A.
141 H4 Floyd, Mount U.S.A.
143 C5 Floydada U.S.A.
108 D2 Fluessen l. Neth.
69 F2 Fly r. P.N.G.
115 H3 Foča Bos.-Herz.
81 H2 Foçha Turkey
103 J3 Fochabers U.K.
125 L2 Fochville S. Africa
114 F4 Focşani Romania
92 D3 Fogang China
114 F4 Foggia Italy
120 □ Fogo i. Cape Verde
133 J4 Fogo Island Canada
83 G4 Fogolevo Rus. Fed.
106 D2 Foinaven hill U.K.
117 E5 Foix France
113 N5 Fokino Rus. Fed.
103 I3 Folda sea chan. Norway
102 K2 Foldereid Norway
115 K6 Folegandros i. Greece
135 F1 Foleyet Canada
114 E3 Foligno Italy
105 I6 Folkestone U.K.
105 F1 Folkingham U.K.
141 F2 Folsom U.S.A.
117 G6 Fomin Rus. Fed.
113 Q4 Fominskaya Rus. Fed.
131 H3 Fond-du-Lac Canada
131 I3 Fond du Lac r. Canada

134 C4 Fond du Lac U.S.A.
111 B2 Fondevila Spain
114 E4 Fondi Italy
69 H2 Fongafale Tuvalu
114 C4 Fonni Sardinia Italy
150 H5 Fonseca, Golfo do b. Central America
133 F3 Fontanges Canada
130 E3 Fontas Canada
130 E3 Fontas r. Canada
154 E4 Fonte Boa Brazil
110 D3 Fontenay-le-Comte France
102 D1 Fontur pt Iceland
135 H3 Foot's Bay Canada
92 C3 Foping China
71 H4 Forbes Australia
138 C1 Forbes, Mount Canada
109 J5 Forchheim Germany
133 G2 Ford r. Canada
134 D2 Ford r. U.S.A.
103 I3 Førde Norway
131 J2 Forde Lake Canada
105 H5 Fordham U.K.
105 F7 Fordingbridge U.K.
73 A4 Ford Range mts Antarctica
71 F2 Fords Bridge Australia
143 E5 Fordyce U.S.A.
120 A4 Forécariah Guinea
105 F7 Foreland hd U.K.
105 D6 Foreland Point U.K.
130 H4 Foresight Mountain Canada
135 G4 Forest Canada
143 F5 Forest MS U.S.A.
146 B4 Forest OH U.S.A.
147 G3 Forest Dale U.S.A.
71 G5 Forest Hill Australia
140 B2 Foresthill U.S.A.
71 H9 Forestier, Cape hd Australia
71 H9 Forestier Peninsula Australia
134 A3 Forest Lake U.S.A.
145 C5 Forest Park U.S.A.
133 G4 Forestville Canada
106 F4 Forfar U.K.
138 C2 Forks U.S.A.
146 E4 Forksville U.S.A.
114 E2 Forlì Italy
104 D4 Formby U.K.
111 G3 Formentera i. Spain
111 H3 Formentor, Cap de pt Spain
158 D3 Formiga Brazil
156 E3 Formosa Arg.
158 C1 Formosa Brazil
155 G6 Formosa, Serra hills Brazil
158 D1 Formoso r. Brazil
106 E3 Forres U.K.
70 E7 Forrest Australia
134 C5 Forrest City U.S.A.
143 F5 Forreston U.S.A.
102 L3 Fors Sweden
68 E3 Forsayth Australia
102 M2 Forsnäs Sweden
103 M3 Forssa Fin.
71 J4 Forster Australia
143 F4 Forsyth MO U.S.A.
138 F2 Forsyth MT U.S.A.
131 I1 Forsythe Canada
88 C5 Fort Abbas Pak.
132 D3 Fort Albany Canada
155 K4 Fortaleza Brazil
141 H5 Fort Apache U.S.A.
130 G4 Fort Assiniboine Canada
134 C4 Fort Atkinson U.S.A.
138 D2 Fort Augustus U.K.
124 G6 Fort Beaufort S. Africa
138 E2 Fort Benton U.S.A.
131 H3 Fort Black Canada
140 A2 Fort Bragg U.S.A.
133 F2 Fort-Chimo Canada see Kuujjuaq
131 G3 Fort Chipewyan Canada
143 D5 Fort Cobb Reservoir U.S.A.
139 F3 Fort Collins U.S.A.
135 I3 Fort-Coulonge Canada
147 F2 Fort Covington U.S.A.
143 C6 Fort Davis U.S.A.
149 L6 Fort-de-France Martinique
145 C5 Fort Deposit U.S.A.
142 E3 Fort Dodge U.S.A.
142 E1 Fort Frances Canada
Fort George Canada see Chisasibi
128 F3 Fort Good Hope Canada
106 D4 Forth r. U.K.
106 E4 Forth, Firth of est. U.K.
141 E2 Fortification Range mts U.S.A.
156 D2 Fortín Capitán Demattei Para.
156 D2 Fortín General Mendoza Para.
156 E2 Fortín Madrejón Para.
156 D2 Fortín Pilcomayo Arg.
154 F7 Fortín Ravelo Bol.
154 F7 Fortín Suárez Arana Bol.
147 I1 Fort Kent U.S.A.
145 D7 Fort Lauderdale U.S.A.
130 E2 Fort Liard Canada
131 G3 Fort Mackay Canada
130 G4 Fort Macleod Canada
131 G3 Fort McMurray Canada
128 E3 Fort McPherson Canada
139 G2 Fort Morgan U.S.A.
145 D7 Fort Myers U.S.A.
130 E2 Fort Nelson Canada
130 E2 Fort Nelson r. Canada
Fort Norman Canada see Tulít'a
145 C5 Fort Payne U.S.A.
138 F2 Fort Peck U.S.A.
138 F2 Fort Peck Reservoir U.S.A.
145 D7 Fort Pierce U.S.A.
142 C2 Fort Pierre U.S.A.
131 I4 Fort Providence Canada
130 G2 Fort Qu'Appelle Canada
130 G2 Fort Resolution Canada
72 B7 Fortrose N.Z.
106 E3 Fortrose U.K.
140 A2 Fort Ross U.S.A.
Fort Rupert Canada see Waskaganish
130 E4 Fort St James Canada
130 E3 Fort St John Canada
130 G4 Fort Saskatchewan Canada
143 E4 Fort Scott U.S.A.
132 C2 Fort Severn Canada
82 B3 Fort-Shevchenko Kazakh.
130 E2 Fort Simpson Canada
131 H3 Fort Smith Canada
143 E5 Fort Smith U.S.A.
143 C6 Fort Stockton U.S.A.
143 B5 Fort Sumner U.S.A.
130 C3 Fort Vermilion Canada
145 C6 Fort Walton Beach U.S.A.
146 C4 Fort Wayne U.S.A.
106 D3 Fort William U.K.
143 D5 Fort Worth U.S.A.
129 F3 Fort Yukon U.S.A.
120 D4 Foumban Cameroon

73 B3 Foundation Ice Stream Antarctica
120 A3 Foundiougne Senegal
134 A4 Fountain U.S.A.
110 G2 Fourches, Mont des hill France
140 D4 Four Corners U.S.A.
125 C4 Fouriesburg S. Africa
110 C4 Fourmies France
115 L6 Fournoi i. Greece
134 C2 Fourteen Mile Point U.S.A.
120 A3 Fouta Djallon reg. Guinea
72 A7 Foveaux Strait N.Z.
145 E7 Fowl Cay i. Bahamas
139 F4 Fowler CO U.S.A.
134 D5 Fowler IN U.S.A.
134 D3 Fowler MI U.S.A.
73 B3 Fowler Ice Rise pen. Antarctica
68 D5 Fowlers Bay Australia
81 L3 Fowman Iran
131 K3 Fox r. Canada
134 K3 Fox r. U.S.A.
130 F4 Fox Creek Canada
104 C3 Foxdale U.K.
129 J3 Foxe Basin g. Canada
129 K3 Foxe Channel Canada
129 K3 Foxe Peninsula Canada
72 E4 Fox Glacier N.Z.
130 E3 Fox Lake Canada
134 C4 Fox Lake U.S.A.
72 E4 Foxton N.Z.
107 D3 Foyle r. Rep. of Ireland/U.K.
107 D2 Foyle, Lough b. Rep. of Ireland/U.K.
107 B5 Foynes Rep. of Ireland
123 B5 Foz do Cunene Angola
158 A4 Foz do Iguaçu Brazil
111 C2 Fraga Spain
73 D4 Framnes Mts Antarctica
158 C3 Franca Brazil
69 G3 Français, Récif des reef New Caledonia
110 F3 France country Europe
70 F3 Frances Australia
130 D2 Frances r. Canada
130 D2 Frances Lake Canada
130 D2 Frances Lake l. Canada
134 D5 Francesville U.S.A.
122 B4 Franceville Gabon
110 D2 Franche-Comté reg. France
142 D3 Francis Case, Lake U.S.A.
150 C2 Francisco I. Madero Mex.
150 C2 Francisco I. Madero Mex.
158 D2 Francisco Sá Brazil
123 C6 Francistown Botswana
130 D4 François Lake Canada
138 E3 Francs Peak mt. U.S.A.
108 D1 Franeker Neth.
109 L4 Frankenberg Germany
109 G3 Frankenberg (Eder) Germany
109 J5 Frankenthal (Pfalz) Germany
109 J4 Frankenwald for. Germany
125 H3 Frankfort S. Africa
146 C4 Frankfort KY U.S.A.
134 C4 Frankfort MI U.S.A.
109 H4 Frankfurt am Main Germany
109 M3 Frankfurt an der Oder Germany
141 E1 Frankin Lake U.S.A.
109 J5 Fränkische Alb reg. Germany
109 J5 Fränkische Schweiz reg. Germany
138 E3 Franklin ID U.S.A.
144 C4 Franklin LA U.S.A.
147 H3 Franklin MA U.S.A.
145 D5 Franklin NC U.S.A.
147 H3 Franklin NH U.S.A.
147 F4 Franklin NJ U.S.A.
145 C5 Franklin PA U.S.A.
145 C5 Franklin TN U.S.A.
146 D5 Franklin VA U.S.A.
146 C4 Franklin WV U.S.A.
128 F3 Franklin Bay Canada
138 C1 Franklin D. Roosevelt Lake U.S.A.
70 B4 Franklin Harbour b. Australia
73 B5 Franklin Island Antarctica
128 G2 Franklin Mountains Canada
72 A6 Franklin Mountains N.Z.
71 G8 Franklin Sound sea chan. Australia
129 I2 Franklin Strait Canada
70 F7 Frankston Australia
102 L3 Fränsta Sweden
76 Frantsa-Iosifa, Zemlya is Rus. Fed.
72 C5 Franz Canada
72 C5 Franz Josef Glacier N.Z.
114 C5 Frasca, Capo della pt Sardinia Italy
114 E4 Frascati Italy
130 E4 Fraser r. B.C. Canada
133 H2 Fraser r. Nfld Canada
124 D5 Fraserburg S. Africa
106 F3 Fraserburgh U.K.
132 D4 Fraserdale Canada
69 F4 Fraser Island Australia
130 E4 Fraser Plateau Canada
72 F3 Frasertown N.Z.
134 E2 Frater Canada
159 E2 Fray Bentos Uruguay
109 G4 Frechen Germany
105 E4 Freckleton U.K.
134 C4 Frederic MI U.S.A.
134 B3 Frederic WI U.S.A.
103 J5 Fredericia Denmark
157 D6 Frederica MD U.S.A.
146 C5 Frederick MD U.S.A.
143 D5 Frederick OK U.S.A.
133 G4 Fredericksburg TX U.S.A.
143 D6 Fredericksburg VA U.S.A.
130 C3 Frederick Sound sea chan. U.S.A.
143 G4 Fredericktown U.S.A.
133 G4 Fredericton Canada
Frederikshåb Greenland see Paamiut
103 J4 Frederikshavn Denmark
103 K5 Frederiksværk Denmark
141 D3 Fredonia AZ U.S.A.
146 D3 Fredonia NY U.S.A.
134 B4 Fredonia WI U.S.A.
102 L2 Fredrika Sweden
103 J4 Fredrikstad Norway
147 F4 Freehold U.S.A.
147 F4 Freeland U.S.A.
71 H8 Freeling Heights mt. Australia
140 C2 Freel Peak mt. U.S.A.
142 D3 Freeman U.S.A.
142 D3 Freeman, Lake U.S.A.
134 C4 Freeport IL U.S.A.
147 H2 Freeport ME U.S.A.
147 G4 Freeport NY U.S.A.
143 D6 Freeport TX U.S.A.
149 I4 Freeport City Bahamas
143 D7 Freer U.S.A.
125 H4 Free State prov. S. Africa
120 A4 Freetown Sierra Leone
111 C3 Fregenal de la Sierra Spain
110 C2 Fréhel, Cap c. France
109 H5 Freiberg Germany
109 G5 Freiberg im Breisgau Germany
108 F5 Freisen Germany
109 K6 Freising Germany
112 F6 Freistadt Austria
110 H5 Fréjus France
70 A5 Fremantle Australia
134 D4 Fremont MI U.S.A.
142 D3 Fremont NE U.S.A.
146 B4 Fremont OH U.S.A.
141 G2 Fremont r. U.S.A.
135 F2 French r. Canada
146 B4 Frenchburg U.S.A.
146 C3 French Creek r. U.S.A.

155 H3 French Guiana terr. S. America
70 F7 French Island Australia
131 H5 Frenchman r. Canada/U.S.A.
140 C2 Frenchman U.S.A.
140 B2 Frenchman Lake U.S.A.
141 E3 Frenchman Lake U.S.A.
107 C4 Frenchpark Rep. of Ireland
72 C4 Frenchman's Cap mt. Australia
67 I5 French Pass N.Z.
French Polynesia terr. Pacific Ocean
65 French Southern and Antarctic Lands terr. Indian Ocean
147 I1 Frenchville U.S.A.
108 F7 Freren Germany
107 B4 Freshford Rep. of Ireland
141 G6 Fresnal Canyon U.S.A.
150 D3 Fresnillo Mex.
140 C3 Fresno U.S.A.
140 C3 Fresno r. U.S.A.
111 H3 Freu, Cap des pt Spain
109 F4 Freudenberg Germany
112 D6 Freudenstadt Germany
71 H4 Freycinet Nat. Park Australia
71 H9 Freycinet Peninsula Australia
109 K1 Freyenstein Germany
110 H2 Freyming-Merlebach France
159 D1 Freyre Arg.
120 A3 Fria Guinea
140 C3 Friant U.S.A.
156 C3 Frías Arg.
112 C7 Fribourg Switz.
109 F1 Friedeburg Germany
112 D7 Friedrichshafen Germany
147 I3 Friendship U.S.A.
109 K2 Friesack Germany
108 D1 Friese Wad tidal flat Neth.
109 F1 Friesoythe Germany
105 I6 Frinton-on-Sea U.K.
158 A4 Frio r. Brazil
143 D6 Frio r. U.S.A.
106 C3 Frisa, Loch l. U.K.
141 F2 Frisco Mountain U.S.A.
129 L3 Frobisher Bay Canada
131 H3 Frobisher Lake Canada
102 J3 Frohavet b. Norway
109 J4 Frohburg Germany
108 A5 Froissy France
117 F6 Frolovo Rus. Fed.
105 E6 Frome U.K.
70 C2 Frome watercourse Australia
70 C2 Frome, Lake salt flat Australia
70 C3 Frome Downs Australia
109 G4 Fröndenberg Germany
151 F4 Frontera Mex.
151 E4 Frontera, Punta pt Mex.
146 D5 Front Royal U.S.A.
114 E3 Frosinone Italy
146 D5 Frostburg U.S.A.
103 J3 Frøya i. Norway
108 A4 Fruges France
141 H2 Fruita U.S.A.
141 G1 Fruitland U.S.A.
83 G4 Frunze Kyrg.
Frunze Kyrg. see Bishkek
112 C7 Frutigen Switz.
113 I6 Frýdek-Místek Czech Rep.
147 H2 Fryeburg U.S.A.
93 D5 Fu'an China
93 D5 Fuchuan China
93 C4 Fuchun Jiang r. China
93 D5 Fude China
93 D5 Fuding China
111 E2 Fuenlabrada Spain
111 D3 Fuente Obejuna Spain
96 D2 Fu'er He r. China
156 E2 Fuerte Olimpo Para.
120 A2 Fuerteventura i. Canary Is
91 G3 Fuga i. Phil.
92 D2 Fugu China
92 C3 Fugu China
84 D4 Fuhaymī Iraq
86 E4 Fujairah U.A.E.
95 F7 Fuji Japan
93 E5 Fujian prov. China
95 C4 Fu Jiang r. China
95 F7 Fuji-Hakone-Izu National Park Japan
94 B1 Fujin China
95 F7 Fujinomiya Japan
94 H3 Fujioka Japan
95 F7 Fujisawa Japan
95 A8 Fukue Japan
95 A8 Fukue-jima i. Japan
95 B8 Fukuoka Japan
95 G6 Fukushima Japan
95 B9 Fukuyama Japan
84 D2 Fūlād Maḥalleh Iran
109 H4 Fulda Germany
109 H4 Fulda r. Germany
105 G6 Fulham U.K.
92 E3 Fuliji China
131 L2 Fullerton, Cape hd Canada
134 B5 Fulton IL U.S.A.
144 B5 Fulton KY U.S.A.
142 F4 Fulton MO U.S.A.
135 F3 Fulton NY U.S.A.
108 C4 Fumay France
110 E4 Fumel France
95 F7 Funabashi Japan
69 H2 Funafuti i. Tuvalu
96 B3 Funan China
120 A1 Funchal Port.
157 C7 Fundación Col.
111 C2 Fundão Port.
151 F5 Fundición Mex.
133 G5 Fundy, Bay of g. Canada
133 G4 Fundy National Park Canada
140 D3 Funeral Peak mt. U.S.A.
Fung Wong Shan hill Hong Kong China see Lantau Peak
123 D6 Funhalouro Moz.
92 E3 Funing Jiangsu China
93 C5 Funing Yunnan China
92 D3 Funiu Shan mts China
120 D3 Funtua Nigeria
93 F5 Fuqing China
94 H3 Furano Japan
113 R3 Furmanov Rus. Fed.
84 E5 Fürgun, Kūh-e mt. Iran
140 D3 Furnace Creek U.S.A.
158 C1 Furnas, Represa resr Brazil
68 E6 Furneaux Group is Australia
109 F3 Fürstenau Germany
109 L1 Fürstenberg Germany
109 M2 Fürstenwalde Germany
109 I5 Fürth Germany
109 K2 Furth im Wald Germany
94 G5 Furukawa Japan
129 K3 Fury and Hecla Strait strait Canada
157 C7 Fusagasugá Col.
93 C7 Fushan Hainan China
94 A5 Fushan Shandong China
96 C3 Fushun Liaoning China
93 B5 Fushun Sichuan China
93 D5 Fusong China
112 D7 Füssen Germany
95 E6 Futago-san vol. Japan
69 H3 Futuna i. Vanuatu
69 H3 Futuna Islands Wallis and Futuna Is
93 E5 Futun r. China
92 C3 Fuxian China
93 B5 Fuxian Hu l. China

96 A2 Fuxin Liaoning China
96 A2 Fuxin Liaoning China
94 F5 Fuya Japan
92 E3 Fuyang Anhui China
93 F4 Fuyang Zhejiang China
92 F2 Fuyang He r. China
90 D2 Fuyu Heilong. China
96 D1 Fuyu Jilin China
93 B5 Fuyuan China
94 A4 Fuyun China
81 K2 Füzuli Azer.
103 J5 Fyn i. Denmark
106 C5 Fyne, Loch inlet U.K.

F.Y.R.O.M. (Former Yugoslav Republic of Macedonia) country Europe see Macedonia

G

114 C6 Gâfour Tunisia
122 F2 Gaalkacyo Somalia
125 F2 Gabane Botswana
140 D2 Gabbs Valley Range mts U.S.A.
123 B5 Gabela Angola
120 D1 Gabès Tunisia
121 □ Gabès, Golfe de g. Tunisia
71 H6 Gabo Island Australia
122 B4 Gabon country Africa
123 C6 Gaborone Botswana
85 E5 Gābrīk Iran
85 E5 Gābrīk watercourse Iran
115 K3 Gabrovo Bulg.
120 A3 Gabú Guinea-Bissau
84 C2 Gach Sār Iran
87 A3 Gachsārān Iran
88 A3 Gadag India
102 K2 Gäddede Sweden
109 J1 Gadebusch Germany
88 B5 Gadra Pak.
88 B4 Gadra Pak.
145 C5 Gadsden U.S.A.
87 B2 Gadwal India
105 D6 Gaer U.K.
114 E3 Gaeta Italy
114 E4 Gaeta, Golfo di g. Italy
160 E5 Gaferut i. Micronesia
145 D5 Gaffney U.S.A.
120 C1 Gafsa Tunisia
116 F4 Gagarin Rus. Fed.
83 H4 Gagarin Uzbek.
116 H4 Gagino Rus. Fed.
120 B4 Gagnoa Côte d'Ivoire
133 G3 Gagnon Canada
117 G2 Gagra Georgia
81 K4 Gahväreh Iran
124 C3 Gaiab watercourse Namibia
89 H6 Gaibandha Bangl.
109 H6 Gaildorf Germany
145 D6 Gainesville FL U.S.A.
145 D5 Gainesville GA U.S.A.
143 D5 Gainesville TX U.S.A.
105 G4 Gainsborough U.K.
70 A3 Gairdner, Lake salt flat Australia
106 D3 Gairloch U.K.
106 C3 Gair Loch inlet U.K.
96 B3 Gaizhou China
85 G5 Gajapatinagaram India
88 B4 Gajar Pak.
124 E4 Gakarosa mt. S. Africa
88 C1 Gakuch Jammu and Kashmir
89 G3 Gala China
83 G4 Galaasiya Uzbek.
122 D4 Galana r. Kenya
161 N6 Galapagos Islands is Pacific Ocean
161 M6 Galapagos Rise sea feature Pacific Ocean
106 F5 Galashiels U.K.
115 L2 Galata, Nos pt Bulg.
115 M2 Galaţi Romania
114 G2 Galatina Italy
146 C6 Galax U.S.A.
107 C5 Galbally Rep. of Ireland
103 J3 Galdhøpiggen mt. Norway
151 D2 Galeana Mex.
84 D4 Galeh Dār Iran
134 B5 Galena U.S.A.
157 E2 Galeota Point Trin. and Tob.
159 B4 Galera, Punta pt Chile
157 E5 Galera, Punta pt Mex.
157 E2 Galera Point Trin. and Tob.
134 B5 Galesburg U.S.A.
124 E5 Galeshewe S. Africa
134 B3 Galesville U.S.A.
117 G7 Gali Georgia
116 G4 Galich Rus. Fed.
116 G2 Galichskaya Vozvyshennost' reg. Rus. Fed.
111 C1 Galicia aut. comm. Spain
80 E5 Galilee, Sea of l. Israel
146 B4 Galion U.S.A.
141 F3 Galiuro Mountains U.S.A.
121 F3 Gallabat Sudan
145 C4 Gallatin r. U.S.A.
138 E2 Gallatin r. U.S.A.
87 C5 Galle Sri Lanka
161 L6 Gallego Rise sea feature Pacific Ocean
156 C8 Gallegos r. Arg.
115 L4 Gallipoli Turkey
114 G4 Gallipoli Italy
146 C5 Gallipolis U.S.A.
102 M2 Gällivare Sweden
102 K3 Gällö Sweden
147 H4 Gallo Island U.S.A.
140 B2 Gallo Mountains U.S.A.
141 H4 Gallup U.S.A.
83 G4 Gallyaaral Uzbek.
106 B4 Galmisdale U.K.
71 H5 Galong Australia
87 C5 Galoya Sri Lanka
87 C5 Gal Oya r. Sri Lanka
104 F4 Galston U.K.
140 B2 Galt U.S.A.
114 C6 Galtat Zemmour W. Sahara
107 C5 Galtee Mountains Rep. of Ireland
107 C5 Galtymore hill Rep. of Ireland
84 E4 Galūgāh-e Āsīyeh Iran
134 B5 Galva U.S.A.
143 E6 Galveston U.S.A.
143 E6 Galveston Bay U.S.A.
159 E3 Galvez Arg.
89 E3 Galwa Nepal
107 B4 Galway Rep. of Ireland
107 B4 Galway Bay b. Rep. of Ireland
91 K6 Gam r. Vietnam
158 D2 Gamá Brazil
89 G3 Gamba China
122 D3 Gambēla Eth.
122 D3 Gambēla National Park Eth.
88 A3 Gambhir r. India
128 A3 Gambell U.S.A.
120 A3 Gambia, The country Africa
161 J6 Gambier, Îles is Fr. Polynesia
70 B5 Gambier Islands Australia
133 J4 Gambo Canada
122 B4 Gamboma Congo
141 H4 Gamerco U.S.A.
103 L4 Gamleby Sweden
125 I5 Gamoep S. Africa
70 C2 Gammon Ranges National Park Australia

124	C4	Gamoep S. Africa
94	B3	Gamova, Mys *pt* Rus. Fed.
87	C5	Gampola Sri Lanka
85	F4	Gamshadzai Küh *mts* Iran
92	A3	Gana China
141	H4	Ganado U.S.A.
135	I3	Gananoque Canada
84	C4	Ganaveh Iran
81	K1	Gäncä Azer.
93	C7	Gancheng China
99	E3	Gandadiwata, Bukit *mt.* Indon.
89	G3	Gandaingoin China
122	C4	Gandajika Dem. Rep. Congo
89	E4	Gandak Dam Nepal
88	B3	Gandari Mountain Pak.
84	A3	Gandava Pak.
133	J4	Gander Canada
100	G1	Ganderkesee Germany
111	G2	Gandesa Spain
88	C5	Gandevi India
88	B5	Gandhidham India
88	C5	Gandhinagar India
88	C4	Gandhi Sagar India
88	C4	Gandhi Sagar Dam India
111	F3	Gandía Spain
85	F4	Gand-i-Zureh *plain* Afgh.
125	E1	Gandu Brazil
88	E4	Ganga *r.* Bangl./India
		alt. Padma,
		conv. Ganges
87	C5	Ganga *r.* Sri Lanka
159	C4	Gangán Arg.
88	C3	Ganganagar India
88	D4	Gangapur India
89	H5	Gangaw Myanmar
87	B3	Gangawati India
92	A2	Gangca China
88	E3	Gangdisê Shan *mts* China
79	G4	Ganges *r.* Bangl./India
		alt. Ganga,
		alt. Padma
110	F5	Ganges France
89	G5	Ganges, Mouths of the *est.* Bangl./India
162	J3	Ganges Cone *sea feature* Indian Ocean
88	D3	Gangoh India
88	D3	Gangotri Group *mt.* India
89	G4	Gangtok India
92	B3	Gangu China
92	B2	Ganjam India
84	C4	Ganjgün Iran
93	E4	Gan Jiang *r.* China
96	B2	Ganjig China
93	B4	Ganluo China
71	G5	Ganmain Australia
110	F3	Gannat France
138	E3	Gannett Peak *mt.* U.S.A.
88	C5	Ganora India
92	C2	Ganquan China
124	C7	Gansbaai S. Africa
92	B3	Gansu *prov.* China
92	B3	Gantang China
70	B6	Gantheaume, Cape *hd* Australia
117	G7	Gant'iadi Georgia
93	E5	Ganxian China
92	F3	Ganyesa S. Africa
82	B3	Ganyushkino Kazakh.
93	E5	Ganzhou China
121	F4	Ganzi Sudan
120	B3	Gao Mali
93	E4	Gao'an China
92	E2	Gaocheng China
92	F4	Gaochun China
92	B2	Gaolan China
92	E3	Gaomi China
93	D5	Gaomutang China
92	D3	Gaoping China
92	A2	Gaotai China
92	E2	Gaotang China
92	C2	Gaotouyao China
120	B3	Gaoua Burkina
120	A3	Gaoual Guinea
93	B4	Gaoxian China
92	E2	Gaoyang China
92	E2	Gaoyi China
92	F3	Gaoyou China
93	F3	Gaoyou Hu *l.* China
93	D6	Gaozhou China
110	H4	Gap France
97	B3	Gapan Phil.
111	F5	Gap Carbon *hd* Alg.
88	E2	Gar China
107	C4	Gara, Lough *l.* Rep. of Ireland
82	F5	Garabekevyul Turkm.
150	J6	Garachiné Panama
85	F4	Garägheh Iran
71	H2	Garah Australia
123	C4	Garamba *r.* Dem. Rep. Congo
155	K5	Garanhuns Brazil
125	G2	Ga-Rankuwa S. Africa
122	D3	Garba Tula Kenya
140	A1	Garberville U.S.A.
84	C3	Garbosh, Küh-e *mt.* Iran
109	H2	Garbsen Germany
158	C3	Garça Brazil
158	B1	Garças, Rio das *r.* Brazil
89	G2	Garco China
114	D2	Garda, Lake *l.* Italy
81	J1	Gardabani Georgia
114	B6	Garden, Cape *hd* Alg.
109	J2	Gardelegen Germany
142	C4	Garden City U.S.A.
134	C3	Garden Corners U.S.A.
140	C5	Garden Grove U.S.A.
134	C4	Garden Hill Canada
134	C3	Garden Island U.S.A.
85	H3	Gardez Afgh.
147	I2	Gardiner *ME* U.S.A.
138	E2	Gardiner *MT* U.S.A.
147	G4	Gardiners Island U.S.A.
134	C5	Gardner U.S.A.
147	G2	Gardner Lake U.S.A.
67	H2	Gardner Pinnacles *is* U.S.A.
140	C2	Gardnerville U.S.A.
106	D4	Garelochhead U.K.
134	E2	Gargantua, Cape Canada
81	L4	Gargar Iran
103	M5	Gargždai Lith.
88	D5	Garhakota India
88	D4	Garhi Khairo Pak.
88	B4	Garhi Malehra India
130	E5	Garibaldi, Mount Canada
130	E5	Garibaldi Provincial Park *nat. park* Canada
125	E5	Gariep Dam S. Africa
124	B5	Garies S. Africa
114	E4	Garigliano *r.* Italy
122	D4	Garissa Kenya
103	N4	Garkalne Latvia
146	D4	Garland *PA* U.S.A.
143	D5	Garland *TX* U.S.A.
84	C2	Garlasco Italy
112	E7	Garmisch-Partenkirchen Germany
83	G5	Garmo, Qullai *mt.* Tajik.
84	D3	Garmsar Iran
85	F4	Garmsel *reg.* Afgh.
142	E4	Garnett U.S.A.
70	E4	Garnpung Lake Australia
89	G4	Garo Hills India
110	D4	Garonne *r.* France
122	D3	Garoowe Somalia
156	A3	Garopaba Brazil
121	D4	Garoua Cameroon
103	D3	Garre Arg.
84	C4	Garrison U.S.A.
107	F2	Garron Point U.K.
84	D4	Garruk Pak.
106	D4	Garry, Loch *l.* U.K.
131	I1	Garry Lake Canada
106	B2	Garrynahine U.K.
122	E4	Garsen Kenya

105	D5	Garth U.K.
109	J1	Gartow Germany
124	B3	Garub Namibia
99	C4	Garut Indon.
107	E3	Garvagh U.K.
106	D3	Garve U.K.
134	D5	Gary U.S.A.
88	E3	Garyarsa China
95	C7	Garyü-zan *mt.* Japan
88	D2	Gar Zangbo *r.* China
90	B3	Garzê China
157	B4	Garzón Col.
		Gascogne, Golfe de *g.* France/Spain *see* Gascony, Gulf of
142	E4	Gasconade *r.* U.S.A.
110	C5	Gascony *reg.* France
110	C5	Gascony, Gulf of France/Spain
68	A4	Gascoyne *r.* Australia
88	D2	Gasherbrum I *mt.* China/Jammu and Kashmir
85	F5	Gasht Iran
120	D3	Gashua Nigeria
85	E3	Gask Iran
99	C3	Gaspar, Selat *sea chan.* Indon.
133	H4	Gaspé Canada
133	H4	Gaspé, Cap *c.* Canada
133	G4	Gaspé, Péninsule de *pen.* Canada
133	G4	Gaspésie, Parc de la *nat. park* Canada
108	E2	Gasselte Neth.
145	D5	Gastonia U.S.A.
159	C4	Gastre Arg.
111	E4	Gata, Cabo de *c.* Spain
80	C4	Gata, Cape Cyprus
116	D3	Gatchina Rus. Fed.
146	B6	Gate City U.S.A.
104	F3	Gatehouse of Fleet U.K.
143	D6	Gatesville U.S.A.
141	H2	Gateway U.S.A.
147	F4	Gateway National Recreational Area *res.* U.S.A.
135	J3	Gatineau Canada
135	J2	Gatineau *r.* Canada
71	J1	Gatton Australia
150	I6	Gatún, Lago *l.* Panama
81	L5	Gatvand Iran
69	H3	Gau *i.* Fiji
131	J3	Gauer Lake Canada
102	J3	Gaula *r.* Norway
146	C5	Gauley Bridge U.S.A.
108	D5	Gaume *reg.* Belgium
89	F4	Gauri Sankar *mt.* China
125	G3	Gauteng *prov.* S. Africa
85	G3	Gauzan Afgh.
85	F5	Gävater Iran
84	D5	Gävbandi Iran
84	C4	Gävbüs, Küh-e *mts* Iran
115	K7	Gavdos *i.* Greece
84	D4	Gävkol Rüd *r.* Iran
81	K4	Gavileh Iran
158	B1	Gavião *r.* Brazil
103	L3	Gävle Sweden
116	F3	Gavrilov-Yam Rus. Fed.
124	B3	Gawachab Namibia
70	C5	Gawler Australia
70	A4	Gawler Ranges *hills* Australia
92	A1	Gaxun Nur *salt l.* China
82	D2	Gay Rus. Fed.
89	F4	Gaya India
120	C3	Gaya Niger
96	E2	Gaya He *r.* China
134	E3	Gaylord U.S.A.
80	D1	Gaza *terr.* Asia
98	B4	Gazik Malaysia
85	E3	Gerineenj Iran
125	J1	Gaza *prov.* Moz.
80	D1	Gaza Gaza
82	E4	Gaz-Achak Turkm.
83	G4	Gazalkent Uzbek.
85	H3	Gazdarra Pass Afgh.
80	D3	Gazipaşa Turkey
85	F3	Gazik Iran
82	E4	Gazli Uzbek.
85	E5	Gaz Mähü Iran
120	A4	Gbangbatok Sierra Leone
120	A4	Gbarnga Liberia
120	C4	Gboko Nigeria
113	I3	Gdańsk Poland
113	I3	Gdańsk, Gulf of Poland/Rus. Fed.
116	C3	Gdov Rus. Fed.
113	I3	Gdynia Poland
106	C1	Gealldruig Mhor *i.* U.K.
109	H4	Gebesee Germany
121	F3	Gedaref Sudan
142	C2	Geddes U.S.A.
108	C5	Gedinne Belgium
80	A2	Gediz *r.* Turkey
105	H5	Gedney Drove End U.K.
103	J3	Gedser Denmark
108	D3	Geel Belgium
70	F7	Geelong Australia
124	D4	Geel Vloer *salt pan* S. Africa
108	E2	Geeste Germany
109	I1	Geesthacht Germany
71	G9	Geeveston Australia
120	D3	Geidam Nigeria
109	H5	Geiersberg *hill* Germany
102	K3	Geilo Norway
108	E4	Geilenkirchen Germany
102	I3	Geilo Norway
103	I3	Geiranger Norway
138	E3	Geist Reservoir U.S.A.
109	K3	Geithain Germany
93	B6	Gejiu China
114	F6	Gela Sicily Italy
122	E3	Geladi Eth.
98	B4	Gelang, Tanjung *pt* Malaysia
82	E2	Ghalkarteniz, Solonchak *salt marsh* Kazakh.
108	D2	Gelderland *prov.* Neth.
108	E3	Geldermalsen Neth.
108	E3	Geldern Germany
85	F5	Gelendzhik Rus. Fed.
117	F6	Gelendzhik Rus. Fed.
		Gelibolu Turkey *see* Gallipoli
80	A1	Gelincik Dağı *mt.* Turkey
84	B3	Gelmord Iran
109	H4	Gelnhausen Germany
108	F3	Gelsenkirchen Germany
99	C5	Gemas Malaysia
108	D2	Gemen Indon.
122	B3	Gemena Dem. Rep. Congo
80	F2	Gemerek Turkey
80	B1	Gemlik Turkey
114	E1	Gemona del Friuli Italy
123	C6	Gemsbok National Park Botswana
124	D3	Gemsbokplein *well* S. Africa
122	E3	Genalē Wenz *r.* Eth.
108	C4	Genappe Belgium
159	E3	General Acha Arg.
		General Alvear Buenos Aires Arg.
159	E1	General Alvear Entre Ríos Arg.
159	D2	General Alvear Mendoza Arg.
159	E3	General Belgrano Arg.
151	E2	General Bravo Mex.
156	B7	General Capdevila Arg.
150	D2	General Cepeda Mex.
159	F3	General Conesa Buenos Aires Arg.
159	D4	General Conesa Río Negro Arg.
159	D4	General Guido Arg.
159	E3	General Juan Madariaga Arg.
159	D2	General La Madrid Arg.
159	E2	General Lavalle Arg.
97	C4	General Luna Phil.
97	C4	General MacArthur Phil.
159	D2	General Pico Arg.
159	C3	General Roca Arg.

97	C5	General Santos Phil.
151	E2	General Terán Mex.
159	D2	General Villegas Arg.
146	E2	Genesee *r.* U.S.A.
134	B5	Geneseo *IL* U.S.A.
146	E3	Geneseo *NY* U.S.A.
125	G3	Geneva S. Africa
112	C7	Geneva Switz.
134	C5	Geneva *IL* U.S.A.
142	D3	Geneva *NE* U.S.A.
146	E3	Geneva *NY* U.S.A.
146	C4	Geneva *OH* U.S.A.
112	C7	Geneva, Lake France/Switz.
134	C4	Geneva, Lake U.S.A.
		Genève Switz. *see* Geneva
111	D4	Genil *r.* Spain
108	D4	Genk Belgium
108	D3	Gennep Neth.
71	H6	Genoa Australia
114	C2	Genoa Italy
114	C2	Genoa, Gulf of *g.* Italy
		Genova Italy *see* Genoa
		Gent Belgium *see* Ghent
109	K2	Genthin Germany
68	B5	Geographe Bay Australia
76	F2	Geografa, Zemlya *i.* Rus. Fed.
133	G2	George *r.* Canada
124	C6	George S. Africa
71	I4	Geneva *IL* U.S.A.
142	D3	Geneva *NY* U.S.A.
146	E3	George, Lake *N.S.W.* Australia
70	C6	George, Lake *S.A.* Australia
145	D6	George, Lake *FL* U.S.A.
147	G3	George, Lake *NY* U.S.A.
72	A6	George Sound *inlet* N.Z.
69	C4	Georgetown Australia
71	G8	George Town Australia
145	F7	George Town Bahamas
135	H4	Georgetown Canada
120	A3	Georgetown Gambia
155	G2	Georgetown Guyana
99	B1	George Town Malaysia
134	D6	Georgetown *DE* U.S.A.
146	C4	Georgetown *KY* U.S.A.
146	C4	Georgetown *OH* U.S.A.
145	E5	Georgetown *SC* U.S.A.
143	D6	Georgetown *TX* U.S.A.
73	B2	George VI Sound *sea chan.* Antarctica
73	B5	George V Land *reg.* Antarctica
143	D6	George West U.S.A.
117	G7	Georgia *country* Asia
145	D5	Georgia *state* U.S.A.
130	E5	Georgia, Strait of Canada
135	G3	Georgian Bay *l.* Canada
135	G3	Georgian Bay Islands National Park Canada
68	D4	Georgina *watercourse* Australia
83	J2	Georgiyevka Vostochnyy Kazakhstan Kazakh.
83	G4	Georgiyevka Yuzhnyy Kazakhstan Kazakh.
117	G6	Georgiyevsk Rus. Fed.
116	H3	Georgiyevskoye Rus. Fed.
109	K4	Gera Germany
108	C4	Geraardsbergen Belgium
155	I6	Geral de Goiás, Serra *hills* Brazil
72	C6	Geraldine N.Z.
158	C1	Geral do Paraná, Serra *hills* Brazil
68	A4	Geraldton Australia
84	D5	Gerāsh Iran
81	H3	Gerçüş Turkey
80	D1	Gerede *r.* Turkey
85	H3	Gereshk Afgh.
98	B4	Geri Malaysia
85	E3	Gerineenj Iran
142	C3	Gering U.S.A.
138	C3	Gerlach U.S.A.
130	E3	Germansen Landing Canada
146	E5	Germantown U.S.A.
112	E5	Germany *country* Europe
102	F3	Germencik Turkey
125	H3	Germiston S. Africa
109	G5	Gernsheim Germany
108	E4	Gerolstein Germany
109	I5	Gerolzhofen Germany
141	G5	Gerona Spain
71	I5	Gerringong Australia
109	H4	Gersfeld (Rhön) Germany
109	I6	Gerstungen Germany
109	J2	Gerwisch Germany
89	F2	Gêrzê China
117	E7	Gerze Turkey
108	F3	Gescher Germany
84	D3	Getcheh, Küh-e *hill* Iran
146	E5	Gettysburg *PA* U.S.A.
142	C2	Gettysburg *SD* U.S.A.
146	E5	Gettysburg National Military Park U.S.A.
93	C5	Getu He *r.* China
73	A4	Getz Ice Shelf Antarctica
99	A2	Geumapang *r.* Indon.
71	H4	Geurie Australia
81	I2	Gevaş Turkey
115	J4	Gevgelija Macedonia
125	I3	Geydorp S. Africa
80	C1	Geyve Turkey
124	F2	Ghaap Plateau S. Africa
81	I5	Ghadaf, Wädi al *watercourse* Iraq
120	D1	Ghadāmis Libya
84	D2	Ghaem Shahr Iran
130	B3	Ghaffron Taj. India
88	C3	Ghaggar, Dry Bed of *watercourse* Pak.
88	E4	Ghaghara *r.* India
82	E2	Ghalkarteniz, Solonchak *salt marsh* Kazakh.
120	B4	Ghana *country* Africa
84	D5	Ghanādah, Rās al *pt* U.A.E.
123	C6	Ghanzi Botswana
123	C6	Ghanzi *admin. dist.* Botswana
84	C5	Ghār, Ras al *pt* Saudi Arabia
80	E6	Gharandal Jordan
120	C1	Ghardaïa Alg.
83	G5	Gharm Tajik.
121	D1	Gharyān Libya
80	F5	Gharz, Wädi al *watercourse* Syria
120	D2	Ghāt Libya
88	D3	Ghauspur Pak.
121	D3	Ghazal, Bahr el *watercourse* Chad
123	B3	Ghazaouet Alg.
88	D3	Ghaziabad India
89	E4	Ghazipur India
88	A3	Ghazluna Pak.
85	H3	Ghazni *r.* Afgh.
85	H3	Ghazni Afgh.
85	H3	Ghazoor Afgh.
108	B3	Ghent Belgium
117	M7	Gheorgheni Romania
117	K7	Gherla Romania
114	C3	Ghisonaccia Corsica France
85	C5	Ghizar Pak.
85	F3	Ghod *r.* India
89	A2	Ghoraghat Bangl.
85	H3	Ghorband *r.* Afgh.
85	H3	Ghorband Pass Afgh.
85	F2	Ghotki Pak.
89	F4	Ghuari *r.* India
88	D5	Ghūdara India
88	D6	Ghugus India
85	H2	Ghulam Mohammed Barrage Pak.
84	D4	Ghūri Iran
85	F3	Ghurian Afgh.

108	A3	Ghyvelde France
98	C3	Gia Đinh Vietnam
117	G6	Giaginskaya Rus. Fed.
115	J4	Giannitsa Greece
125	I4	Giant's Castle *mt.* S. Africa
107	E2	Giant's Causeway U.K.
99	E4	Gianyar Indon.
98	C3	Gia Rai Vietnam
114	F6	Giarre Sicily Italy
114	B2	Giaveno Italy
124	B2	Gibeon Namibia
111	C5	Gibraltar *terr.* Europe
111	C5	Gibraltar, Strait of Morocco/Spain
134	C5	Gibson City U.S.A.
68	C4	Gibson Desert Australia
90	B2	Gichgeniyn Nuruu *mts* Mongolia
87	B3	Gidole Eth.
122	D3	Gidolē Eth.
110	F3	Gien France
109	G4	Gießen Germany
109	I2	Gifhorn Germany
130	F3	Gift Lake Canada
95	E7	Gifu Japan
157	B4	Gigante Col.
106	C5	Gigha *i.* U.K.
111	D1	Gijón Spain
141	F5	Gila *r.* U.S.A.
141	F5	Gila Bend U.S.A.
141	F5	Gila Bend Mountains U.S.A.
141	H5	Gila Mountains U.S.A.
81	J4	Gīlān-e Gharb Iran
81	L1	Gīlāzi Azer.
68	C3	Gil Chashmeh Iran
138	E1	Gildford U.S.A.
130	D4	Gilford Island Canada
71	I2	Gilgai Australia
71	I2	Gilgandra Australia
122	D4	Gilgil Kenya
88	C2	Gilgit Jammu and Kashmir
88	C2	Gilgit *r.* Jammu and Kashmir
71	G4	Gilgunnia Australia
131	K4	Gillam Canada
70	B4	Gilles, Lake *salt flat* Australia
138	F2	Gillette U.S.A.
105	H6	Gillingham *England* U.K.
105	D7	Gillingham *England* U.K.
135	K3	Gills Rock U.S.A.
134	B3	Gilman *IL* U.S.A.
134	A3	Gilman *WI* U.S.A.
132	E2	Gilmour Island Canada
140	B3	Gilroy U.S.A.
147	G3	Gilsum U.S.A.
121	F3	Gimbala, Jebel *mt.* Sudan
122	D3	Gimbi Eth.
131	J4	Gimli Canada
154	E6	Ginebra, Laguna *l.* Bol.
89	G4	Gin Ganga *r.* Sri Lanka
87	B3	Gingee India
122	E3	Ginir Eth.
114	G4	Gioia del Colle Italy
71	G4	Gippsland *reg.* Australia
88	B4	Girab India
85	F4	Girān Rīg *mt.* Iran
146	C3	Girard U.S.A.
81	G2	Giresun Turkey
88	A4	Giral India
71	G4	Girilambone Australia
88	C5	Girna *r.* India
111	H2	Girona Spain
110	D4	Gironde *est.* France
71	G4	Girral Australia
106	D5	Girvan U.K.
116	E2	Girvas Rus. Fed.
88	E4	Girwan Rus. Fed.
57	I2	Gisborne N.Z.
130	E4	Giscome Canada
103	K4	Gislaved Sweden
83	K4	Gissar Range *mts* Tajik./Uzbek.
122	C4	Gitarama Rwanda
114	B3	Gitega Burundi
117	K3	Giurgiu Romania
115	K3	Giuvala, Pasul *pass* Romania
110	G4	Givors France
108	C5	Givry-en-Argonne France
125	I1	Giyani S. Africa
121	F2	Giza Egypt
85	F5	Gīzeh Rūd *r.* Iran
82	F4	Gizhduvan Uzbek.
77	R3	Gizhiga Rus. Fed.
115	I4	Gjirokastër Albania
129	I3	Gjoa Haven Canada
102	J3	Gjøra Norway
103	J3	Gjøvik Norway
133	I4	Glace Bay Canada
130	D2	Glacier Bay National Park and Preserve U.S.A.
130	D3	Glacier National Park Canada
138	D1	Glacier National Park U.S.A.
138	D1	Glacier Peak *vol.* U.S.A.
102	J2	Gladstad Norway
69	F4	Gladstone *Qld* Australia
70	B5	Gladstone *S.A.* Australia
71	H8	Gladstone *Tas.* Australia
134	E4	Gladwin U.S.A.
102	J3	Glama *r.* Germany
97	C5	Glan Phil.
107	B5	Glanaruddery Mountains Rep. of Ireland
109	G2	Glandorf Germany
104	F2	Glanton U.K.
135	G4	Glanworth Canada
106	D5	Glasgow U.K.
144	C4	Glasgow *KY* U.S.A.
138	F1	Glasgow *MT* U.S.A.
146	D5	Glasgow *VA* U.S.A.
71	J1	Glasnevin Australia
140	D3	Glass Mountain U.S.A.
130	D5	Glass Peninsula U.S.A.
136	E6	Glastonbury U.K.
107	C5	Glatt *r.* Switz.
109	K4	Glauchau Germany
76	G4	Glazov Rus. Fed.
117	F4	Glazunovka Rus. Fed.
113	O3	Glębokie Poland
147	H2	Glen U.S.A.
125	G4	Glen Afton *reg.* U.K.
72	E2	Glen Afton N.Z.
85	I1	Glen Afton Canada
122	C3	Glen Alpine Dam S. Africa
107	D4	Glenamaddy Rep. of Ireland
134	C3	Glen Arbor U.S.A.
72	C6	Glenavy N.Z.
106	E4	Glenboig U.K.
106	D5	Glenbuck U.K.
130	G2	Glen Canyon *gorge* U.S.A.
141	G3	Glen Canyon National Recreation Area U.S.A.
106	E4	Glen Clova *valley* U.K.
106	D5	Glencoe Canada
125	I4	Glencoe S. Africa
106	D4	Glen Coe *valley* U.K.
106	D5	Glencolumbkille Rep. of Ireland
141	F5	Glendale *AZ* U.S.A.

140	C4	Glendale *CA* U.S.A.
141	E3	Glendale *NV* U.S.A.
141	F3	Glendale *UT* U.S.A.
146	D4	Glendale Lake U.S.A.
71	I4	Glen Davis Australia
138	F2	Glendive U.S.A.
131	G4	Glendon Canada
98	□	Glendor Canada
70	D6	Glenely *r.* Australia
106	F4	Glen Esk *valley* U.K.
106	A5	Glengad Head Rep. of Ireland
106	C3	Glen Garry *valley* Scotland U.K.
106	D3	Glen Garry *valley* Scotland U.K.
107	D3	Glengavlen Rep. of Ireland
71	I2	Glen Innes Australia
106	D6	Glenluce U.K.
106	D3	Glen Lyon *valley* U.K.
71	H1	Glenmorgan Australia
106	D3	Glen Moriston *valley* U.K.
141	G6	Glenn, Mount U.S.A.
128	C3	Glennallen U.S.A.
106	C4	Glen Nevis *valley* U.K.
135	F3	Glennie U.S.A.
146	E5	Glenns U.S.A.
147	C3	Glenora Canada
147	F2	Glen Robertson Canada
106	E3	Glenrothes U.K.
147	G3	Glens Falls U.S.A.
106	D5	Glen Shee *valley* U.K.
106	C3	Glen Shiel *valley* U.K.
107	C3	Glenties Rep. of Ireland
107	D2	Glenveagh National Park Rep. of Ireland
71	G3	Glengolpan Australia
143	C5	Glenwood *AR* U.S.A.
141	H5	Glenwood *NM* U.S.A.
139	F4	Glenwood Springs U.S.A.
134	B2	Glidden U.S.A.
109	I1	Glinde Germany
113	I5	Gliwice Poland
112	H5	Globe U.S.A.
112	H5	Głogów Poland
102	K2	Glomfjord Norway
103	J4	Glomma *r.* Norway
109	H1	Glückstadt Germany
102	□	Gluggarnir *hill* Faroe Is
104	F5	Glusburn U.K.
117	H5	Gmelinka Rus. Fed.
112	G7	Gmünd Austria
112	F7	Gmunden Austria
103	L3	Gnarp Sweden
109	H1	Gnarrenberg Germany
112	H4	Gniezno Poland
115	I3	Gnjilane Yugo.
87	A3	Goa India
86	B5	Goa Cay *i.* Bahamas
71	I6	Goalen Head *hd* Australia
89	G4	Goalpara India
106	C5	Goat Fell *hill* U.K.
122	E3	Goba Eth.
123	B6	Gobabis Namibia
124	B2	Gobas Namibia
159	E1	Gobernador Crespo Arg.
159	B4	Gobernador Duval Arg.
156	E7	Gobernador Gregores Arg.
90	C2	Gobi *des.* Mongolia
95	D8	Gobö Japan
108	E3	Goch Germany
123	B6	Gochas Namibia
98	C3	Gô Công Vietnam
105	G6	Godalming U.K.
87	C2	Godavari *r.* India
87	C2	Godavari, Mouths of the India
133	G4	Godbout Canada
140	C3	Goddard, Mount U.S.A.
122	E3	Gode Eth.
135	G4	Goderich Canada
88	C5	Godhra India
88	D5	Godhra India
159	C2	Godoy Cruz Arg.
131	K3	Gods *r.* Canada
131	K4	Gods Lake Canada
131	L2	God's Mercy, Bay of Canada
		Godthåb Greenland *see* Nuuk
		Godwin Austen *mt.* China/Jammu and Kashmir *see* K2
108	B3	Goéland, Lac au *l.* Canada
133	F3	Goéland, Lac aux *l.* Canada
108	B3	Goes Neth.
135	F1	Goetville U.S.A.
147	F2	Goffs U.S.A.
135	J2	Gogama Canada
134	C2	Gogebic, Lake U.S.A.
134	C2	Gogebic Range *hills* U.S.A.
88	D4	Gohad India
158	B1	Goianá Brazil
158	B2	Goiandira Brazil
158	B1	Goiânia Brazil
158	B1	Goiás Brazil
158	B1	Goiás *state* Brazil
158	B4	Goio-Erê Brazil
102	J3	Gojra Pak.
87	C7	Gokak India
80	A1	Gökçeada *i.* Turkey
89	G3	Gökçedağ La pass China
80	E2	Gökırmak *r.* Turkey
82	D4	Goklenkuy, Solonchak *salt l.* Turkm.
85	G3	Gokprosh Hills Pak.
80	E2	Göksun Turkey
80	E3	Göksu Nehri *r.* Turkey
123	C5	Gokwe Zimbabwe
103	J3	Gol Norway
88	D3	Gola India
85	E4	Golbaf Iran
85	E3	Golbahar Iran
80	C2	Gölbaşı Turkey
113	K3	Gołdap Poland
109	K1	Goldberg Germany
71	J2	Gold Coast Australia
120	B4	Gold Coast Ghana
130	F4	Golden Canada
72	D5	Golden Bay N.Z.
140	A3	Golden Gate National Recreation Area *res.* U.S.A.
130	D5	Golden Hinde *mt.* Canada
107	C5	Golden Vale *lowland* Rep. of Ireland
140	C2	Goldfield U.S.A.
130	E4	Gold Point U.S.A.
145	E5	Goldsboro U.S.A.
130	D5	Goldstream *r.* Canada
143	D5	Goldthwaite U.S.A.
81	J1	Golämaz Azer.
80	E4	Göle Turkey
130	E5	Golestän Afgh.
140	C4	Goleta U.S.A.
150	I6	Golfito Costa Rica
143	D6	Goliad U.S.A.
96	A1	Golin Baixing China
80	F2	Göksü Turkey
109	F1	Golm Germany
81	J5	Golmänkhäneh Iran
92	A2	Golmud China
92	A2	Golmud He *r.* China
94	I3	Golo *i.* Phil.
94	I3	Golovnino Rus. Fed.
89	H1	Golpäyegän Iran
84	C3	Gölpazarı Turkey
80	C1	Gölpazarı Turkey
106	E3	Golspie U.K.
83	H1	Golubovka Kazakh.

85	F3	Gol Vardeh Iran
115	K4	Golyama Syutkya *mt.* Bulg.
115	K4	Golyam Persenk *mt.* Bulg.
109	K2	Golzow Germany
122	C4	Goma Dem. Rep. Congo
89	G3	Gomang Co *salt l.* China
88	C4	Gomati *r.* India
98	□	Gomati *r.* India
120	D3	Gombe Nigeria
122	D4	Gombe *r.* Tanz.
121	D3	Gombi Nigeria
150	D2	Gómez Palacio Mex.
84	D2	Gomīshān Iran
109	J2	Gommern Germany
89	F2	Gomo Co *salt l.* China
85	C2	Gonäbäd Iran
149	J5	Gonaïves Haiti
125	I1	Gonarezhou National Park Zimbabwe
84	D2	Gonbad-e Kavus Iran
89	E4	Gonda India
88	B5	Gondal India
122	D2	Gonder Eth.
88	E5	Gondia India
80	A1	Gönen Turkey
93	D4	Gong'an China
93	D5	Gongcheng China
92	A3	Gonga Shan *mt.* China
92	A2	Gonghe China
92	E1	Gonghui China
83	J4	Gongliu China
158	E1	Gongogi *r.* Brazil
120	D3	Gongola *r.* Nigeria
71	G3	Gongolgon Australia
93	B5	Gongwang Shan *mts* China
93	B4	Gongxian China
92	D3	Gongyi China
96	C2	Gongzhuling China
125	H6	Gonubie S. Africa
151	E2	Gonzáles Mex.
140	B3	Gonzales *CA* U.S.A.
159	D2	Gonzales *TX* U.S.A.
146	C4	González Moreno Arg.
73	C6	Goodenough, Cape Antarctica
68	F2	Goodenough Island P.N.G.
135	H2	Gooderham Canada
134	C3	Good Harbor Bay U.S.A.
124	C7	Good Hope, Cape of S. Africa
135	C4	Gooding U.S.A.
142	C4	Goodland U.S.A.
71	F2	Goodooga Australia
104	G4	Goole U.K.
71	F5	Goolgowi Australia
71	H4	Gooloma Australia
71	F2	Gooloogong Australia
70	C5	Goolwa Australia
71	F2	Goombalie Australia
71	C4	Goomeri Australia
71	J1	Goondiwindi Australia
133	H3	Goose *r.* Canada
138	B3	Goose Lake U.S.A.
87	B3	Gooty India
112	D6	Göppingen Germany
89	E4	Gorakhpur India
115	H3	Goražde Bos.-Herz.
150	I5	Gorda, Punta *pt* Nicaragua
148	E7	Gorda Cay *i.* Bahamas
80	B2	Gördes Turkey
113	O4	Gordeyevka Rus. Fed.
71	F9	Gordon *r.* Australia
106	F5	Gordon U.K.
71	G9	Gordon, Lake Australia
130	E2	Gordon Lake Canada
146	D5	Gordonsville U.S.A.
121	D4	Goré Chad
122	D3	Gorē Eth.
72	B7	Gore N.Z.
135	F3	Gore Bay Canada
106	F5	Gorebridge U.K.
107	D5	Gorey Rep. of Ireland
85	E4	Gorg Iran
157	A4	Gorgona, Isla *i.* Col.
147	H2	Gorham U.S.A.
117	H7	Gori Georgia
108	D3	Gorinchem Neth.
81	K2	Goris Armenia
114	E2	Gorizia Italy
		Gor'kiy Rus. Fed. *see* Nizhniy Novgorod
117	H5	Gor'ko-Solenoye, Ozero *l.* Rus. Fed.
116	G3	Gor'kovskoye Vodokhranilishche *resr* Rus. Fed.
83	J1	Gor'koye, Ozero *salt l.* Rus. Fed.
113	J6	Gorlice Poland
112	G5	Görlitz Germany
115	K3	Gorna Oryahovitsa Bulg.
115	I2	Gornji Milanovac Yugo.
114	G3	Gornji Vakuf Bos.-Herz.
83	K2	Gorno-Altaysk Rus. Fed.
94	G1	Gornozavodsk Rus. Fed.
83	J4	Gornyak Rus. Fed.
94	C2	Gornyy Klyuchi Rus. Fed.
94	C2	Gornyy Primorskiy Kray Rus. Fed.
82	B1	Gornyy Saratovskaya Oblast' Rus. Fed.
117	H5	Gornyy Balykley Rus. Fed.
116	G3	Gorodets Rus. Fed.
117	H5	Gorodishche Rus. Fed.
117	G6	Gorodovikovsk Rus. Fed.
68	A4	Goroka P.N.G.
122	D3	Gorom Gorom Burkina
125	E6	Gorongosa Moz.
91	E6	Gorontalo Indon.
117	H5	Gorshechnoye Rus. Fed.
107	C4	Gort Rep. of Ireland
155	I5	Gorutuba *r.* Brazil
117	H4	Gorval Iran
109	K2	Görzke Germany
112	H4	Gorzów Wielkopolski Poland
71	I4	Gosford Australia
71	I4	Goshen *IN* U.S.A.
147	G3	Goshen *NY* U.S.A.
94	E6	Goshogawara Japan
109	I3	Goslar Germany
114	F2	Gospić Croatia
105	F7	Gosport U.K.
		Göteborg Sweden *see* Gothenburg
103	K4	Gotha Germany
148	E7	Gothenburg Sweden
142	C3	Gothenburg U.S.A.
103	L4	Gotland *i.* Sweden
115	J4	Gotse Delchev Bulg.
95	C7	Gotsu Japan
109	I3	Göttingen Germany
130	E4	Gott Peak *mt.* Canada
109	H3	Goubangzi China
120	A3	Goudiri Senegal
120	D3	Goudoumaria Niger
134	E1	Goudreau Canada
163	I8	Gough Island S. Atlantic Ocean
132	F4	Gouin, Réservoir Canada
155	J5	Gouianis River Canada
134	E1	Goulburn *r.* N.S.W. Australia
71	I4	Goulburn *r.* Vic. Australia
68	D2	Goulburn Islands Australia
134	G4	Gould City U.S.A.
73	B4	Gould Coast Antarctica
120	B3	Goundam Mali
111	G4	Gouraya Alg.

120	D3	Gouré Niger
124	D7	Gourits r. S. Africa
120	B3	Gourma-Rharous Mali
110	E2	Gournay-en-Bray France
71	H6	Gourock Range mts Australia
108	A5	Goussainville France
147	F2	Gouverneur U.S.A.
131	H5	Govenlock Canada
158	E2	Governador Valadares Brazil
97	C5	Governor Generoso Phil.
145	E7	Governor's Harbour Bahamas
90	B2	Govĭ Altayn Nuruu mts Mongolia
89	E4	Govind Ballash Pant Sagar resr India
88	D3	Govind Sagar resr India
82	F5	Gowārdak Turkm.
146	D3	Gowanda U.S.A.
85	G4	Gowārān Afgh.
84	D4	Gowd-e Aḥmar Iran
84	E3	Gowd-e Hasht Tekkeh waterhole Iran
84	D4	Gowk mt. h. Iran
105	C6	Gower pen. U.K.
135	G2	Gowganda Canada
107	D4	Gowna, Lough l. Rep. of Ireland
156	E3	Goya Arg.
81	K1	Göyçay Azer.
81	H2	Göynük Turkey
94	G5	Goyō-zan mt. Japan
81	L2	Göytäpä Azer.
85	F3	Gōzareh Afgh.
80	G2	Gözene Turkey
88	C2	Gozha Co salt l. China
114	F6	Gozo i. Malta
124	F6	Graaf-Reinet S. Africa
124	C6	Graafwater S. Africa
109	I4	Grabfeld plain Germany
120	B4	Grabo Côte d'Ivoire
124	C7	Grabouw S. Africa
109	G4	Grabow Germany
114	F2	Gračac Croatia
135	I2	Gracefield Canada
82	C1	Grachevka Rus. Fed.
83	I2	Grachi Kazakh.
150	G5	Gracias Hond.
109	K3	Gräfenhainichen Germany
109	J5	Grafenwöhr Germany
71	J2	Grafton Australia
142	D1	Grafton ND U.S.A.
134	D4	Grafton WI U.S.A.
146	C5	Grafton WV U.S.A.
141	E2	Grafton, Mount U.S.A.
143	D5	Graham r. U.S.A.
141	H5	Graham, Mount U.S.A.
		Graham Bell Island Rus. Fed. see Greem-Bell, Ostrov
130	C4	Graham Island B.C. Canada
129	I2	Graham Island Nunavut Canada
147	I2	Graham Lake U.S.A.
73	B2	Graham Land reg. Antarctica
125	G6	Grahamstown S. Africa
107	E5	Graigue Rep. of Ireland
120	A4	Grain Coast Liberia
155	I5	Grajaú Brazil
106	B1	Graisgeir i. U.K.
115	I4	Grammos mt. Greece
106	D4	Grampian Mountains U.K.
124	C5	Graanatboskolk S. Africa
157	B4	Granada Col.
150	H6	Granada Nicaragua
111	E4	Granada Spain
142	C4	Granada U.S.A.
107	C4	Granard Rep. of Ireland
159	C3	Gran Bajo Salitroso salt flat Arg.
132	F4	Granby Canada
120	A2	Gran Canaria i. Canary Is
156	D3	Gran Chaco reg. Arg./Para.
134	D4	Grand r. MI U.S.A.
142	E3	Grand r. MO U.S.A.
145	E7	Grand Bahama i. Bahamas
133	I4	Grand Bank Canada
163	F3	Grand Banks of Newfoundland sea feature N. Atlantic Ocean
120	B4	Grand-Bassam Côte d'Ivoire
133	G4	Grand Bay Canada
135	G4	Grand Bend Canada
		Grand Canal China see Da Yunhe
107	D4	Grand Canal Rep. of Ireland
141	F3	Grand Canyon U.S.A.
141	F3	Grand Canyon gorge U.S.A.
141	F3	Grand Canyon Nat. Park U.S.A.
149	H5	Grand Cayman i. Cayman Is
131	G4	Grand Centre Canada
138	C2	Grand Coulee U.S.A.
159	C3	Grande r. Arg.
154	F7	Grande r. Bol.
155	I6	Grande r. Bahia Brazil
158	B2	Grande r. São Paulo Brazil
156	C8	Grande, Bahía b. Arg.
158	D3	Grande, Ilha i. Brazil
157	E4	Grande, Serra mt. Brazil
130	F4	Grande Cache Canada
		Grande Comore i. Comoros see Njazidja
130	F3	Grande Prairie Canada
121	D3	Grand Erg de Bilma dunes Niger
120	B1	Grand Erg Occidental des. Alg.
120	C2	Grand Erg Oriental des. Alg.
133	H4	Grande-Rivière Canada
136	C4	Grande Ronde r. U.S.A.
133	G4	Grande-Vallée Canada
133	G4	Grand Falls N.B. Canada
133	I4	Grand Falls Nfld Canada
130	F5	Grand Forks Canada
142	D2	Grand Forks U.S.A.
147	F3	Grand Gorge U.S.A.
147	J2	Grand Harbour Canada
134	D4	Grand Haven U.S.A.
130	F2	Grandin, Lac l. Canada
134	D2	Grand Island MI U.S.A.
142	D3	Grand Island NE U.S.A.
143	F5	Grand Isle l. U.S.A.
147	I1	Grand Isle ME U.S.A.
141	H2	Grand Junction U.S.A.
120	B4	Grand-Lahou Côte d'Ivoire
133	H3	Grand Lake Nfld Canada
133	I4	Grand Lake Nfld Canada
143	E6	Grand Lake LA U.S.A.
147	J2	Grand Lake ME U.S.A.
135	F3	Grand Lake MI U.S.A.
147	I1	Grand Lake Matagamon U.S.A.
146	A4	Grand Lake St Marys U.S.A.
147	I1	Grand Lake Seboeis U.S.A.
147	J2	Grand Lake Stream U.S.A.
134	E4	Grand Ledge U.S.A.
133	G5	Grand Manan Island Canada
134	E2	Grand Marais MI U.S.A.
134	B2	Grand Marais MN U.S.A.
133	F4	Grand-Mère Canada
111	B3	Grândola Port.
69	G3	Grand Passage New Caledonia
131	J4	Grand Rapids Canada
134	E4	Grand Rapids MI U.S.A.
142	E2	Grand Rapids MN U.S.A.
69	G4	Grand Récif de Cook reef New Caledonia
69	G4	Grand Récif du Sud reef New Caledonia
138	E3	Grand Teton mt. U.S.A.
138	E3	Grand Teton Nat. Park U.S.A.
134	D3	Grand Traverse Bay U.S.A.
149	J4	Grand Turk Turks and Caicos Is
138	C2	Grandview U.S.A.
141	F3	Grand Wash r. U.S.A.
141	E4	Grand Wash Cliffs U.S.A.
159	B2	Graneros Chile
107	D6	Grange Rep. of Ireland
138	E3	Granger U.S.A.
103	K3	Grängesberg Sweden
138	C2	Grangeville U.S.A.
130	D3	Granisle Canada
142	E2	Granite Falls U.S.A.
133	I4	Granite Lake Canada
141	E4	Granite Mountains U.S.A.
138	E2	Granite Peak mt. MT U.S.A.
141	F1	Granite Peak mt. UT U.S.A.
83	H4	Granitogorsk Kazakh.
114	E6	Granitola, Capo c. Sicily Italy
156	C6	Gran Laguna Salada l. Arg.
103	K4	Gränna Sweden
112	E7	Gran Paradiso mt. Italy
112	E7	Gran Pilastro mt. Austria/Italy
109	K3	Granschütz Germany
109	L1	Gransee Germany
140	C2	Grant, Mount NV U.S.A.
140	D2	Grant, Mount NV U.S.A.
105	G5	Grantham U.K.
73	A4	Grant Island Antarctica
106	F3	Grantown-on-Spey U.K.
141	E2	Grant Range mts U.S.A.
139	F5	Grants U.S.A.
138	B3	Grants Pass U.S.A.
110	D2	Granville France
134	C5	Granville IL U.S.A.
147	G3	Granville NY U.S.A.
131	I3	Granville Lake Canada
158	D2	Grão Mogol Brazil
140	C3	Grapevine U.S.A.
140	D3	Grapevine Mountains U.S.A.
147	G3	Graphite U.S.A.
131	G2	Gras, Lac de l. Canada
125	I2	Graskop S. Africa
147	F2	Grass r. U.S.A.
110	H5	Grasse France
104	F3	Grassington U.K.
131	H5	Grasslands Nat. Park Canada
138	E2	Grassrange U.S.A.
131	I4	Grass River Provincial Park Canada
140	B2	Grass Valley U.S.A.
71	F8	Grassy Australia
145	E7	Grassy Creek r. Bahamas
103	K4	Grästorp Sweden
134	B4	Gratiot U.S.A.
111	G1	Graus Spain
131	I2	Gravel Hill Lake Canada
108	A4	Gravelines France
125	I1	Gravelotte S. Africa
71	I2	Gravesend Australia
105	H6	Gravesend U.K.
114	G4	Gravina in Puglia Italy
134	E3	Grawn U.S.A.
110	G3	Gray France
147	H3	Gray U.S.A.
134	E3	Grayling U.S.A.
105	H6	Grays U.K.
138	A2	Grays Harbor inlet U.S.A.
138	E3	Grays Lake U.S.A.
146	B5	Grayson U.S.A.
134	B3	Grayslake U.S.A.
144	B4	Grayville U.S.A.
112	F2	Graz Austria
145	E7	Great Abaco i. Bahamas
68	C5	Great Australian Bight g. Australia
145	H6	Great Bahama Bank sea feature Bahamas
72	E2	Great Barrier Island N.Z.
68	E3	Great Barrier Reef reef Australia
147	G3	Great Barrington U.S.A.
139	C4	Great Basin U.S.A.
141	E2	Great Basin Nat. Park U.S.A.
147	F5	Great Bay U.S.A.
130	E1	Great Bear r. Canada
130	E1	Great Bear Lake Canada
103	J5	Great Belt sea chan. Denmark
115	I4	Great Bend U.S.A.
72	B2	Great Bernera i. U.K.
107	A5	Great Blasket Island Rep. of Ireland
104	D3	Great Clifton U.K.
106	D4	Great Cumbrae i. U.K.
68	E5	Great Dividing Range mts Australia
135	F3	Great Duck Island Canada
147	F5	Great Egg Harbor Inlet U.S.A.
149	H4	Greater Antilles is Caribbean Sea
84	D5	Greater Tunb i. Iran
149	I4	Great Exuma i. Bahamas
138	E2	Great Falls U.S.A.
125	G6	Great Fish r. S. Africa
125	G6	Great Fish Point S. Africa
89	F4	Great Gandak r. India
145	E7	Great Guana Cay i. Bahamas
145	E7	Great Harbour Cay i. Bahamas
149	J4	Great Inagua i. Bahamas
125	D5	Great Karoo plat. S. Africa
125	H6	Great Kei r. S. Africa
71	G8	Great Lake Australia
105	E6	Great Malvern U.K.
162	C1	Great Meteor Tablemount sea feature N. Atlantic Ocean
124	B3	Great Namaqualand reg. Namibia
		Great Oasis, The Egypt see Khārijah, Wāḩāt al
105	H5	Great Ormes Head U.K.
71	H9	Great Ouse r. U.K.
147	G4	Great Oyster Bay Australia
147	H4	Great Peconic Bay U.S.A.
99	B3	Great Point U.S.A.
105	D5	Great Rhos hill U.K.
122	D4	Great Ruaha r. Tanz.
114	G2	Great Sacandaga Lake U.S.A.
114	B2	Great St Bernard Pass Italy/Switz.
145	E7	Great Sale Cay i. Bahamas
139	D1	Great Salt Lake U.S.A.
141	E2	Great Salt Lake Desert U.S.A.
121	E2	Great Sand Sea des. Egypt/Libya
68	C4	Great Sandy Desert Australia
69	H3	Great Sea Reef reef Fiji
130	E1	Great Slave Lake Canada
145	D5	Great Smoky Mountains U.S.A.
145	D5	Great Smoky Mts National Park U.S.A.
130	D3	Great Snow Mountain Canada
147	G4	Great South Bay U.S.A.
105	I6	Greatstone-on-Sea U.K.
105	I5	Great Stour r. U.K.
68	C4	Great Victoria Desert Australia
73	B1	Great Wall research station Antarctica
92	F1	Great Wall China
105	H6	Great Waltham U.K.
147	J2	Great Wass Island U.S.A.
124	B3	Great Western Tiers mts Australia
104	F3	Great Whernside hill U.K.
105	I5	Great Yarmouth U.K.
114	E4	Greco, Monte mt. Italy
111	D2	Gredos, Sierra de mts Spain
115	I5	Greece country Europe
129	J3	Greely Fiord inlet Canada
76	H1	Greem-Bell, Ostrov i. Rus. Fed.
109	G2	Green r. KY U.S.A.
138	E3	Green r. UT/WY U.S.A.
138	D3	Green r. WY U.S.A.
133	H3	Greenbank Canada
134	C3	Green Bay U.S.A.
134	C3	Green Bay b. U.S.A.
71	I6	Green Cape hd Australia
144	C4	Greencastle U.S.A.
145	E7	Green Cay i. Bahamas
145	D6	Green Cove Springs U.S.A.
134	A4	Greene IA U.S.A.
147	F3	Greene NY U.S.A.
145	D4	Greeneville U.S.A.
140	B3	Greenfield CA U.S.A.
134	E6	Greenfield IN U.S.A.
147	G3	Greenfield MA U.S.A.
146	B5	Greenfield OH U.S.A.
141	F1	Greenfield WI U.S.A.
97	A4	Green Island Bay Phil.
131	H4	Green Lake Canada
134	C4	Green Lake U.S.A.
122	N2	Greenland terr. N. America
164	X2	Greenland Basin sea feature Arctic Ocean
164	X1	Greenland Sea Greenland/Svalbard
106	F5	Greenlaw U.K.
70	A5	Greenly Island Australia
147	G2	Green Mountains U.S.A.
106	D5	Greenock U.K.
107	E3	Greenore Rep. of Ireland
147	F5	Greenport U.S.A.
139	E4	Green River UT U.S.A.
138	E3	Green River WY U.S.A.
145	C4	Greensboro U.S.A.
144	C4	Greensburg IN U.S.A.
143	D4	Greensburg KS U.S.A.
146	D4	Greensburg PA U.S.A.
106	C3	Greenstone Point U.K.
137	K5	Green Swamp U.S.A.
146	B5	Greenup U.S.A.
147	G6	Green Valley Canada
141	G6	Green Valley U.S.A.
134	C5	Greenview U.S.A.
120	B4	Greenville Liberia
145	C6	Greenville AL U.S.A.
140	B1	Greenville CA U.S.A.
145	D6	Greenville FL U.S.A.
147	I2	Greenville ME U.S.A.
134	E4	Greenville MI U.S.A.
145	E5	Greenville MS U.S.A.
145	E5	Greenville NC U.S.A.
147	H3	Greenville NH U.S.A.
146	A4	Greenville OH U.S.A.
146	C4	Greenville PA U.S.A.
143	D5	Greenville SC U.S.A.
143	D5	Greenville TX U.S.A.
131	I4	Greenwater Provincial Park Canada
71	I5	Greenwell Point Australia
147	G4	Greenwich CT U.S.A.
147	G3	Greenwich NY U.S.A.
141	F3	Greenwich UT U.S.A.
143	F5	Greenwood MS U.S.A.
143	D5	Greenwood SC U.S.A.
143	D5	Greers Ferry Lake U.S.A.
142	D3	Gregory r. U.S.A.
70	C2	Gregory, Lake salt flat Australia
68	C4	Gregory, Lake salt flat Australia
68	E3	Gregory Range hills Australia
112	F3	Greifswald Germany
109	K4	Greiz Germany
80	E4	Greko, Cape Cyprus
103	J4	Grená Denmark
157	I1	Grenada country Caribbean Sea
143	F5	Grenada U.S.A.
110	E5	Grenade France
103	J4	Grenen spit Denmark
71	H4	Grenfell Australia
131	I4	Grenfell Canada
110	G4	Grenoble France
157	I1	Grenville Grenada
68	E3	Grenville, Cape hd Australia
138	B2	Gresham U.S.A.
104	F3	Gretna U.K.
106	E6	Gretna U.K.
143	F6	Gretna U.S.A.
109	I3	Greußen Germany
108	B3	Grevelingen sea chan. Neth.
109	G2	Greven Germany
115	I4	Grevena Greece
108	E3	Grevenbroich Germany
108	E5	Grevenmacher Lux.
112	E4	Grevesmühlen Germany
72	E4	Grey r. N.Z.
138	B2	Greybull U.S.A.
130	B2	Grey Hunter Peak mt. Canada
133	I3	Grey Islands Canada
72	C5	Greymouth N.Z.
70	E2	Grey Range hills Australia
157	C2	Greytown N.Z.
125	I4	Greytown S. Africa
108	C4	Grez-Doiceau Belgium
117	G5	Gribanovskiy Rus. Fed.
140	B2	Gridley CA U.S.A.
134	C5	Gridley IL U.S.A.
145	C5	Griffin U.S.A.
71	H5	Griffith Australia
131	H4	Griffith Canada
128	F2	Griffiths Point Canada
71	F8	Grim, Cape Australia
109	K3	Grimma Germany
112	F3	Grimmen Germany
135	H4	Grimsby Canada
105	G5	Grimsby U.K.
102	C1	Grímsey i. Iceland
130	F3	Grimshaw Canada
102	C2	Grímsstaðir Iceland
103	J4	Grimstad Norway
103	J5	Grindavík Iceland
115	M2	Grindul Chituc spit Romania
142	E3	Grinnell U.S.A.
125	H5	Griqualand East reg. S. Africa
124	E5	Griqualand West reg. S. Africa
124	E4	Griquatown S. Africa
129	J2	Grise Fiord Canada
99	B3	Grisik Indon.
105	I7	Gris Nez, Cap pt France
106	F2	Gritley U.K.
114	G2	Grmeč mts Bos.-Herz.
108	B3	Grobbendonk Belgium
125	H2	Groblersdal S. Africa
124	E4	Groblershoop S. Africa
94	B2	Grodekovo Rus. Fed.
		Grodno Belarus see Hrodna
109	J4	Gröditz Germany
124	D3	Groen watercourse N. Cape S. Africa
124	E5	Groen watercourse N. Cape S. Africa
110	C3	Groix, Île de i. France
114	D6	Grombalia Tunisia
108	F2	Gronau (Westfalen) Germany
102	K2	Grong Norway
108	E1	Groningen Neth.
108	E1	Groninger Wad tidal flat Neth.
141	D3	Groom Lake U.S.A.
124	D3	Groot-Aar Pan salt pan S. Africa
124	C6	Groot Berg r. S. Africa
124	E6	Groot Brakrivier S. Africa
125	H3	Grootdraaidam dam S. Africa
125	G5	Grootdrink S. Africa
68	D3	Groote Eylandt i. Australia
123	B5	Grootfontein Namibia
124	C4	Groot Karas Berg plat. Namibia
125	I1	Groot Letaba r. S. Africa
124	D6	Groot Marico S. Africa
125	G4	Groot Swartberg mts S. Africa
124	D7	Grootvloer salt pan S. Africa
125	G6	Groot Winterberg mt. S. Africa
114	E3	Gros Cap U.S.A.
133	I4	Gros Morne National Park Canada
109	L2	Groß Schönebeck Germany
124	C1	Gross Ums Namibia
138	D3	Gros Ventre Range mts U.S.A.
133	I3	Groswater Bay Canada
147	D3	Groton U.S.A.
146	D5	Grottoes U.S.A.
130	F3	Grouard Canada
132	D4	Groundhog r. Canada
108	D1	Grouw Neth.
146	C4	Grove City U.S.A.
145	C6	Grove Hill U.S.A.
140	B3	Groveland U.S.A.
140	B3	Grover Beach U.S.A.
147	H2	Groveton U.S.A.
141	F5	Growler U.S.A.
141	F5	Growler Mountains U.S.A.
117	H7	Groznyy Rus. Fed.
113	I4	Grudziądz Poland
106	C3	Gruinard Bay U.K.
123	B6	Grünau Namibia
102	B2	Grundarfjörður Iceland
146	B6	Grundy U.S.A.
109	G5	Grünstadt Germany
117	F4	Gryazi Rus. Fed.
116	I3	Gryazovets Rus. Fed.
113	G4	Gryfice Poland
112	G4	Gryfino Poland
112	G5	Gryfów Śląski Poland
102	L1	Gryllefjord Norway
156	□	Grytviken Atlantic Ocean
87	D1	Gua India
149	I4	Guacanayabo, Golfo de b. Cuba
157	D2	Guacara Venez.
157	C3	Guacharía r. Col.
111	D4	Guadajoz r. Spain
150	D3	Guadalajara Mex.
111	F2	Guadalajara Spain
69	G2	Guadalcanal i. Solomon Is
111	F2	Guadalete r. Spain
111	F2	Guadalope r. Spain
111	D4	Guadalquivir r. Spain
151	D2	Guadalupe Nuevo León Mex.
150	D3	Guadalupe Zacatecas Mex.
136	C6	Guadalupe i. Mex.
140	B4	Guadalupe r. U.S.A.
111	D6	Guadalupe, Sierra de mts Spain
150	C2	Guadalupe Aguilera Mex.
143	B6	Guadalupe Mountains National Park U.S.A.
143	B6	Guadalupe Peak U.S.A.
150	C2	Guadalupe Victoria Mex.
150	C2	Guadalupe y Calvo Mex.
111	D2	Guadarrama, Sierra de mts Spain
149	L5	Guadeloupe terr. Caribbean Sea
111	C4	Guadiana r. Port./Spain
111	E4	Guadix Spain
156	B6	Guafo, Isla i. Chile
150	H5	Guaimaca Hond.
157	D2	Guaiquinima, Cerro mt. Venez.
156	B6	Guaitecas, Islas is Chile
150	D2	Guaje, Llano de plain Mex.
154	C2	Gualaceo Ecuador
140	A2	Gualala U.S.A.
159	E2	Gualeguay Arg.
159	E2	Gualeguay r. Arg.
159	E2	Gualeguaychu Arg.
91	G5	Guam terr. Pacific Ocean
159	D2	Guaminí Arg.
150	D3	Guamúchil Mex.
157	A4	Guamués r. Col.
98	B4	Gua Musang Malaysia
150	H6	Guanacaste, Parque Nacional nat. park Costa Rica
150	C2	Guanacevi Mex.
159	E2	Guanaco, Cerro hill Arg.
150	D3	Guanaja Hond.
150	D3	Guanajuato Mex.
150	D3	Guanajuato state Mex.
158	D1	Guanambi Brazil
157	D2	Guaname r. Venez.
157	C2	Guanare Venez.
157	C2	Guanare Viejo r. Venez.
157	C2	Guanarito Venez.
157	D3	Guanay, Sierra mts Venez.
92	D2	Guandi Shan mt. China
149	H4	Guane Cuba
92	D3	Guang'an China
93	E5	Guangchang China
93	D6	Guangfeng China
93	D6	Guanghai China
92	D3	Guanghan China
92	B3	Guanghe China
92	B3	Guangling China
96	B4	Guanglu Dao i. China
93	E4	Guangming Ding mt. China
93	D6	Guangnan China
93	D6	Guangning China
92	E4	Guangrao China
92	E4	Guangshan China
93	C6	Guangxi Zhuangzu Zizhiqu aut. reg. China
92	D3	Guangyuan China
93	E5	Guangze China
93	D6	Guangzhou China
158	D2	Guanhães Brazil
158	D2	Guanhães r. Brazil
157	E2	Guanipa r. Venez.
92	A4	Guanling China
87	D1	Guanmian Shan mts China
92	C4	Guannan China
149	I4	Guantánamo Cuba
92	E1	Guanting Shuiku resr China
92	A4	Guanyang China
92	A4	Guanyinqiao China
92	E1	Guanyun China
157	B3	Guapi Col.
150	I6	Guápiles Costa Rica
158	C2	Guaporé r. Bol./Brazil
154	D7	Guaqui Bol.
155	I5	Guará r. Brazil
155	K5	Guarabira Brazil
158	B1	Guaraí Brazil
158	A3	Guarapuava Brazil
158	C3	Guaraqueçaba Brazil
158	C3	Guaratinguetá Brazil
158	D4	Guaratuba, Baía de b. Brazil
111	C2	Guarda Port.
158	C2	Guarda Mor Brazil
157	D2	Guárico r. Venez.
158	C2	Guarujá Brazil
158	C2	Guarulhos Brazil
157	C2	Guasare r. Venez.
150	C3	Guasave Mex.
157	C2	Guasdualito Venez.
157	E2	Guasipati Venez.
158	B2	Guassú r. Brazil
150	G5	Guatemala country Central America
150	F6	Guatemala City Guat.
157	D2	Guatope, Parque Nacional nat. park Venez.
159	C3	Guatrache Arg.
157	C3	Guaviare r. Col.
157	E3	Guaxupé Brazil
157	B4	Guayabero r. Col.
157	D3	Guayapo r. Venez.
154	C4	Guayaquil Ecuador
154	B4	Guayaquil, Golfo de g. Ecuador
154	E6	Guayaramerín Bol.
150	B2	Guaymas Mex.
151	G5	Guazacapán Guat.
122	D2	Guba Eth.
82	D4	Gubadag Turkm.
87	B3	Gubbi India
114	E6	Gubbio Italy
117	F5	Gubkin Rus. Fed.
92	D3	Gucheng China
117	G7	Gudaut'a Georgia
103	J3	Gudbrandsdalen valley Norway
117	H7	Gudermes Rus. Fed.
87	C2	Gudivada India
87	B3	Gudiyattam India
85	G5	Gudri r. Pak.
80	D1	Güdül Turkey
87	B3	Gudur Andhra Pradesh India
87	B3	Gudur Andhra Pradesh India
103	I3	Gudvangen Norway
		Guecho Spain see Algorta
120	A4	Guéckédou Guinea
135	I1	Guégués, Lac l. Canada
157	B4	Güéjar r. Col.
120	C1	Guelma Alg.
120	A2	Guelmine Morocco
135	G4	Guelph Canada
151	E3	Guémez Mex.
157	D2	Güera r. Venez.
135	I1	Guérard, Lac l. Canada
110	E3	Gueret France
105	E7	Guernsey i. U.K.
138	F3	Guernsey U.S.A.
151	E2	Guerrero Mex.
150	D5	Guerrero state Mex.
150	A2	Guerrero Negro Mex.
84	D3	Gügerd, Kūh-e mts Iran
121	D4	Guider Cameroon
114	E4	Guidonia-Montecelio Italy
93	C6	Guiding China
120	B3	Guiglo Côte d'Ivoire
108	B5	Guignicourt France
93	D6	Gui Jiang r. China
93	F5	Guiji Shan mts China
105	G7	Guildford U.K.
147	I2	Guildhall U.S.A.
93	D6	Guilin China
132	E2	Guillaume-Delisle, Lac l. Canada
111	B2	Guimarães Port.
97	B4	Guimaras Strait Phil.
93	E3	Guimeng Ding mt. China
140	A2	Guinda U.S.A.
120	A3	Guinea country Africa
120	A3	Guinea, Gulf of Africa
163	I5	Guinea Basin sea feature N. Atlantic Ocean
120	A3	Guinea-Bissau country Africa
149	H4	Güines Cuba
110	D2	Guingamp France
110	B2	Guipavas France
93	D6	Guiping China
158	B2	Guiratinga Brazil
157	E2	Güiria Venez.
108	B5	Guiscard France
108	B5	Guise France
93	E4	Guixi China
92	B3	Guiyang Guizhou China
93	D5	Guiyang Hunan China
92	B3	Guizhou prov. China
88	B5	Gujarat state India
88	B3	Gujar Khan Pak.
88	C2	Gujranwala Pak.
88	C2	Gujrat Pak.
117	F5	Gukovo Rus. Fed.
81	J3	Gük Tappeh Iran
88	D2	Gulabgarh Jammu and Kashmir
82	D4	Gulabie Uzbek.
92	B4	Gulang China
87	C1	Gulbarga India
103	N4	Gulbene Latvia
83	H4	Gulcha Kyrg.
80	E3	Gülek Turkey
86	D4	Gulf, The Asia
71	H4	Gulgong Australia
92	B3	Gulin China
88	B3	Gulistan Pak.
83	H4	Gulistan Uzbek.
109	J1	Gülitz Germany
134	E1	Gull Island U.S.A.
131	H4	Gull Lake Canada
102	M2	Gullträsk Sweden
80	D3	Gülnar Turkey
85	G5	Gulran Afgh.
117	G7	Gulrip'shi Georgia
80	E3	Gülşehir Turkey
83	H3	Gul'shad Kazakh.
122	D3	Gulu Uganda
88	D3	Gumal r. Pak.
123	C5	Gumare Botswana
82	C5	Gumdag Turkm.
87	D1	Gumia India
88	D3	Gumla India
108	F3	Gummersbach Germany
80	H2	Gümüşhacıköy Turkey
81	H2	Gümüşhane Turkey
71	F5	Guna India
71	H5	Gunbar Australia
71	H5	Gundagai Australia
109	H5	Gundelsheim Germany
80	D3	Güney Turkey
122	B4	Gungu Dem. Rep. Congo
117	H7	Gunib Rus. Fed.
131	J4	Gunisao r. Canada
71	H5	Gunning Australia
146	D5	Gunnison CO U.S.A.
139	F4	Gunnison UT U.S.A.
139	F4	Gunnison r. U.S.A.
88	D2	Gunt r. Tajik.
87	C2	Guntakal India
145	C5	Guntersville U.S.A.
145	C5	Guntersville Lake U.S.A.
87	C2	Guntur India
99	A2	Gunungsitoli Indon.
99	A2	Gunungtua Indon.
109	I5	Gunzenhausen Germany
92	E1	Guojiatun China
92	E1	Guoyang China
92	A2	Gurban Hudag China
92	D1	Gurban Obo China
80	D1	Güre Turkey
80	D3	Güre Turkey
89	H3	Gürdim Iran
88	D4	Gürei India
102	D2	Gurgan Iran
102	K3	Gurk r. Austria
122	D2	Gurk Eth.
155	J5	Gurgueia r. Brazil
122	D2	Gurinhatã Brazil
117	H7	Gurjaani Georgia
85	E4	Gur Khar Iran
82	E4	Gurlen Uzbek.
81	I2	Gürpinar Turkey
123	D5	Gurué Moz.
80	F2	Gürün Turkey
155	I4	Gurupi r. Brazil
88	C4	Guru Sikhar mt. India
116	B4	Gur'yevsk Rus. Fed.
120	C3	Gusau Nigeria
109	J2	Güsen Germany
116	F4	Gusev Rus. Fed.
96	B4	Gushan China
85	F3	Gushgy Turkm.
85	F3	Gushgy r. Turkm.
77	L2	Gusikha Rus. Fed.
116	D4	Gusino Rus. Fed.
77	L4	Gusinoozersk Rus. Fed.
89	F4	Guskara India
116	G4	Gus'-Khrustal'nyy Rus. Fed.
114	C5	Guspini Sardinia Italy
130	B3	Gustavus U.S.A.
109	J2	Güsten Germany
109	L1	Güstrow Germany
109	H2	Gütersloh Germany
141	H5	Guthrie AZ U.S.A.
144	C4	Guthrie KY U.S.A.
143	D5	Guthrie OK U.S.A.
143	C5	Guthrie TX U.S.A.
93	B5	Gutian Fujian China
93	F5	Gutian Fujian China
108	E5	Gutland reg. Germany/Lux.
89	F3	Gutsuo China
134	B4	Guttenberg U.S.A.
123	D5	Gutu Zimbabwe
89	G4	Guwahati India
81	K4	Guwèr Iraq
109	H3	Guxhagen Germany
155	G2	Guyana country S. America
92	D1	Guyang China
143	C4	Guymon U.S.A.
84	D4	Gūyom Iran
71	I3	Guyra Australia
92	E1	Guyuan Hebei China
92	B2	Guyuan Ningxia China
82	F5	Guzar Uzbek.
92	D2	Guzhang China
92	E3	Guzheng China
113	J3	Gvardeysk Rus. Fed.
71	H3	Gwabegar Australia
85	F5	Gwadar Pak.
88	D4	Gwadar West Bay Pak.
88	D4	Gwalior India
123	C6	Gwanda Zimbabwe
85	F5	Gwash Pak.
85	F5	Gwatar Bay Pak.
107	C2	Gweebarra Bay Rep. of Ireland
123	C5	Gweru Zimbabwe
134	D2	Gwinn U.S.A.
121	D3	Gwoza Nigeria
71	H2	Gwydir r. Australia
89	F2	Gyaca China
89	F2	Gyagartang China
89	G3	Gyangnyi Caka salt l. China
89	G3	Gyangrang China
89	G3	Gyangze China
89	G3	Gyaring Co l. China
89	G3	Gyaring Hu l. China
76	I2	Gydan Peninsula pen. Rus. Fed.
		Gydanskiy Poluostrov pen. Rus. Fed. see Gydan Peninsula
89	H3	Gyimda China
89	H3	Gyirong Xizang China
89	F3	Gyirong Xizang China
69	H4	Gympie Australia
113	I7	Gyöngyös Hungary
112	H7	Győr Hungary
131	J4	Gypsumville Canada
115	J6	Gytheio Greece
113	I7	Gyula Hungary
81	I1	Gyumri Armenia
82	D5	Gyzylarbat Turkm.
82	C5	Gyzyletrek Turkm.

H

102	N3	Haapajärvi Fin.
102	N2	Haapavesi Fin.
103	M4	Haapsalu Estonia
108	C2	Haarlem Neth.
124	E6	Haarlem S. Africa
109	G3	Haarstrang ridge Germany
72	B5	Haast N.Z.
88	B4	Hab r. Pak.
122	D3	Habaswein Kenya
130	F3	Habay Canada
86	C7	Habbān Yemen
81	I5	Ḩabbānīyah, Hawr al l. Iraq
85	G5	Hab Chauki Pak.
89	G4	Habiganj Bangl.
92	B3	Habirag China
103	K4	Habo Sweden
159	B3	Hachado, Paso de pass Arg./Chile
95	F5	Hachijō-jima i. Japan
94	G4	Hachinohe Japan
95	F7	Hachiōji Japan
80	H2	Hacıbektaş Turkey
81	H2	Hacıömer Turkey
70	C3	Hack, Mount Australia
123	D6	Hacufera Moz.
84	C6	Hadabat al Budū plain Saudi Arabia
87	A3	Hadagalli India
86	C6	Hadd, Ra's al pt Oman
106	G3	Haddington U.K.
121	D3	Hadejia Nigeria
80	D6	Hadera Israel
103	I5	Haderslev Denmark
105	H5	Hadleigh U.K.
128	H2	Hadley Bay Canada
96	D6	Hadong S. Korea
86	C7	Hadramawt reg. Yemen
103	I4	Hadsten Denmark
117	E5	Hadyach Ukr.
159	F1	Hadyboś, Cuchilla de hills Uruguay
96	C5	Haeju N. Korea
96	C5	Haeju-man b. N. Korea
96	D6	Haenam S. Korea
125	I2	Haenertsburg S. Africa
84	C5	Ḥafar al Bāṭin Saudi Arabia
131	H4	Hafford Canada
80	H2	Hafik Turkey
88	B5	Hafizabad Pak.
89	H4	Haflong India
102	B2	Hafnarfjörður Iceland
102	□	Haforsfljót r. Iceland
135	G2	Hagar Canada
91	1	Hagåtña Guam
122	D2	Hagar Nish Plateau Eritrea
108	C4	Hageland reg. Belgium
68	E2	Hagen, Mount P.N.G.

109 J1 Hagenow Germany
146 E5 Hagerstown U.S.A.
110 D5 Hagetmau France
103 K3 Hagfors Sweden
138 D2 Haggin, Mount U.S.A.
95 B7 Hagi Japan
93 B6 Ha Giang Vietnam
105 E5 Hagley U.K.
107 B5 Hag's Head hd Rep. of Ireland
114 C7 Hague Canada
110 H2 Haguenau France
90 G4 Hahajima-rettō is Japan
122 D4 Hai Tanz.
92 F3 Hai'an China
124 B4 Haib watercourse Namibia
96 B3 Haicheng China
109 I3 Haidenaab r. Germany
93 C6 Hai Duong Vietnam
80 E5 Haifa Israel
80 E5 Haifa, Bay of Israel
93 E6 Haifeng China
109 G4 Haiger Germany
93 D6 Haikou China
90 D2 Hailar China
135 H2 Haileybury Canada
96 E1 Hailin China
105 H7 Hailsham U.K.
102 N2 Hailuoto Fin.
92 F4 Haimen China
93 C7 Hainan prov. China
93 C6 Hainan i. China
93 C6 Hainan Strait China
130 B3 Haines U.S.A.
130 B2 Haines Junction Canada
109 I3 Hainich ridge Germany
109 L4 Hainichen Germany
109 I3 Hainleite ridge Germany
93 C6 Hai Phong Vietnam
92 A2 Hairag China
94 B3 Hairhan Namag China
93 F5 Haitan Dao i. China
142 J5 Haiti country Caribbean Sea
93 C7 Haitou China
141 G5 Haivana Nakya U.S.A.
140 D3 Haiwee Reservoir U.S.A.
92 E2 Haixing China
121 F3 Haiya Sudan
92 A2 Haiyan Qinghai China
92 F4 Haiyan Zhejiang China
96 A5 Haiyang China
96 B4 Haiyang Dao i. China
92 B2 Haiyuan China
92 F3 Haizhou Wan b. China
113 J7 Hajdúböszörmény Hungary
114 C7 Hajeb El Ayoun Tunisia
86 D7 Hajhir mt. Yemen
89 F4 Hajipur India
95 H4 Hajiki-zaki pt Japan
84 D4 Hajjah Yemen
84 D4 Hājjiābād Iran
84 D4 Hājjīābād Iran
89 H5 Haka Myanmar
140 □2 Hakalau U.S.A.
159 C4 Hakelhuincul, Altiplanicie de plat. Arg.
81 I3 Hakkâri Turkey
102 M2 Hakkas Sweden
95 D7 Hakken-zan mt. Japan
95 D7 Hako-dake mt. Japan
94 C4 Hakodate Japan
124 B1 Hakos Mountains Namibia
124 D3 Hakseen Pan salt pan S. Africa
95 E6 Hakui Japan
95 D6 Haku-san vol. Japan
95 D6 Haku-san National Park Japan
88 B4 Hala Pak.
Halab Syria see Aleppo
84 B6 Halabān Saudi Arabia
81 J4 Halabja Iraq
96 C1 Halahai China
96 C1 Halahai China
121 F2 Halaib Sudan
86 E6 Halāniyāt, Juzur al is Oman
84 H4 Halawa U.S.A.
80 F4 Halba Lebanon
90 B2 Halban Mongolia
109 J3 Halberstadt Germany
97 B3 Halcon, Mount Phil.
102 □ Haldarsvík Faroe Is
103 J4 Halden Norway
109 J3 Haldensleben Germany
89 G5 Haldi r. India
89 G5 Haldia India
89 G4 Haldibari India
88 D3 Haldwani India
135 F3 Hale U.S.A.
84 D5 Hāleh Iran
140 □1 Haleiwa U.S.A.
105 I5 Halesowen U.K.
84 C4 Haleyleh Iran
80 F3 Halfeti Turkey
72 B7 Halfmoon Bay N.Z.
130 E3 Halfway r. Canada
107 C6 Halfway Rep. of Ireland
108 C2 Halfweg Neth.
109 G4 Halia India
84 C4 Hālībīyah Syria
135 H3 Haliburton Canada
133 H5 Halifax Canada
104 F4 Halifax U.K.
146 D6 Halifax U.S.A.
92 C1 Haliut China
104 E3 Halkirk U.K.
102 I3 Hälla Sweden
130 D7 Halla-san mt. S. Korea
70 A5 Hall Bay Australia
129 J3 Hall Beach Canada
108 C4 Halle Belgium
108 B3 Halle Neth.
109 J3 Halle (Saale) Germany
103 K3 Hallefors Sweden
112 F7 Hallein Austria
109 J4 Halle-Neustadt Germany
73 A5 Hallett, Cape Antarctica
73 C3 Halley research station Antarctica
66 E2 Hall Islands Micronesia
102 L2 Hällnäs Sweden
122 D1 Hallock U.S.A.
129 L3 Hall Peninsula Canada
103 K4 Hallsberg Sweden
68 C3 Halls Creek Australia
135 H3 Halls Lake Canada
108 B4 Halluin France
102 K3 Hallviken Sweden
91 H4 Halmahera i. Indon.
103 K4 Halmstad Sweden
103 J4 Hals Denmark
102 N3 Halsua Fin.
108 F3 Haltern Germany
104 E3 Haltwhistle U.K.
84 D5 Hālūl i. Qatar
108 F4 Halver Germany
108 B5 Ham France
95 C7 Hamada Japan
120 B2 Hamâda El Haricha des. Mali
120 B2 Hamada Tounassine des. Alg.
80 F4 Hamāh Syria
94 G3 Hamamasu Japan
95 F7 Hamamatsu Japan
103 J3 Hamar Norway
102 K1 Hamarøy Norway
94 H2 Hamatonbetsu Japan
104 F3 Hambantota Sri Lanka
109 H1 Hambergen Germany
104 F3 Hambleton Hills U.K.
109 H1 Hamburg Germany
125 G6 Hamburg S. Africa
143 F5 Hamburg AR U.S.A.
146 D3 Hamburg NY U.S.A.
147 F4 Hamburg PA U.S.A.

109 G1 Hamburgisches Wattenmeer, Nationalpark nat. park Germany
147 G4 Hamden U.S.A.
103 N3 Hämeenlinna Fin.
109 H2 Hameln Germany
68 B4 Hamersley Range mts Australia
96 D4 Hamhŭng N. Korea
88 C2 Hami China
121 F3 Hamid Sudan
70 C4 Hamilton Australia
149 L2 Hamilton Bermuda
135 H4 Hamilton Canada
72 B3 Hamilton N.Z.
106 D3 Hamilton U.K.
145 C5 Hamilton AL U.S.A.
134 B5 Hamilton IL U.S.A.
138 D2 Hamilton MT U.S.A.
147 F3 Hamilton NY U.S.A.
146 A3 Hamilton OH U.S.A.
140 B3 Hamilton, Mount CA U.S.A.
141 E2 Hamilton, Mount NV U.S.A.
140 A2 Hamilton City U.S.A.
103 N3 Hamina Fin.
81 H6 Hāmir, Wādī al watercourse Saudi Arabia
88 D3 Hamirpur India
96 A4 Hamju N. Korea
70 C5 Hamley Bridge Australia
134 D3 Hamlin Lake U.S.A.
109 H3 Hamm Germany
120 B2 Hammada du Drâa plat. Alg.
81 I3 Hammām al 'Alīl Iraq
114 D6 Hammamet Tunisia
114 D6 Hammamet, Golfe de b. Tunisia
81 K6 Hammār, Hawr al l. Iraq
102 L3 Hammarstrand Sweden
109 H4 Hammelburg Germany
102 K3 Hammerdal Sweden
102 M1 Hammerfest Norway
108 F3 Hamminkeln Germany
70 C4 Hammond Australia
138 B3 Hammond IN U.S.A.
143 F6 Hammond LA U.S.A.
138 F2 Hammond MT U.S.A.
135 F2 Hammond Bay U.S.A.
146 D3 Hammondsport U.S.A.
147 F5 Hammonton U.S.A.
108 E5 Hamoir Belgium
72 C6 Hampden N.Z.
105 F6 Hampshire Downs hills U.K.
133 G4 Hampton Canada
143 E5 Hampton AR U.S.A.
147 H3 Hampton NH U.S.A.
147 E6 Hampton VA U.S.A.
81 J4 Hamrin, Jabal mts Iraq
98 A3 Hamta Pass India
93 B4 Hàm Tân Vietnam
85 E5 Hāmūn-e Jaz Mūrīān salt marsh Iran
85 F4 Hamun Helmand salt flat Afgh./Iran
85 G4 Hamun-i-Lora l. Pak.
85 F4 Hamun-i-Mashkel salt flat Pak.
85 G4 Hāmūn Puzak marsh Afgh.
81 I2 Hamur Turkey
108 D4 Han, Grotte de Belgium
140 □2 Hana U.S.A.
124 E1 Hanahai watercourse Botswana/Namibia
140 □2 Hanalei U.S.A.
94 G5 Hanamaki Japan
109 G3 Hanau Germany
92 D3 Hancheng China
146 D5 Hancock MD U.S.A.
134 C2 Hancock MI U.S.A.
147 H4 Hancock WV U.S.A.
106 C2 Handa Island U.K.
92 E2 Handan China
122 D4 Handeni Tanz.
140 D3 Hanford U.S.A.
87 A3 Hangal India
90 D2 Hangayn Nuruu mts Mongolia
92 F2 Hangu China
88 B3 Hangu Pak.
93 D6 Hanguang China
93 F4 Hangzhou China
93 F4 Hangzhou Wan b. China
81 H2 Hani Turkey
84 C5 Hanīdh Saudi Arabia
92 F3 Hanjiang China
109 I2 Hankensbüttel Germany
124 F6 Hankey S. Africa
103 M4 Hanko Fin.
141 G2 Hanksville U.S.A.
88 D2 Hanle Jammu and Kashmir
72 D5 Hanmer Springs N.Z.
131 G4 Hanna Canada
132 D3 Hannah Bay Canada
134 B6 Hannibal U.S.A.
109 H2 Hannover Germany
109 H3 Hannoversch Münden Germany
108 D3 Hannut Belgium
103 K5 Hanöbukten b. Sweden
93 B6 Ha Nôi Vietnam
135 G3 Hanover Canada
124 E6 Hanover S. Africa
147 G4 Hanover NH U.S.A.
146 E5 Hanover PA U.S.A.
73 B4 Hansen Mts Antarctica
93 C4 Hanshou China
92 E4 Han Shui r. China
88 D3 Hansi India
102 L1 Hansnes Norway
70 B3 Hanson, Lake salt flat Australia
103 J4 Hanstholm Denmark
108 E6 Han-sur-Nied France
116 C4 Hantsavichy Belarus
88 C3 Hanumangarh India
71 G5 Hanwood Australia
92 D3 Hanyin China
93 B4 Hanyuan China
85 F5 Hanzaran Iran
92 D3 Hanzhong China
67 J6 Hao atoll Fr. Polynesia
89 G4 Haora India
102 N3 Haparanda Sweden
89 H4 Hapoli India
133 I3 Happy Valley-Goose Bay Canada
96 B3 Hapsu N. Korea
88 D3 Hapur India
84 C5 Haputale Sri Lanka
84 C5 Haraḍ well Saudi Arabia
84 C5 Haraḍh Saudi Arabia
116 D4 Haradok Belarus
86 E6 Harāsīs, Jiddat al des. Oman
90 B2 Har-Ayrag Mongolia
120 A4 Harbel Liberia
94 B3 Harbin China
135 F4 Harbor Beach U.S.A.
133 E4 Harbour Breton Canada
133 F4 Harbour Grace Canada
141 F4 Harcuvar Mountains U.S.A.
88 D5 Harda India
103 I3 Hardangervidda plat. Norway
103 I3 Hardangervidda Nasjonalpark nat. park Norway
124 B2 Hardap admin. reg. Namibia
124 B2 Hardap Dam Namibia
91 I3 Harden, Bukit mt. Indon.
108 E2 Hardenberg Neth.
108 D2 Harderwijk Neth.
124 C5 Hardeveld mts S. Africa
109 H4 Hardheim Germany
138 F3 Hardin U.S.A.
131 H4 Hardisty Canada
130 G2 Hardisty Lake Canada

88 E4 Hardoi India
145 F5 Hardwick, Cape U.S.A.
70 B5 Hardwicke Bay Australia
143 F4 Hardy U.S.A.
72 C7 Hardy, Mount N.Z. see Rangipoua
134 E4 Hardy Reservoir U.S.A.
108 B4 Harelbeke Belgium
108 E1 Haren Neth.
108 F2 Haren (Ems) Germany
122 E3 Härer Eth.
147 F4 Harford U.S.A.
122 E3 Hargeysa Somalia
113 L7 Harghita-Mădăraş, Vârful mt. Romania
81 H2 Harhal Dağları mts Turkey
92 C2 Harhatan China
92 D3 Har Hu l. China
88 D3 Haridwar India
72 C6 Harihari N.Z.
95 F6 Harima-nada b. Japan
89 G5 Haringhat r. Bangl.
108 B3 Haringvliet est. Neth.
85 G3 Hari Rūd r. Afgh./Iran
103 M3 Harjavalta Fin.
142 E3 Harlan IA U.S.A.
146 C5 Harlan KY U.S.A.
105 C5 Harlech U.K.
138 E1 Harlem U.S.A.
105 I5 Harleston U.K.
108 D1 Harlingen Neth.
143 D7 Harlingen U.S.A.
105 H6 Harlow U.K.
138 E2 Harlowton U.S.A.
110 C5 Harly France
147 I2 Harmony ME U.S.A.
134 A4 Harmony MN U.S.A.
109 I1 Harmsdorf Germany
88 A3 Harnai Pak.
108 A4 Harnes France
138 B3 Harney Basin U.S.A.
138 C3 Harney Lake U.S.A.
103 L3 Härnösand Sweden
90 B2 Har Nuur l. Mongolia
106 □ Haroldswick U.K.
120 B4 Harper Liberia
140 D4 Harper U.S.A.
146 E5 Harpers Ferry U.S.A.
109 G2 Harpstedt Germany
81 G2 Harput Turkey
141 F5 Harquahala Mts U.S.A.
81 G3 Harran Turkey
132 E3 Harricanaw r. Canada
145 C5 Harriman U.S.A.
147 F5 Harriman Reservoir U.S.A.
71 J3 Harrington Australia
147 F5 Harrington U.S.A.
133 J3 Harrington Harbour Canada
106 B3 Harris U.K.
70 A3 Harris, Lake salt flat Australia
106 A3 Harris, Sound of sea chan. U.K.
134 B4 Harrisburg IL U.S.A.
146 E4 Harrisburg PA U.S.A.
125 H4 Harrismith S. Africa
143 E4 Harrison AR U.S.A.
134 D3 Harrison MI U.S.A.
133 J3 Harrison, Cape Canada
128 C2 Harrison Bay U.S.A.
146 D5 Harrisonburg U.S.A.
130 E5 Harrison Lake Canada
142 E4 Harrisonville U.S.A.
135 F2 Harrisville MI U.S.A.
146 C5 Harrisville WV U.S.A.
104 F4 Harrogate U.K.
109 H1 Harsefeld Germany
84 B3 Harsin Iran
80 G1 Harşit r. Turkey
115 L2 Hârşova Romania
102 L1 Harstad Norway
109 H2 Harsum Germany
134 C4 Hart U.S.A.
70 B3 Hart, Lake salt flat Australia
96 B2 Hartao China
124 G7 Hartbees watercourse S. Africa
112 G7 Hartberg Austria
106 E5 Hart Fell hill U.K.
147 G4 Hartford CT U.S.A.
134 C4 Hartford MI U.S.A.
142 D3 Hartford SD U.S.A.
134 B3 Hartford WI U.S.A.
105 C7 Hartland U.K.
133 G4 Hartland Canada
147 I2 Hartland U.S.A.
105 C7 Hartland Point U.K.
104 F3 Hartlepool U.K.
130 E3 Hartley Bay Canada
103 N3 Hartola Fin.
130 D3 Hart Ranges mts Canada
112 E6 Härtsfeld hills Germany
124 F3 Hartswater S. Africa
145 D5 Hartwell Reservoir U.S.A.
90 B2 Har Us Nuur l. Mongolia
85 F3 Harut watercourse Afgh.
139 F4 Harvard, Mount U.S.A.
134 D2 Harvey MI U.S.A.
142 D2 Harvey ND U.S.A.
71 J2 Harwood Australia
80 F6 Haşāh, Wādī al watercourse Jordan
83 I5 Hasalbag China
88 C2 Hasan Abdal Pak.
81 H3 Hasan Dağı mts Turkey
81 H3 Hasankeyf Turkey
87 B2 Hasanparti India
84 C2 Hasb, Sha'īb watercourse Iraq
80 E5 Hasbani r. Lebanon
80 F2 Hasbek Turkey
87 C2 Hasdo r. India
109 F2 Haselünne Germany
109 I4 Hasenkopf hill Germany
84 C2 Hashtgerd Iran
84 C2 Hashtpar Iran
84 C2 Hashtrud Iran
143 D5 Haskell U.S.A.
105 H6 Haslemere U.K.
113 L7 Hăşmaşul Mare mt. Romania
109 I3 Hasselfelde Germany
108 E3 Hasselt Belgium
108 D3 Hasselt Neth.
120 C1 Hassi Messaoud Alg.
103 K4 Hässleholm Sweden
108 D4 Hastière-Lavaux Belgium
71 F4 Hastings Australia
72 F3 Hastings N.Z.
105 H7 Hastings U.K.
134 A5 Hastings MN U.S.A.
142 D3 Hastings NE U.S.A.
141 F3 Hatch U.S.A.
130 E3 Hatchet Lake Canada
71 F4 Hatfield Australia
105 G5 Hatfield U.K.
90 C1 Hatgal Mongolia
89 F4 Hatia Nepal
93 C4 Hatia India
98 C1 Ha Tinh Vietnam
81 I4 Hatra Iraq

70 E5 Hattah Australia
145 F5 Hatteras, Cape U.S.A.
163 E4 Hatteras Abyssal Plain sea feature S. Atlantic Ocean
102 K2 Hattfjelldal Norway
87 C2 Hatti r. India
145 B6 Hattiesburg U.S.A.
108 F3 Hattingen Germany
93 B4 Hat Yai Thai.
122 E3 Haud reg. Eth.
103 I4 Haugesund Norway
72 C3 Hauhungaroa mt. N.Z.
103 I4 Haukeligrend Norway
102 N2 Haukipudas Fin.
103 O3 Haukivesi l. Fin.
131 H4 Haultain r. Canada
72 E2 Hauraki Gulf N.Z.
72 A7 Hauroko, Lake N.Z.
147 I3 Haut, Isle au i. U.S.A.
120 B1 Haut Atlas mts Morocco
133 G4 Hauterive Canada
120 B1 Hauts Plateaux Alg.
140 □1 Hauula U.S.A.
149 H4 Havana Cuba
134 B5 Havana U.S.A.
105 G7 Havant U.K.
141 E4 Havasu, Lake U.S.A.
109 K2 Havel r. Germany
108 E4 Havelange Belgium
109 K2 Havelberg Germany
109 K2 Havelländisches Luch marsh Germany
135 I3 Havelock Canada
63 G6 Havelock i. India
72 F3 Havelock North N.Z.
105 C6 Haverfordwest U.K.
105 H5 Haverhill U.K.
87 A3 Haveri India
108 D4 Haversin Belgium
133 H4 Havre Aubert, Île du i. Canada
147 J5 Havre de Grace U.S.A.
133 H3 Havre-St-Pierre Canada
115 L4 Havsa Turkey
80 F3 Havza Turkey
140 □1 Hawaii i. U.S.A.
140 □1 Hawaiian Islands N. Pacific Ocean
160 H4 Hawaiian Ridge sea feature N. Pacific Ocean
140 □2 Hawaii Volcanoes National Park U.S.A.
81 K7 Hawallī Kuwait
105 D4 Hawarden U.K.
130 H3 Hawarden Canada
72 B6 Hawea, Lake N.Z.
72 E3 Hawera N.Z.
140 □2 Hawi U.S.A.
106 F5 Hawick U.K.
81 K6 Hawizah, Hawr al l. Iraq
72 B6 Hawkdun Range mts N.Z.
72 F3 Hawke Bay N.Z.
133 J3 Hawke Island Canada
70 C3 Hawker Australia
70 D2 Hawkers Gate Australia
147 F3 Hawkesbury Canada
141 F3 Hawkins Peak mt. U.S.A.
147 J2 Hawkshaw Canada
81 I5 Hawrān, Wādī watercourse Iraq
84 B6 Hawshah, Jibāl al mts Saudi Arabia
124 C7 Hawston S. Africa
140 C2 Hawthorne U.S.A.
96 C1 Haxat China
104 F3 Haxby U.K.
70 F5 Hay Australia
130 F2 Hay r. Canada
92 B1 Haya China
84 B5 Haydarābād Iran
138 C2 Hayden ID U.S.A.
141 I3 Hayes r. Man. Canada
129 I3 Hayes r. Nunavut Canada
127 G2 Hayes Halvø pen. Greenland
105 B7 Hayle U.K.
86 B7 Haymā' Oman
80 D2 Haymana Turkey
146 E5 Haymarket U.S.A.
147 I2 Haynesville U.S.A.
105 D6 Hay-on-Wye U.K.
116 E5 Hayrabolu Turkey
130 G2 Hay River Canada
142 D4 Hays U.S.A.
117 D5 Haysyn Ukr.
140 A3 Hayward CA U.S.A.
134 B2 Hayward WI U.S.A.
105 G7 Haywards Heath U.K.
85 G4 Hazarajat reg. Afgh.
146 B6 Hazard U.S.A.
89 F5 Hazaribagh India
89 F5 Hazaribagh Range mts India
108 A4 Hazebrouck France
130 D3 Hazelton Canada
128 G2 Hazen Strait Canada
108 C2 Hazerswoude-Rijk Neth.
147 F4 Hazleton U.S.A.
85 G3 Hazrat Sultan Afgh.
81 H2 Hazro Turkey
159 D2 H. Bouchard Arg.
107 B4 Headford Rep. of Ireland
140 A2 Healdsburg U.S.A.
70 F6 Healesville Australia
104 E4 Heanor U.K.
162 I8 Heard Island Indian Ocean
143 D6 Hearne U.S.A.
132 D6 Hearst Canada
73 B2 Hearst Island Antarctica
105 H7 Heathfield U.K.
147 E6 Heathsville U.S.A.
143 D7 Hebbronville U.S.A.
92 E3 Hebei prov. China
136 D3 Heber City U.S.A.
143 D5 Heber Springs U.S.A.
92 E3 Hebi China
133 H2 Hebron Canada
134 D5 Hebron IN U.S.A.
142 C2 Hebron ND U.S.A.
147 G3 Hebron NY U.S.A.
80 E6 Hebron West Bank
133 H2 Hebron Fiord inlet Canada
130 C3 Hecate Strait Canada
151 C5 Hecelchakán Mex.
130 C4 Heceta Island U.S.A.
93 C5 Hechi China
92 C4 Hechuan China
103 K3 Hedemora Sweden
93 E5 Hedi Shuiku resr China
134 A5 Hedrick U.S.A.
108 F2 Heek Germany
108 E2 Heerde Neth.
108 E1 Heerenveen Neth.
108 C2 Heerhugowaard Neth.
108 E4 Heerlen Neth.
80 E5 Hefa Israel see Haifa
92 E4 Hefei China
92 D4 Hefeng China
94 B3 Hegang China
95 E6 Hegura-jima i. Japan
109 J3 Heidberg hill Germany
112 D3 Heide Germany

123 B6 Heide Namibia
109 I5 Heidelberg Germany
125 H3 Heidelberg Gauteng S. Africa
124 D7 Heidelberg W. Cape S. Africa
109 H5 Heidenheim Germany
112 E6 Heiligenhafen Germany
93 □ Hei Ling Chau i. Hong Kong China
96 E1 Heilongjiang prov. China
90 E2 Heilong Jiang r. China/Rus. Fed. alt. Amur
109 I5 Heilsbronn Germany
102 J3 Heimdal Norway
103 N3 Heinola Fin.
98 A2 Heinze Islands Myanmar
96 B3 Heishan China
92 E2 Heishui China
108 C3 Heist-op-den-Berg Belgium
92 E2 Hejian China
93 C5 Hejiang China
93 D6 He Jiang r. China
80 F2 Hejin China
80 F2 Hekimhan Turkey
102 □1 Hekla vol. Iceland
92 B2 Hekou Gansu China
93 C7 Hekou Yunnan China
89 H4 Helem India
140 D3 Helen, Mount U.S.A.
143 F5 Helena AR U.S.A.
138 E2 Helena MT U.S.A.
106 D4 Helensburgh U.K.
80 E6 Helez Israel
72 E2 Helensville N.Z.
112 D3 Helgoländer Bucht b. Germany
71 J1 Helidon Australia
102 □1 Hella Iceland
84 C4 Helleh r. Iran
108 D4 Hellevoetsluis Neth.
111 F4 Hellín Spain
102 N1 Helligskogen Norway
138 C2 Hells Canyon gorge U.S.A.
85 F4 Helmand r. Afgh.
109 I3 Helme r. Germany
108 E3 Helmond Neth.
106 E2 Helmsdale U.K.
106 E2 Helmsdale r. U.K.
104 F4 Helmsley U.K.
109 J3 Helmstedt Germany
96 D2 Helong China
141 G2 Helper U.S.A.
103 K4 Helsingborg Sweden
Helsingfors Fin. see Helsinki
103 K4 Helsingør Denmark
103 N3 Helsinki Fin.
105 B7 Helston U.K.
104 D3 Helvellyn hill U.K.
107 D5 Helvick Head hd Rep. of Ireland
105 G6 Hemel Hempstead U.K.
140 D5 Hemet U.S.A.
109 H2 Hemer Germany
109 H5 Hemmingen Germany
135 I5 Hemmingford Canada
109 H1 Hemmoor Germany
143 D6 Hempstead U.S.A.
105 I5 Hemsby U.K.
103 L4 Hemse Sweden
92 A3 Henan China
92 E3 Henan prov. China
111 E2 Henares r. Spain
94 C1 Henashi-zaki pt Japan
144 C1 Henderson KY U.S.A.
145 E5 Henderson NC U.S.A.
141 E3 Henderson NV U.S.A.
147 E3 Henderson NY U.S.A.
143 E5 Henderson TX U.S.A.
67 J7 Henderson Island Pitcairn Is
145 D5 Hendersonville NC U.S.A.
145 C5 Hendersonville TN U.S.A.
105 G6 Hendon U.K.
85 D5 Hendorābī i. Iran
85 E5 Hengam Iran
90 E4 Hengduan Shan mts China
108 E2 Hengelo Neth.
94 D5 Hengshan Heilong. China
92 D3 Hengshan Hunan China
92 D3 Hengshan Shaanxi China
92 E3 Heng Shan mt. Hunan China
92 D2 Heng Shan mt. Shanxi China
92 D2 Hengshui China
93 C6 Hengxian China
92 D5 Hengyang Hunan China
93 D5 Hengyang Hunan China
117 E6 Heniches'k Ukr.
72 C6 Henley N.Z.
105 G6 Henley-on-Thames U.K.
147 F5 Henlopen, Cape U.S.A.
108 F4 Hennef (Sieg) Germany
109 L2 Hennigsdorf Berlin Germany
143 D4 Hennessey U.S.A.
132 D5 Henrietta Maria, Cape Canada
141 G2 Henrieville U.S.A.
134 B5 Henry U.S.A.
73 B4 Henry Ice Rise Antarctica
129 L3 Henry Kater, Cape hd Canada
141 G2 Henry Mountains U.S.A.
135 G3 Hensall Canada
109 H1 Henstedt-Ulzburg Germany
123 B5 Hentiesbaai Namibia
71 G5 Henty Australia
98 A2 Henzada Myanmar
131 H4 Hepburn Canada
93 C6 Heping China
93 D6 Hepu China
110 F3 Hérault r. France
131 H4 Herbert Canada
109 G4 Herborn Germany
73 B4 Hercules Dome ice feature Antarctica
109 F3 Herdecke Germany
109 G3 Herdorf Germany
150 H6 Heredia Costa Rica
105 E6 Hereford U.K.
143 C5 Hereford U.S.A.
67 J6 Héréhérétué atoll Fr. Polynesia
108 D3 Herent Belgium
109 G2 Herford Germany
109 I4 Herleshausen Germany
147 G3 Herkimer U.S.A.
112 F7 Hermagor Austria
106 □ Hermaness hd U.K.
109 I2 Hermannsburg Germany
124 C7 Hermanus S. Africa
144 C5 Hermann U.S.A.
138 C2 Hermiston U.S.A.
71 H5 Hermidale Australia
66 E2 Hermit Islands P.N.G.
80 E6 Hermon, Mount Lebanon/Syria
150 C3 Hermosillo Mex.
158 D3 Hernandarias Para.
109 G2 Herne Germany
105 I6 Herne Bay U.K.
103 I4 Herning Denmark
134 D1 Heron Bay Canada
158 D3 Herradura Arg.
111 D3 Herrera del Duque Spain
71 G8 Herrick Australia

109 I5 Herrieden Germany
146 E4 Hershey U.S.A.
105 G6 Hertford U.K.
125 G6 Hertzogville S. Africa
108 D4 Herve Belgium
69 F4 Hervey Bay Australia
161 I7 Hervey Islands Cook Is
109 K2 Herzberg Brandenburg Germany
109 L3 Herzberg Brandenburg Germany
109 K1 Herzberg (Harz) Germany
109 K1 Herzogenaurach Germany
109 K1 Herzsprung Germany
81 L4 Heşar Iran
108 C4 Hesbaye reg. Belgium
108 F1 Hesel Germany
93 C6 Heshan China
92 D2 Heshun China
92 D4 Heshui China
130 C2 Hess r. Canada
109 I5 Heßdorf Germany
109 H4 Hesselberg hill Germany
109 H4 Hessen admin. div. Germany
109 H3 Hessisch Lichtenau Germany
93 B6 Het r. Laos
140 B3 Hetch Hetchy Aqueduct canal U.S.A.
108 D3 Heteren Neth.
142 C2 Hettinger U.S.A.
104 E3 Hetton U.K.
109 J3 Hettstedt Germany
104 E3 Hexham U.K.
92 F4 Hexian China
92 B2 Hexipu China
124 C6 Hex River Pass S. Africa
92 D3 Heyang China
85 E5 Heydarābād Iran
104 E3 Heysham U.K.
93 E6 Heyuan China
70 D7 Heywood Australia
104 E4 Heywood U.K.
134 B5 Heyworth U.S.A.
92 B2 Heze China
93 B5 Hezhang China
92 B3 Hezheng China
93 D5 Hezhou China
92 D5 Hezuo China
145 D7 Hialeah U.S.A.
142 E4 Hiawatha U.S.A.
134 A2 Hibbing U.S.A.
72 D5 Hibbs, Point hd Australia
145 D5 Hickory U.S.A.
72 D5 Hicks Bay N.Z.
151 G5 Hicks Cays is Belize
131 J2 Hicks Lake Canada
143 D5 Hico U.S.A.
94 H3 Hidaka-sanmyaku mts Japan
151 E3 Hidalgo Mex.
151 E3 Hidalgo state Mex.
151 E3 Hidalgo del Parral Mex.
158 C2 Hidrolândia Brazil
95 C6 Higashi-Hiroshima Japan
94 G5 Higashine Japan
95 A8 Higashi-suidō sea chan. Japan
143 C4 Higgins U.S.A.
135 F3 Higgins Bay U.S.A.
138 C3 High Desert U.S.A.
134 E3 High Falls Reservoir U.S.A.
134 E3 High Island U.S.A.
93 □ High Island Reservoir Hong Kong China
134 D4 Highland Park U.S.A.
140 D4 Highland Peak mt. CA U.S.A.
141 E3 Highland Peak mt. NV U.S.A.
130 G3 High Level Canada
88 D3 High Level Canal India
145 E5 High Point U.S.A.
130 G4 High Prairie Canada
130 H4 High River Canada
145 E7 High Rock Bahamas
131 J4 Highrock Lake Canada
71 F9 High Rocky Pt hd Australia
104 E3 High Seat hill U.K.
147 F4 Highstown U.S.A.
105 G6 High Wycombe U.K.
150 B2 Higuera de Zaragoza Mex.
157 D2 Higüerote Venez.
103 M4 Hiiumaa i. Estonia
86 A4 Hijaz reg. Saudi Arabia
141 E3 Hiko U.S.A.
95 E7 Hikone Japan
72 F3 Hikurangi mt. N.Z.
73 B5 Hillary Coast Antarctica
141 H2 Hildale U.S.A.
109 I4 Hildburghausen Germany
109 I4 Hilders Germany
109 I2 Hildesheim Germany
81 J5 Hillah Iraq
142 E4 Hill City U.S.A.
103 K5 Hillerød Denmark
147 H3 Hillsboro NH U.S.A.
142 D2 Hillsboro ND U.S.A.
138 B3 Hillsboro OR U.S.A.
143 D5 Hillsboro TX U.S.A.
146 B5 Hillsboro WV U.S.A.
134 E5 Hillsdale MI U.S.A.
147 G3 Hillsdale NY U.S.A.
146 E4 Hillsgrove U.S.A.
68 B4 Hillside Australia
71 G5 Hillston Australia
71 I5 Hilltop Australia
140 □1 Hilo U.S.A.
125 I4 Hilton S. Africa
146 D3 Hilton U.S.A.
135 D5 Hilton Beach Canada
81 H3 Hilvan Turkey
108 D2 Hilversum Neth.
88 D3 Himachal Pradesh state India
89 F3 Himalaya mts Asia
89 E3 Himalchul mt. Nepal
102 M2 Himanka Fin.
115 H4 Himarë Albania
88 C5 Himatnagar India
95 D7 Himeji Japan
94 G4 Himekami-dake mt. Japan
125 H4 Himeville S. Africa
95 E6 Himi Japan
Ḥimş Syria see Homs
97 C4 Hinatuan Phil.
68 C2 Hinchinbrook Island Australia
134 A2 Hinckley MN U.S.A.
141 F2 Hinckley UT U.S.A.
147 G3 Hinckley Reservoir U.S.A.
88 D3 Hindan r. India
104 G3 Hinderwell U.K.
146 B6 Hindman U.S.A.
70 D6 Hindmarsh, Lake Australia
88 D5 Hindol India
85 G3 Hindu Kush mts Afgh./Pak.
87 B3 Hindupur India
130 F3 Hines Creek Canada
88 D5 Hinganghat India
88 B3 Hingol r. Pak.
87 B2 Hingoli India
81 H2 Hinis Turkey
140 D4 Hinkley U.S.A.
102 L1 Hinnøya i. Norway
97 B4 Hinobaan Phil.
111 D4 Hinojosa del Duque Spain
95 C7 Hino-misaki pt Japan
147 G3 Hinsdale U.S.A.

108 F1 Hinte Germany
130 F4 Hinton Canada
146 C6 Hinton U.K.
108 C2 Hippolytushoef Neth.
81 J2 Hirabit Dağ mt. Turkey
95 A8 Hirado Japan
95 A8 Hirado-shima i. Japan
87 C1 Hirakud Reservoir India
94 H3 Hiroo Japan
94 G4 Hirosaki Japan
95 C7 Hiroshima Japan
109 J5 Hirschaid Germany
109 J4 Hirschberg Germany
112 E7 Hirschberg mt. Germany
110 G2 Hirson France
103 J4 Hirtshals Denmark
88 C3 Hisar India
81 L3 Hisar Iran
85 G3 Hisar, Koh-i- mts Afgh.
80 D1 Hisarönü Turkey
81 J6 Hisb, Sha'ib watercourse Iraq
83 G5 Hisor Tajik.
149 J4 Hispaniola i. Caribbean Sea
89 F4 Hissa Japan
81 I5 Hit Iraq
95 G6 Hitachi Japan
95 G6 Hitachi-ōta Japan
95 B8 Hitoyoshi Japan
102 J3 Hitra i. Norway
109 J1 Hitzacker Germany
95 C7 Hiuchi-nada b. Japan
67 J5 Hiva Oa i. Fr. Polynesia
130 E4 Hixon Canada
81 I2 Hizan Turkey
103 K4 Hjälmaren i. Sweden
131 H2 Hjalmar Lake Canada
103 J3 Hjerkinn Norway
103 K4 Hjo Sweden
103 J4 Hjørring Denmark
125 I4 Hlabisa S. Africa
125 I3 Hlatikulu Swaziland
117 E5 Hlobyne Ukr.
125 H4 Hlohlowane S. Africa
125 H4 Hlotse Lesotho
125 J4 Hluhluwe S. Africa
117 E5 Hlukhiv Ukr.
113 N4 Hlusha Belarus
116 C4 Hlybokaye Belarus
120 C4 Ho Ghana
123 B6 Hoachanas Namibia
71 G9 Hobart Australia
143 D5 Hobart U.S.A.
143 C5 Hobbs U.S.A.
73 A4 Hobbs Coast Antarctica
145 D7 Hobe Sound U.S.A.
92 D1 Hobor China
103 J4 Hobro Denmark
122 E3 Hobyo Somalia
109 H5 Höchberg Germany
109 I3 Hochharz nat. park Germany
98 C3 Ho Chi Minh City Vietnam
112 G7 Hochschwab mt. Austria
109 G5 Hockenheim Germany
146 B5 Hocking r. U.S.A.
151 G3 Hoctúm Mex.
88 D4 Hodal India
104 E4 Hodder r. U.K.
105 G6 Hoddesdon U.K.
86 B7 Hodeida Yemen
147 J1 Hodgdon U.S.A.
113 J7 Hódmezővásárhely Hungary
111 I5 Hodna, Chott el salt l. Alg.
96 D4 Hodo-dan pt N. Korea
 Hoek van Holland Neth. see Hook of Holland
108 D4 Hoensbroek Neth.
96 E2 Hoeryŏng N. Korea
96 D4 Hoeyang N. Korea
109 J4 Hof Germany
109 I4 Hofheim in Unterfranken Germany
125 F5 Hofmeyr S. Africa
102 D2 Höfn Iceland
103 L3 Hofors Sweden
102 C2 Hofsjökull ice cap Iceland
95 B9 Hōfu Japan
103 K4 Höganäs Sweden
71 G7 Hogan Group i. Australia
120 C2 Hoggar plat. Alg.
147 F6 Hog Island U.S.A.
103 L4 Högsby Sweden
109 H5 Hohenloher Ebene plain Germany
109 K3 Hohennölsen Germany
109 K2 Hohennauen Germany
109 J4 Hohenwartetalsperre resr Germany
109 H4 Hohe Rhön mts Germany
112 F7 Hohe Tauern mts Austria
108 E4 Hohe Venn moorland Belgium
92 D1 Hohhot China
89 H2 Hoh Sai Hu l. China
89 G2 Hoh Xil Hu salt l. China
89 G2 Hoh Xil Shan mts China
98 D2 Hội An Vietnam
122 D3 Hoima Uganda
93 B6 Hội Xuân Vietnam
89 G8 Hojai India
95 C8 Hōjo Japan
97 D1 Hokianga Harbour N.Z.
72 C5 Hokitika N.Z.
94 H3 Hokkaidō i. Japan
103 J4 Hokksund Norway
81 J1 Hoktemberyan Armenia
103 J3 Hol Norway
87 B3 Holalkere India
103 J5 Holbæk Denmark
105 H5 Holbeach U.K.
105 H5 Holbrook U.S.A.
134 B3 Holcombe Flowage resr U.S.A.
131 G4 Holden Canada
141 F2 Holden U.S.A.
143 D5 Holdenville U.S.A.
142 D3 Holdrege U.S.A.
87 B3 Hole Narsipur India
149 I4 Holguín Cuba
103 K3 Höljes Sweden
134 D4 Holland U.S.A.
73 B2 Hollick-Kenyon Peninsula Antarctica
146 D4 Hollidaysburg U.S.A.
130 C3 Hollis AK U.S.A.
143 D5 Hollis OK U.S.A.
138 C3 Hollister U.S.A.
135 F4 Holly U.S.A.
143 F5 Holly Springs U.S.A.
145 D7 Hollywood U.S.A.
102 K2 Holm Norway
128 C2 Holman Canada
103 J4 Holmestrand Norway
102 M3 Holmön i. Sweden
102 N3 Holmsund Sweden
124 B3 Holoog Namibia
103 J4 Holstebro Denmark
143 D4 Holston r. U.S.A.
146 C6 Holston Lake U.S.A.
105 C7 Holsworthy U.K.
105 I5 Holt U.K.
134 E4 Holt U.S.A.
142 E4 Holton U.S.A.
108 D1 Holwerd Neth.
107 C6 Holycross Rep. of Ireland
105 C4 Holyhead U.K.
105 C4 Holy Island England U.K.
104 F2 Holy Island Wales U.K.
147 G3 Holyoke U.S.A.
105 H6 Holywell U.K.
109 G3 Holzkirchen Germany
112 E5 Holzminden Germany
109 H3 Homberg (Efze) Germany
120 B3 Hombori Mali
108 F5 Homburg Germany
129 L3 Home Bay Canada

108 D5 Homécourt France
143 E5 Homer U.S.A.
145 D6 Homerville U.S.A.
145 D7 Homestead U.S.A.
145 C5 Homewood U.S.A.
87 B2 Homnabad India
97 C4 Homonhon Point Phil.
80 F4 Homs Syria
117 D4 Homyel' Belarus
157 B3 Honavar India
57 A4 Honda Col.
141 H4 Hon Dah U.S.A.
92 C1 Hondlon Ju China
151 B4 Hondo r. Belize/Mex.
143 D6 Hondo U.S.A.
108 E1 Hondsrug reg. Neth.
150 H5 Honduras country Central America
151 B4 Honduras, Gulf of Belize/Hond.
103 J3 Honefoss Norway
147 F4 Honesdale U.S.A.
140 B1 Honey Lake U.S.A.
147 E3 Honeoye Lake U.S.A.
110 E2 Honfleur France
 Hông, Sông r. Vietnam see Red
92 E4 Hong'an China
96 D5 Hongch'ŏn S. Korea
93 C6 Hồng Gai Vietnam
93 B6 Honghai Wan b. China
93 B6 Honghe China
92 E3 Hong He r. China
93 D4 Honghu China
93 C5 Hongjiang Hunan China
93 C5 Hongjiang Hunan China
 Hong Kong China (City Plan 51)
93 □ Hong Kong special admin. reg. China
93 □ Hong Kong Harbour sea chan. Hong Kong China
93 □ Hong Kong Island Hong Kong China
92 C2 Hongliu He r. China
92 D3 Hongliuyuan China
98 C3 Hồng Ngự Vietnam
92 B2 Hongshansi China
92 D2 Hongshi China
93 D6 Hongshui He r. China
92 D2 Hongtong China
133 G4 Honguedo, Détroit d' sea chan. Canada
96 D3 Hongwŏn N. Korea
96 B1 Hongxing China
92 B3 Hongyuan China
92 F3 Hongze China
93 F3 Hongze Hu l. China
69 F2 Honiara Solomon Is
105 D7 Honiton U.K.
98 C3 Honjô r. Japan
103 M3 Honkajoki Fin.
87 A3 Honnali India
102 N1 Honningsvåg Norway
140 □² Honoka'a U.S.A.
140 □¹ Honolulu U.S.A.
95 E7 Honshū i. Japan
138 B2 Hood, Mount vol. U.S.A.
88 B5 Hood Point Australia
108 E2 Hoogeveen Neth.
108 E1 Hoogezand-Sappemeer Neth.
143 C4 Hooker U.S.A.
107 E5 Hook Head hd Rep. of Ireland
71 G6 Hook r. Australia
108 B2 Hook of Holland Neth.
130 B3 Hoonah U.S.A.
128 B3 Hooper Bay U.S.A.
68 B5 Hooper Island U.S.A.
134 D5 Hoopstad S. Africa
125 F3 Höör Sweden
108 D2 Hoorn Neth.
 Hoorn, Îles de is Wallis and Futuna Is see Futuna Islands
147 G3 Hoosick U.S.A.
141 H3 Hoover Dam U.S.A.
146 B4 Hoover Memorial Reservoir U.S.A.
81 H1 Hopa Turkey
147 H4 Hop Bottom U.S.A.
130 E5 Hope Canada
72 C1 Hope r. N.Z.
143 E5 Hope AR U.S.A.
141 F9 Hope AZ U.S.A.
70 C2 Hope, Lake salt flat Australia
128 B3 Hope, Point c. U.S.A.
133 I2 Hopedale Canada
124 C6 Hopefield S. Africa
153 H3 Hope Mountains Canada
76 D2 Hopen i. Svalbard
72 D4 Hope Saddle pass N.Z.
133 G2 Hopes Advance, Baie b. Canada
70 E5 Hopetoun Australia
124 F4 Hopetown S. Africa
146 E6 Hopewell U.S.A.
132 E2 Hopewell Islands Canada
68 C4 Hopkins, Lake salt flat Australia
145 C4 Hopkinsville U.S.A.
140 A2 Hopland U.S.A.
138 B2 Hoquiam U.S.A.
92 A3 Hor China
81 K2 Horadiz Azer.
81 I1 Horasan Turkey
103 K5 Hörby Sweden
150 D4 Horcasitas Mex.
92 B1 Horh Uul mts Mongolia
134 C4 Horicon U.S.A.
109 D1 Horinger China
160 H7 Horizon Deep sea feature S. Pacific Ocean
116 D4 Horki Belarus
73 B4 Horlick Mts Antarctica
117 F5 Horlivka Ukr.
85 F4 Hormak Iran
84 E5 Hormoz i. Iran
84 E5 Hormuz, Strait of strait Iran/Oman
112 G6 Horn Austria
130 F2 Horn r. Canada
102 B1 Horn c. Iceland
156 C9 Horn, Cape Chile
102 L2 Hornavan l. Sweden
154 C5 Hornbeck U.S.A.
109 I2 Hornberg Germany
105 G4 Horncastle U.K.
103 L3 Horndal Sweden
109 H1 Hörnefors Sweden
132 D4 Hornell U.S.A.
132 D4 Hornepayne Canada
145 B6 Horn Island U.S.A.
124 B3 Hornkranz Namibia
159 B4 Hornos, Cabo de c. Chile see Horn, Cape
71 I4 Hornsby Australia
104 F4 Hornsea U.K.
113 L6 Hornslandet pen. Sweden
117 D5 Horodenka Ukr.
117 C5 Horodok Ukr.
117 B5 Horodok Ukr.
94 F4 Horokanai Japan
113 L5 Horokhiv Ukr.
94 H3 Horoshiri-dake mt. Japan
96 A2 Horqin Shadi reg. China
95 C7 Horrabridge U.K.
89 G3 Horru China
131 J4 Horsefly Canada
146 B3 Horseheads U.S.A.
129 I3 Horse Islands Canada
107 C4 Horseleap Rep. of Ireland
146 E5 Horseshoe Bend U.S.A.

163 H3 Horseshoe Seamounts sea feature N. Atlantic Ocean
70 E6 Horsham Australia
105 G6 Horsham U.K.
109 K5 Horšovský Týn Czech Rep.
109 H4 Horst hill Germany
109 H4 Hörstel Germany
103 J4 Horten Norway
128 F3 Horton r. Canada
135 F1 Horwood Lake Canada
113 M5 Horyn' r. Ukr.
122 D3 Hosa'ina Eth.
109 H4 Hösbach Germany
87 B3 Hosdurga India
81 K4 Hoseynābād Iran
84 C3 Hoseynīyeh Iran
85 F5 Hoshab Pak.
88 C3 Hoshangabad India
88 C3 Hoshiarpur India
87 B3 Hospet India
107 C5 Hospital Rep. of Ireland
159 F1 Hospital, Cuchilla del hills Uruguay
156 C9 Hoste, Isla i. Chile
102 K3 Hotagen l. Sweden
83 I5 Hotan China
83 I5 Hotan He watercourse China
124 E3 Hotazel S. Africa
124 G4 Hoteville U.S.A.
71 H4 Hotham, Mount Australia
102 L2 Hoting Sweden
143 E5 Hot Springs AR U.S.A.
142 C3 Hot Springs SD U.S.A.
130 F1 Hottah Lake Canada
108 D4 Houffalize Belgium
98 □ Hougang Sing.
134 C2 Houghton U.S.A.
134 E3 Houghton Lake l. U.S.A.
134 E3 Houghton Lake U.S.A.
104 F3 Houghton le Spring U.K.
147 J1 Houlton U.S.A.
92 D3 Houma China
143 F6 Houma U.S.A.
107 D4 Hourn, Loch inlet U.K.
147 G3 Housatonic r. U.S.A.
141 F2 House Range mts U.S.A.
130 D4 Houston Canada
143 F5 Houston MO U.S.A.
143 F5 Houston MS U.S.A.
143 E6 Houston TX U.S.A.
125 H1 Hout r. S. Africa
107 F4 Hout U.K.
68 B4 Houtman Abrolhos is Australia
124 E5 Houwater S. Africa
90 B2 Hovd Mongolia
105 G6 Hove U.K.
105 I5 Hoveton U.K.
84 C4 Hoveyzeh Iran
103 K4 Hovmantorp Sweden
92 C1 Hövsgöl Mongolia
90 C1 Hövsgöl Nuur l. Mongolia
90 D2 Hövüün Mongolia
121 E3 Howar, Wadi watercourse Sudan
134 E4 Howard City U.S.A.
131 H2 Howard Lake Canada
104 G4 Howden U.K.
71 H6 Howe, Cape hd Australia
135 F4 Howell U.S.A.
142 C2 Howes U.S.A.
147 G2 Howick Canada
125 I4 Howick S. Africa
70 C1 Howitt, Lake salt flat Australia
71 G6 Howitt, Mount Australia
147 I2 Howland U.S.A.
69 I1 Howland Island Pacific Ocean
71 G5 Howlong Australia
107 E4 Howth Rep. of Ireland
84 D3 Howz-e Dūmatu Iran
84 E4 Howz-e Panj Iran
109 H3 Höxter Germany
106 F2 Hoy i. U.K.
109 H2 Hoya Germany
103 I3 Høyanger Norway
109 K5 Hoyerswerda Germany
102 N2 Høylandet Norway
109 G5 Hoym Germany
102 O3 Höytiäinen l. Fin.
81 G2 Hozat Turkey
112 G5 Hradec Králové Czech Rep.
109 L4 Hradiště hill Czech Rep.
115 H3 Hrasnica Bos.-Herz.
81 J1 Hrazdan Armenia
117 E5 Hrebinka Ukr.
116 B4 Hrodna Belarus
93 F5 Hsinchu Taiwan
79 H4 Hsipaw Myanmar
93 F6 Hsüeh Shan mt. Taiwan
93 F5 Hsüeh Shan mt. Taiwan
93 B5 Hua'an China
157 D4 Huachamacarí, Cerro mt. Venez.
92 C2 Huachi China
154 C6 Huacho Peru
94 B1 Huachuan China
141 H6 Huachuca City U.S.A.
159 C1 Huaco Arg.
92 D2 Huade China
96 D2 Huadian China
92 D6 Huaiji China
92 E1 Huai'an Hebei China
92 E3 Huai'an Jiangsu China
92 E3 Huaibin China
92 D2 Huaidezhen China
92 E3 Huai He r. China
93 C6 Huaihua China
92 E3 Huaiji China
93 D6 Huaiji China
93 B7 Huai Luang r. Thai.
92 E3 Huainan China
92 E3 Huairen China
92 E1 Huaiyang Jiangsu China
93 F5 Huaiyin Jiangsu China
92 E3 Huaiyuan Guangxi China
92 E3 Huaiyuan China
92 E3 Huajialing China
151 E4 Huajuápan de León Mex.
141 E7 Huaki Indon.
141 F5 Hualapai Peak mt. U.S.A.
93 F5 Hualien Taiwan
154 C5 Huallaga r. Peru
92 B2 Huama China
123 B5 Huambo Angola
94 B1 Huanan China
154 C4 Huancabamba r. Peru
154 C4 Huancavelica Peru
92 A2 Huangbizhuang Shuiku resr China
92 E3 Huangchuan China
 Huang Hai sea Pacific Ocean see Yellow Sea
 Huang He r. China see Yellow
94 F2 Huanghua China
89 H2 Huanghua China
92 E2 Huangjiabu China
92 C3 Huangling China
93 D6 Huangliu China
92 D2 Huangnihe China
93 E1 Huangpi China
93 D5 Huangping China
92 D1 Huangqi Hai l. China
93 B5 Huangsang China
92 E3 Huangshan China
92 E3 Huang Shui r. China
92 B2 Huangtu Gaoyuan plat. China
92 F2 Huangxian China
93 F3 Huangyan China
92 A2 Huangzhou China
93 C5 Huanjiang China

92 C2 Huan Jiang r. China
96 C3 Huanren China
96 B3 Huanren China
154 E7 Huanuni Bol.
92 C2 Huanxian China
93 G5 Huap'ing Yü i. Taiwan
154 C5 Huaráz Peru
154 C6 Huarmey Peru
93 D4 Huarong China
154 C5 Huascarán, Nevado de mt. Peru
156 B3 Huasco Chile
156 B3 Huasco r. Chile
96 C2 Huashulinzi China
92 A3 Huating China
96 A3 Huatong China
151 E4 Huatusco Mex.
151 E4 Huauchinango Mex.
151 E4 Huautla Mex.
92 C3 Huaxian China
93 C4 Huaying China
93 C4 Huayuan China
154 C5 Huayllay Peru
92 C3 Huazhou China
96 C2 Huch'ang N. Korea
108 D3 Hückelhoven Germany
105 F4 Hucknall U.K.
104 F4 Huddersfield U.K.
146 B6 Huddy U.S.A.
103 L4 Hudiksvall Sweden
134 E5 Hudson r. U.S.A.
147 G3 Hudson NY U.S.A.
134 A3 Hudson WI U.S.A.
144 A3 Hudson r. U.S.A.
129 J4 Hudson Bay sea Canada
131 I4 Hudson Bay Canada
147 G3 Hudson Falls U.S.A.
129 P3 Hudson Land reg. Greenland
130 D3 Hudson's Hope Canada
129 K3 Hudson Strait Canada
98 C1 Huê' Vietnam
159 A4 Huechucuicui, Punta pt Chile
151 G5 Huehuetenango Guat.
150 D3 Huehueto, Cerro mt. Mex.
151 E4 Huejutla Mex.
111 C4 Huelva Spain
159 B1 Huentelauquén Chile
159 B1 Huequi, Volcán vol. Chile
111 C4 Huércal-Overa Spain
111 F1 Huesca Spain
111 E4 Huéscar Spain
150 D4 Huétamo Mex.
151 E4 Hughenden Australia
71 H4 Hughes r. Australia
72 E2 Hugli r. India
143 C5 Hugo U.S.A.
143 C4 Hugoton U.S.A.
92 C3 Huguan China
124 C3 Huhudi S. Africa
93 F5 Hui'an China
92 C2 Hui'anpu China
73 G2 Huiarau Range mts N.Z.
124 B3 Huib-Hoch Plateau Namibia
93 E5 Huichang China
96 D3 Huich'ŏn N. Korea
93 B6 Huidong Guangdong China
93 B5 Huidong Sichuan China
93 F5 Huifa r. China
93 □ Huiji He r. China
109 A2 Huijbergen Neth.
93 D6 Huiji China
157 B4 Huila, Nevado de mt. Col.
93 G6 Huilai China
92 B3 Huili China
151 F4 Huimanguillo Mex.
92 E2 Huimin China
96 D2 Huinahuaca Arg.
159 D2 Huinca Renancó Arg.
92 B3 Huining China
93 C5 Huishui China
89 G2 Huiten Nur l. China
93 C5 Huitong China
103 M3 Huittinen Fin.
151 E4 Huitzuco Mex.
92 C3 Huixian Gansu China
92 D3 Huixian Henan China
151 F5 Huixtla Mex.
92 C3 Huize China
92 C3 Huizhou China
90 D2 Hujirt Mongolia
93 E4 Hukou China
124 D1 Hukuntsi Botswana
138 D2 Hulbert Lake U.S.A.
84 B3 Hulian Iran
92 C3 Hulin China
92 B1 Hulin Gol r. China
135 C3 Hull Canada
103 K4 Hultsfred Sweden
90 D2 Huludao China
121 F2 Hulwan Egypt
117 F6 Hulyaypole Ukr.
90 E1 Hulun Nur l. China
159 C1 Humahuaca Arg.
154 E5 Humaitá Brazil
124 D5 Humansdorp S. Africa
84 B5 Humayyān, Jabal hill Saudi Arabia
104 H4 Humber, Mouth of the est. U.K.
131 H4 Humboldt Canada
138 D2 Humboldt Bay U.S.A.
138 D1 Humboldt Lake U.S.A.
140 C1 Humboldt Range mts U.S.A.
159 F1 Humboldt Salt Marsh U.S.A.
71 F1 Humeburn Australia
79 H3 Hu Men sea chan. China
113 J6 Humenné Slovakia
71 G6 Hume Reservoir Australia
140 C1 Humphreys, Mount U.S.A.
141 G4 Humphreys Peak mt. U.S.A.
102 B2 Húnaflói b. Iceland
93 D5 Hunan prov. China
96 F2 Hunchun China
92 F2 Hunchun He r. China
103 J5 Hundested Denmark
113 J3 Hunedoara Romania
109 H4 Hünfeld Germany
70 F2 Hungary country Europe
70 E2 Hungerford Australia
93 □ Hung Fa Leng hill Hong Kong China
96 D4 Hüngnam N. Korea
138 B3 Hungry Horse Reservoir U.S.A.
93 □ Hung Shui Kiu Hong Kong China
93 C6 Hung Yên Vietnam
86 E7 Hunish, Rubha pt U.K.
77 D4 Hun Jiang r. China
124 B3 Huns Mountains Namibia
105 H5 Hunstanton U.K.
87 B3 Hunsur India
109 H4 Hunsrück reg. Germany
105 H4 Hunt r. U.S.A.
71 H4 Hunter r. Australia
147 F8 Hunter Island Canada
130 D5 Hunter Island New Caledonia
71 F8 Hunter Islands Australia
79 H6 Hunter's Bay Myanmar
147 G3 Huntingdon Canada
105 G5 Huntingdon U.K.
146 B3 Huntingdon U.S.A.
134 E5 Huntington IN U.S.A.
141 F2 Huntington UT U.S.A.
146 C5 Huntington WV U.S.A.
140 D5 Huntington Beach U.S.A.

72 E2 Huntly N.Z.
106 F3 Huntly U.K.
70 B2 Hunt Peninsula ridge Australia
135 H3 Huntsville Canada
145 C5 Huntsville AL U.S.A.
143 E6 Huntsville TX U.S.A.
80 D6 Hunū, Kathib al dunes Egypt
92 D2 Hunyuan China
88 C1 Hunza Pak.
92 C2 Hunza r. Pak.
93 □ Huocheng China
98 C1 Hương Khê Vietnam
98 C1 Hương Thuy Vietnam
68 C2 Huon Peninsula P.N.G.
71 G9 Huonville Australia
92 A3 Huoqiu China
92 D2 Huoshan China
92 D2 Huozhou China
80 D6 Ḩuraydin, Wādī watercourse Egypt
135 D3 Hurd, Cape hd Canada
96 A2 Hure China
92 C1 Hure Jadgai China
134 C1 Hurkett Canada
107 C5 Hurler's Cross Rep. of Ireland
134 B2 Hurley U.S.A.
142 D2 Huron U.S.A.
156 F3 Huron, Lake Canada/U.S.A.
153 F3 Huron, Lake Canada/U.S.A.
134 C2 Huron Bay U.S.A.
134 C2 Huron Mountains hills U.S.A.
141 F3 Hurricane U.S.A.
105 F6 Hursley U.K.
105 H6 Hurst Green U.K.
72 C6 Hurunui r. N.Z.
102 C1 Húsavík Iceland
102 B2 Húsavík Iceland
113 K1 Huşi Romania
103 K4 Huskvarna Sweden
128 C3 Huslia U.S.A.
103 I4 Husnes Norway
89 F4 Hussainabad India
112 D3 Husum Germany
102 L3 Husum Sweden
92 C2 Hutag Mongolia
142 D4 Hutchinson U.S.A.
141 G4 Hutch Mountain U.S.A.
79 A4 Huthi Myanmar
94 C2 Hutou China
146 D5 Huttonsville U.S.A.
92 D2 Hutuo He r. China
92 C3 Huxian China
92 F4 Huzhou China
102 C2 Hvannadalshnúkur mt. Iceland
114 G3 Hvar i. Croatia
117 E6 Hvardiys'ke Ukr.
102 B2 Hveragerði Iceland
103 F4 Hvide Sande Denmark
102 B3 Hvíta r. Iceland
96 E3 Hwadae N. Korea
123 C5 Hwange Zimbabwe
123 C5 Hwange National Park Zimbabwe
96 C4 Hwangju N. Korea
123 C5 Hwedza Zimbabwe
147 H4 Hyannis MA U.S.A.
142 C3 Hyannis NE U.S.A.
90 B2 Hyargas Nuur l. Mongolia
130 C3 Hydaburg U.S.A.
72 C6 Hyde N.Z.
68 B5 Hyden Australia
146 B6 Hyden U.S.A.
145 E5 Hyde Park U.S.A.
87 B2 Hyderabad India
88 B4 Hyderabad Pak.
110 H5 Hyères France
110 H5 Hyères, Îles d' is France
96 E3 Hyesan N. Korea
130 D2 Hyland r. Canada
71 J3 Hyland, Mount Australia
103 I3 Hyllestad Norway
103 K4 Hyltebruk Sweden
70 D6 Hynam Australia
95 D6 Hyōno-sen mt. Japan
102 O3 Hyrynsalmi Fin.
130 F3 Hythe Canada
105 I6 Hythe U.K.
95 B8 Hyūga Japan
103 N3 Hyvinkää Fin.

I

154 E6 Iaco r. Brazil
155 J6 Iaçu Brazil
123 E6 Iakora Madag.
115 L2 Ialomiţa r. Romania
113 K1 Iaşi Romania
97 A3 Iba Phil.
120 C4 Ibadan Nigeria
157 B3 Ibagué Col.
141 F1 Ibapah U.S.A.
154 C4 Ibarra Ecuador
86 B7 Ibb Yemen
109 F2 Ibbenbüren Germany
159 B1 Iberá, Esteros del marsh Arg.
132 F2 Iberville, Lac d' l. Canada
120 A4 Ibi Indon.
120 C4 Ibi Nigeria
158 D1 Ibiá Brazil
158 D1 Ibiapaba, Serra da hills Brazil
159 F1 Ibicuí da Cruz r. Brazil
158 B4 Ibiraçu Brazil
111 G3 Ibiza Spain
111 G3 Ibiza i. Spain
114 F6 Iblei, Monti mts Sicily Italy
84 B5 Ibn Buşayyiş well Saudi Arabia
155 J6 Ibotirama Brazil
86 E6 Ibrā' Oman
86 E5 Ibri Oman
97 B3 Ibuhos i. Phil.
95 B8 Ibusuki Japan
154 C6 Ica Peru
154 E4 Içá r. Brazil
154 D3 Içana Brazil
154 D3 Içana r. Brazil
141 E3 Iceberg Canyon U.S.A.
102 □ Iceland country Europe
163 H2 Iceland Basin sea feature N. Atlantic Ocean
163 I1 Icelandic Plateau sea feature N. Atlantic Ocean
87 A2 Ichalkaranji India
92 D1 Ichchapuram India
95 D6 Ichinoseki Japan
77 Q2 Ichinskaya, Sopka vol. Rus. Fed.
117 E5 Ichnya Ukr.
108 B3 Ichtegem Belgium
109 I4 Ichtershausen Germany
130 B3 Icy Point U.S.A.
130 B2 Icy Strait U.S.A.
143 E5 Idabel U.S.A.
138 D3 Idaho state U.S.A.
138 D2 Idaho City U.S.A.
138 D2 Idaho Falls U.S.A.
109 G4 Idar-Oberstein Germany
121 F2 Idfū Egypt
120 D2 Idhān Awbārī des. Libya
120 D2 Idhān Murzūq des. Libya
80 E4 Idlib Syria
103 K3 Idre Sweden

109 G4 Idstein Germany
125 H6 Idutywa S. Africa
103 I4 Iecava Latvia
108 A4 Ieper Belgium
115 K7 Ierapetra Greece
123 D6 Ifakara Tanz.
120 C4 Ife Nigeria
102 N1 Ifjord Norway
120 C3 Ifôghas, Adrar des reg. Mali
99 D2 Igan Sarawak Malaysia
158 C3 Igarapava Brazil
76 J3 Igarka Rus. Fed.
81 J2 Iğdir Turkey
103 L3 Iggesund Sweden
114 C5 Iglesias Sardinia Italy
131 K3 Igloolik Canada
132 B4 Ignace Canada
117 M7 Ignalina Lith.
115 M4 İğneada Turkey
115 M4 İğneada Burnu pt Turkey
115 I5 Igoumenitsa Greece
76 H3 Igrim Rus. Fed.
158 B4 Iguaçu r. Brazil
156 F3 Iguaçu Falls Arg./Brazil
111 G2 Igualada Spain
151 E4 Iguala Mex.
158 D3 Iguape Brazil
157 B4 Iguaje, Mesa de hills Col.
158 A3 Iguatemi Brazil
158 A3 Iguatemi r. Brazil
155 K5 Iguatu Brazil
122 A4 Iguéla Gabon
123 D6 Igunga Tanz.
123 E6 Iharaña Madag.
90 C2 Ihbulag Mongolia
123 E6 Ihosy Madag.
96 B2 Ih Tal China
95 F6 Iide-san mt. Japan
102 N1 Iijärvi l. Fin.
102 N2 Iijoki r. Fin.
103 N3 Iisalmi Fin.
95 B8 Iizuka Japan
120 C4 Ijebu-Ode Nigeria
108 D2 IJmuiden Neth.
108 D2 IJssel r. Neth.
108 D2 IJsselmeer l. Neth.
158 C4 Ijuí Brazil
122 A4 Ikare Nigeria
115 L6 Ikaria i. Greece
103 J4 Ikast Denmark
94 H3 Ikeda Japan
122 C4 Ikela Dem. Rep. Congo
115 J3 Ikhtiman Bulg.
124 F4 Ikhutseng S. Africa
95 A8 Iki i. Japan
117 H6 Iki-Burul Rus. Fed.
120 C4 Ikom Nigeria
123 E6 Ikongo Madag.
117 H6 Ikryanoye Rus. Fed.
96 D6 Iksan S. Korea
122 D4 Ikungu Tanz.
97 B3 Ilagan Phil.
123 D6 Ilaisamis Kenya
84 B3 Ïlām Iran
89 F4 Ilam Nepal
120 C4 Ilaro Nigeria
113 I4 Iława Poland
77 N3 Ilbenge Rus. Fed.
82 C2 Ilek Kazakh.
82 C2 Ilek r. Rus. Fed.
122 C4 Ilebo Dem. Rep. Congo
80 D1 Ilgaz Turkey
80 D1 Ilgaz Dağları mts Turkey
80 C2 Ilgin Turkey
158 B1 Ilha Grande Brazil
158 B3 Ilha Grande, Baía da b. Brazil
158 B3 Ilha Grande, Represa resr Brazil
158 B3 Ilha Solteira, Represa resr Brazil
111 B2 Ílhavo Port.
158 E1 Ilhéus Brazil
120 □ Ilhéus Secos ou do Rombo i. Cape Verde
128 B4 Iliamna Lake U.S.A.
97 C4 Iligan Phil.
97 C4 Iligan Bay Phil.
80 E2 Ilica Turkey
82 D2 Il'inka Kazakh.
116 H2 Il'insko-Podomskoye Rus. Fed.
147 H3 Ilion U.S.A.
87 B3 Ilkal India
104 F4 Ilkeston U.K.
105 F4 Ilkley U.K.
159 B1 Illapel Chile
158 B1 Illapel r. Chile
112 E7 Iller r. Germany
154 E7 Illimani, Nevado de mt. Bol.
134 C5 Illinois state U.S.A.
134 C4 Illinois r. U.S.A.
117 D5 Illinois and Mississippi Canal U.S.A.
117 D5 Illintsi Ukr.
120 C2 Illizi Alg.
109 J4 Ilm r. Germany
109 I1 Ilmenau Germany
116 D3 Il'men', Ozero l. Rus. Fed.
109 I1 Ilmenau Germany
105 E7 Ilminster U.K.
154 C6 Ilo Peru
97 A4 Iloc i. Phil.
97 B4 Iloilo Phil.
102 O3 Ilomantsi Fin.
120 C4 Ilorin Nigeria
117 G5 Ilovays'k Ukr.
113 I5 Ilovlya Rus. Fed.
113 I5 Ilovlya r. Rus. Fed.
109 I2 Ilsede Germany
129 M3 Ilulissat Greenland
95 F6 Imabari Japan
95 F6 Imaichi Japan
81 J5 Imām al Ḥamzah Iraq
80 E2 İmamoğlu Turkey
81 J6 Imam Mansur Iraq
95 A8 Imari Japan
103 O3 Imatra Fin.
157 D5 Imataca, Serranía de mts Venez.
95 F6 Imazu Japan
122 E3 Īmī Eth.
96 D5 Imja-do i. S. Korea
96 D4 Imjin-gang r. N. Korea
114 D2 Imola Italy
125 H5 Impendle S. Africa
155 H5 Imperatriz Brazil
114 C3 Imperia Italy
140 E5 Imperial Beach U.S.A.
141 E5 Imperial Valley valley U.S.A.

122 B3 Impfondo Congo
89 H4 Imphal India
115 K4 Imroz Turkey
96 D6 Imsil S. Korea
80 F5 Imtän Syria
97 A4 Imuruan Bay Phil.
95 E7 Ina Japan
154 E6 Inambari r. Peru
120 C2 In Aménas Alg.
72 C4 Inangahua Junction N.Z.
91 F7 Inanwatan Indon.
102 N1 Inari Fin.
102 N1 Inarijärvi l. Fin.
102 N1 Inarijoki r. Fin./Norway
111 H4 Inca Spain
117 C7 ince Burnu pt Turkey
117 E7 ince Burun pt Turkey
80 E2 incesu Turkey
107 E5 inch Rep. of Ireland
106 C2 Inchard, Loch b. U.K.
106 E4 Inchkeith i. U.K.
96 D5 Inch'ön S. Korea
125 J2 Incomati r. Moz.
106 B5 Indaal, Loch inlet U.K.
158 D2 Indaiá r. Brazil
158 B2 Indaiá Grande r. Brazil
102 L3 Indalsälven r. Sweden
150 C3 Indalstø Norway
159 C2 Indé Mex.
140 C3 Independence CA U.S.A.
134 E3 Independence IA U.S.A.
143 E4 Independence KS U.S.A.
134 A2 Independence MN U.S.A.
142 E4 Independence MO U.S.A.
146 C6 Independence VA U.S.A.
134 D3 Independence WI U.S.A.
138 C3 Independence Mts U.S.A.
82 B2 Inder, Ozero salt l. Kazakh.
82 B2 Inderborskiy Kazakh.
87 B2 Indi India
79 F4 India country Asia
134 D2 Indian r. U.S.A.
146 D4 Indiana U.S.A.
134 D5 Indiana state U.S.A.
134 D5 Indiana Dunes National Lakeshore res. U.S.A.
163 P9 Indian-Antarctic Basin sea feature Southern Ocean
162 L8 Indian-Antarctic Ridge sea feature Southern Ocean
134 D6 Indianapolis U.S.A.
Indian Desert India/Pak. see Thar Desert
133 I3 Indian Harbour Canada
134 D3 Indian Lake MI U.S.A.
147 F3 Indian Lake NY U.S.A.
146 A4 Indian Lake OH U.S.A.
146 D4 Indian Lake PA U.S.A.
162 Indian Ocean
142 E3 Indianola IA U.S.A.
143 F5 Indianola MS U.S.A.
141 F2 Indian Peak mt. U.S.A.
134 E3 Indian River l. U.S.A.
141 G3 Indian Springs U.S.A.
141 G4 Indian Wells U.S.A.
77 P2 Indiga Rus. Fed.
115 I2 Indija Yugo.
130 F2 Indin Lake Canada
140 D5 Indio U.S.A.
69 G3 Indispensable Reefs reef Solomon Is
91 D7 Indonesia country Asia
88 C5 Indore India
99 C4 Indramayu, Tanjung pt Indon.
99 B3 Indrapura Indon.
87 C2 Indravati r. India
110 E3 Indre r. France
88 B4 Indus r. China/Pak.
alt. Shiquan He (China)
88 A5 Indus, Mouths of the est. Pak.
162 I3 Indus Cone sea feature Indian Ocean
125 G5 Indwe S. Africa
117 E7 inebolu Turkey
80 B1 inegöl Turkey
116 B6 ineu Turkey
124 D7 Infanta, Cape hd S. Africa
150 D4 Infiernillo, Presa Mex.
98 B1 Ing, Nam Mae r. Thai.
134 D3 Ingalls U.S.A.
140 B2 Ingalls, Mount U.S.A.
131 I2 Ingalls Lake Canada
108 B4 Ingelmunster Belgium
153 G4 Ingeniero Jacobacci Arg.
82 F5 Ingichka Uzbek.
104 E3 Ingleborough hill U.K.
129 K2 Inglefield Land reg. Greenland
104 E3 Ingleton U.K.
71 I2 Inglewood Qld Australia
70 E6 Inglewood Vic. Australia
109 H3 Ingolstadt Germany
112 E6 Ingonish Canada
133 H4 Ingonish Canada
89 G4 Ingraj Bazar India
130 F2 Ingray Lake Canada
73 D5 Ingrid Christensen Coast Antarctica
Ingushetia aut. rep. Rus. Fed. see Ingushetiya, Respublika
117 H7 Ingushetiya, Respublika aut. rep. Rus. Fed.
125 J3 Ingwavuma S. Africa
125 J2 Inhaca S. Africa
125 J2 Inhaca, Peninsula pen. Moz.
125 J2 Inhaca e dos Portugueses, Ilhas da S. Africa
123 D6 Inhambane Moz.
125 J1 Inhambane prov. Moz.
125 K2 Inhaminga Moz.
158 A3 Inhanduizinho r. Brazil
158 D1 Inhaúmas Brazil
157 C4 Inírida r. Col.
107 A4 Inishark i. Rep. of Ireland
107 B4 Inishbofin i. Rep. of Ireland
107 A3 Inishkea North i. Rep. of Ireland
107 A3 Inishkea South i. Rep. of Ireland
107 B4 Inishmaan i. Rep. of Ireland
107 B4 Inishmore i. Rep. of Ireland
107 C3 Inishmurray i. Rep. of Ireland
107 D2 Inishowen pen. Rep. of Ireland
107 D2 Inishowen Head Rep. of Ireland
107 D2 Inishtrahull i. Rep. of Ireland
107 D2 Inishtrahull Sound sea chan. Rep. of Ireland
107 A4 Inishturk i. Rep. of Ireland
82 E5 Inkylap Turkm.
72 D5 Inland Kaikoura Range mts N.Z.
129 L2 Innaanganeq c. Greenland
70 D1 Innamincka Australia
102 K2 Inndyr Norway
Inner Mongolia aut. reg. China see Nei Mongol Zizhiqu
106 C3 Inner Sound sea chan. U.K.
68 E3 Innisfail Australia
112 H7 Innisfail Canada
109 D7 Innsbruck Austria
107 D4 Inny r. Rep. of Ireland
122 B4 Inongo Dem. Rep. Congo
119 J4 Inowroclaw Poland
120 C2 In Salah Alg.
116 H4 Insar Rus. Fed.
106 F3 Insch U.K.
76 H3 Inta Rus. Fed.
159 D2 Intendente Alvear Arg.
112 C7 Interlaken Switz.
142 E1 International Falls U.S.A.
95 G7 Inubō-zaki pt Japan
112 E3 Inukjuak Canada
128 E3 Inuvik Canada
106 F4 Inveraray U.K.
72 B7 Invercargill N.Z.

71 I2 Inverell Australia
106 D3 Invergordon U.K.
106 E4 Inverkeithing U.K.
133 H4 Invermere Canada
145 D6 Inverness Canada
106 D3 Inverness U.K.
145 D6 Inverness U.S.A.
106 F3 Inverurie U.K.
162 K5 Investigator Ridge sea feature Indian Ocean
70 B5 Investigator Strait Australia
79 G1 Inya Rus. Fed.
139 C5 Inyokern U.S.A.
140 C3 Inyo Mountains U.S.A.
122 D4 Inyonga Tanz.
116 H4 Inza Rus. Fed.
82 D1 Inzer Rus. Fed.
117 G4 Inzhavino Rus. Fed.
115 I5 Ioannina Greece
95 B9 Iō-jima i. Japan
143 E4 Iola U.S.A.
83 K2 Iolgo, Khrebet mts Rus. Fed.
106 B4 Iona i. U.K.
138 C1 Ione U.S.A.
134 E4 Ionia U.S.A.
115 H5 Ionian Islands Greece
114 G6 Ionian Sea Greece/Italy
Ionioi Nisoi is Greece see Ionian Islands
90 G1 Iony, Ostrov i. Rus. Fed.
81 K1 Iori r. Georgia
115 K6 Ios i. Greece
134 A4 Iowa r. U.S.A.
134 A4 Iowa state U.S.A.
134 A3 Iowa City U.S.A.
142 E3 Iowa Falls U.S.A.
158 C2 Ipameri Brazil
154 D4 Iparía Peru
158 D2 Ipatinga Brazil
117 G6 Ipatovo Rus. Fed.
125 H6 Ipelegeng S. Africa
157 A4 Ipiales Col.
158 E1 Ipiaú Brazil
158 B4 Ipiranga Brazil
99 B2 Ipoh Malaysia
158 B2 Iporá Brazil
122 C3 Ippy Cent. Afr. Rep.
115 L4 Ipsala Turkey
71 J1 Ipswich Australia
105 I5 Ipswich U.K.
129 L3 Iqaluit Canada
156 B2 Iquique Chile
154 D4 Iquitos Peru
95 F7 Iragō-misaki pt Japan
115 K6 Irakleia i. Greece
Irakleio Greece see Iraklion
115 K7 Iraklion Greece
158 E1 Iramaia Brazil
84 D3 Iran country Asia
99 D2 Iran, Pegunungan mts Indon.
84 B2 Īrānshāh Iran
84 E5 Īrānshahr Iran
150 D4 Irapuato Mex.
81 I5 Iraq country Asia
147 G2 Irasville U.S.A.
158 B4 Irati Brazil
80 E5 Irbid Jordan
76 H4 Irbit Rus. Fed.
155 J6 Irecê Brazil
107 C4 Ireland, Republic of country Europe
122 C4 Irema Dem. Rep. Congo
82 E2 Irgiz Kazakh.
82 E2 Irgiz r. Kazakh.
91 F7 Irian Jaya r. Indon.
81 K2 Īrī Dāgh mt. Iran
97 B3 Iriga Phil.
120 B3 Irigui reg. Mali/Mauritania
123 D4 Iringa Tanz.
87 B4 Irinjalakuda India
155 H4 Iriri r. Brazil
104 B5 Irish Sea Rep. of Ireland
155 I4 Irituia Brazil
84 C3 Irj well Saudi Arabia
90 C1 Irkutsk Rus. Fed.
163 G2 Irminger Basin sea feature N. Atlantic Ocean
70 B4 Iron Baron Australia
135 F2 Iron Bridge Canada
146 E3 Irondequoit U.S.A.
70 B4 Iron Knob Australia
134 C3 Iron Mountain MI U.S.A.
141 F3 Iron Mountain UT U.S.A.
89 H4 Itanagar India
134 C2 Iron River U.S.A.
146 B5 Ironton OH U.S.A.
134 B2 Ironwood U.S.A.
147 F2 Iroquois Canada
134 D5 Iroquois r. U.S.A.
97 C3 Irosin Phil.
95 F7 Irō-zaki pt Japan
117 D5 Irpin' Ukr.
84 A5 'Irq al Maghir dunes Saudi Arabia
84 C3 'Irq ath Thāmām dunes Saudi Arabia
84 B5 'Irq Jahām dunes Saudi Arabia
89 H5 Irrawaddy r. China/Myanmar
91 A5 Irrawaddy, Mouths of the est. Myanmar
88 C1 Irshad Pass Afgh./Pak.
116 I2 Irta Rus. Fed.
106 D3 Irthing r. U.K.
76 H3 Irtysh r. Kazakh./Rus. Fed.
83 H1 Irtyshsk Kazakh.
122 C3 Irumu Dem. Rep. Congo
111 F1 Irún Spain
106 D5 Irvine U.K.
140 D5 Irvine CA U.S.A.
146 B6 Irvine KY U.S.A.
143 D6 Irving U.S.A.
155 A1 Isabela Phil.
154 Isabela, Isla i. Galapagos Is Ecuador
150 H5 Isabelia, Cordillera mts Nicaragua
138 A2 Isabella Lake U.S.A.
140 C4 Isabella, Point U.S.A.
102 B1 Ísafjarðardjúp est. Iceland
102 B1 Ísafjörður Iceland
88 B3 Isa Khel Pak.
156 G1 Isakogorka Rus. Fed.
157 A4 Isana r. Col.
106 Isbister U.K.
114 C4 Ischia, Isola d' i. Italy
95 E7 Ise Japan
122 C4 Isengi Dem. Rep. Congo
110 H4 Isère r. France
109 F3 Iserlohn Germany
109 H2 Isernhagen Germany
114 F4 Isernia Italy
95 E7 Isesaki Japan
95 F6 Ise-shima National Park Japan
95 E7 Ise-wan b. Japan
120 C4 Iseyin Nigeria
Esfahān Iran see Eşfahān
83 G5 Isfana Kyrg.
81 J5 Ishāq Iraq
116 H4 Isheyevka Rus. Fed.
94 G3 Ishikari-gawa r. Japan
94 G3 Ishikari-wan b. Japan
83 F2 Ishim r. Kazakh.
82 G1 Ishimskoye Kazakh.
94 G5 Ishinomaki Japan
94 G5 Ishinomaki-wan b. Japan
95 G6 Ishioka Japan
83 I5 Ishkoshim Kazakh.
88 C1 Ishkuman Pak.

134 D2 Ishpeming U.S.A.
83 F5 Ishtykhan Uzbek.
89 G4 Ishwardi Bangl.
154 E7 Isiboro Sécure, Parque Nacional nat. park Bol.
80 B2 Işıklı Turkey
80 B2 Işıklı Baraji resr Turkey
76 I4 Isil'kul' Rus. Fed.
125 I4 Isipingo S. Africa
122 C3 Isiro Dem. Rep. Congo
85 G2 Iskabad Canal Afgh.
80 F3 İskenderun Turkey
80 E1 İskilip Turkey
82 C3 Iskine Kazakh.
90 A1 Iskitim Rus. Fed.
115 K3 Iskŭr r. Bulg.
130 C3 Iskut Canada
130 C3 Iskut r. Canada
80 D3 Islahiye Turkey
88 C2 Islamabad Pak.
88 B4 Islam Barrage Pak.
88 B4 Islamgarh Pak.
88 B4 Islamkot Pak.
145 D7 Islamorada U.S.A.
85 F3 Islam Qala Afgh.
97 A4 Island Bay Phil.
147 I1 Island Falls U.S.A.
70 B3 Island Lagoon salt flat Australia
131 K4 Island Lake l. Canada
131 K4 Island Lake Canada
134 A2 Island Lake U.S.A.
107 F3 Island Magee pen. U.K.
140 A1 Island Mountain U.S.A.
138 E2 Island Park U.S.A.
147 H2 Island Pond U.S.A.
72 B5 Islands, Bay of N.Z.
106 B5 Islay i. U.K.
104 C3 Isle of Man i. Irish Sea
146 E6 Isle of Wight U.K.
134 C2 Isle Royale National Park U.S.A.
81 L1 İsmayıllı Azer.
103 M3 Isojoki Fin.
123 D5 Isoka Zambia
102 N2 Isokylä Fin.
114 G5 Isola di Capo Rizzuto Italy
80 C3 Isparta Turkey
115 L3 Isperikh Bulg.
85 F5 Ispikan Pak.
81 H1 İspir Turkey
80 E5 Israel country Asia
116 H4 Issa Rus. Fed.
108 E3 Isselburg Germany
120 D4 Issia Côte d'Ivoire
110 F4 Issoire France
Issyk-Kul' salt l. Kyrg. see Ysyk-Köl
81 I4 İştablāt Iraq
80 B1 İstanbul Turkey (City Plan 54)
İstanbul Boğazı strait Turkey see Bosporus
84 C3 Istgāh-e Eznā Iran
115 J5 Istiaia Greece
157 A3 Istmina Col.
81 I3 Istik r. Tajik.
145 D7 Istokpoga, Lake U.S.A.
Istra pen. Croatia see Istria
110 G5 Istres France
114 E2 Istria pen. Croatia
89 E2 Iswaripur Bangl.
82 D1 Isyangulovo Rus. Fed.
155 K6 Itabaianinha Brazil
155 J6 Itaberaba Brazil
158 D2 Itabira Brazil
158 D3 Itabirito Brazil
155 L5 Itabuna Brazil
155 H4 Itacajá Brazil
155 G4 Itacoatiara Brazil
158 C2 Itaguajé Brazil
159 C1 Itaí Brazil
155 G4 Itaituba Brazil
158 B4 Itajaí Brazil
158 D3 Itajubá Brazil
114 D2 Italy country Europe
155 K7 Itamaraju Brazil
158 E2 Itamarandiba Brazil
158 E2 Itambacuri Brazil
158 E2 Itambacuri r. Brazil
158 D2 Itambé, Pico de mt. Brazil
123 E6 Itampolo Madag.
89 H4 Itanagar India
158 D1 Itanguari r. Brazil
158 E2 Itanhém Brazil
158 E2 Itanhém r. Brazil
158 E1 Itaobím Brazil
158 C3 Itapajipe Brazil
158 E1 Itapebi Brazil
158 E1 Itapemirim Brazil
158 E3 Itaperuna Brazil
158 E3 Itapetinga Brazil
158 C3 Itapetininga Brazil
158 C3 Itapeva Brazil
155 K6 Itapicuru r. Bahia Brazil
155 J4 Itapicuru r. Maranhão Brazil
155 J4 Itapicuru Mirim Brazil
158 D1 Itapipoca Brazil
158 C3 Itararé r. Brazil
88 D5 Itarsi India
158 B2 Itarumã Brazil
97 B3 Itbayat i. Phil.
130 G1 Itchen Lake Canada
115 J5 Itea Greece
83 I3 Itemgen, Ozero l. Kazakh.
157 C2 Itenz... r. Bol.
134 E4 Ithaca MI U.S.A.
146 E3 Ithaca NY U.S.A.
109 H2 Ith Hils ridge Germany
80 E5 Ithrah Saudi Arabia
95 B8 Itihusa-yama mt. Japan
122 C4 Itimbiri r. Dem. Rep. Congo
158 A2 Itiquira Brazil
158 A2 Itiquira r. Brazil
82 C2 Itmurinkol', Ozero l. Kazakh.
95 F7 Itoigawa Japan
87 B3 Ito Togo
125 F4 Itula Dem. Rep. Congo
158 C2 Itumbiara Brazil
155 I5 Ituni r. Brazil
158 B2 Iturama Brazil
90 G2 Iturup, Ostrov i. Rus. Fed.
159 D2 Ituzaingó Arg.
89 F4 Ituxi r. Brazil
154 F4 Ivaí r. Brazil

116 C4 Ivatsevichy Belarus
115 L4 Ivaylovgrad Bulg.
76 H3 Ivdel' Rus. Fed.
158 B3 Ivinheima Brazil
158 B3 Ivinheima r. Brazil
129 N3 Ivittuut Greenland
123 E6 Ivohibe Madag.
114 B2 Ivrea Italy
115 L5 İvrindi Turkey
117 H7 Ivris Ughelt'ekhili pass Georgia
113 M4 Ivujivik Canada
113 M4 Ivyanyets Belarus
94 G5 Iwaizumi Japan
94 G4 Iwaki Japan
95 C7 Iwakuni Japan
94 G4 Iwamizawa Japan
94 G3 Iwate-san vol. Japan
120 C4 Iwo Nigeria
116 C4 Iwye Belarus
108 C4 Ixelles Belgium
151 E5 Ixmiquilpán Mex.
125 I5 Ixopo S. Africa
150 D3 Ixtlán Mex.
151 E4 Ixtlán Mex.
105 H5 Ixworth U.K.
95 C8 Iyo Japan
95 C8 Iyo-nada b. Japan
151 G5 Izabal, Lago de Guat.
94 G3 Izari-dake mt. Japan
122 D4 Izazi Tanz.
117 H7 Izberbash Rus. Fed.
113 P3 Izdeshkovo Rus. Fed.
108 B4 Izegem Belgium
84 C4 Izeh Iran
76 G4 Izhevsk Rus. Fed.
116 J1 Izhma Rus. Fed.
116 J1 Izhma r. Rus. Fed.
117 H7 Izmalkovo Rus. Fed.
107 D2 Izmayil Ukr.
115 L5 İzmir Turkey
115 L5 İzmir Körfezi g. Turkey
80 B1 İznik Gölü l. Turkey
117 G6 Izobil'nyy Rus. Fed.
95 F7 Izu-hantō pen. Japan
95 A7 Izuhara Japan
95 C7 Izumo Japan
160 E3 Izu-Ogasawara Trench sea feature N. Pacific Ocean
95 F7 Izu-shotō is Japan
117 C5 Izyaslav Ukr.
82 D3 Izyndy Kazakh.
117 F5 Izyum Ukr.

J

84 E3 Jaba watercourse Iran
121 F3 Jabal, Bahr el r. Sudan/Uganda
alt. Abiad, Bahr el, conv. White Nile
84 C6 Jabal Dab Saudi Arabia
111 E3 Jabalón r. Spain
88 D5 Jabalpur India
80 D5 Jabbūl Syria
80 D5 Jabbūl, Sabkhat al l. Syria
68 D3 Jabiru Australia
80 D4 Jablah Syria
114 G3 Jablanica Bos.-Herz.
155 L5 Jaboatão Brazil
158 C3 Jaboticabal Brazil
111 F1 Jaca Spain
155 J6 Jacaré r. Brazil
155 G5 Jacareacanga Brazil
158 C3 Jacarezinho Brazil
159 C1 Jáchal r. Arg.
109 K4 Jáchymov Czech Rep.
158 C2 Jacinto Brazil
154 E7 Jaciparaná r. Brazil
134 D1 Jackfish Canada
135 H3 Jack Lake Canada
147 H2 Jackman U.S.A.
143 D6 Jackson AL U.S.A.
140 B2 Jackson CA U.S.A.
143 G6 Jackson KY U.S.A.
134 E4 Jackson MI U.S.A.
142 E2 Jackson MN U.S.A.
143 F5 Jackson MS U.S.A.
142 E4 Jackson MO U.S.A.
146 B5 Jackson OH U.S.A.
143 C5 Jackson TN U.S.A.
138 E3 Jackson WY U.S.A.
72 B5 Jackson Head hd N.Z.
138 E2 Jackson Lake U.S.A.
134 D3 Jacksonport U.S.A.
143 E5 Jacksonville AR U.S.A.
145 D6 Jacksonville FL U.S.A.
142 F4 Jacksonville IL U.S.A.
145 E5 Jacksonville NC U.S.A.
143 E6 Jacksonville TX U.S.A.
145 D6 Jacksonville Beach U.S.A.
149 J5 Jacmel Haiti
88 B3 Jacobabad Pak.
155 J6 Jacobina Brazil
141 F4 Jacob Lake U.S.A.
124 B4 Jacobsdal S. Africa
133 H4 Jacques-Cartier, Détroit de sea chan. Canada
133 G4 Jacques Cartier, Mont mt. Canada
133 G4 Jacquet River Canada
159 C1 Jacuí r. Brazil
155 K6 Jacuípe r. Brazil
155 G4 Jacundá Brazil
158 C3 Jacupiranga Brazil
157 C2 Jacura Venez.
85 F5 Jaddi, Ras pt Pak.
109 G1 Jadebusen b. Germany
114 G2 Jadovnik mt. Bos.-Herz.
120 C1 Jādū Libya
97 B3 Jaen Phil.
111 E4 Jaén Spain
70 C6 Jaffa, Cape pt Australia
87 C5 Jaffna Sri Lanka
80 E5 Jaffr r. Jordan
88 D3 Jagadhri India
87 C2 Jagdalpur India
125 F4 Jagersfontein S. Africa
85 E5 Jagin watercourse Iran
109 H5 Jagst r. Germany
88 C5 Jagtial India
158 B2 Jaguarão r. Brazil/Uruguay
159 F2 Jaguarão r. Brazil/Uruguay
155 J5 Jaguaribe Brazil
155 K5 Jaguaribe r. Brazil
88 C4 Jahanabad India
84 C4 Jahān Dāgh mt. Iran
88 C4 Jahazpur India
84 C4 Jahrom Iran
88 D3 Jaipur India
88 C4 Jaisalmer India
88 D4 Jaisinghnagar India
88 D5 Jaitgarh mt. India
84 E2 Jajarm Iran
114 G2 Jajce Bos.-Herz.
89 G4 Jakar Bhutan
99 Jakarta Indon. (City Plan 50)
130 C2 Jakes Corner Canada
102 L2 Jäkkvik Sweden

102 M3 Jakobstad Fin.
85 H3 Jalālābād Afgh.
80 C7 Jalālah al Baḥrīyah, Jabal plat. Egypt
81 J4 Jalāmid, Ḥazm al ridge Saudi Arabia
88 C3 Jalandhar India
151 G5 Jalapa Guat.
151 H5 Jalapa Nicaragua
103 M3 Jalasjärvi Fin.
81 J4 Jalawlā' Iraq
89 G4 Jaldhaka r. Bangl.
87 B2 Jaldrug India
88 B5 Jaleshwar India
88 C5 Jalgaon Maharashtra India
88 C5 Jalgaon Maharashtra India
81 K6 Jalibah Iraq
120 D4 Jalingo Nigeria
150 C4 Jalisco state Mex.
85 F5 Jālo Iran
111 F2 Jalón r. Spain
150 D3 Jalostotitlán Mex.
150 D3 Jalpa Mex.
89 G4 Jalpaiguri India
151 E3 Jalpan Mex.
120 D2 Jālū Libya
85 E2 Jām r. Iran
149 I5 Jamaica country Caribbean Sea
149 I5 Jamaica Channel Haiti/Jamaica
81 K3 Jamalabad Iran
89 F4 Jamalpur Bangl.
89 F4 Jamalpur India
99 B3 Jambi Indon.
99 A2 Jamboaye r. Indon.
99 A1 Jambongan i. Sabah Malaysia
99 C1 Jambuair, Tanjung pt Indon.
88 C4 Jambusar India
142 D1 James r. ND U.S.A.
146 E5 James r. VA U.S.A.
88 B4 Jamesabad Pak.
112 E3 James Bay Canada
149 L5 James, Cistern Bahamas
159 C9 James Craik Arg.
129 M2 Jameson Land reg. Greenland
72 B6 James Peak N.Z.
73 B2 James Ross Island Antarctica
129 I3 James Ross Strait Canada
70 C4 Jamestown Australia
125 G5 Jamestown S. Africa
142 D2 Jamestown ND U.S.A.
146 D3 Jamestown NY U.S.A.
87 A2 Jamkhandi India
87 A2 Jamkhed India
87 B3 Jammalamadugu India
88 C2 Jammu Jammu and Kashmir
88 C2 Jammu and Kashmir terr. Asia
88 B5 Jamnagar India
88 C4 Jamni r. India
99 C4 Jampang Kulon Indon.
88 B4 Jampur Pak.
103 N3 Jämsä Fin.
103 N3 Jämsänkoski Fin.
89 F5 Jamshedpur India
89 F4 Jamuna r. Bangl.
158 D1 Janaúba Brazil
84 D3 Jandaq Iran
140 B1 Janesville CA U.S.A.
134 C4 Janesville WI U.S.A.
85 E3 Jangal Iran
89 G4 Jangipur India
83 K2 Jangy-Bazar Kyrg.
81 K2 Jani Beglū Iran
100 C2 Jan Mayen i. Arctic Ocean
109 L2 Jänickendorf Germany
85 K5 Jannatābād Iran
124 F6 Jansenville S. Africa
158 D1 Januária Brazil
84 B4 Janúb, Al Fulayj al watercourse Saudi Arabia
94 C4 Japan country Asia
94 C4 Japan, Sea of Pacific Ocean
160 E3 Japan Basin sea feature Sea of Japan
160 E3 Japan Trench sea feature N. Pacific Ocean
154 E4 Japurá r. Brazil
89 H4 Japvo Mount India
150 J7 Jaqué Panama
80 D3 Jarābulus Syria
158 A3 Jaraguari Brazil
158 B3 Jardim Brazil
84 B3 Jarash Jordan
158 E5 Jardim Brazil
92 B2 Jargalang China
112 H5 Jargalant Mongolia
81 J4 Jarmo Iraq
104 A3 Jarosław Poland
102 K5 Järpen Sweden
92 B2 Jartai China
103 N3 Järvakandi Estonia
103 N3 Järvenpää Fin.
67 I4 Jarvis Island terr. Pacific Ocean
88 C4 Jasdan India
85 E5 Jāsk Iran
113 J6 Jasło Poland
156 E8 Jason Islands Falkland Is
73 B2 Jason Peninsula Antarctica
130 F4 Jasper Canada
145 C5 Jasper AL U.S.A.
143 E5 Jasper AR U.S.A.
145 C6 Jasper FL U.S.A.
142 F4 Jasper IN U.S.A.
147 F3 Jasper NY U.S.A.
146 D4 Jasper OH U.S.A.
143 E6 Jasper TX U.S.A.
130 F4 Jasper National Park Canada
81 J5 Jaşşān Iraq
113 I6 Jastrzębie-Zdrój Poland
88 B2 Jaswantpura India
113 I7 Jászberény Hungary
158 B2 Jataí Brazil
155 G4 Jatapu r. Brazil
88 B4 Jati Pak.
158 C3 Jaú Brazil
154 F4 Jaú r. Brazil
154 F4 Jaú, Parque Nacional do nat. park Brazil
157 D3 Jauaperi r. Brazil
154 E4 Jaua Sarisariñama, Parque Nacional nat. park Venez.
103 M4 Jaunlutrini Latvia
103 N4 Jaunpiebalga Latvia
89 F4 Jaunpur India
92 B2 Java China
Java i. Indon. see Jawa
88 C5 Jawai r. India

99 D3 Java Sea Indon.
162 K5 Java Trench sea feature Indian Ocean
109 J2 Jävenitz Germany
Jawa i. Indon. see Java
88 C5 Jawai r. India
80 B4 Jawb Syria
88 C6 Jawhar India
122 E3 Jawhar Somalia
112 H5 Jawor Poland
91 G7 Jaya, Puncak mt. Indon.
91 G7 Jayapura Indon.
89 F4 Jaynagar India
80 F5 Jayrūd Syria
81 L3 Jazvān Iran
134 D1 J. C. Murphey Lake U.S.A.
141 E4 Jean U.S.A.
130 E2 Jean Marie River Canada
133 G4 Jeannin, Lac l. Canada
133 E4 Jeannin, Lac Canada
121 F4 Jebba Nigeria
122 B3 Jebel Abyad Plateau Sudan
122 B3 Jebel, Bahr el r. Sudan/Uganda
alt. Abiad, Bahr el, conv. White Nile
88 C3 Jech Doab lowland Pak.
106 F5 Jedburgh U.K.
86 A5 Jeddah Saudi Arabia
114 C6 Jedeida Tunisia
109 J1 Jeetze r. Germany
147 G3 Jefferson NY U.S.A.
134 C4 Jefferson WI U.S.A.
138 D2 Jefferson r. U.S.A.
138 B2 Jefferson, Mount vol. U.S.A.
142 F4 Jefferson City U.S.A.
146 A5 Jeffersonville U.S.A.
124 F7 Jeffrey's Bay S. Africa
156 E2 Jejuí Guazú r. Para.
103 N4 Jēkabpils Latvia
112 G5 Jelenia Góra Poland
89 G4 Jelep La pass China
103 M4 Jelgava Latvia
146 A6 Jellico U.S.A.
109 J4 Jena Germany
120 C1 Jendouba Tunisia
Jengish Chokusu mt. China/Kyrg. see Pobeda Peak
80 E5 Jenin West Bank
146 C6 Jenkins U.S.A.
143 E6 Jennings U.S.A.
131 H4 Jenpeg Canada
70 E6 Jeparit Australia
158 D1 Jequié Brazil
158 D2 Jequitaí Brazil
158 D2 Jequitaí r. Brazil
158 E2 Jequitinhonha Brazil
158 E2 Jequitinhonha r. Brazil
99 D1 Jerantut Malaysia
121 F4 Jerbar Sudan
149 J5 Jérémie Haiti
150 D3 Jerez Mex.
111 C4 Jerez de la Frontera Spain
111 C4 Jerez de los Caballeros Spain
115 I5 Jergucat Albania
71 I5 Jerilderie Australia
81 J2 Jermuk Armenia
138 D2 Jerome U.S.A.
107 E5 Jersey i. U.K.
147 F4 Jersey City U.S.A.
146 D4 Jersey Shore U.S.A.
155 J5 Jerumenha Brazil
80 E6 Jerusalem Israel/West Bank (City Plan 54)
71 J5 Jervis Bay b. Australia
71 J5 Jervis Bay Australia
71 J5 Jervis Bay Territory admin. div. Australia
114 F1 Jesenice Slovenia
114 E1 Jesi Italy
109 K3 Jessen Germany
103 J3 Jessheim Norway
89 G5 Jessore Bangl.
145 D6 Jesup U.S.A.
150 H5 Jesús Carranza Mex.
159 C3 Jesús María Arg.
88 B5 Jetalsar India
109 F1 Jever Germany
88 D4 Jha Jha India
88 B3 Jhajjar India
88 C3 Jhajju India
89 G4 Jhalakati Bangl.
85 G5 Jhal Jhao Pak.
88 C5 Jhang India
88 D4 Jhansi India
89 F5 Jharia India
87 D1 Jharsuguda India
88 B3 Jhatpat Pak.
88 B3 Jhelum Pak.
88 C2 Jhelum r. India/Pak.
89 G5 Jhenaidah Bangl.
88 C5 Jhudo Pak.
88 C4 Jhumritilaiya India
88 C4 Jhunjhunun India
92 B2 Jiachuan China
93 C6 Jiading China
93 B4 Jiahe China
93 C4 Jiajiang China
93 C4 Jialing Jiang r. China
94 B1 Jiamusi China
93 E5 Ji'an Jiangxi China
93 E5 Ji'an Jiangxi China
93 F4 Ji'an Jilin China
93 D4 Jianchang China
93 B5 Jianchuan China
92 E3 Jiang'an China
93 F1 Jiangcheng China
93 C4 Jiangchuan China
93 E5 Jiangdu China
92 F2 Jiangjin China
92 E2 Jiangluozhen China
93 D6 Jiangmen China
93 E4 Jiangshan China
93 F4 Jiangsu prov. China
93 E5 Jiangxi prov. China
92 E2 Jiangxian China
93 F4 Jiangyan China
93 B5 Jiangyong China
93 F4 Jianhu China
93 A5 Jiankang China
93 E4 Jianning China
93 F2 Jian'ou China
93 E5 Jianping Liaoning China
93 E4 Jianping Liaoning China
93 B4 Jianshi China
93 B6 Jianshui China
93 E4 Jianyang Fujian China
93 C4 Jianyang Sichuan China
93 F3 Jiaohe China
93 E5 Jiaojiang China see Taizhou
96 A2 Jiaolai He r. Nei Mongol China
92 F2 Jiaolai He r. Shandong China

93 E5 Jiaoling China
92 F3 Jiaonan China
92 F2 Jiaozhou China
92 F2 Jiaozhou Wan b. China
92 E3 Jiaozuo China
98 D2 Jiagpigou China
83 I5 Jiashi China
92 D2 Jiaxian China
92 F4 Jiaxing China
93 D4 Jiayu China
90 B3 Jiayuguan China
93 E6 Jiazi China
150 I7 Jicarón, Isla i. Panama
Jiddah Saudi Arabia see Jeddah
80 D6 Jiddi, Jabal al hill Egypt
96 F1 Jidong China
92 B2 Jieheba China
102 L1 Jiehkkevarri mt. Norway
93 E6 Jieshi China
93 E6 Jieshi Wan b. China
93 E6 Jieshou China
102 N1 Jiešjávri i. Norway
93 E6 Jiexi China
92 D2 Jiexiu China
93 E6 Jieyang China
103 N5 Jieznas Lith.
92 A3 Jigzhi China
112 G6 Jihlava Czech Rep.
85 F3 Jija Sarai Afgh.
122 E3 Jijiga Eth.
93 A4 Jiju China
121 E2 Jilf al Kabīr, Haḍabat al plat. Egypt
85 H3 Jilga r. Afgh.
122 E3 Jilib Somalia
96 D2 Jilin China
96 C2 Jilin prov. China
92 A2 Jiling China
96 C2 Jilin Hada Ling mts China
122 D3 Jima Eth.
150 C2 Jiménez Chihuahua Mex.
150 D1 Jiménez Coahuila Mex.
151 E2 Jiménez Tamaulipas Mex.
92 F2 Jimo China
147 F4 Jim Thorpe U.S.A.
92 E2 Jinan China
92 B2 Jinchang China
92 D3 Jincheng China
92 B4 Jinchuan China
88 D3 Jind India
71 H4 Jindabyne Australia
71 G5 Jindera Australia
112 G6 Jindřichův Hradec Czech Rep.
92 C2 Jing'an China
92 C2 Jingbian China
92 C3 Jingchuan China
92 E2 Jingde China
93 E4 Jingdezhen China
93 E5 Jinggangshan China
93 E4 Jinggongqiao China
92 E2 Jinghai China
92 J3 Jinghe China
92 C3 Jing He r. China
93 C4 Jinghong China
92 F3 Jingjiang China
92 D2 Jingle China
92 D4 Jingmen China
92 B3 Jingning China
92 E1 Jingpeng China
92 C2 Jingpo China
92 C2 Jingpo Hu resr China
92 B2 Jingtai China
93 C6 Jingxi China
93 F4 Jingxian China
96 D2 Jingyu China
92 B2 Jingyuan China
92 D4 Jingzhou Hubei China
93 D4 Jingzhou Hubei China
93 C5 Jingzhou Hunan China
92 F3 Jinhu China
93 F4 Jinhua China
92 D1 Jining Nei Mongol China
92 E3 Jining Shandong China
122 D3 Jinja Uganda
93 F5 Jinjiang China
93 A5 Jin Jiang r. China
122 D3 Jinka Eth.
96 A3 Jinlingji China
93 C7 Jinmu Jiao pt China
150 H5 Jinotega Nicaragua
150 H6 Jinotepe Nicaragua
93 C5 Jinping Guizhou China
93 B6 Jinping Yunnan China
93 A5 Jinping Shan mts China
93 C5 Jinsha China
93 E4 Jinsha Jiang r. China
  alt. Chang Jiang,
  alt. Tongtian He,
  alt. Zhi Qu,
  conv. Yangtze,
  long Yangtze Kiang
92 F1 Jinshan Nei Mongol China
92 F3 Jinshan Shanghai China
93 D4 Jinshi China
92 B4 Jintang China
97 B4 Jintotolo i. Phil.
97 B4 Jintotolo Channel Phil.
88 D6 Jintur India
93 E5 Jinxi China
93 E4 Jinxian China
93 E6 Jinxiang China
93 F5 Jinxiang Shandong China
93 F5 Jinxiang Zhejiang China
93 B5 Jinyang China
93 F4 Jinyun China
92 E4 Jinzhai China
92 D2 Jinzhong China
96 A4 Jinzhou Liaoning China
96 A4 Jinzhou Liaoning China
154 F6 Ji-Paraná Brazil
154 F5 Jiparaná r. Brazil
154 B4 Jipijapa Ecuador
89 H2 Ji Qu r. China
83 G5 Jirgatol Tajik.
85 E4 Jiroft Iran
84 C6 Jirwān Saudi Arabia
84 C6 Jirwan well Saudi Arabia
93 C4 Jishou China
80 F4 Jisr ash Shughūr Syria
84 B4 Jisra Malaysia
92 C2 Jiudengkou China
92 B4 Jiuding Shan mt. China
92 C3 Jiufoping China
93 E4 Jiujiang Jiangxi China
93 E4 Jiujiang Jiangxi China
93 E4 Jiuling Shan mts China
93 A4 Jiulong China
89 A2 Jiumiao China
92 C3 Jiurongcheng China
96 C1 Jiutai China
93 D6 Jiuxu China
93 E4 Jiuzhaigou China
85 F5 Jiwani Pak.
93 F4 Jixi Heilong. China
96 B1 Jixian China
92 D3 Jiyuan China
84 B6 Jīzān Saudi Arabia
95 C7 Jizō-zaki pt Japan
155 L5 João Pessoa Brazil
158 C2 João Pinheiro Brazil
140 C2 Job Peak mt. U.S.A.
109 K4 Jocketa Germany
87 D1 Joda India
88 C4 Jodhpur India
102 O3 Joensuu Fin.
95 D6 Jōetsu Japan
123 D6 Jofane Moz.
103 N4 Jõgeva Estonia
103 N4 Jõgua Estonia
123 G3 Johannesburg S. Africa
125 G3 Johannesburg S. Africa
140 D4 Johannesburg U.S.A.
88 E5 Johilla r. India

138 C2 John Day U.S.A.
138 B2 John Day r. U.S.A.
130 F3 John d'Or Prairie Canada
147 G4 John F. Kennedy airport U.S.A.
146 D6 John H. Kerr Reservoir U.S.A.
106 D2 John o'Groats U.K.
145 D4 Johnson City U.S.A.
130 C2 Johnson's Crossing Canada
145 D5 Johnston U.S.A.
67 H2 Johnston Atoll N. Pacific Ocean
106 D5 Johnstone U.K.
107 D5 Johnstown Rep. of Ireland
147 H3 Johnstown NY U.S.A.
146 D4 Johnstown PA U.S.A.
135 F3 Johnswood U.S.A.
99 B2 Johor Bahru Malaysia
103 N4 Jõhvi Estonia
156 D3 Joinville Brazil
110 G2 Joinville France
73 B2 Joinville Island Antarctica
102 L2 Jokkmokk Sweden
102 □2 Jökulsá á Dál r. Iceland
102 C1 Jökulsá á Fjöllum r. Iceland
102 □2 Jökulsá í Fljótsdal r. Iceland
84 B2 Jolfa Iran
134 C5 Joliet U.S.A.
132 F4 Joliette Canada
97 B5 Jolo Phil.
97 B5 Jolo i. Phil.
98 □ Jombang Indon.
151 G4 Jonathan Pt Belize
103 N5 Jonava Lith.
92 B3 Jonê China
143 E4 Jonesboro AR U.S.A.
147 J2 Jonesboro ME U.S.A.
73 A3 Jones Mts Antarctica
147 J2 Jonesport U.S.A.
129 J2 Jones Sound sea chan. Canada
146 B6 Jonesville U.S.A.
121 F4 Jonglei Canal Sudan
87 C1 Jonk r. India
103 K4 Jönköping Sweden
133 F4 Jonquière Canada
151 F4 Jonuta Mex.
143 E4 Joplin U.S.A.
147 E5 Joppatowne U.S.A.
88 D4 Jora India
80 F6 Jordan country Asia
80 E6 Jordan r. Asia
138 F2 Jordan r. U.S.A.
138 E3 Jordan r. U.S.A.
138 C3 Jordan Valley U.S.A.
158 B4 Jordão r. Brazil
103 K3 Jordet Norway
89 H4 Jorhat India
83 I5 Jor Hu l. China
109 H1 Jork Germany
102 M2 Jörn Sweden
103 N3 Joroinen Fin.
103 I4 Jærpeland Norway
120 C4 Jos Nigeria
97 C5 José Abad Santos Phil.
151 E4 José Cardel Mex.
156 B6 José de San Martín Arg.
158 A2 Joselândia Brazil
159 F2 José Pedro Varela Uruguay
133 G3 Joseph, Lac l. Canada
68 C3 Joseph Bonaparte Gulf Australia
141 G4 Joseph City U.S.A.
95 F6 Jōshinetsu-kōgen National Park Japan
141 E5 Joshua Tree National Park U.S.A.
120 C4 Jos Plateau Nigeria
103 I3 Jostedalsbreen Nasjonalpark nat. park Norway
103 J3 Jotunheimen Nasjonalpark nat. park Norway
124 E6 Joubertina S. Africa
125 G3 Jouberton S. Africa
108 D2 Joure Neth.
103 N3 Joutsa Fin.
103 O3 Joutseno Fin.
108 E5 Jouy-aux-Arches France
89 H4 Jowai India
107 B4 Joyce's Country reg. Rep. of Ireland
150 D2 Juan Aldama Mex.
138 A1 Juan de Fuca Strait U.S.A.
123 E5 Juan de Nova i. Indian Ocean
152 E5 Juan Fernández, Archipiélago is S. Pacific Ocean
102 O3 Juankoski Fin.
150 H6 Juan Santamaria airport Costa Rica
150 D2 Juárez Mex.
155 J5 Juàzeiro Brazil
155 K5 Juàzeiro do Norte Brazil
121 F4 Juba Sudan
73 B2 Jubany research station Antarctica
122 E3 Jubba r. Somalia
140 D3 Jubilee Pass U.S.A.
111 F3 Júcar r. Spain
151 F4 Juchatengo Mex.
150 D3 Juchipila Mex.
151 F4 Juchitán Mex.
150 C3 Juchitlán Mex.
155 I2 Jucuruçu r. Brazil
103 I4 Judaberg Norway
81 H6 Judaidat al Hamir Iraq
81 J4 Judaydah Syria
81 H6 Judayyidat 'Ar'ar well Iraq
112 H2 Judenburg Austria
103 J5 Juelsminde Denmark
92 C2 Juh China
92 F1 Juhua Dao i. China
150 H5 Juigalpa Nicaragua
108 F1 Juist i. Germany
155 K6 Juiz de Fora Brazil
154 E8 Julaca Bol.
142 C3 Julesburg U.S.A.
154 D7 Juliaca Peru
108 D2 Julianadorp Neth.
155 G3 Juliana Top mt. Suriname
117 G6 Jülich Germany
114 E1 Julijske Alpe mts Slovenia
154 C5 Jumbilla Peru
111 F3 Jumilla Spain
89 E3 Jumla Nepal
88 B5 Junagadh India
87 C2 Junagarh India
92 F3 Junan China
156 B4 Juncal, Cerro mt. Chile
158 C3 Jundiaí Brazil
130 C3 Juneau U.S.A.
71 G5 Junee Australia
109 J4 Jungfrau mt. Switz.
82 D2 Junggar Pendi basin China
88 A4 Jungshahi Pak.
159 E2 Junín Arg.
159 D2 Junín de los Andes Arg.
147 J1 Juniper Canada
138 C3 Juniper Serro Peak mt. U.S.A.
93 B4 Junlian China
102 L3 Junsele Sweden
138 C3 Juntura U.S.A.
103 N4 Juodupé Lith.
158 C2 Juquiá Brazil
121 F4 Jur r. Sudan
110 H3 Jura mts France/Switz.
106 D5 Jura i. U.K.
106 C5 Jura, Sound of sea chan. U.K.
80 E6 Jurf ad Darāwīsh Jordan

109 K1 Jürgenstorf Germany
96 A1 Jurh Nei Mongol China
96 A1 Jurh Nei Mongol China
89 G2 Jurhen Ul Shan mts China
103 M4 Jūrmala Latvia
103 N2 Jurmu Fin.
92 F4 Jurong China
98 □ Jurong Sing.
154 E4 Juruá r. Brazil
155 G6 Juruena r. Brazil
102 M3 Jurva Fin.
84 E2 Jūshqān Iran
159 D2 Justo Daract Arg.
154 E4 Jutaí r. Brazil
109 L3 Jüterbog Germany
158 A3 Juti Brazil
151 G5 Jutiapa Guat.
150 H5 Juticalpa Hond.
102 L2 Jutis Sweden
102 O3 Juuka Fin.
85 F4 Juwain Afgh.
92 F3 Juxian China
92 A1 Juyan China
92 E3 Juye China
85 E3 Jūymand Iran
84 D4 Jūyom Iran
123 C6 Jwaneng Botswana
83 I4 Jyrgalang Kyrg.
103 N3 Jyväskylä Fin.

K

88 D2 K2 mt. China/Jammu and Kashmir
140 □1 Kaala mt. U.S.A.
103 M3 Kaarina Fin.
108 E3 Kaarßen Germany
102 O3 Kaarst Germany
68 C2 Kaavi Fin.
82 C5 Kabaena i. Indon.
84 A4 Kabala Sierra Leone
122 C4 Kabale Uganda
122 C4 Kabalo Dem. Rep. Congo
122 C4 Kabambare Dem. Rep. Congo
83 J3 Kabanbay Almatinskaya Oblast' Kazakh.
83 F1 Kabanbay Severnyy Kazakhstan Kazakh.
123 C5 Kabangu Dem. Rep. Congo
98 A5 Kabanjahe Indon.
82 B1 Kabanovka Rus. Fed.
117 G7 Kabardino-Balkarskaya Respublika aut. rep. Rus. Fed.
122 C4 Kabare Dem. Rep. Congo
102 M2 Kåbdalis Sweden
134 C1 Kabenung Lake Canada
132 D4 Kabinakagami Lake Canada
122 C4 Kabinda Dem. Rep. Congo
84 B3 Kabirkūh mts Iran
88 B3 Kabirwala Pak.
122 B3 Kabo Centr. Afr. Rep.
123 C5 Kabompo Zambia
122 C4 Kabongo Dem. Rep. Congo
85 F3 Kabūdeh Iran
85 E2 Kabūd Gonbad Iran
84 E3 Kabūd Rāhang Iran
97 B2 Kabugao Phil.
85 H3 Kabūl Afgh.
85 H3 Kabūl r. Afgh.
97 C6 Kaburuang i. Indon.
123 C5 Kabwe Zambia
82 A2 Kabyrga r. Kazakh.
81 F1 Kabzn' Kazakh.
82 B4 Kaca Kuh mts Iran/Pak.
117 H5 Kachalinskaya Rus. Fed.
88 B5 Kachchh, Gulf of India
88 B4 Kachchh, Rann of marsh India
83 I1 Kachiry Kazakh.
88 C3 Kach Pass Afgh.
90 C1 Kachug Rus. Fed.
81 F3 Kaçkar Dağı mt. Turkey
87 B4 Kadaiyanallur India
84 A3 Kadanai r. Afgh./Pak.
98 A2 Kadan Kyun i. Myanmar
69 D1 Kadavu i. Fiji
69 H3 Kadavu Passage Fiji
120 B4 Kade Ghana
88 C5 Kadi India
80 B1 Kadıköy Turkey
70 B4 Kadina Australia
80 D2 Kadınhanı Turkey
120 B3 Kadiolo Mali
87 B3 Kadiri India
80 D3 Kadirli Turkey
87 A4 Kadmat i. India
96 C4 Ka-do i. N. Korea
142 C3 Kadoka U.S.A.
123 C5 Kadoma Zimbabwe
121 E3 Kadugli Sudan
120 C3 Kaduna Nigeria
120 C3 Kaduna r. Nigeria
89 I3 Kadusam mt. China
116 G3 Kaduy Rus. Fed.
76 G3 Kadzhi-Say Kyrg. see Kajy-Say
96 C4 Kaechon N. Korea
120 A3 Kaédi Mauritania
121 D3 Kaélé Cameroon
140 □1 Kaena Pt U.S.A.
72 D1 Kaeo N.Z.
96 C4 Kaesŏng N. Korea
80 F6 Käf Saudi Arabia
122 C5 Kafakumba Dem. Rep. Congo
84 A2 Kafan Armenia see Kapan
115 K5 Kafireas, Akra pt Greece
80 C6 Kafr ash Shaykh Egypt
123 C5 Kafue Zambia
123 C5 Kafue r. Zambia
123 C5 Kafue National Park Zambia
95 E6 Kaga Japan
122 B3 Kaga Bandoro Centr. Afr. Rep.
117 G6 Kagal'nitskaya Rus. Fed.
82 E1 Kagan Uzbek.
135 F3 Kagawong Canada
102 M2 Kåge Sweden
81 I1 Kağızman Turkey
80 □ Kagologolo Indon.
95 B9 Kagoshima Japan
84 C2 Kahak Iran
120 □1 Kahalu'u U.S.A.
122 D4 Kahama Tanz.
140 □1 Kahana U.S.A.
117 D6 Kaharlyk Ukr.
98 □ Kahayan r. Indon.
122 B4 Kahemba Dem. Rep. Congo
72 H4 Kaherekoau Mountains N.Z.
109 J4 Kahla Germany
85 F4 Kahnūj Iran
142 F3 Kahoka U.S.A.
140 □1 Kaho'olawe i. U.S.A.
80 B3 Kahramanmaraş Turkey
88 B3 Kahror Pak.
80 E3 Kahta Turkey
140 □1 Kahuku U.S.A.
140 □1 Kahuku Pt U.S.A.
140 □2 Kahului U.S.A.
72 D4 Kahurangi Point N.Z.
88 C2 Kahuta Pak.
122 C4 Kahuzi-Biega, Parc National du Dem. Rep. Congo
91 F7 Kai, Kepulauan is Indon.
120 C4 Kaiama Nigeria
72 D5 Kaiapoi N.Z.
139 D4 Kaibab Plat. plat. U.S.A.
141 G3 Kaibito U.S.A.
141 G3 Kaibito Plateau U.S.A.
92 E3 Kaifeng Henan China

92 E3 Kaifeng Henan China
93 F4 Kaihua China
124 D5 Kaiingveld reg. S. Africa
92 C4 Kaijiang China
91 F7 Kai Kecil i. Indon.
93 □ Kai Keung Leng hill Hong Kong China
72 D5 Kaikoura N.Z.
72 D5 Kaikoura Peninsula N.Z.
120 A4 Kailahun Sierra Leone
89 G4 Kailashahar India
93 C5 Kaili China
93 D6 Kaili China
140 □1 Kailua U.S.A.
140 □1 Kailua Kona U.S.A.
72 E2 Kaimai Range hills N.Z.
68 D2 Kaimana Indon.
72 E3 Kaimanawa Mountains N.Z.
89 H2 Kaimar China
88 E4 Kaimur Range hills India
120 C3 Kainji Reservoir Nigeria
120 C3 Kainji Lake National Park Nigeria
72 D2 Kaipara Harbour N.Z.
141 G3 Kaiparowits Plateau U.S.A.
93 D6 Kaiping China
88 D3 Kairana India
120 D1 Kairouan Tunisia
109 F5 Kaiserslautern Germany
73 C5 Kaiser Wilhelm II Land reg. Antarctica
96 E2 Kaishantun China
72 D1 Kaitaia N.Z.
72 F3 Kaitangata N.Z.
88 D3 Kaithal India
102 M2 Kaitum Sweden
92 C4 Kaixian China
93 C5 Kaiyang China
96 A4 Kaiyuan Liaoning China
93 B6 Kaiyuan Yunnan China
102 N2 Kajaani Fin.
68 E4 Kajabbi Australia
85 G3 Kajaki Afgh.
99 B2 Kajang Malaysia
88 B3 Kajanpur Pak.
84 A2 K'ajaran Armenia
85 G3 Kajrān Afgh.
83 I4 Kaju-Say Kyrg.
82 D5 Kaka Turkm.
131 K2 Kakabeka Falls Canada
124 D4 Kakamas S. Africa
122 D3 Kakamega Kenya
72 C6 Kakanui Mountains N.Z.
120 A4 Kakata Liberia
72 E3 Katahi N.Z.
95 C7 Kake Japan
130 C3 Kake U.S.A.
122 C4 Kakenge Dem. Rep. Congo
109 J2 Kakerbeck Germany
117 E6 Kakhovka Ukr.
117 E6 Kakhovs'ke Vodoskhovyshche resr Ukr.
84 C4 Kākī Iran
87 C2 Kakinada India
130 F2 Kakisa Canada
130 F2 Kakisa Lake Canada
95 D7 Kakogawa Japan
122 C4 Kakoswa Dem. Rep. Congo
84 B4 Kakreh Iran
128 D2 Kaktovik U.S.A.
95 G6 Kakuda Japan
130 F4 Kakwa r. Canada
88 B3 Kala Pak.
114 D7 Kalaâ Kebira Tunisia
Kalaallit Nunaat terr. N. America see Greenland
88 C2 Kalabagh Pak.
91 E7 Kalabahi Indon.
97 A5 Kalabakan Sabah Malaysia
70 D3 Kalabity Australia
123 C5 Kalabo Zambia
117 G5 Kalach Rus. Fed.
116 G3 Kalachinsk Rus. Fed.
117 G5 Kalach-na-Donu Rus. Fed.
89 H5 Kaladan r. India/Myanmar
135 J3 Kaladar Canada
140 □2 Ka Lae c. U.S.A.
123 C6 Kalahari Desert Africa
123 B6 Kalahari Gemsbok National Park S. Africa
85 F3 Kala-I-Mor Turkm.
102 M2 Kalajoki Fin.
102 M2 Kalajoki r. Fin.
88 C2 Kalam Pak.
125 J4 Kalamare Botswana
115 J6 Kalamaria Greece
115 J4 Kalamata Greece
134 C4 Kalamazoo U.S.A.
134 C4 Kalamazoo r. U.S.A.
115 I5 Kalampaka Greece
70 C1 Kalamurru, Lake salt flat Australia
88 C2 Kalanaur India
117 D6 Kalanchak Ukr.
85 F4 Kalandi India
68 D6 Kalangadoo Australia
88 C3 Kalanwali India
97 C5 Kalao i. Indon.
85 F5 Kalar watercourse Iran
81 K4 Kalar r. Iraq
98 B1 Kalasin Thai.
85 G4 Kalāt Iran
85 H4 Kalāt Iran
140 □2 Kalaupapa U.S.A.
117 G6 Kalaus r. Rus. Fed.
81 J1 Kalbā U.A.E.
68 A5 Kalbarri Australia
68 A5 Kalbarri National Park Australia
109 □2 Kalbe (Milde) Germany
82 A2 Kalbinskiy Khrebet mts Kazakh.
83 J2 Kaldygayty r. Kazakh.
80 B3 Kale Turkey
80 D1 Kale Turkey
109 □1 Kalecik Turkey
84 D5 Kaleh Sarai Iran
109 L3 Kalefeld Germany
122 C4 Kalema Tanz.
122 C4 Kalemie Dem. Rep. Congo
89 H5 Kalemyo Myanmar
68 C5 Kalgoorlie Australia
114 F2 Kali Croatia
88 D3 Kali r. India/Nepal
97 B4 Kalibo Phil.
122 C4 Kalima Dem. Rep. Congo
98 C3 Kalimantan reg. Indon.
88 E4 Kali Nadi r. India
103 K5 Kaliningrad Rus. Fed.
103 K5 Kaliningradskaya Oblast' admin. div. Rus. Fed.
116 G3 Kalinino Rus. Fed.
82 F2 Kalininabad Tajik.
117 H5 Kalininsk Rus. Fed.
117 H5 Kalinkavichy Belarus
82 C2 Kalinovka Kazakh.
88 D4 Kali Sindh r. India

138 D1 Kalispell U.S.A.
112 I5 Kalisz Poland
84 E4 Kalituyeh Iran
117 G5 Kalitva r. Rus. Fed.
102 M3 Kalix Sweden
102 M2 Kalix r. Sweden
89 H4 Kalkalighat India
80 B4 Kalkan Turkey
134 E3 Kalkaska U.S.A.
123 B6 Kalkfeld Namibia
125 F4 Kalkfontein dam S. Africa
108 E4 Kall Germany
98 □ Kallang Sing.
103 N4 Kallaste Estonia
102 N3 Kallavesi l. Fin.
102 K3 Kallsjön l. Sweden
82 F3 Kalmakkyrgan watercourse Kazakh.
83 J1 Kalmanka Rus. Fed.
103 L4 Kalmar Sweden
103 L4 Kalmarsund sea chan. Sweden
89 H4 Kalmukhi India
87 C5 Kalmunai Sri Lanka
117 H6 Kalmykiya - Khalm'g-Tangch, Respublika aut. rep. Rus. Fed.
89 G4 Kalni r. Bangl.
113 M5 Kalodnaye Belarus
88 C5 Kalol India
97 C6 Kaloma i. Indon.
123 C6 Kalomo Zambia
130 D4 Kalone Peak mt. Canada
84 B2 Kalow r. Iran
88 D3 Kalpa India
87 A4 Kalpeni i. India
88 D4 Kalpi India
83 I4 Kalpin China
84 E3 Kal Safid Iran
128 C3 Kaltag U.S.A.
109 H1 Kaltenkirchen Germany
109 I4 Kaltensundheim Germany
88 C3 Kalu India
113 M5 Kaluga Rus. Fed.
103 J5 Kalundborg Denmark
88 B5 Kalur Kot Pak.
117 C5 Kalush Ukr.
87 B5 Kalutara Sri Lanka
116 E4 Kaluzhskaya Oblast' admin. div. Rus. Fed.
102 M3 Kälviä Fin.
87 A2 Kalyan India
116 G3 Kalyazin Rus. Fed.
115 L6 Kalymnos i. Greece
115 L6 Kalymnos Greece
113 L6 Kalynivka Ukr.
122 C4 Kama Dem. Rep. Congo
94 G5 Kama r. Rus. Fed.
95 G5 Kamaishi Japan
88 B3 Kamalia Pak.
80 D2 Kaman Turkey
123 B5 Kamanjab Namibia
87 B2 Kamareddi India
85 F5 Kamarod Pak.
85 G5 Kamashi Uzbek.
68 C5 Kambalda Australia
88 B3 Kambam India
83 J4 Kambardi China
122 C4 Kambove Dem. Rep. Congo
77 R4 Kamchatka r. Rus. Fed.
160 G2 Kamchatka Basin sea feature Bering Sea
77 Q4 Kamchatka Peninsula Rus. Fed.
115 L3 Kamchiya r. Bulg.
82 B2 Kamelik r. Rus. Fed.
109 F3 Kamen Germany
87 C4 Kamenjak, Rt pt Croatia
82 B2 Kamenka Kazakh.
116 H3 Kamenka Penzenskaya Oblast' Rus. Fed.
94 E2 Kamenka Primorskiy Kray Rus. Fed.
76 J4 Kamen'-na-Obi Rus. Fed.
116 F3 Kamennogorsk Rus. Fed.
117 G6 Kamennomostskiy Rus. Fed.
117 G6 Kamenolomni Rus. Fed.
94 C2 Kamen'-Rybolov Rus. Fed.
77 R3 Kamenskoye Rus. Fed.
117 G5 Kamensk-Shakhtinskiy Rus. Fed.
76 H4 Kamensk-Ural'skiy Rus. Fed.
116 G3 Kameshkovo Rus. Fed.
124 D4 Kamiesberge mts S. Africa
124 D4 Kamieskroon S. Africa
131 I2 Kamilukuak Lake Canada
123 C4 Kamina Dem. Rep. Congo
131 K2 Kaminak Lake Canada
113 L5 Kamin'-Kashyrs'kyy Ukr.
95 H4 Kamishihoro Japan
95 G7 Kamo Japan
81 I1 Kamo Armenia
95 G7 Kamogawa Japan
123 B5 Kamoke Pak.
98 B3 Kamon, Xé r. Laos
108 D2 Kampen Neth.
122 C4 Kampene Dem. Rep. Congo
98 A1 Kamphaeng Phet Thai.
98 C2 Kâmpóng Cham Cambodia
98 C2 Kâmpóng Chhnăng Cambodia
98 C2 Kâmpóng Khleăng Cambodia
98 C2 Kâmpóng Spœ Cambodia
98 C2 Kâmpóng Thum Cambodia
98 C3 Kâmpôt Cambodia
Kampuchea country Asia see Cambodia
84 B2 Kamrau, Teluk b. Indon.
131 J4 Kamsack Canada
76 G4 Kamskoye Vodokhranilishche resr Rus. Fed.
122 E3 Kamsuuma Somalia
131 I3 Kamuchawie Lake Canada
122 D3 Kamuli Uganda
82 B2 Kam''yanets'-Podil's'kyy Ukr.
113 L6 Kam''yanets'-Podil's'kyy Ukr.
117 C5 Kam''yanka-Buz'ka Ukr.
113 L6 Kamyanyets Belarus
84 C3 Kāmyārān Iran
82 C2 Kamyshevatskaya Rus. Fed.
117 H5 Kamyshin Rus. Fed.
82 A2 Kamyslybas, Ozero l. Kazakh.
116 H4 Kamyzyak Rus. Fed.
82 E2 Kamzar Oman
141 F3 Kanab U.S.A.
141 F3 Kanab Creek r. U.S.A.
122 C4 Kananga Dem. Rep. Congo
71 I4 Kanangra-Boyd National Park Australia
82 D1 Kanash Rus. Fed.
141 F3 Kanarraville U.S.A.
146 C5 Kanawha r. U.S.A.
95 F6 Kanazawa Japan
98 A2 Kanchanaburi Thai.
87 B3 Kanchipuram India
85 G4 Kandahār Afgh.
116 E2 Kandalaksha Rus. Fed.
98 A5 Kandang Indon.

88 B2 Kandhura Pak.
120 C3 Kandi Benin
85 G4 Kandiaro Pak.
88 B4 Kandiaro Pak.
80 C1 Kandıra Turkey
71 H4 Kandos Australia
123 E5 Kandreho Madag.
87 B3 Kandukur India
87 C5 Kandy Sri Lanka
82 C2 Kandyagash Kazakh.
146 D4 Kane U.S.A.
Kane Bassin b. Canada/Greenland
84 D5 Kaneh watercourse Iran
140 □1 Kaneohe Bay U.S.A.
117 F6 Kanevskaya Rus. Fed.
123 C6 Kang Botswana
89 G5 Kanga r. Bangl.
129 K2 Kangaarsussuaq c. Greenland
89 G5 Kangaatsiaq Greenland
120 B3 Kangaba Mali
80 D3 Kangal Turkey
85 E5 Kangān Iran
85 E5 Kangān Iran
99 B1 Kangar Malaysia
70 B5 Kangaroo Island Australia
102 O3 Kangasniemi Fin.
103 N3 Kangasniemi Fin.
84 D5 Kangāvar Iran
92 E1 Kangbao China
89 G4 Kangchenjunga mt. India/Nepal
93 A4 Kangding China
96 D5 Kangdong N. Korea
98 □ Kangean, Kepulauan is Indon.
129 L3 Kangeeak Point Canada
129 N3 Kangeq hd Greenland
129 M3 Kangerlussuaq inlet Greenland
129 O3 Kangerlussuatsiaq inlet Greenland
129 M2 Kangersuatsiaq Greenland
129 P2 Kangertittivaq sea chan. Greenland
129 O3 Kangertittivatsiaq inlet Greenland
96 D5 Kanggye N. Korea
96 D5 Kanghwa S. Korea
96 D5 Kanghwa-do i. S. Korea
133 G2 Kangiqsualujjuaq Canada
129 K3 Kangiqsujuaq Canada
133 G1 Kangirsuk Canada
92 B3 Kangle China
89 H3 Kangmar Xizang China
89 G3 Kangmar Xizang China
96 D5 Kangnŭng S. Korea
122 B4 Kango Gabon
96 B2 Kangping China
89 H3 Kangri Karpo Pass India
88 I3 Kangrinboqê Feng mt. China
89 H4 Kangto mt. China
89 H3 Kangtog China
92 B3 Kangxian China
89 E4 Kanhar r. India
122 C5 Kaniama Dem. Rep. Congo
72 C5 Kaniere, Lake N.Z.
87 B3 Kani India
76 F3 Kanin, Poluostrov pen. Rus. Fed.
81 J3 Kāni Rash Iraq
117 D5 Kaniv Ukr.
70 D4 Kaniva Australia
103 M3 Kankaanpää Fin.
134 C5 Kankakee U.S.A.
134 C5 Kankakee r. U.S.A.
120 B3 Kankan Guinea
87 C1 Kanker India
87 C4 Kankesanturai Sri Lanka
98 A3 Kanmaw Kyun i. Myanmar
145 D5 Kannapolis U.S.A.
89 E4 Kannauj India
88 D5 Kanniyakumari India
102 N3 Kannonkoski Fin.
Kannur India see Cannanore
102 M3 Kannus Fin.
120 C3 Kano Nigeria
83 I2 Kanonerka Kazakh.
124 D7 Kanonpunt pt S. Africa
88 D3 Kanor India
95 E6 Kanoya Japan
88 E4 Kanpur India
85 G5 Kanrach reg. Pak.
83 H5 Kansas r. U.S.A.
142 D4 Kansas state U.S.A.
142 E4 Kansas City KS U.S.A.
142 E4 Kansas City MO U.S.A.
90 B1 Kansk Rus. Fed.
83 H5 Kansu China
89 G4 Kantanagar Bangl.
88 A4 Kantang Thai.
88 B3 Kantaralak Thai.
120 C3 Kantchari Burkina
117 F5 Kanthi India
88 C3 Kanti India
69 I2 Kanton i. Kiribati
107 C5 Kanturk Rep. of Ireland
125 I2 KaNyamazane S. Africa
123 C6 Kanye Botswana
93 F5 Kaohsiung Taiwan
123 B5 Kaokoveld plat. Namibia
120 A3 Kaolack Senegal
123 C5 Kaoma Zambia
140 □2 Kapaa U.S.A.
83 I4 Kapal Kazakh.
83 K2 Kapan Armenia
122 C4 Kapanga Dem. Rep. Congo
83 I4 Kapchagay Kazakh.
108 C3 Kapellen Belgium
103 J6 Kapellskär Sweden
80 A1 Kapıdağı Yarımadası pen. Turkey
160 F6 Kapingamarangi atoll Micronesia
160 F5 Kapingamarangi Rise sea feature N. Pacific Ocean
123 B5 Kapiri Mposhi Zambia
129 M3 Kapisillit Greenland
132 D3 Kapiskau Canada
132 D3 Kapiskau r. Canada
135 G2 Kapiskong Lake Canada
72 E4 Kapiti Island N.Z.
121 E4 Kapoeta Sudan
121 H7 Kaposvár Hungary
85 F5 Kappar Pak.
109 H1 Kappeln Germany
122 D3 Kapsabet Kenya
98 □ Kapuas r. Indon.
98 □ Kapuas r. Indon.
70 C5 Kapunda Australia
88 C3 Kapurthala India
132 D3 Kapuskasing Canada
117 H5 Kapustin Yar Rus. Fed.
112 H7 Kapuvár Hungary
116 C4 Kapyl' Belarus

96 D5 Kap'yŏng S. Korea
83 I5 Kaqung China
120 C4 Kara Togo
81 H2 Kara r. Turkey
115 L5 Kara Ada i. Turkey
80 D2 Karaali Turkey
83 H4 Kara-Balta Kyrg.
82 E1 Karabalyk Kazakh.
83 H2 Karabas Kazakh.
82 C2 Karabau Kazakh.
85 F2 Karabil', Vozvyshennost' reg. Turkm.
82 C4 Kara-Bogaz-Gol, Zaliv b. Turkm.
82 C4 Karabogazkel' Turkm.
80 D1 Karabük Turkey
83 I3 Karabulak Almatinskaya Oblast' Kazakh.
83 K3 Karabulak Vostochnyy Kazakhstan Kazakh.
83 H2 Karabulakskaya Kazakh.
82 E2 Karabutak Kazakh.
80 B1 Karacabey Turkey
80 D3 Karacadağ mts Turkey
80 D1 Karacadağ Turkey
81 G3 Karacalı Dağ mt. Turkey
80 B3 Karacasu Turkey
80 C3 Karaca Yarımadası pen. Turkey
117 G7 Karachayevo-Cherkesskaya Respublika aut. rep. Rus. Fed.
117 G7 Karachayevsk Rus. Fed.
116 E4 Karachev Rus. Fed.
85 G3 Karachi Pak. (City Plan 51)
81 I2 Karaçoban Turkey
87 A2 Karad India
80 D3 Kara Dağ mt. Turkey
81 I3 Kara Dağ mt. Turkey
83 H4 Kara-Darya r. Kyrg.
83 H2 Karaganda Kazakh.
83 G2 Karagandinskaya Oblast' admin. div. Kazakh.
83 H2 Karagayly Kazakh.
77 R4 Karaginskiy Zaliv b. Rus. Fed.
82 B4 Karagiye, Vpadina depr. Kazakh.
83 J2 Karaguzhikha Kazakh.
80 D2 Karahallı Turkey
80 E2 Karahasanlı Turkey
87 B4 Karaikal India
87 B4 Karaikkudi India
83 K3 Kara Irtysh r. Kazakh.
80 E3 Karaisalı Turkey
84 C3 Karaj Iran
84 C3 Karak r. Iran
82 D3 Karakalpakiya Uzbek.
82 F4 Karakatinskaya, Vpadina depr. Uzbek.
88 E1 Karakax He r. China
81 G3 Karakeçi Turkey
80 D2 Karakeçili Turkey
91 E6 Karakelong i. Indon.
82 E1 Karakoçan Turkey
82 C2 Karaköl Turkm.
83 H4 Kara-Köl Kyrg.
83 I4 Karakol Kyrg.
83 I4 Karakol Kyrg.
88 D2 Karakoram Pass China/Jammu and Kashmir
79 F3 Kara K'orē Eth.
122 D1 Kara K'orē Eth.
83 G3 Karakoyyn, Ozero salt l. Kazakh.
82 E5 Karakul' Bukharskaya Oblast' Uzbek.
82 E5 Karakul' Bukharskaya Oblast' Uzbek.
82 E1 Karakul'skoye Rus. Fed.
83 I3 Karakum, Peski des. Kazakh.
Karakum, Peski des. Kazakh. see Karakum Desert
82 C3 Karakum Desert des. Kazakh.
85 F2 Karakum Desert Turkm.
82 E5 Karakumskiy Kanal canal Turkm.
82 D5 Kara Kumy des. Turkm.
Karakumy, Peski des. Turkm. see Karakum Desert
81 I1 Karakurt Turkey
103 M4 Karala Estonia
80 D3 Karaman Turkey
80 D3 Karamanlı Turkey
79 G2 Karamay China
88 C1 Karambar Pass Afgh./Pak.
72 D4 Karamea N.Z.
72 C4 Karamea Bight b. N.Z.
82 F2 Karamendy Kazakh.
82 F5 Karamet-Niyaz Turkm.
89 F1 Karamiran China
89 F1 Karamiran Shankou pass China
80 D1 Karamürsel Turkey
116 D4 Karamyshevo Rus. Fed.
84 C5 Karan i. Saudi Arabia
88 D5 Karanja India
87 B2 Karanja r. India
89 F5 Karanja India
88 C3 Karanpura India
83 I1 Karaoba Kazakh.
83 H3 Karaoy Almatinskaya Oblast' Kazakh.
83 H3 Karaoy Almatinskaya Oblast' Kazakh.
82 F3 Karaozek Kazakh.
80 D3 Karapınar Turkey
83 I4 Karaqi China
124 B3 Karas admin. reg. Namibia
124 B3 Karas watercourse Namibia
84 F5 Kara-Say Kyrg.
123 B6 Karasburg Namibia
76 I2 Kara Sea Rus. Fed.
102 N1 Kárášjohka Norway
83 H2 Karasor Kazakh.
83 H2 Karasor, Ozero salt l. Karagandinskaya Oblast' Kazakh.
83 H1 Karasor, Ozero salt l. Pavlodarskaya Oblast' Kazakh.
83 H3 Karasu Karagandinskaya Oblast' Kazakh.
82 F1 Karasu Kustanayskaya Oblast' Kazakh.
83 H1 Karasu Turkey
80 C1 Karasu Turkey
81 I2 Karasu r. Turkey
83 I1 Karasuk Rus. Fed.
83 H4 Kara-Suu Kyrg.
83 K3 Karataş Turkey
80 E3 Karataş Turkey
83 G3 Karataş Burun pt Turkey
83 G3 Karatal r. Kazakh.
88 E2 Karatax Shan mts China
87 A3 Karathuri Myanmar
87 B4 Karativu i. Sri Lanka
82 C2 Karatobe Kazakh.
82 B3 Karatobe, Mys pt Kazakh.
82 D2 Karatogay Kazakh.
83 I3 Karaul Kazakh.
82 E1 Karatomarskoye Vodokhranilishche resr Kazakh.
82 C3 Karaton Kazakh.
82 F2 Karatoya r. Bangl.
83 G4 Karatsu Japan
97 C3 Karatung i. Indon.
82 F2 Kara-Turgay r. Kazakh.
83 I2 Karaul Kazakh.
83 I2 Karaulbazar Uzbek.
88 D4 Karauli India
83 I1 Karawang Indon.
83 J4 Karayilgen China
82 B3 Karazhanbas Kazakh.
82 B3 Karazhanbas Kazakh.
82 D4 Karazhar Uzbek.

83 H3 Karazhingil Kazakh.
81 J5 Karbalā' Iraq
109 G4 Karben Germany
83 H2 Karbushevka Kazakh.
113 J7 Karcag Hungary
108 F4 Karden Germany
115 I5 Karditsa Greece
103 M4 Kärdla Estonia
125 A4 Karee S. Africa
124 D5 Kareeberge mts S. Africa
121 F3 Kareima Sudan
117 H7 K'areli Georgia
88 D5 Kareli India
116 E2 Kareliya, Respublika aut. rep. Rus. Fed.
90 D1 Karenga r. Rus. Fed.
88 M1 Karera India
85 F5 Kārevāndar Iran
82 C2 Kargala Rus. Fed.
117 H7 Kargalinskaya Rus. Fed.
82 D2 Kargalinskoye Kazakh.
83 H2 Kargaly Karagandinskaya Oblast' Kazakh.
83 J2 Kargaly Vostochnyy Kazakhstan Kazakh.
81 H2 Kargapazarı Dağları mts Turkey
80 E1 Kargı Turkey
88 D2 Kargil Jammu and Kashmir
116 E3 Kargopol' Rus. Fed.
84 E5 Kargoshki Iran
102 L3 Karholmsbruk Sweden
123 C5 Kariba Zimbabwe
123 C5 Kariba, Lake resr Zambia/Zimbabwe
94 F3 Kariba-yama vol. Japan
124 E6 Kariega r. S. Africa
102 N1 Karigasniemi Fin.
72 D1 Karikari, Cape N.Z.
84 D3 Karīmābād Iran
99 C3 Karimata, Pulau-pulau is Indon.
99 C3 Karimata, Selat strait Indon.
87 B2 Karīmnagar India
99 D4 Karimunjawa, Pulau-pulau is Indon.
122 E2 Karin Somalia
84 E3 Karin Iran
84 A2 Karjat India
89 F5 Karkai r. India
87 A3 Karkal India
83 H2 Karkaralinsk Kazakh.
97 C5 Karkaralong, Kepulauan is Indon.
68 C2 Karkar Island P.N.G.
84 C4 Karkheh, Rūdkhāneh-ye r. Iran
117 E5 Karkinits'ka Zatoka g. Ukr.
103 N3 Kärkölä Fin.
103 H4 Karksi-Nuia Estonia
117 E5 Karlivka Ukr.
114 F2 Karlovac Croatia
115 K3 Karlovo Bulg.
112 F5 Karlovy Vary Czech Rep.
109 G6 Karlsbad Germany
103 K4 Karlsborg Sweden
103 K4 Karlshamn Sweden
103 K4 Karlskoga Sweden
103 L5 Karlskrona Sweden
109 G5 Karlsruhe Germany
103 K4 Karlstad Sweden
142 D1 Karlstad U.S.A.
109 H5 Karlstadt Germany
116 D4 Karma Belarus
87 A2 Karmala India
82 B2 Karmanovka Kazakh.
103 I4 Karmøy i. Norway
89 H5 Karnafuli Reservoir Bangl.
89 E3 Karnal India
89 E3 Karnali r. Nepal
87 A3 Karnataka state India
85 G5 Karodi Pak.
123 C5 Karoi Zimbabwe
83 G4 Kara La pass China
89 H4 Karong India
123 D4 Karonga Malawi
83 I4 Karool-Döbö Kyrg.
124 E6 Karoo National Park S. Africa
70 C5 Karoonda Australia
88 B3 Karor Pak.
122 D2 Karora Eritrea
109 K1 Karow Germany
115 L7 Karpathos i. Greece
115 L6 Karpathou, Steno sea chan. Greece
115 I5 Karpenisi Greece
116 H1 Karpogory Rus. Fed.
68 M4 Karratha Australia
84 C4 Karri Iran
88 E1 Karrukh Afgh.
81 I1 Kars Turkey
102 N3 Kärsämäki Fin.
103 N4 Kärsava Latvia
82 C4 Karshi Turkm.
82 F5 Karshi Uzbek.
89 G4 Karsiyang India
83 G3 Karskiye Vorota, Proliv strait Rus. Fed.
Karskoye More sea Rus. Fed. see Kara Sea
109 J1 Karstädt Germany
102 N3 Karstula Fin.
80 B1 Kartal Turkey
82 E1 Kartaly Rus. Fed.
84 C4 Karun, Kūh-e hill Iran
84 C4 Kārūn, Rūd-e r. Iran
84 B4 Karur India
103 M3 Karvia Fin.
103 M4 Karvianjoki r. Fin.
87 A3 Karwar India
90 D1 Karymskoye Rus. Fed.
77 M3 Karynzharyk, Peski des. Kazakh.
115 K5 Karystos Greece
80 B3 Kaş Turkey
132 C3 Kasaba Canada
132 C3 Kasabonika Canada
132 B4 Kasabonika Lake Canada
122 B4 Kasai r. Dem. Rep. Congo
123 D5 Kasaji Dem. Rep. Congo
123 D5 Kasama Zambia
82 C4 Kasan Uzbek.
124 B4 Kasane Botswana
123 D5 Kasanga Tanz.
122 C4 Kasangulu Dem. Rep. Congo
88 D4 Kasaragod India
88 D4 Kasganj India
83 I5 Kashgar China see Kashi
83 I5 Kashi China
80 D7 Kashihara Japan
90 B8 Kashima Japan
95 G4 Kashima-nada b. Japan
116 F3 Kashin Rus. Fed.
88 D3 Kashipur India
95 F6 Kashiwazaki Japan
84 E3 Kashkan r. Iran
83 H3 Kashkantengi Kazakh.
84 C2 Kashmar Iran
84 D3 Kashmar-i'iyeh Iran
85 H3 Kashmir, Vale of valley India
85 H3 Kashmor Pak.
85 H3 Kashmund reg. Afgh.

122 C4 Kashyukulu Dem. Rep. Congo
116 G4 Kasimov Rus. Fed.
144 B4 Kaskaskia r. U.S.A.
131 K3 Kaskattama r. Canada
113 J7 Kaskinen Fin.
103 M3 Kaskinen Kazakh.
122 C4 Kasongo Dem. Rep. Congo
122 B4 Kasongo-Lunda Dem. Rep. Congo
115 L7 Kasos i. Greece
115 L7 Kasou, Steno sea chan. Greece
117 H7 Kaspi Georgia
117 H7 Kaspiysk Rus. Fed.
117 O3 Kasplya Rus. Fed.
121 F3 Kassala Sudan
115 J4 Kassandra pen. Greece
115 J4 Kassandras, Kolpos b. Greece
109 H3 Kassel Germany
120 C1 Kasserine Tunisia
134 A3 Kasson U.S.A.
80 D1 Kastamonu Turkey
108 F4 Kastellaun Germany
115 J7 Kastelli Greece
108 C3 Kasterlee Belgium
115 I4 Kastoria Greece
116 E4 Kastsyukovichy Belarus
95 E7 Kasugai Japan
122 D4 Kasulu Tanz.
95 D7 Kasumi Japan
84 C2 Kasumiga-ura l. Japan
117 I7 Kasumkent Rus. Fed.
123 D5 Kasungu Malawi
85 I5 Kasur Pak.
147 I2 Katahdin, Mount U.S.A.
88 D2 Kataklik Jammu and Kashmir
122 C4 Katako-Kombe Dem. Rep. Congo
88 D5 Katangi India
68 D5 Katanning Australia
83 H3 Katawaz Afgh.
122 C4 Katea Dem. Rep. Congo
115 J4 Katerini Greece
130 C3 Kate's Needle mt. Canada/U.S.A.
123 D5 Katete Zambia
87 C1 Katghora India
118 B4 Katha Myanmar
68 D3 Katherine r. Australia
88 B5 Kathiawar pen. India
87 C4 Kathiraveli Sri Lanka
125 H3 Kathlehong S. Africa
89 F3 Kathmandu Nepal
124 E3 Kathu S. Africa
88 C2 Kathua Jammu and Kashmir
120 B3 Kati Mali
89 F4 Katihar India
72 E2 Katikati N.Z.
125 G6 Kati-Kati S. Africa
123 C5 Katima Mulilo Namibia
120 B4 Katiola Côte d'Ivoire
122 D4 Katko Hills reg. S. Africa
115 I5 Katol Greece
88 D5 Katol India
115 J6 Katong Sing.
83 K2 Katon-Karagay Kazakh.
71 I4 Katoomba Australia
113 I5 Katowice Poland
106 D3 Katoya India
103 L4 Katrine, Loch l. U.K.
120 C3 Katrineholm Sweden
120 C3 Katsina Nigeria
95 G7 Katsina-Ala Nigeria
95 E6 Katsuura Japan
133 G2 Katsuyama Japan
82 F5 Kattaktoc, Cap hd Canada
85 J3 Kattakurgan Uzbek.
103 J4 Kattasang Hills Afgh.
83 K1 Kattegat strait Denmark/Sweden
108 C2 Katun' r. Rus. Fed.
109 H5 Katwijk aan Zee Neth.
140 □2 Katzenbuckel hill Germany
140 □2 Kaua'i i. U.S.A.
109 F4 Kauai Channel U.S.A.
103 M3 Kaub Germany
103 M3 Kauhajoki Fin.
102 N2 Kauhava Fin.
140 □2 Kaukonen Fin.
140 □2 Kaula i. U.S.A.
133 H2 Kaulakahi Channel U.S.A.
140 □2 Kaumajet Mountains Canada
103 M5 Kaunakakai U.S.A.
103 N4 Kaunas Lith.
120 C3 Kaunata Latvia
93 □ Kaura-Namoda Nigeria
Kau Sai Chau i. Hong Kong China
102 M3 Kaustinen Fin.
102 M1 Kautokeino Norway
98 A3 Kau-ye Kyun i. Myanmar
115 J4 Kavadarci Macedonia
80 F1 Kavak Turkey
115 K4 Kavala Greece
103 N4 Kavalerovo Rus. Fed.
87 C3 Kavali India
84 D4 Kavār Iran
87 A4 Kavaratti i. India
115 M3 Kavarna Bulg.
87 B4 Kaveri r. India
84 D3 Kavīr salt flat Iran
84 D3 Kavīr salt flat Iran
84 D3 Kavīr, Dasht-e des. Iran
84 D3 Kavīr-e Hāj Alī Qoli salt l. Iran
95 F7 Kawagoe Japan
95 F7 Kawaguchi Japan
140 □2 Kawaihae U.S.A.
72 E1 Kawakawa N.Z.
123 C4 Kawambwa Zambia
123 E5 Kawartha Lakes Canada
95 F7 Kawasaki Japan
72 E3 Kawau Island N.Z.
103 M3 Kawerau N.Z.
72 E3 Kawerau N.Z.
72 E3 Kawhia N.Z.
72 E3 Kawhia Harbour N.Z.
138 C2 Kawich Range mts U.S.A.
140 A2 Kawkareik Myanmar
84 E6 Kawr, Jabal mt. Oman
98 A3 Kawthaung Myanmar
83 I5 Kaxgar He r. China
120 B3 Kaya Burkina
90 F2 Kayabi i. Indon.
72 F4 Kayan r. Indon.
123 D4 Kayanaza Burundi
87 B4 Kayankulam India
115 K5 Kaycee U.S.A.
123 C4 Kayembe-Mukulu Dem. Rep. Congo
141 G3 Kayenta U.S.A.
120 A3 Kayes Mali
82 F2 Kayga Kazakh.
120 B3 Kayima Sierra Leone
83 H1 Kaymanachikha Rus. Fed.
83 I2 Kaynar Vostochnyy Kazakhstan Kazakh.
83 H4 Kaynar Zhambylskaya Oblast' Kazakh.
80 F2 Kaynar Turkey
83 I5 Kayrakty Rus. Fed.
117 H5 Kaysatskoye Rus. Fed.
80 E1 Kayseri Turkey
99 B3 Kayuagung Indon.
89 F5 Kayyerkan Rus. Fed.
83 H4 Kazach'ye Rus. Fed.
84 E2 Kazakh Azer.
83 H2 Kazakhstan country Asia
82 E3 Kazalinsk Kazakh.

131 J2 Kazan r. Canada
116 I4 Kazan' Rus. Fed.
80 D3 Kazancı Turkey
116 I4 Kazanka r. Rus. Fed.
115 K3 Kazanlŭk Bulg.
Kazan-rettō is Japan see Volcano is
117 G5 Kazanskaya Rus. Fed.
83 H4 Kazarman Kyrg.
82 D2 Kazatskiy Kazakh.
117 H7 Kazbek mt. Georgia/Rus. Fed.
115 L5 Kaz Dağı mts Turkey
84 C4 Kāzerūn Iran
116 I2 Kazhim Rus. Fed.
85 F5 Kazhmak r. Pak.
113 J6 Kazincbarcika Hungary
117 H7 Kazret'i Georgia
82 B2 Kaztalovka Kazakh.
94 A4 Kazuno Japan
83 G4 Kazygurt Kazakh.
76 H3 Kazymskiy Mys Rus. Fed.
116 K6 Kea i. Greece
107 E3 Keady U.K.
140 □2 Kealakekua Bay U.S.A.
141 G4 Keams Canyon U.S.A.
142 D3 Kearney U.S.A.
141 F3 Kearny U.S.A.
80 G2 Keban Turkey
80 G2 Keban Barajı resr Turkey
120 A3 Kébémèr Senegal
121 E3 Kebkabiya Sudan
102 L2 Kebnekaise mt. Sweden
106 B2 Kebock Head hd U.K.
122 E3 K'ebrī Dehar Eth.
99 C4 Kebumen Indon.
130 C3 Kechika r. Canada
80 C3 Keçiborlu Turkey
113 I7 Kecskemét Hungary
81 H1 K'eda Georgia
103 M5 Kėdainiai Lith.
88 D3 Kedar Kantha mt. India
88 D3 Kedarnath Peak India
133 G4 Kedgwick Canada
99 C4 Kediri Indon.
120 A3 Kédougou Senegal
130 C2 Keele r. Canada
130 C2 Keele Peak mt. Canada
139 C4 Keeler U.S.A.
Keeling Islands terr. Indian Ocean see Cocos Islands
106 F4 Keen, Mount U.K.
97 A5 Keenapusan i. Phil.
147 I3 Keene U.S.A.
108 C3 Keerbergen Belgium
123 B6 Keetmanshoop Namibia
117 H6 Kegul'ta Rus. Fed.
103 N4 Kehra Estonia
106 F3 Keighley U.K.
103 N4 Keila Estonia
124 D4 Keimoes S. Africa
102 N3 Keitele Fin.
102 N3 Keitele l. Fin.
70 C3 Keith Australia
130 E1 Keith Arm b. Canada
131 J5 Kejimkujik National Park Canada
113 I7 Kékes mt. Hungary
88 E4 Kekri India
79 F6 Kelai i. Maldives
92 B2 Kelan China
99 B2 Kelang Malaysia
98 B1 Kelantan r. Malaysia
82 E5 Keles Uzbek.
109 J6 Kelheim Germany
114 D6 Kelibia Tunisia
82 F5 Kelif Turkm.
109 G4 Kelkheim (Taunus) Germany
80 G1 Kelkit r. Turkey
130 F4 Keller Lake l. Canada
82 F1 Kellerovka Kazakh.
134 B3 Kelleys Island U.S.A.
138 C2 Kellogg U.S.A.
102 O2 Kelloselkä Fin.
107 B6 Kells Rep. of Ireland
103 M5 Kelmė Lith.
108 C4 Kelmis Belgium
121 F4 Kelo Chad
130 F5 Kelowna Canada
138 B2 Kelseyville U.S.A.
106 F5 Kelso U.K.
141 E4 Kelso CA U.S.A.
138 B2 Kelso WA U.S.A.
99 B2 Keluang Malaysia
131 I4 Kelvington Canada
138 B2 Kelvin U.S.A.
131 I4 Kelwood Canada
137 J4 Kem' Rus. Fed.
136 E2 Kemah Turkey
140 A2 Kemaliye Turkey
80 B3 Kemalpaşa Turkey
130 D4 Kemano Canada
130 D4 Kemer Turkey
80 B3 Kemer Turkey
80 C3 Kemer Turkey
80 C3 Kemer Barajı resr Turkey
88 B5 Kemerovo Rus. Fed.
102 N2 Kemi Fin.
102 N2 Kemijärvi Fin.
102 O2 Kemijärvi l. Fin.
102 O2 Kemijoki r. Fin.
102 N2 Keminmaa Fin.
138 F4 Kemmerer U.S.A.
109 J5 Kemnath Germany
143 D6 Kemp, Lake U.S.A.
75 C4 Kemp Land reg. Antarctica
73 D4 Kemp Peninsula Antarctica
145 F7 Kemp's Bay Bahamas
71 J3 Kempsey Australia
133 F4 Kempt, Lac l. Canada
112 F7 Kempten (Allgäu) Germany
71 G9 Kempton Australia
125 H3 Kempton Park S. Africa
135 J3 Kemptville Canada
99 D4 Kemujan i. Indon.
128 C4 Kenai U.S.A.
128 C4 Kenai Mountains U.S.A.
143 F6 Kenansville U.S.A.
104 E3 Kendal U.K.
131 L2 Kendall, Cape hd Canada
134 A2 Kendallville U.S.A.
99 D4 Kendari Indon.
99 C4 Kendawangan Indon.
121 G3 Kendégué Chad
99 J3 Kendrapara India
138 C2 Kendrick U.S.A.
141 G4 Kendrick Peak mt. U.S.A.
83 J4 Kendyktas mts Kazakh.
82 C4 Kendyrli-Kayasanskoye, Plato Kazakh.
82 C4 Kendyrlisor, Solonchak salt l. Kazakh.
71 H3 Kenebri Australia
143 D6 Kenedy U.S.A.

120 A4 Kenema Sierra Leone
82 D4 Keneurgench Turkm.
122 B4 Kenge Dem. Rep. Congo
82 D4 Keng-Peli Uzbek.
91 H6 Kengtung Myanmar
124 D5 Kenhardt S. Africa
120 A3 Kéniéba Mali
120 B1 Kénitra Morocco
92 D2 Kenli China
107 B6 Kenmare Rep. of Ireland
142 C1 Kenmare U.S.A.
107 A6 Kenmare River inlet Rep. of Ireland
108 E5 Kenn Germany
147 I2 Kenna U.S.A.
147 H3 Kennebec r. U.S.A.
143 F6 Kennebunkport U.S.A.
105 F6 Kenner U.S.A.
143 F4 Kennet r. U.K.
143 F4 Kennett U.S.A.
138 B2 Kennewick U.S.A.
130 B2 Keno Canada
135 G1 Kenogami Lake Canada
135 G1 Kenogamissi Lake Canada
131 K5 Kenora Canada
134 C3 Kenosha U.S.A.
116 F2 Kenozero, Ozero l. Rus. Fed.
104 E3 Kent r. U.K.
147 I2 Kent U.S.A.
143 B2 Kent TX U.S.A.
138 B2 Kent WA U.S.A.
71 G7 Kent Group is Australia
134 C5 Kentland U.S.A.
146 A3 Kenton U.S.A.
137 J4 Kentucky r. U.S.A.
145 E4 Kentucky state U.S.A.
145 E4 Kentucky Lake U.S.A.
133 H4 Kentville Canada
143 E4 Kentwood LA U.S.A.
134 E4 Kentwood MI U.S.A.
122 D3 Kenya country Africa
122 D4 Kenya, Mount Kenya
134 A3 Kenyon U.S.A.
83 G2 Kenzharyk Kazakh.
140 □2 Keokea U.S.A.
134 B5 Keokuk U.S.A.
98 C1 Keo Neua, Col de pass Laos/Vietnam
134 B5 Keosauqua U.S.A.
69 □ Keppel Bay Australia
98 □ Keppel Harbour sea chan. Sing.
80 B2 Kepsut Turkey
84 E4 Kerah Iran
87 A4 Kerala state India
70 C5 Kerang Australia
103 N3 Kerava Fin.
111 I4 Kerba Alg.
83 G4 Kerben Kyrg.
117 H6 Kerch Ukr.
69 K1 Kerema P.N.G.
130 F5 Keremeos Canada
117 E7 Kerempe Burun pt Turkey
122 D2 Keren Eritrea
84 B3 Kerend Iran
83 G2 Kerey watercourse Kazakh.
83 G2 Kerey, Ozero salt l. Kazakh.
82 D5 Kergeli Turkm.
162 I8 Kerguélen, Îles is Indian Ocean
162 I8 Kerguelen Plateau sea feature Indian Ocean
122 D3 Kericho Kenya
72 D1 Kerikeri N.Z.
103 O3 Kerimäki Fin.
99 B3 Kerinci, Gunung vol. Indon.
88 E1 Keriya He watercourse China
88 E1 Keriya Shankou pass China
82 F5 Kerki Turkm.
82 F5 Kerkichi Turkm.
115 I5 Kerkinitis, Limni l. Greece
115 H5 Kerkyra Greece
Kerkyra i. Greece see Corfu
121 F3 Kerma Sudan
67 H5 Kermadec Islands S. Pacific Ocean
160 H8 Kermadec Trench sea feature S. Pacific Ocean
84 D4 Kermān Iran
140 B3 Kerman U.S.A.
85 E4 Kermān Desert Iran
84 B3 Kermānshāh Iran
84 C3 Kermānshāhān Iran
143 C6 Kermit U.S.A.
138 C4 Kern r. U.S.A.
140 C4 Kern, South Fork r. U.S.A.
133 G2 Kernertut, Cap pt Canada
138 C4 Kernville U.S.A.
115 K6 Keros i. Greece
116 J3 Keros Rus. Fed.
120 B4 Kérouané Guinea
108 E4 Kerpen Germany
73 B5 Kerr, Cape Antarctica
131 H4 Kerrobert Canada
143 D6 Kerrville U.S.A.
107 B5 Kerry Head Rep. of Ireland
99 B2 Kerteh Malaysia
103 J5 Kerteminde Denmark
Kerulen r. China/Mongolia
Kerynela Cyprus see Kyrenia
116 H3 Kerzhenets r. Rus. Fed.
132 D3 Kesagami Lake Canada
103 O3 Kesälahti Fin.
80 B1 Keşan Turkey
80 G1 Keşap Turkey
94 F5 Kesennuma Japan
85 G3 Keshem Afgh.
85 G3 Keshendeh-ye Bala Afgh.
88 B5 Keshod India
84 C3 Keshvar Iran
80 D2 Keskin Turkey
116 E2 Keskozero Rus. Fed.
108 E2 Kessel Neth.
125 H4 Kestell S. Africa
102 O2 Kesten'ga Rus. Fed.
102 N3 Kestilä Fin.
131 K5 Keswick Canada
106 E3 Keswick U.K.
112 H7 Keszthely Hungary
76 J4 Ket' r. Rus. Fed.
120 C4 Keta Ghana
99 □ Ketapang Indon.
130 C3 Ketchikan U.S.A.
108 D2 Ketelmeer l. Neth.
85 G5 Keti Bandar Pak.
83 J4 Ketmen', Khrebet mts China/Kazakh.
107 G6 Kettering U.K.
146 A3 Kettering U.S.A.
130 G5 Kettle r. Canada
135 J3 Kettle Creek r. U.S.A.
138 C2 Kettleman City U.S.A.
138 C1 Kettle River Range mts U.S.A.
135 G2 Keuka Lake U.S.A.
103 N3 Keuruu Fin.
134 C3 Kewanee U.S.A.
134 C2 Kewaunee U.S.A.
134 C1 Keweenaw Bay U.S.A.
134 C1 Keweenaw Peninsula U.S.A.
134 D1 Keweenaw Point U.S.A.
157 F2 Kewelgi Guyana
130 C4 Key, Lough l. Rep. of Ireland
135 F5 Keyano Canada
135 H2 Key Harbour Canada
135 J4 Keyi China
145 D7 Key Largo U.S.A.
105 H6 Keynsham U.K.
135 J3 Keyser Ridge U.S.A.
146 D5 Keystone Peak mt. U.S.A.
146 D6 Keysville U.S.A.
81 L4 Keytü Iran

145 D7 Key West FL U.S.A.
134 B4 Key West IA U.S.A.
123 C6 Kezi Zimbabwe
113 J6 Kežmarok Slovakia
147 H3 Kezar Falls U.S.A.
124 D2 Kgalagadi admin. dist. Botswana
125 G2 Kgatleng admin. dist. Botswana
124 D1 Kgomofatshe Pan salt pan Botswana
124 D2 Kgoro Pan salt pan Botswana
125 G3 Kgotsong S. Africa
90 F2 Khabarovsk Rus. Fed.
83 I1 Khabary Rus. Fed.
81 H4 Khābūr, Nahr al r. Syria
81 I7 Khadd, Wādī al watercourse Saudi Arabia
84 B6 Khafs Daghrah Saudi Arabia
88 D4 Khaga India
89 G5 Khagrachari Bangl.
88 D3 Khairgarh India
85 H4 Khairpur Pak.
88 D5 Khajuraho India
123 C6 Khakhea Botswana
85 G4 Khakir Afgh.
85 G4 Khak-rēz Afgh.
85 G4 Khakriz reg. Afgh.
84 C2 Khalajestan reg. Iran
88 D2 Khalatse Jammu and Kashmir
85 E3 Khalīfat mt. Pak.
85 E3 Khalilabad Iran
84 C2 Khalkhāl Iran
87 D2 Khallikot India
116 D4 Khalopyenichy Belarus
90 C1 Khamar-Daban, Khrebet mts Rus. Fed.
88 C5 Khambhat India
88 B5 Khambhat, Gulf of India
88 D5 Khamgaon India
84 D5 Khamir Iran
84 B5 Khamir Iran
98 C1 Khamkkeut Laos
84 B5 Khamma well Saudi Arabia
87 B2 Khammam India
84 C2 Khamseh reg. Iran
83 G4 Khamza Uzbek.
98 B1 Khan, Nam r. Laos
85 H2 Khānābād Afgh.
84 A3 Khānaqāh Iran
81 I5 Khān al Baghdādī Iraq
81 J5 Khān al Mahāwīl Iraq
81 J5 Khān al Mashāhidah Iraq
81 J5 Khān al Muşallá Iraq
87 A3 Khanapur India
84 B2 Khānaqāh Iran
81 J6 Khānaqīn Iraq
81 J6 Khān ar Raḥbah Iraq
81 J2 Khanasur Pass Iran/Turkey
80 F6 Khān az Zabīb Jordan
88 C2 Khanbari Pass Jammu and Kashmir
71 H6 Khancoban Australia
88 B2 Khand Pass Afgh./Pak.
85 H3 Khandud Afgh.
77 O3 Khandyga Rus. Fed.
98 D2 Khanewal Pak.
98 D2 Khanh Duong Vietnam
88 C2 Khaniadhana India
94 C2 Khanka, Lake China/Rus. Fed.
88 C2 Khanki Weir Pak.
88 B3 Khanna India
88 B3 Khanpur Pak.
80 F6 Khān Shaykhūn Syria
88 H3 Khantau Kazakh.
76 K3 Khantayskoye, Ozero l. Rus. Fed.
Khan-Tengri mt. Kyrg. see Khan-Tengri, Pik
83 J4 Khan-Tengri, Pik mt. Kyrg.
76 H3 Khanty-Mansiysk Rus. Fed.
80 E6 Khān Yūnis Gaza
98 D3 Khao Chum Thong Thai.
117 H6 Kharabali Rus. Fed.
89 F5 Kharagpur India
84 E2 Kharaki Iran
85 F4 Khārān r. Iran
85 G4 Kharan Pak.
84 D3 Kharānaq Iran
88 B3 Kharbin Pass Afgh.
88 D2 Khardung La pass India
85 F3 Kharez Ilias Afgh.
81 K6 Kharfiyah Iraq
84 C4 Khārg Islands Iran
88 C5 Khargon India
88 C4 Khari r. Rajasthan India
88 C4 Khari r. Rajasthan India
88 C2 Kharian Pak.
121 F2 Khārijah, Wāḥāt al oasis Egypt
117 F5 Kharkiv Ukr.
115 K3 Kharmanli Bulg.
84 C3 Khar Rūd r. Iran
87 D1 Kharsia India
121 F3 Khartoum Sudan
82 C5 Khasardag, Gora mt. Turkm.
117 H7 Khasav'yurt Rus. Fed.
85 F4 Khash Afgh.
85 F4 Khāsh Iran
85 F4 Khash Desert Afgh.
117 G7 Khashuri Georgia
89 G4 Khasi Hills India
115 K3 Khaskovo Bulg.
77 L2 Khatanga Rus. Fed.
80 D6 Khatmia Pass Egypt
77 S3 Khatyrka Rus. Fed.
82 F5 Khavast Uzbek.
88 B5 Khavda India
85 H3 Khāwāk Pass Afgh.
84 E5 Khawr Fakkān U.A.E.
125 F5 Khayamnandi S. Africa
124 C7 Khayelitsha S. Africa
84 C3 Khayrabad Iran
82 E5 Khāzarāsp Uzbek.
98 C2 Khe Bo Vietnam
91 G1 Khē Bo Vietnam
87 A2 Khed India
88 C4 Khedbrahma India
84 C3 Khedri Iran
88 C4 Khela India
111 H4 Khemis Miliana Alg.
98 C1 Khemmarat Thai.
114 C4 Khenchela Alg.
111 H5 Khenchela Alg.
120 B1 Khenifra Morocco
84 C4 Kherāmeh Iran
84 C4 Khersān r. Iran
117 E5 Kherson Ukr.
77 K2 Kheta r. Rus. Fed.
84 C4 Kheyrābād Iran
85 F4 Kheyrābād Iran
84 C2 Khezerābād Iran
88 D4 Khilchipur India
90 C1 Khilok Rus. Fed.
90 D1 Khilok r. Rus. Fed.
117 G6 Khlevnoye Rus. Fed.
117 C5 Khmel'nyts'kyy Ukr.
117 C5 Khmil'nyk Ukr.
98 C3 Khoai, Hon i. Vietnam
82 C2 Khobda Kazakh.

84 B2 Khodā Āfarīn Iran
82 F5 Khodzhambaz Turkm.
82 D4 Khodzheyli Uzbek.
124 D2 Khokhowe Pan salt pan Botswana
88 B4 Khokhropar Pak.
116 G1 Kholmogory Rus. Fed.
90 G2 Kholmsk Rus. Fed.
113 P3 Kholm-Zhirkovskiy Rus. Fed.
81 L3 Khoman Iran
124 B1 Khomas admin. reg. Namibia
124 A1 Khomas Highland reg. Namibia
84 C3 Khomeyn Iran
84 C3 Khomeynishahr Iran
81 L4 Khondāb Iran
117 G7 Khoni Georgia
84 D5 Khonj Iran
98 B1 Khon Kaen Thai.
77 P3 Khonuu Rus. Fed.
117 G5 Khoper r. Rus. Fed.
90 F2 Khor Rus. Fed.
90 F2 Khor r. Rus. Fed.
88 B4 Khora Pak.
89 F5 Khordha India
90 C1 Khorinsk Rus. Fed.
123 B6 Khorixas Namibia
94 C2 Khorol Rus. Fed.
117 E5 Khorol Ukr.
81 K2 Khoroslū Dāgh hills Iran
84 C3 Khorramābād Iran
81 L3 Khorram Darreh Iran
84 C4 Khorramshahr Iran
83 G5 Khorugh Tajik.
85 E3 Khosf Iran
117 H6 Khosheutovo Rus. Fed.
84 C4 Khosravi Iran
85 F5 Khosrowābād Iran
81 L4 Khosrowvī Iran
84 D4 Khowrjān Iran
85 H3 Khowrnag, Kūh-e mt. Iran
81 I1 Khozap'ini, Tba l. Georgia
89 H5 Khreum Myanmar
89 G4 Khri r. India
116 H2 Khristoforovo Rus. Fed.
77 P2 Khroma r. Rus. Fed.
82 D2 Khromtau Rus. Fed.
94 D2 Khrustalnyy Rus. Fed.
113 N6 Khrystynivka Ukr.
85 G5 Khude Hills Pak.
124 F1 Khudumelapye Botswana
84 B5 Khuff Saudi Arabia
85 F5 Khūh Lab, Ra's pt Iran
124 D3 Khuis Botswana
83 G4 Khūjand Tajik.
98 C2 Khu Khan Thai.
85 G3 Khulm r. Afgh.
89 G5 Khulna Bangl.
81 I1 Khulo Georgia
125 G3 Khuma S. Africa
88 C2 Khunjerab Pass China/Jammu and Kashmir
84 C3 Khunsar Iran
89 F5 Khunti India
98 A1 Khun Yuam Thai.
85 E3 Khūr Iran
88 D4 Khurai India
84 D5 Khūran sea chan. Iran
85 G3 Khurd, Koh-i- mt. Afgh.
88 D3 Khurja India
85 F3 Khurmalik Afgh.
81 I6 Khūr, Wādī al watercourse Saudi Arabia
88 C2 Khushab Pak.
81 L3 Khūshāvar Iran
85 E4 Khushk Rud Iran
85 F3 Khuspas Afgh.
117 B5 Khust Ukr.
125 G3 Khutsong S. Africa
85 G5 Khuzdar Pak.
85 F3 Khvāf Iran
116 I4 Khvalynsk Rus. Fed.
84 D3 Khvor Iran
84 E3 Khvord Nārvan Iran
84 C4 Khvormūj Iran
82 B1 Khvorostyanka Rus. Fed.
81 K3 Khvosh Maqām Iran
84 D4 Khvoy Iran
116 E3 Khvoynaya Rus. Fed.
98 A2 Khwae Noi r. Thai.
85 F4 Khwaja Ali Afgh.
85 H2 Khwaja Muhammad Range mts Afgh.
88 B2 Khyber Pass Afgh./Pak.
71 I5 Kiama Australia
97 C5 Kiamba Phil.
122 C4 Kiambi Dem. Rep. Congo
143 E5 Kiamichi r. U.S.A.
102 O2 Kiantajärvi r. Fin.
84 D2 Kiāseh Iran
129 L2 Kiatassuaq i. Greenland
97 C5 Kibawe Phil.
122 D4 Kibaya Tanz.
123 D4 Kibiti Tanz.
122 C4 Kibombo Dem. Rep. Congo
122 D4 Kibondo Tanz.
115 I4 Kičevo Macedonia
116 H3 Kichmengskiy Gorodok Rus. Fed.
120 A3 Kidal Mali
105 E5 Kidderminster U.K.
122 D3 Kidepo Valley National Park Uganda
120 A3 Kidira Senegal
88 D2 Kidmang Jammu and Kashmir
72 F3 Kidnappers, Cape N.Z.
105 E4 Kidsgrove U.K.
112 E5 Kiel Germany
134 C4 Kiel U.S.A.
112 D3 Kiel Canal canal Germany
113 J5 Kielce Poland
104 E2 Kielder Water resr U.K.
112 E3 Kieler Bucht b. Germany
123 C5 Kienge Dem. Rep. Congo
108 F3 Kierspe Germany
117 D5 Kiev Ukr.
120 A3 Kiffa Mauritania
115 J5 Kifisia Greece
81 J4 Kifri Iraq
122 D4 Kigali Rwanda
81 H2 Kiği Turkey
133 H2 Kiglapait Mountains Canada
122 C4 Kigoma Tanz.
102 M2 Kihlanki Fin.
102 N2 Kihniö Fin.
83 H3 Kiik Kazakh.
102 N2 Kiiminki Fin.
95 D8 Kii-sanchi mts Japan
95 D8 Kii-suidō sea chan. Japan
115 I2 Kikinda Yugo.
85 F5 Kikki Pak.
116 H3 Kiknur Rus. Fed.
94 D4 Kikonai Japan
123 C5 Kikondja Dem. Rep. Congo
68 E2 Kikori P.N.G.
68 E2 Kikori r. P.N.G.
122 B4 Kikwit Dem. Rep. Congo
103 I3 Kilafors Sweden
87 B4 Kilakkarai India
88 D2 Kilar India
140 D2 Kilauea U.S.A.
140 D2 Kilauea Crater U.S.A.
100 C5 Kilbrannan Sound sea chan. U.K.
96 E1 Kilchu N. Korea
107 E4 Kilcoole Rep. of Ireland
107 E4 Kilcormac Rep. of Ireland
71 J1 Kilcoy Australia
107 E4 Kildare Rep. of Ireland
102 P1 Kil'dinstroy Rus. Fed.
122 B4 Kilembe Dem. Rep. Congo
106 C5 Kilfinane Rep. of Ireland
143 E5 Kilgore U.S.A.
104 E2 Kilham U.K.
122 D4 Kilifi Kenya

122 D4 Kilimanjaro mt. Tanz.
69 F2 Kilinailau Islands P.N.G.
123 D4 Kilindoni Tanz.
103 N3 Kilingi-Nõmme Estonia
80 F3 Kilis Turkey
117 D6 Kiliya Ukr.
107 B5 Kilkee Rep. of Ireland
107 F3 Kilkeel U.K.
107 D5 Kilkenny Rep. of Ireland
105 C7 Kilkhampton U.K.
115 J4 Kilkis Greece
107 B3 Killala Rep. of Ireland
107 B3 Killala Bay Rep. of Ireland
107 C5 Killaloe Rep. of Ireland
135 I3 Killaloe Station Canada
131 G4 Killam Canada
71 J2 Killarney Australia
135 G3 Killarney Canada
107 B5 Killarney Rep. of Ireland
107 B6 Killarney National Park Rep. of Ireland
135 G2 Killarney Provincial Park Canada
107 B4 Killary Harbour b. Rep. of Ireland
143 D6 Killeen U.S.A.
107 D5 Killenaule Rep. of Ireland
107 C4 Killimor Rep. of Ireland
105 D4 Killin U.K.
107 E5 Killinick Rep. of Ireland
133 H1 Killiniq Canada
133 H1 Killiniq Island Canada
107 B5 Killorglin Rep. of Ireland
107 E5 Killurin Rep. of Ireland
107 C5 Killybegs Rep. of Ireland
107 D2 Kilmacrenan Rep. of Ireland
107 C5 Kilmaine Rep. of Ireland
106 B3 Kilmaluag U.K.
106 C4 Kilmarnock U.K.
116 I3 Kil'mez' Rus. Fed.
116 I3 Kil'mez' r. Rus. Fed.
107 C6 Kilmona Rep. of Ireland
71 H4 Kilmore Australia
107 E5 Kilmore Quay Rep. of Ireland
123 C4 Kilosa Tanz.
102 M1 Kilpisjärvi Fin.
102 P1 Kilp"yavr Rus. Fed.
107 I3 Kilrea U.K.
107 B5 Kilrush Rep. of Ireland
106 D5 Kilsyth U.K.
107 C4 Kiltullagh Rep. of Ireland
123 C4 Kilwa Dem. Rep. Congo
123 C4 Kilwa Masoko Tanz.
106 D5 Kilwinning U.K.
123 D4 Kimambi Tanz.
70 B4 Kimba Australia
122 B4 Kimba Dem. Rep. Congo
142 C3 Kimball U.S.A.
68 F2 Kimbe P.N.G.
130 F5 Kimberley Canada
124 F4 Kimberley S. Africa
68 C3 Kimberley Plateau Australia
72 E4 Kimbolton N.Z.
96 E3 Kimch'aek N. Korea
96 E5 Kimch'ŏn S. Korea
103 M3 Kimito Fin.
96 E5 Kimje S. Korea
129 L3 Kimmirut Canada
115 K6 Kimolos i. Greece
116 F4 Kimovsk Rus. Fed.
122 B4 Kimpese Dem. Rep. Congo
116 F3 Kimry Rus. Fed.
122 B4 Kimvula Dem. Rep. Congo
99 E1 Kinabalu, Gunung mt. Sabah Malaysia
97 A5 Kinabatangan r. Sabah Malaysia
115 L6 Kinaros i. Greece
130 F4 Kinbasket Lake Canada
106 E2 Kinbrace U.K.
135 G3 Kincardine Canada
106 E4 Kincardine U.K.
70 E4 Kincaid... Canada
130 D3 Kincolith Canada
123 C4 Kinda Dem. Rep. Congo
89 H5 Kindat Myanmar
143 E6 Kinder U.S.A.
105 F4 Kinder Scout hill U.K.
131 H4 Kindersley Canada
120 A3 Kindia Guinea
122 C4 Kindu Dem. Rep. Congo
82 B1 Kinel' Rus. Fed.
116 G3 Kineshma Rus. Fed.
71 J1 Kingaroy Australia
140 B3 King City U.S.A.
73 C1 King Edward Point research station Antarctica
146 E3 King Ferry U.S.A.
147 H2 Kingfield U.S.A.
143 D5 Kingfisher U.S.A.
73 B1 King George Island Antarctica
132 E2 King George Islands Canada
116 D3 Kingisepp Rus. Fed.
71 F8 King Island Australia
130 D4 King Island Canada
135 H1 King Kirkland Canada
73 D5 King Leopold and Queen Astrid Coast Antarctica
68 C3 King Leopold Ranges hills Australia
141 E4 Kingman AZ U.S.A.
143 D4 Kingman KS U.S.A.
147 I2 Kingman ME U.S.A.
67 I3 Kingman Reef reef N. Pacific Ocean
130 D3 King Mountain Canada
70 A3 Kingoonya Australia
73 A3 King Peninsula Antarctica
107 D5 Kings r. Rep. of Ireland
140 C3 Kings r. U.S.A.
105 D7 Kingsbridge U.K.
140 C3 Kingsburg U.S.A.
147 I2 Kingsbury U.S.A.
140 C3 Kings Canyon National Park U.S.A.
71 J2 Kingscliff Australia
70 B5 Kingscote Australia
107 E4 Kingscourt Rep. of Ireland
73 B2 King Sejong research station Antarctica
134 C3 Kingsford U.S.A.
145 D6 Kingsland GA U.S.A.
134 C5 Kingsland IN U.S.A.
105 H5 King's Lynn U.K.
69 F2 Kingsmill Group is Kiribati
105 H6 Kingsnorth U.K.
68 C3 King Sound b. Australia
138 E3 Kings Peak mt. U.S.A.
145 D5 Kingsport U.S.A.
135 H3 Kingston Canada
146 E3 Kingston Jamaica
146 F3 Kingston N.Z.
146 B2 Kingston U.S.A.
70 B6 Kingston South East Australia
104 G4 Kingston upon Hull U.K.
149 L6 Kingstown St Vincent
145 D5 Kingstree U.S.A.
130 B3 Kingsville Canada
143 D7 Kingsville U.S.A.
104 E4 Kington U.K.
106 D3 Kingussie U.K.
129 I3 King William Island Canada
125 G6 King William's Town S. Africa
143 E6 Kingwood TX U.S.A.
146 C4 Kingwood WV U.S.A.
131 I4 Kinistino Canada
80 C2 Kınık Turkey
122 B4 Kinkala Congo
135 H3 Kinmount Canada

103 K4 Kinna Sweden
107 D4 Kinnegad Rep. of Ireland
87 C4 Kinniyai Sri Lanka
111 N4 Kinnula Fin.
131 I3 Kinoosao Canada
95 F5 Kinpoku-san mt. Japan
106 E4 Kinross U.K.
107 C6 Kinsale Rep. of Ireland
122 B4 Kinshasa Dem. Rep. Congo
142 D4 Kinsley U.S.A.
145 E5 Kinston U.S.A.
81 H3 Kintai Lith.
120 B4 Kintampo Ghana
106 F3 Kintore U.K.
106 C5 Kintyre pen. U.K.
130 F3 Kinuso Canada
121 F4 Kinyeti mt. Sudan
82 D2 Kinzhaly Kazakh.
109 H4 Kinzig r. Germany
109 I2 Kiosk Canada
132 E4 Kipawa, Lac l. Canada
147 F6 Kiptopeke U.S.A.
123 C5 Kipushi Dem. Rep. Congo
113 I3 Kirakira Solomon Is
87 C2 Kirandul India
116 H4 Kirawsk Belarus
109 G2 Kirchdorf Germany
109 G5 Kirchheim-Bolanden Germany
107 I3 Kircubbin U.K.
90 C1 Kirensk Rus. Fed.
83 H4 Kirghiz Range mts Asia
67 H4 Kiribati country Pacific Ocean
81 H1 Kırık Turkey
80 F3 Kırıkhan Turkey
80 D2 Kırıkkale Turkey
116 F3 Kirillov Rus. Fed.
Kirinyaga mt. Kenya see Kenya, Mount
116 I3 Kirishi Rus. Fed.
95 B9 Kirishima-yama vol. Japan
67 I4 Kiritimati i. Kiribati
80 A2 Kırkağaç Turkey
84 B2 Kırk Bulāğ Dāği mt. Iran
105 F4 Kirkby U.K.
104 E3 Kirkby in Ashfield U.K.
104 E3 Kirkby Lonsdale U.K.
104 E3 Kirkby Stephen U.K.
106 E4 Kirkcaldy U.K.
106 C6 Kirkcolm U.K.
106 D6 Kirkcudbright U.K.
103 K3 Kirkenær Norway
102 O1 Kirkenes Norway
104 E3 Kirkham U.K.
107 C4 Kirkintilloch U.K.
103 N3 Kirkkonummi Fin.
141 F4 Kirkland U.S.A.
141 F4 Kirkland Junction U.S.A.
135 G1 Kirkland Lake Canada
117 C7 Kırklareli Turkey
104 E3 Kirk Michael U.K.
104 E3 Kirkoswald U.K.
132 F1 Kirkpatrick, Mount Antarctica
142 E3 Kirksville U.S.A.
81 J4 Kirkuk Iraq
106 F2 Kirkwall U.K.
125 F6 Kirkwood S. Africa
140 B2 Kirkwood CA U.S.A.
142 F4 Kirkwood MO U.S.A.
80 C1 Kırmır r. Turkey
108 F5 Kirn Germany
116 F4 Kirov Kaluzhskaya Oblast' Rus. Fed.
Kirov Kirovskaya Oblast' Rus. Fed.
81 J1 Kirovabad Azer. see Gäncä
116 I3 Kirovo-Chepetsk Rus. Fed.
116 I3 Kirovohrad Ukr.
81 L2 Kirovsk Azer.
116 D3 Kirovsk Leningradskaya Oblast' Rus. Fed.
102 P2 Kirovsk Murmanskaya Oblast' Rus. Fed.
116 I3 Kirovskaya Oblast' admin. div. Rus. Fed.
94 C2 Kirovskiy Rus. Fed.
82 D5 Kirpili Turkm.
106 E4 Kirriemuir U.K.
116 J3 Kirs Rus. Fed.
116 G4 Kirsanov Rus. Fed.
80 E2 Kırşehir Turkey
85 G5 Kirthar Range mts Pak.
109 H4 Kirtorf Germany
102 M2 Kiruna Sweden
122 C4 Kirundu Dem. Rep. Congo
116 H4 Kirya Rus. Fed.
95 F6 Kiryū Japan
103 K4 Kisa Sweden
122 C3 Kisangani Dem. Rep. Congo
122 B4 Kisantu Dem. Rep. Congo
99 A2 Kisaran Indon.
90 A1 Kiselevsk Rus. Fed.
89 F4 Kishanganj India
88 C4 Kishangarh Rajasthan India
88 C4 Kishangarh Rajasthan India
80 E2 Kishen Ganga r. India/Pak.
95 B9 Kishika-zaki pt Japan
95 D7 Kishiwada Japan
Kishinev Moldova see Chişinău
89 H1 Kishkenekol' Kazakh.
89 G4 Kishorganj Bangl.
88 C2 Kishtwar Jammu and Kashmir
120 C4 Kisi Nigeria
122 D4 Kisii Kenya
131 J4 Kiskittogisu Lake Canada
113 I7 Kiskunfélegyháza Hungary
113 I7 Kiskunhalas Hungary
117 G7 Kislovodsk Rus. Fed.
121 I3 Kismaayo Somalia
122 D3 Kisoro Uganda
95 E7 Kiso-sanmyaku mts Japan
120 A4 Kissidougou Guinea
145 D6 Kissimmee U.S.A.
145 D7 Kissimmee, Lake U.S.A.
122 D4 Kisumu Kenya
120 B3 Kita Mali
95 F5 Kitaibaraki Japan
95 C8 Kitakami Japan
94 G5 Kitakami-gawa r. Japan
95 B8 Kita-Kyūshū Japan
122 D3 Kitale Kenya
94 H4 Kitami Japan
143 C4 Kit Carson U.S.A.
135 G2 Kitchener Canada
102 O3 Kitee Fin.
122 D3 Kitgum Uganda
130 D4 Kitimat Canada
102 N2 Kitinen r. Fin.
122 N2 Kitona Dem. Rep. Congo
70 C2 Kittakittaooloo, Lake salt flat Australia
146 F4 Kittanning U.S.A.
147 I4 Kittatinny Mountains U.S.A.
147 H3 Kittery U.S.A.
102 N2 Kittilä Fin.
122 D4 Kitunda Tanz.
123 C5 Kitwe Zambia
109 I7 Kitzbüheler Alpen mts Austria
109 I3 Kitzingen Germany
102 N3 Kivijärvi Fin.
103 N4 Kiviõli Estonia
122 C4 Kivu, Lake Dem. Rep. Congo/Rwanda
83 G2 Kiyakty, Ozero salt l. Kazakh.
80 B1 Kıyıköy Turkey
83 F2 Kiyma Kazakh.

76 G4 Kizel Rus. Fed.
116 H2 Kizema Rus. Fed.
83 J4 Kizil China
80 D3 Kızılca Dağ mt. Turkey
80 D1 Kızılcahamam Turkey
80 D2 Kızıl Dağı mt. Turkey
80 D1 Kızılırmak Turkey
80 D2 Kızılırmak r. Turkey
80 C3 Kızılkaya Turkey
82 D1 Kizil'skoye Rus. Fed.
81 H5 Kiziltepe Turkey
117 H7 Kizil'yurt Rus. Fed.
117 H7 Kizlyar Rus. Fed.
82 F5 Kizylayak Turkm.
102 N1 Kjøllefjord Norway
102 L1 Kjøpsvik Norway
112 G5 Kladno Czech Rep.
109 G7 Klagenfurt Austria
116 C4 Klaipėda Lith.
103 M5 Klaipėda Lith.
102 □ Klaksvík Faroe Is
138 B3 Klamath r. U.S.A.
138 B3 Klamath Falls U.S.A.
138 B3 Klamath Mountains U.S.A.
103 K4 Klarälven r. Sweden
112 F6 Klatovy Czech Rep.
124 C3 Klawer S. Africa
130 C3 Klawock U.S.A.
108 E2 Klazienaveen Neth.
124 D4 Kleena Kleene Canada
124 D4 Kleinbegin S. Africa
124 B4 Klein Karas Namibia
124 D6 Klein Roggeveldberge mts S. Africa
124 C3 Kleinsee S. Africa
125 G5 Klein Swartberg mts S. Africa
130 D4 Klemtu Canada
125 G3 Klerksdorp S. Africa
116 E4 Kletnya Rus. Fed.
117 G5 Kletskaya Rus. Fed.
108 E3 Kleve Germany
124 F6 Klienpoort S. Africa
116 H4 Klimavichy Belarus
116 F4 Klimovo Rus. Fed.
116 F3 Klin Rus. Fed.
130 □ Klinaklini r. Canada
112 G2 Klingenberg am Main Germany
109 K4 Klingenthal Germany
109 K1 Klink Germany
112 F5 Klinovec mt. Czech Rep.
135 H5 Klintehamn Sweden
117 I5 Klintsovka Rus. Fed.
116 E4 Klintsy Rus. Fed.
124 C5 Kliprand S. Africa
83 G1 Klippan Sweden
114 G2 Ključ Bos.-Herz.
112 H5 Kłodzko Poland
108 E2 Kloosterhaar Neth.
116 H6 Klosterneuburg Austria
132 F1 Klotz, Lac l. Canada
109 J2 Klötze (Altmark) Germany
130 A2 Kluane Game Sanctuary Canada
130 B2 Kluane Lake Canada
130 B2 Kluane National Park Canada
112 I5 Kluczbork Poland
88 B4 Klupro Pak.
116 C4 Klyetsk Belarus
77 R4 Klyuchevskaya, Sopka vol. Rus. Fed.
83 I1 Klyuchi Rus. Fed.
104 F3 Knaresborough U.K.
131 K3 Knee Lake Canada
109 I5 Knetzgau Germany
134 D4 Knife Lake Canada/U.S.A.
130 D4 Knight Inlet inlet Canada
134 E6 Knighton U.K.
134 E6 Knightstown U.S.A.
112 G7 Knittelfeld Austria
115 J3 Knjaževac Yugo.
107 C5 Knock Rep. of Ireland
107 B6 Knockaboy hill Rep. of Ireland
107 B5 Knockacummer hill Rep. of Ireland
107 C7 Knockalongy hill Rep. of Ireland
107 B5 Knockalough Rep. of Ireland
106 C4 Knock Hill U.K.
107 E2 Knocklayd hill U.K.
108 B3 Knokke-Heist Belgium
109 L1 Knorrendorf Germany
73 B2 Knowles, Cape Antarctica
147 I1 Knowles Corner U.S.A.
147 G2 Knowlton Canada
134 D5 Knox U.S.A.
73 C6 Knox Coast Antarctica
134 A5 Knoxville CA U.S.A.
145 D5 Knoxville IL U.S.A.
145 D4 Knoxville TN U.S.A.
106 C4 Knoydart reg. U.K.
129 M1 Knud Rasmussen Land reg. Greenland
124 F7 Knysna S. Africa
95 B9 Kobayashi Japan
102 O1 Kobbfoss Norway
95 D7 Kōbe Japan
København Denmark see Copenhagen
120 B3 Kobenni Mauritania
108 F4 Koblenz Germany
116 I3 Kobra Rus. Fed.
91 F7 Kobroör i. Indon.
116 C4 Kobryn Belarus
81 I1 K'obulet'i Georgia
115 I4 Kočani Macedonia
95 E6 Kočevje Slovenia
89 G4 Koch Bihar India
109 H3 Kocher r. Germany
Kochi India see Cochin
95 D7 Kōchi Japan
117 G6 Kochkor Kyrg.
116 H4 Kochkurovo Rus. Fed.
117 G6 Kochubey Rus. Fed.
117 G6 Kochubeyevskoye Rus. Fed.
87 B4 Kodaikanal India
87 B4 Kodala India
124 D6 Koedoesberg mts S. Africa
95 F7 Kōfu Japan
131 K4 Kogaluc r. Canada
132 F2 Kogaluc, Baie de b. Canada
133 H2 Kogaluk r. Canada
71 I1 Kogan Australia
103 K5 Køge Denmark
85 G4 Kohan Tanz.
88 B2 Kohat Pak.
103 N4 Kohila Estonia
89 H4 Kohima India
85 H3 Kohsan Afgh.
103 N4 Kohtla-Järve Estonia
72 E2 Kohukohunui hill N.Z.

96 D6 Kohŭng S. Korea
95 F6 Koide Japan
130 A2 Koidern Canada
87 C3 Koikuntla India
96 D3 Koin N. Korea
81 J3 Koi Sanjaq Iraq
96 E6 Kŏje-do i. S. Korea
94 F4 Ko-jima i. Japan
95 F8 Ko-jima i. Japan
98 A4 Kok, Nam Mae r. Thai.
147 I2 Kokadjo U.S.A.
82 F2 Kokalat Kazakh.
83 J4 Kokand Uzbek.
103 M4 Kökar i. Fin.
82 E3 Kokaral Kazakh.
83 H4 Kök-Art Kyrg.
83 H4 Kök-Aygyr Kyrg.
85 H2 Kokcha r. Afgh.
103 M3 Kokemäenjoki r. Fin.
123 N3 Kokerboom Namibia
113 N3 Kokhanava Belarus
116 G3 Kokhma Rus. Fed.
83 H4 Kök-Janggak Kyrg.
87 C4 Kokkilai Sri Lanka
102 M3 Kokkola Fin.
140 □¹ Koko Head U.S.A.
134 D5 Kokomo U.S.A.
124 E2 Kokong Botswana
125 G3 Kokosi S. Africa
83 J2 Kokpekti Kazakh.
96 D4 Koksan N. Korea
83 G4 Koksaray Kazakh.
116 H3 Koksharka Rus. Fed.
83 G1 Kökshetau Kazakh.
83 G1 Kökshetauskaya Oblast' admin. div. Kazakh.
133 G2 Koksoak r. Canada
125 H5 Kokstad S. Africa
83 E3 Koksu Almatinskaya Oblast' Kazakh.
83 G4 Koksu Yuzhnyy Kazakhstan Kazakh.
83 I3 Koktal Kazakh.
83 J2 Koktobe Kazakh.
82 D2 Koktubek Kazakh.
83 J3 Koktuma Kazakh.
83 I5 Kokyar China
83 J2 Kokzhayyk Kazakh.
102 P1 Kola Rus. Fed.
76 E3 Kola Peninsula Rus. Fed.
87 B3 Kolar Karnataka India
88 D4 Kolar Madhya Pradesh India
88 D4 Kolaras India
87 B3 Kolar Gold Fields India
102 M2 Kolari Fin.
87 B3 Kolayat India
116 F3 Kol'chugino Rus. Fed.
120 A3 Kolda Senegal
103 J5 Kolding Denmark
122 C4 Kole Dem. Rep. Congo
122 C4 Kole Dem. Rep. Congo
111 I4 Koléa Alg.
102 M2 Koler Sweden
76 F3 Kolguyev, Ostrov i. Rus. Fed.
87 A2 Kolhapur India
103 M4 Kõljala Estonia
89 G5 Kolkata India
87 B4 Kolkhozobod Tajik.
Kollam India see Quilon
108 E1 Kollum Neth.
Köln Germany see Cologne
112 I5 Kołobrzeg Poland
116 H3 Kologriv Rus. Fed.
120 B3 Kolokani Mali
69 F2 Kolombangara i. Solomon Is
116 F4 Kolomna Rus. Fed.
117 C5 Kolomyya Ukr.
120 B4 Kolondiéba Mali
124 D3 Kolonkwaneng Botswana
82 B2 Kolovertnoye Kazakh.
116 F3 Kolp' r. Rus. Fed.
Kol'skiy Poluostrov pen. Rus. Fed. see Kola Peninsula
82 B1 Koltubanovskiy Rus. Fed.
86 B7 Koluli Eritrea
83 G2 Koluton Kazakh.
87 A2 Kolvan India
102 K4 Kolvereid Norway
102 N1 Kolvik Norway
85 G5 Kolwa reg. Pak.
123 C5 Kolwezi Dem. Rep. Congo
77 Q3 Kolyma r. Rus. Fed.
77 Q3 Kolymskaya Nizmennost' lowland Rus. Fed.
77 Q3 Kolymskiy, Khrebet mts Rus. Fed.
94 D4 Komaga-take vol. Japan
124 B4 Komaggas S. Africa
124 B4 Komaggas Mountains S. Africa
77 R4 Komandorskiye Ostrova is Rus. Fed.
112 I7 Komárno Slovakia
125 J3 Komatipoort S. Africa
95 F6 Komatsu Japan
95 E6 Komatsushima Japan
122 C4 Kombe Dem. Rep. Congo
120 B3 Kombissiri Burkina
99 B3 Komering r. Indon.
125 G5 Komga S. Africa
116 I2 Komi, Respublika aut. rep. Rus. Fed.
117 D6 Kominternivs'ke Ukr.
114 G2 Komiža Croatia
113 H7 Komló Hungary
122 B4 Komono Congo
95 F6 Komoro Japan
115 K4 Komotini Greece
124 D6 Komsberg mts S. Africa
77 K1 Komsomolets, Ostrov i. Rus. Fed.
82 C3 Komsomolets, Zaliv b. Kazakh.
116 H3 Komsomol'sk Rus. Fed.
117 D6 Komsomol's'k Ukr.
82 E2 Komsomol'skiy Turkm.
82 E5 Komsomol'skiy Turkm.
116 H4 Komsomol'skiy Rus. Fed.
116 H2 Komsomol'skiy Rus. Fed.
90 F1 Komsomol'sk-na-Amure Rus. Fed.
82 D4 Komsomol'sk-na-Ustyurte Uzbek.
82 B1 Komsomol'skoye Kazakh.

96 D6 Kohŭng S. Korea — see column above
129 O3 Kong Christian IX Land reg. Greenland
129 N3 Kong Frederik VI Kyst reg. Greenland
96 D5 Kongju S. Korea
76 D2 Kong Karls Land is Svalbard
99 E2 Kongkemul mt. Indon.
122 C4 Kongolo Dem. Rep. Congo
129 P2 Kong Oscars Fjord inlet Greenland
120 B3 Kongoussi Burkina
103 J4 Kongsberg Norway
103 K3 Kongsvinger Norway
83 H5 Kongur Shan mt. China
122 D4 Kongwa Tanz.
129 P2 Kong Wilhelm Land reg. Greenland
83 G4 Konibodom Tajik.
109 J4 Königsee Germany
112 I4 Königswinter Germany
103 I4 Konin Poland
115 G3 Konjic Bos.-Herz.
124 B3 Konkiep watercourse Namibia
120 B3 Konna Mali
109 J3 Könnern Germany
102 N3 Konnevesi Fin.
116 G2 Konosha Rus. Fed.
117 E5 Konotop Ukr.
98 D2 Kon Plong Vietnam
109 K5 Konstantinovy Lázně Czech Rep.
112 D7 Konstanz Germany
120 C3 Kontagora Nigeria
102 O3 Kontiolahti Fin.
102 N2 Konttila Fin.
98 D2 Kon Tum Vietnam
98 D2 Kon Tum, Plateau du Vietnam
80 D3 Konya Turkey
83 H3 Konyrat Kazakh.
82 C3 Konystanu Kazakh.
108 E5 Konz Germany
140 □¹ Koolau Range mts U.S.A.
70 F5 Koondrook Australia
146 D5 Koon Lake U.S.A.
71 H5 Koorawatha Australia
138 C2 Kooskia U.S.A.
130 F5 Kootenay r. Canada/U.S.A.
130 F5 Kootenay Lake Canada
130 F4 Kootenay Nat. Park Canada
124 D5 Kootjieskolk S. Africa
83 I3 Kopa Kazakh.
88 D6 Kopargaon India
102 C1 Kópasker Iceland
83 I3 Kopbirlik Kazakh.
114 G2 Koper Slovenia
82 E2 Kopet Dag mts Turkm.
103 L4 Köping Sweden
87 B3 Koppal India
103 K4 Koppang Norway
103 K4 Kopparberg Sweden
102 M2 Köpmanholmen Sweden
125 F2 Kopong Botswana
125 H3 Koppies S. Africa
124 D3 Koppieskraal Pan salt pan S. Africa
114 G1 Koprivnica Croatia
80 C3 Köprü r. Turkey
83 G4 Konibodom Tajik.
87 B2 Korangal Pak.
85 G5 Korak, Baie b. Canada
87 B2 Koraput India
87 C2 Koratla India
89 E5 Korba India
108 G3 Korbach Germany
104 D6 Korbu, Gunung mt. Malaysia
115 I4 Korçë Albania
83 J1 Korchino Rus. Fed.
114 G2 Korčula Croatia
114 G2 Korčula i. Croatia
114 G3 Korčulanski Kanal sea chan. Croatia
83 H4 Korday Kazakh.
81 L4 Kord Khvord Iran
84 D2 Kord Kūy Iran
85 F5 Kords reg. Iran
87 B2 Koregaon India
117 F6 Korenovsk Rus. Fed.
117 C5 Korets' Ukr.
80 B1 Körfez Turkey
73 B3 Korff Ice Rise Antarctica
83 G3 Korgas China
82 F2 Korgasyn Kazakh.
102 K2 Korgen Norway
80 D1 Köroğlu Dağları mts Turkey
80 D1 Köroğlu Tepesi mt. Turkey
122 D4 Korogwe Tanz.
70 F7 Koroit Australia
70 E6 Korong Vale Australia
69 H3 Koronia, Limni l. Greece
69 H3 Koro Sea b. Fiji
117 D5 Korosten' Ukr.
117 D5 Korostyshiv Ukr.
121 E3 Koro Toro Chad
103 N3 Korpilahti Fin.
103 M3 Korpo Fin.
116 I3 Korsakov Rus. Fed.
103 J5 Korser Denmark
117 D5 Korsun'-Shevchenkivs'ky Ukr.
113 J3 Korsze Poland
102 M3 Kortesjärvi Fin.
108 B4 Kortrijk Belgium
115 F6 Korumburra Australia
120 D4 Korup, Parc National de nat. park Cameroon
88 D4 Korwai India
94 F3 Koryakskaya, Sopka vol. Rus. Fed.
77 R3 Koryakskiy Khrebet mts Rus. Fed.
116 H2 Koryazhma Rus. Fed.
96 E4 Koryŏng S. Korea
117 E5 Koryukivka Ukr.
115 L6 Kos i. Greece
82 E2 Kosagal Kazakh.
83 H4 Kosagash Kazakh.
96 C2 Kosan N. Korea
82 E2 Kosay Kazakh.
82 C3 Koschagyl Kazakh.
112 H4 Kościan Poland

M

80	F3	Manbij Syria
105	H4	Manby U.K.
134	E3	Mancelona U.S.A.
105	E4	Manchester U.K.
140	A2	Manchester CA U.S.A.
147	G4	Manchester CT U.S.A.
134	B4	Manchester IA U.S.A.
146	B6	Manchester KY U.S.A.
135	E4	Manchester MI U.S.A.
147	H3	Manchester NH U.S.A.
146	B5	Manchester OH U.S.A.
145	C5	Manchester TN U.S.A.
147	G3	Manchester VT U.S.A.
88	A4	Manchhar Lake Pak.
80	F2	Mancılık Turkey
141	H3	Mancos U.S.A.
141	H3	Mancos r. U.S.A.
85	F5	Mand Pak.
84	D4	Mand, Rūd-e r. Iran
121	D4	Manda, Parc National de nat. park Chad
123	E6	Mandabe Madag.
99	B2	Mandah Indon.
98	⬚	Mandai Sing.
85	F3	Mandal Afgh.
88	C4	Mandal India
103	I4	Mandal Norway
91	G7	Mandala, Puncak mt. Indon.
91	B4	Mandalay Myanmar
90	C2	Mandalgovĭ Mongolia
81	J5	Mandali Iraq
92	D1	Mandalt China
92	D1	Mandalt Sum China
142	C2	Mandan U.S.A.
97	B3	Mandaon Phil.
121	D3	Mandara Mountains Cameroon/Nigeria
114	C4	Mandas Sardinia Italy
122	E3	Mandera Kenya
141	F2	Manderfield U.S.A.
108	E4	Manderscheid Germany
149	I5	Mandeville Jamaica
72	B6	Mandeville N.Z.
88	B4	Mandha India
120	B3	Mandiana Guinea
98	B4	Mandi Angin, Gunung mt. Malaysia
88	C3	Mandi Burewala Pak.
123	D5	Mandié Moz.
123	D5	Mandimba Moz.
125	I4	Mandi S. Africa
89	F5	Mandira Dam India
88	E5	Mandla India
123	E5	Mandritsara Madag.
97	A4	Mandul i. Indon.
68	B5	Mandurah Australia
114	C4	Manduria Italy
88	B5	Mandvi Gujarat India
88	C5	Mandvi Gujarat India
87	B3	Mandya India
87	B2	Maner r. India
114	D2	Manerbio Italy
81	K5	Maneshk Küh mt. Iran
113	L5	Manevychi Ukr.
114	F4	Manfredonia Italy
114	C4	Manfredonia, Golfo di g. Italy
158	D1	Manga Brazil
120	B3	Manga Burkina
122	B4	Mangai Dem. Rep. Congo
67	I5	Mangaia i. Cook Is
73	E3	Mangakino N.Z.
87	C2	Mangalagiri India
89	H4	Mangaldai India
115	M3	Mangalia Romania
87	A3	Mangalore India
87	A2	Mangalvedha India
89	G4	Mangan India
88	A3	Mangapet India
97	C6	Mangarang Indon.
125	G4	Mangaung S. Africa
72	E3	Mangaweka N.Z.
89	G4	Mange Chhu r. Bhutan
107	B6	Mangerton Mountain Rep. of Ireland
99	C3	Manggar Indon.
82	C3	Mangistauskaya Oblast' admin. div. Kazakh.
82	E4	Mangit Uzbek.
90	B3	Mangnai China
123	D5	Mangochi Malawi
91	E7	Mangole i. Indon.
105	E6	Mangotsfield U.K.
88	B5	Mangral India
111	C2	Manguarde Port.
85	G2	Manguchar Pak.
159	G2	Mangueira, Lago l. Brazil
158	E2	Mangueirinha Brazil
121	D2	Mangueni, Plateau du Niger
90	E1	Mangui China
97	C5	Mangupung i. Indon.
82	B3	Mangyshlak, Poluostrov pen. Kazakh.
82	B3	Mangyshlakskiy Zaliv b. Kazakh.
82	B4	Mangystau Kazakh.
142	D4	Manhattan KS U.S.A.
140	D2	Manhattan NV U.S.A.
123	D6	Manhica Moz.
158	D3	Manhoca Moz.
158	D3	Manhuaçu Brazil
158	E2	Manhuaçu r. Brazil
157	B3	Mani Col.
123	E6	Mania r. Madag.
114	F1	Maniago Italy
154	F5	Manicoré Brazil
133	G3	Manicouagan Canada
133	G3	Manicouagan r. Canada
133	G3	Manicouagan, Réservoir resr Canada
84	C5	Manifah Saudi Arabia
67	I4	Manihiki atoll Cook Is
		Manikgarh India see Rajura
88	B4	Manikpur India
97	B3	Manila Phil. (City Plan 50)
138	E3	Manila U.S.A.
71	H4	Manildra Australia
71	I3	Manilla Australia
89	H4	Manipur state India
115	L5	Manisa Turkey
134	E3	Manistee U.S.A.
134	E3	Manistee r. U.S.A.
134	D3	Manistique U.S.A.
134	D3	Manistique Lake U.S.A.
131	J4	Manitoba prov. Canada
131	J5	Manitou Canada
135	G2	Manitou, Lake U.S.A.
146	C6	Manitou Beach U.S.A.
132	C4	Manitou Falls Canada
134	C2	Manitou Island U.S.A.
144	D4	Manitou Islands U.S.A.
135	F3	Manitoulin Island Canada
135	G3	Manitowaning Canada
134	E1	Manitowik Lake Canada
134	D3	Manitowoc U.S.A.
135	J2	Maniwaki Canada
157	B3	Manizales Col.
123	E6	Manja Madag.
125	J2	Manjacaze Moz.
87	B4	Manjeri India
96	D3	Man Jiang r. China
81	L3	Manjil Iran
68	B5	Manjimup Australia
142	E2	Mankato U.S.A.
125	I3	Mankayane Swaziland
120	B4	Mankono Côte d'Ivoire
87	H4	Mankulam Sri Lanka
71	H4	Manly Australia
88	C5	Manmad India
93	D3	Manna Indon.
70	C4	Mannahill Australia
87	B4	Mannar Sri Lanka

87	B4	Mannar, Gulf of India/Sri Lanka
87	B3	Manneru r. India
109	G5	Mannheim Germany
107	A4	Mannin Bay Rep. of Ireland
130	F3	Manning Canada
145	D5	Manning U.S.A.
105	I6	Manningtree U.K.
114	C4	Mannu, Capo pt Sardinia Italy
70	C5	Mannum Australia
91	F7	Manokwari Indon.
122	C4	Manono Dem. Rep. Congo
98	A3	Manoron Myanmar
110	G5	Manosque France
129	K4	Manouane, Lac l. Canada
96	D3	Manp'o N. Korea
69	I2	Manra r. Kiribati
111	G2	Manresa Spain
88	C3	Mansa India
123	C5	Mansa Zambia
120	A3	Mansa Konko Gambia
88	C2	Mansehra Pak.
129	K3	Mansel Island Canada
71	G6	Mansfield Australia
105	F4	Mansfield U.K.
145	E5	Mansfield LA U.S.A.
146	B4	Mansfield OH U.S.A.
146	E3	Mansfield PA U.S.A.
130	E3	Manson Creek Canada
81	L6	Mansūrī Iran
80	E3	Mansuroğlu Turkey
154	B4	Manta Ecuador
154	B4	Manta, Bahía de b. Ecuador
97	A4	Mantalingajan, Mount Phil.
140	B3	Manteca U.S.A.
157	D3	Manteo Venez.
109	K5	Mantel Germany
145	F5	Manteo U.S.A.
110	E2	Mantes-la-Jolie France
81	B2	Manthani India
141	G2	Manti U.S.A.
158	D3	Mantiqueira, Serra da mts Brazil
		Mantova Italy see Mantua
134	E3	Manton U.S.A.
103	N3	Mänttä Fin.
103	N3	Mäntsälä Fin.
114	D2	Mantua Italy
116	H3	Manturovo Rus. Fed.
103	N3	Mäntyharju Fin.
103	N2	Mäntyjärvi Fin.
154	D6	Manu, Parque Nacional nat. park Peru
161	I7	Manuae atoll Fr. Polynesia
67	H4	Manua Islands American Samoa
141	H4	Manuelito U.S.A.
159	F2	Manuel J. Cobo Arg.
158	E1	Manuel Vitorino Brazil
155	H5	Manuelzinho Brazil
91	E7	Manui i. Indon.
85	E5	Manūjān Iran
97	B4	Manukan Phil.
72	E2	Manukau N.Z.
72	E2	Manukau Harbour N.Z.
97	A5	Manuk Manka i. Phil.
70	C4	Manunda watercourse Australia
68	E2	Manus Island P.N.G.
87	B3	Manvi India
125	F2	Manyana Botswana
117	G6	Manych-Gudilo, Ozero l. Rus. Fed.
141	H3	Many Farms U.S.A.
122	D4	Manyoni Tanz.
80	D6	Manzala, Lake l. Egypt
111	E3	Manzanares Spain
149	I4	Manzanillo Cuba
150	C4	Manzanillo Mex.
150	J6	Manzanillo, Punta pt Panama
84	C3	Manzariyeh Iran
90	D2	Manzhouli China
121	D3	Mao Chad
92	D4	Maocifan China
92	D4	Maojiachuan China
91	F7	Maoke, Pegunungan mts Indon.
125	G5	Maokeng S. Africa
96	B2	Maokui Shan hill China
92	B2	Maomao Shan mt. China
93	D6	Maoming China
		Ma On Shan hill Hong Kong China
123	D6	Mapai Moz.
88	E3	Mapam Yumco l. China
88	C2	Mapang India
125	F5	Maphodi S. Africa
150	C2	Mapimí Mex.
151	D2	Mapimí, Bolsón de des. Mex.
97	A5	Mapin i. Phil.
123	D6	Mapinhane Moz.
157	D3	Mapire Venez.
154	E4	Maple r. U.S.A.
131	H5	Maple Creek Canada
160	G4	Mapmakers Seamounts sea feature N. Pacific Ocean
155	G4	Mapuera r. Brazil
123	J2	Mapulanguene Moz.
123	D6	Maputo Moz.
125	J3	Maputo prov. Moz.
125	J3	Maputo r. Moz.
125	G4	Maputsoe Lesotho
81	H6	Maqar an Na'am well Iraq
92	B3	Maqu China
89	E3	Maquan He r. China
122	B4	Maquela do Zombo Angola
159	C6	Maquinchao Arg.
159	C6	Maquinchao r. Arg.
134	B4	Maquoketa r. U.S.A.
85	G4	Mar r. Pak.
158	D3	Mar, Serra do mts Brazil
131	H1	Mara r. Canada
89	H4	Mara India
125	I3	Mara S. Africa
154	E4	Maraã Brazil
155	I5	Maraba Brazil
153	H3	Marabá r. India
157	C2	Maracaibo Venez.
157	C2	Maracaibo, Lake l. Venez.
135	G3	Markdale Canada
158	A3	Maracaju Brazil
158	A3	Maracajú, Serra de hills Brazil
158	E1	Maracás, Chapada de reg. Brazil
157	D2	Maracay Venez.
121	D2	Marādah Libya
120	C3	Maradi Niger
84	B2	Marāgheh Iran
158	E1	Maragogipe Brazil
157	B3	Maragondon Phil.
155	I4	Marajó, Baía de est. Brazil
155	H4	Marajó, Ilha de i. Brazil
85	G4	Mar r. Pak.
158	D3	Mar, Serra do mts Brazil
84	B3	Marãn Iran
116	I3	Mariņš Rus. Fed.

145	D7	Marathon FL U.S.A.
143	C6	Marathon TX U.S.A.
158	E1	Maraú Brazil
99	D3	Marau Indon.
157	D4	Marawá r. Brazil
97	C4	Marawi Phil.
81	L1	Märäzä Azer.
97	B4	Marbella Spain
68	B4	Marble Bar Australia
141	G3	Marble Canyon U.S.A.
141	G3	Marble Canyon gorge U.S.A.
125	H2	Marble Hall S. Africa
147	H3	Marblehead U.S.A.
131	K2	Marble Island Canada
125	I5	Marburg S. Africa
146	E5	Marburg, Lake U.S.A.
109	G4	Marburg an der Lahn Germany
112	H7	Marcali Hungary
105	H5	March U.K.
70	C4	Marchant Hill Australia
108	D4	Marche-en-Famenne Belgium
111	D4	Marchena Spain
154	⬚	Marchena, Isla i. Galapagos Is Ecuador
159	D1	Mar Chiquita, Lago l. Arg.
112	G6	Marchtrenk Austria
145	D7	Marco U.S.A.
108	B4	Marcoing France
132	E2	Marcopeet Islands Canada
159	D2	Marcos Juárez Arg.
147	G2	Marcy, Mount U.S.A.
88	C2	Mardan Pak.
159	F3	Mar del Plata Arg.
81	H3	Mardin Turkey
69	G4	Maré i. New Caledonia
106	C3	Maree, Loch l. U.K.
134	A5	Marengo IA U.S.A.
134	A5	Marengo IL U.S.A.
114	E6	Marettimo, Isola i. Sicily Italy
116	H3	Marevo Rus. Fed.
143	B6	Marfa U.S.A.
70	B2	Margaret watercourse Australia
68	B5	Margaret River Australia
157	E2	Margarita, Isla de i. Venez.
94	D3	Margaritovo Rus. Fed.
71	G9	Margate Australia
125	I5	Margate S. Africa
105	I6	Margate U.K.
83	G4	Margilan Uzbek.
85	F4	Margo, Dasht-i des. Afgh.
108	D5	Margraten Neth.
114	E5	Margherita Canada
73	B2	Marguerite Bay Antarctica
89	G3	Margyang China
81	K5	Marhaj Khalil Iraq
81	I3	Marhan Dāgh hill Iraq
117	E6	Marhanets' Ukr.
161	I7	Maria atoll Fr. Polynesia
156	C2	María Elena Chile
71	H9	Maria Island Australia
159	E3	Maria Ignacia Arg.
68	D3	Maria Island Australia
160	E4	Mariana Ridge sea feature N. Pacific Ocean
160	E5	Mariana Trench sea feature N. Pacific Ocean
89	H4	Mariani India
130	F2	Marian Lake Canada
145	C6	Marianna U.S.A.
112	F6	Mariánské Lázně Czech Rep.
150	D3	Marías, Islas is Mex.
150	I7	Mariato, Punta pt Panama
72	D1	Maria van Diemen, Cape N.Z.
114	F1	Maribor Slovenia
141	F5	Maricopa AZ U.S.A.
140	C4	Maricopa CA U.S.A.
141	F5	Maricopa Mountains U.S.A.
121	F3	Maridi watercourse Sudan
73	A4	Marie Byrd Land reg. Antarctica
149	L5	Marie-Galante i. Guadeloupe
103	L3	Mariehamn Fin.
158	B1	Mariembero r. Brazil
109	K4	Marienberg Germany
108	F1	Marienberg Neth.
123	B6	Mariental Namibia
103	K4	Mariestad Sweden
146	C5	Marietta GA U.S.A.
146	C5	Marietta OH U.S.A.
110	G5	Marignane France
90	G1	Marii, Mys pt Rus. Fed.
90	A1	Mariinsk Rus. Fed.
103	M5	Marijampolė Lith.
158	C3	Marília Brazil
151	D2	Marín Mex.
111	B1	Marín Spain
114	G5	Marina di Gioiosa Ionica Italy
113	N4	Mar"ina Horka Belarus
97	B3	Marinduque i. Phil.
134	D3	Marinette U.S.A.
158	B3	Maringá Brazil
111	B3	Marinha Grande Port.
134	B5	Marion IL U.S.A.
146	B4	Marion IN U.S.A.
145	D5	Marion SC U.S.A.
146	C4	Marion VA U.S.A.
68	D4	Marion Bay Australia
157	D3	Maripa Venez.
157	G3	Maripasoula Fr. Guiana
156	D2	Mariscal Estigarribia Para.
110	H4	Maritime Alps mts France/Italy
115	K3	Maritsa r. Bulg.
117	F6	Mariupol' Ukr.
157	E3	Mariusa, Caño r. Venez.
84	B3	Mariván Iran
116	I3	Mariy El, Respublika aut. rep. Rus. Fed.

80	B3	Marmaris Turkey
142	C2	Marmarth U.S.A.
146	C5	Marmet U.S.A.
132	B4	Marmion Lake Canada
114	D1	Marmolada mt. Italy
84	E6	Maqran, Khalīj b. Oman
84	C4	Masirah i. Oman
81	J1	Masis Armenia
84	C4	Masjed Soleymān Iran
107	A4	Mask, Lough l. Rep. of Ireland
80	G3	Maskanah Syria
85	G4	Maslti Pak.
123	F5	Masoala, Tanjona c. Madag.
134	E2	Mason MI U.S.A.
140	C2	Mason NV U.S.A.
143	D6	Mason TX U.S.A.
72	A7	Mason Bay N.Z.
142	E3	Mason City IA U.S.A.
134	C5	Mason City IL U.S.A.
84	D4	Masqaţ Oman see Muscat
114	D2	Massa Italy
147	G3	Massachusetts state U.S.A.
147	H3	Massachusetts Bay U.S.A.
114	D2	Massafra Italy
121	D3	Massakory Chad
114	D2	Massa Marittimo Italy
123	D6	Massangena Moz.
123	B4	Massango Angola
122	E2	Massawa Eritrea
147	F2	Massena U.S.A.
130	C4	Masset Canada
135	F2	Massey Canada
110	F4	Massif Central mts France
146	C4	Massillon U.S.A.
120	B3	Massina Mali
123	D6	Massinga Moz.
123	D6	Massingir Moz.
125	J*	Massintonto r. Moz./S. Africa
135	J3	Masson Canada
73	D5	Masson Island Antarctica
81	L1	Maştağa Azer.
83	G5	Mastchoh Tajik.
74	G4	Masterton N.Z.
108	C2	Mastdiep sea chan. Neth.
134	C5	Marseilles U.S.A.
88	C1	Mastuj Pak.
85	G4	Mastung Pak.
116	C4	Masty Belarus
95	H7	Masuda Japan
89	L3	Masuleh Iran
123	D6	Masvingo Zimbabwe
80	F3	Maşyāf Syria
135	G2	Matachewan Canada
150	C1	Matachic Mex.
157	D1	Matacuni r. Venez.
122	E4	Matadi Dem. Rep. Congo
150	H5	Matagalpa Nicaragua
132	E4	Matagami Canada
132	E4	Matagami, Lac l. Canada
143	D6	Matagorda Island U.S.A.
147	H1	Matane Canada
72	C5	Matakana Island N.Z.
123	B5	Matala Angola
87	C5	Matale Sri Lanka
120	A3	Matam Senegal
96	I1	Mayi He r. China
83	J4	Mayakum Kazakh.
95	C7	Matsue Japan
95	E6	Matsumoto Japan
95	E6	Matsusaka Japan
93	F5	Matsu Tao i. Taiwan
95	C8	Matsuyama Japan
135	H2	Mattagami r. Canada
147	I2	Mattawamkeag U.S.A.
112	C7	Matterhorn mt. Italy/Switz.
138	D3	Matterhorn mt. U.S.A.
149	K5	Matthew Town Bahamas
84	D6	Matti, Sabkhat salt pan Saudi Arabia
144	C4	Mattoon U.S.A.
87	C5	Matugama Sri Lanka
69	H3	Matuku i. Fiji
157	E2	Maturín Venez.
97	B3	Matutuang i. Indon.
125	G3	Matwabeng S. Africa
134	C2	Mau Aimma India
108	B4	Maubeuge France
110	E5	Mauborguet France
106	D5	Mauchline U.K.
160	J10	Maud Seamount sea feature S. Atlantic Ocean
155	G4	Maués Brazil
147	F4	Mauganj India
140	⬚²	Maui i. U.S.A.
159	B4	Maulbronn Germany
159	C6	Maule admin. reg. Chile
159	B5	Maule r. Chile
159	B4	Maullín Chile
146	B5	Maumee U.S.A.
146	B4	Maumee r. U.S.A.
107	B4	Maumturk Mountains Rep. of Ireland
123	C5	Maun Botswana
140	⬚²	Mauna Kea vol. U.S.A.

140	⬚²	Mauna Loa vol. U.S.A.
140	⬚¹	Maunalua Bay U.S.A.
89	K4	Maunath Bhanjan India
125	F2	Maunatlala Botswana
122	E2	Maunaturoto N.Z.
89	H5	Maungdaw Myanmar
98	A2	Maungmagan Islands Myanmar
128	F3	Maunoir, Lac l. Canada
70	B5	Maupertuis Bay Australia
68	D4	Maurice, Lake salt flat Australia
108	D3	Maurik Neth.
120	A3	Mauritania country Africa
123	□	Mauritius country Indian Ocean
134	B4	Mauston U.S.A.
157	D4	Mavaca r. Venez.
123	C5	Mavinga Angola
125	G5	Mavuya S. Africa
88	D3	Mawana India
122	B4	Ma Wang Dui China
93	D4	Mawdaung Pass Myanmar/Thai.
72	A7	Mawhai Point N.Z.
73	D5	Mawson research station Antarctica
73	D5	Mawson Coast Antarctica
73	D6	Mawson Escarpment Antarctica
73	B6	Mawson Peninsula Antarctica
98	A3	Maw Taung mt. Myanmar
142	C2	Max U.S.A.
151	G3	Maxcanú Mex.
114	C4	Maxia, Punta mt. Sardinia Italy
134	C5	Maxinkuckee, Lake U.S.A.
102	M3	Maxmo Fin.
135	F2	Maxton U.S.A.
140	A2	Maxwell U.S.A.
106	F4	May, Isle of i. U.K.
99	C3	Maya r. Indon.
90	J4	Maya r. Rus. Fed.
149	K5	Mayagüez Puerto Rico
120	C3	Mayahi Niger
85	H3	Mayakovskiy, Qullai mt. Tajik.
83	G4	Mayakum Kazakh.
122	B4	Mayama Congo
84	D2	Mayamey Iran
150	F5	Maya Mountains Belize
93	C5	Mayang China
92	B3	Mayanhe China
94	F5	Maya-san mt. Japan
106	D5	Maybole U.K.
81	L4	Maydān Sarāy Iraq
85	H3	Maydā Shahr Afgh.
71	G9	Maydena Australia
108	F4	Mayen Germany
110	D2	Mayenne France
110	D2	Mayenne r. France
141	F4	Mayer U.S.A.
130	F4	Mayerthorpe Canada
72	C5	Mayfield N.Z.
144	B4	Mayfield U.S.A.
139	F5	Mayhill U.S.A.
96	E1	Mayi He r. China
83	K2	Maykain Kazakh.
83	I3	Maykamys Kazakh.
83	G5	Maykhura Tajik.
117	G6	Maykop Rus. Fed.
82	E3	Maylybas Kazakh.
83	K1	Mayma Rus. Fed.
83	K2	Maymak Kazakh.
91	A2	Maymyo Myanmar
81	L1	Mayna Rus. Fed.
87	A2	Mayni India
135	I3	Maynooth Canada
130	B2	Mayo Canada
97	C5	Mayo Bay Phil.
122	B4	Mayo Congo
130	B2	Mayo Lake Canada
97	B3	Mayon vol. Phil.
159	D3	Mayor Buratovich Arg.
156	D1	Mayor Pablo Lagerenza Para.
123	E5	Mayotte terr. Africa
90	E1	Mayskiy Rus. Fed.
146	E5	Maysville U.S.A.
122	A4	Mayumba Gabon
93	B5	Mayum La pass China
89	H4	Mayuram India
135	F4	Maysville U.S.A.
142	C2	Mayville ND U.S.A.
134	C4	Mayville WI U.S.A.
142	C3	Maywood U.S.A.
159	D3	Maza Arg.
116	F3	Maza Rus. Fed.
123	C5	Mazabuka Zambia
155	H4	Mazagão Brazil
110	F5	Mazamet France
88	D1	Mazar China
85	G4	Mazar, Koh-i- mt. Afgh.
114	E6	Mazara del Vallo Sicily Italy
85	H2	Mazār-e Sharīf Afgh.
157	F3	Mazaruni r. Guyana
150	D3	Mazatán Mex.
150	F6	Mazatenango Guat.
150	C3	Mazatlán Mex.
141	G4	Mazatzal Peak mt. U.S.A.
84	D4	Mazdaj Iran
103	M4	Mažeikiai Lith.
92	E2	Mazgirt Turkey
103	M4	Mazirbe Latvia
122	D4	Mazomora Tanz.
81	L3	Mazr'eh Iran
81	J5	Māzū Iran
123	C6	Mazunga Zimbabwe
117	D4	Mazyr Belarus
125	I3	Mbabane Swaziland
120	B4	Mbahiakro Côte d'Ivoire
121	B4	Mbaïki Centr. Afr. Rep.
123	C5	Mbala Zambia
122	D3	Mbale Uganda
121	B4	Mbalmayo Cameroon
122	B4	Mbandaka Dem. Rep. Congo
120	A4	M'banza Congo Angola
122	B4	Mbanza-Ngungu Dem. Rep. Congo
122	D4	Mbarara Uganda
122	C3	Mbari r. Centr. Afr. Rep.
123	D4	Mbeya Tanz.
123	D5	Mbinga Tanz.
122	B3	Mbizi Zimbabwe
122	B4	Mbomo Congo
120	A3	Mbour Senegal
120	A3	Mbout Mauritania
122	C4	Mbuji-Mayi Dem. Rep. Congo
122	D4	Mbuyuni Tanz.
143	D5	McAdam Canada
143	D5	McAlester U.S.A.
143	D5	McAllen U.S.A.
68	C3	McArthur r. Australia
135	I3	McArthur Mills Canada
146	C5	McArthur Wildlife Sanctuary Canada
130	E4	McBride Canada
138	C3	McCall U.S.A.
143	C6	McCamey U.S.A.
138	D4	McCammon U.S.A.
130	B2	McCauley Island Canada
132	H2	McClintock Channel Canada
128	F2	McClure Strait Canada
143	E5	McComb U.S.A.
142	C3	McConaughy, Lake U.S.A.
146	E5	McConnellsburg U.S.A.
146	C4	McConnelsville U.S.A.
138	E4	McCook U.S.A.
131	J4	McCreary Canada
141	E4	McCullough Range mts U.S.A.

81 G4 Miyāh, Wādī al watercourse Syria
95 F7 Miyake-jima i. Japan
94 G5 Miyako Japan
95 B9 Miyakonojō Japan
82 C2 Miyaly Kazakh.
88 B5 Miyani India
95 B9 Miyanoura-dake mt. Japan
95 B9 Miyazaki Japan
95 D7 Miyazu Japan
93 B5 Miyi China
95 C7 Miyoshi Japan
92 E1 Miyun China
92 E1 Miyun Shuiku resr China
88 G3 Mīzāni Afgh.
122 D3 Mizan Teferi Eth.
121 D1 Mizdah Libya
107 B6 Mizen Head Rep. of Ireland
117 B5 Mizhhir"ya Ukr.
92 D2 Mizhi China
94 G5 Mizoram state India
95 H5 Mizusawa Japan
103 K4 Mjölby Sweden
122 D4 Mkata Tanz.
122 D4 Mkomazi Tanz.
123 C5 Mkushi Zambia
112 G5 Mladá Boleslav Czech Rep.
115 I2 Mladenovac Yugo.
113 J4 Mława Poland
114 G3 Mljet i. Croatia
125 G5 Mlungisi S. Africa
113 L5 Mlyniv Ukr.
125 F2 Mmabatho S. Africa
125 G1 Mmamabula Botswana
125 F2 Mmathethe Botswana
103 I3 Mo Norway
141 H2 Moab U.S.A.
68 E3 Moa Island Australia
69 H3 Moala i. Fiji
84 D3 Mo'alla Iran
125 J2 Moamba Moz.
70 D2 Moanba, Lake salt flat Australia
141 E3 Moapa U.S.A.
107 D4 Moate Rep. of Ireland
122 C4 Moba Dem. Rep. Congo
95 G7 Mobara Japan
84 C3 Mobārakeh Iran
84 D4 Mobārakeh Iran
122 C3 Mobayi-Mbongo Dem. Rep. Congo
142 E4 Moberly U.S.A.
145 B6 Mobile AL U.S.A.
141 F5 Mobile AL U.S.A.
145 B6 Mobile Bay U.S.A.
142 C2 Mobridge U.S.A.
155 I4 Mocajuba Brazil
123 E5 Moçambique Moz.
157 D2 Mocapra r. Venez.
93 B6 Mộc Châu Vietnam
86 B7 Mocha Yemen
157 D2 Mochirma, Parque Nacional nat. park Venez.
123 C6 Mochudi Botswana
123 E5 Mocimboa da Praia Moz.
109 J2 Möckern Germany
109 H5 Möckmühl Germany
102 M2 Mockträsk Sweden
157 A4 Mocoa Col.
158 C3 Mococa Brazil
150 C2 Mocorito Mex.
150 D3 Moctezuma Mex.
123 D5 Mocuba Moz.
110 H4 Modane France
88 C5 Modasa India
124 F4 Modder r. S. Africa
114 D2 Modena Italy
141 F3 Modena U.S.A.
140 B3 Modesto U.S.A.
71 G7 Moe Australia
105 D5 Moel Sych hill U.K.
103 J3 Moelv Norway
102 L1 Moen Norway
141 G3 Moenkopi U.S.A.
72 C6 Moeraki Point N.Z.
108 E3 Moers Germany
106 E5 Moffat U.K.
85 B4 Moga India
122 E3 Mogadishu Somalia
146 C4 Mogadore Reservoir U.S.A.
125 H1 Mogalakwena r. S. Africa
125 H2 Moganyaka S. Africa
109 K2 Mögelin Germany
83 F5 Moghiyon Tajik.
158 C3 Mogi-Mirim Brazil
90 D1 Mogocha Rus. Fed.
114 C6 Mogod mts Tunisia
125 F2 Mogoditshane Botswana
90 B4 Mogok Myanmar
141 H5 Mogollon U.S.A.
141 H5 Mogollon Plateau U.S.A.
125 G2 Mogwase S. Africa
115 H2 Mohács Hungary
72 F3 Mohaka r. N.Z.
125 H5 Mohale's Hoek Lesotho
131 I5 Mohall U.S.A.
85 E3 Mohammad Iran
111 G5 Mohammadia Alg.
88 E3 Mohan r. India/Nepal
141 E4 Mohave, Lake U.S.A.
141 F5 Mohawk U.S.A.
147 F3 Mohawk r. U.S.A.
141 F5 Mohawk Mountains U.S.A.
Mohéli i. Comoros see Mwali
107 C4 Mohill Rep. of Ireland
109 G3 Möhne r. Germany
141 F4 Mohon Peak mt. U.S.A.
123 D4 Mohoro Tanz.
117 C5 Mohyliv Podil's'kyy Ukr.
103 I4 Moi Norway
125 G1 Moijabana Botswana
125 J2 Moine Moz.
113 M7 Moinești Romania
147 F2 Moira U.S.A.
102 K2 Mo i Rana Norway
89 H4 Moirang India
103 N4 Mõisaküla Estonia
159 E1 Moisés Ville Arg.
133 G3 Moisie Canada
133 G3 Moisie r. Canada
110 E4 Moissac France
140 C4 Mojave U.S.A.
141 E4 Mojave r. U.S.A.
141 E4 Mojave Desert U.S.A.
158 C3 Moji das Cruzes Brazil
158 C3 Moji-Guaçu r. Brazil
125 J2 Mojo Moz.
89 H4 Mokama India
72 E3 Mokau N.Z.
72 E3 Mokau r. N.Z.
140 B2 Mokelumne r. U.S.A.
125 H4 Mokhoabong Pass Lesotho
125 I4 Mokhotlong Lesotho
114 C6 Moknine Tunisia
72 E1 Mokohinau Islands N.Z.
121 D3 Mokolo Cameroon
125 G3 Mokolo r. S. Africa
96 D6 Mokp'o S. Korea
116 H4 Moksha r. Rus. Fed.
140 □1 Mokuaula Islands U.S.A.
140 □1 Mokulua Islands U.S.A.
150 D2 Mokumo Mex.
111 F3 Molaten mt. Spain
Moldavia country Europe see Moldova
102 I3 Molde Norway
102 I3 Moldjord Norway
117 D6 Moldova country Europe
115 K2 Moldoveanu, Vârful mt. Romania
105 D7 Mole r. U.K.
120 B4 Mole National Park Ghana
123 C6 Molepolole Botswana
103 N5 Molėtai Lith.

114 G4 Molfetta Italy
111 F2 Molina de Aragón Spain
134 B5 Moline U.S.A.
103 K4 Molkom Sweden
81 L4 Mollā Bodāgh Iran
89 H4 Mol Len mt. India
109 L1 Möllenbeck Germany
154 D7 Mollendo Peru
109 I1 Mölln Germany
103 K4 Mölnlycke Sweden
116 F3 Molochnoye Rus. Fed.
102 P1 Molochnyy Rus. Fed.
73 D4 Molodezhnaya research station Antarctica
83 G1 Molodogvardeyskoye Kazakh.
116 E3 Molodoy Tud Rus. Fed.
140 □2 Molokai i. U.S.A.
116 I3 Moloma r. Rus. Fed.
71 H4 Molong Australia
124 F2 Molopo watercourse Botswana/S. Africa
121 D4 Moloundou Cameroon
131 J4 Molson Lake Canada
91 E7 Moluccas is Indon.
91 E7 Molucca Sea g. Indon.
123 D5 Moma Moz.
70 E3 Momba Australia
122 D4 Mombasa Kenya
89 H4 Mombi New India
155 K6 Mombuca, Serra da hills Brazil
158 B2 Momchilgrad Bulg.
117 C7 Momchilgrad Bulg.
134 D5 Momence U.S.A.
157 B2 Mompós Col.
103 K5 Møn i. Denmark
141 G2 Mona U.S.A.
149 K5 Mona, Isla i. Puerto Rico
106 A3 Monach, Sound of sea chan. U.K.
106 A3 Monach Islands U.K.
110 H5 Monaco country Europe
163 H4 Monaco Basin sea feature N. Atlantic Ocean
106 D3 Monadhliath Mountains U.K.
107 E3 Monaghan Rep. of Ireland
143 C6 Monahans U.S.A.
149 K5 Mona Passage Dom. Rep./Puerto Rico
123 D5 Monapo Moz.
106 C3 Monar, Loch l. U.K.
130 D4 Monarch Mountain Canada
139 F4 Monarch Pass U.S.A.
130 F4 Monashee Mountains Canada
114 B2 Monastir Tunisia
113 D3 Monastyrshchina Rus. Fed.
117 D5 Monastyryshche Ukr.
94 H2 Monbetsu Japan
94 H3 Monbetsu Japan
114 B2 Moncalieri Italy
102 P2 Monchegorsk Rus. Fed.
109 E3 Mönchengladbach Germany
111 B5 Monchique Port.
145 E5 Moncks Corner U.S.A.
150 D2 Monclova Mex.
133 H4 Moncton Canada
111 C2 Mondego r. Port.
125 I3 Mondlo S. Africa
114 B3 Mondovì Italy
114 E4 Mondragone Italy
115 J6 Monemvasia Greece
94 G1 Moneron, Ostrov i. Rus. Fed.
146 D4 Monessen U.S.A.
135 J1 Monett Canada
107 D5 Moneygall Rep. of Ireland
107 E3 Moneymore U.K.
111 E2 Monforte Spain
122 C3 Monga Dem. Rep. Congo
93 B6 Mông Cai Vietnam
96 C3 Mŏnggŭmp'o-ri N. Korea
90 B2 Mŏng Mau Myanmar
88 D2 Mongolia country Asia
123 C5 Mongu Zambia
147 I3 Monhegan Island U.S.A.
106 E5 Moniaive U.K.
140 D2 Monitor Mountain U.S.A.
140 D2 Monitor Range mts U.S.A.
71 I1 Monkira Australia
107 D5 Monkstown Rep. of Ireland
135 G4 Monkton Canada
89 F3 Mon La pass China
105 E6 Monmouth U.K.
134 B5 Monmouth IL U.S.A.
147 I2 Monmouth ME U.S.A.
130 E4 Monmouth Mountain Canada
120 C3 Mono r. Togo
140 C3 Mono Lake U.S.A.
147 H4 Monomoy Point U.S.A.
70 F6 Monon Australia
134 D5 Monona U.S.A.
114 B4 Monopoli Italy
111 G2 Monreal del Campo Spain
114 E5 Monreale Sicily Italy
145 C5 Monroe LA U.S.A.
135 F5 Monroe MI U.S.A.
145 D5 Monroe NC U.S.A.
147 G4 Monroe NY U.S.A.
141 F2 Monroe UT U.S.A.
134 C4 Monroe WI U.S.A.
134 B6 Monroe City U.S.A.
145 C6 Monroeville U.S.A.
120 A4 Monrovia Liberia
108 B4 Mons Belgium
109 H4 Monschau Germany
114 D2 Monselice Italy
109 F4 Montabaur Germany
124 D6 Montagu S. Africa
73 C7 Montagu Island Atlantic Ocean
114 F5 Montalto mt. Italy
114 G5 Montalto Uffugo Italy
115 J3 Montana Bulg.
138 E2 Montana state U.S.A.
150 H5 Montaña de Yoro nat. park Hond.
110 F3 Montargis France
110 E4 Montauban France
147 H4 Montauk U.S.A.
147 H4 Montauk Point U.S.A.
125 H5 Mont-aux-Sources mt. Lesotho
110 G3 Montbard France
111 G2 Montblanc Spain
110 F3 Montbrison France
110 G3 Montceau-les-Mines France
108 C5 Montcornet France
110 D4 Mont-de-Marsan France
110 F2 Montdidier France
155 H4 Monte Alegre Brazil
158 C1 Monte Alegre de Goiás Brazil
158 D1 Monte Azul Brazil
133 G4 Montebello Canada
114 D1 Montebelluna Italy
159 D6 Monte Buey Arg.
110 H5 Monte-Carlo Monaco
159 F1 Monte Caseros Arg.
125 G1 Monte Christo S. Africa
159 D3 Monte Comán Arg.
114 D3 Monte Cristi Dom. Rep.
114 D2 Montecristo, Isola di i. Italy
140 I5 Montélimar France
156 C2 Monte Lindo r. Para.
114 H4 Montella Italy
111 E2 Montello Spain
151 E2 Montemorelos Mex.
111 B3 Montemor-o-Novo Port.
Montenegro aut. rep. Yugo. see Crna Gora
123 D5 Montepuez Moz.
114 D3 Montepulciano Italy
110 F2 Montereau-faut-Yonne France
140 B3 Monterey CA U.S.A.

146 D5 Monterey VA U.S.A.
140 B3 Monterey Bay U.S.A.
157 B2 Montería Col.
154 F7 Montero Bol.
151 D2 Monterrey Mex.
114 F4 Montesano sulla Marcellana Italy
155 K6 Monte Santo Brazil
158 D1 Montes Claros Brazil
114 F3 Montesilvano Italy
114 D3 Montevarchi Italy
159 F2 Montevideo Uruguay
142 D3 Montevideo U.S.A.
143 F6 Monte Vista U.S.A.
139 F4 Monte Vista U.S.A.
134 A5 Montezuma U.S.A.
141 G4 Montezuma Castle National Monument res. U.S.A.
141 H3 Montezuma Creek U.S.A.
140 D3 Montezuma Peak mt. U.S.A.
108 D3 Montfort Neth.
105 D5 Montgomery U.K.
145 C5 Montgomery U.S.A.
112 C7 Monthey Switz.
143 F5 Monticello AR U.S.A.
145 D6 Monticello FL U.S.A.
134 B4 Monticello IA U.S.A.
134 D5 Monticello IN U.S.A.
147 J1 Monticello ME U.S.A.
134 B5 Monticello MO U.S.A.
143 H5 Monticello UT U.S.A.
134 C4 Monticello WI U.S.A.
159 E1 Montiel, Cuchilla de hills Arg.
110 E4 Montignac France
108 C4 Montignies-le-Tilleul Belgium
108 E5 Montigny-lès-Metz France
150 I7 Montijo, Golfo de Panama
111 D4 Montilla Spain
133 G4 Mont-Joli Canada
133 F4 Mont-Laurier Canada
110 E2 Mont Louis Canada
110 F3 Montluçon France
133 F4 Montmagny Canada
108 D5 Montmédy France
110 D5 Montmirail France
134 D5 Montmorenci U.S.A.
133 F4 Montmorency Canada
110 E3 Montmorillon France
108 B6 Montmort-Lucy France
68 F4 Monto Australia
138 D3 Montpelier ID U.S.A.
134 E5 Montpelier IN U.S.A.
144 A4 Montpelier OH U.S.A.
147 G2 Montpelier VT U.S.A.
110 F5 Montpellier France
132 F2 Montréal r. Ont. Canada (City Plan 62)
135 F2 Montreal r. Ont. Canada
135 F2 Montreal r. Ont. Canada
147 G2 Montréal-Dorval Canada
132 E2 Montreal Island Canada
131 H4 Montreal Lake l. Canada
131 H4 Montreal Lake Canada
147 F2 Montréal-Mirabel Canada
134 C2 Montreal River Canada
112 C7 Montreux Switz.
110 D3 Montrose well S. Africa
106 F4 Montrose U.K.
139 F4 Montrose CO U.S.A.
135 F5 Montrose MI U.S.A.
147 F4 Montrose PA U.S.A.
133 G4 Monts, Pointe des pt Canada
149 L5 Montserrat terr. Caribbean Sea
133 F3 Montviel, Lac l. Canada
141 G3 Monument Valley reg. U.S.A.
90 B4 Monywa Myanmar
114 C2 Monza Italy
123 C5 Monze Zambia
111 G2 Monzón Spain
125 I4 Mooi r. S. Africa
124 B3 Mooifontein Namibia
125 I4 Mooirivier S. Africa
125 G1 Mookane Botswana
70 C3 Moolawatana Australia
71 H2 Moomin Cr. r. Australia
70 A3 Moonaree Australia
71 I3 Moonbi Range mts Australia
71 I1 Moonie r. Australia
71 I1 Moonie r. Australia
70 B5 Moonta Australia
138 F2 Moorcroft U.S.A.
68 B4 Moore, Lake salt flat Australia
146 D5 Moorefield U.S.A.
67 B7 Moores Island Bahamas
147 J2 Moores Mills Canada
105 G5 Moorhead U.K.
146 E5 Moorhead U.S.A.
142 D2 Moorhead U.S.A.
70 E4 Moornanyah Lake Australia
70 B6 Moorook Australia
70 F6 Mooroopna Australia
125 G1 Moorreesburg S. Africa
132 D3 Moose r. Canada
132 D3 Moose Factory Canada
147 I2 Moosehead Lake U.S.A.
131 H4 Moose Jaw Canada
134 A2 Moose Lake U.S.A.
147 H2 Mooselookmeguntic Lake U.S.A.
132 D3 Moose River Canada
131 I4 Moosomin Canada
132 D3 Moosonee Canada
70 E3 Mootwingee Australia
125 H1 Mopane S. Africa
120 B3 Mopti Mali
85 G3 Moqor Afgh.
154 D7 Moquegua Peru
154 C1 Mora Cameroon
111 E3 Mora Spain
103 J3 Mora Sweden
159 B2 Mora, Cerro mt. Arg./Chile
88 A3 Morad r. Pak.
88 D3 Moradabad India
123 E5 Morafenobe Madag.
150 G5 Morales Guat.
87 B2 Moram India
123 E5 Moramanga Madag.
134 D3 Moran MI U.S.A.
138 D2 Moran WY U.S.A.
106 C4 Morar, Loch l. U.K.
87 B5 Moratuwa Sri Lanka
112 H6 Morava r. Austria/Slovakia
84 D2 Moraveh Tappeh Iran
147 J3 Moravia U.S.A.
106 E3 Moray Firth est. U.K.
109 F4 Morbach Germany
88 B5 Morbi India
110 D4 Morcenx France
124 D3 Mordaga China
131 J5 Morden Canada
70 F4 Mordialloc Australia
116 I4 Mordoviya, Respublika aut. rep. Rus. Fed.
117 G5 Mordovo Rus. Fed.
104 B4 More, Loch l. U.K.
105 F1 Moreau r. U.S.A.
104 E3 Morecambe U.K.
104 E3 Morecambe Bay U.K.
71 H2 Moree Australia
68 E2 Morehead P.N.G.
145 E5 Morehead City U.S.A.
150 D4 Morelia Mex.
111 F2 Morella Spain
151 E3 Morelos Mex.
151 E5 Morelos state Mex.
88 D3 Morena India
159 C3 Morena, Sierra mts Spain
141 H5 Morenci AZ U.S.A.
134 E5 Morenci MI U.S.A.
115 M2 Moreni Romania
159 E2 Moreno Arg.
150 B1 Moreno Mex.

140 D5 Moreno Valley U.S.A.
130 C4 Moresby Island Canada
124 F1 Moreswe Pan salt pan Botswana
71 J1 Moreton Bay Australia
67 I5 Moreton Island Australia
105 F6 Moreton-in-Marsh U.K.
108 A5 Moreuil France
80 A5 Morfou Cyprus
80 A5 Morfou Bay Cyprus
70 C5 Morgan Australia
140 C3 Morgan, Mount U.S.A.
143 F6 Morgan City U.S.A.
132 H3 Morgan Hill U.S.A.
147 F4 Morgantown PA U.S.A.
146 D5 Morgantown WV U.S.A.
125 H3 Morgenzon S. Africa
94 G3 Mori Japan
141 I4 Moriah, Mount U.S.A.
139 F6 Moriarty U.S.A.
71 F2 Moriarty's Range Australia
84 D3 Morichal Col.
157 E2 Morichal Largo r. Venez.
96 C2 Morihong Shan hill China
125 I3 Morija Lesotho
109 H3 Moringen Germany
116 D3 Morino Rus. Fed.
94 G5 Morioka Japan
71 I4 Morisset Australia
94 G5 Moriyoshi-zan vol. Japan
102 M2 Morjärv Sweden
85 F4 Morjen r. Pak.
116 I3 Morki Rus. Fed.
110 C2 Morlaix France
104 F4 Morley U.K.
141 G4 Mormon Lake U.S.A.
159 B6 Mornington, Isla i. Chile
163 D9 Mornington Abyssal Plain sea feature S. Atlantic Ocean
68 A4 Mornington Island Australia
88 A4 Moro Pak.
68 E2 Morobe P.N.G.
120 B1 Morocco country Africa
72 C5 Morocco U.S.A.
72 C5 Morocco U.S.A.
84 E3 Morogoro Tanz.
97 B5 Moro Gulf Phil.
124 E3 Morojaneng S. Africa
124 E3 Morokweng S. Africa
150 D4 Moroleón Mex.
123 E6 Morombe Madag.
149 I4 Morón Cuba
90 C2 Mörön Mongolia
123 E6 Morondava Madag.
111 D4 Morón de la Frontera Spain
123 E5 Moroni Comoros
91 E6 Morotai i. Indon.
122 D3 Moroto Uganda
117 G5 Morozovsk Rus. Fed.
135 G5 Morpeth Canada
104 F2 Morpeth U.K.
158 C2 Morrinhos Brazil
135 J5 Morris Canada
134 C2 Morris IL U.S.A.
142 D2 Morris MN U.S.A.
134 D3 Morrison U.S.A.
147 F5 Morristown AZ U.S.A.
147 F4 Morristown NJ U.S.A.
147 F3 Morristown NY U.S.A.
145 D4 Morristown TN U.S.A.
73 C6 Morrisville PA U.S.A.
147 G2 Morrisville VT U.S.A.
156 I3 Morro, Punta pt Chile
140 B4 Morro Bay U.S.A.
157 C2 Morrocoy, Parque Nacional nat. park Venez.
150 D4 Morro de Petatlán pt Mex.
155 H4 Morro Grande hill Brazil
157 B2 Morrosquillo, Golfo de b. Col.
109 H3 Morschen Germany
134 D5 Morse Reservoir U.S.A.
116 D4 Morshanka Rus. Fed.
116 H4 Morskaya Masel'ga Rus. Fed.
114 C7 Morsott Alg.
105 F5 Mortagne-au-Perche France
110 D3 Mortagne-sur-Sèvre France
108 C6 Morteloe U.K.
147 I5 Morteros Arg.
155 H6 Mortes, Rio das r. Brazil
70 F7 Mortlake Australia
67 G2 Mortlock Islands Micronesia
105 C5 Morton U.K.
134 C5 Morton IL U.S.A.
138 B2 Morton WA U.S.A.
71 I5 Morton National Park Australia
71 I5 Morundah Australia
125 G1 Morupule Botswana
71 I5 Moruya Australia
106 C4 Morvern reg. U.K.
71 H7 Morwell Australia
109 F4 Mosbach Germany
105 F4 Mosborough U.K.
116 F4 Moscow Rus. Fed. (City Plan 55)
138 C2 Moscow U.S.A.
73 C2 Moscow Univ. Ice Shelf Antarctica
73 B6 Mosel, Cape Antarctica
108 F4 Mosel r. Germany
108 F5 Moselle r. France
121 D3 Moshaweng watercourse S. Africa
122 D4 Moshi Tanz.
134 C4 Mosinee U.S.A.
102 K2 Mosjøen Norway
103 I5 Moskenesøy i. Norway
Moskovskaya Oblast' aut. rep. Rus. Fed. see Moskovskaya Oblast'
Moskva Rus. Fed. see Moscow
115 H7 Mosonmagyaróvár Hungary
157 C2 Mosquera Col.
158 E1 Mosqueiro Brazil
157 J6 Mosquito r. Brazil
131 I2 Mosquito Lake Canada
126 O Mosquitos, Golfo de los b. Indian Ocean
117 H7 Mozdok Rus. Fed.
85 F3 Mozhnābād Iran
122 H5 Mozo Brazil
122 C3 Mpala Dem. Rep. Congo
123 C5 Mpika Zambia
123 D5 Mporokoso Zambia
123 C5 Mporokoso Zambia
125 H2 Mpumalanga prov. S. Africa
114 G2 Mrkonjić-Grad Bos.-Herz.
114 D1 M'Saken Tunisia
116 F3 Mshinskaya Rus. Fed.
115 I5 M'Sila Alg.
116 D3 Mstinskiy Most Rus. Fed.
116 D3 Mstsislaw Belarus
125 J4 Mtubatuba S. Africa
123 D5 Mtunzini S. Africa
123 D5 Mtwara Tanz.
123 C5 Muanda Dem. Rep. Congo
93 B6 Muang Hiam Laos
98 C1 Muang Hôngsa Laos
98 C1 Muang Kasi Laos
106 E5 Muang Khammouan Laos
98 C1 Muang Khao Laos
93 B6 Muang Khôngxédôn Laos
93 B6 Muang Khoua Laos
98 A2 Muang Kirirath r. Thai.

124 E2 Motokwe Botswana
151 F5 Motozintla Mex.
111 E4 Motril Spain
115 J2 Motru Romania
151 I5 Motul Mex.
67 I5 Motu One i. Fr. Polynesia
93 A5 Mouding China
120 A3 Moudjéria Mauritania
115 K5 Moudros Greece
103 M3 Mouhijärvi Fin.
122 B4 Mouila Gabon
70 F5 Moulamein Australia
70 F5 Moulamein Creek r. Australia
122 B4 Moulèngui Binza Gabon
110 F3 Moulins France
145 D6 Moultrie U.S.A.
145 E5 Moultrie, Lake U.S.A.
144 E5 Mound City U.S.A.
142 E3 Mound City MO U.S.A.
121 D4 Moundou Chad
146 C5 Moundsville U.S.A.
88 C4 Mount Abu India
146 C5 Mountain Brook U.S.A.
141 E3 Mountain City U.S.A.
143 E4 Mountain Grove U.S.A.
143 E4 Mountain Home AR U.S.A.
138 D3 Mountain Home ID U.S.A.
125 F6 Mountain Zebra National Park S. Africa
146 C5 Mount Airy U.S.A.
142 E3 Mount Aspiring National Park N.Z.
125 H5 Mount Ayliff S. Africa
142 E3 Mount Ayr U.S.A.
70 C4 Mount Barker Australia
71 G6 Mount Beauty Australia
107 C4 Mount Bellew Rep. of Ireland
71 G6 Mount Buffalo National Park Australia
147 J1 Mount Carleton Provincial Park Canada
141 F3 Mount Carmel Junction U.S.A.
134 C4 Mount Carroll U.S.A.
72 C5 Mount Cook N.Z.
72 C5 Mount Cook National Park N.Z.
123 D6 Mount Darwin Zimbabwe
147 I2 Mount Desert Island U.S.A.
70 A1 Mount Dutton Australia
70 A2 Mount Eba Australia
71 G9 Mount Field Nat. Park Australia
125 H5 Mount Fletcher S. Africa
135 G4 Mount Forest Canada
70 D6 Mount Frere S. Africa
70 C6 Mount Gambier Australia
68 E2 Mount Hagen P.N.G.
71 H4 Mount Hope N.S.W. Australia
70 A5 Mount Hope S.A. Australia
134 C4 Mount Horeb U.S.A.
68 D4 Mount Isa Australia
147 G4 Mount Kisco U.S.A.
71 F5 Mount Lofty Range mts Australia
135 J2 Mount MacDonald Canada
68 E4 Mount Magnet Australia
70 E4 Mount Manara Australia
140 B1 Mount Meadows Reservoir U.S.A.
107 D4 Mountmellick Rep. of Ireland
125 I5 Mount Moorosi Lesotho
70 E3 Mount Murchison Australia
70 C6 Mount Pleasant IA U.S.A.
134 E4 Mount Pleasant MI U.S.A.
144 C3 Mount Pleasant PA U.S.A.
145 E5 Mount Pleasant SC U.S.A.
143 E5 Mount Pleasant TX U.S.A.
141 F2 Mount Pleasant UT U.S.A.
89 H2 Mugu Karnali r. Nepal
89 H2 Mugxung China
68 E4 Moura Australia
154 F4 Moura Brazil
121 E3 Mourdi, Dépression du depr. Chad
107 D3 Mourne r. U.K.
107 E3 Mourne Mountains U.K.
108 B4 Mouscron Belgium
121 D3 Moussoro Chad
91 E6 Moutong Indon.
126 C2 Mouzon France
84 C4 Moveyleh Iran
71 I1 Mowbullan, Mount Australia
145 E4 Moxey Town Bahamas
107 C4 Moy r. Rep. of Ireland
122 D3 Moyale Eth.
120 A4 Moyamba Sierra Leone
87 B4 Moyar r. India
120 B1 Moyen Atlas mts Morocco
125 I5 Moyeni Lesotho
107 E4 Moyer hill Rep. of Ireland
94 A2 Moyu China
83 I5 Moyynkum Kazakh.
83 J3 Moyynkum Kazakh.
83 G3 Moyynkum, Peski des. Kazakh.
83 G3 Moyynkum, Peski des. Yuzhnyy Kazakhstan Kazakh.
83 H3 Moyynty Kazakh.
123 D6 Mozambique country Africa
125 I3 Mozambique Channel strait Africa
162 G6 Mozambique Ridge sea feature Indian Ocean
117 H7 Mozdok Rus. Fed.
116 F3 Mozhaysk Rus. Fed.
85 F3 Mozhnābād Iran
116 H3 Mozhga Rus. Fed.
122 C3 Mpala Dem. Rep. Congo
123 C5 Mpika Zambia
123 D5 Mpoko S. Africa
123 C5 Mporokoso Zambia
125 H2 Mpumalanga prov. S. Africa
114 G2 Mrkonjić-Grad Bos.-Herz.
114 D1 M'Saken Tunisia
116 F3 Mshinskaya Rus. Fed.
115 I5 M'Sila Alg.
116 D3 Mstinskiy Most Rus. Fed.
116 D3 Mstsislaw Belarus
125 J4 Mtubatuba S. Africa
123 D5 Mtunzini S. Africa
123 D5 Mtwara Tanz.
123 C5 Muanda Dem. Rep. Congo
93 B6 Muang Hiam Laos
98 C1 Muang Hôngsa Laos
98 C1 Muang Kasi Laos
106 E5 Muang Khammouan Laos
98 C1 Muang Khao Laos
93 B6 Muang Khôngxédôn Laos
93 B6 Muang Khoua Laos
98 A2 Muang Kirirath r. Thai.

98 C1 Muang Mok Laos
93 B6 Muang Ngoy Laos
98 C1 Muang Nong Laos
98 B1 Muang Ou Nua Laos
98 C1 Muang Pakxan Laos
98 C1 Muang Phalan Laos
98 B1 Muang Phiang Laos
98 C1 Muang Phin Laos
98 B1 Muang Phôn-Hông Laos
98 B1 Muang Souy Laos
93 B6 Muang Va Laos
98 B1 Muang Vangviang Laos
98 B1 Muang Xaignabouri Laos
93 B6 Muang Xay Laos
98 C1 Muang Xon Laos
99 B2 Muar Malaysia
99 B3 Muar r. Malaysia
99 B3 Muarabungo Indon.
99 A3 Muaradua Indon.
99 A3 Muarasiberut Indon.
98 B1 Muarasipongi Indon.
99 B3 Muaratembesi Indon.
99 B3 Muarabakapur India
82 F5 Mubarek Uzbek.
81 H7 Mubarraz well Saudi Arabia
122 D3 Mubende Uganda
121 D3 Mubi Nigeria
157 F4 Mucajaí r. Brazil
157 F4 Mucajaí, Serra do mts Brazil
108 F4 Much Germany
123 D5 Muchinga Escarpment Zambia
93 B4 Muchuan China
106 B4 Muck i. U.K.
106 □ Muckle Roe i. U.K.
157 C5 Muco r. Col.
123 C5 Muconda Angola
157 K4 Mucucuaú r. Brazil
80 E2 Mucur Turkey
158 E2 Mucuri Brazil
158 E2 Mucuri r. Brazil
123 C5 Mucussueje Angola
98 A4 Muda r. Malaysia
87 A3 Mudabidri India
96 E1 Mudanjiang China
96 E1 Mudan Jiang r. China
80 B1 Mudanya Turkey
81 K7 Mudayrah Kuwait
146 C5 Muddlety U.S.A.
102 L2 Muddus nationalpark nat. park Sweden
141 G2 Muddy Creek r. U.S.A.
141 H3 Muddy Peak mt. U.S.A.
109 F4 Mudersbach Germany
71 H4 Mudgee Australia
87 A2 Mudhol India
88 C3 Mudki India
140 D3 Mud Lake U.S.A.
98 A1 Mudon Myanmar
80 C1 Mudurnu Turkey
116 F2 Mud'yuga Rus. Fed.
116 H1 Mufulira Zambia
123 C5 Mufumbwe Zambia
93 C4 Mufu Shan mts China
147 J2 Mugaguadavic Lake Canada
81 L2 Mugan Düzü lowland Azer.
89 F2 Mugarripug China
85 E4 Mughal Sarai India
85 G3 Mughār Iran
80 A7 Mughayrā' Saudi Arabia
80 B3 Muğla Turkey
80 B3 Muğla Turkey
82 D2 Mugodzhary, Gory ridge Kazakh.
89 H2 Mug Qu r. China
89 H2 Mugxung China
121 F2 Muhammad, Ra's c. Egypt
84 B4 Muhammad Ashraf Pak.
81 K7 Muhammad Qol Sudan
84 B5 Muḥayriqah Saudi Arabia
109 K3 Mühlanger Germany
109 G5 Mühlberg Germany
109 K3 Mühlhausen (Thüringen) Germany
102 N2 Muhos Fin.
122 C4 Muhulu Dem. Rep. Congo
98 C3 Mui Ca Mau c. Vietnam
98 D2 Mui Dinh hd Vietnam
98 D2 Mui Nây pt Vietnam
107 E5 Muine Bheag Rep. of Ireland
106 D5 Muirkirk U.K.
106 B2 Muirneag hill U.K.
106 C4 Muir of Ord U.K.
140 A3 Muir Woods National Monument res. U.S.A.
123 D5 Muite Moz.
151 H3 Mujeres, Isla i. Mex.
96 C4 Muju S. Korea
117 B5 Mukacheve Ukr.
99 C2 Mukah Sarawak Malaysia
86 C7 Mukalla Yemen
89 F3 Mükangsar China
98 C1 Mukdahan Thai.
68 D3 Mukinbudin Australia
99 B3 Mukomuko Indon.
82 F5 Mukry Turkm.
88 C3 Mukṭsar India
99 D3 Mukur Indon.
83 J2 Mukur Vostochnyy Kazakhstan Kazakh.
131 J4 Mukutawa r. Canada
134 C4 Mukwonago U.S.A.
88 D5 Mul India
99 B3 Mula r. Indon.
83 I3 Mulaly Kazakh.
94 A2 Mulan China
123 D5 Mulanje Malawi
123 D5 Mulanje, Mount Malawi
84 E5 Mulayḥ Saudi Arabia
143 E5 Mulberry U.S.A.
159 B3 Mulchén Chile
109 K2 Mulde r. Germany
123 D4 Muleba Tanz.
141 H5 Mule Creek NM U.S.A.
138 F3 Mule Creek WY U.S.A.
150 A2 Mulegé Mex.
143 C5 Muleshoe U.S.A.
111 E4 Mulhacén mt. Spain
108 E3 Mülheim an der Ruhr Germany
110 H3 Mulhouse France
93 A5 Muli China
96 F1 Muling Heilong. China
96 G1 Muling He r. China
106 B4 Mull i. U.K.
106 C5 Mull, Sound of sea chan. U.K.
81 L3 Mullā Alī Iran
107 E3 Mullaghareirk Mountains Rep. of Ireland
87 C4 Mullaittivu Sri Lanka
71 H3 Mullaley Australia
68 C4 Mullewa Australia
99 □ Muller, Pegunungan mts Indon.
134 B3 Mullett Lake U.S.A.
68 B4 Mullewa Australia
107 E4 Mullingar Rep. of Ireland
107 F4 Mullion Creek Australia
106 D6 Mull of Galloway c. U.K.
106 C5 Mull of Kintyre hd U.K.
106 B5 Mull of Oa hd U.K.
123 C5 Mulobezi Zambia
87 A2 Mulshi Lake India
88 D5 Multai India
85 F4 Multān Pak.
110 A6 Multien reg. France
85 F5 Mūmān Iran

87 A2 **Mumbai** India (City Plan **54**)
71 H4 **Mumbil** Australia
123 C5 **Mumbwa** Zambia
Mŭ'minobod Tajik. *see* **Leningrad**
117 H6 **Mumra** Rus. Fed.
98 C2 **Mun, Mae Nam** *r.* Thai.
68 C2 **Muna** *i.* Indon.
151 G3 **Muna** Mex.
77 M3 **Muna** *r.* Rus. Fed.
102 B1 **Munaðarnes** Iceland
82 C3 **Munayly** Kazakh.
82 C4 **Munayshy** Kazakh.
109 J4 **Münchberg** Germany
München Germany *see* **Munich**
109 G4 **Münchhausen** Germany
157 A4 **Munchique, Cerro** *mt.* Col.
130 D3 **Muncho Lake** Canada
130 D3 **Muncho Lake Provincial Park** Canada
96 D4 **Munch'ŏn** N. Korea
134 E5 **Muncie** U.S.A.
146 E4 **Muncy** U.S.A.
87 B5 **Mundel Lake** Sri Lanka
105 I5 **Mundesley** U.K.
105 H5 **Mundford** U.K.
68 C5 **Mundrabilla** Australia
88 C4 **Mundwa** India
87 C2 **Muneru** *r.* India
71 G2 **Mungallala Creek** *r.* Australia
88 D4 **Mungaoli** India
122 C3 **Mungbere** Dem. Rep. Congo
87 C1 **Mungeli** India
89 F4 **Munger** India
70 C2 **Mungeranie** Australia
98 D5 **Mungguresak, Tanjung** *pt* Indon.
71 H2 **Mungindi** Australia
96 D5 **Mun'gyŏng** S. Korea
112 E6 **Munich** Germany
155 J4 **Munim** *r.* Brazil
134 D2 **Munising** U.S.A.
158 E3 **Muniz Freire** Brazil
103 J4 **Munkedal** Sweden
102 O1 **Munkelva** Norway
103 K4 **Munkfors** Sweden
109 I4 **Münnerstadt** Germany
125 H1 **Munnik** S. Africa
71 H8 **Munro, Mount** Australia
96 D5 **Munsan** S. Korea
112 C7 **Münsingen** Switz.
109 G5 **Münster** Germany
109 I2 **Münster** Germany
108 F3 **Münster** Germany
108 F3 **Münsterland** *reg.* Germany
102 O2 **Muojärvi** *l.* Fin.
98 C1 **Mương Lam** Vietnam
93 B6 **Mương Nhie** Vietnam
102 M2 **Muonio** Fin.
102 M2 **Muonioälven** *r.* Fin./Sweden
96 A5 **Muping** China
Muqdisho Somalia *see* **Mogadishu**
81 L1 **Müqtädır** Azer.
81 I2 **Muradiye** Turkey
98 □ **Murai Resr.** Sing.
94 F5 **Murakami** Japan
156 B7 **Murallón, Cerro** *mt.* Chile
122 C4 **Muramvya** Burundi
122 D4 **Muranga** Kenya
116 I3 **Murashi** Rus. Fed.
81 H2 **Murat** *r.* Turkey
80 B2 **Murat Dağı** *mts* Turkey
80 A1 **Muratlı** Turkey
94 G5 **Murayama** Japan
84 C3 **Murcheh Khvort** Iran
70 F6 **Murchison** Australia
68 B4 **Murchison** *watercourse* Australia
122 D3 **Murchison Falls National Park** Uganda
111 F4 **Murcia** Spain
111 F4 **Murcia** *aut. comm.* Spain
142 C3 **Murdo** U.S.A.
133 G4 **Murdochville** Canada
123 D5 **Murehwa** Zimbabwe
113 L7 **Mureş** *r.* Romania
110 E5 **Muret** France
145 E4 **Murfreesboro** *NC* U.S.A.
145 C5 **Murfreesboro** *TN* U.S.A.
82 E5 **Murgap** Turkm.
85 F2 **Murgap** *r.* Turkm.
85 G3 **Murghab** *r.* Afgh.
88 B3 **Murgha Kibzai** Pak.
83 H5 **Murghob** Tajik.
83 H5 **Murghob** *r.* Tajik.
85 H3 **Murgh Pass** Afgh.
92 A2 **Muri** China
89 F5 **Muri** India
84 E2 **Mūrī** Iran
158 D3 **Muriaé** Brazil
123 C4 **Muriege** Angola
109 K1 **Müritz** *l.* Germany
109 L1 **Müritz, Nationalpark** *nat. park* Germany
109 K1 **Müritz Seenpark** *res.* Germany
102 P1 **Murmansk** Rus. Fed.
102 O1 **Murmanskaya Oblast'** *admin. div.* Rus. Fed.
114 C4 **Muro, Capo di** *pt Corsica* France
116 G4 **Murom** Rus. Fed.
94 G3 **Muroran** Japan
111 B1 **Muros** Spain
95 D8 **Muroto** Japan
95 D8 **Muroto-zaki** *pt* Japan
138 C3 **Murphy** *ID* U.S.A.
145 D5 **Murphy** *NC* U.S.A.
140 B2 **Murphys** U.S.A.
71 G2 **Murra Murra** Australia
70 D5 **Murray** Australia
130 E3 **Murray** *r.* Canada
144 B4 **Murray** *KY* U.S.A.
138 E3 **Murray** *UT* U.S.A.
68 E2 **Murray, Lake** P.N.G.
145 D5 **Murray, Lake** U.S.A.
70 C5 **Murray Bridge** Australia
124 E5 **Murraysburg** S. Africa
70 D5 **Murrayville** Australia
109 H6 **Murrhardt** Germany
71 H5 **Murringo** Australia
107 B4 **Murrisk** *reg.* Rep. of Ireland
107 B4 **Murroogh** Rep. of Ireland
71 H5 **Murrumbateman** Australia
70 F5 **Murrumbidgee** *r.* Australia
123 D5 **Murrupula** Moz.
71 I3 **Murrurundi** Australia
114 G1 **Murska Sobota** Slovenia
70 D2 **Murteree, Lake** *salt flat* Australia
70 E6 **Murtoa** Australia
87 A2 **Murud** India
96 A2 **Muruin Sum Shuiku** *resr* China
87 C4 **Murunkan** Sri Lanka
72 F3 **Murupara** N.Z.
67 J6 **Mururoa** *atoll* Fr. Polynesia
88 E5 **Murwara** India
71 J2 **Murwillumbah** Australia
82 E5 **Murzechirla** Turkm.
121 D2 **Murzūq** Libya
112 G7 **Mürzzuschlag** Austria
81 H2 **Muş** Turkey
88 B3 **Musa Khel Bazar** Pak.
115 J3 **Musala** *mt.* Bulg.
99 A2 **Musala** *i.* Indon.
96 E2 **Musan** N. Korea
84 E5 **Musandam Peninsula** Oman
85 G3 **Musa Qala** Afgh.
85 G3 **Musa Qala, Rūd-i** *r.* Afgh.
86 E5 **Muscat** Oman
134 B5 **Muscatine** U.S.A.
134 B4 **Muscoda** U.S.A.
147 I3 **Muscongus Bay** U.S.A.
68 D4 **Musgrave Ranges** *mts* Australia
107 C5 **Musheramore** *hill* Rep. of Ireland
122 B4 **Mushie** Dem. Rep. Congo
87 B2 **Musi** *r.* India
99 B3 **Musi** *r.* Indon.
141 F4 **Music Mountain** U.S.A.
141 G2 **Musinia Peak** *mt.* U.S.A.
130 E2 **Muskeg** *r.* Canada
147 H4 **Muskeget Channel** U.S.A.
134 D4 **Muskegon** U.S.A.
134 D4 **Muskegon** *r.* U.S.A.
146 C5 **Muskingum** *r.* U.S.A.
143 E5 **Muskogee** U.S.A.
135 H3 **Muskoka** Canada
135 H3 **Muskoka, Lake** Canada
130 E3 **Muskwa** *r.* Canada
80 F3 **Muslimīyah** Syria
121 F3 **Musmar** Sudan
122 D4 **Musoma** Tanz.
68 E2 **Mussau Island** P.N.G.
106 E5 **Musselburgh** U.K.
108 F2 **Musselkanaal** Neth.
138 E2 **Musselshell** *r.* U.S.A.
80 B1 **Mustafakemalpaşa** Turkey
82 C2 **Mustayevo** Rus. Fed.
103 M4 **Mustjala** Estonia
96 E3 **Musu-dan** *pt* N. Korea
71 I4 **Muswellbrook** Australia
121 E2 **Mūţ** Egypt
80 D3 **Mut** Turkey
158 E1 **Mutá, Ponta do** *pt* Brazil
123 D5 **Mutare** Zimbabwe
91 E7 **Mutis, Gunung** *mt.* Indon.
70 D4 **Mutooroo** Australia
123 D5 **Mutorashanga** Zimbabwe
94 G4 **Mutsu** Japan
94 G4 **Mutsu-wan** *b.* Japan
72 A7 **Muttonbird Islands** N.Z.
107 B5 **Mutton Island** Rep. of Ireland
123 D5 **Mutuali** Moz.
158 C1 **Mutunópolis** Brazil
87 C4 **Mutur** Sri Lanka
102 N1 **Mutusjärvi** *r.* Fin.
102 N2 **Muurola** Fin.
92 C2 **Mu Us Shamo** *des.* China
123 B4 **Muxaluando** Angola
116 E2 **Muyezerskiy** Rus. Fed.
122 D4 **Muyinga** Burundi
82 D4 **Muynak** Uzbek.
122 C4 **Muyumba** Dem. Rep. Congo
92 D4 **Muyuping** China
88 C2 **Muzaffarabad** Pak.
88 B3 **Muzaffargarh** Pak.
88 D3 **Muzaffarnagar** India
89 F4 **Muzaffarpur** India
125 J1 **Muzamane** Moz.
83 J4 **Muzat He** *r.* China
85 F5 **Mūzīn** Iran
130 C4 **Muzon, Cape** U.S.A.
150 D2 **Múzquiz** Mex.
88 E2 **Muztag** *mt. Xinjiang* China
89 F1 **Muztag** *mt. Xinjiang/Xizang* China
83 H5 **Muztagata** *mt.* China
121 E4 **Mvolo** Sudan
122 D4 **Mvomero** Tanz.
123 D5 **Mvuma** Zimbabwe
123 E5 **Mwali** *i.* Comoros
123 C4 **Mwanza** Dem. Rep. Congo
122 D4 **Mwanza** Tanz.
107 B4 **Mweelrea** *hill* Rep. of Ireland
122 C4 **Mweka** Dem. Rep. Congo
123 C5 **Mwenda** Zambia
122 C4 **Mwene-Ditu** Dem. Rep. Congo
123 D6 **Mwenezi** Zimbabwe
123 C4 **Mweru, Lake** Dem. Rep. Congo/Zambia
123 C4 **Mwimba** Dem. Rep. Congo
123 C5 **Mwinilunga** Zambia
116 C4 **Myadzyel** Belarus
92 B4 **Myaglo** China
89 H5 **Myaing** Myanmar
88 B4 **Myajlar** India
71 J4 **Myall Lake** Australia
90 B2 **Myanmar** *country* Asia
106 E2 **Mybster** U.K.
89 H5 **Myebon** Myanmar
91 B4 **Myingyan** Myanmar
98 A2 **Myinmoletkat** *mt.* Myanmar
90 B4 **Myitkyina** Myanmar
98 A2 **Myitta** Myanmar
89 H5 **Myittha** *r.* Myanmar
117 E6 **Mykolayiv** Ukr.
115 K6 **Mykonos** Greece
115 K6 **Mykonos** *i.* Greece
76 G3 **Myla** Rus. Fed.
89 G4 **Mymensingh** Bangl.
103 M3 **Mynämäki** Fin.
83 H3 **Mynaral** Kazakh.
89 H5 **Myohaung** Myanmar
96 E3 **Myŏnggan** N. Korea
116 C4 **Myory** Belarus
102 C3 **Mýrdalsjökull** *ice cap* Iceland
102 K1 **Myre** Norway
102 M2 **Myrheden** Sweden
117 E5 **Myrhorod** Ukr.
117 D5 **Myronivka** Ukr.
145 E5 **Myrtle Beach** U.S.A.
71 G6 **Myrtleford** Australia
138 A3 **Myrtle Point** U.S.A.
83 G4 **Myrzakent** Kazakh.
112 G4 **Myślibórz** Poland
87 B3 **Mysore** India
77 T3 **Mys Shmidta** Rus. Fed.
147 F5 **Mystic Islands** U.S.A.
98 C3 **My Tho** Vietnam
115 L5 **Mytilini** Greece
116 F4 **Mytishchi** Rus. Fed.
125 G5 **Mzamomhle** S. Africa
109 K5 **Mže** *r.* Czech Rep.
123 D5 **Mzimba** Malawi
123 D5 **Mzuzu** Malawi

N

93 B6 **Na, Nam** *r.* China/Vietnam
109 J5 **Naab** *r.* Germany
140 □2 **Naalehu** U.S.A.
103 M3 **Naantali** Fin.
107 E4 **Naas** Rep. of Ireland
124 B4 **Nababeep** S. Africa
87 C2 **Nabarangapur** India
95 E7 **Nabari** Japan
97 B4 **Nabas** Phil.
80 E5 **Nabatiyet et Tahta** Lebanon
109 K5 **Nabburg** Germany
122 D4 **Naberera** Tanz.
76 G4 **Naberezhnyye Chelny** Rus. Fed.
121 D1 **Nabeul** Tunisia
88 D3 **Nabha** India
71 J4 **Nabiac** Australia
91 F7 **Nabire** Indon.
80 E5 **Nāblus** West Bank
125 H2 **Naboomspruit** S. Africa
98 A2 **Nabule** Myanmar
123 E5 **Nacala** Moz.
150 H5 **Nacaome** Hond.
138 B2 **Naches** U.S.A.
88 B4 **Nachna** India
140 B4 **Nacimiento Reservoir** U.S.A.
143 E6 **Nacogdoches** U.S.A.
148 C2 **Nacozari de García** Mex.
88 C5 **Nadiad** India
84 D4 **Nadīk** Iran
120 B1 **Nador** Morocco
84 D3 **Nadūshan** Iran
117 C5 **Nadvirna** Ukr.
76 E3 **Nadvoitsy** Rus. Fed.
76 I3 **Nadym** Rus. Fed.
103 J5 **Næstved** Denmark
115 I5 **Nafpaktos** Greece
115 J6 **Nafplio** Greece
84 C4 **Naft-e Safīd** Iran
81 J5 **Nafţ Khāneh** Iraq
84 B3 **Naft Shahr** Iran
84 B5 **Nafūd al Jur'ā** *dunes* Saudi Arabia
84 A6 **Nafūd as Surrah** *dunes* Saudi Arabia
84 B5 **Nafūd Qunayfidhah** *dunes* Saudi Arabia
84 A5 **Nafy** Saudi Arabia
89 G2 **Nag, Co** *l.* China
97 B3 **Naga** Phil.
132 D4 **Nagagami** *r.* Canada
95 C8 **Nagahama** Japan
89 H4 **Naga Hills** India
95 G5 **Nagai** Japan
89 H4 **Nagaland** *state* India
70 F6 **Nagambie** Australia
95 F6 **Nagano** Japan
95 F6 **Nagaoka** Japan
89 H4 **Nagaon** India
87 B4 **Nagapattinam** India
88 D2 **Nagar** India
87 B2 **Nagarjuna Sagar Reservoir** India
88 B4 **Nagar Parkar** Pak.
89 G3 **Nagarzê** China
95 A8 **Nagasaki** Japan
95 B7 **Nagato** Japan
88 C4 **Nagaur** India
87 C2 **Nagavali** *r.* India
88 C5 **Nagda** India
87 B4 **Nagercoil** India
85 G5 **Nagha Kalat** Pak.
88 D3 **Nagina** India
89 E3 **Nagma** Nepal
116 I3 **Nagorsk** Rus. Fed.
95 E7 **Nagoya** Japan
88 D5 **Nagpur** India
89 H3 **Nagqu** China
97 C3 **Nagumbuaya Point** Phil.
76 F1 **Nagurskoye** Rus. Fed.
114 G1 **Nagyatád** Hungary
112 H7 **Nagykanizsa** Hungary
90 E4 **Naha** Japan
88 D3 **Nahan** India
85 F5 **Nahang** *r.* Iran/Pak.
130 E2 **Nahanni Butte** Canada
130 D2 **Nahanni National Park** Canada
80 E5 **Nahariyya** Israel
84 C3 **Nahāvand** Iran
109 F5 **Nahe** *r.* Germany
159 B3 **Nahuelbuta, Parque Nacional** *nat. park* Chile
159 B4 **Nahuel Huapí, Lago** *l.* Arg.
159 B4 **Nahuel Huapí, Parque Nacional** *nat. park* Arg.
145 D6 **Nahunta** U.S.A.
150 C2 **Naica** Mex.
89 H2 **Naij Tal** China
133 H2 **Nain** Canada
84 D3 **Nā'īn** Iran
88 D3 **Nainital** India
88 E5 **Nainpur** India
106 E3 **Nairn** U.K.
135 G2 **Nairn Centre** Canada
122 D4 **Nairobi** Kenya
122 D4 **Naivasha** Kenya
96 D2 **Naizishan** China
84 B5 **Na'jān** Saudi Arabia
86 B4 **Najd** *reg.* Saudi Arabia
111 E1 **Nájera** Spain
88 D3 **Najibabad** India
96 F2 **Najin** N. Korea
86 B6 **Najrān** Saudi Arabia
95 A8 **Nakadōri-shima** *i.* Japan
98 C1 **Na Kae** Thai.
95 B8 **Nakama** Japan
95 C8 **Nakamura** Japan
77 L3 **Nakanno** Rus. Fed.
95 F6 **Nakano** Japan
95 C6 **Nakano-shima** *i.* Japan
85 H3 **Naka Pass** Afgh.
95 B8 **Nakatsu** Japan
95 E7 **Nakatsugawa** Japan
122 D2 **Nakfa** Eritrea
121 F1 **Nakhl** Egypt
90 F2 **Nakhodka** Rus. Fed.
98 B2 **Nakhon Nayok** Thai.
98 B2 **Nakhon Pathom** Thai.
98 C1 **Nakhon Phanom** Thai.
98 B2 **Nakhon Ratchasima** Thai.
98 B2 **Nakhon Sawan** Thai.
98 A3 **Nakhon Si Thammarat** Thai.
88 B5 **Nakhtarana** India
130 C3 **Nakina** *B.C.* Canada
132 C3 **Nakina** *Ont.* Canada
128 C4 **Naknek** U.S.A.
123 D4 **Nakonde** Zambia
103 J5 **Nakskov** Denmark
96 E6 **Naktong-gang** *r.* S. Korea
122 D4 **Nakuru** Kenya
130 F4 **Nakusp** Canada
85 G5 **Nal** Pak.
85 G5 **Nal** *r.* Pak.
125 J2 **Nalázi** Moz.
89 G4 **Nalbari** India
117 G7 **Nal'chik** Rus. Fed.
87 B2 **Naldurg** India
87 B2 **Nalgonda** India
87 B3 **Nallamala Hills** India
80 C1 **Nallıhan** Turkey
83 G1 **Nalobino** Kazakh.
120 D1 **Nālūt** Libya
125 J2 **Namaacha** Moz.
125 H3 **Namahadi** S. Africa
84 C3 **Namak, Daryācheh-ye** *salt flat* Iran
85 E3 **Namak, Kavīr-i-** *salt flat* Iran
85 E4 **Namakzar-e Shadad** *salt flat* Iran
122 D4 **Namanga** Kenya
83 G4 **Namangan** Uzbek.
123 D5 **Namapa** Moz.
124 B4 **Namaqualand** *reg.* S. Africa
81 J3 **Namashīr** Iran
68 F2 **Namatanai** P.N.G.
71 J1 **Nambour** Australia
71 J3 **Nambucca Heads** Australia
98 C3 **Năm Căn** Vietnam
96 D4 **Namch'ŏn** N. Korea
90 B3 **Nam Co** *l.* China
102 K2 **Namdalen** *valley* Norway
102 J2 **Namdalseid** Norway
93 C6 **Nam Định** Vietnam
134 B3 **Namekagon** *r.* U.S.A.
96 D4 **Nam-gang** *r.* N. Korea
96 E6 **Namhae-do** *i.* S. Korea
123 B6 **Namib Desert** Namibia
123 B5 **Namibe** Angola
123 B6 **Namibia** *country* Africa
163 J8 **Namibia Abyssal Plain** *sea feature* N. Atlantic Ocean
95 G6 **Namie** Japan
89 H3 **Namjagbarwa Feng** *mt.* China
91 E7 **Namlea** Indon.
98 A1 **Nammekon** Myanmar
71 H3 **Namoi** *r.* Australia
130 F3 **Nampa** Canada
88 E3 **Nampa** *mt.* Nepal
138 C3 **Nampa** U.S.A.
120 B3 **Nampala** Mali
98 B1 **Nam Pat** Thai.
98 B1 **Nam Phong** Thai.
96 C4 **Namp'o** N. Korea
123 D5 **Nampula** Moz.
79 H4 **Namrup** India
89 E3 **Namsê La** *pass* Nepal
102 J2 **Namsen** *r.* Norway
89 H4 **Namsi** India
89 G3 **Namsi La** *pass* Bhutan
102 J2 **Namsos** Norway
77 N3 **Namtsy** Rus. Fed.
90 B4 **Namtu** Myanmar
108 C4 **Namur** Belgium
123 C5 **Namwala** Zambia
96 D6 **Namwŏn** S. Korea
98 B1 **Nan** Thai.
98 B2 **Nan, Mae Nam** *r.* Thai.
122 B3 **Nana Bakassa** Centr. Afr. Rep.
130 E5 **Nanaimo** Canada
140 □1 **Nanakuli** U.S.A.
96 E3 **Nanam** N. Korea
93 F5 **Nan'an** China
124 B2 **Nananib Plateau** Namibia
95 E6 **Nanao** Japan
93 E6 **Nan'ao Dao** *i.* China
95 E6 **Nanatsu-shima** *i.* Japan
92 C4 **Nanbu** China
94 A1 **Nancha** China
93 E4 **Nanchang** *Jiangxi* China
93 E4 **Nanchang** *Jiangxi* China
93 E5 **Nancheng** China
93 C4 **Nanchong** China
93 C4 **Nanchuan** China
110 H2 **Nancy** France
88 E3 **Nanda Devi** *mt.* India
88 E3 **Nanda Kot** *mt.* India
93 C5 **Nandan** China
87 B2 **Nanded** India
71 I3 **Nandewar Range** *mts* Australia
88 C5 **Nandgaon** India
93 D6 **Nandu Jiang** *r.* China
88 C5 **Nandurbar** India
87 B3 **Nandyal** India
93 D6 **Nanfeng** *Guangdong* China
93 E5 **Nanfeng** *Jiangxi* China
89 H3 **Nang** China
121 D4 **Nanga Eboko** Cameroon
99 D3 **Nangahpinoh** Indon.
96 E2 **Nangang Shan** *mts* China/N. Korea
88 C2 **Nanga Parbat** *mt.* Jammu and Kashmir
99 D3 **Nangatayap** Indon.
98 A3 **Nangin** Myanmar
96 D3 **Nangnim** N. Korea
96 D3 **Nangnim-sanmaek** *mts* N. Korea
92 E2 **Nangong** China
123 D4 **Nangulangwa** Tanz.
92 A2 **Nanhua** China
92 F4 **Nanhui** China
87 B3 **Nanjangud** India
92 C3 **Nanjiang** China
93 E5 **Nanjing** *Fujian* China
92 F3 **Nanjing** *Jiangsu* China
93 E5 **Nankang** China
Nanking *Jiangsu* China *see* **Nanjing**
95 C8 **Nankoku** Japan
123 B5 **Nankova** Angola
92 E2 **Nanle** China
92 F4 **Nanling** China
93 D5 **Nan Ling** *mts* China
93 C6 **Nanliu Jiang** *r.* China
93 C6 **Nanning** China
98 B1 **Na Noi** Thai.
129 N3 **Nanortalik** Greenland
93 C5 **Nanpan Jiang** *r.* China
96 A3 **Nanpiao** China
93 F5 **Nanping** China
93 F5 **Nanri Dao** *i.* China
Nansei-shotō *is* Japan *see* **Ryukyu Islands**
164 B1 **Nansen Basin** *sea feature* Arctic Ocean
129 I1 **Nansen Sound** *sea chan.* Canada
110 D3 **Nantes** France
108 A5 **Nanteuil-le-Haudouin** France
87 C4 **Nanthi Kadal** *lag.* Sri Lanka
135 G4 **Nanticoke** Canada
147 F5 **Nanticoke** *r.* U.S.A.
130 G4 **Nanton** Canada
92 F4 **Nantong** China
93 F6 **Nant'ou** Taiwan
147 H4 **Nantucket** U.S.A.
147 H4 **Nantucket Island** U.S.A.
147 H4 **Nantucket Sound** *g.* U.S.A.
105 E4 **Nantwich** U.K.
69 H2 **Nanumanga** *i.* Tuvalu
69 H2 **Nanumea** *i.* Tuvalu
158 E2 **Nanuque** Brazil
97 C5 **Nanusa, Kepulauan** *is* Indon.
93 B4 **Nanxi** China
93 D4 **Nanxian** China
93 E5 **Nanxiong** China
92 D3 **Nanyang** China
96 C3 **Nanzamu** China
92 D4 **Nanzhang** China
92 D3 **Nanzhao** China
133 F3 **Naococane, Lac** *l.* Canada
89 G4 **Naogaon** Bangl.
88 B4 **Naokot** Pak.
94 C1 **Naoli He** *r.* China
85 F3 **Naomid, Dasht-e** *des.* Afgh./Iran
88 C2 **Naoshera** Jammu and Kashmir
93 D6 **Naozhou Dao** *i.* China
140 A2 **Napa** U.S.A.
147 J1 **Napadogan** Canada
131 G1 **Napaktulik Lake** Canada
135 I3 **Napanee** Canada
88 C4 **Napasar** India
129 M3 **Napasoq** Greenland
134 C5 **Naperville** U.S.A.
72 F3 **Napier** N.Z.
73 D4 **Napier Mountains** Antarctica
147 G2 **Napierville** Canada
114 F4 **Naples** Italy
145 D7 **Naples** *FL* U.S.A.
147 H3 **Naples** *ME* U.S.A.
93 B6 **Napo** China
154 D4 **Napo** *r.* Ecuador/Peru
146 A4 **Napoleon** U.S.A.
Napoli Italy *see* **Naples**
159 D3 **Naposta** Arg.
159 D3 **Naposta** *r.* Arg.
134 E5 **Nappanee** U.S.A.
81 J3 **Naqadeh** Iran
81 L4 **Naqqash** Iran
95 D7 **Nara** Japan
120 B3 **Nara** Mali
113 M3 **Narach** Belarus
70 D6 **Naracoorte** Australia
71 G4 **Naradhan** Australia
88 C4 **Naraina** India
88 E6 **Narainpur** India
150 B2 **Naranjo** Mex.
151 E3 **Naranjos** Mex.
87 D2 **Narasannapeta** India
87 C2 **Narasapatnam, Point** India
87 C2 **Narasapur** India
87 C2 **Narasaraopet** India
89 F5 **Narasinghapur** India
98 B4 **Narathiwat** Thai.
87 A2 **Narayangaon** India
105 C6 **Narberth** U.K.
110 F5 **Narbonne** France
111 C1 **Narcea** *r.* Spain
84 D2 **Nardin** Iran
114 H4 **Nardò** Italy
159 E1 **Nare** Arg.
88 B3 **Narechi** *r.* Pak.
163 E4 **Nares Abyssal Plain** *sea feature* S. Atlantic Ocean
163 E4 **Nares Deep** *sea feature* N. Atlantic Ocean
129 L1 **Nares Strait** Canada/Greenland
113 J4 **Narew** *r.* Poland
96 D2 **Narhong** China
88 A3 **Nari** *r.* Pak.
123 B6 **Narib** Namibia
124 B5 **Nariep** S. Africa
117 H6 **Narimanov** Rus. Fed.
85 H2 **Narin** Afgh.
85 H3 **Narin** *reg.* Afgh.
80 G3 **Narince** Turkey
89 H1 **Narin Gol** *watercourse* China
95 G7 **Narita** Japan
150 B2 **Narizon, Punta** *pt* Mex.
88 C5 **Narmada** *r.* India
81 H1 **Narman** Turkey
88 D3 **Narnaul** India
114 E3 **Narni** Italy
113 N5 **Narodychi** Ukr.
116 F4 **Naro-Fominsk** Rus. Fed.
71 I6 **Narooma** Australia
116 G4 **Narovchat** Rus. Fed.
117 D5 **Narowlya** Belarus
103 M3 **Närpes** Fin.
71 H3 **Narrabri** Australia
147 H4 **Narragansett Bay** U.S.A.
71 G2 **Narran** *r.* Australia
71 G5 **Narrandera** Australia
71 G2 **Narran Lake** Australia
71 H4 **Narromine** Australia
131 I4 **Narrow Hills Provincial Park** Canada
146 C6 **Narrows** U.S.A.
147 F4 **Narrowsburg** U.S.A.
88 D5 **Narsimhapur** India
89 G5 **Narsingdi** Bangl.
88 D5 **Narsinghgarh** India
87 C2 **Narsipatnam** India
92 E1 **Nart** China
95 D7 **Naruto** Japan
103 O4 **Narva** Estonia
103 N4 **Narva Bay** Estonia/Rus. Fed.
97 B2 **Narvacan** Phil.
103 O4 **Narva veehoidia** *resr* Estonia/Rus. Fed.
102 L1 **Narvik** Norway
88 D3 **Narwana** India
88 D4 **Narwar** India
76 G3 **Nar'yan-Mar** Rus. Fed.
83 K2 **Narymskiy Khrebet** *mts* Kazakh.
83 H4 **Naryn** Kyrg.
83 H4 **Naryn** *r.* Kyrg.
83 J4 **Narynkol** Kazakh.
102 L3 **Näsåker** Sweden
141 H3 **Naschitti** U.S.A.
72 C6 **Naseby** N.Z.
88 C5 **Nashik** India
134 A4 **Nashua** *IA* U.S.A.
147 H3 **Nashua** *NH* U.S.A.
145 C4 **Nashville** U.S.A.
80 F5 **Naşīb** Syria
103 M3 **Näsijärvi** *l.* Fin.
121 F4 **Nasir** Sudan
88 B3 **Nasirabad** Pak.
123 C5 **Nasondoye** Dem. Rep. Congo
80 C6 **Naşr** Egypt
84 C3 **Naşrābād** Iran
85 E3 **Naşrābād** Iran
81 K5 **Naşrīān-e Pā'īn** Iran
130 D3 **Nass** *r.* Canada
145 E7 **Nassau** Bahamas
160 H6 **Nassau** *i.* Cook Is
121 F2 **Nasser, Lake** *resr* Egypt
103 K4 **Nässjö** Sweden
129 M3 **Nassuttooq** *inlet* Greenland
132 E2 **Nastapoca** *r.* Canada
132 E2 **Nastapoka Islands** Canada
95 F6 **Nasu-dake** *vol.* Japan
97 B3 **Nasugbu** Phil.
113 O2 **Nasva** Rus. Fed.
123 C6 **Nata** Botswana
122 D4 **Nata** Tanz.
157 B4 **Natagaima** Col.
155 K5 **Natal** Brazil
Natal *prov.* S. Africa *see* **Kwazulu-Natal**
162 G7 **Natal Basin** *sea feature* Indian Ocean
84 C3 **Naţanz** Iran
133 H3 **Natashquan** Canada
133 H3 **Natashquan** *r.* Canada
143 F6 **Natchez** U.S.A.
143 E6 **Natchitoches** U.S.A.
112 G4 **Natecka, Puszcza** *for.* Poland
70 F6 **Nathalia** Australia
98 B4 **Na Thawi** Thai.
88 C4 **Nathdwara** India
111 H2 **Nati, Punta** *pt* Spain
70 D6 **Natimuk** Australia
140 D5 **National City** U.S.A.
120 C3 **Natitingou** Benin
155 I6 **Natividade** Brazil
150 B1 **Nátora** Mex.
94 G5 **Natori** Japan
122 D4 **Natron, Lake** *salt l.* Tanz.
98 A1 **Nattaung** *mt.* Myanmar
99 C2 **Natuna, Kepulauan** *is* Indon.
99 C2 **Natuna Besar** *i.* Indon.
147 F2 **Natural Bridge** U.S.A.
141 G3 **Natural Bridges National Monument** *res.* U.S.A.
162 L7 **Naturaliste Plateau** *sea feature* Indian Ocean
141 H2 **Naturita** U.S.A.
134 E2 **Naubinway** U.S.A.
123 B6 **Nauchas** Namibia
109 K2 **Nauen** Germany
147 G4 **Naugatuck** U.S.A.
97 B3 **Naujan** Phil.
97 B3 **Naujan, Lake** Phil.
103 M4 **Naujoji Akmenė** Lith.
88 C4 **Naukh** India
109 H3 **Naumburg (Hessen)** Germany
109 J3 **Naumburg (Saale)** Germany
98 A1 **Naungpale** Myanmar
80 E6 **Na'ūr** Jordan
85 G4 **Nauroz Kalat** Pak.
69 G2 **Nauru** *country* Pacific Ocean
88 B4 **Naushara** Pak.
103 I3 **Naustdal** Norway
154 D4 **Nauta** Peru
124 C3 **Naute Dam** Namibia
151 E3 **Nautla** Mex.
85 G3 **Nauzad** Afgh.
89 G5 **Navadwip** India
116 C4 **Navahrudak** Belarus
141 H4 **Navajo** U.S.A.
139 F4 **Navajo Lake** U.S.A.
141 G3 **Navajo Mountain** U.S.A.
97 C4 **Naval** Phil.
111 D3 **Navalmoral de la Mata** Spain
111 D3 **Navalvillar de Pela** Spain
107 E4 **Navan** Rep. of Ireland
116 D4 **Navapolatsk** Belarus
77 S3 **Navarin, Mys** *c.* Rus. Fed.
156 C9 **Navarino, Isla** *i.* Chile
111 F1 **Navarra** *aut. comm.* Spain
70 E6 **Navarre** Australia
140 A2 **Navarro** U.S.A.
116 G4 **Navashino** Rus. Fed.
143 D6 **Navasota** U.S.A.
106 D2 **Naver, Loch** *l.* U.K.
102 K3 **Näverede** Sweden
159 B2 **Navidad** Chile
116 E4 **Navlya** Rus. Fed.
115 M2 **Năvodari** Romania
82 F4 **Navoi** Uzbek.
150 B2 **Navojoa** Mex.
116 G3 **Navoloki** Rus. Fed.
88 C5 **Navsari** India
88 C4 **Nawa** India
80 F5 **Nawá** Syria
89 G4 **Nawabganj** Bangl.
88 B4 **Nawabshah** Pak.
89 F4 **Nawada** India
85 G3 **Nāwah** Afgh.
88 C4 **Nawalgarh** India
81 J2 **Naxçıvan** Azer.
93 B4 **Naxi** China
115 K6 **Naxos** Greece
115 K6 **Naxos** *i.* Greece
157 A4 **Naya** Col.
87 D1 **Nayagarh** India
150 C3 **Nayar** Mex.
150 C3 **Nayarit** *state* Mex.
94 H2 **Nayoro** Japan
87 B3 **Nayudupeta** India
158 E1 **Nazaré** Brazil
87 B4 **Nazareth** India
80 E5 **Nazareth** Israel
143 B7 **Nazas** Mex.
150 C2 **Nazas** *r.* Mex.
154 D6 **Nazca** Peru
161 N7 **Nazca Ridge** *sea feature* S. Pacific Ocean
81 J2 **Nāzīk** Iran
81 I2 **Nazik Gölü** *l.* Turkey
85 F4 **Nāzīl** Iran
80 B3 **Nazilli** Turkey
85 G5 **Nazimabad** Pak.
81 G2 **Nazımiye** Turkey
89 H4 **Nazira** India
130 E4 **Nazko** Canada
130 E4 **Nazko** *r.* Canada
81 J3 **Nāzlū** *r.* Iran
117 H7 **Nazran'** Rus. Fed.
122 D3 **Nazrēt** Eth.
86 E5 **Nazwá** Oman
123 C4 **Nchelenge** Zambia
123 C6 **Ncojane** Botswana
123 B4 **N'dalatando** Angola
122 C3 **Ndélé** Centr. Afr. Rep.
122 B4 **Ndendé** Gabon
69 G3 **Ndeni** *i.* Solomon Is
121 D3 **Ndjamena** Chad
123 C5 **Ndola** Zambia
125 I4 **Ndwedwe** S. Africa
71 G1 **Neabul Cr.** *r.* Australia
107 E3 **Neagh, Lough** *l.* U.K.
138 A1 **Neah Bay** U.S.A.
68 D4 **Neale, Lake** *salt flat* Australia
70 B2 **Neales** *watercourse* Australia
115 J5 **Nea Liosia** Greece
115 J6 **Neapoli** Greece
105 D6 **Neath** U.K.
105 D6 **Neath** *r.* U.K.
71 G1 **Nebine Cr.** *r.* Australia
82 C5 **Nebitdag** Turkm.
157 D4 **Neblina, Pico da** *mt.* Brazil
141 G2 **Nebo, Mount** U.S.A.
116 E3 **Nebolchi** Rus. Fed.
142 C3 **Nebraska** *state* U.S.A.
142 E3 **Nebraska City** U.S.A.
114 F6 **Nebrodi, Monti** *mts Sicily* Italy
143 E6 **Neches** *r.* U.S.A.
157 B3 **Nechí** *r.* Col.
122 D3 **Nechisar National Park** Eth.
109 G5 **Neckar** *r.* Germany
109 H5 **Neckarsulm** Germany
67 H2 **Necker Island** U.S.A.
159 E3 **Necochea** Arg.
109 L1 **Neddemin** Germany
132 F2 **Nedlouc, Lac** *l.* Canada
89 G3 **Nêdong** China
102 M1 **Nedre Soppero** Sweden
141 E4 **Needles** U.S.A.
134 C3 **Neenah** U.S.A.
131 J4 **Neepawa** Canada
129 J2 **Neergaard Lake** Canada
108 D3 **Neerijnen** Neth.
108 D3 **Neerpelt** Belgium
81 L2 **Neftçala** Azer.
82 B1 **Neftegorsk** Rus. Fed.
76 G4 **Neftekamsk** Rus. Fed.
117 H6 **Neftekumsk** Rus. Fed.
76 I3 **Nefteyugansk** Rus. Fed.
105 C5 **Nefyn** U.K.
114 C6 **Nefza** Tunisia
122 B4 **Negage** Angola
122 D3 **Negēlē** Eth.
158 A3 **Negla** *r.* Para.
123 D5 **Negomane** Moz.
87 B5 **Negombo** Sri Lanka
115 J4 **Negotino** Macedonia
154 C5 **Negra, Cordillera** *mts* Peru
154 B5 **Negra, Punta** *pt* Peru
114 B7 **Négrine** Alg.
154 B4 **Negritos** Peru
159 D4 **Negro** *r.* Arg.
158 A2 **Negro** *r.* Brazil
154 F4 **Negro** *r.* S. America
159 F2 **Negro** *r.* Uruguay
97 B4 **Negros** *i.* Phil.
115 M3 **Negru Vodă** Romania
81 L4 **Nehavand** Iran
85 F4 **Nehbandān** Iran
90 E2 **Nehe** China
93 B4 **Neijiang** China
131 H4 **Neilburg** Canada
92 B1 **Nei Mongol Zizhiqu** *aut. reg.* China
109 J3 **Neinstedt** Germany
112 G5 **Neiße** *r.* Germany/Poland
157 B4 **Neiva** Col.
92 D3 **Neixiang** China
131 J3 **Nejanilini Lake** Canada
84 D2 **Neka** Iran
122 D3 **Nek'emtē** Eth.
103 K5 **Neksø** Denmark
88 D3 **Nelang** India
116 E3 **Nelidovo** Rus. Fed.
142 D3 **Neligh** U.S.A.
77 P3 **Nel'kan** Rus. Fed.
90 F1 **Nel'kan** Rus. Fed.
87 B3 **Nellore** India
130 F5 **Nelson** Canada
131 K3 **Nelson** *r.* Canada
72 D4 **Nelson** N.Z.
104 E4 **Nelson** U.K.
141 E4 **Nelson** U.S.A.
70 D7 **Nelson, Cape** Australia
156 B8 **Nelson, Estrecho** *sea chan.* Chile
71 J4 **Nelson Bay** Australia
130 E3 **Nelson Forks** Canada
131 J3 **Nelson House** Canada
125 I2 **Nelspruit** S. Africa
120 B3 **Néma** Mauritania
116 I3 **Nema** Rus. Fed.
134 A2 **Nemadji** *r.* U.S.A.
116 B4 **Neman** Rus. Fed.
85 E4 **Ne'matābād** Iran
116 G3 **Nemda** *r.* Rus. Fed.
116 J2 **Nemed** Rus. Fed.
135 F2 **Nemegos** Canada
102 O1 **Nemetskiy, Mys** *c.* Rus. Fed.
110 F2 **Nemours** France
81 I2 **Nemrut Dağı** *hill* Turkey
94 I3 **Nemuro** Japan
94 I3 **Nemuro-kaikyō** *sea chan.* Japan
117 D5 **Nemyriv** Ukr.
107 C5 **Nenagh** Rep. of Ireland
105 H5 **Nene** *r.* U.K.
90 E2 **Nenjiang** China
108 E5 **Nennig** Germany
116 F1 **Nenoksa** Rus. Fed.
143 E4 **Neosho** U.S.A.
142 E4 **Neosho** *r.* U.S.A.
89 E3 **Nepal** *country* Asia
135 J3 **Nepean** Canada
141 G2 **Nephi** U.S.A.
107 B3 **Nephin** *hill* Rep. of Ireland
107 B3 **Nephin Beg Range** *hills* Rep. of Ireland
122 C3 **Nepoko** *r.* Dem. Rep. Congo
147 F4 **Neptune** U.S.A.
110 E4 **Nérac** France
71 J1 **Nerang** Australia
90 D1 **Nerchinsk** Rus. Fed.
116 G3 **Nerekhta** Rus. Fed.
114 G3 **Neretva** *r.* Bos.-Herz./Croatia
123 C5 **Neriquinha** Angola
103 M5 **Neris** *r.* Lith.
116 F3 **Nerl'** *r.* Rus. Fed.
158 C2 **Nerópolis** Brazil
90 E1 **Neryungri** Rus. Fed.
108 D1 **Nes** Neth.
103 J3 **Nes** Norway
103 J3 **Nesbyen** Norway
102 D2 **Neskaupstaður** Iceland
108 A5 **Nesle** France
102 K2 **Nesna** Norway
106 D3 **Ness, Loch** *l.* U.K.
142 D4 **Ness City** U.S.A.

117 E5 Novomoskovs'k Ukr.
117 D5 Novomyrhorod Ukr.
117 G5 Novonikolayevka Rus. Fed.
83 G1 Novonikolskoye Kazakh.
117 E6 Novooleksiyivka Ukr.
82 D2 Novoorsk Rus. Fed.
82 F1 Novopokrovka Kustanayskaya Oblast' Kazakh.
83 F1 Novopokrovka Severnyy Kazakhstan Kazakh.
83 J2 Novopokrovka Vostochnyy Kazakhstan Kazakh.
94 D2 Novopokrovka Rus. Fed.
117 G6 Novopokrovskaya Rus. Fed.
117 I5 Novorepnoye Rus. Fed.
117 F6 Novorossiysk Rus. Fed.
77 L2 Novorybnaya Rus. Fed.
113 N2 Novorzhev Rus. Fed.
117 E6 Novoselivs'ke Ukr.
113 N1 Novosel'ye Rus. Fed.
82 C1 Novosergiyevka Rus. Fed.
117 F6 Novoshakhtinsk Rus. Fed.
94 C2 Novoshakhtinskiy Rus. Fed.
76 J4 Novosibirsk Rus. Fed.
  Novosibirskiye Ostrova is New Siberia Islands
116 D3 Novosokol'niki Rus. Fed.
116 H4 Novospasskoye Rus. Fed.
82 D2 Novotroitsk Rus. Fed.
117 E6 Novotroyits'ke Ukr.
117 D5 Novoukrayinka Ukr.
82 D2 Novoural'sk Rus. Fed.
117 I5 Novouzensk Rus. Fed.
83 H1 Novovarshavka Rus. Fed.
117 C5 Novovolyns'k Ukr.
117 F5 Novovoronezh Rus. Fed.
83 J2 Novoyer'yevskoye Rus. Fed.
117 D4 Novozybkov Rus. Fed.
112 H6 Nový Jičín Czech Rep.
117 F5 Nový Oskol Rus. Fed.
76 I3 Novyy Port Rus. Fed.
116 I3 Novyy Tor'yal Rus. Fed.
76 I3 Novyy Urengoy Rus. Fed.
90 F1 Novyy Urgal Rus. Fed.
84 D4 Now Iran
143 K4 Nowata U.S.A.
84 C3 Nowbarān Iran
85 E3 Now Deh Iran
81 L3 Nowdī Iran
88 D4 Nowgong India
131 I2 Nowleye Lake Canada
112 G4 Nowogard Poland
71 I5 Nowra Australia
84 C2 Nowshahr Iran
84 C2 Now Shahr Iran
88 C2 Nowshera Pak.
113 J6 Nowy Sącz Poland
113 J6 Nowy Targ Poland
147 E4 Noxen U.S.A.
98 C1 Noy, Xé r. Laos
98 C1 Noy, Xé r. Laos
76 I3 Noyabr'sk r. Rus. Fed.
130 C3 Noyes Island U.S.A.
110 F2 Noyon France
125 F2 Nozizwe S. Africa
125 G6 Nqamakwe S. Africa
125 I4 Nqutu S. Africa
123 D5 Nsanje Malawi
122 B4 Ntandembele Dem. Rep. Congo
125 G3 Ntha S. Africa
122 D4 Ntungamo Uganda
121 F3 Nuba Mountains Sudan
81 J1 Nubarashen Armenia
121 F2 Nubian Desert Sudan
159 B3 Ñuble r. Chile
92 D1 Nüden Mongolia
154 D7 Nudo Coropuna mt. Peru
143 D6 Nueces r. U.S.A.
131 J2 Nueltin Lake Canada
150 H5 Nueva Arcadia Hond.
150 H5 Nueva Armenia Hond.
157 C2 Nueva Florida Venez.
159 F2 Nueva Helvecia Uruguay
159 B3 Nueva Imperial Chile
157 A4 Nueva Loja Ecuador
156 B6 Nueva Lubecka Arg.
151 G5 Nueva Ocotepeque Hond.
150 D2 Nueva Rosita Mex.
151 G5 Nueva San Salvador El Salvador
149 I4 Nuevitas Cuba
159 D4 Nuevo, Golfo g. Arg.
148 C2 Nuevo Casas Grandes Mex.
150 C2 Nuevo Ideal Mex.
151 E2 Nuevo Laredo Mex.
151 E2 Nuevo León state Mex.
122 E3 Nugaal watercourse Somalia
72 B7 Nugget Point N.Z.
69 F2 Nuguria Islands P.N.G.
72 F3 Nuhaka N.Z.
69 H2 Nui i. Tuvalu
98 C2 Nui Ti On mt. Vietnam
  Nu Jiang r. China see Salween
70 A4 Nukey Bluff hill Australia
69 H2 Nukufetau i. Tuvalu
67 J5 Nuku Hiva i. Fr. Polynesia
69 H2 Nukulaelae i. Tuvalu
69 F2 Nukumanu Islands P.N.G.
65 I2 Nukunono i. Pacific Ocean
82 D4 Nukus Uzbek.
68 D4 Nullagine Australia
68 C5 Nullarbor Plain Australia
92 F1 Nulu'erhu Shan mts China
70 F2 Numalla, Lake salt flat Australia
120 D4 Numan Nigeria
95 F6 Numata Japan
95 F7 Numazu Japan
103 J3 Numedal valley Norway
91 F7 Numfoor i. Indon.
71 F6 Numurkah Australia
133 H2 Nunaksaluk Island Canada
129 N3 Nunakuluut i. Greenland
  Nunap Isua c. Greenland see Farewell, Cape
146 E3 Nunda U.S.A.
71 I3 Nundle Australia
105 F5 Nuneaton U.K.
132 B3 Nungesser Lake Canada
128 B2 Nunivak Island U.S.A.
88 D2 Nunkun mt. India
77 T3 Nunligran Rus. Fed.
111 C2 Nuñomoral Spain
108 D2 Nunspeet Neth.
114 C4 Nuoro Sardinia Italy
69 G3 Nupani i. Solomon Is
86 B4 Nuqrah Saudi Arabia
157 A3 Nuquí Col.
88 E1 Nur China
84 D2 Nur r. Iran
83 H2 Nura Kazakh.
82 C1 Nura r. Kazakh.
84 C4 Nūrābād Iran
82 F4 Nurata Uzbek.
83 F4 Nuratau, Khrebet mts Uzbek.
109 J5 Nuremberg Germany
81 I2 Nurettin Turkey
85 H4 Nur Gama Pak.
150 B1 Nuri Mex.
70 C5 Nuriootpa Australia
85 H3 Nuristan reg. Afgh.
116 I4 Nurlaty Rus. Fed.
102 O3 Nurmes Fin.
102 M3 Nurmo Fin.
  Nürnberg Germany see Nuremberg
71 G3 Nurri, Mount Australia
89 H1 Nur Turu China
81 H3 Nusaybin Turkey
85 H4 Nushki Pak.
128 C4 Nutak Canada
141 H5 Nutrioso U.S.A.
88 B3 Nuttal Pak.
164 U2 Nuuk Greenland
102 N2 Nuupas Fin.

129 M2 Nuussuaq Greenland
129 M2 Nuussuaq pen. Greenland
87 C5 Nuwara Eliya Sri Lanka
124 C5 Nuwerus S. Africa
124 D6 Nuweveldberge mts S. Africa
81 J4 Nuzi Iraq
125 I3 Nwanedi Nature Reserve S. Africa
76 H3 Nyagan' Rus. Fed.
70 E5 Nyah West Australia
89 G3 Nyainqêntanglha Feng mt. China
89 G3 Nyainqêntanglha Shan mts China
89 H2 Nyainrong China
102 L3 Nyåker Sweden
121 E3 Nyala Sudan
89 F3 Nyalam China
123 C5 Nyamandhlovu Zimbabwe
116 G2 Nyandoma Rus. Fed.
116 F2 Nyandomskiy Vozvyshennost' reg. Rus. Fed.
122 B4 Nyanga r. Gabon
123 D5 Nyanga Zimbabwe
89 G3 Nyang Qu r. Xizang China
89 H3 Nyang Qu r. Xizang China
88 D3 Nyar r. India
123 D5 Nyasa, Lake Africa
116 C4 Nyasvizh Belarus
103 J5 Nyborg Denmark
102 O1 Nyborg Norway
103 K4 Nybro Sweden
129 M1 Nyeboe Land reg. Greenland
89 G3 Nyêmo China
122 D4 Nyeri Kenya
89 F3 Nyima China
90 B4 Nyingchi China
113 J7 Nyíregyháza Hungary
102 M3 Nykarleby Fin.
103 H5 Nykøbing Denmark
103 J5 Nykøbing Sjælland Denmark
103 L4 Nyköping Sweden
102 L3 Nyland Sweden
125 H2 Nylstroom S. Africa
71 G4 Nymagee Australia
71 J2 Nymboida Australia
71 J2 Nymboida r. Australia
103 L4 Nynäshamn Sweden
71 G3 Nyngan Australia
113 K4 Nyoman r. Belarus/Lith.
112 C7 Nyon Switz.
110 G4 Nyons France
76 G3 Nyrob Rus. Fed.
112 H5 Nysa Poland
116 I2 Nyuchpas Rus. Fed.
94 F5 Nyūdō-zaki pt Japan
122 C4 Nyunzu Dem. Rep. Congo
76 H3 Nyurba Rus. Fed.
116 I2 Nyuvchim Rus. Fed.
117 E6 Nyzhn'ohirs'kyy Ukr.
124 B4 Nzega Tanz.
120 B4 Nzérékoré Guinea
122 B4 N'zeto Angola
125 I1 Nzhelele Dam S. Africa
123 E5 Nzwani i. Comoros

O

142 C2 Oahe, Lake U.S.A.
140 C1 Oahu i. U.S.A.
70 D4 Oakbank Australia
141 F2 Oak City U.S.A.
143 E6 Oakdale U.S.A.
71 I1 Oakey Australia
105 G5 Oakham U.K.
103 N4 Oak Harbor U.S.A.
146 D6 Oak Hill U.S.A.
140 C3 Oakhurst U.S.A.
134 B2 Oak Island U.S.A.
140 A3 Oakland CA U.S.A.
146 D6 Oakland MD U.S.A.
142 D3 Oakland NE U.S.A.
138 B3 Oakland OR U.S.A.
71 G5 Oaklands Australia
134 D5 Oak Lawn U.S.A.
142 C4 Oakley U.S.A.
68 C4 Oakover r. Australia
138 B3 Oakridge U.S.A.
145 C4 Oak Ridge U.S.A.
70 D4 Oakvale Australia
135 H4 Oakville Canada
72 C6 Oamaru N.Z.
72 C6 Oaro N.Z.
97 B3 Oas Phil.
138 D3 Oasis U.S.A.
73 B5 Oates Land reg. Antarctica
71 G9 Oatlands Australia
151 E4 Oatman U.S.A.
151 E4 Oaxaca Mex.
76 H3 Oaxaca state Mex.
120 D4 Ob' r. Rus. Fed.
95 D7 Obala Cameroon
95 E6 Obama Japan
111 C1 Obanazawa Japan
132 F4 O Barco Spain
130 H2 Obatogama Lake Canada
72 B6 Obed Canada
109 H4 Obelisk mt. N.Z.
109 I3 Oberaula Germany
108 D3 Oberdorla Germany
146 C4 Oberhausen Germany
146 B4 Oberlin KS U.S.A.
109 F5 Oberlin OH U.S.A.
70 E6 Obermoschel Germany
109 K5 Oberon Australia
109 H4 Oberpfälzer Wald mts Germany
109 H4 Obersinn Germany
109 G4 Oberthulba Germany
109 H3 Obertshausen Germany
91 E7 Oberwälder Land reg. Germany
155 G4 Obi i. Indon.
83 G5 Óbidos Brazil
94 H3 Obigarm Tajik.
117 H6 Obihiro Japan
157 C2 Obil'noye Rus. Fed.
90 F2 Obluch'ye Rus. Fed.
116 F4 Obninsk Rus. Fed.
122 C3 Obo Centr. Afr. Rep.
122 A2 Obo China
124 E4 Obock Djibouti
96 E3 Ŏbŏk N. Korea
122 C4 Obokote Dem. Rep. Congo
122 B4 Obouya Congo
117 F6 Oboyan' Rus. Fed.
116 G2 Obozerskiy Rus. Fed.
80 D2 Obruk Turkey
82 C2 Obshchiy Syrt hill Rus. Fed.
76 I2 Obskaya Guba sea chan. Rus. Fed.
120 B4 Obuasi Ghana
117 D5 Obukhiv Ukr.
76 G3 Ob"yachevo Rus. Fed.
145 D6 Ocala U.S.A.
157 C4 Ocamo r. Venez.
150 D2 Ocampo Mex.
111 E3 Ocaña Spain
154 C6 Occidental, Cordillera mts Chile
157 A4 Occidental, Cordillera mts Col.
154 C6 Occidental, Cordillera mts Peru
130 B3 Ocean Cape pt U.S.A.
147 F5 Ocean City NJ U.S.A.
130 D4 Ocean Falls Canada

66 Oceania
140 D5 Oceanside U.S.A.
143 F6 Ocean Springs U.S.A.
117 D6 Ochakiv Ukr.
117 G7 Och'amch'ire Georgia
106 E4 Ochil Hills U.K.
88 C1 Ochili Pass Afgh.
109 I5 Ochsenfurt Germany
108 F2 Ochtrup Germany
103 L3 Ockelbo Sweden
113 L7 Ocolaşul Mare, Vârful mt. Romania
137 J5 Oconee r. U.S.A.
134 C4 Oconomowoc U.S.A.
134 D3 Oconto U.S.A.
151 F4 Ocosingo Mex.
150 H5 Ocotal Nicaragua
140 D5 Ocotillo Wells U.S.A.
151 E5 Ocotlán Mex.
120 B4 Oda Ghana
95 C7 Ōda Japan
102 C2 Ódáðahraun lava field Iceland
96 E3 Ódaejin N. Korea
94 G4 Ōdate Japan
95 F7 Odawara Japan
103 I3 Odda Norway
131 J3 Odei r. Canada
134 C5 Odell U.S.A.
111 B4 Odemira Port.
80 A2 Ödemiş Turkey
125 G3 Odendaalsrus S. Africa
103 I5 Odense Denmark
109 G5 Odenwald reg. Germany
109 I3 Oder r. Germany
  alt. Odra (Poland)
112 G3 Oderbucht b. Germany
117 D6 Odesa Ukr.
103 K4 Ödeshog Sweden
143 C6 Odessa U.S.A.
83 H1 Odesskoye Rus. Fed.
111 C4 Odiel r. Spain
120 B4 Odienné Côte d'Ivoire
116 F4 Odintsovo Rus. Fed.
98 C3 Ôdôngk Cambodia
112 G4 Odra r. Poland
  alt. Oder (Germany)
155 K5 Oeiras Brazil
142 C3 Oelrichs U.S.A.
109 K4 Oelsnitz Germany
134 B4 Oelwein U.S.A.
108 D1 Oenkerk Neth.
81 H1 Of Turkey
114 G4 Ofanto r. Italy
109 K4 Offenbach am Main Germany
108 F6 Offenburg Germany
115 L6 Ofidoussa i. Greece
94 G5 Ōfunato Japan
94 F5 Oga Japan
122 E3 Ogadên reg. Eth.
94 F5 Oga-hantō pen. Japan
95 E7 Ōgaki Japan
142 C3 Ogallala U.S.A.
135 H2 Ogascanane, Lac l. Canada
120 C4 Ogbomoso Nigeria
142 E3 Ogden UT U.S.A.
138 E3 Ogden UT U.S.A.
130 C3 Ogden, Mount Canada
147 F2 Ogdensburg U.S.A.
128 E3 Ogilvie r. Canada
128 C2 Ogilvie Mountains Canada
82 C5 Oglanly Turkm.
145 C5 Oglethorpe, Mount U.S.A.
114 D1 Oglio r. Italy
120 C4 Ogoja Nigeria
132 E3 Ogoki r. Canada
132 D3 Ogoki Reservoir Canada
115 J3 Ogosta r. Bulg.
103 N4 Ogre Latvia
114 F2 Ogulin Croatia
82 C5 Ogurchinskiy, Ostrov i. Turkm.
81 K1 Oğuz Azer.
72 B6 Ohai N.Z.
72 E3 Ohakune N.Z.
94 G4 Ōhata Japan
72 B6 Ohau, Lake N.Z.
159 B2 O'Higgins admin. reg. Chile
156 B7 O'Higgins, Lago l. Chile
144 C4 Ohio r. U.S.A.
146 B4 Ohio state U.S.A.
71 C7 Ohre r. Germany
109 I4 Ohre r. Czech Rep.
109 J2 Ohre r. Germany
115 I4 Ohrid Macedonia
115 I4 Ohrid, Lake Albania/Macedonia
125 I2 Ohrigstad S. Africa
109 H5 Öhringen Germany
72 E3 Ohura N.Z.
155 H3 Oiapoque Brazil
73 B3 Oich, Loch l. U.K.
89 H3 Oiga China
108 A4 Oignies France
146 D4 Oil City U.S.A.
140 C4 Oildale U.S.A.
110 F2 Oise r. France
95 B8 Ōita Japan
115 J5 Oiti mt. Greece
140 C4 Ojai U.S.A.
159 D2 Ojeda Arg.
134 B3 Ojibwa U.S.A.
148 D3 Ojinaga Mex.
151 E4 Ojitlán Mex.
95 F6 Ojiya Japan
150 A2 Ojo de Liebre, Lago b. Mex.
150 D5 Ojos del Salado, Nevado mt. Arg.
116 G4 Oka r. Rus. Fed.
123 B6 Okahandja Namibia
72 E3 Okahukura N.Z.
123 B6 Okakarara Namibia
133 H2 Okak Islands Canada
132 F5 Okanagan Falls Canada
132 F5 Okanagan Lake Canada
138 C1 Okanogan U.S.A.
138 B1 Okanogan Range mts U.S.A.
88 C3 Okara Pak.
82 C5 Okarem Turkm.
123 B5 Okaukuejo Namibia
123 C5 Okavango r. Botswana/Namibia
123 C5 Okavango Delta swamp Botswana
95 D6 Okaya Japan
95 D7 Okayama Japan
95 E7 Okazaki Japan
145 D7 Okeechobee U.S.A.
145 D7 Okeechobee, Lake U.S.A.
145 D6 Okefenokee Swamp U.S.A.
105 C7 Okehampton U.K.
89 F4 Okha India
88 B5 Okha India
90 G1 Okha Rus. Fed.
89 G4 Okha Rann marsh India
77 P3 Okhotka r. Rus. Fed.
77 P4 Okhotsk Rus. Fed.
77 P4 Okhotsk, Sea of g. Rus. Fed.
  see Okhotsk, Sea of
117 E5 Okhtyrka Ukr.
95 D5 Okinawa i. Japan
90 E4 Okinawa-guntō is Japan
95 C6 Oki-shotō is Japan
90 E4 Okinoshima i. Japan
95 B6 Oki-shotō is Japan
143 D5 Oklahoma state U.S.A.
143 D5 Oklahoma City U.S.A.
134 B5 Okmulgee U.S.A.
130 D3 Okondja Gabon
130 G4 Okotoks Canada
116 E4 Okovskiy Les for. Rus. Fed.
122 B4 Okoyo Congo
83 J3 Okpety, Gora mt. Kazakh.

102 M1 Øksfjord Norway
116 F2 Oksovskiy Rus. Fed.
83 G5 Oktyabr' Tajik.
116 I4 Oktyabr'sk Rus. Fed.
116 J2 Oktyabr'skiy Rus. Fed.
117 G6 Oktyabr'skiy Rus. Fed.
76 G4 Oktyabr'skiy Rus. Fed.
90 H1 Oktyabr'skiy Rus. Fed.
83 F5 Oktyabr'skiy Uzbek.
82 E1 Oktyabr'skoye Kazakh.
82 C1 Oktyabr'skoye Rus. Fed.
82 E1 Oktyabr'skoye Rus. Fed.
76 H3 Oktyabr'skoye Rus. Fed.
77 K2 Oktyabr'skoy Revolyutsii, Ostrov i. Rus. Fed.
82 D4 Oktyah'sk Turkm.
116 E3 Okulovka Rus. Fed.
94 F3 Okushiri-tō i. Japan
92 B1 Okwa watercourse Botswana
102 B1 Ólafsvík Iceland
140 C3 Olancha U.S.A.
140 C3 Olancha Peak mt. U.S.A.
150 H5 Olanchito Hond.
103 L4 Öland i. Sweden
102 O2 Olanga Rus. Fed.
70 D4 Olary Australia
70 D4 Olary watercourse Australia
142 E4 Olathe U.S.A.
159 E3 Olavarría Arg.
112 H5 Oława Poland
141 G5 Olberg U.S.A.
114 C4 Olbia Sardinia Italy
146 D3 Olcott U.S.A.
71 J3 Old Bar Australia
87 C2 Old Bastar India
107 D4 Oldcastle Rep. of Ireland
128 E3 Old Crow Canada
108 D1 Oldeboorn Neth.
109 G1 Oldenburg Germany
112 D3 Oldenburg in Holstein Germany
108 E2 Oldenzaal Neth.
102 M1 Olderdalen Norway
147 H3 Old Forge NY U.S.A.
147 F4 Old Forge PA U.S.A.
104 E4 Oldham U.K.
107 C6 Old Head of Kinsale Rep. of Ireland
130 H4 Oldman r. Canada
106 F3 Oldmeldrum U.K.
147 H3 Old Orchard Beach U.S.A.
133 H4 Old Perlican Canada
130 G4 Olds Canada
147 I2 Old Town U.S.A.
131 H4 Old Wives Lake Canada
141 H4 Old Woman Mountains U.S.A.
146 D3 Olean U.S.A.
113 K3 Olecko Poland
77 N3 Olekma r. Rus. Fed.
77 N3 Olekminsk Rus. Fed.
117 E5 Oleksandriya Ukr.
77 N2 Olenek Rus. Fed.
103 I4 Ølen Norway
77 M3 Olenek r. Rus. Fed.
77 N2 Olenek Rus. Fed.
77 N2 Olenekskiy Zaliv b. Rus. Fed.
116 E3 Olenino Rus. Fed.
83 H1 Olenti r. Pavlodarskaya Oblast' Kazakh.
82 C2 Olenti r. Zapadnyy Kazakhstan Kazakh.
117 C5 Olevs'k Ukr.
94 D3 Ol'ga Rus. Fed.
111 C4 Olhão Port.
124 C2 Olifants watercourse Namibia
125 I1 Olifants r. S. Africa
124 D6 Olifants r. W. Cape S. Africa
124 C6 Olifants r. W. Cape S. Africa
124 C5 Olifantshoek S. Africa
124 C6 Olifantsrivierberge mts S. Africa
159 F2 Olimar Grande r. Uruguay
158 D3 Olímpia Brazil
151 E5 Olinalá Mex.
155 L5 Olinda Brazil
158 B3 Oliva Arg.
111 F3 Oliva Spain
156 C3 Oliva, Cordillera de mts Arg./Chile
159 C1 Olivares, Cerro de mt. Chile
146 B5 Olive Hill U.S.A.
158 B3 Oliveira Brazil
111 C3 Olivenza Spain
142 E2 Olivia U.S.A.
156 C3 Ollagüe Chile
159 B1 Ollita, Cordillera de mts Arg./Chile
159 B1 Ollitas mt. Arg.
154 C5 Olmos Peru
147 G3 Olmstedville U.S.A.
105 G6 Olney U.K.
144 C4 Olney U.S.A.
103 K4 Olofström Sweden
112 H6 Olomouc Czech Rep.
116 E2 Olonets Rus. Fed.
97 B3 Olongapo Phil.
110 D5 Oloron-Ste-Marie France
111 H1 Olot Spain
90 D1 Olovyannaya Rus. Fed.
109 F3 Olpe Germany
113 J3 Olsztyn Poland
115 L2 Olt r. Romania
112 C7 Olten Switz.
115 L2 Olteniţa Romania
81 H1 Oltu Turkey
97 C4 Olutanga i. Phil.
138 B2 Olympia U.S.A.
115 J6 Olympus, Mount Greece
138 B2 Olympus, Mount U.S.A.
77 R3 Olyutorskiy, Mys c. Rus. Fed.
77 S4 Olyutorskiy Zaliv b. Rus. Fed.
94 G4 Ōma Japan
95 E6 Ōmachi Japan
95 F7 Omae-zaki pt Japan
107 E3 Omagh U.K.
142 E3 Omaha U.S.A.
123 B6 Omaheke admin. reg. Namibia
138 C1 Omak U.S.A.
86 E6 Oman country Asia
85 E5 Oman, Gulf of Asia
72 B6 Omarama N.Z.
123 B5 Omaruru Namibia
123 B5 Omatako watercourse Namibia
154 D7 Omate Peru
123 C6 Omaweneno Botswana
94 G4 Ōma-zaki c. Japan
114 C2 Omegna Italy
124 E5 Omdraaisvlei S. Africa
121 F3 Omdurman Sudan
95 F7 Ōme Japan
150 H5 Ometepe, Isla de i. Nicaragua
122 E2 Om Hajer Eritrea
85 D3 Omīdīyeh Iran
130 D3 Omineca Mountains Canada
94 G4 Ominato Japan
95 F7 Ōmiya Japan
108 E2 Ommen Neth.
81 K2 Ömnögovĭ prov. Mongolia
124 C1 Omo National Park Eth.
124 E2 Omo r. Eth.
96 G4 Omolon Rus. Fed.
77 Q3 Omolon r. Rus. Fed.
77 Q3 Omsukchan Rus. Fed.
82 F1 Omsk Rus. Fed.
94 G5 Omono-gawa r. Japan
94 H2 Ōmū Japan

115 K2 Omu, Vârful mt. Romania
95 B4 Ōmura Japan
134 B4 Onalaska U.S.A.
147 F6 Onancock U.S.A.
132 D4 Onaping Lake Canada
150 B1 Onavas Mex.
135 E3 Onaway U.S.A.
98 A2 Onbingwin Myanmar
159 D1 Oncativo Arg.
104 C3 Onchan U.K.
123 B5 Ondangwa Namibia
123 B5 Ondekaremba Namibia
124 D5 Onderstedorings S. Africa
123 B5 Ondjiva Angola
120 C4 Ondo Nigeria
90 D2 Öndörhaan Mongolia
96 A1 Ondor Had China
92 B1 Ondor Mod China
96 A1 Ondor Sum China
116 E2 Onega Rus. Fed.
124 D1 One Botswana
116 F2 Onega r. Rus. Fed.
116 E2 Onega, Lake Rus. Fed.
147 H2 Oneida U.S.A.
147 H2 Oneida Lake U.S.A.
142 D3 O'Neill U.S.A.
90 H2 Onekotan, Ostrov i. Rus. Fed.
147 H3 Oneonta U.S.A.
113 M7 Oneşti Romania
116 E1 Onezhskaya Guba g. Rus. Fed.
116 E1 Onezhskoye Ozero l. Rus. Fed.
  see Onega, Lake
72 F3 Ongaonga N.Z.
122 A3 Ongo Gabon
124 E4 Ongers watercourse S. Africa
96 C5 Ongjin N. Korea
87 C3 Ongole India
124 B1 Onjati Mountain Namibia
95 E7 Ōno Japan
69 I4 Ono-i-Lau i. Fiji
95 D7 Onomichi Japan
69 H2 Onotoa i. Kiribati
124 C4 Onseepkans S. Africa
68 B4 Onslow Australia
145 E5 Onslow Bay U.S.A.
96 F2 Onsŏng N. Korea
108 E2 Onstwedde Neth.
95 E7 Ontake-san vol. Japan
132 E3 Ontario prov. Canada
138 C2 Ontario U.S.A.
146 E3 Ontario, Lake Canada/U.S.A.
134 C2 Ontonagon U.S.A.
69 F2 Ontong Java Atoll Solomon Is
70 B2 Oodnadatta Australia
70 B3 Oodla Wirra Australia
108 D2 Oostburg Neth.
108 C3 Oosterhout Neth.
108 B3 Oosterschelde est. Neth.
108 D1 Oosterwolde Neth.
108 B4 Oostvleteren Belgium
108 D1 Oost-Vlieland Neth.
130 D4 Ootsa Lake Canada
130 D4 Ootsa Lake l. Canada
122 C4 Opala Dem. Rep. Congo
112 H6 Opava Czech Rep.
145 C6 Opelika U.S.A.
143 E6 Opelousas U.S.A.
138 E1 Opheim U.S.A.
122 C3 Opienge Dem. Rep. Congo
132 F3 Opinaca r. Canada
132 F3 Opinaca, Réservoir resr Canada
132 D3 Opinnagau r. Canada
81 J5 Opis Iraq
133 G3 Opiscotéo, Lac l. Canada
108 C2 Opmeer Neth.
116 D3 Opochka Rus. Fed.
112 H5 Opole Poland
111 B2 Oporto Port.
72 F3 Ōpōtiki N.Z.
145 C6 Opp U.S.A.
102 J3 Oppdal Norway
72 E3 Opunake N.Z.
123 B5 Opuwo Namibia
83 H5 Oqsu r. Tajik.
134 D4 Oquawka U.S.A.
147 H2 Oquossoc U.S.A.
82 D2 Or' r. Rus. Fed.
141 G5 Oracle U.S.A.
141 G5 Oracle Junction U.S.A.
113 J7 Oradea Romania
102 D2 Öræfajökull glacier Iceland
115 I3 Orahovac Yugo.
88 D4 Orai India
120 B3 Oran Alg.
156 D2 Orán Arg.
96 C4 Orang N. Korea
71 H4 Orange Australia
110 G4 Orange France
124 C4 Orange r. Namibia/S. Africa
143 E6 Orange TX U.S.A.
147 I2 Orange MA U.S.A.
147 G3 Orange VA U.S.A.
155 H3 Orange, Cabo c. Brazil
163 J8 Orange Cone sea feature S. Atlantic Ocean
  Orange Free State prov. S. Africa see Free State
135 G3 Orangeville Canada
151 H5 Orange Walk Belize
97 B3 Orani Phil.
109 L2 Oranienburg Germany
123 B6 Oranjemund Namibia
157 L6 Oranjestad Aruba
107 C4 Oranmore Rep. of Ireland
123 C6 Orapa Botswana
115 J2 Orăştie Romania
115 J2 Oraviţa Romania
80 C1 Orbetello Italy
111 D1 Orbigo r. Spain
71 H6 Orbost Australia
102 L3 Örebro Sweden
134 B3 Oregon IL U.S.A.

134 C4 Oregon WI U.S.A.
138 B3 Oregon state U.S.A.
116 B4 Orekhovo-Zuyevo Rus. Fed.
116 F4 Orel Rus. Fed.
90 F1 Orel', Ozero l. Rus. Fed.
141 G1 Orem U.S.A.
80 A2 Ören Turkey
115 L6 Ören Turkey
82 C2 Orenburg Rus. Fed.
82 C2 Orenburgskaya Oblast' admin. div. Rus. Fed.
159 E3 Orense Arg.
72 A7 Orepuki N.Z.
103 K5 Öresund strait Denmark
72 B7 Oreti r. N.Z.
72 E2 Orewa N.Z.
108 D4 Oreye Belgium
105 I5 Orford U.K.
105 I5 Orford Ness spit U.K.
141 F5 Organ Pipe Cactus National Monument res. U.S.A.
85 H3 Orgūn Afgh.
80 B2 Orhaneli Turkey
116 I3 Orhangazi Turkey
116 I3 Orhei Moldova
147 I2 Orient U.S.A.
154 E7 Oriental, Cordillera mts Bol.
154 C5 Oriental, Cordillera mts Col.
154 D6 Oriental, Cordillera mts Peru
159 E3 Oriente Arg.
111 F3 Orihuela Spain
135 H5 Orillia Canada
103 N3 Orimattila Fin.
157 E2 Orinoco r. Col./Venez.
157 E2 Orinoco Delta Venez.
87 D1 Orissa India
103 M4 Orissaare Estonia
114 C4 Oristano Sardinia Italy
103 N3 Orivesi Fin.
103 N3 Orivesi l. Fin.
157 G4 Oriximiná Brazil
151 E4 Orizaba Mex.
151 E4 Orizaba, Pico de vol. Mex.
102 J3 Orkanger Norway
103 K4 Örkelljunga Sweden
102 J3 Orkla r. Norway
125 G3 Orkney S. Africa
106 E6 Orkney Islands U.K.
140 A2 Orland U.S.A.
158 A2 Orlândia Brazil
145 D6 Orlando U.S.A.
110 E3 Orléans France
147 I2 Orleans MA U.S.A.
147 G2 Orleans VT U.S.A.
116 F4 Orlovskaya Oblast' admin. div. Rus. Fed.
117 G6 Orlovskiy Rus. Fed.
97 C4 Ormara Pak.
85 B5 Ormara, Ras hd Pak.
97 C4 Ormoc Phil.
145 D6 Ormond Beach U.S.A.
104 E4 Ormskirk U.K.
137 Q2 Ormstown Canada
110 E3 Orne r. France
102 L3 Örnsköldsvik Sweden
96 N4 Oro N. Korea
157 C3 Orocué Col.
120 B3 Orodara Burkina
138 C2 Orofino U.S.A.
139 F9 Orogrande U.S.A.
133 G4 Oromocto Canada
69 I2 Orona i. Kiribati
147 I2 Orono U.S.A.
106 B4 Oronsay i. U.K.
97 B4 Oroquieta Phil.
155 K5 Orós, Açude resr Brazil
114 C4 Orosei Sardinia Italy
114 C4 Orosei, Golfo di b. Sardinia Italy
113 J7 Orosháza Hungary
141 G5 Oro Valley U.S.A.
140 B2 Oroville CA U.S.A.
138 C1 Oroville WA U.S.A.
140 B1 Oroville, Lake U.S.A.
103 K3 Orsa Sweden
116 D4 Orsha Belarus
82 D2 Orsk Rus. Fed.
103 I3 Ørsta Norway
111 C1 Ortegal, Cabo c. Spain
110 D5 Orthez France
111 C1 Ortigueira Spain
150 B1 Ortiz Mex.
157 D2 Ortiz Venez.
114 D1 Ortles mt. Italy
114 F3 Ortona Italy
142 D2 Ortonville U.S.A.
77 N3 Orulgan, Khrebet mts Rus. Fed.
124 D1 Orumbo Namibia
  Orūmīyeh Iran see Urmia
  Orūmīyeh, Daryācheh-ye salt l. Iran see Urmia, Lake
154 E7 Oruro Bol.
114 E3 Orvieto Italy
73 B3 Orville Coast Antarctica
146 C4 Orwell OH U.S.A.
147 G3 Orwell VT U.S.A.
105 I6 Orwell r. U.K.
150 I6 Osa, Península de Costa Rica
134 A4 Osage r. U.S.A.
95 D7 Osaka Japan
83 H2 Osakarovka Kazakh.
103 K4 Osby Sweden
143 F5 Osceola AR U.S.A.
134 C3 Osceola IA U.S.A.
109 L3 Oschatz Germany
109 L3 Oschersleben (Bode) Germany
114 C4 Oschiri Sardinia Italy
116 F4 Osetr r. Rus. Fed.
135 I3 Osgoode Canada
138 D3 Osgood Mountains U.S.A.
81 O5 Osh Kyrg.
123 B5 Oshakati Namibia
135 H4 Oshawa Canada
94 G5 Oshika-hantō pen. Japan
94 G4 Ō-shima i. Japan
95 F7 Ō-shima i. Japan
142 C3 Oshkosh NE U.S.A.
134 C3 Oshkosh WI U.S.A.
120 C4 Oshogbo Nigeria
85 I5 Oshtorān Kūh mt. Iran
85 I5 Oshtorīnān Iran
122 B4 Oshwe Dem. Rep. Congo
114 G2 Osijek Croatia
88 C4 Osiyan India
125 I3 Osizweni S. Africa
114 E3 Osimo Italy
103 L4 Oskarshamn Sweden
131 J5 Oskélanéo Canada
117 F5 Oskol r. Rus. Fed.
103 J4 Oslo Norway
103 J4 Oslofjorden sea chan. Norway
80 C1 Osmancık Turkey
80 D1 Osmaneli Turkey
80 E3 Osmaniye Turkey
103 O4 Os'mino Rus. Fed.
109 G2 Osnabrück Germany

115 J3 Osogovska Planina mts Bulg./Macedonia
159 B4 Osorno Chile
111 D1 Osorno Spain
159 B4 Osorno, Volcán vol. Chile
130 F5 Osoyoos Canada
103 I3 Øseyri Norway
68 E3 Osprey Reef Coral Sea Is Terr.
108 D3 Oss Neth.
71 G8 Ossa, Mount Australia
134 B3 Osseo U.S.A.
135 F3 Ossineke U.S.A.
147 H3 Ossipee Lake U.S.A.
109 J3 Oßmannstedt Germany
133 H3 Ossokmanuan Lake Canada
116 E3 Ostashkov Rus. Fed.
109 F2 Ostbevern Germany
109 H1 Oste r. Germany
108 A3 Ostend Belgium
113 O5 Øster Norway
109 J2 Osterburg (Altmark) Germany
103 K4 Österbymo Sweden
103 J3 Österdalälven l. Sweden
103 J3 Østerdalen valley Norway
109 J3 Osterfeld Germany
109 G1 Osterholz-Scharmbeck Germany
109 I3 Osterode am Harz Germany
102 K3 Östersund Sweden
109 I3 Osterwieck Germany
72 B7 Ostfriesland reg. Germany
103 L3 Östhammar Sweden
112 I6 Ostrava Czech Rep.
113 I4 Ostróda Poland
117 F5 Ostrogozhsk Rus. Fed.
114 C5 Ostrov Czech Rep.
116 D3 Ostrov Rus. Fed.
113 J5 Ostrowiec Świętokrzyski Poland
113 J4 Ostrów Mazowiecka Poland
112 H5 Ostrów Wielkopolski Poland
113 K3 Osûm r. Bulg.
95 B9 Ōsumi-kaikyō sea chan. Japan
95 B9 Ōsumi-shotō is Japan
124 C5 Osuna Spain
147 F2 Oswegatchie U.S.A.
134 C5 Oswego IL U.S.A.
147 I3 Oswego NY U.S.A.
147 E3 Oswego r. U.S.A.
105 D5 Oswestry U.K.
95 F6 Ōta Japan
72 C6 Otago Peninsula N.Z.
72 E4 Otaki N.Z.
102 N2 Otanmäki Fin.
97 B4 Otar Kazakh.
94 D3 Otaru Japan
72 B7 Otatara N.Z.
154 C3 Otavalo Ecuador
123 B5 Otavi Namibia
95 G6 Ōtawara Japan
83 I4 Otegen Batyr Kazakh.
72 C6 Otematata N.Z.
103 N4 Otepää Estonia
138 C2 Othello U.S.A.
150 C2 Otinapa Mex.
72 C5 Otira N.Z.
147 E3 Otisco Lake U.S.A.
133 F3 Otish, Monts mts Canada
123 B6 Otjiwarongo Namibia
104 F4 Otley U.K.
94 H2 Otoineppu Japan
72 E3 Otorohanga N.Z.
132 C3 Otoskwin r. Canada
82 B3 Otpan, Gora hill Kazakh.
82 B1 Otradnyy Rus. Fed.
115 H4 Otranto Italy
115 H4 Otranto, Strait of Albania/Italy
77 S3 Otrozhnyy Rus. Fed.
134 E4 Otsego U.S.A.
134 E3 Otsego Lake MI U.S.A.
147 F3 Otsego Lake NY U.S.A.
147 F3 Otselic U.S.A.
95 D7 Ōtsu Japan
103 J3 Otta Norway
135 H3 Ottawa r. Canada
135 H2 Ottawa U.S.A.
134 C5 Ottawa IL U.S.A.
134 E4 Ottawa KS U.S.A.
146 A4 Ottawa OH U.S.A.
132 D2 Ottawa Islands Canada
104 E2 Otterburn U.K.
141 G2 Otter Creek Reservoir U.S.A.
134 D1 Otter Island Canada
132 D3 Otter Rapids Canada
109 H1 Ottersberg Germany
105 C7 Ottery r. U.K.
108 C4 Ottignies Belgium
129 J1 Otto Fiord inlet Canada
83 H4 Ottuk Kyrg.
134 A5 Ottumwa U.S.A.
108 F5 Ottweiler Germany
120 C4 Otukpo Nigeria
156 D3 Otumpa Arg.
154 C5 Otuzco Peru
70 E7 Otway, Cape Australia
93 B6 Ou, Nam r. Laos
143 E5 Ouachita r. U.S.A.
143 E5 Ouachita, Lake U.S.A.
143 E5 Ouachita Mountains U.S.A.
122 C3 Ouadda Centr. Afr. Rep.
121 E3 Ouaddaï reg. Chad
120 B3 Ouagadougou Burkina
120 B3 Ouahigouya Burkina
120 B3 Oualâta Mauritania
122 C3 Ouanda-Djallé Centr. Afr. Rep.
120 B2 Ouarâne reg. Mauritania
120 C1 Ouargla Alg.
120 B1 Ouarzazate Morocco
124 F6 Oubergpas pass S. Africa
108 B4 Oudenaarde Belgium
108 F1 Oude Pekela Neth.
124 E8 Oudtshoorn S. Africa
108 C3 Oud-Turnhout Belgium
111 H5 Oued Tlélat Alg.
120 B1 Oued Zem Morocco
114 B6 Ouessant, Île d' i. France
122 B3 Ouesso Congo
120 C4 Ouidah Benin
150 B2 Ouiriego Mex.
120 B1 Oujda Morocco
102 N2 Oulainen Fin.
111 H4 Ouled Farès Alg.
102 N2 Oulu Fin.
102 N2 Oulujärvi l. Fin.
102 N2 Oulujoki r. Fin.
110 H4 Oulx Italy
121 E3 Oum-Chalouba Chad
120 B4 Oumé Côte d'Ivoire
121 D3 Oum-Hadjer Chad
102 N2 Ounasjoki r. Fin.
105 G5 Oundle U.K.
121 E3 Ounianga Kébir Chad
108 B5 Oupeye Belgium
108 F5 Our r. Lux.
139 F4 Ouray CO U.S.A.
141 H1 Ouray UT U.S.A.
111 C1 Ourense Spain
155 J5 Ouricuri Brazil
158 B3 Ourinhos Brazil
158 D1 Ouro r. Brazil
158 D3 Ouro Preto Brazil
108 C4 Ourthe r. Belgium
104 G4 Ouse r. England U.K.
105 H7 Ouse r. England U.K.
131 F4 Outardes r. Canada
106 A2 Outer Hebrides is U.K.
134 C3 Outer Island Canada
140 C5 Outer Santa Barbara Channel U.S.A.
123 B6 Outjo Namibia

128 H4 Outlook Canada
102 O3 Outokumpu Fin.
106 □ Out Skerries is U.K.
69 G4 Ouvéa i. New Caledonia
93 D5 Ouyanghai Shuiku resr China
70 E5 Ouyen Australia
105 G5 Ouzel r. U.K.
114 C4 Ovace, Punta d' mt. Corsica France
81 G2 Ovacık Turkey
114 C2 Ovada Italy
69 H3 Ovalau i. Fiji
159 B1 Ovalle Chile
111 B2 Ovar Port.
159 D2 Oveja mt. Arg.
71 G6 Ovens r. Australia
108 F4 Overath Germany
102 M2 Överkalix Sweden
141 E3 Overton U.S.A.
102 M2 Övertorneå Sweden
103 L4 Överum Sweden
108 C2 Overveen Neth.
134 C4 Ovid U.S.A.
111 D1 Oviedo Spain
102 N1 Øvre Anárjokka Nasjonalpark nat. park Norway
102 L1 Øvre Dividal Nasjonalpark nat. park Norway
103 J3 Øvre Rendal Norway
117 D5 Ovruch Ukr.
72 B7 Owaka N.Z.
122 B4 Owando Congo
95 E7 Owase Japan
142 E2 Owatonna U.S.A.
85 F3 Owbeh Afgh.
147 E3 Owego U.S.A.
107 D3 Owenmore r. Rep. of Ireland
72 D4 Owen River N.Z.
140 C3 Owens r. U.S.A.
134 C4 Owensboro U.S.A.
135 G3 Owen Sound Canada
135 G3 Owen Sound inlet Canada
68 E2 Owen Stanley Range mts P.N.G.
120 C4 Owerri Nigeria
146 B5 Owingsville U.S.A.
147 I2 Owls Head U.S.A.
120 C4 Owo Nigeria
135 E4 Owosso U.S.A.
81 K4 Owrāmān, Kūh-e mts Iran/Iraq
138 C3 Owyhee U.S.A.
138 C3 Owyhee r. U.S.A.
138 C3 Owyhee Mountains U.S.A.
154 C6 Oxapampa Peru
131 I5 Oxbow Canada
147 I1 Oxbow U.S.A.
103 L4 Oxelösund Sweden
72 D5 Oxford N.Z.
105 F6 Oxford U.K.
135 F4 Oxford MI U.S.A.
143 F5 Oxford MS U.S.A.
147 F3 Oxford NY U.S.A.
147 F5 Oxford PA U.S.A.
131 J4 Oxford House Canada
131 J4 Oxford Lake Canada
70 F5 Oxley Australia
71 I3 Oxleys Peak Australia
140 C4 Oxnard U.S.A.
135 H3 Oxtongue Lake Canada
102 K2 Øya Norway
95 F6 Oyama Japan
155 H3 Oyapock r. Brazil/Fr. Guiana
83 J3 Oychilik Kazakh.
122 B3 Oyem Gabon
106 D3 Oykel r. U.K.
89 H5 Oyster Island Myanmar
83 H4 Oy-Tal Kyrg.
81 I2 Ozalp Turkey
97 B4 Ozamiz Phil.
145 C6 Ozark AL U.S.A.
134 E2 Ozark MI U.S.A.
143 E4 Ozark Plateau U.S.A.
142 E4 Ozarks, Lake of the U.S.A.
84 E3 Ozbagū Iran
90 H1 Ozernovskiy Rus. Fed.
82 E1 Ozernoye Kazakh.
82 E2 Ozernoye Rus. Fed.
116 E4 Ozernyy Orenburgskaya Oblast' Rus. Fed.
116 E4 Ozernyy Smolenskaya Oblast' Rus. Fed.
113 K3 Ozersk Rus. Fed.
116 F4 Ozery Rus. Fed.
83 H4 Özgön Kyrg.
114 C4 Ozieri Sardinia Italy
82 B2 Ozinki Rus. Fed.
143 C6 Ozona U.S.A.
95 B7 Ozuki Japan
117 G7 Ozurget'i Georgia

P

129 N3 Paamiut Greenland
98 A1 Pa-an Myanmar
124 C6 Paarl S. Africa
106 A4 Pabbay i. Scotland U.K.
106 A3 Pabbay i. Scotland U.K.
96 B3 P'abal-li N. Korea
113 I5 Pabianice Poland
89 G4 Pabna Bangl.
103 N5 Pabradė Lith.
154 D3 Pacaás Novos, Parque Nacional nat. park Brazil
154 C5 Pacasmayo Peru
139 E6 Pacheco Chihuahua Mex.
150 D2 Pacheco Zacatecas Mex.
116 H2 Pachikha Rus. Fed.
114 C6 Pachino Sicily Italy
87 D1 Pachmarhi India
150 E4 Pachuca Mex.
140 B2 Pacific U.S.A.
161 I9 Pacific-Antarctic Ridge sea feature Pacific Ocean
160 Pacific Ocean
97 C4 Pacijan i. Phil.
158 C1 Pacoval Brazil
158 D2 Pacuí r. Brazil
112 H5 Paczków Poland
97 C5 Padada Phil.
99 B3 Padang Indon.
99 B4 Padang Endau Malaysia
99 B3 Padangpanjang Indon.
99 B3 Padangsidimpuan Indon.
99 C3 Padangtikar i. Indon.
116 E2 Padany Rus. Fed.
81 L5 Padatha, Kūh-e mt. Iran
157 H1 Padauiri r. Brazil
154 F8 Padcaya Bol.
130 F3 Paddle Prairie Canada
109 D3 Paderborn Germany
115 J2 Padeşu, Vârful mt. Romania
154 F8 Padilla Bol.
102 L2 Padjelanta nationalpark nat. park Sweden
89 G5 Padma r. Bangl./India alt. Ganga, conv. Ganges
Padova Italy see Padua
143 D7 Padre Island U.S.A.
114 C3 Padro, Monte mt. Corsica France

105 C7 Padstow U.K.
113 M3 Padsvillye Belarus
70 D6 Padthaway Australia
87 D2 Padua India
114 D2 Padua Italy
144 B4 Paducah KY U.S.A.
143 C5 Paducah TX U.S.A.
88 B2 Padum Jammu and Kashmir
96 E3 Paegam N. Korea
96 C5 Paengnyŏng-do i. N. Korea
72 E2 Paeroa N.Z.
97 B3 Paete Phil.
Pafos Cyprus see Paphos
125 I1 Pafuri Moz.
114 F2 Pag Croatia
114 F2 Pag i. Croatia
97 B5 Pagadian Phil.
99 B3 Pagai Selatan i. Indon.
99 B3 Pagai Utara i. Indon.
91 G5 Pagan i. N. Mariana Is
99 E3 Pagatan Indon.
141 G3 Page U.S.A.
103 M5 Pagegiai Lith.
156 □ Paget, Mount Atlantic Ocean
139 F4 Pagosa Springs U.S.A.
89 G4 Pagri China
132 C3 Pagwa River Canada
140 □2 Pahala U.S.A.
99 B4 Pahang r. Malaysia
88 B2 Paharpur Pak.
72 A7 Pahia Point N.Z.
140 □2 Pahoa U.S.A.
145 D7 Pahokee U.S.A.
85 F3 Pahra Kariz Afgh.
141 E3 Pahranagat Range mts U.S.A.
88 D4 Pahuj r. India
140 D3 Pahute Mesa plat. U.S.A.
98 A1 Pai Thai.
103 N4 Paide Estonia
105 D7 Paignton U.K.
103 N3 Päijänne l. Fin.
89 E3 Paikü Co l. China
98 B2 Pailin Cambodia
159 B5 Paillaco Chile
140 □2 Pailolo Chan. U.S.A.
103 M3 Paimio Fin.
159 B3 Paine Chile
154 C6 Painesville U.S.A.
141 G3 Painted Desert U.S.A.
141 F5 Painted Rock Reservoir U.S.A.
70 C3 Painter, Mount Australia
131 J3 Paint Lake Provincial Recreation Park Canada
146 B6 Paintsville U.S.A.
135 G3 Paisley Canada
106 E5 Paisley U.K.
154 B5 Paita Peru
95 A5 Paitan, Teluk b. Sabah Malaysia
93 D4 Paizhou China
102 M2 Pajala Sweden
155 K5 Pajeú r. Brazil
98 B4 Paka Malaysia
157 E4 Pakaraima Mountains Brazil
151 I6 Pakaraima Mountains Guyana
96 J7 Pakch'ŏn N. Korea
77 R3 Pakhachi Rus. Fed.
82 D7 Pakhar' Kazakh.
83 H4 Pakhtaabad Uzbek.
85 H4 Pakistan country Asia
72 D1 Pakotai N.Z.
88 C2 Pakpattan Pak.
98 A2 Pak Phayun Thai.
103 M5 Pakruojis Lith.
113 I7 Paks Hungary
98 B2 Pak Thong Chai Thai.
85 H3 Paktīkā reg. Afgh.
98 C2 Pakxé Laos
121 D4 Pala Chad
98 A2 Pela Myanmar
99 C4 Palabuhanratu Indon.
99 C4 Palabuhanratu, Teluk b. Indon.
114 G3 Palagruža i. Croatia
115 J7 Palaiochora Greece
110 F2 Palaiseau France
87 D1 Pala Laharha India
124 E1 Palamakoloi Botswana
125 H2 Palamós Spain
88 C4 Palana India
97 Q4 Palana Rus. Fed.
97 B3 Palanan Phil.
84 B3 Palanan Point Phil.
85 F4 Palangān Iran
99 D3 Palangān, Kūh-e mts Iran
99 C3 Palangkaraya Indon.
91 E7 Palanpur India
85 G4 Palanpur Pak.
85 G4 Palantak Pak.
97 C3 Palapag Phil.
123 C6 Palapye Botswana
87 B3 Palasbari India
77 Q3 Palatka Rus. Fed.
145 D6 Palatka U.S.A.
97 B2 Palaui i. Phil.
97 A3 Palauig Phil.
160 D5 Palau country Pacific Ocean
160 D5 Palau Islands Palau
98 A2 Palauk Myanmar
160 D5 Palau Trench sea feature N. Pacific Ocean
98 A2 Palaw Myanmar
97 A4 Palawan i. Phil.
160 C5 Palawan Trough sea feature N. Pacific Ocean
97 B3 Palayan Phil.
103 N4 Paldiski Estonia
89 H5 Pale Myanmar
108 D2 Paleis Het Loo Neth.
99 B3 Palembang Indon.
156 B6 Palena Chile
111 D1 Palencia Spain
151 G4 Palenque Mex.
114 E5 Palermo Sicily Italy
143 E5 Palestine U.S.A.
89 H5 Paletwa Myanmar
87 B2 Palghat India
67 F2 Palikir Micronesia
89 H4 Palin Myanmar
114 F4 Palinuro, Capo c. Italy
108 D5 Paliseul Belgium
88 B5 Palitana India
103 M4 Palivere Estonia
87 D3 Palkohda India
87 B3 Palkonda Range mts India
87 B3 Palk Strait India/Sri Lanka
71 I2 Pallamallawa Australia
107 C5 Pallas Green Rep. of Ireland
102 M1 Pallas ja Ounastunturin kansallispuisto nat. park Fin.
88 C3 Pallavaram India
87 B2 Palleru r. India
72 E4 Palliser Bay N.Z.
72 E4 Palliser, Cape N.Z.
111 D4 Palma del Río Spain
111 H3 Palma de Mallorca Spain
158 C1 Palmares Brazil
157 H3 Palmarito Venez.
120 B4 Palmas, Cape Liberia
158 D1 Palmas de Monte Alto Brazil
145 D7 Palm Bay U.S.A.
155 K5 Palmeira Brazil
158 E1 Palmeirais Brazil
155 J5 Palmeiras Brazil

128 D3 Palmer U.S.A.
73 B2 Palmer Land reg. Antarctica
67 I5 Palmerston atoll Cook Is
72 C6 Palmerston N.Z.
72 E4 Palmerston North N.Z.
147 E7 Palmerton U.S.A.
145 E7 Palmetto Point Bahamas
114 F5 Palmi Italy
151 E3 Palmillas Mex.
157 A4 Palmira Col.
150 D5 Palmito del Verde, Isla i. Mex.
140 D5 Palm Springs U.S.A.
Palmyra Syria see Tadmur
134 B6 Palmyra MO U.S.A.
134 C4 Palmyra NY U.S.A.
67 J5 Palmyra Atoll N. Pacific Ocean
87 F5 Palmyras Point India
140 A3 Palo Alto U.S.A.
121 F3 Paloich Sudan
102 M1 Palojärvi Fin.
102 M1 Palomaa Fin.
140 D5 Palomar Mountain U.S.A.
141 G6 Palomas Mex.
87 C2 Paloncha India
91 E7 Palopo Indon.
111 F4 Palos, Cabo de c. Spain
141 F5 Palo Verde AZ U.S.A.
141 E5 Palo Verde CA U.S.A.
102 N2 Paltamo Fin.
91 D7 Palu Indon.
81 G2 Palu Turkey
82 F5 Pal'vart Turkm.
88 D3 Palwal India
77 S3 Palyavaam r. Rus. Fed.
84 B4 Pamban Channel India
71 H6 Pambula Australia
99 C4 Pameungpeuk Indon.
87 B3 Pamidi India
110 E5 Pamiers France
83 H5 Pamir mts Asia
83 H5 Pamir r. Afgh./Tajik.
145 E5 Pamlico Sound sea chan. U.S.A.
143 C5 Pampa U.S.A.
154 F7 Pampa Grande Bol.
156 D2 Pampas Arg.
97 B3 Pamplona Phil.
111 F1 Pamplona Spain
109 J1 Pampow Germany
80 C1 Pamukova Turkey
146 E6 Pamunkey r. U.S.A.
88 D2 Pamzal Jammu and Kashmir
144 B4 Pana U.S.A.
158 C1 Panabá, Serra do hills Brazil
141 E3 Panaca U.S.A.
97 C5 Panabo Phil.
97 A4 Panaitan i. Indon.
87 A3 Panaji India
146 I6 Panama country Central America
150 J7 Panamá, Bahía de b. Panama
150 J6 Panama, Gulf of g. Panama
150 J6 Panama Canal Panama
150 J6 Panama City Panama
145 C6 Panama City U.S.A.
140 D3 Panamint Range mts U.S.A.
140 D3 Panamint Springs U.S.A.
140 D3 Panamint Valley U.S.A.
97 C5 Panarea, Isola i. Isole Lipari Italy
99 C2 Panarik Indon.
97 B4 Panay i. Phil.
97 C3 Panay Gulf Phil.
115 J2 Pančevo Yugo.
82 E1 Panchevka Kazakh.
109 I1 Panchen Germany
99 D2 Pandan Bay Phil.
99 D2 Pandan Reservoir Sing.
88 E5 Pandaria India
158 D1 Pandeiros r. Minas Gerais Brazil
88 D5 Pandhana India
158 F2 Pando Uruguay
105 E6 Pandy U.K.
103 N5 Panevėžys Lith.
88 D2 Pangi Range mts Pak.
99 A2 Pangkalanbuun Indon.
99 C2 Pangkalansusu Indon.
91 E7 Pangkalpinang, Tanjung pt Indon.
129 L3 Pangnirtung Canada
76 I3 Pangody Rus. Fed.
159 B3 Panguipulli Chile
159 B3 Panguipulli, Lago l. Chile
141 F3 Panguitch U.S.A.
98 A3 Pangururan Indon.
97 B5 Pangutaran Group is Phil.
122 C4 Pania-Mwanga Dem. Rep. Congo
88 B3 Panikoita i. India
117 Q5 Panino Rus. Fed.
88 D3 Panipat India
83 H4 Panj r. Afgh./Tajik.
83 G5 Panj Tajik.
83 H5 Panjāb Afgh.
83 H4 Panjakent Tajik.
85 H3 Panjgur Pak.
94 B2 Panjin China
88 B2 Panjnad r. Pak.
103 O3 Pankakoski Fin.
120 C4 Pankshin Nigeria
96 F2 Pan Ling mts China
68 D4 Panna India
133 G3 Pannawonica Australia
158 B1 Panorama Brazil
83 G4 Panshan China
93 B5 Panxian China
93 A5 Panzhihua China
122 B4 Panzi Dem. Rep. Congo
151 G5 Panzós Guat.
157 E3 Pao r. Venez.
114 F5 Paola Italy
144 C4 Paoli U.S.A.
122 C3 Paoua Centr. Afr. Rep.
83 G4 Pap Uzbek.
113 H7 Pápa Hungary
114 F4 Papa, Monte del mt. Italy
72 D5 Papakura N.Z.
151 F4 Papantla Mex.
106 □ Papa Stour i. U.K.
72 E3 Paparoa Range mts N.Z.
87 C2 Paparhandi India
72 B7 Papatowai N.Z.
106 □ Papa Westray i. U.K.
109 G1 Papenburg Germany
80 D4 Paphos Cyprus
136 E6 Papigochic r. Mex.
73 B2 Papua research station Antarctica

155 G7 Pantanal Matogrossense, Parque Nacional do nat. park Brazil
114 D6 Pantelleria Sicily Italy
114 D6 Pantelleria, Isola di i. Sicily Italy
97 C5 Pantukan Phil.
151 E3 Pánuco Mex.
151 E3 Pánuco r. Mex.

135 J2 Papineau-Labelle, Réserve Faunique de res. Canada
141 E3 Papoose Lake U.S.A.
109 I6 Pappenheim Germany
106 B5 Paps of Jura hills U.K.
68 E2 Papua, Gulf of P.N.G.
68 E2 Papua New Guinea country Oceania
98 A1 Papun Myanmar
105 C7 Par U.K.
158 D2 Pará r. Brazil
116 G4 Para r. Rus. Fed.
155 I4 Pará, Rio do r. Brazil
68 B4 Paraburdoo Australia
97 B3 Paracale Phil.
158 C2 Paracatu Brazil
158 C2 Paracatu r. Brazil
70 C3 Parachilna Australia
85 H3 Parachinar Pak.
115 I3 Paraćin Yugo.
158 D2 Pará de Minas Brazil
135 I1 Paradis Canada
140 B2 Paradise CA U.S.A.
131 H4 Paradise MI U.S.A.
140 D2 Paradise Hill Canada
140 D2 Paradise Peak U.S.A.
133 I3 Paradise River Canada
143 F4 Paragould U.S.A.
154 F6 Paragua r. Bol.
157 A3 Paragua r. Venez.
155 G7 Paraguaçu, Península de pen. Brazil
157 E2 Paraguaipoa Venez.
156 E2 Paraguarí Para.
156 E2 Paraguay country S. America
156 E2 Paraguay r. Arg./Para.
155 K5 Paraíba r. Brazil
155 K5 Paraíba state Brazil
158 D3 Paraíba do Sul r. Brazil
151 F4 Paraíso Mex.
158 E2 Paraíso, Monte hill Brazil
120 C4 Parakou Benin
70 B3 Parakylia Australia
87 D2 Paralakhemundi India
88 B6 Paralakot India
87 B4 Paramakkudi India
155 G2 Paramaribo Suriname
157 B3 Paramillo mt. Col.
157 A3 Paramillo, Parque Nacional nat. park Col.
158 D1 Paramirim Brazil
157 A3 Paramo Frontino mt. Col.
147 F4 Paramus U.S.A.
90 H1 Paramushir, Ostrov i. Rus. Fed.
159 E2 Paraná Arg.
156 I6 Paraná r. Brazil
158 C4 Paraná r. Brazil
158 C1 Paraná r. S. America
158 B2 Paranaíba Brazil
158 B2 Paranaíba r. Brazil
159 E2 Paraná Ibicuy r. Arg.
158 C4 Paranapanema r. Brazil
158 C4 Paranapiacaba, Serra mts Brazil
97 B4 Parang Phil.
88 B4 Parangippettai India
115 J2 Parângul Mare, Vârful mt. Romania
88 C4 Parantij India
158 D2 Paraopeba r. Brazil
72 E4 Paraparaumu N.Z.
150 D2 Paras Mex.
88 D5 Paratwada India
81 K4 Parāū, Kūh-e mt. Iraq
158 B2 Paraúna Brazil
110 G3 Paray-le-Monial France
88 D4 Parbati r. India
87 B2 Parbhani India
109 H1 Parchim Germany
134 C4 Pardeeville U.S.A.
89 G2 Parding China
158 E1 Pardo r. Bahia/Minas Gerais Brazil
158 B3 Pardo r. Mato Grosso do Sul Brazil
158 D1 Pardo r. Minas Gerais Brazil
158 C3 Pardo r. São Paulo Brazil
112 G5 Pardubice Czech Rep.
88 D2 Pare Chu r. China
154 F6 Parecis, Serra dos hills Brazil
150 D2 Paredón Mex.
84 B2 Pareh Iran
72 D1 Parengarenga Harbour N.Z.
132 E4 Parent, Lac l. Canada
72 E3 Pareora N.Z.
159 D2 Parera Arg.
116 G3 Parfen'yevo Rus. Fed.
113 O2 Parfino Rus. Fed.
115 I5 Parga Greece
103 M3 Pargas Fin.
157 E2 Pariaguán Venez.
141 F3 Paria Plateau U.S.A.
103 O3 Parikkala Fin.
157 H4 Parima, Serra mts Brazil
157 D4 Parima-Tapirapecó, Parque Nacional nat. park Venez.
154 D4 Pariñas, Punta pt Peru
155 G4 Parintins Brazil
135 G4 Paris Canada
110 F2 Paris France
110 F2 Paris France (City Plan 58)
146 A5 Paris KY U.S.A.
146 B4 Paris TN U.S.A.
143 E5 Paris TX U.S.A.
134 C2 Parisienne, Île i. Canada
150 I7 Parita Panama
84 D4 Pariz Iran
82 E1 Parizh Rus. Fed.
103 O3 Parkano Fin.
141 G5 Parker U.S.A.
146 E5 Parker U.S.A.
93 □ Parker, Mount Hong Kong China
141 E4 Parker Dam U.S.A.
131 J2 Parker Lake Canada
146 D4 Parkersburg U.S.A.
71 H4 Parkes Australia
134 B3 Park Falls U.S.A.
133 J5 Park Forest U.S.A.
142 C3 Park Rapids U.S.A.
130 E5 Parksville Canada
141 G4 Park Valley U.S.A.
114 D2 Parma Italy
146 C3 Parma ID U.S.A.
146 C4 Parma OH U.S.A.
155 I4 Parnaíba Brazil
155 J4 Parnaíba r. Brazil
72 C6 Parnassus N.Z.
115 J5 Parnassus mt. Greece
71 H5 Parndana Australia
115 J6 Parnon mts Greece
103 N4 Pärnu Estonia
103 N4 Pärnu-Jaagupi Estonia
70 □ Paroo watercourse Australia
85 G3 Paropamisus mts Afgh.
115 K6 Paros Greece
115 K6 Paros i. Greece
157 B4 Pavón Col.
141 F3 Parowan U.S.A.
88 E3 Parowan U.S.A.

159 B3 Parral Chile
147 F6 Parramore Island U.S.A.
150 D2 Parras Mex.
159 D3 Parravicini Arg.
105 E6 Parrett r. U.K.
153 H6 Parrita Costa Rica
131 H5 Parrsboro Canada
128 G2 Parry, Cape Canada
128 G2 Parry Islands Canada
135 G3 Parry Sound Canada
143 E4 Parsons KS U.S.A.
146 D5 Parsons WV U.S.A.
109 H4 Partenstein Germany
110 D3 Parthenay France
105 H4 Partington Rus. Fed.
107 B4 Partry Mountains Rep. of Ireland
155 I4 Paru r. Brazil
87 D3 Parvatipuram India
87 B3 Parwan India
123 F5 Parys S. Africa
140 C4 Pasadena CA U.S.A.
143 E6 Pasadena TX U.S.A.
154 B4 Pasado, Cabo pt Ecuador
92 A4 Pa Sak, Mae Nam r. Thai.
84 D4 Pasargadae Iran
98 A1 Pasarseblat Indon.
98 A1 Pasawng Myanmar
143 F6 Pascagoula U.S.A.
135 I1 Pascaud Canada
113 M7 Paşcani Romania
138 C2 Pasco U.S.A.
158 E2 Pascoal, Monte hill Brazil
Pascua, Isla de i. S. Pacific Ocean see Easter Island
97 B3 Pascual Phil.
Pas de Calais strait France/U.K. see Dover, Strait of
112 G4 Pasewalk Germany
131 H3 Pasfield Lake Canada
116 F2 Pasha Rus. Fed.
97 B3 Pasig Phil.
81 H2 Pasinler Turkey
98 □ Pasir Gudang Malaysia
98 □ Pasir Panjang Sing.
99 B1 Pasir Putih Malaysia
140 A2 Paskenta U.S.A.
85 F5 Paskūh Iran
85 F5 Pasni Pak.
151 I4 Paso Caballos Guat.
159 F2 Paso de los Toros Uruguay
156 B7 Paso Río Mayo Arg.
140 B4 Paso Robles U.S.A.
131 I4 Pasquia Hills Canada
147 I2 Passadumkeag U.S.A.
134 C1 Passage Island U.S.A.
112 F6 Passau Germany
159 F3 Passo Fundo Brazil
158 C3 Passos Brazil
116 C4 Pastavy Belarus
154 C4 Pastaza r. Peru
157 A4 Pasto Col.
141 H3 Pastora Peak mt. U.S.A.
97 B2 Pasuquin Phil.
99 D4 Pasuruan Indon.
103 N5 Pasvalys Lith.
97 B5 Pata i. Phil.
156 D3 Patagonia reg. Arg.
141 G6 Patagonia U.S.A.
89 G4 Patakata India
88 D5 Patan Gujarat India
88 D5 Patan Madhya Pradesh India
89 F4 Patan Nepal
71 I4 Patchewollock Australia
147 G3 Patchogue U.S.A.
72 E3 Patea N.Z.
120 C4 Pategi Nigeria
124 F6 Patensie S. Africa
114 F6 Paternò Sicily Italy
71 I4 Paterson Australia
147 G1 Paterson U.S.A.
147 F4 Paterson U.S.A.
88 C2 Pathankot India
138 F3 Pathfinder Reservoir U.S.A.
98 A3 Pathiu Thai.
87 B2 Pathri India
98 B2 Pathum Thani Thai.
99 D4 Pati Indon.
157 A4 Patía r. Col.
88 D3 Patiala India
115 L5 Patmos i. Greece
89 F4 Patna India
87 C1 Patnagarh India
97 B4 Patnanongan i. Phil.
81 I2 Patnos Turkey
115 H4 Patos Albania
155 K5 Patos Brazil
158 D2 Patos, Lagoa dos l. Brazil
158 C2 Patos de Minas Brazil
159 C1 Patquía Arg.
115 I5 Patras Greece
102 B2 Patreksfjörður Iceland
158 C1 Patrocínio Brazil
102 O1 Patsoyoki r. Europe
98 A2 Pattani Thai.
92 A4 Pattani, Mae Nam r. Thai.
98 B2 Pattaya Thai.
147 I2 Patten U.S.A.
109 H2 Pattensen Germany
140 B3 Patterson U.S.A.
146 D5 Patterson U.S.A.
130 C2 Patterson, Mount Canada
140 C3 Patterson, Point U.S.A.
102 N2 Pättikkä Fin.
87 B3 Pattikonda India
130 D3 Pattullo, Mount Canada
89 G5 Patuakhali Bangl.
131 J4 Patuanak Canada
83 G4 Patuca r. Hond.
150 H5 Patuca, Punta pt Hond.
146 E5 Patuxent Range mts Antarctica
150 D5 Pátzcuaro Mex.
110 D5 Pauillac France
98 A2 Paukkaung Myanmar
141 H3 Paulden U.S.A.
146 A4 Paulding U.S.A.
133 J5 Paul Island Canada
155 J5 Paulistana Brazil
155 J5 Paulo Afonso Brazil
125 I3 Paulpietersburg S. Africa
143 D5 Paul's Valley U.S.A.
147 F1 Paul Smiths U.S.A.
158 E2 Pavão Brazil
84 B3 Pāveh Iran
114 C2 Pavia Italy
103 M4 Pāvilosta Latvia
116 H3 Pavino Rus. Fed.
115 K4 Pavlikeni Bulg.
83 H2 Pavlodar Kazakh.
82 F1 Pavlodarskaya Oblast' admin. div. Kazakh.
83 H1 Pavlohrad Ukr.
83 H2 Pavlovka Kazakh.
117 H6 Pavlovka Rus. Fed.
116 G4 Pavlovo Rus. Fed.
116 F5 Pavlovsk Rus. Fed.
117 F6 Pavlovskaya Rus. Fed.
157 B4 Pavón Col.
88 E3 Pawayan India

120 B3 Pô, Parc National de nat. park Burkina
163 P10 Pobeda Ice Island Antarctica
83 J4 Pobeda Peak China/Kyrg.
146 C5 Pocahontas U.S.A.
146 C5 Pocatalico r. U.S.A.
138 D3 Pocatello U.S.A.
117 O5 Pochayiv Ukr.
116 E4 Pochep Rus. Fed.
116 H4 Pochinki Rus. Fed.
116 E4 Pochinok Rus. Fed.
116 F2 Pocking Germany
104 G4 Pocklington U.K.
158 F4 Poções Brazil
147 F5 Pocomoke City U.S.A.
147 F6 Pocomoke Sound b. U.S.A.
158 A2 Poconé Brazil
147 F4 Pocono Mountains U.S.A.
147 F4 Pocono Summit U.S.A.
158 C3 Poços de Caldas Brazil
117 F5 Poddor'ye Rus. Fed.
115 H3 Podgorica Yugo.
76 J4 Podgornoye Rus. Fed.
87 B3 Podile India
77 K3 Podkamennaya Tunguska r. Rus. Fed.
82 A2 Podlesnoye Rus. Fed.
154 C4 Podocarpus, Parque Nacional nat. park Ecuador
116 F4 Podol'sk Rus. Fed.
116 E2 Podporozh'ye Rus. Fed.
114 C7 Podravina reg. Hungary
115 I3 Podujevo Yugo.
116 H2 Podvoloch'ye Rus. Fed.
116 I2 Podz' Rus. Fed.
135 G2 Pofadder S. Africa
135 G2 Pogamasing Canada
117 E4 Pogar Rus. Fed.
115 I4 Pogradec Albania
158 A2 Poguba r. Brazil
96 E5 P'ohang S. Korea
67 F2 Pohnpei atoll Micronesia
117 D5 Pohrebyshche Ukr.
88 D4 Pohri India
115 J3 Poiana Mare Romania
73 C6 Poie Dem. Rep. Congo
163 C6 Poinsett, Cape Antarctica
140 A2 Point Arena U.S.A.
149 L5 Point-Comfort Canada
155 G3 Pointe au Baril Station Canada
122 B4 Pointe-Noire Congo
53 G3 Point Hope U.S.A.
70 A4 Point Kenny Australia
130 C1 Point Lake Canada
71 J3 Point Lookout U.S.A.
135 F5 Point Pelee National Park Canada
147 F4 Point Pleasant NJ U.S.A.
146 B5 Point Pleasant WV U.S.A.
135 K2 Poisson Blanc, Lac du l. Canada
110 E3 Poitiers France
110 D3 Poitou reg. France
158 E1 Pojuca Brazil
88 B4 Pokaran India
71 H2 Pokataroo Australia
89 E3 Pokhara Nepal
122 C1 Pokhvistnevo Rus. Fed.
73 C6 Poko Dem. Rep. Congo
88 A4 Pokran Pak.
83 G2 Pokrovka Rus. Fed.
82 C1 Pokrovka Primorskiy Kray Rus. Fed.
94 C2 Pokrovka Primorskiy Kray Rus. Fed.
77 N3 Pokrovsk Rus. Fed.
77 F6 Pokrovskoye Rus. Fed.
116 H2 Pokshen'ga r. Rus. Fed.
97 J6 Pola Phil.
141 G4 Polacca U.S.A.
141 G4 Polacca Wash r. U.S.A.
111 D1 Pola de Lena Spain
111 D1 Pola de Siero Spain
112 H4 Poland country Europe
147 F3 Poland U.S.A.
132 D3 Polar Bear Provincial Park Canada
80 D2 Polatlı Turkey
117 B4 Polatsk Belarus
113 M3 Polatskaya Nizina lowland Belarus
87 C2 Polavaram India
102 M2 Polcirkeln Sweden
112 H2 Poldarsa Rus. Fed.
84 B2 Pol Dasht Iran
84 D4 Pol-e Fāsā Iran
85 F2 Pole-Khatum Iran
85 H3 Pol-e Khomri Afgh.
116 B4 Polessk Rus. Fed.
99 E3 Polewali Indon.
121 D4 Poli Cameroon
112 G4 Police Poland
112 G4 Policoro Italy
110 G3 Poligny France
97 B3 Polillo i. Phil.
97 B3 Polillo Islands Phil.
97 B3 Polillo Strait Phil.
80 D4 Polis Cyprus
117 D5 Polis'ke Ukr.
112 H5 Polkowice Poland
87 B4 Pollachi India
109 H3 Polle Germany
111 H3 Pollença Spain
114 G5 Pollino, Monte mt. Italy
102 N1 Polmak Norway
102 O2 Polo Fin.
134 C5 Polo U.S.A.
116 I3 Polohy Ukr.
116 F4 Polom Rus. Fed.
97 C5 Polomoloc Phil.
117 C5 Polonnaruwa Sri Lanka
117 C5 Polonne Ukr.
107 C7 Polperro U.K.
138 D2 Polson U.S.A.
116 I3 Polta r. Ukr.
117 E5 Poltava Ukr.
116 B2 Poltavka Rus. Fed.
117 F6 Poltavskaya Rus. Fed.
103 N4 Põltsamaa Estonia
103 O3 Polva Estonia
103 O3 Polvijärvi Fin.
77 S3 Polyarnyy Murmanskaya Oblast' Rus. Fed.
92 P1 Polyarnyy Murmanskaya Oblast' Rus. Fed.
102 P2 Polyarnyye Zori Rus. Fed.
115 J4 Polygyros Greece
115 J4 Polykastro Greece
160 H6 Polynesia is Oceania
103 M3 Pomarkku Fin.
158 A3 Pomba r. Brazil
111 B3 Pombal Port.
158 B3 Pombo r. Brazil
125 I4 Pomézia Italy
68 F2 Pomio P.N.G.
140 D4 Pomona U.S.A.
115 M3 Pomorie Bulg.
112 G3 Pomorska, Zatoka b. Poland
116 E1 Pomorskiy Bereg coastal area Rus. Fed.
145 D7 Pompano Beach U.S.A.
158 D2 Pompéu Brazil
116 H3 Ponazyrevo Rus. Fed.
143 D5 Ponca City U.S.A.
149 K5 Ponce Puerto Rico
72 E2 Poncheville, Lac l. Canada
87 B4 Pondicherry India
132 J2 Pond Inlet Canada

133 I3 Ponds, Island of Canada
150 H5 Poneloya Nicaragua
111 C1 Ponferrada Spain
72 F4 Pongaroa N.Z.
121 E4 Pongo watercourse Sudan
125 I3 Pongola r. S. Africa
125 I3 Pongolapoort Dam resr S. Africa
113 O3 Ponizov'ye Rus. Fed.
87 B3 Ponnaivar r. India
87 A4 Ponnani India
89 H5 Ponnyadaung Range mts Myanmar
130 G4 Ponoka Canada
82 C1 Ponomarevka Rus. Fed.
120 □ Ponta do Sol Cape Verde
158 B4 Ponta Grossa Brazil
158 C2 Pontalina Brazil
110 H2 Pont-à-Mousson France
158 A3 Ponta Porã Brazil
110 H3 Pontarlier France
143 F6 Pontchartrain, Lake U.S.A.
108 C4 Pont-de-Loup Belgium
111 B3 Ponte de Sor Port.
104 F4 Pontefract U.K.
104 F2 Ponteland U.K.
155 G7 Pontes-e-Lacerda Brazil
111 B1 Pontevedra Spain
134 C5 Pontiac IL U.S.A.
134 C5 Pontiac MI U.S.A.
99 C3 Pontianak Indon.
110 D4 Pontivy France
110 B3 Pont-l'Abbé France
110 F2 Pontoise France
131 J4 Ponton Canada
143 F5 Pontotoc U.S.A.
114 C2 Pontremoli Italy
108 A5 Pont-Ste-Maxence France
71 G9 Pontville Australia
135 H5 Pontypool Canada
105 D6 Pontypool U.K.
105 D6 Pontypridd U.K.
114 E4 Ponza, Isola di i. Italy
114 E4 Ponziane, Isole is Italy
70 A4 Poochera Australia
105 F7 Poole U.K.
Poona India see Pune
70 E4 Pooncarie Australia
70 E3 Poopelloe, Lake salt l. Australia
154 E7 Poopó, Lago de l. Bol.
72 E1 Poor Knights Islands N.Z.
157 A4 Popayán Col.
108 B4 Poperinge Belgium
77 L2 Popigay r. Rus. Fed.
70 D4 Popiltah Australia
70 D4 Popiltah Lake Australia
131 J4 Poplar r. Canada
138 F1 Poplar r. U.S.A.
143 F4 Poplar Bluff U.S.A.
146 C6 Poplar Camp U.S.A.
143 F6 Poplarville U.S.A.
151 F5 Popocatépetl, Volcán vol. Mex.
122 B4 Popokabaka Dem. Rep. Congo
115 J2 Popovo Bulg.
109 I3 Poppenberg hill Germany
113 J6 Poprad Slovakia
85 G5 Porali r. Pak.
72 F4 Porangahau N.Z.
158 C1 Porangatu Brazil
88 B5 Porbandar India
157 B3 Porce r. Col.
130 C4 Porcher Island Canada
128 E3 Porcupine r. Canada/U.S.A.
133 I3 Porcupine, Cape Canada
163 H2 Porcupine Abyssal Plain sea feature N. Atlantic Ocean
131 I4 Porcupine Hills Canada
134 C2 Porcupine Mountains U.S.A.
131 I4 Porcupine Plain Canada
131 J4 Porcupine Provincial Forest res. Canada
157 C3 Pore Col.
114 E2 Poreč Croatia
116 H4 Poretskoye Rus. Fed.
103 M3 Pori Fin.
72 E4 Porirua N.Z.
116 D3 Porkhov Rus. Fed.
157 E2 Porlamar Venez.
110 C3 Pornic France
97 C4 Poro i. Phil.
90 G2 Poronaysk Rus. Fed.
115 J6 Poros Greece
116 E2 Porosozero Rus. Fed.
73 C6 Porpoise Bay Antarctica
102 N1 Porsangen sea chan. Norway
103 J4 Porsgrunn Norway
80 C2 Porsuk r. Turkey
70 C5 Port Adelaide Australia
107 E3 Portadown U.K.
107 F3 Portaferry U.K.
147 I1 Portage ME U.S.A.
134 C4 Portage MI U.S.A.
134 B4 Portage WI U.S.A.
131 J5 Portage la Prairie Canada
142 C1 Portal U.S.A.
130 E5 Port Alberni Canada
71 G7 Port Albert Australia
111 C3 Portalegre Port.
143 C5 Portales U.S.A.
130 C3 Port Alexander U.S.A.
125 G6 Port Alfred S. Africa
130 D4 Port Alice Canada
147 E4 Port Allegany U.S.A.
143 F6 Port Allen U.S.A.
138 B1 Port Angeles U.S.A.
107 D4 Portarlington Rep. of Ireland
71 G9 Port Arthur Australia
143 E6 Port Arthur U.S.A.
106 B5 Port Askaig U.K.
70 B4 Port Augusta Australia
149 J5 Port-au-Prince Haiti
135 F3 Port aux Choix Canada
107 F3 Portavogie U.K.
124 D7 Port Beaufort S. Africa
79 H5 Port Blair India
135 H3 Port Bolster Canada
111 H1 Portbou Spain
135 H4 Port Burwell Canada
70 E7 Port Campbell Australia
135 H3 Port Carling Canada
72 C6 Port Chalmers N.Z.
145 D7 Port Charlotte U.S.A.
147 G4 Port Chester U.S.A.
130 C4 Port Clements Canada
146 B4 Port Clinton U.S.A.
135 H5 Port Colborne Canada
130 E5 Port Coquitlam Canada
135 F4 Port Credit Canada
71 F9 Port Davey b. Australia
149 J5 Port-de-Paix Haiti
98 B5 Port Dickson Malaysia
135 G5 Port Dover Canada
134 D3 Porte des Morts sea chan. U.S.A.
130 C4 Port Edward Canada
125 I5 Port Edward S. Africa
158 D1 Porteirinha Brazil
155 H4 Portel Brazil
135 G3 Port Elgin Canada
125 G6 Port Elizabeth S. Africa
106 B5 Port Ellen U.K.
70 C6 Port Elliot Australia
107 E3 Port Erin U.K.
131 H2 Porter Lake Canada
130 C3 Porter Landing Canada
124 C6 Porterville S. Africa
140 C3 Porterville U.S.A.
72 E2 Port Fairy Australia
72 E7 Port Fitzroy N.Z.
122 A4 Port-Gentil Gabon
70 C4 Port Germein Australia

143 F6 Port Gibson U.S.A.
106 D5 Port Glasgow U.K.
120 C4 Port Harcourt Nigeria
130 D4 Port Hardy Canada
Port Harrison Canada see Inukjuak
133 H4 Port Hawkesbury Canada
105 D6 Porthcawl U.K.
68 B4 Port Hedland Australia
147 G2 Port Henry U.S.A.
105 B7 Porthleven U.K.
105 C5 Porthmadog U.K.
135 H4 Port Hope Canada
133 I3 Port Hope Simpson Canada
105 E6 Porthtowan U.K.
146 B4 Port Huron U.S.A.
81 L2 Port-Iliç Azer.
111 B4 Portimão Port.
93 □ Port Island Hong Kong China
71 I4 Port Jackson inlet Australia
147 G4 Port Jefferson U.S.A.
147 F4 Port Jervis U.S.A.
154 G2 Port Kaituma Guyana
71 I5 Port Kembla Australia
71 H4 Portland N.S.W. Australia
70 D7 Portland Vic. Australia
134 C5 Portland IN U.S.A.
147 H3 Portland ME U.S.A.
138 B2 Portland OR U.S.A.
105 E7 Portland, Isle of pen. U.K.
130 C3 Portland Canal inlet Canada
72 F3 Portland Island N.Z.
70 A5 Port Lincoln Australia
120 A4 Port Loko Sierra Leone
70 D7 Port MacDonnell Australia
71 J3 Port Macquarie Australia
130 D4 Port McNeill Canada
133 H4 Port-Menier Canada
128 B4 Port Moller b. U.S.A.
130 E5 Port Moody Canada
68 E2 Port Moresby P.N.G.
106 B2 Portnaguran U.K.
106 B5 Portnahaven U.K.
70 E4 Port Neill Australia
145 F7 Port Nelson Bahamas
106 B2 Port Ness U.K.
124 B4 Port Nolloth S. Africa
Port-Nouveau-Québec Canada see Kangiqsualujjuaq
Porto Port. see Oporto
154 E5 Porto Acre Brazil
158 B3 Porto Alegre Mato Grosso do Sul Brazil
156 F4 Porto Alegre Brazil
155 G6 Porto Artur Brazil
155 G6 Porto dos Gaúchos Óbidos Brazil
155 G7 Porto Esperidião Brazil
114 D3 Portoferraio Italy
155 I5 Porto Franco Brazil
157 E2 Port of Spain Trin. and Tob.
114 E2 Portogruaro Italy
120 □ Porto Inglês Cape Verde
158 A2 Porto Jofre Brazil
140 A2 Portola U.S.A.
114 D2 Portomaggiore Italy
158 A4 Porto Mendes Para.
155 G8 Porto Murtinho Brazil
155 I6 Porto Nacional Brazil
120 C4 Porto-Novo Benin
158 B3 Porto Primavera, Represa resr Brazil
138 A3 Port Orford U.S.A.
155 H4 Porto Santana Brazil
158 E2 Porto Seguro Brazil
114 E2 Porto Tolle Italy
114 C4 Porto Torres Sardinia Italy
114 C3 Porto-Vecchio Corsica France
154 F5 Porto Velho Brazil
154 B4 Portoviejo Ecuador
106 C6 Portpatrick U.K.
70 F7 Port Phillip Bay Australia
70 B4 Port Pirie Australia
106 B3 Portree U.K.
105 B7 Portreath U.K.
130 E5 Port Renfrew Canada
135 G4 Port Rowan Canada
146 E5 Port Royal U.S.A.
107 E2 Portrush U.K.
121 F1 Port Said Egypt
145 D6 Port St Joe U.S.A.
125 H5 Port St Johns S. Africa
104 C3 Port St Mary U.K.
107 D2 Portsalon Rep. of Ireland
135 H4 Port Sanilac U.S.A.
135 H3 Port Severn Canada
93 □ Port Shelter b. Hong Kong China
125 I5 Port Shepstone S. Africa
130 C4 Port Simpson Canada
105 F7 Portsmouth U.K.
147 H3 Portsmouth NH U.S.A.
146 B5 Portsmouth OH U.S.A.
147 E6 Portsmouth VA U.S.A.
106 F3 Portsoy U.K.
71 J4 Port Stephens b. Australia
107 E2 Portstewart U.K.
121 E3 Port Sudan Sudan
105 D6 Port Talbot U.K.
102 N1 Porttipahdan tekojärvi l. Fin.
111 B3 Portugal country Europe
157 C2 Portuguesa r. Venez.
107 C4 Portumna Rep. of Ireland
110 F5 Port-Vendres France
70 D5 Port Victoria Australia
69 G3 Port Vila Vanuatu
102 P1 Port Vladimir Rus. Fed.
72 E2 Port Waikato N.Z.
70 C5 Port Wakefield Australia
134 C4 Port Washington U.S.A.
134 B2 Port Wing U.S.A.
159 D2 Porvenir Arg.
103 N3 Porvoo Fin.
96 D5 Poryŏng S. Korea
156 E3 Posadas Arg.
115 H4 Posavina reg. Bos.-Herz./Croatia
135 F3 Posen U.S.A.
81 K5 Posht-e Küh mts Iran
101 D6 Posht Küh hill Iran
102 O2 Posio Fin.
99 E3 Poso Indon.
83 J1 Posof Turkey
96 D6 Posŏng S. Korea
103 M4 Pospelikha Rus. Fed.
158 C1 Posse Brazil
109 J4 Pössneck Germany
143 C5 Post U.S.A.
Poste-de-la-Baleine Canada see Kuujjuarapik
124 E4 Postmasburg S. Africa
133 I3 Postville Canada
134 B4 Postville U.S.A.
115 H3 Postojna Slovenia
94 B3 Posyet Rus. Fed.
125 G4 Potchefstroom S. Africa
143 E5 Poteau U.S.A.
155 K5 Potengi r. Brazil
114 F4 Potenza Italy
72 A7 Poteriteri, Lake N.Z.
124 C5 Potfontein S. Africa
94 C2 Pot'i Georgia
87 C2 Potikal India
131 H4 Primrose Lake Canada

120 D3 Potiskum Nigeria
138 D2 Pot Mountain U.S.A.
93 □ Po Toi i. Hong Kong China
146 E5 Potomac r. U.S.A.
146 D5 Potomac, South Branch r. U.S.A.
154 E7 Potosí Bol.
142 F4 Potosi U.S.A.
141 E4 Potosi Mountain U.S.A.
97 B4 Pototan Phil.
151 H5 Potrerillos Hond.
109 L2 Potsdam Germany
147 F2 Potsdam U.S.A.
105 E6 Potterne U.K.
147 F4 Potters Bar U.K.
87 C5 Pottuvil Sri Lanka
146 E4 Pottstown U.S.A.
146 E4 Pottsville U.S.A.
130 E3 Pouce Coupe Canada
133 J4 Pouch Cove Canada
147 G4 Poughkeepsie U.S.A.
147 G3 Poultney U.S.A.
104 E4 Poulton-le-Fylde U.K.
158 D3 Pouso Alegre Brazil
98 B2 Poŭthisăt Cambodia
116 E2 Povenets Rus. Fed.
72 F3 Poverty Bay N.Z.
115 H2 Povlen mt. Yugo.
111 B2 Póvoa de Varzim Port.
117 G5 Povorino Rus. Fed.
94 C3 Povorotnyy, Mys hd Rus. Fed.
140 D5 Poway U.S.A.
138 F3 Powder r. U.S.A.
138 E2 Powder River U.S.A.
138 E2 Powell r. U.S.A.
146 B6 Powell r. U.S.A.
141 G3 Powell, Lake resr U.S.A.
140 C2 Powell Mountain U.S.A.
145 E7 Powell Point Bahamas
130 E5 Powell River Canada
146 E6 Powhatan U.S.A.
158 A1 Poxoréu Brazil
93 E4 Poyang Hu l. China
98 □ Poyan Reservoir Sing.
134 C3 Poygan, Lake l. U.S.A.
114 G2 Požarevac Yugo.
151 E3 Poza Rica Mex.
114 G2 Požega Croatia
115 I3 Požega Yugo.
94 D1 Pozharskoye Rus. Fed.
112 H4 Poznań Poland
111 D3 Pozoblanco Spain
151 E3 Pozo Nuevo Mex.
114 F4 Pozzuoli Italy
98 B2 Prabumulih Indon.
89 F6 Prachin Buri Thai.
98 B2 Prachuap Khiri Khan Thai.
110 F5 Prades France
158 E2 Prado Brazil
112 G5 Prague Czech Rep.
Praha Czech Rep. see Prague
120 □ Praia Cape Verde
125 J2 Praia do Bilene Moz.
158 A1 Praia Rica Brazil
134 C5 Prairie Creek Reservoir U.S.A.
143 C5 Prairie Dog Town Fork r. U.S.A.
134 B4 Prairie du Chien U.S.A.
98 B2 Prakhon Chai Thai.
98 B2 Pran r. Thai.
87 B2 Pranhita r. India
99 A2 Prapat Indon.
115 L7 Prasonisi, Akra pt Greece
158 C2 Prata r. Brazil
158 C2 Prata r. Brazil
114 D3 Prato Italy
143 G5 Prattville U.S.A.
114 F4 Pravara r. Italy
113 J3 Pravdinsk Rus. Fed.
99 E4 Praya Indon.
98 C2 Preăh Vihéar Cambodia
113 P3 Prechistoye Rus. Fed.
76 J4 Predivinsk Rus. Fed.
131 J4 Preeceville Canada
116 B4 Preili Latvia
135 H1 Preissac, Lac l. Canada
71 H3 Premer Australia
110 F3 Prémery France
109 K2 Premnitz Germany
134 C5 Prentice U.S.A.
112 F4 Prenzlau Germany
83 H2 Preobrazheniye Rus. Fed.
112 H6 Přerov Czech Rep.
141 F4 Prescott U.S.A.
141 F4 Prescott Valley U.S.A.
105 C6 Preseli, Mynydd hill U.K.
115 I3 Preševo Yugo.
142 C3 Presho U.S.A.
156 D3 Presidencia Roque Sáenz Peña Arg.
155 J5 Presidente Dutra Brazil
158 C3 Presidente Epitácio Brazil
158 F6 Presidente Hermes Brazil
158 B3 Presidente Prudente Brazil
158 B3 Presidente Venceslau Brazil
143 B6 Presidio U.S.A.
82 F1 Presnogor'kovka Kazakh.
82 F1 Presnovka Kazakh.
113 J6 Prešov Slovakia
115 I4 Prespa, Lake Europe
147 J1 Presque Isle U.S.A.
134 E3 Presque Isle Point U.S.A.
105 E5 Prestatyn U.K.
104 E4 Preston U.K.
138 E3 Preston ID U.S.A.
134 A3 Preston MN U.S.A.
143 E4 Preston MO U.S.A.
141 E2 Preston NV U.S.A.
106 F5 Prestonpans U.K.
146 B6 Prestonsburg U.S.A.
106 E5 Prestwick U.K.
158 C1 Preto r. Bahia Brazil
158 B2 Preto r. Minas Gerais Brazil
125 H2 Pretoria S. Africa
115 I5 Preveza Greece
98 C3 Prey Vêng Cambodia
82 D2 Priaral'skiye Karakumy, Peski des. Kazakh.
115 H4 Priboj Yugo.
112 H6 Příbram Czech Rep.
141 G2 Price U.S.A.
133 G4 Price Canada
130 D4 Price Island Canada
143 F6 Prichard U.S.A.
116 C4 Priekule Latvia
103 M5 Prienai Lith.
124 E5 Prieska S. Africa
138 C1 Priest Lake U.S.A.
138 C1 Priest River U.S.A.
113 I6 Prievidza Slovakia
109 K1 Prignitz reg. Germany
115 H3 Prijepolje Yugo.
115 H2 Prijedor Bos.-Herz.
Prikaspiyskaya Nizmennost' lowland Kazakh./Rus. Fed. see Caspian Lowland
115 I4 Prilep Macedonia
117 H6 Primorsko-Akhtarsk Rus. Fed.
94 C2 Primorskiy Kray admin. div. Rus. Fed.
140 D5 Primo Tapia Mex.
131 H4 Primrose Lake Canada

131 H4 Prince Albert Canada
124 E6 Prince Albert S. Africa
73 B5 Prince Albert Mts Antarctica
131 H4 Prince Albert National Park Canada
128 G2 Prince Albert Peninsula Canada
124 D6 Prince Albert Road S. Africa
128 G2 Prince Albert Sound sea chan. Canada
128 F1 Prince Alfred, Cape Canada
129 K3 Prince Charles Island Canada
73 D4 Prince Charles Mts Antarctica
133 H4 Prince Edward Island prov. Canada
162 G8 Prince Edward Islands Indian Ocean
135 I4 Prince Edward Point Canada
146 E5 Prince Frederick U.S.A.
130 E4 Prince George Canada
128 E3 Prince of Wales Island Australia
129 I2 Prince of Wales Island Canada
130 C3 Prince of Wales Island U.S.A.
128 G2 Prince of Wales Strait Canada
128 F2 Prince Patrick Island Canada
129 I2 Prince Regent Inlet sea chan. Canada
130 C4 Prince Rupert Canada
147 F6 Princess Anne U.S.A.
73 D3 Princess Astrid Coast Antarctica
68 E3 Princess Charlotte Bay Australia
73 D5 Princess Elizabeth Land reg. Antarctica
131 J2 Princess Mary Lake Canada
73 D3 Princess Ragnhild Coast Antarctica
130 D4 Princess Royal Island Canada
130 E5 Princeton Canada
140 A2 Princeton CA U.S.A.
134 C5 Princeton IL U.S.A.
134 C5 Princeton IN U.S.A.
144 C4 Princeton KY U.S.A.
147 J2 Princeton ME U.S.A.
147 F4 Princeton NJ U.S.A.
134 C4 Princeton WI U.S.A.
146 C6 Princeton WV U.S.A.
128 D3 Prince William Sound b. U.S.A.
120 C4 Príncipe i. São Tomé and Príncipe
138 B2 Prineville U.S.A.
76 C2 Prins Karls Forland i. Svalbard
150 I5 Prinzapolka Nicaragua
116 C2 Priozersk Rus. Fed.
113 L5 Pripet r. Belarus/Ukr.
alt. Pryp"yat' (Ukraine), alt. Prypyats' (Belarus)
113 L5 Pripet Marshes Belarus/Ukr.
102 L5 Prirechnyy Rus. Fed.
115 I3 Prishtinë Yugo.
109 J1 Pritzier Germany
109 K1 Pritzwalk Germany
110 G4 Privas France
114 F2 Privlaka Croatia
116 H3 Privolzhsk Rus. Fed.
116 H4 Privolzhskaya Vozvyshennost' reg. Rus. Fed.
82 B1 Priyutovo Rus. Fed.
117 G6 Priyutnoye Rus. Fed.
115 I3 Prizren Yugo.
99 D4 Probolinggo Indon.
109 J4 Probstzella Germany
105 C7 Probus U.K.
134 A2 Proctor MN U.S.A.
147 G3 Proctor VT U.S.A.
155 G3 Professor van Blommestein Meer resr Suriname
151 H5 Progreso Hond.
150 D2 Progreso Coahuila Mex.
151 E3 Progreso Hidalgo Mex.
151 G3 Progreso Yucatán Mex.
117 H7 Prokhladnyy Rus. Fed.
115 I4 Prokuplje Yugo.
116 D3 Proletariy Rus. Fed.
117 G6 Proletarsk Rus. Fed.
158 B3 Promissão Brazil
128 F4 Prophet r. Canada
130 E3 Prophet River Canada
134 C5 Prophetstown U.S.A.
68 E4 Proserpine Australia
147 F3 Prospect U.S.A.
97 C4 Prosperidad Phil.
83 H2 Prostornoye Kazakh.
134 A4 Protivín Czech Rep.
115 L3 Provadiya Bulg.
110 H5 Provence reg. France
147 H4 Providence U.S.A.
72 A7 Providence, Cape N.Z.
135 F3 Providence Bay Canada
150 I5 Providencia, Isla de i. Col.
128 A3 Provideniya Rus. Fed.
147 H3 Provincetown U.S.A.
141 G1 Provo U.S.A.
131 G4 Provost Canada
158 B4 Prudentópolis Brazil
128 D2 Prudhoe Bay U.S.A.
108 E4 Prüm Germany
108 E4 Prüm r. Germany
114 C3 Prunelli-di-Fiumorbo Corsica France
113 J4 Pruszków Poland
117 D6 Prut r. Moldova/Romania
73 D5 Prydz Bay Antarctica
117 E5 Pryluky Ukr.
117 F6 Prymors'k Ukr.
113 L5 Pryp"yat' r. Ukr.
alt. Prypyats' (Belarus), conv. Pripet
113 L5 Prypyats' r. Belarus
alt. Pryp"yat' (Ukraine), conv. Pripet
113 K6 Przemyśl Poland
Przheval'sk Kyrg. see Karakol
115 K5 Psara i. Greece
117 G6 Psebay Rus. Fed.
115 I5 Pshish r. Rus. Fed.
116 D3 Pskov Rus. Fed.
116 D3 Pskov, Lake Estonia/Rus. Fed.
116 D3 Pskovskaya Oblast' admin. div. Rus. Fed.
115 I4 Ptolemaïda Greece
114 F1 Ptuj Slovenia
98 B1 Pua Thai.
159 D3 Pua China
93 D6 Pu'an China
92 D3 Pu'an China
93 H6 Pubei China
154 D5 Pucallpa Peru
93 F5 Pucheng Fujian China
92 D4 Pucheng Shaanxi China
96 D6 Puch'ŏn S. Korea
97 B4 Pucio Point Phil.
112 I3 Puck Poland
159 B3 Pucón Chile
102 O3 Pudasjärvi Fin.
104 F4 Pudsey U.K.
124 D7 Pudimoe S. Africa
84 D3 Pūdanū Iran
87 B4 Pudukkottai India

139 F4 Pueblo U.S.A.
157 C2 Pueblo Nuevo Venez.
151 F4 Pueblo Viejo tourist site Mex.
159 C3 Puelches Arg.
159 C3 Puelén Arg.
159 B2 Puente Alto Chile
151 E4 Puente de Ixtla Mex.
111 D4 Puente-Genil Spain
157 C2 Puente Torres Venez.
156 B7 Puerto Aisén Chile
154 F6 Puerto Alegre Bol.
151 F5 Puerto Ángel Mex.
151 F5 Puerto Arista Mex.
157 A4 Puerto Armuelles Panama
157 A4 Puerto Asís Col.
157 C3 Puerto Ayacucho Venez.
150 G5 Puerto Barrios Guat.
157 B3 Puerto Berrío Col.
157 C2 Puerto Cabello Venez.
150 I5 Puerto Cabezas Nicaragua
150 I5 Puerto Cabo Gracias á Dios Nicaragua
157 C3 Puerto Carreño Col.
156 E2 Puerto Casado Para.
156 B6 Puerto Cisnes Chile
156 A7 Puerto Coig Arg.
150 H5 Puerto Cortés Costa Rica
151 H5 Puerto Cortés Mex.
150 B2 Puerto Cortés Mex.
157 C2 Puerto Cumarebo Venez.
151 H3 Puerto de Morelos Mex.
151 E5 Puerto Escondido Mex.
157 C1 Puerto Estrella Col.
154 F7 Puerto Frey Bol.
156 E1 Puerto Guaraní Para.
154 E6 Puerto Heath Bol.
157 C4 Puerto Inírida Col.
155 G8 Puerto Isabel Bol.
150 H6 Puerto Jesús Costa Rica
157 D2 Puerto La Cruz Venez.
157 C3 Puerto Leguízamo Col.
150 I5 Puerto Lempira Hond.
111 D3 Puertollano Spain
159 D4 Puerto Lobos Arg.
157 B3 Puerto López Col.
151 F5 Puerto Madero Mex.
159 D4 Puerto Madryn Arg.
154 E6 Puerto Maldonado Peru
154 C5 Puerto Máncora Peru
157 C3 Puerto Miranda Venez.
159 B3 Puerto Montt Chile
150 H5 Puerto Morazán Nicaragua
156 B8 Puerto Natales Chile
157 C3 Puerto Nuevo Col.
157 A4 Puerto Obaldía Panama
157 C2 Puerto Ordaz Venez.
157 D3 Puerto Páez Venez.
148 B2 Puerto Peñasco Mex.
156 F2 Puerto Pinasco Para.
159 D4 Puerto Pirámides Arg.
149 J5 Puerto Plata Dom. Rep.
97 A4 Puerto Princesa Phil.
157 B2 Puerto Rey Col.
149 K5 Puerto Rico terr. Caribbean Sea
163 G4 Puerto Rico Trench sea feature Caribbean Sea
150 H5 Puerto San José Guat.
159 C7 Puerto Santa Cruz Arg.
156 E1 Puerto Sastre Para.
157 C3 Puerto Tejado Col.
150 C3 Puerto Vallarta Mex.
159 B3 Puerto Varas Chile
117 H4 Pugachev Rus. Fed.
88 C4 Pugal India
93 H5 Puge China
92 C3 Pu He r. China
84 D5 Pūhāl-e Khamīr, Kūh-e mts Iran
111 H1 Puigmal mt. France/Spain
93 □ Pui O Wan b. Hong Kong China
93 F5 Pujiang China
96 C6 Pujŏn-ho N. Korea
96 C3 Pujŏnryong-sanmaek mts N. Korea
72 E3 Pukaki, Lake N.Z.
134 E1 Pukaskwa r. Canada
134 E1 Pukaskwa National Park Canada
131 J4 Pukatawagan Canada
96 C5 Pukchin N. Korea
96 C3 Pukch'ŏng N. Korea
72 E2 Pukekohe N.Z.
72 E3 Puketeraki Range mts N.Z.
72 C6 Pukeuri Junction N.Z.
113 O3 Pukhnovo Rus. Fed.
116 G2 Puksoozero Rus. Fed.
96 C4 Puksaubaek-san mt. N. Korea
114 F2 Pula Croatia
154 E8 Pulacayo Bol.
96 B4 Pulandian China
97 □ Pulandian Wan b. China
97 C5 Pulangi r. Phil.
147 E3 Pulaski NY U.S.A.
145 C5 Pulaski TN U.S.A.
146 C6 Pulaski VA U.S.A.
134 C4 Pulaski WI U.S.A.
113 J5 Puławy Poland
108 E3 Pulheim Germany
87 B3 Pulicat Lake b. India
87 B4 Puliyangudi India
138 C2 Pullman U.S.A.
102 P1 Pulozero Rus. Fed.
150 D2 Púlpito, Punta pt Mex.
81 E1 Pülümür Turkey
97 C5 Pulutan Indon.
89 G3 Puma Yumco l. China
154 B4 Puná, Isla i. Ecuador
89 G4 Punakha Bhutan
88 C2 Punch Jammu and Kashmir
130 E4 Punchaw Canada
89 G3 Püncogling China
125 I1 Punda Maria S. Africa
87 A2 Pune India
98 □ Punggol Sing.
96 C4 P'ungsan N. Korea
123 D5 Púnguè r. Moz.
122 C4 Punia Dem. Rep. Congo
159 B2 Punitaqui Chile
88 B3 Punjab state India
88 B3 Punjab prov. Pak.
131 □ Punmah Glacier China/Jammu and Kashmir
149 K5 Punta, Cerro de mt. Puerto Rico
159 D3 Punta Alta Arg.
114 C4 Punta Balestrieri mt. Italy
159 B8 Punta Arenas Chile
159 D4 Punta Delgada Arg.
150 G4 Punta Gorda Belize
150 I6 Punta Gorda Nicaragua
145 D7 Punta Gorda U.S.A.
150 H6 Puntarenas Costa Rica
157 C1 Punto Fijo Venez.
102 N2 Puokio Fin.
102 N3 Puolanka Fin.
84 B2 Pūr r. Iran
76 I3 Pur r. Rus. Fed.
157 A4 Puracé, Parque Nacional nat. park Col.
157 A4 Puracé, Volcán de vol. Col.
130 C2 Purcell Mountains Canada
159 B3 Purén Chile
89 F6 Puri India
108 C2 Purmerend Neth.

147 F5 Rehoboth Bay U.S.A.
147 F5 Rehoboth Beach U.S.A.
80 E6 Rehovot Israel
109 K3 Reibitz Germany
109 C4 Reichenbach Germany
109 F6 Reichshoffen France
106 C3 Reidh, Rubha pt U.K.
145 E4 Reidsville U.S.A.
105 G6 Reigate U.K.
141 G5 Reiley Peak mt. U.S.A.
110 G2 Reims France
134 A4 Reinbeck U.S.A.
109 I1 Reinbek Germany
131 J4 Reindeer Island Canada
131 I3 Reindeer Lake Canada
102 K2 Reine Norway
109 I1 Reinfeld (Holstein) Germany
108 C3 Reinga, Cape N.Z.
111 D1 Reinosa Spain
102 B2 Reiphólsfjöll mt. Iceland
102 M1 Reisaelva r. Norway
102 M1 Reisa Nasjonalpark nat. park
    Norway
102 N2 Reisjärvi Fin.
125 H3 Reitz S. Africa
124 F3 Reivilo S. Africa
157 D3 Rejunya Venez.
131 H2 Reken Germany
131 H2 Reliance Canada
120 C1 Relizane Alg.
109 H1 Rellingen Germany
108 E4 Remagen Germany
70 C4 Remarkable, Mount Australia
85 E5 Remeshk Iran
124 B1 Remhoogte Pass Namibia
112 C6 Remiremont France
88 C2 Remo Glacier India
117 G6 Remontnoye Rus. Fed.
108 F3 Remscheid Germany
134 C4 Remus U.S.A.
103 J3 Rena Norway
87 B2 Renapur India
144 B4 Rend Lake U.S.A.
69 F2 Rendova i. Solomon Is
112 D3 Rendsburg Germany
135 I3 Renfrew Canada
106 D5 Renfrew U.K.
159 B2 Rengo Chile
92 C3 Ren He r. China
92 E4 Renheji China
93 D5 Renhua China
93 C5 Renhuai China
117 D6 Reni Ukr.
70 D5 Renmark Australia
69 G3 Rennell i. Solomon Is
69 G4 Rennerod Germany
110 D2 Rennes France
73 B5 Rennick Glacier Antarctica
131 H2 Rennie Lake Canada
114 C2 Reno r. Italy
140 C2 Reno U.S.A.
146 E4 Renovo U.S.A.
92 E2 Renqiu China
93 C4 Renshou China
134 D5 Rensselaer IN U.S.A.
147 G3 Rensselaer NY U.S.A.
108 B2 Renswoude Neth.
138 B2 Renton U.S.A.
89 E4 Renukut India
72 D4 Renwick N.Z.
120 B3 Réo Burkina
91 E7 Reo Indon.
82 E5 Repetek Turkm.
138 C1 Republic U.S.A.
142 D3 Republican r. U.S.A.
129 J3 Repulse Bay Canada
154 D5 Requena Peru
111 F3 Requena Spain
80 F1 Reşadiye Turkey
81 I2 Reşadiye Turkey
158 B4 Reserva Arg.
156 E3 Resistencia Arg.
115 I2 Reşiţa Romania
129 I2 Resolute Bay Canada
129 L3 Resolution Island Canada
72 A6 Resolution Island N.Z.
151 G5 Retalhuleu Guat.
98 □ Retan Laut, Pulau i. Sing.
105 G4 Retford U.K.
110 G2 Rethel France
109 H2 Rethem (Aller) Germany
115 K7 Rethymno Greece
94 C2 Rettikhovka Rus. Fed.
119 I6 Réunion terr. Indian Ocean
109 K1 Reuterstadt Stavenhagen
    Germany
112 D6 Reutlingen Germany
140 D3 Reveille Peak mt. U.S.A.
112 C6 Revel France
130 F4 Revelstoke Canada
148 B5 Revillagigedo, Islas is Mex.
130 C3 Revillagigedo Island U.S.A.
108 D5 Revin France
80 E6 Revivim Israel
88 E4 Rewa India
88 D4 Rewari India
138 E3 Rexburg U.S.A.
134 C4 Rexton Canada
140 A2 Reyes, Point U.S.A.
154 C4 Reyes Peak mt. U.S.A.
80 F3 Reyhanlı Turkey
102 B2 Reykir Iceland
163 G2 Reykjanes Ridge sea feature
    N. Atlantic Ocean
102 B3 Reykjanestá pt Iceland
102 B2 Reykjavík Iceland
151 F2 Reynosa Mex.
81 L3 Rezekne Latvia
81 L3 Rezvānshahr Iran
105 D5 Rhayader U.K.
109 G3 Rheda-Wiedenbrück Germany
108 E3 Rheden Neth.
108 E3 Rhein r. Germany
    alt. Rhin (France),
    conv. Rhine
108 E2 Rheine Germany
108 E4 Rheinisches Schiefergebirge
    hills Germany
108 F5 Rheinland-Pfalz admin. div.
    Germany
109 K1 Rheinsberg Germany
109 G6 Rheinstetten Germany
110 H2 Rhin r. France
    alt. Rhein (Germany),
    conv. Rhine
112 C5 Rhine r. Europe
    alt. Rhein (Germany),
    alt. Rhin (France)
147 G4 Rhinebeck U.S.A.
134 C3 Rhinelander U.S.A.
109 K2 Rhinkanal canal Germany
109 K2 Rhinluch marsh Germany
109 K2 Rhinow Germany
114 C2 Rho Italy
115 M6 Rhode Island state U.S.A.
115 M6 Rhodes Greece
115 M6 Rhodes i. Greece
138 D2 Rhodes Peak mt. U.S.A.
115 K4 Rhodope Mountains
    Bulg./Greece
110 G4 Rhône r. France/Switz.
105 D4 Rhyl U.K.
158 B2 Riacho Brazil
158 D1 Riacho de Santana Brazil
158 C1 Rialma Brazil
158 C1 Rianápolis Brazil
88 C2 Riasi Jammu and Kashmir
99 B2 Riau, Kepulauan is Indon.
111 D1 Ribadeo Spain
111 D1 Ribadesella Spain
158 B3 Ribas do Rio Pardo Brazil

123 D5 Ribáuè Moz.
104 E4 Ribble r. U.K.
103 D3 Ribe Denmark
108 A5 Ribécourt-Dreslincourt France
158 C4 Ribeira r. Brazil
158 C3 Ribeirão Preto Brazil
108 B5 Ribemont France
134 E6 Ribera France
154 E6 Riberalta Bol.
117 D6 Ribnita Moldova
112 F3 Ribnitz-Damgarten Germany
112 G6 Říčany Czech Rep.
141 E4 Rice U.S.A.
135 F2 Rice Lake Canada
134 B3 Rice Lake U.S.A.
134 A4 Riceville IA U.S.A.
146 D4 Riceville PA U.S.A.
125 J4 Richards Bay S. Africa
131 G3 Richardson r. Canada
143 D5 Richardson U.S.A.
147 H2 Richardson Lakes U.S.A.
128 E3 Richardson Mountains Canada
72 B6 Richardson Mountains N.Z.
141 F2 Richfield U.S.A.
147 F3 Richfield Springs U.S.A.
147 G3 Richford NY U.S.A.
147 G2 Richford VT U.S.A.
134 B5 Richland U.S.A.
136 C2 Richland WA U.S.A.
134 B4 Richland Center U.S.A.
146 C6 Richlands U.S.A.
71 I4 Richmond N.S.W. Australia
68 E4 Richmond Qld Australia
135 J3 Richmond Canada
72 D4 Richmond N.Z.
125 I4 Richmond Kwazulu-Natal S. Africa
124 E5 Richmond N. Cape S. Africa
104 F3 Richmond U.K.
134 E6 Richmond IN U.S.A.
146 A6 Richmond KY U.S.A.
134 I2 Richmond MI U.S.A.
135 F4 Richmond MO U.S.A.
146 E5 Richmond VA U.S.A.
147 G2 Richmond VT U.S.A.
72 D4 Richmond, Mount N.Z.
135 H4 Richmond Hill Canada
71 J2 Richmond Range hills Australia
124 B4 Richtersveld National Park
    S. Africa
146 B4 Richwood OH U.S.A.
146 C5 Richwood WV U.S.A.
135 J3 Rideau r. Canada
135 J3 Rideau Lakes Canada
140 D4 Ridgecrest U.S.A.
146 D4 Ridgway U.S.A.
131 I4 Riding Mountain National Park
    Canada
112 D6 Riedlingen Germany
108 D4 Riemst Belgium
109 L3 Riesa Germany
156 B8 Riesco, Isla i. Chile
124 D5 Riet r. S. Africa
103 M5 Rietavas Lith.
124 E5 Rietbron S. Africa
124 D3 Rietfontein S. Africa
114 E3 Rieti Italy
139 F4 Rifle U.S.A.
102 C1 Rifstangi pt Iceland
89 H3 Riga India
103 N4 Riga Latvia
103 M4 Riga, Gulf of Estonia/Latvia
85 E4 Rīgān Iran
147 F2 Rigaud Canada
138 C2 Riggins U.S.A.
133 I3 Rigolet Canada
106 E5 Rigside U.K.
84 E3 Rīgū Iran
89 E4 Rihand r. India
89 E4 Rihand Dam India
103 N3 Riihimäki Fin.
73 C3 Riiser-Larsen Ice Shelf
    Antarctica
73 D3 Riiser-Larsen Sea Antarctica
139 D5 Riito Mex.
114 F2 Rijeka Croatia
94 G5 Rikuzen-takata Japan
115 J3 Rila mts Bulg.
138 C3 Riley U.K.
110 G4 Rillieux-la-Pape France
113 J6 Rimavská Sobota Slovakia
114 E2 Rimini Italy
133 G4 Rimouski Canada
109 H5 Rimpar Germany
106 D2 Rimsdale, Loch l. U.K.
89 D3 Rinbung China
150 D3 Rincón de Romos Mex.
88 E4 Rind r. India
102 J3 Rindal Norway
71 G8 Ringarooma Bay Australia
68 B4 Ringas India
89 G2 Ring Co salt l. China
108 E2 Ringe Germany
103 J3 Ringebu Norway
103 J4 Ringkøbing Denmark
107 D7 Ringsend U.K.
103 G4 Ringsted Denmark
102 L1 Ringvassøy i. Norway
105 F7 Ringwood U.K.
159 B3 Rinihue Chile
159 B3 Riñihue, Lago l. Chile
99 E4 Rinjani, Gunung vol. Indon.
109 H2 Rinteln Germany
134 C4 Rio U.S.A.
134 D7 Riobamba U.S.A.
154 A2 Rio Alegre Brazil
154 C4 Riobamba Ecuador
141 H2 Rio Blanco U.S.A.
154 E6 Rio Branco Brazil
157 B4 Rio Branco, Parque Nacional
    do nat. park Brazil
158 C4 Rio Branco do Sul Brazil
158 A3 Rio Brilhante Brazil
159 B4 Rio Bueno Chile
157 E2 Río Caribe Venez.
159 C4 Río Claro Chile
159 D3 Río Claro Trin. and Tob.
158 D3 Rio Claro Brazil
159 D2 Río Cuarto Arg.
158 D3 Rio de Janeiro Brazil
158 D3 Rio de Janeiro state Brazil
156 I7 Rio de Jesús Panama
156 F5 Río Frío Costa Rica
159 C8 Río Gallegos Arg.
159 C8 Río Grande Arg.
158 C3 Rio Grande Brazil
158 B4 Rio Grande Brazil
151 E2 Rio Grande r. Mex./U.S.A.
    alt. Bravo del Norte, Río
143 D7 Rio Grande City U.S.A.
163 D7 Rio Grande Rise sea feature
    S. Atlantic Ocean
157 B2 Ríohacha Col.
154 C5 Rioja Peru
159 D1 Río Largo Mex.
117 G7 Rioni r. Georgia
159 D1 Río Pardo Brazil
158 D1 Rio Pardo de Minas Brazil
139 F5 Rio Rancho U.S.A.
159 D1 Rio Rico U.S.A.
159 C1 Río Segundo Arg.
157 C3 Ríosucio Col.
159 D2 Río Tercero Arg.
159 E2 Río Tigre Ecuador
97 A4 Rio Tuba Phil.

158 B2 Rio Verde Brazil
151 E3 Río Verde Mex.
151 G4 Río Verde Mex.
158 A2 Rio Verde de Mato Grosso
    Brazil
140 B2 Rio Vista U.S.A.
158 A2 Riozinho r. Brazil
113 O5 Ripky Ukr.
104 F3 Ripley England U.K.
105 F4 Ripley England U.K.
146 B5 Ripley OH U.S.A.
145 B5 Ripley TN U.S.A.
146 C5 Ripley WV U.S.A.
111 H1 Ripoll Spain
104 F3 Ripon U.K.
140 B3 Ripon CA U.S.A.
134 C4 Ripon WI U.S.A.
105 D6 Risca U.K.
94 G2 Rishiri-tō i. Japan
80 E6 Rishon Le Ziyyon Israel
85 F5 Rish Pish Iran
103 J4 Riser Norway
102 J3 Rissa Norway
103 N3 Ristiina Fin.
102 O2 Ristijärvi Fin.
102 O1 Ristikent Rus. Fed.
124 F4 Ritchie S. Africa
102 L2 Ritsem Sweden
139 C4 Ritter, Mount U.S.A.
109 G1 Ritterhude Germany
111 E2 Rituerto r. Spain
138 C2 Ritzville U.S.A.
159 D2 Rivadavia Buenos Aires Arg.
68 B4 Rivadavia Mendoza Arg.
159 C2 Rivadavia Mendoza Arg.
156 D2 Rivadavia Arg.
159 B1 Rivadavia Chile
114 D2 Riva del Garda Italy
150 C1 Riva Palacio Mex.
150 H6 Rivas Nicaragua
85 E3 Rivash Iran
131 J4 Rivera Canada
159 F1 Rivera Uruguay
120 B4 River Cess Liberia
147 G4 Riverhead U.S.A.
146 B6 Riversville U.S.A.
132 B2 Rivers r. Canada
161 N8 Roggeveen Basin sea feature
    S. Pacific Ocean
124 D6 Riverside S. Africa
140 D5 Riverside U.S.A.
70 C5 Riverton Australia
131 J4 Riverton Canada
72 B7 Riverton N.Z.
138 E3 Riverton U.S.A.
133 H4 Riverview Canada
110 F5 Rivesaltes France
135 J3 Rivière-Bleue Canada
135 G4 Rivière-du-Loup Canada
117 C5 Rivne Ukr.
72 D4 Riwaka N.Z.
86 C5 Riyadh Saudi Arabia
84 D3 Riza well Iran
81 H1 Rize Turkey
92 F3 Rizhao China
80 E4 Rizokarpason Cyprus
84 E4 Rīzū'īyeh Iran
103 J4 Rjukan Norway
103 I4 Rjuvbrokkene mt. Norway
120 A3 Rkîz Mauritania
103 J3 Rea Norway
105 G5 Rcade U.K.
102 J2 Roa Norway
158 B3 Rolândia Brazil
142 F4 Rolla U.S.A.
103 J3 Rollag Norway
72 D2 Rolleston N.Z.
135 H2 Rollet Canada
145 D7 Rolleville Bahamas
135 I2 Rolphton Canada
68 E4 Roma Australia
91 E7 Roma i. Indon.
107 B6 Rearingwater Bay
    Rep. of Ireland
150 H4 Röbäck Sweden
102 M3 Röbäck Sweden
85 E4 Robat r. Afgh.
84 E4 Robāt Iran
84 E3 Robāt-e Khān Iran
85 F4 Robat Thana Pak.
71 F8 Robbins Island Australia
70 C6 Robe Australia
70 D3 Robe, r. Rep. of Ireland
109 N1 Röbel Germany
143 K1 Röbel Germany
158 D3 Roberta U.S.A.
71 J2 Roberts, Mount Australia
140 D2 Roberts Creek Mountain U.S.A.
102 M2 Robertsfors Sweden
89 E4 Robertsganj India
124 E6 Robert S. Kerr Reservoir U.S.A.
73 B2 Robertson S. Africa
120 A4 Robertson Island Antarctica
70 C4 Robertsport Liberia
133 F4 Robertstown Australia
129 L1 Roberval Canada
    Robeson Channel
    Canada/Greenland
104 G3 Robin Hood's Bay U.K.
144 C4 Robinson U.S.A.
68 B4 Robinson Range hills Australia
70 E5 Robinvale Australia
141 G5 Robles Junction U.S.A.
141 G5 Robles Pass U.S.A.
131 I4 Roblin Canada
134 C4 Robson, Mount Canada
87 A3 Roc India
104 D4 Robstown U.S.A.
151 F2 Roca Partida, Punta hd Mex.
114 F6 Rocca Busambra mt. Sicily Italy
159 F2 Rocha Uruguay
104 E4 Rochdale U.K.
158 A2 Rochedo Brazil
108 D4 Rochefort Belgium
110 D4 Rochefort France
132 F2 Rochefort, Lac l. Canada
116 B2 Rochegda Rus. Fed.
134 C5 Rochelle U.S.A.
70 F6 Rochester Australia
105 H6 Rochester U.K.
134 E5 Rochester IN U.S.A.
134 A3 Rochester MN U.S.A.
147 H3 Rochester NH U.S.A.
146 E3 Rochester NY U.S.A.
105 H6 Rochford U.K.
109 K3 Rochlitz Germany
110 E3 Roc'h Trévezel hill France
130 D2 Rock r. Canada
134 B5 Rock r. U.S.A.
145 C5 Rock, The Australia
163 H2 Rockall Bank sea feature
    N. Atlantic Ocean
73 B4 Rockefeller Plateau Antarctica
134 C4 Rockford U.S.A.
131 I5 Rockglen Canada
145 D5 Rock Hill U.S.A.
68 D4 Rockingham Australia
145 E5 Rockingham U.S.A.
147 G2 Rock Island Canada
134 B5 Rock Island U.S.A.
142 D1 Rocklake U.S.A.
147 I2 Rockland MA U.S.A.
147 H2 Rockland ME U.S.A.
135 D3 Rockland MI U.S.A.
68 C4 Rockly Point U.S.A.
145 H3 Rockmart U.S.A.
147 H3 Rockport U.S.A.
147 H2 Rock Rapids U.S.A.
158 D1 Rock Springs MT U.S.A.
139 F4 Rock Springs WY U.S.A.
143 C6 Rocksprings U.S.A.
157 E4 Rockstone Guyana
143 D5 Rockville IN U.S.A.
146 E5 Rockville MD U.S.A.
147 I2 Rockwood U.S.A.

139 G4 Rocky Ford U.S.A.
146 B5 Rocky Fork Lake U.S.A.
135 F2 Rocky Island Lake Canada
145 E5 Rocky Mount NC U.S.A.
146 D6 Rocky Mount VA U.S.A.
130 G4 Rocky Mountain House Canada
138 F3 Rocky Mountain National Park
    U.S.A.
136 D2 Rocky Mountains
    Canada/U.S.A.
130 F4 Rocky Mountains Forest
    Reserve Canada
108 B5 Rocourt-St-Martin France
108 C5 Rocroi France
103 J5 Rødberg Norway
103 H4 Rødbyhavn Denmark
133 J3 Roddickton Canada
106 B3 Rodel U.K.
108 E1 Roden Neth.
109 J4 Rödental Germany
159 C1 Rodeo Arg.
150 C1 Rodeo Mex.
141 H6 Rodeo U.S.A.
110 F4 Rodez France
109 K5 Roding Germany
83 J1 Rodino Rus. Fed.
85 G5 Rodkhan Pak.
116 G3 Rodniki Rus. Fed.
82 D2 Rodnikovka Kazakh.
    Rodos Greece see Rhodes
    Rodos i. Greece see Rhodes
162 I6 Rodrigues Island Mauritius
68 B4 Roebourne Australia
68 C3 Roebuck Bay Australia
125 H2 Roedtan S. Africa
108 D3 Roermond Neth.
108 B4 Roeselare Belgium
129 J3 Roes Welcome Sound
    sea chan. Canada
109 J2 Rogätz Germany
143 E4 Rogers U.S.A.
135 F3 Rogers City U.S.A.
140 D4 Rogers Lake U.S.A.
138 D3 Rogerson U.S.A.
146 B6 Rogersville U.S.A.
132 J2 Roggan r. Canada
161 N8 Roggeveen Basin sea feature
    S. Pacific Ocean
124 D6 Roggeveld plat. S. Africa
124 D6 Roggeveldberge esc. S. Africa
102 K2 Rognan Norway
138 A2 Rogue r. U.S.A.
140 A2 Rohnert Park U.S.A.
112 F6 Rohrbach in Oberösterreich
    Austria
108 F5 Rohrbach-lès-Bitche France
85 I4 Rohri Pak.
88 D3 Rohtak India
88 D3 Rohtak India
88 B1 Roi Et Thai.
67 J5 Roi Georges, Îles du
    Fr. Polynesia
108 B5 Roisel France
159 E2 Rojas Arg.
88 B3 Rojhan Pak.
150 C2 Rojo, Cabo Mex.
103 N5 Rokiškis Lith.
103 J3 Rokné Norway
102 M2 Roknäs Sweden
117 C5 Rokytne Ukr.
158 B3 Rolândia Brazil
142 F4 Rolla U.S.A.
103 J3 Rollag Norway
72 D2 Rolleston N.Z.
135 H2 Rollet Canada
145 D7 Rolleville Bahamas
135 I2 Rolphton Canada
68 E4 Roma Australia
91 E7 Roma i. Indon.
125 G4 Roma Lesotho
103 L4 Roma Sweden
145 E5 Romain, Cape U.S.A.
133 H3 Romaine r. Canada
113 M7 Roman Romania
163 H6 Romanche Gap sea feature
    S. Atlantic Ocean
115 K1 Romania country Europe
90 D1 Romanovka Rus. Fed.
117 G5 Romanovka Saratovskaya Oblast'
    Rus. Fed.
83 J1 Romanovo Rus. Fed.
110 H2 Romans-sur-Isère France
128 B3 Romanzof, Cape U.S.A.
110 H2 Rombas France
97 B3 Romblon Phil.
97 B3 Romblon i. Phil.
114 E4 Rome Italy
    (City Plan 62)
147 I2 Rome ME U.S.A.
147 F3 Rome NY U.S.A.
135 F4 Rome NM U.S.A.
105 H6 Romford U.K.
110 F2 Romilly-sur-Seine France
82 B6 Romitan Uzbek.
105 H6 Romney Marsh reg. U.K.
117 E5 Romny Ukr.
103 J5 Rømø i. Denmark
110 E3 Romorantin-Lanthenay France
98 B5 Rompin r. Malaysia
105 F7 Romsey U.K.
87 A3 Ron India
87 A3 Ron India
98 C1 Ron Vietnam
106 C1 Rona i. Scotland U.K.
106 C1 Rona i. Scotland U.K.
106 □ Ronas Hill U.K.
155 H4 Roncador, Serra do hills Brazil
69 F2 Roncador Reef reef Solomon Is
111 D4 Ronda Spain
103 J3 Rondane Nasjonalpark
    nat. park Norway
157 D3 Rondón Col.
157 E4 Rondon, Pico mt. Brazil
158 A2 Rondonópolis Brazil
79 F3 Rondu Jammu and Kashmir
93 B5 Rong'an China
93 C6 Rongchang China
96 B5 Rongcheng China
96 B5 Rongcheng Wan b. China
89 G3 Rong Chu r. China
160 G6 Rongelap atoll Marshall Is
93 C6 Rongjiang China
89 H5 Rongklang Range mts Myanmar
93 C6 Rongxian Guangxi China
93 D6 Rongxian Sichuan China
103 K5 Rønne Denmark
103 K4 Rønne i. Sweden
73 B3 Ronne Entrance strait
    Antarctica
73 B2 Ronne Ice Shelf Antarctica
109 I2 Ronnenberg Germany
108 E5 Ronse Belgium
88 D3 Roorkee India
108 D3 Roosendaal Neth.
141 G5 Roosevelt AZ U.S.A.
139 H1 Roosevelt UT U.S.A.
135 D3 Roosevelt, Mount Canada
73 B6 Roosevelt Island Antarctica
110 E3 Root r. Canada
134 B4 Root r. U.S.A.
116 J2 Ropcha Rus. Fed.
110 D4 Ropczyce Poland
157 F4 Roraima state Brazil
157 F3 Roraima, Mount Guyana
114 D2 Rovereto Italy
103 N3 Rovaniemi Fin.
102 N2 Rovaniemi Fin.
114 D2 Rovigo Italy
114 F2 Rovinj Croatia
113 O6 Ros' r. Ukr.
117 H5 Rovnoye Rus. Fed.

154 □ Rosa, Cabo pt Galapagos Is
    Ecuador
145 D5 Rosa, Lake Bahamas
150 B2 Rosa, Punta pt Mex.
140 C4 Rosamond U.S.A.
140 C4 Rosamond Lake U.S.A.
156 E2 Rosario Arg.
150 A2 Rosario Baja California Mex.
150 C3 Rosario Coahuila Mex.
150 C3 Rosario Sinaloa Mex.
150 C3 Rosario Sonora Mex.
97 B2 Rosario Phil.
97 B3 Rosario Phil.
157 E2 Rosario Venez.
156 E2 Rosário do Tala Arg.
156 F1 Rosário do Sul Brazil
158 A1 Rosário Oeste Brazil
150 A1 Rosarito Baja California Mex.
150 A2 Rosarito Baja California Sur Mex.
114 F5 Rosarno Italy
110 C2 Roscoff France
107 C4 Roscommon Rep. of Ireland
134 E3 Roscommon U.S.A.
107 D5 Roscrea Rep. of Ireland
140 C2 Rose, Mount U.S.A.
131 J5 Roseau Dominica
131 I5 Roseau r. U.S.A.
133 J3 Rose Blanche Canada
133 B3 Roseburg U.S.A.
135 E3 Rose City U.S.A.
105 E3 Rosedale Abbey U.K.
122 C3 Rose Island American Samoa
143 H4 Rosenberg U.S.A.
103 I4 Rosendal Norway
125 G4 Rosendal S. Africa
112 F7 Rosenheim Germany
130 D3 Rose Point Canada
143 I5 Roselle Italy
135 H1 Rose Valley Canada
140 B2 Roseville CA U.S.A.
134 B5 Roseville IL U.S.A.
71 J1 Rosewood Australia
84 D4 Rūd-e Kor watercourse Iran
85 E4 Rūd-i-Shur watercourse Iran
103 J5 Rudkøbing Denmark
116 J3 Rudnaya Pristan' Rus. Fed.
116 J3 Rudnichny Rus. Fed.
85 E5 Rudnyy Iran
124 B3 Rosh Pinah Namibia
83 G5 Roshtqal'a Tajik.
114 D3 Rosignano Marittimo Italy
115 L2 Roşiori de Vede Romania
103 K5 Roskilde Denmark
85 E4 Roslavl' Rus. Fed.
116 D4 Roslavl' Rus. Fed.
116 J3 Roslyakovo Rus. Fed.
130 C2 Ross r. Canada
72 C5 Ross N.Z.
72 C6 Ross, Mount N.Z.
114 G5 Rossano Italy
107 C3 Rosson Point Rep. of Ireland
143 F5 Ross Barnett Reservoir l.
133 B3 Ross Bay Junction Canada
107 B6 Ross Carbery Rep. of Ireland
73 A5 Ross Dependency reg.
    Antarctica
39 F3 Rossel Island P.N.G.
73 B4 Ross Ice Shelf Antarctica
133 H5 Rossignol, Lake Canada
73 B5 Ross Island Antarctica
107 F5 Rosslare Rep. of Ireland
147 F5 Rosslare Harbour
    Rep. of Ireland
120 A3 Rosso Mauritania
114 C3 Rosso, Capo pt Corsica France
105 E6 Ross-on-Wye U.K.
85 F5 Rossosh' Rus. Fed.
134 D1 Rosport Canada
130 C2 Ross River Canada
73 A5 Ross Sea Antarctica
109 I3 Roßtal Germany
102 K2 Røssvatnet l. Norway
109 I3 Rosswood Canada
130 D3 Rosswood Canada
81 J3 Rostāq Afgh.
84 D5 Rostāq Iran
31 H4 Rosthern Canada
112 F3 Rostock Germany
116 F3 Rostov Rus. Fed.
117 G6 Rostov-na-Donu Rus. Fed.
117 G6 Rostovskaya Oblast' admin. div.
    Rus. Fed.
102 M2 Rosvik Sweden
145 D5 Roswell GA U.S.A.
139 F5 Roswell NM U.S.A.
91 J5 Rota i. N. Mariana Is
109 I5 Rot am See Germany
91 E8 Rote i. Indon.
109 H1 Rotenburg (Wümme) Germany
109 J4 Roter Main r. Germany
109 J4 Roth Germany
104 F2 Rothbury U.K.
109 I5 Rothenburg ob der Tauber
    Germany
105 G7 Rother r. U.K.
73 B2 Rothera research station
    Antarctica
72 D4 Rotherham N.Z.
105 F4 Rotherham U.K.
106 E5 Rothes U.K.
134 C3 Rothschild U.S.A.
73 B2 Rothschild Island Antarctica
105 G5 Rothwell U.K.
71 F4 Roto Australia
72 C5 Rotomanu N.Z.
114 C3 Rotondo, Monte mt. Corsica
    France
72 D4 Rotorua N.Z.
72 F3 Rotorua, Lake N.Z.
112 F6 Rott r. Germany
109 J5 Rottendorf Germany
112 E7 Rottenmann Austria
108 C3 Rotterdam Neth.
109 J3 Rottleberode Germany
112 E7 Rottumeroog i. Neth.
112 E6 Rottweil Germany
73 F4 Rotuma i. Fiji
109 K5 Rötz Germany
103 K4 Rötviken Sweden
109 K5 Rötz Germany
110 F1 Roubaix France
110 F2 Rouen France
110 H2 Round Ridge mt. U.S.A.
133 D2 Roundeyed Lake Canada
104 F3 Round Hill U.K.
140 D2 Round Mountain U.S.A.
71 J3 Round Mount Australia
141 H3 Round Rock U.S.A.
147 J2 Rouses Point U.S.A.
110 F5 Roussillon reg. France
125 G4 Rouxville S. Africa
135 H1 Rouyn-Noranda Canada
102 N2 Rovaniemi Fin.
114 D2 Rovereto Italy
98 C2 Rôviěng Tbong Cambodia
114 D2 Rovigo Italy
114 F2 Rovinj Croatia
113 O6 Ros' r. Ukr.
117 H5 Rovnoye Rus. Fed.

71 H2 Rowena Australia
97 A4 Roxas Phil.
97 B2 Roxas Phil.
97 B3 Roxas Phil.
97 B4 Roxas Phil.
97 B3 Roxas Phil.
145 E4 Roxboro U.S.A.
70 B2 Roxburgh N.Z.
139 F4 Roy U.S.A.
107 E4 Royal Canal Rep. of Ireland
134 C1 Royale, Isle i. U.S.A.
125 H4 Royal Natal National Park
    S. Africa
135 F4 Royal Oak U.S.A.
110 D4 Royan France
108 A5 Roye France
105 G5 Royston U.K.
117 F6 Rozdil'ne Ukr.
117 F6 Rozdol'ne Ukr.
83 G2 Rozhdestvenka Kazakh.
117 C6 Rozhniv Ukr.
105 D5 Ruabon U.K.
123 D5 Ruacana Namibia
122 F4 Ruaha National Park Tanz.
72 F3 Ruahine Range mts N.Z.
72 E3 Ruapehu, Mount vol. N.Z.
72 B7 Ruapuke Island N.Z.
72 A6 Ruatoria N.Z.
116 D4 Ruba Belarus
84 D6 Rub' al Khālī des. Saudi Arabia
94 H3 Rubeshibe Japan
140 B2 Rubicon r. U.S.A.
117 F5 Rubizhne Ukr.
83 J2 Rubtsovsk Rus. Fed.
128 C3 Ruby U.S.A.
141 E1 Ruby Lake U.S.A.
141 E1 Ruby Mountains U.S.A.
93 D5 Rucheng China
146 D5 Ruckersville U.S.A.
89 E4 Rudauli India
85 F4 Rudbar Afgh.
81 L3 Rūdbār Iran
84 D4 Rūd-e Kor watercourse Iran
85 E4 Rūd-i-Shur watercourse Iran
103 J5 Rudkøbing Denmark
116 J3 Rudnaya Pristan' Rus. Fed.
116 J3 Rudnichny Rus. Fed.
82 E1 Rudnya Rus. Fed.
82 E1 Rudnyy Kazakh.
94 D2 Rudnyy Rus. Fed.
76 G1 Rudol'fa, Ostrov i. Rus. Fed.
109 J4 Rudolstadt Germany
92 F3 Rudong China
134 E2 Rudyard U.S.A.
123 D4 Rufiji r. Tanz.
159 D2 Rufino Arg.
120 A3 Rufisque Senegal
123 C5 Rufunsa Zambia
92 F3 Rugao China
105 F5 Rugby U.K.
105 F5 Rugby U.S.A.
112 F3 Rügen i. Germany
146 B4 Ruggles U.S.A.
109 I5 Rügland Germany
84 B5 Ruhayyat al Ḥamr'ā' waterhole
    Saudi Arabia
122 F4 Ruhengeri Rwanda
103 M4 Ruhnu i. Estonia
108 F4 Ruhr r. Germany
93 F5 Ruihai China
139 F5 Ruidoso U.S.A.
93 E5 Ruijin China
131 M2 Ruin Point Canada
123 D4 Ruipa Tanz.
150 C3 Ruiz Mex.
157 B3 Ruiz, Nevado del vol. Col.
    Rujayfah, Ḥarrat ar lava field
    Jordan
103 N4 Rūjiena Latvia
84 C5 Rukbah well Saudi Arabia
89 E3 Rukumkot Nepal
122 D4 Rukwa, Lake Tanz.
106 B4 Rùm i. Scotland U.K.
106 B4 Rùm i. Scotland U.K.
115 H2 Ruma Yugo.
84 B5 Rumāh Saudi Arabia
121 E4 Rumbek Sudan
145 F7 Rum Cay i. Bahamas
147 H2 Rumford U.S.A.
110 G4 Rumilly France
68 D3 Rum Jungle Australia
94 H2 Rumoi Japan
93 E4 Runan China
72 C5 Runanga N.Z.
72 F2 Runaway, Cape N.Z.
105 E4 Runcorn U.K.
123 B5 Rundu Namibia
102 L3 Rundvik Sweden
98 C3 Rŭng, Kaôh i. Cambodia
98 B3 Rŭng Sănlŏem, Kaôh i.
    Cambodia
92 E3 Runheji China
103 D3 Ruokolahti Fin.
90 A3 Ruoqiang China
89 H4 Rupa India
159 B4 Rupanco, Lago l. Chile
71 J1 Rupanyup Australia
99 B2 Rupat i. Indon.
132 F3 Rupert r. Canada
132 F3 Rupert Bay Canada
73 A4 Rupert Coast Antarctica
123 D5 Rusape Zimbabwe
115 K3 Ruse Bulg.
105 G5 Rushan China
105 G5 Rushden U.K.
134 B4 Rush Lake U.S.A.
134 C4 Rushville IL U.S.A.
147 F3 Rushville NE U.S.A.
143 F6 Rusk U.S.A.
145 D7 Rusk U.S.A.
131 I4 Russell Man. Canada
147 F2 Russell Ont. Canada
72 E1 Russell N.Z.
142 D4 Russell U.S.A.
129 I2 Russell Island Canada
69 F2 Russell Islands Solomon Is
130 F2 Russel Lake Canada
145 C5 Russellville AL U.S.A.
144 B4 Russellville AR U.S.A.
146 A5 Russellville KY U.S.A.
109 H5 Rüsselsheim Germany
76 G3 Russian Federation country
    Asia/Europe
83 H1 Russkaya-Polyana Rus. Fed.
94 C3 Russkiy, Ostrov i. Rus. Fed.
81 I1 Rustavi Georgia
125 G2 Rustenburg S. Africa
143 E6 Ruston U.S.A.
91 E7 Ruteng Indon.
141 E2 Ruth U.S.A.
109 H3 Rüthen Germany
135 G4 Rutherglen Canada
108 C3 Rutigliano Italy
116 H3 Rutka r. Rus. Fed.
147 G3 Rutland U.S.A.
105 G5 Rutland Water resr U.K.
131 G2 Rutledge Lake Canada
88 D2 Rutog China
146 B5 Rutter Canada
84 G4 Ru'ūs al Jibāl pen. Oman
123 D5 Ruvuma r. Moz./Tanz.
80 F5 Ruwayshid, Wādī watercourse
    Jordan

84	D5	**Ruweis** U.A.E.
93	D5	**Ruyuan** China
83	F1	**Ruzayevka** Kazakh.
116	H4	**Ruzayevka** Rus. Fed.
92	D3	**Ruzhou** China
113	I6	**Ružomberok** Slovakia
122	C4	**Rwanda** country Africa
84	D2	**Ryābād** Iran
116	H2	**Ryadovo** Rus. Fed.
106	C5	**Ryan, Loch** b. U.K.
116	F4	**Ryazan'** Rus. Fed.
116	G4	**Ryazanskaya Oblast'** admin. div. Rus. Fed.
116	G4	**Ryazhsk** Rus. Fed.
76	E2	**Rybachiy, Poluostrov** pen. Rus. Fed.
82	D3	**Rybachiy Poselok** Uzbek.
83	J3	**Rybach'ye** Kazakh.
116	F3	**Rybinsk** Rus. Fed.
116	F3	**Rybinskoye Vodokhranilishche** resr Rus. Fed.
116	I4	**Rybnaya Sloboda** Rus. Fed.
113	I5	**Rybnik** Poland
116	F4	**Rybnoye** Rus. Fed.
130	F3	**Rycroft** Canada
103	K4	**Ryd** Sweden
73		**Rydberg Peninsula** Antarctica
105	F7	**Ryde** U.K.
105	H7	**Rye** r. U.K.
104	G3	**Rye** r. U.K.
117	E5	**Ryl'sk** Rus. Fed.
71	H4	**Rylstone** Australia
82	B3	**Ryn-Peski** des. Kazakh.
95	F5	**Ryōtsu** Japan
90	E4	**Ryukyu Islands** Japan
162	M3	**Ryukyu Trench** sea feature N. Pacific Ocean
113	K5	**Rzeszów** Poland
117	G4	**Rzhaksa** Rus. Fed.
116	E3	**Rzhev** Rus. Fed.

S

84	E3	**Sa'ābād** Iran
84	D4	**Sa'ādatābād** Iran
84	D4	**Sa'ādatābād** Iran
109	J6	**Saal an der Donau** Germany
109	J3	**Saale** r. Germany
109	J4	**Saalfeld** Germany
108	C5	**Saar** r. Germany
108	E5	**Saarbrücken** Germany
103	M4	**Saaremaa** i. Estonia
102	N2	**Saarenkylä** Fin.
109	G2	**Saargau** reg. Germany
102	N3	**Saarijärvi** Fin.
102	N2	**Saari-Kämä** Fin.
102	M1	**Saarikoski** Fin.
108	C5	**Saarland** admin. div. Germany
108	E5	**Saarlouis** Germany
81	L2	**Saatlı** Azer.
159	C3	**Saavedra** Arg.
80	F5	**Sab' Ābār** Syria
115	H2	**Šabac** Yugo.
111	H2	**Sabadell** Spain
95	E7	**Sabae** Japan
99	E1	**Sabah** reg. Malaysia
98	B5	**Sabak** Malaysia
81	K2	**Sabalan, Kūhhā-ye** mts Iran
98	D4	**Sabalana, Kepulauan** is Indon.
88	D4	**Sabalgarh** India
150	H5	**Sabamagrande** Hond.
149	H4	**Sabana, Archipiélago de** is Cuba
157	B2	**Sabanalarga** Col.
80	D1	**Şabanözü** Turkey
158	D2	**Sabará** Brazil
87	C2	**Sabari** r. India
88	C5	**Sabarmati** r. India
114	E4	**Sabaudia** Italy
85	E3	**Sabeh** Iran
124	E5	**Sabelo** S. Africa
121	D2	**Sabhā** Libya
84	B6	**Şabhā'** Saudi Arabia
88	D3	**Sabi** r. India
125	J2	**Sabie** Moz.
125	J2	**Sabie** r. Moz./S. Africa
125	I2	**Sabie** S. Africa
150	D2	**Sabinas** Mex.
151	D2	**Sabinas Hidalgo** Mex.
143	E6	**Sabine Lake** U.S.A.
81	L1	**Sabirabad** Azer.
97	B3	**Sablayan** Phil.
131	L5	**Sable, Cape** Canada
145	D7	**Sable, Cape** U.S.A.
69	F3	**Sable, Île de** i. New Caledonia
129	M5	**Sable Island** Canada
135	F2	**Sables, River aux** r. Canada
73	C6	**Sabrina Coast** Antarctica
97	B1	**Sabtang** i. Phil.
111	C2	**Sabugal** Port.
134	B4	**Sabula** U.S.A.
86	B6	**Şabyā** Saudi Arabia
81	L5	**Sabzevār** Iran
115	M2	**Sacalinul Mare, Insula** i. Romania
115	K2	**Săcele** Romania
123	B5	**Sachanga** Angola
132	B3	**Sachigo** r. Canada
132	B3	**Sachigo Lake** Canada
85	C5	**Sachin** India
96	F3	**Sach'on** S. Korea
96	F3	**Sach'ŏn** S. Korea
88	D2	**Sach Pass** India
109	K3	**Sachsen** admin. div. Germany
109	J3	**Sachsen-Anhalt** admin. div. Germany
109	H6	**Sachsenheim** Germany
128	F2	**Sachs Harbour** Canada
147	E3	**Sackets Harbor** U.S.A.
109	G4	**Sackpfeife** hill Germany
133	H4	**Sackville** Canada
147	H3	**Saco** ME U.S.A.
138	F1	**Saco** MT U.S.A.
97	B5	**Sacol** i. Phil.
140	D2	**Sacramento** U.S.A.
140	B2	**Sacramento** r. U.S.A.
139	F5	**Sacramento Mountains** U.S.A.
138	B3	**Sacramento Valley** valley U.S.A.
125	G6	**Sada** S. Africa
111	F1	**Sádaba** Spain
84	D4	**Sa'dābād** Iran
80	F4	**Şadad** Syria
98	B4	**Sadao** Thai.
81	J5	**Saddat al Hindīyah** Iraq
125	I2	**Saddleback** pass S. Africa
98	C3	**Sa Đec** Vietnam
89	H3	**Sadēng** China
85	E5	**Sadij** watercourse Iran
88	B3	**Sadiqabad** Pak.
88	C1	**Sad Istragh** mt. Afgh./Pak.
81	K5	**Sa'dīyah, Hawr as** l. Iraq
84	B4	**Sa'diyyat** i. U.A.E.
86	E2	**Sad-Kharv** Iran
111	B3	**Sado** r. Port.
95	F6	**Sadoga-shima** i. Japan
95	F6	**Sado-shima** i. Japan
111	H3	**Sa Dragonera** i. Spain
103	J4	**Saeby** Denmark
81	K6	**Safayal Maqūf** well Iraq
85	H2	**Safed Khirs** mts Afgh.
88	G3	**Safed Koh** mts Afgh.
103	K4	**Säffle** Sweden
141	H5	**Safford** U.S.A.
105	H5	**Saffron Walden** U.K.
120	B1	**Safi** Morocco
84	D3	**Safid** r. Iran
84	D3	**Safid** Iran
85	E3	**Safidabeh** Iran
81	L5	**Safid Dasht** Iran
80	F4	**Şāfītā** Syria
76	F3	**Safonovo** Arkhangel'skaya Oblast' Rus. Fed.

102	P1	**Safonovo** Murmanskaya Oblast' Rus. Fed.
116	E4	**Safonovo** Smolenskaya Oblast' Rus. Fed.
84	A5	**Safrā' al Asyāḥ** esc. Saudi Arabia
80	D1	**Safranbolu** Turkey
81	K6	**Safwān** Iraq
89	F3	**Saga** China
95	B8	**Saga** Japan
82	E2	**Saga** Kostanayskaya Oblast' Kazakh.
82	F2	**Saga** Kostanayskaya Oblast' Kazakh.
95	F7	**Sagamihara** Japan
95	F7	**Sagami-nada** g. Japan
95	F7	**Sagami-wan** b. Japan
157	B3	**Sagamoso** r. Col.
83	I4	**Sagankuduk** China
98	A2	**Saganthit Kyun** i. Myanmar
87	B2	**Sagar** Karnataka India
88	D2	**Sagar** Karnataka India
88	D5	**Sagar** Madhya Pradesh India
117	H7	**Sagarejo** Georgia
89	G5	**Sagar Island** India
77	N2	**Sagastyr** Rus. Fed.
84	D3	**Saghand** Iran
85	F3	**Saghar** Afgh.
87	B3	**Sagileru** r. India
135	F4	**Saginaw** U.S.A.
135	F4	**Saginaw Bay** U.S.A.
82	C2	**Sagiz** Kazakh.
133	H2	**Saglek Bay** Canada
114	C3	**Sagone, Golfe de** b. Corsica France
111	B4	**Sagres** Port.
89	H5	**Sagu** Myanmar
139	H4	**Saguache** U.S.A.
145	D5	**Sagua la Grande** Cuba
141	G5	**Saguaro National Park** U.S.A.
133	F4	**Saguenay** r. Canada
111	F3	**Sagunto** Spain
88	B5	**Sagwara** India
82	C2	**Sagyz** r. Kazakh.
157	B2	**Sahagún** Col.
111	D1	**Sahagún** Spain
81	K3	**Sahand, Kūh-e** mt. Iran
120	C2	**Sahara** des. Africa
88	D3	**Saharanpur** India
89	F4	**Saharsa** India
88	D3	**Sahaswan** India
84	C6	**Sabhā', Wādī as** watercourse Saudi Arabia
88	C3	**Sahiwal** Pak.
88	C3	**Sahiwal** Pak.
84	D4	**Sahlābād** Iran
81	K4	**Sahneh** Iran
81	J6	**Şaḥrā al Ḥijārah** reg. Iraq
150	B1	**Sahuaripa** Mex.
141	G6	**Sahuarita** U.S.A.
150	D3	**Sahuayo** Mex.
98	D2	**Sa Huynh** Vietnam
88	E4	**Sai** r. India
88	B4	**Sai Buri** Thai.
98	B4	**Sai Buri, Mae Nam** r. Thai.
		Saïda Lebanon see **Sidon**
98	B2	**Sai Dao Tai, Khao** mt. Thai.
85	F5	**Sa'īdī** Iran
88	B3	**Saidpur** Bangl.
88	C2	**Saido** Pak.
95	C6	**Saigō** Japan
		Saigon Vietnam see **Ho Chi Minh City**
98	C3	**Saiha** India
89	H5	**Saiha** India
92	D1	**Saihan Tal** China
92	A1	**Saihan Toroi** China
95	C8	**Saijō** Japan
95	B8	**Saiki** Japan
93	□	**Sai Kung** Hong Kong China
103	O3	**Saimaa** l. Fin.
80	F2	**Saimbeyli** Turkey
150	B2	**Sain Alto** Mex.
85	F4	**Saindak** Pak.
84	B2	**Sa'indezh** Iran
105	B7	**St Abb's Head** hd U.K.
105	B7	**St Agnes** U.K.
105	A8	**St Agnes** i. U.K.
133	I4	**St Alban's** Canada
105	G6	**St Albans** U.K.
147	G2	**St Albans** VT U.S.A.
146	C5	**St Albans** WV U.S.A.
105	E7	**St Alban's Head** hd U.K.
130	G4	**St Albert** Canada
108	B4	**St-Amand-les-Eaux** France
110	F3	**St-Amand-Montrond** France
110	G3	**St-Amour** France
147	J2	**St Andrews** Canada
106	F4	**St Andrews** U.K.
149	I5	**St Ann's Bay** Jamaica
107	F6	**St Ann's Head** hd U.K.
133	I3	**St Anthony** Canada
138	E3	**St Anthony** U.S.A.
70	E6	**St Arnaud** Australia
72	D5	**St Arnaud Range** mts N.Z.
133	I3	**St-Augustin** Canada
145	D6	**St Augustine** U.S.A.
105	C7	**St Austell** U.K.
110	E3	**St-Avertin** France
108	E5	**St-Avold** France
149	L5	**St-Barthélemy** i. Guadeloupe
104	D3	**St Bees** U.K.
104	D3	**St Bees Head** hd U.K.
105	B6	**St Bride's Bay** U.K.
110	C3	**St-Brieuc** France
135	H4	**St Catharines** Canada
145	D6	**St Catherines Island** U.S.A.
110	E4	**St Catherine's Point** U.K.
147	G2	**St-Céré** France
110	G4	**St-Césaire** Canada
138	E3	**St-Chamond** France
134	A4	**St Charles** ID U.S.A.
134	A4	**St Charles** MN U.S.A.
134	C4	**St Charles** MO U.S.A.
135	F4	**St Clair** U.S.A.
135	F4	**St Clair, Lake** Canada/U.S.A.
110	G3	**St Clair Shores** U.S.A.
105	C6	**St Clears** U.K.
142	C2	**St Cloud** U.S.A.
133	G4	**St Croix** r. Canada
134	C2	**St Croix** r. U.S.A.
149	L5	**St Croix** i. Virgin Is (U.S.A.)
134	A3	**St Croix Falls** U.S.A.
105	A8	**St David's** U.K.
107	F6	**St David's Head** hd U.K.
110	F4	**St-Denis** France
110	H2	**St-Dizier** France
133	J5	**Ste-Anne, Lac** l. Canada
147	H1	**Ste-Anne-de-Beaupré** Canada
147	I1	**Sainte-Anne-de-Madawaska** Canada
110	D3	**Ste-Anne-du-Lac** Canada
147	H1	**Ste-Camille-de-Lellis** Canada
147	H1	**Ste-Justine** Canada
147	I1	**St Elias Mountains** Canada
130	D3	**St Elias Mountains** Canada
110	H5	**Ste-Maxime** France
110	F3	**Saintes** France
110	G4	**Ste-Thérèse** Canada
110	G4	**St-Étienne** France
147	F2	**St Eugene** Canada
147	J2	**St-Eustache** Canada
147	F2	**St-Félicien** Canada
105	F7	**Saintfield** U.K.
114	C3	**St-Florent** Corsica France
110	F3	**St-Florent-sur-Cher** France
122	C3	**St Floris, Parc National** nat. park Centr. Afr. Rep.

135	G4	**St Francis** r. Canada/U.S.A.
142	C4	**St Francis** KS U.S.A.
147	I1	**St Francis** ME U.S.A.
143	F4	**St Francis** r. U.S.A.
133	J4	**St Francis, Cape** Canada
147	I1	**St Froid Lake** U.S.A.
110	E5	**St-Gaudens** France
147	H2	**St-Gédéon** Canada
71	H2	**St George** Australia
147	J2	**St George** Canada
145	D5	**St George** SC U.S.A.
141	F3	**St George** UT U.S.A.
69	F2	**St George, Cape** pt P.N.G.
138	A3	**St George, Point** U.S.A.
145	C6	**St George Island** U.S.A.
133	F4	**St-Georges** Canada
149	L6	**St George's** Grenada
133	I4	**St George's Bay** Canada
68	F2	**St George's Channel** P.N.G.
105	A6	**St George's Channel** Rep. of Ireland/U.K.
112	D7	**St Gotthard Pass** Switz.
105	C7	**St Govan's Head** hd U.K.
134	E3	**St Helena** U.S.A.
118	D6	**St Helena** terr. Atlantic Ocean
140	A2	**St Helena** i. U.S.A.
124	C6	**St Helena Bay** b. S. Africa
124	C6	**St Helena Bay** S. Africa
71	H8	**St Helens** Australia
104	E4	**St Helens** U.K.
138	B2	**St Helens** U.S.A.
138	B2	**St Helens, Mount** vol. U.S.A.
71	H8	**St Helens Pt** Australia
110	C2	**St Helier** Belgium
130	D4	**St-Hubert** Belgium
132	F4	**St-Hyacinthe** Canada
134	E3	**St Ignace** U.S.A.
134	C1	**St Ignace Island** Canada
105	C6	**St Ishmael** U.K.
105	B7	**St Ives** England U.K.
105	G5	**St Ives** England U.K.
147	I1	**St-Jacques** Canada
134	E3	**St James** U.S.A.
130	C4	**St James, Cape** pt Canada
133	F4	**St-Jean, Lac** l. Canada
110	D4	**St-Jean-d'Angély** France
110	C3	**St-Jean-de-Monts** France
132	F4	**St-Jean-sur-Richelieu** France
132	F4	**St-Jérôme** Canada
138	C2	**St Joe** r. U.S.A.
133	G4	**Saint John** Canada
147	J2	**St John** r. Canada/U.S.A.
141	F1	**St John** U.S.A.
149	L5	**St John** i. Virgin Is (U.S.A.)
149	L5	**St John's** Antigua and Barbuda
133	J4	**St John's** Canada
141	H4	**St Johns** AZ U.S.A.
134	E4	**St Johns** MI U.S.A.
145	D6	**St Johns** r. U.S.A.
147	H2	**St Johnsbury** U.S.A.
104	F3	**St John's Chapel** U.K.
142	D4	**St Joseph** MO U.S.A.
134	E4	**St Joseph** MI U.S.A.
133	G3	**St-Joseph-de-Beauce** Canada
135	F2	**St Joseph Island** Canada
143	D7	**St Joseph Island** U.S.A.
132	F4	**St-Junien** France
110	E4	**St-Junien** France
105	A5	**St-Just-en-Chaussée** France
105	B7	**St Keverne** U.K.
149	L5	**St Kitts and Nevis** country Caribbean Sea
		St-Laurent, Golfe du g. Canada/U.S.A. see **St-Laurent, Gulf of**
155	H2	**St-Laurent-du-Maroni** Fr. Guiana
133	J4	**St Lawrence** inlet Canada
133	H4	**St Lawrence, Gulf of** Canada/U.S.A.
128	B3	**St Lawrence Island** U.S.A.
135	J3	**St Lawrence Islands National Park** Canada
147	F2	**St Lawrence Seaway** sea chan. Canada/U.S.A.
133	G4	**St-Léonard** Canada
133	I3	**St Lewis** Canada
133	I3	**St Lewis** r. Canada
110	D2	**St-Lô** France
120	A3	**St Louis** Senegal
134	E4	**St Louis** MI U.S.A.
142	F4	**St Louis** MO U.S.A.
134	A2	**St Louis** r. U.S.A.
149	L6	**St Lucia** country Caribbean Sea
125	J4	**St Lucia, Lake** S. Africa
125	J4	**St Lucia Estuary** S. Africa
106	□	**St Magnus Bay** U.K.
110	D4	**St-Maixent-l'École** France
110	C2	**St-Malo** France
110	C2	**St-Malo, Golfe de** g. France
125	G6	**St Marks** S. Africa
149	L5	**St Martin** i. Guadeloupe
124	B6	**St Martin, Cape** S. Africa
131	J4	**St Martin, Lake** Canada
134	D2	**St Martin Island** U.S.A.
105	A8	**St Martin's** i. U.K.
89	H5	**St Martin's Island** Bangl.
71	H8	**St Mary Peak** Australia
71	H8	**St Marys** Australia
135	G4	**St Mary's** Canada
105	A8	**St Mary's** i. U.K.
105	G5	**St Mary's** U.K.
135	G4	**St Marys** U.S.A.
145	D6	**St Marys** r. U.S.A.
133	J4	**St Mary's, Cape** hd Canada
128	A3	**St Matthew Island** U.S.A.
68	F2	**St Matthias Group** is P.N.G.
110	G4	**St Maurice** r. Canada
105	B7	**St Mawes** U.K.
110	H2	**St-Médard-en-Jalles** France
133	I3	**St Michael's Bay** Canada
110	C2	**St-Nazaire** France
110	H2	**St-Nicolas-de-Port** France
105	H5	**St Neots** U.K.
110	F1	**St-Omer** France
133	G4	**St-Pamphile** Canada
133	G4	**St Paul** Canada
131	K4	**St Paul** U.S.A.
134	A2	**St Paul** MN U.S.A.
147	H2	**St Paul** NE U.S.A.
146	B6	**St Paul** r. U.S.A.
162	J7	**St Paul, Île** i. Indian Ocean
133	H3	**St Peter** Canada
147	H1	**St Peter Port** U.K.
116	D3	**St Petersburg** Rus. Fed. (City Plan 55)
145	D7	**St Petersburg** U.S.A.
110	G5	**St-Pierre** r. America
133	I3	**St-Pierre, Lac** l. Canada
129	M5	**St Pierre and Miquelon** terr. N. America
110	C2	**St-Pierre-d'Oléron** France
147	H1	**St-Pierre-le-Moûtier** France
110	A4	**St-Pol-sur-Ternoise** France
110	F3	**St-Pourçain-sur-Sioule** France
110	H2	**St-Quentin** France
110	H5	**St-Raphaël** France
147	F2	**St Regis Falls** U.S.A.
147	F2	**St-Rémi** Canada
147	F2	**St-Sébastien** Canada
147	J2	**St Simons Island** U.S.A.
147	I2	**St Stephen** Canada
147	E3	**St Stephen** U.S.A.
147	F2	**St-Théophile** Canada
131	K4	**St Theresa Point** Canada

135	G4	**St Thomas** Canada
110	H5	**St-Tropez** France
131	J5	**St Vincent** U.S.A.
71	F9	**St Vincent, Cape** hd Australia
70	B5	**St Vincent, Gulf** Australia
149	L6	**St Vincent and the Grenadines** country Caribbean Sea
108	E4	**St-Vith** Belgium
131	H4	**St Walburg** Canada
135	G4	**St Williams** Canada
110	E4	**St-Yrieix-la-Perche** France
92	C1	**Sain Us** China
111	F1	**Sainsa** mt. Spain
88	E3	**Saipal** mt. Nepal
64	C4	**Saipan** i. N. Mariana Is
91	H5	**Saitai** Myanmar
102	N2	**Saittanulkki** hill Fin.
154	E7	**Sajama, Nevado** mt. Bol.
84	D5	**Sājir** Saudi Arabia
124	D5	**Sak** watercourse S. Africa
95	C7	**Sakai** Japan
95	C7	**Sakaide** Japan
95	C7	**Sakaiminato** Japan
85	G5	**Saka Kalat** Pak.
86	B5	**Sakākah** Saudi Arabia
142	C2	**Sakakawea, Lake** U.S.A.
132	E3	**Sakami** Canada
132	F3	**Sakami** r. Canada
132	E3	**Sakami Lake** Canada
115	I4	**Sakar** mts Bulg.
80	C1	**Sakarya** Turkey
80	C1	**Sakarya** r. Turkey
94	F5	**Sakata** Japan
96	C3	**Sakchu** N. Korea
83	H2	**Saken Seyfullin** Kazakh.
98	A2	**Sa Keo** r. Thai.
120	C4	**Sakété** Benin
90	G1	**Sakhalin** i. Rus. Fed.
90	C1	**Sakhalinskiy Zaliv** b. Rus. Fed.
88	C3	**Sakhi** India
125	H3	**Sakhile** S. Africa
84	C2	**Sakht-Sar** Iran
81	K1	**Şäki** Azer.
117	G6	**Saky** Ukr.
103	M3	**Säkylä** Fin.
88	A3	**Sakir** mt. Pak.
90	E4	**Sakishima-shotō** is Japan
120	□	**Sal** i. Cape Verde
117	G6	**Sal** r. Rus. Fed.
150	H5	**Sal, Punta** pt Hond.
103	L4	**Sala** Sweden
132	F4	**Salaberry-de-Valleyfield** Canada
103	N4	**Salacgrīva** Latvia
114	F4	**Sala Consilina** Italy
141	E5	**Salada, Laguna** salt l. Mex.
159	D2	**Saladillo** r. Arg.
109	Q3	**Salado** r. Arg.
109	J2	**Salado** r. Buenos Aires Arg.
88	B4	**Salado** r. Mendoza/San Luis Arg.
93	B7	**Salado** r. Río Negro Arg.
84	B4	**Salado** r. Santa Fé Arg.
159	E1	**Salado, Quebrada de** r. Chile
120	C4	**Salaga** Ghana
121	F2	**Salajwe** Botswana
86	D6	**Şalālah** Oman
151	H5	**Salamá** Guat.
150	H5	**Salamá** Hond.
150	D4	**Salamanca** Mex.
157	D3	**Salamanca** Spain
99	E3	**Salamanca** U.S.A.
94	D2	**Salamat, Bahr** r. Chad
83	F5	**Salāmatābād** Iran
81	I4	**Salamina** Col.
97	A4	**Salamīyah** Syria
116	I4	**Salamonie** r. U.S.A.
83	J2	**Salandi** r. India
81	L1	**Salantai** Lith.
122	C4	**Salaqi** China
99	E2	**Salas** Spain
99	D3	**Salaspils** Latvia
99	C2	**Salavat** Rus. Fed.
123	F5	**Salawati** i. Indon.
88	D3	**Salaya** India
88	C4	**Salayar, Tanjung** pt Indon.
117	B5	**Salayar** i. Indon.
152	C5	**Sala y Gómez, Isla** i. S. Pacific Ocean
159	D3	**Salazar** Arg.
103	N5	**Šalčininkai** Lith.
157	B4	**Saldaña** Col.
110	C2	**Saldaña** Spain
124	B6	**Saldanha** S. Africa
124	B6	**Saldanha Bay** S. Africa
159	E3	**Saldungaray** Arg.
103	M4	**Saldus** Latvia
71	G7	**Sale** Australia
81	K5	**Şālehābād** Iran
76	H3	**Salekhard** Rus. Fed.
96	E4	**Salem** MA U.S.A.
81	K1	**Şämkir** Azer.
69	I3	**Samoa** country Pacific Ocean
160	H7	**Samoa Basin** sea feature Pacific Ocean
114	F2	**Samobor** Croatia
116	G2	**Samoded** Rus. Fed.
115	J3	**Samokov** Bulg.
112	H6	**Šamorín** Slovakia
115	L6	**Samos** i. Greece
115	K4	**Samothraki** Greece
115	K4	**Samothraki** i. Greece
99	D3	**Sampit** Indon.
99	D3	**Sampit, Teluk** b. Indon.
122	C4	**Sampwe** Dem. Rep. Congo
98	D2	**Sâm Sao, Phou** mts Laos/Vietnam
98	C2	**Sâm Sơn** Vietnam
80	F1	**Samsun** Turkey
117	G7	**Samtredia** Georgia
98	B3	**Samui, Ko** i. Thai.
98	B2	**Samut Prakan** Thai.
98	B2	**Samut Sakhon** Thai.
98	B3	**Samut Songkhram** Thai.
89	G3	**Samyai** China
120	D3	**San** Mali
98	C1	**San, Phou** mt. Laos
98	C2	**San** r. Cambodia
121	D4	**Sanaga** r. Cameroon
97	C5	**San Agustin, Cape** Phil.
81	K4	**Sanandaj** Iran
84	C5	**Sanām** Saudi Arabia
154	C5	**San Ambrosio, Isla** i. S. Pacific Ocean
99	E3	**Sanandaj** Iran
161	N7	**San Félix, Isla** i. S. Pacific Ocean
140	B2	**San Andreas** U.S.A.
159	E2	**San Andrés** Arg.
157	B2	**San Andrés, Isla de** i. Col.
150	I5	**San Andrés, Isla de** i. Col.
111	E3	**San Andrés** Spain
150	D2	**San Andrés Tuxtla** Mex.
151	F5	**San Andrés Tuxtla** Mex.
140	C5	**San Angelo** U.S.A.
157	D3	**San Antonio** Venez.
143	C6	**San Angelo** U.S.A.
129	J4	**San Antonio** Chile
97	B3	**San Antonio** Phil.
143	D6	**San Antonio** U.S.A.
157	D3	**San Antonio** Venez.
140	B3	**San Antonio** r. U.S.A.

159	F3	**San Antonio, Cabo** pt Arg.
149	H4	**San Antonio, Cabo** pt Cuba
140	D4	**San Antonio, Mount** U.S.A.
111	G3	**San Antonio Abad** Spain
156	C7	**San Antonio de los Cobres** Arg.
157	D2	**San Antonio de Tamanaco** Venez.
159	D4	**San Antonio Oeste** Arg.
140	B3	**San Antonio Reservoir** U.S.A.
140	B3	**San Ardo** U.S.A.
159	B3	**San Augustín** Arg.
159	C1	**San Augustín de Valle Fértil** Arg.
88	B3	**Sanawad** India
151	D3	**San Bartolo** Mex.
114	E2	**San Benedetto del Tronto** Italy
148	B5	**San Benedicto, Isla** i. Mex.
143	D7	**San Benito** U.S.A.
140	B3	**San Benito** r. U.S.A.
140	B3	**San Benito Mountain** U.S.A.
140	C3	**San Bernardino** U.S.A.
139	D5	**San Bernardino Mountains** U.S.A.
156	C3	**San Bernardo** Chile
150	C2	**San Bernardo** Mex.
95	C7	**Sanbe-san** vol. Japan
150	C2	**San Blas** Nayarit Mex.
150	C2	**San Blas** Sinaloa Mex.
150	J6	**San Blas, Archipiélago de** is Panama
145	C6	**San Blas, Cape** U.S.A.
150	J6	**San Blas, Cordillera de** mts Panama
154	E6	**San Borja** Bol.
147	H5	**Sanbornville** U.S.A.
150	D2	**San Buenaventura** Mex.
159	B3	**San Carlos** Chile
151	D3	**San Carlos** Coahuila Mex.
150	D1	**San Carlos** Tamaulipas Mex.
150	H6	**San Carlos** Nicaragua
97	B3	**San Carlos** Phil.
97	B4	**San Carlos** Phil.
159	F2	**San Carlos** Uruguay
141	G5	**San Carlos** U.S.A.
157	D2	**San Carlos** Venez.
159	E1	**San Carlos Centro** Arg.
158	B1	**San Carlos de Bariloche** Arg.
159	E3	**San Carlos de Bolívar** Arg.
157	C2	**San Carlos del Zulia** Venez.
141	G5	**San Carlos Lake** U.S.A.
92	C2	**Sancha** Gansu China
92	C5	**Sancha** Shanxi China
93	B5	**Sancha He** r. China
93	I5	**Sanchakou** China
98	C1	**San Chien Pau** mt. Laos
92	D2	**Sanchuan He** r. China
116	J4	**Sanchursk** Rus. Fed.
151	E3	**San Ciro de Acosta** Mex.
159	B2	**San Clemente** Chile
140	C5	**San Clemente** U.S.A.
140	C5	**San Clemente Island** U.S.A.
110	F3	**Sancoins** France
159	E1	**San Cristóbal** Arg.
69	G3	**San Cristobal** i. Solomon Is
157	D3	**San Cristóbal** Venez.
154	□	**San Cristóbal, Isla** i. Galapagos Is Ecuador
151	F5	**San Cristóbal de las Casas** Mex.
141	F5	**San Cristobal Wash** r. U.S.A.
149	I4	**Sancti Spíritus** Cuba
125	H1	**Sand** r. S. Africa
94	D3	**Sandagou** Rus. Fed.
106	C5	**Sanda Island** U.K.
99	E1	**Sandakan** Sabah Malaysia
115	J4	**Sandanski** Bulg.
109	K2	**Sandau** Germany
106	F1	**Sanday** i. U.K.
106	F1	**Sanday Sound** sea chan. U.K.
105	E4	**Sandbach** U.K.
103	J4	**Sandefjord** Norway
73	D4	**Sandercock Nunataks** Antarctica
109	J3	**Sandersleben** Germany
143	C6	**Sanderson** U.S.A.
71	J1	**Sandgate** Australia
106	D6	**Sandhead** U.K.
154	E6	**Sandia** Peru
140	C5	**San Diego** U.S.A.
156	C8	**San Diego, Cabo** c. Arg.
80	C2	**Sandıklı** Turkey
88	D3	**Sandila** India
134	B2	**Sand Island** U.S.A.
134	E2	**Sand Lake** Canada
103	I4	**Sandnes** Norway
102	K2	**Sandnessjøen** Norway
123	C5	**Sandoa** Dem. Rep. Congo
113	J5	**Sandomierz** Poland
114	E2	**San Donà di Piave** Italy
91	B6	**Sandoway** Myanmar
105	F7	**Sandown** U.K.
124	C7	**Sandown Bay** S. Africa
102	□	**Sandoy** i. Faroe Is
138	C1	**Sandpoint** U.S.A.
106	A4	**Sandray** i. U.K.
115	K2	**Sandul Mare, Vârful** mt. Romania
103	K3	**Sandsjö** Sweden
130	C4	**Sandspit** Canada
143	D4	**Sand Springs** U.S.A.
139	G2	**Sand Springs Salt Flat** U.S.A.
68	B5	**Sandstone** Australia
134	A2	**Sandstone** U.S.A.
93	D5	**Sandu** Guizhou China
93	C5	**Sandu** Hunan China
135	F4	**Sandusky** MI U.S.A.
146	C3	**Sandusky** OH U.S.A.
124	C5	**Sandveld** mts S. Africa
124	B2	**Sandverhaar** Namibia
103	I4	**Sandvika** Norway
103	L3	**Sandviken** Sweden
133	I3	**Sandwich Bay** Canada
106	□	**Sandwick** U.K.
89	G5	**Sandwip Channel** Bangl.
147	H2	**Sandy** r. U.S.A.
131	I3	**Sandy Bay** Canada
71	H8	**Sandy Cape** hd Australia
71	F8	**Sandy Cape** hd Australia
147	H2	**Sandy Hook** U.S.A.
146	B5	**Sandy Hook** pt U.S.A.
85	H3	**Sandykachi** Turkm.
131	J3	**Sandy Lake** Canada
132	B3	**Sandy Lake** Canada
147	H3	**Sandy Pond** U.S.A.
159	E2	**San Estanislao** Para.
156	C2	**San Felipe** Chile
150	B2	**San Felipe** Baja California Mex.
150	D4	**San Felipe** Chihuahua Mex.
150	D3	**San Felipe** Guanajuato Mex.
157	D2	**San Felipe** Venez.
140	D5	**San Felipe Creek** r. U.S.A.
145	D6	**Sanford** FL U.S.A.
147	H3	**Sanford** ME U.S.A.

146 D4 Scottdale U.S.A.
73 B4 Scott Glacier Antarctica
129 K2 Scott Inlet Canada
73 A5 Scott Island Antarctica
131 H3 Scott Lake Canada
73 D4 Scott Mountains Antarctica
142 C3 Scottsbluff U.S.A.
145 C5 Scottsboro U.S.A.
144 C4 Scottsburg U.S.A.
71 G8 Scottsdale Australia
139 E5 Scottsdale U.S.A.
140 A3 Scotts Valley U.S.A.
140 C3 Scottville U.S.A.
140 D3 Scotty's Junction U.S.A.
106 C2 Scourie U.K.
106 □ Scousburgh U.K.
106 E2 Scrabster U.K.
147 F4 Scranton U.S.A.
106 B4 Scridain, Loch inlet U.K.
104 G4 Scunthorpe U.K.
105 H7 Seaford U.K.
147 F5 Seaford U.S.A.
135 G4 Seaforth Canada
97 A4 Seahorse Bank sea feature Phil.
131 I4 Seal r. Canada
124 E7 Seal, Cape pt S. Africa
70 E5 Sea Lake Australia
147 I3 Seal Island U.S.A.
133 H3 Seal Lake Canada
124 F7 Seal Point S. Africa
141 E3 Seaman Range mts U.S.A.
104 G3 Seamer U.K.
141 E4 Searchlight U.S.A.
143 F5 Searcy U.S.A.
140 D4 Searles Lake U.S.A.
134 E4 Sears U.S.A.
147 I2 Searsport U.S.A.
140 B3 Seaside CA U.S.A.
138 B2 Seaside OR U.S.A.
106 E6 Seaton U.K.
138 B2 Seattle U.S.A.
130 B3 Seattle, Mount Canada/U.S.A.
147 F5 Seaville U.S.A.
147 H3 Sebago Lake U.S.A.
150 A1 Sebastián Vizcaíno, Bahía b. Mex.
147 I2 Sebasticook r. U.S.A.
99 E2 Sebatik i. Indon.
80 C1 Seben Turkey
115 J2 Sebeş Romania
99 C4 Sebesi i. Indon.
135 F4 Sebewaing U.S.A.
116 D3 Sebezh Rus. Fed.
80 G1 Sebinkarahisar Turkey
147 I2 Seboeis Lake U.S.A.
147 I2 Seboomook U.S.A.
147 I2 Seboomook Lake U.S.A.
145 D7 Sebring U.S.A.
117 G5 Sebrovo Rus. Fed.
154 B5 Sechura Peru
154 B5 Sechura, Bahía de b. Peru
109 H5 Seckach Germany
147 H2 Second Lake U.S.A.
72 A6 Secretary Island N.Z.
125 H3 Secunda S. Africa
87 B2 Secunderabad India
142 E4 Sedalia U.S.A.
87 B2 Sedam India
70 C5 Sedan Australia
110 G2 Sedan France
72 E4 Seddon N.Z.
72 C4 Seddonville N.Z.
85 E4 Sedeh Iran
147 I2 Sedgwick U.S.A.
120 A3 Sédhiou Senegal
112 G6 Sedlčany Czech Rep.
80 E6 Sedom Israel
114 B6 Šeduva Alg.
103 M5 Šeduva Lith.
109 I1 Seedorf Germany
107 D5 Seefin hill Rep. of Ireland
109 J2 Seehausen Germany
109 J2 Seehausen (Altmark) Germany
123 B6 Seeheim Namibia
109 G5 Seeheim-Jugenheim Germany
124 C5 Seekoegat S. Africa
141 E5 Seeley U.S.A.
73 B3 Seelig, Mount Antarctica
109 H2 Seelze Germany
110 E2 Sées France
109 I3 Seesen Germany
109 I1 Seevetal Germany
120 A4 Sefadu Sierra Leone
125 G1 Sefare Botswana
115 L5 Seferihisar Turkey
125 G1 Sefophe Botswana
103 J3 Segalstad Norway
97 A5 Segama r. Sabah Malaysia
99 B2 Segamat Malaysia
109 K2 Segeletz Germany
116 E2 Segezha Rus. Fed.
83 F3 Segiz salt l. Kazakh.
83 F3 Segiz, Ozero salt l. Kazakh.
111 F3 Segorbe Spain
120 B3 Ségou Mali
157 B3 Segovia Col.
111 D2 Segovia Spain
116 E2 Segozerskoye, Ozero resr Rus. Fed.
111 G¹ Segre r. Spain
120 B4 Séguédine Niger
120 B4 Séguéla Côte d'Ivoire
143 D6 Seguin U.S.A.
159 D1 Segundo r. Arg.
111 F3 Segura r. Spain
123 C6 Sehithwa Botswana
125 H4 Sehlabathebe National Park Lesotho
88 D5 Sehore India
102 M1 Seiland i. Norway
143 D4 Seiling U.S.A.
102 M3 Seinäjoki Fin.
131 L2 Seine r. Canada
110 E2 Seine r. France
110 D2 Seine, Baie de b. France
110 E2 Seine, Val de valley France
113 K3 Sejny Poland
99 B3 Sekayu Indon.
120 B4 Sekoma Botswana
120 B4 Sekondi Ghana
85 F4 Seküheh Iran
98 D5 Sekura Indon.
138 B2 Selah U.S.A.
91 F7 Selaru i. Indon.
99 □ Selat, Tanjung pt Indon.
98 □ Selat Johor sea chan. Malaysia/Sing.
98 □ Selat Jurong sea chan. Sing.
98 □ Selat Pandan sea chan. Sing.
128 B3 Selawik U.S.A.
109 K4 Selb Germany
102 J3 Selbekken Norway
102 J3 Selbu Norway
104 F4 Selby U.K.
142 C2 Selby U.S.A.
123 C6 Selebi-Phikwe Botswana
90 F1 Selemdzhinskiy Khrebet mts Rus. Fed.
80 B2 Selendi Turkey
110 H2 Sélestat France
98 □ Seletar Sing.
98 □ Seletar, Pulau i. Sing.
98 □ Seletar Reservoir Sing.
125 G Seletinskoye Kazakh.
142 C2 Selfridge U.S.A.
116 I2 Selib Rus. Fed.
120 A3 Sélibabi Mauritania
109 G4 Seligenstadt Germany
116 E3 Seliger, Ozero l. Rus. Fed.
141 F4 Seligman U.S.A.
121 E2 Selima Oasis Sudan
135 I5 Selinsgrove U.S.A.
113 P2 Selishche Rus. Fed.

117 H6 Selitrennoye Rus. Fed.
113 P2 Selizharovo Rus. Fed.
103 J4 Seljord Norway
109 J3 Selke r. Germany
131 I4 Selkirk Canada
106 F5 Selkirk U.K.
130 F4 Selkirk Mountains Canada
104 D3 Sellafield U.K.
141 G6 Sells U.S.A.
108 F3 Selm Germany
145 C5 Selma AL U.S.A.
140 C3 Selma CA U.S.A.
145 B5 Selmer U.S.A.
85 F4 Selseleh-ye Pīr Shūrān mts Iran
105 G7 Selsey Bill U.K.
98 C4 Seluan i. Indon.
154 D5 Selvas reg. Brazil
158 D2 Sete Lagoas Brazil
102 L1 Setermoen Norway
103 I4 Setesdal valley Norway
89 F4 Seti r. Nepal
88 E3 Seti r. Nepal
120 C1 Sétif Alg.
95 E7 Seto Japan
120 B1 Settat Morocco
104 E3 Settle U.K.
111 B3 Setúbal Port.
111 B3 Setúbal, Baía de b. Port.
132 B3 Seul, Lac l. Canada
129 L5 Seul Choix Point U.S.A.
81 J1 Sevan Armenia
81 J1 Sevan, Lac l. Armenia
Sevana Lich l. Armenia see Sevan
117 E6 Sevastopol' Ukr.
133 H2 Seven Islands Bay Canada
105 H6 Sevenoaks U.K.
110 F4 Sévérac-le-Château France
71 I2 Severn r. Australia
132 B3 Severn r. Canada
124 E3 Severn r. S. Africa
105 E6 Severn r. U.K.
116 G2 Severnaya Dvina r. Rus. Fed.
117 H7 Severnaya Osetiya - Alaniya, Respublika aut. rep. Rus. Fed.
77 L1 Severnaya Zemlya is Rus. Fed.
132 B3 Severn Lake Canada
76 H3 Severnyy Rus. Fed.
82 D3 Severnyy Chink Ustyurta esc. Kazakh.
90 D1 Severo-Baykal'skoye Nagor'ye mts Rus. Fed.
116 F1 Severodvinsk Rus. Fed.
77 Q4 Severo-Kuril'sk Rus. Fed.
102 P1 Severomorsk Rus. Fed.
76 K3 Severo-Yeniseyskiy Rus. Fed.
117 F6 Severskaya Rus. Fed.
139 D4 Sevier r. U.S.A.
141 F2 Sevier Bridge Reservoir U.S.A.
141 F2 Sevier Desert U.S.A.
141 F2 Sevier Lake salt l. U.S.A.
157 B3 Sevilla Col.
Sevilla Spain see Seville
111 D4 Seville Spain
115 K3 Sevlievo Bulg.
88 C3 Sewani India
128 D3 Seward AK U.S.A.
142 D3 Seward NE U.S.A.
128 B3 Seward Peninsula U.S.A.
130 F3 Sexsmith Canada
136 E6 Sextín r. Mex.
85 F3 Seyah Band Koh mts Afgh.
76 I2 Seyakha Rus. Fed.
151 G4 Seybaplaya Mex.
119 I5 Seychelles country Indian Ocean
82 E5 Seydi Turkm.
80 C3 Seydişehir Turkey
102 □ Seyðisfjörður Iceland
84 B2 Seýdvan Iran
80 E3 Seyhan r. Turkey
Seyhan Turkey see Adana
117 E5 Seym r. Rus. Fed.
77 Q3 Seymchan Rus. Fed.
70 F6 Seymour Australia
124 G4 Seymour S. Africa
144 C4 Seymour IN U.S.A.
143 D5 Seymour TX U.S.A.
85 H3 Seyyedābād Afgh.
110 F2 Sézanne France
115 K7 Sfakia Greece
115 J2 Sfântu Gheorghe Romania
120 D1 Sfax Tunisia
115 J4 Sfikia, Limni resr Greece
108 C2 's-Gravenhage Neth. see The Hague
106 B3 Sgurr Alasdair hill U.K.
106 C4 Sgurr Dhomhnuill hill U.K.
106 C3 Sgurr Mor mt. U.K.
92 C3 Shaanxi prov. China
84 B2 Shabestar Iran
115 M3 Shabla, Nos pt Bulg.
133 G3 Shabogamo Lake Canada
122 C4 Shabunda Dem. Rep. Congo
83 I5 Shache China
73 B4 Shackleton Coast Antarctica
73 B4 Shackleton Glacier Antarctica
73 C3 Shackleton Ice Shelf Antarctica
73 C3 Shackleton Range mts Antarctica

159 D1 Serrezuela Arg.
155 K6 Serrinha Brazil
158 D2 Sêrro Brazil
159 B4 Serrucho mt. Arg.
114 C6 Sers Tunisia
158 C3 Sertãozinho Brazil
116 D2 Sertolovo Rus. Fed.
98 A4 Seruai Indon.
99 D3 Seruyan r. Indon.
89 H2 Sêrwolungwa China
90 B3 Sêrxü China
99 E2 Sesayap Indon.
97 A6 Sesayap r. Indon.
132 B3 Seseganaga Lake Canada
135 G1 Sesekinika Canada
123 B5 Sesfontein Namibia
125 I1 Seshego S. Africa
123 C5 Sesheke Zambia
114 E4 Sessa Aurunca Italy
111 H3 Ses Salines, Cap de pt Spain
111 H3 Sestri Levante Italy
116 D2 Sestroretsk Rus. Fed.
98 C2 Set, Phou mt. Laos
94 F3 Setana Japan
110 F5 Sète France
84 A4 Shadadkot Pak.
84 B4 Shādegān Iran
84 A3 Shādīkhak Pass Pak.
84 A3 Shādkām watercourse Iran
134 D5 Shafer, Lake U.S.A.
73 B5 Shafer Peak mt. Antarctica
140 C4 Shafter U.S.A.
105 E6 Shaftesbury U.K.
82 □ Shagan watercourse Aktyubinskaya Oblast' Kazakh.
83 I2 Shagan watercourse Vostochnyy Kazakhstan Kazakh.
128 C3 Shageluk U.S.A.
83 G1 Shaglyteniz, Ozero l. Kazakh.
83 G1 Shaglyteniz, Ozero l. Kazakh.
73 B2 Shag Rocks is Atlantic Ocean
72 C7 Shag Point N.Z.
83 G4 Shagyray, Plato plat. Kazakh.
82 D3 Shagyrlyk Uzbek.
87 B2 Shahabad Karnataka India
88 D4 Shāhābād Uttar Pradesh India
84 E4 Shāhābād Iran
99 B2 Shah Alam Malaysia
85 G5 Shahbaz Kalat Pak.
85 G5 Shahbazpur sea chan. Bangl.
85 E4 Shahdād Iran
88 D4 Shahdol Madhya Pradesh India
88 D4 Shahpura Rajasthan India
85 G3 Shahrak Afgh.

85 F3 Shāhrakht Iran
84 D4 Shahr-e Bābak Iran
84 C3 Shahr-e Kord Iran
84 D3 Shahr-e Rey Iran
83 G5 Shahrtuz Tajik.
84 C2 Shāhrūd, Rūdkhāneh-ye r. Iran
84 D3 Shahrud Bustam reg. Iran
85 H4 Shaikh Husain mt. Pak.
84 C5 Shaj'ah, Jabal hill Saudi Arabia
96 C3 Shajianzi China
81 K3 Shakar Bolāghī Iran
81 K3 Shakaville S. Africa
83 G5 Shakhdara r. Tajik.
85 E3 Shakhen Iran
116 E3 Shakhovskaya Rus. Fed.
83 F5 Shakhrisabz Uzbek.
83 H4 Shakhtinsk Kazakh.
82 D2 Shakhty Kazakh.
117 F5 Shakhty Rus. Fed.
116 H3 Shakhun'ya Rus. Fed.
120 C4 Shaki Nigeria
142 E3 Shakopee U.S.A.
94 F3 Shakotan-hantō pen. Japan
94 F3 Shakotan-misaki c. Japan
116 G2 Shalakusha Rus. Fed.
83 I2 Shalday Kazakh.
83 G3 Shalginskiy Kazakh.
82 D3 Shalkar Kazakh.
82 E2 Shalkar, Ozero salt l. Kazakh.
82 E2 Shalkar Karashatau salt l. Kazakh.
89 D3 Shaluli Shan mts China
89 I3 Shaluni mt. India
131 K3 Shamattawa Canada
93 □ Sham Chun hill Hong Kong China
84 E5 Shamil Iran
84 D3 Shamis U.A.E.
83 H4 Shamokin U.S.A.
143 C5 Shamrock U.S.A.
123 D5 Shamva Zimbabwe
107 B6 Shanacrane Rep. of Ireland
92 C2 Shanchengbu China
85 F4 Shand Afgh.
85 F4 Shāndak Iran
92 A2 Shandan China
84 E1 Shandian He r. China
85 E2 Shandiz Iran
140 B4 Shandon U.S.A.
92 E2 Shandong prov. China
92 E2 Shandong Bandao pen. China
88 C1 Shandur Pass Pak.
123 C5 Shangani r. Zimbabwe
123 C5 Shangani Zimbabwe
93 E5 Shangcheng China
92 E3 Shangcheng China
94 E5 Shangchuan Dao i. China
89 D6 Shangdu China
93 E5 Shangdundu China
92 F4 Shanggao China
92 F4 Shanghai China
92 F4 Shanghai mun. China (City Plan 51)
92 F4 Shanghang China
92 F3 Shanghe China
96 C3 Shanghekou China
93 C6 Shangjin China
93 C6 Shanglin China
92 E3 Shangnan China
93 E4 Shangqiu China
92 E3 Shangrao Jiangxi China
92 E3 Shangrao Jiangxi China
92 F2 Shangshui China
93 C6 Shangsi China
92 D3 Shangtang China
92 D3 Shangyi China
93 E5 Shangyou China
92 F4 Shangyu China
93 F4 Shangyou Shuiku salt flat China
94 A1 Shangzhi China
93 C6 Shangzhou China
92 E3 Shanhetun China
107 C5 Shannon est. Rep. of Ireland
107 C4 Shannon r. Rep. of Ireland
107 B5 Shannon, Mouth of the est. Rep. of Ireland
96 C2 Shansonggang China
89 G5 Shantipur India
93 E6 Shantou China
93 E6 Shanwei China
92 D3 Shanxi prov. China
93 E5 Shanxian China
92 C3 Shanyang China
92 C3 Shanyin China
93 D5 Shaodong China
93 D5 Shaoguan China
93 E5 Shaowu China
92 F4 Shaoxing China
93 D5 Shaoyang Hunan China
93 D5 Shaoyang Hunan China
70 A3 Shapa China
104 F1 Shapinsay i. U.K.
93 D6 Shapa China
106 F1 Shapinsay i. U.K.
86 C4 Shaqrā' Saudi Arabia
81 J2 Shaqqā Syria
89 B4 Shaqpur Bangl.
80 E6 Sharan Jogizai Pak.
117 G5 Sharchino Rus. Fed.
76 A3 Shardara Kazakh.
83 F5 Shargun' Uzbek.
117 D5 Sharhorod Ukr.
81 J4 Shārī, Buḥayrat l. Iraq
94 I3 Shari-dake vol. Japan
84 D4 Sharjah U.A.E.
113 M3 Sharkawshchyna Belarus
68 A4 Shark Bay Australia
82 C1 Sharlouk Turkm.
82 C1 Sharlyk Rus. Fed.
80 G6 Sharm ash Shaykh Egypt
146 C4 Sharon PA U.S.A.
82 E3 Sharqī, Jabal ash mts Lebanon/Syria
85 H2 She'ya Iran
85 H5 Shibar Pass Afgh.
94 I3 Shashemenē Eth.
89 B4 Shashubay Eth.
94 I3 Shibetsu Japan

83 K2 Shebalino Rus. Fed.
117 F5 Shebekino Rus. Fed.
85 G2 Sheberghān Afgh.
134 C3 Sheboygan U.S.A.
120 D4 Shebshi Mountains Nigeria
130 D3 Shediac Canada
130 D3 Shedin Peak mt. Canada
107 D2 Sheelin, Lough l. Rep. of Ireland
107 D2 Sheep Haven b. Rep. of Ireland
125 I3 Sheepmoor S. Africa
141 E3 Sheep Peak mt. U.S.A.
105 H6 Sheerness U.K.
133 H5 Sheet Harbour Canada
71 I8 Sheffield Australia
72 D5 Sheffield N.Z.
105 F4 Sheffield U.K.
145 C5 Sheffield AL U.S.A.
134 C5 Sheffield IL U.S.A.
146 D4 Sheffield PA U.S.A.
143 C6 Sheffield TX U.S.A.
135 G3 Shelburne Canada
92 B4 Shehong China
84 D3 Sheikh, Jebel esh mt. Lebanon/Syria see Hermon, Mount
88 C1 Shekhupura Pak.
93 □ Shek Kwu Chau i. Hong Kong China
93 □ Shek Pik Reservoir Hong Kong China
116 F3 Sheksna Rus. Fed.
93 □ Shek Uk Shan hill Hong Kong China
84 E5 Shelag watercourse Afgh./Iran
77 S2 Shelagskiy, Mys pt Rus. Fed.
134 A6 Shelbina U.S.A.
133 A6 Shelburne N.S. Canada
135 G3 Shelburne Ont. Canada
135 G3 Shelburne Falls U.S.A.
134 D4 Shelby MI U.S.A.
138 F1 Shelby MT U.S.A.
145 D5 Shelby NC U.S.A.
146 C4 Shelby OH U.S.A.
144 C4 Shelbyville IN U.S.A.
134 A6 Shelbyville MO U.S.A.
145 C5 Shelbyville TN U.S.A.
142 E3 Sheldon IA U.S.A.
147 G2 Sheldon Springs U.S.A.
133 H4 Shelldrake Canada
77 Q3 Shelikhova, Zaliv g. Rus. Fed.
128 C4 Shelikof Strait U.S.A.
131 H4 Shellbrook Canada
138 D3 Shelley U.S.A.
71 I5 Shellharbour Australia
93 E6 Shelter Bay Canada
140 A1 Shelter Cove U.S.A.
93 □ Shelter Island Hong Kong China
147 G4 Shelter Island U.S.A.
72 B7 Shelter Point N.Z.
83 J2 Shemonaikha Kazakh.
82 E2 Shenbertal Kazakh.
120 C4 Shendam Nigeria
94 C1 Shending Shan hill China
82 E3 Shengel'dy Kazakh.
92 F4 Shengsi China
92 F4 Shenmu China
92 D2 Shennong Ding mt. China
92 D4 Shennongjia China
92 F4 Shenqiu China
94 A1 Shenshu China
90 E2 Shenwo Shuiku resr China
96 B3 Shenyang China
93 E6 Shenzhen China
93 □ Shenzhen Wan b. Hong Kong China
117 C5 Shepetivka Ukr.
69 G3 Shepherd Islands Vanuatu
71 F6 Shepparton Australia
105 H6 Sheppey, Isle of i. U.K.
83 G5 Sherabad Uzbek.
105 E7 Sherborne U.K.
133 H4 Sherbrooke N.S. Canada
135 I3 Sherbrooke Que. Canada
147 F3 Sherburne U.S.A.
107 C4 Shercock Rep. of Ireland
85 H3 Sher Dahan Pass Afgh.
121 F3 Shereiq Sudan
88 C4 Shergarh India
143 E5 Sheridan AR U.S.A.
138 F2 Sheridan WY U.S.A.
71 H4 Sheringa Australia
105 I5 Sheringham U.K.
143 D5 Sherman U.S.A.
147 I2 Sherman Mills U.S.A.
141 E1 Sherman Mountain U.S.A.
131 I3 Sherridon Canada
108 D3 's-Hertogenbosch Neth.
105 F6 Sherwood Forest reg. U.K.
81 J3 Shor Barsa-Kel'mes salt marsh Uzbek.
81 J3 Shor Gol Iran
82 A3 Shorkot Pak.
82 C3 Shorkozakhly, Solonchak depr. Turkm.
83 H2 Shortandy Kazakh.
94 G2 Shosanbetsu Japan
140 D4 Shoshone CA U.S.A.
138 D3 Shoshone ID U.S.A.
138 E3 Shoshone r. U.S.A.
138 E3 Shoshone Lake U.S.A.
139 C4 Shoshone Mts U.S.A.
125 G1 Shoshong Botswana
138 E3 Shoshoni U.S.A.
117 E5 Shostka Ukr.
93 F5 Shouguang China
93 F5 Shouning China
92 E3 Shouxian China
93 B5 Shouyang China
92 E2 Shouyang Shan mt. China
141 G6 Show Low U.S.A.
117 G6 Shpakovskoye Rus. Fed.
117 D5 Shpola Ukr.
143 E5 Shreveport U.S.A.
105 E5 Shrewsbury U.K.
87 A2 Shrigonda India
88 B3 Shri Mohangarh India
81 K6 Shu'aiba Iraq
92 D1 Shuangcheng China
96 D2 Shuangcheng China
92 E3 Shuanggou China
92 E2 Shuangliao China
92 D1 Shuangyang China
90 A3 Shuangtaizihe Kou b. China
92 C2 Shuangyashan China
82 D2 Shubarkuduk Kazakh.
82 D2 Shubarshi Kazakh.
92 E4 Shucheng China
93 F5 Shufu China
92 F3 Shu He r. China
92 D3 Shuiku China
92 C4 Shuikou China
96 A3 Shuiquan China
96 C2 Shuiyuan China
82 D2 Shula China
92 D1 Shulinzhao China
94 H2 Shumarinai-ko l. Japan
92 E4 Shumba Zimbabwe
95 B8 Shumerlya Rus. Fed.
113 N3 Shumilina Belarus

82 B2 Shil'naya Balka Kazakh.
147 F5 Shiloh U.S.A.
92 D2 Shilou China
116 G4 Shilovo Rus. Fed.
95 F3 Shimabara Japan
94 G5 Shimada Japan
90 E1 Shimanovsk Rus. Fed.
93 B4 Shimian China
95 F5 Shimizu Japan
88 D3 Shimla India
95 F6 Shimoda Japan
88 B3 Shimoga India
122 D4 Shimoni Kenya
95 B8 Shimonoseki Japan
88 C1 Shimshal Jammu and Kashmir
116 D3 Shimsk Rus. Fed.
106 D2 Shin, Loch l. U.K.
88 B3 Shindand Afgh.
88 B3 Shinghar Pak.
88 B3 Shinghshal Pass Pak.
134 D2 Shingleton U.S.A.
83 J3 Shingozha Kazakh.
95 E7 Shingū Japan
125 I1 Shingwedzi S. Africa
125 I1 Shingwedzi r. S. Africa
105 E4 Shining Tor hill U.K.
135 G2 Shining Tree Canada
94 G5 Shinjō Japan
95 F3 Shinkay Afgh.
93 B4 Shinminato Japan
147 I1 Shin Pond U.S.A.
122 D4 Shinyanga Tanz.
94 G5 Shiogama Japan
95 D8 Shiono-misaki c. Japan
95 G4 Shioya-zaki pt Japan
145 E7 Ship Chan Cay i. Bahamas
93 B6 Shiping China
104 F4 Shipley U.K.
133 H4 Shippegan Canada
146 E4 Shippensburg U.S.A.
141 H3 Shiprock U.S.A.
141 H3 Shiprock Peak mt. U.S.A.
93 C5 Shipu China
93 C5 Shipunovo Rus. Fed.
93 C5 Shiquan China
88 B4 Shiquan He r. China conv. Indus
92 C3 Shiquan Shuiku resr China
81 L2 Shīrābād Iran
95 G6 Shirakawa Japan
94 I3 Shirane-san mt. Japan
95 F5 Shirane-san vol. Japan
73 D4 Shirasebreen ice feature Antarctica
73 A4 Shirase Coast Antarctica
84 D4 Shīrāz Iran
80 C6 Shirbīn Egypt
94 I3 Shiretoko-misaki c. Japan
83 I2 Shirikrabat tourist site Kazakh.
85 G4 Shirinab r. Pak.
82 D3 Shiriya-zaki c. Japan
147 H3 Shirley U.S.A.
147 I2 Shirley Mills U.S.A.
95 E7 Shirotori Japan
88 C5 Shirpur India
88 D3 Shirvān Iran
84 D2 Shishaldin Volcano U.S.A.
77 R4 Shiveluch, Sopka mt. Rus. Fed.
144 C4 Shively U.S.A.
85 H2 Shivpuri India
141 F3 Shivwits Plateau U.S.A.
85 H2 Shiwal r. Afgh.
93 C5 Shiwan Dashan mts China
93 E5 Shixing China
92 D3 Shizi China
93 C4 Shizhu China
92 C2 Shizuishan China
95 F6 Shizuoka Japan
116 D4 Shklow Belarus
115 H3 Shkodër Albania
76 J1 Shmidta, Ostrov i. Rus. Fed.
85 G5 Shodpar Tajik.
94 G3 Shokanbetsu-dake mt. Japan
83 J2 Sholakkorgan Kazakh.
82 F2 Sholaksay Kazakh.
87 B3 Sholapur India
116 I2 Shomvukva Rus. Fed.
106 C4 Shona, Eilean i. U.K.
163 J9 Shona Ridge sea feature S. Atlantic Ocean
82 B3 Shoptykol' Kazakh.
82 H2 Shoptykol' Kazakh.
147 I2 Shorancur India
81 K4 Shoranur India
84 E5 Shoranur India
85 G5 Shorapur Bangl.
85 G5 Shorawak reg. Afgh.

141 G4 Shumway U.S.A.
116 E4 Shumyachi Rus. Fed.
83 H3 Shunak, Gora mt. Kazakh.
93 E5 Shunchang China
96 B3 Shunde China
93 D6 Shunde China
128 C3 Shungnak U.S.A.
92 E1 Shunyi China
93 C6 Shuolong China
92 D2 Shuozhou China
86 C7 Shuqrah Yemen
84 D4 Shūr r. Iran
102 N2 Shūr r. Iran
85 F3 Shūr r. Iran
84 D4 Shūr watercourse Iran
84 D5 Shūr watercourse Iran
85 E3 Shūr watercourse Iran
84 C3 Shūr Āb Iran
84 D3 Shūrāb Iran
84 E3 Shūrāb Iran
84 E4 Shūr Āb watercourse Iran
83 F5 Shurchi Uzbek.
84 D4 Shureghestan Iran
85 E4 Shūr Gaz Iran
84 D4 Shūrjestān Iran
83 G4 Shūrob Tajik.
123 D5 Shurugwi Zimbabwe
81 J6 Shuruppak Iraq
85 F4 Shusf Iran
84 C3 Shūsh Iran
84 C3 Shushtar Iran
130 F4 Shuswap Lake Canada
83 H2 Shutar Khun Pass Afgh.
80 F6 Shuwaysh, Tall ash hill Jordan
116 G3 Shuya Rus. Fed.
92 F3 Shuyang China
98 A1 Shwegun Myanmar
83 G3 Shyganak Kazakh.
83 G3 Shygys Konyrat Kazakh.
83 G4 Shymkent Kazakh.
88 D2 Shyok r. India
88 D2 Shyok Jammu and Kashmir
117 F5 Shypuvate Ukr.
117 E6 Shyroke Ukr.
91 F7 Sia Indon.
88 D2 Siachen Glacier India
88 B1 Siahan Range mts Pak.
81 J2 Siah Chashmeh Iran
85 G3 Siah Koh mts Afgh.
84 D3 Siāh Kūh mts Iran
85 G4 Siah Sang Pass Afgh.
88 C2 Sialkot Pak.
98 C1 Siantan i. Indon.
157 H4 Siapa r. Venez.
85 F4 Siāreh Iran
97 J5 Siargao i. Phil.
97 B5 Siasi Phil.
97 B5 Siasi i. Phil.
97 J4 Siaton Phil.
103 M5 Šiauliai Lith.
85 F5 Sib Iran
84 C3 Sibak Iran
125 I1 Sibasa S. Africa
97 B4 Sibay i. Phil.
82 D1 Sibay Rus. Fed.
125 J3 Sibayi, Lake S. Africa
73 B5 Sibbald, Cape Antarctica
114 F3 Šibenik Croatia
77 K3 Siberia reg. Rus. Fed.
99 A3 Siberut i. Indon.
88 A3 Sibi Pak.
122 D3 Sibiloi National Park Kenya
Sibir' Rus. Fed. see Siberia
94 C2 Sibirtsevo Rus. Fed.
122 B4 Sibiti Congo
115 K2 Sibiu Romania
99 A2 Sibolga Indon.
98 A5 Siborongborong Indon.
89 H4 Sibsagar India
97 B5 Sibu Sarawak Malaysia
97 B5 Sibuco Phil.
97 B5 Sibuguey r. Phil.
97 B5 Sibuguey Bay Phil.
122 B3 Sibut Centr. Afr. Rep.
97 A5 Sibutu i. Phil.
97 A5 Sibutu Passage Phil.
97 B3 Sibuyan i. Phil.
97 B3 Sibuyan Sea Phil.
97 B2 Sicapoo mt. Phil.
98 A3 Sichon Thai.
93 B4 Sichuan prov. China
93 B4 Sichuan Pendi basin China
110 G5 Sicié, Cap c. France
114 E6 Sicilian Channel Italy/Tunisia
114 E6 Sicily i. Italy
Sicilia i. Italy see Sicily
154 D6 Sicuani Peru
115 K2 Šid Yugo.
87 B2 Siddipet India
115 L7 Sideros, Akra pt Greece
124 E6 Sidesaviwa S. Africa
111 H5 Sidi Aïssa Alg.
111 G4 Sidi Ali Alg.
120 B1 Sidi Bel Abbès Alg.
114 C7 Sidi Bouzid Tunisia
114 D7 Sidi El Hani, Sebkhet de salt pan Tunisia
120 A2 Sidi Ifni Morocco
120 B1 Sidi Kacem Morocco
98 A5 Sidikalang Indon.
106 A4 Sidlaw Hills U.K.
73 A4 Sidley, Mount Antarctica
105 D7 Sidmouth U.K.
130 E5 Sidney Canada
138 F2 Sidney MT U.S.A.
142 C3 Sidney NE U.S.A.
147 F3 Sidney NY U.S.A.
146 A4 Sidney OH U.S.A.
145 D5 Sidney Lanier, Lake U.S.A.
89 H5 Sidoktaya Myanmar
80 E5 Sidon Lebanon
116 G3 Sidorovo Rus. Fed.
158 A3 Sidrolândia Brazil
125 I3 Sidvokodvo Swaziland
83 G4 Sidzhak Uzbek.
110 F5 Sié, Col de pass France
113 K4 Siedlce Poland
109 C4 Siegen Germany
98 B2 Siěmréab Cambodia
114 D3 Siena Italy
113 I5 Sieradz Poland
159 D4 Sierra, Punta pt Arg.
143 B6 Sierra Blanca U.S.A.
159 C4 Sierra Colorada Arg.
159 D4 Sierra Grande Arg.
120 A4 Sierra Leone country Africa
Sierra Leone Basin sea feature N. Atlantic Ocean
163 Sierra Leone Rise sea feature N. Atlantic Ocean
140 C4 Sierra Madre Mountains U.S.A.
150 D2 Sierra Mojada Mex.
157 C2 Sierra Nevada, Parque nat. park Venez.
157 B2 Sierra Nevada de Santa Marta, Parque Nacional nat. park Col.
140 B2 Sierra Vista U.S.A.
141 G6 Sierraville U.S.A.
112 C7 Sierre Switz.
102 N3 Sievi Fin.
93 C6 Sifang Ling mts China
115 K6 Sifnos i. Greece
111 F5 Sig Alg.
129 M2 Sigguup Nunaa pen. Greenland
113 K7 Sighetu Marmaţiei Romania
113 L7 Sighişoara Romania
98 □ Siglap Sing.
99 A1 Sigli Indon.
102 C1 Siglufjörður Iceland
112 D6 Sigmaringen Germany
109 H4 Signal de Botrange hill Belgium
141 E5 Signal Peak mt. U.S.A.
108 C5 Signy-l'Abbaye France
134 A5 Sigourney U.S.A.

115 K5 Sigri, Akra pt Greece
163 C4 Sigsbee Deep sea feature Gulf of Mexico
151 H5 Siguatepeque Hond.
111 E2 Sigüenza Spain
120 B3 Siguiri Guinea
103 N4 Sigulda Latvia
98 B3 Sihanoukville Cambodia
92 F3 Sihong China
88 E5 Sihora India
93 D6 Sihui China
102 N2 Siikajoki Fin.
102 N3 Siilinjärvi Fin.
81 H3 Siirt Turkey
93 B3 Sijunjung Indon.
88 B5 Sika India
130 E3 Sikanni Chief Canada
130 E3 Sikanni Chief r. Canada
88 C4 Sikar India
85 H3 Sikaram mt. Afgh.
120 B3 Sikasso Mali
83 K3 Sikeshu China
134 B4 Sikeston U.S.A.
90 F2 Sikhote-Alin' mts Rus. Fed.
115 K6 Sikinos i. Greece
89 G4 Sikkim state India
102 L2 Siksjö Sweden
96 B4 Sikuaishi China
99 E1 Sikuati Sabah Malaysia
111 C1 Sil r. Spain
97 C4 Silago Phil.
103 M5 Šilalė Lith.
150 D3 Silao Mex.
97 B4 Silay Phil.
109 H1 Silberberg hill Germany
88 D1 Silchar India
80 B1 Şile Turkey
87 C2 Sileru r. India
81 I1 Sileti r. Kazakh.
83 H1 Siletiteniz, Ozero salt l. Kazakh.
88 E3 Silgarhi Nepal
114 C6 Siliana Tunisia
80 D3 Silifke Turkey
89 G3 Siling Co salt l. China
115 L2 Silistra Bulg.
80 B1 Silivri Turkey
102 D3 Siljan l. Sweden
103 J4 Silkeborg Denmark
103 N4 Sillamäe Estonia
88 E5 Sillod India
125 I3 Silobela S. Africa
89 G3 Silong China
143 E6 Silsbee U.S.A.
102 N2 Siltaharju Fin.
81 H2 Silvan Turkey
88 C5 Silvassa India
134 C1 Silver Bay U.S.A.
139 E5 Silver City U.S.A.
134 C1 Silver Islet Canada
140 C3 Silver Lake l. CA U.S.A.
140 B2 Silver Lake l. MI U.S.A.
138 B3 Silver Lake U.S.A.
107 C5 Silvermine Mountains Rep. of Ireland
140 D3 Silver Peak Range mts U.S.A.
146 E5 Silver Spring U.S.A.
140 C2 Silver Springs U.S.A.
70 D3 Silverton Australia
105 D7 Silverton U.K.
135 F3 Silver Water Canada
150 C3 Silvituc Mex.
135 H2 Simard, Lac l. Canada
85 K5 Şīmareh, Rūdkhāneh-ye r. Iran
99 A3 Simaria Indon.
80 B2 Simav Turkey
80 B2 Simav Dağları mts Turkey
122 C4 Simba Dem. Rep. Congo
135 G4 Simcoe Canada
135 H3 Simcoe, Lake Canada
87 D1 Simdega India
122 D2 Simēn Mountains Eth.
99 A2 Simeuluë i. Indon.
117 E6 Simferopol' Ukr.
89 E3 Simikot Nepal
157 B3 Simiti Col.
140 C4 Simi Valley U.S.A.
139 F4 Simla U.S.A.
113 K7 Şimleu Silvaniei Romania
108 F5 Simmerath Germany
109 C5 Simmern (Hunsrück) Germany
140 C4 Simmler U.S.A.
141 F4 Simmons U.S.A.
145 F7 Simm's Bahamas
81 K2 Simnas Lith.
102 N2 Simo Fin.
150 D2 Simojovel Mex.
130 F4 Simonette r. Canada
131 I4 Simonhouse Canada
112 D7 Simplon Pass Switz.
68 D4 Simpson Desert Australia
131 H4 Simpson Island Canada
140 D2 Simpson Park Mountains U.S.A.
103 M5 Simrishamn Sweden
94 F4 Simushir, Ostrov i. Rus. Fed.
87 A2 Sina r. India
99 A2 Sinabang Indon.
98 A5 Sinabung vol. Indon.
121 F2 Sinai reg. Egypt
110 L7 Sinaia, Mont France
150 B2 Sinaloa state Mex.
114 D2 Sinalunga Italy
93 C5 Sinan China
96 C4 Sinanju N. Korea
89 H5 Sinbyugyun Myanmar
80 E2 Sincan Turkey
157 B2 Sincé Col.
157 B2 Sincelejo Col.
145 D5 Sinclair, Lake U.S.A.
130 E4 Sinclair Mills Canada
124 B2 Sinclair Mine Namibia
106 E2 Sinclair's Bay U.K.
88 C4 Sind r. India
99 C4 Sindangan Indon.
99 C4 Sindangbarang Indon.
109 H1 Sindelfingen Germany
87 B2 Sindgi India
88 B4 Sindh prov. Pak.
87 B3 Sindhnur India
88 B4 Sindkhed India
88 D6 Sindkheda India
116 I2 Sindor Rus. Fed.
89 E5 Sind Sagar Doab lowland Pak.
116 I3 Sindor Rus. Fed.
115 L4 Sinekçi Turkey
111 B4 Sines Port.
111 B4 Sines, Cabo de pt Port.
121 F3 Singa Sudan
88 B3 Singahi India
88 D2 Singa Pass India
98 □ Singapore country Asia
98 B5 Singapore Sing.
(City Plan 50)
98 □ Singapore, Strait of Indon./Sing.
99 C4 Singaraja Indon.
98 B2 Singa Buri Thai.
135 G3 Singhampton Canada
122 D4 Singida Tanz.
68 C2 Singkang Indon.
99 C2 Singkawang Indon.
98 A5 Singkil Indon.
71 J4 Singleton Australia
96 C4 Singŭiho N. Korea
114 C4 Siniscola Sardinia Italy
82 E2 Siniy-Shikhan Rus. Fed.

147 G3 Sinj Croatia
68 C2 Sinjai Indon.
81 H3 Sinjar Iraq
81 H3 Sinjār, Jabal mt. Iraq
121 F3 Sinkat Sudan
96 C4 Sinmi-do i. N. Korea
109 G4 Sinn Germany
155 H2 Sinnamary Fr. Guiana
115 M2 Sinoie, Lacul lag. Romania
117 E7 Sinop Turkey
96 D3 Sinp'a N. Korea
96 E3 Sinp'o N. Korea
96 D4 Sinp'yŏng N. Korea
96 D4 Sinsang N. Korea
109 G5 Sinsheim Germany
99 D2 Sintang Indon.
107 A6 Sint Eustatius i. Neth. Antilles
108 B3 Sint-Laureins Belgium
149 L5 Sint Maarten i. Neth. Antilles
108 B3 Sint-Niklaas Belgium
143 D6 Sinton U.S.A.
108 D4 Sint-Truiden Belgium
157 A2 Sinú r. Col.
96 C3 Sinŭiju N. Korea
108 F4 Sinzig Germany
97 B5 Siocon Phil.
113 H7 Siófok Hungary
112 C7 Sion Switz.
107 D3 Sion Mills U.K.
142 D3 Sioux Center U.S.A.
142 D3 Sioux City U.S.A.
142 D3 Sioux Falls U.S.A.
132 B3 Sioux Lookout Canada
151 G5 Sipacate Guat.
97 B4 Sipalay Phil.
96 C2 Siping China
131 J3 Sipiwesk Canada
131 J3 Sipiwesk Lake Canada
73 A4 Siple, Mount Antarctica
73 B4 Siple Coast Antarctica
87 A3 Sipra r. India
145 C5 Sipsey r. U.S.A.
99 A3 Sipura i. Indon.
150 H5 Siquia r. Nicaragua
97 B4 Siquijor Phil.
97 B4 Siquijor i. Phil.
88 B5 Sir r. Pak.
103 I4 Sira r. Norway
125 I2 Şir Abū Nu'āyr i. U.A.E.
98 B2 Si Racha Thai.
Siracusa Sicily Italy see Syracuse
130 E4 Sir Alexander, Mount Canada
81 G1 Şiran Turkey
85 G5 Şāranda Lake Pak.
125 I2 Şīr Banī Yās i. U.A.E.
81 L3 Sīrdān Iran
68 D3 Sir Edward Pellew Group is Australia
134 A3 Siren U.S.A.
84 E5 Sīrīk Iran
98 B1 Siri Kit Dam Thai.
84 D4 Sīrīz Iran
130 D2 Sir James McBrien, Mount Canada
84 D4 Sīrjān Iran
84 D4 Sīrjān salt flat Iran
70 B5 Sir Joseph Banks Group is Australia
88 E4 Sirmour India
81 I3 Şırnak Turkey
87 C2 Sironcha India
87 B2 Sironj India
89 C4 Sirpur India
88 C3 Sirretta Peak mt. U.S.A.
88 C3 Sirri, Jazīreh-ye i. Iran
88 C3 Sirsa Haryana India
88 B3 Sir Sandford, Mount Canada
87 A3 Sirsi Karnataka India
88 D3 Sirsi Uttar Pradesh India
87 B2 Sirsilla India
121 D1 Sirte Libya
121 D1 Sirte, Gulf of Libya
87 A2 Sirur India
81 J4 Sīrvan r. Turkey
103 N5 Širvintos Lith.
85 K3 Sīrwān r. Iraq
130 F4 Sir Wilfrid Laurier, Mount Canada
114 G2 Sisak Croatia
98 C2 Sisaket Thai.
150 D2 Sisal Mex.
124 E3 Sishen S. Africa
81 K2 Sisian Armenia
134 C2 Siskiwit Bay U.S.A.
98 B2 Sisŏphŏn Cambodia
140 B4 Sisquoc r. U.S.A.
142 D2 Sisseton U.S.A.
147 J1 Sisson Branch Reservoir Canada
85 F4 Sīstān reg. Iran
85 F4 Sīstān, Daryācheh-ye marsh Afgh.
71 F8 Sisters Beach Australia
85 E5 Sīt Iran
88 C5 Sitamau India
97 B4 Sitangkai Phil.
88 E4 Sitapur India
125 I3 Siteki Swaziland
115 J4 Sithonia pen. Greece
158 C1 Sítio da Abadia Brazil
158 D1 Sítio do Mato Brazil
130 C3 Sitka U.S.A.
88 B3 Sitpur Pak.
108 D4 Sittard Neth.
89 H5 Sittaung Myanmar
109 H1 Sittensen Germany
105 H6 Sittingbourne U.K.
89 H5 Sittwe Myanmar
93 □ Siu A Chau i. Hong Kong China
150 H5 Siuna Nicaragua
89 F5 Siuri India
87 B3 Sivaganga India
87 B4 Sivakasi India
84 D4 Sīvand Iran
80 D2 Sivas Turkey
80 B2 Sivasli Turkey
81 G3 Siverek Turkey
80 C2 Sivrihisar Turkey
125 H3 Sivukile S. Africa
114 I2 Siwah Egypt
88 D3 Siwalik Range mts India/Nepal
89 F4 Siwan India
87 A2 Siwana India
110 G5 Six-Fours-les-Plages France
92 E3 Sixian China
105 D5 Six Lakes U.S.A.
105 D3 Sixmilecross U.K.
113 I6 Siyang China
115 I5 Siyäzän Azer.
84 C1 Siyuni Iran
Sjælland i. Denmark see Zealand
115 I3 Sjenica Yugo.
103 I5 Sjøvegan Norway
102 L1 Sjöbo Sweden
102 N2 Skaftafell Iceland
102 C1 Skaftárós est. Iceland
102 C1 Skagafjörður inlet Iceland
103 J4 Skagen Denmark
103 J4 Skagerrak strait Denmark/Norway
130 B3 Skagit r. Canada/U.S.A.
130 B3 Skagway U.S.A.
102 M3 Skaland Norway
102 L1 Skalmodal Sweden
103 J4 Skanderborg Denmark
82 E2 Siniy-Shikhan Rus. Fed.

147 E3 Skaneateles Lake U.S.A.
134 C2 Skanee U.S.A.
115 K5 Skantzoura i. Greece
103 K4 Skara Sweden
103 M4 Skärgårdshavets nationalpark nat. park Fin.
103 J4 Skarnes Norway
113 J5 Skarżysko-Kamienna Poland
102 M2 Skaulo Sweden
113 I6 Skawina Poland
130 D3 Skeena r. Canada
130 D3 Skeena Mountains Canada
105 H4 Skegness U.K.
102 M2 Skellefteå Sweden
102 M2 Skellefteälven r. Sweden
102 M2 Skelleftehamn Sweden
107 A6 Skellig Rocks i. Rep. of Ireland
105 E4 Skelmersdale U.K.
107 E5 Skerries Rep. of Ireland
103 J4 Ski Norway
115 J5 Skiathos i. Greece
102 M1 Skibotn Norway
103 D3 Skiddaw mt. U.K.
103 I4 Skien Norway
113 J5 Skierniewice Poland
120 C1 Skikda Alg.
104 G4 Skipsea U.K.
70 E4 Skipton Australia
102 L2 Skjak Norway
103 J5 Skjern Denmark
103 J5 Skjern r. Denmark
103 I3 Skjolden Norway
102 I3 Skodje Norway
102 N2 Skoganvarre Norway
105 B6 Skokholm Island U.K.
115 K5 Skopelos i. Greece
116 F4 Skopin Rus. Fed.
115 I4 Skopje Macedonia
117 F5 Skorodnoye Rus. Fed.
103 K4 Skövde Sweden
147 I2 Skowhegan U.S.A.
103 M4 Skrunda Latvia
130 D3 Skukum, Mount Canada
125 I2 Skukuza S. Africa
140 D2 Skull Peak mt. U.S.A.
103 M4 Skuodas Lith.
103 L3 Skunk r. U.S.A.
124 F6 Skurweberge mts S. Africa
103 L3 Skutskär Sweden
117 D5 Skvyra Ukr.
106 B3 Skye i. U.K.
115 K5 Skyros Greece
115 K5 Skyros i. Greece
73 B3 Skytrain Ice Rise Antarctica
103 J5 Slagelse Denmark
103 J5 Slagnäs Sweden
99 C2 Slamet, Gunung vol. Indon.
107 E4 Slane Rep. of Ireland
107 E5 Slaney r. Rep. of Ireland
116 D4 Slantsy Rus. Fed.
117 G5 Slashchevskaya Rus. Fed.
114 D1 Slate Islands Canada
114 G2 Slatina Croatia
115 K2 Slatina Romania
131 G2 Slave r. Canada
120 C4 Slave Coast Africa
130 G3 Slave Lake Canada
82 H1 Slavgorod Rus. Fed.
113 N2 Slavkovichi Rus. Fed.
114 G2 Slavonija reg. Croatia
114 G2 Slavonski Brod Croatia
117 C5 Slavuta Ukr.
94 B3 Slavyanka Rus. Fed.
117 F6 Slavyansk-na-Kubani Rus. Fed.
116 D4 Slawharad Belarus
112 H2 Sławno Poland
105 G4 Sleaford U.K.
70 A5 Sleaford Bay Australia
107 A5 Slea Head Rep. of Ireland
106 B4 Sleat pt. U.K.
106 B4 Sleat, Sound of sea chan. U.K.
132 E2 Sleeper Islands Canada
134 C3 Sleeping Bear Dunes National Lakeshore nat. park U.S.A.
134 C3 Sleeping Bear Point U.S.A.
117 H7 Sleptsovskaya Rus. Fed.
73 A2 Slessor Glacier Antarctica
143 F6 Slidell U.S.A.
107 A5 Slievanea Rep. of Ireland
67 I5 Slieve Anierin hill Rep. of Ireland
107 D5 Slieveardagh Hills Rep. of Ireland
107 C4 Slieve Aughty Mountains Rep. of Ireland
107 D3 Slieve Beagh hill Rep. of Ireland/U.K.
107 C5 Slieve Bernagh hill Rep. of Ireland
107 D4 Slieve Bloom Mountains Rep. of Ireland
107 B3 Slieve Car hill Rep. of Ireland
107 B3 Slieve Donard hill U.K.
107 B4 Slieve Elva hill Rep. of Ireland
107 C3 Slieve Gamph hill Rep. of Ireland
107 C3 Slieve League hill Rep. of Ireland
107 B5 Slieve Mish Mountains Rep. of Ireland
107 B3 Slieve Miskish Mountains Rep. of Ireland
107 A3 Slieve na Calliagh hill Rep. of Ireland
107 D5 Slievenamon hill Rep. of Ireland
107 D5 Slieve Snaght hill Rep. of Ireland
106 B3 Sligachan U.K.
107 C3 Sligo Rep. of Ireland
107 C3 Sligo Bay Rep. of Ireland
115 L4 Slite Sweden
115 L3 Sliven Bulg.
116 I2 Sloboda Rus. Fed.
92 A1 Sloboda Rus. Fed.
116 H2 Slobodchikovo Rus. Fed.
115 L2 Slobozia Romania
108 E1 Slochteren Neth.
116 C3 Slonim Belarus
108 C2 Slootdorp Neth.
108 D2 Sloten Neth.
108 D2 Slotermeer l. Neth.
105 G6 Slough U.K.
113 I6 Slovakia country Europe
114 E1 Slovenia country Europe
114 F1 Slovenj Gradec Slovenia
117 F5 Slov"yans'k Ukr.
112 H3 Słupsk Poland
102 L3 Slussfors Sweden
116 C3 Slutsk Belarus
107 A4 Slyne Head Rep. of Ireland
77 L4 Slyudyanka Rus. Fed.
133 H3 Smallwood Reservoir Canada
116 C4 Smalyavichy Belarus
113 M3 Smarhon' Belarus
124 E5 Smart Syndicate Dam resr S. Africa
131 H1 Smeaton Canada
115 I2 Smederevo Yugo.
115 I2 Smederevska Palanka Yugo.
117 D5 Smila Ukr.
108 E2 Smilde Neth.
103 N4 Smiltene Latvia
83 G1 Smirnovo Kazakh.

130 G3 Smith Canada
140 C2 Smith U.S.A.
105 C6 Smith r. U.S.A.
128 B2 Smith Bay U.S.A.
131 G5 Smithers Canada
125 G5 Smithfield S. Africa
145 E5 Smithfield NC U.S.A.
138 E2 Smithfield UT U.S.A.
73 A3 Smith Glacier Antarctica
73 B2 Smith Island Antarctica
147 E5 Smith Island MD U.S.A.
147 F6 Smith Island VA U.S.A.
146 D5 Smith Mountain Lake U.S.A.
130 D3 Smith River Canada
135 I2 Smiths Falls Canada
129 K2 Smith Sound strait Canada/Greenland
71 F8 Smithton Australia
140 C1 Smoke Creek Desert U.S.A.
130 F4 Smoky r. Canada
71 J3 Smoky Cape hd Australia
132 D3 Smoky Falls Canada
142 C4 Smoky Hills r. U.S.A.
142 D4 Smoky Hills U.S.A.
130 G4 Smoky Lake Canada
102 I3 Smøla i. Norway
116 E4 Smolenka Rus. Fed.
116 E4 Smolensk Rus. Fed.
116 E4 Smolenskaya Oblast' admin. div. Rus. Fed.
116 E4 Smolenskoye Rus. Fed.
115 K3 Smolyan Bulg.
94 C3 Smolyoninovo Rus. Fed.
132 D4 Smooth Rock Falls Canada
132 C3 Smoothrock Lake Canada
131 H4 Smoothstone Lake Canada
102 N1 Smørfjord Norway
73 B3 Smyley Island Antarctica
Smyrna Turkey see İzmir
116 H3 Smyrna DE U.S.A.
145 C5 Smyrna GA U.S.A.
146 A4 Smyrna OH U.S.A.
147 I1 Smyrna Mills U.S.A.
102 D2 Snæfell mt. Iceland
104 C3 Snæfell mt. U.K.
130 A2 Snag Canada
138 D3 Snake r. U.S.A.
141 E2 Snake Range mts U.S.A.
138 D3 Snake River Plain U.S.A.
130 D3 Snare Lakes Canada see Wekweeti
69 G6 Snares Islands N.Z.
102 K2 Snåsa Norway
108 D1 Sneek Neth.
107 B6 Sneem Rep. of Ireland
124 F6 Sneeuberge mts S. Africa
133 H3 Snegamook Lake Canada
105 H5 Snettisham U.K.
76 J3 Snezhnogorsk Rus. Fed.
114 F2 Snežnik mt. Slovenia
113 I4 Śniardwy, Jezioro l. Poland
117 E6 Snihurivka Ukr.
106 B3 Snizort, Loch b. U.K.
138 B2 Snoqualmie Pass U.S.A.
130 D5 Snowbird Lake Canada
105 C5 Snowdon mt. U.K.
105 C5 Snowdonia National Park U.K.
141 F4 Snowflake U.S.A.
147 F5 Snow Hill MD U.S.A.
145 E5 Snow Hill NC U.S.A.
131 H4 Snow Lake Canada
70 C4 Snowtown Australia
138 D3 Snowville U.S.A.
71 H6 Snowy r. Australia
71 H6 Snowy Mountains Australia
71 G9 Snug Australia
133 I3 Snug Harbour Nfld Canada
135 G3 Snug Harbour Ont. Canada
98 C2 Snuŏl Cambodia
143 D5 Snyder TX U.S.A.
143 C5 Snyder TX U.S.A.
123 E5 Soalala Madag.
123 E5 Soanierana-Ivongo Madag.
96 D6 Soan-kundo i. S. Korea
157 B3 Soata Col.
107 A4 Soay i. U.K.
96 D6 Sobaek-sanmaek mts S. Korea
121 F4 Sobat r. Sudan
109 F5 Sobernheim Germany
91 G7 Sobger r. Indon.
95 B8 Sobo-san mt. Japan
155 J6 Sobradinho, Barragem de resr Brazil
155 J4 Sobral Brazil
117 F7 Sochi Rus. Fed.
96 E5 Sŏch'ŏn S. Korea
67 I5 Society Islands Fr. Polynesia
158 B3 Socorro Brazil
157 B3 Socorro Col.
139 F5 Socorro U.S.A.
148 B5 Socorro, Isla i. Mex.
86 D7 Socotra i. Yemen
98 C3 Soc Trăng Vietnam
111 E3 Socuéllamos Spain
140 D4 Soda Lake U.S.A.
102 N2 Sodankylä Fin.
88 D2 Soda Plains China/Jammu and Kashmir
138 E3 Soda Springs U.S.A.
103 L3 Söderhamn Sweden
103 L3 Söderköping Sweden
103 L4 Södertälje Sweden
121 F3 Sodiri Sudan
122 D3 Sodo Eth.
103 L3 Södra Kvarken strait Fin./Sweden
125 H1 Soekmekaar S. Africa
108 D2 Soest Neth.
109 D3 Soest Germany
115 H4 Sofala Bulg.
115 H4 Sofia Bulg.
Sofiya Bulg. see Sofia
102 O2 Sofporog Rus. Fed.
95 G10 Sōfu-gan i. Japan
89 G3 Sog China
157 B3 Sogamoso Col.
81 L6 Soğanlı Dağları mts Turkey
108 F2 Sögel Germany
80 C2 Söğüt Turkey
90 D7 Sŏgwip'o S. Korea
88 D2 Sohagpur India
105 H5 Soham U.K.
88 B3 Sohan r. Pak.
69 L2 Sohano P.N.G.
87 C1 Sohela India
96 D2 Sŏho-ri N. Korea
96 D5 Sŏhuksan i. S. Korea
108 C4 Soignies, Forêt de for. Belgium
108 C4 Soignies Belgium
110 F2 Soissons France
88 B4 Sojat India
37 B4 Sojotin Point Phil.
96 C5 Sokcho S. Korea
80 B3 Söke Turkey
83 G4 Sokh Tajik.
81 I5 Sokhumi Georgia
120 C4 Sokodé Togo
116 F3 Sokol Rus. Fed.
113 K3 Sokółka Poland
120 B3 Sokolo Mali
113 G5 Sokolov Czech Rep.
94 D3 Sokolovka Rus. Fed.
113 K4 Sokołów Podlaski Poland

120 C3 Sokoto Nigeria
120 C3 Sokoto r. Nigeria
117 C5 Sokyryany Ukr.
88 D3 Solan India
72 A7 Solander Island N.Z.
87 A2 Solapur India
157 B2 Soledad Col.
140 B3 Soledad U.S.A.
157 E2 Soledad Venez.
151 E4 Soledad de Doblado Mex.
117 G6 Solenoye Rus. Fed.
102 K2 Solfjellsjøen Norway
81 H2 Solhan Turkey
116 G3 Soligalich Rus. Fed.
105 F5 Solihull U.K.
76 G4 Solikamsk Rus. Fed.
82 G2 Sol'-Iletsk Rus. Fed.
151 H4 Solimán, Punta pt Mex.
108 F3 Solingen Germany
124 A1 Solitaire Namibia
81 L1 Sollar Azer.
102 K3 Sollefteå Sweden
109 G3 Söllichau Germany
109 H1 Solling hill Germany
109 I3 Sollstedt Germany
109 G4 Solms Germany
116 F3 Solnechnogorsk Rus. Fed.
99 B3 Solok Indon.
151 G5 Sololá Guat.
Solomon Islands country Pacific Ocean
68 F2 Solomon Sea P.N.G./Solomon Is
83 K2 Soloneshnoye Rus. Fed.
134 B2 Solon Springs U.S.A.
91 E7 Solor, Kepulauan is Indon.
112 C7 Solothurn Switz.
116 E1 Solovetskiye Ostrova is Rus. Fed.
116 H3 Solovetskoye Rus. Fed.
114 G3 Šolta i. Croatia
85 E2 Soltānābād Iran
85 H3 Soltānābād Iran
109 H2 Soltau Germany
116 D3 Sol'tsy Rus. Fed.
147 E3 Solvay U.S.A.
103 K4 Sölvesborg Sweden
106 E6 Solway Firth est. U.K.
123 C5 Solwezi Zambia
95 G6 Sōma Japan
80 A2 Soma Turkey
108 B4 Somain France
122 E3 Somalia country Africa
162 H5 Somali Basin sea feature Indian Ocean
123 C4 Sombo Angola
115 H2 Sombor Yugo.
150 D3 Sombrerete Mex.
88 C4 Somdari India
147 I2 Somerest Junction U.S.A.
147 H3 Somero Fin.
144 C4 Somerset KY U.S.A.
134 E4 Somerset MI U.S.A.
146 D5 Somerset OH U.S.A.
125 F6 Somerset East S. Africa
129 I2 Somerset Island Canada
147 G3 Somerset Reservoir U.S.A.
125 D7 Somerset West S. Africa
147 H3 Somersworth U.S.A.
147 H3 Somerville Reservoir U.S.A.
84 B3 Someydeh Iran
103 K4 Sommen l. Sweden
108 C3 Sömmerda Germany
134 C5 Somonauk U.S.A.
150 H5 Somotillo Nicaragua
150 H5 Somoto Nicaragua
159 C4 Somuncurá, Mesa Volcánica de plat. Arg.
150 I7 Soná Panama
83 G2 Sonaly Karagandinskaya Oblast' Kazakh.
83 G2 Sonaly Karagandinskaya Oblast' Kazakh.
89 F5 Sonamukhi India
89 G5 Sonamura India
88 D4 Sonar r. India
96 C4 Sŏnch'ŏn N. Korea
103 I5 Sønderborg Denmark
109 I3 Sondershausen Germany
114 C1 Sondrio Italy
88 B5 Sonepat India
87 D2 Sonepur India
88 B5 Songad India
92 B4 Songbu China
98 B4 Sông Cau Vietnam
123 C5 Songea Tanz.
96 C1 Songhua Hu resr China
96 C1 Songhuajiang China
92 B1 Songhua Jiang r. China
92 F3 Songjiang Shanghai China
96 C2 Songjianghe China
98 B4 Songkhla Thai.
83 J4 Songköl l. Kyrg.
92 F1 Song Ling mts China
96 C2 Songnim N. Korea
123 B5 Songo Angola
123 D5 Songo Moz.
92 B3 Songpan China
96 D5 Sŏngsan S. Korea
92 E2 Song Shan mt. China
92 D3 Songshuzhen China
93 F5 Songxi China
96 C1 Songyuan China
93 C6 Songzi China
98 A4 Son Ha Vietnam
88 D3 Sonipat India
102 N3 Sonkajärvi Fin.
98 B3 Son La Vietnam
88 B4 Sonmiani Pak.
88 B4 Sonmiani Bay Pak.
109 J4 Sonneberg Germany
158 C2 Sono r. Minas Gerais Brazil
155 I6 Sono r. Brazil
150 B2 Sonoita r. Mex.
150 B2 Sonoita Mex.
140 B3 Sonoma U.S.A.
143 C6 Sonora r. Mex.
150 B2 Sonora state Mex.
143 C6 Sonora TX U.S.A.
140 B3 Sonora CA U.S.A.
157 B3 Sonsón Col.
151 H5 Sonsonate El Salvador
125 H5 Sonwabile S. Africa
159 F1 Sopas r. Uruguay
121 F4 Sopo watercourse Sudan
115 I3 Sopot Bulg.
113 H7 Sopron Hungary
117 J4 Sopu-Korgon Kyrg.
114 E4 Sora Italy
87 D2 Sorada India
103 L3 Söråker Sweden
96 E4 Sŏrak-san mt. S. Korea
82 C2 Sor Donyztau l. Kazakh.
135 G5 Sorel Canada
71 G9 Sorell Australia
71 G9 Sorell, Lake Australia
80 D2 Sorgun Turkey
111 E2 Soria Spain
159 F2 Soriano Uruguay
84 D3 Sorkh, Küh-e mts Iran

84	D3	Sorkheh Iran
102	K2	Sørli Norway
82	C3	Sor Mertvyy Kultuk l. Kazakh.
89	F5	Soro India
117	D5	Soroca Moldova
158	C3	Sorocaba Brazil
82	C1	Sorochinsk Rus. Fed.
83	K1	Sorokino Rus. Fed.
91	G6	Sorol i. Micronesia
91	F7	Sorong Indon.
122	D3	Soroti Uganda
102	M1	Sørøya i. Norway
111	B3	Sorraia r. Port.
102	L1	Sørreisa Norway
70	F7	Sorrento Australia
123	B6	Sorris Sorris Namibia
102	L2	Sorsele Sweden
97	C3	Sorsogon Phil.
116	D2	Sortavala Rus. Fed.
102	K1	Sortland Norway
116	I2	Sortopolovskaya Rus. Fed.
116	I3	Sorvizhi Rus. Fed.
96	D5	Sŏsan S. Korea
125	H2	Soshanguve S. Africa
117	F4	Sosna r. Rus. Fed.
159	C2	Sosneado mt. Arg.
116	J2	Sosnogorsk Rus. Fed.
83	I2	Sosnovka Rus. Fed.
116	H2	Sosnovka Arkhangel'skaya Oblast' Rus. Fed.
76	F3	Sosnovka Murmanskaya Oblast' Rus. Fed.
116	G4	Sosnovka Tambovskaya Oblast' Rus. Fed.
102	P2	Sosnovyy Bor Rus. Fed.
103	O4	Sosnovyy Bor Rus. Fed.
113	I5	Sosnowiec Poland
117	F6	Sosyka r. Rus. Fed.
157	A4	Sotara, Volcán vol. Col.
102	O2	Sotkamo Fin.
159	D1	Soto Arg.
151	E3	Soto la Marina Mex.
151	G3	Sotuta Mex.
122	B3	Souanké Congo
120	C4	Soubré Côte d'Ivoire
147	F4	Souderton U.S.A.
115	L4	Soufli Greece
110	E4	Souillac France
108	D5	Souilly France
120	C1	Souk Ahras Alg.
		Soûl S. Korea see Seoul
110	D5	Soulom France
111	H4	Sour Lebanon see Tyre
		Soûr Lebanon see Tyre
131	I3	Souris Man. Canada
133	H4	Souris P.E.I. Canada
131	I5	Souris r. Canada/U.S.A.
155	K5	Sousa Brazil
120	D1	Sousse Tunisia
110	D5	Soustons France
124	E4	South Africa, Republic of country Africa
152		South America
135	G3	Southampton Canada
105	F7	Southampton U.K.
147	G4	Southampton U.S.A.
131	L2	Southampton Island Canada
146	E6	South Anna r. U.S.A.
105	F4	South Anston U.K.
133	H2	South Aulatsivik Island Canada
68	D5	South Australia state Australia
162	L7	South Australian Basin sea feature Indian Ocean
143	F5	Southaven U.S.A.
139	F5	South Baldy mt. U.S.A.
105	I5	South Bank U.K.
146	B4	South Bass Island U.S.A.
135	F3	South Baymouth Canada
138	D5	South Bend IN U.S.A.
138	B2	South Bend WA U.S.A.
145	E7	South Bight sea chan. Bahamas
146	D6	South Boston U.S.A.
72	D5	Southbridge N.Z.
147	G3	Southbridge U.S.A.
		South Cape U.S.A. see Ka Lae
145	D5	South Carolina state U.S.A.
147	I2	South China U.S.A.
99	C1	South China Sea Pacific Ocean
142	C2	South Dakota state U.S.A.
147	G3	South Deerfield U.S.A.
105	G7	South Downs hills U.K.
122	F2	South-East Admin. dist. Botswana
71	G9	South East Cape Australia
162	J7	Southeast Indian Ridge sea feature Indian Ocean
161	L10	Southeast Pacific Basin sea feature S. Pacific Ocean
131	I3	Southend Canada
106	C5	Southend U.K.
105	H6	Southend-on-Sea U.K.
134	A5	South English U.S.A.
72	C5	Southern Alps mts N.Z.
68	B5	Southern Cross Australia
131	J3	Southern Indian Lake Canada
121	E4	Southern National Park Sudan
145	E5	Southern Pines U.S.A.
73	C1	Southern Thule i. S. Atlantic Ocean
106	D3	Southern Uplands reg. U.K.
106	E4	South Esk r. U.K.
134	B6	South Fabius r. U.S.A.
160	G7	South Fiji Basin sea feature S. Pacific Ocean
139	F4	South Fork U.S.A.
146	D5	South Fork South Branch r. U.S.A.
134	E3	South Fox Island U.S.A.
73	C5	South Geomagnetic Pole Antarctica
156	□	South Georgia terr. S. Atlantic Ocean
153	G7	South Georgia and South Sandwich Islands terr. Atlantic Ocean
106	A3	South Harris i. U.K.
89	G5	South Hatia Island Bangl.
134	D4	South Haven U.S.A.
131	J2	South Henik Lake Canada
147	G2	South Hero U.S.A.
146	D6	South Hill U.S.A.
160	E3	South Honshu Ridge sea feature N. Pacific Ocean
131	J3	South Indian Lake Canada
147	G4	Southington U.S.A.
72	C6	South Island N.Z.
97	A4	South Islet reef Phil.
87	D1	South Koel r. India
96	D5	South Korea country Asia
140	B2	South Lake Tahoe U.S.A.
123	D5	South Luangwa National Park Zambia
73	B6	South Magnetic Pole Antarctica
134	D3	South Manitou Island U.S.A.
105	H4	Southminster U.K.
131	I4	South Moose Lake Canada
146	E5	South Mountains U.S.A.
130	D2	South Nahanni r. Canada
106	□	South Nesting Bay U.K.
69	H5	South Orkney Is Atlantic Ocean
69	H5	South Pacific Ocean
147	H2	South Paris U.S.A.
138	C3	South Platte r. U.S.A.
73	B4	South Pole Antarctica
135	F2	South Porcupine Canada
71	J1	Southport Australia
104	D4	Southport U.K.
147	H3	South Portland U.S.A.
135	H1	South Porcupine Canada
106	F2	South Ronaldsay i. U.K.
125	I5	South Sand Bluff pt S. Africa
163	H9	South Sandwich Islands S. Atlantic Ocean
163	H9	South Sandwich Trench sea feature S. Atlantic Ocean
131	H4	South Saskatchewan r. Canada
131	J3	South Seal r. Canada
73	B2	South Shetland Is Antarctica
163	E10	South Shetland Trough sea feature S. Atlantic Ocean
104	F2	South Shields U.K.
134	A5	South Skunk r. U.S.A.
160	F6	South Solomon Trench sea feature Pacific Ocean
72	E3	South Taranaki Bight b. N.Z.
162	N8	South Tasman Rise sea feature Southern Ocean
141	G2	South Tent U.S.A.
89	E4	South Tons r. India
132	E3	South Twin Island Canada
105	F3	South Tyne r. U.K.
106	A3	South Uist i. U.K.
71	G9	South West Cape hd Australia
72	A7	South West Cape N.Z.
162	G7	Southwest Indian Ridge sea feature Indian Ocean
133	G4	Southwest Miramichi r. Canada
71	G9	South West National Park Australia
161	I8	Southwest Pacific Basin sea feature S. Pacific Ocean
		South-West Peru Ridge sea feature S. Pacific Ocean see Nazca Ridge
71	J3	South West Rocks Australia
134	E5	South Whitley U.S.A.
147	H3	South Windham U.S.A.
105	I5	South Wold U.K.
78	C5	South Yemen governorate Yemen
125	H1	Soutpansberg mts S. Africa
114	G5	Soverato Italy
116	B4	Sovetsk Kaliningradskaya Oblast' Rus. Fed.
116	I3	Sovetsk Kirovskaya Oblast' Rus. Fed.
90	G2	Sovetskaya Gavan' Rus. Fed.
76	H3	Sovetskiy Rus. Fed.
116	D2	Sovetskiy Leningradskaya Oblast' Rus. Fed.
116	I3	Sovetskiy Respublika Mariy El Rus. Fed.
125	G3	Soweto S. Africa
151	F4	Soyaló Mex.
94	G2	Soya-misaki c. Japan
96	D4	Soyang-ho l. S. Korea
113	O4	Sozh r. Belarus
115	L3	Sozopol Bulg.
108	D4	Spa Belgium
73	B3	Spaatz Island Antarctica
111	D2	Spain country Europe
105	G5	Spalding U.K.
105	D6	Span Head hill U.K.
135	F2	Spanish Canada
135	G2	Spanish r. Canada
141	G1	Spanish Fork U.S.A.
149	I5	Spanish Town Jamaica
140	C2	Sparks U.S.A.
146	C6	Sparta NC U.S.A.
134	B4	Sparta WI U.S.A.
145	D5	Spartanburg U.S.A.
115	J6	Sparti Greece
114	G6	Spartivento, Capo c. Italy
130	G5	Sparwood Canada
116	E4	Spas-Demensk Rus. Fed.
116	E2	Spasskaya Guba Rus. Fed.
90	F2	Spassk-Dal'niy Rus. Fed.
115	J7	Spatha, Akra pt Greece
130	B3	Spatsizi Plateau Wilderness Provincial Park Canada
142	C2	Spearfish U.S.A.
143	C4	Spearman U.S.A.
147	H3	Speculator U.S.A.
138	C6	Spencer IA U.S.A.
138	D2	Spencer ID U.S.A.
146	C5	Spencer WV U.S.A.
70	B5	Spencer, Cape hd Australia
70	B5	Spencer, Cape c. U.S.A.
70	B5	Spencer Gulf est. Australia
130	E4	Spences Bridge Canada
107	D3	Spennymoor U.K.
107	D3	Sperrin Mountains hill U.K.
109	H5	Sperryville U.S.A.
109	H5	Spessart reg. Germany
115	J6	Spetses i. Greece
106	E3	Spey r. U.K.
109	G5	Speyer Germany
85	G4	Spezand Pak.
109	F1	Spiekeroog i. Germany
112	C7	Spiez Switz.
108	E1	Spijk Neth.
108	C3	Spijkenisse Neth.
114	E1	Spilimbergo Italy
105	H4	Spilsby U.K.
85	G4	Spīn Būldak Afgh.
88	B3	Spintangi Pak.
130	F3	Spirit River Canada
134	C3	Spirit River Flowage resr U.S.A.
113	H4	Spiritwood Canada
85	G4	Spīrsang Pass Afgh.
113	J6	Spišská Nová Ves Slovakia
81	J1	Spitak Armenia
88	D2	Spiti r. India
76	C2	Spitsbergen i. Svalbard
112	F7	Spittal an der Drau Austria
114	G3	Split Croatia
131	J3	Split Lake l. Canada
131	J3	Split Lake Canada
138	C2	Spokane U.S.A.
114	E3	Spoleto Italy
98	C2	Spong Cambodia
134	B3	Spooner U.S.A.
138	F2	Spornitz Germany
138	F2	Spotted Horse U.S.A.
135	F2	Spragge Canada
130	E4	Spranger, Mount Canada
138	C2	Sprague U.S.A.
112	G5	Spree r. Germany
108	A4	Spremont Belgium
135	F3	Spring Bay Canada
124	B4	Springbok S. Africa
133	I4	Springdale Canada
143	E4	Springdale U.S.A.
109	H2	Springe Germany
139	F4	Springer U.S.A.
141	H4	Springerville U.S.A.
134	C4	Springfield CO U.S.A.
134	C6	Springfield IL U.S.A.
134	E6	Springfield KY U.S.A.
147	H3	Springfield MA U.S.A.
147	I2	Springfield ME U.S.A.
143	E2	Springfield MO U.S.A.
147	G3	Springfield OH U.S.A.
146	B4	Springfield OR U.S.A.
138	B3	Springfield SD U.S.A.
142	D3	Springfield TN U.S.A.
145	C4	Springfield VT U.S.A.
147	G3	Springfield, Lake U.S.A.
134	C6	Springfontein S. Africa
125	F5	Springfontein S. Africa
146	B5	Spring Green U.S.A.
140	C2	Spring Mountains U.S.A.
72	D5	Springs Junction N.Z.
134	A4	Spring Valley U.S.A.
141	G1	Springville UT U.S.A.
105	I5	Sprowston U.K.
130	G4	Spruce Grove Canada
146	D5	Spruce Knob-Seneca Rocks National Recreation Area U.S.A.
138	D3	Spruce Mountain U.S.A.
104	H4	Spurn Head c. U.K.
130	E5	Spuzzum Canada
130	E5	Squamish Canada
147	H3	Squam Lake U.S.A.
147	I1	Squapan Lake U.S.A.
147	I1	Square Lake U.S.A.
114	G5	Squillace, Golfo di g. Italy
115	J3	Srbija aut. rep. Yugo.
98	B3	Srê Âmbêl Cambodia
115	L3	Sredets Bulg.
77	Q4	Sredinnyy Khrebet mts Rus. Fed.
115	J3	Sredna Gora mts Bulg.
77	Q3	Srednekolymsk Rus. Fed.
		Sredne-Russkaya Vozvyshennost' reg. Rus. Fed. see Central Russian Upland
		Sredne-Sibirskoye Ploskogor'ye
102	O2	Sredneye Kuyto, Ozero l. Rus. Fed.
115	K3	Srednogorie Bulg.
98	C2	Srêpok, Tônlé r. Cambodia
90	D1	Sretensk Rus. Fed.
97	D2	Sri Aman Sarawak Malaysia
87	B5	Sriharikota Island India
87	B5	Sri Jayewardenepura Kotte Sri Lanka
87	B4	Srikakulam India
87	B3	Sri Kalahasti India
88	D3	Srikanta mt. India
162	C5	Sri Lanka country Asia
88	C2	Srinagar India
88	C2	Srinagar Jammu and Kashmir
		Sri Pada Sri Lanka see Adam's Peak
87	B4	Srirangam India
98	B1	Sri Thep Thai.
87	B4	Srivaikuntam India
87	A2	Srivardhan India
87	B4	Srivilliputtur India
83	K1	Srostki Rus. Fed.
87	C2	Srungavarapukota India
109	H1	Stade Germany
108	B4	Staden Belgium
108	B4	Stadskanaal Neth.
109	H2	Stadtallendorf Germany
109	H2	Stadthagen Germany
109	J4	Stadtilm Germany
108	E3	Stadtlohn Germany
109	H3	Stadtoldendorf Germany
109	J4	Stadtroda Germany
106	B4	Staffa i. U.K.
109	J4	Staffelberg hill Germany
109	I4	Staffelstein Germany
105	E5	Stafford U.K.
146	E5	Stafford U.S.A.
103	J4	Staicele Latvia
105	G6	Staines U.K.
117	F5	Stakhanov Ukr.
105	E7	Stalbridge U.K.
105	I5	Stalham U.K.
130	E3	Stalin, Mount Canada
		Stalingrad Rus. Fed. see Volgograd
113	K5	Stalowa Wola Poland
115	K3	Stamboliyski Bulg.
105	G5	Stamford U.K.
147	G5	Stamford CT U.S.A.
147	F3	Stamford NY U.S.A.
123	B6	Stampriet Namibia
102	N1	Stamsund Norway
142	E3	Stamford U.S.A.
108	C3	Standdaarbuiten Neth.
125	H3	Standerton S. Africa
134	E4	Standish U.S.A.
144	C4	Stanford U.S.A.
125	I4	Stanger S. Africa
145	E7	Staniard Ck Bahamas
119	J4	Stánishche Rus. Fed.
70	C5	Stanley Australia
147	J1	Stanley Canada
93	□	Stanley Hong Kong China
156	E8	Stanley Falkland Is
104	F3	Stanley U.K.
138	D2	Stanley ID U.S.A.
142	C1	Stanley ND U.S.A.
134	B3	Stanley WI U.S.A.
122	C3	Stanley, Mount Dem. Rep. Congo/Uganda
71	F8	Stanley, Mount Australia
87	B4	Stanley Reservoir India
104	F2	Stannington U.K.
90	D1	Stanovoye Nagor'ye mts Rus. Fed.
71	I2	Stanovoy Khrebet mts Rus. Fed.
71	I2	Stanthorpe Australia
105	H5	Stanton U.K.
146	B6	Stanton KY U.S.A.
134	E4	Stanton MI U.S.A.
142	C3	Stapleton U.S.A.
113	J5	Starachowice Poland
		Stara Planina mts Bulg./Yugo. see Balkan Mts
116	H4	Staraya Kulatka Rus. Fed.
117	H5	Staraya Poltavka Rus. Fed.
116	D3	Staraya Russa Rus. Fed.
116	O2	Staraya Toropa Rus. Fed.
116	I4	Staraya Tumba Rus. Fed.
115	K3	Stara Zagora Bulg.
67	I4	Starbuck Island Kiribati
112	G4	Stargard Szczeciński Poland
116	E3	Staritsa Rus. Fed.
82	D2	Star Karabutak Kazakh.
145	D6	Starke U.S.A.
143	F5	Starkville U.S.A.
112	E7	Starnberger See l. Germany
83	J2	Staroaleyskoye Rus. Fed.
117	F5	Starobil's'k Ukr.
113	P4	Starodub Rus. Fed.
113	I4	Starogard Gdański Poland
117	C5	Starokostyantyniv Ukr.
117	F5	Starominskaya Rus. Fed.
117	F6	Staroshcherbinovskaya Rus. Fed.
82	D1	Starosubkhangulovo Rus. Fed.
140	C1	Start Peak U.S.A.
105	D7	Start Point U.K.
103	N4	Staryya Darohi Belarus
77	L2	Staryy Kayak Rus. Fed.
117	F5	Staryy Oskol Rus. Fed.
109	J3	Staßfurt Germany
146	E3	State College U.S.A.
145	D5	Statesboro U.S.A.
145	D5	Statesville U.S.A.
164	W1	Station Nord Greenland
109	H2	Stauchitz Germany
125	G4	Stauffenberg Germany
146	D5	Staunton U.S.A.
103	I4	Stavanger Norway
117	G6	Stavropol' Rus. Fed.
117	G6	Stavropol'skaya Vozvyshennost' reg. Rus. Fed.
117	G6	Stavropol'skiy Kray admin. div. Rus. Fed.
70	E6	Stawell Australia
125	H4	Steadville S. Africa
140	C2	Steamboat U.S.A.
138	F3	Steamboat Springs U.S.A.
73	B2	Steele Island Antarctica
146	E4	Steelton U.S.A.
134	E3	Steenbergen Neth.
72	D5	Steens Mountains mts S. Africa
130	F3	Steen River Canada
138	C3	Steens Mountain U.S.A.
		Steenstrup Gletscher glacier Greenland see Sermersuaq
108	A4	Steenvoorde France
108	E2	Steenwijk Neth.
73	D4	Stefansson Bay Antarctica
73	D4	Stefansson Island Canada
109	G4	Steigerwald for. Germany
109	J5	Stein Germany
109	J4	Steinach Germany
131	J5	Steinbach Canada
109	G2	Steinfeld (Oldenburg) Germany
123	B6	Steinhausen Namibia
109	H3	Steinheim Germany
109	H2	Steinhuder Meer l. Germany
102	J2	Steinkjer Norway
124	B4	Steinkopf S. Africa
141	H5	Steins U.S.A.
102	J2	Steinsdalen Norway
124	F3	Stella S. Africa
145	E7	Stella Maris Bahamas
124	C6	Stellenbosch S. Africa
114	C3	Stello, Monte mt. Corsica France
108	D5	Stenay France
109	J2	Stendal Germany
93	□	Stenhouse, Mount Hong Kong China
106	E4	Stenhousemuir U.K.
103	J4	Stenungsund Sweden
		Stepanakert Azer. see Xankändi
117	H7	Step'anavan Armenia
131	J4	Stephen U.S.A.
70	D4	Stephens watercourse Australia
70	D3	Stephens, Cape U.S.A.
70	D3	Stephens Creek Australia
130	C3	Stephens Passage U.S.A.
133	I4	Stephenville Canada
143	D5	Stephenville U.S.A.
83	H1	Stepnogorsk Kazakh.
83	H4	Stepnoy Kyrg.
82	E1	Stepnoye Chelyabinskaya Oblast' Rus. Fed.
117	H5	Stepnoye Saratovskaya Oblast' Rus. Fed.
83	G1	Stepnyak Kazakh.
125	F4	Sterkfontein Dam resr S. Africa
125	H5	Sterkstroom S. Africa
82	C1	Sterlibashevo Rus. Fed.
124	D5	Sterling S. Africa
138	F3	Sterling CO U.S.A.
134	C5	Sterling IL U.S.A.
142	C2	Sterling ND U.S.A.
141	G2	Sterling UT U.S.A.
143	C6	Sterling City U.S.A.
135	F4	Sterling Heights U.S.A.
82	C1	Sterlitamak Rus. Fed.
109	J1	Sternberg Germany
130	D4	Stettler Canada
134	D2	Steuben U.S.A.
134	C4	Steubenville U.S.A.
105	G6	Stevenage U.K.
131	J4	Stevenson Lake Canada
134	C3	Stevens Point U.S.A.
128	D3	Stevens Village U.S.A.
130	B3	Stewart r. Canada
130	B2	Stewart Crossing Canada
72	A7	Stewart Island N.Z.
		Stewart Islands Solomon Is. see Sikaiana
129	J3	Stewart Lake Canada
106	D5	Stewarton U.K.
134	A4	Stewartville U.S.A.
125	F5	Steynsburg S. Africa
112	G6	Steyr Austria
124	F6	Steytlerville S. Africa
108	D1	Stiens Neth.
130	C3	Stikine r. Canada/U.S.A.
130	C3	Stikine Plateau mts Canada
124	D7	Stilbaai S. Africa
134	C1	Stillwater MN U.S.A.
140	C2	Stillwater NV U.S.A.
143	D4	Stillwater OK U.S.A.
139	C4	Stillwater Range mts U.S.A.
105	G5	Stilton U.K.
115	J3	Štip Macedonia
70	C5	Stirling Australia
106	E4	Stirling U.K.
140	B2	Stirling City U.S.A.
70	B4	Stirling North Australia
106	E4	Stjerdalshalsen Norway
112	H6	Stockerau Austria
109	J4	Stockheim Germany
103	L3	Stockholm Sweden
147	I1	Stockholm U.S.A.
105	E4	Stockport U.K.
163	G6	Stocks Seamount sea feature S. Atlantic Ocean
140	B3	Stockton CA U.S.A.
142	D4	Stockton KS U.S.A.
141	F1	Stockton UT U.S.A.
143	E4	Stockton Lake U.S.A.
143	E4	Stockton Lake U.S.A.
104	F3	Stockton-on-Tees U.K.
147	I2	Stockton Springs U.S.A.
102	L3	Stöde Sweden
98	C2	Stœng Trêng Cambodia
106	C2	Stoer, Point of U.K.
105	E5	Stoke-on-Trent U.K.
71	E8	Stokesley U.K.
102	B3	Stokkseyri Iceland
102	K2	Stokkvågen Norway
102	K1	Stokmarknes Norway
114	G3	Stolac Bos.-Herz.
108	E4	Stolberg (Rheinland) Germany
83	K2	Stolboukha Kazakh.
117	C5	Stolin Belarus
109	H2	Stolzenau Germany
105	E5	Stone U.K.
135	I2	Stonecliffe Canada
70	F5	Stone Harbor U.S.A.
106	F4	Stonehaven U.K.
130	D3	Stone Mountain Provincial Park Canada
141	H3	Stonewall Canada
147	H4	Stone Ridge U.S.A.
131	J4	Stonewall Canada
146	C5	Stonewall Jackson Lake U.S.A.
135	F4	Stoney Point Canada
147	I2	Stonington U.S.A.
140	A2	Stonyford U.S.A.
140	C3	Stony Point U.S.A.
131	H3	Stony Rapids Canada
102	L2	Storavan l. Sweden
102	L2	Storforshei Norway
102	K2	Storjord Norway
102	L2	Storlien Sweden
125	G5	Stormberg S. Africa
125	G5	Stormberg mts S. Africa
142	E3	Storm Lake U.S.A.
102	L2	Stornoway U.K.
116	J2	Storozhevsk Rus. Fed.
117	C6	Storozhynets' Ukr.
103	L2	Storseleby Sweden
102	L2	Storsjön l. Sweden
105	H5	Stornoway U.K.
121	G3	Storudal swamp Sudan
102	L3	Storvik Sweden
102	K2	Storvorde Denmark
102	K4	Storvreta Sweden
102	L3	Stotfold U.K.
134	C4	Stoughton U.S.A.
105	E7	Stour r. England U.K.
105	H6	Stour r. England U.K.
84	B2	Stûfián Iran
105	E5	Stourbridge U.K.
105	E5	Stourport-on-Severn U.K.
146	E4	Stout Lake Canada
71	J4	Stowbtsy Belarus
116	C4	Stowmarket U.K.
147	F4	Stowe U.S.A.
105	H5	Stowmarket U.K.
107	D3	Strabane U.K.
107	D4	Stradbally Rep. of Ireland
114	I5	Stradella Italy
71	F9	Strahan Australia
141	F9	Straight Cliffs U.S.A.
156	B8	Strait of Magellan sea chan. Chile
112	F6	Strakonice Czech Rep.
112	F3	Stralsund Germany
124	F3	Stella S. Africa
124	C7	Strand S. Africa
102	I3	Stranda Norway
145	E7	Strangers Cay i. Bahamas
107	F3	Strangford U.K.
107	F3	Strangford Lough l. U.K.
105	C5	Stranraer U.K.
110	H2	Strasbourg France
138	C2	Strasburg U.S.A.
71	G6	Stratford Australia
135	G4	Stratford Canada
143	C4	Stratford TX U.S.A.
134	B3	Stratford WI U.S.A.
105	F5	Stratford-upon-Avon U.K.
106	C5	Strathaven U.K.
106	D3	Strathcarron valley U.K.
130	D5	Strathcona Provincial Park Canada
106	C3	Strathconon valley U.K.
106	D3	Strathdearn valley U.K.
106	D2	Strath Fleet valley U.K.
130	E4	Strathmore Canada
106	D2	Strathnaver Canada
106	D2	Strathnaver valley U.K.
130	E4	Strath of Kildonan valley U.K.
135	G4	Strathroy Canada
106	E2	Strathspey valley U.K.
106	D2	Strathy U.K.
106	D2	Strathy Point U.K.
105	C7	Stratton U.K.
147	H2	Stratton U.S.A.
109	K6	Straubing Germany
68	D5	Straumnes pt Iceland
134	B4	Strawberry Point U.S.A.
141	G1	Strawberry Reservoir U.S.A.
70	D5	Streaky Bay b. Australia
68	D5	Streaky Bay Australia
134	C5	Streator U.S.A.
105	E6	Street U.K.
115	L2	Strehaia Romania
109	L3	Strehla Germany
77	O3	Strelka Rus. Fed.
103	N4	Strenči Latvia
109	K5	Stříbro Czech Rep.
106	F3	Strichen U.K.
115	J4	Strimonas r. Greece
159	D4	Stroeder Arg.
107	C4	Strokestown Rep. of Ireland
114	F5	Stromboli, Isola i. Italy
		Isole i Lipari Italy
106	E2	Stromness U.K.
142	D3	Stromsburg U.S.A.
103	J4	Strömstad Sweden
102	K3	Strömsund Sweden
146	C4	Strongsville U.S.A.
106	F1	Stronsay i. U.K.
70	B4	Stroud Australia
105	E6	Stroud U.K.
147	I4	Stroud Road Australia
147	F4	Stroudsburg U.S.A.
103	J4	Struer Denmark
115	I4	Struga Macedonia
116	D3	Strugi-Krasnyye Rus. Fed.
124	D7	Struis Bay S. Africa
109	J5	Strullendorf Germany
115	J4	Struma r. Bulg.
105	B5	Strumble Head U.K.
115	I4	Strumica Macedonia
125	K3	Stryama r. Bulg.
124	E4	Strydenburg S. Africa
117	B5	Stryn Ukr.
70	D2	Strzelecki Creek watercourse Australia
71	H8	Strzelecki Peak hill Australia
145	D7	Stuart FL U.S.A.
146	C6	Stuart VA U.S.A.
130	E4	Stuart Lake Canada
146	D5	Stuarts Draft U.S.A.
71	E4	Stuart Town Australia
72	C6	Studholme Junction N.Z.
102	L3	Studsviken Sweden
131	H3	Stull Lake Canada
116	F4	Stupino Rus. Fed.
73	A6	Sturge Island Antarctica
134	D2	Sturgeon r. U.S.A.
131	J4	Sturgeon Bay Canada
134	D3	Sturgeon Bay U.S.A.
134	D3	Sturgeon Bay b. U.S.A.
134	D3	Sturgeon Bay Canal sea chan. U.S.A.
135	H2	Sturgeon Falls Canada
132	B3	Sturgeon Lake Canada
144	C4	Sturgis KY U.S.A.
134	E5	Sturgis MI U.S.A.
142	C2	Sturgis SD U.S.A.
70	D2	Sturt, Mount Australia
70	B5	Sturt Bay Australia
70	D2	Sturt National Park Australia
70	D2	Sturt Stony Desert Australia
125	G6	Stutterheim S. Africa
112	D6	Stuttgart Germany
143	F5	Stuttgart U.S.A.
102	B2	Stykkishólmur Iceland
113	L5	Styr r. Ukr.
158	D2	Suaçuí Grande r. Brazil
121	G3	Suakin Sudan
93	F5	Suao Taiwan
150	B1	Suaqui Grande Mex.
157	B3	Suárez r. Col.
113	L3	Subačius Lith.
89	F3	Subansiri r. India
89	F5	Subarnarekha r. India
81	G6	Subayḩah Saudi Arabia
99	D1	Subi Besar i. Indon.
115	H1	Subotica Yugo.
113	M7	Suceava Romania
94	C4	Suchan r. Rus. Fed.
107	C4	Suck r. Rep. of Ireland
109	J7	Suckow Germany
152	C6	Sucre Bol.
157	B2	Sucuaro Col.
158	B2	Sucuriú r. Brazil
117	E6	Sudak Ukr.
121	E3	Sudan country Africa
116	G3	Suday Rus. Fed.
109	J1	Sude r. Germany
121	F3	Sudd swamp Sudan
105	H5	Sudbury U.K.
138	F2	Sundance U.S.A.
147	H3	Sudbury U.S.A.
88	D3	Sundarnagar India
162	L4	Sunda Shelf sea feature Indian Ocean
		Sunda Trench sea feature Indian Ocean see Java Trench
105	G5	Sudbury U.K.
104	F3	Sunderland U.K.
109	G3	Sünden (Sauerland) Germany
80	C2	Sündiken Dağları mts Turkey
135	H3	Sundridge Canada
103	L3	Sundsvall Sweden
76	C3	Sundsvall county Sweden
82	E5	Sundukli, Peski des. Turkm.
81	J5	Sümär Iran
99	B3	Sumatera i. Indon. see Sumatra
99	B3	Sumatra i. Indon.
112	F6	Šumava mts Czech Rep.
91	E7	Sumba i. Indon.
99	D2	Sumba, Selat sea chan. Indon.
82	C5	Sumbar r. Turkm.
99	E4	Sumbawa i. Indon.
99	D4	Sumbawa i. Indon.
123	D4	Sumbawanga Tanz.
123	B5	Sumbe Angola
106	□	Sumburgh U.K.
106	□	Sumburgh Head hd U.K.
84	D6	Sumdo China/Jammu and Kashmir
81	L3	Sume'eh Sarā Iran
91	E7	Sumenep Indon.
95	F9	Sumisu-jima i. Japan
81	I3	Summēl Iraq
132	C2	Summer Beaver Canada
133	J4	Summerford Canada
134	D3	Summer Island U.S.A.
146	C5	Summersville U.S.A.
146	C5	Summersville Lake U.S.A.
130	E4	Summit Lake Canada
140	D2	Summit Mountain U.S.A.
72	D5	Sumner N.Z.
146	D2	Sumner, Lake N.Z.
130	C3	Sumner Strait U.S.A.
95	F6	Sumoto Japan
112	H6	Šumperk Czech Rep.
82	A4	Sumqayıt Azer.
81	L1	Sumqayıt Azer.
88	B4	Sumrahu Pak.
145	D5	Sumter U.S.A.
95	E6	Sumy Ukr.
147	I2	Sumy U.S.A.
116	I3	Suna Rus. Fed.
94	G3	Sunagawa Japan
89	G4	Sunamganj Bangl.
96	C4	Sunan N. Korea
106	C4	Sunart, Loch inlet U.K.
84	D6	Şunaynah Oman
135	I3	Sunburst U.S.A.
71	F6	Sunbury Australia
146	B4	Sunbury OH U.S.A.
146	E4	Sunbury PA U.S.A.
159	E1	Sunchales Arg.
96	C4	Sunch'ŏn N. Korea
96	C6	Sunch'ŏn S. Korea
99	C3	Sun City S. Africa
147	H3	Suncook U.S.A.
99	C3	Sunda, Selat sea chan. Indon.

117 G5 Tatsinskiy Rus. Fed.
95 D7 Tatsuno Japan
88 A4 Tatta Pak.
83 H4 Tatti Kazakh.
158 C3 Tatui Brazil
130 E4 Tatuk Mountain Canada
143 C5 Tatum U.S.A.
70 F6 Tatura Australia
81 I2 Tatvan Turkey
103 I4 Tau Norway
155 J5 Taua Brazil
158 D3 Taubaté Brazil
83 F5 Tauber r. Germany
109 H5 Tauberbischofsheim Germany
109 K3 Taucha Germany
82 B3 Tauchik Kazakh.
109 H4 Taufstein hill Germany
83 H3 Taukum, Peski des. Kazakh.
124 F3 Taung S. Africa
91 B4 Taunggyi Myanmar
98 A2 Taungnyo Range mts Myanmar
105 D6 Taunton U.K.
147 H4 Taunton U.S.A.
109 F4 Taunus hill Germany
72 C3 Taupo N.Z.
72 E3 Taupo, Lake N.Z.
103 M5 Tauragé Lith.
72 F2 Tauranga N.Z.
114 G5 Taurianova Italy
72 D1 Tauroa Point N.Z.
80 D3 Taurus Mountains mts Turkey
69 F2 Tauu Islands P.N.G.
80 B3 Tavas Turkey
105 I5 Taverham U.K.
111 C4 Tavira Port.
105 C7 Tavistock U.K.
98 A2 Tavoy Myanmar
98 A2 Tavoy Point Myanmar
94 B3 Tavrichanka Rus. Fed.
80 B2 Tavşanli Turkey
105 C6 Taw r. U.K.
97 A5 Tawai, Bukit mt. Sabah Malaysia
135 F3 Tawas Bay U.S.A.
135 F3 Tawas City U.S.A.
99 E2 Tawau Sabah Malaysia
88 C2 Tawi r. India
97 A5 Tawitawi i. Phil.
93 F6 Tawu Taiwan
151 E4 Taxco Mex.
83 H5 Taxkorgan China
130 C2 Tay r. Canada
106 E4 Tay r. U.K.
106 E4 Tay, Firth of est. U.K.
106 D4 Tay, Loch l. U.K.
97 B3 Tayabas Bay Phil.
102 P1 Taybola Rus. Fed.
106 C5 Tayinloan U.K.
130 E3 Taylor Canada
141 G4 Taylor AZ U.S.A.
135 F4 Taylor MI U.S.A.
134 B6 Taylor MO U.S.A.
142 D3 Taylor NE U.S.A.
143 D8 Taylor TX U.S.A.
147 G5 Taylors Island U.S.A.
144 B4 Taylorville U.S.A.
86 A4 Taymā' Saudi Arabia
77 K3 Taymura r. Rus. Fed.
77 L2 Taymyr, Ozero l. Rus. Fed.
   Taymyr, Poluostrov pen. Rus. Fed. see Taymyr Peninsula
77 K2 Taymyr Peninsula pen. Rus. Fed.
83 G1 Tayncha Kazakh.
98 C3 Tây Ninh Vietnam
150 C2 Tayoltita Mex.
82 B4 Taypak Kazakh.
82 C2 Taysoygan, Peski des. Kazakh.
97 A4 Taytay Phil.
97 B3 Taytay Phil.
97 A4 Taytay Bay Phil.
85 F3 Tayyebād Iran
83 G1 Tayynsha Kazakh.
77 J2 Taz r. Rus. Fed.
120 B1 Taza Morocco
81 J4 Taza Khurmātū Iraq
81 K2 Tazeh Kand Azer.
146 B6 Tazewell TN U.S.A.
146 C6 Tazewell VA U.S.A.
131 H2 Tazin r. Canada
131 H3 Tazin Lake Canada
121 C2 Tāzirbū Libya
111 I4 Tazmalt Alg.
76 I3 Tazovskaya Guba sea chan. Rus. Fed.
117 H7 T'bilisi Georgia
117 H7 Tbilisskaya Rus. Fed.
122 B4 Tchibanga Gabon
121 D2 Tchigaï, Plateau du Niger
121 D4 Tcholliré Cameroon
113 I3 Tczew Poland
150 C3 Teacapán Mex.
72 A6 Te Anau N.Z.
72 A6 Te Anau, Lake N.Z.
151 F4 Teapa Mex.
72 G2 Te Araroa N.Z.
72 F2 Te Aroha N.Z.
72 E3 Te Awamutu N.Z.
104 E3 Tebay U.K.
131 J2 Tebesjuak Lake Canada
120 C1 Tébessa Alg.
114 B7 Tébessa, Monts de mts Alg.
156 E3 Tebicuary r. Para.
99 A2 Tebingtinggi Indon.
99 B3 Tebingtinggi Indon.
114 C6 Tébourba Tunisia
114 C6 Téboursouk Tunisia
117 H7 Tebulos Mt'a Georgia/Rus. Fed.
120 B4 Techiman Ghana
156 B6 Tecka Arg.
82 E3 Tecklenburger Land reg. Germany
151 E3 Tecolutla Mex.
150 D4 Tecomán Mex.
140 D4 Tecopa U.S.A.
150 B3 Tecoripa Mex.
150 D4 Técpan Mex.
113 M7 Tecuci Romania
135 F5 Tecumseh U.S.A.
82 E5 Tedzhen Turkm.
85 F2 Tedzhen r. Turkm.
141 H3 Teec Nos Pos U.S.A.
79 H1 Teeli Rus. Fed.
104 F3 Tees r. U.K.
153 E6 Teesdale reg. U.K.
154 E4 Tefé r. Brazil
80 B3 Tefenni Turkey
99 C4 Tegal Indon.
109 L2 Tegel Germany
105 D5 Tegid, Llyn l. U.K.
150 H5 Tegucigalpa Hond.
120 C3 Teguidda-n-Tessoumt Niger
140 C4 Tehachapi U.S.A.
139 C5 Tehachapi Mountains U.S.A.
140 C4 Tehachapi Pass U.S.A.
131 J2 Tehek Lake Canada
   Teheran Iran see Tehrān
120 B4 Téhini Côte d'Ivoire
84 C3 Tehrān Iran
   (City Plan 54)
88 D3 Tehri India
151 E4 Tehuacán Mex.
151 F5 Tehuantepec, Gulf of g. Mex.
151 F5 Tehuantepec, Istmo de isthmus Mex.
161 M5 Tehuantepec Ridge sea feature N. Pacific Ocean
151 E4 Tehuitzingo Mex.
105 D7 Teifi r. U.K.
105 D7 Teign r. U.K.
111 B3 Teignmouth U.K.
   alt. Tajo (Spain), conv. Tagus

140 C4 Tejon Pass U.S.A.
150 D4 Tejupan, Punta pt Mex.
72 D1 Te Kao N.Z.
72 C5 Tekapo, Lake N.Z.
89 F4 Tekari India
151 G3 Tekax Mex.
83 H1 Teke, Ozero salt l. Kazakh.
82 E2 Tekeli Aktyubinskaya Oblast' Kazakh.
83 I3 Tekeli Almatinskaya Oblast' Kazakh.
83 J4 Tekes China
83 J4 Tekes Kazakh.
83 J3 Tekes He r. China
122 D2 Tekezé Wenz r. Eritrea/Eth.
88 E1 Tekiliktag mt. China
80 A1 Tekirdağ Turkey
87 D2 Tekkali India
81 H2 Tekman Turkey
89 H2 Teknaf Bangl.
134 C4 Tekonsha U.S.A.
78 E3 Te Kuiti N.Z.
87 C2 Tel r. India
150 H5 Tela Hond.
117 H7 T'elavi Georgia
80 E5 Tel Aviv-Yafo Israel
112 G6 Telč Czech Rep.
151 G3 Telchac Puerto Mex.
130 C3 Telegraph Creek Canada
158 B4 Telémaco Borba Brazil
159 D3 Telén Arg.
99 E2 Telen r. Indon.
115 K2 Teleorman r. Romania
140 D3 Telescope Peak mt. U.S.A.
155 G5 Teles Pires r. Brazil
105 E5 Telford U.K.
109 F3 Telgte Germany
116 G3 Telica Nicaragua
120 A3 Télimélé Guinea
128 B3 Telkwa Canada
128 B3 Teller U.S.A.
87 A4 Tellicherry India
108 D4 Tellin Belgium
81 K6 Telloh Iraq
98 □ Telok Blangah Sing.
133 D4 Teloloapan Mex.
103 M5 Telšiai Lith.
109 L2 Teltow Germany
99 B2 Teluk Anson Malaysia
99 A2 Telukdalam Indon.
135 H2 Temagami Canada
135 G2 Temagami Lake Canada
99 D4 Temanggung Indon.
151 G3 Temax Mex.
125 H2 Temba S. Africa
77 K3 Tembenchi r. Rus. Fed.
99 B3 Tembilahan Indon.
125 H3 Tembisa S. Africa
122 B4 Tembo Aluma Angola
105 E5 Teme r. U.K.
140 D5 Temecula U.S.A.
80 D2 Temelli Turkey
76 D4 Temerluh Malaysia
81 L5 Temileh Iran
82 D2 Temir Kazakh.
83 G4 Temirlanovka Kazakh.
83 H2 Temirtau Kazakh.
135 H2 Temiscaming Canada
135 H2 Témiscamingue, Lac l. Canada
133 G4 Témiscouata, Lac l. Canada
71 F8 Temma Australia
102 N2 Temmes Fin.
116 C4 Temnikov Rus. Fed.
71 G5 Temora Australia
150 C1 Temósachic Mex.
141 G5 Tempe U.S.A.
109 L2 Tempelhof airport Germany
114 C4 Tempio Pausania Sardinia Italy
134 E3 Temple MI U.S.A.
143 D6 Temple TX U.S.A.
105 C5 Temple Bar U.K.
107 D5 Templemore Rep. of Ireland
97 A4 Templer Bank sea feature Phil.
115 I3 Temple Sowerby U.K.
109 L1 Templin Germany
117 F6 Temryuk Rus. Fed.
159 B3 Temuco Chile
72 C6 Temuka N.Z.
154 C4 Tena Ecuador
140 D1 Tenabo, Mount U.S.A.
99 □ Tenali India
151 E4 Tenancingo Mex.
98 A2 Tenasserim Myanmar
105 E5 Tenbury Wells U.K.
105 C6 Tenby U.K.
135 F2 Tenby Bay Canada
122 E2 Tendaho Eth.
108 H6 Tende France
79 H6 Ten Degree Channel India
94 G5 Tendō Japan
81 I2 Tendürek Dağı mt. Turkey
120 B3 Ténenkou Mali
154 C4 Ténenbuc Mali
120 D3 Ténéré reg. Niger
120 D3 Ténéré du Tafassâsset des. Niger
120 A2 Tenerife i. Canary Is
111 U4 Ténès Alg.
99 E4 Tengah, Kepulauan is Indon.
98 □ Tenge Kazakh.
98 □ Tengah Reservoir Sing.
92 D2 Tengger Shamo des. China
98 B4 Tenggul i. Malaysia
83 G2 Tengiz, Ozero salt l. Kazakh.
120 B3 Tengréla Côte d'Ivoire
93 C6 Tengxian China
92 E3 Tengzhou China
82 F1 Teniz, Ozero l. Kazakh.
123 C7 Tenke Dem. Rep. Congo
77 P2 Tenkeli Rus. Fed.
120 B3 Tenkodogo Burkina
68 D3 Tennant Creek Australia
145 C5 Tennessee r. U.S.A.
145 C5 Tennessee state U.S.A.
139 F4 Tennessee Pass U.S.A.
102 L1 Tennevoll Norway
159 B2 Teno r. Chile
102 O1 Tenojoki r. Fin./Norway
151 G4 Tenosique Mex.
138 F2 Ten Sleep U.S.A.
68 C2 Tenteno Indon.
71 H2 Tenterden U.K.
71 J2 Tenterfield Australia
158 D1 Ten Thousand Islands U.S.A.
158 E2 Teófilo Otôni Brazil
151 E4 Teotihuacán tourist site Mex.
151 E4 Teotitlán Mex.
150 E6 Tepache Mex.
72 D1 Te Paki N.Z.
151 D5 Tepalcatepec Mex.
150 D4 Tepatitlán Mex.
150 D3 Tepehuanes Mex.
81 H3 Tepe Turkey
81 J3 Tepe Gawra Iraq
150 E2 Tepehuanes Mex.
76 I2 Tepeji Mex.
115 I4 Tepelenë Albania
151 D7 Tepeme de Morelos Mex.
109 K5 Tepelská Vrchovina reg. Czech Rep.
150 D3 Tepic Mex.
112 F5 Teplá Czech Rep.
116 I4 Teplogorka Rus. Fed.
112 F5 Teplice Czech Rep.
114 F4 Teploye Rus. Fed.
98 A3 Te Pirita N.Z.
72 E2 Te Puke N.Z.
151 E3 Tequila Mex.
151 E3 Tequisquiapán Mex.
67 I3 Teraina Kiribati

88 D2 Teram Kangri mt. China/Jammu and Kashmir
114 E3 Teramo Italy
70 E7 Terang Australia
108 F2 Ter Apel Neth.
88 B3 Teratani r. Pak.
117 F4 Terbuny Rus. Fed.
81 H2 Tercan Turkey
113 L6 Terebovlya Ukr.
117 H7 Terek Rus. Fed.
117 H7 Terek r. Rus. Fed.
83 G2 Terekty Karagandinskaya Oblast' Kazakh.
83 K2 Terekty Vostochnyy Kazakhstan Kazakh.
116 I4 Teren'ga Rus. Fed.
158 A3 Terenos Brazil
82 F3 Terenozek Kazakh.
82 D2 Terensay Rus. Fed.
157 C2 Terepaima, Parque Nacional nat. park Venez.
116 H4 Tereshka r. Rus. Fed.
155 J5 Teresina Brazil
158 D3 Teresópolis Brazil
108 B5 Tergnier France
83 F2 Terisakkan r. Kazakh.
80 F1 Terme Turkey
83 F5 Termez Uzbek.
114 E6 Termini Imerese Sicily Italy
151 G4 Términos, Laguna de Mex.
114 F4 Termoli Italy
105 E5 Tern r. U.K.
91 E6 Ternate Indon.
108 B3 Terneuzen Neth.
94 E2 Terney Rus. Fed.
114 E3 Terni Italy
117 D2 Ternopil' Ukr.
70 C4 Terowie Australia
90 G2 Terpeniya, Mys c. Rus. Fed.
90 G2 Terpeniya, Zaliv g. Rus. Fed.
130 D4 Terrace Canada
134 D1 Terrace Bay Canada
124 E2 Terra Firma S. Africa
114 C5 Terralba Sardinia Italy
133 D4 Terra Nova National Park Canada
73 B6 Terre Adélie reg. Antarctica
143 F6 Terrebonne Bay U.S.A.
144 C4 Terre Haute U.S.A.
133 J4 Terrenceville Canada
138 F2 Terry U.S.A.
117 G5 Tersa r. Rus. Fed.
108 D1 Terschelling i. Neth.
83 I4 Terskey Ala-Too mts Kyrg.
114 C5 Tertenia Sardinia Italy
111 F2 Teruel Spain
102 N2 Tervola Fin.
114 G3 Tešanj Bos.-Herz.
122 D2 Teseney Eritrea
116 G4 Tesha r. Rus. Fed.
128 C2 Teshekpuk Lake U.S.A.
94 I3 Teshikaga Japan
94 G2 Teshio Japan
94 H3 Teshio-dake mt. Japan
94 G2 Teshio-gawa r. Japan
150 B2 Tesia Mex.
130 C2 Teslin Canada
130 C2 Teslin r. Canada
130 C2 Teslin Lake Canada
158 B1 Tesouras r. Brazil
158 B2 Tesouro Brazil
120 C3 Tessaoua Niger
105 F6 Test r. U.K.
114 C6 Testour Tunisia
156 B2 Tetas, Punta pt Chile
123 D5 Tete Moz.
72 F3 Te Teko N.Z.
113 O5 Teteriv r. Ukr.
109 K1 Teterow Germany
113 N6 Tetiyiv Ukr.
104 □ Tetney U.K.
138 E2 Teton r. U.S.A.
138 E3 Teton Range mts U.S.A.
70 B5 Tétouan Morocco
115 J5 Tetovo Macedonia
88 B5 Tetpur India
116 I4 Tetyushi Rus. Fed.
156 D2 Teuco r. Arg.
124 B1 Teufelsbach Namibia
109 G1 Teufels Moor reg. Germany
94 G2 Teuri-tō i. Japan
109 G2 Teutoburger Wald hills Germany
103 M3 Teuva Fin.
   Tevere r. Italy see Tiber
   Teverya Israel see Tiberias
106 F5 Teviot r. U.K.
106 F5 Teviotdale valley U.K.
72 A7 Te Waewae Bay N.Z.
125 I3 Tewane Botswana
69 F4 Tewantin Australia
72 E4 Te Wharau N.Z.
105 E6 Tewkesbury U.K.
92 B3 Têwo China
130 E5 Texada Island Canada
143 E5 Texarkana U.S.A.
71 I2 Texas Australia
143 E6 Texas state U.S.A.
143 E6 Texas City U.S.A.
151 E4 Texcoco Mex.
108 D1 Texel i. Neth.
143 C4 Texhoma U.S.A.
143 C5 Texoma, Lake U.S.A.
125 G4 Teyateyaneng Lesotho
116 G3 Teykovo Rus. Fed.
85 G3 Teyvareh Afgh.
116 G3 Teza r. Rus. Fed.
151 E4 Teziutlán Mex.
89 H4 Tezpur India
134 D5 Tezu India
131 J2 Tha-anne r. Canada
125 G4 Thabana-Ntlenyana mt. Lesotho
125 G4 Thaba Nchu S. Africa
125 H4 Thaba Putsoa mt. Lesotho
125 H4 Thaba-Tseka Lesotho
125 G2 Thabazimbi S. Africa
98 B1 Tha Bo Laos
125 G3 Thabong S. Africa
84 B5 Thādiq Saudi Arabia
98 A2 Thagyettaw Myanmar
98 B1 Thai Binh Vietnam
98 A3 Thailand country Asia
98 B3 Thailand, Gulf of Asia
91 □ Thai Muang Thai.
98 B3 Thai Nguyên Vietnam
84 B5 Thaj Saudi Arabia
98 B2 Thakhek Laos
88 B2 Thal Pak.
104 □ Thala Tunisia
98 A3 Thalang Thai.
109 J3 Thale (Harz) Germany
91 H2 Thallon Australia
85 E5 Thalo Pak.
125 F2 Thamaga Botswana
86 D7 Thamar, Jabal mt. Yemen
83 F7 Thamarit Oman
105 G5 Thame r. U.K.
72 E2 Thames N.Z.
105 H6 Thames est. U.K.
105 H6 Thames r. U.K.
134 E3 Thamesville Canada
153 F3 Thandwe Myanmar
98 A3 Thung Song Thai.
84 D2 Thangadh India
93 B6 Thăng Binh Vietnam
98 C1 Thanh Hoa Vietnam
87 C4 Thanjavur India
84 A3 Thano Bula Khan Pak.
88 B4 Thar Desert India/Pak.

70 E1 Thargomindah Australia
81 I5 Tharthār, Buḥayrat ath l. Iraq
115 K4 Thasos i. Greece
93 C6 Thật Khê Vietnam
91 B5 Thaton Myanmar
89 H4 Thaungdut Myanmar
98 A1 Thaungyin r. Myanmar/Thai.
98 C1 Tha Uthen Thai.
91 B5 Thayetmyo Myanmar
72 F2 The Aldermen Islands N.Z.
141 F5 Theba U.S.A.
149 I3 The Bahamas country Caribbean Sea
145 E7 The Bluff Bahamas
104 E2 The Cheviot hill U.K.
70 C5 The Coorong inlet Australia
138 D2 The Dalles U.S.A.
142 C3 Thedford U.S.A.
105 G5 The Fens reg. U.K.
147 I2 The Forks U.S.A.
120 A3 The Gambia country Africa
70 E6 The Grampians mts Australia
86 D4 The Gulf Asia
108 C2 The Hague Neth.
72 C6 The Hunters Hills N.Z.
98 A3 Theinkun Myanmar
72 A6 The Key N.Z.
131 H2 Thekulthili Lake Canada
131 I2 Thelon r. Canada
131 I2 Thelon Game Sanctuary Canada
109 I4 Themar Germany
124 F6 Thembalesizwe S. Africa
125 H3 Thembalihle S. Africa
106 C2 The Minch strait U.K.
105 F7 The Needles stack U.K.
111 H4 Thenia Alg.
111 H5 Theniet El Had Alg.
154 F5 Theodore Roosevelt r. Brazil
141 G5 Theodore Roosevelt Lake U.S.A.
142 C2 Theodore Roosevelt National Park U.S.A.
107 B5 The Paps hills Rep. of Ireland
107 B6 The Pocket hill Rep. of Ireland
108 A5 Thérain r. France
147 F2 Theresa U.S.A.
115 J4 Thermaïkos Kolpos g. Greece
140 B2 Thermalito U.S.A.
138 E3 Thermopolis U.S.A.
108 A4 Thérouanne France
128 F2 Thesiger Bay Canada
105 F7 The Solent strait U.K.
135 J4 Thessalon Canada
115 J4 Thessaloniki Greece
89 H5 The Storr hill U.K.
106 B3 Thet r. U.K.
105 H5 Thetford U.K.
97 A4 The Teeth mt. Phil.
105 H5 Thetford U.K.
133 F4 Thetford Mines Canada
106 C1 Theun r. Laos
98 D2 Theunissen S. Africa
105 H6 The Wash b. U.K.
105 H6 The Weald reg. U.K.
143 F6 Thibodaux U.S.A.
131 J3 Thicket Portage Canada
142 D1 Thief River Falls U.S.A.
79 F2 Thien Shan
103 L3 The Thumb Antarctica
139 L3 Thiers France
151 E4 Thiès Senegal
151 G3 Thika Kenya
87 A5 Thiladhunmathee Atoll Maldives
89 G4 Thimphu Bhutan
121 D4 Thionville France
133 H4 Thira i. Greece
152 C2 Thirasia i. Greece
157 E2 Thirsk U.K.
81 K5 Thiruvananthapuram India see Trivandrum
103 J4 Thisted Denmark
70 B5 Thistle Island Australia
113 J5 Thlewiaza r. Canada
131 J2 Thlewiaza r. Canada
131 H2 Thoa r. Canada
98 B3 Thô Chu, Đao i. Vietnam
125 I1 Thohoyandou S. Africa
108 D2 Tholen Neth.
109 G2 Tholey Germany
146 D5 Thomas U.S.A.
146 D5 Thomaston GA U.S.A.
147 I2 Thomaston ME U.S.A.
147 J2 Thomaston Corner Canada
107 D5 Thomastown Rep. of Ireland
145 D6 Thomasville U.S.A.
108 E4 Thommen Belgium
131 J3 Thompson Canada
130 E4 Thompson r. Canada
134 C2 Thompson r. U.S.A.
134 C2 Thompson MI U.S.A.
147 F4 Thompson PA U.S.A.
134 D3 Thompson r. U.S.A.
138 D2 Thompson Falls U.S.A.
98 C1 Thôn Cư Lai Vietnam
112 C7 Thonon-les-Bains France
98 D3 Thôn Son Hai Vietnam
161 K7 Tiki Basin sea feature Pacific Ocean
139 E5 Thoreau U.S.A.
71 F2 Thorlindah, L. salt flat Australia
72 F3 Tikokino N.Z.
69 G3 Tikopia i. Solomon Is
81 I4 Tikrit Iraq
104 F3 Thornaby-on-Tees U.K.
134 E4 Thornapple r. U.S.A.
77 N2 Tiksi Rus. Fed.
135 H2 Thorne Canada
104 G4 Thorne U.K.
140 C2 Thorne Bay U.S.A.
104 F4 Thornhill U.K.
105 H6 Thornton U.K.
134 B3 Thorp U.S.A.
73 D3 Thorshavnheiane mts Antarctica
125 H4 Thota-ea-Moli Lesotho
110 D3 Thouars France
147 G2 Thousand Islands Canada
141 G2 Thousand Lake Mountain U.S.A.
140 C4 Thousand Oaks U.S.A.
115 K4 Thrakiko Pelagos sea Greece
138 D1 Three Forks U.S.A.
130 G4 Three Hills Canada
71 F8 Three Hummock I. Australia
72 D1 Three Kings Islands N.Z.
134 D5 Three Lakes U.S.A.
134 D5 Three Oaks U.S.A.
98 A2 Three Pagodas Pass Myanmar/Thai.
120 B4 Three Points, Cape Ghana
134 D5 Three Rivers MI U.S.A.
143 D6 Three Rivers TX U.S.A.
138 B2 Three Sisters mt. U.S.A.
   Thrissur India see Trichur
143 D5 Throckmorton U.S.A.
68 B5 Throssell, Lake salt flat Australia
104 E3 Thornbury U.K.

73 A3 Thurston Island Antarctica
109 H2 Thüster Berg hill Germany
104 E3 Thwaite U.K.
73 A3 Thwaites Glacier Tongue Antarctica
103 J4 Thyborøn Denmark
92 A1 Tiancang China
92 A3 Tianchang China
93 C6 Tiandeng China
93 C5 Tiandong China
93 C5 Tian'e China
155 J4 Tianguá Brazil
92 E2 Tianjin China
92 E2 Tianjin mun. China
90 B3 Tianjun China
93 C5 Tianlin China
93 C5 Tianmen China
93 F4 Tianmu Shan mts China
96 E2 Tianqiaoling China
93 B4 Tianquan China
92 C3 Tianshifu China
92 B3 Tianshui China
88 D2 Tianshuihai China/Jammu and Kashmir
93 F4 Tiantai China
92 E1 Tiantaiyong China
93 C6 Tianyang China
92 C1 Tianzhu Gansu China
93 C5 Tianzhu Guizhou China
120 C1 Tiaret Alg.
120 B4 Tiassalé Côte d'Ivoire
158 B4 Tibagi r. Brazil
81 I5 Tibal, Wādī watercourse Iraq
121 D4 Tibati Cameroon
114 E3 Tibel r. Italy
80 E5 Tiberias Israel
   Tiberias, Lake Israel see Galilee, Sea of
138 C3 Tiber Reservoir U.S.A.
121 D2 Tibesti mts Chad
   Tibet aut. reg. China see Xizang Zizhiqu
79 G3 Tibet, Plateau of China
70 E2 Tibooburra Australia
89 E3 Tibrikot Nepal
103 K4 Tibro Sweden
150 A1 Tiburón, Isla i. Mex.
87 B3 Ticao i. Phil.
105 H6 Ticehurst U.K.
135 I3 Tichborne Canada
120 B3 Tichît Mauritania
120 A2 Tichla W. Sahara
112 D7 Ticino r. Switz.
147 G3 Ticonderoga U.S.A.
151 G3 Ticul Mex.
103 K4 Tidaholm Sweden
89 H5 Tiddim Myanmar
120 C2 Tidikelt, Plaine du plain Alg.
120 A3 Tidjikja Mauritania
83 K3 Tiechanggou China
96 B2 Tiefa China
104 D3 Tiel Neth.
96 A1 Tieli China
96 B2 Tieling China
88 D2 Tielongtan China/Jammu and Kashmir
108 B4 Tielt Belgium
108 C4 Tienen Belgium
79 F2 Tien Shan mts China/Kyrg.
   Tientsin China see Tianjin
103 L3 Tierp Sweden
139 F4 Tierra Amarilla U.S.A.
151 E4 Tierra Blanca Mex.
151 E4 Tierra Colorada Mex.
156 C8 Tierra del Fuego, Isla Grande de i. Arg./Chile
111 D2 Tiétar r. Spain
111 D2 Tiétar, Valle de valley Spain
158 C3 Tietê Brazil
158 B3 Tietê r. Brazil
146 C4 Tiffin U.S.A.
145 D6 Tifton U.S.A.
82 B3 Tigen Kazakh.
115 M2 Tighecului, Dealurile hills Moldova
117 D6 Tighina Moldova
83 J2 Tigiretskiy Khrebet mts Kazakh./Rus. Fed.
89 F5 Tigiria India
121 D4 Tignère Cameroon
133 H4 Tignish Canada
152 C2 Tigre r. Ecuador/Peru
157 E2 Tigre r. Venez.
81 K5 Tigris r. Turkey
   alt. Dicle (Turkey), alt. Dijlah, Nahr (Iraq/Syria)
80 D7 Tih, Jabal at plat. Egypt
86 B4 Tihāmah reg. Saudi Arabia
148 A2 Tijuana Mex.
158 B2 Tijuco r. Brazil
151 G4 Tikal tourist site Guat.
88 D4 Tikamgarh India
117 G6 Tikhoretsk Rus. Fed.
116 E3 Tikhvin Rus. Fed.
116 E3 Tikhvinskaya Gryada ridge Rus. Fed.
89 F3 Tila r. Nepal
84 D2 Tilavar Iran
70 E1 Tilbooroo Australia
108 D3 Tilburg Neth.
70 D2 Tilcha Australia
89 H5 Tilin Myanmar
120 C3 Tillabéri Niger
138 B2 Tillamook U.S.A.
106 E4 Tillicoultry U.K.
131 G4 Tillsonburg Canada
115 L6 Tilos i. Greece
70 D3 Tilpa Australia
117 F5 Tim Rus. Fed.
131 J1 Timanskiy Kryazh ridge Rus. Fed.
81 J2 Timar Turkey
72 C6 Timaru N.Z.
117 F6 Timashevsk Rus. Fed.
68 D3 Timber Creek Australia
143 D6 Timber Mountain U.S.A.
146 D5 Timberville U.S.A.
70 E7 Timboon Australia
120 B3 Timbuktu Mali
120 B2 Timimoun Alg.
83 F1 Timiryazev Kazakh.
83 F1 Timiryazevo Kazakh.
115 J2 Timișoara Romania
134 E1 Timmins Canada
116 F3 Timokhino Rus. Fed.
155 J5 Timon Brazil
91 F7 Timor i. Indon.
68 C1 Timor Sea Australia/Indon.
159 D2 Timote Arg.
103 L3 Timrå Sweden
135 I3 Tims Ford Lake U.S.A.

89 F3 Tingri China
103 K4 Tingsryd Sweden
159 B2 Tinguiririca, Volcán vol. Chile
103 J3 Tingvoll Norway
106 E1 Tingwall U.K.
158 E1 Tinharé, Ilha de i. Brazil
98 C1 Tinh Gia Vietnam
91 G5 Tinian i. N. Mariana Is
156 C3 Tinogasta Arg.
115 K6 Tinos Greece
108 B5 Tinqueux France
105 C7 Tintagel U.K.
70 D5 Tintinara Australia
106 E5 Tinto hill U.K.
146 E4 Tioga r. U.S.A.
99 B2 Tioman i. Malaysia
135 F1 Tionaga Canada
146 D4 Tionesta Lake U.S.A.
134 E5 Tippecanoe r. U.S.A.
134 C5 Tippecanoe Lake U.S.A.
107 C5 Tipperary Rep. of Ireland
89 F4 Tiptala Bhanjyang pass Nepal
141 E4 Tipton IA U.S.A.
134 E1 Tipton IN U.S.A.
151 K6 Tipton, Mount U.S.A.
131 I4 Tip Top Hill Canada
105 H6 Tiptree U.K.
157 C4 Tiquié r. Brazil
151 G5 Tiquisate Guat.
155 I4 Tiracambu, Serra do hills Brazil
115 H4 Tirana Albania
   Tiranë Albania see Tirana
117 D6 Tiraspol Moldova
124 C3 Tiraz Mountains Namibia
80 A2 Tire Turkey
106 B4 Tiree i. U.K.
88 B1 Tirich Mir mt. Pak.
87 B2 Tirna r. India
87 A3 Tirthahalli India
87 B4 Tiruchchendur India
87 B4 Tiruchchirappalli India
87 B4 Tiruchengodu India
87 B4 Tirunelveli India
87 B3 Tirupati India
87 B3 Tiruppattur India
87 B3 Tiruppur India
87 B4 Tirutturaippundi India
87 B3 Tiruvannamalai India
87 B4 Tisaiyanvilai India
131 I4 Tisdale Canada
87 C5 Tissamaharama Sri Lanka
111 G5 Tissemsilt Alg.
89 G4 Tista r. India
73 B4 Titan Dome ice feature Antarctica
77 N2 Tit-Ary Rus. Fed.
154 E7 Titicaca, Lake Bol./Peru
87 C1 Titlagarh India
114 C3 Titov Drvar Bos.-Herz.
115 K2 Titu Romania
145 D6 Titusville FL U.S.A.
146 D4 Titusville PA U.S.A.
130 D7 Tiverton Canada
105 D7 Tiverton U.K.
114 E3 Tivoli Italy
151 G3 Tixkokob Mex.
151 E4 Tixtla Mex.
150 D3 Tizapán el Alto Mex.
111 H4 Tizi El Arba hill Alg.
111 H5 Tizi Ouzou Alg.
120 B2 Tiznados r. Venez.
83 I5 Tiznap He r. China
120 B2 Tiznit Morocco
150 D2 Tizoc Mex.
125 I2 Tjaneni Swaziland
102 L2 Tjappsåive Sweden
103 I4 Tjeukemeer l. Neth.
103 I4 Tjorhom Norway
151 E4 Tlacolula Mex.
151 E4 Tlacotalpán Mex.
151 E4 Tlalnepantla Mex.
151 E4 Tlapa Mex.
150 D3 Tlaquepaque Mex.
151 E4 Tlaxcala Mex.
151 E4 Tlaxcala state Mex.
151 E4 Tlaxiaco Mex.
120 B1 Tlemcen Alg.
124 F4 Tlhakalatlou S. Africa
125 H4 Tlholong S. Africa
125 F2 Tlokweng Botswana
98 C3 Tnaôt, Prêk l. Cambodia
130 C4 Toad River Canada
123 E5 Toamasina Madag.
74 □ Toa Payoh Sing.
159 D3 Toay Arg.
95 E6 Toba Japan
99 A5 Toba, Danau l. Indon.
88 A3 Toba and Kakar Ranges mts Pak.
154 F1 Tobago i. Trin. and Tob.
91 E6 Tobelo Indon.
135 F2 Tobermory Canada
106 B4 Tobermory U.K.
140 D1 Tobin, Mount U.S.A.
131 I4 Tobin Lake Canada
147 J1 Tobique r. Canada
94 F5 Tobi-shima i. Japan
99 C2 Toboali Indon.
83 F1 Toboli Kazakh.
76 H4 Tobol r. Kazakh./Rus. Fed.
98 B2 To Bong Vietnam
155 I4 Tocantinópolis Brazil
155 I4 Tocantins r. Brazil
158 C1 Tocantinzinha r. Brazil
145 D5 Toccoa U.S.A.
103 J4 Töcksfors Sweden
159 B2 Tocopilla Chile
71 F5 Tocumwal Australia
154 C2 Tocuyo r. Venez.
114 D3 Todi Italy
112 D7 Todi mt. Switz.
103 J4 Todohokke Japan
94 H5 Todoga-saki pt Japan
151 K2 Todos Santos Bol.
150 B3 Todos Santos Mex.
150 D4 Todos Santos, Bahía de b. Mex.
130 G4 Tofield Canada
130 E5 Tofino Canada
106 □ Toft U.K.
134 D2 Tofte U.S.A.
69 I3 Tofua i. Tonga
120 C4 Togo country Africa
134 C2 Togo U.S.A.
92 D1 Togtoh China
92 D1 Toguz Kazakh.
141 H4 Tohatchi U.S.A.
102 N3 Toholampi Fin.
92 D3 Tohom China
95 E7 Tōi Japan
94 H5 Toi-misaki pt Japan
95 M3 Tōin Japan
140 D2 Toiyabe Range mts U.S.A.
151 K2 Tojikobod Tajik.
82 E4 Tok r. Rus. Fed.
128 D3 Tok U.S.A.
95 J5 Tokamachi Japan
94 N3 Tokanui N.Z.
94 H5 Tokar Sudan
90 E4 Tokara-rettō is Japan
83 H2 Tokarevka Kazakh.

80 F1 **Tokat** Turkey
96 D5 **Tŏkchŏk-to** i. S. Korea
69 I2 **Tokelau** terr. Pacific Ocean
117 E6 **Tokmak** Ukr.
83 H4 **Tokmok** Kyrg.
72 G3 **Tokomaru Bay** N.Z.
72 E3 **Tokoroa** N.Z.
125 H3 **Tokoza** S. Africa
76 J5 **Toksun** China
83 H4 **Toktogul** Kyrg.
83 H4 **Toktogul Suu Saktagychy** resr Kyrg.
83 J3 **Tokty** Kazakh.
95 D7 **Tokushima** Japan
95 B7 **Tokuyama** Japan
95 F7 **Tōkyō** Japan (City Plan **52**)
95 F7 **Tōkyō-wan** b. Japan
85 G3 **Tokzār** Afgh.
72 G3 **Tolaga Bay** N.Z.
123 E6 **Tôlañaro** Madag.
82 C1 **Tolbazy** Rus. Fed.
150 I6 **Tola** Panama
151 E3 **Toleant** tourist site Mex.
158 B4 **Toledo** Brazil
111 D3 **Toledo** Spain
134 A5 **Toledo** IA U.S.A.
146 B4 **Toledo** OH U.S.A.
111 D3 **Toledo, Montes de** mts Spain
143 E6 **Toledo Bend Reservoir** U.S.A.
159 B3 **Tolhuaca, Parque Nacional** nat. park Chile
83 J3 **Toli** China
123 E6 **Toliara** Madag.
157 B3 **Tolima, Nevado del** vol. Col.
91 E6 **Tolitoli** Indon.
76 J3 **Tol'ka** Rus. Fed.
109 L1 **Tollensesee** l. Germany
116 D3 **Tolmachevo** Rus. Fed.
114 E1 **Tolmezzo** Italy
93 □ **Tolo Channel** Hong Kong China
93 □ **Tolo Harbour** b. Hong Kong China
111 E1 **Tolosa** Spain
96 D6 **Tolsan-do** i. S. Korea
135 F3 **Tolsmaville** Canada
106 B2 **Tolsta Head** hd U.K.
157 B2 **Tolú** Col.
151 E4 **Toluca** Mex.
102 O2 **Tolvand, Ozero** l. Rus. Fed.
116 I4 **Tol'yatti** Rus. Fed.
82 E2 **Tolybay** Kazakh.
134 B4 **Tomah** U.S.A.
134 A3 **Tomahawk** U.S.A.
94 G3 **Tomakomai** Japan
69 H3 **Tomanivi** mt. Fiji
157 E5 **Tomar** Brazil
111 B3 **Tomar** Port.
80 F1 **Tomarza** Turkey
159 F1 **Tomás Gomensoro** Uruguay
113 K5 **Tomaszów Lubelski** Poland
113 J5 **Tomaszów Mazowiecki** Poland
106 E3 **Tomatin** U.K.
150 C4 **Tomatlán** Mex.
145 B6 **Tombigbee** r. U.S.A.
122 B4 **Tomboco** Angola
158 D3 **Tombos** Brazil
Tombouctou Mali see Timbuktu
141 G6 **Tombstone** U.S.A.
123 B5 **Tombua** Angola
125 H1 **Tom Burke** S. Africa
159 B3 **Tomé** Chile
125 K1 **Tome** Moz.
103 K5 **Tomelilla** Sweden
111 E3 **Tomelloso** Spain
83 F4 **Tomenaryk** Kazakh.
135 H2 **Tomiko** Canada
71 H4 **Tomingley** Australia
91 E7 **Tomini, Teluk** g. Indon.
120 B3 **Tominian** Mali
106 E3 **Tomintoul** U.K.
114 G3 **Tomislavgrad** Bos.-Herz.
102 K2 **Temmerneset** Norway
77 N4 **Tommot** Rus. Fed.
157 D3 **Tomo** Col.
157 C3 **Tomo** r. Col.
92 D1 **Tomortei** China
77 O3 **Tompo** Rus. Fed.
68 B4 **Tom Price** Australia
90 A1 **Tomsk** Rus. Fed.
103 K4 **Tomtabacken** hill Sweden
77 P3 **Tomtor** Rus. Fed.
94 H3 **Tomuraushi-yama** mt. Japan
117 G6 **Tomuzlovka** r. Rus. Fed.
151 F4 **Tonalá** Mex.
141 G3 **Tonalea** U.S.A.
154 E4 **Tonantins** Brazil
138 C1 **Tonasket** U.S.A.
105 H6 **Tonbridge** U.K.
91 E6 **Tondano** Indon.
103 J5 **Tønder** Denmark
105 E6 **Tone** r. U.K.
69 I4 **Tonga** country Pacific Ocean
125 I4 **Tongaat** S. Africa
70 F6 **Tongala** Australia
93 F5 **Tong'an** China
72 E3 **Tongariro National Park** N.Z.
69 I4 **Tongatapu Group** is Tonga
160 H7 **Tonga Trench** sea feature S. Pacific Ocean
92 D3 **Tongbai** China
92 D3 **Tongbai Shan** mts China
92 E4 **Tongcheng** Anhui China
93 D4 **Tongcheng** Hubei China
96 D4 **T'ongch'ŏn** N. Korea
92 C3 **Tongchuan** China
93 C5 **Tongdao** China
92 A3 **Tongde** China
96 D5 **Tongduch'ŏn** S. Korea
108 D4 **Tongeren** Belgium
93 H4 **Tonggu** China
93 D7 **Tonggu Zui** pt China
96 C5 **Tonghae** S. Korea
93 B5 **Tonghai** China
94 A2 **Tonghe** China
96 D3 **Tonghua** Jilin China
96 D3 **Tonghua** Jilin China
96 E2 **Tongjiang** China
96 B3 **Tongjiangkou** China
96 D4 **Tongjosŏn-man** b. N. Korea
93 C6 **Tongking, Gulf of** China/Vietnam
93 C4 **Tongliang** China
92 D2 **Tongliao** China
92 F4 **Tongling** China
92 F4 **Tonglu** China
96 C6 **Tongnae** S. Korea
93 B4 **Tongnan** China
70 D3 **Tongo** Australia
70 D3 **Tongo Lake** salt flat Australia
97 B5 **Tongquil** i. Phil.
93 D5 **Tongren** Guizhou China
92 A3 **Tongren** Qinghai China
92 E4 **Tongshan** Jiangsu China
93 D4 **Tongshan** Jiangsu China
93 C7 **Tongshi** China
92 D3 **Tongtian He** r. China see Yangtze
106 D2 **Tongue** U.K.
138 F2 **Tongue** r. U.S.A.
145 C7 **Tongue of the Ocean** sea chan. Bahamas
92 A3 **Tongwei** China
92 B2 **Tongwei** China
92 E3 **Tongxin** China
96 E6 **T'ongyŏng** S. Korea
96 B3 **Tongyu** China
96 C5 **Tongyu** China
92 E2 **Tongyuanpu** China
93 D4 **Tongzhou** Beijing China
92 F3 **Tongzhou** Jiangsu China
93 C4 **Tongzi** China
143 C5 **Tonica** U.S.A.

150 B1 **Tónichi** Mex.
88 C4 **Tonk** India
84 C2 **Tonkābon** Iran
92 B5 **Tonkin** reg. Vietnam
116 H3 **Tonkino** Rus. Fed.
98 C2 **Tônlé Repou** r. Laos
98 B2 **Tônlé Sab** l. Cambodia
94 G5 **Tōno** Japan
140 D2 **Tonopah** U.S.A.
157 E2 **Tonoro** r. Venez.
150 I7 **Tonosí** Panama
88 D3 **Tons** r. India
103 I4 **Tønsberg** Norway
103 I4 **Tonstad** Norway
141 G5 **Tonto National Monument** res. U.S.A.
89 H5 **Tonzang** Myanmar
71 H2 **Toobeah** Australia
138 D3 **Tooele** U.S.A.
71 J1 **Toogoolawah** Australia
70 E5 **Tooleybuc** Australia
70a A4 **Tooligie** Australia
71 H6 **Tooma** r. Australia
71 H3 **Toora** Australia
124 F6 **Toorberg** mt. S. Africa
71 H3 **Tooraweenah** Australia
71 I1 **Toowoomba** Australia
141 E1 **Topawa** U.S.A.
140 C2 **Topaz** U.S.A.
83 J1 **Topchikha** Rus. Fed.
142 E4 **Topeka** U.S.A.
150 D2 **Topia** Mex.
130 C3 **Topley Landing** Canada
109 K2 **Töplitz** Germany
159 B2 **Topocalma, Punta** pt Chile
141 E4 **Topock** U.S.A.
112 I6 **Topol'čany** Slovakia
82 B3 **Topoli** Kazakh.
150 C2 **Topolobampo** Mex.
115 L3 **Topolovgrad** Bulg.
102 P2 **Topozero, Ozero** l. Rus. Fed.
147 J2 **Topsfield** U.S.A.
141 F3 **Toquerville** U.S.A.
122 D3 **Tor** Eth.
115 L5 **Torbalı** Turkey
85 E3 **Torbat-e Heydariyeh** Iran
85 E3 **Torbat-e Jām** Iran
116 I4 **Torbeyevo** Rus. Fed.
134 E3 **Torch Lake** U.S.A.
111 D2 **Tordesillas** Spain
102 M2 **Töre** Sweden
111 H1 **Torelló** Spain
108 D2 **Torenberg** hill Neth.
109 K3 **Torgau** Germany
117 H5 **Torgun** r. Rus. Fed.
108 B3 **Torhout** Belgium
Torino Italy see Turin
95 G9 **Tori-shima** i. Japan
121 F4 **Torit** Sudan
158 B2 **Torixoreu** Brazil
81 K3 **Torkamān** Iran
116 G3 **Tor'kovskoye Vodokhranilishche** resr Rus. Fed.
111 D2 **Tormes** r. Spain
102 M2 **Tornio** Fin./Sweden
71 G7 **Toralgon** Australia
89 G4 **Trashigang** Bhutan
114 E3 **Trasimeno, Lago** l. Italy
98 B2 **Trat** Thai.
112 F7 **Traunsee** l. Austria
112 F7 **Traunstein** Germany
70 E4 **Travellers Lake** Australia
72 C5 **Travers, Mount** N.Z.
73 C1 **Traversay Islands** S. Atlantic Ocean
134 E3 **Traverse City** U.S.A.
98 C3 **Tra Vinh** Vietnam
143 D6 **Travis, Lake** U.S.A.
114 G2 **Travnik** Bos.-Herz.
114 F1 **Trbovlje** Slovenia
69 F2 **Treasury Islands** Solomon Is
109 L2 **Trebbin** Germany
112 G6 **Třebíč** Czech Rep.
115 H3 **Trebinje** Bos.-Herz.
112 I6 **Trebišov** Slovakia
114 F2 **Trebnje** Slovenia
109 G5 **Trebur** Germany
109 J5 **Treffurt** Germany
134 B3 **Trego** U.S.A.
159 F2 **Treinta y Tres** Uruguay
156 C6 **Trelew** Arg.
103 K5 **Trelleborg** Sweden
110 F1 **Trélon** France
105 C5 **Tremadog Bay** U.K.
132 □4 **Tremblant, Mont** hill Canada
114 F3 **Tremiti, Isole** is Italy
138 D3 **Tremonton** U.S.A.
111 J1 **Tremp** Spain
134 B3 **Trempealeau** r. U.S.A.
105 B7 **Trenance** U.K.
112 F6 **Trenčín** Slovakia
159 D3 **Trenque Lauquén** Arg.
104 G2 **Trent** r. U.K.
114 D1 **Trento** Italy
135 I3 **Trenton** Canada
142 E3 **Trenton** MO U.S.A.
147 F4 **Trenton** NJ U.S.A.
105 D5 **Treorchy** U.K.
133 J4 **Trepassey** Canada
159 E3 **Tres Arboles** Uruguay
159 E3 **Tres Arroyos** Arg.
105 A8 **Tresco** i. U.K.
158 B4 **Três Corações** Brazil
157 B7 **Três Esquinas** Col.
158 B2 **Três Lagoas** Brazil
156 B7 **Tres Lagos** Arg.
159 B4 **Tres Lomas** Arg.
158 D2 **Três Marias, Represa** resr Brazil
159 B4 **Três Picos** mt. Arg.
159 F5 **Três Picos, Cerro** mt. Arg.
139 F4 **Tres Piedras** U.S.A.
158 D3 **Três Pontas** Brazil
156 C7 **Três Puntas, Cabo** pt Arg.
158 D3 **Três Rios** Brazil
151 F4 **Tres Valles** Mex.
150 **Tres Vírgenes, Volcán Las** vol. Mex.
151 F4 **Tres Zapotes** tourist site Mex.
103 I5 **Tretten** Norway
109 I6 **Treuchtlingen** Germany
109 K2 **Treuenbrietzen** Germany
103 J4 **Treungen** Norway
114 E2 **Treviglio** Italy
114 E2 **Treviso** Italy
105 B7 **Trevose Head** U.K.
71 □7 **Triabunna** Australia
115 L6 **Tria Nisia** i. Greece
115 M6 **Trianta** Greece
88 B3 **Tribal Areas** admin. div. Pak.
114 F5 **Tricase** Italy
88 C4 **Trichur** India
110 F1 **Tricot** France
71 F4 **Trida** Australia
109 I5 **Trier** Germany
114 E2 **Trieste** Italy
114 E2 **Triglav** mt. Slovenia
115 I5 **Trikala** Greece
80 D4 **Trikomon** Cyprus
91 F7 **Trikora, Puncak** mt. Indon.
107 D7 **Trim** Rep. of Ireland
87 C4 **Trincomalee** Sri Lanka
158 C2 **Trindade** Brazil
163 I7 **Trindade, Ilha da** i. S. Atlantic Ocean
154 F6 **Trinidad** Bol.
157 C3 **Trinidad** Col.

149 I4 **Trinidad** Cuba
154 F1 **Trinidad** i. Trin. and Tob.
159 F2 **Trinidad** Uruguay
139 F4 **Trinidad** U.S.A.
157 E2 **Trinidad and Tobago** country Caribbean Sea
133 J4 **Trinity Bay** Canada
145 **Trinity Islands** U.S.A.
140 C1 **Trinity Range** mts U.S.A.
145 C5 **Trion** U.S.A.
109 J1 **Tripkau** Germany
115 J6 **Tripoli** Greece
80 E4 **Tripoli** Lebanon
121 D1 **Tripoli** Libya
121 D1 **Tripolitania** reg. Libya
89 G5 **Tripura** state India
163 I8 **Tristan da Cunha** i. S. Atlantic Ocean
88 D3 **Trisul** mt. India
89 F4 **Trisul Dam** Nepal
109 I1 **Trittau** Germany
109 G5 **Trittenheim** Germany
87 B4 **Trivandrum** India
114 E4 **Trivento** Italy
112 H6 **Trnava** Slovakia
69 **Trobriand Islands** P.N.G.
102 K2 **Trofors** Norway
114 G3 **Trogir** Croatia
114 F4 **Troia** Italy
109 G4 **Troisdorf** Germany
108 D4 **Trois-Ponts** Belgium
133 F4 **Trois-Rivières** Canada
82 E1 **Troitsk** Rus. Fed.
83 K1 **Troitskoye** Altayskiy Kray Rus. Fed.
82 C1 **Troitskoye** Orenburgskaya Oblast' Rus. Fed.
82 D1 **Troitskoye** Respublika Bashkortostan Rus. Fed.
117 H6 **Troitskoye** Respublika Kalmykiya - Khalm'g-Tangch Rus. Fed.
103 K4 **Trollhättan** Sweden
155 G5 **Trombetas** r. Brazil
119 I6 **Tromelin, Île** i. Indian Ocean
159 B3 **Tromen, Volcán** vol. Arg.
125 F5 **Trompsburg** S. Africa
102 L1 **Tromsø** Norway
140 D4 **Trona** U.S.A.
102 J3 **Trondheim** Norway
102 J3 **Trondheimsfjorden** sea chan. Norway
89 G4 **Trongsa Chhu** r. Bhutan
80 G4 **Troödos** Cyprus
80 G4 **Troödos, Mount** Cyprus
115 I5 **Troon** U.K.
158 D1 **Tropeiros, Serra dos** hills Brazil
141 F3 **Tropic** U.S.A.
107 E2 **Trostan** hill U.K.
106 F3 **Trout Head** hd U.K.
130 E3 **Trout** r. Canada
130 D3 **Trout Creek** Canada
135 H3 **Trout Creek** U.S.A.
130 D3 **Trout Lake** l. Alta Canada
130 E3 **Trout Lake** l. N.W.T. Canada
132 B3 **Trout Lake** l. Ont. Canada
130 C2 **Trout Lake** Canada
134 C2 **Trout Lake** U.S.A.
138 E2 **Trout Peak** mt. U.S.A.
146 E6 **Trout Run** U.S.A.
105 F6 **Trowbridge** U.K.
71 □ **Trowutta** Australia
145 G6 **Troy** AL U.S.A.
138 D2 **Troy** MT U.S.A.
147 H3 **Troy** NH U.S.A.
147 G3 **Troy** NY U.S.A.
146 A4 **Troy** OH U.S.A.
146 E4 **Troy** PA U.S.A.
115 K3 **Troyan** Bulg.
110 G2 **Troyes** France
140 D4 **Troy Lake** U.S.A.
115 I3 **Trstenik** Yugo.
117 C1 **Trubchevsk** Rus. Fed.
111 C1 **Truchas** Spain
116 E3 **Trud** Rus. Fed.
116 F3 **Trudovoye** Rus. Fed.
150 H5 **Trujillo** Hond.
154 C5 **Trujillo** Peru
111 D3 **Trujillo** Spain
157 C2 **Trujillo** Venez.
108 F5 **Trulben** Germany
147 G2 **Trumbull** U.S.A.
141 F3 **Trumbull, Mount** U.S.A.
99 A2 **Trumon** Indon.
71 G4 **Trundle** Australia
98 C2 **Trung Hiệp** Vietnam
133 H4 **Truro** Canada
105 B7 **Truro** U.K.
107 C4 **Truskmore** hill Rep. of Ireland
130 D3 **Trutch** Canada
139 F5 **Truth or Consequences** U.S.A.
112 G5 **Trutnov** Czech Rep.
115 K7 **Trypiti, Akra** pt Greece
103 K3 **Trysil** Norway
112 G3 **Trzebiatów** Poland
104 G2 **Trzcianka** Poland
90 A2 **Tsagaannuur** Mongolia
117 H6 **Tsagan Aman** Rus. Fed.
117 H6 **Tsagan-Nur** Rus. Fed.
81 J1 **Ts'ageri** Georgia
123 **Tsaratanana, Massif du** mts Madag.
115 L3 **Tsarevo** Bulg.
124 B4 **Tsaris** Namibia
117 H5 **Tsatsa** Rus. Fed.
124 A3 **Tsaukaib** Namibia
122 D4 **Tsavo East National Park** Kenya
123 B6 **Tses** Namibia
123 C5 **Tsetseng** Botswana
90 C2 **Tsetserleg** Mongolia
123 C6 **Tshabong** Botswana
123 C6 **Tshane** Botswana
117 F6 **Tshekskoye Vodokhranilishche** resr Rus. Fed.
123 C5 **Tshela** Dem. Rep. Congo
122 C4 **Tshibala** Dem. Rep. Congo
122 C4 **Tshikapa** Dem. Rep. Congo
122 C4 **Tshikapa** r. Dem. Rep. Congo
122 C4 **Tshofa** Dem. Rep. Congo
122 C3 **Tshuapa** r. Dem. Rep. Congo
125 I3 **Tshipise** S. Africa
125 G4 **Tshokwane** S. Africa
122 I2 **Tshwane** S. Africa
117 G6 **Tsimlyansk** Rus. Fed.
97 A5 **Tsimlyanskoye Vodokhranilishche** resr Rus. Fed.
124 E3 **Tsineng** S. Africa
93 □ **Tsing Shui Wan** b. Hong Kong China
Tsingtao China see Qingdao
93 □ **Tsing Yi** i. Hong Kong China
123 E6 **Tsiombe** Madag.
123 **Tsiroanomandidy** Madag.
124 E6 **Tsitsikamma Forest and Coastal National Park** S. Africa
116 H4 **Tsivil'sk** Rus. Fed.
81 J1 **Ts'khinvali** Georgia
116 G4 **Tsna** r. Rus. Fed.
88 D2 **Tso Morari Lake** India
117 D7 **Tsomo** S. Africa
93 □ **Tso Chung Wan** b. Hong Kong China
95 E7 **Tsu** Japan

95 G6 **Tsuchiura** Japan
93 □ **Tsuen Wan** Hong Kong China
94 G4 **Tsugaru-kaikyō** strait Japan
123 B5 **Tsumeb** Namibia
123 B6 **Tsumis Park** Namibia
123 C5 **Tsumkwe** Namibia
89 C4 **Tsunthang** India
95 E7 **Tsuruga** Japan
94 F5 **Tsurugi-san** mt. Japan
95 A7 **Tsushima** i. Japan
95 D7 **Tsuyama** Japan
124 D1 **Tswaane** Botswana
125 F4 **Tswaraganang** S. Africa
125 F3 **Tswelelang** S. Africa
113 L4 **Tsyelyakhany** Belarus
102 P1 **Tsyp-Navolok** Rus. Fed.
117 E6 **Tsyurupyns'k** Ukr.
91 F7 **Tual** Indon.
107 C4 **Tuam** Rep. of Ireland
72 D4 **Tuamo, Archipel des** is Fr. Polynesia
67 J5 **Tuamotu Islands** Fr. Polynesia
93 B6 **Tuân Giao** Vietnam
98 A5 **Tuangku** i. Indon.
117 F6 **Tuapse** Rus. Fed.
98 **Tuas** Sing.
72 A7 **Tuatapere** N.Z.
106 A2 **Tuath, Loch a'** b. U.K.
141 G3 **Tuba City** U.S.A.
99 D4 **Tuban** Indon.
155 G5 **Tubarão** Brazil
97 A4 **Tubbataha Reefs** Phil.
107 C4 **Tubbercurry** Rep. of Ireland
112 D6 **Tübingen** Germany
120 B4 **Tubmanburg** Liberia
97 B4 **Tubod** Phil.
121 E1 **Tubruq** Libya
161 J7 **Tubuai** i. Fr. Polynesia
67 I6 **Tubuai Islands** Fr. Polynesia
150 D2 **Tubutama** Mex.
155 K6 **Tucano** Brazil
159 B3 **Tucapel, Punta** pt Chile
155 G7 **Tucavaca** Bol.
109 K1 **Tüchen** Germany
109 K2 **Tuchheim** Germany
130 D2 **Tuchitua** Canada
147 G5 **Tuckerton** U.S.A.
141 G5 **Tucson** U.S.A.
141 G5 **Tucson Mountains** U.S.A.
157 B2 **Tucuco** r. Venez.
139 F4 **Tucumcari** U.S.A.
157 C2 **Tucupido** Venez.
154 G4 **Tucupita** Venez.
155 I4 **Tucuruí** Brazil
155 I4 **Tucuruí, Represa** resr Brazil
81 L5 **Tū Dār** Iran
111 C1 **Tudela** Spain
111 C2 **Tuela** r. Port.
93 □ **Tuen Mun** Hong Kong China
89 H4 **Tuensang** India
84 C5 **Tufayh** Saudi Arabia
161 J2 **Tufts Abyssal Plain** sea feature N. Pacific Ocean
125 I4 **Tugela** r. S. Africa
97 B2 **Tuguegarao** Phil.
77 O4 **Tugur** Rus. Fed.
83 K3 **Tugyl** Kazakh.
92 F2 **Tuhai He** r. China
98 A5 **Tuhemberua** Indon.
111 B1 **Tui** Spain
72 □ **Tuira** r. Panama
84 D3 **Tuleh** Iran
91 E7 **Tukangbesi, Kepulauan** is Indon.
132 D2 **Tukarak Island** Canada
83 H5 **Tükhtamish** Tajik.
72 □ **Tukituki** r. N.Z.
130 C2 **Tuktoyaktuk** Canada
103 M4 **Tukums** Latvia
116 H4 **Tula** r. Rus. Fed.
151 E3 **Tula** Mex.
116 F4 **Tula** Rus. Fed.
89 H1 **Tulagt Ar Gol** r. China
151 E3 **Tulancingo** Mex.
140 C3 **Tulare** U.S.A.
140 C3 **Tulare Lake Bed** U.S.A.
139 F5 **Tularosa** U.S.A.
87 C2 **Tulasi** mt. India
154 C3 **Tulcán** Ecuador
115 M2 **Tulcea** Romania
117 D5 **Tul'chyn** Ukr.
84 D3 **Tuleh** Iran
89 G4 **Tule-la Pass** Bhutan
133 I2 **Tulemalu Lake** Canada
143 C5 **Tulia** U.S.A.
80 E5 **Tulkarm** West Bank
107 E3 **Tullah** Australia
145 C5 **Tullahoma** U.S.A.
71 H4 **Tullamore** Australia
107 D4 **Tullamore** Rep. of Ireland
110 E4 **Tulle** France
71 G4 **Tullibigeal** Australia
107 E5 **Tullow** Rep. of Ireland
68 E3 **Tully** Australia
103 D3 **Tully** r. Australia
147 E3 **Tully** U.S.A.
116 F4 **Tul'skaya Oblast'** admin. div. Rus. Fed.
157 A3 **Tuluá** Col.
128 H3 **Tulsa** U.S.A.
159 C1 **Tulum** tourist site Mex.
151 H4 **Tulum, Valle de** valley Mex.
99 C8 **Tulungagung** Indon.
97 A4 **Tuluran** i. Phil.
125 G3 **Tumahole** S. Africa
154 B4 **Tumaco** Col.
125 G3 **Tumba** S. Africa
103 K4 **Tumba** Sweden
122 B4 **Tumba, Lac** l. Dem. Rep. Congo
99 D3 **Tumbangsamba** Indon.
155 **Tumbes** Brazil
130 D3 **Tumbler Ridge** Canada
70 B5 **Tumby Bay** Australia
102 D2 **Tumcha** r. Fin./Rus. Fed.
96 D3 **Tumen** China
96 D3 **Tumen** r. China/N. Korea
92 B2 **Tumenzi** China
154 G3 **Tumereng** Guyana
97 A5 **Tumindao** i. Phil.
89 G3 **Tum La** pass China
90 E3 **Tumnin** r. Rus. Fed.
87 A3 **Tumkur** India
106 E5 **Tummel, Loch** l. U.K.
88 C4 **Tump** Pak.
120 B3 **Tumu** Ghana
155 G3 **Tumucumaque, Serra** hills Brazil
71 H5 **Tumut** Australia
83 J4 **Tumxuk** China
105 H6 **Tunbridge Wells, Royal** U.K.
85 D1 **Tunceli** Turkey
93 D7 **Tunchang** China
71 H5 **Tuncurry** Australia
88 D1 **Tundla** India
123 D4 **Tunduma** Tanz.
123 D5 **Tunduru** Tanz.
115 L3 **Tundzha** r. Bulg.
87 B3 **Tungabhadra** r. India
87 A3 **Tungabhadra Reservoir** India
89 H3 **Tunga Pass** China/India
93 □ **Tung Chung Wan** b. Hong Kong China

102 C2 **Tungnaá** r. Iceland
93 □ **Tung Pok Liu Hoi Hap** Hong Kong China
130 D2 **Tungsten** Canada
116 E1 **Tunguda** Rus. Fed.
93 □ **Tung Wan** b. Hong Kong China
87 D2 **Tuni** India
120 D1 **Tunis** Tunisia
114 D6 **Tunis, Golfe de** g. Tunisia
120 C1 **Tunisia** country Africa
157 B3 **Tunja** Col.
92 D2 **Tuniu** China
92 F2 **Tuoji Dao** i. China
105 K2 **Tunstall** U.K.
102 O2 **Tuntsa** Fin.
133 G2 **Tunulic** r. Canada
133 H2 **Tunungayualok Island** Canada
159 C2 **Tunuyán** Arg.
159 C2 **Tunuyán** r. Arg.
92 F3 **Tuo He** r. China
98 **Tuoi Khpos** Cambodia
140 D3 **Tuolumne** r. U.S.A.
138 B4 **Tuolumne** U.S.A.
140 C3 **Tuolumne Meadows** U.S.A.
92 D5 **Tuoniang Jiang** r. China
89 H2 **Tuotuo He** r. China
83 I4 **Tüp** Kyrg.
158 B3 **Tupã** Brazil
158 C2 **Tupaciguara** Brazil
81 K3 **Tüp Aghāj** Iran
156 E3 **Tupancireta** Brazil
157 C3 **Tuparro** r. Col.
143 F5 **Tupelo** U.S.A.
154 E8 **Tupiza** Bol.
147 F2 **Tupper Lake** l. U.S.A.
147 F2 **Tupper Lake** U.S.A.
159 C2 **Tupungato** Arg.
159 C2 **Tupungato, Cerro** mt. Arg./Chile
96 A1 **Tuquan** China
157 A4 **Túquerres** Col.
89 G4 **Tura** India
77 L3 **Tura** Rus. Fed.
86 B5 **Turabah** Saudi Arabia
157 D3 **Turagua, Serranía** mt. Venez.
72 E4 **Turakina** N.Z.
84 E3 **Turan** Iran
90 F1 **Turana, Khrebet** mts Rus. Fed.
72 E3 **Turangi** N.Z.
84 E2 **Turan Lowland** Asia
83 G4 **Turar Ryskulov** Kazakh.
80 G4 **Turayf** Saudi Arabia
84 C5 **Turayf** well Saudi Arabia
103 N4 **Turba** Estonia
157 B2 **Turbaco** Col.
85 F5 **Turbat** Pak.
157 A2 **Turbo** Col.
113 K7 **Turda** Romania
84 C3 **Türeh** Iran
Turfan China see Turpan
83 H2 **Turgay** Akmolinskaya Oblast' Kazakh.
82 E2 **Turgay** Kostanayskaya Oblast' Kazakh.
82 E2 **Turgay** r. Kazakh.
82 E2 **Turgayskaya Dolina** valley Kazakh.
82 E2 **Turgayskaya Oblast'** admin. div. Kazakh.
82 E2 **Turgayskaya Stolovaya Strana** reg. Kazakh.
115 L3 **Türgovishte** Bulg.
80 A2 **Turgutlu** Turkey
80 F1 **Turhal** Turkey
103 N4 **Türi** Estonia
111 F3 **Turia** r. Spain
157 D2 **Turiamo** Venez.
114 B2 **Turin** Italy
116 F3 **Turinsk** Rus. Fed.
117 D5 **Turiys'k** Ukr.
122 D3 **Turkana, Lake** salt l. Eth./Kenya
115 L5 **Türkeli Adası** i. Turkey
83 G4 **Turkestan** Kazakh.
88 B2 **Turkestan Range** mts Asia
80 E2 **Turkey** country Asia
134 A3 **Turkey** r. U.S.A.
117 G5 **Turki** Rus. Fed.
80 C2 **Türkmenabat** Turkm.
80 B2 **Türkmenbashi** Turkm.
84 D2 **Turkmenistan** country Asia
80 B2 **Türkmen Dağı** mt. Turkey
80 C2 **Türkmenskiy Zaliv** b. Turkm.
80 F3 **Türkoğlu** Turkey
149 J4 **Turks and Caicos Islands** terr. Caribbean Sea
149 J4 **Turks Islands** Turks and Caicos Is
103 M3 **Turku** Fin.
122 D3 **Turkwel** watercourse Kenya
140 B3 **Turlock** U.S.A.
72 F4 **Turnagain, Cape** N.Z.
106 D5 **Turnberry** U.K.
141 H4 **Turnbull, Mount** U.S.A.
151 H4 **Turneffe Islands** Belize
135 F3 **Turner** U.S.A.
108 C3 **Turnhout** Belgium
71 H4 **Turon** r. Australia
115 K3 **Turnu Măgurele** Romania
113 K3 **Turnu Roşu, Pasul** pass Romania
90 A2 **Turpan** China
150 F5 **Turquino, Pico** mt. Cuba
106 F3 **Turriff** U.K.
81 J5 **Turt'kul'** Uzbek.
134 C2 **Turtle Flambeau Flowage** resr U.S.A.
131 H4 **Turtleford** Canada
134 A2 **Turtle Lake** U.S.A.
83 H4 **Turugart Pass** China/Kyrg.
82 C1 **Turush** Kazakh.
158 B2 **Turvo** r. Goiás Brazil
158 B3 **Turvo** r. São Paulo Brazil
152 **Tuscaloosa** U.S.A.
146 E4 **Tuscarawas** r. U.S.A.
146 E4 **Tuscarora Mountains** U.S.A.
134 C6 **Tuscola** IL U.S.A.
143 D5 **Tuscola** TX U.S.A.
145 C5 **Tusharik** Iran
81 I2 **Tutak** Turkey
87 B4 **Tutayev** Rus. Fed.
87 B4 **Tuticorin** India
112 D7 **Tuttle Creek Reservoir** U.S.A.
112 D7 **Tuttlingen** Germany
66 C2 **Tutuila** i. American Samoa
123 D4 **Tutubu** Tanz.
124 C2 **Tutume** Botswana
151 **Tutotepec** Mex.
96 D3 **Tuun-bong** mt. N. Korea
102 O3 **Tuupovaara** Fin.
102 O3 **Tuusniemi** Fin.
69 **Tuvalu** country Pacific Ocean
84 B5 **Tuwayq, Jabal** hill Saudi Arabia
150 D4 **Tuxpan** Jalisco Mex.
151 G4 **Tuxpan** Veracruz Mex.
151 F4 **Tuxtla Gutiérrez** Mex.
157 F2 **Tuy** r. Venez.
93 B6 **Tuyên Quang** Vietnam
93 **Tuy Hoa** Vietnam
84 C3 **Tüysärkän** Iran
80 D2 **Tuz Gölü** salt l. Turkey see Tuz, Lake
Tuz, Lake

141	F4	**Tuzigoot National Monument** *res.* U.S.A.
81	J4	**Tuz Khurmātū** Iraq
115	H2	**Tuzla** Bos.-Herz.
81	H2	**Tuzla** *r.* Turkey
117	F6	**Tuzlov** *r.* Rus. Fed.
103	J4	**Tvedestrand** Norway
116	E3	**Tver'** Rus. Fed.
116	E3	**Tverskaya Oblast'** *admin. div.* Rus. Fed.
135	I3	**Tweed** Canada
106	F5	**Tweed** *r.* U.K.
71	J2	**Tweed Heads** Australia
130	D4	**Tweedsmuir Provincial Park** Canada
124	C6	**Tweefontein** S. Africa
124	C5	**Twee Rivier** Namibia
108	E2	**Twente** *reg.* Neth.
140	D4	**Twentynine Palms** U.S.A.
133	J4	**Twillingate** Canada
138	D2	**Twin Bridges** U.S.A.
143	H3	**Twin Buttes Reservoir** U.S.A.
133	H3	**Twin Falls** Canada
138	D3	**Twin Falls** U.S.A.
130	F3	**Twin Lakes** Canada
147	H2	**Twin Mountain** U.S.A.
146	C6	**Twin Oaks** U.S.A.
140	B2	**Twin Peak** *mt.* U.S.A.
70	A2	**Twins, The** Australia
109	G2	**Twistringen** Germany
71	H6	**Twofold Bay** Australia
141	G4	**Two Guns** U.S.A.
134	B2	**Two Harbors** U.S.A.
131	G4	**Two Hills** Canada
138	D1	**Two Medicine** *r.* U.S.A.
134	D3	**Two Rivers** U.S.A.
89	H5	**Tyao** *r.* India/Myanmar
102	K3	**Tydal** Norway
146	D5	**Tygart Lake** U.S.A.
146	D5	**Tygart Valley** *valley* U.S.A.
90	E1	**Tygda** Rus. Fed.
143	E5	**Tyler** U.S.A.
143	F6	**Tylertown** U.S.A.
90	E1	**Tynda** Rus. Fed.
130	A2	**Tyndall Glacier** U.S.A.
106	F4	**Tyne** *r.* U.K.
104	F2	**Tynemouth** U.K.
103	J3	**Tynset** Norway
80	E5	**Tyre** Lebanon
102	N2	**Tyrnävä** Fin.
115	J5	**Tyrnavos** Greece
146	D4	**Tyrone** U.S.A.
70	E5	**Tyrrell** *r.* Australia
70	E5	**Tyrrell, Lake** Australia
114	D4	**Tyrrell, Lake** Canada
114	D4	**Tyrrhenian Sea** France/Italy
77	P3	**Tyubelyakh** Rus. Fed.
82	B3	**Tyub-Karagan, Mys** *pt* Kazakh.
76	I4	**Tyukalinsk** Rus. Fed.
82	B3	**Tyulen'i Ostrova** *is* Kazakh.
76	D1	**Tyul'gan** Rus. Fed.
76	H4	**Tyumen'** Rus. Fed.
83	J1	**Tyumentsevo** Rus. Fed.
77	M3	**Tyung** *r.* Rus. Fed.
82	F1	**Tyuntyugur** Kazakh.
105	C6	**Tywi** *r.* U.K.
105	C5	**Tywyn** U.K.
125	I1	**Tzaneen** S. Africa

U

123	C5	**Uamanda** Angola
157	E4	**Uatatás** *r.* Brazil
155	K5	**Uauá** Brazil
157	C4	**Uaupés** *r.* Brazil
157	C4	**Uaupés** *r.* Brazil
151	G4	**Uaxactún** Guat.
84	B4	**U'aywij** *well* Saudi Arabia
81	I7	**U'aywij, Wādī al** *watercourse* Saudi Arabia
158	D3	**Ubá** Brazil
83	J2	**Uba** *r.* Kazakh.
82	F1	**Ubagan** *r.* Kazakh.
158	D2	**Ubaí** Brazil
158	E1	**Ubaitaba** Brazil
122	B3	**Ubangi** *r.* Centr. Afr. Rep./Dem. Rep. Congo
157	B3	**Ubate** Col.
81	I5	**Ubayyiḍ, Wādī al** *watercourse* Iraq/Saudi Arabia
95	B8	**Ube** Japan
111	E3	**Úbeda** Spain
158	C2	**Uberaba** Brazil
155	G7	**Uberaba, Lagoa** *l.* Bol./Brazil
158	C2	**Uberlândia** Brazil
98	□	**Ubin, Pulau** *i.* Sing.
125	J3	**Ubombo** S. Africa
98	B1	**Ubonrat, Angkep Nam** *resr* Thai.
98	C2	**Ubon Ratchathani** Thai.
109	G5	**Ubstadt-Weiher** Germany
122	C4	**Ubundu** Dem. Rep. Congo
81	K1	**Ucar** Azer.
154	D5	**Ucayali** *r.* Peru
88	B3	**Uch** Pak.
82	E5	**Uch-Adzhi** Turkm.
82	D1	**Uchaly** Rus. Fed.
84	C2	**Uchán** Iran
83	J3	**Uchiura-wan** *b.* Japan
94	G3	**Uchiura-wan** *b.* Japan
82	E4	**Uchkuduk** Uzbek.
82	D4	**Uchsay** Uzbek.
109	G2	**Uchte** Germany
109	J2	**Uchte** *r.* Germany
90	F1	**Uchur** *r.* Rus. Fed.
105	H7	**Uckfield** U.K.
130	D5	**Ucluelet** Canada
141	H3	**Ucolo** U.S.A.
138	F2	**Ucross** U.S.A.
77	O4	**Uda** *r.* Rus. Fed.
117	H6	**Udachnoye** Rus. Fed.
77	M3	**Udachnyy** Rus. Fed.
87	B4	**Udagamandalam** India
88	C4	**Udaipur** *Rajasthan* India
89	G5	**Udaipur** *Tripura* India
89	E5	**Udanti** *r.* India/Myanmar
87	B3	**Udayagiri** India
103	J4	**Uddevalla** Sweden
106	D5	**Uddingston** U.K.
102	L2	**Uddjaure** *l.* Sweden
108	D3	**Uden** Neth.
87	B2	**Udgir** India
116	H1	**Udimskiy** Rus. Fed.
114	E1	**Udine** Italy
133	I2	**Udjuktok Bay** Canada
116	E3	**Udomlya** Rus. Fed.
98	B1	**Udon Thani** Thai.
90	F1	**Udskaya Guba** *b.* Rus. Fed.
87	B4	**Udumalaippettai** India
87	A3	**Udupi** India
90	F1	**Udyl', Ozero** *l.* Rus. Fed.
112	G4	**Ueckermünde** Germany
95	F6	**Ueda** Japan
68	C2	**Uekuli** Indon.
122	C3	**Uele** *r.* Dem. Rep. Congo
128	B3	**Uelen** Rus. Fed.
109	I2	**Uelzen** Germany
122	C3	**Uere** *r.* Dem. Rep. Congo
109	H1	**Uetersen** Germany
109	H5	**Uettingen** Germany
109	I2	**Uetze** Germany
76	G4	**Ufa** Rus. Fed.
109	I5	**Uffenheim** Germany
123	B6	**Ugab** *watercourse* Namibia
122	D4	**Ugalla** *r.* Tanz.
125	H5	**Uganda** *country* Africa
125	H5	**Ugie** S. Africa
117	G3	**Uglegorsk** Rus. Fed.
94	C3	**Uglekamensk** Rus. Fed.
116	F3	**Uglich** Rus. Fed.
114	F2	**Ugljan** *i.* Croatia

116	E3	**Uglovka** Rus. Fed.
94	C3	**Uglovoye** Rus. Fed.
83	J2	**Uglovskoye** Rus. Fed.
77	P3	**Ugol'noye** Rus. Fed.
77	S3	**Ugol'nyye Kopi** Rus. Fed.
116	E4	**Ugra** Rus. Fed.
83	H4	**Ügüt** Kyrg.
112	H6	**Uherské Hradiště** Czech Rep.
146	C4	**Uhrichsville** U.S.A.
106	B3	**Uig** U.K.
122	B4	**Uíge** Angola
90	D5	**Uijŏngbu** S. Korea
96	C3	**Ŭiju** N. Korea
82	C2	**Uil** *r.* Kazakh.
82	C2	**Uil** *r.* Kazakh.
102	O3	**Uimaharju** Fin.
141	F3	**Uinkaret Plateau** U.S.A.
138	E3	**Uinta Mountains** U.S.A.
123	B6	**Uis Mine** Namibia
107	D4	**Uisneach** *hill* Rep. of Ireland
96	E5	**Ŭisŏng** S. Africa
125	I3	**Uitenhage** S. Africa
108	C2	**Uithoorn** Neth.
108	E1	**Uithuizen** Neth.
133	H2	**Uivak, Cape** *hd* Canada
95	D7	**Uji** Japan
95	A9	**Uji-guntō** *is* Japan
88	C5	**Ujjain** India
99	E4	**Ujung Pandang** Indon.
81	I5	**Ukhaydir** Iraq
89	H4	**Ukhrul** India
116	J2	**Ukhta** Rus. Fed.
116	J2	**Ukhta** *r.* Rus. Fed.
71	J2	**Uki** Australia
140	A2	**Ukiah** *CA* U.S.A.
138	C2	**Ukiah** *OR* U.S.A.
129	M2	**Ukkusissat** Greenland
103	N5	**Ukmergė** Lith.
117	D5	**Ukraine** *country* Europe
83	J2	**Ukrainka** Kazakh.
116	I2	**Uktym** Rus. Fed.
95	A8	**Uku-jima** *i.* Japan
124	D1	**Ukwi** Botswana
124	D1	**Ukwi Pan** *salt pan* Botswana
		Ulaanbaatar Mongolia *see* Ulan Bator
90	B2	**Ulaangom** Mongolia
71	H4	**Ulan** Australia
92	C2	**Ulan** China
90	C2	**Ulan Bator** Mongolia
83	G3	**Ulanbel'** Kazakh.
92	C1	**Ulan Buh Shamo** *des.* China
117	H6	**Ulan Erge** Rus. Fed.
90	E2	**Ulanhot** China
92	D1	**Ulan Hua** China
117	H6	**Ulan-Khol** Rus. Fed.
92	C1	**Ulansuhai Nur** *l.* China
92	A1	**Ulan Tohoi** China
90	C1	**Ulan-Ude** Rus. Fed.
89	G2	**Ulan Ul Hu** *l.* China
80	F2	**Ulaş** Turkey
69	G2	**Ulawa Island** Solomon Is
84	C2	**Ūläy, Kūh-e** *hill* Iran
83	J2	**Ul'ba** Kazakh.
96	E5	**Ulchin** S. Korea
103	J4	**Ulefoss** Norway
103	N4	**Ülenurme** Estonia
83	F2	**Ul'gili** Kazakh.
87	A2	**Ulhasnagar** India
90	D2	**Uliastai** China
90	B2	**Uliastay** Mongolia
108	C3	**Ulicoten** Neth.
102	P1	**Ulita** *r.* Rus. Fed.
91	F6	**Ulithi** *i.* Micronesia
82	E2	**Ul'kayak** *r.* Kazakh.
83	H4	**Ul'ken Sulutor** Kazakh.
71	I5	**Ulladulla** Australia
103	L4	**Ullapool** U.K.
102	M3	**Ullava** Fin.
104	E3	**Ullswater** *l.* U.K.
96	F5	**Ullŭng-do** *i.* S. Korea
112	D6	**Ulm** Germany
71	J2	**Ulmarra** Australia
108	E4	**Ulmen** Germany
103	K4	**Ulricehamn** Sweden
108	E1	**Ulrum** Neth.
96	E6	**Ulsan** S. Korea
103	J3	**Ulsberg** Norway
107	D3	**Ulster Canal** Rep. of Ireland/U.K.
70	E5	**Ultima** Australia
151	H5	**Ulúa** *r.* Hond.
80	B1	**Ulubat Gölü** *l.* Turkey
80	C2	**Uluborlu** Turkey
80	B1	**Uludağ** *mt.* Turkey
98	B5	**Ulu Kali, Gunung** *mt.* Malaysia
80	E3	**Ulukışla** Turkey
125	I4	**Ulundi** S. Africa
98	□	**Ulu Pandan** Sing.
68	D4	**Uluru** *hill* Australia
106	B4	**Ulva** *i.* U.K.
108	D3	**Ulvenhout** Neth.
71	G8	**Ulverstone** Australia
103	K3	**Ulvsjön** Sweden
83	G4	**Ul'yanovo** Rus. Fed.
116	H4	**Ul'yanovsk** Rus. Fed.
116	H4	**Ul'yanovskaya Oblast'** *admin. div.* Rus. Fed.
83	H2	**Ul'yanovskiy** Kazakh.
143	C4	**Ulysses** U.S.A.
83	F3	**Ulytau** Kazakh.
83	F3	**Ulytau, Gory** *mts* Kazakh.
151	G3	**Umán** Mex.
117	D5	**Uman'** Ukr.
88	B5	**Umarao** Pak.
88	D6	**Umarkhed** India
87	C2	**Umarkot** India
88	B4	**Umarkot** Pak.
138	C2	**Umatilla** U.S.A.
76	J3	**Umba** Rus. Fed.
147	H2	**Umbagog Lake** U.S.A.
68	E2	**Umboi** *i.* P.N.G.
103	M3	**Umeå** Sweden
102	L2	**Umeälven** *r.* Sweden
125	I4	**Umfolozi** *r.* S. Africa
116	I2	**Umba** Rus. Fed.
125	I5	**Umkomaas** S. Africa
125	I4	**Umlazi** S. Africa
115	I3	**Umka** Serbia
81	K6	**Umm al Qaywayn** U.A.E.
84	D5	**Umm Bāb** Qatar
84	C5	**Umm Keddada** Sudan
81	K6	**Umm Qaşr** Iraq
150	B3	**Umm Ruwaba** Sudan
84	D5	**Umm Sa'id** Qatar
155	C5	**Umpqua** *r.* U.S.A.
123	B5	**Umpulo** Angola
88	C5	**Umred** India
88	C5	**Umreth** India
125	I5	**Umtata** S. Africa
125	I5	**Umtentweni** S. Africa
124	B3	**Umuahia** Nigeria
158	B3	**Umuarama** Brazil
125	H5	**Umzimkulu** S. Africa
125	I5	**Umzinto** S. Africa
114	G2	**Una** *r.* Bos.-Herz./Croatia
158	E1	**Una** Brazil
80	F6	**'Unāb, Wādī al** *watercourse* Jordan
155	H5	**Unaí** Brazil
128	B3	**Unalakleet** U.S.A.
128	B4	**Unalaska** U.S.A.
157	D2	**Unare** *r.* Venez.

80	E6	**'Unayzah** Jordan
86	B4	**'Unayzah** Saudi Arabia
81	G5	**'Unayzah, Jabal** *hill* Iraq
139	E4	**Uncompahgre Plateau** U.S.A.
125	H4	**Underberg** S. Africa
70	D5	**Underbool** Australia
142	C2	**Underwood** U.S.A.
116	E4	**Unecha** Rus. Fed.
71	G4	**Ungarie** Australia
70	B5	**Ungarra** Australia
132	F1	**Ungava, Péninsule d'** *pen.* Canada
133	G2	**Ungava Bay** Canada
96	F7	**Unggi** N. Korea
117	C6	**Ungheni** Moldova
82	E5	**Unguz, Solonchakovyye Vpadiny** *salt flat* Turkm.
116	I3	**Uni** Rus. Fed.
158	B4	**União da Vitória** Brazil
154	F4	**Unini** *r.* Brazil
147	I2	**Union** Para.
145	D5	**Union** *SC* U.S.A.
146	C6	**Union** *WV* U.S.A.
141	F4	**Union, Mount** U.S.A.
134	E5	**Union City** *OH* U.S.A.
146	D4	**Union City** *PA* U.S.A.
145	B4	**Union City** *TN* U.S.A.
124	E6	**Uniondale** S. Africa
145	C5	**Union Springs** U.S.A.
146	D5	**Uniontown** U.S.A.
135	F4	**Unionville** U.S.A.
84	D6	**United Arab Emirates** *country* Asia
76	E3	**United Kingdom** *country* Europe
136	D4	**United States of America** *country* N. America
131	H4	**Unity** Canada
147	I2	**Unity** *ME* U.S.A.
138	C2	**Unity** *OR* U.S.A.
88	C5	**Unjha** India
109	F3	**Unna** Germany
88	E4	**Unnao** India
96	C4	**Unp'a** N. Korea
96	C3	**Unsan** N. Korea
96	B4	**Unsan** N. Korea
106	□	**Unst** *i.* U.K.
109	I3	**Unstrut** *r.* Germany
89	G2	**Unuli Horog** China
87	D1	**Upar Ghat** India
157	E2	**Upata** Venez.
123	C4	**Upemba, Lac** *l.* Dem. Rep. Congo
97	C5	**Upi** Phil.
157	B3	**Upia** *r.* Col.
124	D4	**Upington** S. Africa
88	B5	**Upleta** India
102	O2	**Upoloksha** Rus. Fed.
69	I3	**Upolu** *i.* Samoa
138	B3	**Upper Alkali Lake** U.S.A.
146	B4	**Upper Arlington** U.S.A.
130	F4	**Upper Arrow Lake** Canada
72	E4	**Upper Hutt** N.Z.
146	B5	**Upper Iowa** *r.* U.S.A.
147	J1	**Upper Kent** Canada
138	B3	**Upper Klamath Lake** U.S.A.
140	A2	**Upper Lake** U.S.A.
130	D2	**Upper Liard** Canada
107	D3	**Upper Lough Erne** *l.* U.K.
146	E5	**Upper Marlboro** U.S.A.
98	□	**Upper Peirce Reservoir** Sing.
133	I4	**Upper Salmon Reservoir** Canada
146	B4	**Upper Sandusky** U.S.A.
147	F2	**Upper Saranac Lake** U.S.A.
72	D4	**Upper Takaka** N.Z.
103	L4	**Uppsala** Sweden
133	G2	**Upsala** Canada
147	H2	**Upton** U.S.A.
81	K7	**Uqlat al 'Udhaybah** *well* Iraq
81	K6	**Ur** Iraq
157	A2	**Urabá, Golfo de** *b.* Col.
84	E4	**Ūrāf** Iran
94	H3	**Urakawa** Japan
71	G4	**Ural** *hill* Australia
82	B2	**Ural** *r.* Kazakh./Rus. Fed.
71	I3	**Uralla** Australia
76	G4	**Ural Mountains** Rus. Fed.
82	B2	**Ural'sk** Kazakh.
		Ural'skiy Khrebet *mts* Rus. Fed. *see* Ural Mountains
122	D4	**Urambo** Tanz.
71	G5	**Urana** Australia
71	G5	**Urana, Lake** Australia
158	D1	**Urandi** Brazil
131	H3	**Uranium City** Canada
71	G5	**Uranquinty** Australia
157	E4	**Uraricoera** *r.* Brazil
157	E3	**Uraricoera** *r.* Brazil
157	E3	**Uraucaima, Serra** *mt.* Brazil
141	H2	**Uravan** U.S.A.
84	B5	**'Urayq, ad Duḥūl** *dunes* Saudi Arabia
117	C5	**Urazovo** Rus. Fed.
134	C5	**Urbana** *IL* U.S.A.
146	B4	**Urbana** *OH* U.S.A.
71	J2	**Urbenville** Australia
114	E3	**Urbino** Italy
154	D6	**Urcos** Peru
82	A2	**Urda** Kazakh.
116	I2	**Urdoma** Rus. Fed.
83	J3	**Urdzhar** Kazakh.
104	F3	**Ure** *r.* U.K.
116	H3	**Uren'** Rus. Fed.
76	I3	**Urengoy** Rus. Fed.
69	G3	**Uréparapara** *i.* Vanuatu
72	F3	**Urewera National Park** N.Z.
116	H4	**Urga** *r.* Rus. Fed.
88	E4	**Urgench** Uzbek.
80	E3	**Ürgüp** Turkey
83	F5	**Urgut** Uzbek.
157	B4	**Uribia** Col.
70	E2	**Urisino** Australia
103	N3	**Urjala** Fin.
82	E1	**Urk** Neth.
117	H7	**Urkarakh** Rus. Fed.
115	L5	**Urla** Turkey
107	D5	**Urlingford** Rep. of Ireland
83	G5	**Urmetan** Tajik.
84	B2	**Urmia** Iran
84	B2	**Urmia, Lake** *salt l.* Iran
93	□	**Urmston Road** *sea chan.* Hong Kong China
115	I3	**Uroševac** Yugo.
99	I3	**Ŭroteppa** Tajik.
92	A1	**Urt** Mongolia
150	B2	**Uruáchic** Mex.
158	C1	**Uruaçu** Brazil
150	D4	**Uruapan** Mex.
154	D6	**Urubamba** *r.* Peru
155	G4	**Urucara** Brazil
158	J5	**Uruçuí** Brazil
158	D1	**Urucuia** *r.* Brazil
155	J5	**Uruçuí Preto** *r.* Brazil
155	G4	**Urucurituba** Brazil
156	E4	**Uruguaiana** Brazil
159	E4	**Uruguay** *r.* Arg./Uruguay
159	F2	**Uruguay** *country* S. America
92	A2	**Ürümqi** China
71	G6	**Urunga** Australia
117	O6	**Urup** *r.* Rus. Fed.
90	F2	**Urup, Ostrov** *i.* Rus. Fed.
117	H7	**Urus-Martan** Rus. Fed.
83	K2	**Uryl'** Kazakh.
116	H3	**Urzhum** Rus. Fed.
115	L2	**Urziceni** Romania
95	B8	**Usa** Japan
116	I4	**Usa** *r.* Rus. Fed.
80	B2	**Uşak** Turkey

123	B6	**Usakos** Namibia
73	B5	**Usarp Mountains** Antarctica
156	E8	**Usborne, Mount** Falkland Is
76	I1	**Ushakova, Ostrov** *i.* Rus. Fed.
83	J2	**Ushanovo** Kazakh.
83	G4	**Usharal** Kazakh.
95	B8	**Ushibuka** Japan
83	I3	**Ushtobe** Kazakh.
156	C8	**Ushuaia** Arg.
109	G4	**Usingen** Germany
76	G3	**Usinsk** Rus. Fed.
105	E6	**Usk** U.K.
105	E6	**Usk** *r.* U.K.
116	C4	**Uska** India
114	G5	**Uskhodni** Belarus
109	H3	**Uslar** Germany
117	F4	**Usman'** Rus. Fed.
103	M4	**Usmas ezers** *l.* Latvia
116	I2	**Usogorsk** Rus. Fed.
90	C1	**Usol'ye-Sibirskoye** Rus. Fed.
83	I1	**Uspenka** Kazakh.
83	H2	**Uspenskiy** Kazakh.
110	F4	**Ussel** France
94	D1	**Ussuri** *r.* China/Rus. Fed.
90	F2	**Ussuriysk** Rus. Fed.
116	H3	**Usta** *r.* Rus. Fed.
77	L4	**Ust'-Barguzin** Rus. Fed.
117	G5	**Ust'-Buzulukskaya** Rus. Fed.
83	J1	**Ust'-Charyshskaya Pristan'** Rus. Fed.
117	G6	**Ust'-Donetskiy** Rus. Fed.
114	G4	**Ust'-Ilimsk** Rus. Fed.
90	C1	**Ust'-Ilimskiy Vodokhranilishche** *resr* Rus. Fed.
76	G3	**Ust'-Ilych** Rus. Fed.
112	G5	**Ústí nad Labem** Czech Rep.
112	H3	**Ustka** Poland
83	J1	**Ust'-Kalmanka** Rus. Fed.
77	R4	**Ust'-Kamchatsk** Rus. Fed.
83	J2	**Ust'-Kamenogorsk** Kazakh.
83	K2	**Ust'-Kan** Rus. Fed.
83	K2	**Ust'-Koksa** Rus. Fed.
90	C1	**Ust'-Kut** Rus. Fed.
77	O2	**Ust'-Kuyga** Rus. Fed.
117	F6	**Ust'-Labinsk** Rus. Fed.
103	O4	**Ust'-Luga** Rus. Fed.
77	O3	**Ust'-Maya** Rus. Fed.
76	G3	**Ust'-Nem** Rus. Fed.
77	P3	**Ust'-Nera** Rus. Fed.
116	I2	**Ust'-Ocheya** Rus. Fed.
77	M2	**Ust'-Olenek** Rus. Fed.
77	P3	**Ust'-Omchug** Rus. Fed.
90	C1	**Ust'-Ordynskiy** Rus. Fed.
77	O3	**Ust'-Port** Rus. Fed.
76	G3	**Ust'-Shonosha** Rus. Fed.
76	G3	**Ust'-Tsil'ma** Rus. Fed.
116	H2	**Ust'-Ura** Rus. Fed.
82	E1	**Ust'-Uyskoye** Kazakh.
116	E2	**Ust'-Vayen'ga** Rus. Fed.
116	H2	**Ust'-Vyyskaya** Rus. Fed.
77	O2	**Ust'ya** *r.* Rus. Fed.
116	F3	**Ust'ye** Rus. Fed.
116	F3	**Ust'ye** *r.* Rus. Fed.
82	C3	**Ust'yurta** *esc.* Kazakh.
82	C3	**Ust'yurt Plateau** Kazakh./Uzbek.
116	I2	**Ustyuzhna** Rus. Fed.
95	B8	**Usuki** Japan
151	G6	**Usulután** El Salvador
151	G4	**Usumacinta** *r.* Guat./Mex.
116	D4	**Usvyaty** Rus. Fed.
141	G1	**Utah** *state* U.S.A.
141	F2	**Utah Lake** U.S.A.
102	N2	**Utajärvi** Fin.
84	C5	**'Utayyiq** Saudi Arabia
103	N5	**Utena** Lith.
98	B2	**Uthai Thani** Thai.
88	B5	**Uthal** Pak.
98	A2	**U Thong** Thai.
98	C2	**Uthumphon Phisai** Thai.
147	F3	**Utica** U.S.A.
111	F3	**Utiel** Spain
130	F3	**Utikuma Lake** Canada
150	H4	**Utila** Hond.
125	F3	**Utlwanang** S. Africa
89	E4	**Utraula** India
108	D2	**Utrecht** Neth.
125	I3	**Utrecht** S. Africa
111	D4	**Utrera** Spain
102	N1	**Utsjoki** Fin.
95	F6	**Utsunomiya** Japan
117	G6	**Utta** Rus. Fed.
98	B1	**Uttaradit** Thai.
88	D4	**Uttar Pradesh** *state* India
105	F5	**Uttoxeter** U.K.
69	G3	**Utupua** *i.* Solomon Is
82	C2	**Utva** *r.* Kazakh.
		Uummannaq Greenland *see* Dundas
129	M2	**Uummannaq Fjord** *inlet* Greenland
102	N3	**Uurainen** Fin.
103	M3	**Uusikaupunki** Fin.
157	C4	**Uva** *r.* Col.
143	D6	**Uvalde** U.S.A.
82	C4	**Uval Karabaur** *hill* Uzbek.
117	G5	**Uvarovo** Rus. Fed.
82	E1	**Uvel'ka** *r.* Rus. Fed.
122	D4	**Uvinza** Tanz.
122	C4	**Uvira** Dem. Rep. Congo
90	A1	**Uvs Nuur** *l.* Mongolia
95	C8	**Uwajima** Japan
121	F3	**Uweinat, Jebel** *mt.* Sudan
92	D1	**Uxin Ju** China
151	G3	**Uxmal** *tourist site* Mex.
82	E1	**Uy** *r.* Rus. Fed.
90	C1	**Uyar** Rus. Fed.
82	C2	**Uyaly** Kazakh.
124	B3	**Uyo** Nigeria
120	C4	**Uyo** Nigeria
154	E8	**Uyuni, Salar de** *salt flat* Bol.
116	H4	**Uza** *r.* Rus. Fed.
81	J4	**'Uzaym, Nahr al** *r.* Iraq
146	A5	**Uzbekistan** *country* Asia
82	E4	**Uzbek** France
110	F4	**Uzès** France
117	L5	**Uzhhorod** Ukr.
115	H3	**Užice** Yugo.
117	F5	**Uzlovaya** Rus. Fed.
80	C3	**Üzümlü** Turkey
83	G5	**Uzun** Uzbek.
84	C3	**Uzun Darreh** *r.* Iran
117	C7	**Uzunköprü** Turkey
117	D5	**Uzyn** Ukr.
82	E2	**Uzynkair** Kazakh.
82	F1	**Uzynkol'** Kazakh.

V

103	N3	**Vaajakoski** Fin.
124	H3	**Vaal** *r.* S. Africa
102	N2	**Vaala** Fin.
124	F4	**Vaalbos National Park** S. Africa
125	H3	**Vaal Dam** S. Africa
125	H2	**Vaalwater** S. Africa
102	M3	**Vaasa** Fin.
117	G6	**Vác** Hungary
158	D2	**Vacaria** Brazil
158	A3	**Vacaria** *r. Mato Grosso do Sul* Brazil
158	D2	**Vacaria** *r. Minas Gerais* Brazil
158	A3	**Vacaria, Serra** *hills* Brazil
140	B3	**Vacaville** U.S.A.
116	G4	**Vad** *r.* Rus. Fed.

88	C6	**Vada** India
103	I4	**Vadla** Norway
88	C5	**Vadodara** India
112	D7	**Vaduz** Liechtenstein
103	I3	**Vadsø** Norway
103	J3	**Vågåmo** Norway
114	F2	**Vaganski Vrh** *mt.* Croatia
102	□	**Vágar** *i.* Faroe Is
102	L2	**Vågsele** Sweden
102	□	**Vágur** Faroe Is
102	M3	**Vähäkyrö** Fin.
84	E4	**Vahhābi** Iran
103	N4	**Vaida** Estonia
87	B4	**Vaigai** *r.* India
141	G5	**Vail** U.S.A.
108	B5	**Vailly-sur-Aisne** France
69	H2	**Vaitupu** *i.* Tuvalu
83	H5	**Vakhsh** Tajik.
103	N5	**Valachchenai** Sri Lanka
135	J2	**Val-Barrette** Canada
103	J3	**Valbo** Sweden
159	C4	**Valcheta** Arg.
114	D2	**Valdagno** Italy
116	E3	**Valday** Rus. Fed.
116	E3	**Valdayskaya Vozvyshennost'** *reg.* Rus. Fed.
111	D3	**Valdecañas, Embalse de** *resr* Spain
103	M4	**Valdemārpils** Latvia
103	L4	**Valdemarsvik** Sweden
110	G2	**Val-de-Meuse** France
111	E3	**Valdepeñas** Spain
110	E2	**Val-de-Reuil** France
159	C4	**Valdés, Península** *pen.* Arg.
128	D3	**Valdez** U.S.A.
159	B5	**Valdivia** Chile
135	I1	**Val-d'Or** Canada
145	D6	**Valdosta** U.S.A.
103	J3	**Valdres** *valley* Norway
81	I1	**Vale** Georgia
138	C2	**Vale** U.S.A.
130	D5	**Valemount** Canada
158	E1	**Valença** Brazil
110	C4	**Valence** France
111	F3	**Valencia** Spain
111	F3	**Valencia** *aut. comm.* Spain
157	D1	**Valencia** Venez.
111	G3	**Valencia, Golfo de** *g.* Spain
111	C3	**Valencia de Alcántara** Spain
111	D1	**Valencia de Don Juan** Spain
107	A6	**Valencia Island** Rep. of Ireland
110	F1	**Valenciennes** France
94	D3	**Valentin** Rus. Fed.
141	F4	**Valentine** *AZ* U.S.A.
142	C2	**Valentine** *NE* U.S.A.
143	B6	**Valentine** *TX* U.S.A.
97	B3	**Valenzuela** Phil.
103	J3	**Våler** Norway
157	C2	**Valera** Venez.
83	G1	**Valikhanovo** Kazakh.
115	H2	**Valjevo** Yugo.
103	N4	**Valka** Latvia
103	N3	**Valkeakoski** Fin.
108	D3	**Valkenswaard** Neth.
117	E5	**Valky** Ukr.
73	C4	**Valkyrie Dome** *ice feature* Antarctica
151	G3	**Valladolid** Mex.
111	D2	**Valladolid** Spain
111	G3	**Vall de Uxó** Spain
103	I4	**Valle** Norway
157	D2	**Valle de la Pascua** Venez.
150	D3	**Valle de Santiago** Mex.
159	C1	**Valle Grande** Bol.
150	E2	**Valle Hermoso** Mex.
140	A2	**Vallejo** U.S.A.
151	E4	**Valle Nacional** Mex.
114	F7	**Valletta** Malta
105	C4	**Valley** *i.* U.K.
142	D2	**Valley City** U.S.A.
138	B3	**Valley Falls** U.S.A.
146	C5	**Valley Head** U.S.A.
130	E3	**Valleyview** Canada
111	G2	**Valls** Spain
131	H5	**Val Marie** Canada
103	N4	**Valmiera** Latvia
111	E1	**Valnera** *mt.* Spain
103	N3	**Valozhyn** Belarus
158	B2	**Valparaíso** Brazil
159	B4	**Valparaíso** Chile
159	B4	**Valparaíso** *admin. reg.* Chile
150	D3	**Valparaíso** Mex.
134	C5	**Valparaiso** U.S.A.
110	G4	**Valréas** France
91	F7	**Vals, Tanjung** *c.* Indon.
89	□	**Valsad** India
125	G4	**Valspan** S. Africa
116	H1	**Val'tevo** Rus. Fed.
102	O3	**Valtimo** Fin.
117	G6	**Valuyevka** Rus. Fed.
117	F5	**Valuyki** Rus. Fed.
111	C4	**Valverde del Camino** Spain
98	C3	**Vam Co Tay** *r.* Vietnam
103	M3	**Vammala** Fin.
87	C2	**Vamsadhara** *r.* India
81	I2	**Vanadzor** Armenia
143	C5	**Van Buren** *AR* U.S.A.
147	H1	**Van Buren** *ME* U.S.A.
98	D2	**Van Canh** Vietnam
147	E5	**Vanceboro** U.S.A.
146	B5	**Vanceburg** U.S.A.
130	E5	**Vancouver** Canada
138	B2	**Vancouver** U.S.A.
130	A2	**Vancouver, Mount** Canada/U.S.A.
130	D5	**Vancouver Island** Canada
134	D5	**Vandalia** *IL* U.S.A.
146	A4	**Vandalia** *OH* U.S.A.
125	H3	**Vanderbijlpark** S. Africa
134	E3	**Vanderbilt** U.S.A.
146	C4	**Vandergrift** U.S.A.
130	A2	**Vanderhoof** Canada
124	F5	**Vanderkloof Dam** *resr* S. Africa
68	D3	**Vanderlin Island** Australia
141	H4	**Vanderwagen** U.S.A.
68	D3	**Van Diemen Gulf** Australia
103	N3	**Vändra** Estonia
103	L4	**Vänern** *l.* Sweden
103	K4	**Vänersborg** Sweden
146	E3	**Van Etten** U.S.A.
123	E6	**Vangaindrano** Madag.
		Van Gölü *salt l.* Turkey *see* Van, Lake
143	B6	**Van Horn** U.S.A.
135	□	**Vanier** Canada
68	E2	**Vanikoro Islands** Solomon Is
68	E2	**Vanimo** P.N.G.
90	C2	**Vanino** Rus. Fed.
87	B3	**Vanivilasa Sagara** *resr* India
87	B3	**Vaniyambadi** India
124	C5	**Vanrhynsdorp** S. Africa
102	A3	**Vansbro** Sweden
103	N3	**Vantaa** Fin.
69	G3	**Vanua Lava** *i.* Vanuatu
69	H3	**Vanua Levu** *i.* Fiji
69	G3	**Vanuatu** *country* Pacific Ocean
146	A4	**Van Wert** U.S.A.

124	D5	**Vanwyksvlei** S. Africa
124	D5	**Vanwyksvlei** *l.* S. Africa
93	B6	**Văn Yên** Vietnam
124	C3	**Van Zylsrus** S. Africa
87	A3	**Varada** *r.* India
103	N4	**Varakļāni** Latvia
84	C4	**Varāmīn** Iran
89	E4	**Varanasi** India
102	O1	**Varangerfjorden** *sea chan.* Norway
102	O1	**Varangerhalvøya** *pen.* Norway
114	G1	**Varaždin** Croatia
114	C2	**Varazze** Italy
103	J5	**Varberg** Sweden
87	B2	**Vardannapet** India
87	B2	**Vardar** *r.* Macedonia
103	J5	**Varde** Denmark
81	J1	**Vardenis** Armenia
102	O1	**Vardø** Norway
109	G1	**Varel** Germany
159	C2	**Varela** Arg.
105	N5	**Vārkava** Latvia
114	C2	**Varese** Italy
94	C2	**Varfolomeyevka** Rus. Fed.
103	L4	**Vårgårda** Sweden
158	D3	**Varginha** Brazil
108	D3	**Varik** Neth.
102	N3	**Varkaus** Fin.
103	J5	**Varna** Bulg.
82	E1	**Varna** Rus. Fed.
103	L4	**Värnamo** Sweden
103	K3	**Värnäs** Sweden
116	H3	**Varnavino** Rus. Fed.
80	D4	**Varosia** Cyprus
102	N3	**Varpaisjärvi** Fin.
112	I7	**Várpalota** Hungary
85	H2	**Varsaj** Afgh.
81	H2	**Varto** Turkey
89	E4	**Varuna** *r.* India
146	D3	**Varysburg** U.S.A.
84	A2	**Varzaneh** Iran
158	D2	**Várzea da Palma** Brazil
158	D3	**Várzea Paulista** Brazil
116	H2	**Varzino** Rus. Fed.
102	N3	**Vaskivesi** Fin.
113	M7	**Vaslui** Romania
82	E1	**Vassar** U.S.A.
158	E1	**Vassouras** Brazil
103	L4	**Västerås** Sweden
103	L3	**Västerdalälven** *r.* Sweden
103	L4	**Västerhaninge** Sweden
103	L4	**Västervik** Sweden
114	F3	**Vasto** Italy
117	D5	**Vasyl'kiv** Ukr.
110	E3	**Vatan** France
106	A4	**Vatersay** *i.* U.K.
115	L6	**Vathy** Greece
114	E4	**Vatican City** *country* Europe
102	C2	**Vatnajökull** *ice cap* Iceland
113	M7	**Vatra Dornei** Romania
103	K4	**Vättern** *l.* Sweden
139	F5	**Vaughn** U.S.A.
108	B4	**Vaux** Belgium
157	C4	**Vaupés** *r.* Col.
110	G5	**Vauvert** France
69	I3	**Vava'u Group** *is* Tonga
120	B4	**Vavoua** Côte d'Ivoire
87	C4	**Vavuniya** Sri Lanka
103	O5	**Vawkavysk** Belarus
103	K4	**Växjö** Sweden
98	B3	**Vây, Đao** *i.* Vietnam
87	B3	**Vayalpad** India
116	I1	**Vazhgort** Rus. Fed.
123	E5	**Vazobe** *mt.* Madag.
98	B2	**Veal Vêng** Cambodia
108	E2	**Vechte** *r.* Germany
109	H3	**Veckerhagen (Reinhardshagen)** Germany
87	B4	**Vedaranniyam** India
115	K3	**Vedea** *r.* Romania
147	H7	**Vedeno** Rus. Fed.
81	J2	**Vedi** Armenia
159	E2	**Vedia** Arg.
116	E2	**Vedlozero** Rus. Fed.
134	C5	**Veedersburg** U.S.A.
108	E2	**Veendam** Neth.
108	D3	**Veenendaal** Neth.
102	J2	**Vega** *i.* Norway
143	C5	**Vega** U.S.A.
131	H4	**Vegreville** Canada
103	N3	**Vehkalahti** Fin.
88	B3	**Vehoa** *r.* Pak.
88	B4	**Veirwaro** Pak.
109	H3	**Veitshöchheim** Germany
109	F3	**Vejer de la Frontera** Spain
103	J5	**Vejle** Denmark
87	B4	**Velanai Island** Sri Lanka
108	F3	**Velbert** Germany
109	J5	**Velburg** Germany
108	D2	**Veldhoven** Neth.
108	E2	**Velen** Germany
124	C6	**Velddrif** S. Africa
114	G2	**Veldhoven** Neth.
131	I5	**Velva** U.S.A.
163	J8	**Vema Seamount** *sea feature* S. Atlantic Ocean
162	I5	**Vema Trench** *sea feature* Indian Ocean
87	B4	**Vembanad Lake** India
104	F3	**Venachar, Loch** *l.* U.K.
159	C3	**Venado Tuerto** Arg.
114	F4	**Venafro** Italy
157	C4	**Venamo** *r.* Guyana/Venez.
157	E3	**Venamo, Cerro** *mt.* Venez.
110	D3	**Vendôme** France
		Venezia Italy *see* Venice
157	C2	**Venezuela** *country* S. America
157	D2	**Venezuela, Golfo de** *g.* Venez.
163	E4	**Venezuelan Basin** *sea feature* S. Atlantic Ocean

87 A3 Vengurla India
114 E2 Venice Italy
114 E2 Venice U.S.A.
114 E2 Venice, Gulf of Europe
110 G4 Vénissieux France
87 B3 Venkatagiri India
87 C2 Venkatapuram India
108 S3 Venlo Neth.
103 I4 Vennesla Norway
108 D3 Venray Neth.
103 M4 Venta r. Latvia/Lith.
103 M4 Venta Lith.
125 G4 Ventersburg S. Africa
125 G3 Ventersdorp S. Africa
125 F5 Venterstad S. Africa
115 F7 Ventnor U.K.
110 G4 Ventoux, Mont mt. France
103 M4 Ventspils Latvia
157 H3 Venturi r. Venez.
140 C4 Ventucopa U.S.A.
140 C4 Ventura U.S.A.
70 F7 Venus Bay Australia
150 D2 Venustiano Carranza Mex.
156 D3 Vera Arg.
111 F4 Vera Spain
151 E4 Veracruz Mex.
151 E3 Veracruz state Mex.
88 B5 Veraval India
114 C2 Verbania Italy
102 J3 Verdalsøra Norway
158 B2 Verde r. Goiás Brazil
158 B2 Verde r. Goiás Brazil
158 C2 Verde r. Goiás/Minas Gerais Brazil
158 B2 Verde r. Mato Grosso do Sul Brazil
136 E6 Verde r. Mex.
158 B2 Verde r. Para.
141 G4 Verde r. U.S.A.
159 D3 Verde, Peninsula pen. Arg.
158 D1 Verde Grande r. Brazil
97 B3 Verde Island Passage Phil.
109 H2 Verden (Aller) Germany
143 E4 Verdigris r. U.S.A.
110 H5 Verdon r. France
110 G2 Verdun France
125 G3 Vereeniging S. Africa
159 G4 Vergara Uruguay
147 G2 Vergennes U.S.A.
111 C2 Verín Spain
82 D1 Verkhne-Avzyan Rus. Fed.
117 F6 Verkhnebakanskiy Rus. Fed.
113 P3 Verkhnedneprovskiy Rus. Fed.
76 J3 Verkhneimbatsk Rus. Fed.
102 O1 Verkhnetulomskiy Rus. Fed.
82 D1 Verkhneural'sk Rus. Fed.
77 N3 Verkhnevilyuysk Rus. Fed.
116 D1 Verkhnee Kuyto, Ozero l. Rus. Fed.
117 H5 Verkhniy Baskunchak Rus. Fed.
117 I5 Verkhniy Kushum Rus. Fed.
102 P2 Verkhnyaya Pirenga, Ozero l. Rus. Fed.
116 H2 Verkhnyaya Toyma Rus. Fed.
116 G2 Verkhovazh'ye Rus. Fed.
116 F4 Verkhov'ye Rus. Fed.
117 C5 Verkhovyna Ukr.
77 N3 Verkhoyansk Rus. Fed.
77 N3 Verkhoyanskiy Khrebet mts Rus. Fed.
83 J2 Verkhuba Kazakh.
108 B5 Vermand France
158 B1 Vermelho r. Brazil
131 G4 Vermilion Canada
134 C5 Vermilion r. U.S.A.
141 F3 Vermilion Cliffs U.S.A.
134 A2 Vermilion Lake U.S.A.
134 A2 Vermilion Range U.S.A.
142 D3 Vermillion U.S.A.
131 K5 Vermilion Bay Canada
147 G3 Vermont state U.S.A.
73 B2 Vernadsky research station Antarctica
138 E3 Vernal U.S.A.
135 G2 Verner Canada
124 D5 Verneuk Pan salt pan S. Africa
130 F4 Vernon Canada
141 H4 Vernon AZ U.S.A.
143 D5 Vernon TX U.S.A.
141 F1 Vernon UT U.S.A.
145 D7 Vero Beach U.S.A.
115 J4 Veroia Greece
114 D2 Verona Italy
159 F2 Verónica Arg.
70 B4 Verran Australia
110 F2 Versailles France
109 G2 Versmold Germany
110 D3 Vertou France
125 I4 Verulam S. Africa
108 D4 Verviers Belgium
110 F2 Vervins France
108 C5 Verzy France
114 C3 Vescovato Corsica France
76 C4 Veselaya, Gora mt. Rus. Fed.
117 E6 Vesele Ukr.
117 G6 Veselovskoye Vodokhranilishche resr Rus. Fed.
83 J2 Veseloyarsk Rus. Fed.
82 F1 Veselyy Podol Kazakh.
117 G5 Veshenskaya Rus. Fed.
108 B5 Vesle r. France
110 H3 Vesoul France
94 D3 Vesselyy Yar Rus. Fed.
108 D3 Vessem Neth.
102 K1 Vesterålen is Norway
102 K1 Vesterålsfjorden sea chan. Norway
103 J4 Vestfjorddalen valley Norway
102 K2 Vestfjorden sea chan. Norway
102 □ Vestmanna Faroe Is
102 B3 Vestmannaeyjar Iceland
102 B3 Vestmannaeyjar is Iceland
102 I3 Vestnes Norway
102 D2 Vesturhorn hd Iceland
114 F4 Vesuvius vol. Italy
102 K1 Ves'yegonsk Rus. Fed.
112 H7 Veszprém Hungary
102 M3 Veteli Fin.
103 K4 Vetlanda Sweden
116 H3 Vetluga Rus. Fed.
116 H3 Vetluga r. Rus. Fed.
114 E3 Vettore, Monte mt. Italy
108 B4 Veurne Belgium
112 C7 Vevey Switz.
84 D4 Veyo Iran
110 E4 Vézère r. France
80 E1 Vezirköprü Turkey
159 B2 V. Hermosa, Paso de pass Chile
155 A4 Viana r. Brazil
111 B2 Viana do Castelo Port.
108 D3 Vianen Neth.
Viangchan Laos see Vientiane
158 C2 Vianópolis Brazil
114 D3 Viareggio Italy
103 J4 Viborg Denmark
114 G3 Vibo Valentia Italy
111 H2 Vic Spain
150 B2 Vicam Mex.
140 C3 Vicente, Point U.S.A.
150 D2 Vicente Guerrero Mex.
114 D2 Vicenza Italy
157 C3 Vichada r. Col.
116 G3 Vichuga Rus. Fed.
159 B3 Vichuquén Chile
110 F3 Vichy France
141 F5 Vicksburg AZ U.S.A.
143 F5 Vicksburg MS U.S.A.
158 D3 Viçosa Brazil
134 A5 Victor U.S.A.
73 D3 Victor, Mount Antarctica

70 C5 Victor Harbor Australia
159 E2 Victoria Arg.
68 D3 Victoria r. Australia
70 F6 Victoria state Australia
130 E5 Victoria Canada
159 B3 Victoria Chile
114 H5 Victoria Hond.
114 F6 Victoria Malta
143 D6 Victoria U.S.A.
122 D4 Victoria, Lake Africa
70 D4 Victoria, Lake N.S.W. Australia
71 G6 Victoria, Lake Vic. Australia
89 H5 Victoria, Mount Myanmar
68 E2 Victoria, Mount P.N.G.
129 K2 Victoria and Albert Mountains Canada
123 C5 Victoria Falls Zambia/Zimbabwe
129 N1 Victoria Fjord inlet Greenland
128 D2 Victoria Island Canada
133 I4 Victoria Land reg. Antarctica
122 D3 Victoria Nile r. Sudan/Uganda
72 G5 Victoria Range mts N.Z.
68 D3 Victoria River Downs Australia
133 F4 Victoriaville Canada
124 E5 Victoria West S. Africa
159 D3 Victorica Arg.
150 D3 Victor Rosales Mex.
140 D4 Victorville U.S.A.
159 D2 Vicuña Mackenna Arg.
141 E4 Vidal Junction U.S.A.
115 K2 Videle Romania
115 J3 Vidin Bulg.
88 D5 Vidisha India
106 □ Vidlin U.K.
116 E2 Viditsa Rus. Fed.
113 M3 Vidzy Belarus
116 I2 Vidz'yuyar Rus. Fed.
109 K5 Viechtach Germany
159 D4 Viedma Arg.
156 B7 Viedma, Lago l. Arg.
109 J1 Vielank Germany
108 D4 Vielsalm Belgium
109 I3 Vienenburg Germany
112 H6 Vienna Austria
144 B4 Vienna IL U.S.A.
147 F5 Vienna MD U.S.A.
146 C4 Vienna WV U.S.A.
110 E3 Vienne France
110 E3 Vienne r. France
98 B1 Vientiane Laos
159 B3 Viento, Cordillera del mts Arg.
149 K5 Vieques i. Puerto Rico
116 E3 Vieremä Fin.
108 E3 Viersen Germany
112 D7 Vierwaldstätter See l. Switz.
150 D2 Viesca Mex.
103 N4 Viesīte Latvia
114 G4 Vieste Italy
102 L2 Vietas Sweden
98 B1 Vietnam country Asia
93 B6 Viêt Trì Vietnam
97 B2 Vigan Phil.
114 C2 Vigevano Italy
158 C1 Vigia Brazil
151 H4 Vigía Chico Mex.
108 A4 Vignacourt France
110 D5 Vignemale mt. France
114 D2 Vignola Italy
111 B1 Vigo Spain
102 N2 Vihanti Fin.
88 C3 Vihari Pak.
103 N3 Vihti Fin.
102 N3 Viitasaari Fin.
88 C3 Vijainagar India
87 A2 Vijayadurg India
87 C2 Vijayawada India
102 C3 Vík Iceland
103 N5 Vikajärvi Fin.
140 C3 Visalia U.S.A.
131 G4 Viking Canada
102 J2 Vikna i. Norway
103 I3 Vikøyri Norway
109 G2 Visbek Germany
120 □ Vila da Ribeira Brava Cape Verde
120 □ Vila de Sal Rei Cape Verde
120 □ Vila do Tarrafal Cape Verde
111 B3 Vila Franca de Xira Port.
111 B2 Vilagarcía de Arousa Spain
125 J2 Vila Gomes da Costa Moz.
111 C1 Vilalba Spain
123 D5 Vilanandro, Tanjona pt Madag.
111 B3 Vila Nova de Gaia Port.
111 B2 Vilanova i la Geltrú Spain
120 □ Vila Real Port.
111 C2 Vilar Formoso Port.
87 B4 Vilavankod India
158 E3 Vila Velha Brazil
102 L2 Vilhelmina Sweden
154 F6 Vilhena Brazil
103 N4 Viljandi Estonia
125 G3 Viljoenskroon S. Africa
103 M5 Vilkaviškis Lith.
103 M5 Vilkija Lith.
77 K2 Vil'kitskogo, Proliv strait Rus. Fed.
151 E4 Villa Alta Mex.
154 E6 Villa Bella Bol.
111 C1 Villablino Spain
159 C1 Villa Cañás Arg.
112 F7 Villach Austria
114 C5 Villacidro Sardinia Italy
159 E2 Villa Constitución Arg.
150 D4 Villa de Álvarez Mex.
159 C2 Villa de Cos Mex.
151 G4 Villa de Guadalupe Mex.
159 D1 Villa del Rosario Arg.
159 E1 Villa del Totoral Arg.
159 D1 Villa Dolores Arg.
150 E3 Villa Flores Mex.
159 E1 Villa Gesell Arg.
159 D1 Villaguay Arg.
111 F3 Villajoyosa Spain
150 D3 Villaldama Mex.
159 E1 Villalonga Arg.
159 D2 Villa María Arg.
159 E1 Villa María Grande Arg.
125 H1 Villa Nora S. Africa
159 E1 Villanueva Col.
151 E2 Villanueva Mex.
111 D3 Villanueva de la Serena Spain
111 E3 Villanueva de los Infantes Spain
150 C2 Villa Ocampo Mex.
159 E1 Villa Ocampo Arg.
151 G4 Villa Orestes Pereyra Mex.
114 C5 Villaputzu Sardinia Italy
159 E3 Villa Regina Arg.
156 E3 Villarrica Para.
159 B3 Villarrica Chile
159 B3 Villarrica, Lago l. Chile
159 B3 Villarrica, Volcán vol. Chile
111 E3 Villarrobledo Spain
114 F5 Villa San Giovanni Italy
159 E2 Villa San José Arg.
159 B3 Villa Santa Rita de Catuna Arg.
159 D1 Villa Unión Arg.
150 D1 Villa Unión Durango Mex.
150 C3 Villa Unión Sinaloa Mex.
159 C3 Villa Valeria Arg.
154 E8 Villazón Bol.
110 F4 Villefranche-de-Rouergue France

110 G4 Villefranche-sur-Saône France
135 H2 Ville-Marie Canada
111 F3 Villena Spain
110 E4 Villeneuve-sur-Lot France
110 F2 Villeneuve-sur-Yonne France
143 E6 Ville Platte U.S.A.
108 B5 Villers-Cotterêts France
108 D5 Villerupt France
110 G4 Villeurbanne France
125 H3 Villiers S. Africa
112 D6 Villingen Germany
131 G4 Vilna Canada
103 N5 Vilnius Lith.
117 E6 Vil'nyans'k Ukr.
103 N3 Vilppula Fin.
109 J5 Vils r. Germany
108 C4 Vilvoorde Belgium
116 C4 Vilyeyka Belarus
77 N3 Vilyuy r. Rus. Fed.
77 L3 Vilyuyskoye Vodokhranilishche resr Rus. Fed.
103 K4 Vimmerby Sweden
108 A4 Vimy France
140 A2 Vina r. U.S.A.
159 B2 Viña del Mar Chile
147 I2 Vinalhaven U.S.A.
111 G2 Vinarós Spain
144 C4 Vincennes U.S.A.
73 C6 Vincennes Bay Antarctica
102 L3 Vindelälven r. Sweden
102 L3 Vindeln Sweden
88 C5 Vindhya Range hills India
147 F5 Vineland U.S.A.
147 H4 Vineyard Haven U.S.A.
98 C1 Vinh Vietnam
98 C1 Vinh Linh Vietnam
98 C3 Vinh Long Vietnam
93 B6 Vinh Yên Vietnam
143 E4 Vinita U.S.A.
115 H2 Vinkovci Croatia
117 D5 Vinnytsya Ukr.
73 B3 Vinson Massif mt. Antarctica
103 J3 Vinstra Norway
134 A4 Vinton U.S.A.
87 B2 Vinukonda India
114 D1 Vipiteno Italy
109 K1 Vipperow Germany
97 C3 Virac Phil.
88 C5 Viramgam India
81 G3 Viranşehir Turkey
88 B4 Virawah Pak.
131 I5 Virden Canada
110 D2 Vire France
123 B5 Virei Angola
158 D2 Virgem da Lapa Brazil
141 F3 Virginia r. Ireland
107 C4 Virginia Rep. of Ireland
125 A2 Virginia S. Africa
134 A2 Virginia U.S.A.
146 D5 Virginia state U.S.A.
147 E6 Virginia Beach U.S.A.
140 C2 Virginia City U.S.A.
149 L5 Virgin Islands (U.K.) terr. Caribbean Sea
149 L5 Virgin Islands (U.S.A.) terr. Caribbean Sea
103 N3 Virkkala Fin.
98 C4 Virôchey Cambodia
134 B4 Viroqua U.S.A.
115 G2 Virovitica Croatia
103 M3 Virrat Fin.
108 C4 Virton Belgium
103 M4 Virtsu Estonia
122 C3 Virunga, Parc National des nat. park Dem. Rep. Congo
114 G3 Vis i. Croatia
103 N5 Visaginas Lith.
140 C3 Visalia U.S.A.
88 C5 Visavadar India
97 B4 Visayan Sea Phil.
109 G2 Visbek Germany
103 L4 Visby Sweden
128 G2 Viscount Melville Sound strait Canada
108 D4 Visé Belgium
76 I2 Vise, Ostrov i. Rus. Fed.
115 H3 Višegrad Bos.-Herz.
155 I4 Viseu Brazil
111 C2 Viseu Port.
87 C2 Visakhapatnam India
88 C5 Visnagar India
114 F3 Viso, Monte mt. Italy
115 H3 Visoko Bos.-Herz.
112 C7 Visp Switz.
109 H2 Visselhövede Germany
140 D5 Vista U.S.A.
158 A2 Vista Alegre Brazil
115 K4 Vistonida, Limni lag. Greece
113 I4 Vistula r. Poland
157 C3 Vita r. Col.
88 B3 Vitakri Pak.
114 F4 Viterbo Italy
115 G2 Vitez Bos.-Herz.
115 K4 Vithkuqi Albania
69 H3 Viti Levu i. Fiji
90 D1 Vitim r. Rus. Fed.
82 C4 Vitória Chagyllys or hill Turkm.
158 D3 Vitória Brazil
158 B1 Vitória da Conquista Brazil
111 E1 Vitoria-Gasteiz Spain
163 G7 Vitória Seamount sea feature S. Atlantic Ocean
110 D2 Vitré France
108 A4 Vitry-en-Artois France
110 G2 Vitry-le-François France
116 B6 Vitsyebsk Belarus
102 M2 Vittangi Sweden
114 F6 Vittoria Sicily Italy
114 E2 Vittorio Veneto Italy
111 C1 Viveiro Spain
125 H1 Vivo S. Africa
70 B6 Vivonne Bay Australia
150 I3 Vizcaíno, Desierto de des. Mex.
150 A2 Vizcaíno, Sierra mts Mex.
117 D7 Vize Turkey
87 C2 Vizianagaram India
110 G3 Vizille France
115 K7 Vlădeasa, Vârful mt. Romania
117 H7 Vladikavkaz Rus. Fed.
116 F5 Vladimir Primorskiy Kray Rus. Fed.
116 G3 Vladimir Vladimirskaya Oblast' Rus. Fed.
94 C3 Vladimiro-Aleksandrovskoye Rus. Fed.
94 D3 Vladivostok Rus. Fed.
125 H2 Vlakte S. Africa
124 D7 Vleesbaai b. S. Africa
108 C2 Vlieland i. Neth.
108 C3 Vlijmen Neth.
108 B3 Vlissingen Neth.
115 H5 Vlorë Albania
112 G6 Vltava r. Czech Rep.
112 F6 Vöcklabruck Austria
116 D3 Vodlozero, Ozero l. Rus. Fed.
108 D2 Voe U.K.
108 D3 Voerendaal Neth.
109 H2 Vogelsberg hill Germany
114 C2 Voghera Italy
109 K5 Vohenstrauß Germany

123 E6 Vohimena, Tanjona c. Madag.
109 G3 Vöhl Germany
103 N4 Võhma Estonia
122 D4 Voi Kenya
120 B4 Voinjama Liberia
110 F2 Voiron France
103 J5 Vojens Denmark
115 H2 Vojvodina prov. Srbija Yugo.
116 H3 Vokhma Rus. Fed.
116 H3 Vokhma r. Rus. Fed.
138 F2 Volborg U.S.A.
159 B1 Volcán, Cerro del mt. Chile
90 G4 Volcano Islands Japan
83 J1 Volchikha Rus. Fed.
103 I3 Volda Norway
108 D2 Volendam Neth.
117 H5 Volga Rus. Fed.
134 B4 Volga r. U.S.A.
117 H5 Volga r. U.S.A.
117 G6 Volgodonsk Rus. Fed.
76 F4 Volgograd Rus. Fed.
117 H5 Volgogradskaya Oblast' admin. div. Rus. Fed.
112 G7 Völkermarkt Austria
116 D3 Volkhov Rus. Fed.
116 D3 Volkhov r. Rus. Fed.
109 G5 Völklingen Germany
125 H3 Volksrust S. Africa
94 B3 Vol'no-Nadezhdinskoye Rus. Fed.
117 E5 Volnovakha Ukr.
83 K2 Vol'noye Rus. Fed.
117 K2 Volochanka Rus. Fed.
117 C5 Volochys'k Ukr.
117 F6 Volodars'ke Ukr.
113 N5 Volodarskiy Rus. Fed.
117 M5 Volodymyrets' Ukr.
117 C5 Volodymyr-Volyns'kyy Ukr.
116 G3 Vologda Rus. Fed.
116 G3 Vologodskaya Oblast' admin. div. Rus. Fed.
116 G3 Volokonovka Rus. Fed.
115 J5 Volos Greece
116 D3 Volosovo Rus. Fed.
113 O2 Volot Rus. Fed.
116 F4 Volovo Rus. Fed.
117 H4 Vol'sk Rus. Fed.
120 C4 Volta, Lake resr Ghana
158 D3 Volta Redonda Brazil
114 F4 Volturno r. Italy
115 J5 Volvi, Limni l. Greece
116 I4 Volzhsk Rus. Fed.
82 B1 Volzhskiy Samarskaya Oblast' Rus. Fed.
117 H5 Volzhskiy Volgogradskaya Oblast' Rus. Fed.
123 E6 Vondrozo Madag.
116 G1 Vop' r. Rus. Fed.
102 G1 Vopnafjörður Iceland
102 H3 Vopnafjörður b. Iceland
116 B2 Vöra Fin.
116 B3 Voranava Belarus
117 F5 Vorchanka Ukr.
116 E2 Vorenzha Rus. Fed.
163 J1 Voring Plateau sea feature N. Atlantic Ocean
76 H3 Vorkuta Rus. Fed.
103 M4 Vormsi i. Estonia
117 F6 Vorona r. Rus. Fed.
117 F5 Voronezh Rus. Fed.
117 F5 Voronezh r. Rus. Fed.
117 G5 Voronezhskaya Oblast' admin. div. Rus. Fed.
113 P3 Vorot'kovo Rus. Fed.
116 I2 Vorskla r. Rus. Fed.
103 N4 Võrtsjärv l. Estonia
103 N4 Võru Estonia
83 G5 Vorukh Tajik.
124 E5 Vosburg S. Africa
110 H2 Vose Tajik.
110 H2 Vosges mts France
82 D1 Voskresenskoye Rus. Fed.
103 I3 Voss Norway
Vostochno-Sibirskoye More sea Rus. Fed. see East Siberian Sea
82 D4 Vostochnyy Chink Ustyurta esc. Uzbek.
83 J2 Vostochnyy Kazakhstan admin. div. Kazakh.
90 B1 Vostochnyy Sayan mts Rus. Fed.
73 C5 Vostok research station Antarctica
94 D1 Vostok Rus. Fed.
67 I5 Vostok Island Kiribati
94 D3 Vostretsovo Rus. Fed.
76 G4 Votkinsk Rus. Fed.
158 C3 Votuporanga Brazil
110 E2 Vouziers France
110 E2 Voves France
116 I3 Voya r. Rus. Fed.
144 A1 Voyageurs National Park U.S.A.
102 O2 Voynitsa Rus. Fed.
76 G2 Vozhe, Ozero l. Rus. Fed.
116 G2 Vozhega Rus. Fed.
117 D6 Voznesens'k Ukr.
83 D1 Voznesenye Rus. Fed.
82 D3 Vozrozhdeniya, Ostrov i. Uzbek.
82 C4 Vozvnye Uzbek.
94 C2 Vrangel' Rus. Fed.
115 J3 Vranje Yugo.
115 K3 Vratnik pass Bulg.
115 J3 Vratsa Bulg.
114 G2 Vrbas r. Bos.-Herz.
115 H2 Vrbas Yugo.
125 H3 Vrede S. Africa
125 F5 Vredefort S. Africa
124 B6 Vredenburg S. Africa
124 C6 Vredendal S. Africa
108 C3 Vresse Belgium
87 B4 Vriddhachalam India
108 E1 Vries Neth.
103 K4 Vrigstad Sweden
125 I2 Vryburg S. Africa
125 H3 Vryheid S. Africa
117 D5 Vsevolozhsk Rus. Fed.
115 H2 Vučitrn Yugo.
115 H2 Vukovar Croatia
76 H2 Vuktyl' Rus. Fed.
117 K7 Vulcan Romania
114 F5 Vulcano, Isola i. Isole Lipari Italy
103 N3 Vuohijärvi Fin.
102 M2 Vuollerim Sweden
102 N2 Vuostimo Fin.
116 H4 Vurnary Rus. Fed.
123 D4 Vwawa Tanz.
88 B5 Vyara India
116 I3 Vyatka r. Rus. Fed.
116 I3 Vyatka r. Rus. Fed. see Kirov
116 I3 Vyatskiye Polyany Rus. Fed.
94 D2 Vyazemskiy Rus. Fed.
116 E4 Vyaz'ma Rus. Fed.
116 G3 Vyazniki Rus. Fed.
116 D2 Vyborg Rus. Fed.
116 H2 Vychegda r. Rus. Fed.
112 H6 Vyerkhnyadzvinsk Belarus
112 H4 Vyetryna Belarus
116 D2 Vyg, Lake Rus. Fed.
116 I3 Vyksa Rus. Fed.
117 D6 Vylkove Ukr.
113 K6 Vynohradiv Ukr.
116 D2 Vypolzovo Rus. Fed.
116 D2 Vyritsa Rus. Fed.

105 D5 Vyrnwy, Lake U.K.
117 F6 Vysëlki Rus. Fed.
116 G4 Vysha Rus. Fed.
117 D5 Vyshhorod Ukr.
116 E3 Vyshnevolotskaya Gryada ridge Rus. Fed.
116 E3 Vyshniy-Volochek Rus. Fed.
112 H6 Vyškov Czech Rep.
117 D5 Vystupovychi Ukr.
116 F2 Vytegra Rus. Fed.

W

120 B3 Wa Ghana
108 D3 Waal r. Neth.
108 D3 Waalwijk Neth.
132 B3 Wabakimi Lake Canada
130 G3 Wabasca Canada
130 E4 Wabasca-Desmarais Canada
134 E5 Wabash U.S.A.
134 E5 Wabash r. U.S.A.
135 E1 Wabatongushi Lake Canada
122 E1 Wabē Gestro r. Eth.
122 E1 Wabē Shebelē Wenz r. Eth.
131 J4 Wabowden Canada
132 C2 Wabuk Point Canada
133 G3 Wabush Canada
140 C2 Wabuska U.S.A.
145 D6 Waccasassa Bay U.S.A.
109 I3 Wächtersbach Germany
143 D6 Waco U.S.A.
85 B5 Wad Pak.
71 H6 Wadbilliga Nat. Park Australia
121 D2 Waddān Libya
108 C2 Waddenzee sea chan. Neth.
68 B4 Waddamana Australia
130 E4 Waddington, Mount Canada
108 C2 Waddinxveen Neth.
105 C7 Wadebridge U.K.
131 I4 Wadena Canada
134 E2 Wadena U.S.A.
109 E5 Wadern Germany
88 B4 Wadhwan India
121 F3 Wad Hamid Sudan
121 F3 Wad Medani Sudan
140 C2 Wadsworth U.S.A.
84 B4 Wafangdian China
109 H2 Wagenfeld Germany
109 G2 Wagenfeld Germany
130 G2 Wager Bay Canada
70 D5 Wagga Wagga Australia
70 A5 Wagin Australia
140 □1 Wahiawā U.S.A.
109 H3 Wahlhausen Germany
142 D2 Wahoo U.S.A.
142 D2 Wahpeton U.S.A.
91 F7 Wah Wah Mountains U.S.A.
72 A6 Waiau N.Z.
72 A6 Waiau r. N.Z.
91 G7 Waidhofen an der Ybbs Austria
91 F7 Waigeo i. Indon.
72 E2 Waiheke Island N.Z.
72 E2 Waihi N.Z.
72 E2 Waihola N.Z.
72 B6 Waihou r. N.Z.
91 D7 Waikabubak Indon.
40 □1 Waikane U.S.A.
72 E2 Waikari N.Z.
140 □1 Waikele U.S.A.
140 □1 Waikiki Beach U.S.A.
140 □1 Waikoloa U.S.A.
72 D5 Waikouaiti N.Z.
91 D7 Waikabubak Indon.
72 E2 Wailua U.S.A.
140 □1 Waialee U.S.A.
140 □1 Waialua U.S.A.
140 □1 Waialua Bay U.S.A.
140 □1 Wai'anae U.S.A.
140 □1 Wai'anae Range mts U.S.A.
72 D5 Waiau r. N.Z.
72 C4 Waihaora r. N.Z.
91 D7 Waikabubak Indon.
140 □1 Waialee U.S.A.
140 □1 Wailuku U.S.A.
72 D5 Waimakariri r. N.Z.
72 C6 Waimangaroa N.Z.
72 E3 Waimarama N.Z.
72 C6 Waimate N.Z.
88 D6 Wainganga r. India
91 E7 Waingapu Indon.
105 C7 Wainhouse Corner U.K.
94 D1 Wainwright Canada
67 I5 Waiouru N.Z.
72 E2 Waipa r. N.Z.
72 C6 Waipahi N.Z.
72 D6 Waipapa Point N.Z.
72 C5 Waipara N.Z.
72 E3 Waipawa N.Z.
72 E2 Waipu N.Z.
72 E3 Waipukurau N.Z.
72 F3 Wairakei N.Z.
72 E4 Wairarapa, Lake N.Z.
72 D5 Wairau r. N.Z.
72 F3 Wairoa N.Z.
72 E2 Wairoa r. N.Z.
72 F3 Waitahanui N.Z.
72 E2 Waitakaruru N.Z.
72 C6 Waitaki r. N.Z.
72 E3 Waitara N.Z.
72 E2 Waitoa N.Z.
72 E3 Waitotara N.Z.
72 E2 Waiuku N.Z.
72 E2 Waiwera South N.Z.
93 E5 Waiyang China
95 D6 Wajima Japan
95 E6 Wakasa-wan b. Japan
72 B7 Wakatipu, Lake N.Z.
131 H4 Wakaw Canada
95 D7 Wakayama Japan
67 F2 Wake Atoll N. Pacific Ocean
142 D4 WaKeeney U.S.A.
135 J3 Wakefield Canada
105 F4 Wakefield U.K.
134 B2 Wakefield MI U.S.A.
146 E6 Wakefield VA U.S.A.
Wakeham Canada see Kangiqsujuaq
85 H3 Wakhan reg. Afgh.
116 H3 Wakinosawa Japan
94 G2 Wakkanai Japan
125 I3 Wakkerstroom S. Africa
70 F5 Wakool Australia
70 F5 Wakool r. Australia
71 J2 Walcha Australia
116 H4 Walchensee l. Germany
112 E7 Walcott U.S.A.
112 H4 Wałcz Poland
109 G3 Waldbröl Germany
109 G5 Waldkirch Germany
109 K6 Waldkraiburg Germany
146 E5 Waldoff U.S.A.
73 D5 Waldron, Cape Antarctica
105 C6 Wales admin. div. U.K.
71 H2 Walgett Australia
122 C3 Walikale Dem. Rep. Congo
140 C2 Walker Lake U.S.A.

73 A3 Walker Mountains Antarctica
140 C4 Walker Pass U.S.A.
145 G3 Walkerton Canada
142 C2 Wall U.S.A.
138 C2 Wallace U.S.A.
135 F4 Wallaceburg Canada
71 I2 Wallangarra Australia
70 A4 Wallaroo Australia
105 D4 Wallasey U.K.
71 G5 Walla Walla Australia
138 C3 Walla Walla U.S.A.
124 B5 Wallekraal S. Africa
71 H5 Wallendbeen Australia
147 F4 Wallenpaupack, Lake U.S.A.
105 F6 Wallingford U.K.
147 G4 Wallingford U.S.A.
69 I3 Wallis, Îles is Pacific Ocean
69 I3 Wallis and Futuna Islands terr. Pacific Ocean
71 J4 Wallis, Lake inlet Australia
146 E5 Wallops Island U.S.A.
138 C2 Wallowa Mountains U.S.A.
106 □ Walls U.K.
131 H2 Walmsley Lake Canada
104 D3 Walney, Isle of i. U.K.
134 C5 Walnut U.S.A.
141 H4 Walnut Canyon National Monument res. U.S.A.
143 E4 Walnut Ridge U.S.A.
89 I3 Walong India
105 F5 Walsall U.K.
139 F4 Walsenburg U.S.A.
109 H2 Walsrode Germany
87 C2 Waltair India
145 D5 Walterboro U.S.A.
145 C6 Walter F. George Reservoir U.S.A.
70 F2 Walter's Range hills Australia
135 I3 Walton KY U.S.A.
144 C4 Walton KY U.S.A.
147 F3 Walton NY U.S.A.
123 B6 Walvis Bay Namibia
163 I8 Walvis Ridge sea feature S. Atlantic Ocean
122 C3 Wamba Dem. Rep. Congo
85 B5 Wana Pak.
70 F2 Wanaaring Australia
72 B6 Wanaka N.Z.
72 B6 Wanaka, Lake N.Z.
93 C5 Wan'an China
135 G2 Wanapitei Lake Canada
147 F4 Wanaque Reservoir U.S.A.
70 D5 Wanbi Australia
72 C6 Wanbrow, Cape N.Z.
70 C2 Wancoocha, Lake salt flat Australia
94 C2 Wanda Shan mts China
109 I4 Wandersleben Germany
109 L2 Wandlitz Germany
96 D6 Wando S. Korea
98 A1 Wang, Mae Nam r. Thai.
72 B3 Wanganui N.Z.
72 E3 Wanganui r. N.Z.
71 G6 Wangaratta Australia
70 A5 Wangary Australia
93 D4 Wangcang China
109 F1 Wangerooge i. Germany
109 F1 Wangerooge Germany
96 B2 Wangjiang China
96 E2 Wangqing China
88 B5 Wankaner India
109 G1 Wanna Germany
93 E4 Wannian China
92 E1 Wanquan China
108 D3 Wanroij Neth.
93 D6 Wanshan Qundao is China
72 B3 Wanstead N.Z.
105 F6 Wantage U.K.
135 G2 Wanup Canada
93 C4 Wanxian China
93 C4 Wanyuan China
93 E4 Wanzai China
109 K2 Wanze Belgium
146 A4 Wapakoneta U.S.A.
134 B5 Wapello U.S.A.
132 D2 Wapikopa Lake Canada
130 F4 Wapiti r. Canada
143 F4 Wappapello Lake resr U.S.A.
134 A5 Wapsipinicon r. U.S.A.
92 B3 Waqên China
84 A4 Waqr well Saudi Arabia
87 B2 Warah Pak.
87 B2 Warangal India
70 F6 Waranga Reservoir Australia
71 F8 Waraseoni India
71 F8 Waratah Australia
71 H1 Waratah Bay Australia
109 H3 Warburg Germany
68 B4 Warburton Australia
70 B1 Warburton watercourse Australia
131 H2 Warburton Bay l. Canada
72 A6 Ward, Mount N.Z.
70 B5 Wardang Island Australia
109 G1 Wardenburg Germany
88 D5 Wardha India
88 D5 Wardha r. India
130 D3 Ware Canada
147 H3 Ware U.S.A.
108 B4 Waremme Belgium
109 K1 Waren Germany
109 G3 Warendorf Germany
71 J1 Warialda Australia
98 B2 Warin Chamrap Thai.
72 E4 Warkworth N.Z.
104 F3 Warkworth U.K.
108 A4 Warloy-Baillon France
131 H4 Warman Canada
124 C4 Warmbad Namibia
125 H2 Warmbad S. Africa
105 E6 Warminster U.K.
108 D2 Warmond Neth.
140 D2 Warm Springs NV U.S.A.
146 D5 Warm Springs VA U.S.A.
124 D6 Warmwaterberg mts S. Africa
147 H3 Warner U.S.A.
138 C3 Warner Mountains U.S.A.
145 D5 Warner Robins U.S.A.
154 B3 Warnes Bol.
70 A4 Warooka Australia
71 G2 Warracknabeal Australia
68 C4 Warrabri Australia
70 C2 Warrego r. Australia
70 E6 Warracknabeal Australia
71 I5 Warragamba Reservoir Australia
71 H7 Warragul Australia
70 C2 Warrakalanna, Lake salt flat Australia
70 A4 Warramboo Australia
71 G6 Warrambool r. Australia
68 E4 Warrego r. Australia
70 E1 Warrego r. Australia
71 H3 Warren Australia
135 G2 Warren Canada
143 E5 Warren AR U.S.A.
144 D2 Warren MI U.S.A.
142 D1 Warren MN U.S.A.
146 C4 Warren OH U.S.A.
146 E4 Warren PA U.S.A.
107 E3 Warrenpoint U.K.
142 E4 Warrensburg MO U.S.A.
147 G3 Warrensburg NY U.S.A.

124 F4 Warrenton S. Africa
146 E5 Warrenton U.S.A.
120 C4 Warri Nigeria
72 C6 Warrington N.Z.
105 E4 Warrington U.K.
145 C6 Warrington U.S.A.
70 C3 Warriota watercourse Australia
70 E7 Warrnambool Australia
142 E1 Warroad U.S.A.
70 A5 Warrow Australia
71 H3 Warrumbungle Range mts Australia
70 D2 Warry Warry watercourse Australia
113 J4 Warsaw Poland
134 E5 Warsaw IN U.S.A.
142 E4 Warsaw MO U.S.A.
146 D3 Warsaw NY U.S.A.
146 E6 Warsaw VA U.S.A.
109 G3 Warstein Germany
Warszawa Poland see Warsaw
112 G4 Warta r. Poland
71 J2 Warwick Australia
105 F5 Warwick U.K.
147 F4 Warwick NY U.S.A.
147 H4 Warwick RI U.S.A.
139 E4 Wasatch Range mts U.S.A.
125 I4 Wasbank S. Africa
140 C4 Wasco U.S.A.
142 E2 Waseca U.S.A.
85 F5 Washap Pak.
134 C5 Washburn IL U.S.A.
147 I1 Washburn ME U.S.A.
142 C2 Washburn ND U.S.A.
134 B2 Washburn WI U.S.A.
88 D5 Washim India
146 E5 Washington DC U.S.A. (City Plan 62)
145 D3 Washington GA U.S.A.
134 B5 Washington IA U.S.A.
134 C5 Washington IL U.S.A.
144 C4 Washington IN U.S.A.
142 F4 Washington MO U.S.A.
145 E5 Washington NC U.S.A.
147 F4 Washington NJ U.S.A.
146 C4 Washington PA U.S.A.
141 F3 Washington UT U.S.A.
138 B2 Washington state U.S.A.
73 B5 Washington, Cape Antarctica
147 H2 Washington, Mount U.S.A.
146 B5 Washington Court House U.S.A.
134 D3 Washington Island U.S.A.
129 L1 Washington Land reg. Greenland
143 D5 Washita r. U.S.A.
85 G5 Washuk Pak.
84 B5 Wasi' Saudi Arabia
81 K5 Wasit Iraq
132 E3 Waskaganish Canada
131 J3 Waskaiowaka Lake Canada
150 H5 Waspán Nicaragua
108 C2 Wassenaar Neth.
124 C3 Wasser Namibia
109 H4 Wasserkuppe hill Germany
109 I5 Wassertrüdingen Germany
140 C2 Wassuk Range mts U.S.A.
132 E4 Waswanipi, Lac l. Canada
91 E7 Watampone Indon.
147 G4 Waterbury CT U.S.A.
147 G2 Waterbury VT U.S.A.
131 H3 Waterbury Lake Canada
107 D5 Waterford Rep. of Ireland
146 D4 Waterford U.S.A.
107 E5 Waterford Harbour Rep. of Ireland
107 C5 Watergrasshill Rep. of Ireland
108 C4 Waterloo Belgium
135 G4 Waterloo Canada
134 A4 Waterloo ME U.S.A.
147 H3 Waterloo NY U.S.A.
146 E3 Waterloo NY U.S.A.
134 C4 Waterloo WI U.S.A.
105 F7 Waterlooville U.K.
125 H1 Waterpoort S. Africa
134 C2 Watersmeet U.S.A.
138 G5 Waterton Lakes National Park Canada
147 G3 Watertown NY U.S.A.
142 D2 Watertown SD U.S.A.
134 C4 Watertown WI U.S.A.
125 I2 Waterval-Boven S. Africa
70 C4 Watervale Australia
147 I2 Waterville U.S.A.
131 G3 Waterways Canada
105 G4 Watford Canada
105 G6 Watford U.K.
142 C2 Watford City U.S.A.
131 I3 Wathaman r. Canada
109 I2 Wathlingen Germany
146 E3 Watkins Glen U.S.A.
143 D5 Watonga U.S.A.
131 H4 Watrous Canada
122 C3 Watsa Dem. Rep. Congo
134 D5 Watseka U.S.A.
122 C4 Watsi Kengo Dem. Rep. Congo
131 I4 Watson Canada
130 D2 Watson Lake Canada
140 B3 Watsonville U.S.A.
106 E2 Watten U.K.
106 E2 Watten, Loch l. U.K.
131 I2 Watterson Lake Canada
70 A2 Wattiwarriganna watercourse Australia
105 H5 Watton U.K.
134 C2 Watton U.S.A.
68 C2 Watubela, Kepulauan is Indon.
68 E2 Wau P.N.G.
121 F4 Wau Sudan
134 D3 Waucedah U.S.A.
71 J3 Wauchope Australia
145 D7 Wauchula U.S.A.
134 C3 Waukegan U.S.A.
134 C4 Waukesha U.S.A.
134 B4 Waukon U.S.A.
143 C4 Waupaca U.S.A.
134 C4 Waupun U.S.A.
143 D5 Waurika U.S.A.
134 C3 Wausau U.S.A.
146 A4 Wauseon U.S.A.
134 C4 Wautoma U.S.A.
134 C4 Wauwatosa U.S.A.
105 I5 Waveney r. U.K.
134 A4 Waverly IA U.S.A.
146 B5 Waverly OH U.S.A.
145 C5 Waverly TN U.S.A.
146 E6 Waverly VA U.S.A.
108 C4 Wavre Belgium
134 E1 Wawa Canada
120 C4 Wawa Nigeria
134 E5 Wawasee, Lake U.S.A.
140 C3 Wawona U.S.A.
143 D5 Waxahachie U.S.A.
145 D6 Waycross U.S.A.
134 B6 Wayland KY U.S.A.
134 B6 Wayland MO U.S.A.
142 D3 Wayne U.S.A.
145 D5 Waynesboro GA U.S.A.
145 F6 Waynesboro MS U.S.A.
146 E5 Waynesboro PA U.S.A.
146 D5 Waynesboro VA U.S.A.
146 C5 Waynesville U.S.A.
143 D4 Waynoka U.S.A.
121 D4 Waza, Parc National de nat. park Cameroon
88 C2 Wazirabad Pak.
120 D3 W du Niger, Parcs Nationaux du nat. park Niger
99 A1 We, Pulau i. Indon.
132 B3 Weagamow Lake Canada
104 E3 Wear r. U.K.
69 B4 Weary Bay Australia
143 D5 Weatherford U.S.A.
138 B3 Weaverville U.S.A.

135 G2 Webbwood Canada
132 C3 Webequie Canada
130 D3 Weber, Mount Canada
162 M5 Weber Basin sea feature Indon.
122 E3 Webi Shabeelle r. Somalia
147 H3 Webster MA U.S.A.
142 D2 Webster SD U.S.A.
134 A3 Webster WI U.S.A.
142 E3 Webster City U.S.A.
146 C5 Webster Springs U.S.A.
162 B9 Weddell Abyssal Plain sea feature Southern Ocean
156 D8 Weddell Island Falkland Is
73 B2 Weddell Sea Antarctica
70 E6 Wedderburn Australia
109 H1 Wedel (Holstein) Germany
138 B3 Weed U.S.A.
146 D4 Weedville U.S.A.
71 I4 Weemelah Australia
108 F1 Weener Germany
108 D3 Weert Neth.
71 G4 Weethalle Australia
71 H3 Wee Waa Australia
108 E3 Wegberg Germany
113 J3 Wegorzewo Poland
92 E1 Weichang China
109 K4 Weida Germany
109 J5 Weidenberg Germany
109 K5 Weiden in der Oberpfalz Germany
92 F2 Weifang China
96 B5 Weihai China
92 B2 Wei He r. Henan China
92 B2 Wei He r. Shaanxi China
92 E3 Weihui China
96 D2 Weihu Ling mts China
109 G4 Weilburg Germany
71 G2 Weilmoringle Australia
109 J4 Weimar Germany
92 C3 Weinan China
109 G5 Weinheim Germany
93 B5 Weining China
109 H5 Weinsberg Germany
68 E3 Weipa Australia
71 H2 Weir r. Australia
131 K3 Weir River Canada
146 C4 Weirton U.S.A.
138 C2 Weiser U.S.A.
92 E3 Weishan Hu l. China
92 E3 Weishan China
92 E3 Weishi China
109 I5 Weißenburg in Bayern Germany
109 I5 Weißenfels Germany
145 C5 Weiss Lake U.S.A.
124 B2 Weissrand Mountains Namibia
109 G5 Weiterstadt Germany
93 B5 Weixin China
92 B3 Weiyuan Gansu China
93 B4 Weiyuan Sichuan China
112 G7 Weiz Austria
93 C6 Weizhou Dao i. China
96 B3 Weizi China
112 I3 Wejherowo Poland
131 J4 Wekusko Canada
131 J4 Wekusko Lake Canada
130 G2 Wekweti Canada
146 C5 Welch U.S.A.
147 H2 Weld U.S.A.
122 D3 Weldiya Eth.
140 C3 Weldon U.S.A.
122 D3 Welk'it'e Eth.
125 G3 Welkom S. Africa
135 H4 Welland r. Canada
135 H4 Welland Canal Canada
87 C5 Wellawaya Sri Lanka
135 G4 Wellesley Canada
69 B3 Wellesley Islands Australia
130 B2 Wellesley Lake Canada
147 H4 Wellfleet U.S.A.
108 D4 Wellin Belgium
105 G5 Wellingborough U.K.
71 H4 Wellington N.S.W. Australia
70 C5 Wellington S. Australia
72 E4 Wellington N.Z.
124 C6 Wellington S. Africa
105 D7 Wellington England U.K.
105 E6 Wellington England U.K.
138 F3 Wellington CO U.S.A.
143 D4 Wellington KS U.S.A.
140 C2 Wellington NV U.S.A.
146 B4 Wellington OH U.S.A.
143 C5 Wellington TX U.S.A.
141 G2 Wellington UT U.S.A.
156 A7 Wellington, Isla i. Chile
71 G7 Wellington, Lake Australia
134 B5 Wellman U.S.A.
130 E4 Wells Canada
105 E6 Wells U.K.
134 E6 Wells U.S.A.
138 D3 Wells NV U.S.A.
147 F3 Wells NY U.S.A.
68 C4 Wells, Lake salt flat Australia
146 E3 Wellsboro U.S.A.
72 E2 Wellsford N.Z.
130 E4 Wells Gray Provincial Park Canada
105 H5 Wells-next-the-Sea U.K.
146 B5 Wellston U.S.A.
146 E3 Wellsville U.S.A.
141 E5 Wellton U.S.A.
112 G6 Wels Austria
105 D5 Welshpool Canada
105 D5 Welshpool U.K.
109 L3 Welsickendorf Germany
105 G6 Welwyn Garden City U.K.
105 H6 Welzheim Germany
109 F3 Wembley Canada
132 E3 Wemindji Canada
145 E7 Wemyss Bight Bahamas
138 B2 Wenatchee U.S.A.
93 F5 Wencheng China
93 F5 Wenchang China
92 B4 Wenchuan China
109 J5 Wendelstein Germany
109 H4 Wenden Germany
141 F5 Wenden U.S.A.
96 B5 Wendeng China
122 D3 Wendo Eth.
138 D3 Wendover U.S.A.
135 F2 Wenebegon Lake Canada
93 C5 Weng'an China
109 G4 Wengerohr Germany
93 J3 Wengyuan China
92 B4 Wen He r. China
92 B4 Wenjiang China
93 F4 Wenling China
154 □ Wenman, Isla i. Galapagos Is Ecuador
134 C3 Wenona U.S.A.
93 C5 Wenquan China
93 B6 Wenshan China
83 J4 Wensu China
105 H5 Wensum r. U.K.
109 I1 Wentorf bei Hamburg Germany
70 D5 Wentworth Australia
145 D5 Wentworth U.S.A.
92 B3 Wenxian China
93 E5 Wenzhou China
109 K2 Wenzlow Germany
125 G4 Wepener S. Africa
124 D2 Werda Botswana
109 K2 Werdau Germany
109 K2 Werder Germany
109 I3 Werl Germany
109 K5 Wernberg-Köblitz Germany
109 I3 Werne Germany
130 C2 Wernecke Mountains Canada
109 J4 Wernigerode Germany
109 H3 Werra r. Germany
70 D5 Werrimull Australia

71 I3 Werris Creek Australia
109 H5 Wertheim Germany
108 B4 Wervik Belgium
108 E3 Wesel Germany
108 E3 Wesel-Datteln-Kanal canal Germany
109 K1 Wesenberg Germany
109 I2 Wesendorf Germany
109 H2 Weser r. Germany
109 G1 Weser sea chan. Germany
109 H2 Wesergebirge hill Germany
142 C4 Weskan U.S.A.
147 J2 Wesley U.S.A.
133 J4 Wesleyville Canada
68 D3 Wessel, Cape Australia
68 D3 Wessel Islands Australia
125 H3 Wesselton S. Africa
142 D2 Wessington Springs U.S.A.
134 D2 West Allis U.S.A.
73 A4 West Antarctica reg. Antarctica
162 K6 West Australian Basin sea feature Indian Ocean
88 B5 West Banas r. India
80 B5 West Bank terr. Asia
133 I3 West Bay Canada
143 F6 West Bay b. U.S.A.
134 C4 West Bend U.S.A.
89 F5 West Bengal state India
135 E3 West Branch U.S.A.
105 F5 West Bromwich U.K.
147 H3 Westbrook U.S.A.
106 □ West Burra i. U.K.
71 J4 Westbury Australia
105 E6 Westbury U.K.
71 G5 Westby Australia
134 B4 Westby U.S.A.
160 E5 West Caroline Basin sea feature N. Pacific Ocean
147 F5 West Chester U.S.A.
147 G2 West Danville U.S.A.
135 F3 West Duck Island Canada
145 E7 West End Bahamas
140 D4 Westend U.S.A.
145 D7 West End Point Bahamas
109 F4 Westerburg Germany
108 F1 Westerholt Germany
112 D3 Westerland Germany
108 C3 Westerlo Belgium
147 H4 Westerly U.S.A.
147 H1 Western r. Canada
68 C4 Western Australia state Australia
124 D6 Western Cape prov. S. Africa
121 E2 Western Desert Egypt
Western Dvina r. Europe see Zapadnaya Dvina
87 A2 Western Ghats mts India
70 F7 Western Port b. Australia
120 A2 Western Sahara terr. Africa
108 B3 Westerschelde est. Neth.
109 F1 Westerstede Germany
109 F4 Westerwald reg. Germany
156 D8 West Falkland i. Falkland Is
142 D2 West Fargo U.S.A.
134 D5 Westfield IN U.S.A.
147 G3 Westfield MA U.S.A.
147 J1 Westfield ME U.S.A.
146 D3 Westfield NY U.S.A.
108 C1 West Frisian Islands is Neth.
108 E1 Westgat sea chan. Germany
147 G2 West Grand Lake U.S.A.
109 I6 Westhausen Germany
106 F3 Westhill U.K.
142 C1 Westhope U.S.A.
73 D5 West Ice Shelf Antarctica
108 B3 Westkapelle Neth.
93 □ West Lamma Channel Hong Kong China
146 B5 West Lancaster U.S.A.
72 B5 Westland National Park N.Z.
105 I5 Westleton U.K.
140 B3 Westley U.S.A.
146 B6 West Liberty KY U.S.A.
146 C4 West Liberty OH U.S.A.
106 F2 West Linton U.K.
106 B2 West Loch Roag b. U.K.
130 G4 Westlock Canada
135 G4 West Lorne Canada
108 C3 Westmalle Belgium
160 E4 West Mariana Basin sea feature Pacific Ocean
143 F5 West Memphis U.S.A.
146 E5 Westminster MD U.S.A.
145 D5 Westminster SC U.S.A.
146 C5 Weston U.S.A.
105 E6 Weston-super-Mare U.K.
145 D7 West Palm Beach U.S.A.
143 E4 West Plains U.S.A.
70 A5 West Point pt U.S.A.
71 H8 West Point Tas. Australia
143 F5 West Point MS U.S.A.
147 F4 West Point NY U.S.A.
135 I3 Westport Canada
72 C5 Westport N.Z.
107 B4 Westport Rep. of Ireland
140 A2 Westport U.S.A.
131 I4 Westray r. Canada
106 E1 Westray i. U.K.
135 G2 Westree Canada
108 F5 Westrich reg. Germany
130 E4 West Road r. Canada
76 J3 West Siberian Plain plain Rus. Fed.
71 G7 West Sister Island Australia
147 H2 West Stewartstown U.S.A.
108 D1 West-Terschelling Neth.
147 H4 West Tisbury U.S.A.
147 H3 West Townshend U.S.A.
134 B4 West Union IA U.S.A.
146 B5 West Union OH U.S.A.
146 C5 West Union WV U.S.A.
134 C5 Westville U.S.A.
146 C5 West Virginia state U.S.A.
140 C2 West Walker r. U.S.A.
140 B1 Westwood U.S.A.
71 G4 West Wyalong Australia
138 E2 West Yellowstone U.S.A.
108 C2 Westzaan Neth.
91 E7 Wetar i. Indon.
130 G4 Wetaskiwin Canada
135 F2 Wetmore U.S.A.
109 G4 Wetter r. Germany
109 J3 Wettin Germany
109 G5 Wetzlar Germany
68 E2 Wewak P.N.G.
107 E5 Wexford Rep. of Ireland
131 H4 Weyakwin Canada
134 C3 Weyauwega U.S.A.
105 G6 Weybridge U.K.
131 I5 Weyburn Canada
105 D6 Weymouth U.K.
147 H3 Weymouth U.S.A.
72 F2 Whakaari i. N.Z.
72 F2 Whakatane N.Z.
72 F3 Whakatane r. N.Z.
131 I2 Whale Cove Canada
106 □ Whalsay i. U.K.
72 E2 Whangamata N.Z.
72 E3 Whangamomona N.Z.
72 E2 Whangarei N.Z.
132 C3 Whapmagoostui Canada
104 F4 Wharfe r. U.K.
135 F2 Wharncliffe Canada
131 I2 Wharton Lake Canada
130 F2 Wha Ti Canada
138 F3 Wheatland U.S.A.

134 C5 Wheaton U.S.A.
139 F4 Wheeler Peak mt. NM U.S.A.
141 E2 Wheeler Peak mt. NV U.S.A.
146 C4 Wheeling U.S.A.
159 E2 Wheelwright Arg.
104 E3 Whernside hill U.K.
70 A5 Whidbey, Point Australia
138 B3 Whiskeytown Shasta Trinity National Recreation Area res. U.S.A.
106 E5 Whitburn U.K.
135 H4 Whitby Canada
104 F4 Whitby U.K.
105 E5 Whitchurch U.K.
130 A2 White r. Canada/U.S.A.
143 E4 White r. AR U.S.A.
141 G5 White r. CO U.S.A.
134 C4 White r. IN U.S.A.
134 C4 White r. MI U.S.A.
138 E3 White r. NV U.S.A.
142 C3 White r. SD U.S.A.
134 B2 White r. WI U.S.A.
68 C4 White, Lake salt flat Australia
133 I3 White Bay Canada
142 C2 White Butte mt. U.S.A.
70 E3 White Cliffs Australia
138 B3 White Cloud U.S.A.
120 F4 Whitecourt Canada
134 A2 Whiteface Lake U.S.A.
147 H2 Whitefield U.S.A.
135 G2 Whitefish Canada
138 D1 Whitefish U.S.A.
134 D1 Whitefish r. U.S.A.
131 H2 Whitefish Lake Canada
134 E2 Whitefish Point U.S.A.
146 E3 Whitehall r. Rep. of Ireland
106 F1 Whitehall U.K.
147 G3 Whitehall NY U.S.A.
134 B3 Whitehall WI U.S.A.
104 D3 Whitehaven U.K.
107 F3 Whitehead U.K.
105 G6 Whitehill U.K.
130 B2 Whitehorse Canada
70 F6 White Horse, Vale of valley U.K.
141 E1 White Horse Pass U.S.A.
73 D4 White Island Antarctica
143 E6 White Lake LA U.S.A.
134 D4 White Lake MI U.S.A.
140 C3 White Mountain Peak mt. U.S.A.
147 H2 White Mountains U.S.A.
121 F3 White Nile r. Sudan/Uganda
 alt. Abiad, Bahr el,
 alt. Jebel, Bahr el
124 C1 White Nossob watercourse Namibia
141 E2 White Pine Range mts U.S.A.
147 G4 White Plains U.S.A.
132 C4 White River Canada
145 H5 Whiteriver U.S.A.
147 G3 White River Junction U.S.A.
141 F3 White River Valley U.S.A.
141 E2 White Rock Peak mt. U.S.A.
139 F5 White Sands National Monument res. U.S.A.
146 B6 Whitesburg U.S.A.
76 B3 White Sea Rus. Fed.
131 J4 Whiteshell Provincial Park Canada
138 E2 White Sulphur Springs MT U.S.A.
146 C6 White Sulphur Springs WV U.S.A.
145 E5 Whiteville U.S.A.
120 B4 White Volta r. Ghana
134 C4 Whitewater U.S.A.
141 H5 Whitewater Baldy mt. U.S.A.
122 C3 Whitewater Lake Canada
131 I4 Whitewood Canada
71 G6 Whitfield Australia
106 D6 Whithorn U.K.
72 E2 Whitianga N.Z.
147 J2 Whiting U.S.A.
105 C6 Whitland U.K.
147 F2 Whitley Bay U.K.
145 D5 Whitmire U.S.A.
135 H3 Whitney Canada
140 C3 Whitney, Mount U.S.A.
143 D6 Whitney, Lake U.S.A.
105 H6 Whitstable U.K.
68 E4 Whitsunday Island Australia
70 F6 Whittlesea Australia
105 G5 Whittlesey U.K.
71 G5 Whitton Australia
131 H2 Wholdaia Lake Canada
141 F5 Why U.S.A.
70 B4 Whyalla Australia
98 B1 Wiang Sa Thai.
135 G3 Wiarton Canada
108 B3 Wichelen Belgium
143 D4 Wichita U.S.A.
143 D5 Wichita Falls U.S.A.
143 D5 Wichita Mountains U.S.A.
106 E2 Wick U.K.
141 F5 Wickenburg U.S.A.
105 H6 Wickford U.K.
71 E7 Wickham, Cape Australia
107 E5 Wicklow Rep. of Ireland
107 E5 Wicklow Head Rep. of Ireland
107 E5 Wicklow Mountains Rep. of Ireland
107 E4 Wicklow Mountains National Park Rep. of Ireland
71 G2 Widgeegoara watercourse Australia
96 D6 Wi-do i. S. Korea
109 G2 Wiehengebirge hill Germany
108 F4 Wiehl Germany
113 I5 Wieluń Poland
Wien Austria see Vienna
112 H7 Wiener Neustadt Austria
108 E2 Wierden Neth.
108 D2 Wieringermeer Polder Neth.
108 D2 Wieringerwerf Neth.
109 G4 Wiesbaden Germany
109 I5 Wiesenfelden Germany
109 I5 Wiesentheid Germany
109 G5 Wiesloch Germany
109 F1 Wiesmoor Germany
109 H2 Wietze Germany
109 H2 Wietzendorf Germany
112 I3 Więcbork Poland
104 E4 Wigan U.K.
68 E2 Wigina P.N.G.
143 F6 Wiggins U.S.A.
105 F7 Wight, Isle of i. U.K.
104 E4 Wigston U.K.
104 D4 Wigton U.K.
106 D6 Wigtown U.K.
106 D6 Wigtown Bay U.K.
108 E2 Wijhe Neth.
108 D2 Wijnegem Belgium
140 D2 Wildcat Peak mt. U.S.A.
124 D7 Wild Coast S. Africa
109 I5 Wildeshausen Germany
134 C1 Wild Goose Canada
131 G4 Wildhay r. Canada
70 D3 Wilcannia Australia
109 J4 Wildberg Germany
71 F9 Wild Rivers Nat. Park Australia
145 D5 Wildwood FL U.S.A.
147 F5 Wildwood NJ U.S.A.
125 H3 Wilge r. Free State S. Africa

125 H2 Wilge r. Gauteng/Mpumalanga S. Africa
70 A3 Wilgena Australia
146 C4 Wilhelm, Lake P.N.G.
68 E2 Wilhelm, Mount P.N.G.
109 G1 Wilhelmshaven Germany
147 F4 Wilkes-Barre U.S.A.
73 B6 Wilkes Coast Antarctica
73 B6 Wilkes Land reg. Antarctica
131 H4 Wilkie Canada
73 B2 Wilkins Coast Antarctica
73 B2 Wilkins Ice Shelf Antarctica
130 D3 Will, Mount Canada
138 B2 Willamette r. U.S.A.
105 D7 Willand U.K.
70 F4 Willandra Billabong watercourse Australia
138 B1 Willapa Bay U.S.A.
146 B4 Willard U.S.A.
147 F5 Willards U.S.A.
141 H5 Willcox U.S.A.
108 C3 Willebroek Belgium
149 K6 Willemstad Neth. Antilles
131 H3 William r. Canada
70 E6 William, Mount Australia
70 B2 William Creek Australia
141 F4 Williams AZ U.S.A.
140 A2 Williams CA U.S.A.
134 A5 Williamsburg IA U.S.A.
146 A6 Williamsburg KY U.S.A.
134 E3 Williamsburg MI U.S.A.
146 E6 Williamsburg VA U.S.A.
145 E7 Williams Island Bahamas
130 E4 Williams Lake Canada
133 H1 William Smith, Cap c. Canada
146 C5 Williamson U.S.A.
134 D5 Williamsport IN U.S.A.
146 E4 Williamsport PA U.S.A.
145 E5 Williamston U.S.A.
147 H3 Williamstown MA U.S.A.
147 F3 Williamstown NY U.S.A.
146 C5 Williamstown WV U.S.A.
147 G4 Willimantic U.S.A.
130 F4 Willingdon Canada
70 B3 Willochra watercourse Australia
130 E4 Willow r. Canada
131 H5 Willow Bunch Canada
146 E4 Willow Hill U.S.A.
130 F2 Willow Lake Canada
124 C5 Willowmore S. Africa
134 C3 Willow Reservoir U.S.A.
140 A2 Willows U.S.A.
143 F4 Willow Springs U.S.A.
71 I3 Willow Tree Australia
125 H6 Willowvale S. Africa
68 C4 Wills, Lake salt flat Australia
70 C5 Willunga Australia
147 F5 Wilmington DE U.S.A.
145 E5 Wilmington NC U.S.A.
146 B5 Wilmington OH U.S.A.
147 G3 Wilmington VT U.S.A.
105 I4 Wilmslow U.K.
109 G4 Wilnsdorf Germany
142 D2 Wilmot U.S.A.
131 J5 Wilson Canada
147 I2 Winn U.S.A.
68 C4 Wilson, Mount CO U.S.A.
139 F4 Wilson, Mount CO U.S.A.
141 E2 Wilson, Mount NV U.S.A.
73 B5 Wilson Hills Antarctica
142 D4 Wilson Reservoir U.S.A.
147 H2 Wilsons Mills U.S.A.
71 G7 Wilson's Promontory pen.
71 G7 Wilson's Promontory National Park Australia
108 E2 Wilsum Germany
130 C2 Wolf r. Canada
134 C3 Wolf r. U.S.A.
154 □ Wolf, Volcán vol. Galapagos Is Ecuador
138 D2 Wolf Creek U.S.A.
139 F4 Wolf Creek Pass U.S.A.
147 H3 Wolfeboro U.S.A.
135 I3 Wolfe Island Canada
109 K3 Wolfen Germany
109 I2 Wolfenbüttel Germany
109 I4 Wolfhagen Germany
112 G7 Wolfsberg Austria
109 I2 Wolfsburg Germany
108 F5 Wolfstein Germany
133 H4 Wolfville Canada
112 H4 Wolgast Germany
112 G4 Wolin Poland
156 B8 Wollaston, Islas is Chile
131 I3 Wollaston Lake Canada
131 I3 Wollaston Lake l. Canada
128 G3 Wollaston Peninsula Canada
71 I5 Wollongong Australia
125 I3 Wolmaransstad S. Africa
109 J2 Wolmirstedt Germany
70 D6 Wolseley Australia
125 C6 Wolseley S. Africa
105 F6 Wolsingham U.K.
105 F5 Wolverhampton U.K.
105 F5 Wolverton U.K.
134 E3 Wolverine U.S.A.
108 E5 Wommelgem Belgium
109 G3 Womrather Höhe hill Germany
70 D3 Wongalarroo Lake salt l. Australia
71 H4 Wongarbon Australia
89 G4 Wong Chhu r. Bhutan
93 □ Wong Chuk Hang Hong Kong China
96 D5 Wŏnju S. Korea
70 E3 Wonomita watercourse Australia
96 C4 Wŏnsan N. Korea
70 D7 Wonthaggi Australia
70 B3 Woocalla Australia
68 D1 Woodah, Isle i. Australia
105 I5 Woodbridge U.K.
147 F5 Woodbridge U.S.A.
130 G3 Wood Buffalo National Park Canada
71 J2 Woodburn Australia
138 B2 Woodburn U.S.A.
134 E3 Woodbury MI U.S.A.
147 F5 Woodbury NJ U.S.A.
140 A6 Wood Creek Lake U.S.A.
140 B2 Woodfords U.S.A.
140 B2 Woodland U.S.A.
139 F4 Woodland Park U.S.A.
98 □ Woodlands Sing.
69 F2 Woodlark Island P.N.G.
138 E3 Woodruff U.S.A.
68 C4 Woods, Lake salt flat Australia
131 K5 Woods, Lake of the Canada/U.S.A.
146 D5 Woodsfield U.S.A.
71 G6 Woods Point Australia
135 G4 Woodstock Ont. Canada
133 H4 Woodstock N.B. Canada
105 F6 Woodstock U.K.
134 C5 Woodstock IL U.S.A.
146 E5 Woodstock VA U.S.A.
147 G2 Woodsville U.S.A.

72 E4 Woodville N.Z.
146 E3 Woodville NY U.S.A.
143 E5 Woodville TX U.S.A.
143 D4 Woodward U.S.A.
104 E2 Wooler U.K.
71 J3 Woolgoolga Australia
71 J2 Wooli Australia
70 C3 Wooltana Australia
70 B3 Woomera Australia
70 A4 Woomera Prohibited Area res. Australia
147 H4 Woonsocket U.S.A.
146 E4 Wooster U.S.A.
109 I3 Worbis Germany
124 C6 Worcester S. Africa
109 G6 Worcester U.K.
147 H3 Worcester U.S.A.
112 F7 Wörgl Austria
104 D3 Workington U.K.
105 F4 Worksop U.K.
138 F2 Workum Neth.
138 F2 Worland U.S.A.
109 K3 Wörlitz Germany
108 C2 Wormerveer Neth.
123 B5 Worms Germany
105 C6 Worms Head U.K.
124 B1 Wortel Namibia
109 G5 Wörth am Rhein Germany
105 G7 Worthing U.K.
142 E3 Worthington U.S.A.
160 G6 Wotje atoll Marshall Is
81 E7 Wotu Indon.
108 C3 Woudrichem Neth.
142 C3 Wounded Knee U.S.A.
108 F5 Woustviller France
91 E7 Wowoni i. Indon.
77 T4 Wrangel Island Rus. Fed.
130 C3 Wrangell U.S.A.
130 C3 Wrangell Island U.S.A.
128 C4 Wrangell Mountains U.S.A.
105 F5 Wrath, Cape U.K.
142 C3 Wray U.S.A.
105 F5 Wreake r. U.K.
124 B4 Wreck Point S. Africa
109 I2 Wrestedt Germany
105 E4 Wrexham U.K.
97 C4 Wright Phil.
138 F3 Wright U.S.A.
131 E5 Wright Patman Lake U.S.A.
141 G6 Wrightson, Mount U.S.A.
130 E2 Wrigley Canada
112 H5 Wrocław Poland
112 H4 Września Poland
92 E2 Wu'an China
92 D2 Wubu China
90 D1 Wuchang China
92 C4 Wuchuan Guizhou China
92 D1 Wuchuan Nei Mongol China
92 C2 Wuda China
92 F1 Wudan China
92 D3 Wudang Shan mt. China
92 C3 Wudang Shan mts China
96 A4 Wudao China
89 H2 Wudaoliang China
93 B5 Wuding China
92 D2 Wuding He r. China
70 A4 Wudinna Australia
92 B3 Wudu China
93 D4 Wufeng China
93 D5 Wugang China
92 C3 Wugong China
92 E2 Wuhai China
93 E4 Wuhan China
92 E3 Wuhe China
93 E6 Wuhu China
93 E6 Wuhua China
88 D3 Wüjiang China
93 C6 Wujia China
93 C4 Wu Jiang r. China
120 C4 Wukari Nigeria
89 H3 Wular Lake India
88 C2 Wular Lake India
96 B5 Wuleidao Wan i. China
92 F3 Wulian China
93 B4 Wulian Feng mts China
90 C4 Wuliang Shan mts China
91 F7 Wuliaru i. Indon.
93 C4 Wuling Shan mts China
93 B5 Wumeng Shan mts China
93 C6 Wuming China
109 H1 Wümme r. Germany
92 A4 Wungda China
93 E4 Wuning China
109 G3 Wünnenberg Germany
109 K4 Wunsiedel Germany
109 H2 Wunstorf Germany
90 B4 Wuntho Myanmar
141 G4 Wupatki National Monument res. U.S.A.
93 E5 Wuping China
108 F3 Wuppertal Germany
124 C6 Wuppertal S. Africa
92 C2 Wuqi China
83 H5 Wuqia China
92 E2 Wuqiang China
92 E3 Wuqiao China
109 H5 Wuqing China
109 G5 Würzburg Germany
109 K5 Wurzen Germany
92 B3 Wushan Gansu China
92 C4 Wushan Sichuan China
92 D4 Wu Shan mts China
92 C3 Wusheng China
93 B6 Wushi Guangdong China
83 I4 Wushi Xinjiang China
109 H3 Wüstegarten hill Germany
92 D1 Wutai China
68 E2 Wuvulu Island P.N.G.
92 E4 Wuwei Anhui China
92 B2 Wuwei Gansu China
92 F4 Wuxi Jiangsu China
92 C2 Wuxi Sichuan China
Wuxing China see Huzhou
93 C6 Wuxu China
93 C5 Wuxuan China
93 E4 Wuxue China
92 D3 Wuyang China
93 F4 Wuyi China
93 C6 Wuyiling China
93 F5 Wuyishan China
93 E5 Wuyi Shan mts China
93 B3 Wuyuan Jiangxi China
92 C1 Wuyuan Nei Mongol China
92 D4 Wuzhai China
92 D3 Wuzhen China
92 D3 Wuzhong China
93 D6 Wuzhou China
134 B5 Wyaconda U.S.A.
71 H4 Wyalong Australia
135 F4 Wyandotte U.S.A.
134 C5 Wyanet U.S.A.
71 H4 Wyangala Reservoir Australia
70 F2 Wyara, Lake salt flat Australia
70 E6 Wycheproof Australia
105 I6 Wye r. U.K.
105 I6 Wylye r. U.K.
70 C5 Wynbring Australia
105 I5 Wymondham U.K.
70 F6 Wyndham Australia
70 D5 Wyndham-Werribee Australia
143 F5 Wynne U.S.A.
128 C2 Wynniatt Bay Canada
71 H8 Wynyard Australia
131 H4 Wynyard Canada
134 C5 Wyoming IL U.S.A.
135 F4 Wyoming MI U.S.A.
138 E3 Wyoming state U.S.A.
138 E3 Wyoming Peak mt. U.S.A.
71 I4 Wyong Australia
147 I7 Wyperfeld National Park Australia
104 E4 Wyre r. U.K.
147 E4 Wysox U.S.A.
113 J4 Wyszków Poland
105 F5 Wythall U.K.

146 C6 Wytheville U.S.A.
147 I2 Wytopitlock U.S.A.

X

122 F2 Xaafuun Somalia
82 A4 Xaçmaz Azer.
124 E1 Xade Botswana
89 H3 Xagquka China
88 D1 Xaidulla China
89 G3 Xainza China
123 D6 Xai-Xai Moz.
151 G3 Xal, Cerro de hills Mex.
92 C1 Xamba China
91 C4 Xam Hua Laos
98 B1 Xan r. Laos
98 C2 Xan, Xê r. Vietnam
123 C6 Xanagas Botswana
92 B1 Xangd China
92 D1 Xangdin Hural China
89 E2 Xangdoring China
123 B5 Xangongo Angola
81 K2 Xankändi Azer.
115 K4 Xanthi Greece
154 E6 Xapuri Brazil
81 L2 Xaraba Şähär Sayı i. Azer.
89 F3 Xärä Zirä Adası is Azer.
92 D1 Xar Moron r. Nei Mongol China
92 F1 Xar Moron r. Nei Mongol China
111 F3 Xàtiva Spain
123 C6 Xau, Lake Botswana
155 I6 Xavantes, Serra dos hills Brazil
98 C3 Xa Vo Đat Vietnam
83 J4 Xayar China
83 I5 Xekar China
146 B5 Xenia U.S.A.
96 F1 Xiachengzi China
92 D6 Xiachuan Dao i. China
92 B3 Xiahe China
92 E2 Xiajin China
93 F5 Xiamen China
92 C3 Xi'an China
92 C4 Xianfeng China
92 E3 Xiangcheng Henan China
92 D3 Xiangcheng Henan China
92 B3 Xiangfan China
98 B1 Xiangkhoang Laos
93 F4 Xiangshan China
93 D5 Xiangxiang China
93 D4 Xiangyin China
93 D4 Xianju China
93 D4 Xiantao China
93 E5 Xianxia Ling mts China
92 C3 Xianxian China
92 C3 Xianyang China
93 F5 Xianyou China
93 D4 Xiaochang China
93 D4 Xiaodong China
93 D4 Xiaogan China
90 E1 Xiao Hinggan Ling mts China
93 D4 Xiaojin China
92 H2 Xiaonanchuan China
93 E4 Xiaoshan China
93 E5 Xiaoxiang Ling mts China
92 D2 Xiaoyi China
92 F5 Xiapu China
96 A2 Xiawa China
92 D3 Xiayukou China
93 B5 Xichang China
92 C3 Xichong China
93 B6 Xichou China
93 D4 Xichuan China
93 B4 Xide China
157 D4 Xié r. Brazil
93 C6 Xieyang Dao i. China
93 F4 Xifei He r. China
92 C3 Xifeng Gansu China
93 C5 Xifeng Guizhou China
92 F2 Xifeng Liaoning China
79 G4 Xigazê China
93 B3 Xihan Shui r. China
92 C3 Xihe China
96 A3 Xi He r. China
92 A1 Xi He watercourse China
92 B3 Xiji China
93 D1 Xi Jiang r. China
89 G2 Xijir China
92 D1 Xijir Ulan Hu salt l. China
92 B2 Xil China
96 B2 Xiliao He r. China
92 E1 Xilinhot China
92 A1 Ximiao China
92 C2 Xin China
93 F4 Xin'anjiang China
92 F4 Xin'anjiang Shuiku resr China
125 J2 Xinavane Moz.
96 C3 Xinbin China
92 D1 Xin Bulag China
92 E1 Xincai China
92 A2 Xincheng Gansu China
93 C5 Xincheng Guangxi China
92 C2 Xincheng Ningxia China
92 C2 Xingcheng China
92 D6 Xindu Guangdong China
92 B3 Xindu Sichuan China
93 E5 Xinfeng Guangdong China
93 E5 Xinfeng Jiangxi China
93 E5 Xinfengjiang Shuiku resr China
93 D5 Xing'an China
94 A4 Xing'an China
92 F1 Xingcheng China
93 E5 Xingguo China
79 H3 Xinghai China
92 D1 Xinghe China
93 E3 Xinghua China
94 C2 Xingkai Hu l. China/Rus. Fed. see Khanka, Lake
93 E5 Xingning Guangdong China
93 D5 Xingning Hunan China
93 D4 Xingou China
93 A3 Xingren China
93 D4 Xingshan China
92 E2 Xingtai China
155 H6 Xingu, Parque Indígena do nat. park Brazil
93 B4 Xingwen China
93 D2 Xingxian China
93 C6 Xingye China
93 D6 Xingyi China
93 E4 Xingzi China
83 J4 Xinhe China
92 E1 Xin Hot China
93 D5 Xinhua China
92 D5 Xinhuacun China
92 B3 Xinhuang China
93 D6 Xinhui Guangdong China
92 F1 Xinhui Nei Mongol China
92 H2 Xinmenzhuang China
92 E1 Xinji China
93 J4 Xinjian China
92 D3 Xinjie China
89 D1 Xinjiang Uygur Zizhiqu aut. reg. China
92 C2 Xinjie Nei Mongol China
93 B6 Xinjie Yunnan China

93 B4 Xinjin China
96 B1 Xinkai He r. China
96 B3 Xinmin China
93 D5 Xinning China
92 C2 Xinqian China
93 D5 Xinshao China
92 E3 Xintai China
93 D5 Xintian China
92 E4 Xinxian China
92 D3 Xinxiang China
93 D6 Xinxing China
92 E3 Xinyang China
93 F3 Xinyi Guangdong China
92 F3 Xinyi Jiangsu China
93 I He r. China
93 C7 Xinying China
93 E5 Xinyu China
83 J4 Xinyuan China
92 D2 Xinzhou Shanxi China
92 D2 Xinzhou Shanxi China
111 C1 Xinzo de Limia Spain
96 B3 Xiongyuecheng China
92 E3 Xiping Henan China
92 E3 Xiping Henan China
92 A3 Xiqing Shan mts China
155 J6 Xique Xique Brazil
92 C1 Xishanzui China
92 C4 Xishui Guizhou China
93 E4 Xishui Hubei China
93 F4 Xiuning China
93 C4 Xiushan China
93 E4 Xiushui China
92 D3 Xiuwen China
93 D3 Xiuwu China
96 B3 Xiuyan China
93 F3 Xixabangma Feng mt. China
92 E3 Xixia Henan China
92 D2 Xixian Shanxi China
92 C3 Xixiang China
93 F5 Xiyang Dao i. China
93 B5 Xiyang Jiang r. China
89 G3 Xizang Zizhiqu aut. reg. China
93 C4 Xizhong Dao i. China
98 H3 Xoka China
92 H3 Xom An Lôc Vietnam
98 C4 Xom Duc Hanh Vietnam
93 C4 Xuan'en China
92 C4 Xuanhan China
92 B2 Xuanhepu China
92 E1 Xuanhua China
98 C3 Xuân Lôc Vietnam
93 B5 Xuanwei China
92 F4 Xuanzhou China
92 D3 Xuchang China
82 A4 Xudat Azer.
122 E3 Xuddur Somalia
92 C5 Xuefeng Shan mts China
89 H2 Xugui China
92 F3 Xun He r. China
92 E5 Xun Jiang r. China
92 E3 Xunke China
92 E5 Xunwu China
92 C3 Xunyi China
93 D5 Xupu China
89 D6 Xuru Co salt l. China
92 D6 Xuwen China
92 F3 Xuyi China
93 B4 Xuyong China
Xuzhou China see Tongshan

Y

93 B4 Ya'an China
70 E5 Yaapeet Australia
120 C4 Yabassi Cameroon
122 D3 Yabēlo Eth.
90 C1 Yablonovyy Khrebet mts China
92 B2 Yabrai Shan mts China
92 B2 Yabrai Yanchang China
80 F5 Yabrūd Syria
96 E1 Yabuli China
157 C2 Yacambu, Parque Nacional nat. park Venez.
93 C7 Yacheng China
93 C5 Yachi He r. China
154 E6 Yacuma r. Bol.
137 J4 Yadkin r. U.S.A.
116 H4 Yadrin Rus. Fed.
163 E9 Yaghan Basin sea feature S. Atlantic Ocean
94 G2 Yagishiri-tō i. Japan
82 C5 Yagman Turkm.
121 D3 Yagoua Cameroon
92 E3 Yagra China
89 H2 Yagradagzê Shan mt. China
159 F1 Yaguari r. Uruguay
98 A4 Yaha Thai.
80 D2 Yahşihan Turkey
80 E2 Yahyalı Turkey
85 H4 Yahya Wana Afgh.
92 E2 Yaita Japan
95 G2 Yaizu Japan
93 A4 Yajiang China
80 F3 Yakacık Turkey
85 G5 Yakhchāl Afgh.
138 B2 Yakima U.S.A.
138 B2 Yakima r. U.S.A.
85 I1 Yakīnish Iran
85 F5 Yakmach Pak.
120 B3 Yako Burkina
94 G3 Yakumo Japan
94 G3 Yakushima i. Japan
130 B3 Yakutat U.S.A.
130 B3 Yakutat Bay U.S.A.
77 N3 Yakutsk Rus. Fed.
117 E6 Yakymivka Ukr.
98 A4 Yala Thai.
135 F4 Yale U.S.A.
151 G3 Yalkubul, Punta pt Mex.
71 G7 Yallourn Australia
80 A5 Yalova Turkey
117 F6 Yalta Ukr.
96 C3 Yalu Jiang r. China/N. Korea
80 C2 Yalvaç Turkey
94 G5 Yamagata Japan
94 B9 Yamagawa Japan
95 B7 Yamaguchi Japan
Yamal, Poluostrov pen. Rus. Fed. see Yamal Peninsula
76 H2 Yamal Peninsula Rus. Fed.
71 J2 Yamba Australia
71 E7 Yambacoona Australia
131 Q2 Yamba Lake Canada
157 C4 Yambi, Mesa de hills Col.
114 L3 Yambol Bulg.
72 D2 Yamburg Rus. Fed.
91 D8 Yamdena i. Indon.
90 B2 Yamethin Myanmar
91 F7 Yamin, Puncak mt. Indon.
120 B4 Yamoussoukro Côte d'Ivoire
143 F5 Yampa r. U.S.A.
117 D5 Yampil' Ukr.
88 D3 Yamunanagar India

83 I2 Yamyshevo Kazakh.
89 G3 Yamzho Yumco l. China
77 O3 Yana r. Rus. Fed.
70 D6 Yanac Australia
87 C2 Yanam India
92 C2 Yan'an China
154 D6 Yanaoca Peru
86 A5 Yanbu' al Bahr Saudi Arabia
92 F3 Yancheng China
68 B5 Yanchep Australia
92 D2 Yanchuan China
71 G5 Yanco Australia
70 D5 Yanco Glen Australia
71 F3 Yanda watercourse Australia
70 D3 Yandama Creek watercourse Australia
120 B3 Yanfolila Mali
89 H3 Yangbajain China
92 D3 Yangcheng China
93 D6 Yangchun China
92 D1 Yanggao China
92 E2 Yanggu China
92 E1 Yang He r. China
83 G4 Yangjiang China
82 F5 Yangi-Nishan Uzbek.
82 F4 Yangirabad Uzbek.
83 G6 Yangiyul' Uzbek.
89 D6 Yangjiang China
Yangôn Myanmar see Rangoon
92 D2 Yangping China
92 D2 Yangquan China
93 D5 Yangshan China
93 D5 Yangshuo China
89 H2 Yangtze r. Qinghai China
93 E4 Yangtze r. China
alt. Chang Jiang,
alt. Jinsha Jiang,
alt. Tongtian He,
alt. Zhi Qu,
long Yangtze Kiang
Yangtze Kiang r. China see
92 F4 Yangtze, Mouth of the est. China
122 E2 Yangudi Rassa National Park Eth.
93 D6 Yangxi China
96 E5 Yangyang S. Korea
92 E1 Yangyuan China
92 C3 Yanhe China
89 E2 Yanji China
70 A4 Yanimee, Lake salt flat Australia
96 E2 Yanji China
93 B4 Yanjin China
82 A4 Yanliang China
89 H2 Yanling China
77 O2 Yano-Indigirskaya Nizmennost' lowland Rus. Fed.
87 C4 Yan Oya r. Sri Lanka
92 E1 Yanshan Hebei China
93 E4 Yanshan Jiangxi China
93 B6 Yanshan Yunnan China
92 E1 Yan Shan mts China
89 H2 Yanshiping China
92 E1 Yanshou China
77 O2 Yanskiy Zaliv g. Rus. Fed.
71 F2 Yantabulla Australia
76 A5 Yantai China
70 D2 Yantara Lake salt flat Australia
113 I3 Yantarnyy Rus. Fed.
96 D2 Yantongshan China
93 A5 Yanyuan China
92 D4 Yanzhou China
120 D4 Yaoundé Cameroon
98 A3 Yao Yai, Ko i. Thai.
91 F7 Yap i. Micronesia
157 D4 Yapacana, Cerro mt. Venez.
91 F7 Yapen i. Indon.
91 F7 Yapen, Selat sea chan. Indon.
160 E5 Yap Trench sea feature N. Pacific Ocean
150 B1 Yaqui r. Mex.
157 C2 Yaracuy r. Venez.
68 E4 Yaraka Australia
116 H3 Yaransk Rus. Fed.
70 A4 Yardea Australia
80 C3 Yardımcı Burnu pt Turkey
81 L2 Yardımlı Azer.
105 I5 Yare r. U.K.
116 J2 Yarega Rus. Fed.
69 G2 Yaren Nauru
116 I2 Yarensk Rus. Fed.
157 B4 Yari r. Col.
95 E6 Yariga-take mt. Japan
157 C2 Yaritagua Venez.
83 I5 Yarkant He r. China
131 I3 Yarker Canada
85 H3 Yarkhun r. Pak.
89 G4 Yarlung Zangbo r. Asia alt. Dihang (India), conv. Brahmaputra
133 G5 Yarmouth Canada
105 F7 Yarmouth U.K.
147 H4 Yarmouth Port U.S.A.
116 F3 Yaroslavskaya Oblast' admin. div. Rus. Fed.
94 C2 Yaroslavskiy Rus. Fed.
70 F6 Yarra r. Australia
71 G7 Yarram Australia
71 I1 Yarraman Australia
70 E4 Yarrie Australia
116 E4 Yartö Tra La pass China
76 J3 Yartsevo Rus. Fed.
116 E4 Yartsevo Smolenskaya Oblast' Rus. Fed.
157 B3 Yarumal Col.
89 J3 Yasai r. India
69 H3 Yasawa Group is Fiji
117 F6 Yasenskaya Rus. Fed.
117 G6 Yashalta Rus. Fed.
85 H5 Yashilkul l. Tajik.
117 H6 Yashkul' Rus. Fed.
92 C2 Yasothon Thai.
71 H5 Yass Australia
71 H5 Yass r. Australia
84 D4 Yāsūj Iran
69 G4 Yaté New Caledonia
143 E5 Yates Center U.S.A.
131 J2 Yathkyed Lake Canada
95 C8 Yatsushiro Japan
105 E6 Yatton U.K.
93 □ Yau Tong Hong Kong China
95 B8 Yavari r. Brazil/Peru
150 B2 Yávaros Mex.
81 H2 Yavatmal India
157 D3 Yavi, Cerro mt. Venez.
117 B5 Yavoriv Ukr.
95 C8 Yawatahama Japan
90 B1 Yaw Chaung r. Myanmar
80 F3 Yawng-hwe Myanmar
151 F6 Yaxchilan tourist site Guat.
Yaxian China see Sanya
84 D3 Yazd Iran
Yazdān Iran see Samírum
80 D2 Yazihan Turkey
143 F5 Yazoo City U.S.A.
103 J5 Ydby Skovhej hill Denmark
115 J6 Ýdra i. Greece
98 A2 Ye Myanmar
70 F6 Yea Australia

105 D7 Yealmpton U.K.
83 I5 Yecheng China
150 E1 Yécora Mex.
145 D7 Yeehaw Junction U.S.A.
70 A5 Yeelanna Australia
116 F4 Yefremov Rus. Fed.
81 J2 Yeghegnadzor Armenia
83 I2 Yegindybulak Kazakh.
83 G2 Yegindykol' Kazakh.
117 G6 Yegorlyk r. Rus. Fed.
117 G6 Yegorlykskaya Rus. Fed.
94 E2 Yegorova, Mys pt Rus. Fed.
116 F4 Yegor'yevsk Rus. Fed.
121 F4 Yei Sudan
76 H4 Yekaterinburg Rus. Fed.
117 G5 Yelan' Rus. Fed.
71 I2 Yelarbon Australia
82 E5 Yelbarsli Turkm.
117 F4 Yelets Rus. Fed.
120 A3 Yélimané Mali
106 □ Yell i. U.K.
87 C2 Yellandu India
87 A3 Yellapur India
92 E2 Yellow r. China
134 B3 Yellow r. U.S.A.
146 D4 Yellow Creek U.S.A.
128 G3 Yellowknife Canada
71 G4 Yellow Mountain Australia
66 B6 Yellow Sea Pacific Ocean
138 E2 Yellowstone r. U.S.A.
138 E2 Yellowstone Lake U.S.A.
138 E2 Yellowstone Nat. Park U.S.A.
138 E2 Yellowtail Reservoir U.S.A.
105 □ Yell Sound sea chan. U.K.
82 E5 Yeloten Turkm.
117 D5 Yel'sk Belarus
129 J1 Yelverton Bay Canada
122 C7 Yemen country Asia
116 G2 Yemetsk Rus. Fed.
116 I2 Yemva Rus. Fed.
102 O2 Yena Rus. Fed.
117 F5 Yenakiyeve Ukr.
89 H5 Yenangyat Myanmar
89 H5 Yenangyaung Myanmar
90 A1 Yenanma Myanmar
98 B6 Yên Bai Vietnam
71 G5 Yenda Australia
120 B4 Yendi Ghana
122 B4 Yénéganou Congo
81 K3 Yengejeh Iran
83 I5 Yengisar China
80 D1 Yeniçağa Turkey
80 D1 Yenice Turkey
115 L5 Yenice Turkey
80 D1 Yeniceoba Turkey
76 K4 Yenisey r. Rus. Fed.
76 K4 Yeniseysk Rus. Fed.
76 K4 Yeniseyskiy Kryazh ridge Rus. Fed.
77 O2 Yeniseyskiy Zaliv inlet Rus. Fed.
93 B6 Yên Minh Vietnam
117 H6 Yenotayevka Rus. Fed.
88 C5 Yeola India
71 H4 Yeoval Australia
105 E7 Yeovil U.K.
105 E7 Yeovilton U.K.
150 B1 Yepachi Mex.
71 F4 Yeppoon Australia
82 D5 Yerbent Turkm.
77 L3 Yerbogachen Rus. Fed.
83 H2 Yerementau, Gory hills Kazakh.
81 J1 Yerevan Armenia
83 H2 Yereymentau Kazakh.
117 H6 Yergeni hill Rus. Fed.
140 C2 Yerington U.S.A.
87 A2 Yerköy Turkey
164 A1 Yermak Plateau sea feature Arctic Ocean
150 C2 Yermo Mex.
140 D4 Yermo U.S.A.
115 I5 Yershov Rus. Fed.
116 I5 Yertsevo Rus. Fed.
Yerushalayim Israel/West Bank see Jerusalem
96 D5 Yesan S. Korea
83 I4 Yesik Kazakh.
82 F2 Yesil' Kazakh.
80 E1 Yeşilhisar Turkey
80 F1 Yeşilırmak r. Turkey
80 C1 Yeşilova Turkey
117 G6 Yessentuki Rus. Fed.
77 L3 Yessey Rus. Fed.
105 C7 Yes Tor hill U.K.
71 I2 Yetman Australia
90 B4 Yeu Myanmar
110 C3 Yeu, Île d' i. France
81 K1 Yevlax Azer.
117 E6 Yevpatoriya Ukr.
89 E1 Yexian China
117 F6 Yeya r. Rus. Fed.
116 H1 Yezhuga r. Rus. Fed.
116 D4 Yezyaryshcha Belarus
159 F2 Yí r. Uruguay
93 B3 Yibin China
89 F2 Yibug Caka salt l. China
93 D4 Yicheng Hubei China
92 D2 Yicheng Shanxi China
93 E4 Yichun Heilong. China
93 E5 Yichun Jiangxi China
92 C3 Yifeng China
92 D3 Yi He r. Henan China
92 D3 Yi He r. Shandong China
92 D3 Yihuang China
92 C3 Yijun China
94 A1 Yilan China
115 L4 Yıldız Dağları mts Turkey
80 F2 Yıldızeli Turkey
93 B5 Yiliang Yunnan China
93 B5 Yiliang Yunnan China
93 C4 Yilong China
93 B4 Yilong Hu l. China
93 C7 Yima China
92 D3 Yima China
93 B5 Yimen China
93 B4 Yinanpo China
92 E2 Yinan China
92 C2 Yinchuan China
92 C2 Yingchengzi China
92 D3 Yinggehai China
92 D3 Ying He r. China
92 D3 Yingjiang China
93 C7 Yingkou China
92 B2 Yingpanshui China
92 D3 Yingshan Hubei China
92 C3 Yingshan Sichuan China
92 E3 Yingshang China
92 E3 Yingtan China
92 D3 Yingxian China
83 J4 Yining China
96 C1 Yinma He r. China
92 C4 Yin Shan mts China
92 D3 Yipinglang China
122 D3 Yirga Alem Eth.
93 F5 Yi Shan mt. China
92 F2 Yishui China
98 □ Yishun Sing.
115 J4 Yixian Anhui China
96 A3 Yixian Liaoning China

92 F4 Yixing China
93 D4 Yiyang Hunan China
93 E4 Yiyang Jiangxi China
93 C5 Yizhang China
103 M3 Yläne Fin.
102 M3 Ylihärmä Fin.
102 N2 Yli-Ii Fin.
102 N2 Ylikiiminki Fin.
102 O2 Yli-Kitka l. Fin.
102 M3 Ylistaro Fin.
102 M2 Ylitornio Fin.
103 M3 Ylöjärvi Fin.
83 G2 Yntaly Kazakh.
94 D6 Yobetsu-dake vol. Japan
99 Yogyakarta Indon.
130 F4 Yoho National Park Canada
96 D5 Yŏju S. Korea
121 E5 Yokadouma Cameroon
121 D4 Yokkaichi Japan
120 D4 Yoko Cameroon
95 F7 Yokohama Japan
95 F7 Yokosuka Japan
94 G5 Yokote Japan
94 G4 Yokotsu-dake mt. Japan
121 D4 Yola Nigeria
151 E4 Yoloxóchitl Mex.
120 B4 Yom, Mae Nam r. Thai.
95 G6 Yŏnan N. Korea
95 G6 Yonezawa Japan
70 C4 Yongala Australia
96 D6 Yŏng-am S. Korea
93 E5 Yong'an China
92 A2 Yongchang China
92 E3 Yongcheng China
96 E6 Yŏngch'ŏn S. Korea
93 F5 Yongchun China
93 B5 Yongdeng China
96 E5 Yŏngdŏk S. Korea
93 E5 Yongding He r. China
96 E5 Yŏngdŏk S. Korea
93 E5 Yongfeng China
93 C5 Yongfu China
96 D6 Yŏnggwang S. Korea
96 H3 Yŏnghŭng-man b. N. Korea
96 D4 Yŏnghŭng N. Korea
92 B3 Yongji China
92 D2 Yongji China
93 B4 Yongjing China
96 D6 Yŏngju S. Korea
96 E5 Yongkang China
92 C3 Yongnian China
92 C6 Yongning China
93 A5 Yongren China
96 D6 Yŏngsan-gang r. S. Korea
96 D6 Yŏngsanp'o S. Korea
92 C3 Yongshun China
93 F5 Yongtai China
96 E5 Yŏngwŏl S. Korea
93 D4 Yongxing China
93 E5 Yongxiu China
93 D4 Yongzhou China
96 D6 Yŏnhwa-san mt. N. Korea
147 G4 Yonkers U.S.A.
110 F2 Yonne r. France
157 B3 Yopal Col.
83 I5 Yopurga China
104 F3 York U.K.
142 D3 York NE U.S.A.
146 E5 York PA U.S.A.
145 D5 York SC U.S.A.
68 E3 York, Cape Australia
104 F3 York, Vale of valley U.K.
70 B5 Yorke Peninsula Australia
70 B5 Yorketown Australia
104 F3 Yorkshire Dales National Park U.K.
104 G3 Yorkshire Wolds reg. U.K.
131 I4 Yorkton Canada
146 E6 Yorktown U.S.A.
150 H5 York Hond.
120 B3 Yorosso Mali
140 C3 Yosemite National Park U.S.A.
140 C3 Yosemite Village U.S.A.
95 C8 Yoshino-gawa r. Japan
95 D7 Yoshino-Kumano National Park Japan
116 H3 Yoshkar-Ola Rus. Fed.
96 D6 Yŏsu S. Korea
107 D6 Youghal Rep. of Ireland
146 D5 Youghiogheny River Lake U.S.A.
93 C6 You Jiang r. China
71 H5 Young Australia
159 F2 Young Uruguay
70 B3 Younghusband, Lake salt flat Australia
70 C5 Younghusband Peninsula Australia
73 A4 Young Island Antarctica
146 C4 Youngstown U.S.A.
93 D4 Youxi China
120 B3 Youvarou Mali
93 F5 Youxi China
93 C4 Youxian China
93 C4 Youyang China
92 B1 Youyi China
93 G3 Youyu China
71 F1 Yowah watercourse Australia
93 A5 Yozgat Turkey
158 A3 Ypané r. Para.
158 A3 Ypé-Jhú Para.
138 D5 Yreka U.S.A.
Yr Wyddfa mt. U.K. see Snowden
108 A4 Yser r. France
108 D3 Ysselsteyn Neth.
103 K5 Ystad Sweden
105 D5 Ystwyth r. U.K.
Ysyk-Köl Kyrg. see Balykchy
83 I4 Ysyk-Köl salt l. Kyrg.
105 D5 Ythan r. U.K.
106 F3 Ythan r. U.K.
77 O3 Ytyk-Kyuyel' Rus. Fed.
98 A1 Yuam, Nam Mae r. Myanmar/Thai.
92 D4 Yu'an China
90 B1 Yuanbao Shan mt. China
93 D4 Yuanjiang Hunan China
93 B5 Yuanjiang Yunnan China
93 D4 Yuan Jiang r. Hunan China
93 B5 Yuan Jiang r. Yunnan China
93 F5 Yüanli Taiwan
93 B5 Yuanling China
93 B5 Yuanmou China
92 D3 Yuanqu China
92 D3 Yuanquan China
140 B2 Yuba r. U.S.A.
140 B2 Yuba City U.S.A.
94 G3 Yūbari Japan
151 G4 Yucatán pen. Mex.
151 G4 Yucatan state Mex.
148 G5 Yucatan Channel strait Cuba/Mex.
140 E4 Yucca U.S.A.
141 G4 Yucca Lake U.S.A.
141 E4 Yucca Valley U.S.A.
92 E2 Yucheng China
77 O4 Yudoma r. Rus. Fed.
93 E5 Yudu China
93 C4 Yuechi China
68 D5 Yuendumu Australia
93 □ Yuen Long Hong Kong China
93 F4 Yueqing China

ACKNOWLEDGEMENTS

Maps designed and created by
HarperCollins Cartographic, Glasgow

Additional work by Cosmographics, Watford

DESIGN
One O'Clock Gun Design Consultants Ltd, Edinburgh

IMAGES AND PHOTOS

pages 4–15
Remote Sensing Applications Consultants Ltd,
2 Prospect Place, Mill Lane, Alton, Hants. GU34 2SX, UK
pages 16–17
NRSC Ltd/Science Photo Library
pages 38–39
San Andreas Fault: David Parker/Science Photo Library
Kluchevskaya Volcano: NASA
pages 40–41
Okavango Delta: Francois Suchel/Still Pictures
Florida: Earth Satellite Corporation/Science Photo Library
Hurricane Floyd: NASA/Goddard Space Flight Center/Science Photo Library
page 43
Tōkyō: NASA

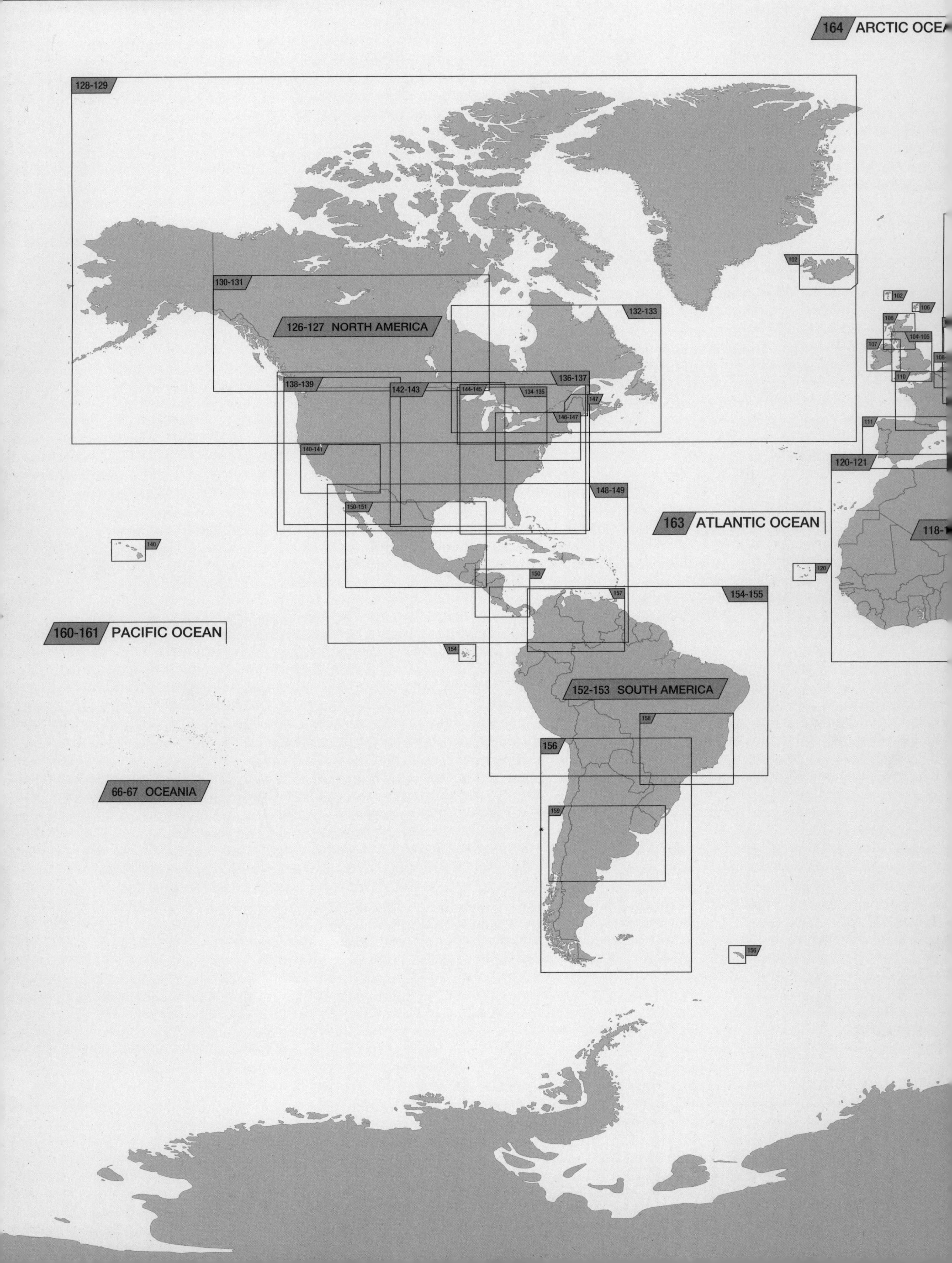

164 ARCTIC OCEA

128-129

102

130-131

102

126-127 NORTH AMERICA

132-133

106

106

107

104-105

110

138-139

142-143

144-145

134-135

136-137

147

146-147

111

120-121

140-141

148-149

118-

163 ATLANTIC OCEAN

150-151

140

120

160-161 PACIFIC OCEAN

150

157

154-155

154

152-153 SOUTH AMERICA

66-67 OCEANIA

158

156

159

156